Music Lib. Ref. ML 128 .S3
S66 1995
Snyder, Lawrence D., 1946-

German poetry in song

MUSIC LIB. Ref. ML128.S3 S66 1995
Snyder, Lawrence D.,
[redacted]

WITHDRAWN

D1710739

DO NOT REMOVE
FROM LIBRARY

GERMAN POETRY IN SONG

Fallen Leaf Reference Books in Music, 30

GERMAN POETRY IN SONG

An Index of Lieder

LAWRENCE D. SNYDER

Fallen Leaf Press
Berkeley, California
1995

Copyright © 1995 by Fallen Leaf Press
All rights reserved

Published by Fallen Leaf Press
P.O. Box 10034
Berkeley, CA 94709 USA

Printed in the United States of America.

Library of Congress Cataloging-in-Publication Data

Snyder, Lawrence D., 1946-
German poetry in song: an index of Lieder / Lawrence D. Snyder.
p. cm. — (Fallen Leaf reference books in music, 30)
Includes bibliographical references (p.) and indexes.
ISBN 0-914913-32-8 (cloth: alk. paper)
1. Songs, German--Indexes. I. Title. II. Series: Fallen Leaf reference books in music; no. 30.
ML128.S3S66 1995
016.78242168'0943--dc20 94-49170
CIP
MN

The paper used in this book meets the minimum requirements of the
American National Standard for Information Services —
Permanence of Paper for Printed Library Materials,
ANSI Z39.48-1984.

In

memoriam

Timothy Tuttle Brown

(1938-1989)

Tim was an Olympic skater, choreographer, and teacher. He began studying piano as an adult, and became a remarkable musician and accompanist. I have known very few people who could exhibit the emotional courage that he brought to his performances, and to his life.

315931

Table of Contents

Introduction ix

Acknowledgments xv

Key to Index Entries xviii

Index of Lieder by Poet, First Line, and Composer

Alphabetical List of Poets 1

Anonymous 453

Volkslieder from *Des Knaben Wunderhorn* 467

Other Volkslieder 476

Not Yet Identified 496

Index of First Lines 499

Index of Lieder by Composer, Poet, and First Line 581

Bibliographies

Indexes of Settings of Individual Poets 711

Biographical Sources 712

Musical Sources 713

Introduction

Meine Ruh' ist hin,
Mein Herz ist schwer;
Ich finde sie nimmer
Und nimmermehr.

No one familiar with Lieder can miss the miraculous invention that sprang from the mind of the seventeen-year-old Franz Schubert as he stared at this narrow column of text in October, 1814. Even a casual listener hears the expansive emotional palette, the rattling and whirring of the old spinning wheel, the sour minor ninth under "Die ganze Welt/ ist mir vergällt," or the way Gretchen stops spinning as she thinks of Faust's kiss and is so disconcerted that it takes her three attempts to get the wheel started again. The song is so compelling, so dominant in the popular history of Lieder, so prevalent on the concert stage, and such a perfect wedding of text and music that Schubert and Goethe may seem inextricably joined in the listener's mind. The identity becomes so complete that one may well overlook other composers, such as Zelter and Loewe, who found the same lines in *Faust* as evocative as did Schubert, and yet whose vision as they read them was so very different. Even more unfortunate is the resultant tendency for the listener to start with Schubert, rather than Goethe, when hearing these other settings for the first time.

Some years ago a local soprano and I decided to give a recital of pairs of songs setting the same text, demonstrating how various composers each approached the starkness of the same lines on the page. I hied myself over to the local university library hoping to locate a single volume that would give me the information I needed to put together such a program, but none such was to be found. The nearest copy, either in original or in reprint, of *Ernst Challier's Grosser Lieder Katalog* was 70 miles away and did not circulate. Moreover, it is hardly a practical work, as most of the songs it lists are long out of print and unavailable even through interlibrary loan, and it gives neither poets nor dates.

I began my own collection of information on available Lieder, during which search I met Ann Basart of Fallen Leaf Press, who asked me to consider making the information more generally accessible. The idea is hardly novel. In addition to *Challier*, there are *The Ring of Words, The Fischer-Dieskau Book of Lieder,* and *The Oxford Book of German Verse,* each of which includes short lists of settings of various poems. There are also individual indexes of settings of the works of Goethe, Heine, Mörike, Hölderlin, Rückert, etc., and even a wonderful index of 131 known settings of Goethe's "Erlkönig." (See Bibliography 1.) The current volume is neither so exhaustive nor so methodical as each of these latter in its own sphere. It does, however, gather information for about 9,800 Lieder, scores to most of which can actually be located by an industrious library patron, into a single resource.

This book is intended as a guide for singers and accompanists who would like to extend their repertoires beyond what is known to be readily available. It is my sincere hope that no search will end with this particular list, but that it will serve instead as an enticement for musicians to locate and perform not only these songs but works I have not managed to catalog as well. Knowing that a setting exists is small excitement beside that of hearing it in rehearsal or recital.

Scope of the Index

As this is a practical volume based on accessible works, compiled by a single person without academic appointment or research budget, it must of necessity be incomplete and curiously regional. The period covered runs roughly from 1770 to the present, with the time from about 1800 to 1930 being best represented. It includes the German songs of all those composers whose entire opus is generally available: Mozart, Beethoven, Schubert, Spohr, Loewe, Robert Schumann, Clara Schumann, Mendelssohn, Franz, Cornelius, Mussorgsky, Liszt, Tchaikovsky, Brahms, Wolf, Strauss, Grieg, Mahler, Griffes, Ives, Schoenberg, Schreker, Marx, Zemlinsky, Berg, Webern, Szymanowski, Pfitzner, Rachmaninoff, Medtner, etc. But this is followed by partial opera and those other single songs or opus numbers that I have been able to locate, primarily in the libraries of the various University of California campuses, with a few additions from the New York Public Library for the Performing Arts, from current publishers, from private collections, and—in a few cases—from archives in Europe. Were I in Minnesota or Boston this would be a rather different list.

To get an idea of how much material is *not* included one need only look at the titles of other works offered on the back covers of late-nineteenth-century sheet music. I have found, for example, only two songs by Eugen Hildach, but the covers of these two list 117 other songs by the same composer. Advertisements for new publications in German and Austrian journals of music and the arts since the early nineteenth century also attest to the truly vast number of Lieder that have been composed, as does a single glance into *Challier*. Though I attempted to exercise little personal preference over the selection, it is often true of library work that one finds what one seeks. After much effort (and ultimately through the courtesy of Christopher Hailey), I obtained a copy of Schreker's Opus 3 Heyse Lieder, for example, but only because I knew to look for it. Anyone with an extraordinary interest in song will inevitably find many wonderful pieces hidden in undeserved obscurity that have been omitted here.

The listing is made yet more idiosyncratic by my decisions on what to exclude, and what sources to draw upon for information. I did not often depend upon catalogs of works unless the works themselves could be located. Thus, though I have a catalog of the works of Franz Lachner, he is unfortunately not well represented in the list because I actually found very few of his songs. I also excluded settings of English translations from the German, which is why Charles Ives' setting of Groth's "Wie Melodien zieht es mir" is included, while his setting of Heine's "My Native Land" ("Ich hatte einst ein schönes Vaterland") is not. This is a wholly arbitrary decision on my part, since I *have* included songs originally set in French and Russian translation. Hence, one will find Mussorgsky here, but not Ethelbert Nevin. Although my intent was to include German-language poets only, a number of others, such as Robert Burns, James Macpherson, and Alexander Pushkin, have found their ways into the index, so long as the poems were originally set in German translation and the composer already appears in the list.

Arrangement of Data

The index is divided into four parts. First is an alphabetical list of the poets, followed by the first lines of the poems by which they are represented. Under each poem are the composers who have set it to music, the title given the song, date of composition or publication, any opus number or other identifier (such as Deutsch numbers for Schubert or Jähns for Weber), and the instrumentation, if other than one unspecified voice and piano. When more than one setting appears in the list, the composers' works are listed in approximate order of composition or publication, depending upon what information was available.

The second section is an index of first lines, identifying each poem by its author. The third is a cross-index by composer, listing each poet and the first line of each setting. The fourth includes the bibliographies and source list.

The book centers around the poetry. For this purpose, the first lines have proven to be a much more consistent and reliable means of identifying each poem or song than either poets' or composers' titles. Composers often use a different title for the song from that given by the poet. Where indexing songs by first lines serves to limit a search, an ordering of material by composer's title does not. A Title Index entry in this book for "Wiegenlied," for example, would need to direct the reader to 44 songs by 31 different composers, setting 38 different poems. Even so, composers often introduce variations into the text itself, so the first line as given here does not always match that in a critical edition of the poetry. When there is but one setting of the poem, the first line is given as it appears in the song. When more than one setting is listed, the poet's version is given, and minor variations are not listed unless they occur near enough to the beginning of the line to upset the index order. If a definitive version of the poem was not available to me, the best known setting was used as the source for the text.

Poets are usually listed by the name under which they are most widely known. When a poet has used a pseudonym consistently, his or her works will be found under that pseudonym, which is always presented in quotation marks. When a pseudonym was used for but some of the works, as with Friedrich Bodenstedt and "Mirza-Schaffy," the poet will be found under the given name, with a referral note to be found under the pseudonym.

Volkslieder present a special problem. Many composers cite the editor of a Volkslied collection as the poet, while others will name the collection, or simply list the verse as a folk poem. One might well find a poem attributed to Herder's *Stimmen der Völker*, to Herder himself, to Uhland, to Brentano and Arnim's *Des Knaben Wunderhorn,* listed as "Anonymous," or merely referred to as "Volkslied." Since most users of this book will often have encountered the poem first in a score, the setting will usually be found under the name to which the composer attributed it, with appropriate cross-references to other settings. There are separate sections following the alphabetical poet listings for "Anonymous," for folk poems stated in the score as being from *Des Knaben Wunderhorn,* and for "Other Volkslieder." Where the same poem is found in more than one section, or under an editor's or translator's name as well, the reader is directed to the other settings.

Composers also frequently list translators as the authors of the poems. Where names of both translator and poet are given, I have listed the song under the name of the original poet. Hence many of both Bethge's and Daumer's translations can be found under the Persian poet Hafis. When the composer lists only the translator as poet, as often with Brahms and Daumer/Hafis, the song is entered under the translator's name, with a cross-reference where necessary. When the works of several foreign poets are known solely through the work of a single translator, as with Gisbert Vincke and the "Maria Stuart" Lieder of Schumann and Raff, they are cited under the translator's name. If there is any question as to where a poem might be located, consult the Index of First Lines. Another problem with translated works is that the same poem might appear in German translation in several different forms. Byron's "Sun of the Sleepless," for example, takes so many forms in German that there was no way to regularize the first lines into a single entry. A similar problem arises from the number of ways nineteenth-century efforts to modernize Walther von der Vogelweide have avoided "da unser zweier bette was."

Poets are sometimes incorrectly identified in the scores, often inadequately identified, and, occasionally, not identified at all. I have corrected misattributions when I could, adding a note of explanation in the text. I have not tried to assign known poets to inadequate attributions unless I could do so with relative certainty, though I should be surprised if I have not made mistakes. Where no poet was given and I was unable to identify the text, I listed the song as "Not Yet Identified" at the end of the Poet Index. Though many of these will prove to be truly anonymous, others may well be reunited ultimately with their proper authors. I do *so* wish that Challier had named names.

The date given is usually the date of composition. When followed by "pub," as in "1914pub," it represents the date of publication of the earliest source available to me either in a reference work or in the score itself. Since many of these songs are somewhat obscure, and could be found only in posthumous anthologies, this date should not be relied upon for anything but an approximation of when the song may have appeared, especially when the song dates from the second half of the nineteenth century or the first decades of the twentieth. There are songs published in *Der Merker* just before the first World

War by composers no longer alive at the time, such as Ferdinand Gumbert, who died in 1896. Yet those appearances may well be the only record of a song that I could find, and hence carry a "1911pub" note or the like in the database. In a few cases where the publisher of the anthology appears to have purchased the copyright, but it seems possible that the songs did not first appear there, the listing will appear as "1914cop."

Most songs included are written for a single voice and piano. When the composer specified a particular vocal range or a different configuration, it will be found following the opus number. A few abbreviation conventions have been adopted for the purpose. Specific solo voice types are partially spelled out, as in "sop, alt, ten," etc. Further abbreviation, as in "satb," refers to choral groups. A single "v" denotes an unspecified voice, "fv" denotes a female voice, "ch" is a chorus, and "mch" is a men's chorus. Other abbreviations used include:

pf	piano	vla	viola	hn	horn
org	organ	vc	cello	str	string ensemble
harm	harmonium	fl	flute	insts	various instruments
vn	violin	cl	clarinet	orch	orchestra

So "sop.sttb.hn.pf" denotes a soprano solo, with a vocal ensemble consisting of sopranos, first and second tenors, basses, a horn and a piano.

Some Statistics

The index lists 9,807 songs by 370 different composers, setting about 7,450 different poems. Of these songs, the texts to 891 of them are Volkslieder, anonymous, or unidentified. The remaining 8,916 songs are settings of texts by 1,115 different poets. Almost half of these poets are represented by but a single song, 164 by two songs, and another 88 poets by only three entries each. On the other end of the scale, the following 12 poets each wrote the texts in more than a hundred settings:

920	Goethe	169	Rückert
446	Heine	152	Geibel
304	Eichendorff	151	Morgenstern
232	Mörike	139	Uhland
179	Lenau	126	Schiller
175	Heyse	124	Hesse

Goethe accounts for over ten percent of the settings to attributable texts, and Heine for about half as many. A single special collection accounts in part for the rather disproportionate Hesse figure, but the remaining names are more representative. The following poets account for 50 or more songs apiece:

98	Brecht	65	Conrad Ferdinand Meyer
91	Hoffmann von Fallersleben	63	Matthisson
87	Dehmel	63	Reinick
87	Wilhelm Müller	63	Ludwig Hölty
86	Hafis (in translation)	60	Rilke
79	Cornelius	56	Osterwald
77	Hölderlin	55	Daumer
72	Chamisso	51	Friedrich Bodenstedt
68	Matthias Claudius		

If Daumer's more than 61 other Hafis settings were indexed under his own name (as Brahms listed them and as perhaps they all should be, given the freedom of the translations), he would certainly appear in the first list. Many poets owe their relatively high representation in the index to a single composer. Certainly Müller would not have appeared so often without Schubert, nor Osterwald without Robert Franz, nor Daumer (again) without Brahms, Brecht without Eisler, nor yet Peter Cornelius without himself. Other poets owe their showing to a pair of champions, as is the case with Meyer, a favorite of both Schoeck and Behn, while still others enjoy a universal appeal.[1]

Because of the unreliable nature of the dates of appearance of many of the Lieder in this index, the following statistics are more fun than informative. Here are a few of the years in which a great many of these songs appeared, and the names of the composers whose works contribute strongly to the figures. It is also a testament to the capricious way statistics can change depending on the manner of the data collection. I made a similar list at a time when there were 2,000 songs fewer in the index, and 1903, 1907, and 1914 were barely noticeable.

1815 – 233 songs	Schubert 169
1907 – 200	Schoeck 25, Streicher 25, Teichmüller 25, Reger 22, Wolff 18
1840 – 180	R. Schumann 157
1816 – 159	Schubert 128
1903 – 150	Reger 38, Streicher 30, Griffes 24, Schönberg 14, Damrosch 10
1888 – 147	Wolf 94
1914 – 146	Wolff 60
1849 – 121	R. Schumann 108

It was in 1914 that the Nachlaß of Erich J. Wolff, who died in 1913, was published, which skews the statistic. But to see 1815 and 1816 dominated by Schubert, or 1840 and 1849 by Schumann, or yet 1888 by Hugo Wolf should surprise no one.

Where to Look for Scores

Not many of these songs are likely to appear on the racks in even a good retail music store, and though seasoned researchers will have little trouble tracking down almost anything they wish, I would ask their indulgence while I offer some hints to others.

Those local music stores will probably have catalogs of current publishers and distributors. Take the time to look through them. The more popular composers such as Schubert or Wolf present little difficulty, but since this is an index of German song, most of the scores originally had European publishers. Bärenreiter, Universal, Schott, and others still list many scores that one might expect to find long out of print. Many items published in the 'forties and earlier are still in the catalogs, often simply because the backstocks have never been sold out. The companies specializing in reprints, such as Kalmus, Da Capo, Gregg International, Georg Olms Verlag, Belwin Mills, and Masters Music Publications have catalogs worth scouring. If the local music retailer doesn't have the catalogs, write the companies for information. Ask also about new releases. When I began this project, I relied upon Nancy Reich's biography of Clara Schumann for information about her songs. Since then Breitkopf has published the complete Lieder in two volumes.

In addition to the mainstream publishers, there are a number of smaller publishers, often specializing in vocal music, with which one may deal directly. Classical Vocal Reprints in New York City is run by Glendower Jones, a singer with a large collection of old vocal editions, long out of copyright, which he reproduces to order for interested performers. He also handles editions from European publishers not often carried in other retail music stores. Similarly, Walter Foster's Recital Publications in Huntsville, Texas, produces a wonderful catalog of vocal scores in reprint, including many works long unavailable

[1]For an overview *al fresco* of the appeal that various poets held for the many composers of the Lied, see Dietrich Fischer-Dieskau: "German Song—an Essay," in *The Fischer-Dieskau Book of Lieder*, London: Victor Gollancz Ltd., 1976; and J. W. Smeed: *German Song and its Poetry, 1740-1900,* London: Croom Helm, 1987, pp. 173-203, "A General Assessment."

outside of archives and libraries. Suzanne Summerville's Arts Venture in Fairbanks, Alaska, is republishing works of Fanny Hensel, Johanna Kinkel, and others, available through distribution by Hildegard Press in Bryn Mawr, Pennsylvania. Both Hildegard and ClarNan Editions in Fayetteville, Arkansas, specialize in the works of women composers.

Many used book stores have sections devoted to music where older collections and editions appear. And be certain to take advantage of friends travelling in Europe to look for music in bookstores and retail outlets abroad.

The most fruitful source, however, is likely to remain the libraries. Check not only the areas devoted to songs, but also the sections containing composers' complete works and collected sets. Series such as *Das Musikwerk* and *Denkmäler der Tonkunst in Österreich* have volumes of Lieder from various historical periods or geographical locations. Many libraries have yet to enter their older books into the electronic databases, so check the card catalogs when the computer fails to produce what you're looking for. When the local resources are exhausted, look elsewhere with online databases such as OCLC, or physical catalogs such as the *The National Union Catalog* or the *Dictionary Catalog of the Music Collection* from the New York Public Library. Not all archives participate in Interlibrary Loan, but many do provide their own photocopying or microfilm service. Some library services may be denied to public users in academic collections, but the same materials may be available by going through the cooperative loan programs in county libraries. Individual librarians often have very different views of both institutional regulations and the functions of the archive, so be prepared to ask a number of people how any particular problem might possibly be solved. When all else fails, write to the archive directly and ask what can be done to obtain a photocopy or microfilm of scores no longer subject to copyright restrictions.

If you have an Internet account there are gophers and online catalogs from collections all over the world at your fingertips. Often a well-placed query in a newsgroup will be returned by some kind soul who will have word of an unusual score. Ask. And if nothing turns up, ask someone else.

My Own Brazen Request

In the spirit of the previous sentence, I would ask any reader who finds grievous errors in my work to contact me. Should anyone be able to name any of the poets in the Not Yet Identified section starting on page 495, I would welcome the information. If there is a song or group of songs anyone feels ought to have been added to this index, I would very much like the chance to rectify the omission. Either a photocopy or complete information as to where the score can be found or purchased would be most appreciated. I can be reached through Fallen Leaf Press, through the postal service at 34977 Colonia Feliz, Davis, CA 95616, or through the Internet at ldsnyder@wheel.dcn.davis.ca.us.

Larry Snyder
Davis, California
December, 1994

Technical Stuff

The data were collected and manipulated in Microsoft's FoxPro 2.6 for DOS, running under IBM's OS/2 version 2.1. A text-based report was generated and then edited using The SemWare Editor, version 2.0, from SemWare Corporation. The manuscript was imported into DeScribe Incorporated's DeScribe 5.0, a versatile native OS/2 word processor, where it was formatted and edited further. The body of the text is in Monotype Corporation's Times New Roman font included with OS/2, altered by Ares Software's FontMonger to include eastern European characters. Without the products developed by these companies and without their respective technical support staffs, this book would not exist.

Acknowledgments

As with any such endeavor as this, my efforts would have been fruitless without the help, generosity, and encouragement of many other people and institutions. With that in mind, my first note of thanks must go to Patty Flowers, head Administrative Officer of the Music Department at the University of California at Davis, who joined the project and for two years, even during a time of great family tragedy, marched over to the library each week and exhausted her Interlibrary Loan privileges on our behalf. No one could have been more diligent or dependable, and I shall always remain grateful and touched by her endless willingness to help.

For the roots of my interest in Lieder in general, I owe my thanks to a small group of performers and teachers in the East Bay region near San Francisco. Among these, Barbara and Allen Shearer, Stephanie Friedmann, Miriam Abramowitsch, Tim Brown, Judith Nelson, Anna Carol Dudley, and Leslie Retallick stand out as I listen in my mind to the music which led me to this project. In addition, my own piano teachers, Barbara Shearer and Karl Ulrich Schnabel, have left me with an appreciation for this stuff of music as strong as any love in life.

I'm grateful to Ann Basart, of Fallen Leaf Press, who was still working as Reference Librarian for the Music Library at the University of California, Berkeley, when I began looking for these materials for my own purposes. It was her later suggestion and assurance that the information might prove of use to more people than I had imagined which has resulted directly in this volume. I must also thank her for her tireless editorial help, her insistence upon my putting the *Chicago Manual of Style* under my pillow each night, and her ready encouragement. Here too I would also especially thank Rachel Kessler, a soprano, singing teacher, and choral director in Davis, whose continual belief in both myself and the project often sustained me during the long effort.

Jim Sylva, who works in Acquisitions and Special Collections at Shields Library, University of California, Davis, is almost single-handedly responsible for dragging me out of my complete computer illiteracy and into the twentieth century at the time that I started the Index. We spent many evenings getting my 3x5-card brain dressed up for a microprocessor world. John Skarstad and Ricki-Ellen Brooke of Special Collections also helped me initially with database design at the suggestion of Don Kunitz, then head of that department. In addition, Randy Young, Mike Forester, Glenn Snyder, John Navas, Lisa Slater, and Walt Kennamer all contributed to helping me understand and overcome computer related problems and questions along the way. In the later stages, the support and development staff of DeScribe, Inc.—Merrylee Croslin, John Serences, and Leslie Allen—all provided invaluable assistance in getting the material from the database into the word processor. Steve Weeks was always ready with new magic with the DeScribe macro language, and Cliff Cullum helped with font alteration and manipulation.

Without the archives and libraries, most of this music would have disappeared long ago, and without the people who work in them, it would remain inaccessible. At the UC Davis Shields Library, the entire staff of Interlibrary Loan busied themselves on my behalf for a very long time. Particular help came from Raleigh Elliott, Christine Alan, and Sandra Leers, but they were quick to tell me that I must not forget those behind the scenes I never met, including Gary Clark, Jason Newborn, and Jeanne Prins. Upstairs at the Reference Desk, Opritsa Popa led me to many biographical resources of which I had been unaware, and Michael Colby was helpful with music reference questions. John Skarstad, now head of Special Collections, made it possible for me to obtain photocopies of important scores of Franz, Weber, and Ritter, and also provided help finding early editions of German poetry not accessible to me elsewhere. My remarkable sister-in-law, Wendy Jones, in Preservation, assisted me in locating and obtaining access to rare volumes. In Copy Services, Debbie Luna produced lovely photocopies of scores in those fragile books while stressing neither signature nor stitch. Lucia MacLean in Circulation was kind enough to relax the limitations normally placed on library use by non-University borrowers for the last few months of the project. Peter Schaeffer of the German Department often volunteered his time and experience to help me milk the archives for hidden information, and Fritz Sammern, formerly of the same department, was equally generous with help interpreting some of the bits the archives were cajoled into giving up.

At the University of California at Berkeley, my sister, Susan Snyder, who worked at the Environmental Design Library and now at The Bancroft, was more help than I can say, both directly with the location of materials common and rare, and indirectly by introducing me to helpful people in other UC Berkeley libraries, including Joe Catelano, Elisabeth Rebman, Leah Emdy, Judy Tsou, and Steve Mendoza in the Music Library.

In the New York Public Library for the Performing Arts I wish to thank Susan Sommer and Joseph Boonin. Heidi Stock in Copy Services took an unusual interest in a temporarily misplaced microfilm order, solving the problem in less time than I expected it to take *without* incident. And I especially want to thank all those who were working as runners in the Music Research wing in the fall of 1993, who for a week carried my many call slips into the bowels of the collection always to return with the scores in what seemed like record time.

Other collections to which I remain ever grateful are the Yolo County Library in Davis, for their Interlibrary Loan efforts; The Musiksammlung in the Österreichische National-Bibliothek in Wien; the Deutsche Musiksammlung in the Staatsbibliothek in Berlin; and all the other institutions which participated in my Interlibrary Loan requests, especially the University of California at Santa Barbara.

A special word goes to Tom White. Of all the retail music stores from Los Angeles and San Francisco to New York that I've been in, only one, Jack's House of Music in Sacramento, can boast of his like. A remarkable accompanist and pianist on his own, Tom's enthusiasm and ingenuity in locating and obtaining uncommon scores still in print both here and in Europe is matched only by his wit and good humor.

I owe another great debt to the owners of three small publishers of vocal music, not only for the services they provide for those of us looking for these songs in reprint or new editions, but for the extraordinary generosity each showed me, outside of any normal business contact. Glendower Jones, of Classical Vocal Reprints in New York, sent not only the many things in his catalog I ordered, but also sent me photocopies of songs by Medtner, Jensen, Griffes, and Meyerbeer not yet reprinted. Walter Foster, of Recital Publications in Huntsville, Texas always managed to find something I had not ordered (but would have had I known) to throw into the parcels at no additional cost, and went out of his way to provide me with original publication information on the works he has reprinted. And Suzanne Summerville, of Arts Venture in Fairbanks, Alaska, sent me photocopies of songs by Johanna Kinkel and Fanny Hensel from her private collection, as well as providing a seemingly endless supply of bits of information about various composers and poets she had performed, studied, and lectured upon.

Though I remain responsible for any and all errors to be found in the volume, without the inestimable proofreading efforts of Eva Einstein, who somehow was born with the patience enough to work through printouts of the entire database, those remaining errors would overwhelm the manuscript.

Many other individuals participated in a myriad of ways. Sherman Stein always took a small list whenever he went to New York and would return with photocopies from the Performing Arts Library of whatever I had requested. Christopher Hailey sent me songs by Schreker and Korngold that I had been unable to find elsewhere. R. Wayne Shoaf searched the archives in the Schoenberg Institute for other Schreker and Zemlinsky scores that had eluded me. The incomparable Paul Moor, enlisting the help of three learned cohorts in Berlin—Helmut Möller, Colman Kraft, and Dagmar Beck—took time out of a busy lecture schedule there and returned with copies of scores of the later songs of Anna Teichmüller not available here. Sylvia Glickman, of Hildegard Press, mailed copies of the texts to Bettina von Arnim's songs long before they were actually released. Carolyn Waggoner helped with the identification of Russian translations of texts by Goethe, Heine, and Uhland, and introduced me to the songs of Eugen Hildach. Rachel Kessler, Carol Plack, Eleanor Yeatman, Jim Elliott, and others all conspired and contributed towards getting me back to New York so I could visit those collections, and Rebecca Plack offered me the use of her living room sofa and the output of her extraordinary *cucina* for the ten days I was there.

I would thank, too, my beloved Livia, the sweetly recalcitrant Queensland Healer, who lay patiently warming my feet as I sat typing away all the hours she would rather I had spent with her on doggie walks. And I will also mention my mother here, for no other reason than that she died before I could show her the results of all this collective effort, and I miss her.

Without the singers who have allowed me to accompany them in performance of some of these songs, my interest would have dwindled many years ago. It is they who give life to what would otherwise be merely a dry and dusty catalog of equally dry and dusty facts.

Haleh Abghari	Jim Elliott	Myrna Scholes	Amanda Serra
Niloofar Abghari	Elizabeth Globus	Rebecca Plack	Robin Treseder
Krista Boone	Rachel Kessler	Leslie Retallick	Eleanor Yeatman
William Courtney	Rodney Kingsnorth	Warren Roberts	Gloria Young

"O danke nicht für diese Lieder, mir ziemt es dankbar dir zu sein!"

(Wolfgang Müller von Königswinter, 1841)

Key to Index Entries

In the Poet Index, an entry may contain any or all of the following information:

(Seldom used first names) Poet's Common Name, née Birth Name ("Pseudonym") (Life Dates)
First line of poem set by the following composers
First Composer's Name, "Composer's Song Title" Date, Opus Number, Instrumentation
Translation information or other short notes
from *Name of Song Cycle or Work* (Position in Cycle)
Second Composer's Name, "This Composer's Title" Date, etc.

If a pseudonym is more well-known than the poet's given name, the first line may be indexed as:

"Pseudonym" (Poet's Given Name) (Life Dates)

In the line giving composer's name, the Date can be either the date of composition or of publication (see Introduction, page xi). The general opus is separated from the individual number by a comma, so that an "Opus 14, number 3" will appear as "Op14,3." See page xii for abbreviations used in the Instrumentation. The name of the cycle is sometimes followed by the number that the particular song is given in the work, so that *Hafis-Lieder* (5) is the fifth song in that composer's group of Hafis settings.

Entries in the Index of First Lines, beginning on page 499, all resemble:

First line of the poem *–Poet's Name*

The Composer Index, page 581, gives the following data:

Composer's Name (Life Dates)
First Poet's Name
First line of poem used in the song
First line of another poem set, in alphabetical order
Second Poet's Name
First line, etc.

Alphabetical order in the various indexes follows the German convention. Articles and spaces are significant, so that "Die Zeit" always precedes "Diese Rose." Umlauted vowels *ä, ö,* and *ü* are ordered as if spelled *ae, oe,* and *ue.* Other characters with diacritics, such as *á, č, è, í, ř,* and *ý,* are indexed the same as their unaccented counterparts. Punctuation is ignored.

Index of Lieder by Poet, First Line, and Composer

Kornél Abrányi

Sei gesegnet, König der Magyaren!
Franz Liszt, "Ungarisches Königslied" 1883

Adil

Wer hätte sie gesehn und nicht auch sie geliebt?
Louis Spohr, "Ghasel" 1826, Op72,3

Friedrich Adler (1857-1938)

Sprich nur, sprich! ich höre die Rede rinnen
Frank van der Stucken, "Dämmerstunde" 1904pub, Op34,2

Erasmus Albers (ca.1500-1555)

O Jesu Christ, wir warten dein
Max Reger, "O Jesu Christ, wir warten dein" 1914, Op137,12, 1v.pf(harm/org)
from *Zwölf geistliche Lieder*

Steht auf, ihr lieben Kinderlein!
Max Reger, "Morgengesang" 1914, Op137,8, 1v.pf(harm/org)
Verses 2&3 by Albers. First is from a Volkslied. See Webern Op15,2
from *Zwölf geistliche Lieder*

Heinrich Albert (1604-1651)

Junges Volk, man rufet euch zu dem Tanz hervor!
Wilhelm Pohl, "Amor im Tanz" 1785pub

Markgraf Albrecht Alcibiades von Brandenburg-Culmbach (1522-1557)

Was mein Gott will, das g'scheh allzeit
Carl Loewe, "Was mein Gott will, das g'scheh allzeit" 1839, Op82,4, 4v
attribution to Albrecht probably spurious.

Sophie Albrecht, née Baumer (1757-1840)

Die ersten Blümchen, die ich fand, Geliebter!
Johann Holzer, "Bei Übersendung eines Blumenstraußes" 1779pub

Thomas Bailey Aldrich (1836-1907)

Einen Ring von Golde steckt' ich an die Hand
Eduard Lassen, "Verlobung" Op62,6

"Willibald Alexis" (Wilhelm Häring) (1798-1871)

Es war einmal ein Schneidergesell, der hatte eine Zauberell'
Carl Loewe, "Schneiderlied" 1836

Fridericus Rex, unser König und Herr
Carl Loewe, "Fredericus Rex" 1837, Op61,1

Liebe Mutter, heut Nacht heulte Regen und Wind
Carl Loewe, "Walpurgisnacht" 1824, Op2,3
Johannes Brahms, "Walpurgisnacht" 1878, Op75,4, 2sop.pf

Mach' auf, mach' auf, mach' auf deine Thür, charmantestes Kind
Carl Loewe, "Wer ist Bär?" 1837, Op64,4

O Lady Judith, spröder Schatz
Johannes Brahms, "Entführung" 1885?, Op97,3

Schwerin ist todt, Schwerin, mein General, ist todt!
Carl Loewe, "General Schwerin" 1837, Op61,2

Sie liebte ihn, Er liebte sie, sie liebten sich beide erstaunlich
Carl Loewe, "Rüberettig" 1837?

Was klopft ans Thor? Über die rothe Heide
Carl Loewe, "Der späte Gast" 1825, Op7,2

Hermann Allmers (1821-1902)

Der graue Nebel tropft so still
Johannes Brahms, "Spätherbst" before 1884, Op92,2, satb.pf

Gern bin ich allein an des Meeres Strand
Eugen d'Albert, "Strandlust" 1898?pub, Op17,3

Hörst du, wie die Stürme sausen durch den blätterlosen Wald?
Robert Kahn, "Novemberfeier" 1894, Op20,i,2

Ich ruhe still im hohen grünen Gras
Johannes Brahms, "Feldeinsamkeit" 1878, Op86,2, 1v(low).pf
Charles Edward Ives, "Feldeinsamkeit" 1900

"Peter Altenberg" (Richard Engländer) (1859-1919)

Und endlich stirbt die Sehnsucht doch
Hanns Eisler, "Und endlich" 1953

Von der Last des Gedankens und der Seele befreit
Alban Berg, "Flötenspielerin" 1906

Was erhoffst du dir, Mädchen, noch?!?
Alban Berg, "Hoffnung" 1906

Weinet, sanfte Mädchen...! So lang ihr weinet
Alban Berg, "Traurigkeit" 1906

"Amalia"

Du gabst mir längst dein schönes Herz
Louis Spohr, "An Rosa Maria" 1826, Op72,5

Amaru (between 6th and 8th centuries)

Sie hatte schüchtern zu ihm aufgesehen
Alexander Zemlinsky, "Die Verschmähte" 1937/38, Op27,5
translated from the Sanskrit by Maurice Wright

"Johanna Ambrosius" (Johanna Voigt) (1854-1938)

Die Liebe ist die Sonne, die Freundschaft sanfter Tau
Ernest Vietor, "Liebe und Freundschaft" Op3,1

Es sind die schlecht'sten Früchte nicht
Ernest Vietor, "Es sind die schlecht'sten Früchte nicht" Op6,5

Mein Herz ging auf die Wanderschaft
Ernest Vietor, "Mein Herz ging auf die Wanderschaft" Op6,3

Mit ausgespannten Armen kommt leis' die Nacht
Richard Kahn, "Sommernacht" 1896?pub

Heinrich Ammann (1864-?)
Sie führten ihn durch den grauen Hof
Arnold Schönberg, "Jane Grey" 1907, Op12,1

Anacreon (572-488BC)
Der sei nicht mein Genoß
Hanns Eisler, "Geselligkeit betreffend" 1943
from *Anakreontische Fragmente*

Die schwarze Erde trinket
Josef Antonín Štěpán, "Die schwarze Erde trinket" 1778-79pub
after Anacreon's 19th Ode

Dir auch wurde Sehnsucht nach der Heimat tödlich
Hanns Eisler, "Dir auch wurde Sehnsucht..." 1943
from *Anakreontische Fragmente*

Du bist glücklich, o Cicade
Carl Loewe, "An die Grille" 1835, Op9,ix,5
translated by Carl von Blankensee. Loewe's setting includes the Greek.

Es sagen mir die Weiber: Anakreon, du greisest
Carl Loewe, "Auf sich selbst" 1815?
after Anacreon's 11th Ode

Gegen Mitternacht schon war es um die Stunde
Anna Teichmüller, "Der Besuch des Eros" 1907pub, Op13,1

Grau bereits sind meine Schläfen
Hanns Eisler, "Die Unwürde des Alterns" 1943
from *Anakreontische Fragmente*

Ich will von den Atriden
Carl Loewe, "An die Leier" 1815?
after Anacreon's 1st Ode

Natur gab Stieren Hörner, Sie gab den Rossen Hufe
Joseph Haydn, "An die Frauen" 1796-1801, satb.bc
after Anacreon's 2nd Ode

Und um die Rippen zog er sich ein kahles Ochsenfell
Hanns Eisler, "Später Triumph" 1942
from *Anakreontische Fragmente*

Vom Dünnkuchen zum Morgenbrot erst ein Stücklein mir brach ich
Hanns Eisler, "In der Frühe" 1943
from *Anakreontische Fragmente*

Weil ich sterblich bin geboren
Carl Loewe, "Auf sich selbst" 1815?
after Anacreon's 24th Ode

Hans Christian Anderson (1805-1875)
Als das Christkind ward zur Welt gebracht
Robert Schumann, "Weihnachtlied" 1849, Op79,16
from *Lieder-Album für die Jugend*

Der Himmel wölbt sich rein und blau
Robert Schumann, "Märzveilchen" 1840, Op40,1
German translation by Adelbert Chamisso

Die Mutter betet herzig und schaut entzückt auf den schlummernden Kleinen
Robert Schumann, "Muttertraum" 1840, Op40,2
German translation by Adelbert Chamisso
Frank van der Stucken, "Muttertraum" 1879, Op5,6
German translation by Adelbert Chamisso

Johann André (1744-1799)
In einem Thal, bei einem Bach, da flog ein bunter Schmetterling
Carl Loewe, "Romanze"

Lou (Louise) von Andreas-Salomé (1861-1937)
Gewiß, so liebt ein Freund den Freund
Friedrich Nietzsche, "Gebet an das Leben" 1882, NWV41

Gabriele d'Annunzio (1863-1938)
Wenn lichter Mondenschein um wald'ge Gipfel schwebet
Max Reger, "Wenn lichter Mondenschein" 1899, Op35,6, 1v(med).pf

Ernst Anschütz (1797-1855)
Es klappert die Mühle am rauschenden Bach
Carl Reinecke, "Die Mühle" Op91, 2v.pf
from *Kinderlieder*

Ha, Priester, zitt're! nicht verhöhnen lässt sich des Königs Machtgebot!
Carl Loewe, "Johann von Nepomuk" 1834, Op35,2

Thomas Aquinas (1225?-1274)
All' mein Leben bist Du! Ohne Dich nur Tod!
Josefine Lang, "Arie" WoO

"Kurt Aram" (Hans Fischer) (1869-1934)
Komm, komm mit nur einen Schritt!
Arnold Schönberg, "Lockung" 1903-05, Op6,7

Ernst Moritz Arndt (1769-1860)
Ade! es muss geschieden sein! reich' mir ein Gläschen kühlen Wein
Friedrich Silcher, "Ade"

Du lieber, frommer, heil'ger Christ
Carl Reinecke, "An den heiligen Christ" 2v.pf
from *Kinderlieder*

Geht nun hin und grabt mein Grab
Max Reger, "Grablied" 1914, Op137,7, 1v.pf(harm/org)
from *Zwölf geistliche Lieder*

Juchhei, Blümelein! dufte und blühe!
Friedrich Silcher, "Frühling"

Lieb' sei ferne, ist doch immer da
Carl Loewe, "Liebesnähe" 1815-16?

Und die Sonne macht den weiten Ritt um die Welt
Eduard Lassen, "Ballade" Op85,2

Wo ist der kleine Jakob geblieben?
Wilhelm Taubert, "Kleiner Jakob"
from *Klänge aus der Kinderwelt*, Vol.2, No1

J. Arndt
Wenn die Erde leise aufgewacht
Robert Franz, "Im Frühling" 1870?pub, Op22,3

Karl Joachim ("Achim") Friedrich Ludwig von Arnim (1781-1831)
Der Kirschbaum blüht, ich sitze da im Stillen
Louise Reichardt, "Unruhiger Schlaf" 1811pub

Ein recht Gemüth springt mit den Nachtigallen
Louise Reichardt, "Ein recht Gemüth" 1811pub

Freunde, weihet den Pokal jener fremden Menschenwelt
Richard Strauss, "Der Pokal" 1918, Op69,2

Ich sehe ihn wieder den lieblichen Stern
Richard Strauss, "Der Stern" 1918, Op69,1

Ihr Mund ist stets derselbe
Richard Strauss, "Einerlei" 1918, Op69,3

Lilie sieh' mich Thau umblinkt dich
Louise Reichardt, "Aus *Ariels Offenbarungen*" 1806pub

O süßer Mai, der Strom ist frei
Johannes Brahms, "O süßer Mai!" 1883?, Op93a,3, satb

Wenn des Frühlings Wachen ziehen
Louise Reichardt, "Kriegslied des Mays" 1819pub

Wenn ich gestorben bin, leg mich aufs Schifflein hin
Louise Reichardt, "Ida" 1806pub

Arthur
Wo ist mein Vater und Mutter hin
Ferdinand Ries, "Die Waisen des Krieges" 1811pub, Op35,1

Elsa Asenijeff (fl.1899)
Amselchen mein, Amselchen mein! Sag an!
Max Reger, "Amselliedchen" 1912
from *Drei Gedichte von Elsa Asenijeff* (3)

Der Himmel ist so weit und hehr
Max Reger, "An eine Mutter" 1912
from *Drei Gedichte von Elsa Asenijeff* (2)

Wo ich bin, fern und nah, fern und nah
Max Reger, "Klage" 1912
from *Drei Gedichte von Elsa Asenijeff* (1)

Auerbach
O Schwarzwald, o Heimat, wie bist du so schön!
Franz Abt, "O Schwarzwald, o Heimat" Op465,2

Anton Alexander Graf von Auersperg: see "Anastasius Grün"

Aurnhammer [possibly Emmerich Jakob Aurnhammer (1772-1817)]
Kennst du das Blümchen auf der Au?
Emilie Zumsteeg, "Beim Abschiede" 1817pub
from *Neun Lieder* (3)

Ferdinand Avenarius (1856-1923)
Ertrage dus, laß schneiden dir den Schmerz
Anton Webern, "Gebet" 1903-04
from *Drei Lieder* (2)

Leise tritt auf... Nicht mehr in tiefem Schlaf
Anton Webern, "Vorfrühling" 1899-1903
from *Drei Gedichte für Gesang und Klavier*

Nun wir uns lieben, rauscht mein stolzes Glück
Anton Webern, "Gefunden" 1903-04
from *Drei Lieder* (1)

Schmerzen und Freuden reift jede Stunde
Anton Webern, "Freunde" 1903-04
from *Drei Lieder* (3)

Weit draussen, einsam im ödem Raum
Anna Teichmüller, "Der Seelchenbaum" 1906pub, Op11

v.Bn**
Kommst spät du liebe Nachtigall!
Johann Rudolf Zumsteeg, "Der Landmann an die Nachtigall" 1803pub
from *Kleine Balladen und Lieder, fünftes Heft*

J. F. A. B–r
Sorgt für die Zukunft! sorgt bei Zeiten!
Johann Rudolf Zumsteeg, "Vorbereitung zum Tode" 1805pub
from *Kleine Balladen und Lieder, siebtes Heft*

Friedrich Bach (1817-1866)
Meine Seele ist still und in sich gekehrt
Johann Vesque von Püttlingen, "Melancholie" 1844-51?, Op43,4

Jens Immanuel Baggesen (1764-1826)
Horch! Leise horch, Geliebte!
Carl Maria von Weber, "Serenade" 1809, J.65

Wenn, Brüder, wie wir täglich sehen
Carl Maria von Weber, "Die Lethe des Lebens" 1809, Op66,6, bass.satb.pf

Eufemia Gräfin Ballestrem (Adlersfeld-Ballestrem) (1854-1941)
Es singt der Schwan am Ufer des Nachts
Adolph Martin Foerster, "Schwanenlied" 1909, Op69,2

Adolf Bartels (1862-1945)
Ich möchte still nach Hause gehn und nimmer wieder fort
Frank van der Stucken, "In der Fremde" 1904pub, Op33,4
Ernest Vietor, "In der Fremde" Op6,2

Wenn sich Liebes von dir lösen will
Hans Pfitzner, "Wenn sich Liebes von dir lösen will" 1931, Op40,2

M. Barthel
Leben gibst du, Leben nimmst du
Emil Mattiesen, “Schicksal” 190-?pub, Op15,1
from *Überwindungen* (1)

Dr. Bartholdy
In Liebe sich begegnen, das ist der Sorge Tod
Carl Loewe, “Polterabendlied” 1859

Über Wolken Herr der Herren, gütig, weise und gerecht
Carl Loewe, “Dem Herrscher” 1859

Rudolf Hans Bartsch (1873-1952)
Es geht, es weht ein Rauch vor dem Wald ins Land hinein
Joseph Marx, “Der Rauch” 1910

Seliges Blümelein, kann Dir so nahe sein!
Viktor Junk, “Volkslied” 1910pub

Karl Johann Friedrich Franz Bassewitz (1809-1907)
Komm in den Garten! ich harre dein
Louis Spohr, “Erwartung” 1853, WoO121

Charles Baudelaire (1821-1867)
Tod, alter Kapitän, nun säum nicht lange!
Erich J. Wolff, “Der Tod” 1914pub, Lieder No.52
translated by E. L. Schellenberg

Ludwig Amandus Bauer (1803-1846)
Gut’ Nacht, gut’ Nacht, ihr Blumen all’ mit eurem bunten Schein
Franz Abt, “Gut’ Nacht, ihr Blumen” 1873pub, Op220,1

Eduard von Bauernfeld (1802-1890)
Dem Vater liegt das Kind im Arm
Franz Schubert, “Der Vater mit dem Kind” 1827, D906

Rudolph Baumbach (1840-1905)
Bin ein fahrender Gesell, kenne keine Sorgen
Ferruccio Busoni, “Bin ein fahrender Gesell” 1880, Op31,2, bass(bar).pf

Dirnlein kommt vom Maientanz
Wilhelm Kienzl, “Triftiger Grund” 189-?, Op37,2

Es pflagen einst drei Knaben der Ruh’ im Waldesraum
Richard Sternfeld, “Die blaue Blume” 1895?pub, Op6

Keinen Tropfen im Becher mehr
Franz Abt, “Die Lindenwirtin”

Zum Hänschen sprach das Gretchen: Mein Lieben mich gereut
Carl Bohm, “Der Schwur” 1887cop, Op310,2
Max Reger, “Der Schwur” 1904, Op76,26, 1v(med).pf
from *Schlichte Weisen, Band 2*

Gabriele von Baumberg (von Bacsanyi) (1768-1839)
Durch eine ganze Nacht sich nah zu sein
Franz Schubert, “Der Morgenkuss” 1815, D264

Erzeugt von heisser Phantasie
Wolfgang Amadeus Mozart, "Als Luise die Briefe" 1787, K520

Ich sass an einer Tempelhalle
Franz Schubert, "Lebenstraum" 1809-10?, D39

Nach so vielen trüben Tagen send' uns wiederum einmal
Franz Schubert, "Cora an die Sonne" 1815, D263

O köstlicher Tokayer, o königlicher Wein
Franz Schubert, "Lob des Tokayers" 1815, D248

Sei sanft wie ihre Seele, und heiter wie ihr Blick
Franz Schubert, "Abendständchen: An Lina" 1815, D265

Sinke, liebe Sonne, sinke
Franz Schubert, "An die Sonne" 1815, D270

Johannes Robert Becher (1891-1958)
Am Fenster sitzend und schon im Genesen
Hanns Eisler, "Genesung" 1957

Ludwig Bechstein (1801-1860)
Unter den rothen Blumen schlumm're, lieb' Vögelein!
Robert Schumann, "Nänie" 1853, Op114,1, 3fv.pf
Frederic Louis Ritter, "Vögleins Begräbniss" 1867pub, Op3,5
from *Kinder-Lieder*
Carl Reinecke, "Vögleins Begräbnis"
from *Kinderlieder*

Karl Isidor Beck (1817-1879)
Gott hilf, Gott hilf! im Wasser wächst das Schiff
Franz von Holstein, "Entsagungslieder IV" 1854, Op11,4

Ich glaubte, die Schwalbe träumte schon vom theuren Nest
Franz von Holstein, "Entsagungslieder II" 1854, Op11,2
Adolf Jensen, "Über Nacht" 1864, Op24,3

Rinne, rinne leise, meine Thräne du
August Bungert, "Eine Thräne" 1889-91pub, Op17,3

Sie spielt mit Blumen im welken Strauss[1]
Franz von Holstein, "Entsagungslieder – Epilog" 1854, Op11,5

Verbleibst ihm dennoch hold gewogen, mein Herz
Franz von Holstein, "Entsagungslieder I" 1854, Op11,1

Wenn Gott auch mir vergönnte
Franz von Holstein, "Entsagungslieder III" 1854, Op11,3

August Becker (1828-1891)
Wenn die Sonne sinkend hinterm Berg sich neigt
Peter Cornelius, "Heimatgedenken" 1866-67, Op16,1, sop.bass.pf

[1]Holstein credits all five of his "Entsagungslieder" texts to one Hugo Staacke. The first four are poems found in Karl Beck's *Stille Lieder*, Leipzig: Wilhelm Engelmann, 1840, in the cycle "Die Entsagende." Only the poem of the "Epilog" is unaccounted for. I have not yet determined whether it is Beck's or Holstein's, or if there is actually a Hugo Staacke. No currently available sources suggest that Beck wrote under a pseudonym.

Cornelius Becker (1521-1604)
Mit meinem Gott geh ich zur Ruh
Max Reger, "Am Abend" 1914, Op137,4, 1v.pf(harm/org)
from *Zwölf geistliche Lieder*

Nikolaus Becker (1809-1845)
Sie sollen ihn nicht haben, den freien deutschen Rhein
Robert Schumann, "Der deutsche Rhein" 1840, 1v.ch.pf

Mathilde Beckmann (Beckmann-Raven) (1817-after 1898)
Über die Wellen zieht zagend und trauernd
Louis Spohr, "Lied aus dem *Mährlein von der Wasserfee*" 1848, Op139,4

Michael Beer (1800-1833)
Armes Kind, südlich weht der Wind
Giacomo Meyerbeer, "Scirocco" 1837

Gegen mich selber in Haß entbrannt
Giacomo Meyerbeer, "Menschenfeindlich" 1837

Komm', Liebchen, komm'! die Nacht ist hell
Giacomo Meyerbeer, "Lied des venezianischen Gondoliers" 1837?

Richard Beer-Hofmann (1866-1945)
Schlaf, mein Kind, der Abendwind weht
Alexander Zemlinsky, "Schlummerlied" 1896?

Schlaf mein Kind, schlaf, es ist spät
Carl Orff, "Schlaflied für Mirjam" 1911, Op6,2
Orff's second verse is Zemlinsky's first

Hermann Behn (1859?-1927)
Es leuchtet die Gottheit aus heiligen Blitzen
Hermann Behn, "Gewitter" 189-?, Op2,3, 1v(med).pf

Hell und sieghaft strahlest du, golderglühend, Stern des Tags!
Hermann Behn, "Sapphische Rhapsodie" 189-?, Op3,2, bar.pf

In dem Frieden heil'ger Nacht schlaf' in süsser Ruh'!
Hermann Behn, "Wiegenlied" 189-?, Op1,i,3, sop.pf

Was hast du mir gestanden, dass mir dein Herz gehört
Hermann Behn, "Geständniss" 189-?, Op1,ii,5

Wissen möchtest du, Geliebter, wie der Schlag der Amsel klinget
Hermann Behn, "Antwort" 189-?, Op4,3, sop.pf
from *Mädchenlieder*

Isakschar (Isachar) Falkensohn Behr (1746-1781)
Holder Frühling, kehre wieder
Karl Friberth, "Sehnsucht nach dem Frühling" 1780pub

Carl Beils
Nach der Heimath möcht' ich wieder
Karl Gottlieb Reissiger, "Heimweh" Op50,1

Gottfried Benn (1886-1956)

Als ob das alles nicht gewesen wäre
Günter Bialas, "Den jungen Leuten" 1988, ten.pf
from *Überblickt man die Jahre* (3)

Erinnerungen, Erinnerungen, Klänge nachtverhangen
Günter Bialas, "Erinnerungen" 1988, ten.pf
from *Überblickt man die Jahre* (1)

Hör zu, so wird der letzte Abend sein
Günter Bialas, "Hör zu" 1988, ten.pf
from *Überblickt man die Jahre* (5)

Überblickt man die Jahre von Ur bis El Alamein
Günter Bialas, "Überblickt man die Jahre" 1988, ten.pf
from *Überblickt man die Jahre* (4)

Wohin können die Götter weinen
Günter Bialas, "Leid der Götter" 1988, ten.pf
from *Überblickt man die Jahre* (2)

Friedrich Benz (1878-1904)

Schlaf wohl, schlaf wohl, über dich hin leuchten rot
Max Reger, "Schlummerlied" 1902
from *Liebeslieder* (7)

Hans Benzmann (1869-1926)

Das ist des Abends Segen
Felix Weingartner, "Abendsegen" 1910, Op51,5
from *Abendlieder*

Pierre Jean de Béranger (1780-1857)

In dieser Rinne will ich sterben!
Franz Liszt, "Der alte Vagabund" before 1849, bass.pf
translated from the French by Theobald Rehbaum

Werner Bergengruen (1892-1964)

Atme, Seele, erhöhter, weil du den Sommer lobst
Ernst Pepping, "Sommer" 1949pub
from *Haus- und Trostbuch* (11)

Es rieseln die Sekunden, an weißen Sand gebunden
Ernst Pepping, "Zum Einschlafen" 1949pub
from *Haus- und Trostbuch* (18)

Hier liegt der Sommer begraben–
Ernst Pepping, "Abgesang" 1949pub
from *Haus- und Trostbuch* (9)

Rüste abendlich die Schale, schütte Milch und bakke Brot
Ernst Pepping, "Die Unsichtbaren" 1949pub
from *Haus- und Trostbuch* (20)

Emilie von Berlepsch (Harms), née von Oppel (1757-1830)

Ruhig ist des Todes Schlummer und der Schoss der Erde kühl!
Carl Loewe, "Lied am Grabe" 1826

Karl von Berlepsch (1882-1955)
Kindlein schlaf' ein. Hoch lodern des Abendfeuers Flammen
Rudi Stephan, "Ein Neues" 1914

Maximilian Bern (1849-1923)
Ich habe mein Kindlein in Schlaf gewiegt
Max Reger, "Mit Rosen bestreut" 1903-04, Op76,12, 1v(med).pf
from *Schlichte Weisen, Band 1*

Was mich zu Dir so mächtig zog
Erik Meyer-Helmund, "Was mich zu Dir so mächtig zog" 1886-88

Josef Karl Bernard (1781-1850)
Ja, ich weiss es, diese treue Liebe
Franz Schubert, "Vergebliche Liebe" 1815, D177

Berndes
Fliege, Vögelein, fliege zu der Geliebten hin
Alexander Fesca, "Liebesbotschaft" 1882pub, Op29,1

Elsa Bernstein: see "Ernst Rosmer"

Max Bernstein (1854-1925)
Die Welt ist schlafen gangen, still ist's in Busch und Baum
Luise Adolpha Le Beau, "Frühlingsnacht" Op18,5

Alexander von Bernus (1880-1965)
Schlaf ein! Die Nacht ist tief und weit
Felix Wolfes, "Schlaf ein!" 1966

Friedrich Anton Franz Bertrand (1757?-1806+)
Hoch, und ehern schier von Dauer, ragt ein Ritterschloß empor
Franz Schubert, "Adelwold und Emma" 1815, D211

Wie treiben die Wolken so finster und schwer
Franz Schubert, "Minona" 1815, D152

Hans Bethge (1876-1946)
An einem Abend, da die Blumen dufteten
Anton Webern, "Die geheimnisvolle Flöte" 1917, Op12,2
translated from Li-Tai-Po

Der volle Mond steigt aus dem Meer herauf
Egon Wellesz, "Mondnacht auf dem Meer" 1914cop
translated from the Chinese

Die Nachtigall sang ohne Ende
Felix Weingartner, "Frühlingsabend" 1910, Op51,4
from *Abendlieder*

Die Sonne scheidet
Felix Weingartner, "In Erwartung des Freundes" 1917pub, Op63,3, sop.ten.pf
from *Blüten aus dem Osten*

Ich pflückte eine kleine Pfirsichblüthe
Richard Strauss, "Liebesgeschenke" 1928, Op77,3
translated in "Die chinesische Flöte"
from *Gesänge des Orients*

Mein Schiff treibt
Felix Weingartner, "Auf dem Flusse" 1917pub, Op63,4, sop.ten.pf
from *Blüten aus dem Osten*

Nicht deshalb lieb ich
Felix Weingartner, "Das Blatt der Frühlingsweide" 1917pub, Op63,2, sop.ten.pf
from *Blüten aus dem Osten*

Noch ist der Glanz der Frühe
Felix Weingartner, "Die wilden Schwäne" 1917pub, Op63,1, sop.ten.pf
from *Blüten aus dem Osten*

So schön sind deine Hände
Felix Weingartner, "Liebeslied" 1917pub, Op63,6, sop.ten.pf
from *Blüten aus dem Osten*

Vom Wind getroffen
Felix Weingartner, "Nächtliches Bild" 1917pub, Op63,7, sop.ten.pf
from *Blüten aus dem Osten*

Wenn ich erführe, daß das Alter mich besuchen möchte
Hanns Eisler, "Wenn ich erführe" 1922, Op2,3

Wenn sich der Abend niedersenkt und Nebel wallen
Harald Genzmer, "Sehnsucht nach der Heimat" 1940-87, bar.pf or sop.pf
translated from Yakamochi
from *Acht Lieder nach verschiedenen Dichtern*

Wo das Reisfeld abgeerntet
Felix Weingartner, "Abendsonne" 1917pub, Op63,5, sop.ten.pf
from *Blüten aus dem Osten*

Zu meiner Flöte, die aus Jade ist
Lise Maria Mayer, "Der Tanz der Götter" 1913pub
translated from the Chinese of Li-Tai-Po

Christoph Bezzel (1692-1740)

Bekehre du mich, Herr, so werd ich wohl bekehret
Carl Loewe, "Bekehre du mich, Herr" 1854, 4v
Carl Loewe, "Bekehre du mich, Herr (2nd version)" 1855, 4v

from the *Bible*

Ach Herr, wie lange willst du mein so ganz vergessen?
Franz Schubert, "Der 13. Psalm" 1819, D663
translated by Moses Mendelssohn

Alsdann kommt Jesus aus Galiläa an den Jordan zu Johannes
Carl Loewe, "Idyll des Gotteslammes" 1861, 4v.pf/organ
from Matthew 3:13 and John 1:29

Denn es gehet dem Menschen wie dem Vieh
Johannes Brahms, "Vier ernste Gesänge (1)" 1896, Op121,1, bass.pf
from Ecclesiastes 3

Der Herr ist mein Hirte
Othmar Schoeck, "Psalm 23" 1907, Op11,2

Der Mensch, vom Weibe geboren, lebt nur kurze Zeit und ist voll Unruhe
Hanns Eisler, "Der Mensch" 1943

Dort werd' ich das im Licht erkennen
Josefine Lang, "Die Augen der Blinden werden aus dem Dunkel und Finsterniss sehen" WoO
from Isaiah 29:18

Gott! Drücke, wenn das Herze bricht
Josefine Lang, "Es ist noch eine Ruhe vorhanden dem Volk Gottes" WoO
from Hebrews 4:9

Gott ist mein Hirt, mir wird nichts mangeln
Franz Schubert, "Der 23. Psalm" 1820, D706, 2s2a.pf
translated by Moses Mendelssohn

Herr, du bist unsre Zuflucht für und für!
Carl Loewe, "Herr, du bist unsre Zuflucht für und für!" 1829, Op30,15
from Psalm 90:1; Acts 4:12; John 14:1,20

Herr, wie lange willst du mein so gar vergessen?
Johannes Brahms, "Der 13. Psalm" 1859, Op27, ssa.pf/org.str

Ich bin ein guter Hirte, und kenne die Meinen
Carl Loewe, "Ich bin ein guter Hirte" 1860, 1v.pf/organ
from John 10:14-16

Ich wandte mich, und sahe an
Johannes Brahms, "Vier ernste Gesänge (2)" 1896, Op121,2, bass.pf
from Ecclesiastes 4

In der Zeit sprach der Herr Jesus zu den Scharen der Juden
Franz Schubert, "Evangelium Johannis" 1818, D607

Israel hat dennoch Gott zum Trost
Carl Loewe, "Israel hat dennoch Gott zum Trost" 1839/40
Psalm 73

Jauchzet dem Herrn, alle Welt!
Othmar Schoeck, "Psalm 100" 1907, Op11,3

Jauchzet Gott, alle, alle Lande!
Reinhard Schwarz-Schilling, "Der 100. Psalm" 1949
from *Drei Geistliche Lieder*

Komm' nur mühselig und gebückt!
Josefine Lang, "Gott sei mir Sünder gnädig" WoO
from Luke 18:13

Magdalena weint am Grabe
Carl Loewe, "Magdalena weint am Grabe" 1825, Op66, 1v.pf/organ
after John 21:13-17, arr. by Loewe from his Oratorio "Die Festzeiten"

Meine Seele ist still zu Gott
Max Reger, "Meine Seele ist still zu Gott" 1907, Op105,2, 1v(med).org(pf)
from Psalm 52
from *Zwei geistliche Lieder* (2)

O Tod, o Tod, wie bitter, wie bitter bist du
Johannes Brahms, "Vier ernste Gesänge (3)" 1896, Op121,3, bass.pf
from the Apocrypha

Und er spützete auf die Erde
Carl Loewe, "Des Blindgeborenen Heilung" 1860, Op131,6&7, 1v.pf/organ
from John 9:6-7. Translated by W. M. L. de Wettes.

Wenn ich mit Menschen- und mit Engelszungen redete
Johannes Brahms, "Vier ernste Gesänge (4)" 1896?, Op121,4, bass.pf
from First Corinthians 12

Zu den Bergen hebet sich ein Augenpaar
Peter Cornelius, "Zu den Bergen hebet sich ein Augenpaar" 1866, sop.bar.pf
after Psalm 121

Freiherr Rüdiger von Biegeleben

Sieh auf dem Meer den Glanz der hohen Sonne liegen
Franz Liszt, "Und sprich" 1874

Karl Bienestein (1869-1927)

Von Porphyr rot
Felix Weingartner, "Das alte Schloß" 1910, Op51,9
from *Abendlieder*

Otto Julius Bierbaum ("Martin Möbius") (1865-1910)

Ach, wie wird mir wohl und weh, süße Dame
Richard Trunk, "Menuett" 1933pub, Op63,3
from *Vier heitere Lieder*

Als Nachts ich überm Gebirge ritt
Richard Strauss, "Junghexenlied" 1898, Op39,2

Auf der fernen See ein Segel steht
Alban Berg, "Lied des Schiffermädels" 1902

Aus dem Rosenstokke vom Grabe des Christ
Paul Graener, "Die schwarze Laute" 1911pub, Op29,2
Erich J. Wolff, "Die schwarze Laute" 1914pub, Lieder No.7

Da nun die Blätter fallen, oh weh
Ernest Vietor, "Im Blätterfallen" 1907?, Op4,3

Der Schmerz ist ein Schmied, sein Hammer ist hart
Max Reger, "Schmied Schmerz" 1900, Op51,6
Karl Weigl, "Schmied Schmerz" 1912cop, Op1,7

Die heiligen drei Könige stehn vorm Haus
Paul Graener, "Lied aus Bethlehem" 1916pub, Op40,4

Eine Wiese voller Margeriten (see also "Nicht im Schlafe...")
Max Reger, "Freundliche Vision" 1902, Op66,2, 1v(med).pf

Es ging ein Wind durch's weite Land
Richard Strauss, "Wir beide wollen springen" 1896

Fräulein Gigerlette lud mich ein zum Tee
Arnold Schönberg, "Gigerlette" 1901?
from *Brettl-Lieder*

"Frauenhaar" trag' ich am Hute
Max Reger, "Frauenhaar" 1899, Op37,4, 1v(med).pf

Gell ja, also Morgen? "Ja freiliwenn's auf stehn"
Ernest Vietor, "Ich freue mich auf morgen" Op3,5

Gib dir weiter keine Mühe, mein Sohn
Ernst Toch, "Die Straßburger Münster-Engelchen" 1928pub, Op41,3

Gott, deine Himmel sind mir aufgetan
Alma Schindler-Mahler, "Ekstase" 1924pub

Hans und Grethe, Grethe und Hans
Ernest Vietor, "Hans und Grethe" Op6,1

Laß mich noch einmal dir ins schwarze Auge sehn
Max Reger, "Letzte Bitte" 1899

Nicht im Schlafe hab ich das geträumt (see also "Eine Wiese...")
Richard Strauss, "Freundliche Vision" 1900, Op48,1

Nun hängt nur noch am Kirchturmknopf
Max Reger, "Gegen Abend" 1902-03, Op70,11

Ringelringelrosenkranz, ich tanz' mit meiner Frau
Alexander Zemlinsky, "Ehetanzlied" 1901?, Op10,1
from *Ehetanzlied und andere Gesänge*

Ringsum dunkle Nacht, hüllt in Schwarz mich ein
Alma Schindler-Mahler, "Licht in der Nacht" 1915pub

Sitz im Sattel, reite, reite auf die Freite
Max Reger, "Ritter rät dem Knappen dies" 1902-03, Op70,3

Sonntagsfriede liegt heilig über der Stadt
Rudi Stephan, "Sonntag" 1913

Stille, träumende Frühlingsnacht
Max Reger, "Flieder" 1899, Op35,4, 1v(med).pf

Über Wiesen und Felder ein Knabe ging
Richard Strauss, "Schlagende Herzen" 1895, Op29,2

Weite Wiesen im Dämmergrau
Richard Strauss, "Traum durch die Dämmerung" 1895, Op29,1
Max Reger, "Traum durch die Dämmerung" 1899, Op35,3, 1v(med).pf
Vítězslav Novák, "Traum durch die Dämmerung" 1912pub, Op46,2
from *Erotikon*

Wenn im braunen Hafen alle Schiffe schlafen
Max Reger, "Aus der Ferne in der Nacht" 1902, Op66,3, 1v(med).pf

Wie ging ich durch mein Leben hin
Ernest Vietor, "Gavotte des Verliebten" 1907?, Op4,1

Wir gingen durch die stille, milde Nacht
Richard Strauss, "Nachtgang" 1895, Op29,3
Max Reger, "Nachtgang" 1900, Op51,7, 1v(med).pf

Franz Rudolf Immanuel Binder (1810-1846+)
Es ziehet den Pilgrim rastlos fort
Carl Loewe, "Das Grab zu Ephesus" 1837, Op75,1, alt.pf

Rudolf Georg Binding (1867-1938)
Alles stirbt. Auch die Freunde, die Freunde sterben
Felix Wolfes, "Grabschrift eines Mannes" 1959

Heut Nacht, mein Lieb, da nehm ich dich in meinen Traum
Helmut Paulsen, "Traumverkündigung"
from *Sieben besinnliche Lieder*

Wenn so stolz im Licht der Sterne Tannenwaldung aufwärts steigt
Erich Riede, "Evangelium der Nacht" Op7,7, sop.pf

Julius Bittner (1874-1939)

Du bist der schimmernd Edelstein
Julius Bittner, "An Sie" 1923pub
from *Sechzehn Lieder von Liebe, Treue, und Erde*, I,2

Du bist wie eine Julinacht, so süß, so weich, so warm!
Julius Bittner, "Du bist wie eine Julinacht" 1923pub
from *Sechzehn Lieder von Liebe, Treue, und Ehre*, IV,1

Du hältst uns, Frau, die heiligste der Flammen!
Julius Bittner, "Mysterium" 1923pub
from *Sechzehn Lieder von Liebe, Treue, und Erde*, II,3

Du kleiner Mensch im Bettlein klein
Julius Bittner, "Wiegenlied eines Vaters" 1923pub
from *Sechzehn Lieder von Liebe, Treue, und Erde*, III,2

Es dunkelt. Friede im Gemach
Julius Bittner, "Es dunkelt" 1910pub

Es ist schon spät, so um die Mitternacht
Julius Bittner, "Nächtliche Stunde" 1923pub
from *Sechzehn Lieder von Liebe, Treue, und Ehre*, IV,2

Ich geh zu Dir in dunkler Nacht, doch in mir ist es hell
Julius Bittner, "Nachtwanderung" 1923pub
from *Sechzehn Lieder von Liebe, Treue, und Erde*, I,4

Ich habe Dich schon längst gekannt
Julius Bittner, "Wiederkunft" 1923pub
from *Sechzehn Lieder von Liebe, Treue, und Erde*, II,1

Ich seh' vor mir ein liebes Bild
Julius Bittner, "Herbstmorgen" 1923pub
from *Sechzehn Lieder von Liebe, Treue, und Ehre*, IV,3

Ich weiß, daß Dir und mir bereitet ist ein Haus
Julius Bittner, "Refugium" 1923pub
from *Sechzehn Lieder von Liebe, Treue, und Erde*, III,3

Und ob auch Sturm das Haus mir umsaust
Julius Bittner, "Zuversicht" 1923pub
from *Sechzehn Lieder von Liebe, Treue, und Erde*, II,2

Wald vor uns, Wies' vor uns und Blütenpracht
Julius Bittner, "Ausblick" 1923pub
from *Sechzehn Lieder von Liebe, Treue, und Erde*, II,4

Weißt Du noch, wie das war? Es war noch früh im Jahr
Julius Bittner, "Aprilsonne" 1923pub
from *Sechzehn Lieder von Liebe, Treue, und Erde*, III,4

Wem säng' ich Lieder, wenn nicht Dir?
Julius Bittner, "Zueignung" 1923pub
from *Sechzehn Lieder von Liebe, Treue, und Erde*, I,1

Wir waren nie getrennt und werden nie getrennt sein
Julius Bittner, "Trost" 1923pub
from *Sechzehn Lieder von Liebe, Treue, und Ehre*, IV,4

Wo ich immer geh' und stehe
Julius Bittner, "Minnelied" 1923pub
from *Sechzehn Lieder von Liebe, Treue, und Erde*, I,3

Zu einem Wesen wurden zwei
Julius Bittner, "Choral" 1923pub
from *Sechzehn Lieder von Liebe, Treue, und Erde*, III,1

Björnstjerne Björnson (1832-1910)
Es sass die Prinzessin im Frau'ngemach
Anna Teichmüller, "Die Prinzessin" 1905pub, Op3,2

Nun habe Dank für alles seit wir klein
Wilhelm Kempff, "Nun habe Dank" 1923pub, Op16,2

Marianne Blaauw
Wie leise scheue Kinder, so geh'n meine einsamen Gedanken
Anna Teichmüller, "Wie leise scheue Kinder" 1906pub, Op7,2

Otto Blankenfeldt
Holder Lenz, mit reichen Gaben schmückst du wieder unsre Flur
Carl Loewe, "Frühlingsweihe" 185-?

Carl von Blankensee
Herz, mein Herz, ermanne dich
Carl Maria von Weber, "Schmerz" 1820, Op80,4

Hoffe, liebe, glaube, ist des Herren Wort
Carl Loewe, "Blumen-Evangelium" 1836

Victor Blüthgen (1844-1920)
Es war ein niedlich' Zeiselein
Alexander Zemlinsky, "Der Traum" 1894-96, Op2,ii,3

Gemäht sind die Felder, der Stoppelwind weht
Franz Abt, "Ach, wer doch das könnte!" 1870?pub
from *Kinderlieder*

Ich war mal in dem Dorfe, da gab es einen Sturm
Max Reger, "Die fünf Hühnerchen" 1909-10, Op76,51, 1v(med).pf
from *Schlichte Weisen, Band 5, "Aus der Kinderwelt"*
Erich Zeisl, "Die fünf Hühnerchen" 1936pub

Nun gute Nacht! Es gab so viel zu schauen
Franz Abt, "Nun gute Nacht" 1870?pub
from *Kinderlieder*
Gustav Lewin, "Gute Nacht" 1912pub

Still, wie so still! 's ist Mitternacht schon
Max Reger, "Strampelchen" 1901, Op62,9, 1v(med).pf

Wer hat das erste Lied erdacht
Ferruccio Busoni, "Wer hat das erste Lied erdacht" 1880, Op31,1, mez(ten).pf

Johannes Alois Blumauer (1755-1798)

Immerdar mit leisem Weben schwebt dein süsses Bild vor mir
Franz Jacob Freystädtler, "Sehnsucht eines Liebenden" 1795
from *Sechs Lieder der besten deutschen Dichter* (4)

Liebe traf mich, meine Augen weinen
Anton Teyber, "Liebesschmerz" 1797

Närrchen, sei nicht spröde
Leopold Kozeluch, "Stutzerlied" 1785?

Theuthold, mein Trauter, ist gangen von hier
Johann Holzer, "In Abwesenheit des Geliebten zu singen" 1779pub
Franz Jacob Freystädtler, "In Abwesenheit des Geliebten zu singen" 1795
from *Sechs Lieder der besten deutschen Dichter* (3)

Wer unter eines Mädchens Hand
Wolfgang Amadeus Mozart, "Lied der Freiheit" 1785, K506

Zwei Augen sinds, aus deren Blikken
Johann Holzer, "Zwei Augen" 1779pub

F. Bobrich

Wo blüht das Thal wo Liebe sich ew'ge Kränze flicht?
Louis Spohr, "Jenseits" 1838, WoO98, sop.ten.pf

Johann Friedrich Ludwig Bobrik (1781-1848)

Der König saß beim frohen Mahle
Franz Schubert, "Die drei Sänger" (fragment), 1815, D329

Marchese Cesare Bocella

Englein hold im Lockengold
Franz Liszt, "Englein hold im Lockengold" 1842pub
translated from the Italian by Peter Cornelius

Curt Bock (1890-1949)

Sieh, an letzten Himmels Saum schwebt die Blume voller Süße
Paul Hindemith, "Die trunkene Tänzerin" 1922, Op18,1

Gustav von Boddien (1814-1870)

Es blinkt der Thau in den Gräsern der Nacht
Anton Rubinstein, "Es blinkt der Thau" 1864, Op72,1

Ich habe ein kleines Lied erdacht und hab' es gesungen
Hans Sommer, "Ganz leise" 1891pub, Op14,2

Vorbei, vorbei durch Feld und Wald
Anton Rubinstein, "Die Waldhexe" 1864, Op72,3

Wie eine Lerch' in blauer Luft
Anton Rubinstein, "Wie eine Lerch' in blauer Luft" 1864, Op72,2

Friedrich Martin von Bodenstedt ("Mirza-Schaffy") (1819-1892)

Deine Finger rühren die Saiten
Louis Spohr, "Fatima beim Saitenspiel" 1850, WoO119,3

Die Gletscher leuchten im Mondenlicht
Eduard Lassen, "Die Gletscher leuchten im Mondenlicht" Op60,2
Ingeborg von Bronsart, "Abschied vom Kaukasus" 189-?pub, Op10,2

Die helle Sonne leuchtet auf's weite Meer hernieder
Anton Rubinstein, "Die helle Sonne leuchtet" 1854, Op34,10
Giacomo Meyerbeer, "Die helle Sonne leuchtet" 1860
Robert Franz, "Die helle Sonne leuchtet" 1870?, Op42,2
Eduard Lassen, "Die helle Sonne leuchtet" Op60,6
Ingeborg von Bronsart, "Die helle Sonne leuchtet" 189-?pub, Op8,5
from *Sechs Lieder des Mirza Schaffy*

Die Weise guter Zecher ist, zu früh' und später Stunde
Anton Rubinstein, "Die Weise guter Zecher ist" 1854, Op34,5

Einst wollt ich einen Kranz dir winden
Franz Liszt, "Einst" 1879pub

Es hat die Rose sich beklagt
Anton Rubinstein, "Die Rose" 1854, Op34,4
Robert Franz, "Es hat die Rose sich beklagt" 1870?, Op42,5

Es ragt der alte Elborus so hoch der Himmel reicht
Robert Franz, "Es ragt der alte Elborus" 1870?, Op43,5

Füllt mir das Trinkhorn! reicht es herum!
Louis Spohr, "Trinklied" 1850, WoO119,2

Gelb rollt mir zu Füssen der brausende Kur
Anton Rubinstein, "Gelb rollt mir zu Füssen" 1854, Op34,9
Ingeborg von Bronsart, "Gelb rollt mir zu Füssen" 189-?pub, Op8,4
from *Sechs Lieder des Mirza Schaffy*

Glücklich lebt, vor Noth geborgen
Ingeborg von Bronsart, "Das Vöglein" 189-?pub, Op10,5
from the Russian

Gott hiess die Sonne glühen
Anton Rubinstein, "Gott hiess die Sonne glühen" 1854, Op34,12

Ich fühle deinen Odem mich überall umweh'n
Anton Rubinstein, "Ich fühle deinen Odem" 1854, Op34,6
Eduard Lassen, "Ich fühle deinen Odem" Op45,4
Ingeborg von Bronsart, "Ich fühle deinen Odem" 189-?pub, Op8,6
from *Sechs Lieder des Mirza Schaffy*

Im Garten klagt die Nachtigall, und hängt das feine Köpfchen nieder
Ingeborg von Bronsart, "Im Garten klagt die Nachtigall" 189-?pub, Op8,2
from *Sechs Lieder des Mirza Schaffy*

In meinem Lebensringe bist du der Edelstein
Franz Liszt, "An Edlitam. Zur silbernen Hochzeit" 1879pub

In Stunden der Entmutigung, wenns gar zu trübe geht
Franz Liszt, "Gebet" 1879pub
after Lermontoff

Mein Herz schmückt sich mit dir
Anton Rubinstein, "Mein Herz schmückt sich mit dir" 1854, Op34,2

Mir träumte einst ein schöner Traum
Edvard Grieg, "Ein Traum" 1889, Op48,6
Ingeborg von Bronsart, "Mir träumte einst ein schöner Traum" 189-?pub, Op10,1

Nachtigall, o Nachtigall! Sangeshelle Nachtigall!
Ingeborg von Bronsart, "Nachtigall, o Nachtigall" 189-?pub, Op10,4
from the Russian

Neig' schöne Knospe, dich zu mir
Anton Rubinstein, "Neig' schöne Knospe" 1854, Op34,8
Otto Lohse, "Neig' schöne Knospe dich zu mir" 1910pub
"Aus Mirza Schaffy's Liederbuche"

Nicht mit Engeln im blauen Himmelszelt
Louis Spohr, "Zuleikha" 1850, WoO119,1
Anton Rubinstein, "Nicht mit Engeln" 1854, Op34,1
Leopold Damrosch, "Zuléikha" Op6,2
Ingeborg von Bronsart, "Zuléikha" 189-?pub, Op8,1
from *Sechs Lieder des Mirza Schaffy*

Schlag' die Tschadra zurück
Anton Rubinstein, "Schlag' die Tschadra zurück" 1854, Op34,7

Seh' ich deine kleinen Händchen an
Leopold Damrosch, "Seh' ich deine kleinen Händchen an" Op6,1

Seh' ich deine zarten Füßchen an
Anton Rubinstein, "Seh' ich deine zarten Füßchen an" 1854, Op34,3

Sing, mit Sonnenaufgang singe, Nachtigall, dein schmetternd Lied!
Ingeborg von Bronsart, "Sing, mit Sonnenaufgang singe" 189-?pub, Op10,6
from the Russian

Thu' nicht so spröde, schönes Kind
Anton Rubinstein, "Thu' nicht so spröde, schönes Kind" 1854, Op34,11

Und was die Sonne glüht, was Wind und Welle singt
Adolph Martin Foerster, "- - -" 1908, Op53,1

Was ist der Wuchs der Pinie, das Auge der Gazelle
Felix Weingartner, "Morgenländisches Ständchen" 1900, Op28,11

Weit über das Feld durch die Lüfte hoch
Johannes Brahms, "Lied" 1853, Op3,4

Wenn der Frühling auf die Berge steigt
Leopold Damrosch, "Frühlingslied" Op6,3
Eduard Lassen, "Wenn der Frühling auf die Berge steigt" Op60,5
Robert Franz, "Wenn der Frühling auf die Berge steigt" 1870?, Op42,6
Oscar Weil, "Frühlingslied" 1888pub, Op10,2, sop.vn.pf
Ingeborg von Bronsart, "Wenn der Frühling auf die Berge steigt" 189-?pub, Op8,3
from *Sechs Lieder des Mirza Schaffy*
Franz Ries, "O wie wunderschön ist die Frühlingszeit" before 1891

Wenn ich dich seh' so lieb und hold auf mich die Blicke lenken
Eduard Lassen, "Wenn ich dich seh'" Op60,4
August Bungert, "Wenn ich dich seh', so lieb und hold" 1889-91pub, Op19,2

Wie lächeln die Augen der Liebe willkommen
Ingeborg von Bronsart, "Wie lächeln die Augen" 189-?pub, Op10,3

Emanuel, Freiherr von Bodmann (1874-1946)

Es ist der Tag, wo jedes Leid vergessen
Richard Strauss, "Gesang der Apollopriesterin" 1896, Op33,2, 1v.orch

Herr Lenz springt heute durch die Stadt
Richard Strauss, "Herr Lenz" 1896, Op37,5

Martin Boelitz (1874-1918)

Auf der schönen, schönen Wiese
Max Reger, "Ein Tänzchen" 1909-10, Op76,49, 1v(med).pf
from *Schlichte Weisen, Band 5, "Aus der Kinderwelt"*

Das dank' ich deiner Güte, nun geh' ich ganz im Licht
Max Reger, "Erlöst" 1902, Op66,9, 1v(med).pf

Deiner Liebe goldene Güte trägst du lächelnd durch meine Tage
Max Reger, "Reinheit" 1901, Op62,6

Draußen weht es bitterkalt
Max Reger, "Knecht Ruprecht" 1909-10, Op76,50, 1v(med).pf
from *Schlichte Weisen, Band 5, "Aus der Kinderwelt"*

Dröhnende Hämmer in rußiger Hand
Max Reger, "Wehe" 1901, Op62,1

Du bist mir gut! Es hat ein heimlich Singen
Max Reger, "Du bist mir gut!" 1902, Op66,4, 1v(med).pf

Ein linder Südhauch sprengt die Riegel
Max Reger, "Ostern" 1902

Ein Müller mahlte Tag und Nacht
Max Reger, "Zwiesprach" 1904, Op76,23, 1v(med).pf
from *Schlichte Weisen, Band 2*

Ein Reiter muß haben ein Rößlein, zu traben
Max Reger, "Reiterlied" 1907, Op76,34, 1v(med).pf
from *Schlichte Weisen, Band 3*

Es blüht ein Blümlein rosenrot
Max Reger, "Es blüht ein Blümlein rosenrot" 1904, Op76,20, 1v(med).pf
from *Schlichte Weisen, Band 2*

Es haben die liebjungen Mädchen die blauen Husaren so gern
Max Reger, "Vorbeimarsch" 1904, Op76,30, 1v(med).pf
from *Schlichte Weisen, Band 2*

Es waren mal zwei Mäuschen ganz allein zu Haus
Max Reger, "Zwei Mäuschen" 1909-10, Op76,48, 1v(med).pf
from *Schlichte Weisen, Band 5, "Aus der Kinderwelt"*

Es zog ein Jäger in den Wald, halli, halli!
Max Reger, "Der verliebte Jäger" 1903-04, Op76,13, 1v(med).pf
from *Schlichte Weisen, Band 1*

Holde Nacht wie still bist du, wie still!
Hugo Kaun, "Holde Nacht, wie still bist du" 1908pub, Op80,3

Ich geh' auf stillen Auen
Max Reger, "Das Wölklein" 1907, Op76,33, 1v(med).pf
from *Schlichte Weisen, Band 3*

Leise tritt der Mond heraus, schlafe, Kindchen, schlafe
Max Reger, "Schlaf ein" 1909-10, Op76,47, 1v(med).pf
from *Schlichte Weisen, Band 5, "Aus der Kinderwelt"*

Liegt ein Dorf im Abendleuchten
Max Reger, "Dämmer" 1903, Op75,4

Lutschemund, Lutschemund, treib's nur nicht gar zu bunt
Max Reger, "Lutschemäulchen" 1909-10, Op76,45, 1v(med).pf
from *Schlichte Weisen, Band 5, "Aus der Kinderwelt"*

Maria sitzt am Rosenhag und wiegt ihr Jesuskind
Max Reger, "Mariä Wiegenlied" 1911-12, Op76,52, 1v(med).pf
from *Schlichte Weisen, Band 6, "Neun Kinderlieder"*

Nebelgrau die weite Welt, Wolken tief und schwer
Max Reger, "Unterwegs" 1902, Op68,2, 1v(med).pf

O du, der ich erblühte, die mich erquickte Tag um Tag
Max Reger, "Mädchenlied" 1907, Op104,6

So ein rechter Soldat fürcht' nicht Kugel und Streit
Max Reger, "Soldatenlied" 1909-10, Op76,46, 1v(med).pf
from *Schlichte Weisen, Band 5, "Aus der Kinderwelt"*

Sturm, wie lieb ich dich, wilden Gesellen
Max Reger, "Präludium" 1902-03, Op70,1

Tragt, blaue Träume, mich ins Land zurück
Max Reger, "Tragt, blaue Träume" 1901

Vor meinem Fenster schläft die Nacht
Max Reger, "Notturno" 1905, Op88,1, 1v(med).pf

Wenn dich die tiefe Sehnsucht rührt
Max Reger, "Vor dem Sterben" 1901, Op62,7, 1v(med).pf

Wer hätte gedacht, daß die Rosen so schnell verwehen!
Gustav Lewin, "Lied der Frau" 1910pub

Wie ist die Nacht voll holder Heimlichkeiten!
Max Reger, "Das Dorf" 1906, Op97,1

Dorothea Böttcher von Schwerin: see "D. B. Schwerin"

Grete Boettcher
Du altes schlafbefang'nes Nest
Wilhelm Kienzl, "Das alte Nest" 1926, Op106,3

Adolf Böttger (1815-1870)
Ich hör' ein Vöglein locken
Felix Mendelssohn, "Ich hör' ein Vöglein" 1841, Nachlass
Hans Pfitzner, "Ich hör' ein Vöglein locken" 1888/89, Op2,5

Christian Heinrich Boie (1744-1806)
Grabet in die junge Rinde, Schäfer
Johann Holzer, "Der verschwiegene Schäfer" 1779pub

Max Bolliger (1929-)
Kehre zurück zur Arbeit, an den Tisch zum schweren Handwerk
Gottfried von Einem, "Kehre zurück" 1983?, Op73,11
from *Tag- und Nachtlieder*

Walter Bollmann

Die Erde ist dunkler und satter in den Farben
Gottfried von Einem, "Die Erde ist dunkler" 1958, Op25,4

Ein jeder leide, auf daß er glücklich werde
Gottfried von Einem, "Ein jeder leide" 1958, Op25,5
Einem lists both Bollmann and Karola Boysen as the authors.

Leise schwindest du hinter Baum und ferner Wolke
Gottfried von Einem, "Leise schwindest du" 1958, Op25,1

Weit aus den Wäldern drängen die Tiere
Gottfried von Einem, "Weit aus den Wäldern" 1954-56, Op19,7

H. Bone

Im tiefen Thale, bei heissem Mittag
Max Bruch, "Im tiefen Thale" 1862, Op15,3

Lausche, lausche! War's ein Säuseln aus der Höh'?
Max Bruch, "Lausche, lausche!" 1862, Op15,1

Über die Bäume möcht' ich mich schwingen
Max Bruch, "Gott!" 1862, Op15,2

Hermann Bonn (Hermann Bonnus) (1504-1548)

Jesus Christus, wahrer Gottes-Sohn
Carl Loewe, "Jesus Christus, wahrer Gottes-Sohn" 1863, Op132,9, 4v
Text may have been edited by Loewe to some extent

Wolfgang Borchert (1921-1947)

Die Apfelblüten tun sich langsam zu beim Abendvers
Gottfried von Einem, "Auf dem Nachhauseweg 1945" 1954-56, Op19,5

Weil nun die Nacht kommt bleib' ich bei dir
Gottfried von Einem, "Liebeslied" 1954-56, Op19,3

Gertrud Emily Borngräber: see "Gerda von Robertus"

Friedrich Bouterwek (1766-1828)

Hüll in deinen Schattenmantel
Johann Rudolf Zumsteeg, "An die Dämmerung" 1805pub
from *Kleine Balladen und Lieder, siebtes Heft*

Wirklich, wirklich bist du schon verschwunden
Johann Rudolf Zumsteeg, "Ergebung" 1802pub
from *Kleine Balladen und Lieder, viertes Heft*

Ludwig Bowitsch (1818-1881)

Und sitz' ich in der Schenke beim vollen Glase Wein
Friedrich Silcher, "Entschuldigung" 4v

Karola Boysen

Du, gib Ruh', ohne dich, ohne dich ertrage ich das Leben nicht
Gottfried von Einem, "Du, gib Ruh'" 1958, Op25,2

Ein jeder leide, auf daß er glücklich werde
Gottfried von Einem, "Ein jeder leide" 1958, Op25,5
Einem lists both Boysen and Walter Bollmann as the authors.

Weh im Herzen, tiefe Schwerzen der Liebe quälen mich
Gottfried von Einem, "Weh im Herzen" 1958, Op25,3

Thelyma Nelly Helene Branco: see "Dilia Helena"

Maximilian Brantl (1881-1951)
Aus schimmernden Zweigen langen und neigen
Max Reger, "Abendgang" 1909, Op111a,3, sop.alt.pf

Ferdinand Braun
Das Körnlein springt, der Vogel singt, der Frühling ist gekommen
Robert Schumann, "Frühlingslied" 1850-1, Op125,1
from *Fünf heitere Gesänge*
Frederic Louis Ritter, "Frühlingslied" 1867pub, Op3,3
from *Kinder-Lieder*
Arno Kleffel, "Frühlingslied" Op14,4

Käthe Braun-Prager (1888-1967)
Streu' ich Zucker auf die Speise
Ernst Pepping, "Köchin in der Fremde" 1949pub
from *Haus- und Trostbuch* (4)

Richard Braungart (1872-1963)
Du brachtest mir deiner Seele Trank
Max Reger, "Du brachtest mir deiner Seele Trank" 1903, Op75,17, 1v(low).pf

Du ewigkalter Himmel, ich schreie auf zu dir
Max Reger, "Gebet" 1901, Op62,8, 1v(med).pf

Kleine Tränen seh' ich zittern
Max Reger, "Tränen" 1902-03, Op70,15

Nun kommt die Nacht gegangen
Max Reger, "Nun kommt die Nacht gegangen (Wiegenlied)" 1903

Nun ruhst du sanft in meinem Arm
Max Reger, "Abendfrieden" 1906

O wie greulich, wie abscheulich ist der Winter, o Not!
Max Reger, "Schlecht' Wetter" 1903-04, Op76,7, 1v(med).pf
from *Schlichte Weisen, Band 1*

Schweigend geht die junge Frau an dem Arm des greisen Gatten
Max Reger, "Ein Paar" 1901, Op55,9, 1v(med).pf

Was tragen wir unsere Leiden in diesen Glanz hinein?
Max Reger, "Mensch und Natur" 1901, Op62,4

Wenn die Buben recht böse sind
Max Reger, "Warte nur!" 1903-04, Op76,10, 1v(med).pf
from *Schlichte Weisen, Band 1*

Karl Johann Ritter Braun von Braunthal (1802-1866)
Immortelle! bring' mein "gute Nacht" ihr hin
Louis Spohr, "Gruss" 1843, WoO110

Pulse, höret auf zu schlagen
Louis Spohr, "An Sie am Klavier" 1848, Op138

Bertolt Brecht (1898-1956)
Aber auch ich auf dem letzten Boot
Hanns Eisler, "Die Landschaft des Exils" 1943
Als ich dich gebar, schrien deine Brüder schon um Suppe
Hanns Eisler, "Als ich dich gebar"
from *Vier Wiegenlieder für Arbeitermütter*
Als ich dich in meinem Leib trug
Hanns Eisler, "Als ich dich in meinem Leib trug"
from *Vier Wiegenlieder für Arbeitermütter*
Als ich nachher von dir ging
Paul Dessau, "Als ich nachher von dir ging" 1951
from *Vier Liebeslieder*
Am See, tief zwischen Tann und Silberpappel
Hanns Eisler, "Im Blumengarten" 1955
An der weißgetünchten Wand steht der schwarze Koffer mit den Manuskripten
Hanns Eisler, "Hotelzimmer 1942" 1942
from *Hollywood Liederbuch*
An einem frühen Morgen, lange vor Morgengraun
Hanns Eisler, "Der Kirschdieb" 1942
from *Hollywood Liederbuch*
An meiner Wand hängt ein japanisches Holzwerk
Hanns Eisler, "Die Maske des Bösen" 1942
Auf der Flucht vor meinen Landsleuten
Hanns Eisler, "Die Flucht" 1942
Auf die Erde voller kaltem Wind kamt ihr alle als ein nacktes Kind
Rudolf Wagner-Régeny, "Von der Freundlichkeit der Welt" 1953pub
from *Lieder auf Worte von Bertolt Brecht*
Rudolf Wagner-Régeny, "Von der Freundlichkeit der Welt und Gegenlied" 1953pub
from *Lieder auf Worte von Bertolt Brecht*
Hanns Eisler, "Von der Freundlichkeit der Welt" 1954
Da ich die Bücher, nach der Grenze hetzend
Hanns Eisler, "Auf der Flucht" 1942
Da war der Lehrer Huber, der war für den Krieg
Hanns Eisler, "Das Lied vom kriegerischen Lehrer" 1950
from *Neue Kinderlieder*
Das ist nun alles und 's ist nicht genug
Hanns Eisler, "Spruch" 1942
Daß er verrekke, ist mein letzter Wille
Hanns Eisler, "Epitaph auf einen in der Flandernschlacht Gefallenen" 1942
Der Herr ist aufs Feld gangen
Hanns Eisler, "Die haltbare Graugans" 1955
Der Schnee beginnt zu treiben
Hanns Eisler, "Winterspruch" 1942
Die Burschen, eh sie ihre Mädchen legen
Hanns Eisler, "Wie der Wind weht" 1955

Die Häuser sollen nicht brennen
Paul Dessau, "Bitten der Kinder"
from *Herrnburger Bericht*

Die Liebste gab mir einen Zweig
Paul Dessau, "Die Liebste gab mir einen Zweig" 1951
from *Vier Liebeslieder*

Die Schlechten fürchten deine Klaue
Hanns Eisler, "Motto: Auf einen chinesischen Theewurzellöwen" 1961

Die Stadt ist nach den Engeln genannt
Hanns Eisler, "Elegie II" 1942
from *Fünf Elegien*

Die Vaterstadt, wie find ich sie doch?
Hanns Eisler, "Die Heimkehr" 1943
from *Hollywood Liederbuch*
Eduard Steuermann, "Die Rückkehr" 1945, 1v(low).pf
from *Brecht-Lieder*

Diese Stadt hat mich belehrt
Hanns Eisler, "Elegie IV" 1942
from *Fünf Elegien*

Du Färberssohn vom Lech, im Klukkerspiele dich messend mit mir
Hanns Eisler, "Panzerschlacht" 1942

Du kleiner Kasten, den ich flüchtend trug
Hanns Eisler, "An den kleinen Radioapparat" 1942
from *Hollywood Liederbuch*

Ein Ruder liegt auf dem Dach
Hanns Eisler, "Zufluchtsstätte" 1939

Eine Pappel steht am Karlsplatz
Hanns Eisler, "Die Pappel vom Karlsplatz" 1950
from *Neue Kinderlieder*

Es war einmal ein Adler, der hatte viele Tadler
Paul Dessau, "Der Adler" 1973
from *Tierverse*

Es war einmal ein Elefant, der hatte keinen Verstand
Paul Dessau, "Der Elefant" 1968pub
from *Tierverse*

Es war einmal ein Igel, der fiel in einen Tiegel
Paul Dessau, "Der Rabe" 1973
from *Tierverse*

Es war einmal ein Kind, das wollte sich nicht waschen
Paul Dessau, "Vom Kind, das sich nicht waschen wollte" 195-?
from *Fünf Kinderlieder*

Es war einmal ein Mann, der fing das Trinken an
Paul Dessau, "Kleines Lied" 1965

Es war einmal ein Pferd, das war nicht sehr viel wert
Paul Dessau, "Das Pferd" 1973
from *Tierverse*

Es war einmal ein Rabe, ein schlauer alter Knabe
Paul Dessau, "Der Rabe" 1973
from *Tierverse*

Es war einmal ein Schwein, das hatte nur ein Bein
Paul Dessau, "Das Schwein" 1968pub
from *Tierverse*

Es war einmal eine Kellerassel, die geriet in ein, ein Schlamassel
Paul Dessau, "Die Kellerassel" 1973
from *Tierverse*

Fischreiche Wässer, schönbäumige Wälder
Hanns Eisler, "Frühling" 1942

Friede auf unserer Erde! Friede auf unserem Feld!
Hanns Eisler, "Friedenslied" 1950
from *Neue Kinderlieder*

General, dein Tank ist ein starker Wagen
Paul Dessau, "General, dein Tank ist ein starker Wagen" 1973

Herr Bäkker, Herr Bäkker, das Brot ist verbakken
Paul Dessau, "Der Gottseibeiuns" 195-?
from *Fünf Kinderlieder*

Herrlich, was im schönsten Feuer nicht zur kalten Asche kehrt!
Hanns Eisler, "Ardens sed virens" 1954

Heute, Ostersonntag früh, ging ein plötzlicher Schneesturm über die Insel
Hanns Eisler, "Ostersonntag" 1942

Höchstes Glück ist doch, zu spenden
Rudolf Wagner-Régeny, "Vom Glück des Gebens" 1953pub
from *Lieder auf Worte von Bertolt Brecht*

Ich hab dich ausgetragen, und das war schon Kampf genug
Hanns Eisler, "Ich hab dich ausgetragen"
from *Vier Wiegenlieder für Arbeitermütter*

Ich zog meine Fuhre trotz meiner Schwäche
Hanns Eisler, "O Falladah, die du hangest!" 1932, 1v.insts

Ihr, die ihr auftauchen werdet aus der Flut
Hanns Eisler, "Elegie II: An die Überlebenden" 1945pub
Hanns Eisler, "An die Nachgeborenen II" 195-?

Ihr, die ihr überlebtet in gestorbenen Städten
Paul Dessau, "An meine Landsleute" 1965

Im Hofe steht ein Pflaumenbaum
Hanns Eisler, "Der Pflaumenbaum" 1937
Paul Dessau, "Der Pflaumenbaum" 195-?
from *Fünf Kinderlieder*
Hanns Eisler, "Der Pflaumenbaum" 1960

In dem grünen Kuddelmuddel sitzt ein Aas mit einer Buddel
Kurt Schwaen, "Über den Schnapsgenuß" 1954

In den finsteren Zeiten, wird da noch gesungen werden?
Hanns Eisler, "Spruch 1939" 1939

In den Hügeln wird Gold gefunden
Hanns Eisler, "Elegie V" 1942
from *Fünf Elegien*

In den Weiden am Sund ruft in diesen Frühlingsnächten oft das Käuzlein
Hanns Eisler, "In den Weiden" 1942
Eduard Steuermann, "Der Totenvogel" 1945, 1v(low).pf
from *Brecht-Lieder*

In die Städte kam ich zu der Zeit der Unordnung
Hanns Eisler, "Elegie I" 1937
Hanns Eisler, "An die Nachgeborenen I" 195-?

In diesem Lande und in dieser Zeit
Hanns Eisler, "Über den Selbstmord" 1942
from *Hollywood Liederbuch*

In Erwägung unser Schwäche machtet ihr Gesetze
Hanns Eisler, "Resolution" 1934?

In Nürnberg machten sie ein Gesetz, darüber weinte manches Weib
Hanns Eisler, "Ballade von der «Judenhure» Marie Sanders" 1935

Jeden Morgen, mein Brot zu verdienen, geh ich zum Markt
Hanns Eisler, "Elegie III" 1942
from *Fünf Elegien*

Keiner plagt sich gerne, doch wir wissen
Paul Dessau, "Aufbaulied der FDJ" 1950, 1v.orch

Laßt euch nicht verführen, es gibt keine Wiederkehr
Rudolf Wagner-Régeny, "Gegen Verführung" 1953pub
from *Lieder auf Worte von Bertolt Brecht*

Mein Bruder war ein Flieger, eines Tags bekam er eine Kart
Paul Dessau, "Mein Bruder war ein Flieger" 1954?
from *Fünf Kinderlieder*

Mein junger Sohn fragt mich: Soll ich Mathematik lernen?
Hanns Eisler, "Der Sohn II" 1942

Mein Sohn, ich hab dir die Stiefel und diese braune Hemd geschenkt
Paul Dessau, "Lied einer deutschen Mutter" 1943

Mein Sohn, was immer auch aus dir werde
Hanns Eisler, "Mein Sohn, was immer auch aus dir werde"
from *Vier Wiegenlieder für Arbeitermütter*

Mutter Beimlein hat ein Holzbein
Hanns Eisler, "Mutter Beimlein" 1935, 1v.insts
from *Kinderlieder*

Oh, schattige Kühle! Einer dunklen Tanne Geruch
Hanns Eisler, "Speisekammer 1942" 1942

Oh Sprengen des Gartens, das Grün zu ermutigen
Hanns Eisler, "Vom Sprengen des Gartens" 1943
from *Hollywood Liederbuch*

Schießgewehr schießt, und das Spießmesser spießt
Hanns Eisler, "Ballade vom Soldaten" 1928, 1v.insts

Schlage keinen Nagel in die Wand
Hanns Eisler, "Über die Dauer des Exils I" 1939
Eduard Steuermann, "Gedanken über die Dauer des Exils" 1945, 1v(low).pf
from *Brecht-Lieder*

Sieben Rosen hat der Strauch, sechs gehör'n dem Wind
Paul Dessau, "Sieben Rosen hat der Strauch" 1951
from *Vier Liebeslieder*

Sieh den Nagel in der Wand
Hanns Eisler, "Über die Dauer des Exils II" 1939

Singt noch ein Lied und denkt euch nur
Paul Dessau, "Kleines Bettellied" 195-?
from *Fünf Kinderlieder*
Hanns Eisler, "Bettellied" 1934
from *Kinderlieder*

Über die vier Städte kreisen die Jagdflieger der Verteidigung
Hanns Eisler, "Die letzte Elegie" 1942

Und es sind die finstern Zeiten in der fremden Stadt
Hanns Eisler, "Und es sind die finstern Zeiten" 1954

Und es waren mächtge Zaren einst im weiten Russenreich
Paul Dessau, "Zukunftslied" 1950?

Und ich werde nicht mehr sehen das Land, aus dem ich gekommen bin
Hanns Eisler, "Und ich werde nicht mehr sehen" 1942-51

Und sie kamen in ihren Hemden von braunem Schirting daher
Hanns Eisler, "Die Ballade vom Baum und den Ästen" 1933

Und weil der Mensch ein Mensch ist
Hanns Eisler, "Das Einheitsfrontlied" 1948, 1v.insts

Unter den grünen Pfefferbäumen
Hanns Eisler, "Elegie I" 1942
from *Fünf Elegien*

Vorwärts und nicht vergessen, worin unsre Stärke besteht
Hanns Eisler, "Solidaritätslied" 1932, 1v.insts

Was meine Mutter mir sagte, das kann wohl wahr nicht sein
Rudolf Wagner-Régeny, "Lied der verderbten Unschuld beim Wäschefalten" 1953pub
from *Lieder auf Worte von Bertolt Brecht*

Wenn du mich lustig machst, lustig machst
Paul Dessau, "Lied einer Liebenden" 1951
from *Vier Liebeslieder*

Wenn sie nachts lag und dachte und ihr Sohn auf der grimmigen See
Hanns Eisler, "Der Sohn I" 1942

Wie viel besser fuhren wir in der Räuberzeit
Rudolf Wagner-Régeny, "Räuberlied" 1953pub
from *Lieder auf Worte von Bertolt Brecht*

Wir liegen allesamt im Kattegat
Hanns Eisler, "Gedenktafel für 4000 Soldaten, die im Krieg gegen Norwegen versenkt wurden" 1942

Wir waren miteinander nicht befreundet
Kurt Schwaen, "Liebeslied aus einer schlechten Zeit" 1954

Wirklich, ich lebe in finsteren Zeiten
Hanns Eisler, "Elegie 1939" 1939

Wirklicher Fortschritt ist nicht
Paul Dessau, "Spruch" 1973

Wohin zieht ihr? Freilich, freilich wo ihr immer hinzieht
Kurt Schwaen, "Wohin zieht ihr?" 1954

Christiane von Breden: see "Ada Christen"

Heinrich Karl Breidenstein (1796-1876)

Was schimmert dort auf dem Berge so schön
Emilie Zumsteeg, "Die Kapelle" 1819pub, Op4,1

Clemens Maria Wenzeslaus Brentano (1778-1842)

Als mir dein Lied erklang
Richard Strauss, "Als mir dein Lied erklang" 1918, Op68,4

An dem Feuer saß das Kind Amor
Richard Strauss, "Amor" 1918, Op68,5

Durch den Wald mit raschen Schritten
Louise Reichardt, "Durch den Wald" 1826pub

Einen kenn ich, wir lieben ihn nicht
Ernst Pepping, "Der Feind" 1949pub
from *Haus- und Trostbuch* (36)

Einsamkeit, du stummer Bronnen
Felix Wolfes, "Nachklänge Beethovenscher Musik" 1952, 1v(med).pf

Es sang vor langen Jahren wohl auch die Nachtigall!
Louise Reichardt, "Der Spinnerin Nachtlied" 1811pub, 1v.guitar
Fanny Hensel, "Altes Lied" 1837
Franz Krause, "Der Spinnerin Lied" 1972?pub, Op51,ii,4
from *Gedichte aus alter Zeit 2*

Heilige Nacht! Heilige Nacht! Sterngeschlossner Himmelsfriede!
Richard Strauss, "An die Nacht" 1918, Op68,1

Hör', es klagt die Flöte wieder und die kühlen Brunnen rauschen
Louise Reichardt, "Duettino" 1819pub, 2v.pf
Johannes Brahms, "Abendständchen" 1859, Op42,1, saatbb
Robert Gund, "Abendständchen" 1904, Op34,5
Ernest Vietor, "Abendständchen" 1937-38, Op16,7
Louis Ferdinand, "Abendständchen" 1955pub

Ich habe allem Leben mit jedem Abendrot
Ernst Pepping, "Ich habe allem Leben" 1949pub
from *Haus- und Trostbuch* (42)

Ich wollt' ein Sträußlein binden
Louise Reichardt, "Für die Laute componiert" 1811pub
Richard Strauss, "Ich wollt ein Sträußlein binden" 1918, Op68,2

Komm heraus, komm heraus, o du schöne, schöne Braut
Armin Knab, "Brautgesang" 1920
Parody by Brentano of a poem in *Des Knaben Wunderhorn*
from *Wunderhorn-Lieder* (3)

Nach Sevilla, nach Sevilla, wo die hohen Prachtgebäude
Louise Reichardt, "Nach Sevilla" 1811pub

O kühler Wald, wo rauschest du, in dem mein Liebchen geht?
Heinrich Marschner, "O kühler Wald" 184-?pub, Op132,2
Johannes Brahms, "O kühler Wald" 1877, Op72,3

Säusle, liebe Myrthe! Wie still ists in der Welt
Richard Strauss, "Säusle, liebe Myrthe" 1918, Op68,3

Singet leise, leise, leise, singt ein flüsternd Wiegenlied
Emil Mattiesen, "Wiegenlied" 1900pub, Op7,1
from *Vier heitere Lieder*

Was reif in diesen Zeilen steht
Ernst Pepping, "Was reif in diesen Zeilen steht" 1949pub
from *Haus- und Trostbuch* (1)
Franz Krause, "Was reif in diesen Zeilen steht" 1972?pub, Op51,ii,3
from *Gedichte aus alter Zeit 2*

Wenn es stürmt auf den Wogen
Richard Strauss, "Lied der Frauen" 1918, Op68,6

Fritz Brentano (1840-1914)
Leise, leise weht ihr Lüfte, denn mein Kind, es geht zur Ruh
Max Reger, "Leise, leise weht ihr Lüfte" 1906, Op97,2

Ch. von Breuning
Auf der weiten Welt ist es schlecht bestellt
Ferdinand Ries, "Wiegenlied" 1835pub, Op180,2

Stephan von Breuning (1774-1827)
Der Hoffnung letzter Schimmer sinkt dahin
Ludwig van Beethoven, "Als die Geliebte sich trennen wollte" 1806, WoO132

Otto von Briesen
Regenwetter ziehen trübe, und der Himmel scheint mir grau
Carl Loewe, "Letzter Seufzer" 184-?

Karl Gustav von Brinckmann: see "Selmar"

Paul Brockhaus (1879-1965)
Es klingt von den Sternen, es singt aus den Fernen
Hugo Distler, "Dankbare Stunde" 1967pub, alt.pf
from *Drei Lieder für tiefe Frauenstimme und Klavier*

Ob noch die alte Geige singt? Fern rauscht das Meer
Hugo Distler, "Erinnerung" 1967pub, alt.pf
from *Drei Lieder für tiefe Frauenstimme und Klavier*

Vom fernen Klang der Uhren abgemessen
Hugo Distler, "Gleichklang" 1967pub, alt.pf
from *Drei Lieder für tiefe Frauenstimme und Klavier*

Franz, Ritter von Bruchmann (1798-1867)

Ich will von Atreus Söhnen, von Kadmus will ich singen!
Franz Schubert, "An die Leyer" 1822-23, D737
after Anakreon

Im Mondenschein' wall' ich auf und ab
Franz Schubert, "Schwestergruss" 1822, D762

In des Sees Wogenspiele
Franz Schubert, "Am See" 1822?, D746

Sonnenstrahlen durch die Tannen
Franz Schubert, "Im Haine" 1822?, D738

Wer wagt's, wer wagt's, wer wagt's, wer will mir die Leier zerbrechen
Franz Schubert, "Der zürnende Barde" 1823, D785

Pauline Brumm

Von der zarten Kinder Händen nimm der Kronen Krone hin!
Carl Loewe, "Brautlied" 185-?

Friederike Brun (Brion) (1765-1835)

Ich denke dein, wenn sich im Blüthenregen der Frühling malt
Carl Friedrich Zelter, "Ich denke dein" 1794
Emilie Zumsteeg, "Ich denke Dein!" 1817pub
from *Neun Lieder* (9)

O selig wer liebt. Ihm tönet der Wald
Johann Friedrich Reichardt, "O selig wer liebt" 1800pub
from *Lieder aus dem Liederspiel, Lieb' und Treue* (6)

Schlaf, Kindlein, schlafe sanft und süß
Johann Abraham Peter Schulz, "Wiegenlied (im Mai zu singen)" 1795pub

Süßes Bild, schwebst mir vor mit leisem Sehnen!
Carl Friedrich Zelter, "Abendphantasie" 1794?

Anton Graf von Brunykowski (fl.1836)

Ich will vor deiner Thüre stehn', bis ich, mein Liebchen, dich gesehn'
Friedrich Kücken, "Maurisches Ständchen"

Georg Karl Immanuel Buddeus (1739-1814)

Helle Silberglöcklein klingen aus der Luft vom Meer
Robert Schumann, "Die Meerfee" 1850-1, Op125,3
from *Fünf heitere Gesänge*

Johann Friedrich Christian Budy (1809-1856)

Deutschlands Adler liegt gebunden, an der Ostsee, an dem Belt
Carl Loewe, "Deutsche Flotte" 1848

Franz Büchler (1904-)

Die Krähen rudern schwer im Blut, das aus dem Hals des Winters fließt
Wolfgang Rihm, "Frühling" 1968-69, Op1,10

Samuel Gottlob Bürde (1753-1831)

Alles, was Odem hat, lobe den Herrn!
Carl Loewe, "Lobgesang" before 1829

Elise (Marie Christine Elisabeth Hahn) Bürger (1769-1833)

Goldene Sonne wie hehr sinkst du im röthenden Glanz
Emilie Zumsteeg, "Der Abend" 1817pub
from *Neun Lieder* (2)

Gottfried August Bürger (1747-1794)

Bist untreu, Wilhelm, oder tot, wie lange willst du säumen?
Friedrich Ludwig Kunzen, "Lenore, ein musikalisches Gemälde" 1788-93?

Der Winter hat mit kalter Hand die Pappel abgelaubt
Johann Abraham Peter Schulz, "Winterlied" 1782-90pub

Du, mein Heil, mein Leben, meine Seele!
Peter Cornelius, "Die Entfernten" 1859

Es blüht ein Blümchen irgendwo
Ludwig van Beethoven, "Das Blümchen Wunderhold" 1805pub, Op52,8

Hast du nicht Liebe zugemessen
Ludwig van Beethoven, "Seufzer eines Ungeliebten" 1794-95, WoO118,1

Herr Bachus ist ein braver Mann
J. J. Grünwald, "Herr Bachus" 1785pub

Ich habe was Liebes, das hab ich zu lieb
Johann Rudolf Zumsteeg, "An die Menschengesichter" 1803pub
from *Kleine Balladen und Lieder, fünftes Heft*

Ich rühme mir mein Dörfchen hier
Franz Schubert, "Das Dörfchen" 1817, D641, 2t2b.pf
Franz Schubert, "Das Dörfchen" 1817, D598, 2t2b

Im Garten des Pfarrers von Taubenhain
Johann Rudolf Zumsteeg, "Des Pfarrers Tochter von Taubenhain" 1796?

Knapp', sattle mir mein Dänenroß
Johann Rudolf Zumsteeg, "Die Entführung" 1793

Lebewohl, du Mann der Lust und Schmerzen
Ludwig van Beethoven, "Mollys Abschied" 1805pub, Op52,5

Lenore fuhr um's Morgenrot
Maria Therese Paradis, "Lenore" 1789
Václav Jan Tomášek, "Lenore" 1806?pub
Johann Friedrich Reichardt, "Lenore" (set in English), 1806?pub
Franz Liszt, "Lenore" 1860, declamation.pf
Johann André, "Lenore (4 versions)" 1775-91

Mädel, schau mir ins Gesicht! Schelmenauge blinzle nicht!
Emilian G. von Jacquin, "Liebeszauber"
Johann Holzer, "Liebeszauber" 1779pub
Johann Abraham Peter Schulz, "Liebeszauber" 1782-90pub
Carl Maria von Weber, "Liebeszauber" 1807, Op13,3, 1v.guit(pf)

Meine Liebe, lange wie die Taube
Peter Cornelius, "Liebe ohne Heimat" 1859

Mir tut's so weh im Herzen! Ich bin so matt, so krank!
Josef Antonín Štěpán, "Schwanenlied" 1778-79pub

O wie öde, sonder Freudenschall
Hans Pfitzner, "Trauerstille" 1916, Op26,4

Schön Suschen kannt' ich lange Zeit
Hans Pfitzner, "Schön Suschen" 1907, Op22,3

Seht mir doch mein schönes Kind
Richard Strauss, "Muttertänderlei" 1899, Op43,2

Trallirum larum höre mich! Trallirum larum leier!
Johann Abraham Peter Schulz, "Ständchen" 1782-90pub

Wann die goldne Frühe, neu geboren
Hans Pfitzner, "Auf die Morgenröte" 1931, Op41,1
After Petrarca, "Quand' io veggio dal ciel scender l'Aurora"
from *Drei Sonette für eine Männerstimme und Klavier*

Wenn, o Mädchen, wenn dein Blut (see also "Wüßt' ich,...")[2]
Hans Pfitzner, "Gegenliebe" 1907, Op22,4

Wie selig, wer sein Liebchen hat
Josef Antonín Štěpán, "Lust am Liebchen" 1778-79pub

Wollt ihr wissen, holde Bienen
Hans Pfitzner, "An die Bienen" 1907, Op22,5

Wonnelohn getreuer Huldigungen
Peter Cornelius, "Verlust (Auf Mollys Tod)" (2 versions) 1859

Wüsst ich, dass du mich lieb (see also "Wenn, o Mädchen...")
Joseph Haydn, "Gegenliebe" 1781/84, XXVIa Nr.16
Ludwig van Beethoven, "Gegenliebe" 1794-95, WoO118,2

Karl Bulcke (1875-1936)

Da droben am Berge, ei, seht doch 'mal an!
Karol Szymanowski, "Einsiedel" 1910, Op22,1

Heinrich Alfred Bulthaupt (1849-1905)

Nun ist ein jeder Nerv in mir und jede Ader voll von dir
Franz von Holstein, "Geständnis" 1880, Op44,3

Wie sich Nebelzüge drängend zu Wolken verdichten
Franz von Holstein, "Im Sturm" 1880, Op43,5

Rudolf Bunge (1836-1907)

Kühl und stille ist die Nacht
Franz Abt, "Serenade" 1873pub, Op296,2

Christian Karl Ernst Wilhelm Buri (1758-1820)

Als noch in jener alten Zeit
Johann Rudolf Zumsteeg, "Hexenballade" 1805pub
from *Kleine Balladen und Lieder, siebtes Heft*

Drei Rosen hielt ich in Händen
Louis Spohr, "Klagelied von den drei Rosen" 1816, Op41,4

Schwand nicht mit Pfeilesschnelle
Johann Rudolf Zumsteeg, "Zeitgesang" 1805pub
from *Kleine Balladen und Lieder, siebtes Heft*

[2]Bürger published several versions of this poem. Only the final quatrain ("Gegengunst erhöhet Gunst") remains fairly constant.

Robert Burns (1759-1796)
Dem rothen Röslein gleicht mein Lieb'
Robert Schumann, "Dem rothen Röslein gleicht mein Lieb'" 1840, Op27,2
translated by Wilhelm Gerhard

Der Sommer ist so schön
Robert Franz, "Der Sommer ist so schön" 1844pub, Op3,5

Die finstre Nacht bricht schnell herein, der Sturmwind heult
Adolf Jensen, "Lebe wohl, mein Ayr!" 1875pub, Op49,7
from *7 Lieder von Robert Burns*

Die süsse Dirn' von Inverness wird nun und nimmer wieder froh
Robert Franz, "Die süsse Dirn' von Inverness" 1845pub, Op4,2
Adolf Jensen, "Die süsse Dirn von Inverness" 1875pub, Op49,4
from *7 Lieder von Robert Burns*

Du hast mich verlassen Jamie!
Robert Franz, "Du hast mich verlassen Jamie!" 1845pub, Op4,6

Durch irr' ich Länder noch so fern
Robert Franz, "Mein Hochland-Kind" 1845pub, Op4,1

Einen schlimmen Weg ging gestern ich
Robert Franz, "Ihr Auge" 1843pub, Op1,1
Adolf Jensen, "Einen schlimmen Weg ging gestern ich" 1875pub, Op49,3
from *7 Lieder von Robert Burns*

Früh mit der Lerche-Sang wandert ich weit
Robert Franz, "Liebliche Maid" 1845pub, Op4,3

Hoch zu Pferd! Stahl auf zartem Leibe
Robert Schumann, "Hauptmann's Weib" 1840, Op25,19
translated by Wilhelm Gerhard
from *Liederkreis*

Ich bin gekommen in's Niederland, o weh, o weh, o weh!
Robert Schumann, "Die Hochländer-Wittwe" 1840, Op25,10
translated by Wilhelm Gerhard
from *Liederkreis*

Ich hab' mein Weib allein, und theil' es, traun, mit Niemand
Robert Schumann, "Niemand" 1840, Op25,22
translated by Wilhelm Gerhard
from *Liederkreis*

Ich schau' über Forth, hinüber nach Nord
Robert Schumann, "Im Westen" 1840, Op25,23
translated by Wilhelm Gerhard
from *Liederkreis*

Ihr Hügel dort am schönen Doon
Robert Franz, "Ihr Hügel dort am schönen Doon" 1845pub, Op4,4

John Anderson, mein Lieb!
Robert Schumann, "John Anderson" 1849, Op67,5, satb
Robert Schumann, "John Anderson" 1849, Op145,4, satb
Adolf Jensen, "John Anderson, mein Lieb!" 1875pub, Op49,5
from *7 Lieder von Robert Burns*

Mein Herz ist betrübt, ich sag' es nicht
Robert Schumann, "Jemand" 1840, Op25,4
translated by Wilhelm Gerhard
from *Liederkreis*

Mein Herz ist im Hochland, mein Herz ist nicht hier!
Robert Schumann, "Hochländers Abschied" 1840, Op25,13
translated by Wilhelm Gerhard
from *Liederkreis*
Adolf Jensen, "Mein Herz ist im Hochland" 1869-73, Op49,1
from *7 Lieder von Robert Burns*
Robert Franz, "Mein Herz ist im Hochland" 1870?pub, Op31,6
Alexander Fesca, "Mein Herz ist im Hochland" 1882pub, Op21,1

Mein Herz ist schwer, Gott sei es geklagt!
Robert Franz, "Für Einen" 1843pub, Op1,8
Adolf Jensen, "Für Einen!" 1875pub, Op49,2
from *7 Lieder von Robert Burns*

Mein Lieb, das ist ein Röslein roth
George Henschel, "Mein Lieb, das ist ein Röslein roth" 187-?, Op12,2

Mein Lieb ist eine rothe Ros'
Robert Franz, "Mein Lieb ist eine rothe Ros'" 1870?pub, Op31,3

Mich zieht es nach dem Dörfchen hin
Robert Schumann, "Mich zieht es nach dem Dörfchen hin" 1846, Op55,3, satb

Nicht Damen tönt von hohem Rang
Robert Schumann, "Das Hochlandmädchen" 1846, Op55,1, satb

Nun holt mir eine Kanne Wein
Robert Franz, "Nun holt mir eine Kanne Wein" 1843pub, Op1,4

Nun, wer klopft an meine Thür?
Carl Loewe, "Findlay" 1836
translated by Ferdinand Freiligrath

O Bänkelsänger Willie, du ziehst zum Jahrmarkt aus
Robert Schumann, "Bänkelsänger Willie" 1849, Op146,2, satb

O, säh' ich auf der Haide dort
Felix Mendelssohn, "Volkslied" 1842, Op63,5, 2sop.pf
Robert Franz, "O säh' ich auf der Haide dort" 1843pub, Op1,5
Adolf Jensen, "O, säh ich auf der Haide dort" 1875pub, Op49,6
from *7 Lieder von Robert Burns*

Schlafe, süsser kleiner Donald
Robert Schumann, "Hochländisches Wiegenlied" 1840, Op25,14
translated by Wilhelm Gerhard
from *Liederkreis*

Schönster Bursch', den je ich traf
Robert Schumann, "Hochlandbursch" 1846, Op55,5, satb(soli)satb(ch)

So trieb sie mich denn grausam fort
Robert Franz, "So weit von hier" 1870?pub, Op22,6

Sonst kam mein Johnnie zur Stadt vom Land
Robert Schumann, "Der Rekrut" 1849, Op75,4, satb

Traurig schau ich von der Klippe auf die Flut
Clara Schumann, "Am Strande" 1841
translated by Wilhelm Gerhard

Wachst du noch, Liebchen, Gruss und Kuss!
Robert Schumann, "Liebhabers Ständchen" 1840, Op34,2, sop.ten.pf

Wär' auch mein Lager jener Moor
Robert Franz, "Montgomery-Gretchen" 1845pub, Op4,5

Was pocht mein Herz so sehr?
Robert Franz, "Was pocht mein Herz so sehr?" 1860?, Op9,1

Wer ist vor meiner Kammerthür?
Robert Schumann, "Unter'm Fenster" 1840, Op34,3, sop.ten.pf

Wer lenkt nicht gern den heitern Blick
Robert Schumann, "Die alte gute Zeit" 1846, Op55,4, satb

Wie du mit gift'gem Stachel fast
Robert Schumann, "Zahnweh" 1846, Op55,2, satb

Wie kann ich froh und munter sein
Robert Schumann, "Weit, weit" 1840, Op25,20
translated by Wilhelm Gerhard
from *Liederkreis*

Wollt' er nur fragen, wollt' er nur fragen?
Karl Goldmark, "Wollt' er nur fragen" 187-?, Op21,3, 1v(low).pf
Carl Bohm, "Wollt' er nur fragen" 1887cop, Op326,20
translated from "Jamie, come try me."

Wilhelm Busch (1832-1908)
Das glaube mir, so sagte er
Othmar Schoeck, "Dilemma" 1907, Op13,3

Es flog einmal ein munt'res Fliegel zu einem vollen Honigtiegel
Erich Zeisl, "Der Unvorsichtige" 1936pub

Es sitzt ein Vogel auf dem Leim
Ernest Vietor, "Es sitzt ein Vogel auf dem Leim" 1939-40, Op17,6

Es stand vor eines Hauses Tor ein Esel mit gespitztem Ohr
Ernst Toch, "Der Esel" 1928pub, Op41,9
Erich Zeisl, "Der Weise" 1935pub

Rotkehlchen auf dem Zweige hupft
Felix Wolfes, "Rotkehlchen" 1964

Carl Busse (1872-1918)
Abendschwärmer zogen um die Linden
Hans Pfitzner, "Michaelskirchplatz" 1905, Op19,2

Bleiche Blüte, Blüte der Liebe, leuchte über dem Laubendach
Richard Strauss, "Weisser Jasmin" 1895, Op31,3
Franz Mittler, "Weisser Jasmin" 1911pub

Ein blauer Sommer glanz- und glutenschwer
Richard Strauss, "Blauer Sommer" 1896, Op31,1

Entfalte des Kelches Pracht, hörst du die lockenden Töne?
Hugo Kaun, "Königin der Nacht" 1898?pub, Op25,3

Es gibt ein stilles Königreich
Alban Berg, "Das stille Königreich" 1908

Hell jubeln die Geigen mit Kling und mit Klang
Alexander Zemlinsky, "Kirchweih" 1901?, Op10,6
from *Ehetanzlied und andere Gesänge*

Ich raun' dir am Bette in schlafloser Nacht
Hans Pfitzner, "Stimme der Sehnsucht" 1905, Op19,1

Mädel, halt die Rökke fest, wenn die Winde blasen!
Max Reger, "Der Sausewind" 1907, Op104,5

Mit den Gänsen, weissen Gänsen, zog ich oft dem Teiche zu
Hugo Kaun, "Mit den Gänsen" 1906?pub, Op68,6

Nun hoch den Kopf und den Thränenfluss
Hugo Kaun, "Ermunterung" 1898?pub, Op25,6

Rebhahnruf und Glokkenlaut, ich und du im Heidekraut
Franz Mittler, "Ich und du" 1911pub

Schönheit, die du im Mädchen blühst
Joseph Marx, "Schönheit" 1905, ten.pf

Sum, sum, der Sandmann geht, ach wie dunkel, ach wie spät
Max Reger, "Schlafliedchen" 1903, Op75,14, 1v(med).pf

Über den Bergen, weit zu wandern
Alban Berg, "Über den Bergen" 1905
Ernest Vietor, "Über den Bergen" 1907?, Op4,2

Und wärst du mein Weib und wärst du mein Lieb
Richard Strauss, "Wenn..." 1895, Op31,2

Vor der Tür, im Sonnenscheine
Hans Pfitzner, "Gretel" 1901, Op11,5

Wenn die Linde blüht, sind die jungen, jungen Gänschen da
Max Reger, "Wenn die Linde blüht" 1903-04, Op76,4, 1v(med).pf
from *Schlichte Weisen, Band 1*
Franz Mittler, "Polnisches Volkslied" 1911pub

Wo der Weiser steht an der Straß'
Hans Pfitzner, "Leierkastenmann" 1904, Op15,1

"Christine Busta" (Christine Dimt) (1915-1987)

Bring mir keine Geschenke. Bring mir nur dich
Gottfried von Einem, "Das Geschenk" 1989pub, Op77,3
from *Inmitten aller Vergänglichkeit* (3)

Dasitzendir gegenüber am Tisch
Gottfried von Einem, "Stilles Wiedersehen" 1989pub, Op77,5
from *Inmitten aller Vergänglichkeit* (5)

Die Erde hat nicht Erde genug, dich in mir zu verschütten
Gottfried von Einem, "Abbitte" 1989pub, Op77,7
from *Inmitten aller Vergänglichkeit* (7)

Die Liebe nimmt an, nicht weg
Gottfried von Einem, "Die Liebe nimmt an" 1989pub, Op77,12
from *Inmitten aller Vergänglichkeit* (12)

Die Stachelfrucht hat sich geöffnet
Gottfried von Einem, "Eine Kastanie auf dem Schreibtisch" 1989pub, Op77,6
from *Inmitten aller Vergänglichkeit* (6)

Die Wege sind fremd und die Finsternis dicht
Gottfried von Einem, "Advent an der burgenländischen Grenze 1956" 1982pub
from *Carmina Gerusena* (2)

Du hast es mir vorgesagt, ich hab' es dir nachgesprochen
Gottfried von Einem, "Já tě miluji" 1989pub, Op77,10
from *Inmitten aller Vergänglichkeit* (10)

Du nicht mehr erhoffter Palmschatten
Gottfried von Einem, "Kleiner Oasenpsalm" 1989pub, Op77,4
from *Inmitten aller Vergänglichkeit* (4)

Einmal wichtig gewesen zu sein, für jemanden
Gottfried von Einem, "Inmitten aller Vergänglichkeit" 1989pub, Op77,8
from *Inmitten aller Vergänglichkeit* (8)

Hänsel, komm in den Wald, wir wollen die Hexen bannen
Gottfried von Einem, "Vaterunserwald" 1989pub, Op77,9
from *Inmitten aller Vergänglichkeit* (9)

Herzlaub, holder Honigmund summend unter lauter Sonnen!
Gottfried von Einem, "Unter einer Linde" 1982pub
from *Carmina Gerusena* (5)

Ich darf dir nicht folgen, ich rufe nur heimlich die Nacht
Gottfried von Einem, "Unter Abendsternen" 1982pub
from *Carmina Gerusena* (3)

Ich kann die Sonne nicht Sonne nennen
Gottfried von Einem, "Wiedergutmachung" 1989pub, Op77,11
from *Inmitten aller Vergänglichkeit* (11)

Ich weiß: sie werden über uns lächeln
Gottfried von Einem, "Unanfechtbar" 1989pub, Op77,1
from *Inmitten aller Vergänglichkeit* (1)

Lang schon umwanderst Du mich, du sagenhaft Treue
Gottfried von Einem, "Der unentrinnbaren Löwin" 1982, Op73,4
from *Tag- und Nachtlieder*

Mondlos hat sich der Teich verdunkelt
Gottfried von Einem, "Nocturno (in u-moll)" 1982, Op73,5
from *Tag- und Nachtlieder*

Ruh' dich aus. Mir brauchst Du das Gras zu schneiden
Gottfried von Einem, "Stille Anweisung" 1989pub, Op77,2
from *Inmitten aller Vergänglichkeit* (2)

Siehe, es scheidet der Tag, hingeht die Nacht mit den Sternen
Gottfried von Einem, "Bitte" 1982pub
from *Carmina Gerusena* (1)

Wer mir jetzt noch die Hand reicht
Gottfried von Einem, "Eine Treppe abwärts steigend" 1983, Op73,6
from *Tag- und Nachtlieder*

George Gordon Noel Lord Byron (1788-1824)

An Babylons Wassern gefangen da weinten wir
Carl Loewe, "An den Wassern zu Babel" 1823, Op4,2
translated from the English by Franz Theremin, 1820

An Babylons Wassern wir weinten und dachten
Ferruccio Busoni, "An Babylons Wassern" 1883, Op15,2

An mir vorüber ging ein Geist: das Bild der Ewigkeit
Carl Loewe, "Eliphas' Gesicht" 1826, Op14,2
translated by Franz Theremin

Auf Jordan's Ufer streifen wilde Horden
Carl Loewe, "Jordan's Ufer" 1825, Op13,4
translated from the English by Franz Theremin, 1820

Beweint die, so geweint in Babels Land!
Carl Loewe, "Weint um Israel!" 1824, Op5,4
translated from the English by Franz Theremin, 1820

Beweint sie, die an Babels Strömen klagen!
Karl Goldmark, "Weinet um sie" 1868pub, Op18,7, 1v(low).pf

Da die Heimath, o Vater, da Gott von der Tochter verlanget den Tod
Robert Schumann, "Die Tochter Jephta's" 1849, Op95,1, 1v.harp/pf
translated from Byron's Hebrew Melodies by Körner

Dein Leben schliesst, dein Ruhm begann
Carl Loewe, "Saul" 1826, Op14,4
translated from the English by Franz Theremin, 1820

Dein Tag ist aus, dein Ruhm fing an
Robert Schumann, "Dem Helden" 1849, Op95,3, 1v.harp/pf
translated from Byron's Hebrew Melodies by Körner

Der König thront; es sitzen die Grossen im Gemach
Carl Loewe, "Balsazar's Gesicht" Op13,2
translated by Franz Theremin

Du, deren Kunst die Todten ruft
Carl Loewe, "Saul und Samuel" 1826, Op14,1
translated by Franz Theremin

Du in der Schönheit strahlendem Schein Entschwundne
Carl Loewe, "Todtenklage" 1823, Op4,5
translated from the English by Franz Theremin, 1820

Es flüstert's der Himmel, es murrt es die Hölle: See Catharine Fanshawe

Es kam des Assyrers gewaltige Macht
Carl Loewe, "Sanherib's Niederlage" 1825, Op13,1
translated from the English by Franz Theremin, 1820

Es waren Ruhm und Weisheit mein
Carl Loewe, "Alles ist eitel, spricht der Prediger" 1823, Op4,4
translated from the English by Franz Theremin, 1820

Gazelle, die so wild und schnell auf Juda's Bergen springt
Carl Loewe, "Die wilde Gazelle" 1824, Op5,3
translated from the English by Franz Theremin, 1820

Ich sah die Thräne groß und schwer
Ferruccio Busoni, "Ich sah die Thräne" 1883, Op15,1

Ich sah die volle Thräne glühn in deines Auges Blau
Carl Loewe, "Thränen und Lächeln" 1823, Op4,6
translated from the English by Franz Theremin, 1820

Keine gleicht von allen Schönen
Hugo Wolf, "Keine gleicht von allen Schönen" 1886
translated by Otto Gildemeister
from *Vier Gedichte nach Heine u.a.*

Keine von der Erde Schönen
Felix Mendelssohn, "Keine von der Erde Schönen" 1833, Nachlass

Krieger und Feldherrn, ereilt mich der Tod
Carl Loewe, "Saul vor seiner letzten Schlacht" 1824, Op5,6
translated from the English by Franz Theremin, 1820

Lebe wohl! Lebe wohl! Lebe wohl! wenn je ein brünstig Flehen
Carl Loewe, "Lebewohl" 1817-18?
translated by Therese von Jacob (Talvj)

Mein Ende zeigt mir jeder Traum!
Josefine Lang, "Erinnerung" WoO

Mein Geist ist trüb'; den Ton der Saiten
Carl Loewe, "Mein Geist ist trüb'" 1824, Op5,5
translated from the English by Franz Theremin, 1820

Mein Herz ist schwer! Auf! von der Wand die Laute
Robert Schumann, "Aus den hebräischen Gesängen" 1840, Op25,15
translated by Körner
from *Liederkreis*

O Harfe, die des Gottgeliebten Hand
Carl Loewe, "Davids Harfe" 1826, Op14,3, 1v.pf or 4v
translated from the English by Franz Theremin, 1820

O höh're Welt, lehrt uns der Schmerz
Carl Loewe, "Die höh're Welt" 1825, Op13,3
translated from the English by Franz Theremin, 1820

O Mariamne, dieses Herz, das dein Herz bluten liess, muss bluten
Carl Loewe, "Herodes' Klage um Mariamne" 1823, Op4,1
translated from the English by Franz Theremin, 1820

O, weint um sie die einst an Babels Strand geweint
Friedrich Nietzsche, "O weint um sie" (fragment), 1865, NWV31
translated by Adolf Boettger

Schlafloser Augen Leuchte, trüber Stern
Felix Mendelssohn, "Schlafloser Augen Leuchte" 1834, Nachlass

Schlafloser Augen Sonne trüber Stern
Friedrich Nietzsche, "Sonne des Schlaflosen" (fragment), NWV30

Schlafloser Augen Sonne, zitternd Licht
Carl Loewe, "Die Sonne der Schlaflosen" 1825, Op13,6
translated from the English by Franz Theremin, 1820

Schlafloser Sonne, melanchol'scher Stern!
Robert Schumann, "An den Mond" 1849, Op95,2, 1v.harp/pf
translated from Byron's Hebrew Melodies by Körner

Sie geht in Schönheit und entzücket, wie Nachts ein heitres Sternenlicht
Carl Loewe, "Sie geht in Schönheit" 1824, Op5,1
translated from the English by Franz Theremin, 1820

Soll nach des Volkes und nach Gottes Willen, o Vater
Carl Loewe, "Jephtha's Tochter" 1824, Op5,2
translated from the English by Franz Theremin, 1820

Sonne der Schlummerlosen, bleicher Stern!
Hugo Wolf, "Sonne der Schlummerlosen" 1886
translated by Otto Gildemeister
from *Vier Gedichte nach Heine u.a.*

Unglücklich Herz, und konnt' es sein
Josefine Lang, "Auf ein zerbrochnes Herz von Carneol" WoO

Von dem Berg, wo zuletzt noch dein Tempel sich zeigt
Carl Loewe, "Jerusalem's Zerstörung durch Titus" 1826, Op14,5
translated from the English by Franz Theremin, 1820

Wär' ich wirklich so falsch, als der Irrthum es glaubt
Carl Loewe, "Wär' ich wirklich so falsch?" 1823, Op4,3
translated from the English by Franz Theremin, 1820

Wohin, o Seele, wirst du eilen
Carl Loewe, "Wohin, o Seele, wirst du eilen?" 1825, Op13,5
translated from the English by Franz Theremin, 1820

Agnes von Calatin

Getäuscht hat mich ein Schimmer
Josefine Lang, "Getäuscht hat mich ein Schimmer" WoO

Wie glänzt so hell dein Auge
Josefine Lang, "Wie glänzt so hell dein Auge" WoO

Pedro Calderón de la Barca y Henao (1600-1681)

Es war ein Bruder Liederlich
Richard Strauss, "Lied der Chispa" 1904, mez.mch.guit.2harp

Hör mein Liebesliedchen ziehn
Richard Strauss, "Liebesliedchen" 1904, 1v.guit.harp

Walter Calé (1881-1904)

Was sich in Zeiten je begeben
Joseph Marx, "Der Denker" 1908, bar.pf

Joachim Heinrich Campe (1746-1818)

Abend ist's, die Sonne ist verschwunden
Wolfgang Amadeus Mozart, "Abendempfindung" 1787, K523

Karl August Candidus (1817-1872)
Aetherische ferne Stimmen
Johannes Brahms, "Lerchengesang" 1877pub, Op70,2

Aus dem dunkeln Thor wallt kein Zug von Mücklein
Robert Schumann, "Husarenabzug" 1850-1, Op125,5
from *Fünf heitere Gesänge*

Den Wirbel schlag ich gar so stark
Johannes Brahms, "Tambourliedchen" 1877, Op69,5

Es kehrt die dunkle Schwalbe
Johannes Brahms, "Alte Liebe" 1876, Op72,1

Jäger, was jagst du die Häselein
Johannes Brahms, "Jägerlied" 1875, Op66,4, 2v.pf

Mir ist so weh ums Herz
Johannes Brahms, "Schwermut" 1871, Op58,5

O Frühlingsabenddämmerung!
Johannes Brahms, "Geheimnis" 1877, Op71,3

Sommerfäden hin und wieder
Johannes Brahms, "Sommerfäden" 1876, Op72,2

Louise Pauline Henriette Carl: see "Louise von Haber"

Hans Carossa (1878-1956)
Finsternisse fallen dichter auf Gebirg und Stadt und Tal
Gottfried von Einem, "Finsternisse fallen dichter" 1954-56, Op19,4

Und wie manche Nacht bin ich aufgewacht
Ernest Vietor, "Und wie manche Nacht" 1939-40, Op17,3
Gottfried von Einem, "Und wie manche Nacht" 1954-56, Op19,1

"Heinrich Carsten:" see Karl Heinrich Carsten Reinecke

Ignaz Franz Castelli (1780-1862)
Brüder! unser Erdenwallen ist ein ew'ges Steigen
Franz Schubert, "Trinklied" 1815, D148, ten.ttb.pf

Ein König einst gefangen sass
Carl Maria von Weber, "Romanze" 1816, J.195, 1v.guit

Herzliebe gute Mutter, o grolle nicht mit mir
Franz Schubert, "Das Echo" 1826-28?, D868
Erik Meyer-Helmund, "Das Echo" 1886-88

Ich bin von lockerem Schlage, geniess ohne Trübsinn die Welt
Franz Schubert, "Frohsinn" 1817, D520

Sohn der Ruhe
Carl Maria von Weber, "Schlummerlied" 1822, Op68,4, 4mv

Wenn ich die Blümlein schau', wünsch' ich mir eine Frau
Carl Maria von Weber, "Wunsch und Entsagung" 1817, Op66,4

from the Catholic Mass
O Lamm Gottes, welches der Welt Sünde trägt
Carl Loewe, "O Lamm Gottes" 1847, 4v

Adelbert von Chamisso (1781-1838)

An meinem Herzen, an meiner Brust
- Carl Loewe, "An meinem Herzen, an meiner Brust" 1836, Op60,7
  - from *Frauenliebe, Liederkranz von Chamisso*
- Robert Schumann, "An meinem Herzen, an meiner Brust" 1840, Op42,7
  - from *Frauenliebe und Leben*
- Louis Ferdinand, "Liebesglück" 1966pub

Auf hohen Burgeszinnen der alte König stand
- Robert Schumann, "Ungewitter" 1849, Op67,4, satb
- Friedrich Nietzsche, "Ungewitter" 1864, NWV25

Da Nachts wir uns küßten o Mädchen
- Robert Schumann, "Verrathene Liebe" 1840, Op40,5
- Peter Cornelius, "Verratene Liebe" 1847-48, 2sop.pf
- Nicolai Rimsky-Korsakov, "Verratene Liebe" (set in Russian), 1868, Op8,3

Den Säugling an der Brust
- Robert Schumann, "Die rothe Hanne" 1840, Op31,3
  - after Béranger

Denke, denke, mein Geliebter, meiner alten Lieb' und Treue
- Adolf Jensen, "Denke, denke, mein Geliebter" 1868, Op30,4
  - from *Dolorosa*
- Robert Franz, "Thränen" 1879, Op50,5
- Moritz Moszkowski, "Thränen (4)" 1888?pub, Op22,4

Der Gang war schwer, der Tag war rauh
- Friedrich Nietzsche, "Gern und gerner" 1864, NWV26

Die Mühle, die dreht ihre Flügel
- Johanna Kinkel, "Der Müllerinn Nachbar" Op10,6
- Johannes Brahms, "Die Müllerin" (fragment), 1853?, sop.pf
- Johannes Brahms, "Die Müllerin" 1859-60?, Op44,5, ssaa.(pf)
- Edvard Grieg, "Die Müllerin" 1861, Op2,1, alt.pf

Du arme, arme Kerze giebst fürder keinen Schein
- Friedrich Nietzsche, "Das Kind an die erloschene Kerze" 1864, NWV27

Du Ring an meinem Finger, mein goldenes Ringelein
- Carl Loewe, "Du Ring an meinem Finger" 1836, Op60,4
  - from *Frauenliebe, Liederkranz von Chamisso*
- Robert Schumann, "Du Ring an meinem Finger" 1840, Op42,4
  - from *Frauenliebe und Leben*

Er, der Herrlichste von allen
- Carl Loewe, "Er, der Herrlichste von allen" 1836, Op60,2
  - from *Frauenliebe, Liederkranz von Chamisso*
- Robert Schumann, "Er, der Herrlichste von Allen" 1840, Op42,2
  - from *Frauenliebe und Leben*

Es geht bei gedämpfter Trommel Klang
- Robert Schumann, "Der Soldat" 1840, Op40,3
  - after H. C. Anderson
- Friedrich Silcher, "Der Soldat"
  - after H. C. Anderson

Robert Franz, “Mitten ins Herzen” 1884, Op52,2
after H. C. Anderson

Es steh’n in unserm Garten der blühenden Rosen genug
Max Reger, “Scherz” 1892, Op8,4

Es steht ein altes Gemäuer hervor aus Waldesnacht
Richard Strauss, “Lass ruhn die Toten” 1877
from *Jugendlieder*

Es wallte so silbernen Scheines nicht immer mein lokkiges Haar
Johann Vesque von Püttlingen, “Die drei Sonnen” 1867

Hab’ oft im Kreise der Lieben in duftigem Grase geruht
Friedrich Silcher, “Frisch Gesungen” 4v
Nikolai Medtner, “Frisch gesungen!” 1925-26, Op46,7

Helft mir, ihr Schwestern, freundlich mich schmücken
Carl Loewe, “Helft mir, ihr Schwestern” 1836, Op60,5
from *Frauenliebe, Liederkranz von Chamisso*
Robert Schumann, “Helft mir, ihr Schwestern” 1840, Op42,5
from *Frauenliebe und Leben*

Ich hab’ ihn im Schlafe zu sehen gemeint
Adolf Jensen, “Ich hab’ ihn im Schlafe zu sehen gemeint” 1868, Op30,5
from *Dolorosa*

Ich habe, bevor der Morgen im Osten noch gegraut
Adolf Jensen, “Ich habe, bevor der Morgen” 1868, Op30,2
from *Dolorosa*
Robert Franz, “Thränen” 1884, Op52,4
Moritz Moszkowski, “Thränen (2)” 1888?pub, Op22,2

Ich kann’s nicht fassen, nicht glauben
Carl Loewe, “Ich kann’s nicht fassen, nicht glauben” 1836, Op60,3
from *Frauenliebe, Liederkranz von Chamisso*
Robert Schumann, “Ich kann’s nicht fassen, nicht glauben” 1840, Op42,3
from *Frauenliebe und Leben*

Ich träume als Kind mich zurücke
Johanna Kinkel, “Das Schloss Boncourt” 1838pub, Op9

Im Städtchen giebt es Jubels viel
Robert Schumann, “Der Spielmann” 1840, Op40,4
translated from H. C. Anderson

Mein Aug’ ist trüb, mein Mund ist stumm
Robert Schumann, “Was soll ich sagen!” 1840, Op27,3
Edvard Grieg, “Was soll ich sagen” 1861, Op2,4, alt.pf

Mit der Myrthe geschmückt und dem Brautgeschmeid
Robert Schumann, “Die Löwenbraut” 1840, Op31,1

Mutter, Mutter, meine Puppe hab’ ich in den Schlaf gewiegt
Richard Kursch, “Mutter, Mutter, meine Puppe” 1905pub, Op5,1

Nicht der Thau und nicht der Regen dringen, Mutter, in dein Grab
Robert Franz, “Thränen” 1846pub, Op6,6
Adolf Jensen, “Nicht der Thau und nicht der Regen” 1868, Op30,3
from *Dolorosa*

Moritz Moszkowski, "Thränen (3)" 1888?pub, Op22,3

Nun hast du mir den ersten Schmerz gethan
Carl Loewe, "Nun hast du mir den ersten Schmerz gethan" 1836
from *Frauenliebe, Liederkranz von Chamisso*
Robert Schumann, "Nun hast du mir den ersten Schmerz gethan" 1840, Op42,8
from *Frauenliebe und Leben*
Ernest Vietor, "Nun hast du mir den ersten Schmerz getan" 1936, Op14,8

's war einer, dem's zu Herzen ging
Johann Vesque von Püttlingen, "Der Zopf" 1844-51?, Op47,6
Hans Pfitzner, "Tragische Geschichte" 1907, Op22,2

's war mal 'ne Katzenkönigin, Ja, ja!
Carl Loewe, "Die Katzenkönigin" 1837, Op64,3

Schlief' die Mutter endlich ein
Robert Schumann, "Die Kartenlegerin" 1840, Op31,2
after Béranger

Seit ich ihn gesehen, glaub' ich blind zu sein
Franz Lachner, "Frauen-Liebe und Leben" 1831, Op82, sop.cl.pf
Carl Loewe, "Seit ich ihn gesehn" 1836, Op60,1
from *Frauenliebe, Liederkranz von Chamisso*
Robert Schumann, "Seit ich ihn gesehen" 1840, Op42,1
from *Frauenliebe und Leben*

Sie haben mich geheißen
Edvard Grieg, "Die Waise" 1863-64, Op4,1

Süsser Freund, du blickest mich verwundert an
Carl Loewe, "Süsser Freund, du blickest mich verwundert an" 1836, Op60,6
from *Frauenliebe, Liederkranz von Chamisso*
Robert Schumann, "Süsser Freund, du blickest" 1840, Op42,6
from *Frauenliebe und Leben*

Traum der eignen Tage, die nun ferne sind
Carl Loewe, "Traum der eignen Tage" 1836
from *Frauenliebe, Liederkranz von Chamisso*

Uns're Quelle kommt im Schatten duft'ger Linden an das Licht
Karl Goldmark, "Die Quelle" 1868pub, Op18,5, 1v(low).pf
Nikolai Medtner, "Die Quelle" 1925-26, Op46,6

Was ist's, o Vater, was ich verbrach?
Louis Spohr, "Thränen" 1842, WoO108
Adolf Jensen, "Was ist's, o Vater, was ich verbrach?" 1868, Op30,1
from *Dolorosa*
Robert Franz, "Thränen" 1879, Op51,2
Moritz Moszkowski, "Thränen (1)" 1888?pub, Op22,1

Wie so bleich ich geworden bin?
Adolf Jensen, "Wie so bleich ich geworden bin?" 1868, Op30,6
from *Dolorosa*
Moritz Moszkowski, "Thränen (5)" 1888?pub, Op22,5

Willkommen, du Gottes Sonne
Friedrich Curschmann, "Willkommen, du Gottes Sonne" 183-?, Op3,1

Wir wollten mit Kosen und Lieben
Edvard Grieg, "Morgentau" 1863-64, Op4,2

Wohl wandert' ich aus in trauriger Stund'
Hugo Wolf, "Auf der Wanderschaft" 1878

Wilhelmine (Helmine) Christiane von Chézy, née Klencke (1783-1856)
Ach, wie ist's möglich dann, daß ich dich lassen kann
Friedrich Silcher, "Ach, wie ist's möglich dann" 4v

Der Vollmond strahlt auf Bergeshöh'n
Charles Edward Ives, "Ballad from *Rosamunde*" 1895?

In tiefster Schlucht, in Waldesschoss
Carl Loewe, "Moosröslein" 1834, Op37,2, alt.pf

Johannes ging am hellen Bach
Carl Loewe, "St. Johannes und das Würmlein" 1843, Op35,1

Wenn auf dem höchsten Fels ich steh'
Franz Schubert, "Der Hirt auf dem Felsen" 1828, D965
First four verses (including this line) and last verse by Wilhelm Müller

"Ada Christen" (Christiane von Breden) (1844-1901)
Daß schon die Maienzeit vorüber
Arnold Schönberg, "Daß schon die Maienzeit vorüber" 189-?

Die Sonne sinkt. Jählings schwebt kühles Dämmern hin durch das Thal
Max Reger, "Abendlied (Adagio)" 1890/91

Hörst auch du die leisen Stimmen
Joseph Marx, "Christbaum" 1908

Sinnend stand ich bei dem Grabe Rabby Löv's, des jüdischen Weisen
Felix Weingartner, "Auf dem alten jüdischen Kirchhof (Prag)" 1893, Op18,1
from *Severa. Sechs ernste Lieder*

So gross, so still, so feierlich ragen die Bäume empor
Felix Weingartner, "Im Walde" 1894, Op19,6
from *Hilaria. Sechs heitere Lieder*

C. Christern
Warum soll ich denn wandern
Robert Schumann, "Ich wand're nicht" 1840, Op51,3

Hermann Claudius (1878-1980)
Das alte Wunder ward wieder wahr:
Karl Marx, "Der Star" 1936, Op26,2

Das Heimlicht zwischen dir und mich
Karl Marx, "Franziska" 1936, Op26,4

Daß zwei sich herzlich lieben
Karl Marx, "Daß zwei sich herzlich lieben" 1936, Op26,5

Der alte Turm und die Schwalben haben einander gern
Karl Marx, "Der alte Turm" 1937, Op29,4

Der Regen, der Regen, der langentbehrte Segen!
Karl Marx, "Hauslied bei Regen" 1936, Op26,13

Der Wind der weht. Alles vergeht im Winde
Karl Marx, "Mein Lied" 1937, Op29,1

Des Nordens Wunder ist der Winter
Karl Marx, "Dezembertag" 1937, Op29,7

Du liebe, liebe Sonne, bescheine mir
Karl Marx, "An die Sonne" 1936, Op26,11

Dunkel war der Zweig, den du mir brachtest
Karl Marx, "Auf ein trauriges Mädchen" 1936, Op26,10

Ein Menschlein ward geboren. Ein Schicksal nimmt den Lauf
Karl Marx, "Ein Menschlein" 1936, Op26,7

Es blinken in der Sonne die grünen Gräser sehr
Karl Marx, "Auf Brümmerhoff" 1937, Op29,5, 1v or 2v.pf

Es drängt sich auf den Beeten, und alles will Gestalt
Karl Marx, "Sommerbeet" 1937, Op29,3

Ich habe sie selber gezogen aus einem winzigen Kern
Karl Marx, "Der alte Gärtner" 1936, Op26,9

Ist das in dir der Mensch oder der Christ
Karl Marx, "Auf eine kranke Rose" 1937, Op29,2

Mann und Weib und Kind. Draußen weht der Wind
Karl Marx, "Ursame Weihnacht" 1936, Op26,6

Mund und Augen wissen ihre Pflicht
Paul Hindemith, "Mund und Augen wissen ihre Pflicht" 1925, Op45,ii,7, 2v.insts
from *Sing-und Spielmusiken für Liebhaber und Musikfreunde*

Sie wiegen schwankend sich in schwerem Schreiten
Karl Marx, "Kühe" 1936, Op26,1

Sonne über Ähren du kannst dich nicht erwehren
Karl Marx, "Ährenlied" 1936, Op26,12

Späte Rose, in dem hohen Glase
Karl Marx, "Späte Rose" 1936, Op26,3

Tage der Gnade brechen herein
Karl Marx, "Oktoberlied" 1937, Op29,6

Tagtäglich bietest du dich dar, so Mond um Mond, so Jahr um Jahr
Karl Marx, "Lied an meinen Tisch" 1937, Op29,9

Wie wandelnde Landschaft gehn über die Erde Gesichter der Menschen
Karl Marx, "Wie wandelnde Landschaft" 1936, Op26,14

Wir tragen alle den Tod im Leib und helfen ihn weitertragen
Karl Marx, "Großstadt-Abend" 1936, Op26,8

Zu den winterkahlen Zweigen
Karl Marx, "Im Januar" 1937, Op29,8

Matthias Claudius (1740-1815)

Ach, es ist so dunkel in des Todes Kammer
Anton Webern, "Der Tod" 1901-04
from *Acht frühe Lieder* (7)
Hanns Eisler, "Ach, es ist so dunkel..." 1922, Op2,2

Othmar Schoeck, "Der Tod" 1937, Op52,16
from *Wandsbecker Liederbuch*
Hermann Reutter, "Der Tod" 1947pub, Op60,2

Bekränzt mit Laub den lieben, vollen Becher
Ernst Pepping, "Rheinweinlied" 1949pub
from *Haus- und Trostbuch* (6)

Das heiss' ich rechte Augenweide
Othmar Schoeck, "Als er sein Weib und 's Kind schlafend fand" 1937, Op52,4
from *Wandsbecker Liederbuch*

Dass ich dich verloren habe
Franz Schubert, "Am Grabe Anselmo's" 1816, D504

Der Mensch lebt und bestehet
Othmar Schoeck, "Spruch" 1937, Op52,17
from *Wandsbecker Liederbuch*

Der Mond ist aufgegangen, die goldnen Sternlein prangen
Johann Friedrich Reichardt, "Abendlied"
Johann Abraham Peter Schulz, "Abendlied" 1782-90pub
Franz Schubert, "Abendlied" 1816, D499
Othmar Schoeck, "Abendlied" 1937, Op52,10
from *Wandsbecker Liederbuch*

Der Säemann säet den Samen, die Erd' erhält ihn
Johann Abraham Peter Schulz, "Beim Tode der Geliebten" 1782-90pub

Der Winter ist ein rechter Mann, kernfest und auf die Dauer
Christof Rheineck, "Ein Lied, hinterm Ofen zu singen" 1784
Othmar Schoeck, "Ein Lied, hinterm Ofen zu singen" 1937, Op52,9
from *Wandsbecker Liederbuch*

Die Liebe hemmet nichts
Othmar Schoeck, "Die Liebe" 1937, Op52,1
from *Wandsbecker Liederbuch*

Die Römer, die, vor vielen hundert Jahren
Othmar Schoeck, "Die Römer" 1937, Op52,12
from *Wandsbecker Liederbuch*

Du kleine grünumwachs'ne Quelle
Franz Schubert, "An eine Quelle" 1817, D530

Empfanget und genähret vom Weibe, wunderbar
Eduard Steuermann, "Der Mensch" 1931, bass.pf
from *Drei Lieder*
Othmar Schoeck, "Der Mensch" 1937, Op52,11
from *Wandsbecker Liederbuch*

Er liegt und schläft an meinem Herzen, mein guter Engel sang ihn ein
Johann Friedrich Reichardt, "Glück"
Franz Schubert, "An die Nachtigall" 1816, D497

Es war einmal 'ne Henne fein, die legte fleißig Eier
Chr. F. Daniel Schubart, "Die Henne" 1786pub

Friede sei um diesen Grabstein her! sanfter Friede Gottes!
Johann Rudolf Zumsteeg, "Am Grabe meines Vaters" 1803pub
from *Kleine Balladen und Lieder, fünftes Heft*
Franz Schubert, "Bei dem Grabe meines Vaters" 1816, D496

Füllt noch einmal die Gläser voll und stoßet herzlich an
Friedrich Silcher, "Auf's Wohl der Frauen" 4v

Heute will ich fröhlich, fröhlich sein, keine Weis' und keine Sitte hören
Franz Schubert, "Am ersten Maimorgen" 1816?, D344
Othmar Schoeck, "Der Frühling" 1937, Op52,6
from *Wandsbecker Liederbuch*
Hermann Reutter, "Der Frühling" 1947pub, Op60,3

Hier liegt der Müller Mayhon!
Ernst Pepping, "Grabschrift" 1949pub
from *Haus- und Trostbuch* (38)

Ich bin ein deutscher Jüngling
Maria Therese Paradis, "Vaterlandslied" 1784-86
from *Zwölf Lieder auf ihrer Reise in Musik gesetzt*

Ich bin vergnügt, im Siegeston verkünd' es mein Gedicht
Franz Schubert, "Lied" 1816, D362
Franz Schubert, "Lied (Zufriedenheit)" 1816, D501

Ich danke Gott und freue mich wie's Kind zur Weihnachtsgabe
Johann Abraham Peter Schulz, "Täglich zu singen" 1782-90pub
Johann Friedrich Reichardt, "Täglich zu singen"
Franz Schubert, "Täglich zu singen" 1817, D533

Ich sehe oft um Mitternacht, wenn ich mein Werk getan
Othmar Schoeck, "Die Sternseherin" 1937, Op52,7
from *Wandsbecker Liederbuch*
Ernst Pepping, "Die Sterne" 1949pub
from *Haus- und Trostbuch* (2)

Ich war erst sechszehn Sommer alt, unschuldig und nichts weiter
Josef Antonín Štěpán, "Phidile" 1778-79pub
Johann Rudolf Zumsteeg, "Phidile" 1805pub
from *Kleine Balladen und Lieder, siebtes Heft*
Franz Schubert, "Phidile" 1816, D500
Othmar Schoeck, "Phidile" 1937, Op52,2
from *Wandsbecker Liederbuch*

Im Anfang war's auf Erden nur finster, wüst und leer
Carl Loewe, "Im Anfang und jetzt" before 1829

Ist gar ein holder Knabe, er! als ob er's Bild der Liebe wär
Johann Abraham Peter Schulz, "Anselmuccio" 1782-90pub

Laßt mich! laßt mich! Ich will klagen
Franz Schubert, "Klage um Ali Bey" 1815, D140, ssa.pf
Franz Schubert, "Klage um Ali Bey" 1816?, D2:496A

Man weiß oft grade denn am meisten
Paul Hindemith, "Man weiß oft grade denn am meisten" 1927, Op43,2, ch
from *Lieder für Singkreise* (3)

O du Land des Wesens und der Wahrheit
Othmar Schoeck, "O du Land" 1954-55, Op70,12, 1v(med).orch
from *Nachhall*

's ist Krieg! 's ist Krieg! O Gottes Engel wehre
Othmar Schoeck, "Der Krieg" 1937, Op52,14
from *Wandsbecker Liederbuch*

Schlaf, holder Knabe, süss und mild!
Carl Loewe, "Die Mutter an der Wiege" 1840

Schön röthlich die Kartoffeln sind
Johann Rudolf Zumsteeg, "Kartoffellied" 1803pub, 3v
from *Kleine Balladen und Lieder, fünftes Heft*

Seht meine lieben Bäume an, wie sie so herrlich stehn
Franz Schubert, "Das Lied vom Reifen" 1817, D532

Sie haben mich dazu beschieden, so bring' ich's denn auch dar
Johann Adam Hiller, "Des alten, lahmen Invaliden Görgels Neujahrswunsch" 1790

Sie machte Frieden! Das ist mein Gedicht
Othmar Schoeck, "Auf den Tod einer Kaiserin" 1937, Op52,15
from *Wandsbecker Liederbuch*

So schlafe nun, du Kleine! Was weinest du?
Hanns Eisler, "So schlafe nun, du Kleine!" 1922, Op2,1
Othmar Schoeck, "Ein Wiegenlied, bei Mondschein zu singen" 1937, Op52,3
from *Wandsbecker Liederbuch*
Hermann Reutter, "Ein Wiegenlied, im Mondenschein zu singen" 1947pub, Op60,1

Tausend Blumen um mich her
Othmar Schoeck, "Die Natur" 1937, Op52,5
from *Wandsbecker Liederbuch*

Victoria! Victoria! der kleine weisse Zahn ist da
Carl Loewe, "Der Zahn"

Vorüber, ach vorüber, geh' wilder Knochenmann!
Franz Schubert, "Der Tod und das Mädchen" 1817, D531

Was meinst du, Kunz, wie groß die Sonne sei?
Paul Hindemith, "Was meinst du, Kunz" 1927, Op43,2, ch
from *Lieder für Singkreise* (4)

Weit von meinem Vaterlande
Johann Rudolf Zumsteeg, "Mohrenlied" 1803pub
from *Kleine Balladen und Lieder, fünftes Heft*
Othmar Schoeck, "Der Schwarze in der Zuckerplantage" 1937, Op52,13
from *Wandsbecker Liederbuch*

Wenn hier nun kahler Boden wär, wo itzt die Bäume stehn
Johann Abraham Peter Schulz, "Serenata, im Walde zu singen" 1782-90pub, ch.pf

Wenn jemand eine Reise thut
Ludwig van Beethoven, "Urians Reise um die Welt" 1792?, Op52,1

Wir Vögel singen nicht egal
Johann Rudolf Zumsteeg, "Kukuk" 1803pub
from *Kleine Balladen und Lieder, fünftes Heft*

Othmar Schoeck, "Kuckuck" 1937, Op52,8
from *Wandsbecker Liederbuch*

Wir ziehn nun unsern Zahn heraus
Johann Abraham Peter Schulz, "Ein Lied in die Haushaltung zu singen, wenn ein Wechselzahn soll ausgezogen werden" 1790pub

Collignon
In dunkler Nacht, wenn's Aug' noch wacht
Franz Abt, "In dunkler Nacht" Op144,4

Heinrich Josef, Edler von Collin (1771-1811)
Hinauf! hinauf! in Sprung und Lauf!
Franz Schubert, "Kaiser Maximilian auf der Martinswand in Tyrol. 1490." 1818?, D2:990A

Vom Meere trennt sich die Welle
Franz Schubert, "Leiden der Trennung" 1816, D509
after Metastasio

Matthäus Kasimir von Collin (1779-1824)
Heil'ge Nacht, du sinkest nieder!
Franz Schubert, "Nacht und Träume" 1822?, D827

Im trüben Licht verschwinden schon die Berge
Franz Schubert, "Der Zwerg" 1822, D771

Liebe ist ein süsses Licht
Franz Schubert, "Licht und Liebe (Nachtgesang)" 1822?, D352

Und nimmer schreibst du?
Franz Schubert, "Epistel: Musikalischer Schwank" 1822, D749

Wenn ich durch Wald und Fluren geh'
Franz Schubert, "Wehmuth" 1822, D772

Colly
Ebenes Paradefeld Kasper in der Mitte hält hoch auf seinem Gaul
Arnold Schönberg, "Jedem das Seine" 1901?
from *Brettl-Lieder*

Michael Georg Conrad (1846-1927)
Nicht unter schwarzer Erdenlast
Adolf Wallnöfer, "Die Flamme" 1911pub, Op98,1

Hermann Conradi (1862-1890)
Im Morgengrauen schritt ich fort
Arnold Schönberg, "Verlassen" 1903-05, Op6,4

Hugo Conrat
Brauner Bursche führt zum Tanze
Johannes Brahms, "Zigeunerlieder (5)" 1887/88, Op103,5, satb.pf or 1v.pf
translated from Hungarian

Brennessel steht an Weges Rand
Johannes Brahms, "Brennessel steht an Weges Rand" 1891, Op112,5, satb.pf or 1v.pf
translated from Hungarian
from *Vier Zigeunerlieder* (3)

He, Zigeuner, greife in die Saiten ein
Johannes Brahms, "Zigeunerlieder (1)" 1887/88, Op103,1, satb.pf or 1v.pf
translated from Hungarian

Himmel strahlt so helle und klar
Johannes Brahms, "Himmel strahlt so helle" 1891, Op112,3, satb.pf or 1v.pf
translated from Hungarian
from *Vier Zigeunerlieder* (1)

Hochgetürmte Rimaflut, wie bist du so trüb
Johannes Brahms, "Zigeunerlieder (2)" 1887/88, Op103,2, satb.pf or 1v.pf
translated from Hungarian

Horch, der Wind klagt in den Zweigen traurig sacht
Johannes Brahms, "Zigeunerlieder (8)" 1887/88, Op103,8, satb.pf or 1v.pf
translated from Hungarian

Kommt dir manchmal in den Sinn
Johannes Brahms, "Zigeunerlieder (7)" 1887/88, Op103,7, satb.pf or 1v.pf
translated from Hungarian

Liebe Schwalbe, kleine Schwalbe
Johannes Brahms, "Liebe Schwalbe, kleine Schwalbe" 1891, Op112,6, satb.pf or 1v.pf
Brahms editions say translated from Hungarian, but see also Gregorovius: Zemlinsky, Op6,1
from *Vier Zigeunerlieder* (4)

Lieber Gott, du weißt, wie oft bereut ich hab
Johannes Brahms, "Zigeunerlieder (4)" 1887/88, Op103,4, satb.pf or 1v.pf
translated from Hungarian

Mond verhüllt sein Angesicht
Johannes Brahms, "Zigeunerlieder (10)" 1887/88, Op103,10, satb.pf or 1v.pf
translated from Hungarian

Röslein dreie in der Reihe blühn so rot
Johannes Brahms, "Zigeunerlieder (6)" 1887/88, Op103,6, satb.pf or 1v.pf
translated from Hungarian

Rote Abendwolken ziehn am Firmament
Johannes Brahms, "Zigeunerlieder (11)" 1887/88, Op103,11, satb.pf or 1v.pf
translated from Hungarian

Rote Rosenknospen künden schon des Lenzes Triebe
Johannes Brahms, "Rote Rosenknospen künden" 1891, Op112,4, satb.pf or 1v.pf
translated from Hungarian
from *Vier Zigeunerlieder* (2)

Weit und breit schaut Niemand mich an
Johannes Brahms, "Zigeunerlieder (9)" 1887/88, Op103,9, satb.pf or 1v.pf
translated from Hungarian

Wißt ihr, wann mein Kindchen am allerschönsten ist?
Johannes Brahms, "Zigeunerlieder (3)" 1887/88, Op103,3, satb.pf or 1v.pf
translated from Hungarian

Karl Philipp Conz (1762-1827)

Es singt ein Vöglein "Witt,witt,witt. Komm mit, komm mit."
Louise Reichardt, "Das Mädchen am Ufer" 1826pub

Neu geschmückt lacht die Natur
Johann Rudolf Zumsteeg, "Frühlingslied eines Trauernden" 1805pub
from *Kleine Balladen und Lieder, siebtes Heft*

Franz Cordes

Hätt' ich nimmer Sie gesehn
Johann Rudolf Zumsteeg, "Macht der Sinne" 1802pub
from *Kleine Balladen und Lieder, viertes Heft*

(Carl August) Peter Cornelius (1824-1874)

Als du auf Erden, Herr, geweilt
Peter Cornelius, "Führe uns nicht in Versuchung" 1854-55, Op2,8
from *Vater unser. Neun geistliche Lieder*

An dem Seegestade düster steht der hohe Tannenbaum
Peter Cornelius, "Am See" 1848

An hellen Tagen, Herz, welch' ein Schlagen
Peter Cornelius, "Liebeslied" 1872, Op20,2, ssatb

Das einst ein Kind auf Erden war
Peter Cornelius, "Christkind" 1856-58, Op8,6
from *Weihnachtslieder* (6)

Das Knäblein nach acht Tagen
Peter Cornelius, "Simeon" 1856-58, Op8,4
from *Weihnachtslieder* (4)

Das sind goldne Himmelspfade
Peter Cornelius, "Zu uns komme dein Reich" 1854-55, Op2,3
from *Vater unser. Neun geistliche Lieder*

Das war vor hundert Jahren
Peter Cornelius, "Beethoven-Lied" 1870, Op10, satb

Das zarte Knäblein ward ein Mann
Peter Cornelius, "Christus der Kinderfreund" 1856-58, Op8,5
from *Weihnachtslieder* (5)

Dein Gedenken lebt in Liedern fort
Peter Cornelius, "Treue" 1854, Op3,5
from *Trauer und Trost*

Der Dichter singt dem Frühling, und Allem, was da lenzt
Eduard Lassen, "Der Sänger" Op67,1

Der du im Feld die Vöglein nährst
Peter Cornelius, "Unser täglich Brot gib uns heute" 1854-55, Op2,5
from *Vater unser. Neun geistliche Lieder*

Der Glükkes Fühle mir verlieh'n
Peter Cornelius, "Trost" 1854, Op3,6
from *Trauer und Trost*

Des lauten Tages wirre Klänge schweigen
Peter Cornelius, "Vater unser, der du bist im Himmel" 1854-55, Op2,1
from *Vater unser. Neun geistliche Lieder*

Die Blümlein auf der Heide
Peter Cornelius, "In der Ferne" 1865, Op15,3
from *An Bertha*

Die Hirten wachen nachts im Feld
Peter Cornelius, "Die Hirten" 1856, Op8,2a
from *Weihnachtslieder* (2a)

Die Nacht vergeht nach süßer Ruh
Peter Cornelius, "Am Morgen" 1856-59
from *Brautlieder* (4)

Die Sterne tönen ewig hohe Weisen
Peter Cornelius, "Geheiliget werde dein Name" 1854-55, Op2,2
from *Vater unser. Neun geistliche Lieder*

Drei Kön'ge wandern aus Morgenland
Peter Cornelius, "Die Könige" 1856, Op8,3a
from *Weihnachtslieder* (3a)
Peter Cornelius, "Die Könige" 1870, Op8,3b
from *Weihnachtslieder* (3b)

Du meiner Seele schönster Traum!
Eduard Lassen, "Du meiner Seele schönster Traum!" Op58,3

Durch die Glut, durch die Öde
Peter Cornelius, "Zug der Juden nach Babylon" 1872, Op20,1, satb

Ein grünes Spinnchen gaukelte
Peter Cornelius, "Denkst du an mich?" 1853, Op1,6

Es lebt ein Schwur in jeder deutschen Brust
Peter Cornelius, "Der deutsche Schwur" 1873, Op12,3, ttbb

Fahren wir froh im Nachen
Peter Cornelius, "Amor im Nachen" 1872, Op20,3, ssatb

Frisch auf in Windeseil
Peter Cornelius, "Reiterlied" 1873, Op17, ttbb

Halb Dämmerschein, halb Kerzenlicht
Peter Cornelius, "Dein Bildnis" 1865, Op15,4
from *An Bertha*

Heil und Freude ward mir verheißen
Peter Cornelius, "Jerusalem" 1872, Op13,3, satb
after Psalm 122

Heil'ge Liebe, flammend Herz
Peter Cornelius, "Erlöse uns vom Übel" 1854-55, Op2,9
from *Vater unser. Neun geistliche Lieder*

Hinaus in das Lustgeschmetter der Vögel von Busch und Baum!
Franz Abt, "Du weisst ja, wo!" 1873pub, Op211,2
Franz Ries, "Hinaus!" before 1891

Hirten wachen im Feld
Peter Cornelius, "Die Hirten" 1870, Op8,2b
from *Weihnachtslieder* (2b)

Ich ersehnt' ein Lied wie die Blume den Tau
Franz Mikorey, "Ich ersehnt' ein Lied"

Ich ging hinaus, um dich zu seh'n
Eugen d'Albert, "Ich ging hinaus" 1889pub, Op9,3

Ich sterbe den Tod des Verräters
Peter Cornelius, "Der Tod des Verräters" 1851, ten.bar.bass.pf

Ich wandle einsam, mein Weg ist lang
Peter Cornelius, "Trauer" 1854, Op3,1
from *Trauer und Trost*

Ich war ein Blatt an grünem Baum
Eugen d'Albert, "Ich war ein Blatt an grünem Baum" 1889pub, Op9,1

Im tiefsten Herzen glüht mir eine Wunde
Peter Cornelius, "Im tiefsten Herzen glüht mir eine Wunde" 1862

In deiner Nähe weil' ich noch
Eduard Lassen, "In deiner Nähe weil' ich noch" Op58,6

In Lust und Schmerzen, in Kampf und Ruh'
Peter Cornelius, "In Lust und Schmerzen" 1854, Op4,1

In meinem Herzen regte der Liebe Wunsch sich leis
Peter Cornelius, "Ein Myrtenreis" 1856-59
from *Brautlieder* (1)

Kehr' ich zum heimischen Rhein
Peter Cornelius, "Gedenken" 1856
from *Rheinische Lieder* (4)

Komm, wir wandeln zusammen im Mondschein
Peter Cornelius, "Komm, wir wandeln zusammen im Mondschein" 1854, Op4,2

Liebendes Wort, dich send' ich fort
Peter Cornelius, "Botschaft" 1856, Op5,1
from *Rheinische Lieder* (2)

Lilienblüthe! Mädchen schön und zart!
Eduard Lassen, "Lilienblüthe" Op58,5

Mein Freund ist mein, und ich bin sein!
Peter Cornelius, "Aus dem hohen Liede" 1856-59
from *Brautlieder* (5)

Mein Lied ist klein, braucht wenig Platz
Peter Cornelius, "Untreu" 1853, Op1,1

Mir klingt ein Ton so wunderbar in Herz und Sinnen immerdar
Peter Cornelius, "Ein Ton" 1854, Op3,3
from *Trauer und Trost*
Charles Edward Ives, "Ein Ton" 1895?

Mit hellem Sang und Harfenspiel möcht' ich die Welt durchreisen
Peter Cornelius, "In der Ferne" 1856
from *Rheinische Lieder* (1)

Möcht' im Walde mit dir geh'n
Peter Cornelius, "Möcht' im Walde mit dir geh'n" 1854, Op4,3

Nachts bin vom Traum schlaftrunken ich erwacht
Peter Cornelius, "Nachts" 1853, Op1,5

Nachts, wenn sich Sturmwind wild erhebt
Peter Cornelius, "Vergib uns unsre Schuld" 1854-55, Op2,6
from *Vater unser. Neun geistliche Lieder*

Nun laß mich träumen, laß mich schwärmen
Peter Cornelius, "Märchenwunder" 1856-59
from *Brautlieder* (6)

Nun lasse ganz der Seele Flug
Peter Cornelius, "Also auch wir vergeben unsern Schuldigern" 1854-55, Op2,7
from *Vater unser. Neun geistliche Lieder*

Nun, Liebster, geh', nun scheide!
Peter Cornelius, "Vorabend" 1856-59
from *Brautlieder* (3)

Nun wollen Knospen sich entfalten
Eduard Lassen, "Der Lenz" Op45,6

O Lust am Rheine, am heimischen Strande!
Peter Cornelius, "Am Rhein" 1856
from *Rheinische Lieder* (3)

O Welt, ich sag' dir gern Ade
Peter Cornelius, "Freund Hein" 1872, satb

Öffne mir die goldne Pforte
Peter Cornelius, "An den Traum" 1854, Op3,4
from *Trauer und Trost*

Pilger auf Erden, so raste am Ziele
Peter Cornelius, "Grablied" 1869, Op9,4, ttbb

Segne, Herz, den Freudentag
Peter Cornelius, "Dein Wille geschehe" 1854-55, Op2,4
from *Vater unser. Neun geistliche Lieder*

Stromflut dahin rauscht durch Babels Gefilde
Peter Cornelius, "An Babels Wasserflüssen" 1872, Op13,2, satb
after Psalm 137

Süß tönt Gesanges Hauch, wenn alles ruht
Peter Cornelius, "Der Liebe Lohn" 1856-59
from *Brautlieder* (2)

Tief im Gemüt mir Liebe glüht
Peter Cornelius, "Sei mein!" 1865, Op15,1
from *An Bertha*

Und sängen die Vögel dir laut meine Lieb'
Peter Cornelius, "Wie lieb ich dich hab'" 1865, Op15,2
from *An Bertha*

Vöglein fliegt dem Nestchen zu
Peter Cornelius, "Wiegenlied" 1853, Op1,3

Von der Wartburg Zinnen nieder
Franz Liszt, "Weimars Volkslied" 1857

Von stillem Ort, von kühler Statt
Peter Cornelius, "Angedenken" 1854, Op3,2
from *Trauer und Trost*

Warum verbirgst du vor mir dein Antlitz
Peter Cornelius, "Bußlied" 1872, Op13,1, satb
after Psalm 88

Weh, daß ich mußte schauen
Peter Cornelius, "Blaue Augen" 1872, satb

Wenn wir hinauszieh'n am Frühlingssonntag
Peter Cornelius, "Das Tanzlied" 1872, Op20,4, satb

Wer hat's doch durchschauet
Peter Cornelius, "Schmetterling" 1853, Op1,4

Wie schön geschmückt der festliche Raum!
Peter Cornelius, "Christbaum" 1856, Op8,1
from *Weihnachtslieder* (1)

Wieder möcht' ich dir begegnen
Franz Liszt, "Wieder möcht' ich dir begegnen" 1860
Leopold Damrosch, "Wieder möcht' ich dir begegnen" Op8,9
Eduard Lassen, "Wieder möcht' ich dir begegnen" Op58,1

Zu dem Duft, der da würzt die Lenzesluft
Peter Cornelius, "Veilchen" 1853, Op1,2

Zur Drossel sprach der Fink: "Komm mit, liebe Drossel"
Luise Adolpha Le Beau, "Ich habe die Blumen so gern" Op45,3, alt.vn.pf
Eugen d'Albert, "Zur Drossel sprach der Fink" 1889pub, Op9,4

Franz Karl Graf Coronini-Cronberg (1818-1910)
Die Fischerstochter sitzt am Strand
Franz Liszt, "Die Fischerstochter" 1871

Paul Nikolaus Cossmann (1869-1942)
Die Bäume wurden gelb, und wir wandelten zusammen im Walde
Hans Pfitzner, "Die Bäume wurden gelb" 1888/89, Op6,5, 1mv.pf

Ohn' Lieb' bist du durchs Leben kommen
Hans Pfitzner, "Widmung" 1888/89, Op6,4, 1mv.pf

Abraham Cowley (1618-1667)
Noch fand von Evens Töchterschaaren ich keine, die mir nicht gefiel
Franz Schubert, "Der Weiberfreund" 1815, D271
translated by J. F. Ratschky

Jacob Nicolaus de Jachelutta Craigher (1797-1855)
O Menschheit, o Leben, was soll's? o was soll's?
Franz Schubert, "Todtengräbers Heimwehe" 1825, D842

O sagt, ihr Lieben, mir einmal, welch Ding ist's, Licht genannt?
Franz Schubert, "Der blinde Knabe" 1825, D833

Wie braust durch die Wipfel der heulende Sturm!
Franz Schubert, "Die junge Nonne" 1824?, D828

Johann Andreas Cramer (1723-1788)
Der Herr ist Gott und keiner mehr, frohlockt ihm, alle Frommen
Carl Loewe, "Der Herr ist Gott" before 1829

Die Himmel rufen: jeder ehret die Grösse Gottes, seine Pracht
Carl Loewe, "Die Himmel rufen" before 1829

Johann Friedrich Freiherr von Cronegk (1731-1758)
Erbarm dich, Herr! mein schwaches Herz strebt oft nach
Johann Abraham Peter Schulz, "Um Besserung des Lebens" 1786pub

Herr, es gescheh dein Wille! Der Körper eilt zur Ruh
Johann Abraham Peter Schulz, "Abendandacht" 1786pub
Franz Jacob Freystädtler, "Abend-Gebet" 1795
from *Sechs Lieder der besten deutschen Dichter* (5)

Wilhelm Czermak
Aus dem finster'n Schooss der Nacht
Wilhelm Kienzl, "Klärung" 188-?, Op16,4
from *Süsses Verzichten* (4)

O, wie meine Lippen beben
Wilhelm Kienzl, "Eine And're!" 188-?, Op16,2
from *Süsses Verzichten* (2)

So gross, so rein, so hehr geklart
Wilhelm Kienzl, "Zum Abschiede" 188-?, Op16,5
from *Süsses Verzichten* (5)

Tief dunkle Nacht! Nur fahler Laternen Schimmer
Wilhelm Kienzl, "Nachtstück" 188-?, Op16,3
from *Süsses Verzichten* (3)

Viel Thränen flossen in herbem Weh
Wilhelm Kienzl, "Ein 'Ade!'" 188-?, Op18,4

Wie hast du dich in's Herz versenkt
Wilhelm Kienzl, "Erwachen" 188-?, Op16,1
from *Süsses Verzichten* (1)

Simon Dach (1605-1659)
Ännchen von Tharau ist, die mir gefällt
Friedrich Silcher, "Ännchen von Tharau"

Felix Dahn ("Ludwig Julius Sophus") (1843-1912)
Aber Epheu nenn' ich jene Mädchen
Richard Strauss, "Epheu" 1888, Op22,3
from *Mädchenblumen*

Ach Lieb, ich muss nun scheiden
Richard Strauss, "Ach Lieb, ich muss nun scheiden!" 1887-88, Op21,3

Ach weh mir unglückhäftem Mann
Richard Strauss, "Ach weh mir unglückhäftem Mann" 1887-88, Op21,4

All mein Gedanken, mein Herz und mein Sinn
Richard Strauss, "All mein Gedanken..." 1887-88, Op21,1
Max Reger, "All' mein Gedanken" 1903, Op75,9, 1v(med).pf

Das ist die sanfte, die heilige
Felix Weingartner, "Sonnenuntergang" 1910, Op51,2
from *Abendlieder*

Die Finken schlagen, der Lenz ist da
Eugen Hildach, "Lenz" 1894pub, Op19,5

Die Frauen sind oft fromm und still
Richard Strauss, "Die Frauen sind oft fromm und still" 1887-88, Op21,5

Du bist die Herrlichste von Allen
Erik Meyer-Helmund, "Du bist die Herrlichste!" 1886-88

Du meines Herzens Krönelein
Richard Strauss, "Du meines Herzens Krönelein" 1887-88, Op21,2
Max Reger, "Du meines Herzens Krönelein" 1903-04, Op76,1, 1v(med).pf
from *Schlichte Weisen, Band 1*

Erschlagen war mit dem halben Heer
George Henschel, "Jung Dieterich" 188-?, Op45

Kennst du die Blume, die märchenhafte
Richard Strauss, "Wasserrose" 1888, Op22,4
from *Mädchenblumen*

Kornblumen nenn' ich die Gestalten
Richard Strauss, "Kornblumen" 1888, Op22,1
from *Mädchenblumen*

Mohnblumen sind die runden
Richard Strauss, "Mohnblumen" 1888, Op22,2
from *Mädchenblumen*

Schlanke Fatme, hohe Palme, sprich!
Anton Rubinstein, "Fatme" 1881

Seit ganz mein Aug' ich durft' in deines tauchen
Max Reger, "Dein Auge" 1899, Op35,1, 1v(med).pf

Dante Alighieri (1265-1321)

Du, des Erbarmens Feind, grausamer Tod
Othmar Schoeck, "Du, des Erbarmens Feind" 1906, Op9,2
German translation of a sonnet from *Vita Nuova* by Richard Zoozmann

Mir ist wie einem, der im Schlafe schaut
Ernst Pepping, "Nachklang" 1949pub
translated by Karl Voßler
from *Haus- und Trostbuch* (21)

Heinrich Danz

Leis' in meines Kindleins Träume klinge, kleines Schlummerlied
Louis Ferdinand, "Wiegenlied" 1953pub

Georg Friedrich Daumer (1800-1875) (see also Daumer's translations under Hafis)

Ach, wende diesen Blick
Johannes Brahms, "Ach, wende diesen Blick" 1871, Op57,4

Alles, alles in den Wind sagst du mir, du Schmeichler
Johannes Brahms, "Neue Liebeslieder (11)" 1875, Op65,11, sop.pf (4-hands)

Am Donaustrande, da steht ein Haus
Johannes Brahms, "Liebeslieder (9)" 1869, Op52,9, satb.pf (4-hands)

Am Gesteine rauscht die Flut
Johannes Brahms, "Liebeslieder (2)" 1869, Op52,2, satb.pf (4-hands)

An jeder Hand die Finger hatt ich bedeckt mit Ringen
Johannes Brahms, "Neue Liebeslieder (3a&b)" 1875, Op65,3a&b, sop.pf (4-hands)

Die grüne Hopfenranke, sie schlängelt auf der Erde hin
Johannes Brahms, "Liebeslieder (5)" 1869, Op52,5, satb.pf (4-hands)

Die Schnur, die Perl an Perlen
Johannes Brahms, "Die Schnur, die Perl an Perlen" 1871, Op57,7

Ein dunkeler Schacht ist Liebe
Johannes Brahms, "Liebeslieder (16)" 1869, Op52,16, satb.pf (4-hands)

Ein kleiner, hübscher Vogel nahm den Flug zum Garten hin
Johannes Brahms, "Liebeslieder (6)" 1869, Op52,6, satb.pf (4-hands)

Eine gute, gute Nacht pflegst du mir zu sagen
Johannes Brahms, "Eine gute, gute Nacht" 1873, Op59,6

Es bebet das Gesträuche, gestreift hat es im Fluge ein Vögelein
Johannes Brahms, "Liebeslieder (18)" 1869, Op52,18, satb.pf (4-hands)

Es träumte mir, ich sei dir teuer
Johannes Brahms, "Es träumte mir" 1871, Op57,3

Finstere Schatten der Nacht
Johannes Brahms, "Neue Liebeslieder (2)" 1875, Op65,2, satb.pf (4-hands)

Flammenauge, dunkles Haar, Knabe wonnig und verwogen
Johannes Brahms, "Neue Liebeslieder (14)" 1875, Op65,14, satb.pf (4-hands)

Hier ob dem Eingang seid befestiget
Johannes Brahms, "Die Kränze" 1868, Op46,1

Holder, leichtbeschwingter Bote den die Liebe wandeln heißt
Bettina von Arnim, "Hafis" 1842?

Ich kose süß mit der und der
Johannes Brahms, "Neue Liebeslieder (10)" 1875, Op65,10, ten.pf (4-hands)

Ich sahe dich im Traume, ich sah dich in Thränen
August Bungert, "Ich sahe dich im Traume" 1889-91pub, Op11,3

Ich thät mich einst vermiethen zu Sankt Marie in den Himmel hinein
Felix Mottl, "Wiegenlied einer alten Magd" 1894?pub

Ihr schwarzen Augen, ihr dürft nur winken
Johannes Brahms, "Neue Liebeslieder (4)" 1875, Op65,4, bass.pf (4-hands)

In meiner Nächte Sehnen, so tief allein
Johannes Brahms, "In meiner Nächte Sehnen" 1871, Op57,5

Komm, falsche Dirne, laß dich küssen!
Frank van der Stucken, "Leidenschaft" 1904pub, Op34,1

Komm Mädchen an dein Fenster, komm wenn die Schatten düstern
George Henschel, "Zigeuner-Ständchen" 187-?, Op20

Mein liebes Herz, was ist dir, was ist dir?
Johannes Brahms, "Fragen" 1874, Op64,3, satb.pf

Nachtigall, sie singt so schön
Johannes Brahms, "Liebeslieder (15)" 1869, Op52,15, satb.pf (4-hands)

Nagen am Herzen fühl ich ein Gift mir
Johannes Brahms, "Neue Liebeslieder (9)" 1875, Op65,9, sop.pf (4-hands)

Nein, es ist nicht auszukommen mit den Leuten
Johannes Brahms, "Liebeslieder (11)" 1869, Op52,11, satb.pf (4-hands)

Nein, Geliebter, setze dich mir so nahe nicht!
Johannes Brahms, "Neue Liebeslieder (13)" 1875, Op65,13, sa.pf (4-hands)

Nicht mehr zu dir zu gehen
Johannes Brahms, "Nicht mehr zu dir zu gehen" 1864, Op32,2

Nicht wandle, mein Licht, dort außen im Flurbereich!
Johannes Brahms, "Liebeslieder (17)" 1869, Op52,17, ten.pf (4-hands)

Nun, ihr Musen, genug!
Johannes Brahms, "Neue Liebeslieder (15): Zum Schluß" 1875, Op65,15, satb.pf (4-hands)

O die Frauen, o die Frauen, wie sie Wonne, Wonne tauen
Johannes Brahms, "Liebeslieder (3a&b)" 1869, Op52,3a&b, tb.pf (4-hands)

O schöne Nacht! Am Himmel märchenhaft erglänzt der Mond
Johannes Brahms, "O schöne Nacht" 1877?, Op92,1, satb.pf

O wie sanft die Quelle sich durch die Wiese windet!
Johannes Brahms, "Liebeslieder (10)" 1869, Op52,10, satb.pf (4-hands)
Johannes Brahms, "O wie sanft!" 1908pub, WoO posth 26, 4fv

Rede, Mädchen, allzu liebes
Johannes Brahms, "Liebeslieder (1)" 1869, Op52,1, satb.pf (4-hands)

Rosen steckt mir an die Mutter
Johannes Brahms, "Neue Liebeslieder (6)" 1875, Op65,6, sop.pf (4-hands)

Sah dem edlen Bildnis in des Auges allzu süßen Wunderschein
Johannes Brahms, "Magyarisch" 1868, Op46,2

Schlosser auf, und mache Schlösser
Johannes Brahms, "Liebeslieder (12)" 1869, Op52,12, satb.pf (4-hands)

Schön war, das ich dir weihte
Johannes Brahms, "Schön war, das ich dir weihte" 1883/84?, Op95,7

Schwarzer Wald, dein Schatten ist so düster!
Johannes Brahms, "Neue Liebeslieder (12)" 1875, Op65,12, satb.pf (4-hands)

Sieh, wie ist die Welle klar
Johannes Brahms, "Liebeslieder (14)" 1869, Op52,14, tb.pf (4-hands)

Strahlt zuweilen auch ein mildes Licht
Johannes Brahms, "Strahlt zuweilen auch ein mildes Licht" 1871, Op57,6

Unbewegte laue Luft, tiefe Ruhe der Natur
Johannes Brahms, "Unbewegte laue Luft" 1871, Op57,8

Verzicht, o Herz, auf Rettung
Johannes Brahms, "Neue Liebeslieder (1)" 1875, Op65,1, satb.pf (4-hands)

Vögelein durchrauscht die Luft
Johannes Brahms, "Liebeslieder (13)" 1869, Op52,13, sa.pf (4-hands)

Vom Gebirge Well auf Well kommen Regengüsse
Johannes Brahms, "Neue Liebeslieder (7)" 1875, Op65,7, satb.pf (4-hands)

Von waldbekränzter Höhe
Johannes Brahms, "Von waldbekränzter Höhe" 1871, Op57,1

Wahre, wahre deinen Sohn, Nachbarin, vor Wehe
Johannes Brahms, "Neue Liebeslieder (5)" 1875, Op65,5, alt.pf (4-hands)

Weiche Gräser im Revier, schöne stille Plätzchen
Johannes Brahms, "Neue Liebeslieder (8)" 1875, Op65,8, satb.pf (4-hands)

Wenn du nur zuweilen lächelst
Johannes Brahms, "Wenn du nur zuweilen lächelst" 1871, Op57,2

Wenn so lind dein Auge mir und so lieblich schauet
Johannes Brahms, "Liebeslieder (8)" 1869, Op52,8, satb.pf (4-hands)

Wie des Abends schöne Röte
Johannes Brahms, "Liebeslieder (4)" 1869, Op52,4, sa.pf (4-hands)

Wir wandelten, wir zwei zusammen
Johannes Brahms, "Wir wandelten" 1884?, Op96,2

Wohl schön bewandt war es vor ehe mit meinem Leben
Johannes Brahms, "Liebeslieder (7)" 1869, Op52,7, sop.pf (4-hands)

Jakob Julius David (1859-1906)

Ich hab' kein Haus, ich hab' kein Nest
Karl Goldmark, "Trutz" 1888/89, Op46,3
Wilhelm Kienzl, "Habenichts" 192-?, Op114,6

Richard Fedor Leopold Dehmel (1863-1920)

Ach! aus Träumen fahr ich in die graue Luft
Karol Szymanowski, "Entführung" 1907, Op17,8

Aprilwind; alle Knospen sind schon aufgesprossen
Arnold Schönberg, "Mädchenfrühling" 1897

Aurikelchen, Aurikelchen stehn auf meinem Beet
Armin Knab, "Aurikelchen" 1905-20
from *Kinderlieder* (23)

Aus dem meergrünen Teiche neben der roten Villa
Arnold Schönberg, "Erwartung" 1899, Op2,1

Aus des Abends weissen Wogen
Anton Webern, "Tief von Fern" 1901-04
from *Acht frühe Lieder* (1)

Bienchen, Bienchen, Bienchen wiegt sich im Sonnenschein
Max Reger, "Wiegenlied" 1899-1900, Op43,5, 1v(med).pf
Richard Strauss, "Wiegenliedchen" 1901, Op49,3
Leo Ornstein, "Wiegenlied" 1915pub, Op33,1, 1v.(vn).pf

Der Abend graut, Herbstfeuer brennen
Richard Strauss, "Stiller Gang" 1895, Op31,4, 1v.vla.pf
Conrad Ansorge, "Stiller Gang" 1895-96pub, Op10,3

Willy Burkhard, "Stiller Gang" 1925, Op9,7, 1v(low).pf
from *Frage*

Der Sturm behorcht mein Vaterhaus
Richard Strauss, "Lied an meinen Sohn" 1898, Op39,5

Der Wald beginnt zu rauschen, den Bäumen naht die Nacht
Richard Strauss, "Waldseligkeit" 1901, Op49,1
Max Reger, "Waldseligkeit" 1901, Op62,2
Conrad Ansorge, "Waldseligkeit" 1904?pub, Op17,2
Joseph Marx, "Waldseligkeit" 1911
Alma Schindler-Mahler, "Waldseligkeit" 1915pub
Leo Ornstein, "Waldseligkeit" 1915pub, Op33,3

Die Rosen leuchten immer noch
Jean Sibelius, "Aus banger Brust" 1906, Op50,4

Die Welt verstummt, dein Blut erklingt
Richard Strauss, "Am Ufer" 1899, Op41a,3
Anton Webern, "Am Ufer" 1906-08
from *Fünf Lieder* (2)

Doch hatte niemals tiefre Macht dein Blick
Conrad Ansorge, "Auf See" 1904?pub, Op17,3

Drum sollst du dulden, Mensch
Erich J. Wolff, "Drum sollst du dulden, Mensch" 1907pub, Op8,1, bar.pf
from *Sechs Gedichte von Richard Dehmel, Op. 8*

Du bist mein Auge! Du durchdringst mich ganz
Richard Strauss, "Mein Auge" 1898, Op37,4

Du hattest einen Glanz auf deiner Stirn
Anton Webern, "Ideale Landschaft" 1906-08
from *Fünf Lieder* (1)

Du mußt nicht meinen, ich hätte Furcht vor dir
Arnold Schönberg, "Mannesbangen" 189-?

Du sahst durch meine Seele in die Welt
Max Reger, "Die Liebe" 1902, Op66,7, 1v(med).pf

Du tatest mir die Tür auf, ernstes Kind
Karol Szymanowski, "Verkündigung" 1907, Op17,6

Du wirst nicht weinen. Leise, leise wirst du lächeln
Richard Strauss, "Befreit" 1898, Op39,4

Eh' wir uns trennen konnten, o wie hielt mich dein Gesicht
Erich J. Wolff, "Immer wieder" 1907pub, Op8,3
from *Sechs Gedichte von Richard Dehmel, Op. 8*

Es klagt im Dunklen irgendwo, ich möchte wissen, was es ist
Erich J. Wolff, "Stimme im Dunkeln" 1907pub, Op8,5
from *Sechs Gedichte von Richard Dehmel, Op. 8*

Es steht ein goldnes Garbenfeld, das geht bis an den Rand der Welt
Wilhelm Kempff, "Erntelied" 1923pub, Op16,4

Fest steht mein flammendes Gebot: Aus Abendrot wächst Morgenrot!
Erich J. Wolff, "Fest steht mein flammendes Gebot" 1907pub, Op8,4
from *Sechs Gedichte von Richard Dehmel, Op. 8*

Gib mir deine Hand, nur den Finger
Arnold Schönberg, "Erhebung" 1899, Op2,3
Erich J. Wolff, "Erhebung" 1907pub, Op8,2
from *Sechs Gedichte von Richard Dehmel, Op. 8*

Hoch hing der Mond; das Schneegefild lag bleich und öde um uns her
Richard Strauss, "Notturno" 1899, Op44,1, bar(low).orch

Ich warf eine Rose ins Meer
Ernest Vietor, "Wellentanzlied" 1939-40, Op17,1

Ich wünsche dir Glück. Ich bring dir die Sonne in meinem Blick
Erich Wolfgang Korngold, "Glückwunsch" 1947, Op38,1

Immer stiller stehn die Bäume, nicht ein Blatt mehr scheint zu leben
Willy Burkhard, "Ruf" 1925, Op9,5, 1v(low).pf
from *Frage*

In die dunkle Bergsschlucht kehrt der Mond zurück
Conrad Ansorge, "Geheimniss" 1895-96pub, Op10,2
Karol Szymanowski, "Geheimnis" 1907, Op17,2

In einem stillen Garten an eines Brunnens Schacht
Richard Strauss, "Leises Lied" 1898, Op39,1

Kinder, kommt, verzählt euch nicht, jeder hat zehn Zehen
Armin Knab, "Käuzchenspiel" 1905-20
from *Kinderlieder* (21)

Komm an mein Feuer, mein Weib, es ist kalt in der Welt
Erich J. Wolff, "Selig mit blutendem Herzen" 1907pub, Op8,6
from *Sechs Gedichte von Richard Dehmel, Op. 8*
Paul Graener, "Selig mit blutendem Herzen" 1916pub, Op40,2
The 1916 Universal ed. lists the poet as "Richard Schmel"
Wilhelm Kienzl, "Am Opferherd" 192-?, Op114,3

Krause, krause Muhme, alte Butterblume
Armin Knab, "Puhstemuhme" 1905-20
from *Kinderlieder* (22)

Lass uns noch die Nacht erwarten
Arnold Schönberg, "Alles" 1903-05, Op6,2

Lege deine Hand auf meine Augen
Conrad Ansorge, "Letzte Bitte" 1904?pub, Op17,5

Lieber Morgenstern, lieber Abendstern, ihr scheint zwei und seid eins
Ernest Vietor, "Zweier Seelen Lied" 1937-38, Op16,6
Richard Trunk, "Zweier Seelen Lied" 1963pub, Op76,3

Liegt eine Stadt im Tale, ein blasser Tag vergeht
Alma Schindler-Mahler, "Die stille Stadt" 1900-01?
Jean Sibelius, "Die stille Stadt" 1906, Op50,5
Hans Pfitzner, "Die stille Stadt" 1921, Op29,4
Felix Wolfes, "Die stille Stadt" 1951

Mädel, laß das Stricken geh
  Arnold Schönberg, "Nicht doch!" 189-?

Mein Hund, du, hat dich bloss beknurrt
  Arnold Schönberg, "Warnung" 1899-1903, Op3,3, 1v(med).pf

O mein Geliebter – in die Kissen
  Anton Webern, "Nachtgebet der Braut" 1899-1903
    from *Drei Gedichte für Gesang und Klavier*

O zürne nicht, wenn mein Begehren dunkel aus seinen Grenzen bricht
  Conrad Ansorge, "Ansturm" 1904?pub, Op17,1
  Alma Schindler-Mahler, "Ansturm" 1915pub

Schenk mir deinen goldenen Kamm
  Arnold Schönberg, "Schenk mir deinen goldenen Kamm" 1899?, Op2,2

Schmück dir das Haar mit wildem Mohn
  Alexander Zemlinsky, "Entbietung" 1900?, Op7,2
    from *Irmelin Rose und andere Gesänge*

Schwebst du nieder aus den Weiten
  Anton Webern, "Himmelfahrt" 1906-08
    from *Fünf Lieder* (3)

Seit wann du mein ich weiß es nicht
  Max Reger, "Jetzt und immer" 1902, Op66,11, 1v(med).pf

Sieh, der Himmel wird blau; die Schwalben jagen sich wie Fische
  Karol Szymanowski, "Nach einem Regen" 1907, Op17,7

Sieh, wie wir zu den Sternen aufsteigen!
  Karol Szymanowski, "Hoch in der Frühe" 1907, Op17,1

Still, es ist ein Tag verflossen
  Conrad Ansorge, "Nacht für Nacht" 1895-96pub, Op10,8

Tauchst du nieder aus den Weiten
  Conrad Ansorge, "Himmelfahrt" 1904?pub, Op17,4

Träume, träume, du mein süsses Leben
  Richard Strauss, "Wiegenlied" 1899, Op41a,1
  Max Reger, "Träume, träume, du mein süßes Leben! Wiegenlied" 1900, Op51,3
  Hans Pfitzner, "Venus mater" 1901, Op11,4
  Franz Salmhofer, "Lied einer jungen Mutter" 1923pub, Op5,1
    from *Vier Lieder*

Über unsre Liebe hängt eine tiefe Trauerweide
  Anton Webern, "Aufblick" 1901-04
    from *Acht frühe Lieder* (2)
  Karol Szymanowski, "Aufblick" 1907, Op17,5

Und du kamest in mein Haus, kamst mit deinen schwarzen Blicken
  Conrad Ansorge, "Gieb mir" 1895-96pub, Op10,6
  Karol Szymanowski, "Werbung" 1907, Op17,3

Und noch im alten Elternhause und noch am Abend keine Ruh?
  Rudi Stephan, "Heimat" 1914

Was will in deinen Augen mir
Alexander Zemlinsky, "Meeraugen" 1900?, Op7,3
from *Irmelin Rose und andere Gesänge*

Wenn der Regen durch die Gosse tropft
Conrad Ansorge, "Dann" 1895-96pub, Op10,7

Wenn die Felder sich verdunkeln, fühl ich wird mein Auge heller
Karol Szymanowski, "Manche Nacht" 1907, Op17,4
Othmar Schoeck, "Manche Nacht" 1911, Op24a,6
Ernest Vietor, "Manche Nacht" 1937-38, Op16,2

Wie das Meer ist die Liebe: unerschöpflich, unergründlich, unermeßlich
Vítězslav Novák, "Lobgesang" 1912pub, Op46,1
from *Erotikon*
Alma Schindler-Mahler, "Lobgesang" 1924pub

Wir haben ein Bett, wir haben ein Kind
Richard Strauss, "Der Arbeitsmann" 1898, Op39,3
Hans Pfitzner, "Der Arbeitsmann" 1922, Op30,4

Zaghaft vom Gewölk ins Land
Anton Webern, "Nächtliche Scheu" 1906-08
from *Fünf Lieder* (4)

Johann Ludwig Ferdinand von Deinhardstein (1794-1859)
Lasst im Morgenstrahl des Mai'n uns der Blume Leben freun
Franz Schubert, "Skolie" 1815, D306

Wie weil' ich so gern, wo die Trauer webt
Louis Spohr, "Lied des verlassenen Mädchens" WoO90

Emmy Destinn (1878-1930)
Es tönt in meinem Ohren ein seltsam müder Klang
Adolph Martin Foerster, "(An Old Melody)" 1908, Op53,4

"Gottl. von Deuern" (Gustav von Ludwiger)
Wenn im letzten Dämmrungsstrahle
Louis Spohr, "Ruhe" 1838, Op108,3, 2sop.pf

Franz Diederich (1865-1921)
Der Mond glüht über'm Garten
Max Reger, "Der Mond glüht über'm Garten" 1900, Op51,1

Georg Christian Dieffenbach (1822-1901)
Abend ists geworden, Dunkel hüllt uns ein
Franz Abt, "Abendlied" 1870?pub
from *Kinderlieder*

An dem Spinnrad sitzt das Mädchen
Franz Abt, "Am Spinnrad" 1870?pub
from *Kinderlieder*

Auf zum Himmel steigt die Lerche
Franz Abt, "Die Lerche" 1870?pub
from *Kinderlieder*

Da ist die liebe Schwalbe wieder!
Franz Abt, "Alte Freundschaft" 1870?pub
from *Kinderlieder*

Der Sommer ist vergangen, der Herbst entschwindet bald
Franz Abt, "Der Vöglein Abschied" 1870?pub
from *Kinderlieder*

Die Blumen all, die Blüthen all, sie müssen rasch verblühn
Franz Abt, "Tannengrün" 1870?pub
from *Kinderlieder*

Frau Schwalbe ist 'ne Schwätzerin, sie schwatzt den ganzen Tag
Engelbert Humperdinck, "Die Schwalbe" 1901
from *Vier Kinderlieder*

Hänschen möcht ein Reiter sein
Franz Abt, "Hänschen möcht ein Reiter sein" 1870?pub
from *Kinderlieder*

Hoch auf Stelzen, hoch auf Stelzen, geht mein Büblein kühn dahin
Franz Abt, "Der kleine Riese Goliath" 1870?pub
from *Kinderlieder*

Hört wie laut, hört wie laut klingt der Vöglein Chor
Franz Abt, "Wohl in dem grünen Wald" 1870?pub
from *Kinderlieder*

Ich kenne einen grossen Garten
Franz Abt, "Der schönste Garten" 1870?pub
from *Kinderlieder*

Mein Pferdchen gallopirt, Hurrah!
Franz Abt, "Der kleine Reiter" 1870?pub
from *Kinderlieder*

Nach Oben steigt die Lerche mit lautem Jubelschall
Franz Abt, "Nach Oben" 1870?pub
from *Kinderlieder*

Vöglein, Vöglein hüte dich, hüte dich!
Franz Abt, "Vöglein, hüte dich!" 1870?pub
from *Kinderlieder*

Vorbei, vorbei die dunkle Nacht, der helle Tag kommt wieder!
Franz Abt, "Morgenlied" 1870?pub
from *Kinderlieder*

Wenn ich ein Vöglein wär, flög ich wohl hin und her
Franz Abt, "Vöglein so klein möcht ich wohl sein" 1870?pub
from *Kinderlieder*

Wo eilst du hin, du Bächlein, du?
Franz Abt, "Zur Ewigkeit" 1870?pub
from *Kinderlieder*

Dietmar von Aiste (fl. ca. 1139-before 1171)

Liebster, Liebster, schläfst du noch? Liebster, Liebster, höre doch!
Richard Stöhr, "Altdeutsches Lied" 1914pub, Op28,2

Schläfst du noch mein Trauter? Man weckt so bald uns leider
Frank van der Stucken, "Unter der Linde" 1904pub, Op33,5

Franz Ferdinand Freiherr von Dingelstedt (1814-1881)
Die Wolken ziehen schwarz und hoch
Louis Spohr, "Mitternacht" 1838, WoO97
Louis Spohr, "Mitternacht" 1838, WoO97, 1v.pf(4-hand)

In die blaue Luft hinaus einen stillen Gruss nach Haus
Louis Spohr, "Unterwegs" 1839, WoO101

Schwebe, schwebe, blaues Auge
Franz Liszt, "Schwebe, schwebe, blaues Auge" 1848
Franz Liszt, "Schwebe, schwebe, blaues Auge" 1860pub

Dionysius
O Muse, mir Vertraute du, lass klingen meine Lieder
Carl Loewe, "An die Muse: Hymne an die Kalliope" 1842

Johann von Döhring
Noch weisst du nicht! wess Kind du bist
Ludwig van Beethoven, "An einen Säugling" 1784?, WoO108

Wie so schmachtend, glücklich Weibchen
Johann Rudolf Zumsteeg, "Er und Sie (als sie die Nachtigall hörten)" 1803pub
from *Kleine Balladen und Lieder, fünftes Heft*

C. Dorr-Ljubljaschtschi
Mutter, draußen ist es Frühling worden
Max Reger, "Mägdleins Frage" 1900, Op51,2

Martin Drescher (1863-1920)
Taufrisch glänzen die Blumen, die der Frühling entbot
Hugo Kaun, "Der Sieger" 1902pub, Op37,1

Vor meinem Fenster klingt ein deutsches Lied
Hugo Kaun, "Heimat" 1908pub, Op80,5

Leberecht Blücher Dreves (1816-1870)
Frühmorgens, wenn die Hähne kräh'n
Franz Abt, "Waldandacht" 1873pub, Op211,3

Annette Elisabeth, Freiin von Droste-Hülshoff (1797-1848)
Wär' ich ein Kind, ein Knäblein klein
Peter Cornelius, "Das Kind" 1862

Wer bist du doch, o Mädchen?
Peter Cornelius, "Gesegnet" 1862

Zum Ossa sprach der Pelion
Peter Cornelius, "Unerhört" 1862, Op5,5

Johann Gustav Droysen (1808-1884)
Fern und ferner schallt der Reigen
Fanny Hensel, "Sehnsucht" 1830pub, Op9,7(FM)

Herr, zu Dir will ich mich retten
Felix Mendelssohn, "Entsagung" 1830pub, Op9,11

In weite Fernen will ich träumen (see also Heine)
Felix Mendelssohn, "Ferne" 1830pub, Op9,9

Ida von Düringsfeld (1815-1876)
Schlafe wohl! Im Thal von Schatten singt das Wasser klar und lind
Franz Abt, "Schlafe wohl!" 1873pub, Op324,3

Alexandre Dumas (père) (1802-1870)
Mein Gott! aus meiner Herden Mitten
Franz Liszt, "Johanna von Arc vor dem Scheiterhaufen" 1874, mez.pf
German translation by M. G. Friedrich

Alexander von Dusch (1789-1876)
Auf die stürm'sche See hinaus
Carl Maria von Weber, "Des Künstlers Abschied" 1810, Op71,6

George von Dyherrn (1847-1878)
Wenn dein ich denk', dann sinn' ich oft in träumerischem Gang
Erik Meyer-Helmund, "Das Zauberlied" 1886-88

Elisabeth Ebeling (1828-1905)
Es schaukeln die Winde das Nest in der Linde
Engelbert Humperdinck, "Wiegenlied" 1900
from *Vier Kinderlieder*

Es spielen leise die Blüthen am duftenden Lindenbaum
Carl Bohm, "Frühlingsnacht" 1887cop, Op230,2

Karl Egon Ebert (1801-1882)
Als ich das erste Veilchen erblickt
Felix Mendelssohn, "Das erste Veilchen" 1834pub, Op19,2

Bringet des treu'sten Herzens Grüsse
Felix Mendelssohn, "Reiselied" 1830, Op19,6

Der Vogel steigt, ein verkörpertes Lied
Louis Spohr, "Ermunterung" 1849, WoO117,1, 2sop.pf

Die Perle, wahrend im Gehäuse
Josefine Lang, "Perle und Lied" WoO

Julius Eberwein (1801-1870)
Das Vöglein singt den ganzen Tag
Louis Spohr, "Sangeslust" 1837, Op101,2, 1v.pf(4-hand)

Marie von Ebner-Eschenbach (1830-1916)
O du des himmlischen Reiches Kind
Felix Weingartner, "Chinesische Rose" 1900, Op28,1

Josef August Eckschläger (1784-?)
Maienblümlein, so schön, mag euch gern blühen sehn!
Carl Maria von Weber, "Maienblümlein" 1811, Op23,3

Edward
Eile auf der Morgenröthe Flügeln
Johann Rudolf Zumsteeg, "Lied" 1803pub
from *Kleine Balladen und Lieder, sechstes Heft*

"Hans Ehlen" (Hanna Kolb) (fl.1892)
Er hat mich im Traum geküßt
Max Reger, "Wenn ich's nur wüßt" 1893, Op12,3

Paul Ehlers
Zum Wasser neigen sich die silbergrauen Weiden
Richard Trunk, "Ammersee" 1963pub, Op76,1

Hans Heinrich Ehrler (1872-1951)
Am Markte lag ein totgestürztes Kind
Hermann Reutter, "Anima" 1948pub, Op65,8
from *Ehrler-Zyklus II*

Augen ihr, durch allen Schein gegangen
Hermann Reutter, "An meine Augen" 1948pub, Op65,3
from *Ehrler-Zyklus II*

Den kurzen Tag umgab die lange Nacht
Hermann Reutter, "Wintersonnwend" 1948pub, Op65,1
from *Ehrler-Zyklus II*

Der den Sterngang maß mit Menschenzeichen
Hermann Reutter, "Johann Kepler. Harmonia mundi" 1948, Op64,5

Gehet nun, gehet nun fort! Lasset mich schließen die Tür!
Hermann Reutter, "Des Mönches Abschied von den Geleite Gebenden" 1948pub, Op65,12
from *Ehrler-Zyklus II*

Heimat, Schoß des Heimeslosen, Wiege dem verlornen Sohn
Hermann Reutter, "An die Heimat" 1948pub, Op65,5
from *Ehrler-Zyklus II*

Ich denk an dich und gehe aus mir auf einem seligen Weg zu dir
Hermann Reutter, "Nachtlied" 1948pub, Op65,7
from *Ehrler-Zyklus II*

Ich möchte einmal so betauet sein, wie dieser Anger in erwachter Frühe
Hermann Reutter, "Wonnen" 1948pub, Op65,6
from *Ehrler-Zyklus II*

Ist der Gang der Uhr nicht ein ganz andrer als ich glaubte
Hermann Reutter, "Die alte Uhr" 1948pub, Op65,4
from *Ehrler-Zyklus II*

O Bruder sag, warum bist du gekommen?
Hermann Reutter, "Die Beiden" 1948pub, Op65,10
from *Ehrler-Zyklus II*

O holder Himmelswind, führ in die Welt die Barke
Hermann Reutter, "Beter am Meer" 1948pub, Op65,11
from *Ehrler-Zyklus II*

Strahl, der durch die Gassen geht, wo du bist, wird's mild
Hermann Reutter, "Barmherzige Schwester" 1948pub, Op65,9
from *Ehrler-Zyklus II*

Wieviel Wege bin ich schon gegangen?
Hermann Reutter, "Frage" 1948pub, Op65,2
from *Ehrler-Zyklus II*

Bernhard Ambros Ehrlich (1765?-1827)

All' mein Wirken, all' mein Leben
 Franz Schubert, "Als ich sie erröthen sah" 1815, D153

Joseph (Karl Benedikt) Freiherr von Eichendorff (1788-1857)

Abendlich schon rauscht der Wald
 Fanny Hensel, "Abendlich schon rauscht der Wald" 1846, Op3,5, satb
 from *Gartenlieder*
 Robert Franz, "Abends" 1856pub, Op16,4
 Christian Fink, "Abschied" 1865pub, Op7,5
 Hans Pfitzner, "Abschied" 1894/95, Op9,5
 Othmar Schoeck, "Abschied" 1909, Op20,7

Ach! wie ist es doch gekommen, daß die ferne Waldespracht
 Fanny Hensel, "Anklänge II" 1841
 from *Anklänge*

Ade, mein Schatz, du mocht'st mich nicht
 Hugo Wolf, "Seemanns Abschied" 1888
 from *Eichendorff Lieder* (17)

Am Himmelsgrund schießen so lustig die Stern'
 Robert Franz, "Der Bote" 1846pub, Op8,1
 Adolf Jensen, "Der Bote" 1878, Op57,4
 Hans Pfitzner, "Der Bote" 1888/89, Op5,3
 Otto Lohse, "Der Bote" 1910pub

Am Kreuzweg da lausche ich
 Hugo Wolf, "Die Zigeunerin" 1887
 from *Eichendorff Lieder* (7)

Auf die Dächer zwischen blassen Wolken scheint der Mond herfür
 Hugo Wolf, "Das Ständchen" 1888
 from *Eichendorff Lieder* (4)
 Erich Wolfgang Korngold, "Das Ständchen" 1911, Op9,3
 Richard Trunk, "Das Ständchen" 1933pub, Op45,7

Aufs Wohlsein meiner Dame
 Hugo Wolf, "Der Schreckenberger" 1888
 from *Eichendorff Lieder* (9)

Aus der Heimat hinter den Blitzen rot
 Robert Schumann, "In der Fremde" 1840, Op39,1
 from *Liederkreis*
 Johannes Brahms, "In der Fremde" 1852, Op3,5
 Hanns Eisler, "Erinnerung an Eichendorff und Schumann" 1943

Aus schweren Träumen
 Othmar Schoeck, "Motto" 1934, Op51,2

Bei dem angenehmsten Wetter
 Hugo Wolf, "Der Scholar" 1888
 from *Eichendorff Lieder* (13)

Berg' und Täler wieder fingen
 Othmar Schoeck, "Angedenken" 1915?, Op36,21
 from *Elegie*

Bevor er in die blaue Flut gesunken
Reinhard Schwarz-Schilling, "Todeslust" 1944

Bin ein Feuer hell, das lodert von dem grünen Felsenkranz
Robert Schumann, "Waldmädchen" 1849, Op69,2, 2sop.2alt.pf
from *Romanzen für Frauenstimmen I*
Hugo Wolf, "Waldmädchen" 1887
from *Eichendorff Lieder* (Anhang, Nr.3)

Bist du manchmal auch verstimmt, drück dich zärtlich an mein Herze
Reinhard Schwarz-Schilling, "Der wandernde Musikant (3)" 1944, bar.pf
from *Der wandernde Musikant. Lieder nach Gedichten von Eichendorff*

Bleib' bei uns! wir haben den Tanzplan im Thal
Charles Griffes, "Elfe" 1903-11?, A21
Joseph Marx, "Die Elfe" 1909
Bruno Walter, "Elfe" 1910pub

Da die Welt zur Ruh gegangen
Johannes Brahms, "Die Nonne und der Ritter" 1860, Op28,1, alt.bar.pf

Da fahr ich still im Wagen, du bist so weit von mir
Hugo Wolf, "In der Fremde (I)" 1881
Othmar Schoeck, "In der Fremde" 1908, Op15,4
Richard Trunk, "Der verliebte Reisende" 1933pub, Op45,6

Dämm'rung will die Flügel spreiten
Robert Schumann, "Zwielicht" 1840, Op39,10
from *Liederkreis*

Das ist der alte Baum nicht mehr der damals hier gestanden
Frank van der Stucken, "Vorbei" 1892pub

Das Kind ruht aus vom Spielen, am Fenster rauscht die Nacht
Max Reger, "Gottes Segen" 1907, Op76,31, 1v(med).pf
from *Schlichte Weisen, Band 3*
Bruno Walter, "Des Kindes Schlaf" 1910pub
Othmar Schoeck, "Gottes Segen" 1928, Op35,3

Dein Bildnis wunderselig hab ich im Herzensgrund
Robert Schumann, "Intermezzo" 1840, Op39,2
from *Liederkreis*
Willy Burkhard, "Andenken" 1925, Op9,3, 1v(low).pf
from *Frage*

Dein Wille, Herr, geschehe! Verdunkelt schweigt das Land
Hugo Wolf, "Ergebung" 1881, satb
from *Sechs geistliche Lieder nach Gedichten von Eichendorff*
Max Reger, "Dein Wille, Herr, geschehe" 1914, Op137,2, 1v.pf(harm/org)
from *Zwölf geistliche Lieder*

Der Herbstwind schüttelt die Linde
Hans Pfitzner, "Zum Abschied meiner Tochter" 1889-1901, Op10,3

Der Hirt bläst seine Weise, von fern ein Schuss noch fällt
Eduard Lassen, "Abendlandschaft"
Othmar Schoeck, "Abendlandschaft" 1914, Op20,10
Arno Kleffel, "Abendlandschaft" Op12,9

Der jagt dahin, daß die Rosse schnaufen
Aribert Reimann, "Trost" 1978, bar.pf
from *Nachtstück II*

Der Strom glitt einsam hin und rauschte
Robert Franz, "Am Strom" 1870?pub, Op30,3

Der Sturm geht lärmend um das Haus
Othmar Schoeck, "Der Sturm geht lärmend um das Haus" 1928, Op42,6, 1v.pf.cl.hn.perc
from *Wandersprüche*

Der Wald wird falb, die Blätter fallen, wie öd und still der Raum
Fanny Hensel, "Im Herbst" 1844
Eduard Lassen, "Im Herbst" Op45,3
Hans Pfitzner, "Im Herbst" 1894/95, Op9,3

Der Wandrer, von der Heimat weit, wenn alle Wipfel lauschen
Peter Cornelius, "Am Meer" 1866, sop.bar.pf
Othmar Schoeck, "Der Wand'rer, von der Heimat weit" 1928, Op42,8, 1v.pf.cl.hn.perc
from *Wandersprüche*

Die Abendglocken klangen
Othmar Schoeck, "Vesper" 1921?, Op36,11
from *Elegie*

Die Höh'n und Wälder schon steigen
Robert Franz, "Gute Nacht!" 1846pub, Op5,7

Die Jäger ziehn in grünen Wald
Hans Pfitzner, "Studentenfahrt" 1901, Op11,3
Robert Gund, "Studentenfahrt" 1922pub, Op40,6

Die Lerche grüßt den ersten Strahl
Othmar Schoeck, "Die Lerche grüßt den ersten Strahl" 1928, Op42,4, 1v.pf.cl.hn.perc
from *Wandersprüche*

Die Nacht war kaum verblühet
Robert Franz, "Sonntag" 1843pub, Op1,7

Die Vöglein, die so fröhlich sangen, der Blumen bunte Pracht
Armin Knab, "Nacht" 1922, alt/bar.pf
from *Eichendorff-Lieder*
Aribert Reimann, "Nachtstück (2)" 1966, bar.pf
from *Nachtstück*

Die Welt ruht still im Hafen, mein Liebchen, gute Nacht!
Richard Trunk, "An die Entfernte" 1933pub, Op45,3

Du liebe, treue Laute, wie manche Sommernacht
Hugo Wolf, "Nachruf" 1880
Othmar Schoeck, "Nachruf" 1914, Op20,14

Dunkle Giebel, hohe Fenster, Türme, tief aus Nebeln sehn
Hans Pfitzner, "In Danzig" 1907, Op22,1
Louis Ferdinand, "In Danzig" 1955pub

Durch Feld und Buchenhallen bald singend, bald fröhlich still
Othmar Schoeck, "Reiselied" 1908, Op12,1
Reinhard Schwarz-Schilling, "Der wandernde Musikant (4)" 1944, bar.pf
from *Der wandernde Musikant. Lieder nach Gedichten von Eichendorff*

Durch schwankende Wipfel schiesst güldener Strahl
Robert Franz, "Jagdlied" 1843pub, Op1,9

Ein Adler saß am Felsenbogen, den lockt ein Sturm weit übers Meer
Richard Stöhr, "Durch" 1914pub, Op28,3

Ein Gems auf dem Stein, ein Vogel im Flug
Johannes Brahms, "Ein Gems auf dem Stein" 1859-63, Op113,8, ssaa
from *13 Kanons für Frauenstimmen*

Ein Wunderland ist oben aufgeschlagen
Othmar Schoeck, "Sonett III" 1952, Op66,3, 1v(high).orch
from *Befreite Sehnsucht*

Eingeschlafen auf der Lauer oben ist der alte Ritter
Robert Schumann, "Auf einer Burg" 1840, Op39,7
from *Liederkreis*
Robert Gund, "Auf einer Burg" 1906, Op40,2
Othmar Schoeck, "Auf einer Burg" 1909, Op17,6, 1v(low).pf

Er reitet nachts auf einem braunen Roß
Hans Pfitzner, "Nachtwanderer" 1888-1900, Op7,2
Erich Wolfgang Korngold, "Nachtwanderer" 1911, Op9,2

Es geht wohl anders, als du meinst
Othmar Schoeck, "Es geht wohl anders, als du meinst" 1928, Op42,1, 1v.pf.cl.hn.perc
from *Wandersprüche*

Es glänzt der Tulpenflor, durchschnitten von Allen
Hans Pfitzner, "Sonst" 1904, Op15,4

Es haben viel Dichter gesungen
Othmar Schoeck, "Trost" 1935, Op51,3

Es ist schon spät, es ist schon kalt
Robert Schumann, "Waldesgespräch" 1840, Op39,3
from *Liederkreis*
Adolf Jensen, "Waldesgespräch" 1860, Op5,4
Hans Pfitzner, "Waldesgespräch" (fragment), 188-?

Es rauschen die Wipfel und schauern
Robert Schumann, "Schöne Fremde" 1840, Op39,6
from *Liederkreis*
Fanny Hensel, "Schöne Fremde" 1846, Op3,2, satb
from *Gartenlieder*
Ernest Vietor, "Schöne Fremde" 1937-38, Op16,9

Es schienen so golden die Sterne, am Fenster ich einsam stand
Othmar Schoeck, "Sehnsucht" 1909, o.op30, ch
Richard Trunk, "Sehnsucht" 1933pub, Op45,4

Es steht ein Berg im Feuer, in feurigem Morgenbrand
Eduard Lassen, "Frühlingsgruss" Op45,2
Wilhelm Kempff, "Frühlingsgruß" 1917, Op7,4

Es wandelt, was wir schauen, Tag sinkt ins Abendrot
Alban Berg, "Es wandelt, was wir schauen" 1904
Othmar Schoeck, "Ergebung" 1918, Op30,6

Ernst Pepping, "Ergebung" 1949pub
from *Haus- und Trostbuch* (39)

Es war, als hätt der Himmel die Erde still geküßt
Robert Schumann, "Mondnacht" 1840, Op39,5
from *Liederkreis*
Johannes Brahms, "Mondnacht" 1853, WoO 21

Es weiss und räth es doch Keiner
Robert Schumann, "Die Stille" 1840, Op39,4
from *Liederkreis*
Felix Mendelssohn, "Es weiss und räth es doch Keiner" 1847, Op99,6

Es zog eine Hochzeit den Berg entlang, ich hörte die Vögel schlagen
Robert Schumann, "Im Walde" 1840, Op39,11
from *Liederkreis*
Robert Schumann, "Im Walde" 1849, Op75,2, satb
Nikolai Medtner, "Im Walde" 1925-26, Op46,4
Wilhelm Petersen, "Im Walde" 1956pub, Op44,4

Es zogen zwei rüst'ge Gesellen
Robert Schumann, "Frühlingsfahrt" 1840, Op45,2
Johann Vesque von Püttlingen, "Die zwei Gesellen" 185-?, Op52,3

Ewig muntres Spiel der Wogen!
Othmar Schoeck, "Ewig muntres Spiel der Wogen!" 1928, Op42,7, 1v.pf.cl.hn.perc
from *Wandersprüche*

Fliegt der erste Morgenstrahl durch das stille Nebeltal
Eduard Lassen, "Der Morgen" Op81,3

Für alle muß vor Freuden
Othmar Schoeck, "Dichterlos" 1922pub, Op36,23

Gedenk ich noch der Frühlingsnächte
Armin Knab, "Morgendämmerung" 1922, alt/bar.pf
from *Eichendorff-Lieder*

Genug gemeistert nun die Weltgeschichte!
Othmar Schoeck, "Mahnung" 1933, Op49,6, bar.mch.cham orch
from *Kantate. Nach Gedichten von Eichendorff*

Gleich wie Echo frohen Liedern fröhlich Antwort geben muß
Johannes Brahms, "Tafellied" 1884, Op93b, saatbb.pf

Grüss euch aus Herzensgrund
Hugo Wolf, "Erwartung" 1880
from *Eichendorff Lieder* (Anhang, Nr.1)

Herz, in deinen sonnenhellen Tagen
Othmar Schoeck, "Herz, in deinen sonnenhellen Tagen" 1928, Op42,2, 1v.pf.cl.hn.perc
from *Wandersprüche*

Herz, mein Herz, warum so fröhlich
Wilhelm Kienzl, "Neue Liebe" 187-?, Op8,6
Hans Pfitzner, "Neue Liebe" 1916, Op26,3

Hier bin ich, Herr! Gegrüßt das Licht
Othmar Schoeck, "Umkehr" 1914, Op20,12

Hier unter dieser Linde saß ich viel tausendmal
Franz von Holstein, "Sonst und jetzt" 1877, Op37,4
Bruno Walter, "Der junge Ehemann" 1910pub

Hoch mit den Wolken geht der Vögel Reise
Hans Pfitzner, "Das Alter" 1931, Op41,3
from *Drei Sonette für eine Männerstimme und Klavier*

Hoch über stillen Höhen stand in dem Wald ein Haus
Johannes Brahms, "Anklänge" 1853, Op7,3

Hochweiser Rat, geehrte Kollegen!
Othmar Schoeck, "Ratskollegium" 1933, Op49,4, bar.mch.cham orch
from *Kantate. Nach Gedichten von Eichendorff*

Hörst du die Gründe rufen in Träumen halb verwacht?
Othmar Schoeck, "Nacht" 1917, Op30,9
Aribert Reimann, "Nachtstück (4)" 1966, bar.pf
from *Nachtstück*

Hörst du nicht die Bäume rauschen draußen durch die stille Rund?
Joseph Dessauer, "Lockung"
Fanny Hensel, "Hörst du nicht die Bäume rauschen" 1846, Op3,1, satb
from *Gartenlieder*
Bernhard Hopffer, "Lockung" 1872, Op22,1
Hans Pfitzner, "Lockung" 1888-1900, Op7,4

Hörst du nicht die Quellen gehen zwischen Stein und Blumen weit
Hugo Wolf, "Nachtzauber" 1887
from *Eichendorff Lieder* (8)
Richard Trunk, "Nachtzauber" 1933pub, Op45,1

Ich geh durch die dunkeln Gassen
Hugo Wolf, "In der Fremde (II)" 1883

Ich ging bei Nacht einst über Land
Hugo Wolf, "Unfall" 1888
from *Eichendorff Lieder* (15)

Ich hab' ein Liebchen lieb recht von Herzen
Hugo Wolf, "Liebesglück" 1888
from *Eichendorff Lieder* (16)

Ich hör' die Bächlein rauschen im Walde her und hi
Robert Schumann, "In der Fremde" 1840, Op39,8
from *Liederkreis*
Joseph Marx, "Erinnerung" 1909, 1v(med).pf
Othmar Schoeck, "Erinnerung" 1909, Op17,7, 1v(high).pf

Ich kann hier nicht singen, aus dieser Mauern dunklen Ringen
Bruno Walter, "Die Lerche" 1910pub

Ich kann wohl manchmal singen, als ob ich fröhlich sei
Robert Schumann, "Wehmuth" 1840, Op39,9
from *Liederkreis*
Fanny Hensel, "Ich kann wohl manchmal singen" 1846
Adolph Martin Foerster, "Wehmut" 1878, Op6,2
Othmar Schoeck, "Wehmut" 1922, Op36,1
from *Elegie*

Ich rufe vom Ufer verlorenes Glück
  Joachim Raff, "Vom Strande" 1855-63, Op98,25
    from *Sanges-Frühling*
  Johannes Brahms, "Vom Strande" 1877, Op69,6
    after the Spanish

Ich seh' von des Schiffes Rande
  Robert Franz, "Meeresstille" 1846pub, Op8,2

Ich stehe in Waldesschatten wie an des Lebens Rand
  Hans Pfitzner, "Nachts" 1916, Op26,2

Ich wandre durch die stille Nacht
  Friedrich Curschmann, "Bild der Nacht" 1838, Op18,2
  Fanny Hensel, "Nachtwanderer" 1843, Op7,1
  Robert Franz, "Ich wandre durch die stille Nacht" 1862?, Op35,2
  Theodor Kirchner, "Ich wandre durch die stille Nacht" 1890pub, Op95
  Max Reger, "Nachts" 1894, Op14,1, sop.alt.pf
  Armin Knab, "Nachts" 1918, alt/bar.pf
    from *Eichendorff-Lieder*
  Erich Zeisl, "Nachts" 1935pub
  Wilhelm Petersen, "Nachts" 1956pub, Op44,1
  Aribert Reimann, "Nachts" 1978, bar.pf
    from *Nachtstück II*

Ihr habt den Vogel gefangen
  Johann Vesque von Püttlingen, "Der Unverbesserliche" 1855

Im Winde fächeln, Mutter, die Blätter
  Otto Lohse, "Seliges Vergessen" 1910pub
    translated from the Spanish

In den Wipfeln frische Lüfte, fern melod'scher Quellen Fall
  Fanny Hensel, "Morgenständchen" 1846pub, Op1,5
  Wilhelm Petersen, "Morgenständchen" 1956pub, Op44,2

In einem kühlen Grunde, da geht ein Mühlenrad
  Friedrich Glück, "Untreue" 1814
  Friedrich Silcher, "Untreue"
  Friedrich Silcher, "Untreue" 4v
  Friedrich Nietzsche, "Das zerbrochene Ringlein" 1863, NWV14, declamation.pf
  Alexis Holländer, "Das zerbrochene Ringlein" 1864pub, Op6,5

In stiller Bucht, bei finstrer Nacht
  Robert Schumann, "Der Eidgenossen Nachtwache" 1847, Op62,1, ttbb

Ist auch schmuck nicht mein Rößlein, so ist's doch recht klug
  Hugo Wolf, "Der Soldat (I)" 1887
    from *Eichendorff Lieder* (5)
  Josef V. Wöss, "Der Soldat" 1910pub, Op18,4
  Bruno Walter, "Der Soldat" 1910pub

Juchheisa! und ich führ' den Zug
  Othmar Schoeck, "Der neue Rattenfänger" 1933, Op49,3, bar.mch.cham orch
    from *Kantate. Nach Gedichten von Eichendorff*

Kaiserkron' und Päonien rot, die müssen verzaubert sein
  Wilhelm Petersen, "Der alte Garten" 1956pub, Op44,3

Könnt ich zu den Wäldern flüchten, mit dem Grün in frischer Lust
Fanny Hensel, "Anklänge III" 1841
from *Anklänge*

Komm, Trost der Welt, du stille Nacht!
Joseph Dessauer, "Der Einsiedler"
Karl Reinthaler, "Der Einsiedler"
Robert Schumann, "Der Einsiedler" 1850, Op83,3
Hugo Wolf, "Resignation" 1881, satb
from *Sechs geistliche Lieder nach Gedichten von Eichendorff*
Othmar Schoeck, "Der Einsame" 1922, Op36,24
Felix Wolfes, "Der Einsiedler" 1953, 1v(med).pf

Komm zum Garten denn, du Holde!
Nikolai Medtner, "Aussicht" 1925-26, Op46,3

Kühle auf dem schönen Rheine
Othmar Schoeck, "Auf dem Rhein" 1917, Op30,12

Läuten kaum die Maienglocken
Robert Franz, "Der Schalk" 1844pub, Op3,1
Fanny Hensel, "Mayenlied" 1846pub, Op1,4

Laue Luft kommt blau geflossen, Frühling, Frühling soll es sein!
Felix Mendelssohn, "Wanderlied" 1841, Op57,6
Ernst Rudorff, "Frische Fahrt" Op16,2

Lieb Vöglein, vor Blüten sieht man dich kaum!
Wilhelm Petersen, "Die Zeit geht schnell" 1956pub, Op44,5

Lindes Rauschen in den Wipfeln
Johannes Brahms, "Lied" 1852, Op3,6
Othmar Schoeck, "Erinnerung" 1907, Op10,1

Lust'ge Vögel in dem Wald
Othmar Schoeck, "Nachklang" 1917, Op30,7

Magst du zu dem Alten halten
Othmar Schoeck, "Spruch" 1933, Op49,7, bar.mch.cham orch
from *Kantate. Nach Gedichten von Eichendorff*

Markt und Straßen steh'n verlassen
Wilhelm Kienzl, "Weihnachten" 190-?, Op61,1

Mit meinem Saitenspiele, das schön geklungen hat
Hugo Wolf, "Rückkehr" 1883

Möcht' wissen, was sie schlagen so schön bei der Nacht
Robert Franz, "Möcht' wissen, was sie schlagen" 1860?pub, Op18,5
Hans Pfitzner, "Die Nachtigallen" 1907, Op21,2

Mürrisch sitzen sie und maulen auf den Bänken stumm und breit
Hermann Grädener, "Der wandernde Musikant" 1896?pub, Op29

Nach Süden nun sich lenken
Othmar Schoeck, "Wanderlied der Prager Studenten" 1907, Op12,2

Nacht ist wie ein stilles Meer, Leid und Lust und Liebesklagen
Fanny Hensel, "Nacht ist wie ein stilles Meer" 1846
Joseph Rheinberger, "Die Nachtblume" 1861?pub, Op22,2

Hugo Wolf, "Die Nacht" 1880
from *Eichendorff Lieder* (Anhang, Nr.2)
Josef V. Wöss, "Die Nacht" 1910cop, Op18,3
Ernst Bacon, "Die Nachtblume" 1928pub

Nachts durch die stille Runde rauschte des Rheines Lauf
Joachim Raff, "Die Hochzeitsnacht" 1855-63, Op98,16
from *Sanges-Frühling*

Nächtlich dehnen sich die Stunden
Othmar Schoeck, "Geistesgruß" 1933, Op49,2, bar.mch.cham orch
from *Kantate. Nach Gedichten von Eichendorff*

Nächtlich macht der Herr die Rund
Hans Pfitzner, "Der Weckruf" 1931, Op40,6

Nun legen sich die Wogen, und die Gewitter schwül'
Othmar Schoeck, "Sterbeglocken" 1918, Op30,5
Wilhelm Petersen, "Sterbeglocken" 1956pub, Op44,8

O Lust vom Berg zu schauen weit über Wald und Strom
Fanny Hensel, "Bergeslust" 1850pub, Op10,5

O Maria, meine Liebe, denk ich recht im Herzen dein
Reinhard Schwarz-Schilling, "O Maria, meine Liebe" 1949
from *Drei Geistliche Lieder*

Ochse, wie bist du so stattlich, bedachtsam, fleißig und nützlich!
Ernst Pepping, "Spaziergang" 1949pub
from *Haus- und Trostbuch* (5)

Posthorn, wie so keck und fröhlich
Othmar Schoeck, "Kurze Fahrt" 1918, Op30,2
Reinhard Schwarz-Schilling, "Kurze Fahrt" 1943
from *Drei Lieder*

's war doch wie ein leises Singen
Erich Wolfgang Korngold, "Schneeglöckchen" 1911, Op9,1

Schlafe, Liebchen, weil's auf Erden nun so still und seltsam wird!
Robert Gund, "Abendständchen" 1922pub, Op40,3

Schon kehren die Vögel wieder ein
Othmar Schoeck, "Nachklang" 1921, Op36,14
from *Elegie*

Schweigt der Menschen laute Lust
Paul Hindemith, "Der Abend" 1925, Op35,ii,2, sop.ob.vla.vc
from *Die Serenaden*

Schwirrend Tambourin, schwirrend Tambourin, dich schwing' ich
Robert Schumann, "Tamburinschlägerin" 1849, Op69,1, ssaa.pf
from the Spanish
from *Romanzen für Frauenstimmen I*
Eduard Lassen, "Die Musikantin"

Seh' ich im verfall'nen dunklen Haus
Hans Pfitzner, "Zorn" 1904, Op15,2, bar.pf

Sie stand wohl am Fensterbogen
Johannes Brahms, "Parole" 1852, Op7,2

So eitel künstlich haben sie verwoben
Othmar Schoeck, "Sonett II" 1952, Op66,2, 1v(high).orch
from *Befreite Sehnsucht*

So lass' herein nun brechen die Brandung, wie sie will
Hugo Wolf, "Erhebung" 1881, satb
from *Sechs geistliche Lieder nach Gedichten von Eichendorff*

So ruhig geh' ich meinen Pfad
Othmar Schoeck, "Im Wandern" 1918, Op30,4

So viele Quellen von den Bergen rauschen
Othmar Schoeck, "Sonett I" 1952, Op66,1, 1v(high).orch
from *Befreite Sehnsucht*

Soldat sein ist gefährlich
Hugo Wolf, "Lieber alles" 1888
from *Eichendorff Lieder* (11)

Soll ich dich denn nun verlassen, Erde, heit'res Vaterhaus?
Othmar Schoeck, "Der Kranke" 1913, Op20,9
Erich Wolfgang Korngold, "Der Kranke" 194-?, Op38,2

Springer, der in luft'gem Schreiten
Othmar Schoeck, "Guter Rat" 1907, Op10,3

Still bei Nacht fährt manches Schiff
Robert Schumann, "Meerfey" 1849, Op69,5, 3sop.2alt.pf
from *Romanzen für Frauenstimmen I*

Studieren will nichts bringen
Hugo Wolf, "Der verzweifelte Liebhaber" 1888
from *Eichendorff Lieder* (14)

Tag und Regung war entflohen
Othmar Schoeck, "Vision" 1933, Op49,5, bar.mch.cham orch
from *Kantate. Nach Gedichten von Eichendorff*

Über gelb' und rote Streifen
Othmar Schoeck, "Lockung" 1917, Op30,10

Über Wipfel und Saaten in den Glanz hinein
Hugo Wolf, "Verschwiegene Liebe" 1888
from *Eichendorff Lieder* (3)

Über'n Garten durch die Lüfte hört' ich Wandervögel zieh'n
Friedrich Curschmann, "Frühlingsnacht" 1839, Op20,4
Robert Schumann, "Frühlingsnacht" 1840, Op39,12
from *Liederkreis*
Fanny Hensel, "Frühling" 1848pub, Op7,3
Adolf Jensen, "Frühlingsnacht" 1856, Op1,6
Ernest Vietor, "Frühlingsnacht" 1934-35, Op12,6
from *Frühlingslieder*

Und wenn es einst dunkelt
Peter Cornelius, "Der alte Soldat" 1873, Op12,1, 6t3b

Und wo noch kein Wandrer gegangen
Robert Franz, "Romanze" 1862?, Op35,4
Hans Pfitzner, "Der Kühne" 1894/95, Op9,4

Vergangen ist der lichte Tag, von ferne kommt der Glokken Schlag
Friedrich Curschmann, "Nachtlied" 1840, Op23,4
Felix Mendelssohn, "Nachtlied" 1847, Op71,6
Othmar Schoeck, "Nachtlied" 1914, Op20,13
Wilhelm Petersen, "Nachtlied" 1956pub, Op44,9

Vergeht mir der Himmel vor Staube schier
Hugo Wolf, "Aufblick" 1881, satb
from *Sechs geistliche Lieder nach Gedichten von Eichendorff*

Verschneit liegt rings die ganze Welt, ich hab' nichts was mich freuet
Othmar Schoeck, "Winternacht" 1918, Op30,3
Nikolai Medtner, "Winternacht" 1925-26, Op46,5

Vöglein in den sonn'gen Tagen, Lüfte blau, die mich verführen!
Fanny Hensel, "Anklänge I" 1841
from *Anklänge*

Von allen Bergen nieder so fröhlich Grüßen schallt
Johannes Brahms, "Der Bräutigam" 1860, Op44,2, ssaa.(pf)

Von fern die Uhren schlagen
Othmar Schoeck, "Aud meines Kindes Tod" 1914, Op20,8

Vor dem Schloss in den Bäumen es rauschend weht
Aribert Reimann, "Nachtstück (3)" 1966, bar.pf
from *Nachtstück*

Vorüber ist der blut'ge Strauß
Peter Cornelius, "Die Räuberbrüder" 1868-69

Wär's dunkel, ich läg' im Walde
Hans Pfitzner, "Die Einsame" 1894/95, Op9,2
Othmar Schoeck, "Die Einsame" 1907, Op10,2

Wagen musst du und flüchtig erbeuten
Peter Cornelius, "Reiterlied" 1872-73, Op12,2, 2(ttbb)
Hugo Wolf, "Der Soldat (II)" 1886
from *Eichendorff Lieder* (6)

Waldeinsamkeit! Du grünes Revier!
Philipp Spitta, "Waldeinsamkeit" 1860
Anton Rubinstein, "Waldeinsamkeit" 1867, Op76,1
Othmar Schoeck, "Waldeinsamkeit" 1918, Op30,1

Wandern lieb' ich für mein Leben, lebe eben, wie ich kann
Hugo Wolf, "Der Musikant" 1888
from *Eichendorff Lieder* (2)
Reinhard Schwarz-Schilling, "Der wandernde Musikant (1)" 1944, bar.pf
from *Der wandernde Musikant. Lieder nach Gedichten von Eichendorff*

Was ich wollte, liegt zerschlagen
Aribert Reimann, "Der Umkehrende (III)" 1978, bar.pf
from *Nachtstück II*

Was ist mir denn so wehe? Es liegt mir wie im Traum
Max Reger, "Traum" 1894, Op15,4, 1v(med).pf
Armin Knab, "Was ist mir denn so wehe?" 1922, alt/bar.pf
from *Eichendorff-Lieder*

Ernst Bacon, "Was ist mir denn so wehe?" 1928pub
Aribert Reimann, "Auf meines Kindes Tod (III)" 1978, bar.pf
from *Nachtstück II*

Was willst auf dieser Station?
Othmar Schoeck, "Was willst auf dieser Station?" 1928, Op42,3, 1v.pf.cl.hn.perc
from *Wandersprüche*

Weil jetzo alles stille ist und alle Menschen schlafen
Hugo Wolf, "Einkehr" 1881, satb
from *Sechs geistliche Lieder nach Gedichten von Eichendorff*
Othmar Schoeck, "Nachtgruß" 1931, Op51,1
Wilhelm Petersen, "Nachtgruß" 1956pub, Op44,6

Wem Gott will rechte Gunst erweisen
Robert Schumann, "Der frohe Wandersmann" 1840, Op77,1
Othmar Schoeck, "Der frohe Wandersmann" 1909, Op17,8, 1v(high).pf

Wenn alle Wälder schliefen, er an zu graben hub
Robert Schumann, "Der Schatzgräber" 1840, Op45,1

Wenn der Hahn kräht auf dem Dache
Othmar Schoeck, "Wenn der Hahn kräht auf dem Dache" 1928, Op42,5, 1v.pf.cl.hn.perc
from *Wandersprüche*

Wenn die Klänge nahn und fliehen
Johannes Brahms, "Wenn die Klänge nahn und fliehen" 1891pub, Op113,7, 3fv
from *13 Kanons für Frauenstimmen*

Wenn die Sonne lieblich schiene wie in Welschland lau und blau
Felix Mendelssohn, "Pagenlied" 1835, Nachlass
Richard Trunk, "Der wandernde Musikant" 1933pub, Op45,2
Reinhard Schwarz-Schilling, "Der wandernde Musikant (2)" 1944, bar.pf
from *Der wandernde Musikant. Lieder nach Gedichten von Eichendorff*

Wenn die Wogen unten toben, Menschenwitz zu Schanden wird
Wilhelm Petersen, "Spruch" 1956pub, Op44,7

Wenn Fortuna spröde tut, lass' ich sie in Ruh
Hugo Wolf, "Der Glücksritter" 1888
from *Eichendorff Lieder* (10)

Wenn ins Land die Wetter hängen und der Mensch erschrocken steht
Reinhard Schwarz-Schilling, "Marienlied" 1941

Wer auf den Wogen schliefe
Hugo Wolf, "Der Freund" 1888
from *Eichendorff Lieder* (1)

Wer einmal tief und durstig hat getrunken
Othmar Schoeck, "Sonett IV" 1952, Op66,4, 1v(high).orch
from *Befreite Sehnsucht*

Wer in die Fremde will wandern
Hugo Wolf, "Heimweh" 1888
from *Eichendorff Lieder* (12)

Wetterleuchten fern im Dunkeln
Aribert Reimann, "Wetterleuchten" 1978, bar.pf
from *Nachtstück II*

Wie dem Wanderer in Träumen, daß er still im Schlafe weint
Louis Ferdinand, "Treue" 1955pub

Wie ein todeswunder Streiter
Hugo Wolf, "Letzte Bitte" 1881, satb
from *Sechs geistliche Lieder nach Gedichten von Eichendorff*

Wir sind durch Not und Freude gegangen Hand in Hand
Richard Strauss, "Im Abendrot" 1948, sop.orch
from *Vier letzte Lieder*
Ernst Pepping, "Im Abendrot" 1949pub
from *Haus- und Trostbuch* (35)

Wir ziehen treulich auf die Wacht
Aribert Reimann, "Nachtstück (1)" 1966, bar.pf
from *Nachtstück*

Wo aber werd ich sein im künft'gen Lenze?
Othmar Schoeck, "Der verspätete Wanderer" 1917, Op30,8
Hans Pfitzner, "Der verspätete Wanderer" 1931, Op41,2
from *Drei Sonette für eine Männerstimme und Klavier*

Wo noch kein Wand'rer gegangen
Felix Mendelssohn, "Das Waldschloss" 1835, Nachlass

Wo ruhig sich und wilder unstäte Wellen teilen
Othmar Schoeck, "Motto" 1933, Op49,1, bar.mch.cham orch
from *Kantate. Nach Gedichten von Eichendorff*

Wohin ich geh' und schaue, in Feld und Wald und Tal
Felix Mendelssohn, "Gruß" 1845pub, Op63,3, 2sop.pf
Robert Franz, "Der vielschönen Fraue" 1860pub, Op10,4
Hans Pfitzner, "Der Gärtner" 1894/95, Op9,1
Othmar Schoeck, "Der Gärtner" 1914, Op20,11
Armin Knab, "Der Gärtner" 1920, alt/bar.pf
from *Eichendorff-Lieder*

Wolken, wälderwärts gegangen
Hugo Wolf, "In der Fremde (VI)" 1883

Wunderliche Spießgesellen
Othmar Schoeck, "An die Lützowschen Jäger" 1917, Op30,11

Zur ew'gen Ruh' sie sangen die schöne Müllerin
Robert Franz, "Romanze (Der traurige Jäger)" 1879, Op51,9
Robert Schumann, "Der traurige Jäger" 1849, Op75,3, satb

Zwei Musikanten zieh'n daher vom Wald aus weiter Ferne
Alexander Zemlinsky, "Vor der Stadt" 1894-96, Op2,i,7
Bruno Walter, "Musikantengruß" 1910pub
Richard Trunk, "Vor der Stadt" 1933pub, Op45,5
Louis Ferdinand, "Musikantengruß" 1953pub

Zwischen Bergen, liebe Mutter, weit den Wald entlang
Franz von Holstein, "Die Kleine" 1877, Op37,1
Hugo Wolf, "Die Kleine" 1887

Franz Eichert (1857-1926)
Ich bin mein Lied, mein Lied bin ich
Emil Mattiesen, "Der Dichter spricht" 190-?pub, Op15,7
from *Überwindungen* (7)

Walther Eidlitz (1892-)
Eine wilde Lokomotive schrie in der Nacht
Erich Zeisl, "Schrei" 1935pub

Wolrad Eigenbrodt (1860-1921)
Die Sonne sengt und dörrt das Land
Anna Teichmüller, "Elfenarbeit" 1907pub, Op17,4
from *Lieder Kindern gesungen*

Ein Rößlein möcht' ich haben und reiten in die weite Welt
Anna Teichmüller, "Ein Rößlein möcht' ich haben" 1910pub, Op19,4

Kleiner blauer Schmetterling, Schmetterling auf der roten Heide
Anna Teichmüller, "Auf der roten Heide" 1907pub, Op17,6
from *Lieder Kindern gesungen*

Sanft und lind geht der liebe Abendwind durch den Blütenbaum
Anna Teichmüller, "Abendwind" 1910pub, Op19,5

Summ! summ! summ! summ! so schwirrt es um das Bienenhaus
Anna Teichmüller, "Bienchen" 1910pub, Op19,1

W. Eisenmayer
Was ich mir still gelobte, will's halten treu und fest
Eduard Lassen, "Meine Devise" Op52,6

Anselm Karl Elwert (1761-1825)
Es stehen drei Stern' am Himmel (see also Volkslied)
Louise Reichardt, "Vaters Klage"

Hugo Emsmann
König Wilhelm, unsre Sonne, Hohenzollern, unser Stern!
Carl Loewe, "König Wilhelm" 1861, Op139

Franz Engel
Verlassen hab' ich mein Lieb
Max Reger, "Verlassen hab' ich mein Lieb" 1894, Op15,9, 1v(med).pf

Johann Jakob Engel (1741-1802)
Schon fesselt Lieb' und Ehre mich
Joseph Haydn, "Minna" 1781/84, XXVIa Nr.23

Magdelena Philippine Engelhard (1756-1831)
Ach, die entzückenden Töne der Saiten
Johann Rudolf Zumsteeg, "Lied" 1805pub
from *Kleine Balladen und Lieder, siebtes Heft*

Du blickst herab und scheinst zu fragen
Johann Rudolf Zumsteeg, "An den Mond" 1803pub
from *Kleine Balladen und Lieder, fünftes Heft*

Karl August Engelhardt ("Richard Roos") (1768-1834)
Dort ist ihr Grab, die einst im Schmelz der Jugend glühte
Franz Schubert, "Ihr Grab" 1822, D736

Karl Wilhelm Ferdinand Enslin (1819-1875)
Bist ja noch ganz allein!
Carl Loewe, "Der Abendstern" 1850

Der Abend dämmert, der Schmied, er hämmert
Carl Loewe, "Der Schmied" 1850?, 2v.pf

Du sagst, mein liebes Mütterlein
Max Reger, "Herzenstausch" 1903-04, Op76,5, 1v(med).pf
from *Schlichte Weisen, Band 1*

Herbei, heran, auf die glänzende Bahn!
Carl Loewe, "Schlittschuhlauf" 1850

Kling' Glöckchen kling'! klinge Glöckchen kling ling ling
Carl Reinecke, "Christkindchens Einlass"
from *Kinderlieder*

O Freude, o Wonne, wie scheinet die Sonne
Carl Loewe, "Der Schwimmer" 1850

Wir hatten uns ein Haus gebaut von Sand
Carl Loewe, "Das Sandkorn" 1850

Hermann Erler (1844-1918)
Blaue Augen, holde Sterne, sinkt in Schlummer
Franz Ries, "Gute Nacht" Op37,3

Mir tönt aus fernen Zeiten ein Wort, so wunderbar
Erik Meyer-Helmund, "Die Jugendzeit" 1886-88

"Ermin:" see Johann Gottfried Kumpf

"Ernst" (Jakob Matthias Schleiden) (1804-1881)
Die ersten Tropfen fallen aus trübem Morgenroth
Eduard Lassen, "Trüber Morgen" Op75,4

In deine Augen will ich schauen, wenn ich dir nahe bin
Eduard Lassen, "Immer bei dir" Op68,1
Joachim Raff, "Immer bei dir" 1855-63, Op98,9
from *Sanges-Frühling*

Längst schon flog zu Nest der Vogel
Joachim Raff, "Abendlied" 1855-63, Op98,7
from *Sanges-Frühling*

Leis sinkt der Dämmerung Schleier auf Wiese, Feld und Wald
Joachim Raff, "Ave Maria" 1855-63, Op98,17
from *Sanges-Frühling*

Seid mir gegrüsst ihr Wellen, du trautes Wasserlein
Joachim Raff, "Ihr Bild" 1855-63, Op98,20
from *Sanges-Frühling*

So still und mild der Tag und feierlich
Eduard Lassen, "Sonntagsruhe" Op62,3

Hans Eschelbach (1868-1948)
Es war ein Tag im Maien, da zog mein Alles fort
Frank van der Stucken, "Es war ein Tag im Maien" 1904pub, Op33,2

Johann Joachim Eschenburg (1743-1820)
Sollt' ich voller Sorg' und Pein
Joseph Haydn, "Der Gleichsinn" 1781/84, XXVIa Nr.6
translated from George Wither (1588-1667)

Tora zu Eulenburg
Heissa, heia! Stosset an, seht, wie das Leben lacht!
Erich J. Wolff, "Trinklied" 1907pub, Op11,4
from *Zwei Gedichte von Tora zu Eulenburg*

Verlangend dehntest du dich aus nach allem
Erich J. Wolff, "Sturmflut" 1907pub, Op11,3
from *Zwei Gedichte von Tora zu Eulenburg*

Franz Evers (1871-1947)
Das Fenster klang im Winde
Max Reger, "Das Fenster klang im Winde" 1903, Op75,16, 1v(med).pf

Der Mond streut durch die Zweige sein silberblaues Licht
Max Reger, "Sommernacht" 1902-03, Op70,17

Die andern Mädchen wissen's nicht
Max Reger, "Geheimnis" 1900, Op51,4

Die blaue Nacht geht leuchtend über'n See
Alexander Zemlinsky, "Nach dem Gewitter" 1897?, Op5,ii,3

Die Lande durchträumt der Schlaf
Max Reger, "Nachtsegen" 1901, Op55,12, 1v(med).pf

Die Sommernacht ist sanft und milde, unendlich milde ist die Nacht
Erich J. Wolff, "Andacht" 1907pub, Op11,1
from *Zwei Gedichte von Franz Evers*

Die Sterne sind so hell
Felix Weingartner, "Nacht" 1910, Op51,10
from *Abendlieder*

Er sitzt am Weg und klopft die harten Steine
Erich J. Wolff, "Der Steinklopfer" 1907pub, Op11,2
from *Zwei Gedichte von Franz Evers*

Es ist ein seliges Prangen und eine wilde Pracht
Max Reger, "Mondnacht" 1903, Op75,2

Hältst mich nun ganz in den Armen
Max Reger, "Ruhe" 1901, Op62,3

Meine Seele, die hat weite Flügel
Max Reger, "Meine Seele" 1902-03, Op70,7

Mich umduftet deine Seele süß wie eine Mondennacht
Max Reger, "Nachtseele" 1902, Op68,5, 1v(med).pf

Nachts wenn die Bäume rauschen
Max Reger, "Märchenland" 1902, Op68,3, 1v(med).pf

Nun du wie Licht durch meine Träume gehst
Max Reger, "Traum" 1901, Op55,2

Oh, das Korn, das wogte so
Alexander Zemlinsky, "Im Korn" 1897?, Op5,ii,4

Weiche Flötentöne, tiefverträumtes Girren
Max Reger, "Flötenspielerin" 1905, Op88,3

Wie geheimes Lispeln rieselt's durch die Nacht
Max Reger, "Nachtgeflüster" 1900
from *Liebeslieder* (3)

A. Faber

Schaukle auf den grünen Wellen
Franz Abt, "Schifferständchen" 1873pub, Op225,4

Emil Faktor (1876-after 1941?)[3]

Der Frühling starb im Dufte der Syringen
Erich J. Wolff, "Der tote Lenz" 1914pub, Lieder No.13

Du bist mein Schicksal, das ich wild begehre
Erich J. Wolff, "Bekenntnis" 1914pub, Lieder No.15

Glaub' es mir, jubelnde Kinderschar, all die schönen Märchen sind wahr
Erich J. Wolff, "Märchen" 1914pub, Lieder No.23

Heute summte mir im Ohr stundenlang die Weise
Erich J. Wolff, "Frühlingskinder" 1914pub, Lieder No.24

Ich bin so müd' und weiß nicht mehr wovon
Erich J. Wolff, "Der Wanderer" 1914pub, Lieder No.28

Ich weiß ihr liebt das Dunkel nicht
Karol Szymanowski, "An kleine Mädchen" 1910, Op22,3

In der Seele ein Wachsen und Keimen
Erich J. Wolff, "Wüßt' ich nur..." 1914pub, Lieder No.32

In tiefem Rausch hab' ich mein Glück gesegnet
Erich J. Wolff, "Entsagung" 1914pub, Lieder No.34

Schön wie die Sünden bist du, Kind
Erich J. Wolff, "Dir" 1914pub, Lieder No.46

Johannes Daniel Falk (1768-1826)

Nach dem Sturme fahren wir sicher durch die Wellen
Carl Loewe, "Nordisches Seelied" before 1829

Thoms saß am hallenden See
Carl Friedrich Zelter, "Der arme Thoms" 1796
Niklas von Krufft, "Der arme Thoms" 1812pub

Gustav Falke (1853-1916)

Aus der Tiefe tauchte sie nach oben
Max Reger, "Die Nixe" 1901, Op62,10, 1v(med).pf

Dämmerung löscht die letzten Lichter
Karol Szymanowski, "Seele" 1907, Op17,10

[3]Faktor was deported to Łódź Ghetto in Poland in 1941.

Das war der Junker Übermut
Max Reger, "Gute Nacht" 1901, Op55,13, 1v(med).pf

Der ganze Himmel glüht in hellen Morgenrosen
Alma Schindler-Mahler, "Erntelied" 1915pub

Der Mond scheint auf mein Lager, ich schlafe nicht
Anton Webern, "Fromm" 1899-1903
from *Drei Gedichte für Gesang und Klavier*
Max Reger, "Fromm" 1901, Op62,11, 1v(med).pf
Hugo Kaun, "Fromm" 1903pub, Op46,4

Der Morgen steigt und glüht und steigt
Max Reger, "Zwischen zwei Nächten" 1899, Op43,1

Drei bunte Kühe in guter Ruh
Max Reger, "Die bunten Kühe" 1902-03, Op70,4

Du hast in meinem Herzen ein reines Feuer erwekt
Josef Bohuslav Foerster, "Du hast in meinem Herzen..." 1913pub, Op43,2

Du schläfst, und sachte neig' ich mich
Max Reger, "Meinem Kinde" 1899-1900, Op43,3
Richard Strauss, "Meinem Kinde" 1897, Op37,3

Ein kühler Hauch. Die Linde träumt
Max Reger, "Müde" 1899-1900, Op43,2

Hat der junge Geigenmacher mit dem Tagwerk aufgeräumt
Hugo Kaun, "Abendlied" 1903pub, Op49,1, 1v.vn.pf

Herr, laß mich hungern dann und wann
Joseph Marx, "Gebet" 1910, 1v(med).pf

Holde Königin der Geigen, der die Liebe Namen lieh
Max Reger, "Viola d'amour" 1901, Op55,11, 1v(med).pf

Ich habe lieb die helle Sonne
Max Reger, "Heimat" 1907, Op76,37, 1v(med).pf
from *Schlichte Weisen, Band 4*

Ich wollt', ich wär' ein Held
Max Reger, "Der tapfere Schneider" 1901, Op55,3

Im Frühling, als der Märzwind ging
Alban Berg, "Die Sorglichen" 1907

Immer bleibst du lieblich mir, immer hold im Herzen
Max Reger, "An die Geliebte" 1902, Op68,6, 1v(med).pf

Jahrelang sehnten wir uns einen Garten unser zu nennen
Hugo Kaun, "Späte Rosen" 1903pub, Op46,6

Komm' ich längs der grünen Wiese
Max Reger, "Die Verschmähte" 1902-03, Op70,8

Laue Sommernacht, am Himmel stand kein Stern
Alma Schindler-Mahler, "Laue Sommernacht" 1900-01?

Nun steh' ich über Grat und Kluft
Max Reger, "Der Alte" 1901, Op55,15, 1v(med).pf

Reglos steht der alte Baum, alles Leid verwehet
Rudi Stephan, "Abendlied" 1914

Schlitten vorm Haus, steig ein, kleine Maus!
Richard Trunk, "Schlittenfahrt" 1933pub, Op63,1
from *Vier heitere Lieder*

Still, still! 'sist nur ein Traum
Max Reger, "Trost" 1894, Op15,10, 1v(med).pf

Tollt der Wind über Feld und Wiese
Max Reger, "Wäsche im Wind" 1903, Op75,8

Trug mein Herz ich auf der Hand, wehte ein Wind her übers Land
Max von Schillings, "Das mitleidige Mädel" 1901cop, Op13,1
Hugo Kaun, "Das mitleidige Mädel" 1903pub, Op46,5

Windräder gehn die Herbstesharfen sind
Joseph Marx, "Windräder" 1906
Universal Ed. list the poet as Oskar Falke. Schuberthaus Verlag as G. Falke.

Wir haben oft beim Wein gesessen und öfter beim Grog
Max Reger, "Wir Zwei" 1901, Op62,5

Wo die Wälder Wache halten um dein weisses Haus
Hugo Kaun, "Heimweh" 1903pub, Op46,3

Über die verhüllten Abendhügel
Siegfried Drescher, "Aus den Liedern Gustav Falkes" 1911pub

Alfred Fankhauser (1890-1973)
In meinem Herzen ruft ein groß Verlangen
Willy Burkhard, "Nach einer alten Melodie" 1925, Op9,4, 1v(low).pf
from *Frage*

Nun da der heiße Tag versank
Willy Burkhard, "Trost" 1925, Op9,9, 1v(low).pf
from *Frage*

Catherine Maria Fanshawe (1765-1834)
Es flüstert's der Himmel, es murrt es die Hölle
Robert Schumann, "Räthsel" 1840, Op25,16
translated by K. Kannegiesser. Poem misattributed to Byron as early as 1818.
from *Liederkreis*

Jakob Feis (1842-1900)
'S ist nicht dein holdes Angesicht
Eduard Lassen, "'s ist nicht dein holdes Angesicht" Op66,6
after R. Burns

L. Feldmann
Der Winter ist ein böser Gast
Josefine Lang, "Der Winter" 1834, Op15,5

Carl Felix
Die Sonne sank, die Möve zieht nicht mehr
Adolph Martin Foerster, "Am Meeresgestade" 1897, Op42,3

Kühl in dem Schatten, geküsst von dem Thau
Adolph Martin Foerster, "Wildröslein" 1897, Op42,2

Johann Georg Fellinger (1781-1816)
Die erste Liebe füllt das Herz
Franz Schubert, "Die erste Liebe" 1815, D182

Oben drehen sich die grossen unbekannten Welten dort
Franz Schubert, "Die Sternenwelten" 1815, D307
translated from the Sovene poet Urban Jarník

Was funkelt ihr so mild mich an? ihr Sterne, hold und hehr!
Franz Schubert, "Die Sterne" 1815, D176

"P. von Fels:" see Johann Christian Glücklich

"Eduard Ferrand" (B. Eduard Schulz) (1813-1842)
Das Kind schläft unter dem Rosenstrauch
Louis Spohr, "Der Rosenstrauch" 1838, Op105,2
Gustave Bley, "Der Rosenstrauch" 1896?pub, Op22,2

Ein Mägdlein saß am Meeresstrand
Johannes Brahms, "Treue Liebe" 1852, Op7,1

Afanasij Fet (1806-1892)
Ruhe, heilige Nacht! Dämmerig scheint der Mond
Alexander Zemlinsky, "Heilige Nacht" 1894-96, Op2,i,1
German translation by Friedrich von Bodenstedt

Ernst, Freiherr von Feuchtersleben (1806-1849)
Es ist bestimmt in Gottes Rat
Felix Mendelssohn, "Volkslied" 1839, Op47,4
Richard Wagner, "Es ist bestimmt in Gottes Rat" 1858, WWV 92
Ferruccio Busoni, "Es ist bestimmt in Gottes Rat" 1879, Op24,2, 1v(low).pf
Othmar Schoeck, "Es ist bestimmt in Gottes Rat" 1906, o.op24, ch

Heinrich Fick
Des Jünglings Blick erkennt der Liebe Zeichen
Carl Loewe, "Die Begegnung am Meeresstrande" 1847,after, Op120

K. Fick
Die Erde schläft, des Mondes Schein verklärend sie bedeckt
Max Reger, "Der Bote" 1902-03, Op70,14

Immer schwitzend, immer sitzend
Max Reger, "Des Durstes Erklärung" 1902-03, Op70,16

Ludwig Finckh (1876-1964)
Ich hab' es nicht gewußt, was Liebe ist
Alban Berg, "Fraue, du Süße" 1906

Gottfried Wilhelm Fink (1783-1847)
Dem Ew'gen unsre Lieder! was auch das Herz bewegt
Carl Loewe, "Dem Ew'gen" before 1829

Hans Fischer: see "Kurt Aram"

Johann Georg Fischer (1816-1897)

Das Mägdlein sprach: "Lieb Knabe, sag mir, was ist mein und dein?"
Max Reger, "Mein und Dein" 1902-03, Op70,13

Gestern ein Rieseln im weichen Eise
Ernest Vietor, "Ans Ziel" 1936, Op14,3

Ich sah am liebsten hoch im Turm
Alban Berg, "Eure Weisheit" 1906

Wo fliehst du armes Blättchen hin
Emilie Zumsteeg, "Das Epheüblättchen" 1817pub
from *Neun Lieder* (8)

Wo zweie sich küssen zum ersten Mal
Ernest Vietor, "Geweihte Stätte" 1939-40, Op17,4

Arthur (Heinrich Wilhelm) Fitger (1840-1909)

Seid gegrüsst, ihr grünen Hallen frühlingsheller Waldespracht
Jean Sibelius, "Lenzgesang" 1906, Op50,1

Heinrich Fitzau (1810-1859)

Im Abendgolde glänzet zu Bärenburg das Schloss
Carl Loewe, "Der alte Dessauer" 1868, Op141

Cäsar Flaischlen (1864-1920)

Es ist mitunter, als wären alle Fäden abgeschnitten
Karl Höller, "Graue Tage" 1926, 1v(med).pf
from *Cäsar Flaischlen-Zyklus*

Februarschnee, Februarschnee tut mir nicht weh
Ernest Vietor, "Februarschnee" 1936, Op14,2

Ganz still zuweilen, wie im Traum
Karl Höller, "Ganz still zuweilen" 1926, 1v(med).pf
from *Cäsar Flaischlen-Zyklus*

Ich möchte still am Wege stehn
Karl Höller, "Ich möchte still am Wege stehn" 1926, 1v(med).pf
from *Cäsar Flaischlen-Zyklus*

Schlafe, müde Seele! Daß dich nichts mehr quäle!
Karl Höller, "Schlafe, müde Seele" 1926, 1v(med).pf
from *Cäsar Flaischlen-Zyklus*

So regnet es sich langsam ein
Alban Berg, "So regnet es sich langsam ein" 1906

Siegfried Fleischer (1856-1924)

Verwelkte Blätter, entseelte Götter
Alban Berg, "Herbstgefühl" 1901

Bernhard Flemes (1875-1940)

Aus dunkler Nacht ein Brunnenlied klang hell
Max Reger, "Brunnensang" 1907, Op76,43, 1v(med).pf
from *Schlichte Weisen, Band 4*

Paul Flemming (1609-1640)

Laß dich nur nichts nicht dauern, mit Trauern sei stille!
Felix Mendelssohn, "Pilgerspruch" 1828pub, Op8,5
Johannes Brahms, "Geistliches Lied" 1856, Op30, satb.org/pf(3-4hd)
Max Reger, "Laß dich nur nichts nicht dauern" 1914, Op137,9, 1v.pf(harm/org)
from *Zwölf geistliche Lieder*

O liebliche Wangen, ihr macht mir Verlangen
Johannes Brahms, "O liebliche Wangen" 1868, Op47,4

Sei dennoch unverzagt. Gib dennoch unverloren
Ernst Krenek, "An sich" 1927, Op53,4
from *Vier Gesänge nach alten Gedichten*

Und gleichwohl kann ich anders nicht
Johannes Brahms, "An die Stolze" 1886, Op107,1

Florian

Wie lieb' ich euch ihr Nachtigallen
Johann Friedrich Reichardt, "Wie lieb' ich euch ihr Nachtigallen" 1800pub
after a Romanze from Florian's *Estelle*
from *Lieder aus dem Liederspiel, Lieb' und Treue* (1)

Wilhelm Floto (1812-1869)

Es blühet das Blümchen voll Glanz und voll Duft
Franz Abt, "Es blühet das Blümchen" 1873pub, Op124,4

Ernst Foerster

Du bist betroffen, daß in deinen Händen die Blumen welken
Adolph Martin Foerster, "Welke Blumen" 1909, Op69,7

Friedrich Förster (1791-1868)

Ach, wär' doch zu dieser Stund'
Carl Maria von Weber, "Mein Verlangen" 1816, Op47,5

Als ich ein junger Geselle war
Carl Loewe, "Der alte Goethe" 1835, Op9,ix,2

Die Wolken zieh'n vorüber, und Keiner hört sie geh'n
Friedrich Curschmann, "Die stillen Wanderer" 1833, Op5,5

Du trauter Stern! Warum so fern?
Friedrich Curschmann, "Trost in der Ferne" 1836, Op14,4

Ich bin ein lust'ger Wandersmann
Friedrich Curschmann, "Der lustige Wanderer" 1836, Op14,5

Ihr holden Augensterne, wie möcht ich doch so gerne
Friedrich Curschmann, "Gegenwärtiges Glück" 1836, Op14,1

In dunkler Felsenbucht am Rhein
Karl Gottlieb Reissiger, "Lurley" Op140,4, bar.pf

Keine Lust ohn' treues Lieben!
Carl Maria von Weber, "Triolett" 1819, Op71,1

Nein, ich will's nicht länger leiden
Friedrich Curschmann, "Der kleine Hans" 1836, Op11,6

Vöglein hüpfet in dem Haine
Carl Maria von Weber, "Die freien Sänger" 1816, Op47,2

Wach' auf, du gold'nes Morgenroth
Friedrich Curschmann, "An Rose" 1837, Op15,1

Wie mir geschah, ich weiss es nicht
Friedrich Curschmann, "Wie mir geschah!" 1838, Op18,1

Theodor Fontane (1819-1898)
Alles still! es tanzt den Reigen Mondesstrahl in Wald und Flur
Erich J. Wolff, "Alles still!" 1914pub, Lieder No.5

Das Kind ist krank zu Sterben, die Lampe giebt trägen Schein
Hugo Kaun, "Der Gast" 1903pub, Op46,2
Joseph Marx, "Der Gast" 1907, 1v(med).pf

Der Reimer Thomas lag am Bach
Carl Loewe, "Thomas der Reimer" 1860?, Op135

Es zieht sich eine blut'ge Spur
Ferruccio Busoni, "Lied des Monmouth" 1879, Op24,1, 1v(low).pf

Halte dich still, halte dich stumm
Ernest Vietor, "Die Frage bleibt" 1937-38, Op16,5

Ich hab' es getragen sieben Jahr
Carl Loewe, "Archibald Douglas" 1857, Op128, 1v(low).pf

Immer enger, leise, leise ziehen sich die Lebenskreise
Ernest Vietor, "Ausgang" 1936, Op14,11

Fouqué: see La Motte-Fouqué

Hans Franck (1879-1964)
Über alle Weiten weht der gleiche Wind
Louis Ferdinand, "Über alle Weiten" 1966pub

Michael Franck (1609-1667)
Ach, wie nichtig, ach, wie flüchtig
Peter Cornelius, "Ach, wie nichtig, ach, wie flüchtig" 1869, Op9,1, t(a).t.3b

Francke
Reizender Schmetterling, flüchtiges, kleines Ding
Franz Abt, "Schmetterling, setz' dich" Op294,3

Sage mir, Vogel im grünen Wald, Kuckuck, Kuckuck, Kuckuck!
Franz Abt, "Kuckuck wie alt?" Op237,4

Bruno Frank (1887-1945)
Sonn' auf Sonn' sich hellt, Schnee und Regen fällt
Joseph Marx, "Isolde" 1915, 1v(med).pf

Ludwig August Frankl (1810-1894)
Vom Himmel zogen rauschend viel runde Tropfen sacht
Carl Loewe, "Menschenlose" 1844, Op103,2

(Hermann) Ferdinand Freiligrath (1810-1876)
Auf dem stillen, schwülen Pfuhle tanzt die dünne Wasserspinne
Carl Loewe, "Schwalbenmärchen" 1839, Op68,1

Auf der Messe, da zieht es, da stürmt es hinan zum Cirkus
Carl Loewe, "Der Mohrenfürst auf der Messe" 1844, Op97,3

Auf des Lagers weichem Kissen
Carl Loewe, "Der Blumen Rache" 1839, Op68,3

Auf Jordan's grünen Borden
Carl Loewe, "Nebo" 1860, Op136(135b)

Da schwimm ich allein auf dem stillen Meer
Carl Loewe, "Meerfahrt" 1843?, Op93

Die Fürstin zog zu Walde mit Jägern und Marschalk
Carl Loewe, "Der Edelfalk" 1839, Op68,2

Fern tobt der Kampf im Palmenthal!
Carl Loewe, "Die Mohrenfürstin" 1844, Op97,2

O lieb, o lieb, so lang du lieben kannst
Franz Liszt, "O lieb" 1850pub

Sein Heer durchwogte das Palmenthal
Carl Loewe, "Der Mohrenfürst" 1844, Op97,1

So lass mich sitzen ohne Ende, so lass mich sitzen für und für!
Frederic Louis Ritter, "Ruhe in der Geliebten" 1876pub, Op10,2

Und nun kam die Nacht, und wir ritten hindann
Franz Liszt, "Und wir dachten der Toten"

Zelte, Posten, Werda-Rufer! Lust'ge Nacht am Donauufer!
Carl Loewe, "Prinz Eugen, der edle Ritter" 1844, Op92

Käte Freiligrath (Freiligrath-Kroeker) (?-1845)

Drei süsse kleine Dirnen sassen auf dem Zaun
Carl Reinecke, "Der wunderschöne Tag im September"
after Kate Greenawey
from *Kinderlieder*

Es waren fünf fette Gänse, die gingen eben vorbei
Carl Reinecke, "Von den fünf fetten Gänsen"
after Kate Greenawey
from *Kinderlieder*

Mariechen sitzt sinnend unter dem Baum
Carl Reinecke, "Mariechen unterm Baum" Op154b
after Kate Greenawey
from *Kinderlieder*

Prinz Sisi und die Frau Mama
Carl Reinecke, "Prinz Sisi und die Frau Mama"
after Kate Greenawey
from *Kinderlieder*

Ringel Reihe Rosenkranz, wir fünf Stumpfnäschen geh'n zum Tanz
Carl Reinecke, "Ringel Reihe Rosenkranz"
after Kate Greenawey
from *Kinderlieder*

Freudenberg

Das war die junge Königsbraut, die zog wohl über's Meer
Joachim Raff, "Höchster Lohn" 1855-63, Op98,11
from *Sanges-Frühling*

Der Knabe eilt durch den düstern Hain
Joachim Raff, "Die Winde wehen so kalt" 1855-63, Op98,6
from *Sanges-Frühling*

Die Sonne strahlt auf Wald und Feld
Joachim Raff, "Der Ungetreuen" 1855-63, Op98,12
from *Sanges-Frühling*

Adolf Frey (1855-1920)

I bi=n i d'Beeri gange dur d'Büsch und Stude=n i
Paul Hindemith, "Zur Unzeit" 1914-16, Op5,2
from *Lustige Lieder in Aargauer Mundart*

Im Gefild zum Strauße wand' wilde Blüt' ich sonder Acht
Max Reger, "Unvergessen" 1900, Op48,7, 1v(med).pf

In begrünter Sommerlaube
Othmar Schoeck, "Das Schlummerlied" 1907, Op14,2

Klingend schlagen hier die Finken
Othmar Schoeck, "Schöner Ort" 1907, Op14,3

's alt Bäni, heißt's, seig gwüss e Häx
Paul Hindemith, "Die Hexe" 1914-16, Op5,3
from *Lustige Lieder in Aargauer Mundart*

Was git's denn do? Was g'seh=n i do?
Paul Hindemith, "Kindchen" 1914-16, Op5,5
from *Lustige Lieder in Aargauer Mundart*

Wenn mein Herz beginnt zu klingen
Johannes Brahms, "Meine Lieder" 1888, Op106,4

Friedrich Hermann Frey: see "Martin Greif"

Daniel Friderici (1584-1638)

In einem Rosengärtelein
Max Reger, "In einem Rosengärtelein" 1904, Op76,18, 1v(med).pf
from *Schlichte Weisen, Band 2*

Friedelberg (?-1800)

Ein grosses deutsches Volk sind wir
Ludwig van Beethoven, "Kriegslied der Österreicher" 1797, WoO122

Keine Klage soll erschallen
Ludwig van Beethoven, "Abschiedsgesang an Wiens Bürger" 1796, WoO121

Hans Friedrich

Wenn ich müde bin einmal, führe, Mutter Erde, meine Seele
Paul Graener, "Nacht in der Heimat" 1916pub, Op40,1

von Fröhlich

Es regnet, es regnet, der Kukuk wird nass
Carl Reinecke, "Regenlied"
from *Kinderlieder*

Im Garten steht die Nonne bei Rosen in der Sonne
Robert Schumann, "Die Nonne" 1840, Op49,3

Schnick, schnack, Dud'lsack, unser Kind will tanzen
Carl Reinecke, "Tanzlied"
from *Kinderlieder*

Gottlieb Fuchs (1721-1799)

Hier, wo ich Abendröte und Tag verlöschen sah
Leopold Kozeluch, "Die Mitternacht" 1785?
Johann Christoph Hackel, "An die Mitternacht" 1786pub

Ludwig Fulda (1862-1939)

Dieser Tag verglüht nun auch
Paul Graener, "Abend" 1909pub, Op21,3

Friedrich Funcke (1642-1699)

Zeuch uns nach dir, nur für und für
Carl Loewe, "Himmelfahrtsgesang" 1835?, 4v

G.

Sanft, wie deine Seele, Lotte, sei dein Schlummer in der Gruft!
Johann Rudolf Zumsteeg, "An Lottchens frühem Grabe" 1803pub
from *Kleine Balladen und Lieder, fünftes Heft*

v.G.

Umflattre mir des liebsten Mädchens Wangen
Johann Rudolf Zumsteeg, "An die schlafende Psycharion" 1802pub
from *Kleine Balladen und Lieder, viertes Heft*

Eugenie Tugendreich (von Loos) Galli (1849-after 1917)

Nun, da sie Alle eingeschlafen
Max Reger, "Verlorne Liebe" 1900, Op51,10, 1v(med).pf

Gustav Gamper (1873-1948)

Führe mich zum Rosenhaine
Othmar Schoeck, "Jünger des Weins I" 1915, Op24b,2

Laut gesungen sei das Feuer
Othmar Schoeck, "Jünger des Weins II" 1915, Op24b,3

Federico García Lorca (1898-1936)

Die Zigeunernonne. Schweigsamkeit von Kalk und Myrthe
Hermann Reutter, "Die Zigeunernonne" 1956

Durch die Straßen von Sevilla tanzt und tanzet Carmen
Hermann Reutter, "Tanz" 1953

(Franz) Emanuel August Geibel (1815-1884)

Ach, wie lang die Seele schlummert!
Hugo Wolf, "Ach, wie lang die Seele schlummert!" 1889
from *Spanisches Liederbuch* (Geistliche Lieder, 8)

Alle gingen, Herz, zur Ruh'
Robert Schumann, "In der Nacht" 1849, Op74,4, sop.ten.pf
from *Spanisches Liederspiel*
Hugo Wolf, "Alle gingen, Herz, zur Ruh" 1889
from *Spanisches Liederbuch* (Weltliche Lieder, 21)

Also lieb' ich Euch, Geliebte
Robert Schumann, "Geständnis" 1849, Op74,7, ten.pf
from *Spanisches Liederspiel*

Am Ufer des Flusses, des Manzanares
Adolf Jensen, "Am Ufer des Flusses, des Manzanares" 1864, Op21,6
Leopold Damrosch, "Am Manzanares" 1903?pub, Op11,10

An den Ufern jenes Wassers sah ich Rosen stehn in Knospen
Max Bruch, "Von den Rosen komm' ich" 186-?, Op17,ii,1
translated from the Spanish
from *Vier weltliche Lieder aus dem Spanischen und Italienischen*

Auf des Gartens Mauerzinne
Fanny Hensel, "Im Herbste" 1846, Op10,4

Auf Flügeln rauscht der Wind daher, es rinnen und rauschen die Quellen
Joachim Raff, "Betrogen" 1855-63, Op98,8
from *Sanges-Frühling*

Ave Maria! Meer und Himmel ruh'n
Robert Franz, "Ave Maria" 1860?pub, Op17,1

Bedeckt mich mit Blumen, ich sterbe vor Liebe
Robert Schumann, "Duett" 1849, Op138,4, sop.alt.pf(4-hand)
from *Spanische Liebes-Lieder*
Hugo Wolf, "Bedeckt mich mit Blumen" 1889
from *Spanisches Liederbuch* (Weltliche Lieder, 26)
Leopold Damrosch, "Bedeckt mich mit Blumen" 1903?pub, Op11,7
Anton Rubinstein, "Bedeckt mich mit Rosen" 1867, Op76,5

Blaue Augen hat das Mädchen
Robert Schumann, "Duett" 1849, Op138,9, ten.bas.pf(4-hand)
from *Spanische Liebes-Lieder*

Da ich nun entsagen müssen Allem, was mein Herz erbeten
Robert Schumann, "Der Page" 1840, Op30,2

Dass die Luft mit leisem Wehen nicht den süssen Duft entführe
Leopold Damrosch, "Bedeckt mich mit Blumen" 1903?pub, Op11,3

Dass ihr steht in Liebesglut
Robert Schumann, "Es ist verraten" 1849, Op74,5, satb.pf
from *Spanisches Liederspiel*

Der Blumen wollt' ich warten
Joseph Marx, "Neugriechisches Mädchenlied" 1909

Der du am Sternenbogen, als Erstling kommst gezogen
Joachim Raff, "Mädchenlied" 1855-63, Op98,22
from *Sanges-Frühling*

Der Mai ist gekommen, die Bäume schlagen aus
Friedrich Silcher, "Burschenlust"

Der Mond kommt still gegangen mit seinem goldnen Schein
Johanna Kinkel, "Nachtlied" Op7,1
Clara Schumann, "Der Mond kommt still gegangen" 1842, Op13,4
Joachim Raff, "Der Mond kommt still gegangen" 1855-63, Op98,19
from *Sanges-Frühling*
Robert Franz, "Nachtlied" 1870?pub, Op28,3
Edward MacDowell, "Nachtlied" 1885pub, Op12,1
Charles Griffes, "Nachtlied" 1912, A28
Werner Josten, "Mondesstille" 1926pub
from *Fünf Lieder* (2)

Der Wald wird dichter mit jedem Schritt
Karl Goldmark, "Der Wald wird dichter" 1868pub, Op18,4, 1v(low).pf

Dereinst, dereinst Gedanke mein, wirst ruhig sein
Robert Schumann, "Liebesgram" 1849, Op74,3, sop.alt.pf
from *Spanisches Liederspiel*
Adolf Jensen, "Dereinst, Gedanke mein" 1860, Op4,7
Edvard Grieg, "Dereinst, Gedanke mein" 1889, Op48,2
Hugo Wolf, "Dereinst, dereinst Gedanke mein" 1890
from *Spanisches Liederbuch* (Weltliche Lieder, 22)
Leopold Damrosch, "Dereinst, dereinst" 1903?pub, Op11,4

Die ihr schwebet um diese Palmen (see also Lope da Vega: "Die ihr dort…")
Johannes Brahms, "Geistliches Wiegenlied" 1863/64?, Op91,2, alt.vla.pf
from the *Spanisches Liederbuch*, after Lope da Vega
Hugo Wolf, "Die ihr schwebet um diese Palmen" 1889
from *Spanisches Liederbuch* (Geistliche Lieder, 4)

Die Liebe saß als Nachtigall im Rosenbusch und sang
Clara Schumann, "Liebeszauber" 1842, Op13,3
Richard Strauss, "Waldesgesang" 1879
from *Jugendlieder*

Die Nacht war schwarz, die Luft war schwül
Felix Weingartner, "Reue" 1893, Op18,5
from *Severa. Sechs ernste Lieder*

Die stille Lotusblume steigt aus dem blauen See
Clara Schumann, "Die stille Lotusblume" 1842, Op13,6
Robert Franz, "Die Lotusblume" 1843pub, Op1,3

Die stille Wasserrose steigt aus dem blauen See
Franz Liszt, "Die stille Wasserrose" 1860

Du feuchter Frühlingsabend, wie hab' ich dich so gern
Adolf Jensen, "Du feuchter Frühlingsabend" 1862, Op6,1
Eduard Lassen, "Im April" Op46,2
Anton Bruckner, "Im April" 1868?
Max Reger, "Im April" 1891, Op4,4, 1v(med).pf
Alban Berg, "Am Abend" 1903

Du fragst mich, du mein blondes Lieb, warum so stumm mein Mund?
Eduard Lassen, "Schweigsamkeit" Op65,3

Dunkler Lichtglanz, blinder Blick
Robert Schumann, "Quartett" 1849, Op138,10, satb.pf(4-hand)
from *Spanische Liebes-Lieder*

Es fliegt manch' Vöglein in das Nest
Friedrich Silcher, "An die Treulose"
Hugo Kaun, "Geh' du nur immer hin" 1905pub, Op27,2

Es hat die Mutter mir gesagt: Dort hinter jenem Berge
Eugen Hildach, "Das Kraut Vergessenheit" 1898pub, Op9,3

Es ist das Glück ein flüchtig Ding
Werner Josten, "Das Glück" 1926pub
from *Fünf Lieder* (3)

Es ist so süss, zu scherzen mit Liedern und mit Herzen
Robert Schumann, "Der Hidalgo" 1840, Op30,3

Es rauscht das rote Laub zu meinen Füssen
Robert Franz, "Im Herbst" 1865?pub, Op20,6

Fern im Süd' das schöne Spanien, Spanien ist mein Heimathland
Eduard Lassen, "Zigeunerbub' im Norden" Op52,5
Karl Gottlieb Reissiger, "Der Zigeunerbube im Norden" Op206,2

Fluthenreicher Ebro, blühendes Ufer
Robert Schumann, "Romanze" 1849, Op138,5, bar.pf(4-hand)
from *Spanische Liebes-Lieder*

Geh, Geliebter, geh jetzt! Sieh', der Morgen dämmert
Hugo Wolf, "Geh, Geliebter, geh jetzt!" 1890
from *Spanisches Liederbuch* (Weltliche Lieder, 34)
Leopold Damrosch, "Geh', Geliebter, geh' jetzt!" 1903?pub, Op11,6

Goldne Brücken seien alle Lieder mir
Max Bruch, "Goldne Brücken" 1862, Op15,4

Gute Nacht, mein Herz, und schlumm're ein
Robert Franz, "Gute Nacht, mein Herz" 1860?, Op12,5

Hast einsam mich verlassen in dieser Öde!
Max Bruch, "Verlassen" 186-?, Op17,ii,3
translated from the Spanish
from *Vier weltliche Lieder aus dem Spanischen und Italienischen*

Herbstlich sonnige Tage, mir beschieden zur Lust
Friedrich Nietzsche, "Herbstlich sonnige Tage" 1867, NWV33, satb.pf

Hoch, hoch sind die Berge und steil ist ihr Pfad
Robert Schumann, "Lied" 1849, Op138,8, alt.pf(4-hand)
from *Spanische Liebes-Lieder*

Horch', im Winde säuseln sacht, Mutter, die Blätter
Leopold Damrosch, "Unter dem Schatten" 1903?pub, Op11,1

Ich bin der Contrabandiste, weiss wohl
Robert Schumann, "Der Contrabandiste" 1849, Op74,Anhang, bar.pf
from *Spanisches Liederspiel*

Ich bin ein lust'ger Geselle, wer könnt' auf Erden fröhlicher sein
Robert Schumann, "Der Knabe mit dem Wunderhorn" 1840, Op30,1

Joachim Raff, "Der Knabe mit dem Wunderhorn" 1855-63, Op98,28
from *Sanges-Frühling*

Ich blick' in mein Herz und ich blick' in die Welt
Louis Spohr, "Sehnsucht" 1837, Op103,3, sop.cl.pf
Robert Schumann, "Sehnsucht" 1840, Op51,1
Johanna Kinkel, "Sehnsucht nach Griechenland" Op6,1

Ich weiß nicht, säuselt in den Bäumen
Anton Rubinstein, "Frühmorgens" 1864, Op57,1

Ich weiß nicht, wie's geschieht, daß, was mein Herz auch singt
Werner Josten, "Lied" 1926pub
from *Fünf Lieder* (4)

Im Schatten des Waldes, im Buchengezweig
Johanna Kinkel, "Die Zigeuner" Op7,6
Robert Schumann, "Zigeunerleben" 1840, Op29,3, satb.pf.(perc.)

Im Wald, im hellen Sonnenschein wenn alle Knospen springen
Fanny Hensel, "Im Wald" 1846, Op3,6, satb
from *Gartenlieder*
Richard Strauss, "Im Walde" 1878
from *Jugendlieder*

In den Wassern der Laguna schwimmt das goldne Bild der Luna
Louis Spohr, "Gondelfahrt" 1837, Op101,6, 1v.pf(4-hand)

In meinem Garten die Nelken mit ihrem Purpurstern
Robert Schumann, "Lied" 1840, Op29,2, 3sop.pf
Robert Franz, "In meinem Garten die Nelken" 1843pub, Op1,12
Eduard Lassen, "Lied eines Mädchens" Op83,1
Arnold Schönberg, "Mädchenlied" 189-?
Franz Ries, "In meinem Garten" before 1891

Jeden Morgen, in der Frühe, wenn mich weckt das Tageslicht
Robert Schumann, "Zigeunerliedchen (2)" 1849, Op79,7,ii
translated from the Spanish
from *Lieder-Album für die Jugend*

Klinge, klinge mein Pandero
Adolf Jensen, "Klinge, klinge mein Pandero" 1864, Op21,1
translated from the Spanish of Alvaro Fernandez de Almeida
Anton Rubinstein, "Klinge, klinge" 1867, Op76,6
Hugo Wolf, "Klinge, klinge, mein Pandero" 1889
from *Spanisches Liederbuch* (Weltliche Lieder, 1)

Komm, o Tod, von Nacht umgeben
Hugo Wolf, "Komm, o Tod, von Nacht umgeben" 1890
from *Spanisches Liederbuch* (Weltliche Lieder, 24)

Kornblumen flecht' ich dir zum Kranz
Wilhelm Kienzl, "Im Glücke" 188-?, Op18,3

Laß schlafen mich und träumen was hab ich zu versäumen
Otto Lohse, "Lied des Mädchens" 1910pub

Mag auch heiss das Scheiden brennen
Friedrich Silcher, "Das Gedenken"

Mein Herz ist schwer, mein Auge wacht
Johannes Brahms, "Mein Herz ist schwer" 1883/84, Op94,3, 1v(low).pf

Mein Herz ist wie die dunkle Nacht
Eduard Lassen, "Mein Herz ist wie die dunkle Nacht"
Felix Mendelssohn, "Der Mond" 1851pub, Op86,5
Hans Pfitzner, "Mein Herz ist wie die dunkle Nacht" 1888/89, Op3,3, 1v(med).pf
Charles Griffes, "Mein Herz ist wie die dunkle Nacht" 1903-11?, A.Add1

Mit geheimnisvollen Düften grüßt vom Hang der Wald mich schon
Johannes Brahms, "Frühlingslied" 1878, Op85,5

Mögen alle bösen Zungen immer sprechen, was beliebt
Robert Schumann, "Ich bin geliebt" 1849, Op74,9, satb.pf
from *Spanisches Liederspiel*
Hugo Wolf, "Mögen alle bösen Zungen" 1890
from *Spanisches Liederbuch* (Weltliche Lieder, 13)

Mühvoll komm' ich und beladen
Hugo Wolf, "Mühvoll komm' ich und beladen" 1890
from *Spanisches Liederbuch* (Geistliche Lieder, 7)

Nelken wind' ich und Jasmin
Robert Schumann, "Botschaft" 1849, Op74,8, sop.alt.pf
from *Spanisches Liederspiel*
Leopold Damrosch, "Nelken wind' ich und Jasmin" 1903?pub, Op11,5

Nun die Schatten dunkeln, Stern an Stern erwacht
Johann Wenzeslaus Kalliwoda, "Abschiedsständchen" Nachlaß
Robert Franz, "Für Musik" 1860pub, Op10,1
Adolf Jensen, "Nun die Schatten dunkeln" 1862, Op6,2
Anton Rubinstein, "Nun die Schatten dunkeln" 1864, Op57,2
Hermann Behn, "Nun die Schatten dunkeln" 189-?, Op1,ii,7

Nun rauscht im Morgenwinde sacht so Busch als Waldrevier
Adolf Jensen, "Im Gebirg" 1862, Op6,5

Nun wollen Berg' und Thale wieder blüh'n
Robert Franz, "Wasserfahrt" 1860?, Op9,2

O schneller, mein Ross, mit Hast, mit Hast!
Adolf Jensen, "O schneller, mein Ross, mit Hast, mit Hast!" 1862, Op6,6
Hans Pfitzner, "O schneller, mein Roß" 1884-86?

O Sommerfrühe blau und hold!
Joseph Marx, "Sommerlied" 1909

O wie lieblich ist das Mädchen
Robert Schumann, "Lied" 1849, Op138,3, ten.pf(4-hand)
from *Spanische Liebes-Lieder*

Schlage nicht die feuchten Augen
Karl Goldmark, "Schlage nicht die feuchten Augen nieder" 1868pub, Op18,6, 1v(low).pf

Schmerzliche Wonnen und wonnige Schmerzen
Hugo Wolf, "Schmerzliche Wonnen und wonnige Schmerzen" 1890
from *Spanisches Liederbuch* (Weltliche Lieder, 18)

Seltsam ist Juanas Weise
Hugo Wolf, "Seltsam ist Juanas Weise" 1889
from *Spanisches Liederbuch* (Weltliche Lieder, 3)

Siehst du das Meer? Es glänzt auf seiner Fluth
George Henschel, "Siehst du das Meer?" 187-?, Op19,3
Frank van der Stucken, "Siehst du das Meer" 1879, Op5,2

So halt' ich endlich dich umfangen
Charles Griffes, "So halt' ich endlich dich umfangen" 1903-11?, A8

Tief im grünen Frühlingshag
Franz Ries, "Tief im grünen Frühlingshag" before 1891

Tief im Herzen trag' ich Pein
Robert Schumann, "Lied" 1849, Op138,2, sop.pf(4-hand)
from *Spanische Liebes-Lieder*
Hugo Wolf, "Tief im Herzen trag' ich Pein" 1890
from *Spanisches Liederbuch* (Weltliche Lieder, 23)

Und schläfst du, mein Mädchen, auf!
Robert Schumann, "Intermezzo" 1849, Op74,2, ten.bass.pf
from *Spanisches Liederspiel*
Adolf Jensen, "Und schläfst du, mein Mädchen" 1864, Op21,3
Hugo Wolf, "Und schläfst du, mein Mädchen" 1889
from *Spanisches Liederbuch* (Weltliche Lieder, 27)

Und wenn die Primel schneeweiß blickt am Bach
Robert Schumann, "Ländliches Lied" 1840, Op29,1, 2sop.pf

Unter den Bäumen, unter den Bäumen ruht das Mädchen
Leopold Damrosch, "Unter den Bäumen" 1903?pub, Op11,9

Unter die Soldaten ist ein Zigeunerbub' gegangen
Robert Schumann, "Zigeunerliedchen (1)" 1849, Op79,7,i
translated from the Spanish
from *Lieder-Album für die Jugend*

Verglommen ist das Abendrot
Robert Franz, "Des Müden Abendlied" 1870?pub, Op26,4
Charles Griffes, "Des Müden Abendlied" 1903-11?, A19

Vöglein, wohin so schnell?
Eduard Lassen, "Vöglein, wohin so schnell?"
Robert Franz, "Vöglein, wohin so schnell?" 1843pub, Op1,11

Von dem Rosenbusch, o Mutter
Robert Schumann, "Erste Begegnung" 1849, Op74,1, sop.alt.pf
from *Spanisches Liederspiel*
Leopold Damrosch, "Von dem Rosenbusch, o Mutter" 1903?pub, Op11,2

Wann erscheint der Morgen, wann denn, wann denn
Robert Schumann, "Melancholie" 1849, Op74,6, sop.pf
from *Spanisches Liederspiel*
Leopold Damrosch, "Wann erscheint der Morgen?" 1903?pub, Op11,8

Weh, wie zornig ist das Mädchen
Robert Schumann, "Lied" 1849, Op138,7, ten.pf(4-hand)
from *Spanische Liebes-Lieder*

Wenn sich auf dieses Blatt dein Auge senkt
Max Reger, "In ein Stammbuch" 1890/91

Wenn sich zwei Herzen scheiden, die sich dereinst geliebt
Felix Mendelssohn, "Wenn sich zwei Herzen scheiden" 1845, Op99,5
Robert Franz, "Wenn sich zwei Herzen scheiden" 1862?, Op35,5
Friedrich Kücken, "Wenn sich zwei Herzen scheiden"

Wer that deinem Füsslein weh?
Hugo Wolf, "Wer that deinem Füsslein weh?" 1889
from *Spanisches Liederbuch* (Weltliche Lieder, 30)

Wie doch so still dir am Herzen ruhet das Kind!
Max Reger, "Das sterbende Kind" 1898, Op23,3, 1v(med).pf
Charles Griffes, "Das sterbende Kind" 1903-11?, A.Add2

Wo am Herd ein Brautpaar siedelt
Max Reger, "Hütet Euch!" 1900, Op48,1, 1v(med).pf

Wohl lag ich einst in Gram und Schmerz
Charles Griffes, "Wohl lag ich einst in Gram und Schmerz" 1903-09?, A7

Wohl waren es Tage der Sonne
Robert Franz, "Wohl waren es Tage der Sonne" 1867?, Op41,3

Wolle Keiner mich fragen warun mein Herz so schlägt?
Louis Spohr, "Wolle Keiner mich fragen" 1842, WoO106
Robert Franz, "Wolle Keiner mich fragen" 1884, Op52,3

Wunden trägst du mein Geliebter
Hugo Wolf, "Wunden trägst du mein Geliebter" 1889
from *Spanisches Liederbuch* (Geistliche Lieder, 10)

Zwei Könige sassen auf Orkadal
Charles Griffes, "Zwei Könige sassen auf Orkadal" 1903-10?, A20

Max Geissler (1868-1945)

Auf dem Herd kein Feuer, kein Rößlein zum Ritt
Joseph Marx, "Wanderliedchen" 1911

Mein brauner Liebster, sage mir
Joseph Marx, "Zigeuner" 1911

So durch die Gassen im Silberlicht
Joseph Marx, "Piemontesisches Volkslied" 1911

Christian Fürchtegott Gellert (1715-1769)

An dir allein, an dir hab' ich gesündigt
Ludwig van Beethoven, "Busslied" 1802, Op48,6

Der Jüngling hofft des Greises Ziel
Joseph Haydn, "Betrachtung des Todes" 1796-1801, satb.bc

Die Himmel rühmen des Ewigen Ehre
Ludwig van Beethoven, "Die Ehre Gottes aus der Natur" 1802, Op48,4

Du bist's, dem Ruhm und Ehre gebühret
Joseph Haydn, "Aus dem Danklied zu Gott" 1796-1801, satb.bc

Gott, deine Güte reicht so weit
Carl Philipp Emanuel Bach, "Bitten" 1758

Ludwig van Beethoven, "Bitten" 1802, Op48,1

Gott ist mein Lied! Er ist der Gott der Stärke
Ludwig van Beethoven, "Gottes Macht und Vorsehung" 1802, Op48,5
Carl Loewe, "Gott ist mein Lied" 1826

Herr! Herr! der du mir das Leben bis diesen Tag gegeben
Joseph Haydn, "Abendlied zu Gott" 1796-1801, satb.bc

Ich komme vor dein Angesicht
Carl Loewe, "Busslied" 1829, Op22,i,4

Meine Lebenszeit verstreicht
Ludwig van Beethoven, "Vom Tode" 1802, Op48,3

So Jemand spricht: Ich liebe Gott!
Ludwig van Beethoven, "Die Liebe des Nächsten" 1802, Op48,2

Was ist mein Stand, mein Glück und jede gute Gabe
Joseph Haydn, "Wider den Übermut" 1796-1801, satb.bc

Wenn ich, o Schöpfer, deine Macht, die Weisheit deiner Wege
Carl Loewe, "Wenn ich, o Schöpfer, deine Macht" before 1829

Wie gross ist des Allmächt'gen Güte!
Carl Loewe, "Wie gross ist des Allmächt'gen Güte!" 1831, Op22,ii,4, 4v
Carl Loewe, "Wie gross ist des Allmächt'gen Güte! (later version)" 1850, 4v

Otto Franz Gensichen (1874-1933)

Unter blühenden Bäumen hab' bei schweigender Nacht
Ludwig Thuille, "Gruss" 189-?pub, Op4,1
Alexander Zemlinsky, "Unter blühenden Bäumen" 1897?, Op5,ii,1
Max Reger, "Gruß" 1902-03, Op70,5

Stefan Anton George (1868-1933)

Als neuling trat ich ein in dein gehege
Arnold Schönberg, "Als neuling trat ich ein in dein gehege" 1908-09, Op15,3
from *Das Buch der hängenden Gärten*

Als wir hinter dem beblümten tore
Arnold Schönberg, "Als wir hinter dem beblümten tore" 1908-09, Op15,11
from *Das Buch der hängenden Gärten*

An baches ranft die einzigen frühen die hasel blühen
Anton Webern, "An baches ranft" 1908-09, Op3,3
Wolfgang Rihm, "Lied" 1969, Op1,9

Angst und hoffen wechselnd mich beklemmen
Arnold Schönberg, "Angst und hoffen wechselnd mich beklemmen" 1908-09, Op15,7
from *Das Buch der hängenden Gärten*

Da meine lippen reglos sind und brennen
Arnold Schönberg, "Da meine lippen reglos sind und brennen" 1908-09, Op15,4
from *Das Buch der hängenden Gärten*

Das ist ein Lied für dich allein
Egon Wellesz, "Das ist ein Lied für dich allein" 1917
from *Lieder nach Dichtungen von Stefan George* (1)

Das lockere saatgefilde lechzet krank
  Anton Webern, "Das lockere saatgefilde lechzet krank" 1908-09
    from *Vier Lieder* (4)

Das schöne beet betracht ich mir im harren
  Arnold Schönberg, "Das schöne beet betracht ich mir im harren" 1908-09, Op15,10
    from *Das Buch der hängenden Gärten*

Dem bist du kind, dem freund
  Anton Webern, "Kunfttag I" 1908-09
    from *Vier Lieder* (2)

Dies ist ein lied für dich allein
  Anton Webern, "Dies ist ein lied" 1908-09, Op3,1

Du lehnest wider eine silberweide
  Arnold Schönberg, "Du lehnest wider eine silberweide" 1908-09, Op15,13
    from *Das Buch der hängenden Gärten*

Entflieht auf leichten Kähnen
  Anton Webern, "Entflieht auf leichten Kähnen" 1908, Op2, satb.harm.pf qt

Erwachen aus dem tiefsten traumes-schoosse
  Anton Webern, "Erwachen aus dem tiefsten traumes-schoosse" 1908-09
    from *Vier Lieder* (1)

Fenster wo ich einst mit dir Abends in die Landschaft sah
  Egon Wellesz, "Fenster wo ich einst mit dir" 1917
    from *Lieder nach Dichtungen von Stefan George* (6)

Gib ein Lied mir wieder
  Alexander Zemlinsky, "Gib ein Lied mir wieder" 1937/38, Op27,10

Hain in diesen paradiesen
  Arnold Schönberg, "Hain in diesen paradiesen" 1908-09, Op15,2
    from *Das Buch der hängenden Gärten*

Ich darf nicht dankend an dir niedersinken
  Arnold Schönberg, "Ich darf nicht dankend" 1907-08, Op14,1

Ihr tratet zu dem herde
  Anton Webern, "Ihr tratet zu dem herde" 1908-09, Op4,5

Im morgen-taun trittst du hervor
  Anton Webern, "Im morgen-taun" 1908-09, Op3,4
  Egon Wellesz, "Im Morgentaun trittst du hervor" 1917
    from *Lieder nach Dichtungen von Stefan George* (3)

Im windes-weben war meine frage
  Anton Webern, "Im windes-weben" 1908-09, Op3,2
  Egon Wellesz, "Im Windesweben war meine Frage nur Träumerei" 1917
    from *Lieder nach Dichtungen von Stefan George* (2)

Ja heil und dank dir die den segen brachte!
  Anton Webern, "Ja heil und dank dir die den segen brachte!" 1908-09, Op4,3

Jedem werke bin ich fürder tot
  Arnold Schönberg, "Jedem werke bin ich fürder tot" 1908-09, Op15,6
    from *Das Buch der hängenden Gärten*

Kahl reckt der baum im winterdunst
Anton Webern, "Kahl reckt der baum" 1908-09, Op3,5
Egon Wellesz, "Kahl reckt der Baum im Winterdunst" 1917
from *Lieder nach Dichtungen von Stefan George* (4)

Kreuz der Straße wir sind am End'
Egon Wellesz, "Kreuz der Straße" 1917
from *Lieder nach Dichtungen von Stefan George* (5)

Lilie der Auen! Herrin im Rosenhag!
Harald Genzmer, "Lilie der Auen" 1940-87, bar.pf or sop.pf
from *Acht Lieder nach verschiedenen Dichtern*

Mich erfreute der flug aller tiefdunklen pracht
Hans Erich Apostel, "Nachtgesang II" 1948, Op15,2, 1v(med).pf

Mild und trüb ist mir fern Saum und fahrt mein geschick
Hans Erich Apostel, "Nachtgesang I" 1948, Op15,1, 1v(med).pf
from *Drei Gesänge*

Noch zwingt mich treue über dir zu wachen
Anton Webern, "Noch zwingt mich treue über dir zu wachen" 1908-09, Op4,2

Saget mir, auf welchem pfade
Arnold Schönberg, "Saget mir, auf welchem pfade" 1908-09, Op15,5
from *Das Buch der hängenden Gärten*

Sei rebe die blümt Sei frucht die betört
Hans Erich Apostel, "Nachtgesang III" 1948, Op15,3, 1v(med).pf

So ich traurig bin weiss ich nur ein ding
Anton Webern, "So ich traurig bin" 1908-09, Op4,4

So wart bis ich dies dir noch künde
Anton Webern, "Trauer I" 1908-09
from *Vier Lieder* (3)

Sprich nicht immer von dem laub
Arnold Schönberg, "Sprich nicht immer von dem laub" 1908-09, Op15,14
from *Das Buch der hängenden Gärten*

Streng ist uns das glück und spröde
Arnold Schönberg, "Streng ist uns das glück und spröde" 1908-09, Op15,9
from *Das Buch der hängenden Gärten*

Unterm schutz von dichten blättergründen
Arnold Schönberg, "Unterm schutz von dichten blättergründen" 1908-09, Op15,1
from *Das Buch der hängenden Gärten*

Welt der gestalten lang lebewohl!
Anton Webern, "Eingang" 1908-09, Op4,1

Wenn ich heut nicht deinen leib berühre
Arnold Schönberg, "Wenn ich heut nicht deinen leib berühre" 1908-09, Op15,8
from *Das Buch der hängenden Gärten*

Wenn sich bei heiliger ruh in tiefen matten
Arnold Schönberg, "Wenn sich bei heiliger ruh in tiefen matten" 1908-09, Op15,12
from *Das Buch der hängenden Gärten*

Wir bevölkerten die abend-düstern
Arnold Schönberg, "Wir bevölkerten die abend-düstern" 1908-09, Op15,15
from *Das Buch der hängenden Gärten*

Zieh mit mir, geliebtes Kind, in die Wälder ferner Kunde
Alexander Zemlinsky, "Entführung" 1937/38, Op27,1
Franz Schreker, "Entführung" 1909?

Geppert

Nimm sie willig und geduldig diese Leiden, diese Schmerzen
Carl Loewe, "Engelsstimmen am Krankenbette" 1830, Op22,ii,2, 4v

Paul Gerhardt (1607-1676)

Alle, die ihr Gott zu Ehren unsre Christlust wollt vermehren
Ernst Pepping, "Christwiegenlied" 1945-46
from *Liederbuch nach Gedichten von Paul Gerhardt* (6)

Befiehl du deine Wege und was dein Herze kränkt
Ernst Pepping, "Befiehl du deine Wege" 1945-46
from *Liederbuch nach Gedichten von Paul Gerhardt* (11)

Die güldne Sonne voll Freud und Wonne
Ernst Pepping, "Die güldne Sonne" 1945-46
from *Liederbuch nach Gedichten von Paul Gerhardt* (3)

Fröhlich soll mein Herze springen dieser Zeit
Ernst Pepping, "Fröhlich soll mein Herze springen" 1945-46
from *Liederbuch nach Gedichten von Paul Gerhardt* (4)

Geh aus, mein Herz, und suche Freud
Ernst Pepping, "Geh aus, mein Herz, und suche Freud (duplicate)" 1945-46
This song also appears in *Haus und Trostbuch*
from *Liederbuch nach Gedichten von Paul Gerhardt* (10)
Ernst Pepping, "Sommergesang" 1949pub
from *Haus- und Trostbuch* (10)

Gib dich zufrieden und sei stille
Ernst Pepping, "Gib dich zufrieden" 1945-46
from *Liederbuch nach Gedichten von Paul Gerhardt* (9)

Ich bin ein Gast auf Erden
Ernst Pepping, "Ich bin ein Gast auf Erden" 1945-46
from *Liederbuch nach Gedichten von Paul Gerhardt* (8)

Ich steh an deiner Krippen hier
Ernst Pepping, "Ich steh an deiner Krippen hier" 1945-46
from *Liederbuch nach Gedichten von Paul Gerhardt* (5)

Jedes Ding in jeder Sache, was mir träumet für und für
Carl Friedrich Zelter, "Sonett" 1803

Kommt und laßt uns Christum ehren
Ernst Pepping, "Kommt und laßt uns Christum ehren" 1945-46
from *Liederbuch nach Gedichten von Paul Gerhardt* (7)

Nicht so traurig, nicht so sehr, meine Seele, sei betrübt
Ernst Pepping, "Nicht so traurig" 1945-46
from *Liederbuch nach Gedichten von Paul Gerhardt* (2)

Nun laßt uns gehn und treten mit Singen und mit Beten
Ernst Pepping, "Zum neuen Jahr" 1945-46
from *Liederbuch nach Gedichten von Paul Gerhardt* (1)

O Haupt voll Blut und Wunden
Ernst Pepping, "O Haupt voll Blut und Wunden" 1945-46
from *Liederbuch nach Gedichten von Paul Gerhardt* (12)

Rosa Gerheusser

Der Maien ist gestorben in seiner Blütenpracht!
Max Reger, "Der Maien ist gestorben" 1906

Rudolf Gernss

Trenn mich nicht vom Blätterthrone, gib mich nicht dem Tode hin
Luise Adolpha Le Beau, "Der Rose Bitte" Op39

(Friedrich) Karl von Gerok (1815-1890)

Einsamer Garten, öde und leer
Felix Weingartner, "Der öde Garten" 1904, Op31,1

Müder Glanz der Sonne! Blasses Himmelblau!
Josefine Lang, "Herbst-Gefühl" WoO

Julius Gersdorf (1849-1907)

An dem Brünnele, an dem Brünnele hab' ich oft gelauscht
Max Reger, "Am Brünnele" 1903-04, Op76,9, 1v(med).pf
from *Schlichte Weisen, Band 1*

von Gerstenberg[4]

Auch das schönste Blumenleben
Carl Loewe, "Himmelsblüthen" 1836, Op69,2

Dich blendet Kerzenlicht! Mich nicht!
Carl Loewe, "Kerzen und Augen" 1836, Op69,5

Die mich recht erkennen, Gott! erhalte sie mir
Carl Loewe, "Abendgebet, nach einer erlittenen Kränkung" 1836, Op69,3

Liebes Haus auf Berges Höh'!
Carl Loewe, "Gruss an Züllchow" 1836, Op69,1

Noch einmal muss ich vor dir stehn
Carl Loewe, "Abschied (Proömium)" 1819, Op9,iv,2

So viel Blumen allwärts blühen
Carl Loewe, "Der Fernen" 1836, Op9,ix,6

Welch Leuchten auf den Wogen, im Haus welch Himmelslicht!
Carl Loewe, "Die Sterne" 1836, Op69,4

Wo kommst du her? wo kommst du her?
Carl Loewe, "Der Komet" 1836, Op69,6

[4]For a discussion of the possible identity of this Gerstenberg (or these Gerstenbergs, since "Abschied" may be the work of yet another poet), see Maximilian Runze in *Carl Loewes Werke: Gesamtausgabe der Balladen, Legenden, Lieder und Gesänge.* Band XVII: Liederkreise; Leipzig: Breitkopf und Härtel, 1904. Forword, pp.xii-xiv. Reprinted Aldershot: Gregg International, 1970. Runze writes it is most unlikely that either Schubert's and Weber's Müller-Gerstenberg, or Zumsteeg's and Kuhlau's Heinrich Wilhelm von Gerstenberg is the author in question, at least for the Loewe songs from 1836.

Heinrich (Hans) Wilhelm von Gerstenberg (1737-1823)

Darachna! komm, mein Wunsch, mein Lied!
Johann Rudolf Zumsteeg, "Lied eines Mohren" 1805pub
from *Kleine Balladen und Lieder, siebtes Heft*

Der erste Tag im Monat Mai war mir der schönste Tag von allen
Friedrich Kuhlau, "Der erste Mai" 1820?
from *Drey Gedichte aus Gerstenbergs poetischem Wäldchen*

Ich sah ein Mädchen ohne Mangel
Friedrich Kuhlau, "Der Traum" 1820?
from *Drey Gedichte aus Gerstenbergs poëtischem Wäldchen*

Orpheus, als du mit Thränen deine Geliebte sangest
Friedrich Kuhlau, "Orpheus" 1820?
from *Drey Gedichte aus Gerstenbergs poetischem Wäldchen*

Stillen Geists will ich dir flehen!
Johann Rudolf Zumsteeg, "Anselmo" 1803pub
from *Kleine Balladen und Lieder, fünftes Heft*

Georg Friedrich Konrad Ludwig Gerstenbergk (Müller von Gerstenbergk) (1780-1838)

Lasst mich, ob ich auch still verglüh'
Franz Schubert, "Hippolit's Lied" 1826, D890
poem often misattributed to Johanna Schopenhauer

Was bricht hervor, wie Blüthen weiss
Carl Maria von Weber, "Das Mädchen an das erste Schneeglöckchen" 1819, Op71,3

Guido Gezelle (1830-1899)

Weh mir nun sachte, du seufzender Wind
Paul Hindemith, "Schlaflied" 1917, alt.pf
from *Zwei Lieder für Alt und Klavier*

(Heinrich) Ludwig Theodor Giesebrecht (1792-1873)

Als Weibesarm in jungen Jahren
Carl Loewe, "Als Weibesarm in jungen Jahren" 1839, Op39
from *Der Bergmann* (5)

Bienen summen, wie schwer zu tragen, und die ämsige Spinne webt
Carl Loewe, "Bienenweben" 1862-63

Bleib, mein Bruder, bleib noch eine Stunde!
Carl Loewe, "Scholastica" 1838, Op76,2, alt.ch.pf

Der König auf dem gold'nen Stuhle hat dich gesehn
Carl Loewe, "Der König auf dem gold'nen Stuhle" 1835, Op52,2
from *Esther: Ein Liederkreis in Balladenform* 2

Der Sabbath hebt, ein gröss'rer Sabbath an
Carl Loewe, "Sang des Moses" bass.pf

Ein Wasser in Oberpommern, der Virchowsee benannt
Carl Loewe, "Der Wurl" 184-?, 1v.ch.pf

Es hat der schimmernde Sonnenstrahl
Carl Loewe, "Frühlings Seele" 1844

Es steht ein Kelch in der Kapelle
Carl Loewe, "Es steht ein Kelch in der Kapelle" 1839, Op39
from *Der Bergmann* (4)

Euer Herz erschrecke nicht
Carl Loewe, "Der Friedhof" 1824

Euern Helfer, euern Sieger suchet droben, nicht in mir
Carl Loewe, "Des Meisters Phönix-Sang" 1843
from the Oratorio *Der Meister von Avis*

Glaubst du in Gott, den Vater, Sohn und Geist?
Carl Loewe, "Des Polus Taufe" 1856-59, bar.t.ch.pf
from *Gesangskreis* (8)

Gott sei mit euch! Uns ist es nicht beschieden
Carl Loewe, "Gott sei mit euch!" 1832-33, Op46,22, alt.orch
from the oratorio *Die sieben Schläfer*

Hat mit frischem Birkenlaube
Carl Loewe, "Taubenlied" 1844

Ich der Arzt, ich der Arzt, ich der Arzt für so viel Kranke
Carl Loewe, "Gesang des Polus" 1856-59, ten.pf
from *Gesangskreis* (3)

Im Schacht der Adern und der Stufen fahr' ich hinab
Carl Loewe, "Im Schacht der Adern und der Stufen" 1839, Op39
from *Der Bergmann* (1)

In dieses Thal, in diese Stille
Carl Loewe, "Gesang des Bischofs nebst Kyrie" 1856-59, bar.alt.pf
from *Gesangskreis* (4)

Jung stritt ich einst um Accons Schloss
Carl Loewe, "Sankt Mariens Ritter" 1834, Op36,2

Kann ich fürchten, zweifeln, meinen?
Carl Loewe, "Gesang des Persis" 1856-59, sop.pf
from *Gesangskreis* (7)

Lasst sich der Höhle Thor erschliessen
Carl Loewe, "Lasst sich der Höhle Thor erschliessen" 1832-33, Op46,4
from the oratorio *Die sieben Schläfer*

Lazarus ward auferwecket, aufgethan der Gräber Nacht
Carl Loewe, "Lazarus ward auferwecket" 1832-33, Op46,16
from the oratorio *Die sieben Schläfer*

Nach Jerusalem, der klaren Mutterstadt der Christenwelt
Carl Loewe, "Franz von Assisi" 1862, bass.satb.ch.pf

Neige, neige dich herab, unser Flehn zu hören
Carl Loewe, "Neige, neige dich herab" 1833, Op46,12, 4v

Nun auf dem fremden Boden mehret und baut euch, Israels Geschlecht
Carl Loewe, "Nun auf dem fremden Boden" 1835, Op52,3
from *Esther: Ein Liederkreis in Balladenform* 3

O Lämmlein bleibt, gedenkt an diesen Tag
Carl Loewe, "Einsegnungslied" 184-?, mch

Polus, beginne rasch und kühn dein Werk!
Carl Loewe, "Gesang des Kaisers" 1856-59, bass.pf
from *Gesangskreis* (2)

Schatten deckt, vom Thau befeuchtet
Carl Loewe, "Abendlied" 1844

Schlägt hier ein Menschenherz, wie meines, bange?
Carl Loewe, "Wechselgesang des Polus und Bischofs nebst Kyrie" 1856-59, satb.ch.pf
from *Gesangskreis* (6)

Spielt, Mägdlein, unter eurer Weide
Carl Loewe, "Spielt, Mägdlein, unter eurer Weide!" 1835, Op52,4
from *Esther: Ein Liederkreis in Balladenform* 4

Staunend schreit' ich durch die Gassen
Carl Loewe, "Staunend schreit' ich durch die Gassen" 1832-33, Op46,13, sop.orch
from the oratorio *Die sieben Schläfer*

Unser Herzog hat herrliche Thaten vollbracht
Carl Loewe, "Unser Herzog hat herrliche Thaten vollbracht" 1839, Op39
from *Der Bergmann* (3)

Voll banger Sorge hab ich längst bemerkt
Carl Loewe, "Gesang des Kaisers" 1856-59, bass.pf
from *Gesangskreis* (1)

Von meines Hauses engen Wänden
Carl Loewe, "Von meines Hauses engen Wänden" 1839, Op39
from *Der Bergmann* (2)

Wie früh das enge Pförtchen knarre
Carl Loewe, "Wie früh das enge Pförtchen knarre" 1835, Op52,1
from *Esther: Ein Liederkreis in Balladenform* 1

Wie still, wie einsam! aber meine Brust wird hier nicht stiller
Carl Loewe, "Gesang des Polus" 1856-59, ten.bar.pf
from *Gesangskreis* (5)

Wie wohnst du in des Reiches Städten
Carl Loewe, "Wie wohnst du in des Reiches Städten" 1835, Op52,5
from *Esther: Ein Liederkreis in Balladenform* 5

Wir graben tief in Trauer ein Grab hier in den Sand
Carl Loewe, "Des Meisters Geistersang" 1843, satb.ch.pf

Wolke lichtweiss in dem Blauen, reiner Schwan im Äthermeer!
Carl Loewe, "Das heilige Haus in Loretto" 1834, Op33,2

Hermann von Gilm zu Rosenegg (1812-1864)

Auf frisch gemähtem Weideplatz
Richard Strauss, "Die Zeitlose" 1882-83pub, Op10,7

Aus dem Walde tritt die Nacht
Richard Strauss, "Die Nacht" 1882-83pub, Op10,3
Ernest Vietor, "Die Nacht" 1907?, Op4,4

Es lokket und zwitschert von Haus zu Haus
Max Reger, "Das arme Vögelein" 1893, Op12,2

Es steht ein Lied in Nacht und Frost, die alles Leben tödten
Richard Strauss, "Wer hat's gethan" 1885, Op10,6a
Originally Op10,6. Dropped from final publication.

Geduld, sagst du und zeigst mit weißem Finger
Richard Strauss, "Geduld" 1882-83pub, Op10,5

Ich hab drei Kränze gewunden
Felix Weingartner, "Drei Kränze" 1904, Op32,1

Ich habe wohl, es sei hier laut vor aller Welt verkündigt
Richard Strauss, "Die Verschwiegenen" 1882-83pub, Op10,6

Ja, du weisst es teure Seele
Richard Strauss, "Zueignung" 1882-83pub, Op10,1

Küss' ich die Mutter Abends aus meines Herzens Grund
Felix Weingartner, "Küss' ich die Mutter Abends" 1904, Op32,3

Nennen soll ich, sagt ihr, meine Königin im Liederreich?
Richard Strauss, "Nichts" 1882-83pub, Op10,2

Stell' auf den Tisch die duftenden Reseden
Richard Strauss, "Allerseelen" 1882-83pub, Op10,8
Ludwig Thuille, "Allerseelen" 189-?pub, Op4,4

Warum so spät erst, Georgine?
Richard Strauss, "Die Georgine" 1882-83pub, Op10,4

Franz Karl Ginzkey (1871-1963)
Schrieb die schöne Adelheid
Max Reger, "Von der Liebe" 1907, Op76,32, 1v(med).pf
from *Schlichte Weisen, Band 3*

Frau E. von Girardin
Nein, nein, ich liebt' ihn nicht!
Franz Liszt, "Er liebte mich so sehr!" 1843pub
translated from the French by M. G. Friedrich and Th. Rehbaum

Albert Giraud (1860-1929)
Den Wein, den man mit Augen trinkt
Arnold Schönberg, "Mondestrunken" 1912, Op21,1, sprechstimme.cham
translated by Otto Erich Hartleben
from *Pierrot lunaire*

Der Mond, ein blankes Türkenschwert
Arnold Schönberg, "Enthauptung" 1912, Op21,13, sprechstimme.cham
translated by Otto Erich Hartleben
from *Pierrot lunaire*

Der Mondstrahl ist das Ruder
Arnold Schönberg, "Heimfahrt" 1912, Op21,20, sprechstimme.cham
translated by Otto Erich Hartleben
from *Pierrot lunaire*

Der Violine zarte Seele voll schweigend reger Harmonien
Joseph Marx, "Die Violine" 1909, 1v(med).pf

Des Mondlichts bleiche Blüten, die weißen Wunderrosen
Joseph Marx, "Kolumbine" 1909, 1v(med).pf

Arnold Schönberg, "Colombine" 1912, Op21,2, sprechstimme.cham
translated by Otto Erich Hartleben
from *Pierrot lunaire*

Die dürre Dirne mit langem Halse
Arnold Schönberg, "Galgenlied" 1912, Op21,12, sprechstimme.cham
translated by Otto Erich Hartleben
from *Pierrot lunaire*

Du nächtig todeskranker Mond
Arnold Schönberg, "Der kranke Mond" 1912, Op21,7, sprechstimme.cham
translated by Otto Erich Hartleben
from *Pierrot lunaire*

Eine blasse Wäscherin
Arnold Schönberg, "Eine blasse Wäscherin" 1912, Op21,4, sprechstimme.cham
translated by Otto Erich Hartleben
from *Pierrot lunaire*

Einen weissen Fleck des hellen Mondes
Arnold Schönberg, "Der Mondfleck" 1912, Op21,18, sprechstimme.cham
translated by Otto Erich Hartleben
from *Pierrot lunaire*

Finstre, schwarze Riesenfalter töteten der Sonne Glanz
Arnold Schönberg, "Nacht" 1912, Op21,8, sprechstimme.cham
translated by Otto Erich Hartleben
from *Pierrot lunaire*

Heilge Kreuze sind die Verse
Arnold Schönberg, "Die Kreuze" 1912, Op21,14, sprechstimme.cham
translated by Otto Erich Hartleben
from *Pierrot lunaire*

Im phantast'schen Mondenstrahle
Joseph Marx, "Pierrot Dandy" 1909

In den blanken Kopf Cassanders
Arnold Schönberg, "Gemeinheit!" 1912, Op21,16, sprechstimme.cham
translated by Otto Erich Hartleben
from *Pierrot lunaire*

Lieblich klagend – ein kristallnes Seufzen
Arnold Schönberg, "Heimweh" 1912, Op21,15, sprechstimme.cham
translated by Otto Erich Hartleben
from *Pierrot lunaire*

Mit einem phantastischen Lichtstrahl
Arnold Schönberg, "Der Dandy" 1912, Op21,3, sprechstimme.cham
translated by Otto Erich Hartleben
from *Pierrot lunaire*

Mit groteskem Riesenbogen
Arnold Schönberg, "Serenade" 1912, Op21,19, sprechstimme.cham
translated by Otto Erich Hartleben
from *Pierrot lunaire*

O alter Duft der Märchenzeit
Arnold Schönberg, "O alter Duft" 1912, Op21,21, sprechstimme.cham
translated by Otto Erich Hartleben
from *Pierrot lunaire*

Pierrot! Mein Lachen hab ich verlernt!
Ernest Vietor, "Gebet an Pierrot" Op5,4
Arnold Schönberg, "Gebet an Pierrot" 1912, Op21,9, sprechstimme.cham
translated by Otto Erich Hartleben
from *Pierrot lunaire*

Rote, fürstliche Rubine
Arnold Schönberg, "Raub" 1912, Op21,10, sprechstimme.cham
translated by Otto Erich Hartleben
from *Pierrot lunaire*

Steig, o Mutter aller Schmerzen
Arnold Schönberg, "Madonna" 1912, Op21,6, sprechstimme.cham
translated by Otto Erich Hartleben
from *Pierrot lunaire*

Stricknadeln, blank und blinkend
Arnold Schönberg, "Parodie" 1912, Op21,17, sprechstimme.cham
translated by Otto Erich Hartleben
from *Pierrot lunaire*

Wie ein blasser Tropfen Blut's
Joseph Marx, "Valse de Chopin" 1909, 1v(med).pf
Arnold Schönberg, "Valse de Chopin" 1912, Op21,5, sprechstimme.cham
translated by Otto Erich Hartleben
from *Pierrot lunaire*

Zu grausem Abendmahle
Arnold Schönberg, "Rote Messe" 1912, Op21,11, sprechstimme.cham
translated by Otto Erich Hartleben
from *Pierrot lunaire*

R. Glaser

Des Lebens Schönheit mußt ich tief empfinden
Gottfried Herrmann, "Erfüllung" 1843, 1v.cl.pf

Johann Wilhelm Ludwig Gleim (1719-1803)

Das arme Veilchen, sieh' o sieh'
Josef Antonín Štěpán, "Das Veilchen im Hornung" 1778-79pub

Das Leben ist ein Traum
Joseph Haydn, "Das Leben ist ein Traum" 1781/84, XXVIa Nr.21

Erhalt uns den König
Carl Friedrich Zelter, "Lied für preußische Patrioten" 1792

Gute Nacht! Mädchen, das der Liebe lacht
Emil Mattiesen, "Ständchen" 1900pub, Op7,3
from *Vier heitere Lieder*

Hin ist alle meine Kraft, alt und schwach bin ich
Joseph Haydn, "Der Greis" 1796-1801, satb.bc

Ich bin vergnügt, will ich was mehr?
Joseph Haydn, "Zufriedenheit" 1781/84, XXVIa Nr.20

Ich, der mit flatterndem Sinn
Ludwig van Beethoven, "Selbstgespräch" 1792?, WoO114

Ich hab' ein kleines Hüttchen nur
Carl Friedrich Zelter, "Das Hüttchen" 1791-92?

Ich möchte wohl der Kaiser sein!
Johann Holzer, "Der Kaiser" 1779pub
Wolfgang Amadeus Mozart, "Ein deutsches Kriegslied" 1788

Ob ich dich liebe weiss ich nicht
Johann Rudolf Zumsteeg, "Nach Hans Hadloub" 1803pub
from *Kleine Balladen und Lieder, fünftes Heft*

Phyllis, unter diesen Buchen
Paul Hindemith, "Corrente" 1925, Op35,i,3, sop.ob.vla.vc
from *Die Serenaden*

Rosen pflücke, Rosen blühn, morgen ist nicht heut!
Alban Berg, "Leukon" 1908

Wilhelm Gleim d. J.
Da kommt ja der liebliche Mai
Carl Loewe, "Naturgenuss" before 1826
The poet is probably a nephew of J. W. L. Gleim

Barbara Elisabeth Glück: see "Betty Paoli"

(Johann) Christian Glücklich ("P. von Fels") (1839-1920)
Du, der die Menschheit stolz und kühn
Max Reger, "An Zeppelin" 1909

Unendlich dehnt sich das brausende Meer
Max Reger, "Am Meer" 1894

H. Goeble
Wenn die Sonne nieder sinket
Ludwig van Beethoven, "Abendlied unterm gestirnten Himmel" 1820, WoO150

Karl Emil Konstantin von Goechhausen (1778-1855)
Eya popeya, so leise, so lind, wieg dich in Schlummer
Louis Spohr, "Wiegenlied" 1809, Op25,1

Leopold Friedrich Günther von Goekingk (1748-1828)
Meine Tränen sind geweint!
Karl Friberth, "Als er seinem Tode entgegen sah" 1780pub

Gerd Hans Goering
Du ewig Wandelbare, sieh, du bist die Brükke
Ernst Krenek, "Rätselspiel" 1922, Op9,6

Es war ein König Lobesam
Ernst Krenek, "Die Ballade vom König Lobesam" 1924pub, Op9,7

Groß wuchsen alle Räume; wie enge wird es nun
Ernst Krenek, "Räume" 1921, Op9,2

Und oft war's nur ein Hauch, der Blätter streifte
Ernst Krenek, "Erinnerungen" 1922, Op9,4

Wir sind nicht droben, doch wir sind am Ziel
Ernst Krenek, "Im Spiegel" 1921, Op9,1

Reinhard Goering (1887-1936)
Die wir dem Licht in Liebe dienen
Paul Hindemith, "Die wir dem Licht in Liebe dienen" 1925, Op45,ii,3, 2v.insts
from *Sing-und Spielmusiken für Liebhaber und Musikfreunde*

Albrecht Goes (1908-)
Du haderst wohl zuweilen, Liebster, sag'
Erich Riede, "Geburt der Liebe" Op10,2, sop.pf

Klein ist, mein Kind, dein erster Schritt, klein wird dein letzter sein
Erich Riede, "Die Schritte" Op10,4, sop.pf
Felix Wolfes, "Die Schritte" 1960

Johann Wolfgang von Goethe (1749-1832)
Aber abseits, wer ist's? Ins Gebüsch verliert sich sein Pfad
Johannes Brahms, "Rhapsodie" 1869, Op53, alt.ttbb.orch

Ach daß die innre Schöpfungskraft
Johann Friedrich Reichardt, "Künstlers Abendlied" 1794pub, 1v.pf or 4v
Carl Friedrich Zelter, "Künstlers Abendlied" 1807

Ach neige, du Schmerzenreiche
Bernhard Klein, "Gretchen"
Franz Schubert, "Gretchens Bitte" (fragment), 1817, D564
Richard Wagner, "Melodram" 1831, WWV 15, declamation.pf
from *Sieben Kompositionen zu Goethes "Faust"* (7)
Carl Loewe, "Scene aus *Faust*" 1835 or 1836, Op9,ix,1
Giuseppe Verdi, "Deh, pietoso, oh Addolorata" 1838
translated into Italian by Luigi Balestra
from *Sei romanze*
Hugo Wolf, "Gretchen vor dem Andachtsbild der Mater Dolorosa" 1878

Ach! um deine feuchten Schwingen: See Marianne von Willemer

Ach, was soll der Mensch verlangen?
Hugo Wolf, "Beherzigung" 1888
from *Goethe Lieder* (18)
Winfried Zillig, "Beherzigung" 1941
from *Zehn Lieder nach Gedichten von Goethe*

Ach, wer bringt die schönen Tage, jene Tage der ersten Liebe
Johann Friedrich Reichardt, "Erster Verlust" 1794pub
Hans Georg Nägeli, "Erster Verlust" 1797
Carl Friedrich Zelter, "Erster Verlust" 1807
Franz Schubert, "Erster Verlust" 1815, D226
Václav Jan Tomášek, "Erster Verlust" 1815?, Op56,3
from *Gedichte von Goethe:* IV,3
Felix Mendelssohn, "Erster Verlust" 1841, Op99,1
Hugo Wolf, "Erster Verlust" 1876, Op9,3
Alban Berg, "Erster Verlust" 1904
Nikolai Medtner, "Erster Verlust" 1904-05, Op6,8

Othmar Schoeck, "Erster Verlust" 1908, Op15,5
Armin Knab, "Erster Verlust" 1924-46
from *Zwölf Lieder nach Gedichten von J. W. von Goethe*
Pierre-Octave Ferroud, "Erster Verlust" 1932pub
from *Drei traute Gesänge*
Cor de Groot, "Erster Verlust" 194-?pub
from *7 Goethe Lieder* (4)

Ach wer heilet die Schmerzen
Johann Friedrich Reichardt, "Rhapsodie (Aus der Harzreise)" 1794pub

Alle Menschen groß und klein
Richard Strauss, "Sinnspruch" 1919

Alles geben die Götter, die unendlichen
Othmar Schoeck, "Dithyrambe" 1911, Op22, 2ch.orch.organ

Alles kündet Dich an! Erscheinet die herrliche Sonne
Fanny Hensel, "Gegenwart" 1833
Robert Franz, "Gegenwart" 1864pub, Op33,2

Als er, Sami, mit dir jüngst Blumen brach in dem Garten
Carl Loewe, "An Sami" 1844, Op104,2, ss.pf

Als ich auf dem Euphrat schiffte
Johanna Kinkel, "Traumdeutung" Op10,5
Hugo Wolf, "Als ich auf dem Euphrat schiffte" 1889
from *Goethe Lieder* (41)

Als ich noch ein Knabe war, sperrte man mich ein
Corona Schröter, "Jugendlied" 1786
Johann Friedrich Reichardt, "Der neue Amadis" 1809pub
Hugo Wolf, "Der neue Amadis" 1889
from *Goethe Lieder* (23)
Armin Knab, "Der neue Amadis" 1924-46
from *Zwölf Lieder nach Gedichten von J. W. von Goethe*
Ernst Krenek, "Der neue Amadis" 1927, Op56,2

Als ich still und ruhig spann, ohne nur zu stocken
Johann Friedrich Reichardt, "Die Spinnerin" 1809pub
Ferdinand Ries, "Die Spinnerin" 1811pub, Op36,5
Franz Schubert, "Die Spinnerin" 1815, D247
Václav Jan Tomášek, "Die Spinnerin" 1815?, Op55,2
from *Gedichte von Goethe:* III,2

Am Ziele! ich fühle die Nähe, die Nähe des Lieben
Siegmund Seckendorff, "Am Ziele: Schlußarie aus *Lila*" 1776

Amor, nicht das Kind: der Jüngling, der Psychen verführte
Carl Friedrich Zelter, "Der neue Amor" 1820?

An ä Bergli bin i gesässe (see also "Uf'm Bergli…")
Johann Friedrich Reichardt, "Nach einem Schweizervolkslied" 1811pub, 1v.pf or 4v

An dem reinsten Frühlingsmorgen ging die Schäferin und sang
Domenico Cimarosa, "Die Spröde und die Bekehrte" 1797pub
Cimarosa sets both poems together in the same strophic song
Carl Friedrich Zelter, "Die Spröde" 1807

Václav Jan Tomášek, "Die Spröde" 1815?, Op54,2
from *Gedichte von Goethe:* II,2
Hugo Wolf, "Die Spröde" 1889
from *Goethe Lieder* (26)
Richard Kahn, "Die Spröde" 1896?pub
Nikolai Medtner, "Die Spröde" 1908-09, Op18,1
Armin Knab, "Die Spröde" 1924-46
from *Zwölf Lieder nach Gedichten von J. W. von Goethe*
Wilhelm Petersen, "Die Spröde" 1941pub, Op40,1
from *Goethe Lieder*

An des lust'gen Brunnens Rand
Fanny Hensel, "Suleika und Hatem" 1828pub, Op8,12(FM), sop.ten.pf
Othmar Schoeck, "Suleika und Hatem" 1915, Op19b,2

An die Thüren will ich schleichen
Johann Friedrich Reichardt, "Letztes Lied des Harfenspielers" 1809pub
Franz Schubert, "An die Thüren will ich schleichen" 1816, D479
Carl Friedrich Zelter, "Harfenspieler 2" 1818
Norbert Burgmüller, "Harfenspieler I" 1827-36?, Op3,6
Robert Schumann, "An die Thüren will ich schleichen" 1849, Op98a,8
Modest Mussorgsky, "Lied des Harfenspielers" (set in Russian), 1863
Hugo Wolf, "Harfenspieler (II)" 1888
from *Goethe Lieder* (2)
Victor August Loser, "Gesang des Harfners aus *Wilhelm Meister*" 1899?pub, Op15,2
Nikolai Medtner, "Aus *Wilhelm Meister*" 1907-08, Op15,2

An vollen Büschelzweigen, Geliebte, sieh nur hin!
Ernst Pepping, "An vollen Büschelzweigen" 1949pub
from *Haus- und Trostbuch* (22)

Arm am Beutel, krank am Herzen, schleppt' ich meine langen Tage
Johann Friedrich Reichardt, "Der Schatzgräber" 1811pub
Franz Schubert, "Der Schatzgräber" 1815, D256
Carl Loewe, "Der Schatzgräber" 1836, Op59,3
Hanns Eisler, "Der Schatzgräber" 1942

Auch in der Ferne dir so nah! Und unerwartet kommt die Qual
Fanny Hensel, "An Suleika" 1825

Auf aus der Ruh! auf aus der Ruh!
Siegmund Seckendorff, "Szene aus *Lila*" 1776, 3v.pf

Auf dem Land und in der Stadt
Herzogin Anna Amalia, "Auf dem Land und in der Stadt" 1776

Auf Kieseln im Bache da lieg' ich, wie helle!
Johann Friedrich Reichardt, "Wechsel" 1809pub
Carl Loewe, "Wechsel" 1835

Augen, sagt mir, sagt, was sagt ihr?
Fanny Hensel, "April" 1836, sop.alt.pf
Ernst Pepping, "April" 1949pub
from *Haus- und Trostbuch* (24)

Bedecke deinen Himmel, Zeus, mit Wolkendunst
Johann Friedrich Reichardt, "Prometheus" 1809pub, 1v(low).pf

Franz Schubert, "Prometheus" 1819, D674
Hugo Wolf, "Prometheus" 1889
from *Goethe Lieder* (49)

Bei dem Glanze der Abendröte ging ich still den Wald entlang
Carl Friedrich Zelter, "Die Bekehrte" 1807
Václav Jan Tomášek, "Die Bekehrte" 1815?, Op54,3
from *Gedichte von Goethe:* II,3
Hugo Wolf, "Die Bekehrte" 1889
from *Goethe Lieder* (27)
Nikolai Medtner, "Die Bekehrte" 1908-09, Op18,2
Ferruccio Busoni, "Die Bekehrte" 1921, 1fv.pf
Armin Knab, "Die Bekehrte" 1924-46
from *Zwölf Lieder nach Gedichten von J. W. von Goethe*

Bilder der Hoffnung, täuschet mein Herz!
Johann Friedrich Reichardt, "Aus *Alexis und Dora*" 1805-06pub

Bist du aus einem Traum erwacht?
Johann Friedrich Reichardt, "Monolog des Tasso" 1791

Bleibe, bleibe bei mir, holder Fremdling, süße Liebe
Armin Knab, "Bleibe, bleibe bei mir" 1924-46
from *Zwölf Lieder nach Gedichten von J. W. von Goethe*

Blumen der Wiese, dürfen auch diese hoffen und wähnen?
Johann Friedrich Reichardt, "An ***" 1780pub

Bulbuls Nachtlied durch die Schauer
Wilhelm Petersen, "Bulbul (Die Nachtigall)" 1941pub, Op40,6
from *Goethe Lieder*

Burgen mit hohen Mauern und Zinnen
Richard Wagner, "Lied der Soldaten" 1831, WWV 15, 4v.pf
from *Sieben Kompositionen zu Goethes "Faust"* (1)

Christ ist erstanden! Christ ist erstanden!
Franz Schubert, "Chor der Engel aus Goethe's *Faust*" 1816, D439, satb

Cupido, loser, eigensinniger Knabe
Robert Franz, "Cupido, loser Knabe" 1864pub, Op33,4

Da droben auf jenem Berge, da steh' ich tausendmal
Moriz von Dietrichstein, "Schäfers Klagelied"
Wilhelm Ehlers, "Schäfers-Klage" 1801
Carl Friedrich Zelter, "Schäfers Klagelied" 1802
Johann Friedrich Reichardt, "Schäfers Klage" 1805-06pub
Franz Schubert, "Schäfers Klagelied" 1814, D121
Václav Jan Tomášek, "Schäfers Klagelied" 1815?, Op56,1
from *Gedichte von Goethe:* IV,1

Da droben auf jenem Berge, da steht ein altes Schloß
Johann Friedrich Reichardt, "Bergschloß" 1811pub

Da flattert um die Quelle
Bernhard Theodor Breitkopf, "Die Freuden" 1770pub

Da sind sie nun! Da habt ihr sie!
Bernhard Theodor Breitkopf, "Zueignung" 1770pub

Da wächst der Wein, wos Faß ist
Karl Marx, "Da wächst der Wein" 1949, Op49,3

Dämmrung senkte sich von oben, schon ist alle Nähe fern
Fanny Hensel, "Dämmrung senkte sich von oben" 1843
Johannes Brahms, "Dämmrung senkte sich von oben" 1873, Op59,1
Othmar Schoeck, "Dämmrung senkte sich von oben" 1911, Op19a,2

Das Beet, schon lockert sich's in die Höh'
Carl Loewe, "Frühling über's Jahr" 1836, Op79,5
Hugo Wolf, "Frühling übers Jahr" 1888
from *Goethe Lieder* (28)

Das ist die wahre Liebe
Johann Friedrich Reichardt, "Kanon" 1811pub, 2desc.ten.bass

Das Veilchen auf der Wiese stand (see also "Ein Veilchen...")

Das Wasser rauscht', das Wasser schwoll, ein Fischer saß daran
Anton Eberl, "Der Fischer"
Siegmund Seckendorff, "Der Fischer" 1779
Johann Friedrich Reichardt, "Der Fischer" 1794pub
Carl Friedrich Zelter, "Der Fischer" 1809
C. Moltke, "Der Fischer" before 1815
Franz Schubert, "Der Fischer" 1815, D225
Václav Jan Tomášek, "Der Fischer" 1815?, Op59,3
from *Gedichte von Goethe:* VII,3
Friedrich Curschmann, "Der Fischer" 1832, Op4,3
Carl Loewe, "Der Fischer" 1835, Op43,1
Johann Vesque von Püttlingen, "Der Fischer" 1865
Hugo Wolf, "Der Fischer" 1875, Op3,3
Richard Strauss, "Der Fischer" 1877
from *Jugendlieder*

Deinem Blick mich zu bequemen
Othmar Schoeck, "Suleika" 1915, Op19b,3

Dem Schnee, dem Regen, dem Wind entgegen
Johann Friedrich Reichardt, "Rastlose Liebe" 1794pub
Johann Friedrich Reichardt, "Rastlose Liebe (2nd version)" 1808pub
Carl Friedrich Zelter, "Rastlose Liebe" 1812
Franz Schubert, "Rastlose Liebe" 1815, D138
Václav Jan Tomášek, "Rastlose Liebe" 1815?, Op58,1
from *Gedichte von Goethe:* VI,1
Robert Schumann, "Rastlose Liebe" 1840, Op33,5, ttbb
Joachim Raff, "Rastlose Liebe" 1855-63, Op98,23
from *Sanges-Frühling*
Robert Franz, "Rastlose Liebe" 1864pub, Op33,6
Othmar Schoeck, "Rastlose Liebe" 1912, Op19a,5
Ernest Vietor, "Rastlose Liebe" 1933, Op10,5

Dem Schützen, doch dem alten nicht
Karl Marx, "Novemberlied" 1949, Op49,5

Den einzigen Psyche, welchen du lieben kannst
Johann Friedrich Reichardt, "An Lida" 1794pub

Den künft'gen Tag und Stunden
Johann Friedrich Reichardt, "Bundeslied" 1781pub

Der Damm zerreißt, das Feld erbraust
Johann Friedrich Reichardt, "Johanna Sebus" 1811pub
Franz Schubert, "Johanna Sebus" (fragment), 1821, D728

Der du von dem Himmel bist, alles Leid und Schmerzen stillest
Philipp Christoph Kayser, "Um Friede" 1777
Friedrich Wilhelm Rust, "Lied" before 1781
Johann Friedrich Reichardt, "Wandrers Nachtlied" 1794pub
Carl Friedrich Zelter, "Wandrers Nachtlied" 1807
Johann Friedrich Reichardt, "Wandrers Nachtlied (2nd version)" 1809pub, satb
Franz Schubert, "Wandrers Nachtlied" 1815, D224
Václav Jan Tomášek, "Wanderers Nachtlied" 1815?, Op58,4
from *Gedichte von Goethe:* VI,4
Carl Loewe, "Wandrers Nachtlied" 1828, Op9,i,3b
Fanny Hensel, "Wandrers Nachtlied"
Bettina von Arnim, "Wandrers Nachtlied" 1842?
Franz Liszt, "Der du von dem Himmel bist" 1843pub
Franz Liszt, "Der du von dem Himmel bist" 1856pub
Franz Liszt, "Der du von dem Himmel bist" 1860pub
Hermann Goetz, "Wandrers Nachtlied" 1862-63, Op19,6
Philip Wolfrum, "Wanderers Nachtlied" 1885?, Op16,5
Hugo Wolf, "Wanderers Nachtlied" 1887
from *Sechs Gedichte von Scheffel u.a.*
Hermann Behn, "Wandrers Nachtlied" 189-?, Op1,ii,6
Joseph Marx, "Wanderers Nachtlied" 1906, 1v(med).pf
Nikolai Medtner, "Wandrers Nachtlied I" 1907-08, Op15,1
Ernst Bacon, "Der Du von dem Himmel bist" 1928pub
Hans Pfitzner, "Wanderers Nachtlied" 1931, Op40,5
Eduard Steuermann, "Wandrers Nachtlied" 1931, bass.pf
from *Drei Lieder*
Alexander Zemlinsky, "Wandrers Nachtlied" 1937/38, Op27,12
Cor de Groot, "Wanderers Nachtlied" 194-?pub
from *7 Goethe Lieder* (1)
Winfried Zillig, "Wanderers Nachtlied" 1941
from *Zehn Lieder nach Gedichten von Goethe*
Harald Genzmer, "Der du von dem Himmel bist" 1940-87, bar.pf
from *Acht Lieder nach verschiedenen Dichtern*
Ernst Pepping, "Wandrers Nachtlied" 1949pub
from *Haus- und Trostbuch* (33)

Der edle Mensch sei hülfreich und gut
Ludwig van Beethoven, "Der edle Mensch sei hülfreich und gut" 1823, WoO151

Der Schäfer putzte sich zum Tanz
Richard Wagner, "Bauer unter der Linde" 1831, WWV 15, ten.sop.4v.pf
from *Sieben Kompositionen zu Goethes "Faust"* (2)

Der Spiegel sagt mir ich bin schön!
Fartein Valen, "Suleika" 1925-7, Op6,3
Wilhelm Petersen, "Suleika spricht" 1941pub, Op40,8
from *Goethe Lieder*

Luigi Dallapiccola, "Der Spiegel sagt mir ich bin schön!" 1953, mez.2cl
from *Goethe-Lieder*

Der Strauß, den ich gepflücket, grüße dich viel tausendmal
Carl Friedrich Zelter, "Willkommen" 1810, 1v.satb.pf
Johann Friedrich Reichardt, "Der Strauß" 1811pub
Friedrich Curschmann, "Blumengruß" 1839, Op22, 3sop.pf
Hugo Wolf, "Blumengruß" 1888
from *Goethe Lieder* (24)
Anton Webern, "Blumengruß" 1901-04
from *Acht frühe Lieder* (3)
Armin Knab, "Blumengruß" 1924-46
from *Zwölf Lieder nach Gedichten von J. W. von Goethe*
Cor de Groot, "Blumengruss" 194-?pub
from *7 Goethe Lieder* (6)

Der Tempel ist euch aufgebaut
Johann Friedrich Reichardt, "Künstlers Morgenlied" 1809pub, 1v.pf or 4v

Der Thürmer, der schaut zu mitten der Nacht
Carl Friedrich Zelter, "Todtentanz" 1814
Carl Loewe, "Der Todtentanz" 1835, Op44,3

Der Vorhang schwebet hin und her bei meiner Nachbarin
Johann Friedrich Reichardt, "Selbstbetrug" 1809pub
Václav Jan Tomášek, "Selbstbetrug" 1815?, Op56,2
from *Gedichte von Goethe:* IV,2
Nikolai Medtner, "Selbstbetrug" 1907-08, Op15,3

Des Maurers Wandeln, es gleicht dem Leben
Gottfried von Einem, "Symbolum" 1983, Op73,1
from *Tag- und Nachtlieder*

Des Menschen Seele gleicht dem Wasser
Franz Schubert, "Gesang der Geister über den Wassern" 1817, D538, 2t2b
Franz Schubert, "Gesang der Geister über den Wassern" (unfinished), 1820, D705, 2t2b.pf
Franz Schubert, "Gesang der Geister über den Wassern" 1821, D714, 4t4b.str
Carl Loewe, "Gesang der Geister über den Wassern" 1840, Op88, satb.pf
Eduard Steuermann, "Gesang der Geister über den Wassern" 1931, bass.pf
from *Drei Lieder*

Dich ergriff mit Gewalt der alte Herrscher des Flusses
Johann Friedrich Reichardt, "Herzog Leopold von Braunschweig" 1809pub, 4v

Dich hat Amor gewiß, o Sängerin
Johann Friedrich Reichardt, "Philomele" 1809pub, 4v

Die heilgen drei König mit ihrem Stern
Hugo Wolf, "Epiphanias" 1888
from *Goethe Lieder* (19)
Ernst Pepping, "Epiphaniasfest" 1949pub
from *Haus- und Trostbuch* (17)

Die ihr Felsen und Bäume bewohnt, o heilsame Nymphen
Johann Friedrich Reichardt, "Einsamkeit" 1794pub
Max Reger, "Einsamkeit" 1903, Op75,18, 1v(low).pf
Nikolai Medtner, "Einsamkeit" 1908-09, Op18,3

Pierre-Octave Ferroud, "Einsamkeit" 1932pub
from *Drei traute Gesänge*
Winfried Zillig, "Einsamkeit" 1941
from *Zehn Lieder nach Gedichten von Goethe*

Die Königin steht im hohen Saal
Carl Loewe, "Wirkung in die Ferne" 1837, Op59,1

Die Nachtigall, sie war entfernt
Felix Mendelssohn, "Die Nachtigall" 1843, Op59,4, satb

Die Nebel zerreißen, der Himmel ist helle
Johann Friedrich Reichardt, "Glückliche Fahrt" 1796pub
Václav Jan Tomášek, "Glückliche Fahrt" 1815?, Op61,4, ssb.pf or ttb.pf
from *Gedichte von Goethe:* IX,4
Nikolai Medtner, "Glückliche Fahrt" 1907-08, Op15,8

Die Sonne kommt! Ein Prachterscheinen!
Luigi Dallapiccola, "Die Sonne kommt! Ein Prachterscheinen!" 1953, mez.cl
from *Goethe-Lieder*

Die Trommel gerühret! Das Pfeifchen gespielt!
Johann Friedrich Reichardt, "Klärchens Lied aus Egmont" 1804pub

Dies zu deuten bin erbötig!
Hugo Wolf, "Dies zu deuten bin erbötig" 1889
from *Goethe Lieder* (42)

Diese Federn, weiß' und schwarze
Johann Friedrich Reichardt, "Der Federschmuck" 1796pub

Diese Gondel vergleich' ich der sanft einschaukelnden Wiege
Othmar Schoeck, "Diese Gondel vergleich' ich" 1906, Op19b,7/V
from *Fünf Venezianische Epigramme*

Dir zu eröffnen mein Herz verlangt mich
Carl Friedrich Zelter, "Aus der Fernen" 1816
Robert Schumann, "Liebeslied" 1850, Op51,5

Du Bächlein silberhell und klar, du eilst vorüber immerdar
Johann Wenzeslaus Kalliwoda, "Das Bächlein" 184-pub, sop.vn.pf
Richard Strauss, "Das Bächlein" 1933, (Op88,1)
poem possibly spurious, but see Kalliwoda's attribution in 184-

Du gefällst mir so wohl, mein liebes Kind
Václav Jan Tomášek, "Vorschlag zur Güte" 1815?, Op60,2
from *Gedichte von Goethe:* VIII,2

Du hast uns oft im Traum gesehen
Bernhard Theodor Breitkopf, "Das Glück" 1770pub

Du prophet'scher Vogel du
Johann Friedrich Reichardt, "Frühlings-Orakel" 1805-06pub

Du siehst mich, Königin, zurück
Carl Loewe, "Lynceus, der Helena seine Schätze darbietend" 1833, Op9,viii,2
from *Faust* part 2: Drei Lieder des Thurmwächter Lynceus

Du verklagest das Weib, sie schwanke von einem zum andern
Johann Friedrich Reichardt, "Kanon" 1811pub, desc.ten.bass

Durch allen Schall und Klang
Richard Strauss, "Durch allen Schall und Klang" 1925

Durch Feld und Wald zu schweifen, mein Liedchen wegzupfeifen
Carl Friedrich Zelter, "Der Musensohn" 1807
Johann Friedrich Reichardt, "Der Musensohn" 1809pub
Franz Schubert, "Der Musensohn" 1822, D764

Ein armes Mädchen! vergebt, vergebet!
Philipp Christoph Kayser, "Scene aus *Scherz, List und Rache*" 1785

Ein Blick von deinen Augen in die meinen
Franz Schubert, "Die Liebende schreibt" 1819, D673
Felix Mendelssohn, "Die Liebende schreibt" 1831, Op86,3
Johannes Brahms, "Die Liebende schreibt" 1868, Op47,5

Ein Blumenglöckchen vom Boden hervor
Carl Friedrich Zelter, "Gleich und gleich" 1819
Robert Franz, "Gleich und Gleich" 1870?pub, Op22,1
Hugo Wolf, "Gleich und Gleich" 1888
from *Goethe Lieder* (25)
Nikolai Medtner, "Gleich und Gleich" 1907-08, Op15,11
Anton Webern, "Gleich und gleich" 1917, Op12,4

Ein Veilchen auf der Wiese stand, gebückt in sich und unbekannt
Johann André, "Das Veilchen" 1774
Herzogin Anna Amalia, "Das Veilchen" 1776
Philipp Christoph Kayser, "Romanze" 1776
Josef Antonín Štěpán, "Das Veilchen auf der Wiese" 1778-79pub
Johann Friedrich Reichardt, "Aus *Erwin und Elmire*" 1780pub
Wolfgang Amadeus Mozart, "Das Veilchen" 1785, K476
Johann Friedrich Reichardt, "Das Veilchen" 1788pub, 1v.pf or 4v
Václav Jan Tomášek, "Das Veilchen" 1815?, Op57,1
from *Gedichte von Goethe:* V,1
Clara Schumann, "Das Veilchen" 1853
Nikolai Medtner, "Das Veilchen" 1908-09, Op18,5
Othmar Schoeck, "Aus *Erwin und Elmire*" 1919pub, Op25,5, sop.orch

Eine einzige Nacht an deinem Herzen!
Othmar Schoeck, "Eine einzige Nacht an deinem Herzen!" 1907, Op19b,7/II
from *Fünf Venezianische Epigramme*

Einst gieng ich meinem Mädchen nach
Bernhard Theodor Breitkopf, "Das Schreyen" 1770pub

Einziger Augenblick, in welchem ich lebte!
Johann Friedrich Reichardt, "Aus *Alexis und Dora*" 1805-06pub

Erst sitzt er eine Weile, die Stirn von Wolken frei
Bernhard Theodor Breitkopf, "Der Misanthrop" 1770pub
Carl Friedrich Zelter, "Der Misantrop" 1812?

Erwache Friedericke, vertreib die Nacht
Johann Valentin Görner, "Erwache, Friedericke" 1744

Es fing ein Knab' ein Vögelein, hm hm, so so,
Carl Reinecke, "Lied des Georg im *Götz von Berlichingen*"
from *Kinderlieder*

Paul Hindemith, "Georgslied" 1908/09
from *7 Lieder für Sopran oder Tenor mit Klavierbegleitung*

Es flattert um die Quelle die wechselnde Libelle
Carl Loewe, "Die Freude" 1844, Op104,1, ss.pf

Es fürchte die Götter das Menschengeschlecht!
Johann Friedrich Reichardt, "Lied der Parzen" 1809pub, 4v

Es ist doch meine Nachbarin ein allerliebstes Mädchen!
Franz Schubert, "Der Goldschmiedsgesell" 1817, D560

Es ist ein Schnee gefallen, denn es ist noch nicht Zeit
Fanny Hensel, "März" 1836, sop.alt.pf
Carl Loewe, "März" 1844, Op104,3, ss.pf
Armin Knab, "März" 1924-46
from *Zwölf Lieder nach Gedichten von J. W. von Goethe*
Ernst Pepping, "März" 1949pub
from *Haus- und Trostbuch* (23)

Es ist ein Schuß gefallen! Mein! sagt, wer schoß da draus?
Carl Friedrich Zelter, "Der junge Jäger" 1810pub
Johann Friedrich Reichardt, "Schneiderschreck" 1811pub

Es klingt so prächtig, wenn der Dichter
Othmar Schoeck, "Nachklang" 1915, Op19b,1
Ernst Pepping, "Nachklang" 1949pub
from *Haus- und Trostbuch* (31)

Es lacht der Mai! Der Wald ist frei
Carl Loewe, "Die erste Walpurgisnacht" 1833, Op25, soli.ch.pf

Es lohnet mich heute mit doppelter Beute
Johann Friedrich Reichardt, "Der Jäger" 1799pub
Ferdinand Ries, "Es lohnet mich heute" 1811pub, Op32,5

Es rauschet das Wasser und bleibet nicht stehn
Johannes Brahms, "Es rauschet das Wasser" 1862, Op28,3, alt.bar.pf

Es schlug mein Herz, geschwind zu Pferde!
Johann Friedrich Reichardt, "Willkommen und Abschied" 1794pub
Franz Schubert, "Willkommen und Abschied" 1822, D767
Hans Pfitzner, "Willkommen und Abschied" 1921, Op29,3

Es war ein Buhle frech genung
Siegmund Seckendorff, "Romanze" 1779

Es war ein fauler Schäfer, ein rechter Siebenschläfer
Hugo Wolf, "Der Schäfer" 1888
from *Goethe Lieder* (22)
Armin Knab, "Der Schäfer" 1924-46
from *Zwölf Lieder nach Gedichten von J. W. von Goethe*
Erich Zeisl, "Der Schäfer" 1936pub

Es war ein Kind, das wollte nie zur Kirche sich bequemen
Carl Loewe, "Die wandelnde Glocke" 1832, Op20,3
Robert Schumann, "Die wandelnde Glocke" 1849, Op79,17
from *Lieder-Album für die Jugend*

Es war ein Knabe frech genug, war erst aus Frankreich kommen
Johann Friedrich Reichardt, "Der untreue Knabe" 1805-06pub
Nikolai Medtner, "Der untreue Knabe" 1907-08, Op15,10

Es war ein König in Thule, ein goldnen Becher er hätt
Siegmund Seckendorff, "Der König von Thule" 1782

Es war ein König in Thule, gar treu bis an das Grab
Johann Friedrich Reichardt, "Der König von Thule" 1805-06pub
Carl Friedrich Zelter, "Der König von Thule" 1811
Václav Jan Tomášek, "Der König in Thule" 1815?, Op59,2
from *Gedichte von Goethe:* VII,2
Franz Schubert, "Der König in Thule" 1816, D367
Karl Eckert, "Der König in Thule" 1828
Hector Berlioz, "Le Roi de Thulé" (set in French), 1829
Franz Liszt, "Es war ein König in Thule" 1843pub
Robert Schumann, "Der König von Thule" 1849, Op67,1, ten.satb
Franz Liszt, "Es war ein König in Thule" 1856pub
Friedrich Silcher, "Der König von Thule" 4v
Hermann Behn, "Der König in Thule" 189-?, Op2,1, 1v(med).pf

Es war eine Ratt' im Kellernest
Fürst Anton Radziwill, "Es war eine Ratt' im Kellernest" 1809-19
Richard Wagner, "Branders Lied" 1831, WWV 15, bass.unis ch.pf
from *Sieben Kompositionen zu Goethes "Faust"* (3)
Ferruccio Busoni, "Lied des Brander" 1938, bar.pf

Es war einmal ein König, der hat einen Skorpion
Ignatz Walter, "Gesang des Leviathan" 1797

Es war einmal ein König, der hatt' einen großen Floh
Ludwig van Beethoven, "Aus Goethe's *Faust*" 1809, Op75,3
Hector Berlioz, "Histoire d'une Puce" (set in French), 1829
Richard Wagner, "Lied des Mephistopheles" 1831, WWV 15, bass.unis ch.pf
from *Sieben Kompositionen zu Goethes "Faust"* (4)
Modest Mussorgsky, "Lied des Mephistopheles im Auerbachs Keller" (set in Russian), 1878
Ferruccio Busoni, "Lied des Mephistopheles aus Goethes *Faust*" 1918, bar.pf

Euch bedaur' ich, unglücksel'ge Sterne
Winfried Zillig, "Nachtgedanken" 1941
from *Zehn Lieder nach Gedichten von Goethe*

Feiger Gedanken, bängliches Schwanken, weibisches Zagen, ängstliches Klagen
Johann Friedrich Reichardt, "Aus *Lila*" 1809pub
Johannes Brahms, "Beherzigung" 1883?, Op93a,6, satb
Hugo Wolf, "Beherzigung" 1887
from *Sechs Gedichte von Scheffel u.a.*
Hermann H. Wetzler, "Beherzigung" 1907
Ernest Vietor, "Feiger Gedanken bängliches Schwanken" 1933, Op10,3
Alexander Zemlinsky, "Feiger Gedanken bängliches Schwanken" 1934, Op22,3
Cor de Groot, "Beherzigung" 194-?pub
from *7 Goethe Lieder* (7)

Felsen sollten nicht Felsen und Wüsten Wüsten nicht bleiben
Karl Marx, "Felsen sollten nicht" 1949, Op49,4

Felsen stehen gegründet
Johann Friedrich Reichardt, "Aus *Euphrosyne*" 1809pub, 4v

Fetter grüne, du Laub am Rebengeländer hier mein Fenster herauf!
Johann Friedrich Reichardt, "Herbstgefühl" 1794pub
Othmar Schoeck, "Herbstgefühl" 1909, Op19a,1
Wilhelm Petersen, "Herbstgefühl" 1941pub, Op40,3
from *Goethe Lieder*

Freudig war vor vielen Jahren
Othmar Schoeck, "Parabase" 1914, Op19a,8

Freudvoll und leidvoll, gedankenvoll sein
Carl Friedrich Zelter, "Clärchen" 1804
Johann Friedrich Reichardt, "Klärchens Lied aus Egmont" 1804pub
Johann Christoph Kienlen, "Freudvoll und leidvoll" 1810
Franz Schubert, "Die Liebe" 1815, D210
Franz Liszt, "Freudvoll und leidvoll" 1844
Franz Liszt, "Freudvoll und leidvoll" 1848pub
Franz Liszt, "Freudvoll und leidvoll" 1860
Anton Rubinstein, "Clärchens Lied" 1864, Op57,4
Ernest Vietor, "Aus *Egmont*" 1933, Op10,1
Cor de Groot, "Wonne der Liebe" 194-?pub
from *7 Goethe Lieder* (2)

Frisch, der Wein soll reichlich fließen
Johann Friedrich Reichardt, "Rechenschaft" 1811pub, 1v(low).mch.(pf)

Früh, wenn Tal, Gebirg' und Garten
Winfried Zillig, "Früh, wenn Tal, Gebirg' und Garten" 1941
from *Zehn Lieder nach Gedichten von Goethe*

Füllest wieder Busch und Tal still mit Nebelglanz
Siegmund Seckendorff, "Füllest wieder 's liebe Thal" 1778
Andreas Romberg, "An den Mond" 1793
Johann Friedrich Reichardt, "An den Mond" 1794pub
Friedrich Heinrich Himmel, "An den Mond" 1807?, Op26,1
Carl Friedrich Zelter, "An den Mond" 1811?
Franz Schubert, "An den Mond (1)" 1815, D259
Václav Jan Tomášek, "An den Mond" 1815?, Op56,4
from *Gedichte von Goethe:* IV,4
Franz Schubert, "An den Mond (2)" 1819?, D296
Moritz Hauptmann, "An den Mond" 1834pub, Op22,5
Johanna Kinkel, "An den Mond" 184-?pub, Op7,5
Leopold Damrosch, "An den Mond" Op17,4
Hans Pfitzner, "An den Mond" 1906, Op18

Für Männer uns zu plagen, uns zu plagen sind leider
Corona Schröter, "Für Männer uns zu plagen" 1782

Geh! gehorche meinen Winken, nutze deine jungen Tage
Johann Friedrich Reichardt, "Kophtisches Lied" 1796pub, bass.pf
Hugo Wolf, "Cophtisches Lied (II)" 1888
from *Goethe Lieder* (15)
Max Bruch, "Zweites Kophtisches Lied" 1892, Op59,3, bar.pf
Ernest Vietor, "Koptisches Lied" 1933, Op10,4

Gern in stillen Melancholieen
Carl Loewe, "Die verliebte Schäferin Scapine" 1835, Op9,ix,3

Gern verlaß ich diese Hütte
Bernhard Theodor Breitkopf, "Die Nacht" 1770pub

Göttlicher Morpheus, umsonst bewegst du
Johannes Brahms, "Göttlicher Morpheus, umsonst bewegst du" 1891pub, Op113,1, 4fv
from *13 Kanons für Frauenstimmen*

Gottes ist der Orient! Gottes ist der Occident!
Carl Loewe, "Gottes ist der Orient!" 1829, Op22,i,5, 1v.pf or 4v
Robert Schumann, "Talismane" 1840, Op25,8
from *Liederkreis*
Robert Schumann, "Talismane" 1849, Op141,4, 2ch(satb).pf
from *Vier doppelchörige Gesänge*

Grausam erweiset sich Amor an mir
Johannes Brahms, "Grausam erweiset sich Amor" 1863-?, WoO posth 24, 4fv
Johannes Brahms, "Grausam erweiset sich Amor an mir" 1891pub, Op113,2, 4fv
from *13 Kanons für Frauenstimmen*

Grosser Brama, Herr der Mächte!
Carl Loewe, "Gebet des Paria" 1836, Op58
from *Paria* (1)

Großer Brahma! nun erkenn ich
Carl Loewe, "Dank des Paria" 1836, Op58
from *Paria* (3)
Hugo Wolf, "Dank des Paria" 1888
from *Goethe Lieder* (30)

Ha, ich bin der Herr der Welt!
Hugo Wolf, "Königlich Gebet" 1889
from *Goethe Lieder* (31)
Harald Genzmer, "Königlich Gebet" 1940-87, bar.pf
from *Acht Lieder nach verschiedenen Dichtern*

Hab ich euch denn je geraten
Richard Strauss, "Hab ich euch denn je geraten" 1918, Op67,5
from *Drei Lieder aus den Büchern des Unmuts des Rendsch Nameh*

Hab ich tausendmal geschworen
Johannes Brahms, "Unüberwindlich" 1876, Op72,5

Hab' oft einen dummen düstern Sinn
Johann Friedrich Reichardt, "Christel" 1809pub
Carl Friedrich Zelter, "Der Verliebte" 1810

Haben sie von deinen Fehlen
Othmar Schoeck, "Haben sie von deinen Fehlen" 1915, Op19b,4/I
from *Drei Lieder aus dem Buch der Betrachtungen*

Hätt ich irgend wohl Bedenken
Hugo Wolf, "Hätt ich irgend wohl Bedenken" 1889
from *Goethe Lieder* (43)

Hand in Hand und Lipp' auf Lippe!
Johann Friedrich Reichardt, "An die Erwählte" 1809pub

Ferdinand Ries, "Hand in Hand und Lipp' auf Lippe" 1811pub, Op32,1

Hans Adam war ein Erdenkloß
Hugo Wolf, "Erschaffen und Beleben" 1889
from *Goethe Lieder* (33)
Richard Strauss, "Erschaffen und Beleben" 1922, (Op87,2), bass.pf

Hat der alte Hexenmeister sich doch einmal wegbegeben!
Carl Friedrich Zelter, "Der Zauberlehrling" 1799
Johann Rudolf Zumsteeg, "Der Zauberlehrling" 1805pub
from *Kleine Balladen und Lieder, siebtes Heft*
Carl Loewe, "Der Zauberlehrling" 1832, Op20,2

Heiß mich nicht reden, heiß mich schweigen
Johann Friedrich Reichardt, "Das Geheimnis" 1795-96pub
Johann Rudolf Zumsteeg, "Aus *Meister Wilhelms Lehrjahren*" 1805pub
from *Kleine Balladen und Lieder, siebtes Heft*
Carl Friedrich Zelter, "Geheimnis" 1811
Václav Jan Tomášek, "Das Geheimniß" 1815?, Op58,3
from *Gedichte von Goethe:* VI,3
Franz Schubert, "Heiss mich nicht reden (1)" 1821, D726
Franz Schubert, "Heiss mich nicht reden (2)" 1826, D877,2
Robert Schumann, "Heiss' mich nicht reden, heiss' mich schweigen" 1849, Op98a,5
Pyotr Il'yich Tchaikovsky, "Heiss mich nicht reden" (set in Russian), 1885, Op57,3
Hugo Wolf, "Mignon (I)" 1888
from *Goethe Lieder* (5)

Heraus in eure Schatten, rege Wipfel
Johann Friedrich Reichardt, "Monolog der Iphigenia" 1798pub, 1v.ch.pf

Herein, o du Guter! du Alter herein!
Carl Loewe, "Ballade vom vertriebenen und zurückkehrenden Grafen" 1835, Op44,1

Herr! ein Mädchen, Herr ein Weibchen
Philipp Christoph Kayser, "Scene aus *Scherz, List und Rache*" 1785, 2v.pf

Herr, laß dir gefallen dieses kleine Haus!
Karl Marx, "Herr, laß dir gefallen dieses kleine Haus!" 1949, Op49,12

Herrin! sag was heißt das Flüstern?
Wilhelm Petersen, "Vollmondnacht" 1941pub, Op40,7
from *Goethe Lieder*

Herz, mein Herz, was soll das geben, was bedränget dich so sehr?
Johann Friedrich Reichardt, "Neue Liebe, neues Leben" 1794pub
Ludwig van Beethoven, "Neue Liebe, neues Leben" 1798/99, WoO127
Ludwig van Beethoven, "Neue Liebe, neues Leben" 1809, Op75,2
Johann Friedrich Reichardt, "Neue Liebe, neues Leben (2nd version)" 1809pub
Carl Friedrich Zelter, "Neue Liebe neues Leben" 1812
Fanny Hensel, "Neue Liebe, neues Leben" 1836
Louis Spohr, "Neue Liebe, neues Leben" 1858, WoO127

Hielte diesen frühen Segen
Johann Friedrich Reichardt, "Dauer im Wechsel" 1809pub

Hier hilft nun weiter kein Bemühn!
Karl Marx, "Hier hilft nun weiter kein Bemühn" 1949, Op49,2

Hier klag' ich verborgen, dem tauenden Morgen
Johann Friedrich Reichardt, "Der Schmachtende" 1798pub
Ferdinand Ries, "Hier klag' ich verborgen" 1811pub, Op32,4

Hier muß ich sie finden
Johann Friedrich Reichardt, "Der Jüngling" 1798pub
Ferdinand Ries, "Hier muss ich sie finden" 1811pub, Op32,3

Hier sind wir versammelt zu löblichem Tun
Max Eberwein, "Ergo bibamus" 1813

Hin und wieder fliegen die Pfeile
Franz Schubert, "Hin und wieder fliegen die Pfeile" 1815, D239,3
from the Singspiel, "Claudine von Villa Bella"

Hoch auf dem alten Thurme steht des Helden edler Geist
Johann Friedrich Reichardt, "Geistes-Gruß" 1794pub
Carl Friedrich Zelter, "Geistesgruß" 1810
Franz Schubert, "Geistes-Gruss" 1815, D142
Václav Jan Tomášek, "Geistesgruß" 1815?, Op57,2
from *Gedichte von Goethe:* V,2
Hugo Wolf, "Geistesgruß" 1876, Op13,2, ttbb
Nikolai Medtner, "Geistergruss" 1907-08, Op15,12

Hochbeglückt in deiner Liebe: See Marianne von Willemer

Höchste Herrscherin der Welt!
Hermann Simon, "Die Lobpreisung des Doctor Marianus" 1935, bar.harp.perc
from *Drei Goethe-Gesänge* (3)

Höre den Rat, den die Leier tönt!
Othmar Schoeck, "Höre den Rat, den die Leier tönt!" 1915, Op19b,4/II
from *Drei Lieder aus dem Buch der Betrachtungen*

Ich armer Teufel, Herr Baron
Hugo Wolf, "Spottlied aus *Wilhelm Meister*" 1888
from *Goethe Lieder* (4)

Ich bin der wohlbekannte Sänger, der vielgereis'te Rattenfänger
Anonymous, "Der Rattenfänger" 1810
Franz Schubert, "Der Rattenfänger" 1815, D255
Václav Jan Tomášek, "Der Rattenfänger" 1815?, Op54,5
from *Gedichte von Goethe:* II,5
Hugo Wolf, "Der Rattenfänger" 1888
from *Goethe Lieder* (11)

Ich denke dein, wenn mir der Sonne Schimmer vom Meere strahlt
Johann Friedrich Reichardt, "Nähe des Geliebten" 1795?
Johann Friedrich Reichardt, "Nähe des Geliebten" 1803pub
Friedrich Heinrich Himmel, "Nähe des Geliebten" 1807?
Carl Friedrich Zelter, "Nähe des Geliebten" 1808
Franz Schubert, "Nähe des Geliebten" 1815, D162
Václav Jan Tomášek, "Nähe des Geliebten" 1815?, Op53,2
from *Gedichte von Goethe:* I,2
Carl Loewe, "Ich denke dein" 1817?, Op9,iii,1
Carl Loewe, "Ich denke dein" 1823, satb
Josefine Lang, "Nähe des Geliebten" 1830?, Op5,1

Stephen Heller, "Nähe des Geliebten" 1830-38?
Robert Schumann, "Ich denke dein" 1849, Op78,3, sop.ten.pf
Eduard Lassen, "Nähe des Geliebten" Op62,1
Leopold Damrosch, "Nähe des Geliebten" Op17,1
Nikolai Medtner, "Nähe des Geliebten" 1907-08, Op15,9
Paul Hindemith, "Nähe des Geliebten" 1914
Winfried Zillig, "Nähe des Geliebten" 1941
from *Zehn Lieder nach Gedichten von Goethe*

Ich ging im Felde so für mich hin
Carl Loewe, "Im Vorübergehen" 1836, Op81,1
Nikolai Medtner, "Im Vorübergehn" 1904-05, Op6,4

Ich ging im Wald so für mich hin
Carl Friedrich Zelter, "Auch mein Sinn" 1814
Alexis Holländer, "Gefunden" 1864pub, Op6,6
Wilhelm Kienzl, "Gefunden" 187-?, Op6,8
Hermann Behn, "Gefunden" 189-?, Op1,i,1, sop.pf
Richard Strauss, "Gefunden" 1903, Op56,1
Nikolai Medtner, "Gefunden (Epithalamion)" 1904-05, Op6,9
Werner Josten, "Gefunden" 1926pub
from *Fünf Lieder* (5)
Ernest Vietor, "Gefunden" 1933, Op10,2
Wilhelm Petersen, "Gefunden" 1941pub, Op40,2
from *Goethe Lieder*

Ich hab' ihn gesehen! wie ist mir geschehen?
Johann Friedrich Reichardt, "Das Mädchen" 1798pub
Ferdinand Ries, "Ich hab' ihn gesehen!" 1811pub, Op32,2

Ich hab' mein Sach auf nichts gestellt, Juche, Juche, Juche!
Carl Friedrich Zelter, "Vanitas! vanitatum vanitas" 1806
Johann Friedrich Reichardt, "Vanitas! vanitatum vanitas" 1809pub
Louis Spohr, "Vanitas! Vanitatum vanitas" 1816, Op41,6

Ich habe geliebet, nun lieb ich erst recht!
Carl Friedrich Zelter, "Gewohnt, getan" 1813

Ich kenn' ein Blümlein Wunderschön
Johann Rudolf Zumsteeg, "Das Blümlein Wunderschön. Lied des gefangenen Grafen" 1801pub
from *Kleine Balladen und Lieder, drittes Heft*
Johann Friedrich Reichardt, "Das Blümlein Wunderschön: Lied des gefangenen Grafen" 1805pub

Ich kenn', o Jüngling, deine Freude
Bernhard Theodor Breitkopf, "Die Reliquie" 1770pub

Ich komme schon durch manches Land
Ludwig van Beethoven, "Marmotte" 1790-92?, Op52,7

Ich liebte sie mit innigem Gefühle
Johann Friedrich Reichardt, "Klage" 1804pub

Ich weiß es wohl, und spotte viel
Bernhard Theodor Breitkopf, "Die Liebe wider Willen" 1770pub

Ich weiß nicht was mir hier gefällt
Johann Friedrich Reichardt, "Einschränkung" 1796pub

Ich wollt' ich wär' ein Fisch, so hurtig und frisch!
Carl Friedrich Zelter, "Duettino" 1810, 2v.zither.pf
Franz Schubert, "Liebhaber in allen Gestalten" 1817, D558

Ihr guten Herrn, ihr schönen Frauen
Conradin Kreutzer, "Ein Bettler vor dem Thor"

Ihr verblühet, süße Rosen, meine Liebe trug euch nicht
Philipp Christoph Kayser, "Arie aus *Erwin und Elmire*" 1775
Johann Friedrich Reichardt, "Aus *Erwin und Elmire*" 1780pub
Fanny Hensel, "Erwin" 1846, Op7,2
Edvard Grieg, "Zur Rosenzeit" 1889, Op48,5
Othmar Schoeck, "Aus *Erwin und Elmire*" 1919pub, Op25,9, ten.orch
Armin Knab, "Wehmut" 1924-46
from *Zwölf Lieder nach Gedichten von J. W. von Goethe*

Im Felde schleich' ich still und wild, gespannt mein Feuerrohr (see also "Im Walde...")
Philipp Christoph Kayser, "Jägers Nachtlied" 1777
Johann Friedrich Reichardt, "Jägers Nachtlied" 1794pub
Carl Friedrich Zelter, "Jägers Abendlied" 1807
Friedrich Heinrich Himmel, "Jägers Abendlied" 1807?
Franz Schubert, "Jägers Abendlied (1)" 1815, D215
Václav Jan Tomášek, "Jägers Abendlied" 1815?, Op57,5
from *Gedichte von Goethe:* V,5
Franz Schubert, "Jägers Abendlied (2)" 1816, D368
Nikolai Medtner, "Jägers Abendlied" 1908-09, Op18,6

Im Nebelgeriesel, im tiefen Schnee
Louis Spohr, "Zigeuner Lied" 1809, Op25,5
Ferruccio Busoni, "Zigeunerlied" 1923pub, Op55,2, bar.pf

Im Schlafgemach, entfernt vom Feste
Bernhard Theodor Breitkopf, "Hochzeitslied" 1770pub

Im spielenden Bache da lieg ich wie helle!
Bernhard Theodor Breitkopf, "Unbeständigkeit" 1770pub

Im Walde schleich ich still und wild (see also "Im Felde...")
Johann Friedrich Reichardt, "Im Walde schleich ich still und wild" 1800pub
from *Lieder aus dem Liederspiel, Lieb' und Treue* (4)
Bernhard Anselm Weber, "Jägers Abendlied" 1814-?

Immer wieder in die Weite
Othmar Schoeck, "Ungeduld" 1914, Op19a,7

In allen guten Stunden, erhöht von Lieb' und Wein
Johann Friedrich Reichardt, "Bundeslied" 1796pub, 3v
Johann Friedrich Reichardt, "Bundeslied (2nd version)" 1809pub
Franz Schubert, "Bundeslied" 1815, D258

In dem stillen Mondenscheine
Johann Friedrich Reichardt, "Mondenschein-Szene aus *Claudine von Villa Bella*" 1805-06pub

In des Pappillons Gestalt
Bernhard Theodor Breitkopf, "Der Schmetterling" 1770pub

In großen Städten lernen früh
Bernhard Theodor Breitkopf, "Kinderverstand" 1770pub

In tausend Formen magst du dich verstekken
Carl Friedrich Zelter, "Aus dem westöstlichen Divan" 1823
Luigi Dallapiccola, "In tausend Formen magst du dich verstecken" 1953, mez.3cl
from *Goethe-Lieder*

Inneres Wühlen ewig zu finden, immer verlangen, nimmer erlangen
Nikolai Medtner, "Aus *Erwin und Elmira* –Inneres Wühlen..." 1904-05, Op6,6
Othmar Schoeck, "Aus *Erwin und Elmire*" 1919pub, Op25,10, ten.orch
from *Gesänge zu dem Singspiel von Goethe*

Ist's möglich, dass ich, Liebchen, dich kose
Luigi Dallapiccola, "Ist's möglich, dass ich, Liebchen, dich kose" 1953, mez.3cl
from *Goethe-Lieder*

Kaum an dem blaueren Himmel erblickt' ich die glänzende Sonne
Othmar Schoeck, "Epigramm" 1906, Op31,5

Kaum dass ich dich wieder habe
Luigi Dallapiccola, "Kaum dass ich dich wieder habe" 1953, mez.cl
from *Goethe-Lieder*

Kehre nicht in diesem Kreise neu und immer neu zurück!
Johann Friedrich Reichardt, "Sorge" 1794pub
Václav Jan Tomášek, "Sorge" 1815?, Op57,4
from *Gedichte von Goethe:* V,4
Othmar Schoeck, "Sorge" 1910, Op19a,6

Keinen Reimer wird man finden
Othmar Schoeck, "Unmut" 1915, Op19b,5
Ferruccio Busoni, "Lied des Unmuts" 1918, bar.pf

Kennst du das Land, wo die Citronen blühn
Carl Friedrich Zelter, "Kennst du das Land" 1795
Johann Friedrich Reichardt, "Italien" 1795-96pub
Ludwig van Beethoven, "Mignon" 1809, Op75,1
Hélène Riese Liebmann, "Kennst du das Land?" 1811pub, Op4
Franz Schubert, "Kennst du das Land" 1815, D321
Václav Jan Tomášek, "Mignon's Sehnsucht" 1815?, Op54,1
from *Gedichte von Goethe:* II,1
Louis Spohr, "Mignons Lied" 1816, Op37,1
Fanny Hensel, "Sehnsucht nach Italien" 1822
Gasparo Spontini, "Mignon" 1830?
Franz Liszt, "Mignons Lied" 1842
Robert Schumann, "Mignon" 1849, Op79,28;98a,1
from *Lieder-Album für die Jugend*
Moritz Hauptmann, "Mignon" 1852?pub, Op37,1
Franz Liszt, "Mignons Lied" 1860
Leopold Damrosch, "Mignon" Op17,2
Pyotr Il'yich Tchaikovsky, "Kennst du das Land" (set in Russian), 1874-75, Op25,3
Hugo Wolf, "Mignon" 1888
from *Goethe Lieder* (9)
Alban Berg, "Mignon" 1907

Kleine Blumen, kleine Blätter streuen mir mit leichter Hand
Johann Friedrich Reichardt, "Mit einem gemalten Bande" 1794pub, 1v.pf or 4v
Ludwig van Beethoven, "Mit einem gemalten Band" 1810, Op83,3

Václav Jan Tomášek, "Mit einem gemahlten Bande" 1815?, Op55,4
from *Gedichte von Goethe:* III,4
Othmar Schoeck, "Mit einem gemalten Bande" 1912, Op19a,4
Armin Knab, "Mit einem gemalten Band" 1924-46
from *Zwölf Lieder nach Gedichten von J. W. von Goethe*
Ernst Pepping, "Mit einem gemalten Band" 1949pub
from *Haus- und Trostbuch* (25)

Knabe saß ich Fischerknabe
Richard Strauss, "Lust und Qual" 1877
from *Jugendlieder*

Komm, Liebchen, komm! umwinde mir die Mütze!
Hugo Wolf, "Komm, Liebchen, komm" 1889
from *Goethe Lieder* (44)

Komm mit, o Schöne, komm mit mir zum Tanze
Johann Friedrich Reichardt, "Wechsellied zum Tanze" 1794pub
Johannes Brahms, "Wechsellied zum Tanze" 1859, Op31,1, satb.pf

Lass deinen süssen Rubinenmund
Luigi Dallapiccola, "Lass deinen süssen Rubinenmund" 1953, mez.2cl
from *Goethe-Lieder*

Laß dich genießen, freundliche Frucht
Johann Friedrich Reichardt, "Aus *Proserpina*" 1800/01

Laß mein Aug' den Abschied sagen
Johann Friedrich Reichardt, "Der Abschied" 1794pub

Lass mich knieen, lass mich schauen
Carl Loewe, "Thurmwächter Lynceus zu den Füssen der Helena" 1833, Op9,viii,1
from *Faust* part 2: Drei Lieder des Thurmwächter Lynceus

Laß Neid und Mißgunst sich verzehren
Karl Marx, "Laß Neid und Mißgunst sich verzehren" 1949, Op49,9

Lasset Gelehrte sich zanken und streiten
Hugo Wolf, "Cophtisches Lied (I)" 1888
from *Goethe Lieder* (14)
Max Bruch, "Kophtisches Lied" 1892, Op59,2, bar.pf
Harald Genzmer, "Kopthisches Lied" 1940-87, bar.pf
from *Acht Lieder nach verschiedenen Dichtern*

Lasset heut im edlen Kreis meine Warnung gelten!
Wilhelm Ehlers, "Generalbeichte" 1810?

Laßt fahren hin das Allzuflüchtige
Johann Nepomuk Hummel, "Zur Logenfeier" 1825

Lasst mich nur auf meinem Sattel gelten!
Robert Schumann, "Freisinn" 1840, Op25,2
from *Liederkreis*
Anton Rubinstein, "(Freisinn)" (set in Russian) 1864, Op57,5

Leere Zeiten der Jugend!
Johann Friedrich Reichardt, "Aus *Alexis und Dora*" 1805-06pub

Leichte Silberwolken schweben durch die erst erwärmten Lüfte
Fanny Hensel, "Mai" 1836, sop.alt.pf

Lichtlein schwimmen auf dem Strome
Hugo Wolf, "St. Nepomuks Vorabend" 1888
from *Goethe Lieder* (20)

Lieb' um Liebe, Stund' um Stunde, Wort um Worte und Blick um Blick
Franz Wüllner, "Lieb' um Liebe" 1857pub

Liebchen, kommen diese Lieder jemals wieder dir zur Hand
Johann Friedrich Reichardt, "An Lina" 1804pub
Václav Jan Tomášek, "An Linna" 1815?, Op58,5
from *Gedichte von Goethe:* VI,5
Leopold Damrosch, "An Lina" Op17,5

Liebe schwärmt auf allen Wegen
Franz Schubert, "Liebe schwärmt auf allen Wegen" 1815, D239,6

Liebesqual verschmäht mein Herz
Hugo Wolf, "Frech und froh (II)" 1889
from *Goethe Lieder* (17)

Liebliches Kind, kannst du mir sagen
Christian Gottlob Neefe, "Serenate, aus Claudine von Villa Bella" 1777
Johann Friedrich Reichardt, "Aus *Claudine von Villa Bella*" 1781pub
Johann Friedrich Reichardt, "Aus *Claudine von Villa Bella* (2nd version)" 1781pub
Johannes Brahms, "Serenade" 1876, Op70,3
Max Bruch, "Frage" 1882, Op49,i,1
Nikolai Medtner, "Aus *Claudine von Villa-Bella*" 1904-05, Op6,5

Lokken, haltet mich gefangen
Hugo Wolf, "Lokken, haltet mich gefangen" 1889
from *Goethe Lieder* (47)

Mädchen, als du kamst ans Licht
Carl Loewe, "Mädchen, als du kamst ans Licht" 1836
from *Faust* part 2

Mahadöh, der Herr der Erde, kommt herab zum sechsten Mal
Carl Friedrich Zelter, "Der Gott und die Bajadere" 1797
Franz Schubert, "Der Gott und die Bajadere" 1815, D254
Carl Loewe, "Der Gott und die Bajadere" 1835, Op45,2
Othmar Schoeck, "Der Gott und die Bajadere" 1921, Op34, 1v(low).pf

Mein Haus hat kein' Thür, mein Thür hat ke' Haus
Carl Loewe, "Freibeuter" 1836
Text is a parody of "Aus ist es mit mir" from *Des Knaben Wunderhorn*

Mein Mädel ward mir ungetreu
Johann Friedrich Reichardt, "Rettung" 1809pub

Meine Ruh' ist hin, mein Herz ist schwer
Louis Spohr, "Gretchen" 1809, Op25,3
Carl Friedrich Zelter, "Margarethe" 1809?
Franz Schubert, "Gretchen am Spinnrade" 1814, D118
Carl Loewe, "Meine Ruh' ist hin" 1822, Op9,iii,2
Richard Wagner, "Gretchen am Spinnrade" 1831, WWV 15, sop.pf
from *Sieben Kompositionen zu Goethes "Faust"* (6)
Friedrich Curschmann, "Meine Ruh' ist hin" 1836, Op11,5

Giuseppe Verdi, "Perduta ho la pace" 1838
translated into Italian by Luigi Balestra
from *Sei romanze*
Mikhail Glinka, "Gretchen am Spinnrade " (set in Russian), 1848
translated into Russian by Huber

Mich ergreift, ich weiß nicht wie, himmlisches Behagen
Carl Friedrich Zelter, "Tischlied" 1807
Johann Friedrich Reichardt, "Tischlied" 1809pub
Max Eberwein, "Tischlied" 1810
Ferdinand Ries, "Mich ergreift ich weiss nicht wie" 1811pub, Op32,6
Franz Schubert, "Tischlied" 1815, D234
Parody of "Mihi est propositum in taberna mori," a medieval drinking song

Mit des Bräutigams Behagen
Johann Friedrich Reichardt, "Ritter Curts Brautfahrt" 1811pub
Hugo Wolf, "Ritter Kurts Brautfahrt" 1888
from *Goethe Lieder* (12)

Mit Mädeln sich vertragen, mit Männern rumgeschlagen
Johann Friedrich Reichardt, "Aus *Claudine* (von Villa Bella)"
Hugo Wolf, "Frech und froh (I)" 1888
from *Goethe Lieder* (16)

Mit vollen Atemzügen saug ich, Natur, aus dir
Johann Friedrich Reichardt, "Aus *Erwin und Elmire*" 1780pub

Mitternachts weint und schluchzt ich
Ferruccio Busoni, "Schlechter Trost" 1924, bar.pf
Ernst Pepping, "Schlechter Trost" 1949pub
from *Haus- und Trostbuch* (29)

Möge Wasser, springend, wallend
Luigi Dallapiccola, "Möge Wasser, springend, wallend" 1953, mez.3cl
from *Goethe-Lieder*
verse from the poem "An des lustgen Brunnens Rand"

Morgennebel, Lila, hüllen deinen Thurm ein
Richard Strauss, "Pilgers Morgenlied (An Lila)" 1897, Op33,4, 1v.orch

Nach Corinthus von Athen gezogen
Carl Loewe, "Die Braut von Corinth" 1830, Op29

Nach diesem Frühlingsregen, den wir, so warm, erfleht
Johann Friedrich Reichardt, "Die glücklichen Gatten" 1809pub
Johann Friedrich Reichardt, "Die glücklichen Gatten (2nd version)" 1809pub, satb

Nach Mittage saßen wir junges Volk im Kühlen
Carl Friedrich Zelter, "Stirbt der Fuchs, so gilt der Balg" 1807
Václav Jan Tomášek, "Stirbt der Fuchs, so gilt der Balg" 1815?, Op58,2
from *Gedichte von Goethe:* VI,2

Nicht Gelegenheit macht Diebe
Hugo Wolf, "Nicht Gelegenheit macht Diebe" 1889
from *Goethe Lieder* (39)

Nicht mehr auf Seidenblatt schreib' ich symmetrische Reime
Ernst Pepping, "Nicht mehr auf Seidenblatt" 1949pub
from *Haus- und Trostbuch* (30)

Nichts vom Vergänglichen wie's auch geschah!
Richard Strauss, "Xenion" 1942

Nimmer will ich dich verlieren: See Marianne von Willemer

Nun ihr Musen, genug! Vergebens strebt ihr zu schildern
Johann Friedrich Reichardt, "Aus *Alexis und Dora*" 1809pub

Nun verlaß' ich diese Hütte
Johann Friedrich Reichardt, "Die schöne Nacht" 1809pub
Ferdinand Ries, "Die schöne Nacht" 1811pub, Op36,3

Nur fort, du braune Hexe
Johann Friedrich Reichardt, "Der Müllerin Reue" 1809pub

Nur Platz, nur Blösse! wir brauchen Räume
Carl Loewe, "Nur Platz, nur Blösse!" 1836, 2v.pf
from *Faust* part 2

Nur wer die Sehnsucht kennt, weiß, was ich leide!
Carl Friedrich Zelter, "Sehnsucht" 1795
Johann Friedrich Reichardt, "Sehnsucht" 1795-96pub
Johann Friedrich Reichardt, "Sehnsucht" 1805-06pub
Ludwig van Beethoven, "Sehnsucht (4 versions)" 1807-08, WoO134
Carl Friedrich Zelter, "Sehnsucht" 1812
Franz Schubert, "Nur wer die Sehnsucht kennt (1)" 1815, D310
Franz Schubert, "Nur wer die Sehnsucht kennt (2)" 1816, D359
Franz Schubert, "Nur wer die Sehnsucht kennt (3)" 1816, D481
Carl Loewe, "Sehnsucht" 1818?, Op9,iii,5
Franz Schubert, "Sehnsucht" 1819, D656, 2t3b
Carl Friedrich Zelter, "Sehnsucht" 1821pub
Franz Schubert, "Nur wer die Sehnsucht kennt (4)" 1826, D877,4
Franz Schubert, "Nur wer die Sehnsucht kennt (5)" 1826, D877,1, 2v.pf
Fanny Hensel, "Mignon" 1826
Robert Schumann, "Nur wer die Sehnsucht kennt" 1849, Op98a,3
Pyotr Il'yich Tchaikovsky, "Nur wer die Sehnsucht kennt" (set in Russian), 1869, Op6,6
Hugo Wolf, "Mignon (II)" 1888
from *Goethe Lieder* (6)
Nikolai Medtner, "Mignon" 1908-09, Op18,4

O fände für mich ein Bräutigam sich!
Bernhard Theodor Breitkopf, "Wunsch eines jungen Mädchen" 1770pub
Carl Loewe, "Mädchenwünsche" 1833, Op9,viii,4

O gieb vom weichen Pfühle, träumend ein halb Gehör!
Carl Friedrich Zelter, "Nachtgesang" 1804
Johann Friedrich Reichardt, "Nachtgesang" 1809pub
Franz Schubert, "Nachtgesang" 1814, D119
Carl Loewe, "Nachtgesang" 1836, Op79,2, saat
Leopold Damrosch, "Nachtgesang" Op17,3
Walter von Goethe, "Nachtgesang"
Wilhelm Petersen, "Nachtgesang" 1941pub, Op40,4
from *Goethe Lieder*

O Magdeburg, die Stadt, die schöne Mädchen hat
Ernst Krenek, "Die Zerstörung Magdeburgs" 1927, Op56,1

O Mutter, guten Rat mir leiht
Corona Schröter, "O Mutter, guten Rat mir leiht" 1782

O schaudre nicht, laß diesen Blick
Bettina von Arnim, "Aus *Faust*" 1842

O schönes Mädchen du, du mit dem schwarzen Haar
Johann Friedrich Reichardt, "Anliegen" 1809pub

O wären wir weiter, o wär' ich zu Haus!
Carl Loewe, "Der getreue Eckart" 1835, Op44,2

Ob der Koran von Ewigkeit sei?
Hugo Wolf, "Ob der Koran von Ewigkeit sei" 1889
from *Goethe Lieder* (34)

Ros' und Lilie morgenthaulich blüht im Garten meiner Nähe
Franz Schubert, "In Gegenwärtigen Vergangenes" 1821?, D710, 2t2b.pf

Sagt es niemand, nur den Weisen, weil die Menge gleich verhöhnet
Othmar Schoeck, "Selige Sehnsucht" 1911, Op19b,6
Wilhelm Petersen, "Selige Sehnsucht" 1941pub, Op40,9
from *Goethe Lieder*
Ernst Pepping, "Selige Sehnsucht" 1949pub
from *Haus- und Trostbuch* (12)

Sah ein Knab' ein Röslein stehn, Röslein auf der Heiden
Peter Grønland, "Heidenröslein"
Johann Friedrich Reichardt, "Heidenröslein" 1792pub
Franz Schubert, "Heidenröslein" 1815, D257
Václav Jan Tomášek, "Heidenröslein" 1815?, Op53,1
from *Gedichte von Goethe:* I,1
Johann Christoph Kienlen, "Heidenröslein" 1820
Robert Schumann, "Heidenröslein" 1849, Op67,3, satb
Johannes Brahms, "Heidenröslein" 1857, WoO 31,6
from *Volks-Kinderlieder* (6)

Schaff', das Tagwerk meiner Hände
Franz Schubert, "Hoffnung" 1819?, D295

Schlange, halt stille! Halt stille, Schlange!
Alexander Zemlinsky, "Brasilianisch" 1910pub

Schönste Tugend einer Seele
Bernhard Theodor Breitkopf, "An die Unschuld" 1770pub

Schwester von dem ersten Licht
Johanna Kinkel, "An Luna" Op6,4
Bernhard Theodor Breitkopf, "An den Mond" 1770pub

Seh ich den Pilgrim, so kann ich mich nie der Tränen enthalten
Johann Friedrich Reichardt, "Kanon" 1811pub, 2desc.ten.bass
Othmar Schoeck, "Seh' ich den Pilgrim" 1906, Op19b,7/IV
from *Fünf Venezianische Epigramme*

Seht den Felsenquell, freudehell
Franz Schubert, "Mahomets Gesang (1)" (fragment), 1817, D549
Franz Schubert, "Mahomets Gesang (2)" (fragment), 1821, D721, bass.pf
Carl Loewe, "Mahomet's Gesang" 1840, Op85

Sei mir heute nichts zuwider
Carl Loewe, "Sei mir heute nichts zuwider!" 1836
from *Faust* part 2

Setze mir nicht, du Grobian, mir den Krug so derb vor die Nase!
Robert Schumann, "Lieder aus dem Schenkenbuch im Westöstlichen Divan von Goethe. II" 1840, Op25,6
from *Liederkreis*

Sie haben wegen der Trunkenheit
Hugo Wolf, "Sie haben wegen der Trunkenheit" 1889
from *Goethe Lieder* (37)

Sie liebt mich! Sie liebt mich! Welch' schrekkliches Beben!
Josefine Lang, "Sie liebt mich" 1840, Op33,4
Nikolai Medtner, "Aus *Erwin und Elmire*" 1907-08, Op15,4
Othmar Schoeck, "Aus *Erwin und Elmire*" 1919pub, Op25,16, ten.bass.orch
from *Gesänge zu dem Singspiel von Goethe*

Sie saugt mit Gier verrätrisches Getränke
Ernst Pepping, "Fliegentod" 1949pub
from *Haus- und Trostbuch* (7)

Sie scheinen zu spielen voll Leichtsinn und Trug
Herzogin Anna Amalia, "Sie scheinen zu spielen" 1776

Sieh mich, Heil'ger, wie ich bin, eine arme Sünderin
Herzogin Anna Amalia, "Sieh mich, Heil'ger, wie ich bin" 1776
Philipp Christoph Kayser, "Bußlied" 1777
Johann Friedrich Reichardt, "Lied aus *Erwin und Elmire*" 1791pub
Nikolai Medtner, "Aus *Erwin und Elmire*" 1904-05, Op6,7

Singet nicht in Trauertönen von der Einsamkeit der Nacht
Johann Friedrich Reichardt, "Die Nacht" 1795-96pub
Václav Jan Tomášek, "Die Nacht" 1815?, Op55,5
from *Gedichte von Goethe:* III,5
Robert Schumann, "Singet nicht in Trauertönen" 1849, Op98a,7
Hugo Wolf, "Philine" 1888
from *Goethe Lieder* (8)
Cor de Groot, "Philine (aus *Wilhelm Meister*)" 194-?pub
from *7 Goethe Lieder* (3)

Sitz' ich allein. wo kann ich besser sein?
Robert Schumann, "Lieder aus dem Schenkenbuch im Westöstlichen Divan von Goethe. I" 1840, Op25,5
from *Liederkreis*

So hab' ich wirklich dich verloren?
Ludwig Berger, "An die Entfernte"
Johann Friedrich Reichardt, "An die Entfernte" 1794pub
Carl Friedrich Zelter, "An die Entfernte" 1807
Václav Jan Tomášek, "An die Entfernte" 1815?, Op55,1
from *Gedichte von Goethe:* III,1
Franz Schubert, "An die Entfernte" 1822, D765

So lang man nüchtern ist
Hugo Wolf, "So lang man nüchtern ist" 1889
from *Goethe Lieder* (36)

So laßt mich scheinen bis ich werde
Johann Friedrich Reichardt, "Mignons letzter Gesang" 1796pub
Franz Schubert, "So lasst mich scheinen (1&2)" (fragments), 1816, D469(a&b)
Franz Schubert, "So lasst mich scheinen (3)" 1821, D727
Franz Schubert, "So lasst mich scheinen (4)" 1826, D877,3
Robert Schumann, "So lasst mich scheinen, bis ich werde" 1849, Op98a,9
Hugo Wolf, "Mignon (III)" 1888
from *Goethe Lieder* (7)

So tanzet und springet in Reihen und Kranz
Nikolai Medtner, "Aus *Lila*" 1907-08, Op15,5

So wälz ich ohne Unterlaß
Hugo Wolf, "Genialisch Treiben" 1888
from *Goethe Lieder* (21)

So weit gebracht, daß wir bei Nacht
Felix Mendelssohn, "Aus der *ersten Walpurgisnacht*" 1831-33,43, 1v(low).ch.pf

Sorglos über die Fläche weg
Johann Friedrich Reichardt, "Mut" 1809pub

Spute dich, Kronos! Fort, den rasselnden Trott!
Franz Schubert, "An Schwager Kronos" 1816?, D369

Süße Freundin, noch Einen, nur Einen Kuß
Johann Friedrich Reichardt, "Das Wiedersehn" 1811pub

Tage der Wonne kommt ihr so bald?
Carl Friedrich Zelter, "Frühzeitiger Frühling" 1802
Johann Friedrich Reichardt, "Frühzeitiger Frühling" 1805-06pub
Václav Jan Tomášek, "Frühzeitiger Frühling" 1815?, Op54,4
from *Gedichte von Goethe:* II,4
Josefine Lang, "Frühzeitiger Frühling" 1830?, WoO
Carl Loewe, "Frühzeitiger Frühling" 1836, Op79,1
Adolph Martin Foerster, "Frühzeitiger Frühling" 1909, Op57,4

Tiefe Stille herrscht im Wasser, ohne Regung ruht das Meer
Johann Friedrich Reichardt, "Meeresstille" 1796pub
Franz Schubert, "Meeres Stille (1)" 1815, D2:215A
Franz Schubert, "Meeres Stille (2)" 1815, D216
Václav Jan Tomášek, "Meeresstille" 1815?, Op61,3, ssb.pf or ttb.pf
from *Gedichte von Goethe:* IX,3
Adolph Martin Foerster, "Meeresstille" 1878, Op6,5
Charles Griffes, "Tiefe Stille herrscht im Wasser" 1903-11?, A13
Nikolai Medtner, "Meeresstille" 1907-08, Op15,7

Tiefer liegt die Nacht um mich her
Johann Friedrich Reichardt, "Aus *Euphrosyne*" 1809pub

Trink, o Jüngling, heilges Glücke
Bernhard Theodor Breitkopf, "Das Glück der Liebe" 1770pub

Trocknet nicht, trocknet nicht, Tränen der ewigen Liebe!
Johann Friedrich Reichardt, "Wonne der Wehmut" 1788pub
Carl Friedrich Zelter, "Wonne der Wehmut" 1807
Ludwig van Beethoven, "Wonne der Wehmuth" 1810, Op83,1
Moriz von Dietrichstein, "Wonne der Wehmuth" 1811-?

Franz Schubert, "Wonne der Wehmut" 1815, D260
Václav Jan Tomášek, "Wonne der Wehmuth" 1815?, Op61,1, ssb.pf or ttb.pf
from *Gedichte von Goethe:* IX,1
Robert Franz, "Wonne der Wehmuth" 1864pub, Op33,1
Frank van der Stucken, "Wonne der Wehmuth" 1879, Op5,5
Franz Salmhofer, "Wonne der Wehmut" 1923pub, Op5,3
from *Vier Lieder*
Winfried Zillig, "Wonne der Wehmut" 1941
from *Zehn Lieder nach Gedichten von Goethe*

Trunken müssen wir alle sein!
Hugo Wolf, "Trunken müssen wir alle sein" 1889
from *Goethe Lieder* (35)

Über allen Gipfeln ist Ruh', in allen Wipfeln spürest du kaum einen Hauch
Carl Friedrich Zelter, "Ruhe" 1814
Carl Loewe, "Wandrers Nachtlied" 1817?, Op9,i,3a
Franz Schubert, "Wandrers Nachtlied" 1822?, D768
Ferdinand Hiller, "Wandrers Nachtlied" 1827
Fanny Hensel, "Über allen Gipfeln ist Ruh" 1835
Aleksandr Varlamov, "Über allen Gipfeln" (set in Russian), before 1848
translated by Lermontov
Franz Liszt, "Über allen Gipfeln ist Ruh" 1848/1860
Robert Schumann, "Nachtlied" 1850, Op96,1
Hermann Behn, "Wandrers Nachtlied" 189-?, Op2,4, 1v(med).pf
Max Reger, "Abendlied" 1894, Op14,2, sop.alt.pf
Charles Edward Ives, "Ilmenau" 1902
Nikolai Medtner, "Wandrers Nachtlied II" 1904-05, Op6,1
Ernst Bacon, "Wanderers Nachtlied" 1928pub
Cor de Groot, "Über allen Gipfeln ist Ruh" 194-?pub
from *7 Goethe Lieder* (5)
Ernst Pepping, "Ein gleiches" 1949pub
from *Haus- und Trostbuch* (34)
Harald Genzmer, "Über allen Gipfeln" 1940-87, bar.pf
from *Acht Lieder nach verschiedenen Dichtern*

Über meines Liebchens Äugeln
Franz Schubert, "Geheimes" 1821, D719

Über Tal und Fluß getragen ziehet rein der Sonne Wagen
Carl Friedrich Zelter, "An Mignon" 1797
Johann Friedrich Reichardt, "An Mignon" 1798pub
Johann Rudolf Zumsteeg, "An Mignon" 1800pub
from *Kleine Balladen und Lieder, zweites Heft*
Johann Friedrich Reichardt, "An Mignon (2nd version)" 1809pub
Franz Schubert, "An Mignon" 1815, D161
Louis Spohr, "An Mignon" 1816, Op41,3

Übers Niederträchtige niemand sich beklage
Richard Strauss, "Wanderers Gemütsruhe" 1918, Op67,6
from *Drei Lieder aus den Büchern des Unmuts des Rendsch Nameh*

Uf'm Bergli bin i g'sässe, ha de Vögle zugeschaut (see also "An ä Bergli...")
Carl Friedrich Zelter, "Schweitzer Lied" 1811
Franz Schubert, "Schweizerlied" 1817, D559

Robert Franz, "Schweizerlied" 1864pub, Op33,5
Friedrich Silcher, "Schweizerlied"
George Henschel, "Schweitzerlied" 187-?, Op24,7
Adolf Jensen, "Schweitzerlied" 1875-77, Op57,6

Ullin trat auf mit der Harfe, und gab uns Alpin's Gesang
Carl Loewe, "Alpin's Klage um Morar" 1844, Op95(94)
free translation from Ossian's (Macpherson's) "Colma"

Um Mitternacht ging ich, nicht eben gerne
Carl Friedrich Zelter, "Um Mitternacht" 1818
Ernst Pepping, "Um Mitternacht" 1949pub
from *Haus- und Trostbuch* (3)

Um Mitternacht, ich schlief, im Busen wachte das liebevolle Herz
Winfried Zillig, "Der Bräutigam" 1941
from *Zehn Lieder nach Gedichten von Goethe*

Um Mitternacht, wenn die Menschen erst schlafen
Nikolai Medtner, "Elfenliedchen" 1904-05, Op6,3
Alexander Zemlinsky, "Elfenlied" 1934, Op22,4

Umsonst, daß du ein Herz zu lenken
Bernhard Theodor Breitkopf, "Der wahre Genuß" 1770pub

Und frische Nahrung, neues Blut saug ich aus freier Welt
Johann Friedrich Reichardt, "Auf dem See" 1794pub
Hans Georg Nägeli, "Auf dem See" 1799
Václav Jan Tomášek, "Auf dem See" 1815?, Op57,3
from *Gedichte von Goethe:* V,3
Franz Schubert, "Auf dem See" 1817, D543
Carl Loewe, "Auf dem See" 1836, Op80,i,2, 4v
Fanny Hensel, "Auf dem See" 1841
Hugo Wolf, "Auf dem See" 1875, Op3,5
Nikolai Medtner, "Auf dem See" 1903, Op3,3
translated by Fet

Und Morgen fällt Sanct Martins Fest
Carl Loewe, "Gutmann und Gutweib" 1833, Op9,viii,5
Hugo Wolf, "Gutmann und Gutweib" 1888
from *Goethe Lieder* (13)

Verfließet, vielgeliebte Lieder, zum Meere der Vergessenheit!
Johann Friedrich Reichardt, "Am Flusse" 1809pub
Franz Schubert, "Am Flusse (1)" 1815, D160
Václav Jan Tomášek, "Am Fluße" 1815?, Op55,3
from *Gedichte von Goethe:* III,3
Franz Schubert, "Am Flusse (2)" 1822, D766
Moritz Hauptmann, "Am Flusse" 1834pub, Op22,6

Verteilet Euch nach allen Regionen
Johann Friedrich Reichardt, "Weltseele" 1809pub

Viele der Blümlein zusammengeknüpfet
Carl Loewe, "Meisters Schlusswort" 1836, sat.pf
poem from "Vier Jahrezeiten, Frühling," adapted by Loewe
from *Canon-Kranz*

Viele Gäste wünsch ich heut' mir zu meinem Tische!
Carl Friedrich Zelter, "Das Gastmahl" 1814, 1v.ttb

Voll Locken kraus ein Haupt so rund
Franz Schubert, "Versunken" 1821, D715

Von allen schönen Waaren, zum Markte hergefahren
Carl Friedrich Zelter, "Wer kauft Liebes-Götter" 1802, 1v.3vn.pf
Johann Friedrich Reichardt, "Wer kauft Liebesgötter" 1809pub
Franz Schubert, "Wer kauft Liebesgötter?" 1815, D261
Václav Jan Tomášek, "Wer kauft Liebesgötter?" 1815?, Op53,6
from *Gedichte von Goethe:* I,6

Von den Bergen zu den Hügeln
Fanny Hensel, "Wanderlied" 1837, Op1,2

Von mehr als einer Seite verwaist
Ernst Krenek, "Fragment" 1927, Op56,3

Von wem ich's habe, das sag' ich euch nicht
Nikolai Medtner, "Vor Gericht" 1907-08, Op15,6

Von Wolken streifenhaft befangen
Hanns Eisler, "Goethe-Fragmente" 1953?

War schöner als der schönste Tag
Carl Loewe, "Canzonette" 1835

Warum doch erschallen himmelwärts die Lieder!
Johann Friedrich Reichardt, "Aus dem Vorspiel: Was wir bringen" 1802pub, 3fv.pf(or harp)
Johannes Brahms, "Warum?" before 1884, Op92,4, satb.pf

Warum leckst du dein Mäulchen, indem du mir eilig begegnest?
Othmar Schoeck, "Warum leckst du dein Mäulchen" 1906, Op19b,7/I
from *Fünf Venezianische Epigramme*

Warum ziehst du mich unwiderstehlich
Johann Friedrich Reichardt, "An Belinden" 1794pub
Johann Friedrich Reichardt, "An Belinden (2nd version)" 1809pub

Was bedeutet die Bewegung: See Marianne von Willemer

Was die Großen Gutes taten, sah ich oft in meinem Leben
Karl Marx, "Was die Großen Gutes taten" 1949, Op49,8

Was die gute Natur weislich nur vielen verteilet
Johann Friedrich Reichardt, "Erkanntes Glück" 1794pub

Was hör' ich draußen vor dem Thor, was auf der Brücke schallen?
Johann Friedrich Reichardt, "Der Sänger" 1795-96pub
Carl Friedrich Zelter, "Der Sänger" 1803
Franz Schubert, "Der Sänger" 1815, D149
Carl Loewe, "Der Sänger" 1836, Op59,2
Robert Schumann, "Ballade des Harfners" 1849, Op98a,2
Hugo Wolf, "Der Sänger" 1888
from *Goethe Lieder* (10)

Was ich dort gelebt, genossen
Hanns Eisler, "Was ich dort gelebt" 1954

Was in der Schenke waren heute
Hugo Wolf, "Was in der Schenke waren heute" 1889
from *Goethe Lieder* (38)

Was machst du mir vor Liebchens Tür
Richard Wagner, "Lied des Mephistopheles" 1831, WWV 15, bass.unis ch.pf
from *Sieben Kompositionen zu Goethes "Faust"* (5)

Was zieht mir das Herz so, was zieht mich hinaus?
Johann Friedrich Reichardt, "Sehnsucht" 1805pub
Ludwig van Beethoven, "Sehnsucht" 1810, Op83,2
Franz Schubert, "Sehnsucht" 1814, D123
Fanny Hensel, "Sehnsucht" 1839
Hugo Wolf, "Sehnsucht" 1875, Op3,2

Wasser holen geht die reine, schöne Frau des hohen Bramen
Carl Loewe, "Legende" 1836, Op58
from *Paria* (2)

Weichet, Sorgen, von mir! doch ach!
Johann Friedrich Reichardt, "Süße Sorgen" 1794pub
Winfried Zillig, "Süße Sorgen" 1941
from *Zehn Lieder nach Gedichten von Goethe*

Weint, Mädchen, hier bei Amors Grabe!
Bernhard Theodor Breitkopf, "Amors Grab" 1770pub
Armin Knab, "Scheintod" 1924-46
from *Zwölf Lieder nach Gedichten von J. W. von Goethe*

Weiß wie Lilien, reine Kerzen, Sternen gleich bescheidner Beugung
Fartein Valen, "Weiss wie Lilien" 1925-7, Op6,2
Anton Webern, "Weiß wie Lilien, reine Kerzen" 1926, Op19,1, satb.cham
from *Zwei Lieder* (1)

Wekke den Amor nicht auf
Johann Friedrich Reichardt, "Warnung" 1809pub, 4v

Wenn der Blüten Frühlingsregen
Carl Loewe, "Wenn der Blüthen Frühlingsregen" 1836
from *Faust* part 2, Eingang und Maskenzug. (Scene)
Fanny Hensel, "Szene aus *Faust*" 1843, sop.ssaa.pf
from Faust, Part II, lines 4612-4665

Wenn der uralte heilige Vater
Franz Schubert, "Grenzen der Menschheit" 1821, D716
Hugo Wolf, "Grenzen der Menschheit" 1889
from *Goethe Lieder* (51)
Alban Berg, "Grenzen der Menschheit" 1902

Wenn die Reben wieder blühen, rühret sich der Wein im Fasse
Carl Friedrich Zelter, "Nachgefühl" 1798
Johann Rudolf Zumsteeg, "Erinnerung" 1805pub
from *Kleine Balladen und Lieder, siebtes Heft*
Johann Friedrich Reichardt, "Nachgefühl" 1809pub
Václav Jan Tomášek, "Nachtgefühl" 1815?, Op53,4
from *Gedichte von Goethe:* I,4
Louis Spohr, "Nachgefühl" 1819, WoO91

Johanna Kinkel, "Nachgefühl" Op10,1

Wenn dirs in Kopf und Herzen schwirrt
Karl Marx, "Das Beste" 1949, Op49,7

Wenn du dich im Spiegel besiehst
Winfried Zillig, "Blick um Blick" 1941
from *Zehn Lieder nach Gedichten von Goethe*

Wenn einem Mädgen das uns liebt
Bernhard Theodor Breitkopf, "Liebe und Tugend" 1770pub

Wenn ich dein gedenke, fragt mich gleich der Schenke
Hugo Wolf, "Wenn ich dein gedenke" 1889
from *Goethe Lieder* (46)

Wenn ich, liebe Lili, dich nicht liebte
Johann Friedrich Reichardt, "Vom Berge" 1794pub

Wenn ich 'mal ungeduldig werde, denk' ich an die Geduld der Erde
Pierre-Octave Ferroud, "Beispiel" 1932pub
from *Drei traute Gesänge*

Wenn im Unendlichen dasselbe sich wiederholend ewig fließt
Nikolai Medtner, "Praeludium" 1925-26, Op46,1

Wenn zu den Reihen der Nymphen, versammelt in heiliger Mondnacht
Nikolai Medtner, "Geweihter Platz" 1925-26, Op46,2

Wenn zu der Regenwand Phöbus sich gattet
Johannes Brahms, "Phänomen" 1873/74, Op61,3, 2v.pf
Hugo Wolf, "Phänomen" 1889
from *Goethe Lieder* (32)

Wer darf ihn nennen? und wer bekennen
Johann Friedrich Reichardt, "Gott (Aus dem *Faust*)" 1809pub

Wer kömmt! wer kauft von meiner Waar!
Georg Simon Löhlein, "Neujahrslied" 1769
Bernhard Theodor Breitkopf, "Neujahrslied" 1770pub

Wer nie sein Brod mit Thränen aß
Carl Friedrich Zelter, "Klage" 1795
Johann Friedrich Reichardt, "Klage" 1795-96pub
Carl Friedrich Zelter, "Klage" 1816
Franz Schubert, "Wer nie sein Brod mit Thränen ass (1)" 1816, D480,1
Franz Schubert, "Wer nie sein Brod mit Tränen ass (2)" 1816, D480,2
Franz Schubert, "Wer nie sein Brod mit Tränen ass (3)" 1822, D480,3
Norbert Burgmüller, "Harfenspieler II" 1827-36?, Op6,1
Wilhelm Stade, "Aus *Wilhelm Meister*" 1842pub
from "Aus Wilhelm Meister," *Lieder, Heft 1* (3)
Franz Liszt, "Wer nie sein Brot mit Tränen aß" 1848/1860
Robert Schumann, "Wer nie sein Brod mit Thränen ass" 1849, Op98a,4
Franz Liszt, "Wer nie sein Brod mit Tränen aß" 1862
Hugo Wolf, "Harfenspieler (III)" 1888
from *Goethe Lieder* (3)

Wer reitet so spät, durch Nacht und Wind
Corona Schröter, "Der Erlkönig" 1782

Andreas Romberg, "Erlkönig" 1793pub
Johann Friedrich Reichardt, "Erlkönig" 1794pub
Carl Friedrich Zelter, "Der Erlkönig" 1797
Gottlob Bachmann, "Erlkönig" 1798/99?pub, Op43
Ludwig van Beethoven, "Erlkönig" (sketch), 180?
Sketch completed 1897 by Reinhold Becker
Franz Schubert, "Erlkönig" 1815, D328
Václav Jan Tomášek, "Erlkönig" 1815?, Op59,1
from *Gedichte von Goethe:* VII,1
Bernhard Klein, "Der Erlkönig" 1815?pub
Carl Loewe, "Erlkönig" 1818, Op1,3
Julius Schneider, "Erlkönig" 1828
Anselm Hüttenbrenner, "Erlkönig" 1829
Louis Spohr, "Erlkönig" 1856, Op154,4, bar.vn.pf
Louis Schlottmann, "Erlkönig" 1878?pub, Op44,8

Wer sich der Einsamkeit ergibt, ach, der ist bald allein
Carl Friedrich Zelter, "Einsamkeit" 1795
Johann Friedrich Reichardt, "Einsamkeit" 1795-96pub
Franz Schubert, "Wer sich der Einsamkeit ergiebt (1)" 1815, D325
Franz Schubert, "Wer sich der Einsamkeit ergibt (2)" 1816, D478
Fanny Hensel, "Harfners Lied" 1825
Robert Schumann, "Wer sich der Einsamkeit ergiebt" 1849, Op98a,6
Hugo Wolf, "Harfenspieler (I)" 1888
from *Goethe Lieder* (1)

Wer, wer kann gebieten den Vögeln
Karl Marx, "Unvermeidlich" 1949, Op49,6

Wer will denn alles gleich ergründen!
Karl Marx, "Kommt Zeit, kommt Rat" 1949, Op49,1

Wer wird von der Welt verlangen
Richard Strauss, "Wer wird von der Welt verlangen" 1918, Op67,4
from *Drei Lieder aus den Büchern des Unmuts des Rendsch Nameh*

Wie an dem Tag, der dich der Welt verliehen
Hermann Simon, "Urworte–Dämon" 1935, bar.perc
from *Drei Goethe-Gesänge* (1)

Wie anders, Gretchen, war dir's
Franz Schubert, "Scene aus Goethe's *Faust*" 1814, D126

Wie du mir oft, geliebtes Kind
Johann Friedrich Reichardt, "Nähe" 1794pub

Wie Feld und Au so blinkend im Tau: See Johann Georg Jacobi[5]

Wie herrlich leuchtet mir die Natur!
Johann Friedrich Reichardt, "Mailied" 1781pub, 1v.pf or 4v
Ludwig van Beethoven, "Mailied" 1796?, Op52,4
Christian August Gabler, "Mailied" 1798

[5]Goethe inadvertently included this poem in his works in 1815, according to Max Friedlaender in *Das deutsche Lied im 18. Jahrhundert*, Stuttgart: J. G. Cotta'sche Buchhandlung Nachfolger, 1902. Reprint. Hildesheim: Georg Olms Verlagsbuchhandlung, 1962. Several composers, among them Wolf and Franz, remained unaware of the correct attribution.

Václav Jan Tomášek, "Maylied" 1815?, Op53,3
from *Gedichte von Goethe:* I,3
Bernhard Klein, "Mailied" 1827, Op15,6
Carl Loewe, "Mailied" 1836, Op79,4
Othmar Schoeck, "Mailied" 1910, Op19a,3
Hans Pfitzner, "Mailied" 1916, Op26,5
Armin Knab, "Mailied" 1924-46
from *Zwölf Lieder nach Gedichten von J. W. von Goethe*

Wie ich so ehrlich war
Othmar Schoeck, "Wie ich so ehrlich war" 1915, Op19b,4/III
from *Drei Lieder aus dem Buch der Betrachtungen*

Wie im Morgenglanze du rings mich anglühst
Johann Friedrich Reichardt, "Ganymed" 1794pub
Franz Schubert, "Ganymed" 1817, D544
Carl Loewe, "Ganymed" 1836-7, Op81,5, 4v
Hugo Wolf, "Ganymed" 1889
from *Goethe Lieder* (50)

Wie kommt's, daß du so traurig bist, da alles froh erscheint? (Parody. See Wunderhorn)
Ludwig Berger, "Trost in Thränen" Op33,2
Carl Friedrich Zelter, "Trost in Tränen" 1803
Johann Friedrich Reichardt, "Trost in Tränen" 1805-06pub
Franz Schubert, "Trost in Thränen" 1814, D120
Václav Jan Tomášek, "Trost in Tränen" 1815?, Op53,5
from *Gedichte von Goethe:* I,5
Carl Loewe, "Trost in Thränen" 1836, Op80,ii,2, ssa
Johannes Brahms, "Trost in Tränen" 1868, Op48,5
Peter Cornelius, "Trost in Tränen" 1872, Op14, bar.mez.t2b(pf)

Wie kühl schweift sichs bei nächt'ger Stunde
Fanny Hensel, "Liebe in der Ferne" 1844

Wie mit innigstem Behagen: See Marianne von Willemer

Wie sie klingeln, die Pfaffen! Wie angelegen sie's machen
Othmar Schoeck, "Wie sie klingeln, die Pfaffen!" 1906, Op19b,7/III
from *Fünf Venezianische Epigramme*

Wie sollt' ich heiter bleiben
Hugo Wolf, "Wie sollt' ich heiter bleiben" 1889
from *Goethe Lieder* (45)

Wilkommen schöner froher Tag
Johann Friedrich Reichardt, "Willkommen schöner froher Tag" 1800pub
from *Lieder aus dem Liederspiel, Lieb' und Treue* (7)

Willst du die Blüten des frühen, der Früchte des späteren Jahres
Fartein Valen, "Sakontola" 1925-7, Op6,1

Willst du immer weiter schweifen? sieh, das Gute liegt so nah'
Johann Friedrich Reichardt, "Erinnerung" 1809pub
Václav Jan Tomášek, "Erinnerung" 1815?, Op61,2, stb.pf
from *Gedichte von Goethe:* IX,2

Wir helfen gerne, sind nimmer ferne
Johann Friedrich Reichardt, "Aus *Lila*" 1809pub, 3fv

Wir reiten in die Kreuz und Quer
Karl Marx, "Kläffer" 1949, Op49,10

Wir singen und sagen vom Grafen so gern
Carl Friedrich Zelter, "Hochzeitlied" 1802
Johann Friedrich Reichardt, "Hochzeitlied" 1802
Václav Jan Tomášek, "Hochzeitlied" 1815?, Op56,5
from *Gedichte von Goethe:* IV,5
Carl Loewe, "Hochzeitlied" 1832, Op20,1

Wo die Rose hier blüht, wo Reben um Lorbeer sich schlingen
Hugo Wolf, "Anakreons Grab" 1888
from *Goethe Lieder* (29)
Fartein Valen, "Anakreons Grab" 1939, Op31,2

Wo willst du, klares Bächlein, hin so munter
Carl Friedrich Zelter, "Der Junggesell und der Mühlbach" 1799
Johann Friedrich Reichardt, "Der Junggesell und der Mühlbach" 1805-06pub
Václav Jan Tomášek, "Der Junggesell und der Mühlbach" 1815?, Op60,3
from *Gedichte von Goethe:* VIII,3

Woher der Freund so früh und schnelle
Johann Friedrich Reichardt, "Der Müllerin Verrat" 1809pub

Wohin, wohin? schöne Müllerin! wie heißt du? "Liese."
Johann Friedrich Reichardt, "Der Edelknabe und die Müllerin" 1806pub
Václav Jan Tomášek, "Der Edelknabe und die Müllerin" 1815?, Op60,1
from *Gedichte von Goethe:* VIII,1

Wohl, ich weiß es, da durchschleicht uns innen
Johann Friedrich Reichardt, "An Lotte" 1804pub

Wohl! wer auf rechter Spur sich in der Stille siedelt
Karl Marx, "Wohl! wer auf rechter Spur" 1949, Op49,11

Wunderlichstes Buch der Bücher ist das Buch der Liebe
Ernst Pepping, "Lesebuch" 1949pub
from *Haus- und Trostbuch* (28)

Ziehn die Schafe von der Wiese
Anton Webern, "Ziehn die Schafe von der Wiese" 1926, Op19,2, satb.cham
from *Zwei Lieder* (2)

Zu lieblich ists, ein Wort zu brechen
Johann Friedrich Reichardt, "Abschied" 1805-06pub
Mauro Giuliani, "Abschied" 1817pub, Op89,1, v.pf./guitar

Zugemessne Rhythmen reizen freilich
Richard Strauss, "Zugemessne Rhythmen" 1935

Zum Sehen geboren, zum Schauen bestellt
Carl Loewe, "Lynceus, der Thürmer, auf Faust's Sternwarte singend" 1833, Op9,viii,3
from *Faust* part 2: Drei Lieder des Thurmwächter Lynceus
Robert Schumann, "Lied Lynceus des Thürmers" 1849, Op79,27
from *Lieder-Album für die Jugend*
Hermann Simon, "Lynceus der Türmer" 1935, bar.horn
from *Drei Goethe-Gesänge* (2)

Zwischen dem Alten, zwischen dem Neuen
Johann Friedrich Reichardt, "Zum neuen Jahr" 1809pub, 2v.pf

Zwischen oben, zwischen unten schweb ich hin zu muntrer Schau
Wilhelm Petersen, "Schwebender Genius über der Erdkugel" 1941pub, Op40,5
from *Goethe Lieder*

Zwischen Waizen und Korn, zwischen Hecken und Dorn
Carl Friedrich Zelter, "Wo gehts Liebchen" 1810
Robert Franz, "Mailied" 1864pub, Op33,3
Hugo Wolf, "Mailied" 1876, Op13,3, ttbb
Arnold Schönberg, "Mailied" 189-?
Alexander Zemlinsky, "Mailied" 1894-96, Op2,i,5
Nikolai Medtner, "Mailied" 1904-05, Op6,2

Bruno Goetz (1885-1954)
Mich rief ein Ton aus weiter Ferne
Rudi Stephan, "Im Einschlafen" 1914

Johann Nikolaus Götz (1721-1781)
Nie hält sich Zephyrus bei einem Vorwurf auf
Maria Therese Paradis, "Die Schäferin" 1786pub

O wunderbare Harmonie, was Er will, will auch Sie
Joseph Haydn, "Die Harmonie in der Ehe" 1796-1801, satb.bc

Sie hat das Auge, die Hand, den Mund der schönen Psyche
Joseph Haydn, "Daphnens einziger Fehler" 1796-1801, satb.bc

Christian Gottlieb Goez (1746-1803)
Still und ruhig ist des Todes Schlummer
Johann Rudolf Zumsteeg, "Das Grab" 1803pub
from *Kleine Balladen und Lieder, sechstes Heft*

Alfred Gold (1874-?)
In hellen Träumen hab ich Dich oft geschaut
Arnold Schönberg, "In hellen Träumen hab ich Dich oft geschaut" 189-?

Fr. Goldtammer
Ein Kränzlein sollst du tragen, kein Perlendiadem
Carl Loewe, "Brautkranzlied" 1820?

Generalin Freifrau Emilie von der Goltz (?-1893)
In des Südens heissen Zonen Blumen giebt es köstlich schön
Carl Loewe, "Spirito Sancto" 1864, Op143

Wilhelm Conrad Gomoll (1877-?)
Am murmelnden Bach, unter schattigen, flüsternden Bäumen
Hugo Kaun, "Am murmelnden Bach" 1908pub, Op79,2

Du, silbernes Mondenlicht, schleich dich zu ihr!
Ernő Dohnányi, "Du, silbernes Mondenlicht" 1909pub, Op16,2
from *Im Lebenslenz*

Helles Klingen in den Lüften mischt sich mit dem Frühlingslicht
Hugo Kaun, "Lerchenlieder" 1908pub, Op79,3

Hört ihr's nicht klingen? Leis ganz leis?
Ernő Dohnányi, "Fernes Klingen" 1909pub, Op16,1
from *Im Lebenslenz*
Hugo Kaun, "Fernes Klingen" 1908pub, Op80,2

Komm', komm' zu mir, Lieb', komm' zur Nacht
Ernő Dohnányi, "Serenade" 1909pub, Op16,6
from *Im Lebenslenz*

Nach deinen Lippen sehnen die meinen, Geliebte!
Ernő Dohnányi, "Grüsse zur Nacht" 1909pub, Op16,3
from *Im Lebenslenz*

Um deine Liebe, zu allen Zeiten
Ernő Dohnányi, "Um deine Liebe" 1909pub, Op16,5
from *Im Lebenslenz*

Wie leis die Schwäne gleiten auf dunkler Flut
Ernő Dohnányi, "Im Traum" 1909pub, Op16,4
from *Im Lebenslenz*

Friedrich Wilhelm Gotter (1746-1797)
Ach, was ist die Liebe für ein süßes Ding
Anton Eberl, "Die Liebe"
Johann Rudolf Zumsteeg, "Die Liebe" 1803pub
from *Kleine Balladen und Lieder, sechstes Heft*

Auch die sprödeste der Schönen
Joseph Haydn, "Auch die sprödeste der Schönen" 1781/84, XXVIa Nr.18
Leopold Kozeluch, "Der Langmut Lohn" 1785?

Du, der ewig um mich trauert
Franz Schubert, "Pflicht und Liebe" 1816, D467

Ludwig Andreas Gotter (1661-1735)
Herr Jesu, Gnadensonne, wahrhaftes Lebenslicht
Carl Loewe, "Herr Jesu, Gnadensonne" 1860, Op131,8, 4v

Wie der Tag mir schleichet ohne dich vollbracht
Carl Loewe, "An die Geliebte" 1817, Op9,iii,3
translated from J. J. Rousseau
Norbert Burgmüller, "Wie der Tag mir schleichet" 1827-36?, Op12,2

Rudolph von Gottschall (1823-1909)
Da welkt am Fenster die letzte Rose
Robert Franz, "Die letzte Rose" 1865?pub, Op20,2

Marie, am Fenster sitzest du, du liebes, süßes Kind
Adolf Jensen, "Marie" 1849pub, Op1,2
Robert Franz, "Marie" 1860?pub, Op18,1
Charles Edward Ives, "Marie" 1896

Christian Dietrich Grabbe (1801-1836)
Wie ein Goldadler reißt der Blitz
Alban Berg, "Ich liebe dich!" 1903

R. Graf

Acht der winzigen Perlen enthält das goldene Kettlein
Joseph Marx, "Ein goldenes Kettlein" 1908

Die Quellen sangen in tiefer Nacht
Joseph Marx, "Serenata" 1908

Tod mit Blumen laß dein Tor bereiten
Joseph Marx, "Der Gefangene" 1907

Mary Graf-Bartholemew (1832-?)

Mir bist du tot, ob auch deine Wange
Hans Pfitzner, "Mir bist du tot" 1884

Gerhard Anton Hermann Gramberg (1772-1816)

Es schauet der Morgen mit funkelndem Schein
Carl Loewe, "Frühlingserwachen" 1819, Op9,iv,3

H. Grassmann (1809-1877)

O dolce far niente, du bist doch auch etwas!
Carl Loewe, "Das «Dolce far niente»" 185-?, mch or 1v.pf

Ferdinand Gregorovius (1821-1891)

Blaues Sternlein, du sollst schweigen
Alexander Zemlinsky, "Blaues Sternlein" 1898, Op6,5
from *Walzer Gesänge nach toskanischen Volkliedern*

Briefchen schrieb und warf in den Wind ich
Alexander Zemlinsky, "Briefchen schrieb ich" 1898, Op6,6
from *Walzer Gesänge nach toskanischen Volkliedern*

Fensterlein, nachts bist du zu
Alexander Zemlinsky, "Fensterlein, nachts bist du zu" 1898, Op6,3
from *Walzer Gesänge nach toskanischen Volkliedern*

Ich gehe des Nachts, wie der Mond thut gehn
Alexander Zemlinsky, "Ich geh' des Nachts" 1898, Op6,4
from *Walzer Gesänge nach toskanischen Volkliedern*

Klagen ist der Mond gekommen
Alexander Zemlinsky, "Klagen ist der Mond gekommen" 1898, Op6,2
from *Walzer Gesänge nach toskanischen Volkliedern*

Liebe Schwalbe, kleine Schwalbe
Alexander Zemlinsky, "Liebe Schwalbe" 1898, Op6,1
from *Walzer Gesänge nach toskanischen Volkliedern*
same poem as Brahms Op112,6, attributed to Hugo Conrat's translation from the Hungarian

Wenn ich wüsste, du würdest mein eigen
August Bungert, "Wenn ich wüsste, du würdest mein eigen" 1889-91pub, Op19,5

"Martin Greif" (Friedrich Hermann Frey) (1839-1911)

Am Barbaratage holt' ich drei Zweiglein
Felix Weingartner, "Barbarazweige" 1904, Op32,2

Auf luft'ger Höh' alleine ein Wanderbursche steht
Fried. Mayer, "Des Wanderburschen Abschied" 1910pub

Der Himmel strahlend ausgespannt, die Erde zu umfangen
Lise Maria Mayer, "Frühlingsankunft" 1911pub

Glokken klingen, Scharen dringen durch den Markt im Sonntagsstaat
Siegfried Drescher, "Sonntagsfreuden" 1910

Ich geh' auf stillen Wegen frühtags ins grüne Feld
Emil Mattiesen, "Morgengang" 190-?pub, Op11,4
from *Stille Lieder* (4)
Vítězslav Novák, "Morgengang" 1912pub, Op46,5
from *Erotikon*

Ich hab' zum Brunnen ein Krüglein gebracht
Arnold Schönberg, "Das zerbrochene Krüglein" 189-?, sop.pf

Legt mir unters Haupt Melissen
Alban Berg, "Schlummerlose Nächte" 1903

Naht die jubelvolle Zeit, kommt auch mir ein Sehnen
Richard Strauss, "Weihnachtsgefühl" 1899
from *Jugendlieder*
Rudi Stephan, "Weihnachtsgefühl" 1905

Nun rühret die Ähren im Felde ein leiser Hauch
Ernest Vietor, "Vor der Ernte" 1936, Op14,9

O weile, süßer Geliebter! Es trügt dich nur
Karol Szymanowski, "Liebesnacht" 1907, Op17,12

Sprach eine wilde Ros' am Zaun
Felix Weingartner, "Falter und Rosen" 1893, Op18,2
from *Severa. Sechs ernste Lieder*

Still ist's, wo die Gräber sind meiner Liebe
Alban Berg, "Schattenleben" 1903

Stille ruht die weite Welt, Schlummer fällt des Mondes Horn
Joseph Marx, "Hochsommernacht" 1908
Ernest Vietor, "Hochsommernacht" 1936, Op14,6

Von Wald umgeben ein Blütenbaum
Anton Webern, "Bild der Liebe" 1901-04
from *Acht frühe Lieder* (4)

Vor einem grünen Walde, da liegt ein sanfter Rain
Ernest Vietor, "Die Schnitterin" 1936, Op14,7

Wenn am feuchten Maienmorgen Wälder leuchten
Ernest Vietor, "Maienfrühe" Op6,4

Wie ferne Tritte hörst du's schallen
Hans Pfitzner, "Herbstgefühl" 1931, Op40,4

Wohin, o Bächlein, schnelle? "Hinab ins Tal."
Ernest Vietor, "Der Wanderer und der Bach" Op5,5

Leo Greiner (1876-1928)

Still schwebt die Nacht in hehrer Größe
Rudi Stephan, "Mitternacht" 1904

Wären wir zwei kleine, kleine Vögel
Max Reger, "Wären wir zwei kleine Vögel..." 1901, Op55,10, 1v(med).pf
translated from the Rumanian by Leo Greiner

Georg August von Griesinger
Es grünten die Bäume, es dufteten fein
Johann Rudolf Zumsteeg, "Die Zeit der Liebe" 1802pub
from *Kleine Balladen und Lieder, viertes Heft*

Franz (Seraphicus) Grillparzer (1791-1872)
Nacht umhüllt mit wehendem Flügel
Franz Schubert, "Berta's Lied in der Nacht" 1819, D653

Rührt die Cymbel, schlagt die Saiten
Franz Schubert, "Mirjam's Siegesgesang" 1828, D942, sop.satb.pf

Schöner und schöner schmückt sich der Plan
Fanny Hensel, "Italien" 1828pub, Op8,3(FM)

Wo ich bin, fern und nah, stehn zwei Augen da
Johann Vesque von Püttlingen, "Allgegenwart" 1845
from *Album für Gesang* IV

Zögernd, leise, in des Dunkels nächt'ger Stille
Franz Schubert, "Ständchen" 1827, D920, alt.2t2b.pf
Franz Schubert, "Ständchen" 1827, D921, alt.2s2a.pf
Grillparzer's original poem reads "Zögernd, stille, in des Dunkels nächt'ger Hülle"

Eduard Rudolf Grisebach (1845-1906)
Auf einer Wiese sah ich holde Frauen
Paul Graener, "Madrigal" 1911pub, Op29,3

Melchior Grohe (1829-1906)
O komme, holde Sommernacht
Johannes Brahms, "O komme, holde Sommernacht" 1871, Op58,4

E. Gross
Rauschet, ihr Meere, und wehet ihr Winde!
Louis Spohr, "Lied der Freude" 1809, Op25,4

Julius Waldemar Grosse (1828-1902)
Die Nächte stürmen, doch die Seele singt
Adolf Jensen, "Bei dir" 1863pub, Op13,5, 1v(low).pf

So hat noch niemand mir gethan: an beiden Händen fasst' er mich an
Johannes Doebber, "Erste Liebe" 1894?pub, Op22,4
August Bungert, "Erste Liebe" 1889-91pub, Op19,1

Klaus Groth (1819-1899)
Ade, ade, der Sommer zieht, der Sommer zieht, ade, ade, bis künftig Jahr
Karl Goldmark, "Wenn die Lerche zieht" 1868pub, Op18,2, 1v(low).pf

As ik hier dit Jaar weer, as ik hier dit Jaar weer
Ernst Pepping, "Swulkenleed" 1946
from *As ik hier dit Jaar weer* (12)

Auf dem Kirchhof unter'm Lindenbaum
Karl Goldmark, "Das kahle Grab" 1868pub, Op18,3, 1v(low).pf

Aus der Erde quellen Blumen
Johannes Brahms, "Klänge (I)" before 1875, Op66,1, 2v.pf

Avends, wenn wi to Bette gaat, veertein Engel bi mi staat (see also Wunderhorn: "Abends wenn...")
Ernst Pepping, "Slaapleed II" 1946
from *As ik hier dit Jaar weer* (6)

Da geht ein Bach das Thal entlang, wohin er wohl nur will?
Friedrich Nietzsche, "Da geht ein Bach" 1862, NWV10b

Dar gung en Mann un gung en Fro
Ernst Pepping, "Op'e Reis" 1946
from *As ik hier dit Jaar weer* (3)

Dar kummt en Herr to Peer, he ritt bet anne Döör
Ernst Pepping, "Warnung" 1946
from *As ik hier dit Jaar weer* (5)

De Dag, de graut, de Katt, de maut
Ernst Pepping, "Opstaan" 1946
from *As ik hier dit Jaar weer* (1)

De Wächter geit to blasen alleen in'e Nacht
Ernst Pepping, "Nachtleed" 1946
from *As ik hier dit Jaar weer* (11)

Dein blaues Auge hält so still
Johannes Brahms, "Dein blaues Auge" 1873, Op59,8

Der Weg an unserm Zaun entlang, wie wunderschön war das!
Friedrich Nietzsche, "Mein Platz vor der Thür" 1861, NWV1
Eugen Hildach, "Der Weg an unser'm Zaun entlang" before 1898, Op28,2

Die Ruhe zieht durch Haus und Stall
Karl Goldmark, "Sonntagsruhe" 1868pub, Op18,1, 1v(low).pf

Er sagt' mir so viel und ich sagt' ihm kein Wort
Karl Goldmark, "Er sagt' mir so viel" 1868pub, Op18,10, 1v(med).pf

Ernst ist der Herbst. Und wenn die Blätter fallen
Johannes Brahms, "Im Herbst" 1886, Op104,5, satb

Es hing der Reif im Lindenbaum
Johannes Brahms, "Es hing der Reif" 1888, Op106,3

Ich sah als Knabe Blumen blühn
Johannes Brahms, "Heimweh (III)" 1873, Op63,9

Ich sass und träumte Lieder am flüsternden Klavier
Leopold Damrosch, "Am Clavier" Op8,10

Im Schnee von Blüthenflocken, da spielt der Morgenwind
Leopold Damrosch, "Lenzes Lust" Op8,7

Inne Buurstraten dar steit en glatt Huus
Ernst Pepping, "Schöön Anna" 1946
from *As ik hier dit Jaar weer* (8)

Jehann, nu spann de Schimmels an!
Richard Kursch, "Jehann, nu spann de Schimmels an!" 1905pub, Op5,4

Kein Graben so breit, kein Mauer so hoch
Joachim Raff, "Keine Sorg um den Weg" 1855-63, Op98,10
translated by "Ernst" (Matthias Jakob Schleiden)
from *Sanges-Frühling*

Lüttje Finger, gollne Ringer, lange Meier, Puttenslikker, Lüüschenknikker
Ernst Pepping, "Lütt Fingerleed" 1946
from *As ik hier dit Jaar weer* (10)

Mein wundes Herz verlangt nach milder Ruh
Johannes Brahms, "Mein wundes Herz" 1873, Op59,7

Mien leve Hanne Gnegelputt hett allens, wat he will
Ernst Pepping, "Gnegelputt" 1946
from *As ik hier dit Jaar weer* (9)

Nun mach' mir nicht das Herz
Karl Goldmark, "So lach' doch einmal" 1868pub, Op18,8, 1v(med).pf

O wüßt ich doch den Weg zurück
Johannes Brahms, "Heimweh (II)" 1873, Op63,8

Regen, Regen druus, wi sitt hier warm in Huus!
Ernst Pepping, "Regenleed" 1946
from *As ik hier dit Jaar weer* (7)

Regentropfen aus den Bäumen fallen in das grüne Gras
Johannes Brahms, "Nachklang" 1873, Op59,4
Johannes Brahms, "Regenlied" 1908pub, WoO posth 23

Still min Hanne, hör mi to!
Ernst Pepping, "Slaapleed I" 1946
from *As ik hier dit Jaar weer* (4)

Sünn, Sünn, schiene, kiek ut dien Gardine
Ernst Pepping, "De Sünnschien" 1946
from *As ik hier dit Jaar weer* (2)

Vom Dorfe ab am Raine, da steht ein kleines Haus
Leopold Damrosch, "Bei Mondenschein" Op7,1

Walle, Regen, walle nieder
Johannes Brahms, "Regenlied" 1873, Op59,3

Warum denn warten von Tag zu Tag?
Johannes Brahms, "Komm bald" 1885?, Op97,5

Wenn ein müder Leib begraben
Johannes Brahms, "Klänge (II)" before 1875, Op66,2, 2v.pf

Wie Melodien zieht es mir leise durch den Sinn
Johannes Brahms, "Wie Melodien zieht es mir" 1886, Op105,1, 1v(low).pf
Charles Edward Ives, "Wie Melodien zieht es mir" 1898?

Wie traulich war das Fleckchen
Johannes Brahms, "Heimweh (I)" 1873, Op63,7

Wir gingen zusammen zu Feld, mein Hans
Karl Goldmark, "Wir gingen zusammen" 1868pub, Op18,9, 1v(med).pf

"Anastasius Grün" (Anton Alexander Graf von Auersperg) (1806-1876)

Als Lenz die Erde wieder mit erstem Kuss umschloss
Carl Loewe, "Die Reigerbaize" 1843-44?, Op106

Aus Sanct Justi Klosterhallen tönt ein träges Todtenlied
Carl Loewe, "Die Leiche zu St. Just" 1844, Op99,4
from *Kaiser Karl V* (4)

Du Grabesrose wurzelst wohl in ihres Herzens Schoss
Carl Loewe, "Die Grabrose" 1846?

Es hat das Herz des Menschen ganz eigne Länderkarten!
Carl Loewe, "Max in Augsburg.(1518)" 1853, Op124,1
from *Der letzte Ritter* (1)

Es steht eine gold'ne Wiege am Fuss des Herrscherthrons
Carl Loewe, "Das Wiegenfest zu Gent" 1844, Op99,1
from *Kaiser Karl V* (1)

Frühling ist's in allen Räumen, Blüth und Blume taucht empor
Joachim Raff, "Blätter und Lieder" 1855-63, Op98,4
from *Sanges-Frühling*

Fürst, Trossbub, Ritter, Gauner durchwimmeln Augsburgs Gassen
Carl Loewe, "Max und Dürer" 1853, Op124,2
from *Der letzte Ritter* (2)

Großvater und Großmutter, die saßen im Gartenhag
Robert Schumann, "Familien-Gemälde" 1840, Op34,4, sop.ten.pf

Ich hab' eine alte Muhme, die ein altes Büchlein hat
Franz Ries, "Das Blatt im Buche" before 1891
Max Reger, "Das Blatt im Buche" 1894, Op15,2, 1v(med).pf
Otto Lohse, "Das Blatt im Buche" 1910pub

Max wollt' aus Augsburg reiten
Carl Loewe, "Max' Abschied von Augsburg" 1853, Op124,3
from *Der letzte Ritter* (3)

James Grun

Morgenwölkchen, leichte, weben märchenhaft um Herz und Sinn
Hans Pfitzner, "Frieden" 1888/89, Op5,1

Schlaf ein, gewieget an meiner Brust
Hans Pfitzner, "Wiegenlied" 1888/89, Op5,2

Schon will der Abend sinken aufs weite, brausende Meer
Hans Pfitzner, "Zugvogel" 1888/89, Op6,3, 1mv.pf

Wie Frühlingsahnung weht es durch die Lande
Hans Pfitzner, "Wie Frühlingsahnung weht es durch die Lande" 1888-1900, Op7,5

Otto Friedrich Gruppe (1804-1876)

Der Löw' ist los! der Löw' ist frei!
Carl Loewe, "Landgraf Ludwig" 1837, Op67,3

Die Trepp' hinunter geschwungen komm' ich in vollem Lauf
Carl Loewe, "Niemand hat's gesehn" 1838, Op9,x,4
Richard Strauss, "Begegnung" 1880

Es weicht die Nacht, und über'm Hügel
Felix Weingartner, "Ein Begräbnis" 1904, Op31,2

Im Walde rollt der Wagen bei tiefer, stiller Nacht
Felix Weingartner, "Post im Walde" 1894, Op19,2
from *Hilaria. Sechs heitere Lieder*

Klein Lieschen, klein Lieschen, ich hab' dich so lieb
Carl Loewe, "Einrichtung" 1835?, Op9,x,5

O lass, Geliebter, dich erflehen
Carl Loewe, "Der Feldherr" 1837, Op67,1

's ist wahr, mit blanken Scheiben ist Apothekers Haus
Carl Loewe, "Der Apotheker als Nebenbuhler" 1838, Op9,x,6

Schwalbe, sag mir an, ists dein alter Mann
Johannes Brahms, "Das Mädchen spricht" 1886, Op107,3

Wie pocht mir vor Lust das Herz in der Brust!
Carl Loewe, "Der Bräutigam" 1838, Op9,x,3

Friedrich Wilhelm Gubitz (1786-1870)

Alles in mir glühet, zu lieben
Carl Maria von Weber, "Gebet um die Geliebte" 1814, Op47,6

In der Berge Riesenschatten, rasch enteilt dem Mondenlicht
Carl Maria von Weber, "Liebe-Glühen" 1812, Op25,1

Lust entfloh und hin ist hin!
Carl Maria von Weber, "Der Leichtmüthige" 1815, Op46,1
from *Die vier Temperamente bei dem Verlust der Geliebten*

Nun, bin ich befreit! Wie behäglich!
Carl Maria von Weber, "Der Gleichmüthige" 1815, Op46,4
from *Die vier Temperamente bei dem Verlust der Geliebten*

Sel'ge Zeiten sah ich prangen
Carl Maria von Weber, "Der Schwermüthige" 1815, Op46,2
from *Die vier Temperamente bei dem Verlust der Geliebten*

Verrathen! Verschmähet! Wer drängte mich aus?!
Carl Maria von Weber, "Der Liebewüthige" 1815, Op46,3
from *Die vier Temperamente bei dem Verlust der Geliebten*

Weile Kind, ich will nicht rauben!
Carl Maria von Weber, "Der Jüngling und die Spröde" 1816, Op47,4

Wer stets hinter'n Ofen kroch
Carl Maria von Weber, "Lied" 1815, J.186, bar.ttb.orch

Wie wir voll Glut uns hier zusammenfinden
Carl Maria von Weber, "Lied" 1815, J.187, ten.orch

Friedrich Güll (1812-1879)

Bäuerlein, Bäuerlein, tik, tik, tak, hast'nen grossen Hafersack
Wilhelm Taubert, "Wie das Finklein das Bäuerlein im Scheuerlein besucht"
from *Klänge aus der Kinderwelt*, Vol.3, No6

Der Bauer hat ein Taubenhaus
Wilhelm Taubert, "Vom Bauern und den Tauben. Darf's Büble Alles glauben."
from *Klänge aus der Kinderwelt*, Vol.2, No3

Der Schnitzelmann von Nürenberg hält feil in seiner Buden
Carl Reinecke, "Der Schnitzelmann von Nürenberg"
from *Kinderlieder*

Ei wie langsam, ei wie langsam kommt der Schneck von seinem Fleck
Wilhelm Taubert, "Von dem kleinen Schnecklein unterm Rosenstöcklein..."
from *Klänge aus der Kinderwelt*, Vol.3, No4

Glöcklein, Abendglöcklein, läute Frieden
Wilhelm Taubert, "Abendglöcklein"
from *Klänge aus der Kinderwelt*, Vol.3, No8

Hast viel gespielt und viel gelacht
Wilhelm Taubert, "Walt' Gott"
from *Klänge aus der Kinderwelt*, Vol.5, No5

Klaus ist in den Wald gegangen, weil er will die Vöglein fangen
Wilhelm Taubert, "Vom listigen Grasmücklein. Ein lustiges Stücklein."
from *Klänge aus der Kinderwelt*, Vol.3, No3

Sag mir, du Siebenschläferlein: Wie träumt das Maienkäferlein?
Wilhelm Taubert, "Vom Maienkäferlein"
from *Klänge aus der Kinderwelt*, Vol.2, No6

Johann Christian Günther (1695-1723)

Abermal ein Teil vom Jahre, abermal ein Tag vollbracht
Rudi Stephan, "Am Abend" 1914?, bar.pf
from *Zwei ernste Gesänge*

Brecht die schwangern Anmutsnelken
Armin Knab, "Aria zu einer Nachtmusik vor der Brautkammer" 1907
from *Wunderhorn-Lieder* (5)

Man lauert, sitzt und sinnt, verändert, schreibt, durchstreicht
Ernst Krenek, "Das unerkannte Gedicht" 1927, Op53,1
from *Vier Gesänge nach alten Gedichten*

Wenn des Mondes bleiches Licht
Hugo Wolf, "Ein Grab" 1876

Agnes Emerita Gyr (Geyer) (1787-?)

Schwebe, mein tanzender Kahn
Louis Spohr, "Das Schiffermädchen" 1809, Op25,6

J. L. Haase

Singe, Vöglein, singe, singe, Vöglein, singe
Franz Abt, "Naturfreuden" 1870?pub
from *Kinderlieder*

"Louise von Haber" (Louise Pauline Henriette Carl) (1880-?)

Du Baum an meinem Fenster, was nickst du und grüssest mir zu?
Hermann Behn, "Du Baum an meinem Fenster" 189-?, Op4,2, sop.pf
from *Mädchenlieder*

"Wilhelm Habermann:" see Johannes Öhquist

Sofie Hämmerli-Marti (1868-1942)

Gärtner, chum cho d'Schlößli bschnyde!
Paul Hindemith, "Schlössli bschnyde" 1914-16, Op5,1
from *Lustige Lieder in Aargauer Mundart*

Wilhelm Häring: see "Willibald Alexis"

"Hafis" (Mohammed Schemsed-din) (ca.1327-1390)

Ach, wie richtete, so klagt' ich
Othmar Schoeck, "Ach, wie richtete, so klagt' ich" 1919pub, Op33,4
from *Zwölf Hafis-Lieder*

Ach, wie schön ist Nacht und Dämmerschein!
Othmar Schoeck, "Ach, wie schön ist Nacht und Dämmerschein!" 1919pub, Op33,1
from *Zwölf Hafis-Lieder*

Ach, wie süß, wie süß sie duftet
Theodor Streicher, "Ach, wie süß, wie süß sie duftet" 1907-08pub
translated by Georg Friedrich Daumer
from *Hafis-Lieder* (17)
Erich J. Wolff, "Ach, wie süß, wie süß sie duftet!" 1914pub, Lieder No.4
translated by Georg Friedrich Daumer

Als einst von deiner Schöne
Adolf Jensen, "Als einst von deiner Schöne" 1863, Op11,1
translated from the Persian by Georg Friedrich Daumer
from *Lieder des Hafis*

Als ich zum ersten Male dein Angesicht erblickte
Frederic Louis Ritter, "Als ich zum ersten Male" 1866pub, Op1,1

Bitteres zu sagen denkst du
Johannes Brahms, "Bitteres zu sagen denkst du" 1864, Op32,7
translated by Georg Friedrich Daumer
Erich J. Wolff, "Bittres mir zu sagen, denkst du" 1914pub, Lieder No.9
translated by Georg Friedrich Daumer

Das Gescheh'ne, nicht bereut's Hafis
Othmar Schoeck, "Das Gescheh'ne, nicht bereut's Hafis" 1919pub, Op33,3
from *Zwölf Hafis-Lieder*

Deine gewölbten Brauen, o Geliebte
Richard Strauss, "Ihre Augen" 1928, Op77,1
translated by Hans Bethge
from *Gesänge des Orients*

Der du mich mit gutem Rate
Theodor Streicher, "Der du mich mit gutem Rate" 1907-08pub
translated by Georg Friedrich Daumer
from *Hafis-Lieder* (9)

Der Frühling ist erschienen. Hyazinten und Tulpen und Narzissen
Karol Szymanowski, "Trauriger Frühling" 1911, Op24,6
German paraphrase by Hans Bethge
from *Des Hafis Liebeslieder*

Der Schah von Ormus sah mich nie
Theodor Streicher, "Der Schah von Ormus sah mich nie" 1907-08pub
translated by Georg Friedrich Daumer
from *Hafis-Lieder* (3)

Die Flamme hier, die wilde, zu verhehlen
Johannes Brahms, "Liebesglut" 1868, Op47,2
translated by Georg Friedrich Daumer

Die höchste Macht der Erde sitzt auf keinem Thron
Richard Strauss, "Die Allmächtige" 1928, Op77,4
translated by Hans Bethge
from *Gesänge des Orients*

Die Liebe, sie zerbreche mich
Theodor Streicher, "Die Liebe, sie zerbreche mich" 1907-08pub
translated by Georg Friedrich Daumer
from *Hafis-Lieder* (11)

Die Perlen meiner Seele haben keinen andern Sinn
Richard Strauss, "Huldigung" 1928, Op77,5
translated by Hans Bethge
from *Gesänge des Orients*

Durstig sind wir, lieber Wirt
Theodor Streicher, "Durstig sind wir, lieber Wirt" 1907-08pub
translated by Georg Friedrich Daumer
from *Hafis-Lieder* (4)

Ein solcher ist mein Freund
Erich J. Wolff, "Ein solcher ist mein Freund" 1914pub, Lieder No.17
translated by Georg Friedrich Daumer

Eine Fürstin ist die Schönheit
Theodor Streicher, "Eine Fürstin ist die Schönheit" 1907-08pub
translated by Georg Friedrich Daumer
from *Hafis-Lieder* (24)

Einst aus meinem Grabe werden ungezählte rote Tulpen
Karol Szymanowski, "Die brennenden Tulpen" 1911, Op24,3
German paraphrase by Hans Bethge
from *Des Hafis Liebeslieder*

Entzükket dich ein Wunderhauch
Erich J. Wolff, "Entzücket dich ein Wunderhauch?" 1914pub, Lieder No.18
translated by Georg Friedrich Daumer

Es hält der Ost, der eitle, sich
Theodor Streicher, "Es hält der Ost, der eitle" 1907-08pub
translated by Georg Friedrich Daumer
from *Hafis-Lieder* (7)

Es werde Licht! So tönete der Ruf Gottes in die dumpfe Nacht
Erich J. Wolff, "Es werde Licht!" 1914pub, Lieder No.21
translated by Georg Friedrich Daumer

Fern sei die Ros' und ihre Pracht!
    Theodor Streicher, "Fern sei die Ros' und ihre Pracht!" 1907-08pub
        translated by Georg Friedrich Daumer
        from *Hafis-Lieder* (13)

Freue dich, o Seelenvogel!
    George Henschel, "Freue dich, o Seelenvogel!" 188-?, Op34,2
        translated by Georg Friedrich Daumer

Führer auf dem Weg des Heiles
    Theodor Streicher, "Führer auf dem Weg des Heiles" 1907-08pub
        translated by Georg Friedrich Daumer
        from *Hafis-Lieder* (14)

Gebt mir meinen Becher!
    Richard Strauss, "Schwung" 1928, Op77,2
        translated by Hans Bethge
        from *Gesänge des Orients*

Heute tanzt alles, alles, alles tanzt! Göttlich ist Tanz
    Karol Szymanowski, "Tanz" 1911, Op24,4
        German paraphrase by Hans Bethge
        from *Des Hafis Liebeslieder*

Höre mir den Prediger
    Othmar Schoeck, "Höre mir den Prediger" 1919pub, Op33,2
        from *Zwölf Hafis-Lieder*

Horch, hörst du nicht vom Himmel her
    Erich J. Wolff, "Horch, hörst du nicht vom Himmel her" 1914pub, Lieder No.25
        translated by Georg Friedrich Daumer
    Othmar Schoeck, "Horch, hörst du nicht vom Himmel her" 1919pub, Op33,10
        from *Zwölf Hafis-Lieder*

Ich bin ein armes Lämpchen nur
    Adolf Jensen, "Ich bin ein armes Lämpchen nur" 1863, Op11,2
        translated from the Persian by Georg Friedrich Daumer
        from *Lieder des Hafis*

Ich dachte dein in tiefer Nacht, da leuchtete mit heller Macht
    Frederic Louis Ritter, "Ich dachte dein in tiefer Nacht" 1866pub, Op1,3
    August Bungert, "Der Mensch ist doch Nichts als Begehren sich zu fühlen im Andern!"
            1891pub, Op26,3
        Poem translated by Georg Friedrich Daumer. Title from Bettine von Arnim's *Die Günderode.*
        from *An eine schöne Frau: Liebesbriefe in Liedern*
    Theodor Streicher, "Ich dachte dein in tiefer Nacht" 1907-08pub
        translated by Georg Friedrich Daumer
        from *Hafis-Lieder* (5)

Ich habe mich dem Heil entschworen
    Theodor Streicher, "Ich habe mich dem Heil entschworen" 1907-08pub
        translated by Georg Friedrich Daumer
        from *Hafis-Lieder* (12)
    Othmar Schoeck, "Ich habe mich dem Heil entschworen" 1919pub, Op33,8
        from *Zwölf Hafis-Lieder*

Ich roch der Liebe himmlisches Arom
Othmar Schoeck, "Ich roch der Liebe himmlisches Arom" 1919pub, Op33,7
from *Zwölf Hafis-Lieder*

Ich Unglückseliger! Wer gibt mir Nachricht von meiner Liebsten?
Karol Szymanowski, "Der verliebte Ostwind" 1911, Op24,5
German paraphrase by Hans Bethge
from *Des Hafis Liebeslieder*

Ich will bis in die Sterne die Fahne der Liebe tragen
Adolf Jensen, "Ich will bis in die Sterne" 1863, Op11,3
translated from the Persian by Georg Friedrich Daumer
from *Lieder des Hafis*

Ich wollt', ich wär' ein morgenklarer See und du die Sonne
Karol Szymanowski, "Wünsche" 1911, Op24,1
German paraphrase by Hans Bethge
from *Des Hafis Liebeslieder*

Ist dir ein getreues, liebevolles Kind bescheert
Frederic Louis Ritter, "Ist dir ein getreues..." 1866pub, Op1,6
Theodor Streicher, "Ist dir ein getreues liebevolles Kind beschert" 1907-08pub
translated by Georg Friedrich Daumer
from *Hafis-Lieder* (20)

Ja, ich bin krank, ich weiss, ich weiss, doch lasst mich!
Karol Szymanowski, "Die einzige Arzenei" 1911, Op24,2
German paraphrase by Hans Bethge
from *Des Hafis Liebeslieder*

Keine Sorge verzehre mich um das Künftige
Theodor Streicher, "Keine Sorge verzehre mich um das Künftige" 1907-08pub
translated by Georg Friedrich Daumer
from *Hafis-Lieder* (10)

Lieblich in der Rosenzeit
Theodor Streicher, "Lieblich in der Rosenzeit" 1907-08pub
translated by Georg Friedrich Daumer
from *Hafis-Lieder* (21)
Othmar Schoeck, "Lieblich in der Rosenzeit" 1919pub, Op33,9
from *Zwölf Hafis-Lieder*

Lilie hat der Zungen zehne
Theodor Streicher, "Lilie hat der Zungen zehne" 1907-08pub
translated by Georg Friedrich Daumer
from *Hafis-Lieder* (19)

Lockenstricke sollst du wissen
Adolf Jensen, "Lockenstricke sollst du wissen" 1863, Op11,5
translated from the Persian by Georg Friedrich Daumer
from *Lieder des Hafis*

Mein süßer Schatz! du bist zu gut
Theodor Streicher, "Mein süßer Schatz! du bist zu gut" 1907-08pub
translated by Georg Friedrich Daumer
from *Hafis-Lieder* (6)

Meine Lebenszeit verstreicht
Erich J. Wolff, "Meine Lebenszeit verstreicht" 1914pub, Lieder No.38
Daumer's free translation mimics Gellert's "Vom Tode" in the 1st stanza.
Othmar Schoeck, "Meine Lebenszeit verstreicht" 1919pub, Op33,6
Daumer mimics Gellert's "Vom Tode" in the 1st stanza.
from *Zwölf Hafis-Lieder*

Nicht düstre, Theosoph, so tief!
Othmar Schoeck, "Nicht düstre, Theosoph, so tief!" 1919pub, Op33,11
from *Zwölf Hafis-Lieder*

O hättest du, begrüßend des Lebens erste Sonnen
Erich J. Wolff, "O hättest du!" 1914pub, Lieder No.42
translated by Georg Friedrich Daumer

O harte Sterne! Nie versöhnte, rauhe Welt!
Theodor Streicher, "O harte Sterne!" 1907-08pub
translated by Georg Friedrich Daumer
from *Hafis-Lieder* (15)

O wie süß ein Duft von oben meinen Geist umwittert!
Erich J. Wolff, "O wie süß ein Duft von oben" 1914pub, Lieder No.43
translated by Georg Friedrich Daumer

Rosen im Haare, den Becher zur Hand
Carl Maria von Weber, "Rosen im Haare" 1818, Op66,2
translated by Breuner

Schön wie Thirza bist du
Erich J. Wolff, "Schön wie Thirza bist du" 1914pub, Lieder No.47
translated by Georg Friedrich Daumer

Sie sagen, Hafis, du sei'st ein gar so gewalt'ger Geist
Theodor Streicher, "Sie sagen, Hafis, du sei'st ein gar so gewalt'ger Geist" 1907-08pub
translated by Georg Friedrich Daumer
from *Hafis-Lieder* (25)

Sing', o lieblicher Sängermund
Othmar Schoeck, "Sing', o lieblicher Sängermund" 1919pub, Op33,12
from *Zwölf Hafis-Lieder*

So stehn wir, ich und meine Weide
Johannes Brahms, "So stehn wir, ich und meine Weide" 1864, Op32,8
translated by Georg Friedrich Daumer

Stark wie der Tod ist die Liebe
Erich J. Wolff, "Stark wie der Tod ist die Liebe" 1914pub, Lieder No.50
translated by Georg Friedrich Daumer

Viel bin ich umhergewandert
Erich J. Wolff, "Viel bin ich umhergewandert" 1914pub, Lieder No.54
translated by Georg Friedrich Daumer

Vor den Mauern von Schiras liegt das schöne Mosella
Karol Szymanowski, "Das Grab des Hafis" 191-?, Op. posth.
German paraphrase by Hans Bethge

Was du forderst, es gescheh'!
Theodor Streicher, "Was du forderst, es gescheh'!" 1907-08pub
translated by Georg Friedrich Daumer
from *Hafis-Lieder* (2)

Wehe, Lüftchen, lind und lieblich
Johannes Brahms, "Botschaft" 1868, Op47,1
translated by Georg Friedrich Daumer
Theodor Streicher, "Wehe Lüftchen, lind und lieblich" 1907-08pub
translated by Georg Friedrich Daumer
from *Hafis-Lieder* (23)

Wehe mir, mein Rosenkränzlein, weh
Adolf Jensen, "Wehe mir, mein Rosenkränzlein, weh" 1863, Op11,7
translated from the Persian by Georg Friedrich Daumer
from *Lieder des Hafis*

Weh'n im Garten die Arome
Theodor Streicher, "Weh'n im Garten die Arome" 1907-08pub
translated by Georg Friedrich Daumer
from *Hafis-Lieder* (18)

Wehre nicht, o Lieb, wühlen in den Locken deines holden Hauptes
Adolf Jensen, "Wehre nicht, o Lieb" 1863, Op11,4
translated from the Persian by Georg Friedrich Daumer
from *Lieder des Hafis*

Weißt du noch, mein süßes Herz
Robert Franz, "Weisst du noch?" 1870?, Op42,4
Theodor Streicher, "Weißt du noch, mein süßes Herz" 1907-08pub
translated by Georg Friedrich Daumer
from *Hafis-Lieder* (16)

Wenn dereinst, wo sie versinken
Theodor Streicher, "Wenn dereinst, wo sie versinken" 1907-08pub
translated by Georg Friedrich Daumer
from *Hafis-Lieder* (22)

Wenn du lächelst, wenn du blickst, wenn du grüssest, wenn du sprichst
Frederic Louis Ritter, "Wenn du lächelst" 1866pub, Op1,5

Wenn einer mäßig trinket, so soll ihm das gedeihlich sein
Theodor Streicher, "Wenn einer mäßig trinket" 1907-08pub
translated by Georg Friedrich Daumer
from *Hafis-Lieder* (1)

Wie bist du, meine Königin
Johannes Brahms, "Wie bist du, meine Königin" 1864, Op32,9
translated by Georg Friedrich Daumer

Wie glücklich ist der Morgenwind!
Theodor Streicher, "Wie glücklich ist der Morgenwind!" 1907-08pub
translated by Georg Friedrich Daumer
from *Hafis-Lieder* (8)

Wie Melodie aus reiner Sphäre hör' ich
George Henschel, "Wie Melodie aus reiner Sphäre" 188-?, Op43,3
translated from the Persian by Georg Friedrich Daumer

Erich J. Wolff, "Wie Melodie aus reiner Sphäre hör' ich" 1914pub, Lieder No.57
translated by Georg Friedrich Daumer

Wie stimmst du mich zur Andacht
Othmar Schoeck, "Wie stimmst du mich zur Andacht" 1921, Op33,5
from *Zwölf Hafis-Lieder*

Wo Engel hausen, da ist der Himmel, und sei's auch mitten im Weltgetümmel
Frederic Louis Ritter, "Wo Engel hausen" 1866pub, Op1,4
George Henschel, "Wo Engel hausen" 188-?, Op34,3
translated by Georg Friedrich Daumer

Wo ist der Ort, an dem du weilst?
Erich J. Wolff, "Wo ist der Ort, an dem du weilst?" 1914pub, Lieder No.59
translated by Georg Friedrich Daumer

Zu der Rose, zu dem Weine komm!
Adolf Jensen, "Zu der Rose, zu dem Weine komm!" 1863, Op11,6
translated from the Persian by Georg Friedrich Daumer
from *Lieder des Hafis*

Zwei Paradieseslauben, sind, Liebste, deine Brauen
Frederic Louis Ritter, "Zwei Paradieseslauben" 1866pub, Op1,2

Friedrich von Hagedorn (1708-1754)

Als mich die Mama Hänschen küssen sah, strafte sie mich ab
Paul Hindemith, "Das Kind" 1922, sop.pf

Der Uhu, der Kauz und zwo Eulen
Johann Rudolf Zumsteeg, "Die Eulen" 1805pub
from *Kleine Balladen und Lieder, siebtes Heft*

Zu meiner Zeit bestand noch Recht und Billigkeit
Josef Antonín Štěpán, "Die Alte" 1778-79pub
Wolfgang Amadeus Mozart, "Die Alte" 1787, K517

Charlotte von Hagn (1809-1891)

Dichter! was Liebe sei, mir nicht verhehle!
Franz Liszt, "Was Liebe sei?" 1844pub
Franz Liszt, "Was Liebe sei?" 1855
Franz Liszt, "Was Liebe sei?" 1879pub

Ida Marie Luise Sophie Friederike Gustava Hahn-Hahn (1805-1880)

Es steht in der Bibel geschrieben
Robert Franz, "Ich bin bis zum Tode betrübet" 1878, Op48,5

In den Abgrund lass mich schauen
Robert Franz, "Am Rheinfall" 1870?, Op44,6

In der Nacht, in der Nacht da rauschen die Bäume so traurig
Robert Franz, "Nachtlied" 1843pub, Op1,2

Gerhard Anton von Halem (1752-1819)

Das Leben gleichet der Blume! So sagen die Weisen. Wohlan!
Franz Jacob Freystädtler, "Trinklied" 1795
from *Sechs Lieder der besten deutschen Dichter* (1)

Mit Liebesblick und Spiel und Sang
Ludwig van Beethoven, "Gretels Warnung" 1810pub, Op75,4

Albrecht von Haller (1708-1777)
Des Tages Licht hat sich verdunkelt
Josef Antonín Štěpán, "Doris" 1778-79pub

"Friedrich Halm" (Eligius Franz Joseph Freiherr von Münch-Bellinghausen) (1806-1871)
Bei dir sind meine Gedanken
Johannes Brahms, "Bei dir sind meine Gedanken" 1883/84?, Op95,2

Ich müh mich ab und kann nicht verschmerzen
Johannes Brahms, "Beim Abschied" 1883/84?, Op95,3a&b

Kein Haus, keine Heimat, kein Weib und kein Kind
Johannes Brahms, "Kein Haus, keine Heimat" 1883/84, Op94,5, 1v(low).pf

Mein Herz, ich will dich fragen, was ist denn Liebe? sag'!
Carl Loewe, "Mein Herz, ich will dich fragen" 1842, Op86

Mein Lieb ist ein Jäger, und grün ist sein Kleid
Johannes Brahms, "Der Jäger" 1883/84?, Op95,4

Steig auf, geliebter Schatten
Johannes Brahms, "Steig auf, geliebter Schatten" 1883/84, Op94,2, 1v(low).pf

Was weht um meine Schläfe wie laue Frühlingsnacht
Robert Schumann, "Geisternähe" 1850, Op77,3

Ludwig Hamann (1867-1930/36?)
Hoch am dunklen Himmelsbogen glänzt ein Stern
Max Reger, "Ehre sei Gott in der Höhe!" 1905, 1v.pf(harm/org)

Robert Hamerling (1830-1889)
An den Höhen, an den Wäldern
George Henschel, "Wanderlied" 187-?, Op17,2

Auf schweigendem Bergesgipfel der Knabe vom Thale ruh't
Ludwig Thuille, "Ganymed" 189-?pub, Op4,5

Augenblicke gibt es, zage, wo so grabesstill die Heide
Alban Berg, "Augenblicke" 1904

Die Todten haben Einen in ihrer Einsamkeit
Felix Weingartner, "Allerseelentag" 1893, Op18,6
from *Severa. Sechs ernste Lieder*

Einst träumt' ich im Waldgrün, nun träum' ich am Meer
Franz von Holstein, "Einst träumt' ich im Waldgrün" 1880, Op44,2

Es flimmert der Kranz der Sterne, der Mond aus Wolken bricht
Eduard Lassen, "Meine Lilie" Op67,4

Es rauschen die Tannen und Föhren
Felix Weingartner, "Rübezahl" 1891pub, Op17,1

Es ziehen die Wolken, es wandern die Sterne
Eduard Lassen, "Die Lerchen" Op59,4

Hinter jenen Epheuranken
Felix Weingartner, "Der Traumgott" 1891pub, Op17,2

Lächeln ist des Mundes Sache
George Henschel, "Mund und Auge" 187-?, Op21,3
Eduard Lassen, "Mund und Auge" Op67,6

Lass' die Rose schlummern, und die Wellen auch
Eduard Lassen, "Lass' die Rose schlummern" Op59,6

Nur ein Wörtchen sprich, o Mädchen
Eduard Lassen, "Sei nur ruhig, lieber Robin" Op66,3

O sehne dich nicht an's graue Meer, im Walde, da rauschen die Tannen
Franz von Holstein, "O sehne dich nicht an's graue Meer" 1880, Op44,1
August Bungert, "O sehne dich nicht an's graue Meer" 1889-91pub, Op12,1

O selig, wem in stiller Nacht erscheint ein liebes Bild
Franz von Holstein, "O selig" 1880, Op42,6

O sieh, wie golden die Blümlein die thauige Wiese durchsticken
Eduard Lassen, "Reisebild" Op72,4

O wie so rein oft rieselt ein Wunderklang aus tiefer Stromflut
August Bungert, "Verlor'ne Klänge" 1889-91pub, Op8,1

Saßen zwei Liebende kosend
Felix Weingartner, "Liebe im Schnee" 1891pub, Op17,3

Sieh', Liebchen, hier im Waldestal das Plätzchen unvergessen
Felix Weingartner, "Die Primeln" 1894, Op19,1
from *Hilaria. Sechs heitere Lieder*
Max Reger, "Die Primeln" 1902, Op66,6, 1v(med).pf

Viel Vögel sind geflogen, viel Blumen sind verblüht
George Henschel, "Viel Träume" 187-?, Op21,4

Wandl' ich sinnend über den lauten Marktplatz
August Bungert, "Segen der Schönheit" 1889-91pub, Op8,2

Wie's aussieht im ew'gen Freudenhain
Max Reger, "Das kleinste Lied" 1898, Op23,1

Zwitschert nicht vor meinem Fenster, liebe Vögelein!
Franz von Holstein, "An die Vögel" 1880, Op42,2

(Friedrich) Julius Hammer (1810-1862)
Vertraue dich dem Licht der Sterne
Josefine Lang, "Blick' nach Oben" WoO

Knut Hamsun (1859-1952)
Es singt in tiefem Tone in mir so schwer und an Gold so reich
Joseph Marx, "Der Ton" 1911, 1v(med).pf

Friedrich Leopold Freiherr von Hardenberg: see "Novalis"

Jakob Haringer (1883-1948)
Es leuchtet so schön die Sonne
Arnold Schönberg, "Mädchenlied" 1907-08, Op48,3, 1v(low).pf

Ist alles eins, was liegt daran!
Arnold Schönberg, "Tot" 1907-08, Op48,2, 1v(low).pf

Wenn du schon glaubst, es ist ewige Nacht
Arnold Schönberg, "Sommermüd" 1907-08, Op48,1, 1v(low).pf

Julius Hart (1859-1930)
Nacht fließt in Tag und Tag in Nacht
Arnold Schönberg, "Natur" 1903-05, Op8,1, 1v.orch
from *Six Orchestral Songs, Opus 8* (Piano acc. by Anton Webern)

Um meinen Nakken schliesst sich ein blüthenweisser Arm
Arnold Schönberg, "Traumleben" 1903-05, Op6,1

Wenn du es wüßtest, was träumen heißt
Richard Strauss, "Cäcilie" 1894, Op27,2

Otto Erich Hartleben (1864-1905)
Das Erste sei, daß man der Welt sich freue
Joseph Marx, "Toskanischer Frühling" 1908, 1v(med).orch

Groß ist das Leben und reich!
Joseph Marx, "Gesang des Lebens" 1909, 1v(med).pf

Im Arm der Liebe schliefen wir selig ein
Max Reger, "Im Arm der Liebe" 1900, Op48,3, 1v(med).pf
Alban Berg, "Liebesode" 1907
from *Sieben frühe Lieder*
Joseph Marx, "Selige Nacht" 1915pub

Im Zaune klagt die Nachtigall, im Winde bebt der Flieder
Paul Graener, "Im Zaune klagt die Nachtigall" 1909pub, Op30,1

In meines Vaters Garten blühe, mein Herz, blüh' auf
Alma Schindler-Mahler, "In meines Vaters Garten" 1900-01?

Siehst du die Perlen springen im kristallenen Glase
Vítězslav Novák, "Liebesfeier" 1912pub, Op46,6
from *Erotikon*

Süß duftende Lindenblüte in quellender Juninacht
Joseph Marx, "Nocturne" 1911

Wladimir, Freiherr von Hartlieb (1887-1951)
Du dunkle Sehnsucht meiner Tage
Joseph Marx, "Lied eines Mädchens" 1910, 1v(med).pf

Wald du, fieberdurchglutet, stehst du in schweigendem Schmerz
Joseph Marx, "An einen Herbstwald" 1910, 1v(med).pf

Gottlob David Hartmann (1752-1775)
Eures Sophrons Seele, Freunde, trübt in Schwermuth sich
Johann Rudolf Zumsteeg, "An meine Freunde" 1803pub
from *Kleine Balladen und Lieder, fünftes Heft*

Dora Hartwig
Mein Auge schließ' mit deinem Kusse zu
Max Reger, "Mutter, tote Mutter" 1907, Op104,3

Lorenz Leopold Haschka (1749-1827)
Gott! erhalte Franz der Kaiser
Joseph Haydn, "Das Kaiserlied" 1796-97, XXVIa Nr.43

Hans Leo von Hassler (1564-1612)
Mein G'müth ist mir verwirret
Friedrich Silcher, "An Maria"

Wilhelm Hauch
Morgenroth, Morgenroth, leuchtest mir zum frühen Tod?
Friedrich Silcher, "Reiters Morgengesang"

Steh' ich in finst'rer Mitternacht
Friedrich Silcher, "Treue Liebe"

(Richard) Georg von Hauenschild: see "Max Waldau"

(Johann Christoph) Friedrich Haug (1761-1829)
Ach, der Tag – wie so lang! und mein Herz, wie so bang
Johann Rudolf Zumsteeg, "Lenorens Lied" 1801pub
from *Kleine Balladen und Lieder, drittes Heft*

Du kömmst vom Kloster Walsingham
Johann Rudolf Zumsteeg, "Was ist Liebe?" 1800pub
from the English
from *Kleine Balladen und Lieder, zweites Heft*

Hold bin ich einer Holden
Johann Rudolf Zumsteeg, "Wahre Minne" 1802pub
after Milon von Sevelingen
from *Kleine Balladen und Lieder, viertes Heft*

Hold lächelten die Maienhoren
Johann Rudolf Zumsteeg, "Adelaide" 1803pub
from *Kleine Balladen und Lieder, fünftes Heft*

Im Sonnenschimmer, in Luna's flimmer
Johann Rudolf Zumsteeg, "Antwort" 1801pub
from *Kleine Balladen und Lieder, drittes Heft*

Könnt ihr die Göttin Freude zwingen
Johann Rudolf Zumsteeg, "Rundgesang" 1802pub
from *Kleine Balladen und Lieder, viertes Heft*

Komm, aller Wesen Freude! im bunten Schimmerkleide
Johann Rudolf Zumsteeg, "An den Mai" 1805pub, 2v.pf
from *Kleine Balladen und Lieder, siebtes Heft*

Liebchen und der Saft der Reben theilen meines Herzens Glut
Franz Schubert, "Wein und Liebe" 1827, D901, 2t2b

Mädchen und Jünglinge, Männer und Frauen
Johann Rudolf Zumsteeg, "Rundgesang" 1800pub
from *Kleine Balladen und Lieder, erstes Heft*

Nichts rundum erforschen des Endlichen Blikke
Johann Rudolf Zumsteeg, "Liebe" 1800pub
from *Kleine Balladen und Lieder, erstes Heft*

Noch sass im schwarzen Kleide Fernando's Wittwe da
Johann Rudolf Zumsteeg, "Die Wittwe" 1801pub
from *Kleine Balladen und Lieder, drittes Heft*

O Geliebte! dein vergessen – nein, bei Gott!
Johann Rudolf Zumsteeg, "An Lenoren" 1801pub
from *Kleine Balladen und Lieder, drittes Heft*

Rings walten Todesstille, und Schlaf und Mitternacht
Johann Rudolf Zumsteeg, "Ständchen an Feodoren" 1801pub
from *Kleine Balladen und Lieder, drittes Heft*

Schauet, Priester! schauet, Laien!
Johann Rudolf Zumsteeg, "Mailied" 1802pub
after Walter von der Vogelweide
from *Kleine Balladen und Lieder, viertes Heft*

Schön Klare, zwanzig Sommer alt, glich Raphaels Madonne
Johann Rudolf Zumsteeg, "Fernando's Lied" 1803pub
from *Kleine Balladen und Lieder, fünftes Heft*

Solch ein göttliches Vergnügen
Johann Rudolf Zumsteeg, "Minneglück" 1801pub
after Heinrich von Morunge
from *Kleine Balladen und Lieder, drittes Heft*

Traurig, einsam welkst du hin, Blume!
Carl Maria von Weber, "Rhapsodie" 1809, Op23,2

Vertraue mir, Yoduno! o sage was dir ist
Johann Rudolf Zumsteeg, "Yoduno" 1803pub
from *Kleine Balladen und Lieder, sechstes Heft*
Johann Rudolf Zumsteeg, "Yoduno (2nd setting)" 1805pub
from *Kleine Balladen und Lieder, siebtes Heft*

Vor allen Leinster Schönen pries
Johann Rudolf Zumsteeg, "Richard und Mathilde" 1800pub
from *Kleine Balladen und Lieder, zweites Heft*

Wie trübst du, Geliebter! wie trübst du mein Herz!
Johann Rudolf Zumsteeg, "Antwort" 1802pub
from *Kleine Balladen und Lieder, viertes Heft*

Wohl alle Gedanken des Herzens vereine ich ohne Wanken
Johann Rudolf Zumsteeg, "Minnelied" 1800pub
from *Kleine Balladen und Lieder, erstes Heft*

Wohlauf! im trauten Reih'n zum lieblichsten Verein
Johann Rudolf Zumsteeg, "Canon a tre" 1805pub, 3v.pf
from *Kleine Balladen und Lieder, siebtes Heft*

Paul Graf von Haugwitz (1791-1856)
Lisch aus, lisch aus, mein Licht!
Ludwig van Beethoven, "Resignation" 1817, WoO149

Carl (Ferdinand Max) Hauptmann (1858-1921)
Blütenblätter wehen, holde Zeit!
Anna Teichmüller, "Frühlingslied" 1906pub, Op8,4

Dämmern Wolken über Nacht und Tal
Alban Berg, "Nacht" 1907
from *Sieben frühe Lieder*

Draussen wirbeln viel Blätter im Schein
Anna Teichmüller, "Herbst" 1907pub, Op9,5

Du Kindlein weich, im Erdenreich
Anna Teichmüller, "Erdenkindleins Wiegenlied" 1906pub, Op7,1

Ein Gras vom Felsen, eine Blume, vielleicht toter Stein
Anna Teichmüller, "Annel's Lied" 1910pub, Op24,1

Ein wunderbares Rätselreich die Nacht
Anna Teichmüller, "Am Wachtfeuer" 1907pub, Op12,4

Einsam bin ich nicht, einzeln! Einzeln bin ich, wie Felsen
Anna Teichmüller, "Die einsame Macht" 1910pub, Op25,3

Es schläft ein stiller Garten auf tiefstem Seelengrund
Max Reger, "Es schläft ein stiller Garten" 1906, Op98,4, 1v(low).pf

Flamme in Nächten, selig allein, strahlende Flamme, schwebender Schein!
Anna Teichmüller, "Flamme in Nächten" 1907pub, Op9,3

Frau Nachtigall, sagt ihr, "Königin!"
Anna Teichmüller, "Frau Nachtigall" 1905pub, Op3,4

Gott grüß'! in die Nachtsee! du kleines Licht, du meine Seele
Anna Teichmüller, "Nächtlicher Auslug" 1910pub, Op25,1

Im Dämmer der Nacht, in Mondesluft
Anna Teichmüller, "Im Dämmer der Nacht" 1906pub, Op8,2

In den Wind, in den Wind sing' ich mein Lied
Anna Teichmüller, "Windlied" 1904pub, Op1,2

In meiner Träume Heimat barg ich dich
Anna Teichmüller, "In meiner Träume Heimat" 1905pub, Op5,2

Mir immer wieder unbegreiflich, wenn ich in meinem Dorfe geh'
Anna Teichmüller, "Unbegreiflich" 1906pub, Op7,3

Nacht... Nacht... in Nacht sanken wir. Urgestein sind wir geworden
Erich J. Wolff, "Felsenstimmen" 1907pub, Op10,2
from *Zwei Gesänge*

Schäumende Woge rollt immer zum Strande her
Anna Teichmüller, "Der Fischerfrau Lied" 1907pub, Op9,6

Sehnsucht aus einsamer Seele auffliehht!
Anna Teichmüller, "Sehnsucht" 1904pub, Op1,4

Stiller Abend sinkt, Sterne blinken leise, weisse Wolken zieh'n
Anna Teichmüller, "Stiller Abend" 1904pub, Op2,2

Tausend Tannenwipfel drohen brausend hin und wider
Anna Teichmüller, "Stillung" 1904pub, Op1,3

Über mir in wolkigen Lüften wogen Lerchen traumverloren
Anna Teichmüller, "Erdgeboren" 1904pub, Op1,5

Verfallen liegt ein Tempeltor in einem Rosengarten
Anna Teichmüller, "Frühlingswinde" 1907pub, Op12,1

Verlass dich singend auf deine heimlichen Feuer!
Anna Teichmüller, "Berghäuer's Lichter" 1907pub, Op15,1

Weisst du warum der Tod im Menschenland
Anna Teichmüller, "Der Tod" 1904pub, Op1,1

Gerhart (Johann Robert) Hauptmann (1862-1946)
Purpurschimmer tränket die Rebenhügel
Robert Kahn, "Purpurschimmer tränket die Rebenhügel" 1897, Op27,5

's ist ein so stiller heil'ger Tag
Robert Kahn, "'s ist ein so stiller heil'ger Tag" 1897, Op27,2

Wie eine Windesharfe sei deine Seele
Robert Kahn, "Wie eine Windesharfe" 1897, Op27,1

Felix Hausdorff: see "Paul Mongré"

Manfred Hausmann (1898-1986)
Die weiten Wiesen schweigen im Duft von Gold und Grau
Louis Ferdinand, "Oktoberlied" 1966pub

Qual über Qual ist uns gesetzt insgesamt
Felix Wolfes, "Die Hölle" 1962

Wir befanden uns, so träumt' ich, wieder
Felix Wolfes, "Traumboot" 1960

(Christian) Friedrich Hebbel (1813-1863)
Als du frühmorgens gingst und an der Sonne hingst
Paul Hindemith, "Die Rosen" 1908/09
from *7 Lieder für Sopran oder Tenor mit Klavierbegleitung*

Der Knabe träumt, man schicke ihn fort
Robert Schumann, "Ballade vom Haideknaben" 1852-3, Op122,1, declamation.pf

Die Dämmerung war längst hereingebrochen
Peter Cornelius, "Auf eine Unbekannte" 1861

Die du, über die Sterne weg mit der geleerten Schale aufschwebst
Hugo Brückler, "Gebet" 187-?pub, Nachlass
August Bungert, "Gebet an die Glücksgöttin" 1889-91pub, Op8,3
Max Reger, "Gebet" 1890, Op4,1, 1v(med).pf
Hermann Behn, "Gebet" 189-?, Op2,5, 1v(med).pf
Hans Pfitzner, "Gebet" 1916, Op26,1

Dies ist ein Herbsttag, wie ich keinen sah!
Hans Pfitzner, "Herbstbild" 1907, Op21,1
Felix Wolfes, "Herbstbild" 1960

Dort bläht ein Schiff die Segel
August Brunetti-Pisano, "Der junge Schiffer" 1910pub

Frau Amme, Frau Amme, das Kind ist erwacht!
Hugo Wolf, "Das Kind am Brunnen" 1878

Friedlich bekämpfen Nacht sich und Tag
Peter Cornelius, "Abendgefühl" 1862
Peter Cornelius, "Abendgefühl (2nd version)" 1863
Johannes Brahms, "Abendlied" before 1884, Op92,3, satb.pf
Anna Teichmüller, "Abendgefühl" 1907pub, Op15,4
Fritz Schreiber, "Abendgefühl" 1920pub, Op13,1

Hat sie's dir denn angetan im Vorüberschweben
Peter Cornelius, "Der beste Liebesbrief" 1861, Op6,2, sop.bar.pf

Ich blicke hinab in die Gasse
Johannes Brahms, "In der Gasse" 1871, Op58,6

Ich legte mich unter den Lindenbaum
Johannes Brahms, "Vorüber" 1871, Op58,7

Ich ritt einmal im Dunkeln spät durch ein enges Tal
Rudi Stephan, "Memento vivere" 1914?, bar.pf
from *Zwei ernste Gesänge*

Ich sah des Sommers letzte Rose blühn
Paul Hindemith, "Sommerbild" 1908/09
from *7 Lieder für Sopran oder Tenor mit Klavierbegleitung*

Im Kreise der Vasallen sitzt der Ritter, jung und kühn
Robert Schumann, "Schön Hedwig" 1849, Op106, declamation.pf

In Frühlings Heiligtume, wenn dir ein Duft an's Tiefste rührt
Franz Liszt, "Blume und Duft" 1862

Laß den Jüngling, der dich liebt, eine Lilie pflükken
Peter Cornelius, "Liebesprobe" 1861, Op6,1, sop.bar.pf

Millionen öder Jahre lag ich schon in dumpfem Schlaf
Peter Cornelius, "Reminiszenz" 1862

Quellende, schwellende Nacht, voll von Lichtern und Sternen
Eugen d'Albert, "Nachtlied" 1889pub, Op9,2
Paul Hindemith, "Nachtlied" 1908/09
from *7 Lieder für Sopran oder Tenor mit Klavierbegleitung*
Werner Josten, "Nachtlied" 1926pub
from *Fünf Lieder* (1)

Rausche nur vorüber
Felix Weingartner, "Sturmabend" 1910, Op51,6
from *Abendlieder*

Sag' an, o lieber Vogel mein
Robert Schumann, "Sag' an, o lieber Vogel mein" 1840, Op27,1

Schlaf', Kindlein, schlaf', wie du schläfst, so bist du brav
Robert Schumann, "Wiegenlied am Lager eines kranken Kindes" 1849, Op78,4, sop.ten.pf

Schlafen, schlafen, nichts als schlafen! Kein Erwachen, keinen Traum!
Othmar Schoeck, "Schlafen, schlafen, nichts als schlafen!" 1907, Op14,4
Alban Berg, "Dem Schmerz sein Recht" 1909-10?, Op2,1
Anna Teichmüller, "Schlafen, schlafen" 1910pub, Op24,5

Seele, vergiß sie nicht, Seele, vergiß nicht die Toten!
Peter Cornelius, "Requiem" 1872, ssatbb.str

Vöglein vom Zweig gaukelt hernieder
Robert Schumann, "Das Glück" 1849, Op79,15, 2v.pf
from *Lieder-Album für die Jugend*
Hugo Wolf, "Das Vöglein" 1878
from *Sechs Lieder für eine Frauenstimme*

Vom Berg der Knab, der zieht hinab in heißen Sommertagen
Hugo Wolf, "Knabentod" 1878

Was treibt mich hier von hinnen?
Peter Cornelius, "Dämmerempfindung" 1861

Wenn die Rosen ewig blühten, die man nicht vom Stock gebrochen
Richard Kahn, "Wenn die Rosen ewig blühten" 1896?pub

Wenn ich, o Kindlein, vor dir stehe
Peter Cornelius, "Auf ein schlummerndes Kind" 1861

Wenn zwei sich ineinander still versenken
Othmar Schoeck, "Das Heiligste" 1914, Op24a,5

Wir träumten von einander und sind davon erwacht
Peter Cornelius, "Ich und du" 1861, sop.bar.pf
Hans Pfitzner, "Ich und Du" 1901, Op11,1
Vítězslav Novák, "Ich und Du" 1912pub, Op46,3
from *Erotikon*

Johann Peter Hebel (1760-1826)

Es g'fallt mer nummen eini, und selli g'fallt mer g'wiss!
Friedrich Silcher, "Hans und Verene"

Loset, was i euch will sage!
Friedrich Silcher, "Wächterruf"

Steh' ich im Feld, mein ist die Welt!
Friedrich Silcher, "Grenadier-Lied"

Lydia Hecker, née Paalzow (1802-?, pub. 1842)

Schaust so freundlich aus, Gretelein, nimm den Blumenstrauß, er sei dein!
Friedrich Kücken, "Gretelein"

Johannes Heermann (1585-1647)

O Jesu Christe, wahres Licht, erleuchte, die dich kennen nicht
Carl Loewe, "O Jesu Christe, wahres Licht" 1860, Op131,19, 4v

Johann Ludwig Heiberg (1791-1860)

Süsse Nacht! Wie schweiget rings die Luft so lau!
Adolf Jensen, "Barcarole" 1865, Op23,2

Cäsar Max Heigel (1783-ca.1847)

Umringt vom mutherfüllten Heere
Carl Maria von Weber, "Umringt vom mutherfüllten Heere" 1811, Op25,5, 1v.mch.guit

Victor Heindl

Ich will, ein junger Lenzhusar
Ernő Dohnányi, "Ich will, ein junger Lenzhusar" 1908pub, Op14,3
from *Sechs Gedichte von Victor Heindl*

König Baumbart, der alte Tann, der schüttelt sich heut' vor Lachen
Ernő Dohnányi, "König Baumbart" 1908pub, Op14,5
from *Sechs Gedichte von Victor Heindl*

O Wand'rer, geh' nicht nach dem Abendstein
Ernő Dohnányi, "Bergtrolls Braut" 1908pub, Op14,4
from *Sechs Gedichte von Victor Heindl*

So fügt sich Blüt'- an Blütezeit
Ernő Dohnányi, "So fügt sich Blüt'- an Blütezeit" 1908pub, Op14,2
from *Sechs Gedichte von Victor Heindl*

Sonnenfädchen spinnt Nixlein im Wald
Ernő Dohnányi, "Waldelfelein" 1905

Vergessene Lieder, vergessene Lieb'
Ernő Dohnányi, "Vergessene Lieder, vergessene Lieb'" 1908pub, Op14,6
from *Sechs Gedichte von Victor Heindl*

Was weinst du, meine Geige?
Ernő Dohnányi, "Was weinst du, meine Geige?" 1908pub, Op14,1
from *Sechs Gedichte von Victor Heindl*

C. Heine

Ferne, ferne flammenhelle Sterne
Franz Schubert, "Mein Frieden"

Heinrich Heine (1797-1856)

Ach! die Augen sind es wieder, die mich einst so freundlich grüßten
Fanny Hensel, "Ach, die Augen sind es wieder" 1837

Ach ich sehnte mich nach Thränen
Karl Gottlieb Reissiger, "Erfüllte Ahnung" Op117,3, sop.hn.pf

Ach wüssten's die Blumen, die kleinen (see "Und wüssten's...")

Allnächtlich im Traume seh' ich dich
Robert Schumann, "Allnächtlich im Traume" 1840, Op48,14
from *Dichterliebe*
Felix Mendelssohn, "Allnächtlich im Traume seh' ich dich" 1851pub, Op86,4
Robert Franz, "Allnächtlich im Traume" 1860?, Op9,4

Als meine Großmutter die Liese behext
Wilhelm Kempff, "Lied des Gefangenen" 1923pub, Op16,3

Am einsamen Strande plätschert die Flut
Johann Vesque von Püttlingen, "Die Nixen" 1844-51?, Op39,4

Am fernen Horizonte erscheint, wie ein Nebelbild
Franz Schubert, "Die Stadt" 1827-8, D957,11
from *Heine Lieder*
Robert Franz, "Am fernen Horizonte" 1866?, Op37,3

Am Kreutzweg wird begraben wer selbst sich brachte um
Frank van der Stucken, "Blumen IV" 1879, Op4,4
Joseph Guy Ropartz, "Ceux qui, parmi les morts d'amour" (set in French), 1899
translated by J. Guy Ropartz and P. R. Hirsch
Charles Griffes, "Am Kreuzweg wird begraben" 1903-11?, A16

Am leuchtenden Sommermorgen geh' ich im Garten herum
Robert Schumann, "Am leuchtenden Sommermorgen" 1840, Op48,12
from *Dichterliebe*
Robert Franz, "Am leuchtenden Sommermorgen" 1865?, Op11,2
Aleksandr Glazunov, "Romanze" (set in Russian), 1882, Op4,1

An die blaue Himmelsdecke
Robert Franz, "Auf dem Meere" 1846pub, Op6,3

An die bretterne Schiffswand
Robert Franz, "Auf dem Meere" 1870?pub, Op25,6

And're beten zur Madonna, and're auch zu Paul und Peter
Ludwig Rottenberg, "And're beten zur Madonna" 1914?pub

Anfangs wollt' ich fast verzagen
Robert Schumann, "Anfangs wollt' ich fast verzagen" 1840, Op24,8
from *Liederkreis*
Franz Liszt, "Anfangs wollt ich fast verzagen" 1860pub

Auf den Wällen Salamankas sind die Lüfte lind und labend
Johann Vesque von Püttlingen, "Auf den Wällen Salamankas" 1851pub
from *Heimkehr* (80)

Auf Flügeln des Gesanges, Herzliebchen, trag' ich dich fort
Felix Mendelssohn, "Auf Flügeln des Gesanges" 1836pub, Op34,2
Franz Lachner, "Lyrisches Intermezzo" 1832, sop.cl.pf

Auf ihrem Grab da steht eine Linde
Robert Schumann, "Tragödie III" 1841, Op64,3,iii, sop.ten.pf
Charles Griffes, "Tragödie III" 1903-11?, A12
Frank van der Stucken, "Tragödie (3rd verse)" 1904pub, Op30
Stucken's "Tragödie" concatenates three Heine poems
Thorvald Otterström, "Auf ihrem Grab da steht eine Linde" 1907pub
from *Neun Lieder* (3)

Aus alten Märchen winkt es hervor mit weisser Hand
Robert Schumann, "Aus alten Märchen winkt es" 1840, Op48,15
from *Dichterliebe*

Aus den Himmelsaugen droben fallen zitternd goldne Funken
Robert Franz, "Auf dem Meer" 1846pub, Op5,3
Hermann Behn, "Aus den Himmelsaugen droben" 189-?, Op2,2, 1v(med).pf
Max Reger, "Aus den Himmelsaugen" 1906, Op98,1, 1v(med).pf

Aus meinen großen Schmerzen
Robert Franz, "Aus meinen grossen Schmerzen" 1846pub, Op5,1
Hugo Wolf, "Aus meinen großen Schmerzen" 1878

Aus meinen Thränen sprießen viel blühende Blumen hervor
Fanny Hensel, "Aus meinen Tränen sprießen" 1838, sop.mez.pf
Robert Schumann, "Aus meinen Thränen spriessen" 1840, Op48,2
from *Dichterliebe*
Nicolai Rimsky-Korsakov, "Aus meinen Tränen sprießen" (set in Russian), 1866, Op2,4
Modest Mussorgsky, "Aus meinen Tränen spriessen" (set in Russian), 1866
Aleksandr Borodin, "Aus meinen Tränen spriessen" (set in Russian), 1870
Frank van der Stucken, "Blumen I" 1879, Op4,1

Aus meiner Erinn'rung erblüh'n
Robert Franz, "Aus meiner Erinn'rung" 1860?, Op12,4

Berg' und Burgen schau'n herunter
Robert Schumann, "Berg' und Burgen schau'n herunter" 1840, Op24,7
from *Liederkreis*

Da hab' ich viel blasse Leichen
Johanna Kinkel, "Die Geister haben's vernommen" Op6,3

Dämmernd liegt der Sommerabend
Johannes Brahms, "Sommerabend" 1878, Op85,1
Othmar Schoeck, "Sommerabend" 1904, Op4,1

Das gelbe Laub erzittert, es fallen die Blätter herab
Johann Vesque von Püttlingen, "Der scheidende Sommer" 1844-51?, Op40,5
Edvard Grieg, "Abschied" 1863-64, Op4,3
Robert Franz, "Abschied" 1870?pub, Op31,5
Carl Reinecke, "Herbst" Op81,6

Das Herz ist mir bedrückt und sehnlich gedenke ich der alten Zeit
Ludwig Rottenberg, "Das Herz ist mir bedrückt" 1914?pub

Das ist des Frühlings traurige Lust!
Robert Franz, "Frühlingsfeier" 1867?, Op39,1
Richard Strauss, "Frühlingsfeier" 1906, Op56,5

Das ist ein Brausen und Heulen
Robert Franz, "Das ist ein Brausen und Heulen" 1846pub, Op8,4
Hugo Wolf, "Das ist ein Brausen und Heulen" 1878
Charles Griffes, "Das ist ein Brausen und Heulen" 1903-11?, A9

Das ist ein Flöten und Geigen
Robert Schumann, "Das ist ein Flöten und Geigen" 1840, Op48,9
from *Dichterliebe*

Das ist ein schlechtes Wetter, es regnet und stürmt und schneit
Ludwig Rottenberg, "Das ist ein schlechtes Wetter" 1914?pub
Richard Strauss, "Schlechtes Wetter" 1918, Op69,5

Das Meer erglänzte weit hinaus im letzten Abendscheine
Franz Schubert, "Am Meer" 1827-8, D957,12
from *Heine Lieder*

Das Meer erstrahlt im Sonnenschein
Leopold Damrosch, "Das Meer erstrahlt im Sonnenschein" Op16,1
Robert Franz, "Das Meer erstrahlt im Sonnenschein" 1867?, Op39,3

Das Meer hat seine Perlen, der Himmel hat seine Sterne
Robert Franz, "Auf dem Meere" 1862?, Op36,1

Dein Angesicht, so lieb und schön
Robert Schumann, "Dein Angesicht" 1840, Op127,2
Gustav Hasse, "Dein Angesicht so lieb und schön" 1877pub, Op27,4

Deine weißen Lilienfinger, könnt ich sie noch einmal küssen
Robert Franz, "Deine weissen Lilienfinger" 1861?, Op34,2
Johann Vesque von Püttlingen, "Was bedeuten diese Rätsel?" 1851pub, Op41,2
from *Heimkehr* (31/2)

Den König Wiswamitra, den treibt's ohne Rast und Ruh
Johann Vesque von Püttlingen, "Den König Wiswamitra" 1851pub
from *Heimkehr* (45)
Lord Berners, "König Wiswamitra" 1913-18
from *Lieder Album* (2)

Den Tag, den ich so himmlisch verbracht
Johann Vesque von Püttlingen, "Ketty" 1844-51?, Op40,3

Der arme Peter wankt vorbei
Robert Schumann, "Der arme Peter (III)" 1840, Op53,3,iii

Der Hans und die Grete tanzen herum
Robert Schumann, "Der arme Peter (I)" 1840, Op53,3,i

Der Herbstwind rüttelt die Bäume
Felix Mendelssohn, "Reiselied" 1836pub, Op34,6

Der Mond ist aufgegangen und überstrahlt die Well'n
Johann Vesque von Püttlingen, "Der Seejungfern Gesang" 1851pub, Op11,2
from *Heimkehr* (9)

Der Schmetterling ist in die Rose verliebt
Robert Franz, "Der Schmetterling ist in die Rose verliebt" 1867?, Op38,2

Der Tod, das ist die kühle Nacht
Peter Cornelius, "Der Tod, das ist die kühle Nacht" 1871, Op11,1, 2s2a2t2b
Johannes Brahms, "Der Tod, das ist die kühle Nacht" 1884?, Op96,1
August Bungert, "Schwanengesang" 1889-91pub, Op32,6
from *Verlorne Liebe, verlornes Leben*
Max Reger, "Der Tod, das ist die kühle Nacht" 1899
Frances Allitsen, "Der Tod, das ist die kühle Nacht" 1900pub

Die alten, bösen Lieder, die Träume bös' und arg
Robert Schumann, "Die alten, bösen Lieder" 1840, Op48,16
from *Dichterliebe*

Die blauen Frühlingsaugen schau'n aus dem Gras hervor
Anton Rubinstein, "Frühlingslied" 1856, Op32,2
Robert Franz, "Die blauen Frühlingsaugen" 1865?pub, Op20,1
Leopold Damrosch, "Die blauen Frühlingsaugen" Op13,3
Pyotr Il'yich Tchaikovsky, "Die blauen Frühlingsaugen" (set in Russian), 1873
Franz Ries, "Die blauen Frühlingsaugen" before 1891
Frank van der Stucken, "Blumen II" 1879, Op4,2
Charles Edward Ives, "Frühlingslied" 1896

Die du bist so schön und rein
Robert Franz, "Die du bist so schön und rein" 1866?, Op37,1
Leopold Damrosch, "Die du bist so schön und rein" Op10,3
Léander Schlegel, "Die du bist so schön und rein" 1900, Op20,2
from *Deutsche Liebeslieder*

Die heil'gen drei Kön'ge aus Morgenland
Johann Vesque von Püttlingen, "Die Heil'gen drei Könige" 1851pub, Op38,1
from *Heimkehr* (37)
Richard Strauss, "Die heiligen drei Könige aus Morgenland" 1906, Op56,6
Lord Berners, "Weihnachtslied" 1913-18
from *Lieder Album* (3)

Die Jahre kommen und gehen
Johann Vesque von Püttlingen, "Madam, ich liebe Sie" 1851pub, Op41,3
from *Heimkehr* (25)

Die Jungfrau schläft in der Kammer
Johann Vesque von Püttlingen, "Der Tänzer" 1851pub, Op7,3
from *Heimkehr* (22)

Die Lotusblume ängstigt sich vor der Sonne Pracht
Carl Loewe, "Die Lotusblume" 1828, Op9,i,1
Robert Schumann, "Die Lotusblume" 1840, Op25,7
from *Liederkreis*
Robert Schumann, "Die Lotusblume" 1840, Op33,3, ttbb
Robert Franz, "Die Lotusblume" 1870?pub, Op25,1
Wilhelm Kienzl, "Die Lotusblume" 187-?, Op8,1

Die Mitternacht zog näher schon
Robert Schumann, "Belsatzar" 1840, Op57

Die Nacht ist feucht und stürmisch
Johann Vesque von Püttlingen, "Das Jägerhaus" 1851pub, Op36,2
from *Heimkehr* (5)

Die Rose, die Lilie, die Taube, die Sonne
Giacomo Meyerbeer, "Die Rose, die Lilie, die Taube" 1838
Robert Schumann, "Die Rose, die Lilie, die Taube, die Sonne" 1840, Op48,3
from *Dichterliebe*
Robert Franz, "Die Rose, die Lilie" 1861?, Op34,5

Die schlanke Wasserlilie schaut träumend empor aus dem See
Carl Loewe, "Die schlanke Wasserlilie" 1847
Robert Franz, "Die schlanke Wasserlilie" 1879, Op51,7
Frank van der Stucken, "Blumen III" 1879, Op4,3
Hans Pfitzner, "Die schlanke Wasserlilie" 1884-86?
Sergei Rachmaninoff, "(Die schlanke Wasserlilie)" (set in Russian), 1893, Op8,1, 1v(med).pf
translated into Russian by A. Pleshtchejev

Die Söhne des Glückes beneid ich nicht
Günter Bialas, "Miserere" 1983, bar.pf
from *O Miserere* (3)

Die Wellen blinken und fließen dahin
Leopold Damrosch, "Frühling" Op16,2
Robert Franz, "Frühling" 1867?, Op38,1
Johannes Brahms, "Es liebt sich so lieblich im Lenze!" 1877, Op71,1

Du bist gestorben und weisst es nicht
Robert Franz, "Altes Lied" 1867?, Op39,6

Du bist wie eine Blume, so hold und schön und rein
Norbert Burgmüller, "Lied" 1827-36?, Op3,3
Robert Schumann, "Du bist wie eine Blume" 1840, Op25,24
from *Liederkreis*
Gottfried Herrmann, "Du bist wie eine Blume" 1843, 1v.cl.pf
Franz Liszt, "Du bist wie eine Blume" 1844/1860
Friedrich Kücken, "Du bist wie eine Blume"
Aleksandr Varlamov, "Du bist wie eine Blume" (set in Russian), before 1848
Anton Rubinstein, "Lied" 1856, Op32,5
Hugo Wolf, "Du bist wie eine Blume" 1876
Adolph Martin Foerster, "Du bist wie eine Blume" 1877, Op1,1
Charles Edward Ives, "Du bist wie eine Blume" 1891?
Sergei Rachmaninoff, "(Du bist wie eine Blume)" (set in Russian), 1893, Op8,2, 1v(med).pf
translated into Russian by A. Pleshtchejev

Léander Schlegel, "Du bist wie eine Blume" 1900, Op20,3
from *Deutsche Liebeslieder*
Frank van der Stucken, "Wie eine Blume" 1904pub, Op29,2
Thorvald Otterström, "Du bist wie eine Blume" 1907pub
from *Neun Lieder* (5)
Lord Berners, "Du bist wie eine Blume" 1913-18
from *Lieder Album* (1)

Du hast Diamanten und Perlen, hast alles, was Menschenbegehr
Giorgio Stigelli, "Die schönsten Augen"
Frances Allitsen, "Du hast Diamanten und Perlen" 1900pub

Du liebst mich nicht, du liebst mich nicht
Edward MacDowell, "Du liebst mich nicht" 1881, Op11,2

Du schönes Fischermädchen, treibe den Kahn ans Land
Franz Schubert, "Das Fischermädchen" 1827-8, D957,10
from *Heine Lieder*
Stephen Heller, "Das Fischermädchen" 1830-38?, 1v.pf.(vc)
Carl Loewe, "Du schönes Fischermädchen" 1832, Op9,vii,5
Giacomo Meyerbeer, "Komm!" 1837
Aleksandr Varlamov, "Du schönes Fischermädchen" (set in Russian), before 1848
Aleksandr Borodin, "Du schönes Fischermädchen" (set in Russian), 1854, 1v.vc.pf
Adolph Martin Foerster, "Das Fischermädchen" 1877, Op1,2
Alexis Holländer, "Am Strande" 1895?pub, Op51,8

Durch den Wald im Mondenscheine
Robert Franz, "Durch den Wald im Mondenscheine" 1846pub, Op8,3

Ei! kennt ihr noch das alte Lied
Eduard Lassen, "Das alte Lied"

Ein Fichtenbaum steht einsam im Norden auf kahler Höh'
Fanny Hensel, "Fichtenbaum und Palme" 1838
Eduard Lassen, "Der Fichtenbaum"
Robert Franz, "Der Fichtenbaum" 1856pub, Op16,3
Franz Liszt, "Ein Fichtenbaum steht einsam" 1860pub
Franz Liszt, "Ein Fichtenbaum steht einsam (2nd version)" 1860pub
Nicolai Rimsky-Korsakov, "Ein Fichtenbaum steht einsam" (set in Russian), 1866, Op3,1
Johann Vesque von Püttlingen, "Fichtenbaum und Palme" 1869?, Op56
Hans Pfitzner, "Ein Fichtenbaum steht einsam" 1884-86?
Nicolai Rimsky-Korsakov, "Ein Fichtenbaum steht einsam" (set in Russian), 1888, Op3,1a
Vilhelm Stenhammar, "Ein Fichtenbaum steht einsam" 1890?, Op17,2
Hermann Behn, "Ein Fichtenbaum steht einsam" 189-?, Op1,ii,4
Edvard Grieg, "Der Fichtenbaum" (set in Norwegian), 1893-94, Op59,2
Frances Allitsen, "Der Fichtenbaum" 1900pub
Nikolai Medtner, "Lyrisches Intermezzo (Fichtenbaum)" 1907-08, Op12,2
Joseph Marx, "Ein Fichtenbaum steht einsam" 1908, 1v(med).pf
Adolph Martin Foerster, "Ein Fichtenbaum" 1909, Op57,2
Wilhelm Kempff, "Der Fichtenbaum" 1923pub, Op16,1
from *Drei Lieder von Heinrich Heine*

Ein Jeder hat zu diesem Feste sein liebes Liebchen mitgebracht
Robert Franz, "Mir fehlt das Beste" 1867?, Op39,5

Ein Jüngling liebt ein Mädchen, die hat einen andern erwählt
Robert Schumann, "Ein Jüngling liebt ein Mädchen" 1840, Op48,11
from *Dichterliebe*
Johann Vesque von Püttlingen, "Eine alte Geschichte" 1844-51?, Op41,1

Ein Reiter durch das Bergthal zieht
Nikolai Medtner, "Bergstimme" 1907-08, Op12,3

Ein schöner Stern geht auf in meiner Nacht
Robert Franz, "O lüge nicht!" 1870?pub, Op25,2
Franz von Holstein, "O lüge nicht!" 1880, Op42,5
Frances Allitsen, "Katharine" 1900pub

Eine starke, schwarze Barke segelt trauervoll dahin
Eduard Lassen, "Childe Harold"
Robert Franz, "Childe Harold" 1867?, Op38,3

Eingehüllt in graue Wolken
Edvard Grieg, "Eingehüllt in graue Wolken" 1861, Op2,2, alt.pf

Eingewiegt von Meereswellen
Robert Franz, "Auf dem Meere" 1860?, Op9,6

Entflieh' mit mir und sei mein Weib und ruh an meinem Herzen aus
Robert Schumann, "Tragödie I" 1841, Op64,3,i
Charles Griffes, "Tragödie I" 1903-11?, A10
Frank van der Stucken, "Tragödie" 1904pub, Op30
Stucken's "Tragödie" concatenates three Heine poems
Thorvald Otterström, "Entflieh' mit mir" 1907pub
from *Neun Lieder* (1)

Ernst ist der Frühling, seine Träume sind traurig
Hugo Wolf, "Ernst ist der Frühling" 1878
Alban Berg, "Geliebte Schöne" 1903

Erstorben ist in meiner Brust
Günter Bialas, "Der Scheidende" 1983, bar.pf
from *O Miserere* (2)

Es blasen die blauen Husaren
Hugo Wolf, "Es blasen die blauen Husaren" 1878
Ludwig Rottenberg, "Es blasen die blauen Husaren" 1914?pub

Es fällt ein Stern herunter
Fanny Hensel, "Schwanenlied" 1846pub, Op1,1
Robert Franz, "Es fällt ein Stern herunter" 1870?, Op44,4
Hans Pfitzner, "Es fällt ein Stern herunter" 1888/89, Op4,3, 1v(med).pf

Es faßt mich wieder der alte Mut
Hans Pfitzner, "Es faßt mich wieder der alte Mut" 1888/89, Op4,4, 1v(med).pf

Es fiel ein Reif in der Frühlingsnacht (see also Volkslied)
Clara Schumann, "Volkslied" 1840
Heine refers to this as a genuine Volkslied that he heard at the Rhine.
Robert Schumann, "Tragödie II" 1841, Op64,3,ii
Charles Griffes, "Tragödie II" 1903-11?, A11
Frank van der Stucken, "Tragödie (2nd verse)" 1904pub, Op30
Stucken's "Tragödie" concatenates three Heine poems

Thorvald Otterström, "Es fiel ein Reif" 1907pub
from *Neun Lieder* (2)

Es glänzt so schön die sinkende Sonne
Hans Pfitzner, "Es glänzt so schön die sinkende Sonne" 1888/89, Op4,1, 1v(med).pf

Es leuchtet meine Liebe in ihrer dunkeln Pracht
Robert Schumann, "Es leuchtet meine Liebe" 1840, Op127,3

Es liegt der heiße Sommer auf deinen Wängelein
Thorvald Otterström, "Es liegt der heiße Sommer" 1907pub
from *Neun Lieder* (6)

Es ragt in's Meer der Runenstein
Edvard Grieg, "Wo sind sie hin?" 1863-64, Op4,6
Robert Franz, "Es ragt in's Meer der Runenstein" 1867?, Op39,2

Es schauen die Blumen alle, zur leuchtenden Sonne hinauf
Johannes Brahms, "Es schauen die Blumen" 1884?, Op96,3
Ignaz Brüll, "Es schauen die Blumen alle" 186-?, Op5,i,1
from *Sechs Lieder nach Gedichten von Heinrich Heine*

Es stehen unbeweglich die Sterne in ihrer Höh'
Johanna Kinkel, "Die Sprache der Sterne" Op6,6

Es träumte mir von einer weiten Haide
Robert Franz, "Auf dem Meer" 1865?, Op11,5

Es treibt fort von Ort zu Ort
Robert Franz, "In der Fremde" 1867?, Op38,6

Es treibt mich hin, es treibt mich her!
Robert Schumann, "Es treibt mich hin" 1840, Op24,2
from *Liederkreis*
Robert Franz, "Es treibt mich hin, es treibt mich her!" 1861?, Op34,4

Es war ein alter König, sein Herz war schwer, sein Heupt war grau
Peter Cornelius, "Es war ein alter König" 1843, ttbb
Johann Vesque von Püttlingen, "Königin und Page" 1844-51?, Op46,6
Anton Rubinstein, "Lied" 1856, Op32,4
Edvard Grieg, "Das alte Lied" 1863-64, Op4,5
Leopold Damrosch, "Es war ein alter König" Op10,4
Hugo Wolf, "Es war ein alter König" 1878

Es ziehn die brausenden Wellen
Robert Franz, "Es ziehn die brausenden Wellen" 1867?, Op40,2

Gekommen ist der Maie, die Blumen und Bäume blüh'n
Othmar Schoeck, "Gekommen ist der Maie" 1904, Op17,5, 1v(low).pf
Robert Franz, "Gekommen ist der Maie" 1861?, Op34,6

Güldne Sternlein schauen nieder
Robert Franz, "Güldne Sternlein schauen nieder" 1867?, Op38,5

Herz, mein Herz, sei nicht beklommen
Carl Loewe, "Neuer Frühling" 1832, Op9,vii,4
Franz Ries, "Herz, mein Herz, sei nicht beklommen" before 1891

Hör' ich das Liedchen klingen
Giacomo Meyerbeer, "Hör' ich das Liedchen klingen" 1837

Robert Schumann, "Hör' ich das Liedchen klingen" 1840, Op48,10
from *Dichterliebe*
Robert Franz, "Hör' ich das Liedchen klingen" 1846pub, Op5,11
Leopold Damrosch, "Hör' ich das Liedchen klingen" Op10,2
Adolph Martin Foerster, "Hör' ich das Liedchen klingen" 1878, Op6,4

Ich grolle nicht, und wenn das Herz auch bricht
Robert Schumann, "Ich grolle nicht" 1840, Op48,7
from *Dichterliebe*
Charles Edward Ives, "Ich grolle nicht" 1899

Ich hab' im Traum geweinet, mir träumte, du lägest im Grab
Carl Loewe, "Ich hab' im Traume geweinet" 1832, Op9,vii,6
Robert Schumann, "Ich hab' im Traum geweinet" 1840, Op48,13
from *Dichterliebe*
Eduard Lassen, "Ich hab' im Traum geweinet" Op48,2
César Cui, "Ich hab im Traum geweinet" (set in Russian), 1870-74, Op9,3
Robert Franz, "Ich hab' im Traume geweinet" 1870?pub, Op25,3

Ich hab' mir lang' den Kopf zerbrochen
Ernst Otto Nodnagel, "Ich hab' mir lang' den Kopf zerbrochen" 1895, Op21,1

Ich halte ihr die Augen zu
Leopold Damrosch, "Ich halte ihr die Augen zu" Op16,4

Ich hatte einst ein schönes Vaterland
Eduard Lassen, "Ich hatte einst ein schönes Vaterland"
Leopold Damrosch, "Ich hatte einst ein schönes Vaterland" Op13,2
Sergei Rachmaninoff, "(The Dream)" (set in Russian), 1893, Op8,5
translated into Russian by A. Pleshtchejev from "In der Fremde, Nr.3"

Ich lieb' eine Blume, doch weiß ich nicht welche
Robert Franz, "Ich lieb' eine Blume" 1870?pub, Op28,1
Vilhelm Stenhammar, "Ich lieb' eine Blume" 1890?, Op17,1
from *Drei Lieder von Heinrich Heine*

Ich stand gelehnet an den Mast und zählte jede Welle
Felix Mendelssohn, "Wasserfahrt" 2sop.pf
Friedrich Kücken, "Wasserfahrt"
Franz Commer, "Lied" 1842?pub, Op25,2
Robert Franz, "Wasserfahrt" 1878, Op48,3
Hans Pfitzner, "Wasserfahrt" 1888/89, Op6,6, 1mv.pf

Ich stand in dunkeln Träumen und starrt' ihr Bildnis an
Franz Schubert, "Ihr Bild" 1827-8, D957,9
from *Heine Lieder*
Clara Schumann, "Ich stand in dunkeln Träumen" 1840, Op13,1
Edvard Grieg, "Ich stand in dunkeln Träumen" 1861, Op2,3, alt.pf
Hugo Wolf, "Ich stand in dunkeln Träumen" 1878

Ich unglücksel'ger Atlas
Franz Schubert, "Der Atlas" 1827-8, D957,8
from *Heine Lieder*

Ich wandelte unter den Bäumen
Robert Schumann, "Ich wandelte unter den Bäumen" 1840, Op24,3
from *Liederkreis*

Ich wandle unter Blumen und blühe selber mit
Alma Schindler-Mahler, "Ich wandle unter Blumen" 1900-01?

Ich weiß nicht, was soll es bedeuten, daß ich so traurig bin
Friedrich Silcher, "Lore-Ley"
Johanna Kinkel, "Die Lorelei" Op7,4
Franz Liszt, "Die Loreley" 1841
Clara Schumann, "Lorelei" 1843
Joachim Raff, "Loreley" 1855-63, Op98,26
from *Sanges-Frühling*

Ich will meine Seele tauchen
Johanna Kinkel, "Der Kuss" Op10,2
Robert Schumann, "Ich will meine Seele tauchen" 1840, Op48,5
from *Dichterliebe*
Arno Kleffel, "Ich will meine Seele tauchen" Op12,5
Robert Franz, "Ich will meine Seele tauchen" 1870?, Op43,4

Ich will mich im grünen Wald ergehn
Hans Pfitzner, "Ich will mich im grünen Wald ergehn" 1888/89, Op6,2, 1mv.pf

Ich wollt, meine Lieb ergösse sich
Felix Mendelssohn, "Ich wollt, meine Lieb ergösse sich" 1836, Op63,1, 2sop.pf

Ich wollt', meine Schmerzen ergössen
Alexander Fesca, "Ich wollt', meine Schmerzen" 1844pub, Op32,5
Ignaz Brüll, "Ich wollt' meine Schmerzen ergössen" 186-?, Op5,i,5
from *Sechs Lieder nach Gedichten von Heinrich Heine*
Modest Mussorgsky, "Ich wollt', meine Schmerzen ergössen" (set in Russian) (2 versions), 1866
Pyotr Il'yich Tchaikovsky, "Ich wollt' meine Schmerzen ergössen" (set in Russian), 1875

Im Mondenglanze ruht das Meer
Moritz Bauer, "Im Mondenglanze ruht das Meer"
from *Zwei Lieder* (1)

Im Rhein, im schönen Strome
Robert Schumann, "Im Rhein, im heiligen Strome" 1840, Op48,6
from *Dichterliebe*
Franz Liszt, "Im Rhein, im schönen Strome" 1843pub
Franz Liszt, "Im Rhein, im schönen Strome" 1856pub
Robert Franz, "Im Rhein, im heiligen Strome" 1860?pub, Op18,2
Adolph Martin Foerster, "Im Rhein, im heiligen Strome" 1878, Op6,3
Hermann Behn, "Im Rhein, im schönen Strome" 189-?, Op3,1, bar.pf

Im Traum sah ich die Geliebte
Carl Loewe, "Im Traum sah ich die Geliebte" 1832, Op9,vii,2

Im Walde wandl' ich und weine
Adolph Martin Foerster, "Im Walde wandl' ich und weine" 1877, Op1,3

Im wunderschönen Monat Mai
Fanny Hensel, "Im wunderschönen Monat Mai" 1837, sop.mez.pf
Robert Schumann, "Im wunderschönen Monat Mai" 1840, Op48,1
from *Dichterliebe*
Robert Franz, "Im wunderschönen Monat Mai" 1870?pub, Op25,5

In dem Mondenschein im Walde sah ich jüngst die Elfen reiten
Felix Mendelssohn, "Neue Liebe" 1834pub, Op19,4

In dem Traum siehst du die stillen fabelhaften Blumen prangen
Robert Franz, "Ach, wie komm ich da hinüber?" 1867?, Op41,2

In den Walde spriesst's und grünt es
Anton Rubinstein, "Frühlingslied" 1856, Op32,3

In mein gar zu dunkles Leben
Stephen Heller, "In mein gar zu dunkles Leben" 1830-38?
Ludwig Rottenberg, "In mein gar zu dunkles Leben" 1914?pub

In meiner Brust, da sitzt ein Weh
Robert Schumann, "Der arme Peter (II)" 1840, Op53,3,ii

In weite Ferne will ich träumen!
Josefine Lang, "In weite Ferne" 1832, Op15,3
No such first line found in Heine's works. See J. G. Droysen.

Ja, du bist elend, und ich grolle nicht
Robert Franz, "Ja, du bist elend" 1846pub, Op7,6
Othmar Schoeck, "Ja, du bist elend" 1907, Op13,2

Jedweder Geselle, sein Mädel am Arm
Leopold Damrosch, "Jedweder Geselle, sein Mädel am Arm" Op16,5
Ignaz Brüll, "Jedweder Geselle sein Mädel am Arm" 186-?, Op5,i,3
from *Sechs Lieder nach Gedichten von Heinrich Heine*

Lächelnd scheidet der Despot, denn er weiß, nach seinem Tod
Arnold Mendelssohn, "König David" 1914cop

Lehn' deine Wang' an meine Wang'
Robert Schumann, "Lehn' deine Wang'" 1840, Op142,2
Adolf Jensen, "Lehn' deine Wang' an meine Wang'" 1856, Op1,1
Nicolai Rimsky-Korsakov, "Lehn' deine Wang an meine Wang" (set in Russian), 1865, Op2,1
Frank van der Stucken, "Lehn' deine Wang'" 1878, Op5,4
August Bungert, "Lehn' deine Wang' an meine Wang" 1889-91pub, Op33,1
Richard Sternfeld, "Lehn' deine Wang' an meine Wang'" 1895?pub, Op7,2

Leise zieht durch mein Gemüth liebliches Geläute
Felix Mendelssohn, "Gruss" 1834pub, Op19,5
Carl Loewe, "Leise zieht durch mein Gemüth" 1838
Anton Rubinstein, "Frühlingslied" 1856, Op32,1
Robert Franz, "Leise zieht durch mein Gemüth" 1867?, Op41,1
Edvard Grieg, "Gruss" 1889, Op48,1
Charles Edward Ives, "Gruss" 1895?
Ernest Vietor, "Frühlingsbotschaft" 1934-35, Op12,2
from *Frühlingslieder*

Lieb' Liebchen, leg's Händchen auf's Herze mein
Robert Schumann, "Lieb' Liebchen" 1840, Op24,4
from *Liederkreis*
Robert Franz, "Lieb' Liebchen" 1860?pub, Op17,3
Frank van der Stucken, "Lieb Liebchen, leg's Händchen auf's Herze mein" 1879, Op5,3
Alfred Reisenauer, "Lieb' Liebchen, leg's Händchen" 1896pub
from *Traurige Lieder*, (3)
Nikolai Medtner, "Lieb Liebchen" 1907-08, Op12,1

Mädchen mit dem roten Mündchen, mit dem Äuglein lieb und klar
Robert Franz, "Mädchen mit dem roten Mündchen" 1846pub, Op5,5

Leopold Damrosch, "Mädchen mit dem rothen Mündchen" Op10,6
Hugo Wolf, "Mädchen mit dem roten Mündchen" 1876
Jan Gall, "Mädchen mit dem roten Mündchen" Op1,3
Erik Meyer-Helmund, "Mädchen mit dem rothen Mündchen" 1886-88

Mag da draussen Schnee sich thürmen
Josefine Lang, "Lied" 1834, Op15,2
second and third verses by E. Meier
Frances Allitsen, "Mag da draussen Schnee sich thürmen" 1900pub

Manch' Bild vergess'ner Zeiten, steigt auf seinem Grab
Ignaz Brüll, "Manch' Bild vergess'ner Zeiten" 186-?, Op5,i,6
from *Sechs Lieder nach Gedichten von Heinrich Heine*

Mein Herz, mein Herz ist traurig, doch lustig leuchtet der Mai
Johann Vesque von Püttlingen, "Auf der Bastei" 1851pub, Op39,5
from *Heimkehr* (3)
Ludwig Rottenberg, "Mein Herz, mein Herz ist traurig" 1914?pub

Mein Knecht! steh' auf, und sattle schnell
Nicolai Rimsky-Korsakov, "Die Botschaft" (set in Russian), 1866, Op4,2
Frances Allitsen, "Die Botschaft" 1900pub

Mein Liebchen, wir saßen beisammen traulich im leichten Kahn
Robert Franz, "Meerfahrt" 1860?pub, Op18,4
Hugo Wolf, "Mein Liebchen wir saßen beisammen" 1878
Edward MacDowell, "Mein Liebchen" 1881, Op11,1
Johannes Brahms, "Meerfahrt" 1884?, Op96,4
Erik Meyer-Helmund, "Mein Liebchen wir sassen beisammen" 1886-88
Joseph Guy Ropartz, "Tendrement enlacés, ma chère bienaimée" (set in French), 1899
translated by J. Guy Ropartz and P. R. Hirsch

Mein Wagen rollet langsam durch lustiges Waldesgrün
Robert Schumann, "Mein Wagen rollet langsam" 1840, Op142,4
Richard Strauss, "Waldesfahrt" 1918, Op69,4

Mir träumt', ich bin der liebe Gott
Johann Vesque von Püttlingen, "Mir träumt', ich bin der liebe Gott" 1851pub
from *Heimkehr* (66)

Mir träumte einst von wildem Liebesglüh'n
Robert Franz, "Traumbild" 1861?, Op34,3
Nicolai Rimsky-Korsakov, "Traumbilder 1" (set in Russian), 1870, Op25,1

Mir träumte: traurig schaute der Mond
Alban Berg, "Sehnsucht II" 1902

Mir träumte von einem Königskind mit nassen, blassen Wangen
Johann Vesque von Püttlingen, "Des Königs Kind" 1844-51?, Op54,4
Arno Kleffel, "Mir träumte von einem Königskind" Op14,5
Hugo Wolf, "Mir träumte von einem Königskind" 1878

Mit deinen blauen Augen siehst du mich lieblich an
Eduard Lassen, "Mit deinen blauen Augen"
César Cui, "Mit deinen blauen Augen" (set in Russian), 1877, Op11,4
Richard Strauss, "Mit deinen blauen Augen" 1906, Op56,4

Mit Myrthen und Rosen, lieblich und hold
Robert Schumann, "Mit Myrthen und Rosen" 1840, Op24,9
from *Liederkreis*

Mit schwarzen Segeln segelt mein Schiff
Gustav Eggers, "Mit schwarzen Segeln segelt mein Schiff" 1857pub, Op3,2
Robert Franz, "Mit schwarzen Segeln" 1860?pub, Op18,6
Hugo Wolf, "Mit schwarzen Segeln" 1878
Charles Griffes, "Mit schwarzen Segeln" 1903-11?, A15

Morgens steh' ich auf und frage
Robert Schumann, "Morgens steh' ich auf und frage" 1840, Op24,1
from *Liederkreis*
Franz Liszt, "Morgens steh ich auf und frage" 1844pub
Franz Liszt, "Morgens steh ich auf und frage" 1860pub
Robert Franz, "Kommt feins Liebchen heut'?" 1870?pub, Op25,4

Mutter zum Bienelein: "Hüt dich vor Kerzenschein!"
Robert Franz, "Lehre" 1867?, Op41,5
Frank van der Stucken, "Die Lehre" 1904pub, Op29,3

Nach Frankreich zogen zwei Grenadier'
Karl Gottlieb Reissiger, "Die Grenadiere" Op95,1, bass.pf
Richard Wagner, "Les deux grenadiers" (set in French), 1839-40, WWV 60
Robert Schumann, "Die beiden Grenadiere" 1840, Op49,1

Nacht liegt auf den fremden Wegen
Johannes Brahms, "Mondenschein" 1878, Op85,2
Charles Griffes, "Nacht liegt auf den fremden Wegen" 1903-09?, A5
John H. Powell, "Mondfriede" 1910pub

Neben wohnt Don Henriques
Johann Vesque von Püttlingen, "Der Nachbar" 1851pub, Op41,4
from *Heimkehr* (81)

Nicht gedacht soll seiner werden!
Günter Bialas, "Nicht gedacht soll seiner werden" 1983, bar.pf
from *O Miserere* (1)

Nun ist es Zeit, daß ich mit Verstand mich aller Torheit entled'ge
August Bungert, "Nun ist es Zeit, dass ich mit Verstand" 1889-91pub, Op11,4
Ludwig Rottenberg, "Nun ist es Zeit" 1914?pub

Oben auf des Berges Spitze liegt das Schloss in Nacht gehüllt
Robert Schumann, "Die feindlichen Brüder" 1840, Op49,2

Oben, wo die Sterne glühen, müssen uns die Freuden blühen
Edward MacDowell, "Oben wo die Sterne glühen" 1881, Op11,3

Sag mir, wer einst die Uhren erfund
Robert Franz, "Sag mir!" 1867?, Op38,4

Saphire sind die Augen dein, die lieblichen, die süssen
Frances Allitsen, "Saphire sind die Augen dein" 1900pub

Schöne Wiege meiner Leiden, schönes Grabmal meiner Ruh
Robert Schumann, "Schöne Wiege meiner Leiden" 1840, Op24,5
from *Liederkreis*
Johanna Kinkel, "Abschied" Op19,5, 1v.guit

Seit die Liebste war entfernt, hätt' ich's Lachen ganz verlernt
Frances Allitsen, "Seit die Liebste war entfernt" 1900pub

Sie floh vor mir wie'n Reh so scheu
Robert Franz, "Sie floh vor mir" 1867?, Op40,6

Sie haben heut' Abend Gesellschaft
Hugo Wolf, "Sie haben heut' Abend Gesellschaft" 1878
Hans Pfitzner, "Sie haben heut' Abend Gesellschaft" 1888/89, Op4,2, 1v(med).pf

Sie liebten sich beide, doch keiner wollt' es dem andern gestehn
Carl Loewe, "Erste Liebe" 1832, Op9,vii,3
Clara Schumann, "Sie liebten sich Beide" 1842, Op13,2
Ignaz Brüll, "Sie liebten sich beide" 186-?, Op5,i,4
from *Sechs Lieder nach Gedichten von Heinrich Heine*
Robert Franz, "Sie liebten sich beide" 1870?pub, Op31,4
Vilhelm Stenhammar, "Sie liebten sich beide" 1890?, Op17,3
from *Drei Lieder von Heinrich Heine*
Bernhard Stavenhagen, "Sie liebten sich beide" 1906pub, Op9,1
Ludwig Rottenberg, "Sie liebten sich Beide" 1914?pub

Sie saßen und tranken am Teetisch und sprachen von Liebe viel
Johann Vesque von Püttlingen, "Am Teetisch" 1854

So wandl' ich wieder den alten Weg, die wohlbekannten Gassen
Adolph Martin Foerster, "So wandl' ich wieder den alten Weg" 1878, Op6,6
Ludwig Rottenberg, "So wandl' ich wieder den alten Weg" 1914?pub

Spätherbstnebel, kalte Träume
Hugo Wolf, "Spätherbstnebel, kalte Träume" 1878
Alban Berg, "Vielgeliebte schöne Frau" 1902

Sterne mit den goldnen Füßchen
Robert Franz, "Sterne mit den goldnen Füsschen" 1870?pub, Op30,1
Franz von Holstein, "Sterne mit den goldnen Füßchen" 1877, Op37,3
Hugo Wolf, "Sterne mit den goldnen Füßchen" 1880

Still ist die Nacht, es ruhen die Gassen
Franz Schubert, "Der Doppelgänger" 1827-8, D957,13
from *Heine Lieder*
Johann Vesque von Püttlingen, "Der Doppelgänger" 1851pub
from *Heimkehr* (20)
Thorvald Otterström, "Der Doppelgänger" 1907pub
from *Neun Lieder* (4)

Täglich ging die wunderschöne Sultanstochter auf und nieder
Anton Rubinstein, "Der Asra" 1856, Op32,6
Carl Loewe, "Der Asra" 1863, Op133
Max Renner, "Der Asra" 1899pub, Op3,1

Über die Berge steigt schon die Sonne
Felix Mendelssohn, "Morgengruss" 1840?pub, Op47,2

Und wüssten's die Blumen, die kleinen
Fanny Hensel, "Verlust" 1830pub, Op9,10(FM)
Robert Schumann, "Und wüssten's die Blumen, die kleinen" 1840, Op48,8
from *Dichterliebe*
Josefine Lang, "Und wüssten's die Blumen" Op40,5

Karl Gottlieb Reissiger, "Ach wüssten's die Blumen" Op89,3
Robert Franz, "Und wüssten's die Blumen" 1860?, Op12,6
Moritz Moszkowski, "Und wüssten's die Blumen" 1877pub, Op13,2, bar.pf

Unten Schlacht, doch oben schossen
Johann Vesque von Püttlingen, "Die Walküren" 1846

Unter'm weissen Baume sitzend
Robert Franz, "Unter'm weissen Baume sitzend" 1867?, Op40,3

Vergiftet sind meine Lieder
Franz Liszt, "Vergiftet sind meine Lieder" 1844/1860
Aleksandr Borodin, "Vergiftet sind meine Lieder" (set in Russian), 1868
Aleksandr Glazunov, "Vergiftet sind meine Lieder" (set in Russian), 1882
Othmar Schoeck, "Vergiftet sind meine Lieder" 1907, Op13,1

Verriet mein blasses Angesicht
Stephen Heller, "Verriet mein blasses Angesicht" 1830-38?

Verstummt sind die Pauken, Posaunen und Zinken
Arnold Mendelssohn, "Salomo" 1914cop

Wandl' ich in dem Wald des Abends
Eduard Lassen, "Im Wald"
Leopold Damrosch, "Wandl' ich in dem Wald des Abends" Op16,3
Robert Franz, "Wandl' ich in dem Wald des Abends" 1867?, Op39,4

Warte, warte, wilder Schiffsmann
Robert Schumann, "Warte, warte, wilder Schiffsmann" 1840, Op24,6
from *Liederkreis*

Warum sind denn die Rosen so blaß?
Fanny Hensel, "Warum sind denn die Rosen so blaß" 1837, Op1,3
Peter Cornelius, "Warum sind denn die Rosen so blaß?" 1862
Pyotr Il'yich Tchaikovsky, "Warum sind die Rosen so blass?" (set in Russian), 1869, Op6,5
August Bungert, "Warum sind denn die Rosen so blass?" 1889-91pub, Op11,1
Joseph Guy Ropartz, "Pourquoi vois-je pâlir la rose parfumée?" (set in French), 1899
translated by J. Guy Ropartz and P. R. Hirsch
Othmar Schoeck, "Warum sind denn die Rosen so blaß?" 1906, Op4,2
Ludwig Rottenberg, "Warum sind denn die Rosen so blass" 1914?pub

Was will die einsame Thräne? sie trübt mir ja den Blick
Stephen Heller, "Was will die einsame Träne?" 1830-38?
Robert Schumann, "Was will die einsame Thräne?" 1840, Op25,21
Peter Cornelius, "Die Heimkehr" 1848
Robert Franz, "Was will die einsame Thräne?" 1861?, Op34,1
Frank van der Stucken, "Einsame Thräne" 1892pub

Wenn ich auf dem Lager liege, in Nacht und Kissen gehüllt
Felix Mendelssohn, "Abendlied" 2sop.pf
Josefine Lang, "Traumbild" 1834, Op28,1, 1v.vc.pf
Leopold Damrosch, "Wenn ich auf dem Lager liege" Op10,5
Ignaz Brüll, "Wenn ich auf dem Lager liege" 186-?, Op5,i,2
from *Sechs Lieder nach Gedichten von Heinrich Heine*
Robert Franz, "Wenn ich auf dem Lager liege" 1866?, Op37,6

Wenn ich in deine Augen seh', so schwindet all' mein Leid und Weh
Fanny Hensel, "Wenn ich in deine Augen sehe" 1838, sop.mez.pf

Friedrich Curschmann, "An sie" 1837, Op16,1,ii
Robert Schumann, "Wenn ich in deine Augen seh'" 1840, Op48,4
from *Dichterliebe*
Robert Franz, "Wenn ich in deine Augen seh'" 1870?, Op44,5
Hugo Wolf, "Wenn ich in deine Augen seh" 1876
Nicolai Rimsky-Korsakov, "Wenn ich in deine Augen seh" (set in Russian), 1876, Op25,2
Aleksandr Glazunov, "Wenn ich in deine Augen seh" (set in Russian), 1882, Op4,3

Wenn zwei voneinander scheiden
Josefine Lang, "Wenn zwei von einander scheiden" Op33,6
Robert Franz, "Wenn Zwei voneinander scheiden" 1878, Op48,1

Werdet nur nicht ungeduldig
Ludwig Rottenberg, "Werdet nur nicht ungeduldig" 1914?pub

Wie der Mond sich leuchtend dränget
Ludwig Rottenberg, "Wie der Mond sich leuchtend" 1914?pub

Wie des Mondes Abbild zittert in den wilden Meereswogen
Bertold Damcke, "Das Abbild" 1838pub, Op11,3
Robert Franz, "Wie des Mondes Abbild" 1846pub, Op6,2
Hugo Wolf, "Wie des Mondes Abbild zittert" 1880

Wie kannst du ruhig schlafen
Stephen Heller, "Wie kannst du ruhig schlafen" 1830-38?

Wir saßen am Fischerhause und schauten nach der See
Robert Schumann, "Abends am Strand" 1840, Op45,3
Johann Vesque von Püttlingen, "Am Meere" 1851pub, Op22,2
from *Heimkehr* (7)

Wo ich bin, mich rings umdunkelt Finsternis so dumpf und dicht
Hugo Wolf, "Wo ich bin, mich rings umdunkelt" 1878
Joseph Guy Ropartz, "Depuis que nul rayon de tes yeux bienaimée" (set in French), 1899
translated by J. Guy Ropartz and P. R. Hirsch
Charles Griffes, "Wo ich bin, mich rings umdunkelt" 1903-11?, A18
Richard Strauss, "Der Einsame" 1906, Op51,2, bass.orch (or pf)
Adolph Martin Foerster, "Wo ich bin" 1909, Op69,8

Wo wird einst des Wandermüden
Hugo Wolf, "Wo wird einst..." 1888
from *Vier Gedichte nach Heine u.a.*
Othmar Schoeck, "Wo?" 1906, Op4,3

Wo wird einst des Wandermüden letzte Ruhestätte sein?
Günter Bialas, "Wo?" 1983, bar.pf
from *O Miserere* (4)

Zu dem Wettgesange schreiten Minnesänger jetzt herbei
Robert Schumann, "Die Minnesänger" 1840, Op33,2, ttbb

Zu fragmentarisch ist Welt und Leben
Johann Vesque von Püttlingen, "Der deutsche Professor" 1851pub
from *Heimkehr* (58)

Zuweilen dünkt es mich, als trübe geheime Sehsucht Deinen Blick
Robert Franz, "Verfehlte Liebe, verfehltes Leben!" 1865?pub, Op20,3
Hanns Eisler, "Verfehlte Liebe" 1953

Erna Heinemann

Säulen, Säulen, immer neue Gänge
Viktor Junk, "Moschee in Cordoba" 1910pub

Heinrich der tugendhafte Schreiber (fl.1208-28)

Es ist in den Wald gesungen
Felix Mendelssohn, "Altdeutsches Lied" 1843pub, Op57,1

Heinrich von Stretlingen (13th century)

Der ich von den Frauen allen bis an meines Endes Ziel dienen will
Carl Loewe, "Der Treuergebene" 1817, Op9,iii,4
Loewe's text is modern German version by von Münchhausen

"Dilia Helena" (Thelyma Nelly Helene Branco) (1818-1894)

Blättlein so fein und rund, Blümchen im grünen Grund
Carl Loewe, "Allmacht Gottes" 1842, Op89,3
from *Waldblumen: Eine Liedergabe von Dilia Helena*

Das Glockenspiel der Phantasie hat zauberhafte Harmonie
Carl Loewe, "Vorspiel" 1842, Op89,1
from *Waldblumen: Eine Liedergabe von Dilia Helena*

Der Frühling begrüsset die junge Natur
Carl Loewe, "Frühling" 1842, Op107,3
from *Waldblumen: Eine Liedergabe von Dilia Helena*

Du giebst die Freude, du giebst das Leid
Carl Loewe, "Alles in dir" 1842, Op107,2
from *Waldblumen: Eine Liedergabe von Dilia Helena*

Ein Himmelreich dein Auge ist, ein Engel jeder Blick
Carl Loewe, "Dein Auge" 1842, Op89,2
from *Waldblumen: Eine Liedergabe von Dilia Helena*

Ich sinke dir ans volle Herz
Carl Loewe, "Du Geist der reinsten Güte" 1842, Op89,5
from *Waldblumen: Eine Liedergabe von Dilia Helena*

Komm Mägdelein' ohne Bangen, ich schiff' auf sichrer Bahn
Joachim Raff, "Elfenschiffer" 1855-63, Op98,3
from *Sanges-Frühling*

Mit jedem Pulsschlag leb' ich dir
Carl Loewe, "Mit jedem Pulsschlag leb' ich dir" 1842, Op89,6
from *Waldblumen: Eine Liedergabe von Dilia Helena*

O nimm mich an als deine Magd!
Carl Loewe, "Des Mädchens Wunsch und Geständnis" 1842, Op89,4
from *Waldblumen: Eine Liedergabe von Dilia Helena*

Wenn meine Blicke hangen, du Lichtgestalt, an dir
Joachim Raff, "Vor dem Muttergottesbild" 1855-63, Op98,2
from *Sanges-Frühling*

Wie ein Schwan still die Bahn zieht der Mond mit blassem Glanz
Carl Loewe, "Mondlicht" 1842, Op107,1
from *Waldblumen: Eine Liedergabe von Dilia Helena*

Helene, Herzogin von Orléans (1814-1858)
Wer einsam steht im bunten Lebenskreise
Carl Loewe, "Musik" 184-?
Franz Liszt, "Die Macht der Musik" 1849pub

"Theodor Hell" (Karl Gottfried Theodor Winkler) (1775-1856)
Einsam? Nein, das bin ich nicht
Emilie Zumsteeg, "Lied in der Ferne" 1819pub, Op4,6

Ihr fragt, was Großes ich erdenke
Felix Weingartner, "Der Liebe Erwachen" 1900, Op28,10

Oft in einsam stillen Stunden
Franz Schubert, "Das Heimweh" 1816, D456

Ludwig Helmbold (1532-1598)
Der heilig Geist vom Himmel kam
Carl Loewe, "Pfingstlied"

Amalia von Helvig, née Freiin von Imhoff (1776-1831)
Als vom Schlummer leis beschlichen
Johann Rudolf Zumsteeg, "Mein Traum" 1803pub
from *Kleine Balladen und Lieder, sechstes Heft*

Lasset die Rosenumkränzeten Stunden
Johann Rudolf Zumsteeg, "Die Freuden der Gegenwart" 1803pub
from *Kleine Balladen und Lieder, fünftes Heft*

Felicia Dorothea (Browne) Hemans (1793-1835)
Mutter, o sing' mich zur Ruh'!
Robert Franz, "Mutter, o sing' mich zur Ruh'!" 1860pub, Op10,3

Karl Friedrich Henckell (1864-1929)
Deiner hellen Stimme fröhlicher Klang
Hermann H. Wetzler, "Deiner hellen Stimme" 1905

Der Sonne entgegen in Liebesgluten
Richard Strauss, "Winterliebe" 1900, Op48,5

Die dunklen Wolken sausen, weiss glänzt der Alpen Schnee
Ernest Vietor, "Ich wollt, ich wär ein Ruderknecht" Op3,3

Die Sonne sank. Noch schimmert in meinem Aug' ihr Glanz
Hermann H. Wetzler, "Die Sonne sank" 1905

Heil jenem Tag, der dich geboren
Richard Strauss, "Liebeshymnus" 1896, Op32,3

Ich bin kein Minister, ich bin kein König
Richard Strauss, "Das Lied des Steinklopfers" 1901, Op49,4

Ich schwebe wie auf Engelsschwingen
Max Reger, "Ich schwebe" 1901, Op62,14, 1v(med).pf
Richard Strauss, "Ich schwebe" 1900, Op48,2

Ich trage meine Minne vor Wonne
Richard Strauss, "Ich trage meine Minne" 1896, Op32,1

In diesen Wintertagen, nun sich das Licht verhüllt
Richard Strauss, "Winterweihe" 1900, Op48,4

Arnold Schönberg, "In diesen Wintertagen" 1907-08, Op14,2
Schoenberg lists the poet as "Georg Henckel"

Kling! Meine Seele gibt reinen Ton
Richard Strauss, "Kling!" 1900, Op48,3

Komm in den Wald, Marie!
Vítězslav Novák, "Komm in den Wald, Marie!" 1912pub, Op46,4
from *Erotikon*

Nicht ein Lüftchen regt sich leise
Richard Strauss, "Ruhe, meine Seele!" 1894, Op27,1

O süsser Mai, o habe du Erbarmen
Richard Strauss, "O süsser Mai!" 1896, Op32,4

Was fällt ihm ein, dem edlen Herrn und Ritter?
Emil Nikolaus von Rezniček, "Schelmische Abwehr" 1920pub

Wenn ich dich frage, dem das Leben blüht
Richard Strauss, "Blindenklage" 1903, Op56,2

Alfred Henschke: see "Jucundus Fröhlich Klabund"

Luise Hensel (1798-1876)

Müde bin ich, geh' zur Ruh'
Carl Reinecke, "Gebet zur Nacht"
from *Kinderlieder*

Wilhelm Hensel (1794-1861)

Es rauschen die Bäume, es wallen die Düfte
Fanny Hensel, "Nachtreigen" 1829, 8v

Schnell fliehen die Schatten der Nacht
Fanny Hensel, "Morgengruß" 1846, Op3,4, satb
from *Gartenlieder*

Carl Hepp ("Pater Profundus") (1841-1912)

Die Sterne sah ich am Himmel stehn
Adolph Martin Foerster, "Sterne überall" 1908, Op53,7

Ein Reif ist gefallen ganz über Nacht
Adolph Martin Foerster, "Ein Reif ist gefallen" 1910, Op72,2

Ich habe ein Röschen gefunden, vor deinem Fensterlein
Adolph Martin Foerster, "Träumerei" 1908, Op53,3

Schöne Zeiten, trübe Zeiten sind gekommen und gegangen
Adolph Martin Foerster, "Gefangen" 1910, Op72,1

Tautröpfchen blinkt am Blatt, Buchfinke trinkt sich satt
Adolph Martin Foerster, "Im März" 1909, Op69,ii,5

Überm Strohhut flattern Bänder
Adolph Martin Foerster, "Anfrage" 1909, Op69,ii,6

Johann Gottfried Herder (1744-1803)

Ach, könnt ich, könnte vergessen sie!
Carl Friedrich Zelter, "Sonett aus dem 13. Jahrhundert" 1802
translated from Thibaut IV. Graf von Champagne und König von Navarra

Johannes Brahms, "Ein Sonett (Aus dem 13. Jahrhundert)" 1858, Op14,4
translation from the French of Thibaut IV (1201-1253)

Alle Winde schlafen auf dem Spiegel der Flut
Johannes Brahms, "Die Meere" 1860, Op20,3, sop.alt.pf

An des Baches stillen Weiden
Wilhelm Pohl, "Die Echo" 1785pub

Dein Schwert, wie ist's von Blut so roth, Edward!
Josef Antonín Štěpán, "Edward und seine Mutter" 1778-79pub
Carl Loewe, "Edward" 1818, Op1,1
translated from the Scottish ballade
Franz Schubert, "Eine altschottische Ballade" 1827, D923
Johannes Brahms, "Edward" 1877, Op75,1, alt.ten.pf

Den gordischen Knoten, den Liebe sich band
Johannes Brahms, "Weg der Liebe (Zweiter Teil)" 1858, Op20,2, sop.alt.pf

Ein neues Lied!
Carl Maria von Weber, "Das neue Lied" 1810, J.92

Ein Traum, ein Traum ist unser Leben auf Erden hier
Ernst Pepping, "Unser Leben" 1949pub
from *Haus- und Trostbuch* (32)
Felix Wolfes, "Ein Traum ist unser Leben" 1956, 1v(med).pf

Erde, du meine Mutter, und du mein Vater, der Lufthauch
Ernst Pepping, "Abschied" 1949pub
from *Haus- und Trostbuch* (41)

Es kam zu ihr, leis an die Thür, ihr Lieb um Mitternacht
Carl Loewe, "Das nussbraune Mädchen" 1835, Op43,3

Flattre, flattr' um deine Quelle, kleine, farbige Libelle
Christian Gottlob Neefe, "Die Wassernymphe" 1780

Gott des Schlafes, Freund der Ruh
Johann Rudolf Zumsteeg, "An den Schlaf" 1803pub
from *Kleine Balladen und Lieder, fünftes Heft*

Herr Oluf reitet spät und weit
Carl Loewe, "Herr Oluf" 1821, Op2,2

Höre, die Nachtigall singt
Ludwig van Beethoven, "Der Gesang der Nachtigall" 1813, WoO141

Hoffnung, Hoffnung immer grün! wenn dem Armen alles fehlet
Johann Friedrich Reichardt, "Hoffnung, Hoffnung immer grün" 1800pub
from *Lieder aus dem Liederspiel, Lieb' und Treue* (10)

Ich legte mein Haupt auf Elvershöh, meine Augen begannen zu sinken
Carl Loewe, "Elvershöh" 1820, Op3,2

Im säuselnden Winde, am murmelnden Bach
Josef Antonín Štěpán, "Das Mädchen am Ufer" 1778-79pub
Wilhelm Pohl, "Das Mädchen am Ufer" 1785pub

In der Ruhe Thal geboren, wer verliesse je das Thal?
Carl Loewe, "Lied der Königin Elisabeth" Op119
translated from William Shenstone (1714-1763)

Liebes, leichtes, luftges Ding, Schmetterling!
Wilhelm Pohl, "Das Lied vom Schmetterlinge" 1785pub
Carl Loewe, "Die Sylphide" 1838, Op9,x,2

Mein Freund Antonius, der Vater mir und Lehrer war
Carl Loewe, "Das Paradies in der Wüste" 1834, Op37,3, ten.mch.pf

Meine Schäfchen, morgens früh
Josef Antonín Štěpán, "Landlied" 1778-79pub

O Hochland und o Südland! Was ist auf euch geschehn!
Johannes Brahms, "Murrays Ermordung" 1858, Op14,3
translated from a Scottish folk poem

Turteltaube, du klagest so laut
Ludwig van Beethoven, "Die laute Klage" 1815?, WoO135

Über die Berge, über die Wellen
Johannes Brahms, "Weg der Liebe (Erster Teil)" 1858, Op20,1, sop.alt.pf

Und hörst du, kleine Phylis nicht der Vöglein süßes Lied?
Josef Antonín Štěpán, "Das strickende Mädchen" 1778-79pub
Joseph Haydn, "Das strickende Mädchen" 1781/84, XXVIa Nr.1
translated from Sir Charles Sedley (1639-1701)

Verschwunden ist meinem Blick
Johann Friedrich Reichardt, "Verschwunden ist meinem Blick" 1800pub
from *Lieder aus dem Liederspiel, Lieb' und Treue* (9)

(Borromäus Sebastian Georg) Karl Reginald Herloßsohn (1802-1849)
Wenn die Schwalben heimwärts ziehn
Franz Abt, "Agathe" Op39,1
Hugo Wolf, "Der Schwalben Heimkehr" 1877

Nikolaus Herman (ca. 1480-1561)
Wenn mein Stündlein fürhanden ist
Max Reger, "Bitte um einen seligen Tod" 1914, Op137,1, 1v.pf(harm/org)
from *Zwölf geistliche Lieder*

Franz Rudolf Hermann (1787-1823)
Dort auf dem hohen Felsen sang
Ludwig van Beethoven, "Der Bardengeist" 1813, WoO142

Johann Timotheus Hermes (1738-1821)
Endlich winkt der Freund der Müden mir Erlösung zu
Maria Therese Paradis, "Sophie an Siegwart" 1784-86
from *Zwölf Lieder auf ihrer Reise in Musik gesetzt*

Ich seh durch Tränenbäche
Franz Anton Hoffmeister, "An den Mond"

Ich würd' auf meinem Pfad
Wolfgang Amadeus Mozart, "Ich würd' auf meinem Pfad" 1781-82, K390

Sei du mein Trost, verschwiegne Traurigkeit!
Wolfgang Amadeus Mozart, "Sei du mein Trost" 1781-82, K391

Sey mir gegrüßt mein schmeichelndes Klavier
Maria Therese Paradis, "An das Klavier" 1784-86
from *Zwölf Lieder auf ihrer Reise in Musik gesetzt*

Verdankt sei es dem Glanz
Wolfgang Amadeus Mozart, "Verdankt sei es dem Glanz" 1781-82, K392

Weckst du mich zum neuen Jammer
Maria Therese Paradis, "Morgenlied eines armen Mannes" 1784-86
from *Zwölf Lieder auf ihrer Reise in Musik gesetzt*

[David Friedrich?] Herrmann
Für Maria, meines Lebens Leben
Johann Rudolf Zumsteeg, "Für Maria" 1802pub
from *Kleine Balladen und Lieder, viertes Heft*

K. F. Herrosee
Ich liebe dich, so wie du mich
Ludwig van Beethoven, "Ich liebe dich" 1795?, WoO123

Hersch
Flieg' auf, flieg auf, Frau Schwalbe mein
Franz Abt, "Flieg' auf, flieg auf, Frau Schwalbe mein" Op165,1

Rings Stille herrscht, es schweigt der Wald
Franz Abt, "Schlaf' wohl, du süßer Engel du" Op213,3

H. Hertz
Mein Vater war ein Gärtner, der pflog der Blumen lind
Franz von Holstein, "Glückliche Abkunft" 1880, Op42,3

Wilhelm Hertz (1835-1902)
Auf der Haide ist ein Platz
Eugen d'Albert, "Auf der Haide ist ein Platz" 1898?pub, Op17,5

Auf des Berges höchstem Scheitel steh' ich allezeit so gerne
Adolf Jensen, "Fernsicht" 1864, Op14,2

Mein Schatz will Hochzeit halten
Adolf Jensen, "Letzter Wunsch" 1864, Op14,1

Und weil ich denn von dannen muss
Felix Weingartner, "Scheidende Liebe" 1904, Op32,4

Und willst du von mir scheiden, muss ich verlassen sein
Franz Abt, "Mein Engel hüte dein!" 1873pub, Op164,3
Max Reger, "Daz iuwer min engel walte!" 1903-04, Op76,2, 1v(med).pf
from *Schlichte Weisen, Band 1*

Vergangen ist der lange Tag
Felix Weingartner, "Des Mägdeleins Nachtgebet" 1904, Op32,6

Georg Herwegh (1817-1875)
Ich möchte hingehn wie das Abendrot
Franz Liszt, "Ich möchte hingehn" 1860pub

E. H. Hess
O sähst du mich jetzt beten
Joseph Marx, "Nachtgebet" 1910, ten.pf

Hermann Hesse (1877-1962)
Abends gehn die Liebespaare langsam durch das Feld
Othmar Schoeck, "Abends" 1929, Op44,4

An dem Gedanken bin ich oft erwacht
Rudolf Brömel, "In der Nacht"

Auch zu mir kommst Du einmal, Du vergißt mich nicht
Faber-Krause, "Der Wanderer an den Tod" 1946pub

Auf dem Tisch ein kleiner Strauß von Levkoyen und Reseden
Rudolf Brömel, "Levkoyen und Reseden"

Auf der Strasse und in allen Fabriken
Othmar Schoeck, "Maschinenschlacht" 1953, Op67a, mch

Aus dunkler Brandung gährend des Lebens bunter Braus
Felix Wolfes, "Symphonie" 1964

Bist allein im Leeren, glühst einsam, Herz
Helmut Paulsen, "Blume, Baum, Vogel"
from *Sieben besinnliche Lieder*
Faber-Krause, "Blume, Baum, Vogel" 1946pub

Bleich blickt die föhnige Nacht herein
Gottfried von Einem, "Wache Nacht" 1974, Op43,4, 1v,med.pf
from *Leb wohl, Frau Welt*

Das Geld ist aus, die Flasche leer
Rudolf Brömel, "Handwerksburschenpenne"

Daß du bei mir magst weilen
Othmar Schoeck, "Für Ninon" 1929, Op44,9

Der Föhn schreit jede Nacht, sein feuchter Flügel flattert schwer
Gottfried von Einem, "Vorfrühling" 1974, Op43,2, 1v,med.pf
from *Leb wohl, Frau Welt*

Der Garten trauert, Kühl sinkt in die Blumen der Regen
Richard Strauss, "September" 1948, sop.orch
from *Vier letzte Lieder*

Der Herbst streut weiße Nebel aus, es kann nicht immer Sommer sein!
Rudolf Brömel, "Herbstbeginn"

Der müde Sommer senkt das Haupt
Yrjö Kilpinen, "Jugendflucht" 1942, Op98,1
from *Herbst*

Der Schneewind packt mich jäh von vorn
Yrjö Kilpinen, "Schlittenfahrt" 1954, Op99,4
from *Hochgebirgswinter*

Die Bäume tropfen vom Gewitterguß
Othmar Schoeck, "Sommernacht" 1929, Op44,8

Die ihr meine Brüder seid, arme Menschen nah und ferne
Rudolf Brömel, "Einsame Nacht"

Die mir noch gestern glühten, sind heut dem Tod geweiht
Gottfried von Einem, "Traurigkeit" 1974, Op43,5, 1v,med.pf
from *Leb wohl, Frau Welt*

Die Stunden eilen — Mitternacht
Yrjö Kilpinen, "Gebet der Fischer" 1942, Op98,3
from *Herbst*

Die Vögel im Gesträuch
Yrjö Kilpinen, "Herbst" 1942, Op98,2
from *Herbst*

Drüben überm Berge streut sein Licht der fahle Mond
Yrjö Kilpinen, "Drüben überm Berge streut sein Licht der fahle Mond" 1942, Op98,5
from *Herbst*

Du bist mein fernes Tal, verzaubert
Othmar Schoeck, "Die Kindheit" 1914, Op31,2
Yrjö Kilpinen, "Die Kindheit" 1942, Op98,7
from *Herbst*

Ein starker Geist hält seine weiße Hand
Yrjö Kilpinen, "Berggeist" 1954, Op99,3
from *Hochgebirgswinter*

Ein Wändeviereck, blaß, vergilbt und alt
Othmar Schoeck, "Im Kreuzgang von St. Stefano" 1917, Op31,3

Eine Glocke läutet im Grund fernab
Othmar Schoeck, "Aus zwei Tälern" 1906, Op8,2
Yrjö Kilpinen, "Aus zwei Tälern" 1942, Op98,4
from *Herbst*

Eine rote Sonne liegt in des Teiches tiefen Fluten
Rudolf Brömel, "Sommerruhe"

Eines Dichters Traumgerank mag sich feiner nicht verzweigen
Felix Wolfes, "Die Birke" 1951

Einmal in Kindertagen ging ich die Wiese lang
Felix Wolfes, "Verlorener Klang" 1962

Es führen über die Erde Straßen und Wege viel
Yrjö Kilpinen, "Allein" 1942+?, Op97,5
from *Liederfolge nach Gedichten von Hermann Hesse*
Felix Wolfes, "Allein" 1945
Faber-Krause, "Allein" 1946pub

Es geht ein Wind von Westen, die Linden stöhnen sehr
Casimir von Pászthory, "Der Brief" 1936pub
Gottfried von Einem, "Der Brief" 1974, Op43,3, 1v,med.pf
from *Leb wohl, Frau Welt*

Es hält der blaue Tag für eine Stunde
Othmar Schoeck, "Mittag im September" 1929, Op44,5

Es ist immer derselbe Traum
Yrjö Kilpinen, "Traum" 1942+?, Op97,7
from *Liederfolge nach Gedichten von Hermann Hesse*

Es ist kein Tag so streng und heiß
Rudolf Brömel, "Vergiß es nicht"

Es liegt die Welt in Scherben, einst liebten wir sie sehr
Gottfried von Einem, "Leb wohl, Frau Welt" 1974, Op43,7, 1v,med.pf
from *Leb wohl, Frau Welt*

Es schlug vom Turm die Mitternacht
Rudolf Brömel, "Nacht im Odenwald"

Flügelt ein kleiner blauer Falter vom Wind geweht
Othmar Schoeck, "Blauer Schmetterling" 1929, Op44,6
Franz Krause, "Schmetterling" 196-?pub, Op30,4
from *Sieben Gedichte von Hermann Hesse*
Gottfried von Einem, "Blauer Schmetterling" 1983, Op73,2
from *Tag- und Nachtlieder*

Freund meiner Jugend, zu dir kehr ich voll Dankbarkeit
Franz Krause, "Ode an Hölderlin" 196-?pub, Op15,5, bar.pf
from *Fünf Gedichte von Hermann Hesse*

Frühlinge und Sommer steigen grün herauf und singen Lieder
Rudolf Brömel, "Spielmann"

Gib uns deine milde Hand! Von der Mutter Hand gerissen
Rudolf Brömel, "An die Schönheit"
Franz Krause, "Gebet an die Schönheit" 196-?pub, Op15,2
from *Fünf Gedichte von Hermann Hesse*

Gleichtönig, leis und klagend rinnt
Rudolf Brömel, "Sommers Ende"

Gottes Atem hin und wieder
Othmar Schoeck, "Magie der Farben" 1929, Op44,2

Holder Schein, an deine Spiele sieh mich willig hingegeben
Emil Mattiesen, "Bekenntnis" 190-?pub, Op15,6
from *Überwindungen* (6)

Ich bin auch in Ravenna gewesen
Othmar Schoeck, "Ravenna" 1913, Op24b,9
Franz Krause, "Ravenna" 196-?pub, Op30,1, bar.pf
from *Sieben Gedichte von Hermann Hesse*

Ich fragte dich, warum dein Auge
Yrjö Kilpinen, "Ich fragte dich, warum dein Auge" 1942+?, Op97,4
from *Liederfolge nach Gedichten von Hermann Hesse*

Ich habe meine Kerze ausgelöscht
Gottfried von Einem, "Nacht" 1974, Op43,6, 1v,med.pf
from *Leb wohl, Frau Welt*

Ich weiß: an irgend einem fernen Tag
Rudolf Brömel, "Vollendung"

Ich wollt', ich wär' eine Blume
Yrjö Kilpinen, "Liebeslied" 1942+?, Op97,1
from *Liederfolge nach Gedichten von Hermann Hesse*

Im alten loderlohen Glanze
Othmar Schoeck, "Jahrestag" 1906, Op8,4

Im Garten meiner Mutter steht ein weißer Birkenbaum
Rudolf Brömel, "Im Garten meiner Mutter steht"

Im Grase hingestreckt lausch' ich der Halme zartem Wald
Felix Wolfes, "Im Grase hingestreckt" 1962

Im Kastanienbaum der Wind, der Wind
Rudolf Brömel, "Frühlingsnacht"

Im Walde blüht der Seidelbast, im Graben liegt der Schnee
Robert Gund, "Wanderschaft" 1911cop, Op36,3

Im Welschland, wo die braunen Buben
Othmar Schoeck, "Auskunft" 1906, Op8,3

Immer bin ich ohne Ziel gegangen
Othmar Schoeck, "Das Ziel" 1914, Op24b,8

In dämmrigen Grüften träumte ich lang
Jos. A. Dasatièl, "Frühling" 1921pub
Richard Strauss, "Frühling" 1948, sop.orch
from *Vier letzte Lieder*

Jede Blüte will zur Frucht, jeder Morgen Abend werden
Rudolf Brömel, "Welkes Blatt"

Kennst du das auch, daß manches Mal
Othmar Schoeck, "Kennst du das auch?" 1906, Op24b,4

Klavier und Geige, die ich wahrlich schätze
Othmar Schoeck, "Pfeifen" 1929, Op44,7

Lange waren meine Augen müd'
Franz Krause, "Genesung" 196-?pub, Op15,3
from *Fünf Gedichte von Hermann Hesse*

Mein Heimweh und meine Liebe
Yrjö Kilpinen, "Dunkle Augen" 1942+?, Op97,3
from *Liederfolge nach Gedichten von Hermann Hesse*

Meine fröhliche Liebe hat mich verlassen
Casimir von Pászthory, "Meine fröhliche Liebe" 1936pub

Mir zittern die Saiten und stimmen die Weise an
Joseph Marx, "Con sordino" 1904, ten.pf

Möchten viele Seelen dies verstehen
Othmar Schoeck, "Verwelkende Rosen" 1929, Op44,3

Musik des Weltalls und Musik der Meister
Franz Krause, "Das Glasperlenspiel" 196-?pub, Op30,7
from *Sieben Gedichte von Hermann Hesse*

Nachtwandler, tast' ich mich durch Wald und Schlucht
Felix Wolfes, "Verlorenheit" 1967

Nächtelang, die Stirn in heißer Hand
Rudolf Brömel, "Nächtelang"

Nun der Tag mich müd' gemacht
Rudolf Brömel, "Beim Schlafengehen"
Richard Strauss, "Beim Schlafengehn" 1948, sop.orch
from *Vier letzte Lieder*

O reine, wundervolle Schau, wenn du aus Purpurrot
Felix Wolfes, "Spätblau" 1964

O schau, sie schweben wieder wie leise Melodien
Emil Mattiesen, "Weiße Wolken" 190-?pub, Op11,1
from *Stille Lieder* (1)
Felix Wolfes, "Weisse Wolken" 1963

Rote Nelke blüht im Garten
Rudolf Brömel, "Nelke"

Schon manche selige Nacht hat über mir geblaut
Yrjö Kilpinen, "Grindelwald" 1954, Op99,2
from *Hochgebirgswinter*

Schuh um Schuh im Finstern setz ich
Franz Krause, "Nächtlicher Weg" 196-?pub, Op30,5
from *Sieben Gedichte von Hermann Hesse*

Seele, banger Vogel du
Othmar Schoeck, "Keine Rast" 1914, Op24b,7

Sei nicht traurig! Bald ist es Nacht
Casimir von Pászthory, "Sei nicht traurig" 1936pub
Faber-Krause, "Auf Wanderung" 1946pub

Seltsam, im Nebel zu wandern! Einsam ist jeder Busch und Stein
Casimir von Pászthory, "Im Nebel" 1936pub
Felix Wolfes, "Im Nebel" 1941
Othmar Schoeck, "Im Nebel" 1952, o.op45
Franz Krause, "Im Nebel" 196-?pub, Op15,4, bar.pf
from *Fünf Gedichte von Hermann Hesse*
Gottfried von Einem, "Im Nebel" 1974, Op43,1, 1v,med.pf
from *Leb wohl, Frau Welt*

Seltsam schöne Hügelfluchten, dunkle Berge, helle Matten
Rudolf Brömel, "Schwarzwald"

So mußt Du allen Dingen Bruder und Schwester sein
Faber-Krause, "Spruch" 1946pub

Solang du nach dem Glücke jagst
Rudolf Brömel, "Glück"
Yrjö Kilpinen, "Glück" 1942+?, Op97,6
from *Liederfolge nach Gedichten von Hermann Hesse*

Tief mit blauer Nachtgewalt
Othmar Schoeck, "Nachtgefühl" 1929, Op44,1

Traurig lehnst du dein Gesicht übers Laub, dem Tod ergeben
Franz Krause, "Weiße Rose in der Dämmerung" 196-?pub, Op15,1
from *Fünf Gedichte von Hermann Hesse*

Über den Himmel Wolken ziehn, über die Felder geht der Wind
Rudolf Brömel, "Über die Felder"
Faber-Krause, "Über die Felder" 1946pub
Felix Wolfes, "Über die Felder" 1951

Über mir im Blauen reisen Wolken
Franz Krause, "Fiesole" 196-?pub, Op30,2
from *Sieben Gedichte von Hermann Hesse*

Und ringsum Schnee und Gletschereis
Yrjö Kilpinen, "Aufstieg" 1954, Op99,1
from *Hochgebirgswinter*

Uns ist kein Sein vergönnt. Wir sind nur Strom
Franz Krause, "Klage" 196-?pub, Op30,6
from *Sieben Gedichte von Hermann Hesse*

Voll Blüten steht der Pfirsichbaum
Rudolf Brömel, "Voll Blüten"

Vom Baum des Lebens fällt mir Blatt und Blatt
Othmar Schoeck, "Vergänglichkeit" 1929, Op44,10
Yrjö Kilpinen, "Vergänglichkeit" 1942, Op98,8
from *Herbst*

Von der Tafel rinnt der Wein
Yrjö Kilpinen, "Nach dem Fest" 1942, Op98,6
from *Herbst*

Was blickst du träumend ins verwölkte Land
Felix Wolfes, "Abendgespräch" 1966

Was lachst du so? Mich schmerzt der gelle Ton
Othmar Schoeck, "Was lachst du so?" 1906, Op24b,5

Weit aus allen dunklen Talen kommt der süße Amselschlag
Rudolf Brömel, "Eine Geige in den Garten"

Wenn alle Nachbarn schlafen gangen
Rudolf Brömel, "Königskind"

Wenn du die kleine Hand mir gibst
Joseph Marx, "Bitte" 1907, 1v(med).pf
Casimir von Pászthory, "Bitte" 1936pub

Wer den Weg nach innen fand
Helmut Paulsen, "Weg nach innen"
from *Sieben besinnliche Lieder*

Wetterleuchten fiebert fern, der Jasmin mit sonderbaren Lichtern
Rudolf Brömel, "Wetterleuchten"

Wie eine weiße Wolke
Othmar Schoeck, "Elisabeth" 1906, Op8,1

Wie fremd und wunderlich das ist
Casimir von Pászthory, "Landstreicherherberge" 1936pub

Wie haben sie dich, Baum, verschnitten
Othmar Schoeck, "Gestutzte Eiche" 1953, Op67b, mch

Wie sind die Tage schwer! An keinem Feuer kann ich erwarmen
Rudolf Brömel, "Wie sind die Tage"

Wieder schreitet er den braunen Pfad
Othmar Schoeck, "Frühling" 1911, Op24b,6
Franz Krause, "Frühling" 196-?pub, Op30,3
from *Sieben Gedichte von Hermann Hesse*

Wo mag meine Heimat sein
Yrjö Kilpinen, "Wo mag meine Heimat sein" 1942+?, Op97,2
from *Liederfolge nach Gedichten von Hermann Hesse*

(Johann) Wilhelm Hey (1789-1854)

Armes Bäumchen, dauerst mich: wie so bald bist du alt!
Wilhelm Taubert, "Armes Bäumchen"
from *Klänge aus der Kinderwelt,* Vol.1, No5

Aus dem Himmel ferne, wo die Eng'lein sind
Carl Reinecke, "Der liebe Gott im Himmel" Op75
from *Kinderlieder*

Es ist kein Mäuschen so jung und klein
Wilhelm Taubert, "Wer hat das Alles so gemacht?"
from *Klänge aus der Kinderwelt,* Vol.1, No7

Wo sind all' die Blumen hin?
Wilhelm Taubert, "Wo sind all' die Blumen hin?"
from *Klänge aus der Kinderwelt,* Vol.1, No6

Karl Heinrich Heydenreich (1764-1801)

Wiege mich ein, du Mutter süßen Trostes
Wilhelm Kienzl, "Die Stille" 192-?, Op114,2

Georg Heym (1887-1912)

Er meckert vor sich hin. Die Augen starren ins Wagenstroh
Wolfgang Rihm, "Robespierre" 1969, Op1,12

Paul von Heyse (1830-1914)

Ach, des Knaben Augen sind mir so schön und klar
Hugo Wolf, "Ach, des Knaben Augen" 1889
from *Spanisches Liederbuch* (Geistliche Lieder, 6)

Ach, ihr lieben Äugelein
Adolf Jensen, "Ach, ihr lieben Äugelein" 1864, Op21,2

Ach im Maien war's im Maien wo die warmen Lüfte wehen
Hugo Wolf, "Ach im Maien war's" 1890
from *Spanisches Liederbuch* (Weltliche Lieder, 20)

Ach, was bin ich aufgewacht?
Adolf Jensen, "Schlaf nur ein" 1864, Op22,10
from *Zwölf Gesänge von Paul Heyse*
Alexander Zemlinsky, "Schlaf nur ein!" 1897?, Op5,i,1

Ach, wie schön ist Carmosenella
Max Bruch, "Carmosenella" 186-?, Op17,ii,2
translated from the Italian
from *Vier weltliche Lieder aus dem Spanischen und Italienischen*

Ach, wie so gerne bleib' ich euch ferne
Alexander von Fielitz, "Ach, wie so gerne bleib' ich euch ferne" 1895?pub, Op40,8
from *Acht Mädchenlieder von Paul Heyse*

All' meine Herzgedanken sind immerdar bei dir
Arno Kleffel, "All' meine Herzgedanken" Op7,1
Johannes Brahms, "All meine Herzgedanken" 1874, Op62,5, saatbb

Als wir beiden mussten scheiden, eine Nelke gab sie mir
Adolf Jensen, "Abschied" 1864, Op22,9
from *Zwölf Gesänge von Paul Heyse*

Am jüngsten Tag ich aufersteh
Johannes Brahms, "Mädchenlied" 1883/84?, Op95,6
after the Italian

Am Sonntag Morgen zierlich angetan (see also Volkslied)
Johannes Brahms, "Am Sonntag Morgen" 1868, Op49,1
from the Italienisches Liederbuch

Am Wildbach die Weiden, die schwanken Tag und Nacht
Johannes Brahms, "Vier Lieder aus dem Jungbrunnen (3)" 1859-60?, Op44,9, ssaa.(pf)

An Dich verschwendet hat mein Herz sein bestes Gut und Blut
Franz Schreker, "Umsonst" 1902pub, Op3,5
from *Fünf Lieder nach Paul Heyse*

Auch kleine Dinge können uns entzücken
Hugo Wolf, "Auch kleine Dinge" 1890
from *Italienisches Liederbuch* (1)

Auf dem Dorf' in den Spinnstuben sind lustig die Mädchen (see also "Auf die Nacht...")
Robert Schumann, "Die Spinnerin" 1851-52, Op107,4
Eugen Hildach, "Auf dem Dorf in den Spinnstuben" 1898pub, Op9,1

Auf dem grünen Balcon
Hugo Wolf, "Auf dem grünen Balcon" 1889
from *Spanisches Liederbuch* (Weltliche Lieder, 5)

Auf die Nacht in den Spinnstuben da singen die Mädchen (see also "Auf dem Dorf'...")
Adolf Jensen, "Die Einsame" 1864, Op22,6
from *Zwölf Gesänge von Paul Heyse*
Johannes Brahms, "Mädchenlied" 1886?, Op107,5

Bald stösst vom Lande das Schiff geschwinde
Max Bruch, "Parte la nave" 186-?, Op17,ii,4
translated from the Italian
from *Vier weltliche Lieder aus dem Spanischen und Italienischen*

Benedeit die sel'ge Mutter
Hugo Wolf, "Benedeit die sel'ge Mutter" 1896
from *Italienisches Liederbuch* (35)

Bitt' ihn, o Mutter, bitte den Knaben
Hugo Wolf, "Bitt' ihn, o Mutter, bitte den Knaben" 1889
from *Spanisches Liederbuch* (Weltliche Lieder, 16)

Blindes Schauen, dunkle Leuchte
Hugo Wolf, "Blindes Schauen, dunkle Leuchte" 1889
from *Spanisches Liederbuch* (Weltliche Lieder, 9)

Blühendes Heidekraut, dein Duft ist wie der Hauch von Kinderlippen
Ernest Vietor, "Heimkehr" 1937-38, Op16,1

Da nur Leid und Leidenschaft
Hugo Wolf, "Da nur Leid und Leidenschaft" 1890
from *Spanisches Liederbuch* (Weltliche Lieder, 32)

Das Meer ist für die Fischer auf der Welt
Joseph Marx, "Wofür" 1912, 1v(med).pf
from *Italienisches Liederbuch* (8)

Dass doch gemalt all' deine Reize wären
Hugo Wolf, "Dass doch gemalt all' deine Reize wären" 1891
from *Italienisches Liederbuch* (9)

Dein Herzlein mild, du liebes Bild
Johannes Brahms, "Dein Herzlein mild" 1874, Op62,4, satb
Adolf Jensen, "Über Nacht" 1864, Op22,7
from *Zwölf Gesänge von Paul Heyse*

Deine Mutter, süsses Kind
Hugo Wolf, "Deine Mutter, süsses Kind" 1890
from *Spanisches Liederbuch* (Weltliche Lieder, 31)

Der Himmel hat keine Sterne so klar
Alexander Zemlinsky, "Der Himmel hat keine Sterne" 1894-96, Op2,i,2
Robert Kahn, "Mädchenlied" 1895, Op22,1
Alexander von Fielitz, "Der Himmel hat keine Sterne so klar" 1895?pub, Op40,3
from *Acht Mädchenlieder von Paul Heyse*

Der Mond hat eine schwere Klag' erhoben
Hugo Wolf, "Der Mond hat eine schwere Klag' erhoben" 1890
from *Italienisches Liederbuch* (7)

Der Tag wird kühl, der Tag wird blass
Alexander von Fielitz, "Der Tag wird kühl" 1895?pub, Op40,1
from *Acht Mädchenlieder von Paul Heyse*

Die Berge sind spitz und die Berge sind kalt
Johannes Brahms, "Vier Lieder aus dem Jungbrunnen (2)" 1859-60?, Op44,8, ssaa.(pf)

Die du Gott gebarst, du Reine
Hugo Wolf, "Die du Gott gebarst, du Reine" 1889
from *Spanisches Liederbuch* (Geistliche Lieder, 2)

Drunten auf der Gassen stand ich
Adolf Jensen, "Mädchenlied" 1864, Op22,8
from *Zwölf Gesänge von Paul Heyse*
Alexander von Fielitz, "Drunten auf der Gassen stand ich" 1895?pub, Op40,6
from *Acht Mädchenlieder von Paul Heyse*

Du denkst mit einem Fädchen mich zu fangen
Hugo Wolf, "Du denkst mit einem Fädchen mich zu fangen" 1891
from *Italienisches Liederbuch* (10)

Du sagst mir, dass ich keine Fürstin sei
Hugo Wolf, "Du sagst mir, dass ich keine Fürstin sei" 1896
from *Italienisches Liederbuch* (28)

Dulde, gedulde dich fein! Über ein Stündelein
Hans Pfitzner, "Über ein Stündlein" 1888-1900, Op7,3
Felix Weingartner, "Über ein Stündlein" 1899, Op25,6

Eide, so die Liebe schwur
Hugo Wolf, "Eide, so die Liebe schwur" 1890
from *Spanisches Liederbuch* (Weltliche Lieder, 10)

Ein Ständchen Euch zu bringen kam ich her
Hugo Wolf, "Ein Ständchen Euch zu bringen" 1891
from *Italienisches Liederbuch* (22)

Ein Stündlein sind sie beisammen gewes't
Alexander Zemlinsky, "Hütet euch!" 1897?, Op5,i,2

Einst warst du meiner Seele Hoffnungstern
Adolf Jensen, "Vergangnes Glück" 1864?, Nachlaß

Es geht ein Wehen durch den Wald
Johannes Brahms, "Es geht ein Wehen" 1874-?, Op62,6, satb or 4fv

Es kommen Blätter, es kommen Blüten
Franz Schreker, "Es kommen Blätter" 1902pub, Op3,4
from *Fünf Lieder nach Paul Heyse*

Es zürnt das Meer, es zürnt die Felsenküste
Joseph Marx, "Es zürnt das Meer" 1907, mez.pf
from *Italienisches Liederbuch* (10)

Führ mich, Kind, nach Bethlehem!
Hugo Wolf, "Führ mich, Kind, nach Bethlehem" 1889
from *Spanisches Liederbuch* (Geistliche Lieder, 5)

Geh' schlafen, Liebste, lege dich zur Ruh
Joseph Marx, "Abends" 1912, bar.pf
from *Italienisches Liederbuch* (6)

Gesegnet sei das Grün und wer es trägt!
Hugo Wolf, "Gesegnet sei das Grün" 1896
from *Italienisches Liederbuch* (39)

Gesegnet sei, durch den die Welt entstund
Hugo Wolf, "Gesegnet sei, durch den die Welt entstund" 1890
from *Italienisches Liederbuch* (4)

Geselle, woll'n wir uns in Kutten hüllen
Hugo Wolf, "Geselle, woll'n wir uns in Kutten hüllen" 1891
from *Italienisches Liederbuch* (14)

Gott woll' dass ich daheime wär'
Max Bruch, "Duett" 1891?, Op54,3, ten.bar.vn.pf
from *Siechentrost*

Gute Nacht, geliebtes Leben, ruf' ich dir in's Fensterlein
Joseph Marx, "Ständchen" 1912, 1v(med).pf
from *Italienisches Liederbuch* (2)

Hab Erbarmen, hab Erbarmen! Um mich selbst bin ich gebracht
Adolf Jensen, "Durch die Ferne, durch die Nacht" 1864, Op22,11
from *Zwölf Gesänge von Paul Heyse*

Hat dich die Liebe berührt
Joseph Marx, "Hat dich die Liebe berührt" 1908

Heb' auf dein blondes Haupt
Hugo Wolf, "Heb' auf dein blondes Haupt" 1891
from *Italienisches Liederbuch* (18)

Herr, was trägt der Boden hier
Hugo Wolf, "Herr, was trägt der Boden hier" 1889
from *Spanisches Liederbuch* (Geistliche Lieder, 9)

Herz verzage nicht geschwind
Hugo Wolf, "Herz verzage nicht geschwind" 1889
from *Spanisches Liederbuch* (Weltliche Lieder, 11)

Heut Nacht erhob ich mich um Mitternacht
Hugo Wolf, "Heut Nacht erhob ich mich um Mitternacht" 1896
from *Italienisches Liederbuch* (41)

Hoffährtig seid Ihr, schönes Kind
Hugo Wolf, "Hoffährtig seid Ihr, schönes Kind" 1891
from *Italienisches Liederbuch* (13)

Holde, schattenreiche Bäume, neiget, neigt die Zweige dicht
Adolf Jensen, "Holde, schattenreiche Bäume" 1860, Op4,1

Ich bin durch einen schönen Wald gekommen
Joseph Marx, "Die Begegnung" 1912, mez.pf
from *Italienisches Liederbuch* (11)

Ich esse nun mein Brod nicht trocken mehr
Hugo Wolf, "Ich esse nun mein Brod nicht trocken mehr" 1896
from *Italienisches Liederbuch* (24)

Ich fuhr über Meer, ich zog über Land
Hugo Wolf, "Ich fuhr über Meer" 1889
from *Spanisches Liederbuch* (Weltliche Lieder, 8)

Ich glaube in alten Tagen, da liebt ich ein Mägdelein
Franz Schreker, "In alten Tagen" 1902pub, Op3,1
from *Fünf Lieder nach Paul Heyse*

Ich hab' empor gesehen und geglaubt
Joseph Marx, "Am Fenster" 1912, 1v(med).pf
from *Italienisches Liederbuch* (14)

Ich hab' in Penna einen Liebsten wohnen
Hugo Wolf, "Ich hab' in Penna einen Liebsten wohnen" 1896
from *Italienisches Liederbuch* (46)

Ich liess mir sagen und mir ward erzählt
Hugo Wolf, "Ich liess mir sagen und mir ward erzählt" 1896
from *Italienisches Liederbuch* (26)

Ich sah' mein Glück vorüber geh'n
Franz Schreker, "Das Glück" 1902pub, Op3,3
from *Fünf Lieder nach Paul Heyse*

Ich stellt' ein Lilienstäudlein an mein Fenster
Joseph Marx, "Die Lilie" 1912, mez.pf
from *Italienisches Liederbuch* (7)

Ich will nur ihn! Und doch, kommt er zu mir
Joseph Marx, "Liebe" 1907, sop.pf
from *Italienisches Liederbuch* (1)

Ihr jungen Leute, die ihr zieht in's Feld
Hugo Wolf, "Ihr jungen Leute" 1891
from *Italienisches Liederbuch* (16)

Ihr seid die Allerschönste
Hugo Wolf, "Ihr seid die Allerschönste" 1890
from *Italienisches Liederbuch* (3)

Im Föhrenwald wie schwüle! Kein Vogel singt im Feld
Felix Weingartner, "Hochsommer" 1904, Op31,4

Im Lenz, im Lenz, wenn Veilchen blüh'n zu Hauf'
Peter Cornelius, "Im Lenz" 1848
Alexander Zemlinsky, "Im Lenz" 1894-96, Op2,ii,4
Franz Schreker, "Im Lenz" 1902pub, Op3,2
from *Fünf Lieder nach Paul Heyse*

In dem Schatten meiner Locken
Johannes Brahms, "Spanisches Lied" 1852, Op6,1
from the *Spanisches Liederbuch*
Adolf Jensen, "In dem Schatten meiner Locken" 1856, Op1,4
Hugo Wolf, "In dem Schatten meiner Locken" 1889
from *Spanisches Liederbuch* (Weltliche Lieder, 2)

In der Mondnacht, in der Frühlingsmondnacht
Peter Cornelius, "In der Mondnacht" 1848

In Sternennacht, wenn's dämmert sacht
Peter Cornelius, "In Sternennacht" 1847-48, 2sop.pf

Köpfchen, Köpfchen, nicht gewimmert
Peter Cornelius, "Preziosas Sprüchlein gegen Kopfweh" 1854-55
translated from Cervantes' "Cabezita, cabezita"
Hugo Wolf, "Preciosas Sprüchlein gegen Kopfweh" 1889
from *Spanisches Liederbuch* (Weltliche Lieder, 14)

Lass sie nur gehn, die so die Stolze spielt
Hugo Wolf, "Lass sie nur gehn, die so die Stolze spielt" 1896
from *Italienisches Liederbuch* (30)

Lass uns leise bekennen, dass wir uns kennen
Adolf Jensen, "Geheimnis" 1864, Op22,12
from *Zwölf Gesänge von Paul Heyse*

Liebe mir im Busen zündet einen Brand
Hugo Wolf, "Liebe mir im Busen zündet einen Brand" 1890
from *Spanisches Liederbuch* (Weltliche Lieder, 17)

Mai, Mai, Mai! die wunderschöne Zeit giebt Freuden weit und breit!
Max Bruch, "Lied" 1891?, Op54,2, bar.vn.pf
from *Siechentrost*

Man sagt mir, deine Mutter woll' es nicht
Hugo Wolf, "Man sagt mir, deine Mutter woll' es nicht" 1891
from *Italienisches Liederbuch* (21)

Mein Liebster hat zu Tische mich geladen
Hugo Wolf, "Mein Liebster hat zu Tische mich geladen" 1896
from *Italienisches Liederbuch* (25)

Mein Liebster ist so klein
Hugo Wolf, "Mein Liebster ist so klein" 1891
from *Italienisches Liederbuch* (15)

Mein Liebster singt am Haus
Hugo Wolf, "Mein Liebster singt am Haus" 1891
from *Italienisches Liederbuch* (20)

Mir träumte von einem Myrthenbaum
Alexander von Fielitz, "Mir träumte von einem Myrthenbaum" 1895?pub, Op40,2
from *Acht Mädchenlieder von Paul Heyse*

Mir ward gesagt, du reisest in die Ferne
Hugo Wolf, "Mir ward gesagt" 1890
from *Italienisches Liederbuch* (2)

Mühlen still die Flügel drehn
Adolf Jensen, "Sonnenschein" 1864, Op22,2
from *Zwölf Gesänge von Paul Heyse*

Murmelndes Lüftchen, Blüthenwind
Adolf Jensen, "Murmelndes Lüftchen" 1864, Op21,4

Mutter, ich hab' zwei Äugelein
Adolf Jensen, "Mutter, ich hab' zwei Äugelein" 1860, Op4,2

Nein, junger Herr, so treibt man's nicht, für wahr
Hugo Wolf, "Nein, junger Herr" 1891
from *Italienisches Liederbuch* (12)

Nicht länger kann ich singen
Hugo Wolf, "Nicht länger kann ich singen" 1896
from *Italienisches Liederbuch* (42)

Nimm dir ein schönes Weib, doch schön mit Maßen
Joseph Marx, "Nimm dir ein schönes Weib" 1912, 1v(med).pf
from *Italienisches Liederbuch* (16)

Nina, ninana will ich dir singen
Joseph Marx, "Venetianisches Wiegenlied" 1912, 1v(med).pf
from *Italienisches Liederbuch* (17)

Nun bin ich dein, du aller Blumen Blume
Hugo Wolf, "Nun bin ich dein" 1890
from *Spanisches Liederbuch* (Geistliche Lieder, 1)

Nun lass uns Frieden schliessen
Hugo Wolf, "Nun lass uns Frieden schliessen" 1890
from *Italienisches Liederbuch* (8)

Nun stehn die Rosen in Blüthe
Robert Schumann, "Frühlingslust" 1850-1, Op125,2
from *Fünf heitere Gesänge*
Johannes Brahms, "Vier Lieder aus dem Jungbrunnen (1)" 1859-60?, Op44,7, ssaa.(pf)
Adolf Jensen, "Rosenzcit" 1864, Op22,1
from *Zwölf Gesänge von Paul Heyse*

Nun wandre, Maria, nun wandre nur fort
Hugo Wolf, "Nun wandre, Maria" 1889
from *Spanisches Liederbuch* (Geistliche Lieder, 3)

O schick' mich nicht allein zum Brunnen fort
Joseph Marx, "Am Brunnen" 1912, mez.pf
from *Italienisches Liederbuch* (4)

O wär' dein Haus durchsichtig wie ein Glas
Hugo Wolf, "O wär' dein Haus durchsichtig wie ein Glas" 1896
from *Italienisches Liederbuch* (40)

O wüsstest du, wie viel ich deinetwegen
Hugo Wolf, "O wüsstest du, wie viel ich deinetwegen" 1896
from *Italienisches Liederbuch* (44)

Ob auch finstre Blicke glitten
Adolf Jensen, "Ob auch finstere Blicke glitten" 1864, Op21,7
Hugo Wolf, "Ob auch finstre Blicke glitten" 1890
from *Spanisches Liederbuch* (Weltliche Lieder, 25)

Sagt ihm, dass er zu mir komme
Hugo Wolf, "Sagt ihm, dass er zu mir komme" 1890
from *Spanisches Liederbuch* (Weltliche Lieder, 15)

Sagt, seid Ihr es, feiner Herr
Hugo Wolf, "Sagt, seid Ihr es, feiner Herr" 1889
from *Spanisches Liederbuch* (Weltliche Lieder, 12)

Sang ein Bettlerpärlein am Schenkentor
Arnold Schönberg, "Mädchenlied" 189-?

Schon streckt' ich aus im Bett
Hugo Wolf, "Schon streckt' ich aus im Bett" 1896
from *Italienisches Liederbuch* (27)

Schweig' einmal still, du garst'ger Schwätzer dort!
Hugo Wolf, "Schweig' einmal still" 1896
from *Italienisches Liederbuch* (43)

Selig ihr Blinden, die ihr nicht zu schauen vermögt
Hugo Wolf, "Selig ihr Blinden" 1890
from *Italienisches Liederbuch* (5)

Sie blasen zum Abmarsch, lieb Mütterlein
Adolf Jensen, "Sie blasen zum Abmarsch" 1860, Op4,4
Hugo Wolf, "Sie blasen zum Abmarsch" 1889
from *Spanisches Liederbuch* (Weltliche Lieder, 28)

Sie sagen mir, daß meine Wangen schwarz sind
Joseph Marx, "Die Liebste spricht" 1912, mez.pf
from *Italienisches Liederbuch* (5)

So weich so warm hegt dich kein Arm
Peter Cornelius, "So weich und warm" 1848, sop.alt
Peter Cornelius, "So weich und warm" 1874, satb

Soll ich ihn lieben, soll ich ihn lassen
Erik Meyer-Helmund, "Guter Rath" 1886-88
Alexander von Fielitz, "Soll ich lieben" 1895?pub, Op40,7
from *Acht Mädchenlieder von Paul Heyse*

Sonst plaudert ich mit Euch die Zeit entfloh
Joseph Marx, "Die Verlassene" 1912, mez.pf
from *Italienisches Liederbuch* (15)

Sterb' ich, so hüllt in Blumen meine Glieder
Hugo Wolf, "Sterb' ich, so hüllt in Blumen meine Glieder" 1896
from *Italienisches Liederbuch* (33)

Trau nicht der Liebe, mein Liebster, gib Acht!
Hugo Wolf, "Trau nicht der Liebe" 1890
from *Spanisches Liederbuch* (Weltliche Lieder, 19)

Treibe nur mit Lieben Spott
Hugo Wolf, "Treibe nur mit Lieben Spott" 1889
from *Spanisches Liederbuch* (Weltliche Lieder, 4)

Über die Welt kommt Stille, das Dunkel wiegt sie ein
Adolf Jensen, "Über die Welt kommt Stille" 1864, Op22,5
from *Zwölf Gesänge von Paul Heyse*

Über'm dunklen Walde steigt der Mond empor
Franz von Holstein, "Klage" 1877, Op37,5

Und bild' dir nur im Traum nichts ein
Alexander von Fielitz, "Und bild' dir nur im Traum nichts ein" 1895?pub, Op40,4
from *Acht Mädchenlieder von Paul Heyse*
Gustav Trautmann, "Trutzliedchen" 1896?pub, Op1,8

Und bist du jung an Jahren
Peter Cornelius, "Schäfers Nachtlied" 1848

Und gehst du über den Kirchhof
Johannes Brahms, "Vier Lieder aus dem Jungbrunnen (4)" 1859-60?, Op44,10, ssaa.(pf)

Und steht Ihr früh am Morgen auf
Hugo Wolf, "Und steht Ihr früh am Morgen auf" 1896
from *Italienisches Liederbuch* (34)

Und wenn ich werd' im Sarg gebettet liegen (see also Volkslied)
Joseph Marx, "Die tote Braut" 1912, mez.pf
from *Italienisches Liederbuch* (12)

Und wie sie kam zur Hexe, Dornröschen hold, Dornröschen gut
Alexander von Fielitz, "Und wie sie kam zur Hexe" 1895?pub, Op40,5
from *Acht Mädchenlieder von Paul Heyse*

Und willst du deinen Liebsten sterben sehen
Hugo Wolf, "Und willst du deinen Liebsten sterben sehen" 1891
from *Italienisches Liederbuch* (17)

Und wollen mich die klugen Leute fragen
Joseph Marx, "Der Dichter" 1912, bar.pf
from *Italienisches Liederbuch* (3)

Unter den Zweigen in tiefer Nacht
Adolf Jensen, "Unter den Zweigen in tiefer Nacht" 1864, Op22,3
from *Zwölf Gesänge von Paul Heyse*

Verschling' der Abgrund meines Liebsten Hütte
Hugo Wolf, "Verschling' der Abgrund meines Liebsten Hütte" 1896
from *Italienisches Liederbuch* (45)

Vier Grüße send' ich zu dir auf die Reise
Joseph Marx, "Sendung" 1912, 1v(med).pf
from *Italienisches Liederbuch* (9)

Vor Tage weckte mich mein klopfend Herz
George Henschel, "Vor Tage" 188-?, Op43,2

Waldesnacht, du wunderkühle, die ich tausendmale grüss'
Adolf Jensen, "Im Walde" 1864, Op22,4
from *Zwölf Gesänge von Paul Heyse*
Johannes Brahms, "Waldesnacht" 1874, Op62,3, satb
Arnold Schönberg, "Waldesnacht" 189-?

Was für ein Lied soll dir gesungen werden
Hugo Wolf, "Was für ein Lied soll dir gesungen werden" 1896
from *Italienisches Liederbuch* (23)

Was soll der Zorn, mein Schatz
Hugo Wolf, "Was soll der Zorn, mein Schatz" 1896
from *Italienisches Liederbuch* (32)

Wehe der, die mir verstrickte meinen Geliebten!
Hugo Wolf, "Wehe der, die mir verstrickte" 1890
from *Spanisches Liederbuch* (Weltliche Lieder, 33)

Weint nicht, ihr Äuglein!
Hugo Wolf, "Weint nicht, ihr Äuglein" 1890
from *Spanisches Liederbuch* (Weltliche Lieder, 29)

Wenn die Hahnen frühe krähen
Peter Cornelius, "Morgenwind" 1848

Wenn Du, mein Liebster, steigst zum Himmel auf
Hugo Wolf, "Wenn Du, mein Liebster, steigst zum Himmel auf" 1896
from *Italienisches Liederbuch* (36)

Wenn du mich mit den Augen streifst und lachst
Hugo Wolf, "Wenn du mich mit den Augen streifst und lachst" 1896
from *Italienisches Liederbuch* (38)

Wenn du zu den Blumen gehst
Arno Kleffel, "Spanisches Lied" Op14,6
Adolf Jensen, "Wenn du zu den Blumen gehst" 1864, Op21,5
Hugo Wolf, "Wenn du zu den Blumen gehst" 1889
from *Spanisches Liederbuch* (Weltliche Lieder, 6)

Wer da lebt in Liebesqual, Abschied nimmt er tausend Mal
Leopold Damrosch, "Wer da lebt in Liebesqual" Op14,3
translated from the Spanish

Wer rief dich denn? wer hat dich herbestellt?
Hugo Wolf, "Wer rief dich denn?" 1890
from *Italienisches Liederbuch* (6)

Wer sein holdes Lieb verloren
Hugo Wolf, "Wer sein holdes Lieb verloren" 1889
from *Spanisches Liederbuch* (Weltliche Lieder, 7)

Wer weiss, woher das Brünnlein quillt
Max Bruch, "Duett" 1891?, Op54,4, ten.bass.vn.pf
from *Siechentrost*

Wie lange schon war immer mein Verlangen (see also Volkslied)
Hugo Wolf, "Wie lange schon war immer mein Verlangen" 1891
from *Italienisches Liederbuch* (11)

Wie mochte je mir wohler sein
Max Bruch, "Lied (Im Volkston)" 1891?, Op54,1, bass.vn.pf
from *Siechentrost*
Max Bruch, "Schlussgesang" 1891?, Op54,5, satb.vn.pf
from *Siechentrost*

Wie reizend bist du Montag morgens immer
Joseph Marx, "Wie reizend bist du" 1912, 1v(med).pf
from *Italienisches Liederbuch* (13)

Wie soll ich fröhlich sein
Hugo Wolf, "Wie soll ich fröhlich sein" 1896
from *Italienisches Liederbuch* (31)

Wie trag ich doch in Sinne
Peter Cornelius, "Musje Morgenrots Lied" 1848

Wie viele Zeit verlor ich, dich zu lieben!
Hugo Wolf, "Wie viele Zeit verlor ich, dich zu lieben!" 1896
from *Italienisches Liederbuch* (37)

Wir haben Beide lange Zeit geschwiegen
Hugo Wolf, "Wir haben Beide lange Zeit geschwiegen" 1891
from *Italienisches Liederbuch* (19)

Wohl kenn' ich Eueren Stand
Hugo Wolf, "Wohl kenn' ich Eueren Stand" 1896
from *Italienisches Liederbuch* (29)

Franz Karl Hiemer (1768-1822)
Endlich hatte Damon sie gefunden
Carl Maria von Weber, "Die Schäferstunde (Damon und Chloe)" 1810, Op13,1, 1v.guit(pf)

Schlaf', Herzenssöhnchen, mein Liebling bist du!
Carl Maria von Weber, "Wiegenlied" 1810, Op13,2, 1v.guit

Hildebrandt
Auf, Preussenherz, mit deinen Jubeltönen
Carl Loewe, "Dem Könige" 1861

C. Himer
Der Mensch soll nicht stolz sein auf Glück und auf Geld
Max Reger, "Unter der Erde" 1890/91

Franz Himmelbauer (1871-1918)
Nun bin ich schon damit versöhnt
Josef Reiter, "Früher Abend" 1910pub

Hinrich Hinrichs
Meine Seele ist nun stillgeworden
Rudi Stephan, "Dir" 1913

F. Hirsch
Verblichen ist der grüne Wald, mein Herze thut mir weh
Franz von Holstein, "Mädchen's Sehnsucht" 1880, Op42,1

Gustav Hochstetter (1873-1944)
Mädel sei kein eitles Ding
Arnold Schönberg, "Mahnung" 1901?
from *Brettl-Lieder*

Alb. vom Hochwald
Der Regen rasselt, es saust der Sturm
Louis Spohr, "Trostlos" 1837, Op101,4, 1v.pf(4-hand)

R. J. Hodel
Nacht muß es sein, wenn ich sterben will
Paul Hindemith, "Mein Sterben" 1908/09
from *7 Lieder für Sopran oder Tenor mit Klavierbegleitung*

Edmund Hoefer (1819-1882)
Glücklich, wer zum Liebchen zieht
Hugo Wolf, "Fröhliche Fahrt" 1876, Op17,1, satb

Friedrich Hölderlin (1770-1843)
Aber ich will nimmer leben
Wolfgang Rihm, "Fragment 4" 1976-77
from *Hölderlin-Fragmente*

Aber nun ruhet er eine Weile
Wolfgang Rihm, "Fragment 14" 1976-77
from *Hölderlin-Fragmente*

Ähnlich dem Manne, der Menschen frisset
Wolfgang Rihm, "Fragment 57" 1976-77
from *Hölderlin-Fragmente*

Alles ist innig
Wolfgang Rihm, "Fragment 22" 1976-77
from *Hölderlin-Fragmente*

am stürzenden Strom, die Städte
Wolfgang Rihm, "Fragment 27" 1976-77
from *Hölderlin-Fragmente*

Da ich ein Knabe war, rettet' ein Gott mich oft
Benjamin Britten, "Die Jugend" 1963pub, Op61,4

Das Angenehme dieser Welt hab ich genossen
Paul Hindemith, "Fragment" 1933, ten.pf

Den Götterverächter schalten sie dich?
Josef Matthias Hauer, "Vanini" 1914, Op6,4

Denn nirgend bleibt er. Es fesselt kein Zeichen
Wolfgang Rihm, "Empedokles auf dem Ätna – Fragment 17" 1976-77
from *Hölderlin-Fragmente*

Der Nordost weht, der liebste unter den Winden mir
Hanns Eisler, "Andenken" 1943
from *Hölderlin-Fragmente* II

Die Linien des Lebens sind verschieden
Benjamin Britten, "Die Linien des Lebens" 1963pub, Op61,6

Du schweigst und duldest, und sie verstehn dich nicht
Franz Alfons Wolpert, "Diotima" 1943

Einen vergänglichen Tag lebt' ich und wuchs mit den Meinen
Lothar Windsperger, "Die Entschlafenen" 1922, Op25,4

Ewig trägt im Mutterschoße, süße Königin der Flur
Philipp Jarnach, "An eine Rose" 1913, Op7,2
Armin Knab, "An eine Rose" 1945

Froh der süssen Augenweide
Richard Strauss, "Hymne an die Liebe" 1921, Op71,1, 1v.orch
from *Drei Hymnen von Friedrich Hölderlin*

Froh kehrt der Schiffer heim an den stillen Strom
Josef Matthias Hauer, "Die Heimat" 1915, Op12,3
Hanns Eisler, "Die Heimat" 1943
from *Hölderlin-Fragmente* IV
Benjamin Britten, "Die Heimat" 1963pub, Op61,2

Geh unter, schöne Sonne, sie achteten nur wenig Dein
Paul von Klenau, "Am Abend" 1942
from *Vier Lieder nach Gedichten von Hölderlin* (3)

Goldene Leier Appolons und der dunkel gelockten Beistimmendes
Peter Mieg, "An die Leier Apollons" 1946

Heilig Wesen! gestört hab ich die goldene Götterruhe dir oft
Josef Matthias Hauer, "Abbitte" 1914, Op12,2
Hans Pfitzner, "Abbitte" 1921, Op29,1
Wolfgang Fortner, "Abbitte" 1934
from *Vier Gesänge nach Worten von Friedrich Hölderlin*
Josef Bohuslav Foerster, "Abbitte" 1939
Hermann Heiss, "Abbitte"

Hochauf strebte mein Geist, aber die Liebe zog bald ihn nieder
Josef Matthias Hauer, "Lebenslauf" 1914, Op6,5

Ihr, ihr Herrlichen! steht wie ein Volk von Titanen
Max Reger, "Ihr, ihr Herrlichen!" 1903, Op75,6

Ihr linden Lüfte, Boten Italiens und du mit deinen Pappeln
Richard Strauss, "Rückkehr in die Heimat" 1921, Op71,2, 1v.orch
from *Drei Hymnen von Friedrich Hölderlin*

Ihr milden Lüfte, Boten Italiens!
Theodor Fröhlich, "Rückkehr in die Heimat" 1830

Ihr Wälder schön an der Seite
Stefan Wolpe, "Der Spaziergang" 1924, Op1,4, alt.pf
from *Fünf Lieder nach Friedrich Hölderlin*

Ihr wandelt droben im Licht auf weichem Boden, selige Genien!
Erich J. Wolff, "Hyperions Schicksalslied" 1907pub, Op10,1
from *Zwei Gesänge*
Josef Matthias Hauer, "Hyperions Schicksalslied" 1914, Op6,2

Wolfgang Fortner, "Hyperions Schicksalslied" 1934
from *Vier Gesänge nach Worten von Friedrich Hölderlin*

In jüngern Tagen war ich des Morgens froh
Josef Matthias Hauer, "Ehmals und jetzt" 1914, Op12,1
Paul Hindemith, "Ehmals und jetzt" 1935, ten.pf

Ist nicht heilig mein Herz, schöneren Lebens voll, seit ich liebe?
Paul von Klenau, "Ist nicht heilig mein Herz..." 1942
from *Vier Lieder nach Gedichten von Hölderlin* (2)
Ernst-Lothar von Knorr, "Menschenbeifall" 1952
Benjamin Britten, "Menschenbeifall" 1963pub, Op61,1

Komm und besänftige mir, die du einst Elemente versöhntest
Stefan Wolpe, "Diotima" 1924, Op1,3, alt.pf
from *Fünf Lieder nach Friedrich Hölderlin*

Lange lieb ich dich schon, möchte dich, mir zur Lust
Hanns Eisler, "An eine Stadt" 1943
from *Hölderlin-Fragmente* V

Meine geliebten Tale lächeln mich an
Josef Matthias Hauer, "Meine geliebten Tale" 1949

Mit gelben Birnen hänget und voll mit wilden Rosen
Stefan Wolpe, "Hälfte des Lebens" 1924, Op1,1, alt.pf
from *Fünf Lieder nach Friedrich Hölderlin*
Harald Genzmer, "Hälfte des Lebens" 1940-90?, sop.pf
from *Zwei Hölderlin-Lieder*
Benjamin Britten, "Hälfte des Lebens" 1963pub, Op61,5
Wolfgang Rihm, "Hälfte des Lebens" 1969, Op1,3

Nur einen Sommer gönnt, ihr Gewaltigen!
Josef Matthias Hauer, "An die Parzen" 1929pub, Op23,4, bar.pf
Wolfgang Fortner, "An die Parzen" 1934
from *Vier Gesänge nach Worten von Friedrich Hölderlin*
Paul Hindemith, "An die Parzen" 1935, ten.pf
Paul von Klenau, "An die Parzen" 1942
from *Vier Lieder nach Gedichten von Hölderlin* (4)

O heilig Herz der Völker, o Vaterland!
Hanns Eisler, "Erinnerung" 1943
from *Hölderlin-Fragmente* VI

O Hoffnung! Holde, gütiggeschäftige!
Hanns Eisler, "An die Hoffnung" 1943
from *Hölderlin-Fragmente* I
Max Reger, "An die Hoffnung" 1912, Op124, alt(mez).orch

Ringsum ruhet die Stadt; still wird die erleuchtete Gasse
Hermann Reutter, "Die Nacht" 1947, Op67,2

Schönes Leben! Du liegst krank, und das Herz ist mir müd vom Weinen
Josef Matthias Hauer, "Der gute Glaube" 1914, Op6,1

Send' ihr Blumen und Frücht' aus nie versiegender Fülle
Harald Genzmer, "An ihren Genius" 1940-90?, sop.pf
from *Zwei Hölderlin-Lieder*

Übernacht ich im Dorf Albluft Straße hinunter Haus Wiedersehen
Wolfgang Rihm, "An meine Schwester – Fragment 19" 1976-77
from *Hölderlin-Fragmente*

Um meine Weisheit unbekümmert
Hanns Eisler, "Um meine Weisheit unbekümmert" 1959

Vom Taue glänzt der Rasen; beweglicher eilt schon die wache Quelle
Josef Matthias Hauer, "Des Morgens" 1929pub, Op23,3, bar.pf
Paul Hindemith, "Des Morgens" 1935, ten.pf

Vor seiner Hütte ruhig im Schatten sitzt der Pflüger
Josef Matthias Hauer, "Abendphantasie" 1929pub, Op23,1, bar.pf
Paul Hindemith, "Abendphantasie" 1933, ten.pf
Viktor Ullmann, "Abendphantasie" 1943

Warum huldigest du, heiliger Sokrates
Benjamin Britten, "Sokrates und Alcibiades" 1963pub, Op61,3

Was schläfst und träumst du, Jüngling! gehüllt in dich
Josef Matthias Hauer, "Der gefesselte Strom" 1929pub, Op23,2, bar.pf

Wenn auf Gefilden neues Entzükken keimt
Viktor Ullmann, "Der Frühling" 1943

Wenn aus dem Leben kann ein Mensch sich finden
Stefan Wolpe, "Zufriedenheit" 1924, Op1,5, alt.pf
from *Fünf Lieder nach Friedrich Hölderlin*

Wenn aus der Ferne, da wir geschieden sind
Stefan Wolpe, "An Diotima" 1927, Op1,2, alt.pf
from *Fünf Lieder nach Friedrich Hölderlin*

Wenn ihr Freunde vergeßt wenn ihr die Euren all
Richard Strauss, "Die Liebe" 1921, Op71,3, 1v.orch
from *Drei Hymnen von Friedrich Hölderlin*
Karl Machael Komma, "Die Liebe" 1954

Wie wenn die alten Wasser, in anderen Zorn
Hanns Eisler, "Elegie 1943" 1943
from *Hölderlin-Fragmente* III

Wie Wolken um die Zeit legt
Wolfgang Rihm, "Fragment 92" 1976-77
from *Hölderlin-Fragmente*

Wo bist du? Trunken dämmert die Seele mir von aller deiner Wonne
Peter Cornelius, "Sonnenuntergang" 1862
Josef Matthias Hauer, "Sonnenuntergang" 1914, Op6,3
Paul Hindemith, "Sonnenuntergang" 1935, ten.pf
Paul von Klenau, "Dem Sonnengott" 1942
from *Vier Lieder nach Gedichten von Hölderlin* (1)
Hermann Reutter, "Sonnenuntergang" 1947, Op67,1

Hermann Hölty (1828-1887)

Es sprechen und blicken die Wellen
Johannes Brahms, "Am Strande" 1875, Op66,3, 2v.pf

Sie scheidet. Wie der Mutter Abschiedsblick auf's Kind
Hans Sommer, "Sonnenuntergang" 1891pub, Op14,3

Ludwig Heinrich Christoph Hölty (1748-1776)

Beglückt, beglückt, wer dich erblickt, und deinen Himmel trinket
Franz Schubert, "Der Liebende" 1815, D207

Bekränzet die Tonnen und zapfet mir Wein
Franz Schubert, "Trinklied im Mai" 1816, D427, ttb

Birg, o Veilchen, in deinem blauen Kelche
Johannes Brahms, "An ein Veilchen" 1868, Op49,2

Brächte dich meinem Arm
Fanny Hensel, "Die Ersehnte" 1827, Op9,1

Das Glas gefüllt! der Nordwind brüllt
Franz Schubert, "Trinklied im Winter" 1815, D242, ttb

Dein Silber schien durch Eichengrün
Ludwig van Beethoven, "Klage" 1790?, WoO113
Johann Rudolf Zumsteeg, "Klage" 1803pub
from *Kleine Balladen und Lieder, fünftes Heft*
Franz Schubert, "Klage" 1816, D436
Jan Bedřich Kittl, "Klage" 1844pub, Op16,2

Der Schnee zerrinnt, der Mai beginnt
Franz Schubert, "Der Schnee zerrinnt" 1815?, D130, 3v
Franz Schubert, "Mailied" 1815, D202, 2v

Die Luft ist blau, das Tal ist grün, die kleinen Maienglocken blühn
Franz Schubert, "Frühlingslied" 1815, D243, ttb
Franz Schubert, "Frühlingslied" 1816, D398

Die Nachtigall singt überall auf grünen Reisen
Franz Schubert, "Seufzer" 1815, D198
Fanny Hensel, "Seufzer" 1827

Die Schwalbe fliegt, der Frühling siegt
Felix Mendelssohn, "And'res Maienlied (Hexenlied)" 1828pub, Op8,8

Ein heilig Säuseln und ein Gesangeston
Franz Schubert, "An die Apfelbäume, wo ich Julien erblickte" 1815, D197

Eine Schale des Stroms
Johannes Brahms, "Die Schale der Vergessenheit" 1868, Op46,3

Es ist ein halbes Himmelreich, wenn, Paradiesesblumen gleich
Franz Schubert, "Blumenlied" 1816, D431

Es liebt' in Welschland irgendwo
Franz Schubert, "Die Nonne" 1815, D208;D212

Freuden sonder Zahl blüh'n im Himmelssaal
Franz Schubert, "Seligkeit" 1816, D433

Geuß, lieber Mond, geuß deine Silberflimmer
Franz Schubert, "An den Mond (I)" 1815, D193

Geuß nicht so laut der liebentflammten Lieder tonreichen Schall
Franz Schubert, "An die Nachtigall" 1815, D196
Johannes Brahms, "An die Nachtigall" 1868, Op46,4

Grabe, Spaden, grabe, alles, was ich habe, dank' ich Spaten, dir!
J. J. Grünwald, "Das Totengräberlied" 1785pub

Franz Schubert, "Todtengräberlied" 1813?, D38, ttb
Franz Schubert, "Todtengräberlied" 1813, D44

Grüner wird die Au, und der Himmel blau
Johann Friedrich Reichardt, "Mailied"
Franz Schubert, "Mailied" 1815?, D129, ttb
Franz Schubert, "Mailied" 1815, D199, 2v
Franz Schubert, "Mailied" 1816, D503

Holder klingt der Vogelsang, wann die Engelreine
Franz Schubert, "Minnelied" 1816, D429
Felix Mendelssohn, "Minnelied im Mai" 1828pub, Op8,1
Johannes Brahms, "Minnelied" 1877, Op71,5
Charles Edward Ives, "Minnelied" 1892?
poem altered by J. H. Voss

Ihr Freunde, hänget, wenn ich gestorben bin
Peter Cornelius, "Auftrag" 1862, Op5,6

Ihr in der Ferne seid mir so nah
Fanny Hensel, "In die Ferne" 1833

Kein Blick der Hoffnung heitert mit trübem Licht
Fanny Hensel, "Kein Blick der Hoffnung" 1827

Keine Blumen blühn, nur das Wintergrün blickt durch Silberhüllen
Johann Friedrich Reichardt, "Winterlied"
The Nagel Reichardt attributes the poem to Voss, an editor of Hölty's works.
Franz Schubert, "Winterlied" 1816, D401

Liebe säuseln die Blätter
Franz Schubert, "Liebe säuseln die Blätter" D988, 3v

Mir träumt', ich war ein Vögelein, und flog auf ihren Schoss
Franz Schubert, "Der Traum" 1815, D213

Nimmer werd' ich, nimmer dein vergessen, kühle grüne Dunkelheit
Johann Friedrich Reichardt, "Die Liebe"
Franz Schubert, "Die Laube" 1815, D214

O wunderschön ist Gottes Erde
Carl Loewe, "O wunderschön ist Gottes Erde" before 1826

Rosen auf den Weg gestreut, und des Harms vergessen!
Johann Friedrich Reichardt, "Lebenspflichten" 1796
from *Lieder geselliger Freude*

Schon im bunten Knabenkleide pflegten hübsche Mägdelein
Franz Schubert, "Die frühe Liebe" 1816, D430

Sicheln schallen, Ähren fallen unter Sichelschall
Franz Schubert, "Erntelied" 1816, D434

Sie ist dahin, die Maienlieder tönte
Franz Schubert, "Auf den Tod einer Nachtigall" (sketch), 1815, D201
Franz Schubert, "Auf den Tod einer Nachtigall" 1816, D399

Sie wankt dahin, die Abendwinde spielen
Fanny Hensel, "Die Schiffende" 1837

Unter Blüten des Mai's spielt ich mit ihrer Hand
Johannes Brahms, "Der Kuß" 1858, Op19,1

Wann der silberne Mond durch die Gesträuche blinkt
Franz Schubert, "Die Mainacht" 1815, D194
Fanny Hensel, "Die Mainacht" 1838, Op9,6
Johannes Brahms, "Die Mainacht" 1866, Op43,2

Was schauest du so hell und klar durch diese Apfelbäume
Franz Schubert, "An den Mond (II)" 1816, D468

Wenn der silberne Mond (see "Wann der...")

Wie glücklich, wem das Knabenkleid noch um die Schultern fliegt!
Franz Schubert, "Die Knabenzeit" 1816, D400

Willkommen, lieber schöner Mai, der unsre Flur verjüngt
Johann Abraham Peter Schulz, "Mailied" 1782-90pub
Franz Schubert, "Willkommen, lieber schöner Mai" 1815?, D244, 3v

Wo bist du, Bild, das vor mir stand, als ich im Garten träumte
Wolfgang Amadeus Mozart, "Das Traumbild" 1787, K530
Johann Rudolf Zumsteeg, "Das Traumbild" 1803pub
from *Kleine Balladen und Lieder, fünftes Heft*

Ludwig von Hörmann

Husch, husch, husch, husch! es kommt wer, lauf geschwind
Max Reger, "Stelldichein" 1905, Op88,2

August Heinrich Hoffmann von Fallersleben (1798-1874)

Alles still in süsser Ruh, d'rum mein Kind so schlaf auch du!
Friedrich Kücken, "Schlummerlied"
Louis Spohr, "Wiegenlied (In drei Tönen)" 1837, Op103,4, sop.cl.pf

An der Rose Busen schmiegt sich
Anton Rubinstein, "Lied" 1856, Op33,2

Das ist der Dank für jene Lieder
Arno Kleffel, "* * *" Op12,12

Der Frühling kehret wieder, und Alles freuet sich
Robert Schumann, "Die Waise" 1849, Op79,14
from *Lieder-Album für die Jugend*

Der Sonntag ist gekommen, ein Sträusschen auf dem Hut
Robert Schumann, "Sonntag" 1849, Op79,6
from *Lieder-Album für die Jugend*

Die Ähren nur noch nikken das Haupt ist ihnen schwer
Richard Strauss, "Wiegenlied" 1878
from *Jugendlieder*

Die Bäume grünen überall, die Blumen blühen wieder
Heinrich Marschner, "Die Bäume grünen überall" 1851?pub, Op155,3

Die duftenden Gräser auf der Au
Peter Cornelius, "Scheiden" 1866, Op16,4, sop.bass.pf

Die duftenden Kräuter auf der Au'
Franz Liszt, "Ich scheide" 1860

Die Mükke sitzt am Fenster im goldnen Abendschein
Richard Strauss, "Abend- und Morgenrot" 1878
from *Jugendlieder*

Die Sonne sank, der Abend naht, und stiller wird's auf Strass' und Pfad
Carl Reinecke, "Am Abend"
from *Kinderlieder*

Die Trommeln und Pfeifen, die schallen in's Haus
Richard Strauss, "Soldatenlied" 1878
from *Jugendlieder*

Die Wasserlilie einsam träumet tief unten in dem grünen See
Frederic Louis Ritter, "Die Wasserlilie" 1871pub, Op6,4

Draussen blinket in silbernem Schein
Franz von Holstein, "Wiegenlied" 1880, Op44,4

Du lieblicher Stern, du leuchtest so fern
Carl Reinecke, "An den Abendstern"
from *Kinderlieder*
Robert Schumann, "Der Abendstern" 1849, Op79,1
from *Lieder-Album für die Jugend*

Du siehst mich an und kennst mich nicht
Friedrich Curschmann, "Du siehst mich an" 1836, Op13

Dunkel sind nun alle Gassen
Hugo Wolf, "Nach dem Abschiede" 1878

Ei, was blüht so heimlich am Sonnenstrahl?
Wilhelm Taubert, "Die ersten Veilchen"
from *Klänge aus der Kinderwelt*, Vol.5, No2

Ein Leben war's im Ährenfeld
Felix Mendelssohn, "Das Ährenfeld" 1847, Op77,2, 2sop.pf

Ein Röslein zog ich mir im Garten
Richard Strauss, "Ein Röslein zog ich mir im Garten" 1878
from *Jugendlieder*

Ein scheckiges Pferd, ein blankes Gewehr
Wilhelm Taubert, "Soldatenlied"
from *Klänge aus der Kinderwelt*, Vol.1, No2
Robert Schumann, "Soldatenlied" 1844

Eine kleine Geige möcht' ich haben
Carl Reinecke, "Eine kleine Geige möcht' ich haben" Op138
from *Kinderlieder*

Erscheine noch einmal, erscheine!
Friedrich Curschmann, "Erscheine noch einmal!" 1840?, Op26,1

Es blüht ein schönes Blümchen auf unsrer grünen Au
Johann Wenzeslaus Kalliwoda, "Vergissmeinnicht" 1842/43, Op112,3
Carl Reinecke, "Das Vergissmeinnicht"
from *Kinderlieder*

Es freut sich Alles weit und breit
Felix Mendelssohn, "Seemanns Scheidelied" 1831, Nachlass

Es steht ein Baum in jenem Tal
Wilhelm Taubert, "In der Fremde" 1846pub, Op67,2

Es steht ein Blümchen an jenem Rain
Frank van der Stucken, "Es steht ein Blümchen" 1878, Op3,1

Es webte schön Aennchen ohn' Unterlass
Joachim Raff, "Schön Aennchen" 1855-63, Op98,24
from *Sanges-Frühling*

Frohe Lieder will ich singen und vergessen meinen Schmerz
Arno Kleffel, "Frühlingslied" Op7,6
Franz Ries, "Frohe Lieder will ich singen" before 1891

Grün ist das Eiland, weiss der Strand
Robert Franz, "Die Farben Helgolands" 1844pub, Op3,2

Hänselein, willst du tanzen? ich geb' dir auch ein Ei
Wilhelm Taubert, "Hänselein"
from *Klänge aus der Kinderwelt*, Vol.3, No12

Husaren müssen reiten überall durch Stadt und Land
Richard Strauss, "Husarenlied" 1873
from *Jugendlieder*

Ich gehe nie vorüber an ihrem Gartenhag
Joachim Raff, "Schön Elschen" 1855-63, Op98,29
from *Sanges-Frühling*

Ich muß hinaus, ich muß zu dir
Johannes Brahms, "Liebe und Frühling II" 1853, Op3,3

Ihr lichten Sterne habt gebracht
Friedrich Curschmann, "Ihr lichten Sterne" 1836, Op14,3

Im Rosenbusch die Liebe schlief
Robert Franz, "Frühling und Liebe" 1844pub, Op3,3

In Liebeslust, in Sehnsuchtsqual
Franz Liszt, "In Liebeslust" 1860pub

Ist nicht der Himmel so blau?
Johannes Brahms, "Der Jäger und sein Liebchen" 1860, Op28,4, alt.bar.pf

Ja, die Schönst! ich sagt es offen
Hugo Wolf, "Ja, die Schönst! ich sagt es offen" 1878

Ja, du bist mein! Ja, du bist mein! Ich will's dem blauen Himmel sagen
Heinrich Marschner, "Ja, du bist mein!" 1851?pub, Op155,1

Jugend, dich hab' ich so lieb!
Carl Loewe, "Jugend und Alter" 183-?, Op9,x,1

Komm' zum Garten, zu dem wohlbekannten
Robert Franz, "Frühlingsliebe" 1844pub, Op3,4

Kommt, wir wollen uns begeben jetzo in's Schlaraffenland!
Robert Schumann, "Vom Schlaraffenland" 1849, Op79,5
from *Lieder-Album für die Jugend*

Kuckuk, Kuckuk ruft aus dem Wald
Robert Schumann, "Frühlingsbotschaft" 1849, Op79,3
from *Lieder-Album für die Jugend*

Laßt mich ruhen, laßt mich träumen
Franz Liszt, "Laßt mich ruhen" 1860pub
Franz Ries, "Lasst mich ruhen!" before 1891

Maiglöckchen läutet in dem Tal, das klingt so hell und fein
Felix Mendelssohn, "Maiglöckchen und die Blümelein" 1844, Op63,6, 2sop.pf
Carl Reinecke, "Maiglöckchen und die Blümchen"
from *Kinderlieder*
Wilhelm Kempff, "Maienglöckchen und die Blümelein" 1917, Op7,2

Maikäfer, summ, summ, summ, nun sag' mir an: warum?
Wilhelm Taubert, "Kind und Maikäfer"
from *Klänge aus der Kinderwelt*, Vol.1, No11

Mein Lied ist wie der Abendhauch, der durch die Blumen fächelt
Frederic Louis Ritter, "Mein Lied ist wie der Abendhauch" 1871pub, Op6,1

Nach diesen trüben Tagen, wie ist so hell das Feld
Robert Schumann, "Frühlings Ankunft" 1849, Op79,19
from *Lieder-Album für die Jugend*

Nachtigallen schwingen lustig ihr Gefieder
Johannes Brahms, "Nachtigallen schwingen" 1853, Op6,6

O Schmetterling sprich, was fliehest du mich?
Robert Schumann, "Schmetterling" 1849, Op79,2
from *Lieder-Album für die Jugend*

Schlaf, mein Kind, schlaf ein! Schliess deine Äugelein
Friedrich Curschmann, "Wiegenlied" 1837, Op16,2,ii

Schneeglöckchen klingen wieder
Robert Schumann, "Frühlingslied" 1849, Op79,18, 2v.pf
from *Lieder-Album für die Jugend*

Schon sank die Sonne nieder
Richard Strauss, "Der müde Wanderer" 1873
from *Jugendlieder*

Siehe, der Frühling währet nicht lang
Anton Rubinstein, "Lied" 1856, Op33,5

So lange Schönheit wird bestehn
Johannes Brahms, "So lange Schönheit wird bestehn" 1891pub, Op113,6, ssaa
from *13 Kanons für Frauenstimmen*

So schlaf in Ruh'! so schlaf in Ruh'!
Friedrich Curschmann, "Wiegenlied" 1834, Op9,3

So sei gegrüsst viel tausendmal
Robert Schumann, "Frühlingsgruss" 1849, Op79,4
from *Lieder-Album für die Jugend*

Summ, summ, summ, Bienchen, summ herum
Carl Reinecke, "An die Biene"
from *Kinderlieder*

Treue Liebe bis zum Grabe schwör' ich dir mit Herz und Hand
  Louis Spohr, "Mein Vaterland" 1844, WoO111

Über die hellen funkelnden Wellen
  Robert Franz, "Wasserfahrt" 1846pub, Op6,1

Über die Hügel und über die Berge hin
  Hugo Wolf, "Auf der Wanderung" 1878

Unsre lieben Hühnerchen verloren ihren Hahn
  Carl Reinecke, "Der liebe Hahnemann"
    from *Kinderlieder*

Veilchen, Rosmarin, Mimosen, Engelsüss und Immergrün
  Robert Schumann, "Mein Garten" 1850, Op77,2

Veilchen unter Gras versteckt
  Franz Ries, "Veilchen freue dich mit mir" before 1891

Veilchen, wie so schweigend, wie so still dich neigend
  Arno Kleffel, "Das Veilchen" Op7,4

Wart', Vöglein, wart'! Jetzt bist du mein, jetzt hab' ich dich gefangen
  Wilhelm Taubert, "Der kleine Vogelfänger"
    from *Klänge aus der Kinderwelt*, Vol.6, No8

Was mir wohl übrig bliebe
  Louis Spohr, "Was mir wohl übrig bliebe" 1836, Op139,5

Wer hat die schönsten Schäfchen?
  Carl Reinecke, "Wer hat die schönsten Schäfchen?"
    from *Kinderlieder*

Wer singet im Walde so heimlich allein?
  Friedrich Silcher, "Herr Ulrich"

Werde heiter, mein Gemüthe
  Felix Mendelssohn, "Tröstung" 1845, Op71,1

Wie aber soll ich dir erwiedern
  Arno Kleffel, "Lied im Volkston" Op12,11

Wie blüht es im Thale, wie grünt's auf den Höh'n!
  Robert Schumann, "Hinaus in's Freie" 1849, Op79,11
    from *Lieder-Album für die Jugend*

Wie die jungen Blüthen leise träumen
  Arno Kleffel, "Frühlingslied" Op7,5
  Leopold Damrosch, "Wie die jungen Blüthen leise träumen"
    from *Three Songs without Opus-number, by various authors* (1)

Wie die Wolke nach der Sonne
  Johannes Brahms, "Wie die Wolke nach der Sonne" 1853, Op6,5

Wie oft schon ward es Frühling wieder für die erstorbne öde Welt!
  Hugo Wolf, "Liebesfrühling" 1878

Wie sich Rebenranken schwingen in der linden Lüfte Hauch
  Johannes Brahms, "Liebe und Frühling I" 1853, Op3,2a&b
  Friedrich Nietzsche, "Wie sich Rebenranken" 1863, NWV16

Wie singt die Lerche schön
Franz Liszt, "Wie singt die Lerche schön" 1856pub

Wie war so schön doch Wald und Feld!
Felix Mendelssohn, "Abschiedslied der Zugvögel" 1845pub, Op63,2, 2sop.pf

Zum Frühling sprach ich: weile!
Robert Franz, "Doppelwandlung" 1870?, Op44,3

Zum Reigen herbei im fröhlichen Mai!
Robert Franz, "Tanzlied im Mai" 1843pub, Op1,6

Hugo von Hofmannsthal (1874-1929)

Sie trug den Becher in der Hand
Arnold Schönberg, "Die Beiden (1. Fassung)" 189-?

Was ist die Welt? Ein ewiges Gedicht
Felix Wolfes, "Was ist die Welt?" 1962

Christian Hofmann von Hofmannswaldau (1616-1679)

Niemand weiß, wie schwer mirs fällt
Franz Krause, "Strophe" 1972?pub, Op51,ii,2
from *Gedichte aus alter Zeit 2*

Wo sind die Stunden der süßen Zeit
Franz Krause, "Wo sind die Stunden" 1972?pub, Op51,ii,1
from *Gedichte aus alter Zeit 2*

Paul Hohenberg

Hier in der öden Fremde, ach so fern von dir
Alban Berg, "Sehnsucht I" 1902

Nun ziehen Tage über die Welt
Alban Berg, "Sommertage" 1907
from *Sieben frühe Lieder*

Wenn die Nacht sich über die Welt
Alban Berg, "Sehnsucht III" 1902

Prinzessin Therese von Hohenlohe

Ich bin des Meeres zartweiße Tochter
Franz Liszt, "Die Perle" 1876
translated from the Italian by Theobald Rehbaum

Christoph Christian Hohlfeld (1776-1849)

Ernst ritt der Kaiser in die heil'gen Hallen
Carl Loewe, "Kaiser Karl V. in Wittenberg" 1844, Op99,2
from *Kaiser Karl V* (2)

Franz Ignatz Holbein, Edler von Holbeinsberg (1797-1855)

Sei gegrüsst, Frau Sonne, mir
Carl Maria von Weber, "Sei gegrüsst, Frau Sonne, mir" 1818, J.225, tb

Mia Holm, née von Hedenström (1845-1912)

Daß er ganz ein Engel werde, legt den kleinen Leib zur Ruh'
Franz Schreker, "Daß er ganz ein Engel werde" before 1898, Op5,2
from *Zwei Lieder auf den Tod eines Kindes*

O Glokken, böse Glokken, habt schweren, dumpfen Klang
Franz Schreker, "O Glocken, böse Glocken" before 1898, Op5,1
from *Zwei Lieder auf den Tod eines Kindes*

Adolf Holst (1867-1945)
Alle Sternelein, die am Himmel steh'n
Max Reger, "Bitte" 1915, Op142,5
from *Fünf neue Kinderlieder*

Meine scheuen Lieder die sind wie wilde Schwäne
Richard Stöhr, "Wanderschwäne" 1914pub, Op28,4

Franz (Friedrich) von Holstein (1826-1878)
Liegt die Frühlingssonne so goldenhell auf dem traulichen Gartenplätzchen
Franz von Holstein, "Frühlingswunsch" 1877, Op37,2

Arno Holz (1863-1929)
Die Ammer flötet tief im Grund
Ernest Vietor, "Frühling" 1934-35, Op12,5
from *Frühlingslieder*

Die Sonne sank, ich wartete lange
Joseph Marx, "Vergessen" 1911, 1v(med).pf

Kleine Blumen wie aus Glas seh' ich gar zu gerne
Alban Berg, "Er klagt, daß der Frühling so kurtz blüht" 1905

Schenk ein, liebe Sonne, dein Licht
Conrad Ansorge, "Schenk ein" 1895-96pub, Op10,4

Vor meinem Fenster singt ein Vogel
Erich Zeisl, "Vor meinem Fenster" 1936pub

E. Honold
Fern von dir denk' ich dein
Erich Wolfgang Korngold, "Liebesbriefchen" 1913, Op9,4

Thomas Hood (1799-1845)
Mein Liebchen ist nicht Heliotrop
Peter Cornelius, "Mein Liebchen ist nicht Heliotrop" 1854, sop.alt
translated by Cornelius from "I will not have the mad Clystie"

Hans von Hopfen (1835-1904)
Lieb' Seelchen, lass' das Fragen sein: Was wird der Frühling bringen?
Max Renner, "Lieb' Seelchen, lass' das Fragen" 1899pub, Op3,4

Moritz Horn (1814-1874)
Ei Mühle, liebe Mühle, wie schaust so schmuck du heut
Robert Schumann, "Ei Mühle, liebe Mühle" Op112,20, sop.alt.pf

P. Horváth
Lebe wohl! Lebe wohl! in weite Ferne zieh' ich fort von dir!
Franz Liszt, "Lebe wohl!" 1847/1879
translated from the Hungarian by G. F. Zerffi

Hoschek
Du Frühlingsbote, laue Luft, was wekest du mein Herz?
Jan Bedřich Kittl, "Das todte Herz" 183-?, Op4,5

Friedrich Wilhelm von Hoven (1759-1838)

O die du rund, wie meiner Väter Schild
Johann Rudolf Zumsteeg, "Ossians Sonnengesang" 1803pub
from *Kleine Balladen und Lieder, sechstes Heft*

Hozze

Vor Gottes Aug', dem Abendroth, gab sie mir Ring und Schwur
Louis Spohr, "Der Spielmann und seine Geige" 1856, Op154,5, bar.vn.pf

Felix Hubalek (1908-1958)

Der Mond, der dort am Himmel steht, ist bleich wie mein Gesicht
Gottfried von Einem, "Verzweiflung" 1954-56, Op19,6

Berta Huber

Alles dunkel, alles still
Yrjö Kilpinen, "Nacht" 1942, Op95,i,1
from *Lieder um eine kleine Stadt*

Der Marktplatz liegt vom Mond erhellt
Yrjö Kilpinen, "Kleinstadt im Frühling" 1942, Op95,i,8
from *Lieder um eine kleine Stadt*

Draußen im Winde
Yrjö Kilpinen, "Am Fenster" 1942, Op95,i,2
from *Lieder um eine kleine Stadt*

Du wunderbare Frühlingszeit
Yrjö Kilpinen, "Frühling" 1942, Op95,i,4
from *Lieder um eine kleine Stadt*

Es löst ein Blatt sich welk und matt
Yrjö Kilpinen, "Das Ende" 1942, Op95,ii,5
from *Lieder um eine kleine Stadt*

Es tropft auf die Dächer
Yrjö Kilpinen, "Regen I" 1942, Op95,ii,3
from *Lieder um eine kleine Stadt*

Es wälzt der Strom die dunklen Wogen
Yrjö Kilpinen, "Strom bei Nacht" 1942, Op95,ii,1
from *Lieder um eine kleine Stadt*

Feldblumen, zarte, kleine
Yrjö Kilpinen, "Feldblumen" 1942, Op95,i,7
from *Lieder um eine kleine Stadt*

Ich stand in deiner Straße
Yrjö Kilpinen, "Das Licht" 1942, Op95,i,3
from *Lieder um eine kleine Stadt*

In frohen Tagen such' ich dich
Yrjö Kilpinen, "Verbundenheit" 1942, Op95,i,6
from *Lieder um eine kleine Stadt*

Leise geht der Tag zu Ende
Yrjö Kilpinen, "Mein Stübchen" 1942, Op95,i,5
from *Lieder um eine kleine Stadt*

Mein Weg ist weit
Yrjö Kilpinen, "Der Ruhelose" 1942, Op95,ii,2
from *Lieder um eine kleine Stadt*

Regen falle, härter pralle
Yrjö Kilpinen, "Regen II" 1942, Op95,ii,4
from *Lieder um eine kleine Stadt*

Regungslos, ein großer Schweiger
Yrjö Kilpinen, "Der Kirchturm" 1942, Op95,ii,7
from *Lieder um eine kleine Stadt*

Wenn du am Abend müde bist
Yrjö Kilpinen, "Ausklang" 1942, Op95,ii,6
from *Lieder um eine kleine Stadt*

Victor Aimé Huber (1800-1869)

Durch die Strassen von Granada einst der Maurenkönig ritte
Carl Loewe, "Der Sturm von Alhama" 1834, Op54
Spanish Ballade from the Arabian

Ricarda Octavia Huch (1864-1947)

Denn unsre Liebe hat zu heiß geflammt
Hans Pfitzner, "Denn unsre Liebe hat zu heiß geflammt" 1924, Op35,6

Du warst in dieser götterlosen Zeit
Erich Riede, "Du warst in dieser götterlosen Zeit" Op9,3, sop.pf

Eine Melodie singt mein Herz
Hans Pfitzner, "Eine Melodie singt mein Herz" 1924, Op35,5

Ich werde nicht an deinem Herzen satt
Hans Pfitzner, "Ich werde nicht an deinem Herzen satt" 1924, Op35,2

Mit meinem Liebchen Hand in Hand
Emil Mattiesen, "Mit meinem Liebchen Hand in Hand" 190-?pub, Op11,2
from *Stille Lieder* (2)

Schwill an, mein Strom, schwill über deine Weide
Hans Pfitzner, "Schwill an, mein Strom" 1924, Op35,4

Um bei dir zu sein, trüg ich Not und Fährde
Erich Riede, "Sehnsucht" Op9,2, sop.pf
Hans Pfitzner, "Sehnsucht" 1931, Op40,3

Was ist in deiner Seele, was ist in meiner Brust
Karol Szymanowski, "Bestimmung" 1910, Op22,5
Hans Pfitzner, "Bestimmung" 1924, Op35,1

Wo hast du all die Schönheit hergenommen
Hans Pfitzner, "Wo hast du all die Schönheit hergenommen" 1924, Op35,3

Peter Huchel (1903-1981)

Von Nacht übergraut, von Frühe betaut
Gottfried von Einem, "Von Nacht übergraut" 1983, Op73,8
from *Tag- und Nachtlieder*

Wenn sie reiten zur Schwemme aus dem steinernen Tor
Gottfried von Einem, "Sommerabend" 1983, Op73,9
from *Tag- und Nachtlieder*

Heinrich Hüttenbrenner (fl.1820)

Die Abendglocke tönet, vom Himmel sinkt die Ruh'
Franz Schubert, "Wehmut" 1825?, D825,1, 2t2b

Ein Jüngling auf dem Hügel mit seinem Kummer sass
Franz Schubert, "Der Jüngling auf dem Hügel" 1820, D702

Joseph Huggenberger (1865-1938?)

Auf mondbeschienenen Wegen geh' ich bergein
Max Reger, "Auf mondbeschienenen Wegen" 1903, Op79c,ii,3

Ein Schmeichelkätzchen nenn' ich mein
Max Reger, "Schmeichelkätzchen" 1904, Op76,29, 1v(med).pf
from *Schlichte Weisen, Band 2*

Jüngst lasest du – ich merkt' es wohl
Max Reger, "Züge" 1901-03?, Op79c,iii,3

Mein Schätzelein ist ein gar köstliches Ding
Max Reger, "Mein Schätzelein" 1903-04, Op76,14, 1v(med).pf
from *Schlichte Weisen, Band 1*

Schon dämmert's leise; durch's Geäst die letzten Schatten fliehen
Eugen d'Albert, "Erwachen" 1898?pub, Op17,1

Tief im Talgrund überm Bach sich die Weiden neigen
Max Reger, "Friede" 1903, Op79c,ii,2
Max Reger, "Friede" 1904, Op76,25, 1v(med).pf
from *Schlichte Weisen, Band 2*

Langston Hughes (1902-1967)

Grollen die Tomtoms, rollen die Tomtoms
Alexander Zemlinsky, "Afrikanischer Tanz" 1937/38, Op27,9
translated by Maurice Wright

Spielt die Blues für mich
Alexander Zemlinsky, "Elend" 1937/38, Op27,7
translated by Maurice Wright

Tief im Süden Dixies– mein Herz erträgt es kaum
Hermann Reutter, "Lied für ein dunkles Mädchen" 1958
German translation by Paridam von dem Knesebeck

Wisse, Herz: Der Tod trommelt hier, schlägt unentwegt
Hermann Reutter, "Trommel" 1958
German translation by Paridam von dem Knesebeck

Victor Marie Hugo (1802-1885)

Das Grab, es sprach zur Rose
Franz Liszt, "Das Grab und dic Rosc" 1844pub
translated from the French by Theobald Rehbaum

Gastibelza, der greise, kühne Jäger
Franz Liszt, "Gastibelza" 1844pub
translated from the French by Theobald Rehbaum

Gibt es wo einen Rasen grün
Franz Liszt, "Gibt es wo einen Rasen grün" 1844pub
Franz Liszt, "Gibt es wo einen Rasen grün" 1860pub
translated from the French by Peter Cornelius

Immer mag verklingen muntrer Vögel Sang
Louis Spohr, "An die Geliebte" 1839, WoO100

Mein Kind, wär ich König, glänzend und reich vor Allem
Franz Liszt, "Mein Kind, wär ich König" 1844pub
Franz Liszt, "Mein Kind, wär ich König" 1860pub
translated from the French by Peter Cornelius

O komm im Traum, komm in stillester Stunde
Franz Liszt, "O komm im Traum" 1844pub
Franz Liszt, "O komm im Traum" 1860pub
translated from the French by Peter Cornelius

Wie kann, sagten sie, versteckt hier im Nachen
Franz Liszt, "Was tun?" 1843
translated from the French by Theobald Rehbaum

Wozu der Vöglein Chöre belauschen fern und nah?
Felix Mendelssohn, "Lied aus *Ruy Blas*" 1839, Op77,3, 2sop.pf
translated by Dräxler-Manfred
Frank van der Stucken, "Serenade" 1892pub

Hedwig Humperdinck
Ein Sternlein funkelt am Himmelszelt
Engelbert Humperdinck, "Der Stern von Bethlehem" 1900

Johannes (Jan) Hus (1369?-1415)
Jesus ist mein Hirt, auf Jesum will ich bauen
Carl Loewe, "Jesus ist mein Hirt"

Husserl
Deine Sehnsucht ist leer. Einst tönnte sie weit über das wogende Meer
Franz Salmhofer, "Deine Sehnsucht ist leer" 1923pub, Op5,4
from *Vier Lieder*

Henrik Johann Ibsen (1828-1906)
Zu ihr stand all' mein Sehnen
Alban Berg, "Spielleute" 1902

August Wilhelm Iffland (1759-1814)
Ein Gott, ein wahrer Gott ist nur
Johann Rudolf Zumsteeg, "Chor der Derwische" 1802pub, solo.3v
from *Kleine Balladen und Lieder, viertes Heft*

Heilig ist mir Dankbarkeit!
Johann Rudolf Zumsteeg, "(Ina)" 1802pub
from *Kleine Balladen und Lieder, viertes Heft*

Liebe, die sonst stets mit Myrten krönet
Johann Rudolf Zumsteeg, "Ina" 1802pub
from *Kleine Balladen und Lieder, viertes Heft*

Henri Illaire

Schmückt das Haus mit grünen Zweigen

Carl Maria von Weber, "Festlied" 1818, J.228, 4mv

Immerman

Steh' balde still und rühr' dich nicht

Léander Schlegel, "Steh' balde still und rühr' dich nicht" 1900, Op20,14

from *Deutsche Liebeslieder*

Karl Leberecht Immermann (1769-1840)

Auf deinem Grunde haben sie an verborg'nem Ort

Robert Schumann, "Auf dem Rhein" 1846, Op51,4

Leg' in den Sarg mir mein grünes Gewand, Trubor, Trubor!

Felix Mendelssohn, "Todeslied der Bojaren" 1841

Mein Liebe, mein' Lieb' ist ein Segelschiff

Franz Wüllner, "Mein Liebe, mein' Lieb' ist ein Segelschiff" 1857pub

Lotte Ingrisch (Charlotte von Einem) (1930-)

Aus weißen Bildern wachsen deine Flügel

Gottfried von Einem, "Frühling" 1982, Op69,2, 1v(med).pf

from *Lebenstanz*

Brennend rot und schwarz gefleckt hast am Tag du mich erschreckt

Gottfried von Einem, "Mohnlied" 1983, Op71,7, 1v(med).pf

from *Waldviertler Lieder* (7)

Der Stein zerfließt, der Wald ertrinkt, mein Haus versinkt

Gottfried von Einem, "Nebellied" 1983, Op71,5, 1v(med).pf

from *Waldviertler Lieder* (5)

Die Arbeit ist getan. Der Nebel steigt

Gottfried von Einem, "Winter" 1982, Op69,5, 1v(med).pf

from *Lebenstanz*

Die Zeit ist ein Lied, im Herzen entsprungen

Gottfried von Einem, "Die Zeit ist ein Lied" 1988, Op79,4

from *Bald sing' ich das Schweigen* (4)

Du gehst und kommst dir aus dem Sinn

Gottfried von Einem, "Sommer" 1982, Op69,3, 1v(med).pf

from *Lebenstanz*

Einmal noch will ich die Kirschenblüten fallen seh'n

Gottfried von Einem, "Einmal noch" 1988, Op79,3

from *Bald sing' ich das Schweigen* (3)

Frau Erde schläft, Frau Erde träumt, der Mond küßt ihr grünes Haar

Gottfried von Einem, "Wie das Waldviertel zur Welt kam" 1983, Op71,1, 1v(med).pf

from *Waldviertler Lieder* (1)

Großvater, Großvater, Großvater Stein, alter Zauberer, düster und grau

Gottfried von Einem, "Steinlied" 1983, Op71,3, 1v(med).pf

from *Waldviertler Lieder* (3)

Ich atme dich mit allen Sternen aus

Gottfried von Einem, "...zwischen Seele und Gott" 1982, Op69,6, 1v(med).pf

from *Lebenstanz*

Ich habe dich erlöst, ich habe deinen Namen gerufen
Gottfried von Einem, "Diese alte Liebesgeschichte" 1982, Op69,1, 1v(med).pf
from *Lebenstanz*

Ist das der Tod? Als wäre nichts geschehen
Gottfried von Einem, "Ist das der Tod?" 1988, Op79,7
from *Bald sing' ich das Schweigen* (7)

Mein ganzer Leib ist Traurigkeit, ich hab' die Welt verloren
Gottfried von Einem, "Jetzt weiß ich, daß ich glücklich war" 1988, Op79,5
from *Bald sing' ich das Schweigen* (5)

Mein Haus steht unter Birken, der Kupfermond schläft auf dem Dach
Gottfried von Einem, "Mein liebes Haus" 1983, Op71,6, 1v(med).pf
from *Waldviertler Lieder* (6)

Noch hundert Jahre? Nicht ein einz'ges mehr!
Gottfried von Einem, "Warum gerade ich?" 1988, Op79,2
from *Bald sing' ich das Schweigen* (2)

Schau dich im Spiegel der Teiche, uraltes Elbenreich, an
Gottfried von Einem, "Waldviertler Botschaft" 1983, Op71,8, 1v(med).pf
from *Waldviertler Lieder* (8)

Schnee, du stille weiße Braut im einsamen Hochzeitsbett
Gottfried von Einem, "Schneelied" 1983, Op71,4, 1v(med).pf
from *Waldviertler Lieder* (4)

Sie sagten, ich soll nicht erschrekken, und ich erschrak
Gottfried von Einem, "Sie sagten, ich soll nicht erschrekken" 1988, Op79,1
from *Bald sing' ich das Schweigen* (1)

Stumm wächst die Einsamkeit
Gottfried von Einem, "Herbst" 1982, Op69,4, 1v(med).pf
from *Lebenstanz*

Vorüber ist der Kampf, vorbei die Trauer
Gottfried von Einem, "Vorüber ist der Kampf" 1988, Op79,6
from *Bald sing' ich das Schweigen* (6)

Was tut ein Baum den Ganzen Tag?
Gottfried von Einem, "Waldlied" 1983, Op71,2, 1v(med).pf
from *Waldviertler Lieder* (2)

Otto Inkermann: see "C. O. Sternau"

Marie Itzerott (1857-?)

Deine Seele hat die meine einst so wunderbar berührt
Max Reger, "An dich" 1902, Op66,8, 1v(med).pf

Eine Schale blühender Rosen duftet mir entgegen
Max Reger, "Rosen" 1901, Op55,4

Leise deinen Namen flüstern
Max Reger, "Verklärung" 1901, Op55,6

Quellen rauschen, Lüfte schweigen
Max Reger, "Sehnsucht" 1902, Op66,1, 1v(med).pf

Wenn Gott es hätt' gewollt, daß wir zusammen kämen
Max Reger, "Volkslied" 1901, Op79c,ii,1

Therese Albertine L. von Jacob (Therese Robinson) ("Talvj") (1797-1870)

Ach! mein kühler Wasserquell! Ach! meine Rose, rosenroth!
Carl Loewe, "Mädchen und Rose" 1824, Op15,1
translated from the Serbian, from Wuk Stephanowitsch Karadschitsch

Herr Dÿring ritt wohl durch das Land
Carl Loewe, "Der Mutter Geist" 1824, Op8,2

Hinterm Berge dort, dem grünen, tönt ein heller Schrei zu Zeiten
Carl Loewe, "Kapitulation" 1824, Op15,6
translated from the Serbian, from Wuk Stephanowitsch Karadschitsch

Komm, o Bruder, in die helle Sonne
Carl Loewe, "Überraschung" 1824, Op15,3
translated from the Serbian, from Wuk Stephanowitsch Karadschitsch

Singt ein Falk' all die Nacht durch, dicht vor den Fenstern des Milan
Carl Loewe, "Des Jünglings Segen" 1824, Op15,4
translated from the Serbian, from Wuk Stephanowitsch Karadschitsch

Trallallala, mein Liebchen, was hast du mir nicht gesagt
Carl Loewe, "Beim Tanze" 1824, Op15,2
translated from the Serbian, from Wuk Stephanowitsch Karadschitsch

Will die Holde sich ergehen
Carl Loewe, "Ihr Spaziergang" 1819, Op9,iv,4

Winter vorbei, Herzchen, mein Liebchen!
Carl Loewe, "Des Jünglings Segen" 1824, Op15,5
translated from the Serbian, from Wuk Stephanowitsch Karadschitsch

Johann Georg Jacobi (1740-1814)

Bei der Liebe reinsten Flammen glänzt das arme Hüttendach
Franz Schubert, "An Chloen" 1816, D462

Da wo die Tausendschönchen blühn
Johann Rudolf Zumsteeg, "Das Marienlied" 1802pub
from *Kleine Balladen und Lieder, viertes Heft*

Es ging ein Mann zur Frühlingszeit
Franz Schubert, "Die Perle" 1816, D466

Holdes Mädchen! unser Leben war ein frohes Hirtenspiel
Johann Holzer, "An Chloe" 1779pub
Leopold Kozeluch, "An Chloen" 1785?

Leiser nannt' ich deinen Namen
Josef Antonín Štěpán, "Liebesbund" 1778-79pub
Joseph Haydn, "Der erste Kuß" 1781/84, XXVIa Nr.3

Ruh'n in Frieden alle Seelen
Franz Schubert, "Litaney auf das Fest Aller Seelen" 1816, D343

Sagt wo sind die Veilchen hin?
Johann Abraham Peter Schulz, "Vergänglichkeit" 1782-90pub
J. J. Grünwald, "Nach einem alten Liede" 1785pub
Josefine Lang, "Die Veilchen" Op4,2

Todesstille deckt das Thal
Franz Schubert, "In der Mitternacht" 1816, D464

Wälze dich hinweg, du wildes Feuer!
Franz Schubert, "Lied des Orpheus, als er in die Hölle ging" 1816, D474

Wenn die Lieb' aus deinen blauen
Wolfgang Amadeus Mozart, "An Chloe" 1787, K524

Wie Feld und Au' so blinkend im Thau! (see note under Goethe: "Wie Feld und Au'...")
Johann Friedrich Reichardt, "Im Sommer" 1781pub
Robert Franz, "Im Sommer" 1856pub, Op16,2
Hugo Wolf, "Im Sommer" 1876, Op13,1, ttbb
Robert Kahn, "Im Sommer" 1896, Op23,2
Othmar Schoeck, "Im Sommer" 1907, Op17,1, 1v(med).pf

Will singen euch im alten Ton ein Lied von Lieb' und Treu'
Franz Schubert, "Hochzeitlied" 1816, D463

Wo die Taub' in stillen Buchen ihren Tauber sich erwählt
Franz Schubert, "Trauer der Liebe" 1816, D465

Ludwig Jacobowski (1868-1900)

Ach, uns're leuchtenden Tage glänzen wie ewige Sterne
Joseph Marx, "Leuchtende Tage" 1902, 1v(med).pf
Hermann Zilcher, "Leuchtende Tage" 1904?pub, Op12,3
Hans Pfitzner, "Leuchtende Tage" 1931, Op40,1

Alte Gruben schaufle um, tiefer werden sie und breiter
Max Reger, "Sehnsucht" 1902-03, Op70,9

Auf deinem Bild in schwarzem Rahmen
Max Reger, "Dein Bild" 1902-03, Op70,12

Dem Auge fern, dem Herzen nah!
Alban Berg, "Grabschrift" 1904

Duld' es still, wenn von den Zweigen
Max Reger, "Maienblüten" 1902, Op66,5, 1v(med).pf
Joseph Marx, "Maienblüten" 1909

Es ist ein Ring gebogen, der ist nicht blank von Glück!
Max Reger, "Das Ringlein" 1903, Op75,13, 1v(med).pf

Höre mich, Ewiger, höre mich, Ewiger, Allerbarmer
Max Reger, "Hymnus der Liebe" 1914, Op136, bar(alt).orch

Ich aber weiß, ich seh dich manche Nacht
Hans Pfitzner, "Ich aber weiß" 1901, Op11,2

Ich weiß, ich träume im Grabe schon viele tausend Jahre
Max Reger, "Totensprache" 1901, Op62,12, 1v(med).pf

In deinen Liedern lebt mein Leben
Max Reger, "Eine Seele" 1902, Op68,1, 1v(med).pf

Keinen Vater, der das Kinn mir hebt
Max Reger, "Der Narr" 1901, Op55,5

Und der Nachbarssohn, der Ruprecht
Max Reger, "Kindergeschichte" 1902, Op66,12, 1v(med).pf

Jens Peter Jacobsen (1847-1885)

Meine Braut führ' ich heim
Alexander Zemlinsky, "Meine Braut führ' ich heim" 1901?, Op10,4
from *Ehetanzlied und andere Gesänge*

Nacht ist es jetzt, und das Gestirn, das Gott gesetzt
Alexander Zemlinsky, "Turmwächterlied" 1900?, Op8,1
translated by Robert F. Arnold
from *Turmwächterlied und andere Gesänge*

Rosen senken ihr Haupt so schwer von Tau und Duft
Paul von Klenau, "Im Garten des Serail" 1914pub
translated by Stefan George

Schweige, geliebteste Fraue, leis' laß uns schreiten zu zwein
Paul von Klenau, "Landschaft" 1914pub
German translation by A. M.

Seht, es war einmal ein König
Alexander Zemlinsky, "Irmelin Rose" 1900?, Op7,4
translated by Robert F. Arnold
from *Irmelin Rose und andere Gesänge*

So voll und reich wand noch das Leben nimmer euch seinen Kranz
Arnold Schönberg, "Hochzeitslied" 1899-1903, Op3,4, 1v(med).pf

Und hat der Tag all seine Qual
Alexander Zemlinsky, "Und hat der Tag all seine Qual" 1900?, Op8,2
translated by Robert F. Arnold
from *Turmwächterlied und andere Gesänge*

Johannes Jaeger

Mein liebes Kind schlaf ein!
Othmar Schoeck, "Wiegenlied" 1947, o.op44

Maria Jäger (1817-1856)

Dass ich an Dich denke immerdar
Robert Franz, "Denk' ich dein!" 1865?pub, Op21,2

O, Mond, o lösch' dein gold'nes Licht
Robert Franz, "O, Mond, o lösch' dein gold'nes Licht" 1865?pub, Op21,3

Vorüber der Mai, die selige Zeit
Robert Franz, "Vorüber der Mai" 1870?pub, Op22,2

Jakob von Warte (2nd half 13th century)

Man soll hören süsses Singen
Felix Mendelssohn, "Maienlied" 1828pub, Op8,7

Janke

Begrüßet mit Tönen und Liedern den Tag
Carl Friedrich Zelter, "Gesang zum Jahresfeste der Luisenstiftung" 3v.ch

"Jean Paul" (Johann Paul Friedrich Richter) (1763-1825)

Wach' auf Geliebte, der Morgen schimmert
Jan Bedřich Kittl, "Ständchen" 183-?, Op4,1

Aloys (Isidor) Jeitteles (1794-1858)
Auf dem Hügel sitz' ich spähend
Ludwig van Beethoven, "Auf dem Hügel sitz' ich spähend" 1815-16, Op98,1
from *An die ferne Geliebte*

Diese Wolken in den Höhen
Ludwig van Beethoven, "Diese Wolken in den Höhen" 1815-16, Op98,4
from *An die ferne Geliebte*

Es kehret der Maien, es blühet die Au'
Ludwig van Beethoven, "Es kehret der Maien, es blühet die Au'" 1815-16, Op98,5
from *An die ferne Geliebte*

Leichte Segler in den Höhen
Ludwig van Beethoven, "Leichte Segler in den Höhen" 1815-16, Op98,3
from *An die ferne Geliebte*

Nimm sie hin denn, diese Lieder
Ludwig van Beethoven, "Nimm sie hin denn, diese Lieder" 1815-16, Op98,6
from *An die ferne Geliebte*

Wo die Berge so blau aus dem nebligen Grau
Ludwig van Beethoven, "Wo die Berge so blau aus dem nebligen Grau" 1815-16, Op98,2
from *An die ferne Geliebte*

Friedrike Magdalena Jerusalem (1756-1836)
Da eben seinen Lauf vollbracht
Maria Therese Paradis, "Da eben seinen Lauf vollbracht" 1784-86
from *Zwölf Lieder auf ihrer Reise in Musik gesetzt*

O Elise, nicht nur für die Freuden
Johann Rudolf Zumsteeg, "An Elisen" 1803pub
from *Kleine Balladen und Lieder, sechstes Heft*

Lionel Pigot Johnson (1867-1902)
Ein Wort in den Winden, ein Wort auf den Wassern
Harald Genzmer, "Auf Morfydd" 1990, sop.pf
from *Sechs Lieder nach angelsächsischen Dichtern* (5)

Moritz Jókai (1825-1904)
Der Hain widerhallt von der Nachtigall Sang
Franz Liszt, "Des toten Dichters Liebe" 1874, declamation.pf
translated from the Hungarian by Adolf Dux

Friedrich Georg Jünger (1898-1977)
Das Geistige ist wie das Blütenleben, das sich in Lüften regt
Ernst Pepping, "Gleichnisse" 1949pub
from *Haus- und Trostbuch* (13)
Ernst Pepping, "Gleichnisse" 1949pub
from *Vaterland* (4)

Dem Fürsten und dem Bettler ziemt nicht und nicht dem Weisen
Ernst Pepping, "Epilog" 1949pub
from *Vaterland* (2)

Der Kuckuck ruft nicht mehr, der stete Rufer
Ernst Pepping, "An Lotte" 1949pub
from *Vaterland* (8)

Ein Körnchen Ambra lasse ich gelten
Ernst Pepping, "Ambra und Moschus" 1949pub
from *Haus- und Trostbuch* (14)

Fährmann, ahoi! Ahoi! Hinunter treibt es das Boot
Ernst Pepping, "Der Fährmann" 1949pub
from *Vaterland* (9)

Gibt es denn wohl bangere Mienen als die Deinen?
Ernst Pepping, "Die Schüchterne" 1949pub
from *Haus- und Trostbuch* (26)

Ihr Stimmen! Was denn ruft ihr mir, Flüsterer?
Ernst Pepping, "Der Frühling" 1949pub
from *Vaterland* (7)

Man sagt, daß Rosen, die bei Tannen gepflanzt sind
Ernst Pepping, "Rosen und Tannen" 1949pub
from *Haus- und Trostbuch* (27)

Rufst du, Kuckuck? So ganz zur Unzeit rufst du
Ernst Pepping, "Der erste Kuckuck" 1949pub
from *Vaterland* (6)

Tage, wie geht ihr dahin, o Tage, wie schnell doch enteilt ihr!
Ernst Pepping, "Flucht der Tage" 1949pub
from *Vaterland* (3)

Urnen füllen sich und Krüge
Ernst Pepping, "Alter Friedhof" 1949pub
from *Haus- und Trostbuch* (37)

Vaterland ist mir das Lied, ist der offne helle Gesang mir
Ernst Pepping, "Motto" 1949pub
from *Vaterland* (1)

Wer Kastor ruft, muß Polydeukos nennen
Ernst Pepping, "Die Dioskuren" 1949pub
from *Haus- und Trostbuch* (16)

Wie silbernes Geschirr sich stößt, so klingen
Ernst Pepping, "Wintermorgen" 1949pub
from *Haus- und Trostbuch* (8)

Wie Uferland, das in der Feuchte blühet, lieb ich das Leben
Ernst Pepping, "Lebensgefühl" 1949pub
from *Vaterland* (5)

Walther Jung

Des Abends Rosen sind abgeblüht
Eduard Lassen, "Grüssen" Op52,3

Karl Wilhelm Justi (1767-1846)

Es pranget ein Garten im westlichen Strahl
Ferdinand Ries, "Der Garten der Jugend" 1835pub, Op180,1

Was drückt, O Holde, dich für Last?
Ferdinand Ries, "Der Jäger und die Hirten" 1829/30pub, Op154,6

J. C. K.

Wein' aus deine Freude! Wein' aus deinen Schmerz!
Josefine Lang, "Wein' aus deine Freude" WoO

Franz Kafka (1883-1924)

Ach, was wird uns hier bereitet?
Ernst Krenek, "Ach, was wird uns hier bereitet?" 1937-38, Op82,5

Darauf kommt es an, wenn einem ein Schwert in die Seele schneidet
Alexander Goehr, "Darauf kommt es an" 1979, Op41,7, 1v(low).pf
from *Das Gesetz der Quadrille*

Das Gesetz der Quadrille ist klar
Alexander Goehr, "Das Gesetz der Quadrille" 1979, Op41,1, 1v(low).pf
from *Das Gesetz der Quadrille*

Das Gesetz der Quadrille ist klar . . . Aber . . .
Alexander Goehr, "Das Gesetz der Quadrille (2)" 1979, Op41,8, 1v(low).pf
from *Das Gesetz der Quadrille*

Das Trauerjahr war vorüber
Alexander Goehr, "Das Trauerjahr war vorüber" 1979, Op41,9, 1v(low).pf
from *Das Gesetz der Quadrille*

Der Neger, der von der Weltausstellung
Alexander Goehr, "Der Neger" 1979, Op41,4, 1v(low).pf
from *Das Gesetz der Quadrille*

Du kannst dich zurückhalten von den Leiden der Welt
Ernst Krenek, "Du kannst dich zurückhalten von den Leiden der Welt" 1937-38, Op82,4

Du Rabe, sagte ich, du alter Unglücksrabe
Alexander Goehr, "Du Rabe" 1979, Op41,6, 1v(low).pf
from *Das Gesetz der Quadrille*

Kämpfte er nicht genug?
Ernst Krenek, "Kämpfte er nicht genug?" 1937-38, Op82,2

Noch spielen die Jagdhunde im Hof
Ernst Krenek, "Noch spielen die Jagdhunde im Hof" 1937-38, Op82,3
Alexander Goehr, "Noch spielen die Jagdhunde im Hof" 1979, Op41,2, 1v(low).pf
from *Das Gesetz der Quadrille*

Nur ein Wort, nur eine Bitte
Ernst Krenek, "Nur ein Wort, nur eine Bitte" 1937-38, Op82,1

So fest wie die Hand den Stein hält
Alexander Goehr, "So fest wie die Hand" 1979, Op41,5, 1v(low).pf
from *Das Gesetz der Quadrille*

Staunend sahen wir das grosse Pferd
Alexander Goehr, "Staunend sahen wir das grosse Pferd" 1979, Op41,3, 1v(low).pf
from *Das Gesetz der Quadrille*

Karl August Timotheus Kahlert (1807-1864)

Hier steh' ich einsam auf dem Fels im Meer
Carl Loewe, "Sanct Helena" 1853, Op126

Max Kalbeck (1850-1921)

Leblos gleitet Blatt um Blatt still und traurig von den Bäumen
Johannes Brahms, "Letztes Glück" 1877?, Op104,3, saatbb

Störe nicht den leisen Schlummer
Johannes Brahms, "Nachtwandler" 1877?, Op86,3, 1v(low).pf

Johann Nepomuk Ritter von Kalchberg (1765-1827)

Die ihr an süsser Lieder Schall
J. J. Grünwald, "Die tote Nachtigall" 1785pub

Überall, wohin mein Auge blicket, herrschet Liebe
Franz Schubert, "Die Macht der Liebe" 1815, D308

Kalidasa (Indian, 5th century)

Beschwert von Blüten beugen sich
Alexander Zemlinsky, "Regenzeit" 1937/38, Op27,11
translated by Maurice Wright

Der Duft nach Sandel, den die seidenen Fächer
Alexander Zemlinsky, "Sommer" 1937/38, Op27,2
translated by Maurice Wright

Der Wind des Herbstes weht den feinen Duft
Alexander Zemlinsky, "Der Wind des Herbstes" 1937/38, Op27,6
translated by Maurice Wright

Jetzt ist die Zeit, die um die grünen Ränder der Teiche
Alexander Zemlinsky, "Jetzt ist die Zeit" 1937/38, Op27,4
translated by Maurice Wright

Nun liegen Kränze um die schönen Brüste der Mädchen
Alexander Zemlinsky, "Frühling" 1937/38, Op27,3
translated by Maurice Wright

Hans Kaltneker (1895-1919)

Du reine Frau aus Licht und Elfenbein
Erich Wolfgang Korngold, "Versuchung" 1924, Op18,3

In meine innige Nacht geh' ich ein
Erich Wolfgang Korngold, "In meine innige Nacht" 1924, Op18,1

Tu ab den Schmerz, entflieh, Verlangen!
Erich Wolfgang Korngold, "Tu ab den Schmerz" 1924, Op18,2

Kurt Kamlah (1866-1928)

Blasse Blüten neigen ihre duftende Pracht
Erich J. Wolff, "Im Entschlafen" 1914pub, Lieder No.10

Ich bin häßlich, liebe Mutter, sagen mir die Leute täglich
Erich J. Wolff, "Das kranke Kind" 1914pub, Lieder No.27

Silberne Mondesstrahlen glänzen auf tiefblauer Flut
Erich J. Wolff, "Venedig" 1914pub, Lieder No.48

Käthe Lotte Kamossa (1911-)

Die du dich an uns verschwendest
Louis Ferdinand, "An die Sonne" 1966pub

Komm' in aller Tage stille Dunkelheit
Louis Ferdinand, "Kleines Abendlied" 1953pub

Mein sind blaue Himmelsstrahlen
Louis Ferdinand, "Ein Schmetterling singt" 1966pub

Nebel wallen über kahles Land
Louis Ferdinand, "Nebel" 1966pub

Karl Friedrich Ludwig Kannegiesser (1781-1861)

Bald heisst es wieder
Carl Maria von Weber, "Gute Nacht" 1819, Op68,5, 4mv

Ein Kind ist uns geboren!
Carl Maria von Weber, "Freiheitslied" 1819, Op68,3, 4mv

Ich tumm'le mich auf der Haide
Carl Maria von Weber, "Elfenlied" 1819, Op80,3

Ja, freue dich
Carl Maria von Weber, "Ermunterung" 1819, Op68,2, 4mv

Judäa, hochgelobtes Land, und Bethlehem, beglückte Stätte
Carl Maria von Weber, "Sehnsucht (Weihnachtslied)" 1819, Op80,2

Otto von Kapff (1855-?)

Die Luft ist trübe, der Wind weht kalt
Ferruccio Busoni, "Lied der Klage" 1878, Op38, alt.pf

Siegfried Kapper (1821-1879)

Ach, und du mein kühles Wasser!
Johannes Brahms, "Mädchenlied" 1878, Op85,3

Hebt ein Falke sich empor
Johannes Brahms, "Der Falke" 1883?, Op93a,5, satb

Ruft die Mutter, ruft der Tochter über drei Gebirge
Johannes Brahms, "Mädchenfluch" 1877, Op69,9
after the Serbian

Schwor ein junges Mädchen: Blumen nie zu tragen
Johannes Brahms, "Vorschneller Schwur" 1883/84?, Op95,5

Stand das Mädchen, stand am Bergesabhang
Johannes Brahms, "Das Mädchen" 1883?, Op93a,2, satb
Johannes Brahms, "Das Mädchen" 1883, Op95,1

"Karlopago:" see Karl Ziegler

Hella Karstein

Nun zieht mit seinem goldnen Schein das liebe Christkind wieder ein
Engelbert Humperdinck, "An das Christkind" 1905

Moritz Kartscher (1793?-1834)

Die Lippe brennt, die Wange glüht
Louis Spohr, "Der erste Kuss" 1816, Op41,5

Gustav Kastropp (1844-1925)

Der Nebel auf dem Weiher spinnt langsam sich über das Land
Hugo Kaun, "Abend" 1905pub, Op27,1

Im zitternden Mondlicht wiegen schlummernde Blumen sich sacht
Eugen d'Albert, "Strandlust" 1898?pub, Op17,4

Lass mich in den dunklen Grund deiner Augen schauen
Franz Ries, "Trennung" before 1891

Eduard Ernst Heinrich Kauffer (1824-1874)
Du bist im Strahlenkleide die Sonne, lieb und mild
Franz Abt, "Blau-Äugelein" 1873pub, Op158,4

Alexander Kaufmann (1817-1893)
Die Wasserlilie kichert leis': ich muss euch ein Ding verraten
Hugo Brückler, "Verrat" 187-?pub, Nachlass
Erik Meyer-Helmund, "Verrath" 1886-88
Hans Pfitzner, "Verrat" 1888/89, Op2,7

Es schliesst der dunkle Wald uns ein
Johanna Kinkel, "In der Bucht" Op17,5

(Johann) Philipp Kaufmann (1802-1846)
Du arme, kleine Nachtigall
Franz Liszt, "Die tote Nachtigall" 1844pub
Franz Liszt, "Die tote Nachtigall" 1878

Wie kann ich froh und lustig sein?
Felix Mendelssohn, "Wie kann ich froh und lustig sein?" 2sop.pf

Agnes Kayser-Langerhannß (1818-1902)
Der Abend schaut durchs Fensterlein
Franz Ries, "Wiegenlied" before 1891

Gottfried Keller (1819-1890)
Aber auch den Föhrenwald
Othmar Schoeck, "Aus den Waldliedern II" 1943, Op55,9, 1v(med).pf
from *Unter Sternen*

Aber ein kleiner goldener Stern
Othmar Schoeck, "Aus: Ein Tagewerk II" 1941-43, Op55,25, 1v(med).pf
from *Unter Sternen*

Alle meine Weisheit hing in meinen Haaren
Felix Weingartner, "Alle meine Weisheit" 1896pub, Op22,4

Als endlich sie den Sarg hier abgesetzt
Othmar Schoeck, "Als endlich sie den Sarg hier abgesetzt" 1926, Op40,6, bar.orch
from *Lebendig begraben*

Arm in Arm und Kron' an Krone steht der Eichenwald verschlungen
Othmar Schoeck, "Aus den Waldliedern I" 1941-43, Op55,8, 1v(med).pf
from *Unter Sternen*

Augen, meine lieben Fensterlein
Wilhelm Kempff, "Abendlied" 1917, Op7,1
Othmar Schoeck, "Abendlied" 1941-43, Op55,12, 1v(med).pf
from *Unter Sternen*

Berge dein Haupt, wenn ein König vorbeigeht
Othmar Schoeck, "Berge dein Haupt" 1923, Op38,8
from *Gaselen*

Da hab ich gar die Rose aufgegessen
Othmar Schoeck, "Da hab ich gar die Rose aufgegessen" 1926, Op40,8, bar.orch
from *Lebendig begraben*

Da lieg' ich denn, ohnmächtiger Geselle
Othmar Schoeck, "Da lieg' ich denn, ohnmächtiger Geselle" 1926, Op40,2, bar.orch
from *Lebendig begraben*

Das Gärtlein dicht verschlossen
Felix Weingartner, "Das Gärtlein dicht verschlossen" 1896pub, Op22,11

Das Köhlerweib ist trunken, und singt im Wald
Hugo Wolf, "Das Köhlerweib ist trunken" 1890
from *Alte Weisen, Sechs Gedichte von Keller*
Hans Sommer, "Das Köhlerweib ist trunken" 1893?pub, Op16,3
from *Gedichte von Gottfried Keller*
Ernest Vietor, "Das Köhlerweib ist Trunken" 1936, Op15,1

Deiner bunten Blasen Kinderfreude
Othmar Schoeck, "Tod und Dichter" 1941-43, Op55,22, 1v(med).pf
from *Unter Sternen*

Den Linden ist zu Füßen tief
Othmar Schoeck, "Fahrewohl" 1928, Op35,1

Der erste Tannenbaum, den ich gesehen
Othmar Schoeck, "Der erste Tannenbaum, den ich gesehen" 1926, Op40,12, bar.orch
from *Lebendig begraben*

Der Herr gab dir ein gutes Augenpaar
Othmar Schoeck, "Der Herr gab dir ein gutes Augenpaar" 1923, Op38,3
from *Gaselen*

Der schönste Tannenbaum, den ich gesehn
Othmar Schoeck, "Der schönste Tannenbaum, den ich gesehn" 1926, Op40,13, bar.orch
from *Lebendig begraben*

Die Lor' sitzt im Garten, kehrt den Rücken zu mal
Hans Sommer, "Die Lor' sitzt im Garten" 1893?pub, Op16,5
from *Gedichte von Gottfried Keller*

Die Zeit geht nicht, sie stehet still
Othmar Schoeck, "Die Zeit geht nicht" 1941-43, Op55,15, 1v(med).pf
from *Unter Sternen*

Du milchjunger Knabe, wie siehst du mich an?
Johannes Brahms, "Therese" 1878, Op86,1, 1v(low).pf
Hugo Wolf, "Du milchjunger Knabe" 1890
from *Alte Weisen, Sechs Gedichte von Keller*
Hans Sommer, "Du milchjunger Knabe" 1893?pub, Op16,6
from *Gedichte von Gottfried Keller*
Hans Pfitzner, "Du milchjunger Knabe" 1923, Op33,3

Durch Bäume dringt ein leiser Ton
Othmar Schoeck, "Stilleben (aus den Rheinbildern)" 1941-43, Op55,10, 1v(med).pf
from *Unter Sternen*

Ein armer Teufel ist der Schuft
Felix Weingartner, "Lied vom Schuft" 1896pub, Op22,7

Ein Häuptling ritt geehrt im Land, gleich einem der Propheten
Anna Teichmüller, "Ein Berittener" 1910pub, Op25,2

Ein Meister bin ich worden
Othmar Schoeck, "In der Trauer" 1941-43, Op55,19, 1v(med).pf
from *Unter Sternen*

Es donnert über die Pfaffengaß'
Othmar Schoeck, "Frühgesicht (aus den Rheinbildern)" 1941-43, Op55,17, 1v(med).pf
from *Unter Sternen*

Es ist ein stiller Regentag
Othmar Schoeck, "Trübes Wetter" 1941-43, Op55,16, 1v(med).pf
from *Unter Sternen*

Es ist nicht Selbstsucht und nicht Eitelkeit
Othmar Schoeck, "Den Zweifellosen II" 1941-43, Op55,21, 1v(med).pf
from *Unter Sternen*

Es wandert eine schöne Sage
Othmar Schoeck, "Frühlingsglaube" 1941-43, Op55,18, 1v(med).pf
from *Unter Sternen*

Flack're, ew'ges Licht im Tal
Othmar Schoeck, "Flack're, ew'ges Licht im Tal" 1941-43, Op55,14, 1v(med).pf
from *Unter Sternen*

Ha! was ist das? Die Sehnen zucken wieder
Othmar Schoeck, "Ha! was ist das?" 1926, Op40,3, bar.orch
from *Lebendig begraben*

Heerwagen, mächtig Sternbild der Germanen
Othmar Schoeck, "Heerwagen, mächtig Sternbild der Germanen" 1931-33, Op47,Ve, bar.4str
from *Notturno*

Horch – endlich zittert es durch meine Bretter!
Othmar Schoeck, "Horch – endlich zittert es durch meine Bretter!" 1926, Op40,7, bar.orch
from *Lebendig begraben*

Horch! Stimmen und Geschrei, doch kaum zu hören
Othmar Schoeck, "Horch! Stimmen und Geschrei, doch kaum zu hören" 1926, Op40,5, bar.orch
from *Lebendig begraben*

Hüll ein mich in die grünen Dekken
Othmar Schoeck, "Abendlied an die Natur" 1941-43, Op55,6, 1v(med).pf
from *Unter Sternen*

Ich denke oft an's blaue Meer
Felix Weingartner, "Ich denke oft an's blaue Meer" 1900pub, Op27,2
from *Drei Gedichte aus Gottfried Kellers Jugendzeit*

Ich fürcht' nit Gespenster, keine Hexen und Feen
Felix Weingartner, "Ich fürcht' nit Gespenster" 1896pub, Op22,3
Hans Pfitzner, "Ich fürcht' nit Gespenster" 1923, Op33,2

Ich halte dich in meinem Arm, du hältst die Rose zart
Arnold Schönberg, "Ghasel" 1903-05, Op6,5
Othmar Schoeck, "Ich halte dich in meinem Arm" 1923, Op38,7
from *Gaselen*

Ich will spiegeln mich in jenen Tagen
Othmar Schoeck, "Jugendgedenken" 1914, Op24b,10

Im Herbst verblichen liegt das Land
Othmar Schoeck, "Vision" 1949, Op63, mch.orch

In Gold und Purpur tief verhüllt
Othmar Schoeck, "Sonnenuntergang" 1941-43, Op55,2, 1v(med).pf
from *Unter Sternen*

Ja, hätt' ich ein verlass'nes Liebchen nun
Othmar Schoeck, "Ja, hätt' ich ein verlass'nes Liebchen nun" 1926, Op40,10, bar.orch
from *Lebendig begraben*

Jetzt ist des Winters grimmer Frost
Othmar Schoeck, "Für ein Gesangfest im Frühling" 1942, Op54, mch.orch

Klagt mich nicht an, dass ich vor Leid
Anna Teichmüller, "Klagt mich nicht an" 1907pub, Op12,2

Läg' ich, wo es Hyänen gibt, im Sand
Othmar Schoeck, "Läg' ich, wo es Hyänen gibt, im Sand" 1926, Op40,4, bar.orch
from *Lebendig begraben*

Langsam und schimmernd fiel ein Regen
Johannes Brahms, "Abendregen" 1875, Op70,4

Mann merkt, dass der Wein geraten war
Ernest Vietor, "Der Bettler" 1936, Op15,2

Mich tadelt der Fanatiker, in deinen Armen weich zu ruh'n
Othmar Schoeck, "Mich tadelt der Fanatiker" 1923, Op38,9
from *Gaselen*

Mir glänzen die Augen wie der Himmel so klar
Hans Sommer, "Mir glänzen die Augen" 1893?pub, Op16,1
from *Gedichte von Gottfried Keller*
Hans Pfitzner, "Mir glänzen die Augen" 1923, Op33,1

Mit dem grauen Felsensaal
Othmar Schoeck, "Das Tal (aus den Rheinbildern)" 1941-43, Op55,11, 1v(med).pf
from *Unter Sternen*

Nicht ein Flügelschlag ging durch die Welt
Felix Weingartner, "Winternacht" 1896pub, Op22,8
Robert Gund, "Winternacht" 1919, Op39,1

Nun bin ich untreu worden
Felix Weingartner, "Unruhe der Nacht" 1905, Op35,1, 1v(low).orch
Othmar Schoeck, "Unruhe der Nacht" 1941-43, Op55,7, 1v(med).pf
from *Unter Sternen*

Nun schmücke mir dein dunkles Haar mit Rosen
Othmar Schoeck, "Nun schmücke mir dein dunkles Haar mit Rosen" 1923, Op38,5
from *Gaselen*

O ein Glöcklein klingelt mir früh und spät
Felix Weingartner, "Doppelgleichniss" 1896pub, Op22,10

O heiliger Augustin im Himmelssaal
Othmar Schoeck, "O heiliger Augustin im Himmelssaal" 1923, Op38,2
from *Gaselen*

Perlen der Weisheit sind mir deine Zähne!
Othmar Schoeck, "Perlen der Weisheit sind mir deine Zähne!" 1923, Op38,6
from *Gaselen*

Röschen biß den Apfel an
Hans Pfitzner, "Röschen biß den Apfel an" 1923, Op33,6

Schon hat die Nacht den Silberschrein des Himmels aufgetan
Felix Weingartner, "Schifferliedchen" 1896pub, Op22,6
Othmar Schoeck, "Schifferliedchen" 1906, Op6,2
Hugo Kaun, "Schifferliedchen" 1908pub, Op79,1

Schon war die letzte Schwalbe fort
Hans Sommer, "Die Begegnung" 1893?pub, Op16,7
from *Gedichte von Gottfried Keller*

Seht ihr die zwei Kirschenbäumchen
Felix Weingartner, "Plauderwäsche" 1900pub, Op27,1
from *Drei Gedichte aus Gottfried Kellers Jugendzeit*

Sieh den Abendstern erblinken tief im Westen
Felix Weingartner, "Nachhall" 1896pub, Op22,9

Siehst du den Stern im fernsten Blau
Othmar Schoeck, "Siehst du den Stern" 1941-43, Op55,3, 1v(med).pf
from *Unter Sternen*

Singt mein Schatz wie ein Fink, sing ich Nachtigallensang
Johannes Brahms, "Salome" 1877, Op69,8
Hugo Wolf, "Singt mein Schatz wie ein Fink" 1890
from *Alte Weisen, Sechs Gedichte von Keller*
Hans Sommer, "Singt mein Schatz wie ein Fink" 1893?pub, Op16,4
from *Gedichte von Gottfried Keller*
Hans Pfitzner, "Singt mein Schatz wie ein Fink" 1923, Op33,5

Tretet ein, hoher Krieger
Hugo Wolf, "Tretet ein, hoher Krieger" 1890
from *Alte Weisen, Sechs Gedichte von Keller*
Hans Pfitzner, "Tretet ein, hoher Krieger" 1923, Op33,7

Und wieder schlägt's – ein Viertel erst und zwölfe!
Othmar Schoeck, "Und wieder schlägt's – ein Viertel erst und zwölfe!" 1926, Op40,14, bar.orch
from *Lebendig begraben*

Unser ist das Los der Epigonen
Othmar Schoeck, "Unser ist das Los der Epigonen" 1923, Op38,1
from *Gaselen*

Verbogen und zerkniffen war der vordre Rand an meinem Hut
Othmar Schoeck, "Verbogen und zerkniffen" 1923, Op38,10
from *Gaselen*

Vom Lager stand ich mit dem Frühlicht auf
Othmar Schoeck, "Aus: Ein Tagewerk I" 1941-43, Op55,24, 1v(med).pf
from *Unter Sternen*

Wandl' ich in dem Morgentau
Hugo Wolf, "Wandl' ich in dem Morgenthau" 1890
from *Alte Weisen, Sechs Gedichte von Keller*
Hans Sommer, "Wandl' ich in dem Morgenthau" 1893?pub, Op16,2
from *Gedichte von Gottfried Keller*
Hans Pfitzner, "Wandl' ich in dem Morgentau" 1923, Op33,4

War ein heimathloser Wand'rer
Felix Weingartner, "Irrlichter" 1900pub, Op27,3
from *Drei Gedichte aus Gottfried Kellers Jugendzeit*

Weise nicht von dir mein schlichtes Herz
Felix Weingartner, "Geübtes Herz" 1896pub, Op22,1
Arnold Schönberg, "Geübtes Herz" 1899-1903, Op3,5, 1v(med).pf

Welche tiefbewegten Lebensläufchen
Arnold Schönberg, "Die Aufgeregten" 1899-1903, Op3,2, 1v(med).pf

Wende dich, du kleiner Stern
Felix Weingartner, "Unter Sternen" 1896pub, Op22,12
Othmar Schoeck, "Unter Sternen" 1941-43, Op55,5, 1v(med).pf
from *Unter Sternen*

Wenn schlanke Lilien wandelten, vom Weste leis geschwungen
Felix Weingartner, "Wenn schlanke Lilien wandelten" 1896pub, Op22,2
Othmar Schoeck, "Wenn schlanke Lilien wandelten" 1923, Op38,4
from *Gaselen*

Wer ohne Leid, der ist auch ohne Liebe
Othmar Schoeck, "Den Zweifellosen I" 1941-43, Op55,20, 1v(med).pf
from *Unter Sternen*

Wie glänzt der helle Mond so kalt und fern
Hugo Wolf, "Wie glänzt der helle Mond" 1890
from *Alte Weisen, Sechs Gedichte von Keller*
Felix Weingartner, "Wie glänzt der helle Mond" 1896pub, Op22,5
Hans Pfitzner, "Wie glänzt der helle Mond" 1923, Op33,8

Wie herrlich wär's, zerschnittner Tannenbaum
Othmar Schoeck, "Wie herrlich wär's, zerschnittner Tannenbaum" 1926, Op40,11, bar.orch
from *Lebendig begraben*

Wie nun alles stirbt und endet
Paul Hindemith, "Erster Schnee" 1939, 4mv

Wie poltert es! - Abscheuliches Geroll
Othmar Schoeck, "Wie poltert es! – Abscheuliches Geroll" 1926, Op40,1, bar.orch
from *Lebendig begraben*

Wie schlafend unterm Flügel ein Pfau den Schnabel hält
Othmar Schoeck, "Trost der Kreatur" 1941-43, Op55,1, 1v(med).pf
from *Unter Sternen*

Willkommen klare Sommernacht
Felix Weingartner, "Stille der Nacht" 1905, Op35,2, 1v(low).orch
Othmar Schoeck, "Stille der Nacht" 1941-43, Op55,4, 1v(med).pf
from *Unter Sternen*

Willst du nicht dich schließen
Othmar Schoeck, "An das Herz" 1941-43, Op55,23, 1v(med).pf
from *Unter Sternen*

Wir wähnten lange recht zu leben
Othmar Schoeck, "Wir wähnten lange recht zu leben" 1941-43, Op55,13, 1v(med).pf
from *Unter Sternen*

Zwei Geliebte, treu verbunden, gehen durch die Welt spazieren
Johannes Brahms, "Kleine Hochzeits-Kantate" 1874, WoO 16, satb.pf

Zwölf hat's geschlagen – warum denn Mittag?
Othmar Schoeck, "Zwölf hat's geschlagen – warum denn Mittag?" 1926, Op40,9, bar.orch
from *Lebendig begraben*

Frederike Kempner (1836-1904)

Wenn der holde Frühling lenzt und man sich mit Veilchen kränzt
Felix Wolfes, "Frühlingslied" 1965

Josef Kenner (1794-1868)

Ein Fräulein schaut vom hohen Thurm
Franz Schubert, "Ballade" 1815, D134

Er fiel den Tod fürs Vaterland, den süssen der Befreiungsschlacht
Franz Schubert, "Grablied" 1815, D218

Gieb, Schwester, mir die Harf' herab
Franz Schubert, "Der Liedler" 1815, D209

Susanne Kerckhoff (1918-1950)

Der Abend schließt die samtne Tür
Louis Ferdinand, "Der Heimatlose" 1981pub

E. Kern

Du holder Lenz, du Blüthenduft, du süsser Nachtigallenton
Leopold Damrosch, "Dich lieb' ich inniglich" Op7,3

Justinus (Andreas Christian) Kerner (1786-1862)

Ach, ach, ich armes Klosterfräulein! (see also "Ich armes…")
Friedrich Silcher, "Das Klosterfräulein"
Johannes Brahms, "Klosterfräulein" 1852, Op61,2, 2v.pf
Richard Kursch, "Das Klosterfräulein" 1905pub, Op5,2

Dass du so krank geworden
Robert Schumann, "Wer machte dich so krank?" 1840, Op35,11

Dem Wandrer, dem verschwunden so Sonn' als Mondenlicht
Robert Schumann, "Trost im Gesang" 1840, Op142,1

Die Straßen, die ich gehe, so oft ich um mich sehe
Clara Schumann, "Der Wandrer" 1831?
Robert Gund, "Die Strassen, die ich gehe" 1894?, Op10,5

Dort unten in der Mühle saß ich in guter Ruh
Clara Schumann, "Der Wanderer in der Sägemühle" 1831?

Du bist vom Schlaf erstanden
Robert Schumann, "Stille Thränen" 1840, Op35,10

Du herrlich Glas, nun stehst du leer
Robert Schumann, "Auf das Trinkglas eines verstorbenen Freundes" 1840, Op35,6

Du junges Grün, du frisches Gras
Robert Schumann, "Erstes Grün" 1840, Op35,4

Ein Alphorn hör' ich schallen
Richard Strauss, "Alphorn" 1878, 1v.horn.pf
from *Jugendlieder*

Es war in des Maien mildem Glanz
Robert Schumann, "Der Wassermann" 1849, Op91,3, ssaa.pf(ad lib)
from *Romanzen für Frauenstimmen II*

Hörst du den Vogel singen?
Robert Schumann, "Alte Laute" 1840, Op35,12

Ich armes Klosterfräulein, o Mutter! (see also "Ach, ach, ich armes…")
Robert Schumann, "Klosterfräulein" 1849, Op69,3, ssaa.pf
from *Romanzen für Frauenstimmen I*

Könnt' ich dich in Liedern preisen
Robert Schumann, "Stille Liebe" 1840, Op35,8

Lass dich belauschen, du stille Nacht!
Luise Adolpha Le Beau, "In der Mondnacht" Op45,2, alt.vn.pf

Mir träumt', ich flög gar bange weit in die Welt hinaus
Johann Vesque von Püttlingen, "Der schwere Traum" 1863

Seh ich in das stille Thal
Robert Schumann, "Er und Sie" 1849, Op78,2, sop.ten.pf

Wär' ich nie aus euch gegangen, Wälder, hehr und wunderbar!
Robert Schumann, "Sehnsucht nach der Waldgegend" 1840, Op35,5

Wärst du nicht, heil'ger Abendschein!
Robert Schumann, "Frage" 1840, Op35,9

Weint auch einst kein Liebchen
Robert Schumann, "Sängers Trost" 1840, Op127,1

Weiss nicht, woher ich bin gekommen
Ernest Vietor, "Ein Spruch" 1937-38, Op16,3

Wenn durch Berg' und Thale draussen
Robert Schumann, "Lust der Sturmnacht" 1840, Op35,1

Wie dir geschah, so soll's auch mir geschehn
Luise Adolpha Le Beau, "Wie dir, so mir" Op45,1, alt.vn.pf

Wohlauf noch getrunken den funkelnden Wein!
Robert Schumann, "Wanderlust" 1840, Op35,3

Wohlauf und frisch gewandert in's unbekannte Land!
Robert Schumann, "Wanderung" 1840, Op35,7

Zu Augsburg steht ein hohes Haus
Louis Spohr, "Die Himmelsbraut" 1838, Op105,1
Robert Schumann, "Stirb, Lieb' und Freud'!" 1840, Op35,2

Zur Ruh', zur Ruh'! ihr müden Glieder
Hugo Wolf, "Zur Ruh', zur Ruh'!" 1883
from *Sechs Gedichte von Scheffel u.a.*

Alfred Kerr (1867-1948)

Die Händler und die Macher
Richard Strauss, "Die Händler und die Macher" 1918, Op66,11
from *Krämerspiegel*

Die Künstler sind die Schöpfer
Richard Strauss, "Die Künstler sind die Schöpfer" 1918, Op66,10
from *Krämerspiegel*

Drei Masken sah ich am Himmel stehn
Richard Strauss, "Drei Masken sah ich am Himmel stehn" 1918, Op66,4
from *Krämerspiegel*

Einst kam der Bock als Bote
Richard Strauss, "Einst kam der Bock als Bote" 1918, Op66,2
from *Krämerspiegel*

Es liebte einst ein Hase
Richard Strauss, "Es liebte einst ein Hase" 1918, Op66,3
from *Krämerspiegel*

Es war einmal ein Bock
Richard Strauss, "Es war einmal ein Bock" 1918, Op66,1
from *Krämerspiegel*

Es war mal eine Wanze
Richard Strauss, "Es war mal eine Wanze" 1918, Op66,9
from *Krämerspiegel*

Hast du ein Tongedicht vollbracht
Richard Strauss, "Hast du ein Tongedicht vollbracht" 1918, Op66,5
from *Krämerspiegel*

Laß Liebster, wenn ich tot bin, laß du von Klagen ab
Erich Wolfgang Korngold, "Sterbelied" 1918, Op14,1
after Christina Georgina Rossetti (1830-1894)
from *Lieder des Abschieds*

O lieber Künstler sei ermahnt
Richard Strauss, "O lieber Künstler sei ermahnt" 1918, Op66,6
from *Krämerspiegel*

O Schröpferschwarm, o Händlerkreis
Richard Strauss, "O Schröpferschwarm, o Händlerkreis" 1918, Op66,12
from *Krämerspiegel*

Unser Feind ist, grosser Gott
Richard Strauss, "Unser Feind ist, grosser Gott" 1918, Op66,7
from *Krämerspiegel*

Von Händlern wird die Kunst bedroht
Richard Strauss, "Von Händlern wird die Kunst bedroht" 1918, Op66,8
from *Krämerspiegel*

Wilhelm Kienzl (1857-1941)
Mein Lieb hat mich verlassen
Wilhelm Kienzl, "Vorbei!" 188-?, Op18,7

Hedwig Kiesekamp: see "Ludwig Rafael"

(Johann) Friedrich Kind (1768-1843)
Ahidi, ich liebe, ahidi, ich liebe!
Franz Schubert, "Hänflings Liebeswerbung" 1817, D552

Das Herz ist gewachsen. Es pocht in der Brust
Louis Spohr, "Des Mädchens Sehnsucht" 1816, Op41,1

Das Mädchen ging die Wies' entlang
Carl Maria von Weber, "Bach, Echo und Kuss" 1818, Op71,2, 1v.guit

Der Geisshirt steht am Felsenrand
Carl Maria von Weber, "Das Licht im Thale" 1822, J.286

Ein Veilchen blüht im Thale
Carl Maria von Weber, "Das Veilchen im Thale" 1817, Op66,1

Leise weht' es, leise wallte rings der Thau umher
Carl Maria von Weber, "Romanze" 1818, J.223, 1v.guit

Offerus war ein Lanzenknecht
Carl Loewe, "Der grosse Christoph" 1834, Op34

Phöbus, mit lokkerem Zügel
Carl Friedrich Zelter, "Abendlied im Freien" 3ten

Wenn die Maien grün sich kleiden
Carl Maria von Weber, "Lied der Hirtin" 1818, Op71,5

(Johann) Gottfried Kinkel (1815-1882)
Es ist so still geworden
Robert Schumann, "Abendlied" 1851-52, Op107,6

Ringsum auf allen Plätzen schläft unbewegt die Nacht
Johanna Kinkel, "Römische Nacht" 184-?, Op15,1

Johanna Kinkel, née Mockel (Johanna Mathieux) (1810-1858)
Ihr Liebe flüsternden Linden!
Johanna Kinkel, "Vorüberfahrt" Op7,3

O… du hast es gar zu gut, lieb Herzenskind
Johanna Kinkel, "Wiegenlied" Op10,4

Sitze hier an lieber Stelle
Johanna Kinkel, "Verlornes Glück" Op6,5

Heinrich Kipper (1875-1959)?
Ich hab ein kleines Gärtchen
Erich Wolfgang Korngold, "Das Heldengrab am Pruth" 1916, Op9,5

"Jucundus Fröhlich Klabund" (Alfred Henschke) (1890-1928)
Blond ist mein Haar, blau ist mein Blick
Carl Orff, "Blond ist mein Haar" 1919

Der Mond wird oft noch über den Syringen der Schwermut
Hanns Eisler, "Der Mond wird oft noch…" 1923, Op2,5

Du gabst mir immer wieder dein Herz und deine Lieder
Carl Orff, "Zwiegespräch" 1919

Erhebt euch, Freunde, tanzt mit meinem Wort!
Hanns Eisler, "Erhebt euch, Freunde" 1923, Op2,4

Herr, ich liebte aller Dinge Niederstes, Beflecktestes
Carl Orff, "Herr, ich liebte" 1919

Ich habe nie vermeint, mich selber zu erkennen
Hanns Eisler, "Ich habe nie vermeint" 1923, Op2,6

(August) Albert Theodor Kleinschmidt (1847-1924)
Tiefes, tiefes Schweigen waltet ringsum
Max Reger, "Friedhofsgang" 1893, Op12,1

Friedrich August Kleinschmidt (1749-?)
Du sagtest, Freund, an diesen Ort komm' ich zurück
Ludwig van Beethoven, "Der Mann von Wort" 1816, Op99

Wär' ich ein muntres Vögelein
Johann Rudolf Zumsteeg, "Liedchen" 1802pub
from *Kleine Balladen und Lieder, viertes Heft*

Ewald Christian von Kleist (1715-1759)
Groß ist der Herr! die Himmel ohne Zahl sind seine Wohnungen
Johann Abraham Peter Schulz, "Hymne" 1784pub
Carl Loewe, "Gross ist der Herr" 1820
Franz Schubert, "Gott in der Natur" 1822, D757, 2s2a.pf
Original edition credited the poem to J. W. L. Gleim

Ja treuster Damon, ich bin überwunden!
Josef Antonín Štěpán, "Philis an Damon" 1778-79pub

Sie fliehet fort! Es ist um mich geschehen!
Josef Antonín Štěpán, "Amynt" 1778-79pub

Otto Klemperer (1885-1973)
Ungesucht gefunden preis ich meinen Stern
Otto Klemperer, "Lied" 1915pub

Viktor Klemperer (1881-1960)
Trinkt aus, ihr zechtet zum letztenmal
Arnold Schönberg, "Der verlorene Haufen" 1907, Op12,2

Karoline Louise von Klenke (1754-1802)
O du, wenn deine Lippen mich berühren
Franz Schubert, "Heimliches Lieben" 1827, D922

(Gustav) Hermann Kletke (1813-1886)
Frau Elster hat den Schatz entdeckt
Wilhelm Taubert, "Frau Elster"
from *Klänge aus der Kinderwelt*, Vol.5, No10

Ich flüstre deinen Namen in stiller Nacht
Friedrich Kücken, "Immortelle"

Rings waltet heil'ges Schweigen, nur frommer Chöre Reigen
Giacomo Meyerbeer, "Sonntagslied" 1841

Siehst du am Abend die Wolken ziehn
Carl Loewe, "In die Ferne" 1837
Franz Lachner, "In die Ferne" 1837, Op56,1
First edition (München: J. Aibl) lists the poet as "K. Klätke"
Johann Wenzeslaus Kalliwoda, "In die Ferne" 184-pub, sop.vn.pf

Wandervöglein, leichtes Blut, das zur Ferne fliegt
Hermann Goetz, "Wandervöglein" 1868-76, Op12,3

Zwei feine Stieflein hab' ich an
Robert Schumann, "Der Sandmann" 1849, Op79,12
from *Lieder-Album für die Jugend*

C. Klingemann

Ach, wie schnell die Tage fliehen
Felix Mendelssohn, "Im Herbst" 1830pub, Op9,5

Ach, wie so bald verhallet der Reigen
Felix Mendelssohn, "Herbstlied" 1845pub, Op63,4, 2sop.pf

Der Frühling naht mit Brausen
Felix Mendelssohn, "Frühlingslied" 1845, Op71,2

Es brechen im schallenden Reigen
Felix Mendelssohn, "Frühlingslied" 1836pub, Op34,3

Es lauschte das Laub so dunkelgrün
Felix Mendelssohn, "Es lauschte das Laub so dunkelgrün" 1851pub, Op86,1

Im Walde rauschen dürre Blätter
Felix Mendelssohn, "Herbstlied" 1839, Op84,2

Ringsum erschallt in Wald und Flur
Felix Mendelssohn, "Sonntagslied" 1834, Op34,5

Schlummre! Schlummre und träume von kommender Zeit
Felix Mendelssohn, "Bei der Wiege" 1840?pub, Op47,6

Sie wandelt im Blumengarten
Felix Mendelssohn, "Der Blumenstrauss" 1832, Op47,5

Johann Aegidius Klöntrup: see "Rosemann"

Friedrich Gottlieb Klopstock (1724-1803)

Begrabt den Leib in seiner Gruft
Franz Schubert, "Nun lasst uns den Leib begraben" 1815, D168, satb.pf

Cidli, du weinest, und ich schlumm're sicher
Franz Schubert, "Furcht der Geliebten" 1815, D285
Gottfried Emil Fischer, "An Cidli" 1820
from *Zwölf Lieder* (2)

Dein süßes Bild o Lyda! Schwebt stets vor meinem Blick
Josef Antonín Štěpán, "Dein süßes Bild" 1778-79pub
Johann Rudolf Zumsteeg, "Lida" 1803pub
from *Kleine Balladen und Lieder, fünftes Heft*
Franz Schubert, "Edone" 1816, D445

Ehre sei der Hocherhab'nen
Franz Schubert, "Das grosse Halleluja" 1816, D442

Es tönet sein Lob Feld und Wald
Franz Schubert, "Die Gestirne" 1816, D444

Grabt mein verwesliches geheim
Ferdinand Ries, "Nun lasset uns den Leib begraben" 1812pub, Op44,1, 5v.cham

Ha! dort kömmt er mit Schweiß, mit Römerblut
Christian Gottlob Neefe, "Hermann und Thusnelda" 1779
Franz Schubert, "Hermann und Thusnelda" 1815, D322

Ich bin ein deutsches Mädchen
Christoph Willibald von Gluck, "Vaterlandslied" 1786
Franz Schubert, "Vaterlandslied" 1815, D287

Im Frühlingsschatten fand ich sie, da band ich sie mit Rosenbändern
Josef Antonín Štěpán, "Die Cidly" 1778-79pub
Carl Friedrich Zelter, "Das Rosenband" 1810pub
Franz Schubert, "Das Rosenband" 1815, D280
Edward MacDowell, "Das Rosenband" 1880-81, Op12,2
Richard Strauss, "Das Rosenband" 1897, Op36,1

Mit unserm Arm ist nichts gethan
Franz Schubert, "Schlachtgesang" 1816, D443
Franz Schubert, "Schlachtlied" 1827, D912, 2t2b.2t2b
Robert Schumann, "Schlachtgesang" 1847, Op62,3, ttbb

Nein, ich wiederstrebe nicht mehr
Christoph Willibald von Gluck, "Die Neigung" 1786

Preis ihm! Er schuf und er erhält seine wundervolle Welt!
Carl Loewe, "Dem Dreieinigen" before 1829

Schweigend sahe der May die bekränzte
Christoph Willibald von Gluck, "Der Jüngling" 1786

Überwunden hat der Herr den Tod!
Franz Schubert, "Jesus Christus unser Heiland, der den Tod überwand" 1815, D2:168A, satb..pf

Was that dir, Thor, dein Vaterland?
Christoph Willibald von Gluck, "Wir und Sie" 1786

Weine du nicht, o, die ich innig liebe
Franz Schubert, "Selma und Selmar" 1815, D286

Wenn der Schimmer von dem Monde nun herab in die Wälder sich ergiesst
Christoph Willibald von Gluck, "Die Sommernacht" 1786
Franz Schubert, "Die Sommernacht" 1815, D289

Wenn einst ich tot bin
Carl Loewe, "Wenn einst ich tot bin" 1820

Wenn ich einst von jenem Schlummer, welcher Tod heißt, aufersteh'
Maria Therese Paradis, "Der Auferstehungsmorgen" 1784-86
from *Zwölf Lieder auf ihrer Reise in Musik gesetzt*
Franz Lachner, "Morgen Lied" 1837, Op56,3

Wie erhebt sich das Herz, wenn es dich, Unendlicher, denkt!
Franz Schubert, "Dem Unendlichen" 1815, D291

Wie erscholl der Gang des lauten Heers
Christoph Willibald von Gluck, "Schlachtgesang" 1786

Willkommen, o silberner Mond, schöner, stiller Gefährte der Nacht!
Christoph Willibald von Gluck, "Die frühen Gräber" 1786
Franz Schubert, "Die frühen Gräber" 1815, D290
Fanny Hensel, "Die frühen Gräber" 1828, Op9,4
Ernst Krenek, "Die frühen Gräber" 1923, Op19,5

Zeit, Verkündigerin der besten Freuden, nahe selige Zeit
Johann Rudolf Zumsteeg, "An Cidli" 1800pub
from *Kleine Balladen und Lieder, erstes Heft*
Franz Schubert, "An Sie" 1815, D288
Richard Strauss, "An Sie" 1899, Op43,1

Rosemarie Klotz-Burr (1934-)
Allen Schmerz hat Gott gezählet
Louis Ferdinand, "Allen Schmerz hat Gott gezählet" 1981pub

Es trat ein Himmel in mich ein
Louis Ferdinand, "Hoffnung" 1981pub

Albert Knapp (1798-1864)
Ein frommer Landmann in der Kirche saß
Carl Loewe, "Die Einladung" 1837, Op76,1, alt.pf

Himmelsluft vom Morgenlande die zu uns herüber weht
Giacomo Meyerbeer, "Luft von Morgen" 1841

Jakob Kneip (1881-1958)
Das weiß ich und hab ich erlebt
Paul Hindemith, "Das weiß ich und hab ich erlebt" 1925, Op45,ii,6, 2v.insts
from *Sing-und Spielmusiken für Liebhaber und Musikfreunde*

Karl Ernst Knodt (1856-1917)
Nacht auf Nacht steh ich am Meere
Hugo Kaun, "Der eine Reim" 1906?pub, Op68,7

Süß sind mir die Schollen des Tales
Alban Berg, "Süß sind mir die Schollen des Tales" 1904

Karl Kobald (1876-1957)
Mit Dir zu schweigen still im Dunkel
Erich Wolfgang Korngold, "Mit Dir zu schweigen..." 1928-29, Op22,2

Welt ist stille eingeschlafen, ruht im Mondenschein
Erich Wolfgang Korngold, "Welt ist stille eingeschlafen" 1928-29, Op22,3

Koch
Steht ein Mädchen an dem Fenster
Erich Wolfgang Korngold, "Alt-spanisch" 194-?, Op38,3

Ernst Koch (1808-1858)
Der Tag hat sich zur Ruh' gelegt
Louis Spohr, "Abendstille" 1856, Op154,6, bar.vn.pf

Es giebt geheime Schmerzen
Louis Spohr, "Das heimliche Lied" 1837, Op103,5, sop.cl.pf

Was treibt mich hin zu dir mit Macht?
Louis Spohr, "An ***" 1838, Op105,4

Franz Joseph (Xaver) von Königsbrunn-Schaup (1857-1916)
Der Kuckuck ruft Ku-ku-ku-ku
Joseph Marx, "Der Kuckuck ruft" 1907

Friedrich von Köpken (1737-1811)
Freude, die im frühen Lenze meinem Haupte Blumen wand
Franz Schubert, "Freude der Kinderjahre" 1816, D455

(Karl) Theodor Körner (1791-1813)
Alles wiegt die stille Nacht tief in süßen Schlummer
Hugo Wolf, "Ständchen" 1877

Das Volk steht auf, der Sturm bricht los
Carl Maria von Weber, "Männer und Buben" 1814, Op42,4, 4mv or 1v.pf
from *Leyer und Schwert, Heft 2*

Der Spielmann saß am Felsen und blickte hinunter in's Meer
Richard Strauss, "Spielmann und Zither" 1878
from *Jugendlieder*

Die Wunde brennt, die bleichen Lippen beben
Carl Maria von Weber, "Abschied vom Leben" 1814, Op41,2
from *Leyer und Schwert, Heft 1*

Dir, Mädchen, schlägt mit leisem Beben
Franz Schubert, "Liebesrausch" 1815, D179

Du Schwert an meiner Linken, was soll dein heit'res Blinken?
Carl Maria von Weber, "Schwertlied" 1814, Op42,6, 4mv or 1v.pf
from *Leyer und Schwert, Heft 2*
Franz Schubert, "Schwertlied" 1815, D170, 2mch?

Düst're Harmonieen hör' ich klingen
Carl Maria von Weber, "Bei der Musik des Prinzen Louis Ferdinand" 1816, Op43
from *Leyer und Schwert, Heft 3*

Es war ein Jäger wohl keck und kühn
Carl Loewe, "Treuröschen" 1820, Op2,1

Frisch auf, frisch auf mit raschem Flug!
Carl Maria von Weber, "Reiterlied" 1814, Op42,1, 4mv or 1v.pf
from *Leyer und Schwert, Heft 2*

Frisch auf, ihr Jäger, frei und flink!
Franz Schubert, "Jägerlied" 1815, D204, 2v

Herz, lass dich nicht zerspalten
Carl Maria von Weber, "Trost" 1814, Op41,3
from *Leyer und Schwert, Heft 1*

Hoch auf dem Gipfel deiner Gebirge steh' ich und staun' ich
Franz Schubert, "Auf der Riesenkoppe" 1818, D611

Hör' uns, Allmächtiger! Hör' uns, Allgütiger!
Carl Maria von Weber, "Gebet vor der Schlacht" 1814, Op42,3, 4mv or 1v.pf
from *Leyer und Schwert, Heft 2*

Ich bin erwacht! Im Rosenschimmer strahlt mir der junge Frühlingstag
Emilie Zumsteeg, "Morgenfreude" 1819pub, Op4,2

Ich hab' ein heisses junges Blut, wie ihr wohl alle wisst
Franz Schubert, "Das gestörte Glück" 1815, D309

Im Wald', im Wald' ist's frisch und grün
Robert Franz, "Waldfahrt" 1860?, Op14,3

Jüngst träumte mir, ich sah auf lichten Höhen
Franz Schubert, "Das war ich" 1815, D174

Schlacht, du brichst an!
Carl Maria von Weber, "Trinklied vor der Schlacht" 1814, Op42,5, 4mv or 1v.pf
from *Leyer und Schwert, Heft 2*
Franz Schubert, "Trinklied vor der Schlacht" 1815, D169, 2ch(unison).pf

Schlumm're sanft! Noch an dem Mutterherzen
Franz Schubert, "Wiegenlied" 1815, D304

Singe in heiliger Nacht, du meines Herzens Vertraute
Emilie Zumsteeg, "An meine Zither" 1819pub, Op4,4

Stern der Liebe, Glanzgebilde!
Franz Schubert, "Der Morgenstern" (fragment completed by Reinhard van Hoorickx), 1815, D172
Franz Schubert, "Der Morgenstern" 1815, D203, 2v

Süsses Licht! aus goldenen Pforten brichst du siegend durch die Nacht
Franz Schubert, "Sängers Morgenlied (1)" 1815, D163
Franz Schubert, "Sängers Morgenlied (2)" 1815, D165

Süsses Liebchen! Komm zu mir! Tausend Küsse geb' ich dir
Franz Schubert, "Liebeständelei" 1815, D206

Vater, ich rufe Dich! Brüllend umwölkt mich der Dampf der Geschütze
Carl Maria von Weber, "Gebet während der Schlacht" 1814, Op41,1
from *Leyer und Schwert, Heft 1*
Franz Schubert, "Gebet während der Schlacht" 1815, D171

Vor Thebens siebenfach gähnenden Toren
Franz Schubert, "Amphiaraos" 1815, D166

Was glänzt dort vom Walde im Sonnenschein?
Carl Maria von Weber, "Lützow's wilde Jagd" 1814, Op42,2, 4mv or 1v.pf
from *Leyer und Schwert, Heft 2*
Franz Schubert, "Lützows wilde Jagd" 1815, D205, 2v

Was ist des Sängers Vaterland?
Carl Maria von Weber, "Mein Vaterland" 1814, Op41,4
from *Leyer und Schwert, Heft 1*

Wie die Nacht mit heil'gem Beben auf der stillen Erde liegt!
Franz Schubert, "Sehnsucht der Liebe" 1815, D180

Wo dort die alten Gemäuer stehn
Carl Loewe, "Wallhaide" 1819, Op6

Christian Reinhold Köstlin: see "Christian Reinhold"

Benedict Joseph Maria von Koller (1769-1798?)

Der trotzige Mahomet stürzte mit Wut
Franz Jacob Freystädtler, "Mahomet der Zweite" 1795
from *Sechs Lieder der besten deutschen Dichter* (6)

Hanna Kolb: see "Hans Ehlen"

Kolumban Schnitzer von Meerau

Es redet und träumet die Jugend so viel
Franz Schubert, "Der Tanz" 1828, D826, satb.pf

Kolzow

Nächtig schwarze Wälder lichtet Euch!
Anna Teichmüller, "Das ungestüme Mädchen" 1907pub, Op15,5

August Kopisch (1799-1853)

Als Noah aus dem Kasten war, da trat zu ihm der Herre dar
Karl Gottlieb Reissiger, "Noah" bar.pf
attribution to Reissiger uncertain
Hans Pfitzner, "Historie von Noah" (fragment), 1886

Es tönt des Nöcken Harfenschall
Carl Loewe, "Der Nöck" 1859, Op129,2
after a Norse saga

Freunde sagt, was wollt ihr trinken?
Johanna Kinkel, "Wasser und Wein" Op6,2

Ich sahe eine Tigrin im dunklen Haine
Johannes Brahms, "Die Spröde" 1871, Op58,3

Im Finstern geh ich suchen
Johannes Brahms, "Blinde Kuh" 1871, Op58,1

Im Meere möcht' ich fahren, mit Dir, mit Dir allein
Johanna Kinkel, "Wunsch" 184-?pub, Op7,2

Lass stehn die Blume, geh' nicht ins Korn
Carl Reinecke, "Die Roggenmuhme" 2v.pf
from *Kinderlieder*

O wehe, Heinz von Lüder, wie ist um dich mir leid!
Carl Loewe, "Landgraf Philipp der Grossmüthige" 1856, Op125,1

Voller, dichter tropft ums Dach da
Johannes Brahms, "Während des Regens" 1871, Op58,2

Wenn man beim Wein sitzt, was ist da das Beste?
Franz Abt, "Soldatenart" Op204,3

Wie war zu Cölln es doch vordem mit Heinzelmännchen so bequem!
Carl Loewe, "Die Heinzelmännchen" 1841, Op83

Curt Koschnick

Du Wunder, das der Herr uns gab, schließ nun die Äuglein zu
Louis Ferdinand, "Berceuse" 1981pub

Herr, in dieser Weihestunde, da sich Herz zum Herzen fand
Louis Ferdinand, "Traugebet" 1966pub

Ich hab' nichts auf Erden, ob nah oder fern
Louis Ferdinand, "Kindergebet" 1981pub

Wenn zum hellen Glokkenklang fromm miteinstimmt unser Sang
Louis Ferdinand, "Geistliches Lied" 1981pub

Ludwig Gotthard (Theobul) Kosegarten (1758-1818)

Der Abend blüht, der Westen glüht!
Franz Schubert, "Das Abendroth" 1815, D236, ssb.pf

Der Abend blüht, Temora glüht
Franz Schubert, "Der Abend" 1815, D221

Der Morgen blüht; der Osten glüht; es lächelt aus dem dünnen Flor
Franz Schubert, "Von Ida" 1815, D228

Durch Nacht zum Licht! und wenn das grause Dunkel
Johann Rudolf Zumsteeg, "Via crucis, via lucis" 1800pub
from *Kleine Balladen und Lieder, zweites Heft*

Endlich steh'n die Pforten offen, endlich winkt das kühle Grab
Franz Schubert, "Schwangesang" 1815, D318

Ganz verloren, ganz versunken in dein Anschaun, Lieblingin
Franz Schubert, "Huldigung" 1815, D240

Ich hab' ein Mädchen funden, sanft, edel, deutsch und gut
Franz Schubert, "Das Finden" 1815, D219

Ich lag auf grünen Matten, an klarer Quelle Rand
Johann Rudolf Zumsteeg, "Die Erscheinung" 1801pub
from *Kleine Balladen und Lieder, drittes Heft*
Sophia Maria Westenholz, "Die Erscheinung" 1806pub, Op4,?
from *Zwölf Deutsche Lieder*
Franz Schubert, "Die Erscheinung" 1815, D229

Im Erlenbusch, im Tannenhain, in Sonn- und Mond- und Sternenschein
Franz Schubert, "Die Täuschung" 1815, D230

Meine Blüten sind zernagt von der Schwermut Sturme
Carl Friedrich Zelter, "Lied" 1802pub

O Abendsonn', o Holde, woher so bleich und blass?
Johann Rudolf Zumsteeg, "Ahndung" 1800pub
from *Kleine Balladen und Lieder, erstes Heft*

Rosa, denkst du an mich? Innig gedenk' ich dein!
Franz Schubert, "An Rosa II" 1815, D316

Schöne Himmelssonne, mild und hold und hehr
Johann Rudolf Zumsteeg, "Melancholikon" 1800pub
from *Kleine Balladen und Lieder, erstes Heft*

Schwellen nicht Seufzer, meine süsse Ida
Johann Rudolf Zumsteeg, "An Ida" 1800pub
from *Kleine Balladen und Lieder, erstes Heft*

Siehe, wie die Mondesstrahlen
Franz Schubert, "Die Mondnacht" 1815, D238

Sonne, du sinkst, Sonne, du sinkst
Franz Schubert, "An die untergehende Sonne" 1816-7, D457

Theures Mädchen, wenn ein andrer Himmel
Johann Rudolf Zumsteeg, "An Ellwina" 1802pub
from *Kleine Balladen und Lieder, viertes Heft*

Tiefe Feier schauert um die Welt
Johann Rudolf Zumsteeg, "Nachtgesang" 1800pub
from *Kleine Balladen und Lieder, erstes Heft*
Franz Schubert, "Nachtgesang" 1815, D314

Vernimm es, Nacht, was Ida dir vertrauet
Franz Schubert, "Idens Nachtgesang" 1815, D227

Warum bist du nicht hier, meine Geliebteste
Franz Schubert, "An Rosa I" 1815, D315

Was ist es, das die Seele füllt?
Johann Rudolf Zumsteeg, "Alles um Liebe" 1800pub
from *Kleine Balladen und Lieder, erstes Heft*
Franz Schubert, "Alles um Liebe" 1815, D241

Wehmuth, die mich hüllt, welche Gottheit stillt mein unendlich Sehnen?
Franz Schubert, "Das Sehnen" 1815, D231

Wenn du wärst mein eigen
Carl Loewe, "Wenn du wärst mein eigen" 1819, Op9,iv,1
after the Scottish

Wer bist du, Geist der Liebe, der durch das Weltall webt
Franz Schubert, "Geist der Liebe" 1815, D233

Wie erscholl der Gang des lauten Heers
Johann Rudolf Zumsteeg, "Schlachtgesang" 1800pub
from *Kleine Balladen und Lieder, erstes Heft*

Wie schaust du aus dem Nebelflor, o Sonne, bleich und müde!
Franz Schubert, "Idens Schwanenlied" 1815, D317

Wie wohl ist mir im Dunkeln! Wie weht die laue Nacht!
Johann Rudolf Zumsteeg, "Die Sterne" 1801pub
from *Kleine Balladen und Lieder, drittes Heft*
Franz Schubert, "Die Sterne" 1815, D313

Woher, o namenloses Sehnen, das den beklemmten Busen presst?
Franz Schubert, "Abends unter der Linde" 1815, D235
Franz Schubert, "Abends unter der Linde (2)" 1815, D237

Wohl weinen Gottes Engel
Franz Schubert, "Luisens Antwort" 1815, D319

"Kosten"

Auf einem hohen Berge, da steht ein altes Schloß
Johann Vesque von Püttlingen, "Zwei Fräulein" 1843

A. Kotsch

Ich suchte eine Melodie seit vierzehn Tagen schon
Ernest Vietor, "Die neue Melodie" Op6,6

August von Kotzebue (1761-1819)

Das war ein Thier, mein Mauleselein!
Carl Loewe, "Ariette" 1816

Ein Kind an Mutterbrust
Carl Loewe, "Romanze" 1816

Es klingt eine Regel zwar wunderlich
Carl Loewe, "Canzone" 1816

Hier, wo seine fetten Herden in dem üpp'gen Grase ruh'n
Carl Loewe, "Lied" 1816

Komm' fein's Liebchen, komm an's Fenster
Hermann Grädener, "Vor dem Fenster" 1896?pub, Op27,5

Lass mich schlummern, Herzlein, schweige
Carl Maria von Weber, "Lass mich schlummern, Herzlein, schweige" 1811, Op25,3, 1v.guit

Mit langem Barte, bleich und blass
Carl Loewe, "Romanze" 1816

Mitten im Sturm, der mich umbrüllte
Carl Loewe, "Cavatine" 1816

Rase, Sturmwind, blase
Carl Maria von Weber, "Rase, Sturmwind, blase" 1811, J.111, 1v.guit

Über die Berge mit Ungestüm
Carl Maria von Weber, "Über die Berge mit Ungestüm" 1812?, Op25,2

Wir weichen Sklavenbrod in bittre Thränen ein!
Johann Rudolf Zumsteeg, "Lied der Negersklaven" 1805pub
from *Kleine Balladen und Lieder, siebtes Heft*

A. Krafft

Ich denke dein, ob auch getrennt in weiter Ferne
Gottfried Herrmann, "Ich denke dein" 1843, 1v.cl.pf

Kraft

Lasst uns mit ehrfurchtvollem Dank
Carl Loewe, "Lasst uns mit ehrfurchtvollem Dank" 1847

(Friedrich) Julius Krais (1807-1878)

Dein Schlaf ist sanft wie dein Gemüt
Emilie Zumsteeg, "Schlafliedchen"

Karl Kraus (1874-1936)

Ihr Menschenkinder, seid ihr nicht Laub
Ernst Krenek, "Die Nachtigall: aus «Worte in Versen»" 1931, Op68

Nun weiß ich doch, 's ist Frühling wieder
Hanns Eisler, "Printemps allemand" 1956

Johann Christoph Krauseneck (1738-1799)

Kleine Spinnerin hinter deinem Rädchen
Carl Loewe, "An die fliessige Spinnerin" 1819, Op9,v,5

Friedrich Wilhelm Krummacher (1796-1868)

Wie schön bist du, freundliche Stille
Franz Schubert, "Die Nacht" 1823pub, D983,4, 2t2b
Attribution to Krummacher uncertain

Friedrich Adolf Krummacher (1767-1845)

Auf hoher Alp wohnt auch der liebe Gott
Carl Loewe, "Alplied" before 1829

Der Sonntag ist da! Er kommt uns gesendet vom Himmel
Carl Loewe, "Sonntagslied" before 1829

Hört die Lerche, sie singt!
Carl Loewe, "Die Lerche" before 1826

Mag auch die Liebe weinen!
Carl Loewe, "Die Auferstehung" 1826

Wenn einst mein Lebenstag sich neiget
Carl Loewe, "Gebet" 1826

Ottfried Kryzanowski (1891-1918)
Ein einfaches lichtes Kleid, ein leichter Gang
Ernst Krenek, "Wunsch" 1923, Op19,4

Ein Weib zu suchen! Wozu
Ernst Krenek, "Der Individualist" 1923, Op19,2

Es will kein Baum so wie die Linde blühen!
Ernst Krenek, "Erinnerung" 1923, Op19,1

Kurt Kuberzig (1912-1971)
Und ihre Augen irren rings umher
Helmut Paulsen, "Die Blinde"
from *Sieben besinnliche Lieder*

Ludwiga Kuckuck
Du bist so reich als du tränenreich bist
Ernst Toch, "Spruch" 1928pub, Op41,5

Spätnachmittag. Die kleine Straße liegt leblos und leer
Ernst Toch, "Spätnachmittag" 1928pub, Op41,4

(Ferdinand) Gustav Kühne (1806-1888)
Was nennst du deine Liebe schwer und gross
Adolf Jensen, "Was nennst du deine Liebe schwer und gross" 1863pub, Op13,6, 1v(low).pf

Elieser Gottlieb Küster (1732-1799)
Vater unser beten wir, der du in dem Himmel wohnest
Carl Loewe, "Vater unser" 1826

Christoph Johann Anton Kuffner (1780-1846)
Glaube, hoffe, liebe!
Franz Schubert, "Gaube, Hoffnung und Liebe" 1828, D955

Franz Theodor Kugler (1808-1858)
Da draussen auf der Aue da steh'n die Blümelein
Wilhelm Taubert, "Wiegenlied"
Taubert credits the poem to "W. Kugler"
from *Klänge aus der Kinderwelt*, Vol.6, No10
Friedrich Kücken, "Schlummerlied"

Der junge König und sein Gemahl
Carl Loewe, "Der junge König und sein Gemahl" 1834, Op38
from *Gregor auf dem Stein* (3)

Der Mond steht über dem Berge
Johannes Brahms, "Ständchen" 1888, Op106,1

Ein Klippeneiland liegt im Meer
Carl Loewe, "Ein Klippeneiland liegt im Meer" 1834, Op38
from *Gregor auf dem Stein* (4)

Es rinnen die Wasser Tag und Nacht
Johannes Brahms, "Sehnsucht" 1891, Op112,1, satb.pf

Guten Morgen, du Sonnstagsglockenschall!
Carl Loewe, "Jungfrau Lorenz" 1834, Op33,1

Herolde ritten von Ort zu Ort
Carl Loewe, "Herolde ritten von Ort zu Ort" 1834, Op38
from *Gregor auf dem Stein* (1)

Im Schloss, da brennen der Kerzen viel
Carl Loewe, "Im Schloss, da brennen der Kerzen viel" 1834, Op38
from *Gregor auf dem Stein* (2)

Nächtens wachen auf die irren, lügenmächt'gen Spukgestalten
Johannes Brahms, "Nächtens" 1891, Op112,2, satb.pf

Wie bräutlich glänzt das heilige Rom!
Carl Loewe, "Wie bräutlich glänzt das heilige Rom!" 1834, Op38
from *Gregor auf dem Stein* (5)

Wie ist so heiss im Busen mir
Carl Loewe, "Die Jungfrau und der Tod" 1827, Op9,ii,5

Wissen es die blauen Blumen
Arno Kleffel, "Liebesahnung" Op12,4

Johann C. Kugler

Als noch dem blinden Heiden wahn die Pommern waren unterthan
Carl Loewe, "Otto-Lied" 1840

Durch die Freundschaft fest verbunden
Carl Loewe, "Letztes Lied" 1836

Wehmuth weckt der fernen Wolkenwand'rer Gruss
Carl Loewe, "Beim Scheiden" 1836

Emil Kuh (1828-1876)

Das ist die schönste Stunde, wo du mich still bewegst
Peter Cornelius, "Frühling im Sommer" 1859

Du kleine Biene, verfolg' mich nicht
Peter Cornelius, "Du kleine Biene, verfolg' mich nicht" 1859

Hirschlein ging im Wald spazieren
Peter Cornelius, "Hirschlein ging im Wald spazieren" 1859

Ihr Glokken von Marling, wie brauset ihr so hell
Franz Liszt, "Ihr Glokken von Marling" 1874

Mir ist, als zögen Arme mich schaurig himmelwärts
Peter Cornelius, "Mir ist, als zögen Arme mich schaurig himmelwärts" 1859

Elisabeth Kulmann (1808-1825)

Bleibe hier und singe, liebe Nachtigall!
Carl Reinecke, "An die Nachtigall"
from *Kinderlieder*

Robert Schumann, "An die Nachtigall" 1851, Op103,3, 2sop.pf (or sa.pf)

Der Frühling kehret wieder, und schmücket Berg und Thal
Robert Schumann, "Frühlingslied" 1851, Op103,2, 2sop.pf

Die letzten Blumen starben
Robert Schumann, "Die letzten Blumen starben" 1851, Op104,6

Du nennst mich armes Mädchen
Robert Schumann, "Du nennst mich armes Mädchen" 1851, Op104,3

Gekämpft hat meine Barke
Robert Schumann, "Gekämpft hat meine Barke" 1851, Op104,7

Mond, meiner Seele Liebling
Robert Schumann, "Mond, meiner Seele Liebling" 1851, Op104,1

Pflücket Rosen, um das Haar schön
Robert Schumann, "Mailied" 1851, Op103,1, 2sop.pf

Reich' mir die Hand, o Wolke
Robert Schumann, "Reich' mir die Hand, o Wolke" 1851, Op104,5

Schweb empor am Himmel, schöner Abendstern
Robert Schumann, "An den Abendstern" 1851, Op103,4, 2sop.pf (or sa.pf)

Steig' empor am Himmel, schöner Abendstern
Carl Reinecke, "An den Abendstern"
from *Kinderlieder*

Viel Glück zur Reise, Schwalben!
Robert Schumann, "Viel Glück zur Reise, Schwalben" 1851, Op104,2

Wir sind ja, Kind, im Maie, wirf Buch und Heft von dir!
Robert Schumann, "Der Zeisig" 1851, Op104,4

Johann Gottfried Kumpf ("Ermin") (1781-1862)

Rein und freundlich lacht der Himmel nieder auf die dunkle Erde
Franz Schubert, "Der Mondabend" 1815, D141

Sei mir gegrüsst, o Mai, mit deinem Blüthenhimmel
Franz Schubert, "Mein Gruss an den Mai" 1815, D305

Kunde

Du gleichst dem klaren blauen See
Josefine Lang, "Du gleichst dem klaren blauen See" 1860, Op33,1

(Karl Anton Bernhard) Friedrich von Kurowski-Eichen (1780-1853)

Der Hahn hat gekräht, die Lerche singt
Carl Loewe, "Wach auf!" 1824, Op9,vi,1

Die Nacht ist so dunkel, der Sturm so laut
Carl Loewe, "Der grosse Kurfürst und die Spreejungfrau" 1826, Op7,1

Freiwillige vor! Auch du, lieb Mädchen, mit Büchse und Schwert
Carl Loewe, "Die Heldenbraut" 1825

Hermann Kurz (1813-1873)

Der Himmel lacht und heit're Lüfte spielen
Friedrich Silcher, "Trinklied im Frühling" 4v

Isolde (Maria Clara) Kurz (1853-1944)
Was hat des Schlummers Band zerrissen
Max Reger, "Um Dich" 1893, Op12,5

Charles L'Égru
Nicht so schnelle, nicht so schnelle!
Robert Schumann, "Aufträge" 1850, Op77,5

Senkt die Nacht den sanften Fittig nieder
Robert Schumann, "Triolett" 1853, Op114,2, 3fv.pf

Friedrich Heinrich Karl, Freiherr de La Motte-Fouqué (1777-1843)
Ach, wär' ich nur ein Vögelein!
Louis Spohr, "Lied aus Aslauga's *Ritter*" 1816, Op41,2

An dem jungen Morgenhimmel
Franz Schubert, "Don Gayseros III" 1815?, D93,3

Don Gayseros, Don Gayseros, wunderlicher, schöner Ritter
Franz Schubert, "Don Gayseros I" 1815?, D93,1

Du Urquell aller Güte, du Urquell aller Macht
Franz Schubert, "Gebet" 1824, D815, satb.pf

Ein Schäfer sass im Grünen
Franz Schubert, "Der Schäfer und der Reiter" 1817, D517

Mutter geht durch ihre Kammern, räumt die Schränke ein und aus
Franz Schubert, "Lied" 1816, D373

Nächtens klang die süsse Laute
Franz Schubert, "Don Gayseros II" 1815?, D93,2

Wenn alles eben käme, wie du gewollt es hast
Ernst Pepping, "Trost" 1949pub
from *Haus- und Trostbuch* (40)

(Marie) Sophie (Gutermann) von La Roche (1731-1807)
Meiner lieben trauten Linde, die mir freundlich Schatten gab
Maria Therese Paradis, "Erinnerung ans Schiksal" 1784-86, 1v.vn.pf
from *Zwölf Lieder auf ihrer Reise in Musik gesetzt*

Karl von Lackner
Seid munter, ihr Mädchen, frohlokket ihr Brüder
J. J. Grünwald, "Der Frühling" 1785pub

August Heinrich Julius Lafontaine (1758-1831)
Der Morgen glüht, die Rose blüht
Johann Rudolf Zumsteeg, "Der Mohrin Gesang" 1800pub
from *Kleine Balladen und Lieder, zweites Heft*

Stille Thränen liebt mein Herz, blasse, nassgeweinte Wangen
Johann Rudolf Zumsteeg, "Agnes" 1805pub
from *Kleine Balladen und Lieder, siebtes Heft*

Georg Ludwig Heinrich Lang (1836-1920)
Da sitz ich in der Stube, da sitz ich in dem Haus
Franz Abt, "Wär ich ein Hirtenbube" 1870?pub
from *Kinderlieder*

Ein lockerer Zeisig, der bin ich, das weiss ich
Franz Abt, "Ein lockerer Zeisig" 1870?pub
from *Kinderlieder*

Es führen mich die Wege wohl durch die weite Welt
Franz Abt, "Heimath so traut!" 1870?pub
from *Kinderlieder*

Liebes Häschen, willst du morgen uns für Ostereier sorgen?
Franz Abt, "Osterhäschen" 1870?pub
from *Kinderlieder*

Hugo Lang

Frühling- Frühling- Frühlingswind, wir alle deine Kinder sind
Armin Knab, "Frühlingswind" 1905-20
from *Kinderlieder* (12)

Adolph Lange

Feierlicher Glockenklang hallet durch die stillen Felder
Louis Spohr, "Sonntagsfrühe" 1849, WoO117,2, 2sop.pf

Carl Lange

Abend, lege deine Hände leise
Louis Ferdinand, "Abendfrieden" 1955pub

Ein Vöglein singt sein erstes Lied: Wach auf!
Louis Ferdinand, "Liebesbotschaft" 1966pub

Schlaf, mein liebes Kindlein, schlafe ein
Louis Ferdinand, "Schlummerlied" 1981pub

Karl Gottlieb Lappe (1773-1843)

In der Freie will ich leben
Franz Schubert, "Flucht" 1825, D825,3, 2t2b

Nord oder Süd! Wenn nur im warmen Busen
Ludwig van Beethoven, "So oder so" 1817, WoO148
Robert Schumann, "Nord oder Süd" 1846, Op59,1, satb

O, wie schön ist deine Welt
Franz Schubert, "Im Abendroth" 1825?, D799

Wann meine Grillen schwirren, bei Nacht, am spät erwärmten Herd
Franz Schubert, "Der Einsame" 1825?, D800

(Ignaz) Julius Lasker (1811-1876)

Als ich von deinem Grabe ging
Leopold Damrosch, "Zuversicht" Op5,3

Die süsse Rede hallet noch
Leopold Damrosch, "Nachhall" Op5,2

Hinaus, hinaus! in freie Luft
Carl Loewe, "Hinaus! Hinauf! Hinab!" 1840

Else Lasker-Schüler (1869-1945)

Bin so müde. Alle Nächte trag ich dich auf dem Rükken
Paul Hindemith, "Du machst mich traurig – hör" 1922, Op18,6

Der Schlaf entführte mich in deine Gärten
Paul Hindemith, "Traum" 1922, Op18,3

Fänd' ich den Schatten eines süßen Herzens
Paul Hindemith, "Ich bin so allein" 1917, alt.pf
from *Zwei Lieder für Alt und Klavier*

Frieda Laubsch
Der goldne Morgen kommt herauf mit Glut und Duft und Sonnenschein
Max Reger, "Süße Ruh'" 1900
from *Liebeslieder* (4)

Adolf Julius Freiherr Laur von Münchhofen
Ade nun, liebes junges Weib!
Johann Holzer, "Abschied eines Seefahrers" 1779pub

"Richard Leander" (Richard Volkmann) (1830-1889)
Es klopft an das Fenster der Lindenbaum
Gustav Mahler, "Frühlingsmorgen" 1880-87

Es wecket meine Liebe die Lieder immer wieder!
Gustav Mahler, "Erinnerung" 1880-87

In der Früh', wenn die Sonne kommen will
Hans Pfitzner, "In der Früh', wenn die Sonne kommen will" 1888/89, Op2,1

Ist der Himmel darum im Lenz so blau?
Hans Pfitzner, "Ist der Himmel darum im Lenz so blau?" 1888/89, Op2,2

Lebret [possibly Karl August Lebret (1809-1855)]
Nun wird es wieder grün auf allen Wiesen
Robert Franz, "Frühlingsklage" 1879, Op50,2

Helene Lecher
Du milder, Du schöner, Du herrlicher Geist
Ernst Bacon, "Gebet" 1928pub

"Dora Leen" (Dora Pollack) (d. 194-?)[6]
Du rote Rose, die du in schimmernder Vase
Franz Schreker, "Rosentod" 1900?, Op7,5

Im Mondgeflimmer, im Zauberschimmer
Franz Schreker, "Spuk" 1900?, Op7,4

Mich grüßte erstrahlender Schein
Franz Schreker, "Traum" 1900?, Op7,3

Wenn die Sommerzeiten enden, wandelt licht im Abendschein
Franz Schreker, "Sommerfäden" 1901+, Op2,1

R. Lehmann
Viel schöne Blumen stehen
George Henschel, "Junger Wunsch" 187-?, Op27,1

Lehr
Ein Echo kenn' ich, ist weit von hier
Carl Maria von Weber, "Er an Sie" 1808, Op15,6

[6]Christopher Hailey traces Dora Pollack to the gates of Auschwitz. The rest is silence.

Weil es also Gott gefügt
Carl Maria von Weber, "Trinklied" 1809, J.80

Wollt ihr sie kennen, soll ich sie nennen
Carl Maria von Weber, "Meine Farben" 1808, Op23,1

Karl Gottfried (Leopold) Ritter von Leitner (1800-1890)

Auf meinen heimischen Bergen da sind die Wolken zu Haus
Franz Schubert, "Wolke und Quelle" 1827?, D2:896B

Das also, das ist der enge Schrein
Franz Schubert, "Vor meiner Wiege" 1827, D927

Dort blinket durch Weiden und winket ein Schimmer
Franz Schubert, "Des Fischers Liebesglück" 1827, D933

Ein Münich steht in seiner Zell' am Fenstergitter grau
Franz Schubert, "Der Kreuzzug" 1827, D932

Es ist so still, so heimlich um mich
Franz Schubert, "Der Winterabend" 1828, D938

Gar fröhlich kann ich scheiden, ich hätt' es nicht gemeint
Franz Schubert, "Fröhliches Scheiden" (fragment), 1827, D896

Gar tröstlich kommt geronnen der Thränen heil'ger Quell
Franz Schubert, "Das Weinen" 1827, D926

He! schenket mir im Helme ein!
Franz Schubert, "Der Wallensteiner Lanzknecht beim Trunk" 1827, D931

Nehm ich die Harfe, folgend dem Drange süsser Gefühle
Franz Schubert, "Sie in jedem Liede" (fragment), 1827, D2:896A

Vater, du glaubst es nicht, wie's mir zum Herzen spricht
Franz Schubert, "Drang in die Ferne" 1823?, D770

Wie blitzen die Sterne so hell durch die Nacht!
Franz Schubert, "Die Sterne" 1828, D939

Otto von Leixner (von Grünberg) (1847-1907)

Ich ahnte nicht vor kurzer Zeit
Ernst Otto Nodnagel, "Ich ahnte nicht vor kurzer Zeit" 1894, Op20,1

Ich sitze manchen langen Tag
Alexander Zemlinsky, "Das verlassene Mädchen" 1894-96, Op2,ii,5

Ob dein ich bin? Was fragst du mich?
Ernst Otto Nodnagel, "Ob dein ich bin" 1894, Op20,2

Karl Freiherr von Lemayer

Frühling schimmert in den Lüften
Franz Schreker, "Frühling" 189-?, Op4,2

Karl von Lemcke (1831-1913)

Auf den Bergen, den Bergen hab' ich gejauchzt
Adolf Jensen, "Auf den Bergen" 1875-79, Op61,4

Auf der Heide weht der Wind
Johannes Brahms, "Willst du, daß ich geh?" 1877, Op71,4

Es saß ein Salamander auf einem kühlen Stein
Johannes Brahms, "Salamander" 1888, Op107,2

Freiwillige her! Freiwillige her!
Johannes Brahms, "Freiwillige her!" 1861/62?, Op41,2, ttbb

Gebt acht! Gebt acht! Es harrt der Feind
Johannes Brahms, "Gebt acht!" 1861/62?, Op41,5, ttbb

Ich hatte eine Nachtigall, die sang so schön
Anton Rubinstein, "Verlust" 1864, Op72,6

Ich saß zu deinen Füßen in Waldeseinsamkeit
Johannes Brahms, "In Waldeseinsamkeit" 1878, Op85,6

Ich sitz am Strande der rauschenden See
Johannes Brahms, "Verzagen" 1877, Op72,4

Ich stand in einer lauen Nacht
Johannes Brahms, "Verrat" 1886, Op105,5, 1v(low).pf

Im Garten am Seegestade uralte Bäume stehn
Johannes Brahms, "Im Garten am Seegestade" 1877, Op70,1

Jetzt hab ich schon zwei Jahre lang
Johannes Brahms, "Marschieren" 1861/62?, Op41,4, ttbb

Über die See, fern über die See
Johannes Brahms, "Über die See" 1877, Op69,7

Veilchen vom Berg, woran mahnest du mich?
Franz Abt, "Veilchen vom Berg" 1873pub, Op211,1

Was freut einen alten Soldaten?
Johannes Brahms, "Geleit" 1861/62?, Op41,3, ttbb

Nikolaus Lenau (1802-1850)

Ach wärst du mein, es wär' ein schönes Leben
Leopold Damrosch, "An *" Op8,5

Ach, wer möchte einsam trinken
Othmar Schoeck, "Ach, wer möchte einsam trinken" 1931-33, Op47,Va, bar.4str
from *Notturno*

Als ein unergründlich Wonnemeer strahlte mir dein tiefer Seelenblick
Josefine Lang, "Scheideblick" 1839?, Op10,5
Hugo Wolf, "Scheideblick" 1876

Als sie vom Paradiese ward gezwungen
Othmar Schoeck, "Heimatklang" 1954-55, Op70,10, 1v(med).orch
from *Nachhall*

Am Himmelsantlitz wandelt ein Gedanke
Othmar Schoeck, "Himmelstrauer" 1905, Op5,1

An der duftverlor'nen Gränze jener Berge
Anna Teichmüller, "An der duftverlor'nen Gränze jener Berge" 1904pub, Op2,3

An ihren bunten Liedern klettert
Robert Franz, "Liebesfeier" 1865?pub, Op21,4
Felix Weingartner, "Liebesfeier" 1891pub, Op16,2

Auf dem Teich, dem regungslosen
Felix Mendelssohn, "Schilflied" 1842, Op71,4
Robert Franz, "Auf dem Teich, dem regungslosen" 1844pub, Op2,5
from *"Schilflieder" von Nicolaus Lenau*
Charles Griffes, "Auf dem Teich, dem regungslosen" 1903-09?, A3
Henri Marteau, "Auf dem Teich, dem regungslosen" 1925pub, Op31,5
from *Fünf Schilflieder*
Ernst Bacon, "Schilflied" 1928pub

Auf geheimem Waldespfade schleich ich gern im Abendschein
Robert Franz, "Auf geheimem Waldespfade" 1844pub, Op2,1
from *"Schilflieder" von Nicolaus Lenau*
Hans Pfitzner, "Auf geheimem Waldespfade" (fragment), 188-?
Charles Griffes, "Auf geheimem Waldespfade" 1903-09?, A4
Othmar Schoeck, "Auf geheimem Waldespfade" 1905, Op2,3
from *Drei Schilflieder*
Alban Berg, "Schilflied" 1907
from *Sieben frühe Lieder*
Henri Marteau, "Auf geheimem Waldespfade" 1925pub, Op31,3
from *Fünf Schilflieder*

Bin mit dir im Wald gegangen; ach! wie war der Wald so froh!
Fanny Hensel, "Traurige Wege" 1841
Hugo Wolf, "Traurige Wege" 1878
Léander Schlegel, "Traurige Wege" 1900, Op20,9
from *Deutsche Liebeslieder*

Blumen, Vögel, duftend, singend, seid doch nicht so ausgelassen
Ignaz Brüll, "Trauer" 186-?, Op5,iii,3

Da liegt der Feinde gestreckte Schaar
Robert Schumann, "Vier Husarenlieder (4)" 1851, Op117,4, bar.pf

Dein gedenkend irr' ich einsam
Othmar Schoeck, "Das Mondlicht" 1922pub, Op36,16
from *Elegie*

Dein ist mein Herz, mein Schmerz dein eigen
Fanny Hensel, "Dein ist mein Herz" 1846, Op7,6

Den grünen Zeigern, den rothen Wangen
Robert Schumann, "Vier Husarenlieder (3)" 1851, Op117,3, bar.pf

Der Buchenwald ist herbstlich schon gerötet
Othmar Schoeck, "Herbstgefühl" 1922, Op36,15
from *Elegie*

Der holden Lenzgeschmeide, der Rose meiner Freude
Robert Schumann, "Meine Rose" 1850, Op90,2

Der Husar, trara! was ist die Gefahr?
Robert Schumann, "Vier Husarenlieder (1)" 1851, Op117,1, bar.pf

Der leidige Frieden hat lange gewährt
Robert Schumann, "Vier Husarenlieder (2)" 1851, Op117,2, bar.pf

Der Traum war so wild, der Traum war so schaurig
Othmar Schoeck, "Der Traum war so wild" 1931-33, Op47,IIb, bar.4str
from *Notturno*

Der Wind ist fremd, du kannst ihn nicht umfassen
Othmar Schoeck, "Einsamkeit I/II" 1954-55, Op70,2, 1v(med).orch
from *Nachhall*

Des Berges Gipfel war erschwungen
Othmar Schoeck, "Die Ferne" 1930, Op45,7
from *Wanderung im Gebirge*

Des Himmels frohes Antlitz
Othmar Schoeck, "Aufbruch" 1930, Op45,2
from *Wanderung im Gebirge*

Die Bäche rauschen der Frühlingssonne
Leopold Damrosch, "Neid der Sehnsucht" Op8,3

Die Bäume blüh'n, die Vöglein singen
Robert Franz, "Lenz" 1860?, Op14,2
Othmar Schoeck, "Lenz" 1910, Op24a,1

Die Bäume rauschen hier noch immer
Othmar Schoeck, "Verlorenes Glück" 1922pub, Op36,20
from *Elegie*

Die dunkeln Wolken hingen herab so bang und schwer
Robert Schumann, "Der schwere Abend" 1850, Op90,6
Ignaz Brüll, "Der schwere Abend" 186-?, Op5,iii,2
Robert Franz, "Der schwere Abend" 1866?, Op37,4
Frederic Louis Ritter, "Der schwere Abend" 1876pub, Op10,1
Othmar Schoeck, "Die dunklen Wolken hingen" 1931-33, Op47,Id, bar.4str
from *Notturno*

Die Menschheit ist dahinter kommen
Othmar Schoeck, "Veränderte Welt" 1954-55, Op70,4, 1v(med).orch
from *Nachhall*

Die Nacht ist finster, schwül und bang
Hugo Wolf, "Nächtliche Wanderung" 1878

Die Vögel flieh'n geschwind
Othmar Schoeck, "Waldlied" 1922pub, Op36,18
from *Elegie*

Die Wolken waren fortgezogen
Othmar Schoeck, "Der Abend" 1930, Op45,10
from *Wanderung im Gebirge*

Diese Rose pflück' ich dir in der weiten Ferne
Johann Vesque von Püttlingen, "An die Entfernte" 1838/39
Josefine Lang, "An die Entfernte" 1843?, Op13,5
Felix Mendelssohn, "An die Entfernte" 1847, Op71,3
Felix Weingartner, "An die Entfernte" 1891pub, Op16,1
Emil Mattiesen, "An die Entfernte" 190-?pub, Op11,3
from *Stille Lieder* (3)
Othmar Schoeck, "An die Entfernte" 1914, Op24a,3

Drei Reiter nach verlorner Schlacht
Othmar Schoeck, "Die Drei" 1931, o.op39, mch

Drei Seelen hab' ich offenbar
Felix Weingartner, "Trias harmonica" 1891pub, Op16,7

Drei Zigeuner fand ich einmal liegen an einer Weide
Franz Liszt, "Die drei Zigeuner" 1860
Othmar Schoeck, "Die drei Zigeuner" 1914, Op24a,4

Drüben geht die Sonne scheiden und der müde Tag entschlief
Robert Franz, "Drüben geht die Sonne scheiden" 1844pub, Op2,2
from *"Schilflieder" von Nicolaus Lenau*
Johann Vesque von Püttlingen, "Schilflied I" 1856
Arnold Schönberg, "Drüben geht die Sonne scheiden" 189-?
Othmar Schoeck, "Drüben geht die Sonne scheiden" 1905, Op2,1
from *Drei Schilflieder*
Henri Marteau, "Drüben ging die Sonne scheiden" 1925pub, Op31,1
from *Fünf Schilflieder*

Du klagst, daß bange Wehmut dich beschleicht
Fanny Hensel, "Vorwurf" 1850pub, Op10,2

Du trüber Nebel, hüllest mir das Thal mit seinem Fluss
Robert Franz, "Nebel" 1870?pub, Op28,4
Richard Strauss, "Nebel" 1878
from *Jugendlieder*
Heinrich von Herzogenberg, "Nebel" 1881pub, Op29,2
Adolph Martin Foerster, "Nebel" 188?, Op12,2
Felix Weingartner, "Nebel" 1893, Op18,3
from *Severa. Sechs ernste Lieder*

Du warst mir ein gar trauter, lieber
Othmar Schoeck, "Erinnerung" 1930, Op45,1
from *Wanderung im Gebirge*

Durch den Hain mit bangem Stoße
Othmar Schoeck, "Waldlied" 1922pub, Op36,7

Durch den Wald, den dunkeln, geht holde Frühlingsmorgenstunde
Felix Mendelssohn, "Frühlingslied" 1839, Op47,3
Robert Franz, "Frühlingsblick" 1884, Op52,6
Othmar Schoeck, "Frühlingsblick" 1907, Op5,3

Ein Greis trat lächelnd mir entgegen
Othmar Schoeck, "Der Schlaf" 1930, Op45,9
from *Wanderung im Gebirge*

Ein schlafend Kind! o still, o still!
Hugo Wolf, "Die Stimme des Kindes" 1876, Op10, ssaatb.pf

Ein Wand'rer läßt sein helles Lied erklingen
Othmar Schoeck, "Nachhall" 1954-55, Op70,1, 1v(med).orch
from *Nachhall*

Es weht der Wind so kühl, entlaubend rings die Äste
Othmar Schoeck, "Es weht der Wind so kühl" 1931-33, Op47,III, bar.4str
from *Notturno*

Fein Rösslein, ich beschlage dich
Robert Schumann, "Lied eines Schmiedes" 1850, Op90,1

Friedlicher Abend senkt sich aufs Gefilde
Fanny Hensel, "Abendbild" 1846, Op10,3
Hugo Wolf, "Abendbilder" 1877

Froh summte nach der süßen Beute
Othmar Schoeck, "Die Lerche" 1930, Op45,3
from *Wanderung im Gebirge*

Frühlingskinder im bunten Gedränge
Robert Franz, "Frühlingsgedränge" 1846pub, Op7,5
Richard Strauss, "Frühlingsgedränge" 1891, Op26,1
Max von Schillings, "Frühlingsgedränge" 1896?pub

Gespielt mit Regen, Blitz und Sturm
Franz Liszt, "Der traurige Mönch" 1860, declamation.pf

Hast du dich je schon ganz allein gefunden
Othmar Schoeck, "Einsamkeit I/II" 1954-55, Op70,2, 1v(med).orch
from *Nachhall*

Hesperus, der blasse Funken
Othmar Schoeck, "Vergangenheit" 1904, o.op14
Felix Weingartner, "Vergangenheit" 1910, Op51,8
from *Abendlieder*
Othmar Schoeck, "Vergangenheit" 1922pub, Op36,17
from *Elegie*

Holder Lenz, du bist dahin!
Othmar Schoeck, "Herbstklage" 1922pub, Op36,12
from *Elegie*

Horch, wie still es wird im dunkeln Hain
Robert Franz, "Stille Sicherheit" 1860pub, Op10,2
Hugo Wolf, "Stille Sicherheit" 1876
Othmar Schoeck, "Stille Sicherheit" 1922pub, Op36,3

Ich ging an deiner Seite
Othmar Schoeck, "Waldgang" 1922pub, Op36,8

Ich sah den Lenz einmal, erwacht im schönsten Tal
Leopold Damrosch, "Liebesfrühling" Op5,5
Robert Franz, "Liebesfrühling" 1860?, Op14,5
Hugo Wolf, "Liebesfrühling" 1876, Op9,2
Othmar Schoeck, "Liebesfrühling" 1922, Op36,2
from *Elegie*

Ich trat in einen heilig düstern Eichwald
Robert Franz, "Der Eichwald" 1879, Op51,1
Othmar Schoeck, "Der Eichwald" 1930, Op45,4
from *Wanderung im Gebirge*

Ich wandre fort in's ferne Land
Felix Mendelssohn, "Auf der Wanderschaft" 1847, Op71,5
Wilhelm Kienzl, "An den Wind" 187-?, Op8,4
Robert Franz, "An den Wind" 1870?pub, Op26,6
Charles Griffes, "An den Wind" 1903-11?, A17
Othmar Schoeck, "An den Wind" 1922pub, Op36,9

In einem Buche blätternd
Felix Weingartner, "Welke Rose" 1891pub, Op16,3
Othmar Schoeck, "Welke Rose" 1922pub, Op36,22
from *Elegie*

In Schlummer ist der dunkle Wald gesunken
Othmar Schoeck, "Stimme des Windes" 1954-55, Op70,7, 1v(med).orch
from *Nachhall*

Klar und wie die Jugend heiter
Othmar Schoeck, "Niagara" 1954-55, Op70,9, 1v(med).orch
from *Nachhall*

Lebe nicht so schnell und stürmisch
Othmar Schoeck, "Warnung und Wunsch" 1922pub, Op36,5

Lebe wohl! Ach, jene Abendstunde
Othmar Schoeck, "Lebewohl!" 1905, o.op19

Lethe! brich die Fesseln des Ufers
Wilhelm Kienzl, "Sehnsucht nach Vergessen" 188-?, Op39,1
Moritz Bauer, "Sehnsucht nach Vergessen"
from *Zwei Lieder* (2)
Hans Pfitzner, "Sehnsucht nach Vergessen" 1922, Op30,1

Lieblich war die Maiennacht
Othmar Schoeck, "Der Postillon" 1909, Op18, ten.mch.orch(pf)

Ließe doch ein hold Geschick
Othmar Schoeck, "Stumme Liebe" 1913, Op24a,2

Mädchen, sieh am Wiesenhang
Felix Weingartner, "Sommerfäden" 1891pub, Op16,5

Mein Pfeifchen traut, mir ist dein Rauch
Felix Weingartner, "Mein Türkenkopf" 1891pub, Op16,4

Müde schleichen hier die Bäche
Othmar Schoeck, "Auf eine holländische Landschaft" 1954-55, Op70,6, 1v(med).orch
from *Nachhall*

Mürrisch braust der Eichenwald
Léander Schlegel, "Herbstgefühl" Op24,3
Othmar Schoeck, "Herbstgefühl" 1922, Op36,13
from *Elegie*

Nach langem Frost, wie weht die Luft so lind!
Hugo Wolf, "Frühlingsgrüsse" 1876

Noch immer lag ein tiefes Schweigen
Othmar Schoeck, "Das Gewitter" 1930, Op45,8
from *Wanderung im Gebirge*

Nun ist es Herbst, die Blätter fallen
Hugo Wolf, "Herbst" 1879

O Einsamkeit! wie trink' ich gerne
Othmar Schoeck, "O Einsamkeit! wie trink' ich gerne" 1931-33, Op47,Vc, bar.4str
from *Notturno*

O Menschenherz, was ist dein Glück?
Willy Burkhard, "Frage (1)" 1925, Op9,1, 1v(low).pf
from *Frage*
Willy Burkhard, "Frage (2)" 1925, Op9,8, 1v(low).pf
from *Frage*

"O sei mein Freund!" so schallt's vom Heuchelmunde
Othmar Schoeck, "Der falsche Freund" 1954-55, Op70,8, 1v(med).orch
from *Nachhall*

O stürzt, ihr Wolkenbrüche, zum Abgrund nur hinab!
Leopold Damrosch, "Meine Furcht" Op8,2

O wärst du mein, es wär' ein schön'res Leben
Richard Strauss, "O wärst du mein!" 1891, Op26,2

O wag' es nicht, mit mir zu scherzen
Hugo Wolf, "An *" 1877

Rings ein Verstummen, ein Entfärben
Othmar Schoeck, "Rings ein Verstummen, ein Entfärben" 1931-33, Op47,IV, bar.4str
from *Notturno*

Rosen fliehen nicht allein
Othmar Schoeck, "An die Entfernte" 1907, Op5,2

Sahst du ein Glück vorübergehn
Felix Weingartner, "Blick in den Strom" 1891pub, Op16,8
Othmar Schoeck, "Sahst du ein Glück vorübergehn" 1931-33, Op47,Ie, bar.4str
from *Notturno*

Schlaflose Nacht, der Regen rauscht
Othmar Schoeck, "Mein Herz" 1954-55, Op70,3, 1v(med).orch
from *Nachhall*

Schöne Sennin, noch einmal singe deinen Ruf in's Thal
Robert Schumann, "Die Sennin" 1850, Op90,4

Schon seh' ich Hirt' und Herde nimmer
Othmar Schoeck, "Einsamkeit" 1930, Op45,6
from *Wanderung im Gebirge*

Schon zog vom Walde ich ferne wieder
Othmar Schoeck, "Der Hirte" 1930, Op45,5
from *Wanderung im Gebirge*

Sein Bündel Holz am Rücken bringt
Othmar Schoeck, "Abendheimkehr" 1954-55, Op70,5, 1v(med).orch
from *Nachhall*

Sieh' dort den Berg mit seinem Wiesenhange
Othmar Schoeck, "Sieh' dort den Berg mit seinem Wiesenhange" 1931-33, Op47,Ia, bar.4str
from *Notturno*

Sieh' hier den Bach, anbei die Waldesrose
Othmar Schoeck, "Sieh' hier den Bach, anbei die Waldesrose" 1931-33, Op47,Ib, bar.4str
from *Notturno*

So oft sie kam, erschien mir die Gestalt
Leopold Damrosch, "Kommen und Scheiden" Op5,4
Robert Schumann, "Kommen und Scheiden" 1850, Op90,3

Othmar Schoeck, "Kommen und Scheiden" 1922pub, Op36,10
from *Elegie*

Sonnenuntergang, schwarze Wolken zieh'n
Robert Franz, "Sonnenuntergang" 1844pub, Op2,4
from *"Schilflieder" von Nicolaus Lenau*
Henri Marteau, "Sonnenuntergang" 1925pub, Op31,4
from *Fünf Schilflieder*

Stoppelfeld, die Wälder leer
Othmar Schoeck, "Der Kranich" 1954-55, Op70,11, 1v(med).orch
from *Nachhall*

Sturm mit seinen Donnerschlägen kann mir nicht wie du
Hugo Wolf, "Meeresstille" 1876, Op9,1

Trübe wird's die Wolken jagen, und der Regen niederbricht
Robert Franz, "Trübe wird's die Wolken jagen" 1844pub, Op2,3
from *"Schilflieder" von Nicolaus Lenau*
Othmar Schoeck, "Trübe wird's, die Wolken jagen" 1905, Op2,2
from *Drei Schilflieder*
Henri Marteau, "Trübe wirds, die Wolken jagen" 1925pub, Op31,2
from *Fünf Schilflieder*

Trübe Wolken, Herbstesluft
Hugo Wolf, "Herbstentschluss" 1879
Othmar Schoeck, "Herbstentschluß" 1922pub, Op36,19
from *Elegie*

Vor Kälte ist die Luft erstarrt
Robert Franz, "Winternacht" 1865?pub, Op21,5

Weil' auf mir, du dunkles Auge
Carl Loewe, "Das dunkle Auge" 1839
Johann Vesque von Püttlingen, "Bitte" 1844-51?, Op43,2
Fanny Hensel, "Bitte" 1846, Op7,5
Robert Franz, "Bitte" 1860?, Op9,3
Leopold Damrosch, "Bitte" Op5,1
Moritz Moszkowski, "Bitte" 1877pub, Op13,1, bar.pf
Adolf Hoffmann, "Gebet" 1884pub, Op5,3
Max Reger, "Bitte" 1890/91
Felix Weingartner, "Bitte" 1891pub, Op16,6
Léander Schlegel, "Bitte" 1900, Op20,6
from *Deutsche Liebeslieder*
Charles Edward Ives, "Weil' auf mir" 1902
Carl Orff, "Bitte" 1919?

Wenn Worte dir vom Rosenmunde wehen
Oskar Dietrich, "Zweifelnder Wunsch" 1910pub
Othmar Schoeck, "Zweifelnder Wunsch" 1922, Op36,6

Wie die Ros' in deinem Haare, Mädchen, bist du bald verblüht
Leopold Damrosch, "An ein schönes Mädchen" Op8,4

Wie sehr ich Dein, soll ich Dir sagen?
Robert Franz, "Frage nicht" 1860?, Op14,6
Hugo Wolf, "Frage nicht" 1879

Othmar Schoeck, "Frage nicht" 1922pub, Op36,4
Willy Burkhard, "Frage nicht" 1925, Op9,2, 1v(low).pf
from *Frage*

Wild verwachsne dunkle Fichten
Robert Schumann, "Einsamkeit" 1850, Op90,5

Wo kein Strahl des Lichts hinblinket
Anna Teichmüller, "Wo kein Strahl des Lichts" 1906pub, Op8,3

Zieh' nicht so schnell vorüber an dieser stillen Haide
Robert Franz, "An die Wolke" 1870?pub, Op30,6

Willy (Wilhelm) Lentrodt (1864-1914)
Es ist so still. Alles schläft
Eugen d'Albert, "Sehnsucht in der Nacht" 1900?pub, Op22,1

Gustav Lenz (1808-1891)
Major! Ihr habt zu allen Zeiten
Carl Loewe, "Die fünf Sinne" 182-?, 4soli.ch.pf

Ludwig Friedrich Lenz (1717-1780)
O heiliges Band der Freundschaft
Wolfgang Amadeus Mozart, "Lobegesang auf die feierliche Johannisloge" 1775-76?, K148

Friedrich August Leo (1820-1898)
Die Wipfel säuseln Abendruh', die Sonne sinkt dem Meere zu
Eduard Lassen, "Schlummerlied" Op75,2

Was ist des Vögleins Dach, wenn draussen Sturm wird wach?
Eduard Lassen, "Das Nest" Op75,3

Wenn kein Windchen weht, wenn kein Wölkchen geht
Eduard Lassen, "Blaue Augen" Op75,1

Gottlieb von Leon (1757-1830)
Ein blondiges Mägdelein, rosig und zart
Johann Rudolf Zumsteeg, "Vernunft und Liebe" 1803pub
from *Kleine Balladen und Lieder, fünftes Heft*

Mond, sei Zeuge meiner Leiden!
Karl Friberth, "An den Mond" 1780pub

Sobald Damötas Chloen sieht
Johann Rudolf Zumsteeg, "Die Verschwiegenheit" 1803pub
from *Kleine Balladen und Lieder, sechstes Heft*

Solang, ach! schon solang erfüllt
Johann Holzer, "Liebeslied" 1779pub
Joseph Haydn, "Liebeslied" 1781/84, XXVIa Nr.11

Weißt du, mein kleines Mägdelein
Johann Holzer, "Kupido" 1779pub
Joseph Haydn, "Cupido" 1781/84, XXVIa Nr.2

Wo weht der Liebe hoher Geist?
Franz Schubert, "Die Liebe" 1817, D522

Giacomo Leopardi (1798-1837)

Nichts gibt's, was würdig wäre deiner Bemühungen
Hanns Eisler, "Faustus' Verzweiflung" 1953
translated by Robert Hamerling, 1866

O lieblich klarer Mond, ich denke dran
Eugen d'Albert, "An den Mond" 1898?pub, Op17,2
German translation by Paul Heyse

Mikhail Yurevich Lermontov (1814-1841)

Schlaf', mein Kindchen, ruhig liege, schlaf', mein Kind, schlaf' ein
Leopold Damrosch, "Der Kosaken Wiegenlied" Op14,2
German translation by Friedrich Bodenstedt
George Henschel, "Der Kosakin Wiegenlied" 188-?, Op43,1

Gotthold Ephraim Lessing (1729-1781)

Der Neid, o Kind, zählt unsre Küsse
Sigfrid Karg-Elert, "Geschwind" 1907pub, Op56,5
from *Zehn Epigramme von Lessing*

Du, dem kein Epigramm gefällt
Sigfrid Karg-Elert, "Als Prolog für den Hörer" 1907pub, Op56,1
from *Zehn Epigramme von Lessing*

Du Diebin mit der Rosenwange
George Henschel, "Du Diebin mit der Rosenwange" 186-?, Op1,1

Faulheit, endlich muß ich Dir
Joseph Haydn, "Lob der Faulheit" 1781/84, XXVIa Nr.22

Frau X besucht sehr oft den jungen Doctor Klette
Sigfrid Karg-Elert, "Auf Frau X" 1907pub, Op56,2
from *Zehn Epigramme von Lessing*

Freunde, Wasser machet stumm
Joseph Haydn, "Die Beredsamkeit" 1796-1801, satb.bc

Gestern liebt' ich, heute leid' ich, morgen sterb' ich
Sigfrid Karg-Elert, "Aus dem Spanischen" 1907pub, Op56,7
from *Zehn Epigramme von Lessing*

Ich habe nicht stets Lust zu lesen
Sigfrid Karg-Elert, "Auf sich selbst" 1907pub, Op56,3
from *Zehn Epigramme von Lessing*

Kleine Schöne, küsse mich, kleine Schöne, schämst du dich?
Leopold Kozeluch, "An die kleine Schöne" 1785?
Sigfrid Karg-Elert, "An eine sechsjährige Schöne" 1907pub, Op56,9
from *Zehn Epigramme von Lessing*

Mein Esel sicherlich muss klüger sein als ich!
Sigfrid Karg-Elert, "Mein Esel" 1907pub, Op56,4
from *Zehn Epigramme von Lessing*

Ohne Liebe lebe, wer da kann
Ludwig van Beethoven, "Lied" 1792?, Op52,6

So bringst du mich um meine Liebe
Sigfrid Karg-Elert, "An den Genuss" 1907pub, Op56,6
from *Zehn Epigramme von Lessing*

Wenn du von allem dem, was diese Blätter füllt
Sigfrid Karg-Elert, "Als Epilog für den Hörer" 1907pub, Op56,10
from *Zehn Epigramme von Lessing*

Wenn ich, Augenlust zu finden, unter schattig grünen Linden
Sigfrid Karg-Elert, "Ein Unterschied" 1907pub, Op56,8
from *Zehn Epigramme von Lessing*

Zankst du schon wieder, sprach Hans Lau zu seiner lieben Ehefrau
Erich Zeisl, "Stilleben" 1935pub

Heinrich Leuthold (1827-1879)

Deine süßen, süßen Schauer, o Waldesruh'
Ignaz Brüll, "Waldeinsamkeit" 186-?, Op5,ii,3
Ludwig Thuille, "Waldeinsamkeit" 1898cop, Op12,1

Der Lenz ist da und fern und nah
Othmar Schoeck, "Liederfrühling" 1944, Op57,3
from *Der Sänger*

Dich vor allem, heilige Muttersprache
Othmar Schoeck, "Muttersprache" 1944, Op57,2
from *Der Sänger*

Die Ströme zieh'n zum fernen Meer
Othmar Schoeck, "Die Ströme zieh'n zum fernen Meer" 1944, Op56,2, 1v.harp or pf
from *Spielmannsweisen*

Du sahst mich schwelgen oft im Tonregister
Othmar Schoeck, "Unmut" 1944, Op57,25
from *Der Sänger*

Ein guter Ruf ist wie ein wohnlich Haus
Othmar Schoeck, "Spruch" 1944, Op57,24
from *Der Sänger*

Ein unbezwingbar dunkler Hang
Othmar Schoeck, "Trauer" 1944, Op57,19
from *Der Sänger*

Greift zum Becher und laßt das Schelten
Othmar Schoeck, "Trinklied" 1944, Op57,22
from *Der Sänger*

Hier pflegt Natur mit ihren goldnen Auen
Othmar Schoeck, "Heimweh" 1944, Op57,15
from *Der Sänger*

Hier scheidet die Klosterpforte
Othmar Schoeck, "Im Klosterkeller" 1944, Op57,21
from *Der Sänger*

Ich bin ein Spielmann von Beruf
Othmar Schoeck, "Ich bin ein Spielmann von Beruf" 1944, Op56,3, 1v.harp or pf
from *Spielmannsweisen*

Ihr Bilder, die die Zeit begrub
Othmar Schoeck, "Einst" 1944, Op57,17
from *Der Sänger*

In diesen Silberhainen von Oliven
Othmar Schoeck, "Riviera" 1944, Op57,10
from *Der Sänger*

Komm, ambrosische Nacht, ströme dein Silberlicht
Othmar Schoeck, "Nacht, Muse und Tod" 1944, Op57,11
from *Der Sänger*

Leise, windverwehte Lieder, mögt ihr fallen in den Sand
Robert Kahn, "Blätterfall" 1895, Op22,ii,4

Mein Herz ist wie ein Saitenspiel
Othmar Schoeck, "Mein Herz ist wie ein Saitenspiel" 1944, Op56,5, 1v.harp or pf
from *Spielmannsweisen*

Mein Liebster keck ist ein Matros'
Ignaz Brüll, "Ligurisches Volkslied" 186-?, Op5,ii,2
Robert Kahn, "Ligurisches Lied" 1891, Op12,3

Nach Westen zieht der Wind dahin, er fächelt leis' und lind dahin
Karl Lafite, "Ghasel" 1911cop

Nicht allein in Rathaussälen
Othmar Schoeck, "Aus dem Süden" 1944, Op57,9
from *Der Sänger*

Nicht, daß ich dies Bestreben nicht erfasse
Othmar Schoeck, "Rechtfertigung" 1944, Op57,6
from *Der Sänger*

Nun laß das Lamentieren und halte Maß!
Othmar Schoeck, "Trost" 1944, Op57,26
from *Der Sänger*

O Frühlingshauch, o Liederlust
Othmar Schoeck, "O Frühlingshauch, o Liederlust" 1944, Op56,1, 1v.harp or pf
from *Spielmannsweisen*

O Lebensfrühling, Blütendrang
Othmar Schoeck, "O Lebensfrühling, Blütendrang" 1944, Op56,6, 1v.harp or pf
from *Spielmannsweisen*

O wie träumt es sich süß am myrtenumbuschten Gestade
Othmar Schoeck, "Sonnenuntergang" 1944, Op57,13
from *Der Sänger*

Schon verstummt das Lied der Grille
Othmar Schoeck, "Rückkehr" 1944, Op57,16
from *Der Sänger*

Schweigen rings; im Garten der Villa plaudert
Othmar Schoeck, "Sapphische Strophe" 1944, Op57,12
from *Der Sänger*

Selbstzweck sei sich die Kunst, die göttliche deine der Zeit nicht?
Othmar Schoeck, "Distichen" 1944, Op57,23
from *Der Sänger*

Und wieder nehm' ich die Harfe zur Hand
Othmar Schoeck, "Und wieder nehm' ich die Harfe zur Hand" 1944, Op56,4, 1v.harp or pf
from *Spielmannsweisen*

Waldvögelein, wohin ziehst du?
Othmar Schoeck, "Waldvögelein" 1944, Op57,8
from *Der Sänger*

Was immer mir die Feindschaft unterschoben
Othmar Schoeck, "Leidenschaft" 1944, Op57,1
from *Der Sänger*

Wenn ein Gott dir gab fürs Schöne
Othmar Schoeck, "Warnung" 1944, Op57,14
from *Der Sänger*

Wie bist du schön, du tiefer, blauer See!
Othmar Schoeck, "Der Waldsee" 1907, Op15,1
Othmar Schoeck, "Der Waldsee" 1944, Op57,20
from *Der Sänger*

Wie einst den Knaben lacht ihr noch heut mich an
Othmar Schoeck, "Abkehr" 1944, Op57,7
from *Der Sänger*

Wie floß von deiner Lippe milde Güte!
Othmar Schoeck, "An meine Großmutter" 1944, Op57,18
from *Der Sänger*

Wo über mir die Waldnacht finster
Othmar Schoeck, "Waldeinsamkeit" 1944, Op57,4
from *Der Sänger*

Wohl ist es schön, auf fauler Haut
Othmar Schoeck, "Vorwurf" 1944, Op57,5
from *Der Sänger*

Karl Michael Freiherr von Levetzow (1871-1945)

Aus den Trümmern einer hohen Schönheit
Arnold Schönberg, "Abschied" 1898?, Op1,2, bar.pf

Grosses hast Du mir gegeben in jenen Hochstunden
Arnold Schönberg, "Dank" 1898?, Op1,1, bar.pf

Li-Tai-Pe

Vor mein Bett wirft der Mond einen grellen Schein
Othmar Schoeck, "In der Herberge" 1907, Op7,3
from the *Schi-King*

L. Liber

Wenn der Duft quillt aus der Knospe Schoos
Hermann Goetz, "Frühlings Wiederkehr" 1862-63, Op19,3

Felix Maria Vincenz Andreas, Fürst von Lichnowsky (1814-1848)

Ach, nun taucht die Klosterzelle
Franz Liszt, "Nonnenwerth" 1843/1862

Adolf Licht (1811-1885)

Treibe, treibe, Schifflein

Paul Hindemith, "Barcarole" 1925, Op35,i,1, sop.ob.vla.vc

from *Die Serenaden*

Meinrad Lienert (1865-1933)

I weiß äs Seeli, bodelos

Othmar Schoeck, "'s Seeli" 1905, o.op21, ch

Nüd schöiners, as wänn's dimm'red

Othmar Schoeck, "'s Liedli" 1915, o.op34, ch

Friedrich Lienhard (1865-1929)

Mir ist nach einer Heimat weh

Hans Pfitzner, "Abendrot" 1909, Op24,4

Frau von Lieven

Ich stehe hoch überm See

Max Reger, "Ich stehe hoch überm See" 1892-94?, Op14b, bass.pf

Detlev von Liliencron (1844-1909)

Auf dem Wege vom Tanzsaal nach Haus

Hans Pfitzner, "Müde" 1889-1901, Op10,2

Der Abend war so dunkel schwer, und schwer durch's Dunkel schnitt der Kahn

Eugen d'Albert, "Stromüber" 1904pub, Op27,3

Der Tag ging regenschwer und sturmbewegt

Johannes Brahms, "Auf dem Kirchhofe" 1888?, Op105,4, 1v(low).pf

Die Feder am Sturmhut in Spiel und Gefahren, Halli

Richard Strauss, "Bruder Liederlich" 1899, Op41a,4

Du junge, schöne Bleicherin, wo fährst du denn dein Leinen hin

Eugen d'Albert, "Die kleine Bleicherin" 1904pub, Op27,4

Flatternde Fahnen und frohes Gedränge

Ernest Vietor, "Siegesfest" Op3,2

Ich ging den Weg entlang, der einsam lag

Hans Pfitzner, "Sehnsucht" 1889-1901, Op10,1

Richard Strauss, "Sehnsucht" 1896, Op32,2

Ich kann das Wort nicht vergessen, es klang so traurig und schwer

Ernest Vietor, "Zu spät" Op3,4

Hermann Zilcher, "Zu spät" 1904?pub, Op12,2

Im Weizenfeld, im Korn und Mohn

Alexander Zemlinsky, "Tod in Ähren" 1900?, Op8,4

from *Turmwächterlied und andere Gesänge*

In der Dämmerung, um Glock zwei, Glock dreie

Anton Webern, "Heimgang in der Frühe" 1901-04

from *Acht frühe Lieder* (8)

Maienkätzchen, erster Gruß

Johannes Brahms, "Maienkätzchen" 1886?, Op107,4

Alexander Zemlinsky, "Tiefe Sehnsucht" 1897?, Op5,ii,2

Alban Berg, "Tiefe Sehnsucht" 1905

Mit Trommeln und Pfeifen bin ich oft marschiert
Alexander Zemlinsky, "Mit Trommeln und Pfeifen" 1900?, Op8,3
from *Turmwächterlied und andere Gesänge*

O wär es doch! Hinaus in dunkle Wälder
Emil Mattiesen, "Schrei" 190-?pub, Op15,2
from *Überwindungen* (2)

Über eine Wiege schaukelt ein blauer Schmetterling
Alexander Zemlinsky, "Über eine Wiege" 1910pub

Vier adlige Rosse voran unserm Wagen
Richard Strauss, "Ich liebe dich" 1898, Op37,2

War der schönste Sommermorgen, war der Wald so grün und jung
Eugen d'Albert, "Ach, jung..." 1904pub, Op27,5

Wenn sanft du mir im Arme schliefst, ich deinen Atem hören konnte
Richard Strauss, "Glückes genug" 1898, Op37,1
Max Reger, "Glückes genug" 1899, Op37,3, 1v(med).pf
Hermann Zilcher, "Glückes genug" 1904?pub, Op12,4

Wir wandeln durch die stumme Nacht, der Tamtam ist verklungen
Hermann Zilcher, "Frühgang" 1904?pub, Op12,1

Anton Lindner (1874-1915)
Laß Akaziendüfte schaukeln
Richard Strauss, "Hochzeitlich Lied" 1898, Op37,6

Wie Seide war ihr leiser Tritt, ein Flügelschlagen war ihr Gang
Rudi Stephan, "Auf den Tod einer jungen Frau" 1906

Thekla Lingen (1866-1931)
Ach gestern hat er mir Rosen gebracht
Joseph Marx, "Und gestern hat er mir Rosen gebracht" 1909

Sieh', ich steh' vor deiner Thür, laß mich ein!
Alexander Zemlinsky, "Klopfet, so wird euch aufgethan" 1901?, Op10,5
from *Ehetanzlied und andere Gesänge*

Zur Ruhe, mein Herz zur Ruh, schliess deine Augen zu
Hugo Kaun, "Schlummerlied" 1903pub, Op46,1

Hermann von Lingg (1820-1905)
Blumen an den Wegen, Blumen um den Rain
Max Bruch, "Klosterlied" 186-?, Op17,iii,3
from *Drei Lieder gedichtet von Hermann Lingg*

Düster brennt und trüb' die Flamme
Robert Kahn, "Feuerbestattung" 1899pub

Dunkelnd über den See dämmert das Abendrot
Arnold Schönberg, "Gruß in die Ferne" 1900, 1v(low).pf

Ein Wolkengebirg' umfließt die Sonne
Erich Zeisl, "Die Nacht bricht an" 1935pub

Frau Venus, Frau Venus, o lass mich gehn geschwinde
Max Bruch, "Tannhäuser" 186-?, Op17,iii,1
from *Drei Lieder gedichtet von Hermann Lingg*

Geheimnisvoller Klang, für Geister der Luft besaitet
Max Reger, "Aeolsharfe" 1903, Op75,11, 1v(med).pf

Immer leiser wird mein Schlummer, nur wie Schleier liegt mein Kummer
Johannes Brahms, "Immer leiser wird mein Schlummer" 1886, Op105,2, 1v(low).pf
Hans Pfitzner, "Immer leiser wird mein Schlummer" 1888/89, Op2,6
Wilhelm Kienzl, "Immer leiser wird mein Schlummer" 189-?, Op24,2
Ludwig Thuille, "Die Verlassene" 189-?pub, Op4,2
Carl Orff, "Immer leiser wird mein Schlummer" 1911, Op8,2

Kalt und schneidend weht der Wind, und mein Herz ist bang und leidend
Franz Wüllner, "Lied" 1857pub
Leopold Damrosch, "Kalt und schneidend weht der Wind" Op8,8
Hans Pfitzner, "Lied" 1888/89, Op2,3

Leb' wohl, du guter Reiterdienst, zu Fuss muss ich nun wandern
Max Bruch, "Der junge Invalide" 186-?, Op17,iii,2
from *Drei Lieder gedichtet von Hermann Lingg*

Man sagt, durch's Zimmer walle ein schönes Engelskind
Felix Mottl, "Märchen" 1896?pub

Mein Herz, aus goldnen Jugendtagen
Hugo Brückler, "Frühlingssegen" 187-?pub, Nachlass

Schwüle, schwüle Julinacht, Südwind küsst die Zweige
Robert Gund, "Julinacht" 1893, Op10,1

Soviel Raben nachts auffliegen
Arnold Schönberg, "Freihold" 1899-1903, Op3,6, 1v(med).pf

Wenn etwas leise in dir spricht, dass dir mein Herz ergeben
Franz Wüllner, "Wenn etwas leise in dir spricht" 1857pub

Hermann Löns (1866-1914)
Rose Marie, Rose Marie, sieben Jahre mein Herz nach dir schrie
Ernest Vietor, "Abendlied" 1939-40, Op17,2

Lina Löper
Es lag auf meiner Stirn einst eine Wolke so schwer und trüb
Carl Loewe, "Wolkenbild" 1847, Op110,2

Oskar Loerke (1884-1941)
Aus der Glockenstube überm Dom quillt ein kupferroter Lavastrom
Wolfgang Rihm, "Hochsommerbann" 1970, Op1,4

(Johann) Carl Gottfried Loewe (1796-1869)
Habe ich dir nicht gesagt, so du glauben würdest
Carl Loewe, "Lazarus' Todtenerweckung" 1863, Op132,15&16, bar.alt.ch.org/pf
after John 11

Segne den König, ihn, unsern gütigen
Carl Loewe, "Salvum fac regem" 1850
free translation from the Latin

Carl Loewe and [Rechtskandidat] Vocke
Als ich, ein Knabe noch, das heil'ge Land zuerst
Carl Loewe, "Der Ritterschwur" 1825
from the Opera *Rudolf, der deutsche Herr*

Dank, grausender Dank sei dir gebracht
Carl Loewe, "Des Cerivaglia Rachesang" 1823, 1v.orch

Der Mann ist geboren zur Liebe!
Carl Loewe, "Trinklied des deutschen Kriegers" 1823

O falle, mein Schleier, o liege, mein Schleier
Carl Loewe, "Schleier-Romanze" 1825
from the Opera *Rudolf, der deutsche Herr*

's ist wahrlich besser in Kampf und Schlacht
Carl Loewe, "Wachtpostenlied" 1825

Helene Loewe
Steigt empor, ihr Wünsche mein
Carl Loewe, "Ida's Wunsch" 1850-60

Stille, stille, dass ich höre, was das blaue Blümchen spricht!
Carl Loewe, "Das Blümlein" 1850-60

Rudolf Löwenstein (1819-1891)
Ach, Vater, sprich, wie fang' ich's an
Carl Reinecke, "Hans und die Spatzen"
from *Kinderlieder*

Es ist schon dunkel um mich her
Wilhelm Taubert, "Guten Abend"
from *Klänge aus der Kinderwelt*, Vol.3, No7

Hänschen will ein Tischler werden, ist zu schwer der Hobel
Wilhelm Taubert, "Die traurige Geschichte vom dummen Hänschen"
from *Klänge aus der Kinderwelt*, Vol.2, No11

Möcht' wissen, wo der Kerl nur steckt
Carl Reinecke, "Peter und das Echo"
from *Kinderlieder*

Nun reibet euch die Äuglein wach!
Wilhelm Taubert, "Guten Morgen"
from *Klänge aus der Kinderwelt*, Vol.4, No1

Trom to tom, tom, tom, trom to tom, tom! Ich bin der beste Trommler
Wilhelm Taubert, "Trommellied"
from *Klänge aus der Kinderwelt*, Vol.2, No9

Wer klappert am Dache, mein Kindlein? horch, horch!
Wilhelm Taubert, "Der Vöglein Abschied"
from *Klänge aus der Kinderwelt*, Vol.2, No5

Wohin sind all' die Raritäten
Carl Reinecke, "Drei Wochen nach Weihnachten"
from *Kinderlieder*

Wilhelm Graf von Löwenstein-Werthheim
Meine Lieder, meine Sänge sind dem Augenblick geweiht
Carl Maria von Weber, "Meine Lieder, meine Sänge" 1809, Op15,1

(Johann) Karl Philipp Lohbauer (1777-1809)
Der Fluren Grün, das Abendgold
Emilie Zumsteeg, "Natur und Tugend" 1817pub
from *Neun Lieder* (1)

Oft in meiner Kindheit süssen Träumen
Johann Rudolf Zumsteeg, "Die Welt ohne Sie" 1800pub
from *Kleine Balladen und Lieder, zweites Heft*

Wo lebt' ich glücklicher verborgen
Johann Rudolf Zumsteeg, "Der Einsiedler" 1803pub
from *Kleine Balladen und Lieder, sechstes Heft*

(Karl) Julius Lohmeyer (1835-1903)
Guten Morgen! sollt' ich sagen und ein schönes Kompliment
Carl Reinecke, "Der Geburtstagsgratulant"
from *Kinderlieder*

Sebastian Longard
Ach, in dem funklenden, träumerisch dunkelnden Aug'
Johanna Kinkel, "Schwarze Augen" Op17,2

(Auguste) Wilhelmine Lorenz (1784-1861)
Es flüstern und rauschen die Wogen
Robert Schumann, "Loreley" 1840, Op53,2

F. Lorenz
Eh' wir weiter gehen, laß uns stille stehen
Alban Berg, "Wo der Goldregen steht" 1902

Lenz Lorenzi
Wach' auf, erwache wieder
Hugo Wolf, "Grablied" 1876, satb

Ernst Lothar (Müller) (1890-1974)
Mond, so gehst du wieder auf
Erich Wolfgang Korngold, "Mond, so gehst du wieder auf" 1918, Op14,3
from *Lieder des Abschieds*

Weine nicht, daß ich jetzt gehe
Erich Wolfgang Korngold, "Gefaßter Abschied" 1918, Op14,4
from *Lieder des Abschieds*

August Ludwig Lua (1819-1876)
Die Lerche singt ihr Morgenlied froh auf dem weiten Feld
Carl Loewe, "Wanderlied" 1847

Sommer entschwand, Herbstluft durchwehet das Land
Louis Spohr, "Herbst" 1847, WoO115

Michael Lubi (1757-1807)
Am hohen, hohen Thurm, da weht ein kalter Sturm
Franz Schubert, "Ammenlied" 1814, D122

Gustav von Ludwiger: see "Gottl. von Deuern"

(Elisabetha Cordula) Carolina von der Lühe, née Brandenstein (1754-1813)
Wenn im Hauch der Abend kühle
Carl Friedrich Zelter, "Die unsichtbare Welt" 1805

Martin Luther (1483-1546)
Mit Fried und Freud ich fahr dahin
Carl Loewe, "Mit Fried und Freud ich fahr dahin" 1863, Op132,6b, 4v

Mitten wir im Leben sind
Peter Cornelius, "Mitten wir im Leben sind" 1869, Op9,3, ttbb
translated from Notker Balbulus

Tod, Sünd, Leben und Gnad, alles, alles in Händen er hat
Carl Loewe, "Tod, Sünd, Leben und Gnad" 1863, Op132,1, 4v

Wer nicht liebt Weib, Wein und Gesang
Johann Rudolf Zumsteeg, "Canon a 4" 1803pub, 4v
from *Kleine Balladen und Lieder, fünftes Heft*

Wer sich die Musik erkiest
Paul Hindemith, "Wer sich die Musik erkiest" 1925, Op45,ii,2, 2v.insts
from *Sing-und Spielmusiken für Liebhaber und Musikfreunde*

Arthur Lutze (1813-1870)
Ein Engel zog durch Flur und Haus und streute Gaben der Liebe
Carl Loewe, "Gottesbote" 1859, ch

Sag an, was hinauf zur Drachenkluft
Carl Loewe, "Der Drachenfels" 1838, Op121,2, 1v(high).pf

Johann Peter Lyser (1804-1870)
Horch! Welch ein süßes harmonisches Klingen
Clara Schumann, "Walzer" 1834

John Henry Mackay (1864-1933)
Auf, hebe die funkelnde Schale empor zum Mund
Richard Strauss, "Heimliche Aufforderung" 1894, Op27,3

Der Tag, der schwüle, verblasst
Richard Strauss, "Verführung" 1896, Op33,1, 1v.orch

Ich grüsse die Sonne, die dort versinkt
Richard Strauss, "In der Campagna" 1899, Op41a,2

Tausend Menschen ziehen vorüber den ich ersehne, er ist nicht dabei!
Arnold Schönberg, "Am Wegrand" 1903-05, Op6,6

Und morgen wird die Sonne wieder scheinen
Richard Strauss, "Morgen!" 1894, Op27,4
Max Reger, "Morgen" 1902, Op66,10, 1v(med).pf

James Macpherson ("Ossian") (1736-1796)
Beugt euch aus euren Wolken nieder, ihr Geister meiner Väter
Franz Schubert, "Ossians Lied nach dem Falle Nathos'" 1815, D278
translated into German from Ossian's "Dar-Thule" by Edmund von Harold

Der bleiche, kalte Mond erhob sich in Osten
Franz Schubert, "Loda's Gespenst" 1816, D150
translated into German from Ossian's "Carric-Thure" by Edmund von Harold

Die Nacht ist dumpfig und finster
Franz Schubert, "Die Nacht" 1817, D534
translated into German from Ossian's "Croma" by Edmund von Harold

Ich sitz' bei der moosigten Quelle
Franz Schubert, "Cronnan" 1815, D282

Lorma sass in der Halle von Aldo
Franz Schubert, "Lorma (1)" (fragment), 1815, D327
Franz Schubert, "Lorma (2)" (fragment), 1816, D376

Mädchen Inistores, wein' auf dem Felsen der stürmischen Winde
Franz Schubert, "Das Mädchen von Inistore" 1815, D281

Mädchen von Kola, du schläfst!
Johannes Brahms, "Darthulas Grabesgesang" 1861, Op42,3, saatbb
translated into German from Ossian's "Darthula" by Herder

Mein Geliebter ist ein Sohn des Hügels
Franz Schubert, "Shilrik und Vinvela" 1815, D293
translated into German from Ossian's "Carric-Thura" by Edmund von Harold

Rolle, du strömigter Carun
Franz Schubert, "Bardengesang" 1816?, D147, ttb
translated from Ossian's "Comola" by Edmund von Harold

Rund um mich Nacht, ich irr' allein, verloren am stürmischen Hügel
Franz Schubert, "Kolma's Klage" 1815, D217
translated into German from Ossian's "Songs of Selma" by Edmund von Harold

Um mich ist Nacht! Nacht! Verirret steh' ich hier am stürm'schen Hügel
Carl Friedrich Zelter, "Colma" 1812?

Warum öffnest du wieder, Erzeugter von Alpin
Franz Schubert, "Der Tod Oscars" 1816, D375

Marie Madeleine (von Puttkammer, née Günther) (1881-1944)

Die fernen, fernen Berge mit ihren Nebelschleiern
Max Reger, "Mädchenlied" 1901
from *Liebeslieder* (5)

Wie ist mein zitterndes Herz entbrannt
Felix Weingartner, "Der Sklave" 1909, Op46,3

Franz Mäding (1876-?)

Goldiger, sonniger Maientag
Wilhelm Kienzl, "Mai" 1906pub, Op73,5

Maurice Maeterlinck (1862-1949)

Allen weinenden Seelen, aller nahenden Schuld
Alexander Zemlinsky, "Lied der Jungfrau" 1910, Op13,3
translated by Friedrich von Oppeln-Bronikowski
from *Sechs Gesänge nach Gedichten von Maeterlinck*

Als ihr Geliebter schied
Alexander Zemlinsky, "Als ihr Geliebter schied" 1913, Op13,4
translated by Friedrich von Oppeln-Bronikowski
from *Sechs Gesänge nach Gedichten von Maeterlinck*

Die drei Schwestern wollten sterben
Alexander Zemlinsky, "Die drei Schwestern" 1910, Op13,1
translated by Friedrich von Oppeln-Bronikowski
from *Sechs Gesänge nach Gedichten von Maeterlinck*

Die Mädchen mit den verbundenen Augen
Alexander Zemlinsky, "Die Mädchen mit den verbundenen Augen" 1910, Op13,2
translated by Friedrich von Oppeln-Bronikowski
from *Sechs Gesänge nach Gedichten von Maeterlinck*

Sie kam zum Schloß gegangen
Alexander Zemlinsky, "Sie kam zum Schloß gegangen" 1913, Op13,6
translated by Friedrich von Oppeln-Bronikowski
from *Sechs Gesänge nach Gedichten von Maeterlinck*

Und kehrt er einst heim
Alexander Zemlinsky, "Und kehrt er einst heim" 1910, Op13,5
translated by Friedrich von Oppeln-Bronikowski
from *Sechs Gesänge nach Gedichten von Maeterlinck*

Rudolf Friedrich Heinrich von Magenau (1767-1846)
Gott! wie herrlich glänzt der Abendhimmel
Emilie Zumsteeg, "Der Sternenhimmel" 1819pub, Op4,5

Gustav Mahler (1860-1911)
Die zwei blauen Augen von meinem Schatz
Gustav Mahler, "Die zwei blauen Augen" 1884-85, 1v(low).orch(pf)
from *Lieder eines fahrenden Gesellen*

Ging heut' Morgen über's Feld
Gustav Mahler, "Ging heut' Morgen über's Feld" 1884-85, 1v(low).orch(pf)
from *Lieder eines fahrenden Gesellen*

Ich hab' ein glühend Messer
Gustav Mahler, "Ich hab' ein glühend Messer" 1884-85, 1v(low).orch(pf)
from *Lieder eines fahrenden Gesellen*

Ringel, ringel Reih'n! Wer fröhlich ist, der schlinge sich ein!
Gustav Mahler, "Hans und Grete" 1880-87

Sag' an, du Träumer am lichten Tag
Gustav Mahler, "Im Lenz" 1880

Über Berg und Tal mit lautem Schall
Gustav Mahler, "Winterlied" 1880

Wenn mein Schatz Hochzeit macht
Gustav Mahler, "Wenn mein Schatz Hochzeit macht" 1884-85, 1v(low).orch(pf)
after "Wann mein Schatz" from *Des Knaben Wunderhorn*
from *Lieder eines fahrenden Gesellen*

Siegfried August Mahlmann (1771-1826)
Allah giebt Licht in Nächten
Johann Rudolf Zumsteeg, "Thirza" 1800pub
from *Kleine Balladen und Lieder, zweites Heft*

Als mein Leben voll Blumen hieng
Johann Rudolf Zumsteeg, "Schwermuth" 1800pub
from *Kleine Balladen und Lieder, zweites Heft*

Louis Spohr, "Schwermuth" 1835-36, Op94,5

An Himmelshöh'n die Sterne geh'n in fester, stiller Bahn
Hugo Wolf, "Gottvertrauen" 1876, satb

Das Laub fällt von den Bäumen
Robert Schumann, "Herbstlied" 1840, Op43,2, sop.alt.pf

Die Erde ruht, das Herz erwacht
Carl Loewe, "Die Nacht" before 1829

Die Quelle rauscht, die Mükke schwirrt
Johann Rudolf Zumsteeg, "Thirza" 1800pub
from *Kleine Balladen und Lieder, zweites Heft*

Gott sendet Licht in Nächten
Johann Rudolf Zumsteeg, "Licht in Nächten"

Gute Nacht! Liebchen sieh
Paul Hindemith, "Gute Nacht" 1925, Op35,iii,2, sop.ob.vla.vc
from *Die Serenaden*

Ich wand mir einst einen Veilchenkranz
Johann Rudolf Zumsteeg, "Der Veilchenkranz" 1802pub
from *Kleine Balladen und Lieder, viertes Heft*

Was ist es das im Mutterschoose
Emilie Zumsteeg, "Die Unschuld" 1817pub
from *Neun Lieder* (4)

Wo kommst du her, so bleich und blass
Johann Rudolf Zumsteeg, "Lied" 1802pub
from *Kleine Balladen und Lieder, viertes Heft*

Wort des Trostes, o wie schön tönst du vom geliebten Munde
Johann Rudolf Zumsteeg, "Wiedersehn" 1800pub
from *Kleine Balladen und Lieder, zweites Heft*

H. Mahn

Leise schleich' ich mich am Abend
Louis Spohr, "Abend-Feier" 1856, Op154,1, bar.vn.pf

Johann, Graf von Majláth (1786-1855)

Wie tönt es mir so schaurig, des Lenzes erstes Wehn
Franz Schubert, "Der Blumen Schmerz" 1821, D731

Ernst Friedrich Georg Otto Freiherr von der Malsburg (1786-1824)

Helf' mir Gott, wie fliegen die Gänse
Robert Schumann, "Romanze vom Gänsebuben" 1849, Op145,5, satb
translated from the Spanish

Gottfried August, Freiherr von Maltitz (1794-1837)

Auf den Bergen nur wohnet die Freiheit
Karl Gottlieb Reissiger, "Die Berge" Op140,5

Adolf von Marées (1801-1874)

Im Wirthshaus geht es aus und ein
Louis Spohr, "Das Wirthshaus zu…" 1836, WoO93

Prinzessin Margarethe von Oesterreich (1480-1530)
Mein Herzlein hat allzeit Verlangen nach Dir
Edgar Istel, "Minnelied" 1910pub

Rudolf Marggraff (1805-1880)
Durch Schneegestöber und eisigen Wind
Carl Loewe, "Der Lappländer" 1837, Op63,2

Ein Sternlein fiel vom Himmel her
Carl Loewe, "Die Schneeflocke" 1837, Op63,1

Karl Maria
Abendruhe liegt über dem Land
Erich J. Wolff, "Friede" 1914pub, Lieder No.1

Toni Mark
Schweig still, du dummes Menschenherz
Richard Stöhr, "Trost" 1914pub, Op28,1

Friedrich Marx (1830-1905)
Vom Wassergrunde helle grüßt mich das Sterngebild
Felix Weingartner, "Dein Bild" 1899, Op25,3

Wenn du noch schläfst, erwach' mein Lieb'
Wilhelm Kienzl, "Portugiesisches Volkslied" 187-?, Op6,7

Theophile Marzials (1850-1920)
Duft'ge Mispelblume, zartes Blüthenmeer
Frank van der Stucken, "Ein Schäferlied" 1892pub

Von schön Sicilien war mein Traum
Frank van der Stucken, "Von schön Sicilien war mein Traum" 1892pub

Karl Mastalier (1731-1795)
Auf in das Feld zum Streite!
Josef Antonín Štěpán, "Schlachtgesang" 1778-79pub

Hans von Matt
Voll Farben glüht der Garten, hinausgebaut aufs Meer
Paul Hindemith, "Heimatklänge" 1908/09
from *7 Lieder für Sopran oder Tenor mit Klavierbegleitung*

Friedrich von Matthisson (1761-1831)
Abendgewölke schweben hell
Franz Schubert, "Stimme der Liebe (1)" 1815, D187
Franz Schubert, "Stimme der Liebe (2)" 1816, D418

Am Seegestad', in lauen Vollmondsnächten
Franz Schubert, "Erinnerungen" 1814, D98

Auch des Edlen schlummernde Gebeine
Johann Rudolf Zumsteeg, "Grablied" 1803pub
from *Kleine Balladen und Lieder, sechstes Heft*

Der Abend schleiert Flur und Hain
Johann Rudolf Zumsteeg, "Abendlied" 1805pub
from *Kleine Balladen und Lieder, siebtes Heft*
Franz Schubert, "Geist der Liebe" 1816, D414

Franz Schubert, "Geist der Liebe" 1822, D747, 2t2b.pf

Der Dämmrung Schein durchblinkt den Hain
Johann Rudolf Zumsteeg, "Geisternähe" 1801pub
from *Kleine Balladen und Lieder, drittes Heft*
Franz Schubert, "Geisternähe" 1814, D100

Die bretterne Kammer der Todten erbebt
Franz Schubert, "Der Geistertanz (1)" (fragment), 1812?, D15
Franz Schubert, "Der Geistertanz (2)" (fragment), 1812?, D2:15A
Franz Schubert, "Der Geistertanz (3)" 1814, D116
Franz Schubert, "Der Geistertanz" 1816, D494, 2t3b

Die Flamme lodert, milder Schein
Ludwig van Beethoven, "Opferlied" 1794/1801-02, WoO126
Carl Friedrich Zelter, "Opferlied" 1807

Die silbernen Glöckchen der Blume des Mai's
Josefine Lang, "Fee'n-Reigen" 1830?, Op3,4

Die Sonne steigt, die Sonne sinkt
Franz Schubert, "Klage" 1816, D415

Durch Fichten am Hügel, durch Erlen am Bach
Johann Rudolf Zumsteeg, "Lied der Liebe" 1802pub
from *Kleine Balladen und Lieder, viertes Heft*
Franz Schubert, "Lied der Liebe" 1814, D109
Johann Wenzeslaus Kalliwoda, "Lied der Liebe" 1852, Op177,3

Ein Fräulein klagt' im finstern Thurm
Franz Schubert, "Romanze" 1814, D114

Einsam wandelt dein Freund im Frühlingsgarten
Ludwig van Beethoven, "Adelaide" 1794-95, Op46
Franz Schubert, "Adelaide" 1814, D95

Freud' umblühe dich auf allen Wegen
Ludwig van Beethoven, "An Laura" 1792?, WoO112

Freude jubelt, Liebe waltet, auf, beginnt den Maientanz!
Johann Friedrich Reichardt, "Mailied" 1796

Freunde, deren Grüfte sich schon bemoosten!
Franz Schubert, "Die Schatten" 1813, D50

Goldner Schein deckt den Hain
Hans Georg Nägeli, "Abendlandschaft" 1797
Franz Schubert, "Goldner Schein" 1816, D357, 3v

Hast du's in meinem Auge nicht gelesen
Sophia Maria Westenholz, "Der Bund" 1806pub, Op4,?
from *Zwölf Deutsche Lieder*

Heil! dies ist die letzte Zähre, die der Müden Aug' entfällt!
Franz Schubert, "Die Sterbende" 1815, D186

Herzen, die gen Himmel sich erheben
Franz Schubert, "An Laura" 1814, D115

Ich denke dein, wenn durch den Hain
    Johann Rudolf Zumsteeg, "Andenken" 1801pub
        from *Kleine Balladen und Lieder, drittes Heft*
    Carl Maria von Weber, "Ich denke dein!" 1806, Op66,3
    Ludwig van Beethoven, "Andenken" 1809, WoO136
    Ferdinand Ries, "Ich denke dein" 1810pub, Op7,2
    Franz Schubert, "Andenken" 1814, D99
    Hugo Wolf, "Andenken" 1877

Im Abendschimmer wallt der Quell
    Franz Schubert, "Naturgenuss" 1815?, D188
    Franz Schubert, "Naturgenuss" 1816, D422, 2t2b.pf

Kein Rosenschimmer leuchtet dem Tag zur Ruh'!
    Franz Schubert, "Todtenopfer" 1814, D101

Kommen und Scheiden, Suchen und Meiden
    Franz Schubert, "Lebenslied" 1816, D508

Laura betet! Engelharfen hallen Frieden Gottes
    Carl Friedrich Zelter, "Die Betende" 1794
    Ferdinand Ries, "Das Betende" 1811pub, Op36,4
    Franz Schubert, "Die Betende" 1814, D102

Lehnst du deine bleichgehärmte Wange
    Franz Schubert, "Trost an Elisa" 1814, D97

Mädchen entsiegelten, Brüder! die Flaschen
    Johann Rudolf Zumsteeg, "Skolie" 1803pub
        from *Kleine Balladen und Lieder, fünftes Heft*
    Franz Schubert, "Skolie" 1816, D507

Nichts unterm Monde gleicht uns Elfen flink und leicht
    Carl Loewe, "Die Elfenkönigin" 1824, Op9,i,5

Nimmer, nimmer darf ich dir gestehen
    Franz Schubert, "Julius an Theone" 1816, D419

Purpur malt die Tannenhügel nach der Sonne Scheideblick
    Franz Schubert, "Der Abend" 1814, D108

Sanft wehn, im Hauch der Abendluft
    Franz Schubert, "Todtenkranz für ein Kind" 1815, D275

So lang im deutschen Eichenthale
    Franz Schubert, "Jünglingswonne" 1823pub, D983,1, 2t2b

Stern der Liebe! bleich und trübe
    Johann Rudolf Zumsteeg, "An den Abendstern" 1805pub
        from *Kleine Balladen und Lieder, siebtes Heft*

Tag voll Himmel! da aus Laura's Blicken
    Franz Schubert, "Entzückung" 1816, D413

Wann in des Abends letztem Scheine
    Carl Friedrich Zelter, "Lied aus der Ferne" 1794

Was unterm Monde gleicht uns Elfen flink und leicht
    Niklas von Krufft, "Die Elfenkönigin" 1812pub

Wenn ich einst das Ziel errungen habe
Franz Schubert, "Vollendung" 1817, D2:579A

Wenn in des Abends letztem Scheine dir eine lächelnde Gestal
Ferdinand Ries, "Lied aus der Ferne" 1811pub, Op35,6
Franz Schubert, "Lied aus der Ferne" 1814, D107
Mauro Giuliani, "Lied aus der Ferne" 1817pub, Op89,2, v.pf./guitar

Wenn sanft entzückt mein Auge sieht
Franz Schubert, "Die Erde" 1817, D2:579B

Wo der Mond mit bleichem Schimmer
Carl Friedrich Zelter, "Beruhigung" 1796

Wo durch dunkle Buchengänge
Johann Rudolf Zumsteeg, "Beruhigung" 1805pub
from *Kleine Balladen und Lieder, siebtes Heft*

Dr. Mayer

Die schönen Augen der Frühlingsnacht
Robert Franz, "Die schönen Augen der Frühlingsnacht" 1879, Op51,5

Das Vöglein auf dem Baum schaut munter um und singt
Robert Franz, "O Herz in meiner Brust" 1879, Op51,4

Von deinem Bilde nur umschwebet
Carl Loewe, "Nachtständchen" 1847

Georg Josef Mayerhofer

Schwebst du im nächtlichen Raum?
Richard Trunk, "Erscheinung" 1963pub, Op76,2

A. Mayr

Es liegt ein alter Mühlenstein im Schatten einer Linde
Max Reger, "Abgeguckt" 1904, Op76,24, 1v(med).pf
from *Schlichte Weisen, Band 2*

Johann Baptist Mayrhofer (1787-1836)

Alte Liebe rostet nie
Franz Schubert, "Alte Liebe rostet nie" 1816, D477

Auf den Blumen flimmern Perlen
Franz Schubert, "Nach einem Gewitter" 1817, D561

Auf der Wellen Spiegel schwimmt der Kahn
Franz Schubert, "Auf der Donau" 1817, D553

Auf hohem Bergesrücken, wo frischer alles grünt
Franz Schubert, "Der Alpenjäger" 1817, D524

Auf seinen gold'nen Throne der graue König sitzt
Franz Schubert, "Liedesend" 1816, D473

Blüht denn hier an Tauris Strande
Franz Schubert, "Iphigenia" 1817, D573

Da sitz' ich ohne Bogen, und starre in den Sand
Franz Schubert, "Philoktet" 1817, D540

Den Tag hindurch nur einmal mag ich sprechen
Franz Schubert, "Memnon" 1817, D541

Der Abend röthet nun das Thal, mild schimmert Hesperus
Franz Schubert, "Abendlied der Fürstin" 1816?, D495

Der Knabe seufzt über's grüne Meer
Franz Schubert, "Atys" 1817, D585

Der Lerche wolkennahe Lieder
Franz Schubert, "Sehnsucht" 1817?, D516

Der Nachen dröhnt, Cypressen flüstern
Franz Schubert, "Fahrt zum Hades" 1817, D526

Die Angel zuckt, die Ruthe bebt
Franz Schubert, "Wie Ulfru fischt" 1817, D525

Dioskuren, Zwillingssterne, die ihr leuchtet meinem Nachen
Franz Schubert, "Lied eines Schiffers an die Dioskuren" 1822, D360

Du Thurm! zu meinem Leide ragst du so hoch empor
Franz Schubert, "Der Hirt" 1816, D490

Es mahnt der Wald, es ruft der Strom
Franz Schubert, "Schlaflied" 1817, D527

Es tanzen Mond und Sterne den flücht'gen Geisterreih'n
Franz Schubert, "Gondelfahrer" 1824, D808
Franz Schubert, "Der Gondelfahrer" 1824, D809, 2t2b.pf

Es träumen die Wolken, die Sterne, der Mond
Franz Schubert, "Beim Winde" 1819, D669

Fels auf Felsen hingewälzet
Franz Schubert, "Aus *Heliopolis* II" 1822, D754

Gib mir die Fülle der Einsamkeit!
Franz Schubert, "Einsamkeit" 1818, D620

"Hast du Lianen nicht gesehen?" "Ich sah sie zu dem Teiche gehn."
Franz Schubert, "Liane" 1815, D298

Hörnerklänge rufen klagend aus des Forstes grüner Nacht
Franz Schubert, "Trost" 1819, D671

Ihr hohen Himmlischen, erhöret der Tochter herzentströmtes Flehen
Franz Schubert, "Antigone und Oedip" 1817, D542

Im kalten, rauhen Norden ist Kunde mir geworden
Franz Schubert, "Aus *Heliopolis* I" 1822, D753

Im Wald, im Wald da grabt mich ein
Franz Schubert, "An die Freunde" 1819, D654

Im Winde, im Sturme befahr' ich den Fluss
Franz Schubert, "Der Schiffer" 1817?, D536

In monderhellten Nächten mit dem Geschick zu rechten
Franz Schubert, "Die Sternennächte" 1819, D670

Ist dies Tauris, wo der Eumeniden Wuth
Franz Schubert, "Orest auf Tauris" 1817, D548

Ist mir's doch, als sei mein Leben
Franz Schubert, "Am Strome" 1817, D539

Ja, spanne nur den Bogen mich zu tödten
Franz Schubert, "Der zürnenden Diana" 1820, D707

Lasst uns, ihr Himmlischen, ein Fest begehen!
Franz Schubert, "Uraniens Flucht" 1817, D554

Mir ist so wohl, so weh' am stillen Erlafsee
Franz Schubert, "Erlafsee" 1817, D586

Nachtviolen, Nachtviolen!
Franz Schubert, "Nachtviolen" 1822, D752

O unbewölktes Leben! so rein und tief und klar
Franz Schubert, "Der Sieg" 1824, D805

Sag an, wer lehrt dich Lieder
Franz Schubert, "Geheimniss" 1816, D491

Sie hüpfte mit mir auf grünem Plan
Franz Schubert, "Über allen Zauber Liebe" 1819, D682

Sitz' ich im Gras am glatten See
Franz Schubert, "Am See" 1814, D124

So wird der Mann, der sonder Zwang gerecht ist
Franz Schubert, "Fragment aus dem Aeschylus" 1816, D450
translated from *Eumenedes*

Süsse Augen, klare Bronnen!
Franz Schubert, "Augenlied" 1817?, D297

Über die Berge zieht ihr fort
Franz Schubert, "Abschied. Nach einer Wallfahrtsarie" 1816, D475

Verbirg dich, Sonne, denn die Gluthen der Wonne versengen mein Gebein
Franz Schubert, "Auflösung" 1824, D807

Was weilst du einsam an dem Himmel, o schöner Stern?
Franz Schubert, "Abendstern" 1824, D806

Wenn über Berge sich der Nebel breitet
Franz Schubert, "Nachtstück" 1819, D672

Woget brausend, Harmonien, kehre wieder, alte Zeit
Franz Schubert, "Zum Punsche" 1816, D492

Wohin? o Helios! wohin?
Franz Schubert, "Freiwilliges Versinken" 1817?, D700

Zu meinen Füssen brichst du dich, o heimathliches Meer
Franz Schubert, "Der entsühnte Orest" 1817?, D699

Zum Donaustrom, zur Kaiserstadt geh' ich in Bangigkeit
Franz Schubert, "Rückweg" 1815, D163

Friederike Mayröcker (1924-)

Erträumter einsamer blauer Engel
Gottfried von Einem, "Erträumter einsamer blauer Engel" 1982pub
from *Carmina Gerusena* (8)

Es sprießen immerfort die sanften Toten aus
Gottfried von Einem, "Dreizeiler am 21. 2. 1978" 1982pub
from *Carmina Gerusena* (4)

Ich werde in Ostia sein, ich werde dich dort erwarten
Gottfried von Einem, "Ostia wird dich empfangen" 1982pub
from *Carmina Gerusena* (6)

Mein federäugiger Liebling!
Gottfried von Einem, "Mein federäugiger Liebling!" 1982pub
from *Carmina Gerusena* (7)

Claude McKay (1890-1948)
Dirnen und Burschen hört' ich Beifall rasen
Alexander Zemlinsky, "Harlem Tänzerin" 1937/38, Op27,8
translated by Maurice Wright

Karl von Mecklenburg-Strelitz
Wo reiner Liebe gold'ne Strahlen
Louis Spohr, "Mein Heimathland" 1847, WoO116, 2sop.pf

Daniel Eduard (?) Meier
Überall in dem All, mag ich liegen oder stehen
Louis Spohr, "Sehnsucht" 1845, WoO114
attribution of poem uncertain

J. Wilhelm Meinhold (1797-1851)
Wie das Gewürm aus unermeßnem Meer
Paul Hindemith, "Der Wurm am Meer" 1925, Op35,ii,3, sop.ob.vla.vc
from *Die Serenaden*

Alfred von Meissner (1822-1885)
Dass ich dein auf ewig bliebe
Léander Schlegel, "Dass ich dein auf ewig bliebe" 1900, Op20,10
from *Deutsche Liebeslieder*

Lass im Geheim mich zu Dir kommen
Léander Schlegel, "Lass im Geheim mich zu Dir kommen" 1900, Op20,4
from *Deutsche Liebeslieder*

O Meer im Abendstrahl in deiner stillen Flut
Franz Liszt, "O Meer im Abendstrahl" 1883, sop.alt.pf

Sie ist gegangen, die Wonnen versanken
Johannes Brahms, "Nachwirkung" 1852, Op6,3

Friedrich Melzer and Friedrich Hanser
Jetzt erklang die Sterbestunde
Carl Loewe, "Jetzt erklang die Sterbestunde" 1842
Cavatine from the Opera *Emmy*, written after Scott's *Kenilworth*

War einst ein hübsch Mädchen voll Feuer und Gluth
Carl Loewe, "Das Geheimnis" 1842
from the Opera *Emmy*

Moses Mendelssohn (1729-1786)
Der Ewige segnet der Frommen Tage
Johann Rudolf Zumsteeg, "Canon a 3" 1803pub
from *Kleine Balladen und Lieder, sechstes Heft*

Sophie Mereau (1770-1806)
Es rauscht der Strom, es weht der Wind
Carl Friedrich Zelter, "Es rauscht der Strom" 1800

Ich weiss eine Farbe, der bin ich so hold
Ludwig van Beethoven, "Feuerfarb'" 1792/1793-94, Op52,2

Eva Merkel
Sieben kleine Rosenstökke stehn im Garten auf dem Beete
Richard Stöhr, "Die süsse Sieben" 1914pub, Op28,5

Fürst Elim Metschorsky
Mild wie ein Lufthauch, ein Lufthauch im Mai
Franz Liszt, "Bist du!" 1844/1879

Klemens Wenzel Lothar, Fürst von Metternich (1773-1859)
Leise streichen Nebelschleier über Flur und Wiesen hin
Max Reger, "Maiennacht" 1903-04, Op76,15, 1v(med).pf
from *Schlichte Weisen, Band 1*

Conrad Ferdinand Meyer (1825-1898)
Am Himmel wächst der Sonne Glut
Joseph Marx, "Lenzfahrt" 1909, ten.pf
Othmar Schoeck, "Lenzfahrt" 1946, Op60,8, 1v(med).pf
from *Das stille Leuchten (Geheimnis und Gleichnis)*

An wolkenreinem Himmel geht
Othmar Schoeck, "Vor der Ernte" 1905, Op6,3

Auf das Feuer mit dem goldnen Strahle
Hermann Behn, "Das heilige Feuer" 189-?, Op3,5, bar.pf
Othmar Schoeck, "Das Heilige Feuer" 1946, Op60,1, 1v(med).pf
from *Das stille Leuchten (Geheimnis und Gleichnis)*

Aufsteigt der Strahl und fallend gießt
Othmar Schoeck, "Der römische Brunnen" 1946, Op60,14, 1v(med).pf
from *Das stille Leuchten (Geheimnis und Gleichnis)*

Aus der Eltern Macht und Haus
Othmar Schoeck, "Hochzeitslied" 1946, Op60,12, 1v(med).pf
from *Das stille Leuchten (Geheimnis und Gleichnis)*

Aus der Schiffsbank mach' ich meinen Pfühl
Richard Strauss, "Im Spätboot" 1903, Op56,3

Bei der Abendsonne Wandern wann im Dorf den Strahl verlor
Othmar Schoeck, "Requiem" 1946, Op60,25, 1v(med).pf
from *Das stille Leuchten (Berg und See)*
Hermann Behn, "Requiem" 189-?, Op9,5, 1v(med).pf

Bemeßt den Schritt! Bemeßt den Schwung! die Erde bleibt noch lange jung!
Anna Teichmüller, "Säerspruch" 1907pub, Op15,3
Hans Pfitzner, "Säerspruch" 1923, Op32,2, bar/bass.pf

Da mit Sokrates die Freunde tranken
Othmar Schoeck, "Das Ende des Festes" 1946, Op60,15, 1v(med).pf
from *Das stille Leuchten (Geheimnis und Gleichnis)*
Felix Wolfes, "Das Ende des Festes" 1963

Die Mutter mahnt mich Abends: "Trag' Sorg' zur Ampel, Kind!"
Hermann Behn, "Liebesflämmchen" 189-?, Op4,1, sop.pf
from *Mädchenlieder*

Die Rechte streckt' ich schmerzlich oft
Othmar Schoeck, "In Harmesnächten" 1946, Op60,7, 1v(med).pf
from *Das stille Leuchten (Geheimnis und Gleichnis)*

Don Fadrique bringt ein Ständchen seiner drolligen Pepita
Felix Mottl, "Don Fadrique" 1896?pub

Du warest mir ein täglich Wanderziel
Hermann Behn, "Jetzt rede du" 189-?, Op9,2, 1v(med).pf
Wilhelm Kienzl, "Jetzt rede du!" 192-?, Op114,5
Othmar Schoeck, "Jetzt rede du!" 1946, Op60,28, 1v(med).pf
from *Das stille Leuchten (Berg und See)*

Ein betrogen Mägdlein irrt im Walde
Hermann Behn, "Das bittere Trünklein" 189-?, Op9,1, 1v(med).pf

Ein blendendes Spitzchen blickt über den Wald
Othmar Schoeck, "Das weiße Spitzchen" 1946, Op60,20, 1v(med).pf
from *Das stille Leuchten (Berg und See)*

Entgegen wandeln wir dem Dorf im Sonnenkuß
Hermann Behn, "Die tote Liebe" 189-?, Op9,3, 1v(med).pf

Es fährt der Wind gewaltig durch die Nacht
Othmar Schoeck, "In einer Sturmnacht" 1946, Op60,6, 1v(med).pf
from *Das stille Leuchten (Geheimnis und Gleichnis)*

Es geht mit mir zu Ende, mein' Sach' und Spruch
Emil Mattiesen, "Hussens Kerker" 190-?pub, Op15,5
from *Überwindungen* (5)
Hans Pfitzner, "Hussens Kerker" 1923, Op32,1, bar/bass.pf

Es herrscht' ein König irgendwo
Hermann Behn, "Die gefesselten Musen" 189-?, Op8,4, bar.pf

Es sprach der Geist: Sieh auf! Es war im Traume
Othmar Schoeck, "Alle" 1946, Op60,18, 1v(med).pf
from *Das stille Leuchten (Geheimnis und Gleichnis)*

Frau Berte, hört: Ihr dürftet nun
Hermann Behn, "Die drei gemalten Ritter" 189-?, Op8,1, bar.pf

Frühling, der die Welt umblaut
Othmar Schoeck, "Frühling Triumphator" 1946, Op60,9, 1v(med).pf
from *Das stille Leuchten (Geheimnis und Gleichnis)*

Geh nicht, die Gott für mich erschuf!
Hermann Behn, "Lass scharren deiner Rosse Huf!" 189-?, Op7,3, bar.pf
Hans Pfitzner, "Laß scharren deiner Rosse Huf..." 1923, Op32,4, bar/bass.pf

Gestern fand ich, räumend eines lang vergessnen Schrankes Fächer
Othmar Schoeck, "Der Reisebecher" 1946, Op60,19, 1v(med).pf
from *Das stille Leuchten (Berg und See)*

Greif' aus, du mein junges, mein feuriges Thier!
Hermann Behn, "Der Ritt in den Tod" 189-?, Op3,4, bar.pf

Heut ward mir bis zum jungen Tag
Hermann Behn, "Unruhige Nacht" 189-?, Op5,2, 1v(med).pf
Othmar Schoeck, "Unruhige Nacht" 1946, Op60,10, 1v(med).pf
from *Das stille Leuchten (Geheimnis und Gleichnis)*

Hier – doch keinem darfst du's zeigen
Othmar Schoeck, "Mit einem Jugendbildnis" 1946, Op60,4, 1v(med).pf
from *Das stille Leuchten (Geheimnis und Gleichnis)*

In den Lüften schwellendes Gedröhne
Othmar Schoeck, "Neujahrsglocken" 1946, Op60,17, 1v(med).pf
from *Das stille Leuchten (Geheimnis und Gleichnis)*

In den Wald bin ich geflüchtet
Hermann Behn, "Abendrot im Walde" 189-?, Op7,2, bar.pf

In der Nacht, die die Bäume mit Blüten deckt
Hermann Behn, "Liederseelen" 189-?, Op5,4, 1v(med).pf
Othmar Schoeck, "Liederseelen" 1946, Op60,2, 1v(med).pf
from *Das stille Leuchten (Geheimnis und Gleichnis)*

Ins Museum bin zu später Stunde heut ich noch gegangen
Hermann Behn, "Auf Goldgrund" 189-?, Op7,4, bar.pf

Läg' dort ich unterm Firneschein
Hermann Behn, "Ich würd' es hören" 189-?, Op7,1, bar.pf
Othmar Schoeck, "Ich würd' es hören" 1946, Op60,22, 1v(med).pf
from *Das stille Leuchten (Berg und See)*

Liebchen fand ich spielend. Einen Kasten hatte sie entdeckt
Hermann Behn, "Spielzeug" 189-?, Op7,5, bar.pf

Meine eingelegten Ruder triefen
Hermann Behn, "Eingelegte Ruder" 189-?, Op5,3, 1v(med).pf
Hans Pfitzner, "Eingelegte Ruder" 1923, Op32,3, bar/bass.pf
Felix Wolfes, "Eingelegte Ruder" 1963, 1v(med).pf

Melde mir die Nachtgeräusche, Muse
Othmar Schoeck, "Nachtgeräusche" 1946, Op60,27, 1v(med).pf
from *Das stille Leuchten (Berg und See)*

Mir träumt', ich komm an's Himmelsthor
Hermann Behn, "Am Himmelsthor" 189-?, Op3,3, bar.pf
Othmar Schoeck, "Am Himmelstor" 1946, Op60,5, 1v(med).pf
from *Das stille Leuchten (Geheimnis und Gleichnis)*

Mit edeln Purpurröten und hellem Amselschlag
Hermann Behn, "Morgenlied" 189-?, Op9,4, 1v(med).pf

Mittagsruhe haltend auf den Matten
Othmar Schoeck, "Reisephantasie" 1946, Op60,3, 1v(med).pf
from *Das stille Leuchten (Geheimnis und Gleichnis)*

Schwarzschattende Kastanie
Othmar Schoeck, "Schwarzschattende Kastanie" 1946, Op60,24, 1v(med).pf
from *Das stille Leuchten (Berg und See)*

Sehnsucht ist Qual! Der Herrin wag ich's nicht zu sagen
Hermann Behn, "Ein Lied Chastelards" 189-?, Op8,2, bar.pf

So stille ruht im Hafen
Hermann Behn, "Abendwolke" 189-?, Op5,1, 1v(med).pf
Othmar Schoeck, "Abendwolke" 1946, Op60,26, 1v(med).pf
from *Das stille Leuchten (Berg und See)*

Trüb verglomm der schwüle Sommertag
Anna Teichmüller, "Schwüle" 1904pub, Op2,5

Was treibst du, Wind, du himmlisches Kind?
Othmar Schoeck, "Was treibst du, Wind" 1946, Op60,11, 1v(med).pf
from *Das stille Leuchten (Geheimnis und Gleichnis)*

Wer in der Sonne kämpft, ein Sohn der Erde
Felix Wolfes, "Unter den Sternen" 1948
Hermann Behn, "Unter den Sternen" 189-?, Op8,3, bar.pf

Wie pocht' das Herz mir in der Brust
Othmar Schoeck, "Firnelicht" 1946, Op60,23, 1v(med).pf
from *Das stille Leuchten (Berg und See)*

Wo die Tannen finstre Schatten werfen
Othmar Schoeck, "Göttermahl" 1946, Op60,21, 1v(med).pf
from *Das stille Leuchten (Berg und See)*

Wo sah ich, Mädchen, deine Züge
Othmar Schoeck, "Die Jungfrau" 1946, Op60,16, 1v(med).pf
from *Das stille Leuchten (Geheimnis und Gleichnis)*

Wolken, meine Kinder, wandern gehen wollt ihr?
Othmar Schoeck, "Der Gesang des Meeres" 1946, Op60,13, 1v(med).pf
from *Das stille Leuchten (Geheimnis und Gleichnis)*

Friedrich Ludwig (Wilhelm) Meyer (1759-1840)
Bleich flimmert in stürmender Nacht
Johann Rudolf Zumsteeg, "Una" 1800pub
from *Kleine Balladen und Lieder, erstes Heft*

Karl Meyer
Auf dem Dache sitzt der Spatz
Max Reger, "Spatz und Spätzin" 1905, Op88,4

Erik Meyer-Helmund (1861-1932)
Die Schmetterlinge, die fliegen von einer Blume zur andern
Erik Meyer-Helmund, "Gefangen" 1886-88

Du sagst,ich hätte die Nachbarn geweckt
Erik Meyer-Helmund, "Entschuldigung" 1886-88

Ich bin auf Dich böse, du Liebchen mein
Erik Meyer-Helmund, "Das Fensterlein" 1886-88

Ich hab' mein Herz verloren an ein blondes Mägdelein
Erik Meyer-Helmund, "Leichter Verlust" 1886-88

Ihr Mägdelein, nehmt euch in Acht
Erik Meyer-Helmund, "Warnung" 1886-88

Mutter, Mütterchen, ach sei nicht böse
Erik Meyer-Helmund, "Mädchenlied" 1886-88

Alice Christiana Thompson Meynell (1847-1922)
Horch! Horch, in der wehenden Nacht, im bebenden Turm
Harald Genzmer, "Einklang" 1990, sop.pf
from *Sechs Lieder nach angelsächsischen Dichtern* (4)

Otto Michaeli (1870-1941)
Am Kirchhof ging ich jüngst vorbei
Max Reger, "Gruß" 1893, Op12,4

Mein Liedlein ward ein Büblein
Max Reger, "Wunsch" 1907, Op76,40, 1v(med).pf
from *Schlichte Weisen, Band 4*

Nikolai von Michalewski (1931-)
Ach, alle Blumen neigen das Haupt so bang, so schwer
Louis Ferdinand, "Russische Romanze" 1955pub

All meine reinen Gedanken, alles, was gut ist an mir
Louis Ferdinand, "Dank" 1953pub

Das Meer ist wie flüssige Jade
Louis Ferdinand, "Meeressehnsucht" 1955pub

Der Wind aus dem Osten soll mich nicht erschrekken
Louis Ferdinand, "Ostwind" 1981pub

Die Nacht ist so hell, ach laß uns zieh'n hinaus
Louis Ferdinand, "Lebenslust" 1981pub

Es preisen dich die Glokken wohl durch den Lauf der Zeit
Louis Ferdinand, "Es preisen dich dic Glocken" 1981pub

Musik ist alles, was ich sage
Louis Ferdinand, "Musik ist alles" 1981pub

Traum, den du verwebst mit dem Alltagsbild
Louis Ferdinand, "Emigrant" 1981pub

Michelangelo Buonarotti (1475-1564)
Alles endet, was entstehet
Hugo Wolf, "Alles endet, was entstehet" 1897
translated by Walter Robert-Tornow
from *Drei Gedichte von Michelangelo*

An dieser Stelle war's, wo Herz
Erich J. Wolff, "An dieser Stätte war's" 1914pub, Lieder No.6

Bring' ich der Schönheit, da ich sie erblickt'
Erich J. Wolff, "Bring' ich der Schönheit die Seele nah" 1914pub, Lieder No.11

Da deiner Schönheit Glanz mich hat besiegt
Erich J. Wolff, "Da deiner Schönheit Glanz mich hat besiegt" 1914pub, Lieder No.12

Es spricht ein Mann, es spricht ein Gott mit Kraft
Josef Schelb, "An Vittoria Colonna" 1920pub, Op5,3
translated by Sophie Hasenclever
from *Drei Sonette Michelangelos*

Fühlt meine Seele das ersehnte Licht von Gott, der sie erschuf?
Hugo Wolf, "Fühlt meine Seele" 1897
translated by Walter Robert-Tornow
from *Drei Gedichte von Michelangelo*

Gemahnt dein Name mich an deine Züge
Erich J. Wolff, "Gemahnt dein Name mich an deine Züge" 1914pub, Lieder No.22

Ich leb' der Sünde, leb' um mir zu sterben
Josef Schelb, "Ich leb' der Sünde" 1920pub, Op5,2
translated by Sophie Hasenclever
from *Drei Sonette Michelangelos*

In mir nur Tod, in dir mein Leben ruht
Othmar Schoeck, "Die Verklärende" 1907, Op9,1

In schwerer Schuld nur, die sie dumpf bedrückt
Erich J. Wolff, "In schwerer Schuld nur" 1914pub, Lieder No.33

In's Joch beug' ich den Nacken demutvoll
Richard Strauss, "Madrigal" 1886, Op15,1, 1v(med).pf
Othmar Schoeck, "Madrigal" 1917, Op31,1

Kleinodien, Zierat, Perlen und Korallen
Erich J. Wolff, "Kleinodien, Zierat, Perlen und Korallen" 1914pub, Lieder No.35

Täuscht euch, ihr Augen, nicht
Erich J. Wolff, "Täuscht euch, ihr Augen, nicht" 1914pub, Lieder No.51

Wer geboren wird, muß sterben in der Zeiten Flucht
Josef Schelb, "Gesang der Toten" 1920pub, Op5,1
translated by Bettina Jakobson
from *Drei Sonette Michelangelos*

Wie soll den Mut ich finden
Erich J. Wolff, "Wie soll den Mut ich finden?" 1914pub, Lieder No.58

Wohl denk' ich oft an mein vergang'nes Leben
Hugo Wolf, "Wohl denk' ich oft" 1897
translated by Walter Robert-Tornow
from *Drei Gedichte von Michelangelo*

Gustav Michell

Mir ist die Welt so freudenleer
Franz Liszt, "Verlassen" 1880

Adam Mickiewicz (1798-1855) (see also Odyniec)

Ei, das tanzt, das lärmt und trinket!
Carl Loewe, "Frau Twardowska" 1835, (Op50,II,3)
translated by Carl von Blankensee

In den Schlosshof hernieder rief Held Budris die Brüder
Carl Loewe, "Die drei Budrisse" 1835, Op49,3
translated by Carl von Blankensee

Lerche zu des Frühlings Ruhme hat ihr Erstlingslied gesungen
Carl Loewe, "Die Schlüsselblume" 1835, Op49,2
translated by Carl von Blankensee

Von dem Gartenaltan keucht zum Schlosse heran der Woywode
Carl Loewe, "Der Woywode" 1835, Op49,1
translated by Carl von Blankensee

Wer ist der Jüngling, lieblich zu schauen?
Carl Loewe, "Das Switesmädchen" 1835, Op51
translated by Carl von Blankensee

Wilia, sie, der unsre Ström' entsprangen
Carl Loewe, "Wilia und das Mädchen" 1835, Op50,1
translated by Carl von Blankensee

Agnes Miegel (1879-1964)
Ich hörte heute morgen am Klippenhang die Stare schon
Gottfried von Einem, "Heimweh" 1983, Op73,3
from *Tag- und Nachtlieder*

Johann Christian Mikan (1769-1844)
Sie sind in Paris! Die Helden, Europa's Befreier!
Franz Schubert, "Die Befreier Europa's in Paris" 1814, D104

Johann Martin Miller (1750-1814)
Er, dem ich einst alles war
Josef Antonín Štěpán, "Er, dem ich einst alles war" 1778-79pub

Es war einmal ein Gärtner, der sang ein traurig Lied
Maria Therese Paradis, "Das Gärtnerliedchen aus dem Siegwart" 1784-86
from *Zwölf Lieder auf ihrer Reise in Musik gesetzt*

Rosenknöspchen, schön bist du
Johann Vesque von Püttlingen, "An ein Rosenknöspchen (Lied im Rokokostil)" 185-?, Op56,4

Schlaf, Schwester, sanft im Erdenschoos!
Johann Rudolf Zumsteeg, "Grablied" 1803pub
from *Kleine Balladen und Lieder, fünftes Heft*

Siehe, mein Röschen, der Frühling ist da
Josef Antonín Štěpán, "Der Frühling" 1778-79pub

Was frag' ich viel nach Geld und Gut
Wolfgang Amadeus Mozart, "Zufriedenheit" 1780-81, K349
Johann Rudolf Zumsteeg, "Lied" 1803pub
from *Kleine Balladen und Lieder, fünftes Heft*

Wohl und immer wohl dem Mann
Maria Therese Paradis, "Aus *Siegwart*" 1784-86
from *Zwölf Lieder auf ihrer Reise in Musik gesetzt*

"Stefan Milow" (Stefan von Millenkovics) (1836-1915)
Wunderbare Abendhelle, rings die Welt so klar, so frei!
Wilhelm Kienzl, "Abendhelle" 1894?, Op44,2

"Mirza-Schaffy:" see Friedrich Bodenstedt

Gabriela Mistral (1889-1957)
Die kleinen Hunde öffneten die Augen
Harald Genzmer, "Acht kleine Hunde" 1990, sop.pf
from *Sechs Lieder nach angelsächsischen Dichtern* (6)

Mittler
Maria wollt' zur Kirche gehn, da kam sie an den tiefen See (see also Volkslied)
Erich J. Wolff, "Maria und der Schiffer" 1914pub, Lieder No.37

Johann Jakob Mnioch (1765-1804)
Wohlauf zum frohen Rundgesang
Johann Rudolf Zumsteeg, "Rundgesang beim Schlusse des Jahrs" 1803pub
from *Kleine Balladen und Lieder, fünftes Heft*

Moehrcke
Ich bin der Trommelschläger laut, dem zittern Thür und Fenster
Carl Loewe, "Trommel-Ständchen" 1852, Op132,2

Eduard Friedrich Mörike (1804-1875)
Ach, wenn's nur der König auch wüsst'
Friedrich Silcher, "Die Soldatenbraut"
Robert Schumann, "Die Soldatenbraut" 1847, Op64,1
Robert Schumann, "Soldatenbraut" 1849, Op69,4, ssaa.pf
from *Romanzen für Frauenstimmen I*
Hugo Distler, "Die Soldatenbraut" 1939, Op19,ii,6, fch
from *Mörike-Chorliederbuch*

Als der Winter die Rosen geraubt
Felix Weingartner, "Anakreon" 1906pub, Op41,10
from *Frühlings- und Liebeslieder*

Am frisch geschnittnen Wanderstab
Hugo Wolf, "Fussreise" 1888
from *Mörike Lieder* (10)

Am langsamsten von allen Göttern wandeln wir
Felix Wolfes, "Inschrift auf eine Uhr mit den drei Horen" 1965, 1v(med).pf

Am Waldsaum kann ich lange Nachmittage
Othmar Schoeck, "Am Walde" 1948-49, Op62,4
from *Das holde Bescheiden (Natur)*

Anders wird die Welt mit jedem Schritt
Hugo Wolf, "Heimweh" 1888
from *Mörike Lieder* (37)

Angelehnt an die Epheuwand dieser alten Terrasse
Johannes Brahms, "An eine Aeolsharfe" 1858, Op19,5
Hugo Wolf, "An eine Aeolsharfe" 1888
from *Mörike Lieder* (11)

Aninka tanzte vor uns im Grase
Felix Weingartner, "Jedem das Seine" 1906pub, Op41,6
from *Frühlings- und Liebeslieder*
Hugo Distler, "Jedem das Seine" 1939, Op19,i,3, ch
from *Mörike-Chorliederbuch*

Auf ihrem Leibrößlein, so weiß wie der Schnee
Robert Schumann, "Der Gärtner" 1851-52, Op107,3
Hugo Wolf, "Der Gärtner" 1888
from *Mörike Lieder* (17)
Robert Kahn, "Der Gärtner" 1892, Op16,1

Hugo Distler, "Der Gärtner" 1939, Op19,i,7, ch
from *Mörike-Chorliederbuch*
Hugo Distler, "Der Gärtner" 1939, Op19,ii,8, fch
from *Mörike-Chorliederbuch*
Hugo Distler, "Der Gärtner" 1939, Op19,iii,2, mch
from *Mörike-Chorliederbuch*

Aufgeschmückt ist der Freudensaal
Othmar Schoeck, "Peregrina" 1948-49, Op62,14
from *Das holde Bescheiden (Liebe)*

Bedächtig stieg die Nacht an's Land (see "Gelassen stieg…")
Robert Franz, "Um Mitternacht" 1870?pub, Op28,6

Bei euren Taten, euren Siegen
Othmar Schoeck, "Nach dem Kriege" 1948-49, Op62,25
from *Das holde Bescheiden (Betrachtung)*

Bei jeder Wendung deiner Lebensbahn
Othmar Schoeck, "Zu einer Konfirmation" 1948-49, Op62,36
from *Das holde Bescheiden (Glaube)*

Bei Nacht im Dorf der Wächter rief: Elfe!
Hugo Wolf, "Elfenlied" 1888
from *Mörike Lieder* (16)

Bin jung gewesen, kann auch mitreden
Hugo Wolf, "Rath einer Alten" 1888
from *Mörike Lieder* (41)

Da droben auf dem Markte spazier' ich auf und ab
Hugo Distler, "Lammwirts Klagelied" 1939, Op19,iii,8, mch
from *Mörike-Chorliederbuch*

Das süße Zeug ohne Saft und Kraft!
Othmar Schoeck, "Restauration (Nach Durchlesung eines Manuskripts mit Gedichten)" 1948-49, Op62,32
from *Das holde Bescheiden (Betrachtung)*

Dein Liebesfeuer, ach Herr! wie theuer wollt' ich es hegen
Hugo Wolf, "Seufzer" 1888
from *Mörike Lieder* (22)

Der Himmel glänzt vom reinsten Frühlingslichte
Othmar Schoeck, "Zu viel" 1948-49, Op62,15
from *Das holde Bescheiden (Liebe)*

Der Spiegel dieser treuen, braunen Augen
Hugo Wolf, "Peregrina (I)" 1888
from *Mörike Lieder* (33)

Derweil ich schlafend lag, ein Stündlein wohl vor Tag
Wilhelm Speidel, "Ein Stündlein wohl vor Tag" 1854pub, Op9,3
Otto Scherzer, "Ein Stündlein wohl vor Tag" 1860
from *XXV Lieder*, (15)
Robert Franz, "Ein Stündlein wohl vor Tag" 1870?pub, Op28,2
Hugo Wolf, "Ein Stündlein wohl vor Tag" 1888
from *Mörike Lieder* (3)
Richard Kursch, "Ein Stündlein wohl vor Tag" 1905pub, Op5,3

Felix Weingartner, "Ein Stündlein wohl vor Tag" 1906pub, Op41,8
from *Frühlings- und Liebeslieder*
Erich Zeisl, "Ein Stündlein wohl vor Tag" 1935pub
Hugo Distler, "Ein Stündlein wohl vor Tag" 1939, Op19,i,2, ch
from *Mörike-Chorliederbuch*

Des Schäfers sein Haus und das steht auf zwei Rad
Hugo Wolf, "Storchenbotschaft" 1888
from *Mörike Lieder* (48)
Hugo Distler, "Storchenbotschaft" 1939, Op19,i,18, ch
from *Mörike-Chorliederbuch*

Des Wassermanns sein Töchterlein
Hugo Wolf, "Nixe Binsefuss" 1888
from *Mörike Lieder* (45)

Die ganz' Welt ist in dich verliebt
Othmar Schoeck, "Impromptu (An Mörikes Hündchen Joli)" 1948-49, Op62,27
from *Das holde Bescheiden (Betrachtung)*

Die kleine Welt, mit deren Glanzgestalten
Othmar Schoeck, "Widmung" 1948-49, Op62,1
from *Das holde Bescheiden*

Die Liebe, sagt man, steht am Pfahl gebunden
Joseph Marx, "Peregrina V" 1904, ten.pf
Othmar Schoeck, "Peregrina" 1908, Op15,6

Die Welt wär' ein Sumpf, faul und matt
Othmar Schoeck, "Die Enthusiasten" 1948-49, Op62,28
from *Das holde Bescheiden (Betrachtung)*

Dir angetrauet am Altare, o Vaterland
Hugo Wolf, "Der König bei der Krönung" 1886
from *Sechs Gedichte von Scheffel u.a.*
Max Reger, "Der König bei der Krönung" 1902-03, Op70,2

Dort an der Kirchhofmauer, da sitz' ich auf der Lauer
Hugo Distler, "Kinderlied. Für Agnes" 1939, Op19,i,9, ch
from *Mörike-Chorliederbuch*

Drei Tage Regen fort und fort
Hugo Wolf, "Der Jäger" 1888
from *Mörike Lieder* (40)

Du bist Orplid, mein Land! das ferne leuchtet
Hugo Wolf, "Gesang Weyla's" 1888
from *Mörike Lieder* (46)

Du heilest den und tröstest jenen
Hugo Distler, "Der Liebhaber an die heiße Quelle zu B." 1939, Op19,iii,7, mch
from *Mörike-Chorliederbuch*

Ein Irrsal kam in die Mondscheingärten
Othmar Schoeck, "Peregrina" 1909, Op17,4, 1v(med).pf

Ein Tännlein grünet wo, wer weiß, im Walde
Robert Franz, "Ein Tännlein grünet wo" 1870?pub, Op27,6

Hugo Wolf, "Denk' es, o Seele!" 1888
from *Mörike Lieder* (39)
Felix Draeseke, "Denk es, o Seele" 1906pub, Op81,4
Hans Pfitzner, "Denk es, o Seele" 1922, Op30,3
Hugo Distler, "Denk' es, o Seele" 1939, Op19,i,21, ch
from *Mörike-Chorliederbuch*
Fartein Valen, "Denk' es, o Seele" 1941, Op39,1
from *Zwei Lieder*

Eine Liebe kenn' ich, die ist treu
Hugo Wolf, "Wo find' ich Trost" 1888
from *Mörike Lieder* (31)

Einmal nach einer lustigen Nacht
Hugo Wolf, "Zur Warnung" 1888
from *Mörike Lieder* (49)

Entflohn sind wir der Stadt Gedränge
Hugo Distler, "Wanderlied" 1939, Op19,i,20, ch
from *Mörike-Chorliederbuch*

Es graut vom Morgenreif in Dämmerung das Feld
Heimo Erbse, "Früh im Wagen" 1959pub, Op17,2
Felix Wolfes, "Früh im Wagen" 1967, 1v(med).pf

Es ist doch im April fürwahr
Othmar Schoeck, "Das Mädchen an den Mai" 1948-49, Op62,7
from *Das holde Bescheiden (Natur)*

Es ist zwar sonsten nicht der Brauch
Felix Weingartner, "Vogellied" 1906pub, Op41,4
from *Frühlings- und Liebeslieder*

Es war ein König Milesint, von dem will ich euch sagen
Hugo Distler, "Die traurige Krönung" 1939, Op19,i,5, ch
from *Mörike-Chorliederbuch*

Fragst du mich woher die bange Liebe mir zum Herzen kam
Franz von Holstein, "Frage und Antwort" 1870, Op24,1
Hugo Wolf, "Frage und Antwort" 1888
from *Mörike Lieder* (35)
Hugo Distler, "Frage und Antwort" 1939, Op19,i,24, ch
from *Mörike-Chorliederbuch*
Hugo Distler, "Frage und Antwort" 1939, Op19,iii,3, mch
from *Mörike-Chorliederbuch*

Früh, wann die Hähne kräh'n, eh' die Sternlein schwindenn
Robert Schumann, "Das verlassne Mägdelein" 1847, Op64,2
Robert Schumann, "Das verlassene Mägdlein" 1849, Op91,4, ssaa.pf(ad lib)
from *Romanzen für Frauenstimmen II*
Gustav Eggers, "Das verlassene Mägdlein" 1857pub, Op2,3
Ignaz Brüll, "Das verlassene Mägdlein" 186-?, Op5,ii,1
Hermann Goetz, "Das verlassene Mägdelein" 1868-76, Op12,5
Robert Franz, "In Leid versunken" 1870?pub, Op27,4
Erik Meyer-Helmund, "Das verlassene Mädchen" 1886-88
Hans Pfitzner, "Das verlassene Mägdelein" 1887?

Hugo Wolf, "Das verlassene Mägdlein" 1888
from *Mörike Lieder* (7)
Hans Pfitzner, "Das verlassene Mägdlein" 1922, Op30,2
Hugo Distler, "Das verlassene Mägdlein" 1939, Op19,ii,10, fch
from *Mörike-Chorliederbuch*

Frühling läßt ein blaues Band wieder flattern durch die Lüfte
Robert Schumann, "Er ist's" 1849, Op79,23
from *Lieder-Album für die Jugend*
Eduard Lassen, "Frühling"
Robert Franz, "Er ist's!" 1870?pub, Op27,2
Hugo Wolf, "Er ist's" 1888
from *Mörike Lieder* (6)
Felix Weingartner, "Er ist's" 1906pub, Op41,3
from *Frühlings- und Liebeslieder*
Othmar Schoeck, "Er ist's" 1937, Op51,4
Hugo Distler, "Er ist's" 1939, Op19,ii,2, fch
from *Mörike-Chorliederbuch*
Louis Ferdinand, "Frühling" 1966pub

Gelassen stieg die Nacht an's Land, lehnt träumend an der Berge Wand
Hugo Wolf, "Um Mitternacht" 1888
from *Mörike Lieder* (19)
Max Bruch, "Um Mitternacht" 1892, Op59,1, bar.pf
Hugo Distler, "Um Mitternacht" 1939, Op19,i,10, ch
from *Mörike-Chorliederbuch*
Heimo Erbse, "Um Mitternacht" 1959pub, Op17,2
Peter Jona Korn, "Um Mitternacht" 1964pub, Op24,2

Gestern, als ich vom nächtlichen Lager den Stern mir in Osten
Othmar Schoeck, "Johann Kepler" 1948-49, Op62,23
from *Das holde Bescheiden (Betrachtung)*

Gleichwie ein Vogel am Fenster vorbei
Othmar Schoeck, "Auf dem Krankenbette" 1948-49, Op62,38
from *Das holde Bescheiden (Glaube)*

Grausame Frühlingssonne, du weckst mich vor der Zeit
Hugo Wolf, "Citronenfalter im April" 1888
from *Mörike Lieder* (18)
Felix Weingartner, "Zitronenfalter im April" 1906pub, Op41,1
from *Frühlings- und Liebeslieder*

Herr, schicke was du willt, ein Liebes oder Leides
Hugo Wolf, "Gebet" 1888
from *Mörike Lieder* (28)
Felix Weingartner, "Gebet" 1908, Op44,2, mch
Hugo Distler, "Gebet" 1939, Op19,ii,7, fch
from *Mörike-Chorliederbuch*
Hugo Distler, "Gebet" 1939, Op19,ii,9, fch
from *Mörike-Chorliederbuch*
Othmar Schoeck, "Gebet" 1948-49, Op62,33
from *Das holde Bescheiden (Glaube)*

Herz! und weisst du selber denn zu sagen
Robert Franz, "Herz, ich habe schwer an dir zu tragen" 1870?pub, Op27,3

Hier im Schatten, o Batyllos
Othmar Schoeck, "Ruheplatz" 1915, Op31,4
translated from Anacreon

Hier ist Freude, hier ist Lust
Othmar Schoeck, "Auf der Teck (Rauhe Alb)" 1948-49, Op62,6
from *Das holde Bescheiden (Natur)*

Hier lieg' ich auf dem Frühlingshügel
Hugo Wolf, "Im Frühling" 1888
from *Mörike Lieder* (13)

Hört ihn und seht sein dürftig Instrument!
Othmar Schoeck, "Auf einen Klavierspieler" 1948-49, Op62,31
from *Das holde Bescheiden (Betrachtung)*

Horch! Auf der Erde feuchtem Grund gelegen
Othmar Schoeck, "Nachts" 1948-49, Op62,20
from *Das holde Bescheiden (Betrachtung)*

Ich bin meiner Mutter einzig Kind
Hugo Wolf, "Selbstgeständnis" 1888
from *Mörike Lieder* (52)

Ich hätte wohl, dein Haar zu zieren
Felix Weingartner, "Zu Lottchens Geburtstag" 1906pub, Op41,2
from *Frühlings- und Liebeslieder*

Ich hatt ein Vöglein, ach wie fein!
Hugo Wolf, "Suschens Vogel" 1880
Hugo Distler, "Suschens Vogel" 1939, Op19,i,8, ch
from *Mörike-Chorliederbuch*
Hugo Distler, "Suschens Vogel" 1939, Op19,i,16, ch
from *Mörike-Chorliederbuch*

Ich sah den Helikon in Wolkendunst
Othmar Schoeck, "Antike Poesie (An Goethe)" 1948-49, Op62,21
from *Das holde Bescheiden (Betrachtung)*

Ich sah eben ein jugendlich Paar
Felix Weingartner, "Datura suaveolens" 1906pub, Op41,9
from *Frühlings- und Liebeslieder*

Im Nebel ruhet noch die Welt, noch träumen Wald und Wiesen
Othmar Schoeck, "Septembermorgen" 1905, Op7,2
Joseph Marx, "September-Morgen" 1906
Othmar Schoeck, "Septembermorgen" 1937, Op51,5
Ernest Vietor, "Septembermorgen" 1937-38, Op16,8
Felix Wolfes, "Septembermorgen" 1955, 1v(med).pf
Heimo Erbse, "September-Morgen" 1959pub, Op17,1

Im Weinberg auf der Höhe ein Häuslein steht so windebang
Hugo Wolf, "Der Knabe und das Immlein" 1888
from *Mörike Lieder* (2)
Hugo Distler, "Der Knabe und das Immelein" 1939, Op19,i,17, ch
from *Mörike-Chorliederbuch*

Im Winterboden schläft, ein Blumenkeim, der Schmetterling
Hugo Wolf, "Auf eine Christblume II" 1888
from *Mörike Lieder* (21)

In aller Früh, ach, lang vor Tag
Hugo Wolf, "Lied eines Verliebten" 1888
from *Mörike Lieder* (43)
Hugo Distler, "Lied eines Verliebten" 1939, Op19,iii,9, mch
from *Mörike-Chorliederbuch*

In dieser Winterfrühe wie ist mir doch zumut!
Hugo Distler, "Sehnsucht" 1939, Op19,i,22, ch
from *Mörike-Chorliederbuch*

In ein freundliches Städtchen tret' ich ein
Hugo Wolf, "Auf einer Wanderung" 1888
from *Mörike Lieder* (15)

In grüner Landschaft Sommerflor
Hugo Wolf, "Auf ein altes Bild" 1888
from *Mörike Lieder* (23)

In poetischer Epistel ruft ein desperater Wicht
Hugo Wolf, "Auftrag" 1888
from *Mörike Lieder* (50)

Ist's möglich? sieht ein Mann so heiter aus
Othmar Schoeck, "Der Geprüfte" 1948-49, Op62,39
from *Das holde Bescheiden (Glaube)*

Ja, mein Glück, das langgewohnte
Othmar Schoeck, "Trost" 1948-49, Op62,29
from *Das holde Bescheiden (Betrachtung)*

Jung Volker das ist unser Räuberhauptmann
Robert Franz, "Volker spielt auf!" 1870?pub, Op27,1
Felix Weingartner, "Gesang der Räuber" 1908, Op44,3, mch
Hugo Distler, "Jung Volker (Gesang der Räuber)" 1939, Op19,iii,10, mch
from *Mörike-Chorliederbuch*

Kann auch ein Mensch des andern auf der Erde ganz
Hugo Wolf, "Neue Liebe" 1888
from *Mörike Lieder* (30)

Kein Schlaf noch kühlt das Auge mir
Hugo Wolf, "In der Frühe" 1888
from *Mörike Lieder* (24)
Max Reger, "In der Frühe" 1907
Peter Jona Korn, "In der Frühe" 1964pub, Op24,6

Kleine Gäste, kleines Haus. Liebe Mäusin oder Maus
Hugo Wolf, "Mausfallen-Sprüchlein" 1882
from *Sechs Lieder für eine Frauenstimme*
Hugo Distler, "Mausfallensprüchlein" 1939, Op19,ii,5, fch
from *Mörike-Chorliederbuch*

Krank nun vollends und matt! Und du, o Himmlische
Othmar Schoeck, "Muse und Dichter" 1948-49, Op62,37
from *Das holde Bescheiden (Glaube)*

Kunst! o in deine Arme wie gern entflöh' ich dem Eros!
Othmar Schoeck, "Keine Rettung" 1948-49, Op62,24
from *Das holde Bescheiden (Betrachtung)*

Laß, o Welt, o laß mich sein! Lokket nicht mit Liebesgaben
Robert Franz, "Verborgenheit" 1870?pub, Op28,5
Hugo Wolf, "Verborgenheit" 1888
from *Mörike Lieder* (12)
Hugo Distler, "Verborgenheit" 1939, Op19,ii,4, fch
from *Mörike-Chorliederbuch*
Hugo Distler, "Verborgenheit" 1939, Op19,iii,6, mch
from *Mörike-Chorliederbuch*
Peter Jona Korn, "Verborgenheit" 1964pub, Op24,4

"Lebe wohl" Du fühlest nicht, was es heißt, dies Wort der Schmerzen
Hugo Wolf, "Lebe wohl" 1888
from *Mörike Lieder* (36)
Hugo Distler, "Lebewohl" 1939, Op19,i,23, ch
from *Mörike-Chorliederbuch*

Mein Kind, in welchem Krieg hast du
Othmar Schoeck, "Auf ein Kind (das mir eine ausgerissene Haarlocke vorwies)" 1948-49, Op62,35
from *Das holde Bescheiden (Glaube)*

Mein Wappen ist nicht adelig
Othmar Schoeck, "In ein Autographen-Album" 1948-49, Op62,26
from *Das holde Bescheiden (Betrachtung)*

Noch unverrückt, o schöne Lampe, schmückest du
Othmar Schoeck, "Auf eine Lampe" 1948-49, Op62,19
from *Das holde Bescheiden (Betrachtung)*
Felix Wolfes, "Auf eine Lampe" 1968

Nur fast so wie im Traum ist mir's geschehen
Othmar Schoeck, "Besuch in Urach" 1948-49, Op62,40
from *Das holde Bescheiden (Rückblick)*

O flaumenleichte Zeit der dunkeln Frühe!
Othmar Schoeck, "An einem Wintermorgen, vor Sonnenaufgang" 1948-49, Op62,2
from *Das holde Bescheiden (Natur)*

O Fluß, mein Fluß im Morgenstrahl!
Othmar Schoeck, "Mein Fluß" 1948-49, Op62,9
from *Das holde Bescheiden (Natur)*

O Woche, Zeugin heiliger Beschwerde!
Hugo Wolf, "Charwoche" 1888
from *Mörike Lieder* (26)

Ohne das Schöne, was soll der Gewinn?
Othmar Schoeck, "Spruch" 1944, Op51,6

Ostern ist zwar schon vorbei
Othmar Schoeck, "Auf ein Ei geschreiben" 1948-49, Op62,30
from *Das holde Bescheiden (Betrachtung)*

Primel und Stern und Syringe, von einsamer Kerze beleuchtet
Othmar Schoeck, "Nachts am Schreibepult" 1948-49, Op62,16
from *Das holde Bescheiden (Liebe)*

Rosenzeit! wie schnell vorbei
Ferdinand Hiller, "Agnes" 1850?, Op46,2
Robert Franz, "Rosenzeit!" 1870?pub, Op27,5
Johannes Brahms, "Agnes" 1873, Op59,5
Hugo Wolf, "Agnes" 1888
from *Mörike Lieder* (14)
Othmar Schoeck, "Agnes" 1905, o.op20, ch
Hugo Distler, "Agnes" 1939, Op19,iii,5, mch
from *Mörike-Chorliederbuch*

Sausewind, Brausewind! dort und hier!
Hugo Wolf, "Lied vom Winde" 1888
from *Mörike Lieder* (38)
Hugo Distler, "Lied vom Winde" 1939, Op19,ii,11, fch
from *Mörike-Chorliederbuch*

Schlaf! süsser Schlaf! obwohl dem Tod wie du nichts gleicht
Hugo Wolf, "An den Schlaf" 1888
from *Mörike Lieder* (29)
Hanns Eisler, "An den Schlaf" 1940

Schön prangt im Silbertau die junge Rose
Othmar Schoeck, "Nur zu!" 1948-49, Op62,18
from *Das holde Bescheiden (Liebe)*

Sehet ihr am Fensterlein dort die rote Mütze wieder?
Hugo Wolf, "Der Feuerreiter" 1888
from *Mörike Lieder* (44)
Hugo Distler, "Der Feuerreiter" 1939, Op19,i,13, ch
from *Mörike-Chorliederbuch*

Seid ihr beisammen all'? Ihr Freund', auf allen Fall
Hugo Distler, "Handwerkerlied" 1939, Op19,i,12, 1v.ch
from *Mörike-Chorliederbuch*

Sieh, der Kastanie kindliches Laub
Othmar Schoeck, "Im Park" 1948-49, Op62,8
from *Das holde Bescheiden (Natur)*

Siehe von allen den Liedern, nicht eines gilt dir, o Mutter
Felix Weingartner, "An meine Mutter" 1906pub, Op41,12
from *Frühlings- und Liebeslieder*
Othmar Schoeck, "An meine Mutter" 1907, Op14,1

So ist die Lieb'! So ist die Lieb'!
Hugo Wolf, "Nimmersatte Liebe" 1888
from *Mörike Lieder* (9)
Hugo Distler, "Nimmersatte Liebe" 1939, Op19,i,19, ch
from *Mörike-Chorliederbuch*

Sohn der Jungfrau, Himmelskind!
Hugo Wolf, "Schlafendes Jesuskind" 1888
from *Mörike Lieder* (25)

Tinte! Tinte, wer braucht! Schöne schwarze Tinte verkauf ich
Othmar Schoeck, "Lose Ware" 1948-49, Op62,10
from *Das holde Bescheiden (Liebe)*

Tochter des Walds, du Lilienverwandte
Hugo Wolf, "Auf eine Christblume I" 1888
from *Mörike Lieder* (20)

Tödtlich graute mir der Morgen
Hugo Wolf, "Der Genesene an die Hoffnung" 1888
from *Mörike Lieder* (1)

Tonleiterähnlich steiget dein Klaggesang vollschwellend auf
Hugo Distler, "An Philomele" 1939, Op19,iii,12, mch
from *Mörike-Chorliederbuch*
Othmar Schoeck, "An Philomele" 1948-49, Op62,5
from *Das holde Bescheiden (Natur)*

Uffem Kirchhof, am Chor blüeht e Blo-Holder-Strauß
Hugo Distler, "Lieb' in den Tod" 1939, Op19,i,4, ch
from *Mörike-Chorliederbuch*

Unangeklopft ein Herr tritt Abends bei mir ein
Hugo Wolf, "Abschied" 1888
from *Mörike Lieder* (53)

Und die mich trug im Mutterleib
Robert Schumann, "Jung Volkers Lied" 1850-1, Op125,4
from *Fünf heitere Gesänge*
Hugo Distler, "Jung Volkers Lied" 1939, Op19,iii,11, mch
from *Mörike-Chorliederbuch*
Peter Jona Korn, "Jung Volkers Lied" 1964pub, Op24,1

Vesperzeit, Betgeläut' aus den Dörfern weit und breit
Othmar Schoeck, "Der Hirtenknabe (Zu einer Zeichnung L. Richters)" 1948-49, Op62,34
from *Das holde Bescheiden (Glaube)*

Vielfach sind zum Hades die Pfade
Othmar Schoeck, "Erinna an Sappho" 1948-49, Op62,22
from *Das holde Bescheiden (Betrachtung)*

Vierfach Kleeblatt! Selt'ner Fund!
Hugo Distler, "Auf dem Spaziergang" 1939, Op19,i,6, ch
from *Mörike-Chorliederbuch*

Vom Berge was kommt dort um Mitternacht spät
Hugo Wolf, "Die Geister am Mummelsee" 1888
from *Mörike Lieder* (47)

Vor lauter hochadligen Zeugen
Hugo Wolf, "Bei einer Trauung" 1888
from *Mörike Lieder* (51)

Warum, Geliebte, denk' ich dein
Hugo Wolf, "Peregrina (II)" 1888
from *Mörike Lieder* (34)

Was doch heut Nacht ein Sturm gewesen
Hugo Wolf, "Begegnung" 1888
from *Mörike Lieder* (8)
Max Reger, "Begegnung" 1901, Op62,13, 1v(med).pf
Peter Jona Korn, "Begegnung" 1964pub, Op24,5

Was im Netze? Schau einmal! Ach, aber ich bin bange
Hugo Wolf, "Erstes Liebeslied eines Mädchens" 1888
from *Mörike Lieder* (42)
Hugo Distler, "Erstes Liebeslied eines Mädchens" 1939, Op19,ii,12, fch
from *Mörike-Chorliederbuch*

Wasch dich, mein Schwesterchen, wasch dich!
Hugo Wolf, "Die Tochter der Heide" 1884
Hugo Distler, "Die Tochter der Heide" 1939, Op19,i,15, ch
from *Mörike-Chorliederbuch*
Hugo Distler, "Die Tochter der Heide" 1939, Op19,ii,1, fch
from *Mörike-Chorliederbuch*

Weht, o wehet, liebe Morgenwinde!
Othmar Schoeck, "Aus der Ferne" 1948-49, Op62,17
from *Das holde Bescheiden (Liebe)*

Wenn ich von deinem Anschaun tief gestillt
Felix Weingartner, "An die Geliebte" 1906pub, Op41,11
from *Frühlings- und Liebeslieder*
Hugo Wolf, "An die Geliebte" 1888
from *Mörike Lieder* (32)

Wenn meine Mutter hexen könnt'
Hugo Wolf, "Der Tambour" 1888
from *Mörike Lieder* (5)
Hugo Distler, "Der Tambour" 1939, Op19,iii,1, mch
from *Mörike-Chorliederbuch*

Wer die Musik sich erkiest, hat ein himmlisch Gut bekommen
Hugo Distler, "Vorspruch" 1939, Op19,i,1, ch
from *Mörike-Chorliederbuch*

Wie heimlicher Weise ein Engelein leise
Hugo Wolf, "Zum neuen Jahr" 1888
from *Mörike Lieder* (27)
Felix Weingartner, "Zum neuen Jahr" 1908, Op44,1, mch

Wie heißt König Ringangs Töchterlein?
Robert Schumann, "Schön-Rohtraut" 1849, Op67,2, satb
Hugo Distler, "Schön Rohtraut" 1939, Op19,i,14, ch
from *Mörike-Chorliederbuch*
Othmar Schoeck, "Schön-Rohtraut" 1948-49, Op62,13
from *Das holde Bescheiden (Liebe)*

Wie süß der Nachtwind nun die Wiese streift
Othmar Schoeck, "Gesang zu zweien in der Nacht" 1948-49, Op62,3
from *Das holde Bescheiden (Natur)*

Wir Schwestern zwei, wir schönen
Johannes Brahms, "Die Schwestern" before 1860, Op61,1, 2v.pf
Othmar Schoeck, "Die Schwestern" 1948-49, Op62,12
from *Das holde Bescheiden (Liebe)*

Wo gehst du hin, du schönes Kind
Felix Weingartner, "Ritterliche Werbung" 1906pub, Op41,7
from *Frühlings- und Liebeslieder*

Hugo Distler, "Ritterliche Werbung" 1939, Op19,i,11, 2v.ch
from *Mörike-Chorliederbuch*
Othmar Schoeck, "Ritterliche Werbung" 1948-49, Op62,11
from *Das holde Bescheiden (Liebe)*

Zierlich ist des Vogels Tritt im Schnee
Robert Schumann, "Jägerlied" 1846, Op59,3, satb
Hugo Wolf, "Jägerlied" 1888
from *Mörike Lieder* (4)
Robert Kahn, "Jägerlied" 1891, Op12,1
Felix Weingartner, "Jägerlied" 1906pub, Op41,5
from *Frühlings- und Liebeslieder*
Hugo Distler, "Jägerlied" 1939, Op19,ii,3, fch
from *Mörike-Chorliederbuch*
Hugo Distler, "Jägerlied" 1939, Op19,iii,4, mch
from *Mörike-Chorliederbuch*
Peter Jona Korn, "Jägerlied" 1964pub, Op24,3

Chr. F. K. Molbech
Was faßt dich an, o Tochter mein, was drückt dich nieder, Kind?
Adolf Jensen, "Frieden" 1865pub, Op23,2

Tirso de Molina (1571?-1648)
Das Mägdlein trat aus dem Fischerhaus
Gustav Mahler, "Phantasie" 1880-87
translated by L. Braunfels

Ist's dein Wille, süsse Maid, meinem heissen Liebesstreben
Gustav Mahler, "Serenade" 1880-87
translated by L. Braunfels

Alfred Mombert (1872-1942)
Leise fällt ein Schnee auf das Land
Karol Szymanowski, "Schlummerlied" 1907, Op17,9

Leise hör' ich dich singen Sankta Maria
Joseph Marx, "Sankta Maria" 1911

Nun ich der Riesen Stärksten überwand
Alban Berg, "Nun ich der Riesen..." 1909-10?, Op2,3
from *Drei Lieder aus "Der Glühende"*

Schlafend trägt man mich in mein Heimatland
Karol Szymanowski, "Fragment (Der Glühende)" 1907, Op17,11
Alban Berg, "Schlafend trägt man mich" 1909-10?, Op2,2
from *Drei Lieder aus "Der Glühende"*
Joseph Marx, "Schlafend trägt man mich in mein Heimatland" 1911, 1v(med).pf

Sie wandeln durch das Waldes Grün
Alban Berg, "Spaziergang" 1906
Ernest Vietor, "Spaziergang" 1936, Op14,4

Warm die Lüfte, es sprießt Gras
Alban Berg, "Warm die Lüfte" 1909-10?, Op2,4
from *Drei Lieder aus "Der Glühende"*

Theodor Mommsen (1817-1903)
Die Saiten weiß ich zu rühren
Ernst Krenek, "Die Saiten weiß ich zu rühren" 1930, Op64,6
from *Fiedellieder aus dem "Liederbuch dreier Freunde"*

Im Walde, im Walde, im tiefgrünen Wald
Ernst Krenek, "Im Walde, im Walde" 1930, Op64,3
from *Fiedellieder aus dem "Liederbuch dreier Freunde"*

Meine Laute nehm' ich wieder, Laute mit dem grünen Band
Ernst Krenek, "Meine Laute nehm' ich wieder" 1930, Op64,1
from *Fiedellieder aus dem "Liederbuch dreier Freunde"*

Und so laßt mich weiter wandern
Ernst Krenek, "Und so laßt mich weiter wandern" 1930, Op64,4
from *Fiedellieder aus dem "Liederbuch dreier Freunde"*

Wiederum lebt wohl, ihr Brüder
Ernst Krenek, "Wiederum lebt wohl, ihr Brüder" 1930, Op64,7
from *Fiedellieder aus dem "Liederbuch dreier Freunde"*

"Paul Mongré" (Felix Hausdorff) (1868-1942)
Das ist so süß, das unser rascher Bund
Joseph Marx, "Dem Genius des Augenblicks" 1910, 1v(med).pf

Dies Augenpaar von dunklem Glanz betaut
Joseph Marx, "Dein Blick" 1909

Elimar von Monsterberg-Muenckenau (1877-?)
Ein Spielmann, der muss reisen, das ist ein alter Brauch
Alban Berg, "Abschied" 1902

Thomas Moore (1779-1852)
An Celia's Baum in stiller Nacht hängt
Felix Mendelssohn, "Der Blumenkranz" 1829, Nachlass

Die Bowle fort! und schäume sie noch so glänzend heut!
Adolf Jensen, "Die Bowle fort!" 1876, Op50,5
translated by Ferdinand Freiligrath

Leis' rudern hier, mein Gondolier, leis', leis'!
Robert Schumann, "Zwei Venetianische Lieder I" 1840, Op25,17
translated by Ferdinand Freiligrath
from *Liederkreis*
Adolf Jensen, "Leis, rudern hier, mein Gondolier!" 1874, Op50,4
translated by Ferdinand Freiligrath

Nicht die Träne kann es sagen
Peter Cornelius, "Nicht die Träne kann es sagen" 1869, Op9,2, ttbb
translated by Peter Cornelius

Wenn durch die Piazetta die Abendluft weht
Robert Schumann, "Zwei Venetianische Lieder II" 1840, Op25,18
translated by Ferdinand Freiligrath
from *Liederkreis*
Felix Mendelssohn, "Venetianisches Gondellied" 1842, Op57,5
Adolf Jensen, "Wenn durch die Piazzetta" 1874, Op50,3
August Bungert, "Entführung" 1889-91pub, Op33,2

Giorgio Stigelli, "Ninetta (Venetianisches Gondellied)"
translated by Ferdinand Freiligrath

Willst kommen zur Laube, so schattig und kühl?
Carl Reinecke, "Willst du kommen, mein Lieb?" Op81,4
translated by Ferdinand Freiligrath

Zum Friedhof schien der Mond herab, und eisig war die Mitternacht
Anton Rubinstein, "Die Thräne" Op83,8

Christian Morgenstern (1871-1914)

Abendkelch voll Sonnenlicht
Alexander Zemlinsky, "Abendkelch voll Sonnenlicht" 1934, Op22,2

Als wie ein Feld, das erstes Licht ereilt
Felix Weingartner, "Evas Haar" 1909, Op47,1

Also ihr lebt noch, alle, alle, ihr, am Bach ihr Weiden
Yrjö Kilpinen, "Siehe, auch ich– lebe" 1928, Op59,5
Ernest Vietor, "Siehe, auch ich – Lebe" 1933-34, Op11,17

Am Himmel der Wolken er dunkelnder Kranz
Ernest Vietor, "Auf dem Strome" 1933-34, Op11,16

Am Morgen spricht die Magd ganz wild
Ernest Vietor, "Traum der Magd (with apologies to Dr. Richard Strauss)" Op7,8
from *Galgenlieder* (8)

Auf a folgt
Paul Hindemith, "Auf a folgt" 1925, Op45,ii,4, 2v.insts
from *Sing-und Spielmusiken für Liebhaber und Musikfreunde*

Auf braunen Sammetschuhen geht der Abend durch das müde Land
Yrjö Kilpinen, "Der Abend" 1928
Ernest Vietor, "Der Abend" 1933-34, Op11,5
Alexander Zemlinsky, "Auf braunen Sammetschuhen" 1934, Op22,1

Auf dem Meere meiner Seele
Alexander Zemlinsky, "Auf dem Meere meiner Seele" 1934, Op22,(6)

Auf den Schwingen des Windes
Ernest Vietor, "Zeit und Ewigkeit" 1932, Op9,1

Auf der Bank im Walde han sich gestern zwei geküßt
Max Reger, "Anmutiger Vertrag" 1901, Op62,16, 1v(med).pf
Yrjö Kilpinen, "Anmutiger Vertrag" 1928, Op61,5
from *Lieder der Liebe II*
Richard Trunk, "Vertrag" 1933pub, Op63,2
from *Vier heitere Lieder*
Ernest Vietor, "Anmutiger Vertrag" 1933-34, Op11,15

Auf der Treppe sitzen meine Öhrchen
Paul Hindemith, "Auf der Treppe sitzen meine Öhrchen" 1922, Op18,4
Ernest Vietor, "Auf der Treppe" 1933-34, Op11,13

Aus ihrem Bette stürzt sie bleich
Ernest Vietor, "Die wiederhergestellte Ruhe" 1930-31, Op8,8

Aus silbergrauen Gründen tritt ein schlankes Reh
Erich J. Wolff, "Erster Schnee" 1914pub, Lieder No.8

Ernest Vietor, “Erster Schnee” 1933-34, Op11,6

Bau mir die Stadt aus Elfenbein, die Silberflut umschäume!
Ernest Vietor, “Die Stadt aus Elfenbein” 1933-34, Op11,4

Da waren zwei Kinder, jung und gut
Alexander Zemlinsky, “Da waren zwei Kinder” 1900?, Op7,1
from *Irmelin Rose und andere Gesänge*

Das ist eine Nacht! Eine Wacht!
Yrjö Kilpinen, “Sturmnacht” 1928

Das Mondschaf sagt sich selbst gut Nacht
Ernest Vietor, “Das Mondschaf” 1930-31, Op8,6

Dein Wunsch, nicht mehr zu leiden
Walter Schulthess, “Dein Wunsch, nicht mehr zu leiden” 1941-43
from *Lieder nach Gedichten von Christian Morgenstern*

Dein Wunsch war immer fliegen!
Yrjö Kilpinen, “Mit-Erwacht” 1928

Deine Rosen an der Brust
Felix Weingartner, “Deine Rosen an der Brust” 1909, Op48,5
Yrjö Kilpinen, “Deine Rosen an der Brust” 1928, Op61,3
from *Lieder der Liebe II*

Der monddurchbleichte Wald liegt totenstumm
Yrjö Kilpinen, “Der Wind als Liebender” 1928

Der Rabe Ralf will will hu hu
Ernest Vietor, “Der Rabe Ralf” Op7,4
from *Galgenlieder* (4)

Die Primeln blühn und grüssen
Ernest Vietor, “Die Primeln blühn und grüssen” 1932, Op9,3

Die Schleiche singt ihr Nachtgebet
Ernest Vietor, “Geiss und Schleiche” Op7,9
from *Galgenlieder* (9)

Die stillen Stunden sind es
Walter Schulthess, “Die stillen Stunden sind es” 1941-43
from *Lieder nach Gedichten von Christian Morgenstern*

Diese Rose von heimlichen Küssen schwer
Yrjö Kilpinen, “Unsere Liebe” 1928, Op60,3
from *Lieder der Liebe I*

Dinge gehen vor im Mond, die das Kalb selbst nicht gewohnt
Ernest Vietor, “Mondendinge” Op7,7
from *Galgenlieder* (7)

Draußen im weiten Krieg ist blieben mein armer Schatz
Max Reger, “Mädchenlied” 1900, Op51,5

Drinnen im Saal eine Geige sang, sie sang von Liebe so wild
Yrjö Kilpinen, “Wind und Geige” 1928

Du bist ja ein Hamster, ein Hamster bist du
Franz Tischhauser, “In der Strassenbahn” 1937, sop.pf
from *Klein Irmchen* (3)

Du bist mein Land
Felix Weingartner, "Du bist mein Land" 1909, Op48,2

Du dunkler Frühlingsgarten, durch den ich wandre jede Nacht
Yrjö Kilpinen, "Du dunkler Frühlingsgarten" 1928

Du gabst mir deine Kette
Alexander Zemlinsky, "Volkslied" 1934, Op22,5

Du trüber Tag mit deinen stillen, grauen Farben
Yrjö Kilpinen, "Du trüber Tag" 1928

Durch die Lande auf und ab
Yrjö Kilpinen, "Der Säemann" 1928, Op62,5
from *Lieder um den Tod*

Ein Bauernknabe liegt im Wald und liest
Ernest Vietor, "Der Bauernknabe" 1933-34, Op11,8

Ein finstrer Esel sprach einmal zu seinem ehlichen Gemahl
Felix Wolfes, "Die beiden Esel" 1963, 1v(med).pf

Ein Hecht, vom heiligen Anton bekehrt
Felix Wolfes, "Der Hecht" 1963

Ein kleiner Hund mit Namen Fips erhielt vom Onkel einen Schlips
Franz Tischhauser, "Fips" 1937, sop.pf
from *Klein Irmchen* (5)

Ein Rabe sass auf einem Meilenstein und rief
Ernest Vietor, "KM 21" Op7,12
from *Galgenlieder* (12)

Ein Schmetterling fliegt über mir
Yrjö Kilpinen, "Der Schmetterling" 1928

Ein schwarzes Vögelein fliegt über die Welt
Alexander Zemlinsky, "Vöglein Schwermut" 1901?, Op10,3
from *Ehetanzlied und andere Gesänge*
Erich J. Wolff, "Vöglein Schwermut" 1914pub, Lieder No.16
Ernest Vietor, "Vöglein Schwermut" Op5,2
Felix Weingartner, "Vöglein Schwermut" 1906, Op39,2, 1v(med).orch/pf
Yrjö Kilpinen, "Vöglein Schwermut" 1928, Op62,1
from *Lieder um den Tod*
Harald Genzmer, "Vöglein Schwermut" 1940-87, bar.pf or sop.pf
from *Acht Lieder nach verschiedenen Dichtern*

Ein Wiesel sass auf einem Kiesel inmitten Bachgeriesel
Ernest Vietor, "Das aesthetische Wiesel" Op7,11
from *Galgenlieder* (11)

Eine Hütte und ein Stück Wald ganz für mich allein
Yrjö Kilpinen, "Einsiedlerwunsch" 1928

Eines gibt's, darauf ich mich freuen darf
Yrjö Kilpinen, "Unverlierbare Gewähr" 1928, Op62,6
from *Lieder um den Tod*

Erde, die uns dies gebracht
Paul Hindemith, "Erde, die uns dies gebracht" 1925, Op45,ii,8, 2v.insts
from *Sing-und Spielmusiken für Liebhaber und Musikfreunde*

Othmar Schoeck, “Spruch” 1941, Op69,1, 2v.pf
from *Zwei zweistimmige Lieder für Kinder- oder Frauenchor*

Es ist Nacht, und mein Herz kommt zu dir
Yrjö Kilpinen, “Es ist Nacht” 1928, Op60,2
from *Lieder der Liebe I*

Es kommt der Schmerz gegangen
Felix Weingartner, “Es kommt der Schmerz gegangen” 1909, Op48,4

Es lebt ein Ries’ im Wald, der hat ein Ohr so gross
Franz Tischhauser, “Waldmärchen” 1937, sop.pf
from *Klein Irmchen* (4)

Es leiht mir wunderbare Stärke
Walter Schulthess, “Es leiht mir wunderbare Stärke” 1941-43
from *Lieder nach Gedichten von Christian Morgenstern*

Es pfeift der Wind. Was pfeift er wohl?
Ernest Vietor, “Es pfeift der Wind” 1930-31, Op8,1

Es stürzen der Jugend Altäre zusammen
Yrjö Kilpinen, “Thalatta” 1928, Op59,6

Es war einmal ein Lattenzaun, mit Zwischenraum, hindurch zu schaun
Ernest Vietor, “Der Lattenzaun” Op7,5
from *Galgenlieder* (5)

Es war einmal ein Papagei
Ernest Vietor, “Der Papagei” 1930-31, Op8,3

Flockendichte Winternacht
Yrjö Kilpinen, “Winternacht” 1928, Op62,4
from *Lieder um den Tod*

Gleich einer versunkenen Melodie
Max Reger, “Gleich einer versunkenen Melodie” 1900, Op51,8, 1v(med).pf
Yrjö Kilpinen, “Gleich einer versunkenen Melodie” 1928

Glück ist wie Blütenduft, der dir vorüberfliegt
Walter Schulthess, “Glück ist wie Blütenduft” 1941-43
from *Lieder nach Gedichten von Christian Morgenstern*

Glühend zwischen dir und mir Julinächte brüten
Walter Schulthess, “Geheime Verabredung” 1941-43
from *Lieder nach Gedichten von Christian Morgenstern*

Grab tausend Klafter hinab
Felix Weingartner, “Erdriese” 1906, Op39,3, 1v(med).orch/pf

Guten Abend, mein Freund!
Yrjö Kilpinen, “Der Tod und der einsame Trinker (eine Mitternachtsszene)” 1928, Op62,3
from *Lieder um den Tod*

Heil dir, der du hassen kannst, dem im reichen Mark
Max Reger, “Hymnus des Hasses” 1901, Op55,1

Ich bin ein einsamer Schaukelstuhl
Ernest Vietor, “Der Schaukelstuhl auf der Verlassenen Terrasse” Op7,6
from *Galgenlieder* (6)

Ich bin eine Harfe mit goldenen Seiten
Ernest Vietor, "Traum" 1933-34, Op11,3

Ich danke dir, du stummer Stein
Yrjö Kilpinen, "Die Fußwaschung" 1928, Op59,1

Ich liebe die graden Alleen mit ihrer stolzen Flucht
Ernest Vietor, "Die Allee" 1932, Op9,6

Ich sah uns alle und empfand
Ernest Vietor, "Ich sah uns alle" 1933-34, Op11,9

Ich wache noch in später Nacht und sinne
Walter Schulthess, "Ich wache noch" 1941-43
from *Lieder nach Gedichten von Christian Morgenstern*

Im Garten Gottes wirft ein Born
Felix Weingartner, "Der Born" 1906, Op39,1, 1v(med).orch/pf

Im Inselwald, "Zum stillen Kauz," da lebt der heilige Pardauz
Ernest Vietor, "Der heilige Pardauz" 1930-31, Op8,5

Im Süden war's. Zur Nachtzeit. Eine Gast
Felix Weingartner, "Ein Rosenzweig" 1909, Op47,2

In deine langen Wellen, tiefe Glocke
Felix Weingartner, "Abendläuten" 1910, Op51,1
from *Abendlieder*
Ernest Vietor, "Abendläuten" 1933-34, Op11,7

In den Wipfeln des Waldes
Felix Weingartner, "Mondaufgang" 1906, Op39,4, 1v(med).orch/pf

In einem leeren Haselstrauch da sitzen drei Spatzen Bauch an Bauch
Franz Tischhauser, "Die drei Spatzen" 1937, sop.pf
from *Klein Irmchen* (2)

Jetzt bist du da, dann bist du dort
Felix Weingartner, "Schauder" 1909, Op47,3
Ernest Vietor, "Schauder" 1932, Op9,4

Klabautermann, Klabauterfrau, Klabauterkind im Schiffe sind
Ernest Vietor, "Klabautermann" 1930-31, Op8,7

Leise Lieder sing' ich dir bei Nacht
Richard Strauss, "Leise Lieder" 1899, Op41a,5
Robert Kahn, "Leise Lieder sing' ich dir bei Nacht" 1899, Op31,5
Max Reger, "Leise Lieder" 1900, Op48,2, 1v(med).pf
Hugo Kaun, "Leise Lieder" 1903pub, Op47,1
Walter Schulthess, "Leise Lieder" 1941-43
from *Lieder nach Gedichten von Christian Morgenstern*

Litt einst ein Fähnlein große Not
Ernst Toch, "Kleine Geschichte" 1928pub, Op41,6

Mein Herz ist leer, ich liebe dich nicht mehr
Yrjö Kilpinen, "Mein Herz ist leer" 1928, Op60,1
from *Lieder der Liebe I*

Mein lieber und vertrauter Mann
Ernest Vietor, "Brief einer Klabauterfrau" 1930-31, Op8,4

Mit dir, wer weiß, würd' ich noch manche Pfade
Felix Weingartner, "Mit dir, wer weiß, würd' ich" 1909, Op48,1

Mit wilden Atemstössen wirft der Sturm des Turms Geläut mir
Yrjö Kilpinen, "Windglück" 1928

Nach all dem Menschenlärm
Yrjö Kilpinen, "Heimat" 1928, Op61,1
from *Lieder der Liebe II*

Nebel, stiller Nebel über Meer und Land
Ernest Vietor, "Nebel am Wattenmeer" 1932, Op9,5

Nun bevölkert sich das hohe Drüben
Walter Schulthess, "Beim Tode Nahestehender" 1941-43
from *Lieder nach Gedichten von Christian Morgenstern*

Nun schweben Dach und Decke
Felix Weingartner, "Wiegenlied" 1909, Op47,4
after Ibsen

Nun wollen wir uns still die Hände geben
Walter Schulthess, "Nun wollen wir uns still die Hände geben" 1941-43
from *Lieder nach Gedichten von Christian Morgenstern*

O Nacht, du Sternenbronnen, ich bade Leib und Geist
Yrjö Kilpinen, "O Nacht" 1928, Op59,2
Ernest Vietor, "O Nacht" 1933-34, Op11,14

O schauerliche Lebenswirrn, wir hängen hier am roten Zwirn
Ernest Vietor, "Bundeslied der Galgenbrüder" Op7,1
from *Galgenlieder* (1)

Ob Sie mir je Erfüllung wird, die Lust, in alle Höhn
Yrjö Kilpinen, "Ob Sie mir je Erfüllung wird..." 1928

Oh, wer um alle Rosen wüsste
Ernest Vietor, "Von den heimlichen Rosen" 1933-34, Op11,10

Pfeift der Sturm? Keift ein Wurm?
Ernest Vietor, "Nein!" Op7,3
from *Galgenlieder* (3)

Regne, regne, Frühlingsregen, weine durch die stille Nacht!
Max Reger, "Frühlingsregen" 1900, Op51,9, 1v(med).pf
Yrjö Kilpinen, "Frühlingsregen" 1928

Schlaf, Kindlein, schlaf, am Himmel steht ein Schaf
Ernest Vietor, "Galgenkindes Wiegenlied" 1930-31, Op8,2

Schlaf, Kindlein, schlaf! Es war einmal ein Schaf
Franz Tischhauser, "Schlummerliedchen" 1937, sop.pf
from *Klein Irmchen* (6)

Schwalben durch den Abend treibend
Felix Weingartner, "Schwalben" 1910, Op51,3
from *Abendlieder*

So still zu liegen und an dich zu denken
Wilhelm Kienzl, "Schneefall" 190-?, Op61,3

Sophie, mein Henker Mädel, komm, küsse mir den Schädel!
Ernest Vietor, "Galgenbruders Lied an Sophie, die Henkersmaid" Op7,2
from *Galgenlieder* (2)

Spann dein kleines Schirmchen auf; denn es möchte regnen drauf
Ernest Vietor, "Ein Kindergedicht" 1932, Op9,2
Franz Tischhauser, "Klein Irmchen" 1937, sop.pf
from *Klein Irmchen* (1)

Steht ein Häuschen an der Bahn
Ernst Toch, "Das Häuschen an der Bahn" 1928pub, Op41,8

Über der Erde Stirne, durch Tag und Nacht
Max Reger, "Pflügerin Sorge" 1901, Op62,15, 1v(med).pf

Über die tausend Berge
Yrjö Kilpinen, "Über die tausend Berge" 1928, Op61,4
from *Lieder der Liebe II*

Um stille Stübel schleicht des Monds barbarisches Gefunkel
Ernest Vietor, "Das Weiblein mit der Kunkel" Op7,10
from *Galgenlieder* (10)

Und werden wir uns nie besitzen
Yrjö Kilpinen, "Kleines Lied" 1928, Op61,2
from *Lieder der Liebe II*

Und wir werden zusammen schweigen
Felix Weingartner, "Und wir werden zusammen schweigen" 1909, Op48,3

Von dir schein' ich aufgewacht
Paul Hindemith, "Von dir schein' ich aufgewacht" 1922, Op18,5

Von zwei Rosen duftet eine anders
Yrjö Kilpinen, "Von zwei Rosen" 1928, Op59,3

Vorfrühling seufzt in weiter Nacht
Ernest Vietor, "Vorfrühling" 1934-35, Op12,4
from *Frühlingslieder*

War das die Liebe, die mich gestern streifte
Walter Schulthess, "War das die Liebe" 1941-43
from *Lieder nach Gedichten von Christian Morgenstern*

Warrrrrrte nur... wie viel schon riss ich ab von dir
Ernest Vietor, "Meeresbrandung" 1933-34, Op11,1

Warum versankst du mir so ganz?
Ernest Vietor, "Brief an Fega" 1933-34, Op11,11

Was denkst du jetzt? Ach, hinter diese Stirne zu dringen
Ernst Toch, "Was denkst du jetzt?" 1928pub, Op41,7

Was gehst du, armer bleicher Kopf, mich an
Yrjö Kilpinen, "Auf einem verfallenen Kirchhof" 1928, Op62,2
from *Lieder um den Tod*

Was kannst du, Süße, wider dies
Felix Weingartner, "Deine Schönheit" 1909, Op48,6

Weiße Tauben fliegen durch blaue Morgenluft
Max Reger, "Weiße Tauben" 1900, Op51,12, 1v(med).pf

Ernest Vietor, "Weisse Tauben" 1933-34, Op11,2
Walter Schulthess, "Weiße Tauben" 1941-43
from *Lieder nach Gedichten von Christian Morgenstern*

Wem so die Nacht die treugewölbten Hände
Walter Schulthess, "Morgenstimmung" 1941-43
from *Lieder nach Gedichten von Christian Morgenstern*

Wenn die Abendschatten steigen, überhaucht von Zeit zu Zeit
Walter Schulthess, "Sei bereit" 1941-43
from *Lieder nach Gedichten von Christian Morgenstern*

Wer kann schlagen-außer der Liebe
Walter Schulthess, "Wer kann schlagen-außer der Liebe" 1941-43
from *Lieder nach Gedichten von Christian Morgenstern*

Wie Sankt Franciscus schweb' ich in der Luft
Paul Hindemith, "Wie Sankt Franciscus schweb' ich in der Luft" 1922, Op18,2

Wie vieles ist denn Wort geworden
Yrjö Kilpinen, "Wie vieles ist denn Wort geworden" 1928, Op59,4

Wir sind zwei Rosen
Yrjö Kilpinen, "Schicksal der Liebe" 1928, Op60,5
from *Lieder der Liebe I*

Wir sitzen im Dunkeln
Yrjö Kilpinen, "Wir sitzen im Dunkeln" 1928, Op60,4
from *Lieder der Liebe I*

Zu Golde ward die Welt; zu lange traf der Sonne
Ernest Vietor, "Herbst" 1933-34, Op11,12

Zwei goldne Ringe hängen an seidnen Frauenhaaren
Walter Schulthess, "Die Eheringe" 1941-43
from *Lieder nach Gedichten von Christian Morgenstern*

Zwei Tannenwurzeln gross und alt unterhalten sich im Wald
Ernest Vietor, "Die zwei Wurzeln" Op7,13
from *Galgenlieder* (13)

Julius Mosen (1803-1867)

Der See ruht tief im blauen Traum
Robert Schumann, "Der träumende See" 1840, Op33,1, ttbb
Hugo Brückler, "Der träumende See" 187-?pub, Nachlass
Robert Kahn, "Der träumende See" 1894, Op20,i,1
Charles Griffes, "Der träumende See" 1903-09?, A6

Es grünet ein Nussbaum vor dem Haus
Robert Schumann, "Der Nussbaum" 1840, Op25,3
from *Liederkreis*

In meinem Garten lachet manch Blümlein blau und rot
Peter Cornelius, "Brennende Liebe" 1866, Op16,2, sop.bass.pf

Könnt' ich mit dir dort oben gehn
Charles Griffes, "Könnt' ich mit dir dort oben gehn" 1903-11?, A22

Wär' ich der Regen, ich wollte mich legen der Erde
Hugo Brückler, "Sehnsucht" 187-?pub, Nachlass

Was quälte dir dein banges Herz?
Robert Schumann, "Der Zecher als Doctrinair" 1840, Op33,4, ttbb

Salomon Hermann, Ritter von Mosenthal (1821-1877)
Ich sah' dich einmal, und ich seh' dich immer
Anton Rubinstein, "Nachhall" 1856, Op33,6

Ich will hier am Portale steh'n
Felix Weingartner, "Das Blumenmädchen" 1904, Op32,5

Wenn zwei sich lieben von ganzem Herzen
Karl Goldmark, "Wenn zwei sich lieben" 1888/89, Op46,5

Wolfgang Amadeus Mozart (1756-1791)
Du wirst im Ehstand viel erfahren, was Dir ein halbes Rätsel war
Felix Wolfes, "Kleiner Rat (an seine Schwester Nannerl)" 1961

Liebes Mandel, wo ist's Bandel?
Wolfgang Amadeus Mozart, "Terzett: Das Bandel" sop.ten.bass.pf

Karl Friedrich Müchler (1763-1857)
Ein steter Kampf ist unser Leben
Carl Maria von Weber, "Klage" 1808, Op15,2

Es muß das Herz an etwas hangen
Johann Fuss, "Die Verlassne an ihr Kind"
Musical arrangement by Franz

Ich sah ein Röschen am Wege stehn
Carl Maria von Weber, "Das Röschen" 1809, Op15,5

In des Meeres kühle Wogen taucht die Sonn ihr Flammenhaupt
Carl Friedrich Zelter, "Abendlied" 1796?

Was zieht zu deinem Zauberkreise
Carl Maria von Weber, "Was zieht zu deinem Zauberkreise" 1809, Op15,4

Ernst Adolf von Mühlbach
Kam ein Schmetterling geflogen in der schönsten Zaub'rin Reich
Carl Loewe, "Das Zaubernetz" 1832
from the comic Opera *Neckereien*

Heinrich (Gottlob) von Mühler (1813-1874)
Zu Quedlinburg im Dome ertönet Glockenklang
Carl Loewe, "Kaiser Otto's Weihnachtsfeier" 1853, Op121,1

Clara Müller (1861-1905)
Vom Himmel ist der Frühlingsregen herabgerauscht die ganze Nacht
Max Reger, "Frühlingsmorgen" 1900, Op51,11, 1v(med).pf

(Johann) Friedrich Müller (1749-1825)
Heute scheid' ich, heute wander' ich, keine Seele weint um mich
Friedrich Silcher, "Soldaten-Abschied"

Wo irr' ich um des Meeresstrand
Johann Rudolf Zumsteeg, "Verlangen und Sehnsucht" 1803pub
from *Kleine Balladen und Lieder, fünftes Heft*

Joseph Müller (1802-1872)
Dort am grünen Hügel glänzen schmucke Blümchen
Franz Liszt, "Die Schlüsselblumen" 1860pub
from *Muttergottes-Sträußlein zum Maimonate* (2)

Spende, Veilchen, deine Düfte
Franz Liszt, "Das Veilchen" 1860pub
from *Muttergottes-Sträußlein zum Maimonate* (1)

Wilhelm Müller (1794-1827)
Am Bach viel kleine Blumen steh'n, aus hellen blauen Augen sehn
Franz Schubert, "Des Müllers Blumen" 1823, D795,9
from *Die schöne Müllerin*
Fanny Hensel, "Des Müllers Blumen" 1823

Am Brunnen vor dem Thore, da steht ein Lindenbaum
Friedrich Silcher, "Der Lindenbaum"
Franz Schubert, "Der Lindenbaum" 1827, D911,5
from *Winterreise*
Reiner Bredemeyer, "Der Lindenbaum" 1984, bar.horn.pf
from *Die Winterreise*

Auf einen Todtenacker hat mich mein Weg gebracht
Franz Schubert, "Das Wirtshaus" 1827, D911,21
from *Winterreise*
Reiner Bredemeyer, "Das Wirtshaus" 1984, bar.horn.pf
from *Die Winterreise*

Aus des Meeres tiefem, tiefem Grunde
Johannes Brahms, "Vineta" 1860, Op42,2, saatbb

Bächlein, lass dein Rauschen sein, Räder, stellt eu'r Brausen ein
Franz Schubert, "Mein!" 1823, D795,11
from *Die schöne Müllerin*
Friedrich Curschmann, "Mein" 183-?, Op3,4

Das Wandern ist des Müllers Lust, das Wandern
Franz Schubert, "Das Wandern" 1823, D795,1
from *Die schöne Müllerin*

Der du so lustig rauschtest, du heller, wilder Fluß
Franz Schubert, "Auf dem Flusse" 1827, D911,7
from *Winterreise*
Reiner Bredemeyer, "Auf dem Flusse" 1984, bar.horn.pf
from *Die Winterreise*

Der Mai ist auf dem Wege
Fanny Hensel, "Einsamkeit" 1823

Der Reif hat einen weißen Schein mir über's Haupt gestreuet
Franz Schubert, "Der greise Kopf" 1827, D911,14
from *Winterreise*
Reiner Bredemeyer, "Der greise Kopf" 1984, bar.horn.pf
from *Die Winterreise*

Der Wind spielt mit der Wetterfahne
Franz Schubert, "Die Wetterfahne" 1827, D911,2
from *Winterreise*

Reiner Bredemeyer, "Die Wetterfahne" 1984, bar.horn.pf
from *Die Winterreise*

Drei Sonnen sah ich am Himmel steh'n
Franz Schubert, "Die Nebensonnen" 1827, D911,23
from *Winterreise*
Reiner Bredemeyer, "Die Nebensonnen" 1984, bar.horn.pf
from *Die Winterreise*

D'rüben hinter'm Dorfe steht ein Leiermann
Franz Schubert, "Der Leiermann" 1827, D911,24
from *Winterreise*
Wilhelm Kienzl, "Der Leiermann" 1904pub
Reiner Bredemeyer, "Der Leiermann" 1984, bar.horn.pf
from *Die Winterreise*

Ein Licht tanzt freundlich vor mir her
Franz Schubert, "Täuschung" 1827, D911,19
from *Winterreise*
Reiner Bredemeyer, "Täuschung" 1984, bar.horn.pf
from *Die Winterreise*

Eine blaue Schürze hast du mir gegeben
Johannes Brahms, "Die Braut (Von der Insel Rügen)" 1859-60?, Op44,11, ssaa.(pf)

Eine Krähe war mit mir aus der Stadt gezogen
Franz Schubert, "Die Krähe" 1827, D911,15
from *Winterreise*
Reiner Bredemeyer, "Die Krähe" 1984, bar.horn.pf
from *Die Winterreise*

Eine Mühle seh' ich blinken aus den Erlen heraus
Franz Schubert, "Halt!" 1823, D795,3
from *Die schöne Müllerin*

Es bellen die Hunde, es rasseln die Ketten
Franz Schubert, "Im Dorfe" 1827, D911,17
from *Winterreise*
Reiner Bredemeyer, "Im Dorfe" 1984, bar.horn.pf
from *Die Winterreise*

Es brennt mir unter beiden Sohlen
Franz Schubert, "Rückblick" 1827, D911,8
from *Winterreise*
Reiner Bredemeyer, "Rückblick" 1984, bar.horn.pf
from *Die Winterreise*

Fliegt der Schnee mir in's Gesicht
Franz Schubert, "Muth" 1827, D911,22
from *Winterreise*
Reiner Bredemeyer, "Mut" 1984, bar.horn.pf
from *Die Winterreise*

Fremd bin ich eingezogen, fremd zieh' ich wieder aus
Franz Schubert, "Gute Nacht" 1827, D911,1
from *Winterreise*

Reiner Bredemeyer, "Gute Nacht" 1984, bar.horn.pf
from *Die Winterreise*

Gefror'ne Tropfen fallen von meinen Wangen ab
Franz Schubert, "Gefror'ne Thränen" 1827, D911,3
from *Winterreise*
Reiner Bredemeyer, "Gefrorne Tränen" 1984, bar.horn.pf
from *Die Winterreise*

Gute Ruh', gute Ruh', thu' die Augen zu
Franz Schubert, "Des Baches Wiegenlied" 1823, D795,20
from *Die schöne Müllerin*

Guten Abend, lieber Mondenschein!
Fanny Hensel, "Abendreihn" 1823

Guten Morgen, schöne Müllerin
Franz Schubert, "Morgengruss" 1823, D795,8
from *Die schöne Müllerin*

Hätt' ich tausend Arme zu rühren
Franz Schubert, "Am Feierabend" 1823, D795,5
from *Die schöne Müllerin*

Hier und da ist an den Bäumen manches bunte Blatt zu seh'n
Franz Schubert, "Letzte Hoffnung" 1827, D911,16
from *Winterreise*
Reiner Bredemeyer, "Letzte Hoffnung" 1984, bar.horn.pf
from *Die Winterreise*

Ich frage keine Blume, ich frage keinen Stern
Franz Schubert, "Der Neugierige" 1823, D795,6
from *Die schöne Müllerin*
Fanny Hensel, "Die Neugierige" 1823

Ich hört' ein Bächlein rauschen wohl aus dem Felsenquell
Franz Schubert, "Wohin?" 1823, D795,2
from *Die schöne Müllerin*

Ich möchte zieh'n in die Welt hinaus
Franz Schubert, "Die böse Farbe" 1823, D795,17
from *Die schöne Müllerin*

Ich schnitt' es gern in alle Rinden ein
Franz Schubert, "Ungeduld" 1823, D795,7
from *Die schöne Müllerin*
Friedrich Curschmann, "Ungeduld" 183-?, Op3,6
Louis Spohr, "Ungeduld" 1835-36, Op94,4

Ich such' im Schnee vergebens nach ihrer Tritte Spur
Franz Schubert, "Erstarrung" 1827, D911,4
from *Winterreise*
Reiner Bredemeyer, "Erstarrung" 1984, bar.horn.pf
from *Die Winterreise*

Ich träumte von bunten Blumen, so wie sie wohl blühen im Mai
Franz Schubert, "Frühlingstraum" 1827, D911,11
from *Winterreise*

Reiner Bredemeyer, "Frühlingstraum" 1984, bar.horn.pf
from *Die Winterreise*

Ihr Blümlein alle, die sie mir gab
Franz Schubert, "Trockne Blumen" 1823, D795,18
from *Die schöne Müllerin*

In die tiefsten Felsengründe lockte mich ein Irrlicht hin
Franz Schubert, "Irrlicht" 1827, D911,9
from *Winterreise*
Reiner Bredemeyer, "Irrlicht" 1984, bar.horn.pf
from *Die Winterreise*

In Grün will ich mich kleiden, in grüne Thränenweiden
Franz Schubert, "Die liebe Farbe" 1823, D795,16
from *Die schöne Müllerin*
Fanny Hensel, "Die liebe Farbe" 1823

In meines Herzens Mitte
Giacomo Meyerbeer, "Der Garten des Herzens" 1839

Je höher die Glocke, je heller der Klang
Carl Loewe, "Liebesgedanken" 1823, Op9,vi,2

Manche Thrän' aus meinen Augen ist gefallen in den Schnee
Franz Schubert, "Wasserfluth" 1827, D911,6
from *Winterreise*
Reiner Bredemeyer, "Wasserflut" 1984, bar.horn.pf
from *Die Winterreise*

Meine Laute hab' ich gehängt an die Wand
Franz Schubert, "Pause" 1823, D795,12
from *Die schöne Müllerin*

Nun merk' ich erst, wie müd' ich bin
Franz Schubert, "Rast" 1827, D911,10
from *Winterreise*
Reiner Bredemeyer, "Rast" 1984, bar.horn.pf
from *Die Winterreise*

O Liebe, die am Kreuze rang, O Liebe, die den Tod bezwang
Fanny Hensel, "Gebet in der Christnacht" 1823

Schad' um das schöne grüne Band
Franz Schubert, "Mit dem grünen Lautenbande" 1823, D795,13
from *Die schöne Müllerin*

Sie stand im Boot und fischte, ich sah's vom Ufer her
Fanny Hensel, "Die glückliche Fischerin" 1823

Von der Straße her ein Posthorn klingt
Franz Schubert, "Die Post" 1827, D911,13
from *Winterreise*
Reiner Bredemeyer, "Die Post" 1984, bar.horn.pf
from *Die Winterreise*

War es also gemeint, mein rauschender Freund
Franz Schubert, "Danksagung an den Bach" 1823, D795,4
from *Die schöne Müllerin*

Friedrich Curschmann, "Danksagung an den Bach" 1833, Op5,1

Was sucht denn der Jäger am Mühlbach hier?
Franz Schubert, "Der Jäger" 1823, D795,14
from *Die schöne Müllerin*

Was vermeid' ich denn die Wege, wo die andern Wandrer gehn
Franz Schubert, "Der Wegweiser" 1827, D911,20
from *Winterreise*
Reiner Bredemeyer, "Der Wegweiser" 1984, bar.horn.pf
from *Die Winterreise*

Wenn auf dem höchsten Fels ich steh'
Franz Schubert, "Der Hirt auf dem Felsen" 1828, D965
middle verses ("In tiefem Gram…") probably by Helmina von Chézy

Wie eine trübe Wolke durch heit're Lüfte geht
Franz Schubert, "Einsamkeit" 1827, D911,12
from *Winterreise*
Reiner Bredemeyer, "Einsamkeit" 1984, bar.horn.pf
from *Die Winterreise*

Wie hat der Sturm zerrissen des Himmels graues Kleid!
Franz Schubert, "Der stürmische Morgen" 1827, D911,18
from *Winterreise*
Reiner Bredemeyer, "Der stürmische Morgen" 1984, bar.horn.pf
from *Die Winterreise*

Wir sassen so traulich beisammen
Franz Schubert, "Thränenregen" 1823, D795,10
from *Die schöne Müllerin*

Wirf Rosenblätter in die Flut
Giacomo Meyerbeer, "Die Rosenblätter" 1838

Wo ein treues Herze in Liebe vergeht
Franz Schubert, "Der Müller und der Bach" 1823, D795,19
from *Die schöne Müllerin*

Wohin so schnell, so kraus und wild, mein lieber Bach?
Franz Schubert, "Eifersucht und Stolz" 1823, D795,15
from *Die schöne Müllerin*

Friedrich Konrad Müller von der Werre (1823-1881)
Im Palmenhain weht Frieden, wo Memphis sank und fiel
Franz von Holstein, "Salem, Marie" 1871, Op27,1

Müller von Gerstenbergk: see Gerstenbergk

(Karl) Wolfgang Müller von Königswinter (1816-1873)
Die Heide ist braun, einst blühte sie rot
Robert Franz, "Im Herbst" 1860?pub, Op17,6

Die kolossale Flut dehnt sich hinaus
August Bungert, "Die kolossale Flut dehnt sich hinaus" 1889-91pub, Op12,3

Es streckt der Wald die Zweige so grün
Robert Franz, "Im Walde" 1860?, Op12,3

Hast du den Fischerkindern das alte Märchen vernommen
Hans Pfitzner, "Hast du den Fischerkindern das alte Märchen vernommen" 1888-1900, Op7,1

Ich zieh' so allein in den Wald hinein!
Robert Schumann, "Im Wald" 1851-52, Op107,5

O danke nicht für diese Lieder, mir ziemt es dankbar dir zu sein
Robert Franz, "Widmung" 1860?, Op14,1
Charles Edward Ives, "Widmung" 1897?

Karl Müller-Rastatt (1861-1931)
Rote Flammen so glüht der Mohn
Hugo Kaun, "Roter Mohn" 1898?pub, Op25,4

Eligius Franz Joseph Freiherr von Münch-Bellinghausen: see "Friedrich Halm"

Börries, Freiherr von Münchhausen (1874-1945)
Ich bin durch's Leben auf dich zugegangen
Erich Riede, "Lebensweg" Op7,5, sop.pf

Karl Ludwig August Heino Freiherr von Münchhausen (1759-1836)
Es wächst ein Blümchen irgendwo
Johann Rudolf Zumsteeg, "Blümchen Tausendschön" 1801pub
from *Kleine Balladen und Lieder, drittes Heft*

Je länger du dort bist, um so mehr bist du hier
Emil Mattiesen, "Über ein Grab hin" 190-?pub, Op15,4
from *Überwindungen* (4)

Balthasar Münter (1735-1793)
Er ist erstanden, Jesus Christ, der unser Gott und Heiland ist!
Carl Loewe, "Unsere Auferstehung durch Christum" 1820, vv.orch

Alfred de Musset (1810-1857)
Daferns geschah, das wir begraben
Joseph Marx, "Lied" 1905, ten.pf

Ich verlor die Kraft und das Leben
Franz Liszt, "Ich verlor die Kraft und das Leben" 1872
translated from the French by Alfred Meissner

Franz Alfred Muth (1839-1890)
Wenn alle Blumen träumen, träumt auch mein liebes Kind
Max Reger, "Engelwacht" 1902, Op68,4, 1v(med).pf

A.v.N
Was steht ihr am Wege so müssig
Johann Rudolf Zumsteeg, "Zuruf an Jünglinge" 1803pub
from *Kleine Balladen und Lieder, fünftes Heft*

Bernhard Christoph Ludwig Natorp (1774-1846)
In meinen Armen wieg' ich dich
Robert Franz, "In meinen Armen wieg' ich dich" 1846pub, Op7,4

L. G. Naumann
Sei willkommen, Frühlingswehen
Carl Loewe, "Frühlingslust" 1844?

Rudolf Nawrocki (1858-?)
O frage nicht in bitt'rem Harm
Max Reger, "O frage nicht!" 1894, Op14,5, sop.alt.pf

Neidhart von Reuenthal (1180/90-1237/46)
Wohlauf! Wohlauf! der kühle Winter ist vergangen
Ferruccio Busoni, "Wohlauf! Wohlauf!" 1885, Op18,1

"Wilfried von der Neun" (Friedrich Wilhelm Traugott Schöpff) (1826-1916)
Durch die Tannen und die Linden spinnt
Robert Schumann, "Herbst-Lied" 1850, Op89,3

Es stürmet am Abendhimmel
Robert Schumann, "Es stürmet am Abendhimmel" 1850, Op89,1

Hört ihr im Laube des Regens starke Schläge?
Robert Schumann, "Gesungen" 1850, Op96,4

Mir ist's so eng allüberall!
Robert Schumann, "In's Freie" 1850, Op89,5

Nachts zu unbekannter Stunde flieht
Robert Schumann, "Heimliches Verschwinden" 1850, Op89,2

Nun scheidet vom sterbenden Walde
Robert Schumann, "Abschied vom Walde" 1850, Op89,4

Röselein, Röselein! müssen denn Dornen sein?
Robert Schumann, "Röselein, Röselein" 1850, Op89,6

Wie der Bäume kühne Wipfel
Robert Schumann, "Himmel und Erde" 1850, Op96,5

Jakob Neus (1767-1846)
Wir beten an, hier unter Brot- und Weingestalten
Carl Loewe, "Abendmahlslied" 1837, 3v(ch).organ

Gustav Alexander Wilhelm Nicolai (1795-after 1843)
Der Heiland ist für uns gestorben
Carl Loewe, "Der Heiland ist für uns gestorben" 1829, Op30,(15), 4v

Ihr Söhne Abrahams, seid einig!
Carl Loewe, "Gesänge des Hohenpriesters bei Jerusalem's Zerstörung" 1829, Op30,9&27

's is nichts mit den alten Weibern
Carl Maria von Weber, "Alte Weiber" 1817, Op54,5

August Hermann Niemeyer (1754-1828)
Warum dein Blick so trübe, warum dein Herz so schwer
Carl Loewe, "Werfet alle eure Sorgen auf ihn!" 1830, Op22,ii,1, 4v

Wenn immer trüber deine Morgen tagen
Carl Loewe, "Der nahe Retter" 1830, Op22,ii,3, 4v

Friedrich Wilhelm Nietzsche (1844-1900)
An der Brükke stand jüngst ich in brauner Nacht
Gustav Grube, "Venedig" 1912pub, 1v.vn.pf
Felix Wolfes, "Venedig" 1961

Das war ein Tag der Schmerzen, als ich einst Abschied nahm
Nikolai Medtner, "Heimkehr" 1910pub, Op19a,1

Der Tag klingt ab, es gilbt sich Glück
Ernest Vietor, "Der Tag klingt ab" 1935-36, Op13,2

Des Morgens still ich träume und schau den Wolken nach
Friedrich Nietzsche, "Junge Fischerin" 1865, NWV29

Die Krähen schrein und ziehen schwirren Flugs zur Stadt
Ernest Vietor, "Vereinsamt" 1935-36, Op13,5

Dorthin will ich; und ich traue mir fortan und meinem Griff
Frederick Delius, "Nach neuen Meeren" 1898, 1v(med).pf
from *Lieder nach Gedichten von Friedrich Nietzsche*

Es geht ein Wandrer durch die Nacht mit gutem Schritt
Arnold Schönberg, "Der Wanderer" 1903-05, Op6,8

Hier sass ich, wartend, wartend, doch auf nichts
Ernest Vietor, "Sils-Maria" Op5,1

In Sonnenglut, in Mittagsruh liegt stumm das Hospital
Nikolai Medtner, "Alt Mütterlein" 1910?pub, Op19,2

Kein Pfad mehr! Abgrund rings und Totenstille!
Frederick Delius, "Der Wandrer" 1898, 1v(med).pf
from *Lieder nach Gedichten von Friedrich Nietzsche*

Mein Herz ist wie ein See so weit
Anton Webern, "Heiter" 1901-04
from *Acht frühe Lieder* (6)
Carl Orff, "Mein Herz ist wie ein See so weit" 1919

Nicht mehr zurück? und nicht hinan?
Frederick Delius, "Der Wandrer und sein Schatten" 1898, 1v(med).pf
from *Lieder nach Gedichten von Friedrich Nietzsche*

Nun da der Tag des Tages müde ward
Ernest Vietor, "Der Einsamste" 1935-36, Op13,4
Paul Hindemith, "Nun da der Tag des Tages müde ward" 1939, 4mv
from *Drei Chöre* (2)
Ernst Pepping, "Der Einsamste" 1949pub
from *Haus- und Trostbuch* (15)

O! A! Kirchengeschichte hör ich nicht bei Overbeck
Friedrich Nietzsche, "Kirchengeschichtliches Responsorium" 1871, NWV37, mch(unis).pf

O Mensch! Gib acht! Was spricht die tiefe Mitternacht?
Ernest Vietor, "Um Mitternacht" 1935-36, Op13,3
Felix Wolfes, "Das trunkne Lied" 1961, 1v(med).pf

Tag meines Lebens! die Sonne sinkt
Conrad Ansorge, "Die Sonne sinkt" 1895-96pub, Op10,5
Ernest Vietor, "Die Sonne sinkt" 1935-36, Op13,1

Verhaßt ist mir das Folgen und das Führen
Frederick Delius, "Der Einsame" 1898, 1v(med).pf
from *Lieder nach Gedichten von Friedrich Nietzsche*

Von Ferne tönt der Glokkenschlag, die Nacht, sie rauscht so dumpf daher
Nikolai Medtner, "Verzweiflung" 1910pub, Op19a,2

Johann Niklos
Durchs Schlüsselloch einkehrt am häuslichen Herd
Gottfried von Einem, "Am Abend" 1983, Op73,7
from *Tag- und Nachtlieder*

Nikolai
Zum Sterben bin i verliebet in di (see also Wunderhorn)
Erich J. Wolff, "Wer hat's Lieben erdacht?" 1914pub, Lieder No.60

Richard Noehring
Ich sehe Winterblaß ein Land durch Wintertrübe Scheiben
Louis Ferdinand, "Stille" 1966pub

"Henriette Nordheim:" see Henriette Wilhelmine Auguste von Schorn

Johannes Nordmann (Johann Rumpelmeyer) (1820-1887)
Kling leise, mein Lied, durch die schweigende Nacht
Franz Liszt, "Kling leise, mein Lied (Ständchen)" 1848
Franz Liszt, "Kling leise, mein Lied" 1860pub

Klothilde Septimie Nostitz und Jänkendorf (1801-1852)
Wenn Kindlein süssen Schlummers Ruh'
Carl Maria von Weber, "Lied von Clotilde" 1821, Op80,1

"Novalis" (Friedrich Leopold Freiherr von Hardenberg) (1772-1801)
Bricht das matte Herz noch immer
Louise Reichardt, "Sehnsucht nach dem Vaterlande" 1819pub

Der Sänger geht auf rauhen Pfaden
Louise Reichardt, "Der Sänger geht" 1811pub

Es färbte sich die Wiese grün
Louise Reichardt, "Frühlingslied" 1819pub

Hinüber wall' ich, und jede Pein
Louise Reichardt, "Aus *Hymnen an die Nacht*" 1811pub
Franz Schubert, "Nachthymne" 1820, D687
Alma Schindler-Mahler, "Hymne an die Nacht" 1924pub

Ich kenne wo ein festes Schloß
Louise Reichardt, "Bergmannslied" 1819pub

Ich sag' es jedem, dass er lebt und auferstanden ist
Franz Schubert, "Hymne IV" 1819, D662

Ich sehe dich in tausend Bildern, Maria, lieblich ausgedrückt
Franz Schubert, "Marie" 1819?, D658
Louise Reichardt, "An Maria" 1819pub
Max Reger, "Ich sehe dich in tausend Bildern" 1907, Op105,1, 1v(med).org(pf)
from *Zwei geistliche Lieder* (1)
Othmar Schoeck, "Marienlied" 1907, Op6,5
Joseph Marx, "Marienlied" 1909
Erich Riede, "Marienlied" Op7,8, sop.pf

Lobt doch unsre stillen Feste
Louise Reichardt, "Er besucht den Klostergarten" 1819pub

Wenige wissen das Geheimnis der Liebe
Franz Schubert, "Hymne I" 1819, D659
Alma Schindler-Mahler, "Hymne" 1924pub

Wenn alle untreu werden, so bleib ich dir doch treu
Franz Schubert, "Hymne III" 1819, D661
Carl Loewe, "Wenn alle untreu werden" 1822, Op22,i,2, 4v
Carl Loewe, "Wenn alle untreu werden (later version)" 1855, 4v

Wenn ich ihn nur habe, lass' ich alles gern
Franz Schubert, "Hymne II" 1819, D660
Louise Reichardt, "Geistliches Lied" 1819pub, 1v.pf or 4v
Carl Loewe, "Wenn ich ihn nur habe" 1821, Op22,i,1, 4v
Leopold Damrosch, "Wenn ich ihn nur habe" Op7,2
Reinhard Schwarz-Schilling, "Wenn ich ihn nur habe" 1949
from *Drei Geistliche Lieder*

Wenn in bangen, trüben Stunden unser Herz beinah verzagt
Max Reger, "Wenn in bangen, trüben Stunden" 1900, 1v(med).organ
from *Zwei geistliche Lieder* (1)

Willibald Obst
In meinem Herzen ist's öd' und leer
Max Reger, "Hoffnungslos" 1901
from *Liebeslieder* (6)

G. H. von Oder
Und weil Du bist ein Röslein
George Henschel, "Und weil Du bist ein Röslein" 186-?, Op3,2

Anton Odyniec & Adam Mickiewicz
Mägdlein pflücket Beeren in des Waldes Mitten
Carl Loewe, "Der junge Herr und das Mädchen" 1835, Op50,2
translated by Carl von Blankensee

Johannes Öhquist ("Wilhelm Habermann") (1861-1949)
Hoch über mir endlos
Felix Weingartner, "Im Moose" 1913, Op55,3

Hermann Oelschläger (1839-?)
Wie bist du nur, mein Herzensschatz
Anton Rubinstein, "Mein Herzensschatz"

Max(imilian), Freiherr von Oer (1806-1846)
Zu Lüttich, im letzten Häuselein
Carl Loewe, "Die Glocken zu Speier" 1837, Op67,2

Friedrich Oldenberg (1820-1895)
Adieu, Mama, Adieu, Mama, wir fahren auf dem Eise
Carl Reinecke, "Schlittenfahrt in der Stube"
from *Kinderlieder*

Johannes Olearius (1611-1684)
Wunderbarer Gnadenthron
Carl Loewe, "Wunderbarer Gnadenthron" 1847

Johannes Olorinus
Was haben doch die Gänse getan
Paul Hindemith, "Was haben doch die Gänse getan" 1925, Op45,v, 1v.insts
from *Sing-und Spielmusiken für Liebhaber und Musikfreunde*

Martin Opitz (1597-1639)
Ach Liebste laß uns eilen wir haben Zeit
Franz Krause, "Eile zum Lieben" 1972?pub, Op51,ii,6
from *Gedichte aus alter Zeit 2*

Auf, auf, wer deutsche Freiheit liebet
Johann Rudolf Zumsteeg, "Kriegslied" 1801pub
from *Kleine Balladen und Lieder, drittes Heft*

Ich empfinde fast ein Grauen
Carl Maria von Weber, "Gelahrtheit" 1818, Op64,4

Jezzund kömmt die Nacht herbei
Johann Rudolf Zumsteeg, "Nachtgesang" 1801pub
from *Kleine Balladen und Lieder, drittes Heft*

Ernst Ortlepp (1800-1864)
Das Mädchen steht im Grabe
Ferdinand Ries, "Todtenstill" 1835pub, WoO56

Friedrich Heinrich Oser (1820-1891)
O du mein Alles, mein Alles auf der Welt
Franz Abt, "O du mein Alles, mein Alles auf der Welt" 1873pub, Op282,1

O sag' es noch einmal, noch tausend-, tausendmal
Franz Abt, "O sag' es noch einmal" 1873pub, Op249,1

Sachte will's dämmern, mit seinen Lämmern
Franz Abt, "Wiegenlied" 1873pub, Op282,4

Heinrich August Ossenfelder (1725-1801)
Hört an, ihr Mütter alt und jung!
Josef Antonín Štěpán, "Philander und Pedrille" 1778-79pub

"Ossian:" see James Macpherson

(Karl) Wilhelm Osterwald (1820-1887)
Ach dass du kamst, ach dass du kamst in Freuden einst gegangen
Robert Franz, "Ach dass du kamst" 1845pub, Op4,12

Ach! musstest du denn scheiden
Robert Franz, "Kurzes Wiedersehen" 1845pub, Op4,8

Ach, wenn ich doch ein Immchen wär'
Robert Franz, "Ach, wenn ich doch ein Immchen wär'" 1844pub, Op3,6

Ade denn, du stolze blitzaugige Magd
Robert Franz, "Ade denn, du stolze!" 1870?pub, Op31,2

Als die Linden trieben, weckte süsse Hoffnung
Robert Franz, "Bei der Linde" 1862?, Op36,4

Aus bangen Träumen der Winternacht
Robert Franz, "Zu spät" 1866?, Op37,2

Aus der Ferne schallen Gesänge
Robert Franz, "Frühe Klage" 1870?pub, Op22,4

Da der Sommer kommen ist, Blüten auszustreuen
Robert Franz, "Im Sommer" 1865?, Op11,4

Da die Stunde kam, dass ich Abschied nahm
Robert Franz, "Da die Stunde kam" 1846pub, Op7,3

Den Strauss, den sie gewunden zur schönsten aller Stunden
Robert Franz, "Vergiss mein nicht!" 1870?pub, Op26,3

Der junge Tag erwacht, der schöne Morgen lacht
Robert Franz, "Der junge Tag erwacht" 1846pub, Op7,1

Der Mond ist schlafen gangen
Robert Franz, "Ständchen" 1860?pub, Op17,2

Der Schnee ist zergangen
Robert Franz, "Der Schnee ist zergangen" 1846pub, Op6,5

Der Sommer ist zu Ende, ach Liebchen gehst auch du
Robert Franz, "Sonnenwende" 1866?, Op37,5

Der Tag beginnt zu dunkeln
Robert Franz, "Abends" 1865?pub, Op20,4

Des Waldes Sänger singen, die rothe Rose blüht
Robert Franz, "Umsonst" 1860pub, Op10,6

Des Waldes Wipfel rauschen unheimlich hin und her
Robert Franz, "Die Liebe hat gelogen!" 1846pub, Op6,4

Die braune Heide starrt mich an
Max Reger, "Die braune Heide starrt mich an" 1888?

Die Lüfte werden heller
Robert Franz, "Aufbruch" 1862?, Op35,6

Die Nachtigall hat mich vom Schlaf erweckt
Léander Schlegel, "Die Nachtigall hat mich vom Schlaf erweckt" 1900, Op20,11
from *Deutsche Liebeslieder*

Die Schwalbe zieht, der Sommer flieht
Robert Franz, "Verlass' mich nicht!" 1865?pub, Op21,6

Die Sterne flimmern und prangen
Robert Franz, "Erinnerung" 1879, Op51,10

Dornröschen schlägt zum erstenmal die Augen auf nach langer Ruh
Robert Franz, "Dornröschen" 1879, Op51,3

Dort unter'm Lindenbaume in linder Somernacht
Robert Franz, "Dort unter'm Lindenbaume" 1870?pub, Op31,1

Du grüne Rast im Haine
Robert Franz, "Du grüne Rast im Haine" 1867?, Op41,6

Du wunderholde Maid, ich bin meinem Leben so herzlich dir ergeben
Friedrich Kücken, "Du wunderholde Maid!"

Durch säuselnde Bäume im Mondenschein
Robert Franz, "Durch säuselnde Bäume" 1845pub, Op4,9

Gestern hielt er mich im Arme
Robert Franz, "Erster Verlust" 1862?, Op36,2

Gleich eines Herzens bangen Fieberträumen
Robert Franz, "Herbstsorge" 1845pub, Op4,10

Gleich wie der Mond so keusch und rein
Robert Franz, "Gleich wie der Mond so keusch und rein" 1870?, Op43,2

Grolle lauter, zürnend Gewitter
Robert Franz, "Gewitternacht" 1846pub, Op8,6

Hör' ich ein Vöglein singen
Robert Franz, "Die Harrende" 1862?, Op35,1

Ich lobe mir die Vögelein
Robert Franz, "Ich lobe mir die Vögelein" 1846pub, Op5,8

Im Grase lieg' ich manche Stunde
Robert Franz, "Im Frühling" 1860?pub, Op17,5

In dem Dornbusch blüht ein Röslein
Robert Franz, "Lieber Schatz, sei wieder gut mir" 1870?pub, Op26,2

Jetzt steh' ich auf der höchsten Höh'
Robert Franz, "Vom Berge" 1860?, Op9,5

Liebchen, was willst du? komm ich oft, so schiltst du
Robert Franz, "Aprillaunen" 1870?, Op44,2

Lieblich blühn die Bäume voller Schmelz und Duft
Robert Franz, "Träume" 1870?, Op43,1

Lieblich wallen durch die Lüfte
Léander Schlegel, "Lieblich wallen durch die Lüfte" Op21,?

Mein Schatz ist auf der Wanderschaft so lange
Robert Franz, "Mein Schatz ist auf der Wanderschaft" 1867?, Op40,1

Musst nicht allein im Freien, selbander musst du gehn
Robert Franz, "Im Mai" 1870?pub, Op22,5

Nun da die Bäum' in Blüthen stehn
Robert Franz, "In Blüthen" 1870?, Op43,6

Nun grünt der Berg, nun blüht das Thal
Robert Franz, "Im Mai" 1865?, Op11,3
Ludwig Thuille, "Im Mai" 189-?pub, Op4,3

Nun hat das Leid ein Ende
Robert Franz, "Nun hat das Leid ein Ende" 1860?pub, Op18,3

Nun hat mein Stecken gute Rast
Robert Franz, "Nun hat mein Stecken gute Rast" 1862?, Op36,6

O banger Traum, was flatterst du
Robert Franz, "Erinnerung (Vergessen)" 1846pub, Op5,10

Scheust dich noch immer, seliges Leben
Robert Franz, "Entschluss" 1870?, Op43,3

Schöner Mai, bist über Nacht
Robert Franz, "Schöner Mai, bist über Nacht" 1870?pub, Op30,4

Treibt der Sommer seinen Rosen
Robert Franz, "Treibt der Sommer seinen Rosen" 1846pub, Op8,5

Um Mitternacht ruht die ganze Erde nun
Robert Franz, "Um Mitternacht" 1856pub, Op16,6

Und die Rosen, die prangen
Robert Franz, "Und die Rosen, die prangen" 1860pub, Op10,5

Und kommt der Frühling wieder her
Robert Franz, "Wanderlied" 1845pub, Op4,11

Und welche Rose Blüthen treibt
Robert Franz, "Und welche Rose Blüthen treibt" 1860?, Op12,1

Vor meinem Fenster regt die alte Linde
Robert Franz, "Wenn ich's nur wüsste" 1870?pub, Op26,1

Will über Nacht wohl durch das Thal
Robert Franz, "Will über Nacht wohl durch das Thal" 1846pub, Op5,4

A. Ott

Ich bin erwacht, ich bin erwacht aus einem Traum von der Frühlingsnacht
Paul Hindemith, "Frühlingstraum" 1908/09
from *7 Lieder für Sopran oder Tenor mit Klavierbegleitung*

Anton Ottenwalt (1789-1845)

Er schläft so süss, der Mutter Blicke hangen
Franz Schubert, "Der Knabe in der Wiege" 1817, D579

R. Otto

Worte hab' ich nicht, um dir zu sagen
Louis Spohr, "Töne" 1856, Op154,3, bar.vn.pf

Christian Adolf Overbeck (1775-1821)

Blühe, liebes Veilchen, das ich selbst erzog
Johann Abraham Peter Schulz, "Der Knabe an ein Veilchen" 1782-90pub

Komm, lieber Mai, und mache die Bäume wieder grün
Wolfgang Amadeus Mozart, "Sehnsucht nach dem Frühlinge" 1791, K596
Robert Schumann, "Mailied" 1849, Op79,9, 2v.pf
from *Lieder-Album für die Jugend*

Preis ihm, der alle Dinge mit unerforschter Kraft erhält!
Johann Rudolf Zumsteeg, "Hochgesang" 1803pub
from *Kleine Balladen und Lieder, fünftes Heft*

Warum bin ich noch so klein?
Johann Rudolf Zumsteeg, "Die kleine Hirtin" 1803pub
from *Kleine Balladen und Lieder, sechstes Heft*

Warum sind der Tränen unterm Mond so viel?
Johann Abraham Peter Schulz, "Beherzigung" 1782-90pub

Wir Kinder, wir schmecken
Wolfgang Amadeus Mozart, "Das Kinderspiel" 1791, K598

B. P.
Der Heidebusch voll Knospen stand
Paul Graener, "Der Heidebusch" 1909pub, Op21,2

Paalzow
Verstummt ist die Harfe, die Saiten entzwei
Friedrich Kücken, "Das Mädchen von Juda"

Oskar (Oscar) Panizza (1853-1921)
Es wohnt ein kleines Vögelein auf grünem Baum, im grünen Licht
Richard Strauss, "Sie wissen's nicht" 1901, Op49,5

"Betty Paoli" (Barbara Elisabeth Glück) (1814-1894)
Im tiefsten Innern ein süss' Erinnern
Robert Franz, "Gute Nacht!" 1862?, Op36,5

Samuel Christian Pape (1774-1817)
Das Fischermädchen harret am Ufer auf und ab
Johann Rudolf Zumsteeg, "Das Fischermädchen" 1802pub
from *Kleine Balladen und Lieder, viertes Heft*

Wohl an dem Rasenhügel hin
Johann Rudolf Zumsteeg, "Lieb Mary" 1802pub
from *Kleine Balladen und Lieder, viertes Heft*

Alfons Hermann Paquet (1881-1944)
Ein Wand'rer in der Gassen, der acht' mein Fenster gar so wohl
Karol Szymanowski, "Lied des Mädchens am Fenster" 1910, Op22,2

"Jean Paul:" see "Jean..."

Bishop Thomas Percy (1729-1811
Ein Bettelmann, schon lange blind
Carl Loewe, "Des Bettlers Tochter von Bednall Green" 1834
translated by Grossherzog Carl von Mecklenburg

Sándor Petőfi (1823-1849)
Blätter läßt die Blume fallen
Robert Franz, "Blätter läßt die Blume fallen" 1870?pub, Op30,2

Du nur bist, du liebes Mädchen, Licht des Auges, Licht der Seele
Friedrich Nietzsche, "Unendlich!" 1864, NWV23

Du warst ja meine einzge Blume
Friedrich Nietzsche, "Verwelkt!" 1864, NWV24

Es winkt und neigt sich seltsam am Fenster die Rebe roth
Friedrich Nietzsche, "Es winkt und neigt sich" 1864, NWV28
poem's attribution to Petőfi uncertain

Herab läßt sich der Wolke Saum
Friedrich Nietzsche, "Ständchen" 1864, NWV22

Hinweg, Kleinmütige, Hinweg, Kleinmütige
Franz Liszt, "Ungarns Gott" 1881, bar.mch(3t3b).pf
translated from the Hungarian by Ladislaus Neugebauer

Ich möchte lassen diese glanzumspielte Welt
Friedrich Nietzsche, "Nachspiel" 1864, NV21

Selige Nacht! Ich bin nun bei der Liebsten hier
Robert Franz, "Selige Nacht!" 1870?, Op42,3

Francesco Petrarca (1304-1374)

Allein, nachdenklich, wie gelähmt vom Krampfe
Franz Schubert, "Sonett II" 1818, D629
translated by A. W. von Schlegel

Apollo, lebet noch dein hold Verlangen
Franz Schubert, "Sonett I" 1818, D628
translated by A. W. von Schlegel

Fried' ist versagt mir, vergebens träum' ich Schlachten
Franz Liszt, "Sonett XC (104)" 1883
translated from the Italian by Peter Cornelius
from *Drei Sonette von Petrarca*

Nie ward ich, Herrin, müd, um Euch zu minnen
Arnold Schönberg, "Nie ward ich, Herrin, müd" 1903-05, Op8,4, 1v.orch
from *Six Orchestral Songs, Opus 8* (Piano acc. by Anton Webern)

Nunmehr, da Himmel, Erde schweigt und Winde
Franz Schubert, "Sonett III" 1818, D630
translated by Johann Diederich Gries

Sei gesegnet immerdar von allen Tagen
Franz Liszt, "Sonett XXXIX (47)" 1883
translated from the Italian by Peter Cornelius
from *Drei Sonette von Petrarca*

So sah ich denn auf Erden Engelsfrieden
Franz Liszt, "Sonett CV (123)" 1883
translated from the Italian by Peter Cornelius
from *Drei Sonette von Petrarca*

Voll jener Süße, die, nicht auszudrükken
Arnold Schönberg, "Voll jener Süße" 1903-05, Op8,5, 1v.orch
from *Six Orchestral Songs, Opus 8* (Piano acc. by Anton Webern)
Hans Pfitzner, "92. Sonett" 1909, Op24,3

Wenn Vöglein klagen, und in grünen Zweigen
Arnold Schönberg, "Wenn Vöglein klagen" 1903-05, Op8,6, 1v.orch
from *Six Orchestral Songs, Opus 8* (Piano acc. by Anton Webern)

Alfons Petzold (1882-1923)

Ein feuriges Männlein reit' über die Welt
Franz Schreker, "Das feurige Männlein" 1915, bar.pf

Gustav Pfarrius (1800-1884)

Birke, Birke, des Waldes Zier
Robert Schumann, "Der Bräutigam und die Birke" 1851, Op119,3

Es geht der Tag zur Neige, der Licht und Freiheit bot
Johann Vesque von Püttlingen, "Warnung" 185-?, Op56,5
Robert Schumann, "Warnung" 1851, Op119,2
Schumann's attribution reads "aus dem Waldliedern von S. Pfarrius"

Im Wald, in grüner Runde, wo Wipfel über Wipfel schaut
Robert Schumann, "Die Hütte" 1851, Op119,1

Sass ein Fink' in dunkler Hecke
Carl Reinecke, "Vom armen Finken im Baumeszweig"
from *Kinderlieder*

(Karl) Ludwig Pfau (1821-1894)

Da sitz' ich und weine und harre allein
Frederic Louis Ritter, "Da sitz' ich und weine" 1871pub, Op6,3

Der Pflanze, die dort über dem Abgrund schwebt
Arnold Schönberg, "Der Pflanze, die dort über dem Abgrund schwebt" 189-?

Du kehrst mir den Rücken
Arnold Schönberg, "Du kehrst mir den Rücken" 189-?

Du Kleine bist so lieb und hold und schaust mich an so lind
Arnold Schönberg, "Zweifler" 189-?

Einsam bin ich und alleine
Arnold Schönberg, "Einsam bin ich und alleine" 189-?

Einst hat vor deines Vaters Haus
Arnold Schönberg, "Einst hat vor deines Vaters Haus" 189-?

Gott grüß dich, Marie!
Arnold Schönberg, "Gott grüß dich, Marie" 189-?

Könnt' ich zu dir, mein Licht
Arnold Schönberg, "Könnt' ich zu dir, mein Licht" 189-?

Laß deine Sichel rauschen
Arnold Schönberg, "Lied der Schnitterin" 189-?

Mein Schatz ist wie ein Schneck
Arnold Schönberg, "Mein Schatz ist wie ein Schneck" 189-?

O Blätter, dürre Blätter! Wie trauert ihr so sehr!
Alexander Zemlinsky, "O Blätter, dürre Blätter!" 1897?, Op5,i,3
Max Renner, "O Blätter, dürre Blätter" 1899pub, Op3,3
Hugo Kaun, "O Blätter, dürre Blätter" 1908pub, Op80,4

O, du lieber Schatz, wir müssen scheiden
Heinrich Marschner, "Trennung" 185-?, Op184,4

O Sterne, goldene Sterne! Wohl scheint ihr so wunderlicht
Franz Abt, "Unermesslich" 1873pub, Op149,2
Alexander Zemlinsky, "O Sterne, goldene Sterne" 1897?, Op5,i,4

War ein Blümlein wunderfein, hieß Vergißmeinnicht
Arnold Schönberg, "Vergißmeinnicht" 189-?

Warum bist du aufgewacht erst im Sternenscheine
Arnold Schönberg, "Warum bist du aufgewacht" 189-?

Wenn ich im stillen Friedhof geh'
Hugo Wolf, "Im stillen Friedhof" 1876, satb.pf

Gottlieb Conrad Pfeffel (1736-1809)
Ein Vater starb von des Sohnes Hand
Franz Schubert, "Der Vatermörder" 1811, D10

Sieh Doris wie vom Mond bestrahlt
Maria Therese Paradis, "Die Tanne" 1784-86
from *Zwölf Lieder auf ihrer Reise in Musik gesetzt*

Wer, wer ist ein freier Mann?
Ludwig van Beethoven, "Der freie Mann" 1792-94, WoO117

Zween Mönche von des Indus Strand
Johann Rudolf Zumsteeg, "Die beiden Bonzen" 1805pub
from *Kleine Balladen und Lieder, siebtes Heft*

Pfeil
Ich bin so gern, so gern daheim, daheim in meiner stillen Klause
Franz Abt, "Mein Himmel auf der Erde" Op360,3

Paul Pfitzner
Es waren einst zwei Brüder, die liebten sich bis an den Tod
Felix Wolfes, "Die zwei Brüder" 1959

Wohl in der letzten Stunde, da öffnet sich die Wunde
Felix Wolfes, "In der letzten Stunde" 1959

Gustav Pfizer (1807-1890)
Ich bin ein leichter Junggesell und wandre durch die Welt
Carl Loewe, "Der Junggesell" 1842

Karoline Pichler (1769-1843)
Die Nacht bricht an, mit leisen Lüften sinket sie
Franz Schubert, "Der Unglückliche" 1821, D713

Dort, wo in reine Lüfte der Karmel sich erhebt
Carl Loewe, "Karmel-Legende" 1832, sop.orch

Ferne von der grossen Stadt, nimm mich auf in deine Stille
Franz Schubert, "Lied" 1816, D483

Klage, meine Flöte, klage
Franz Schubert, "Der Sänger am Felsen" 1816, D482

Karl August Graf von Platen-Hallermünde (1796-1835)
Am Felsenvorgebirge schroff
Peter Cornelius, "Vision" 1865

Der Strom, der neben mir verrauschte
Johannes Brahms, "Der Strom, der neben mir verrauschte" 1864, Op32,4

Des Abendsterns ersehnter Schein
Norbert Burgmüller, "Fischerknabe" 1827-36?, Op3,5

Die Liebe hat gelogen, die Sorge lastet schwer
Franz Schubert, "Die Liebe hat gelogen" 1822, D751

Du sprichst, daß ich mich täuschte
Johannes Brahms, "Du sprichst, daß ich mich täuschte" 1864, Op32,6

Duften nicht die Laubengänge
Josefine Lang, "Sehnsucht" Op4,4

Ein jedes Band
Paul Hindemith, "Ein jedes Band" 1927, Op43,2, ch
from *Lieder für Singkreise* (1)

Ich schleich' umher betrübt und stumm
Norbert Burgmüller, "Lied" 1838pub, Op6,3
Johannes Brahms, "Ich schleich umher betrübt und stumm" 1864, Op32,3

Lange begehrten wir ruhig allein zu sein
Peter Cornelius, "Ode" 1861, Op5,4

Laß tief in dir mich lesen, verhehl auch dies mir nicht
Friedrich Curschmann, "Lass tief in dir mich lesen" 1834, Op9,4
Johanna Kinkel, "Die Stimme der Geliebten" Op17,4
Johann Vesque von Püttlingen, "Mein Herz und deine Stimme" 185-?, Op55,2
Robert Schumann, "Ihre Stimme" 1850, Op96,3

Mein Herz ist zerrissen, du liebst mich nicht!
Franz Schubert, "Du liebst mich nicht" 1822, D756

Nacht ist's, und Stürme sausen für und für
Carl Loewe, "Der Pilgrim vor St. Just" 1832, Op99,3
from *Kaiser Karl V* (3)
Carl Loewe, "Der Pilgrim vor St. Just" 1832, Op9,vii,1
from *Kaiser Karl V* (3)

O süßer Tod, der alle Menschen schrekket
Joseph Marx, "O süßer Tod" 1909, 1v(med).pf

Schwelle die Segel, günstiger Wind!
Robert Schumann, "Am Bodensee (I)" 1846, Op59,2,i, satb

Wehe, so willst du mich wieder
Johannes Brahms, "Wehe, so willst du mich wieder" 1864, Op32,5

Wie rafft ich mich auf in der Nacht
Johannes Brahms, "Wie rafft ich mich auf in der Nacht" 1864, Op32,1

Wiederkehrend nach dem Vaterlande
Robert Schumann, "Am Bodensee (II)" 1846, Op59,2,ii, satb

Anton Platner (1787-1855)
Es deuten die Blumen des Herzens Gefühle
Franz Schubert, "Die Blumensprache" 1817, D519
attribution to Platner questionable

Luise von Plönnies, née Leisler (1803-1872)
Die Königstochter sticket ein gülden Gewand in Ruh'
Carl Loewe, "Der kleine Schiffer" 1857, Op127

Es schaute in die Wogen die Maid im Abendschein
Carl Loewe, "Agnete (I)" 1846-50?, Op134
translated from Danish into "Agnete und der Meermann"

Sie ist herauf gestiegen aus der Kristallnen Gruft
Carl Loewe, "Agnete (III)" 1846-50?, Op134
translated from Danish into "Agnete und der Meermann"

Sie stürzt dem Neck zu Füssen
Carl Loewe, "Agnete (II)" 1846-50?, Op134
translated from Danish into "Agnete und der Meermann"

Und heller und heller quollen die Hymnen, der Orgel Sang
Carl Loewe, "Agnete (IV)" 1846-50?, Op134
translated from Danish into "Agnete und der Meermann"

Franz, Graf von Pocci (1807-1876)
Hoch in Lüften Vöglein schweben
Carl Reinecke, "Vöglein und Englein"
from *Kinderlieder*

Edgar Allan Poe (1809-1849)
Am Morgen, am Mittag, im Abendlicht
Louis Ferdinand, "Gebet" 1953pub

H. E. Poeschl
Die Spindel dreht sich auf und ab
Jan Bedřich Kittl, "Die Spinnerin" 183-?, Op4,4

Richard (Georg) Pohl (1826-1896)
Ich flüsterte leis in den einsamen Bach
Hermann Goetz, "Geheimnis" 1868-76, Op12,1

O süßer Zauber im Jugendmut
Franz Liszt, "Jugendglück" 1862

Aaron Pollak
Geöffnet sind des Winters Riegel
Franz Schubert, "Frühlingslied" 1827, D914, 2t2b
Franz Schubert, "Frühlingslied" 1827?, D919

Alexander Pope (1688-1744)
Lebensfunke vom Himmel entglüht
Franz Schubert, "Verklärung" 1813, D59
translated and German title by J. G. Herder

Martin Josef Prandstetter (1760-1798)
Wess' Adern leichtes Blut durchspringt
Franz Schubert, "Die Fröhlichkeit" 1815, D262

Adolf von Pratobevera (1806-1875)
Leb' wohl du schöne Erde
Franz Schubert, "Abschied von der Erde" 1826, D829, declamation.pf

(Johann) Otto Prechtler (1813-1881)
Ich sitze hier in dunkler Nacht, und flechte meine Locken
Alexander Fesca, "Das Zigeunermädchen" 1882pub, Op37

Steure, Fährmann, deine Barke in den Golf
Johann Vesque von Püttlingen, "Barcarola" 184-?, Op42,5

Wellen säuseln, Winde locken, und das Schiff wiegt sich am Strand
Carl Loewe, “Deutsche Barcarole” 1844, Op103,3

Karl Heinrich Preller (1830-1890)
Voll glühender Liebeswonne
Franz Abt, “Mein ewiges Lied bist du” 1873pub, Op124,2

Weiche nicht, o süsser Traum!
Franz Abt, “Weiche nicht, o süsser Traum!” 1873pub, Op124,1

Konrad von Prittwitz und Gaffron (1826-1906)
Auf goldnem Wagen
Felix Weingartner, “Sesostris” 1913, Op55,4

Robert Eduard Prutz (1816-1872)
Ich will dir’s nimmer sagen
Eduard Lassen, “Vorsatz” Op48,4

Mond, hast du auch gesehen
Max Reger, “Das Mädchen spricht” 1894, Op15,5, 1v(med).pf

Wohl viele Tausend Vögelein
Ferdinand Gumbert, “O bitt’ euch, liebe Vögelein”
Robert Franz, “Wohl viele Tausend Vögelein” 1884, Op52,1

Aleksandr Sergeevich Pushkin (1799-1837)
Du Wolke, du Letzte des Sturms, der zerstoben!
Louis Ferdinand, “Die Wolke” 1966pub

Nächtlicher Duft weht durch die Luft
Adolf Jensen, “Nächtlicher Duft” 1871, Op39,2
translated by Friedrich Bodenstedt

O sing, du Schöne, sing mir nicht...
Adolf Jensen, “O sing, du Schöne, sing mir nicht...” 1871, Op39,1
translated by Friedrich von Bodenstedt

O wenn es wahr, daß in der Nacht, wann alle ruhen die da leben
Friedrich Nietzsche, “Beschwörung” 1864, NWV20
Karl Goldmark, “Beschwörung” 187-?, Op20, 1v(low).pf

Eugen von Puttkamer-Plauth (1800-1874)
Da, wo des Tajo grünlich blauer Strom
Carl Loewe, “Die Gruft der Liebenden” 1832, Op21[7]

Johann Baptist Ladislaus Pyrker (von Oberwart, Graf von Felsö-Eör) (1772-1847)
Ach, der Gebirgssohn hängt mit kindlicher Lieb’ an der Heimath
Franz Schubert, “Das Heimweh” 1825, D851

Gross ist Jehovah, der Herr
Franz Schubert, “Die Allmacht” 1825, D852

[7]The poem had no attribution when given to Loewe, who later added the “Herr von Puttkamer” to the score. For a discussion of other possible authors, including several Puttkamers, see note by Maximilian Runze in *Carl Loewes Werke: Gesamtausgabe der Balladen, Legenden, Lieder und Gesänge.* Band VI: Französische, spanische und orientalische Balladen; Leipzig: Breitkopf und Härtel, 1904. Forword, pp.viii. Reprinted Aldershot: Gregg International, 1970.

Wilhelm Raabe (1831-1910)

Schaukeln und Gaukeln, halb wachender Traum!
Josef Reiter, "Wiegenlied" 1912pub, Op92,6

"Ludwig Rafael" (Hedwig Kiesekamp) (1844-1919)

Ich werde Mama: und Kinder sind da!
Max Reger, "Das Schwesterchen" 1911-12, Op76,54, 1v(med).pf
from *Schlichte Weisen, Band 6, "Neun Kinderlieder"*

Ich werde Soldat, ich werde Soldat!
Max Reger, "Das Brüderchen" 1911-12, Op76,53, 1v(med).pf
from *Schlichte Weisen, Band 6, "Neun Kinderlieder"*

Kaum sind die ersten Blüten da
Max Reger, "Die Bienen" 1911-12, Op76,57, 1v(med).pf
from *Schlichte Weisen, Band 6, "Neun Kinderlieder"*

Regen, linder Frühlingsregen
Max Reger, "An den Frühlingsregen" 1907, Op76,41, 1v(med).pf
from *Schlichte Weisen, Band 4*

Trara, trara, mein Hörnlein hell
Max Reger, "Der Postillon" 1907, Op76,42, 1v(med).pf
from *Schlichte Weisen, Band 4*

Und haben auch im grünen Wald
Max Reger, "Waldesstille" 1909, Op111a,1, sop.alt.pf

Wenn die kleinen Kinder beten, hören all die Sternlein zu
Max Reger, "Des Kindes Gebet" 1904, Op76,22, 1v(med).pf
from *Schlichte Weisen, Band 2*

Wenn mein Kindlein in der Wiegen lächelt still in süßem Traum
Max Reger, "Kindeslächeln" 1904, Op76,27, 1v(med).pf
from *Schlichte Weisen, Band 2*

Karl Wilhelm Ramler (1725-1798)

Inbrunst, Zärtlichkeit, Verstand
Joseph Haydn, "Der Augenblick" 1796-1801, satb.bc

Ja, Vetter, ja! Ja, Vetter, ja: ich fall' euch bei
Joseph Haydn, "An den Vetter" 1796-1801, satb.bc

Mädchen, seht den Zephyr streichen
Karl Friberth, "Warnung an die Mädchen" 1780pub

Carl Randow & Carl Loewe

Ihr deutschen Länder alle, folgt unserm Ruf und Schalle
Carl Loewe, "Preussisches Marinelied" 1856
Poem by Carl Randow completed by Loewe

Friedrich Rasche (1900-1965)

Der Spiegel rief den Mond herein
Gottfried von Einem, "Mondbesuch" 1983?, Op73,12
from *Tag- und Nachtlieder*

Gustav Rasmus (1817-1900)

Die Wolken ziehen so silbern
Karl Gottlieb Reissiger, "Des deutschen Schiffers Heimat" Op117,2, sop.hn.pf

Schlumm're du mein Leben, schlumm're ruhig ein!
Karl Gottlieb Reissiger, "Abendständchen" Op117,4, sop.hn.pf

Fritz Rassow (1882-1916)
O, konntest du es nicht erraten weshalb ich die Blumen so liebte
Eugen d'Albert, "Im Garten" 1904pub, Op27,1

Sagte ein goldener Schmetterling zu seiner silbernen Frau
Eugen d'Albert, "Möchte wohl gerne ein Schmetterling sein" 1904pub, Op27,2

Josef Franz von Ratschky (1757-1810)
Die ihr einem neuen Grade
Wolfgang Amadeus Mozart, "Lied zur Gesellenreise" 1785, K486

Die Schwermut senkt mit bräunlichem Gefieder
Johann Holzer, "Trennungslied" 1779pub

Schön sind die blumichten Matten, mild sind die Lüfte des Mai's
Franz Jacob Freystädtler, "Lied der Treue" 1795
from *Sechs Lieder der besten deutschen Dichter* (2)

Ernst Benjamin Salomo Raupach (1784-1852)
Ihr Thoren wollt das Glück euch wählen
Carl Loewe, "Basslied" 1833, Op42,12, bass.pf
from the comic Singspiel *Die drei Wünsche*

Liebe, Liebe, deine Schmerzen hab' ich nicht gekannt
Carl Loewe, "Romanze" 1833, Op42,3
from the comic Singspiel *Die drei Wünsche*

Philosophie oder Liebe? das ist die Frage
Carl Loewe, "Cavatine für Tenor" 1833, Op42,16
from the comic Singspiel *Die drei Wünsche*

Wer möchte noch einmnal durchlaufen des Lebens rauhe Bahn?
Carl Loewe, "Basslied" 1833, Op42,19

Elisa (Elisabeth) Charlotte Konstantia von der Recke (1756-1833)
Der Mond schon wandelt am Himmelszelt
Emil Sjögren, "Der Mond schon wandelt am Himmelszelt" 1884, 1v.cl.pf

Mit tausendfacher Schöne begrüsst der Lenz die Flur
Carl Loewe, "Rundgesang im Freien" before 1829

Mitten unter deinen Schmerzen blicktest tröstend du herab
Carl Loewe, "Christi Huld gegen Petrus" 1832?

Oskar von Redwitz (-Schmölz) (1823-1891)
Der Wald ist schwarz, die Luft ist klar
Carl Loewe, "Reiterlied" 1859?, Op145,5
from *Liederkranz für die Bassstimme*

Du, der Du bist der Geister Hort
Carl Loewe, "Sängers Gebet" 1852, Op123,1

Es muß was Wunderbares sein um's Lieben zweier Seelen!
Franz Liszt, "Es muß ein Wunderbares sein" 1852
Carl Bohm, "Es muss was Wunderbares sein" 1887cop, Op326,10
Adolph Martin Foerster, "Es muß was Wunderbares sein" 1909, Op57,3

Ich will die lauten Freuden nicht
Carl Loewe, "Brautlied" 1850?

Nun, da so warm der Sonnenschein
Hans Pfitzner, "Nun, da so warm der Sonnenschein" 1887?

Nur das tut mir so bitterweh'
Arnold Schönberg, "Nur das tut mir so bitterweh'" 189-?

Was ist nun doch in mir erwacht!
Franz Ries, "Es muss was Wunderbares sein" before 1891

Max Reger (1873-1916)

Veilchen wollt' ich pflükken
Max Reger, "Der Schelm" 1894, Op15,7, 1v(med).pf
attribution to Reger conjectural

Johann Joseph Reiff (1793-1864)

Mein Schifflien schwimmt so wunderschön
Ferdinand Ries, "Die Lebensfahrt" 1833pub, WoO44, 1v.(ch).pf

Johann Anton Friedrich Reil (1773-1843)

Gott! lass die Glocke glücklich steigen
Franz Schubert, "Glaube, Hoffnung und Liebe" 1828, D954, sa2t2b.orch/pf

Ins Grüne, ins Grüne, da lockt uns der Frühling
Franz Schubert, "Das Lied im Grünen" 1827, D917

Georg von Reinbeck (1766-1849)

Sanftes Licht, weiche nicht
Carl Maria von Weber, "An den Mond" 1809, Op13,4, 1v.guit(pf)

Süsse Ahnung dehnt den Busen
Carl Maria von Weber, "Romanze" 1809, J.71, 1v.guit

Was stürmet die Haide herauf?
Carl Maria von Weber, "Ballade" 1816, Op47,3, 1v.harp

Karl Heinrich Carsten Reinecke ("Heinrich Carsten") (1824-1910)

Bin ein kleiner Stöpsel noch
Carl Reinecke, "Selbstbetrachtung"
from *Kinderlieder*

Den Stab zur Hand genommen, ein Sträusschen auf den Hut
Carl Reinecke, "Pfingstwanderung"
from *Kinderlieder*

Die allerkleinste Schwester ist ein zuckersüsses Mädchen
Carl Reinecke, "Ein Serenädchen"
from *Kinderlieder*

Die Glocken gehen bim bam bum im festlichen Geläute
Carl Reinecke, "Ostern"
from *Kinderlieder*

Einst am diesem Tage hat der Storch ganz sacht
Carl Reinecke, "Am Geburtstage der Mutter" 2v.pf
from *Kinderlieder*

Glück und Segen allerwegen wünschen wir dir heut'
Carl Reinecke, "Ein Anderes" 2v.pf
from *Kinderlieder*

Goldgrüne Libelle, was fliehest du mich!
Carl Reinecke, "Goldgrüne Libelle"
from *Kinderlieder*

Ich seh' ein Schifflein fahren
Carl Reinecke, "Das Schifflein"
from *Kinderlieder*

Kannst du rathen wer ich sei?
Carl Reinecke, "Räthsel"
from *Kinderlieder*

Mein Bruder ist ein ganzer Mann
Carl Reinecke, "Lustiges Musiciren"
from *Kinderlieder*

Wenn ich dich recht schön bäte
Carl Reinecke, "Das Kind und der Kukuk"
from *Kinderlieder*

Paul Reiner

Aus einem dunklen Forste drängt sich ein Hüttlein klein
Eugen d'Albert, "Die Hütte" 1900?pub, Op22,2

Nebel trauern über dem See, Kranichruf aus dunkler Höh!
Eugen d'Albert, "Herbstgang" 1900?pub, Op22,4

Karl Friedrich Graf von Reinhardt (1761-1837)

In verschwundnen Rosentagen
Johann Rudolf Zumsteeg, "Unsre Liebe" 1803pub
from *Kleine Balladen und Lieder, sechstes Heft*

Josef Reinhart (1875-1957)

Chumm über's Mätteli. chumm über e Hag!
Paul Hindemith, "Dä liess ig y!" 1914-16, Op5,4
from *Lustige Lieder in Aargauer Mundart*

Gygeli, Gygeli Brotisbei! Lüpfet 's Füessli, lüpfet d'Bei!
Paul Hindemith, "Tanzliedli" 1914-16, Op5,7
from *Lustige Lieder in Aargauer Mundart*

Mys Büebli isch erwachet, der Morgen isch im Land!
Paul Hindemith, "Erwachen" 1914-16, Op5,6
from *Lustige Lieder in Aargauer Mundart*

"Christian Reinhold" (Christian Reinhold Köstlin) (1813-1856)

Ach, ich denke und versenke
Robert Franz, "Ach, ich denke" 1879, Op51,6

An dies Schifflein schmiege, holder See, dich sacht!
Johannes Brahms, "Auf dem See" 1885, Op106,2

Auf dem See in tausend Sterne
Josefine Lang, "Auf dem See in tausend Sterne" 1841, Op14,6

Auf langer Haide wallt die Wolke hin und her
Josefine Lang, "Die wandernde Wolke" 1843, Op12,6

Die Sonne kam, im reinsten Glanze
Josefine Lang, "O wärst du da" 1841, Op12,4

Eilende Wellen, spielend im Licht
Josefine Lang, "Am Flusse" 1841, Op14,2

Ein Vögelein fliegt über den Rhein
Johannes Brahms, "Auf dem Schiffe" 1885?, Op97,2

Frühling ist gekommen, wie so lieb und hold!
Josefine Lang, "Frühling ist gekommen" 1841, Op27,4

Gedenke mein! die lieben Augen lenke
Josefine Lang, "Gedenke mein" 1840, Op14,3

Hier wo sich die Straßen scheiden
Johannes Brahms, "Ein Wanderer" 1885, Op106,5

Liebster Freund, und kann's denn sein
Josefine Lang, "Zu Tod möcht ich mich lieben" 1841, Op27,6

Nur den Abschied schnell genommen
Josefine Lang, "Den Abschied schnell genommen" 1838, Op15,1

O Nachtigall, dein süßer Schall
Johannes Brahms, "Nachtigall" 1885?, Op97,1

O sehntest Du dich so nach mir
Josefine Lang, "O sehntest Du dich so nach mir" 1840?, Op14,1

Ob ich manchmal Dein gedenke?
Josefine Lang, "Ob ich manchmal Dein gedenke" 1841, Op27,3

Sie hat mich still zum Abschied angeblickt
Josefine Lang, "Abschied" 1843, Op13,1

Um dies Schifflein schmiege, holder See, dich sacht
Josefine Lang, "An den See" 1840, Op14,4

Robert Reinick (1805-1852)

Ach du klar blauer Himmel, und wie schön bist du heut'!
Friedrich Silcher, "Wohin mit der Freud'"
Hugo Wolf, "Wohin mit der Freud?" 1882-83

Als ich zuerst dich hab' gesehn
Louis Spohr, "Nichts Schöneres" 1837, Op101,3
Robert Schumann, "Nichts Schöneres" 1840, Op36,3

Bald ist der Nacht ein End' gemacht
George Henschel, "Morgen-Hymne" 188-?, Op46,4
Hugo Wolf, "Morgenstimmung" 1886
from *Drei Gedichte von Robert Reinick*

Bleiche, bleiche weisses Lein
Robert Schumann, "Der Bleicherin Nachtlied" 1849, Op91,5, ssaa.pf(ad lib)
from *Romanzen für Frauenstimmen II*

Der Förster ging zu Fest und Schmaus!
Heinrich Marschner, "Die Monduhr" 1839?, Op102,2

Der Hans, der spricht zum Hahn:"Zur Schule mit mir, was lernen wollen wir!"
Wilhelm Taubert, "Merkt euch das! Lernt was!"
from *Klänge aus der Kinderwelt*, Vol.4, No10

Der Himmel da oben, der freut mich sehr, möcht wohl einmal hinauf
Heinrich Marschner, "Der Himmel im Thale" 1839?, Op101,5

Des Sonntags in der Morgenstund' wie wandert's sich so schön
Robert Schumann, "Sonntags am Rhein" 1840, Op36,1

Die Liebe ist ein Rosenstrauch. Wo blüht er?
Heinrich Marschner, "Liebesgarten" 1839?, Op101,1
Robert Schumann, "Liebesgarten" 1840, Op34,1, sop.ten.pf

Durch den Wald, wie schimmert es sonnig im Grün
Adolph Martin Foerster, "Durch den Wald" 1909, Op69,ii,4

"Eia popeia," das ist ein altes Lied
Alexis Holländer, "Im Frühling (Wiegenlied)" 1895?pub, Op51,3

Ein Maler vor dem Zaune sass, aha!
Leopold Damrosch, "Zaunstudien" Op8,12

Glühwürmchen, steck's Laternchen an!
Carl Loewe, "Der verliebte Maikäfer" 1837, Op64,1

Hänschen will reiten, setzt sich zu Rosse hin
Wilhelm Taubert, "Der tapfere Reiter"
from *Klänge aus der Kinderwelt*, Vol.6, No12

Hielt die allerschönste Herrin einst mein Herz so eng gefesselt
Hugo Wolf, "Frohe Botschaft" 1890

Ich bin einmal etwas hinaus spaziert
Karl Gottlieb Reissiger, "Kuriose Geschichte" Op114,2
Hans Pfitzner, "Kuriose Geschichte" 1884/5
Wilhelm Kienzl, "Curiose Geschichte" 1904pub, Op28

Ich bin hinausgegangen des Morgens in der Früh
Robert Schumann, "Schön Blümelein" 1840, Op43,3, sop.alt.pf

Ich hab' dich geliebt, du ahntest es nicht
Franz Wüllner, "Ich hab' dich geliebt" 1857pub

Im Fliederbusch ein Vöglein saß in der stillen, schönen Maiennacht
Carl Reinecke, "Zwiegesang"
from *Kinderlieder*
Louis Spohr, "Zwiegesang" 1837, Op103,2, sop.cl.pf
Arnold Schönberg, "Im Fliederbusch ein Vöglein saß" 189-?

Im Schnee und Eis in kalter Nacht ein Grenadier steht auf der Wacht
Adolph Martin Foerster, "Die Ablösung" 1909, Op69,4

In dem Himmel ruht die Erde, Mond und Sterne halten Wacht
Hugo Wolf, "Nachtgruss" 1883
Alexis Holländer, "Ständchen" 1895?pub, Op51,6

Kaninchen, Karnickelchen, was bist du doch so stumm!
Carl Reinecke, "Kaninchen, Karnickelchen"
from *Kinderlieder*

Kein Meister fällt vom Himmel
Hugo Wolf, "Gesellenlied" 1888
from *Drei Gedichte von Robert Reinick*

Komm' in die stille Nacht, Liebchen, was zögerst du?
Robert Schumann, "Ständchen" 1840, Op36,2
Eduard Lassen, "Ständchen"
Hugo Wolf, "Ständchen" 1883

Mädel trug des Wegs daher einen Korb voll Blüten
Heinrich Marschner, "Diebstahl" 184-?pub, Op114,2

Mein Liebster ist ein Jäger, trägt einen grünen Hut
Alexis Holländer, "Des Jägers Heimkehr" 1895?pub, Op51,1

Morgens als Lerche möcht' ich begrüssen der Sonne Strahl
George Henschel, "Morgens als Lerche" 188-?, Op46,1
Alexander Fesca, "Ständchen" 1882pub, Op29,2

O Sonnenschein, o Sonnenschein! wie scheinst du mir in's Herz hinein
Robert Schumann, "An den Sonnenschein" 1840, Op36,4

O versenk, o versenk dein Leid, mein Kind
Johannes Brahms, "Liebestreu" 1853, Op3,1

Reich' den Pokal mir schäumenden Weines voll
Hugo Wolf, "Skolie" 1889
from *Drei Gedichte von Robert Reinick*

Schlaf' ein, schlaf' ein, schlaf' ein, mein süsses Kind
Hugo Wolf, "Wiegenlied im Winter" 1882
from *Sechs Lieder für eine Frauenstimme*

Schneeglöckchen thut läuten: klinglingling!
Louis Spohr, "Frühlingsglocken" 1837, Op101,1
Robert Schumann, "Frühlingsglocken" 1840, Op33,6, ttbb
Hugo Wolf, "Frühlingsglocken" 1883

Schwalbenmütterlein, Schwalbenmütterlein!
Max Reger, "Schwalbenmütterlein" 1915, Op142,2
from *Fünf neue Kinderlieder*

Schweigen ist ein schönes Ding
Louis Spohr, "Schweigen ist ein schönes Ding" 1837, Op101,5

Sonne hat sich müd gelaufen, spricht: "Nun lass ich's sein!"
Wilhelm Taubert, "Wiegenlied"
from *Klänge aus der Kinderwelt*, Vol.4, No4

Täubchen, ihr lieben, lieben Täubchen im Sonnenschein
Wilhelm Taubert, "Täubchen im Sonnenschein"
from *Klänge aus der Kinderwelt*, Vol.6, No3

Und wieder hatt' ich der Schönsten gedacht
Robert Schumann, "Dichters Genesung" 1840, Op36,5

Vom Berg hinabgestiegen ist nun des Tages Rest
Hugo Wolf, "Wiegenlied im Sommer" 1882
from *Sechs Lieder für eine Frauenstimme*
Leo Blech, "Wiegenlied" 1913pub, Op21,5

Wellen blinkten durch die Nacht
Louis Spohr, "Der Bleicherin Nachtlied" 1835-36, Op94,3

Wie ist doch die Erde so schön, so schön!
Heinrich Marschner, "Juchhe!" 1839?, Op101,4
Johannes Brahms, "Juchhe" 1852, Op6,4
Wilhelm Kienzl, "Wie ist doch die Erde so schön" 1894, Op44,3

Wolken, die ihr nach Osten eilt
Robert Schumann, "Liebesbotschaft" 1840, Op36,6
Hugo Wolf, "Liebesbotschaft" 1883
Arno Kleffel, "Liebesbotschaft" Op12,10

Zaubrer bin ich, doch was frommt es?
Heinrich Marschner, "Liebchen, wo bist du?" 1839?pub, Op101,2
Hugo Wolf, "Liebchen, wo bist du?" 1883

Ludwig Johann Reinwald

Wandelst du auch fern von mir, fern von mir auch in Gedanken
Richard Trunk, "Gedankennähe" 1963pub, Op76,4

Hans Reisiger (1884-1968)

All' deine Anmut hab' ich aufgeweckt, dunkles und scheues zart zugedeckt
Anna Teichmüller, "All' deine Anmut" 1910pub, Op24,2

Christian Ludwig Reissig (1783-after 1822)

Als mir noch die Thräne
Ludwig van Beethoven, "Lied aus der Ferne" 1809, WoO137

Der Frühling entblühet dem Schoos der Natur
Ludwig van Beethoven, "Der Jüngling in der Fremde" 1809, WoO138

Die stille Nacht umdunkelt erquickend Thal und Höh'
Ludwig van Beethoven, "Sehnsucht" 1815-16, WoO146
Carl Loewe, "Sehnsucht"

Einst wohnten süsse Ruh und goldner Frieden in meiner Brust
Ludwig van Beethoven, "An den fernen Geliebten" 1809, Op75,5

Höre Schicksal, was ich heische, höre mich zum letzten Mahl!
Mauro Giuliani, "An das Schicksal" 1817pub, Op89,6, v.pf./guitar

Ich zieh' in's Feld von Lieb' entbrannt
Ludwig van Beethoven, "Des Kriegers Abschied" 1814, WoO143

Komm ans Fenster, holde Schöne
Niklas von Krufft, "Serenade" 1812pub

Mild umschattet von der Dämmrung Schleier
Niklas von Krufft, "Wehmut"

Welch ein wunderbares Leben
Ludwig van Beethoven, "Der Liebende" 1809, WoO139

Zwar schuf das Glück hienieden mich weder reich noch gross
Ludwig van Beethoven, "Der Zufriedene" 1809, Op75,6
Franz Schubert, "Der Zufriedene" 1815, D320

Johann Heinrich Freiherr von Reitzenstein (1722-1780)
Ausgelitten hast du, ausgerungen
Martin Ruprecht, "Lotte bey Werthers Grabe" 1785?

(Heinrich Friedrich) Ludwig Rellstab (1799-1860)
Ade! du muntre, du fröhliche Stadt, Ade!
Franz Schubert, "Abschied" 1827-8, D957,7
from *Rellstab Lieder*

Es rauschen die Winde so herbstlich und kalt
Franz Liszt, "Es rauschen die Winde" 1845-56
Franz Liszt, "Es rauschen die Winde" 1860pub
Franz Schubert, "Herbst" 1828, D945

Fröhlicher Lebensmut braust in dem raschen Blut
Franz Schubert, "Lebensmuth" (incomplete), 1827?, D937

In tiefer Ruh liegt um mich her der Waffenbrüder Kreis
Franz Schubert, "Kriegers Ahnung" 1827-8, D957,2
from *Rellstab Lieder*

Leise flehen meine Lieder durch die Nacht zu dir
Franz Schubert, "Ständchen" 1827-8, D957,4
from *Rellstab Lieder*

Nimm die letzten Abschiedsküsse
Franz Schubert, "Auf dem Strom" 1828, D943, 1v.hn.pf

Nimm einen Strahl der Sonne, vom Abendstern das Licht
Franz Liszt, "Ihr Auge" 1860pub

Rauschender Strom, brausender Wald, starrender Fels mein Aufenthalt
Franz Schubert, "Aufenthalt" 1827-8, D957,5
from *Rellstab Lieder*

Rauschendes Bächlein, so silbern und hell
Franz Schubert, "Liebesbotschaft" 1827-8, D957,1
from *Rellstab Lieder*

Säuselnde Lüfte wehend so mild
Franz Schubert, "Frühlingssehnsucht" 1827-8, D957,3
from *Rellstab Lieder*

Wehe dem Fliehenden, Welt hinaus Ziehenden!
Franz Schubert, "In der Ferne" 1827-8, D957,6
from *Rellstab Lieder*

Wo weilt er? Im kalten, im schaurigen Land
Franz Liszt, "Wo weilt er?" 1860pub

Paul Remer (1867-1943)
Ach, wenn es nun die Mutter wüsst', wie du so wild mich hast geküsst
Arnold Schönberg, "Mädchenlied" 1903-05, Op6,3

Wir schreiten in goldener Fülle
Richard Strauss, "In goldener Fülle" 1901, Op49,2
Leo Ornstein, "In goldener Fülle" 1915pub, Op33,2

Fr. Richter
Drauss ist alles so prächtig, und es ist mer so wohl
Friedrich Silcher, "Im Mai"

Georg Karl Alexander Richter (1760-1806)
Kennst du den Fluss, auf dessen schwarzen Wellen
Johann Rudolf Zumsteeg, "Sehnsucht, an W." 1800pub
from *Kleine Balladen und Lieder, erstes Heft*

Johann Riedinger
Ihr Lieben, die ich Schwermuthsvoll an meinen Busen sehne
Maria Therese Paradis, "An meine entfernten Lieben" 1784-86
from *Zwölf Lieder auf ihrer Reise in Musik gesetzt*

Rainer Maria Rilke (1875-1926)
Alle Mädchen erwarten wen, wenn die Bäume in Blüten stehn
Alban Berg, "Die Näherin" 1904

Am Berge weiß ich trutzen ein Kirchlein mit rostigem Knauf
Karl Prohaska, "Casabianca" 1914cop

Bei dir ist es traut
Alma Schindler-Mahler, "Bei dir ist es traut" 1900-01?

Das ist die Sehnsucht: wohnen im Gewoge
Karl Marx, "Das ist die Sehnsucht" 1943, Op45,1

Das sind die Stunden, da ich mich finde
Franz Krause, "Das sind die Stunden" 1972?pub, Op47,2
from *Sechs Gedichte von Rainer Maria Rilke*

Das war der Tag der weißen Chrysanthemen
Alban Berg, "Traumgekrönt" 1907
from *Sieben frühe Lieder*

Der Abend ist mein Buch. Ihm prangen die Deckel purpurn im Damast
Ernst Toch, "Der Abend" 1928pub, Op41,1

Der Bach hat leise Melodien
George Perle, "Der Bach hat leise Melodien" 1941
from *Two Rilke Songs*

Der Sommer summt. Der Nachmittag macht müde
Léon Orthel, "Übung am Klavier" 1934, Op16,1
from *Twee Liederen*

Der Tod ist groß. Wir sind die Seinen lachenden Munds
Helmut Paulsen, "Der Tod"
from *Sieben besinnliche Lieder*
Ernest Vietor, "Schlussstück" 1939-40, Op17,5

Derselbe große Engel
Paul Hindemith, "Vom Tode Mariä I" 1922-23, Op27,13
from *Das Marienleben*

Die Blätter fallen, fallen wie von weit
Ignace Lilien, "Herbst" 1923
Franz Krause, "Herbst" 1972?pub, Op47,5
from *Sechs Gedichte von Rainer Maria Rilke*

Die falben Felder schlafen schon, mein Herz nur wacht allein
Karl Prohaska, "Die falben Felder schlafen schon (aus Vigilien)" 1914cop
Franz Salmhofer, "Vigilie" 1923pub, Op5,2
from *Vier Lieder*

Diese, die noch eben atemlos flohen mitten aus dem Kindermorden
Paul Hindemith, "Rast auf der Fluch nach Ägypten" 1922-23, Op27,8
from *Das Marienleben*

Doch vor dem Apostel Thomas
Paul Hindemith, "Vom Tode Mariä III" 1922-23, Op27,15
from *Das Marienleben*

Du, der ichs nicht sage, daß ich bei Nacht weinend liege
Anton Webern, "Du, der ichs nicht sage" 1910, Op8,1, mez.cham
Viktor Junk, "Du, der ich's nicht sage" 1911pub

Du machst mich allein. Dich einzig kann ich vertauschen
Anton Webern, "Du machst mich allein" 1910, Op8,2, mez.cham

Du meine heilige Einsamkeit
George Perle, "Du meine heilige Einsamkeit" 1941
from *Two Rilke Songs*

Einsam hinterm letzten Haus geht die rote Sonne schlafen
Franz Krause, "Abend" 1972?pub, Op47,3
from *Sechs Gedichte von Rainer Maria Rilke*

Er wußte nur vom Tod, was alle wissen:
Siegfried Thiele, "Der Tod der Geliebten" 1978

Es gibt so wundervolle Nächte
Joseph Marx, "Traumgekrönt" 1910

Es treibt der Wind im Winterwalde die Flokkenherde wie ein Hirt
Franz Krause, "Advent" 1972?pub, Op47,6
from *Sechs Gedichte von Rainer Maria Rilke*

Große Heilige und kleine feiert jegliche Gemeine
Ernst Toch, "Heilige" 1928pub, Op41,2

Härte schwand. Auf einmal legt sich Schonung
Wolfgang Rihm, "Vorfrühling" 1970, Op1,13

Hättest du der Einfalt nicht
Paul Hindemith, "Geburt Christi" 1922-23, Op27,7
from *Das Marienleben*

Ich bin die Laute. Willst du meinen Leib beschreiben
Donald Martino, "Die Laute" 1961, mez.pf
from *Two Rilke Songs*

Ich möchte einer werden so wie die, die durch die Nacht
Harald Genzmer, "Der Knabe" 1940-87, bar.pf or sop.pf
from *Acht Lieder nach verschiedenen Dichtern*

Ihr Mädchen seid wie die Gärten
Karl Marx, "Ihr Mädchen seid wie die Gärten" 1943, Op45,2

In solchen Nächten wächst mein Schwesterlein
Donald Martino, "Aus einer Sturmnacht VIII" 1961, mez.pf
from *Two Rilke Songs*

Jetzt wird mein Elend voll
Paul Hindemith, "Pietà" 1922-23, Op27,11
from *Das Marienleben*

Konnte sie denn anders, als auf ihn stolz sein
Paul Hindemith, "Vor der Hochzeit zu Kana" 1922-23, Op27,9
from *Das Marienleben*

Lauschende Wolke über dem Wald
Karl Marx, "Lauschende Wolke über dem Wald" 1943, Op45,3

Manchmal geschieht es in tiefer Nacht
Karl Marx, "Manchmal geschieht es in tiefer Nacht" 1943, Op45,4

Maria! Du weinst ich weiss
Anna Teichmüller, "Maria" 1904pub, Op2,4

Mich rührt so sehr böhmischen Volkes Weise
Franz Mittler, "Volksweise" 1911pub
Franz Krause, "Mich rührt so sehr" 1972?pub, Op47,1
from *Sechs Gedichte von Rainer Maria Rilke*

Möchte mir ein blondes Glück erkiesen
Franz Krause, "Möchte mir ein blondes Glück" 1972?pub, Op47,4
from *Sechs Gedichte von Rainer Maria Rilke*

Nicht daß ein Engel eintrat (das erkenn), erschreckte sie
Paul Hindemith, "Mariä Verkündigung" 1922-23, Op27,3
from *Das Marienleben*

Noch erging sie's leicht im Anbeginne
Paul Hindemith, "Mariä Heimsuchung" 1922-23, Op27,4
from *Das Marienleben*

O hast du dies gewollt
Paul Hindemith, "Vor der Passion" 1922-23, Op27,10
from *Das Marienleben*

O Herr, gib jedem seinen eignen Tod
Paul Hindemith, "O Herr, gib jedem seinen eignen Tod" 1927, Op43,2, ch
from *Lieder für Singkreise* (2)

O was muß es die Engel gekostet haben
Paul Hindemith, "Geburt Mariä" 1922-23, Op27,1
from *Das Marienleben*

Oft fühl ich in scheuen Schauern
Karl Marx, "Oft fühl ich in scheuen Schauern" 1943, Op45,5

Oft war sie als Kind ihren Dienerinnen entwichen
Léon Orthel, "Die Entführung" 1934, Op16,2
from *Twee Liederen*

Seht auf, ihr Männer
Paul Hindemith, "Verkündigung über die Hirten" 1922-23, Op27,6
from *Das Marienleben*

Um zu begreifen, wie sie damals war
Paul Hindemith, "Die Darstellung Mariä im Tempel" 1922-23, Op27,2
from *Das Marienleben*

Und der Engel sprach und gab sich Müh an dem Mann
Paul Hindemith, "Argwohn Josephs" 1922-23, Op27,5
from *Das Marienleben*

Und wie mag die Liebe dir kommen sein?
Alban Berg, "Liebe" 1904
Franz Schreker, "Und wie mag die Liebe..." 1919
Siegfried Thiele, "Und wie mag die Liebe" 1978

Uraltes Wehn vom Meer, Meerwind bei Nacht
Helmut Paulsen, "Lied vom Meer"
from *Sieben besinnliche Lieder*

Vorüber die Flut. Noch braust es fern
Arnold Schönberg, "Am Strande" 1909?

Was sie damals empfanden
Paul Hindemith, "Stillung Mariä mit dem Auferstandenen" 1922-23, Op27,12
from *Das Marienleben*

Wer hat bedacht, daß bis zu ihrem Kommen
Paul Hindemith, "Vom Tode Mariä II (Thema mit Variationen)" 1922-23, Op27,14
from *Das Marienleben*

Wie soll ich meine Seele halten
Siegfried Thiele, "Liebeslied" 1978

Bartolomäus Ringwald(t) (1532?-1599)
Eine fromme Magd von gutem Stand
Carl Maria von Weber, "Die fromme Magd" 1818, Op54,1

Johann Rist (1607-1667)
Bleiches Antlitz, sei gegrüsset
Carl Loewe, "Bleiches Antlitz, sei gegrüsset"

Anna (Nuhn) Ritter (1865-1921)
Als über den Flieder das Mondlicht rann
Max Reger, "Brautring" 1900
from *Liebeslieder* (1)
Mathieu Neumann, "Brautring" 1904pub, Op55,2
from *Aus seliger Zeit*

Da kennt so ein Mann nun die halbe Welt
Mathieu Neumann, "Der Papa" 1904pub, Op55,7
from *Aus seliger Zeit*

Das ist ein lieb Beisammen sein, wenn über uns die Wanduhr tickt
Mathieu Neumann, "Im Lampenschein" 1904pub, Op55,5
from *Aus seliger Zeit*

Die ihr den Äther mit seligen Schwingen durchschneidet
Max Reger, "Sterne" 1901, Op55,7, 1v(med).pf

Die Nacht ist keines Menschen Freund!
Karol Szymanowski, "Das hat die Sommernacht getan" 1910, Op22,4

Die Nacht war tief, und die Mutter schlief
Max Reger, "Die Betrogene spricht" 1899-1900, Op43,6, 1v(med).pf

Die Tage rinnen leise hin, ein jeder bringt ein liebes Glück
Mathieu Neumann, "Stille Zeit" 1904pub, Op55,8
from *Aus seliger Zeit*

Ein Brünnlein im Felde, sechs Linden im Kreis
Ernest Vietor, "Frühlingsmärchen" Op5,3

"Ein Mädchen!" "Ein Mädchen!" Wir waren ein bischen erschrocken
Mathieu Neumann, "Ein Mädchen" 1904pub, Op55,6
from *Aus seliger Zeit*

Ein Vöglein singt im Wald, singt Lieb' und Leiden
Max Reger, "Volkslied" 1899, Op37,2, 1v(med).pf
Frank van der Stucken, "Ein Vöglein singt im Wald" 1904pub, Op33,3
Othmar Schoeck, "Ein Vöglein singt im Wald" 1906, o.op23, ch

Es stand eine Rose im tieftiefen Grund
Max Reger, "Unbegehrt" 1898, Op31,3, 1v(med).pf

Hat einmal ein Mädel die Muhme gefragt
Max Reger, "Pythia" 1898, Op23,2

Ich gehe fremd durch die Menge hin
Max Reger, "Sonnenregen" 1902
from *Liebeslieder* (8)

Ich hab' kein' Mutter, die mich hegt
Max Reger, "Und hab' so große Sehnsucht doch" 1898, Op31,4, 1v(med).pf
Hugo Kaun, "Und hab' so große Sehnsucht doch" 1904pub, Op55,7

Ich komme heim aus dem Sonnenland!
Joseph Marx, "Sonnenland" 1910, 1v(med).pf

Ich lauscht' dem Fink im grünen Haag
Paul Graener, "Schelmenlied" 1909pub, Op30,3

Ich trag' ein glückselig Geheimnis mit mir herum
Max Reger, "Geheimnis" 1900
from *Liebeslieder* (2)
Mathieu Neumann, "Geheimnis" 1904pub, Op55,1
from *Aus seliger Zeit*

Ich weiß nicht, was mir gar so bang
Paul Graener, "Das fremde Lied" 1916pub, Op40,3

In deinem Arm, an deinem Herzen o sag', o sag'
Mathieu Neumann, "Sieghafte Lust" 1904pub, Op55,4
from *Aus seliger Zeit*

In verschwiegener Nacht hab' ich deiner gedacht
Max Reger, "In verschwiegener Nacht" 1898

Junge Hände halfen mich schmücken, alte Lippen segneten mich
Mathieu Neumann, "Brautgang" 1904pub, Op55,3
from *Aus seliger Zeit*

Leise wie ein Hauch, zärtlich wie ein Lied
Paul Graener, "Liebe" 1909pub, Op21,1

Liegt nun so still die weite Welt
Max Reger, "Mein Traum" 1898, Op31,5, 1v(med).pf

Mußt's auch grad' so dunkel sein an der Weißdornhekke!
Max Reger, "Schlimme Geschichte" 1898, Op31,6, 1v(med).pf

Und dürft' ich dich wekken zum Sonnenlicht
Franz Mittler, "Schlafe, ach, schlafe" 1911pub

Unter den blühenden Linden weißt du's noch?
Max Reger, "Ich glaub', lieber Schatz" 1898, Op31,2, 1v(med).pf
Frank van der Stucken, "Ich glaub', lieber Schatz..." 1904pub, Op34,3

Viele Glokken hör' ich läuten
Max Reger, "Die Glocke des Glücks" 1903, Op79c,iii,1

War ich gar so jung und dumm
Max Reger, "Vom Küssen!" 1898, Op23,4, 1v(med).pf

Wie zerrißner Saiten Klingen
Max Reger, "Allein" 1898, Op31,1, 1v(med).pf

Wir senkten die Wurzeln in Moos und Gestein
Jean Sibelius, "Rosenlied" 1906, Op50,6

Emil Rittershaus (1834-1897)

Mit Rheinwein füllt den Becher! Der perlt so klar und frisch!
Franz Ries, "Am Rhein und beim Wein" before 1891

Friederike Robert (1795-1832)

Jetzt kommt der Frühling, der Himmel isch blau
Felix Mendelssohn, "Frühlingslied" 1824, Op8,6

Was ist's, das mir den Athem hemmet
Fanny Hensel, "Das Heimweh" 1828pub, Op8,2(FM)

Wisst ihr, wo ich gerne weil' in der Abendkühle?
Felix Mendelssohn, "Lieblingsplätzchen" 184-?, Op99,3

"Gerda von Robertus" (Gertrud Emily Borngräber, née von Schlieban) (1873-?)

Das Sonnenfeuer starb Rubingepränge
Rudi Stephan, "Abendfrieden" 1913
from *Ich will dir singen ein Hohelied...*

Der Rosen Düfte liebeatmend schwingen in weichen Wellen
Rudi Stephan, "Kythere" 1913
from *Ich will dir singen ein Hohelied...*

Geschmeidig und wild wie ein junger Panther
Rudi Stephan, "Patherlied" 1914
from *Ich will dir singen ein Hohelied...*

In Nachbars Garten duftet die Lindenblüte schwül
Rudi Stephan, "In Nachbars Garten" 1914
from *Ich will dir singen ein Hohelied...*

Wir haben im Lärm der Menge im Gleichempfinden geschwiegen
Rudi Stephan, "Glück zu Zweien" 1913?
from *Ich will dir singen ein Hohelied...*

Zwei Tage reichen sich die Hand der eine schied
Rudi Stephan, "Das Hohelied der Nacht" 1914
from *Ich will dir singen ein Hohelied...*

(Johann) Friedrich Rochlitz (1796-1842)

Die Sonne sinkt in's tiefe Meer, da wollte sie kommen
Franz Schubert, "Alinde" 1827, D904

Die stille Nacht heisst niedre Sorgen schweigen
Louis Spohr, "Abendlied" 1838, Op108,1, 2sop.pf

Es stürmt auf der Flur
Carl Maria von Weber, "Es stürmt auf der Flur" 1814, Op30,2

Horcht auf! Es schlägt die Stunde
Franz Schubert, "Zur guten Nacht" 1827, D903, bar.2t2b.pf

Leiser, leiser, kleine Laute! Flüstre, was ich dir vertraute
Franz Schubert, "An die Laute" 1827, D905
Josef Bohuslav Foerster, "An die Laute" 1914pub, Op60,1

Meine Ruh' ist dahin, meine Freud' ist entfloh'n
Franz Schubert, "Klaglied" 1812, D23

Julius von Rodenberg (1831-1914)

Alles stille, nur zuweilen
Felix Weingartner, "Alles stille" 1899, Op25,2

Bächlein am Wiesenrand, rinnst du noch immer?
Heinrich Marschner, "So weit" 185-?pub, Op173,3

Ein Vöglein sang die ganze Nacht
Franz Ries, "Ein Vöglein sang die ganze Nacht" before 1891

Hier in dem Dunkel, auf pfadlosen Mooren
Felix Weingartner, "Ultima Thule" 1899, Op25,1

Nun bricht aus allen Zweigen das maien frische Grün
Joseph Marx, "Im Maien" 1908, 1v.orch

Nun ruht und schlummert Alles
Alexander Zemlinsky, "Um Mitternacht" 1894-96, Op2,i,6

Wach' auf, du schöne Träumerin, wach' auf
Franz Abt, "Wach' auf, du schöne Träumerin" 1873pub, Op124,3
Franz Ries, "Wach' auf, du schöne Träumerin!" before 1891

Otto Röser

Ich sass am einsamen Weiher, der Abend war schweigend und kühl
Robert Franz, "Als trüg' man die Liebe zu Grab'" 1867?, Op40,4

In dem frischen grünen Walde streif' ich leicht und froh herum
Robert Franz, "Stille Liebe" 1867?, Op41,4

Kurt von Rohrscheidt (1857-1935)

Es ruht mit ernstem Sinnen auf mir dein Blick
Max Reger, "Glück" 1894, Op15,1, 1v(med).pf

Hermann Rollet (1819-1904)

An einem lichten Morgen, da klingt es hell im Tal
Clara Schumann, "An einem lichten Morgen" 1853, Op23,2

Auf einem grünen Hügel, da steht ein Röslein hell
Clara Schumann, "Auf einem grünen Hügel" 1853, Op23,4

Das ist ein Tag, der klingen mag
Clara Schumann, "Das ist ein Tag" 1853, Op23,5

Das Vöglein sang vom grünen Baum sein Lied der ew'gen Liebe
Arno Kleffel, "Liebesandacht" Op12,7

Geheimes Flüstern hier und dort
Clara Schumann, "Geheimes Flüstern hier und dort" 1853, Op23,3

Ist der Frühling über Nacht
Arno Kleffel, "Ist der Frühling über Nacht" Op12,3

O Lust, o Lust, vom Berg ein Lied
Clara Schumann, "O Lust, o Lust" 1853, Op23,6

Und wenn es dunkel werden will in meinem Kämmerlein
Frederic Louis Ritter, "Liebe" 1871pub, Op6,2

Was weinst du, Blümlein, im Morgenschein?
Clara Schumann, "Was weinst du, Blümlein?" 1853, Op23,1
Arno Kleffel, "Stille Liebe" Op12,8

Lily Rona

Die Augen fielen meinem Liebsten zu, von Liebe müd
Erich Zeisl, "Liebeslied" 1936pub

Edith Ronsperger

Die Dunkelheit sinkt schwer wie Blei
Franz Schreker, "Die Dunkelheit sinkt schwer wie Blei" 1909
from *Fünf Gesänge*

Dies aber kann mein Sehnen nimmer fassen
Franz Schreker, "Dies aber kann mein Sehnen nimmer fassen" 1909
from *Fünf Gesänge*
Erich Wolfgang Korngold, "Dies eine kann mein Sehnen nimmer fassen" 1918, Op14,2
from *Lieder des Abschieds*

Einst gibt ein Tag mir alles Glück zu eigen
Franz Schreker, "Einst gibt ein Tag mir alles Glück" 1909
from *Fünf Gesänge*

Sie sind so schön, die milden, sonnenreichen, verträumten Tage
Franz Schreker, "Sie sind so schön, die milden, sonnenreichen" 1909
from *Fünf Gesänge*

"Richard Roos:" see Karl August Engelhardt

Otto Roquette (1824-1896)

Ach Gott, das druckt das Herz mir ab
Erik Meyer-Helmund, "Herzbeklemmung" 1886-88

Bei den Bienenkörben im Garten, wo der Flieder in Düften steht
Adolf Jensen, "Unruhe" 1863pub, Op13,2, 1v(low).pf

Das beste Bier im ganzen Nest
Adolf Jensen, "Margreth am Thore" 1870, Op35,5

Das macht das dunkelgrüne Laub
Robert Franz, "Das macht das dunkelgrüne Laub" 1865?pub, Op20,5

Die Sonn' ist hin, wie Lust der Minn'
Robert Franz, "Die Sonn' ist hin" 1862?, Op35,3

Du kleines blitzendes Sternelein, nun sage mir, was willst du?
Friedrich Kücken, "Du kleines blitzendes Sternelain"
Adolph Martin Foerster, "Gleich und Gleich" 1878, Op6,1

Du liebes Auge willst dich tauchen
Robert Franz, "Du liebes Auge" 1856pub, Op16,1
Hugo Wolf, "Perlenfischer" 1876
Max Reger, "Du liebes Auge" 1899, Op35,5, 1v(med).pf

Er kam in der Frühe wie der Morgenwind
Adolf Jensen, "Morgens am Brunnen" 1870pub, Op35,2

Noch ist die blühende, goldene Zeit
Eduard Lassen, "Noch ist die blühende, goldene Zeit" Op84,6
Adolf Jensen, "Noch ist die blühende goldene Zeit" 1875-79, Op55,2

O lass dich halten, gold'ne Stunde, die nie so schön sich wieder beut!
Adolf Jensen, "O lass dich halten, gold'ne Stunde" 1870, Op35,3
Frank van der Stucken, "Seligkeit" 1892pub

O wär ich am Nekkar, o wär ich am Rhein
Franz Abt, "Am Neckar, am Rhein" 1851+?, Op89

So viel Laub an der Linden ist
Adolf Jensen, "An der Linden" 1870, Op35,4

Weißt du noch, wie ich am Felsen bei den Veilchen dich belauschte
Robert Franz, "Weisst du noch?" 1856pub, Op16,5
Adolf Jensen, "Weißt du noch?" 1864, Op24,5
Arno Kleffel, "Weisst du noch?" Op14,1

Willkommen, mein Wald, grünschattiges Haus!
Robert Franz, "Willkommen, mein Wald!" 1865?pub, Op21,1

K. Rose
Die Amsel flötet, es rieselt der Bach
Carl Loewe, "Abendstunde" 1859, Op130,3

Peter Rosegger (1843-1918)
O Vögerl, wia singst du lusti
Wilhelm Kienzl, "Aus'n unglücklan Buam seini Liada" 189-?, Op31,3

"Rosemann" (Johann Aegidius Klöntrup) (1755-1830)
Der Garten des Lebens ist lieblich und schön
Carl Friedrich Zelter, "Der Garten des Lebens" 1791
Carl Loewe, "Der Garten des Lebens" before 1826

Christian Knorr von Rosenroth (1636-1689)
Morgenglanz der Ewigkeit, Licht, vom Licht aus Gott geboren
Carl Loewe, "Morgenglanz der Ewigkeit" 1860, Op131,3, 4v

Fr. Rosenthal

Nun ist der Tag verronnen

Felix Weingartner, "Ein geistlich Nachtlied" 1910, Op51,7

from *Abendlieder*

"Ernst Rosmer" (Elsa Bernstein) (1866-1949)

Roter Ringelrosenbusch hat mein Hemd zerrissen

Engelbert Humperdinck, "Rosenringel" 1895

from *Vier Kinderlieder*

Christina Georgina Rossetti (1830-1894)

Wenn ich gestorben, Liebchen, sing' nicht ein Klagelied

Frank van der Stucken, "Gedenken - Vergessen" 1892pub

Jean-Baptist Rousseau (1802-1867)

Auf das Maines grünen Auen

Ferdinand Ries, "Gesang für den Frankfurter Liederkranz" 1834pub, Op173,5, 4mv

Es lockt und säuselt um den Baum

Johannes Brahms, "Der Frühling" 1852, Op6,2

Liebe recht tief gehegt

Ferdinand Ries, "Liebe duldet" 1834pub, Op173,4, 4mv

Was trinket ihr? Schenkt lustig ein

Ferdinand Ries, "Was trinket ihr? Schenkt lustig ein" 1834pub, Op173,1, 4mv

Wenn die Fluthen blau, wenn die Lüfte lau

Ferdinand Ries, "Barcarole" 1835pub, Op180,3

Anton Rubinstein (1829-1894)

Es schmachtet eine Blume nach einem hellen Stern

Anton Rubinstein, "Räthsel" 1856, Op33,4

Karoline Christiane Louise Rudolphi (1754-1811)

Auf, Brüder, auf! der Tag bricht an

Carl Loewe, "Morgenlied" before 1829

Willkommen süsse Kleine, in unsrem Blütenhaine

Franz Anton Hoffmeister, "An die Nachtigall"

Friedrich Rückert (1788-1866)

Als Maria heut' entwich, heut' vor Jahren

Carl Loewe, "Der Weichdorn" 1837, Op75,2, alt.pf

Ans Auge des Liebsten

Johannes Brahms, "Ans Auge des Liebsten" 1891pub, Op113,9, ssaa

from *13 Kanons für Frauenstimmen*

Auf der Bank, wo sie sonst sitzet

Carl Loewe, "In der Kirche" 1837, Op62,ii,2

Auf jener Flucht, von welcher nun

Carl Loewe, "Das Wunder auf der Flucht" 1837, Op75,4, alt.pf

Aus der Jugendzeit, aus der Jugendzeit klingt ein Lied mir immerdar

Friedrich Nietzsche, "Aus der Jugendzeit" 1862, NWV8

Blicke mir nicht in die Lieder!

Gustav Mahler, "Blicke mir nicht in die Lieder" 1901, 1v.orch(pf)

Blüth' oder Schnee! Lust oder Weh!
Robert Schumann, "Blüth' oder Schnee!" 1847, Op65,3, 3ten.ttbb
from *Ritornelle in canonischen Weisen*

Da ich dich einmal gefunden, kann ich dich nicht mehr verlieren
Adolf Jensen, "Da ich dich einmal gefunden" 1863pub, Op13,1, 1v(low).pf
Wilhelm Kienzl, "II. Aus dem I. Strauss: *Erwacht.*" 187-?, Op11,2
from *Liebesfrühling*

Das ganze, nicht das einzelne
Paul Hindemith, "Das ganze, nicht das einzelne" 1933

Das war die Schlacht von Waterloo, die Schlacht von Bellalliangs
Carl Loewe, "Der Papagei" 1847, Op111

Daß der Ostwind Düfte hauchet in die Lüfte
Franz Schubert, "Dass sie hier gewesen" 1822-23, D775
Giacomo Meyerbeer, "Sie und ich" 1835

Der alte Barbarosse, der Kaiser Friederich
Friedrich Silcher, "Barbarossa" 4v

Der Frost hat mir bereifet des Hauses Dach
Franz Schubert, "Greisengesang" 1822, D778
Richard Strauss, "Vom künftigen Alter" 1929, (Op87,1), bass.pf

Der Himmel hat eine Thräne geweint
Robert Schumann, "Der Himmel hat eine Thräne geweint" 1840, Op37,1
from *12 Gedichte aus Rückert's "Liebesfrühling"*
Robert Franz, "Die Perle" 1878, Op48,4
Max Reger, "Der Himmel hat eine Träne geweint" 1899, Op35,2, 1v(med).pf

Der Schiffer fährt zu Land
Friedrich Curschmann, "Der Schiffer fährt zu Land" 1837, Op15,3

Der Schnee, der gestern noch in Flöckchen
Robert Schumann, "Schneeglöckchen" 1849, Op79,26
from *Lieder-Album für die Jugend*

Die Fahnen flattern im Mitternachtssturm
Richard Strauss, "Nächtlicher Gang" 1899, Op44,2, bar(high).orch

Die gute Nacht, die ich dir sage, Freund hörest du!
Clara Schumann, "Die gute Nacht, die ich dir sage" 1841
Robert Schumann, "Gute Nacht" 1846, Op59,4, sop.satb
Wilhelm Kienzl, "V. Aus dem IV. Strauss: *Wiedergewonnen.*" 187-?, Op11,5
from *Liebesfrühling*

Die Liebste fragt, warum ich liebe?
Arno Kleffel, "Die Liebste fragt, warum ich liebe?" Op14,2

Die Liebste steht mir vor den Gedanken
Richard Strauss, "Anbetung" 1898, Op36,4

Die mich hält am Fädchen
Carl Loewe, "Kind und Mädchen" 1837, Op62,ii,5

Die Rose stand im Thau, es waren Perlen grau
Robert Schumann, "Die Rose stand im Thau" 1847, Op65,1, ttbbb
from *Ritornelle in canonischen Weisen*

Die Stunde sei gesegnet, wo ich dir bin begegnet
Frank van der Stucken, "Die Stunde sei gesegnet" 1892?pub, Op16,2
from *Fünf Liebeslieder*

Die tausend Grüsse, die wir dir senden
Robert Schumann, "Duett" 1849, Op101,7, sop.ten.pf
from *Minnespiel aus Rückert's Liebesfrühling*

Dort, wo der Morgenstern hergeht
Richard Strauss, "Morgenrot" 1900, Op46,4

Du bist die Ruh, der Friede mild
Franz Schubert, "Du bist die Ruh" 1823, D776
Friedrich Curschmann, "Ruhe der Liebe" 1837, Op16,2,i
Fanny Hensel, "Du bist die Ruh" 1848pub, Op7,4

Du meine Seele, du mein Herz
Robert Schumann, "Widmung" 1840, Op25,1
from *Liederkreis*

Durch schöne Augen hab' ich in ein schönes Herz geschaut
Robert Franz, "Vom Auge zum Herzen" 1870?pub, Op26,5

Eia, wie flattert der Kranz
Robert Schumann, "Tanzlied" 1849, Op78,1, sop.ten.pf

Ein Licht im Traum hat mich besucht
Carl Loewe, "Traumlicht" 1842

Ein Liebchen hatt' ich, das auf einem Aug' schielte
Carl Loewe, "Hinkende Jamben" 1837, Op62,i,5

Ein Obdach gegen Sturm und Regen
Robert Kahn, "Obdach der Liebe" 188-?, Op6,5
Richard Strauss, "Ein Obdach gegen Sturm und Regen" 1900, Op46,1

Einen Haushalt klein und fein hab' ich angestellt
Carl Loewe, "Kleiner Haushalt" 1838-39, Op71

Einförmig ist der Liebe Gram
Johannes Brahms, "Einförmig ist der Liebe Gram" 1891pub, Op113,13, 4s2a
from *13 Kanons für Frauenstimmen*

Er ist gekommen in Sturm und Regen, ihm schlug beklommen mein Herz entgegen
Clara Schumann, "Er ist gekommen in Sturm und Regen" 1840, Op12,2
from *12 Gedichte aus Rückert's "Liebesfrühling"*
Robert Franz, "Er ist gekommen" 1845pub, Op4,7
Wilhelm Kienzl, "III. Aus dem II. Strauss: *Entflohen.*" 187-?, Op11,3
from *Liebesfrühling*

Es ging die Riesentochter, zu haben einen Spass
Carl Loewe, "Die Riesen und die Zwerge" 1837

Es läuft ein fremdes Kind am Abend vor Weihnachten
Carl Loewe, "Des fremden Kindes heiliger Christ" 1834, Op33,3

Fahr wohl, o Vöglein, das nun wandern soll
Johannes Brahms, "Fahr wohl!" 1883?, Op93a,4, satb

Flügel! Flügel! um zu fliegen über Berg und Thal
Robert Schumann, "Flügel! Flügel! um zu fliegen" 1840, Op37,8
from *12 Gedichte aus Rückert's "Liebesfrühling"*

Gebt mir zu trinken! Was in den Sternen steht
Robert Schumann, "Gebt mir zu trinken!" 1847, Op65,4, bbb
from *Ritornelle in canonischen Weisen*

Gestern war ich Atlas, der den Himmel trug
Richard Strauss, "Gestern war ich Atlas" 1899, Op46,2

Grün ist der Jasminenstrauch Abends eingeschlafen
Robert Schumann, "Jasminenstrauch" 1840, Op27,4

Herr! Herr, der du alles wohl gemacht
Carl Loewe, "Jünglings Gebet" 1859

Herr Pfarrer hat zwei Fräulchen
Carl Loewe, "Das Pfarrjüngferchen" 1837, Op62,ii,4

Herz, nun so alt und noch immer nicht klug
Hans Pfitzner, "Herbsthauch" 1921, Op29,2

Hier bring' ich dir ein Blümchen
Friedrich Curschmann, "Huldigung" 1838, Op18,4

Hier in diesen erdbeklommnen Lüften
Robert Schumann, "Zum Schluss" 1840, Op25,26
from *Liederkreis*

Hoher Berge Schatten liegen auf dem Meer
Modest Mussorgsky, "Hoher Berge Schatten liegen auf dem Meer" (set in Russian), 1878

Hüttelein, still und klein, blinke sanft im Sternenschein
Friedrich Curschmann, "Ständchen" 1838, Op18,3
Robert Franz, "Ständchen" 1846pub, Op7,2

Ich atmet' einen Linden Duft
Gustav Mahler, "Ich atmet' einen Linden Duft" 1901, 1v.orch(pf)

Ich bin dein Baum, o Gärtner
Robert Schumann, "Duett" 1849, Op101,3, alt.bass.pf
from *Minnespiel aus Rückert's Liebesfrühling*

Ich bin der Welt abhanden gekommen
Gustav Mahler, "Ich bin der Welt abhanden gekommen" 1901, 1v.orch(pf)

Ich bin die Blum' im Garten
Carl Loewe, "Die Blume der Ergebung" 1837, Op62,ii,6
Robert Schumann, "Die Blume der Ergebung" 1850, Op83,2

Ich hab' in deinem Auge den Strahl der ewigen Liebe gesehen
Robert Franz, "Ich hab' in Deinem Auge" 1846pub, Op5,6
Clara Schumann, "Ich hab' in deinem Auge" 1843, Op13,5

Ich hab' in mich gesogen den Frühling treu und lieb
Robert Schumann, "Ich hab' in mich gesogen" 1840, Op37,5
from *12 Gedichte aus Rückert's "Liebesfrühling"*
Robert Franz, "Liebesfrühling" 1879, Op50,6

Ich habe dich mit Rosen so zugedeckt
August Bungert, "Auf ein Grab" 1889-91pub, Op32,3
from *Verlorne Liebe, verlornes Leben*

Ich lag von sanftem Traum umflossen, und fühlte selig mich in dir
Wilhelm Kienzl, "VI. Aus dem IV. Strauss: *Wiedergewonnen.*" 187-?, Op11,6
from *Liebesfrühling*

Ich liebe dich, weil ich dich lieben muß
Franz Liszt, "Ich liebe dich" 1862
Leopold Damrosch, "Ich liebe dich!" Op8,1
Ernst Bacon, "Ich liebe Dich" 1928pub

Ich sah sie nur ein einzigmal
Richard Strauss, "Und dann nicht mehr" 1929, (Op87,3), bass.pf

Ich sehe wie in einem Spiegel
Richard Strauss, "Ich sehe wie in einem Spiegel" 1900, Op46,5

Ich sende einen Gruss wie Duft der Rosen
Robert Schumann, "Aus den östlichen Rosen" 1840, Op25,25
from *Liederkreis*
August Bungert, "Sweets to the sweet!" 1891pub, Op26,1
Bungert attributes the title to *Romeo und Julie*. It is, of course, from *Hamlet.*
from *An eine schöne Frau: Liebesbriefe in Liedern*

Ich stand auf Berges Halde, als heim die Sonne ging
Carl Loewe, "Abendlied" 1837, Op62,ii,1

Ich weiß nicht, was im Hain die Taube girret
Johannes Brahms, "Ich weiß nicht" 1859-63, Op113,11, 4fv
from *13 Kanons für Frauenstimmen*

Ich will die Fluren meiden
Alban Berg, "Ich will die Fluren meiden" 1903

In Basra eine Wittwe war mit ihren beiden Söhnen
Carl Loewe, "Der Traum der Wittwe" 1860, Op142

In diesem Wetter, in diesem Braus
Gustav Mahler, "In diesem Wetter, in diesem Braus" 1901-04, 1v.orch(pf)
from *Kindertotenlieder*

In goldnen Abendschein getauchet
Johannes Brahms, "Gestillte Sehnsucht" 1884?, Op91,1, alt.vla.pf

In Meeres Mitten ist ein offner Laden
Robert Schumann, "In Meeres Mitten ist ein offner Laden" 1847, Op65,7, ttbb
from *Ritornelle in canonischen Weisen*
Robert Schumann, "In Meeres Mitten" 1849, Op91,6, 3sop.3alt.pf
from *Romanzen für Frauenstimmen II*

In Sommertagen rüste den Schlitten
Robert Schumann, "In Sommertagen" 1847, Op65,6, ttbb
from *Ritornelle in canonischen Weisen*

Irrlichter, die Knaben, die laufen und traben
Carl Loewe, "Irrlichter" 1837, Op62,i,6

Jugend, Rausch und Liebe sind gleich drei schönen Frühlingstagen
Peter Cornelius, "Die drei Frühlingstage" 1871, Op11,3, ssattb

Jungfräulein Annika sass an dem Brückenrande
Carl Loewe, "Jungfräulein Annika" 1839, Op78,1

Komm, verhüllte Schöne! Komm! aus deinem Haus
Wilhelm Kienzl, "IV. Aus dem III. Strauss: *Entfremdet.*" 187-?, Op11,4
from *Liebesfrühling*
Thorvald Otterström, "Ständchen" 1907pub
from *Neun Lieder* (7)

Lachen und Weinen zu jeglicher Stunde
Franz Schubert, "Lachen und Weinen" 1822-23?, D777

Lass mich ihm am Busen hangen, Mutter, Mutter!
Robert Schumann, "Lieder der Braut II" 1840, Op25,12
from *Liederkreis*

Lasst Lautenspiel und Becherklang nicht rasten
Robert Schumann, "Lasst Lautenspiel und Becherklang nicht rasten" 1847, Op65,2, bbb
from *Ritornelle in canonischen Weisen*

Leb' wohl und sehen wir uns wieder
Robert Franz, "Wiedersehen" 1879, Op51,8

Leise Töne der Brust, geweckt vom Odem der Liebe
Johannes Brahms, "Leise Töne der Brust" 1859-63, Op113,10, 4fv
from *13 Kanons für Frauenstimmen*
Johannes Brahms, "Nachtwache Nr.1" 1888-?, Op104,1, saatbb

Liebst du um Schönheit, o nicht mich liebe!
Clara Schumann, "Liebst du um Schönheit" 1840, Op12,4
from *12 Gedichte aus Rückert's "Liebesfrühling"*
Gustav Mahler, "Liebst du um Schönheit" 1902, 1v.orch(pf)

Liebste! nur dich seh'n, dich hören
Frank van der Stucken, "Liebste! nur dich seh'n" 1892?pub, Op16,4
from *Fünf Liebeslieder*

Liebste, was kann denn uns scheiden?
Robert Schumann, "Liebste, was kann denn uns scheiden?" 1840, Op37,6
from *12 Gedichte aus Rückert's "Liebesfrühling"*

Liebster, deine Worte stehlen aus dem Busen mir das Herz
Robert Schumann, "Gesang" 1849, Op101,2, sop.pf
from *Minnespiel aus Rückert's Liebesfrühling*

Mächtiger, der du die Wipfel dir beugst
Carl Loewe, "Dem Allmächtigen" 1840?
Peter Cornelius, "An den Sturmwind" 1871, Op11,2, 2(satb)

Mein Gemüthe blühte gleich der frischen Maienrose
Carl Loewe, "Die Herzensrose" 1859, Op130,2
after Goethe's *Neugriechische Liebe-Skolien*, "Von der Rose..."

Mein hochgeborenes Schätzelein, des Glockenthürmers Töchterlein
Carl Loewe, "Des Glockenthürmers Töchterlein" 1850, Op112A

Mein schöner Stern! ich bitte dich
Robert Schumann, "Lied" 1849, Op101,4, ten.pf
from *Minnespiel aus Rückert's Liebesfrühling*

Meine Töne still und heiter
Robert Schumann, "Lied" 1849, Op101,1, ten.pf
from *Minnespiel aus Rückert's Liebesfrühling*

Meine Tränen im Bußgewand
Franz Schubert, "Die Wallfahrt" 1822?, D2:778A

Mich hat der Herbst betrogen
Max Reger, "Winterahnung" 1891, Op4,3, 1v(med).pf

Mir ist, nun ich dich habe, als müßt ich sterben
Wilhelm Kienzl, "VII. Aus dem V. Strauss: *Verbunden.*" 187-?, Op11,7
from *Liebesfrühling*
Max Reger, "Widmung" 1891, Op4,2, 1v(med).pf
Frank van der Stucken, "Mir ist, nun ich dich habe" 1892?pub, Op16,3
from *Fünf Liebeslieder*
Léander Schlegel, "Mir ist, nun ich Dich habe" 1900, Op20,7
from *Deutsche Liebeslieder*

Mit vierzig Jahren ist der Berg erstiegen
Johannes Brahms, "Mit vierzig Jahren" 1883/84, Op94,1, 1v(low).pf

Mutter, Mutter! glaube nicht
Robert Schumann, "Lieder der Braut I" 1840, Op25,11
from *Liederkreis*

Noch eine Stunde laßt mich hier
Richard Strauss, "Im Sonnenschein" 1935, (Op87,4), bass.pf

Nun seh' ich wohl, warum so dunkle Flammen
Gustav Mahler, "Nun seh' ich wohl, warum so dunkle Flammen" 1901-04, 1v.orch(pf)
from *Kindertotenlieder*

Nun will die Sonn' so hell aufgeh'n
Gustav Mahler, "Nun will die Sonn' so hell aufgeh'n" 1901-04, 1v.orch(pf)
from *Kindertotenlieder*

O blicke, wenn den Sinn dir will die Welt verwirren
Robert Schumann, "Spruch" 1853, Op114,3, 3fv.pf

O du Entriss'ne mir und meinem Kusse!
Franz Schubert, "Sei mir gegrüsst" 1822, D741

O Freund, mein Schirm, mein Schutz
Robert Schumann, "Lied" 1849, Op101,6, alt(sop).pf
from *Minnespiel aus Rückert's Liebesfrühling*

O ihr Herren, o ihr werthen grossen reichen Herren all'!
Robert Schumann, "O ihr Herren" 1840, Op37,3
from *12 Gedichte aus Rückert's "Liebesfrühling"*

O Mutter, wie stürmen die Flocken vom Himmel
Carl Loewe, "Die Gottesmauer" 1850, Op140

O Sonn', o Meer, o Rose! Wie wenn die Sonne triumphirend
Robert Schumann, "O Sonn', o Meer, o Rose!" 1840, Op37,10
from *12 Gedichte aus Rückert's "Liebesfrühling"*

O süsse Mutter, ich kann nicht spinnen
Carl Loewe, "O süsse Mutter" 1837, Op62,i,3

Hugo Wolf, "Die Spinnerin" 1878
from *Sechs Lieder für eine Frauenstimme*

Oft denk' ich, sie sind nur ausgegangen!
Gustav Mahler, "Oft denk' ich, sie sind nur ausgegangen!" 1901-04, 1v.orch(pf)
from *Kindertotenlieder*

Oh weh des Scheidens, das er tat, da er mich ließ im Sehnen
Clara Schumann, "Oh weh des Scheidens, das er tat" 1843

Rose, Meer, und Sonne sind ein Bild der Liebsten mein
Robert Schumann, "Rose, Meer, und Sonne" 1840, Op37,9
from *12 Gedichte aus Rückert's "Liebesfrühling"*

Rosen! Ein Zypressenhain, alte Brunnen fließen
Alban Berg, "Ferne Lieder" 1903

Ruhn sie? Ruhn sie? rufet das Horn des Wächters drüben aus Westen
Johannes Brahms, "Nachtwache Nr.2" 1888-?, Op104,2, saatbb

Sage nicht, ich sei dein Leben, ich will deine Seele sein
Leopold Damrosch, "Dein auf ewig" Op8,11

Schäferin, ach, wie haben sie dich so süss begraben
Carl Loewe, "Süsses Begräbnis" 1837, Op62,i,4

Schön ist das Fest des Lenzes
Robert Schumann, "Schön ist das Fest des Lenzes" 1840, Op37,7
from *12 Gedichte aus Rückert's "Liebesfrühling"*
Robert Schumann, "Quartett" 1849, Op101,5, satb.pf
from *Minnespiel aus Rückert's Liebesfrühling*

Sei bescheiden, nimm fürliebe
Carl Loewe, "Bescheidung" 1837, Op62,i,2

Seinen Traum, Lind' wob, Frühling kaum, Wind schnob
Robert Schumann, "Sommerlied" 1849, Op146,4, satb

So lang ich werde: "Liebst du mich, o Liebster"
Joseph Marx, "Frage und Antwort" 1909, sop.pf

So oft der Herbst die Rosen stahl
Oscar Weil, "Herbstfrühlingslied" 1888pub, Op10,1, sop.vn.pf

So wahr die Sonne scheinet, so wahr die Flamme sprüht
Johanna Kinkel, "So wahr die Sonne scheinet" Op10,3
Robert Schumann, "So wahr die Sonne scheinet" 1840, Op37,12
from *12 Gedichte aus Rückert's "Liebesfrühling"*
Robert Schumann, "Quartett" 1849, Op101,8, satb.pf
from *Minnespiel aus Rückert's Liebesfrühling*
Wilhelm Kienzl, "I. Aus dem I. Strauss: *Erwacht.*" 187-?, Op11,1
from *Liebesfrühling*
Hugo Wolf, "So wahr die Sonne scheinet" 1878

Stern, in des Himmels Ferne!
Robert Schumann, "An die Sterne" 1849, Op141,1, 2ch(satb).pf
from *Vier doppelchörige Gesänge*

Um Mitternacht hab' ich gewacht und aufgeblickt zum Himmel
Gustav Mahler, "Um Mitternacht" 1901, 1v.orch(pf)

Verwelkte Blume, Menschenkind
Josef Bohuslav Foerster, "Auf das letzte Blatt meiner Lieder" 1909pub, Op67,20

Wär' ich der gold'ne Sonnenschein
Arno Kleffel, "Wär' ich der gold'ne Sonnenschein" Op12,1

Wann die Rosen aufgeblüht, geht der Lenz zu Ende
Frank van der Stucken, "Wann die Rosen aufgeblüht" 1892?pub, Op16,1
from *Fünf Liebeslieder*

Warum sind deine Augen denn so naß?
Hans Pfitzner, "Warum sind deine Augen denn so naß?" 1888/89, Op3,1, 1v(med).pf

Warum willst du and're fragen
Clara Schumann, "Warum willst du and're fragen" 1840, Op12,11
from *12 Gedichte aus Rückert's "Liebesfrühling"*

Was singt ihr und sagt ihr mir, Vögelein von Liebe?
Arno Kleffel, "Liebespredigt" Op14,3

Weil ich dich nicht legen kann
Richard Strauss, "Die sieben Siegel" 1899, Op46,3

Welche chaotische Haushälterei, welches erotische Tausenderlei
Carl Loewe, "Die Göttin im Putzzimmer" 1838-39, Op73

Wenn dein Mütterlein tritt zur Tür herein
Gustav Mahler, "Wenn dein Mütterlein" 1901-04, 1v.orch(pf)
from *Kindertotenlieder*

Wenn die Vöglein sich gepaart, dürfen sie gleich nisten
Frank van der Stucken, "Wenn die Vöglein sich gepaart" 1892?pub, Op16,5
from *Fünf Liebeslieder*

Wenn ich früh in den Garten geh'
Robert Schumann, "Volksliedchen" 1840, Op51,2

Wenn Kummer hätte zu töten
Johannes Brahms, "Wenn Kummer hätte zu töten" 1859-63, Op113,12, 3fv
from *13 Kanons für Frauenstimmen*

Wissen möcht' ich nur wie lange
Léander Schlegel, "Wissen möcht' ich nur wie lange" 1900, Op20,5
from *Deutsche Liebeslieder*

Wohl endet Tod des Lebens Not
Emil Mattiesen, "Stirb und werde" 190-?pub, Op15,3
translated from the Persian poet Dschelâl ed-dîn Rûmi
from *Überwindungen* (3)

Zeislein, Zeislein, Zeislein, wo ist dein Häuslein?
Carl Loewe, "Zeislein" 1837, Op62,i,1

Zittr', o Erde, dunkle Macht
Robert Schumann, "Freiheitslied" 1847, Op62,2, ttbb

Zu Rauch, zu Rauch muß werden der Erde Schmelz
Johannes Brahms, "Zu Rauch" 186-?, satb

Zürne nicht des Herbstes Wind
Robert Schumann, "Zürne nicht des Herbstes Wind" 1847, Op65,5, ttbb
from *Ritornelle in canonischen Weisen*

Zwei wunderliche Gevattern, die immer mit 'nander flattern
Carl Loewe, "Ich und mein Gevatter" 1837, Op62,ii,3

Armin Rüeger
Es gehen zur Kirche die Leute
Othmar Schoeck, "Bei der Kirche" 1905, Op7,1

Georg Ernst von Rüling (1748-1807)
Dich soll mein Lied erheben
Carl Loewe, "Dich soll mein Lied erheben" 1832

Weine nicht; es ist der Sieg erkämpfet
Martin Ruprecht, "Werthers Geist an Lotte" 1785?

Phillip Otto Runge (1777-1810)
Es blüht eine schöne Blume in einem weiten Land
Louise Reichardt, "Die Blume der Blumen" 1819pub

Johann Baptist Rupprecht (1776-1846)
Merkenstein! Wo ich wandle denk' ich dein
Ludwig van Beethoven, "Merkenstein" 1814, WoO144
Ludwig van Beethoven, "Merkenstein" 1814, WoO100, 2v.pf

Ferdinand von Saar (1833-1906)
Des Tages laute Stimmen schweigen
Franz Liszt, "Des Tages laute Stimmen schweigen" 1880

Lang war die Nacht; wie auf stygischem Nachen
Franz Schreker, "Stimmen des Tages" 1901+, Op2,2

Über kahle, fahle Hügel streicht der Dämmrung kühler Flügel
Robert Gund, "Landschaft im Spätherbst" 1900pub, Op29,1

Th. von Sacken
Lerche steiget im Gesang
Anton Rubinstein, "Die Lerche" 1856, Op33,3

Edith von Salburg-Falkenstein (1868-1942)
Heiliges Rätsel, ewige Macht
Robert Fischhof, "Hymne" 1914cop

Johann Gaudenz von Salis-Seewis (1762-1834)
Abendglockenhalle zittern dumpf durch Moorgedüfte hin
Franz Schubert, "Der Herbstabend" 1816, D405
Johann Vesque von Püttlingen, "Der Herbstabend" 1831?, Op8,2

Arbeitsam und wacker, pflügen wir den Acker, singend auf und ab
Franz Schubert, "Pflügerlied" 1816, D392

Auf! es dunkelt; silbern funkelt dort der Mond ob Tannenhöhn!
Louis Spohr, "Lied beim Rundetanz" 1816, Op37,6
Franz Schubert, "Zum Rundtanz" 1823pub, D983,3, 2t2b

Bunt sind schon die Wälder, gelb die Stoppelfelder
Franz Schubert, "Herbstlied" 1816, D502

Das Fischergewerbe giebt rüstigen Muth!
Franz Schubert, "Fischerlied (1)" 1816?, D351
Franz Schubert, "Fischerlied (2)" 1817, D562

Franz Schubert, "Fischerlied" 1816?, D364, 2t2b
Carl Loewe, "Das Fischergewerbe" before 1826

Das Grab ist tief und stille, und schauderhaft sein Rand
Johann Rudolf Zumsteeg, "Das Grab" 1802pub
from *Kleine Balladen und Lieder, viertes Heft*
Franz Schubert, "Das Grab (1)" 1815, D330, ch.pf
Franz Schubert, "Das Grab (2)" 1816, D377, 2t2b.pf
Franz Schubert, "Das Grab (3)" 1817, D569, unis(mch).pf
Franz Schubert, "Das Grab (4)" 1819, D2:643A, satb.pf

Es rieselt, klar und wehend, ein Quell im Eichenwald
Franz Schubert, "Die Einsiedelei" 1816?, D337, 2t2b
Franz Schubert, "Die Einsiedelei (1)" 1816, D393
Franz Schubert, "Die Einsiedelei (2)" 1817, D563

In's stille Land! Wer leitet uns hinüber?
Franz Schubert, "Lied" 1816, D403
Jan Bedřich Kittl, "In's stille Land!" 183-?, Op4,6

Leise, rieselnder Quell, ihr wallenden, flispernden Pappeln
Franz Schubert, "Der Jüngling an der Quelle" 1821, D300

Mit leisen Harfentönen sei, Wehmut, mir gegrüsst!
Franz Schubert, "Die Herbstnacht (Die Wehmuth)" 1816, D404

Noch einmal tön', o Harfe, die nur Gefühlte tönt
Franz Schubert, "Abschied von der Harfe" 1816, D406

Schöpferin beseelter Töne! Nachklang dem Olymp enthallt!
Franz Schubert, "Gesang an die Harmonie" 1816, D394

Seht wie die Tage sich sonnig verklären
Johann Friedrich Reichardt, "Seht wie die Tage sich sonnig verklären" 1800pub
from *Lieder aus dem Liederspiel, Lieb' und Treue* (11)
Johann Rudolf Zumsteeg, "Ermunterung" 1801pub
from *Kleine Balladen und Lieder, drittes Heft*

Wann, o Schicksal, wann wird endlich
Johann Friedrich Reichardt, "Wann, o Schicksal, wann wird endlich" 1800pub
from *Lieder aus dem Liederspiel, Lieb' und Treue* (5)

Wie schön ist's im Freien, bei grünenden Maien
Franz Schubert, "Lied im Freien" 1817, D572, 2t2b

Wohl denk' ich allenthalben, o du Entfernte, dein!
Franz Schubert, "Der Entfernten" 1816?, D331, 2t2b
Franz Schubert, "Der Entfernten" 1816, D350

Friedrich von Sallet (1812-1843)

Die Knospe träumte von Sonnenschein
Richard Strauss, "Die erwachte Rose" 1880

Durch die Wälder streif' ich munter
Hans Pfitzner, "Herbstlied" 1888/89, Op3,2, 1v(med).pf

Hugo Salus (1866-1929)
König ist spazieren gangen
Arnold Schönberg, “Einfältiges Lied” 1901?
from *Brettl-Lieder*

Meine Freundin hat eine schwarze Katze
Arnold Schönberg, “Der genügsame Liebhaber” 1901?
from *Brettl-Lieder*

Sao-han
Der Mond steigt aufwärts, ein verliebter Träumer
Joseph Marx, “Ein junger Dichter denkt an die Geliebte” 1909, 1v(med).pf
translated from the Chinese

Sappho (fl.600 BC)
Goldenthronend, ewige Aphrodite
Carl Loewe, “An Aphrodite” 1835, Op9,ix,4
translated by Carl von Blankensee. Loewe’s setting includes the Greek.

D. Saul [possibly Daniel Johannes Saul (1854-1903)]
Noch immer halt’ ich dich umfaßt
Max Reger, “Scheiden” 1894, Op15,6, 1v(med).pf

Tausend goldne Sterne, glänzen an des Abendhimmels Pracht
Max Reger, “Sommernacht” 1894, Op14,3, sop.alt.pf

Wo du triffst ein Mündlein hold
Max Reger, “Leichtsinniger Rat” 1894, Op15,8, 1v(med).pf

Samuel Friedrich Sauter (1766-1846)
Ach mir schallt’s dorten so lieblich hervor: Fürchte Gott!
Ludwig van Beethoven, “Der Wachtelschlag” 1803, WoO129
Franz Schubert, “Der Wachtelschlag” 1822?, D742

Geiger und Pfeifer, hier habt ihr Geld darauf
Carl Maria von Weber, “Schwäbisches Tanzlied” 1812, J.135, sttb.(pf)

Adolf Friedrich, Graf von Schack (1815-1894)
Breit’ über mein Haupt dein schwarzes Haar
Richard Strauss, “Breit’ über mein Haupt…” 1887-88, Op19,2

Dem Herzen ähnlich, wenn es lang
Richard Strauss, “Aus den Liedern der Trauer” 1886, Op15,4, 1v(med).pf

Du frag’st mich, Mädchen, was flüsternd der West
Richard Strauss, “Das Geheimnis” 1887, Op17,3

Hoffen und wieder verzagen
Richard Strauss, “Hoffen und wieder verzagen” 1887-88, Op19,5

Lass’ das Zagen, trage mutig deine Sorgen, deine Qual
Richard Strauss, “Nur Mut!” 1887, Op17,5

Leise, um dich nicht zu wecken
Johannes Brahms, “Serenade” 1871, Op58,8

Leiser schwanken die Äste, der Kahn fliegt uferwärts
Richard Strauss, “Heimkehr” 1886, Op15,5, 1v(med).pf

Mach' auf, mach' auf, doch leise, mein Kind
Hans Pfitzner, "Ständchen" 1884-86?
Richard Strauss, "Ständchen" 1887, Op17,2
Robert Kahn, "Ständchen" 1891, Op12,2

Mein Herz ist stumm, mein Herz ist kalt
Richard Strauss, "Mein Herz ist stumm…" 1887-88, Op19,6

Mit Regen und Sturmgebrause sei mir wilkommen, Dezembermond
Richard Strauss, "Winternacht" 1886, Op15,2, 1v(med).pf

O schmäht des Lebens Leiden nicht!
Richard Strauss, "Lob des Leidens" 1886, Op15,3, 1v(med).pf

Schön sind, doch kalt die Himmelssterne
Richard Strauss, "Schön sind, doch kalt die Himmelssterne" 1887-88, Op19,3

Sei willkommen, Zwielichtstunde!
Johannes Brahms, "Abenddämmerung" 1868, Op49,5

Seitdem dein Aug' in meines schaute
Richard Strauss, "Seitdem dein Aug' in meines schaute" 1887, Op17,1

Um der fallenden Ruder Spitzen
Richard Strauss, "Barkarole" 1887, Op17,6
Joseph Marx, "Barkarole" 1909

Von dunklem Schleier umsponnen
Richard Strauss, "Aus den Liedern der Trauer" 1887, Op17,4

Wie sollten wir geheim sie halten
Richard Strauss, "Wie sollten wir gchcim sic halten" 1887-88, Op19,4

Wie wenn im frostgen Windhauch tötlich
Johannes Brahms, "Herbstgefühl" 1868, Op48,7

Wozu noch, Mädchen, soll es frommen
Richard Strauss, "Wozu noch, Mädchen…" 1887-88, Op19,1

Christian Konrad Schad (1821-1871)

Sommerruh, wie schön bist du!
Robert Schumann, "Sommerruh" 1849, sop.alt.pf

Karl (Leonhard) Schaefer (1849-1915)

Kein Laut erschallt im öden Wald. Die Blätter sind gefallen
Adolph Martin Foerster, "Herbstblätter" 1897, Op42,1

Mädchen, sieh', der Lenz ist da!
Adolph Martin Foerster, "Das Lenz ist da!" 1909, Op57,6

Mädchen, was trauerst du? Lass dir was sagen
Adolph Martin Foerster, "Vorschlag" 1908, Op53,8

Müde labend naht der Abend. Mühvoll ist der Tag vollbracht
Adolph Martin Foerster, "Ein Abendlied" 1911, Op76,3

Theo Schäfer (1872-?)

Eine stille Melodie, voll von süßer Lust
Max Reger, "Erinnerung" 1906-07, Op79c,iii,2

Es blüht um mich des Abends Stille
Max Reger, "Abend" 1903, Op79c,i,1

Friedrich Schäffer (1772-1800)
Freunde, sammelt Euch im Kreise
Franz Schubert, "Trinklied" 1813, D75, bass.2t2b.pf

Johann Eberhard Friedrich Schall (1742-1790)
Es war einmal, ihr Leutchen
Wolfgang Amadeus Mozart, "Des kleinen Friedrichs Geburtstag" 1787, K529

Josef Schanderl (1874-1959?)
Ein stilles Wiesental von Schwalben überflogen
Rudi Stephan, "Pappel im Strahl" 1913

J. Schantz
Horch! Rossgestampf! Muss in den Kampf, in Schlachtensturm
Frederic Louis Ritter, "Kriegertod" 1871pub, Op6,6

L. Scharrer
Zersplittert lag des Schiffes Mast
Johann Wenzeslaus Kalliwoda, "Des Lotsen Rückkehr" 1842/43, Op113,3

Schatz
Hier ein Weilchen, dort ein Weilchen!
Max Reger, "Der gute Rat" 1906, Op98,2, 1v(med).pf

Richard von Schaukal (1874-1942)
Als der Gesandte schied, ging meine Königin
Otto Ball, "Der Gesandte" 1912pub, Op4

Ein schwarzer Ritter, Herrin, hält im Burghof mit verhüllter Miene
Karl Lafite, "Meldung" 1911cop

Ein Spielmann auf seiner Geige strich
Erich Zeisl, "Der Fiedler" 1936pub

Halte mir einer von euch Laffen mein Pferd
Otto Ball, "Porträt des Marquis de ..." 1911pub, Op4,2

Ich sah dich nachts am Fenster stehn und weinen
Theodor Streicher, "An Fanny" 1910pub

Nun ist die Nacht gekommen mit sanftem Schritt
Theodor Streicher, "Der Nachen" 1910pub

Vergißmeinnicht hab' ich im Fichtenwald gepflückt
Erich Zeisl, "Vergiss mein micht" 1936pub

(Gottlob) Leopold (Immanuel) Schefer (1784-1862)
Ich habe mich neben die Welt gesetzt in meine Rosenlaube
August Bungert, "Die Rosenlaube" 1889-91pub, Op33,3

Joseph Viktor von Scheffel (1826-1886)
Als wir mit deutschen Klingen geführt manch guten Streich
Franz Liszt, "Wolfram von Eschenbach" 1872, bar.ch.pf
from *Wartburglieder* (1)

Alt Heidelberg, du feine, du Stadt an Ehrenreich
Adolf Jensen, "Alt Heidelberg, du feine" 1867, Op34

Am grünen See von Nemi ein alter Ahorn steht
George Henschel, "Am grünen See von Nemi" 187-?, Op25,8

Am Ufer blies ich ein lustig Stück
Josefine Lang, "Lied des jungen Werner" 1870-71, Op45,2

An dem Ende seiner Tage steht der Kater Hiddigeigei
Josefine Lang, "Lied des Katers Hiddegeigei" 1870-71, Op45,5

Beim Scheiden der Sonne erschimmert der Metilstein
Franz Liszt, "Walther von der Vogelweide" 1872, ten.pf
from *Wartburglieder* (3)

Berggipfel erglühen, Waldwipfel erblühen vom Lenzhauch geschwellt
Adolf Jensen, "Ausfahrt" 1870, Op40,1, bar.pf
from *Gaudeamus*

Das ist im Leben häßlich eingerichtet
Franz Abt, "Es hat nicht sollen sein" Op213,2
Erik Meyer-Helmund, "Es hat nicht sollen sein" 1886-88
Hans Pfitzner, "Lied Werners aus dem *Trompeter von Säckingen*" 1884-86?

Der Pfarrer von Assmannshausen sprach
Adolf Jensen, "Die Heimkehr" 1870, Op40,6, bar.pf
from *Gaudeamus*

Die Erde ist erschlossen, die Blumen sind entsprossen
Franz Liszt, "Anfang" 1872, satb.pf
from *Wartburglieder* (Anfangschor)

Die Sommernacht hat mir's angethan
George Henschel, "Die Sommernacht" 187-?, Op25,3

Hab ich geträumt? Klang hier nicht meine Laute?
Franz Liszt, "Heinrich von Ofterdingen" 1872, ten.pf
from *Wartburglieder* (2)

Heut' schwirren Schelmenlieder, niemand bleibt verschont!
Hugo Brückler, "Dem aufgehenden Mond" 187-?pub, Nachlass

Ich schreib allzeit nur wenig
Franz Liszt, "Der tugendhafte Schreiber" 1872, bar(bass).pf
from *Wartburglieder* (4)

Im heil'gen Land, im Wüstensand bin ich zu Feld gelegen
Franz von Holstein, "Biterolf's Thüringer Waldlied" 1871, Op27,2

Im schwarzen Wallfisch zu Ascalon
Adolf Jensen, "Altassyrisch" 1870, Op40,3, bar.pf
from *Gaudeamus*

Jetzt ist er hinaus in die weite Welt
Frank van der Stucken, "Margarethas Lied" 1904pub, Op29,1

Kampfmüd' und sonnverbrannt, fern an der Heiden Strand
Max Bruch, "Biterolf im Lager vor Akkon. (1190)" 1870pub, Op33,1
from *Vier Lieder von J. V. Scheffel*
Hugo Wolf, "Biterolf" 1886
from *Sechs Gedichte von Scheffel u.a.*

Lind duftig hält die Maiennacht jetzt Berg und Thal umfangen
Max Bruch, "Lind duftig hält die Maiennacht" 1870pub, Op33,4
from *Vier Lieder von J. V. Scheffel*

Nun schreit' ich aus dem Thore in's weite öde Feld
George Henschel, "Nun schreit' ich aus dem Thore" 187-?, Op25,6

Schweigsam treibt mein morscher Einbaum
Ignaz Brüll, "Am Traunsee" 186-?, Op5,iii,1
Hugo Brückler, "Auf dem See" 187-?pub, Nachlass

Schwingt euch auf, Posaunenchöre
Hugo Wolf, "Wächterlied auf der Wartburg" 1887
from *Sechs Gedichte von Scheffel u.a.*

Sonne taucht in Meeresfluthen, Himmel strahlt in letzten Gluthen
George Henschel, "Sonne taucht in Meeresfluthen" 187-?, Op25,5
Max Bruch, "Dein gedenk' ich, Margaretha" 1870pub, Op33,3
from *Vier Lieder von J. V. Scheffel*
Erik Meyer-Helmund, "Dein gedenk' ich, Margaretha" 1886-88
Wilhelm Kienzl, "Jung Werner's Lied" 189-?, Op32,1
Gustav Trautmann, "Margaretha" 1890?pub, Op2,5

Thüringens Wälder senden den Waidmann und den Schmied
Franz Liszt, "Biterolf und der Schmied von Ruhla" 1872, bar.pf
from *Wartburglieder* (5)

Wo liebende Herzen sich innig vermählt
Franz Liszt, "Reimar der Alte" 1872, ten.pf
from *Wartburglieder* (6)

Wohlauf ihr zieren Frauen, lasst euch noch einmal schauen
Max Bruch, "Altdeutscher Herbstreigen" 1870pub, Op33,2
from *Vier Lieder von J. V. Scheffel*

Johannes Scheffler ("Angelus Silesius") (1624-1677)
Ich will dich lieben, meine Krone!
Peter Cornelius, "Liebe II" 1872, Op18,2, saatbb

Liebe, die du mich zum Bilde deiner Gottheit hast gemacht
Peter Cornelius, "Liebe I (Liebe, dir ergeb' ich mich)" 1872, Op18,1, ssaattbb

Thron der Liebe, Stern der Güte!
Peter Cornelius, "Liebe III" 1872, Op18,3, ssaattbb

Ernst Ludwig Schellenberg (1883-1964)
Das machte dein stiller keuscher Blick
Max Reger, "Glück" 1904, Op76,16, 1v(med).pf
from *Schlichte Weisen, Band 2*

Der Igel, der Igel, der ist ein schlimmer Mann
Max Reger, "Der Igel" 1911-12, Op76,56, 1v(med).pf
from *Schlichte Weisen, Band 6, "Neun Kinderlieder"*

Eins, zwei, drei, eins, zwei, drei, was raschelt da im Heu?
Max Reger, "Mausefangen" 1911-12, Op76,58, 1v(med).pf
from *Schlichte Weisen, Band 6, "Neun Kinderlieder"*

Ich bin der König vom Morgenland
Max Reger, "Der König aus dem Morgenland" 1911-12, Op76,60, 1v(med).pf
from *Schlichte Weisen, Band 6, "Neun Kinderlieder"*

Ich bin ein Dieb geworden, ein bitterböser Dieb
Max Reger, "Der Dieb" 1906?

Maria sitzt am Rosenbusch und wiegt den Jesusknaben
Max Reger, "Maria am Rosenstrauch" 1915, Op142,3
from *Fünf neue Kinderlieder*

Mutter, liebe Mutter, komm rasch einmal her
Max Reger, "Furchthäschen" 1911-12, Op76,55, 1v(med).pf
from *Schlichte Weisen, Band 6, "Neun Kinderlieder"*

Oben in dem Birnenbaum sitzt ein Vögelein
Max Reger, "Zum Schlafen" 1911-12, Op76,59, 1v(med).pf
from *Schlichte Weisen, Band 6, "Neun Kinderlieder"*

Wenn hell die liebe Sonne lacht
Max Reger, "Schelmenliedchen" 1907, Op76,36, 1v(med).pf
from *Schlichte Weisen, Band 3*

Zwischen Mohn und Rittersporn
Max Reger, "Mittag" 1907, Op76,35, 1v(med).pf
from *Schlichte Weisen, Band 3*

(Gottlob Ferdinand) Max(imilian) Gottfried von Schenkendorf (1783-1817)

Ach, wer nimmt von meiner Seele
Johannes Brahms, "Todessehnen" 1878, Op86,6, 1v(low).pf

Es weht um mich Narzissenduft
Johannes Brahms, "Frühlingstrost" 1873, Op63,1

Fliegt nur aus, geliebte Tauben!
Johannes Brahms, "An die Tauben" 1873, Op63,4

Ihr wunderschönen Augenblicke
Johannes Brahms, "Erinnerung" 1873, Op63,2

Vöglein einsam in dem Bauer
Carl Maria von Weber, "Die gefangenen Sänger" 1816, Op47,1

Was schaust du mich so freundlich an
Johannes Brahms, "An ein Bild" 1873, Op63,3

Wer spenget auf dem stolzen Ross
Josefine Lang, "Dem Königs-Sohn" WoO

Christian Friedrich Scherenberg (1798-1881)

Eine Blume weiss ich, hegt die Erd' wider jede Wund!
Hermann Goetz, "Eine Blume weiss ich" 1862-63, Op19,1

O Lieb', o Lieb', du Wonnemeer!
Hermann Goetz, "O Lieb', o Lieb', du Wonnemeer!" 1862-63, Op19,2

Ernst Scherenberg (1839-1905)

Ach, noch so jung und schon so verblüht
Franz Schreker, "Ach, noch so jung..." 1900?, Op7,6

Als wollte Winterqual nicht enden
Franz Schreker, "Lenzzauber" 189-?, Op4,5

Der Adler lauscht auf seinem Horst
Carl Loewe, "Der Feind" 1850+?, Op145,2

Heimlich durch's Fenster kam er geflogen
Franz Schreker, "Rosengruss" 1900?, Op7,7

Georg Scherer (1824-1909)
Der Tag ist längst geschieden, und von dem Sternenzelt
Carl Reinecke, "Frieden der Nacht"
from *Kinderlieder*

Die Stunde sei gesegnet in Zeit und Ewigkeit
Carl Reinecke, "Erfüllung" Op81,5

Ich saß am Strand und hub an
Alban Berg, "Am Strand" 1905

Loser, leichter, luft'ger Wind, bist ein recht verwöhntes Kind
Carl Reinecke, "Intermezzo" Op81,3

Nun schwirren die Schwalben in Lüften
Carl Reinecke, "Hinein in das blühende Land" Op81,1

Georg Scheurlin (1802-1872)
Der Tannenbaum steht schweigend, einsam auf grauer Höh'
Richard Wagner, "Der Tannenbaum" 1838, WWV 50

Die Fenster sonnen, der Winter ist aus
Louis Spohr, "Frühlingslied" 1849, WoO117,3, 2sop.pf

Emanuel Schikaneder (1751-1812)
Seit ich so viele Weiber sah
Arnold Schönberg, "Aus dem Spiegel von Arkadien" 1901?
from *Brettl-Lieder*

(Johann Christoph) Friedrich von Schiller (1759-1805)
Ach aus dieses Thales Gründen
Ferdinand Ries, "Sehnsucht" 1811pub, Op35,4
Franz Schubert, "Sehnsucht (1)" 1813, D52
Franz Schubert, "Sehnsucht (2)" 1821?, D636

Am Abgrund leitet der schwindliche Steg
Carl Friedrich Zelter, "Berglied" 1804
Johann Friedrich Reichardt, "Berglied" 1809?pub

An der Quelle sass der Knabe, Blumen wand er sich zum Kranz
Johann Friedrich Reichardt, "Der Jüngling am Bache" 1809?pub
Franz Schubert, "Der Jüngling am Bache (1)" 1812, D30
Franz Schubert, "Der Jüngling am Bache (2)" 1815, D192
Franz Schubert, "Der Jüngling am Bache (3)" 1819, D638

Auf der Berge freien Höhen, in der Mittagssonne Schein
Johann Friedrich Reichardt, "Punschlied. Im Norden zu singen" 1809?pub, 1v
Franz Schubert, "Punschlied (Im Norden zu singen)" 1815, D253

Das edle Bild der Menschheit zu verhöhnen
Johann Friedrich Reichardt, "Das Mädchen von Orleans" 1809?pub

Dass du mein Auge wecktest zu diesem goldenen Lichte
  Richard Strauss, "Hymnus" 1897, Op33,3, 1v.orch

Dem dunkeln Schoß der heilgen Erde
  Johannes Brahms, "Dem dunkeln Schoß der heilgen Erde" 1880-?, satb

Der bessre Mensch tritt in die Welt mit fröhlichem Vertrauen
  Johann Friedrich Reichardt, "Licht und Wärme" 1809?pub

Der Eichwald brauset, die Wolken ziehn
  Carl Friedrich Zelter, "Das Mädchens Klage" 1799
  Johann Rudolf Zumsteeg, "Thekla" 1801pub
    from *Kleine Balladen und Lieder, drittes Heft*
  Franz Schubert, "Des Mädchens Klage (1)" 1811, D6
  Niklas von Krufft, "Des Mädchens Klage" 1812pub
  Franz Schubert, "Des Mädchens Klage (2)" 1815, D191
  Franz Schubert, "Des Mädchens Klage (3)" 1816, D389
  Fanny Hensel, "Der Eichwald brauset" 1826
  Mikhail Glinka, "Des Mädchens Klage " (set in Russian), 1834
    translated into Russian by Zhukovsky
  Felix Mendelssohn, "Des Mädchens Klage" 184-?, Nachlass

Dessen Fahne Donnerstürme wallte
  Franz Schubert, "Dessen Fahne Donnerstürme wallte" 1813, D58, ttb

Dreifach ist der Schritt der Zeit
  Franz Schubert, "Dreifach ist der Schritt der Zeit. Spruch des Konfuzius" 1813, D43, ttb
  Franz Schubert, "Dreifach ist der Schritt der Zeit, Spruch des Konfuzius" 1813, D69, 3v

Ein frommer Knecht war Fridolin
  Carl Loewe, "Der Gang nach dem Eisenhammer" 1829, Op17

Ein jugendlicher Maienschwung
  Franz Schubert, "Ein jugendlicher Maienschwung" 1813, D61, 3v

Es donnern die Höhen, es zittert der Steg
  Václav Jan Tomášek, "Alpenjäger" 1825-?
  Franz Liszt, "Der Alpenjäger" 1845
    from *Drei Lieder aus Schillers "Wilhelm Tell"*
  Franz Liszt, "Der Alpenjäger" 1860pub
    from *Drei Lieder aus Schillers "Wilhelm Tell"*

Es ist so angenehm, so süss, um einen lieben Mann zu spielen
  Franz Schubert, "Lied" 1815, D284
    Attribution to Schiller doubtful. Poem possibly by Karoline von Wolzogen.

Es lächelt der See, er ladet zum Bade
  Friedrich Curschmann, "Es lächelt der See" 183-?, Op2,4
  Franz Liszt, "Der Fischerknabe" 1845
    from *Drei Lieder aus Schillers "Wilhelm Tell"*
  Franz Liszt, "Der Fischerknabe" 1860pub
    from *Drei Lieder aus Schillers "Wilhelm Tell"*
  Leopold Damrosch, "Lied des Fischerknaben"
    from *Three Songs without Opus-number, by various authors* (2)

Es reden und träumen die Menschen viel
  Johann Friedrich Reichardt, "Hoffnung"
  Franz Schubert, "Hoffnung (1)" 1815, D251

Franz Schubert, "Hoffnung (2)" 1817?, D637

Freude! schöner Götterfunken, Tochter aus Elysium!
Johann Rudolf Zumsteeg, "An die Freude" 1803pub, 1v.ch.pf
from *Kleine Balladen und Lieder, sechstes Heft*
Franz Schubert, "An die Freude" 1815, D189

Frisch athmet des Morgens lebendiger Hauch
Franz Schubert, "Der Flüchtling" 1816, D402
Johann Rudolf Zumsteeg, "Morgenfantasie" 1803pub
from *Kleine Balladen und Lieder, fünftes Heft*
Franz Schubert, "Frisch athmet des Morgens lebendiger Hauch" 1813, D67, ttb

Hier strecket der wallende Pilger
Franz Schubert, "Hier strecket der wallende Pilger" 1813, D57, ttb

Hier umarmen sich getreue Gatten
Franz Schubert, "Hier umarmen sich getreue Gatten" 1813, D60, ttb

Hör' ich das Pförtchen nicht gehen? Hat nicht der Riegel geklirrt?
Johann Rudolf Zumsteeg, "Die Erwartung" 1800pub
from *Kleine Balladen und Lieder, zweites Heft*
Niklas von Krufft, "Die Erwartung" 1812pub
Franz Schubert, "Die Erwartung" 1816, D159

Horch, wie Murmeln des empörten Meeres
Franz Schubert, "Gruppe aus dem Tartarus" 1817, D583
Fartein Valen, "Horch wie Murmeln des empörten Meeres ('Gruppe aus dem Tartarus')" 1939, Op31,1

Ihr Matten, lebt wohl, ihr sonnigen Weiden!
Franz Liszt, "Der Hirt" 1845
from *Drei Lieder aus Schillers "Wilhelm Tell"*
Robert Schumann, "Des Sennen Abschied" 1849, Op79,22
from *Lieder-Album für die Jugend*
Franz Liszt, "Der Hirt" 1860pub
from *Drei Lieder aus Schillers "Wilhelm Tell"*

In einem Tal bei armen Hirt erschien mit jedem jungen Jahr
Johann Friedrich Reichardt, "Das Mädchen aus der Fremde"
Franz Schubert, "Das Mädchen aus der Fremde (1)" 1814, D117
Franz Schubert, "Das Mädchen aus der Fremde (2)" 1815, D252

Ist der holde Lenz erschienen? hat die Erde sich verjüngt?
Franz Schubert, "Klage der Ceres" 1815-16, D323

Laura, über diese Welt zu flüchten wähn' ich
Johann Friedrich Reichardt, "Die Entzükkung an Laura" 1809?pub
Franz Schubert, "Die Entzückung an Laura (1)" 1816, D390
Franz Schubert, "Die Entzückung an Laura (2)" (fragment), 1817, D577

Laura, Welt und Himmel weggeronnen
Johann Rudolf Zumsteeg, "Die Entzückung. An Laura" 1803pub
from *Kleine Balladen und Lieder, sechstes Heft*

Lebt wohl ihr Berge, ihr geliebten Triften
Johann Rudolf Zumsteeg, "Johanna" 1803pub
from *Kleine Balladen und Lieder, fünftes Heft*
Johann Friedrich Reichardt, "Erster Monolog der Johanna" 1809?pub

Liebe rauscht der Silberbach
Carl Loewe, "Liebe rauscht der Silberbach" 1817, 2disc.tb.pf
from *Canon-Kranz*
Franz Schubert, "Liebe" 1823pub, D983,2, 2t2b

Lieben Freunde! Es gab schön're Zeiten
Johann Friedrich Reichardt, "An die Freunde" 1809?pub

Majestät'sche Sonnenrosse
Franz Schubert, "Majestät'sche Sonnenrosse" 1813, D64, ttb

Mit dem Pfeil, dem Bogen, durch Gebirg' und Thal
Robert Schumann, "Des Buben Schützenlied" 1849, Op79,25
from *Lieder-Album für die Jugend*

Mit erstorbnem Scheinen steht der Mond auf todtenstillen Hainen
Franz Schubert, "Leichenfantasie" 1811, D7

Nehmt hin die Welt! rief Zeus von seinen Höhen
Carl Friedrich Zelter, "Die Theilung der Erde" 1806

Nein, länger werd' ich diesen Kampf nicht kämpfen
Franz Schubert, "Der Kampf" 1817, D594

Nimmer, das glaubt mir, erscheinen die Götter
Johann Friedrich Reichardt, "Dithyrambe" 1809?pub
Franz Schubert, "Dithyrambe" 1824, D801

Noch in meines Lebens Lenze war ich
Johann Friedrich Reichardt, "Der Pilgrim" 1809?pub
Franz Schubert, "Der Pilgrim" 1823, D794

O Dank, Dank diesen freundlich grünen Bäumen
Johann Rudolf Zumsteeg, "Maria Stuart" 1801pub
from *Kleine Balladen und Lieder, drittes Heft*

Ritter, treue Schwesterliebe widmet euch dies Herz
Johann Rudolf Zumsteeg, "Ritter Toggenburg" 1800pub
from *Kleine Balladen und Lieder, erstes Heft*
Johann Friedrich Reichardt, "Ritter Toggenburg" 1809?pub
Franz Schubert, "Ritter Toggenburg" 1816, D397

Schön wie Engel voll Walhalla's Wonne
Johann Friedrich Reichardt, "Amalia" 1809?pub
Franz Schubert, "Amalia" 1815, D195

Schöne Welt, wo bist du? Kehre wieder, holdes Blüthenalter der Natur
Franz Schubert, "Die Götter Griechenlands" 1819, D677
Schubert used Schiller's 12th verse only

Schwer und Dumpfig, eine Wetterwolke
Franz Schubert, "Die Schlacht" (sketch), 1816, D387, soli.ch.pf

Seht! da sitzt er auf der Matte aufrecht sitzt er da
Johann Rudolf Zumsteeg, "Nadowessische Todtenklage" 1801pub
from *Kleine Balladen und Lieder, drittes Heft*

Selig durch die Liebe Götter
Franz Schubert, "Selig durch die Liebe" 1813, D55, ttb

Senke, strahlender Gott, die Fluren dürsten
Johannes Brahms, "Der Abend" 1874, Op64,2, satb.pf

Sie konnte mir kein Wörtchen sagen, zu viele Lauscher waren wach
Franz Schubert, "Das Geheimniss (1)" 1815, D250
Franz Schubert, "Das Geheimniss (2)" 1823, D793

So willst du treulos von mir scheiden
Johann Friedrich Reichardt, "Die Ideale"
Carl Friedrich Zelter, "Die Ideale" 1797

Thronend auf erhabnem Sitz
Franz Schubert, "Thronend auf erhabnem Sitz" 1813, D62, ttb

Und so finden wir uns wieder
Ferdinand Ries, "Die Gunst des Augenblicks" 1811pub, Op35,2

Unendliche Freude durchwallet das Herz
Franz Schubert, "Unendliche Freude" 1813, D51, ttb
Franz Schubert, "Unendliche Freude" 1813, D54, 3mv

Vier Elemente, innig gesellt
Franz Schubert, "Punschlied" 1815, D277, ttb.pf

Von dem Dome schwer und bang
Peter Cornelius, "Von dem Dome schwer und bang" 1869, Op9,5, ttbb

Vor seinem Löwengarten, das Kampfspiel zu erwarten
Carl Friedrich Zelter, "Der Handschuh" 1800pub
Robert Schumann, "Der Handschuh" 1850, Op87

Vorüber die stöhnende Klage!
Franz Schubert, "Vorüber die stöhnende Klage" 1813, D53, ttb
Franz Schubert, "Elysium" 1817, D584

Was ist der Mensch? halb Thier, halb Engel
Ferdinand Ries, "Was ist Der Mensch?" 1810pub, Op7,1

Weit in nebelgrauer Ferne liegt mir das vergangne Glück
Franz Schubert, "An Emma" 1814, D113
Niklas von Krufft, "An Emma"

Wenn dein Finger durch die Saiten meistert
Franz Schubert, "Laura am Klavier" 1816, D388

Wer die steile Sternenbahn
Franz Schubert, "Wer die steile Sternenbahn" 1813, D63, ttb

Wer wagt es, Rittersmann oder Knapp', zu tauchen in dieser Schlund?
Franz Schubert, "Der Taucher" 1813-14, D77

Will sich Hektor ewig von mir wenden
Franz Schubert, "Hektors Abschied" 1815, D312

Willkommen, schöner Jüngling, du Wonne der Natur
Johann Friedrich Reichardt, "An den Frühling"
Ferdinand Ries, "Willkommen, schöner Jüngling" 1810pub, Op7,6
Franz Schubert, "An den Frühling (1)" 1815, D283
Franz Schubert, "An den Frühling" 1816?, D338, 2t2b
Franz Schubert, "An den Frühling (2)" 1817, D587

Willst du nicht das Lämmlein hüten?
Johann Friedrich Reichardt, "Der Alpenjäger" 1809?pub
Franz Schubert, "Der Alpenjäger" 1817, D588

Wo ich sei, und wo mich hingewendet
Franz Schubert, "Thekla: eine Geisterstimme (1)" 1813, D73
Franz Schubert, "Thekla: eine Geisterstimme (2)" 1817, D595

Wohl auf Kameraden, aufs Pferd, aufs Pferd!
Johann Rudolf Zumsteeg, "Reiterlied" 1802pub
from *Kleine Balladen und Lieder, viertes Heft*

Wohl perlet im Glase der purpurne Wein
Franz Schubert, "Die vier Weltalter" 1816, D391

Zu Aachen in seiner Kaiserpracht, im altertümlichen Saale
Johann Friedrich Reichardt, "Der Graf von Habsburg" 1809?pub
Franz Schubert, "Der Graf von Habsburg" (fragment), 1818?, D990
Carl Loewe, "Der Graf von Habsburg" 1843-44?, Op98

Zu Dionys, dem Tyrannen, schlich Möros, den Dolch im Gewande
Franz Schubert, "Die Bürgschaft" 1815, D246

Zwei sind der Wege, auf welchen der Mensch zur Tugend emporstrebt
Franz Schubert, "Die zwei Tugendwege" 1813, D71, ttb

Zwischen Himmel und Erd' hoch in der Lüfte Meer
Franz Schubert, "Hymne an den Unendlichen" 1815, D232, satb.pf

Heinar Schilling (1894-1955)

Durch die abendlichen Gärten, über glänzende Asphalte
Paul Hindemith, "Durch die abendlichen Gärten" 1922, Op18,7

Johannes Schlaf (1862-1941)

Der schönste Cherub kommt
Alban Berg, "Winter" 1905

Geht ein grauer Mann durch den stillen Wald
Alban Berg, "Regen" 1906

Herbstsonnenschein. Der liebe Abend blickt so still herein
Alban Berg, "Im Zimmer" 1907
from *Sieben frühe Lieder*
Robert Gund, "Im Zimmer" 1910, Op39,2

Ich kam zu einer Wiese im roten Abendschein
Robert Gund, "Der einsame Pfeifer" 1910, Op36,4

In die braunen, rauschenden Nächte flittert ein Licht hinein
Arnold Schönberg, "Waldsonne" 1899?, Op2,4

Franz Xaver Freiherr von Schlechta (-Wssehrd) (1796-1875)

Den Fischer fechten Sorgen und Gram und Leid nicht an
Franz Schubert, "Fischerweise" 1826, D881

Harrt ein Fischer auf der Brücke
Franz Schubert, "Widerschein" 1819/1820, D639,D949

Hier unten steht ein Ritter im hellen Mondenstrahl
Franz Schubert, "Liebeslauschen" 1820, D698

Nicht so düster und so bleich, Schläfer in der Truhe
Franz Schubert, "Todtengräberweise" 1826, D869

Schlagt mein ganzes Glück in Splitter, nehmt mir alle Habe gleich
Franz Schubert, "Des Sängers Habe" 1825, D832

Sei gegrüsst, geweihte Stille, die mir sanfte Trauer weckt
Franz Schubert, "Auf einen Kirchhof" 1815, D151

Wo irrst du durch einsame Schatten der Nacht
Franz Schubert, "Aus *Diego Manazares:* Ilmerine" 1816, D458

August Wilhelm von Schlegel (1767-1845)
Auf den Wassern wohnt mein stilles Leben
Franz Schubert, "Lebensmelodien" 1816, D395

Der Frühlingssonne holdes Lächeln
Franz Schubert, "Wiedersehn" 1825, D855

Hinaus mein Blick! hinaus in's Thal!
Franz Schubert, "Abendlied für die Entfernte" 1825, D856

Hörst du von den Nachtigallen die Gebüsche widerhallen?
Franz Schubert, "Die gefangenen Sänger" 1821, D712

Lass dich mit gelinden Schlägen rühren
Franz Schubert, "Sprache der Liebe" 1816, D410

Laue Lüfte, Blumendüfte
Franz Schubert, "Lob der Thränen" 1818?, D711

Quälend ungestilltes Sehnen pocht mir in empörter Brust
Franz Schubert, "Die verfehlte Stunde" 1816, D409

Wenn fremde Blikke wachsam uns umgeben
Carl Friedrich Zelter, "Gesang und Kuß" 1798

(Karl Wilhelm) Friedrich von Schlegel (1772-1829)
Als bei dem Kreuz Maria stand
Franz Schubert, "Vom Mitleiden Mariä" 1818, D632

Du staunest, o Mensch, was heilig wir strahlen?
Franz Schubert, "Die Sterne" 1819?, D684

Ein sehnend Streben theilt mir das Herz
Franz Schubert, "Fülle der Liebe" 1825, D854

Es lockte schöne Wärme, mich an das Licht zu wagen
Franz Schubert, "Die Rose" 1820, D745

Es wehet kühl und leise
Franz Schubert, "Die Gebüsche" 1819, D646

Friedlich lieg' ich hingegossen
Franz Schubert, "Der Schiffer" 1820, D694

Sanfte Ebbe und hohe Flut tief im Mut
Ernest Vietor, "Der Wanderer" 1936, Op14,5

Sieht uns der Blick gehoben
Franz Schubert, "Die Berge" 1820, D634

Tiefer sinket schon die Sonne
Franz Schubert, "Abendröthe" 1820?, D690

Wenn ich nur ein Vöglein wäre
Franz Schubert, "Der Knabe" 1820, D692

Wenn mich einsam Lüfte fächeln, muss ich lächeln
Franz Schubert, "Blanka" 1818, D631

Wie deutlich des Mondes Licht zu mir spricht
Franz Schubert, "Der Wanderer" 1819, D649

Wie lieblich und fröhlich, zu schweben, zu singen
Franz Schubert, "Die Vögel" 1820, D691

Wie rein Gesang sich windet
Franz Schubert, "Der Fluss" 1820, D693

Wie so innig, möcht' ich sagen, sich der Meine mir ergiebt
Franz Schubert, "Das Mädchen" 1819, D652

Wie soll ich nicht tanzen, es macht keine Mühe
Franz Schubert, "Der Schmetterling" 1820?, D633

Windes Rauschen, Gottes Flügel, tief in kühler Waldesnacht
Franz Schubert, "Im Walde" 1820, D708

Jakob Matthias Schleiden: see "Ernst"

Matthias Leopold Schleifer (1771-1842)

Leon und Castilien waffnen
Carl Loewe, "Zumalacarregui" 1837

Graff von Schlieben (fl.1766)

Ich liebte nur Ismenen, Ismenen liebte mich
Karl Friberth, "Das ungetreue Mädchen" 1780pub
DTÖ 54 lists poet as "Graf von Schlieben od. Putbus(?)"

Albert (Ernst Ludwig Karl) Graf von Schlippenbach (1800-1886)

Die Sterne schau'n in stiller Nacht
Felix Mendelssohn, "Die Sterne schau'n in stiller Nacht" 184-?, Op99,2

Johann Friedrich von Schlotterbeck (1765-1840)

Hört! ich hatt' einmal ein Blümchen
Johann Rudolf Zumsteeg, "Der Verlust" 1803pub
from *Kleine Balladen und Lieder, sechstes Heft*

Konrad Arnold Schmid (1716-1789)

Der Herr erscheint in seiner Höhe
Johann Abraham Peter Schulz, "Der Segen des Erlösers" 1784pub

Erhöhet die prächtigen Pforten der Siege!
Carl Loewe, "Der Siegesfürst (Ein Osterlied)" 1820, vv.orch

(Philipp) Siegfried Schmid(t) (1774-1859)

Wie klingt's so bänglich drüben?
Johann Rudolf Zumsteeg, "Sängers Einsamkeit" 1803pub
from *Kleine Balladen und Lieder, fünftes Heft*

Anton Adolph Schmidl (1802-1863)
Herr, unser Gott! erhöre unser Flehen
Franz Schubert, "Hymne" 1828, D964, 2t2b.mch.winds

Komm heil'ger Geist, erhöre unser Flehen
Franz Schubert, "Hymnus an den heiligen Geist" 1828, D948, 2t2b(soli)2t2b(ch)

Friederike Schmidt (1801-1837)
Deinem sanft flötenden Ton, Philomele
Carl Loewe, "An die Nachtigall"

Georg Philipp Schmidt (von Lübeck) (1766-1849)
Ich hab eine Wiege so schmuck und nett
Carl Friedrich Zelter, "Todes Wiegenlied" 1806

Ich komme vom Gebirge her
Franz Schubert, "Der Wanderer" 1816, D493

Hans Schmidt (1856-1923)
Geh schlafen, Tochter, schlafen!
Johannes Brahms, "Sommerabend" 1881?, Op84,1, 1or2v.pf

Liebster Schatz, i bitt' di schön: wann wir uns nit werden seh'n
Carl Bohm, "Bitte" 1887cop, Op318,1

Mutter, hilf mir armen Tochter
Johannes Brahms, "Der Kranz" 1881?, Op84,2, 1or2v.pf

Rosen brach ich Nachts mir am dunklen Hage
Johannes Brahms, "Sapphische Ode" 1883/84, Op94,4, 1v(low).pf

Singe, Mädchen, hell und klar
Johannes Brahms, "In den Beeren" 1881?, Op84,3, 1or2v.pf

Heinrich Schmidt (1779-1857)
Bitte, bitte! einen Blick aus den holden blauen Augen
Louis Spohr, "Bitte, bitte!" 1835-36, Op94,2

Der Liebe bangen Sorgen erbleicht der Freude Strahl!
Louis Spohr, "Getrennte Liebe" 1816, Op37,4

Schnell geniesst die schnellen Stunden
Louis Spohr, "Lebenslied" 1816, Op37,2

Klamer Eberhard Karl Schmidt (1764-1824)
Das Glück ist rund, zur guten Stunde
Johann Holzer, "Die gute Stunde" 1779pub

Die Engel Gottes weinen
Wolfgang Amadeus Mozart, "Das Lied der Trennung" 1787, K519

(Ferdinand Alexander) August Schnezler (1809-1853)
Im Mummelsee, im dunkeln See, da blüh'n der Lilien viele
Carl Loewe, "Der Mummelsee" 1849?, Op116,3

Franz von Schober (1798-1882)
Als der Frühling sich vom Herzen der erblühten Erde riss
Franz Schubert, "Vergissmeinnicht" 1823, D792

Braust des Unglücks Sturm empor
Franz Schubert, "Trost im Liede" 1817, D546

"Der Friede sei mit euch!" das war dein Abschiedssegen
Franz Schubert, "Pax Vobiscum" 1817, D551

Des Mondes Zauberblume lacht
Franz Schubert, "Mondenschein" 1826, D875, ten.t.3b

Die Wogen am Gestade schwellen
Franz Schubert, "Schiffers Scheidelied" 1827, D910

Dort raget ein Berg aus den Wolken hehr
Franz Schubert, "Genügsamkeit" 1815, D143

Du brachst sie nun, die kalte Rinde
Franz Schubert, "Am Bach im Frühling" 1816?, D361

Du holde Kunst, in wieviel grauen Stunden
Franz Schubert, "An die Musik" 1817, D547

Ich bin ein Waller auf der Erde
Franz Schubert, "Pilgerweise" 1823, D789

Ich schiess' den Hirsch im grünen Forst
Franz Schubert, "Jägers Liebeslied" 1827, D909

In des Todes Feierstunde, wenn ich einst von hinnen scheide
Franz Schubert, "Todesmusik" 1822, D758
Felix Wolfes, "Todesmusik" 1960

In tiefster Erde ruht ein alt Gesetz
Franz Schubert, "Schatzgräbers Begehr" 1822, D761

Schmücket die Locken mit duftigen Kränzen
Franz Schubert, "Frühlingsgesang" 1822, D740, 2t2b.pf
Franz Schubert, "Frühlingsgesang" 1822, D709, 2t2b

Schneeglöcklein, o Schneeglöcklein, in den Auen läutest du
Franz Schubert, "Viola" 1823, D786

Weimars Toten will ich's bringen
Franz Liszt, "Weimars Toten (Dithyrambe)" 1849pub

Paul Schoeck (1882-1952)

Alle meine Wünsche schweigen
Othmar Schoeck, "Alle meine Wünsche schweigen" 1906, Op6,4

Liebe ist Wahrheit!
Othmar Schoeck, "Psalm" 1906, Op11,1

Nun quill aus meiner Seele immerfort
Othmar Schoeck, "Nun quill aus meiner Seele" 1907, Op15,2

Emil Rudolf Osman, Prinz von Schönaich-Carolath (1852-1908)

Drei Rosen gab sie mir, drei Küsse
Felix Weingartner, "Spielmannslied" 1900, Op28,9

Ein Weg durch Korn und rothen Klee
Hugo Kaun, "Daheim" 1900pub, Op33,2

O gib mir nicht die voll erblühte Rose
Joseph Marx, "Herbstzeitlose" 1909, 1v(med).pf

Seid'ne Gewänder, Spangen von Gold
Felix Weingartner, "Lied der Ghawâze" 1899, Op25,5

Friedrich Wilhelm Traugott Schöpff: see "Wilfried von der Neun"

Bernhard Scholz (1831-1971)
Das ist die Zeit der Rosenpracht
Eduard Lassen, "Sommerabend" Op61,4

Dein Auge ist mein Himmel
Eduard Lassen, "Dein Auge ist mein Himmel" Op62,5

Maria Scholz: see "Maria Stona"

Wilhelm von Scholz (1874-1969)
Ich war erlöst, jetzt hab ich stark und leise
Felix Wolfes, "Ein Mönch spricht zu Gott" 1966

Johanna Schopenhauer (1766-1838)
Wundes Herz, hör auf zu klagen
Norbert Burgmüller, "Sehnsucht nach Ruhe" 1827-36?, Op6,4

Henriette Wilhelmine Auguste von Schorn ("Henriette Nordheim") (1807-1869)
Ach! was ist leben doch so schwer, wenn, was du lieb hast
Eduard Lassen, "Sei stille" Op71,2
Franz Liszt, "Sei still" 1877

Alois Schreiber (1761-1841)
Du heilig, glühend Abendroth!
Franz Schubert, "Das Abendroth" 1818, D627

Dunkel rauscht des Stromes Welle
Friedrich Silcher, "Der Strom der Zeit" 4v

Euch Blümlein will ich senden zur schönen Jungfrau dort
Franz Schubert, "Der Blumenbrief" 1818, D622

Freundlich ist dein Antlitz
Franz Schubert, "An den Mond in einer Herbstnacht" 1818, D614

Maria kam auf ihrer Flucht gen Mittag in ein ödes Thal
Carl Loewe, "Maria und das Milchmädchen" 1834, Op36,1

Meister Oluf, der Schmied auf Helgoland
Carl Loewe, "Odin's Meeres-Ritt, oder Der Schmied auf Helgoland" 1851, Op118

Sei gegrüsst, du Frau der Huld und der reinen, schönen Minne
Franz Schubert, "Das Marienbild" 1818, D623

Von des Hügels kahlem Rücken wankt ein hagrer Greis herab
Carl Loewe, "Der ewige Jude" 1834, Op36,3

Was dich ergreift, wenn betend zu den Sternen
Emilie Zumsteeg, "Religion" 1819pub, Op4,3

Leopold von Schroeder (1851-1920)
Wo du nicht bist und deiner Augen Schimmer
Anna Teichmüller, "Wo du nicht bist–" 1905pub, Op5,1
translated from the Indian of Bhartrihari

J. Schröer

Blümlein im Garten, schaut euch doch um
Robert Franz, "Liebchen ist da!" 1846pub, Op5,2

Sel'ge Abende nieder steigen
Robert Franz, "Stiller Abend" 1846pub, Op5,9

Und nun ein End' dem Trauern
Robert Franz, "Genesung" 1846pub, Op5,12

Christian Friedrich Daniel Schubart (1739-1791)

Auf, auf, ihr Brüder und seid stark
Chr. F. Daniel Schubart, "Kaplied" 1783

Da liegt, ach Gott, da drunten liegt
Chr. F. Daniel Schubart, "Am Grabe der Mutter" 1783

Da steht der Mond! Verweile, verweile lieber Mond
Chr. F. Daniel Schubart, "An den Mond" 1783

Gefang'ner Mann, ein armer Mann!
Chr. F. Daniel Schubart, "Der Gefangene" 1783

Gute Nacht! gute Nacht! Unser Tagwerk ist vollbracht
Carl Loewe, "Gute Nacht" before 1826
author of 2nd and 3rd verses unknown

Ich hatt' einmal ein Mädchen, es war im ganzen Städtchen
Chr. F. Daniel Schubart, "Ballade" 1783

Ich lebe immer heiter und flieh' die Traurigkeit
Chr. F. Daniel Schubart, "Der Kohlenbrenner" 1783

Ich Mädchen bin aus Schwaben und schön ist mein Gesicht
Chr. F. Daniel Schubart, "Lied eines Schwabenmädchens" 1783

In einem Bächlein helle, da schoß in froher Eil'
Chr. F. Daniel Schubart, "Die Forelle" 1783
Franz Schubert, "Die Forelle" 1817?, D550

Kühlender Abend, steige vom Hügel
Chr. F. Daniel Schubart, "Der Frühlingsabend" 1783

Mädle 's ist Winter; der wollige Schnee
Chr. F. Daniel Schubart, "Winterlied" 1783

Sanftes Clavier, sanftes Clavier, welche Entzückungen schaffest du mir!
Franz Schubert, "An mein Clavier" 1816?, D342

Schlaf wohl, du Himmelsknabe du, schlaf wohl, du süßes Kind
Chr. F. Daniel Schubart, "Weihnachtslied der Hirten" 1786
Carl Loewe, "Der Hirten Lied am Krippelein" 1828, Op22,i,3, 4v
Richard Strauss, "Weihnachtslied" 1870
from *Jugendlieder*

Sträußchen wem zu Ehren duftest du so süß
Chr. F. Daniel Schubart, "Luise an Wilhelm" 1783

Tod, du Schrecken der Natur! immer rieselt deine Uhr
Franz Schubert, "An den Tod" 1817?, D518

Was will dies Klopfen sagen
Chr. F. Daniel Schubart, "Liebesklage" 1783

Wenn aus deinen sanften Blikken
Chr. F. Daniel Schubart, "An die Geliebte" 1783

Wenn des Abends Rosenflügel kühlend über Tal und Hügel
Chr. F. Daniel Schubart, "Abendlied eines Mädchens" 1783

Wo find ich den Liebling der Seele
Chr. F. Daniel Schubart, "Die Erscheinung" 1783

Zieh hin, du braver Krieger du! Wir gleiten dich zur Grabesruh'
Franz Schubert, "Grablied auf einen Soldaten" 1816, D454

Ludwig Albrecht Schubart (1765-1811)
Horch, grausig heult draussen der Mitternachtwind
Johann Rudolf Zumsteeg, "Lied (in einer Winternacht zu singen)" 1803pub
from *Kleine Balladen und Lieder, sechstes Heft*

Franz Peter Schubert (1797-1828)
Gütigster, Bester! Weisester, Größter!
Franz Schubert, "Beitrag zur fünfzigjährigen Jubelfeier des Herrn von Salieri" 1816, D407, 2t2b;ten.pf;3v
Franz Schubert, "Cantata zur 50 jährigen Jubelfeier Salieris" 1816, D441, ttb.pf

Lebe wohl! lebe wohl! Du lieber Freund!
Franz Schubert, "Abschied von einem Freunde" 1817, D578

Tiefer Sehnsucht heil'ges Bangen
Wilhelm Kienzl, "Mein Gebet" 192-?, Op114,1

Clemens August Schücking (1759-1790)
Hier am Hügel heissen Sandes sitz' ich
Franz Schubert, "Hagars Klage" 1811, D5

Gustav Schüler (1868-1938)
Das Schilf bückt sich hernieder und hebt sich auf
Rudolf Bella, "Im Schilf am See" 1913pub

Christian Wilhelm von Schütz (1776-1847)
Ach, was soll ich beginnen vor Liebe?
Franz Schubert, "Delphine" 1825, D857,2

Nun, da Schatten niedergleiten
Franz Schubert, "Florio" 1825, D857,1

H. Schütz
Das Mühlrad brauset, das Wasser zerstiebt zu eitel Blasen und Schaum
Alexander Fesca, "Des Jägers Klage" 1882pub, Op30,1

Johann Stephen Schütze (1771-1839)
Warum ich bleibe, warum ich traurig bin?
Carl Friedrich Zelter, "Seufzer des Gefangnen" 1810?

E. v. d. Schulenburg
Wenn der Sturm die Blätter jaget
Eduard Lassen, "Herbstgefühl" Op52,2

Walter Schulte vom Brühl (1858-1921)
Sollt' man's denken, ist's zu glauben
Wilhelm Kienzl, "Die Urgrossmutter" 189-?, Op42,2

Adolf Schults (1820-1858)
Ei Veilchen, liebes Veilchen, so sag' doch einmal an
Carl Reinecke, "Das Veilchen" Op63
from *Kinderlieder*

Mutteraug', in deine Bläue möcht' ich all' mein Lebtag seh'n
Carl Reinecke, "Das Mutterauge"
from *Kinderlieder*

Und könnt ich auch erwecken dich, ich wollt' es doch nicht thun
Carl Reinecke, "Der Entschlafenen" Op81,7

Eduard Schulz: see "Eduard Ferrand"

H. Schulz
Sag wie kann man Lieb' erkennen?
Louis Spohr, "Liebesfragen" 1838, Op107,1, sop.ten.pf

Johann Gottlob Schulz (1762-1810)
Der Herbst beginnt, schon saust der Wind
Carl Loewe, "Der Herbst" before 1826

Ernst Konrad Friedrich Schulze (1789-1817)
Die Winde sausen am Tannenhang
Franz Schubert, "Über Wildemann" 1826, D884

Ertönet, ihr Saiten, in nächtlicher Ruh'
Franz Schubert, "Ewige Liebe" 1825?, D825,2, 2t2b

Frisch trabe sonder Ruh' und Rast
Franz Schubert, "Auf der Brücke" 1825?, D853

Ich bin von aller Ruh' geschieden
Franz Schubert, "Tiefes Leid" 1826, D876

Ich wandre über Berg und Thal
Franz Schubert, "Im Walde" 1816, D834

Ihr Sternlein, still in der Höhe, ihr Sternlein, spielend im Meer
Franz Schubert, "Der liebliche Stern" 1825, D861

Keine Stimme hör' ich schallen
Franz Schubert, "Um Mitternacht" 1825, D862

O Herz, sei endlich stille! was schlägst du so unruhvoll?
Franz Schubert, "An mein Herz" 1825, D860

O Quell, was strömst du rasch und wild
Franz Schubert, "O Quell, was strömst du rasch und wild" 1826, D874

O wie dringt das junge Leben kräftig mir durch Sinn und Herz!
Franz Schubert, "Lebensmuth" 1826, D883

Still sitz' ich an des Hügels Hang, der Himmel ist so klar
Franz Schubert, "Im Frühling" 1826, D882

Hans Schumacher (1910-)
Als wir noch die Drachen steigen liessen
Gottfried von Einem, "Die Drachen" 1987, Op78,2
from *Meridiane* (2)
Der Bahnhof steht im Nebel. Leis' tickt es in der Uhr
Gottfried von Einem, "Der letzte Zug" 1987, Op78,5
from *Meridiane* (5)
Eines Tags, am Rand der Felder, fehlten auf der Welt die Wälder
Gottfried von Einem, "Der Traum vom neuen Baum" 1987, Op78,4
from *Meridiane* (4)
Geh'n der Nacht die Sterne aus, ängstige dich nicht
Gottfried von Einem, "Stern und Lampe" 1987, Op78,1
from *Meridiane* (1)
Im Fensterausschnitt mir gegenüber der Baum kahl
Gottfried von Einem, "Notation" 1987, Op78,3
from *Meridiane* (3)

Felix Schumann (1854-1879)
Es brausen der Liebe Wogen
Johannes Brahms, "Versunken" 1878, Op86,5, 1v(low).pf
Meine Liebe ist grün wie der Fliederbusch
Johannes Brahms, "Junge Lieder (I)" 1873, Op63,5
Wenn um den Hollunder der Abendwind kost
Johannes Brahms, "Junge Lieder (II)" 1873, Op63,6

Gustav Schwab (1792-1850)
Der junge König Heinrich schlief
Carl Loewe, "Kaiser Heinrich's Waffenweihe" 1853?, Op122

Friedrich, Fürst von Schwarzenberg (1800-1870)
Sei mir gegrüsst in deiner Pracht
Carl Loewe, "Gruss vom Meere" 1844, Op103,1

Karl Friedrich, Freiherr von Schweizer (1797-1847)
Freudig zum Himmel auf blikke mein Herz!
Louis Spohr, "Ermuthigung" 1845, WoO112
Ich bin so bleich, du bist so roth
Louis Spohr, "Des Mädchens Klage" 1838, Op105,5
Ich wahrte die Hoffnung tief in der Brust
Louis Spohr, "Sei still mein Herz" 1837, Op103,1, sop.cl.pf
Ich wollte in die Fremde gehn
Johann Vesque von Püttlingen, "Ich wollte in die Fremde gehn" 184-?, Op30,5

"D. B. Schwerin" (Dorothea Böttcher von Schwerin)
Aus deinen Augen fliessen meine Lieder
Franz Ries, "Aus deinen Augen fliessen meine Lieder"

Grafin Schwerin-Schwerinburg
Vöglein, ihr schlauen, darf ich euch trauen?
Max von Schillings, "Wanderlied" 1896

Sir Walter Scott (1771-1832)

Ave Maria! Jungfrau mild! Erhöre einer Jungfrau Flehen!
Franz Schubert, "Ellens Gesang III" 1825, D839
translated by Adam Storck
Karl Gottlieb Reissiger, "Ave Maria" Op50,5

Die Nacht bricht bald herein, dann leg' ich mich zur Ruh
Franz Schubert, "Norman's Gesang" 1825, D846
translated by Adam Storck from "The Lady of the Lake"

Er ist uns geschieden vom Berg und vom Walde
Franz Schubert, "Coronach" 1825, D836, ssa.pf
translated by Adam Storck from "The Lady of the Lake"

Grosser Thaten that der Ritter fern im heil'gen Lande viel
Franz Schubert, "Romanze des Richard Löwenherz" 1826?, D907
translated by Karl Ludwig Müller from *Ivanhoe:* "The Crusader's Return"

Jäger, ruhe von der Jagd!
Franz Schubert, "Ellens Gesang II" 1825, D838
translated by Adam Storck

Mein Ross so müd' in dem Stalle sich steht
Franz Schubert, "Lied des gefangenen Jägers" 1825, D843
translated by Adam Storck from "The Lady of the Lake"

Mich führt mein Weg wohl meilenlang
Franz Schubert, "Gesang der Norna" 1825, D831
translated by S. H. Spiker

Raste, Krieger, Krieg ist aus
Franz Schubert, "Ellens Gesang I" 1825, D837
translated by Adam Storck from "The Lady of the Lake"

Schlaf, Söhnchen! Dein Vater war eisenumhüllt
Adolf Jensen, "Wiegenlied" 1873-75, Op52,2
translated by Ferdinand Freiligrath

Sprich, Fräulein, warum härmst du dich?
Adolf Jensen, "Jock von Hazeldean" 1873-75, Op52,1
translated by Ferdinand Freiligrath

Triumph er naht, Heil, Heil dem Helden
Franz Schubert, "Bootgesang" 1825, D835, 2t2b.pf
translated by Adam Storck from "The Lady of the Lake"

Wärst du bei mir im Lebensthal
Franz Schubert, "Lied der Anne Lyle" 1825?, D830
Poem quoted in "Montrose" by Scott, who attributes the poem to Andrew

Karl Sigmund Freiherr von Seckendorf (1744-1785)

Wir stimmen dir mit Flötensang
Franz Schubert, "Nachtmusik" 1825, D848, 2t2b

Christian Friedrich Segelbach (1763-after 1834)

Wir spielen und hüpfen so munter
Carl Loewe, "Wir spielen und hüpfen" 1826

Franz Eugen Joseph Freiherr von Seida und Landenberg (1772-?)
Entfliehet schnell von mir
Carl Maria von Weber, "Entfliehet schnell von mir" 1803, J.38

Seidel
Auf einer Meierei da war einmal ein braves Huhn
Emil Mattiesen, "Das Huhn und der Karpfen" 1900pub, Op7,4
from *Vier heitere Lieder*

Wie tönt an Frühlingstagen so schwermutreich und hold
Wilhelm Kempff, "Die Amsel" 1917, Op7,3

Heinrich Seidel (1842-1906)
Der Abendthau– es sind die Thränen
Hugo Kaun, "Der Abendthau– es sind die Thränen" 1898?pub, Op25,1

Es ist kein Thal so wüst und leer
Hugo Kaun, "Es ist kein Thal so wüst und leer" 1898?pub, Op25,5

Horchend über schroffe Mauern auf die Nachtigallenlieder
Hugo Kaun, "Das Posthorn" 1900pub, Op25,2

Mein Gretchen ist so kugelrund
Hugo Kaun, "Mein Schwesterchen" 1905pub, Op27,3

Mein lieber Herr Reiter, nun stoss' er mal an
Carl Reinecke, "Der Reiter"
from *Kinderlieder*

Mein Täubchen fliegt in Glanz und Duft
Carl Reinecke, "Mein Täubchen"
from *Kinderlieder*

Wie schön sich zu wiegen, die Luft zu durchfliegen
Carl Reinecke, "Die Schaukel" Op196
from *Kinderlieder*

Ina Seidel (1885-1974)
Ich bin dir nie so nah als nachts, wenn rings um uns das Dunkel schweigt
Erich Riede, "Die Mutter sinnt bei der Wiege (II)" Op8,3, sop.pf

O tiefstes Wunder, daß mein Leben in der Kraft geworden ist
Erich Riede, "Die Mutter sinnt bei der Wiege (I)" Op8,2, sop.pf

Oh, daß ich dich fand einzig warm und fest
Erich Riede, "Ehe" Op8,1, sop.pf

Johann Gabriel Seidl (1804-1875)
Bei dir allein empfind' ich, dass ich lebe
Franz Schubert, "Bei dir allein" 1828, D866,2
from *Vier Refrain Lieder*

Die Mutter hat mich jüngst gescholten
Franz Schubert, "Die Unterscheidung" 1828?, D866,1
from *Vier Refrain Lieder*

Die Nacht ist heiter und ist rein
Franz Schubert, "Nachthelle" 1826, D892, ten.2t2b.pf

Die Scheibe friert, der Wind ist rauh
Franz Schubert, "Sehnsucht" 1826, D879

Draussen in der weiten Nacht steh' ich wieder nun
Franz Schubert, "Im Freien" 1826, D880

Du sagtest mir es, Mutter: Er ist ein Springinsfeld!
Franz Schubert, "Die Männer sind méchant" 1828?, D866,3
from *Vier Refrain Lieder*

Ich auf der Erd', am Himmel du, wir wandern beide rüstig zu
Franz Schubert, "Der Wanderer an den Mond" 1826?, D870

Ich hab' eine Brieftaub' in meinem Sold
Franz Schubert, "Die Taubenpost" 1828, D957,14

Ich trage, wo ich gehe, stets eine Uhr bei mir
Carl Loewe, "Die Uhr" 1852, Op123,3
Johann Vesque von Püttlingen, "Die Uhr" 1855?, Op52,2

Ihr lieben Mauern hold und traut, die ihr mich kühl umschließt
Franz Schubert, "Am Fenster" 1826, D878

Kling' die Nacht durch, klinge, süssen Frieden bringe
Franz Schubert, "Das Zügenglöcklein" 1826?, D871

Sei uns stets gegrüsst, o Nacht!
Franz Schubert, "Nachtgesang im Walde" 1827, D913, 2t2b.4hn

Silberblauer Mondenschein fällt herab
Franz Schubert, "Grab und Mond" 1826, D893, 2t2b

So Mancher sieht mit finstrer Miene
Franz Schubert, "Irdisches Glück" 1828, D866,4
from *Vier Refrain Lieder*

Spähend nach dem Eisengitter
Robert Schumann, "Blondel's Lied" 1840, Op53,1

Wenn ich durch Busch und Zweig brech auf beschränktem Steig
Franz Schubert, "Widerspruch" 1826?, D865, 2t2b.pf

Wie sich der Äuglein kindlicher Himmel
Franz Schubert, "Wiegenlied" 1826, D867

Zu des Mondes sanftem Schimmer schickt sich wohl ein sanftes Lied
Giacomo Meyerbeer, "Ständchen" 1841, ten.pf

"Selmar" (Karl Gustav von Brinckmann) (1764-1847)

Vergiss mein nicht! so lispelt Dir die kleine Blüte
Johann Rudolf Zumsteeg, "An Doris" 1805pub
from *Kleine Balladen und Lieder, siebtes Heft*

Frida Semler

Der Mondschein lag auf dem Wasser
Alban Berg, "Traum" 1904

Heinrich Christian Ludwig (Leberecht?) Senf (?-1793)

Nacht und Still ist um mich her
Franz Anton Hoffmeister, "Am Fenster, bei Mondschein"
Johann Christoph Hackel, "Die Zufriedenheit" 1786pub

Johann Chrysostomus Senn (1792-1857)
Ich treibe auf des Lebens Meer
Franz Schubert, "Selige Welt" 1822, D743

Wie klag' ich's aus das Sterbegefühl
Franz Schubert, "Schwanengesang" 1822?, D744

Albert Sergel (1876-1946)
Das war des Frühlings warmer Hauch
Yrjö Kilpinen, "Mein Herz, der wilde Rosenstrauch" 1932-33, Op75,4
from *Sommersegen*

Der Frost in letzter Nacht
Yrjö Kilpinen, "Vor Tau und Tag" 1932-33, Op77,6
from *Spielmannslieder*

Eingeschneite stille Felder
Yrjö Kilpinen, "Eingeschneite stille Felder" 1932-33, Op77,2
from *Spielmannslieder*

Ich sang mich durch das deutsche Land
Yrjö Kilpinen, "Ich sang mich durch das deutsche Land" 1932-33, Op77,8
from *Spielmannslieder*

Ich weiß es nicht, was es wohl war
Yrjö Kilpinen, "Heiligendamm" 1932-33, Op75,3
from *Sommersegen*

Ihr ewigen Sterne
Yrjö Kilpinen, "Ihr ewigen Sterne" 1932-33, Op77,1
from *Spielmannslieder*

Im Walde liegt ein stiller See
Yrjö Kilpinen, "Im Walde liegt ein stiller See" 1932-33, Op75,1
from *Sommersegen*

Küssen und Kosen steht euch an
Yrjö Kilpinen, "Spielmannssehnen" 1932-33, Op77,5
from *Spielmannslieder*

Langsam wird mein Kindchen müde
Max Reger, "Abendlied" 1907, Op76,39, 1v(med).pf
from *Schlichte Weisen, Band 4*

"Nimm mich! Nimm mich!" Was kriegst denn du?
Richard Trunk, "Brautwerbung" 1933pub, Op63,4
from *Vier heitere Lieder*

Nun wind um deine Stirne
Yrjö Kilpinen, "Tanzlied" 1932-33, Op77,4
from *Spielmannslieder*

Rings weiße Blütendolden
Yrjö Kilpinen, "Unter Blüten" 1932-33, Op75,6
from *Sommersegen*

Spiel ich wo zum Tanze auf
Yrjö Kilpinen, "Spiel ich wo zum Tanze auf" 1932-33, Op77,3
from *Spielmannslieder*

Tausend stille weiße, blaue Blumen
Yrjö Kilpinen, "Tausend stille weiße, blaue Blumen" 1932-33, Op75,2
from *Sommersegen*

Wenn der Wein nicht wär
Yrjö Kilpinen, "Wenn der Wein nicht wär" 1932-33, Op77,7
from *Spielmannslieder*

Wir gehen durch goldenes Ährenfeld
Yrjö Kilpinen, "Sommersegen" 1932-33, Op75,5
from *Sommersegen*

Friedrich Anton Serre (1789-1863)

O du mein Stern, schau dich so gern
Clara Schumann, "Mein Stern" 1846

Purpurgluten leuchten ferne, golden sinkt der lichte Tag
Clara Schumann, "Beim Abschied" 1846

Sofie Seyboth

Hab' Singen für mein Leben gern
Max Reger, "Darum" 1903, Op75,15, 1v(med).pf

Liebes Töchterlein, liebes Töchterlein
Max Reger, "Die Mutter spricht" 1904, Op76,28, 1v(med).pf
from *Schlichte Weisen, Band 2*

Mein Schatz ist auf die Wanderschaft wohl
Max Reger, "Schwäbische Treue" 1903, Op75,10, 1v(med).pf

Seyffardt

All Abend, bevor ich zur Ruhe geh
Franz Abt, "Gute Nacht, du mein herziges Kind" Op137,2

William Shakespeare (1564-1616)

Auf morgen ist Sankt Valentin's Tag
Johannes Brahms, "Ophelia-Lieder (3)" 1873, WoO posth 22
translated by August Wilhelm Schlegel, from *Hamlet*

Bacchus, feister Fürst des Weins
Franz Schubert, "Trinklied" 1826, D888
translated by A. W. von Schlegel from "Antony and Cleopatra," Act II, scene vii

Das arme Kind! sie sass und sang, an einem Baum sass sie
Johann Rudolf Zumsteeg, "Aus Shakespeare's *Othello*" 1803pub
from *Kleine Balladen und Lieder, fünftes Heft*

Der Britte ist der Stern der Nationen
Johann Rudolf Zumsteeg, "Aus Shakespeare's *Othello*" 1803pub, 1v.ch.pf
from *Kleine Balladen und Lieder, fünftes Heft*

Die Arme, am Lebensbaum seufzte sie
Wolfgang Fortner, "Lied vom Weidenbaum" 1946
from *Songs nach Texten von William Shakespeare*

Die Arme, wie seufzend am Ahorn sass sie!
Carl Loewe, "Lied der Desdemona" 1827, Op9,ii,2

Die einst'ge Sehnsucht, sie liegt nun tot und kalt
Boris Blacher, "Drei Chansons (2)" 1963pub
from *Drei Chansons aus Shakespeares Romeo und Juliet*

Die Schwalbe, die den Sommer bringt
Hugo Wolf, "Lied des transferierten Zettel" 1889
translated from *Midsummer-Night's Dream* by A. W. Schlegel
from *Vier Gedichte nach Heine u.a.*

Ein junger Bursch durchs Kornfeld ging
Oscar Weil, "Ein junger Bursch durchs Kornfeld ging" 1902pub, Op32,1
translated by F. H. Schneider
from *Drei Lieder von Shakespeare* (1)

Guten Morgen, 's ist Sankt Valentinstag
Richard Strauss, "Zweites Lied der Ophelia" 1918, Op67,2
translated by Karl Simrock, from *Hamlet*
from *Drei Lieder der Ophelia*

Horch, horch! die Lerch' im Ätherblau
Franz Schubert, "Ständchen" 1826, D889
translated by A. W. von Schlegel from *Cymbeline*, Act II, Scene iii

In meiner Jugend als ich liebte, wie dünkte mich das so süss!
Carl Loewe, "Todtengräberlied (aus *Hamlet*)" 1827, Op9,ii,1

Kein Sonnenglanz im Auge meiner Frau
Erich Wolfgang Korngold, "Kein Sonnenglanz" 194-?, Op38,5
translated from Sonnet 130

Komm herbei, komm herbei, Tod
Carl Loewe, "Komm herbei, komm herbei, Tod!" 1836
Peter Cornelius, "Komm herbei, Tod" 1847, 2sop.pf
German translation by August Wilhelm von Schlegel
Peter Cornelius, "Komm herbei, Tod" 1854, sop.alt
German translation by August Wilhelm von Schlegel
Franz Wüllner, "Komm herbei, komm herbei Tod" 1857pub
Peter Cornelius, "Komm herbei, Tod" 1866, sop.bass.pf
German translation by August Wilhelm von Schlegel
Peter Cornelius, "Komm herbei, Tod" 1866-73, Op16,3, sop.bass.pf
German translation by August Wilhelm von Schlegel
Oscar Weil, "Komm herbei, Tod" 1902pub, Op32,2
translated by F. H. Schneider
from *Drei Lieder von Shakespeare* (2)
Harald Genzmer, "Liebestod" 1990, sop.pf
from *Sechs Lieder nach angelsächsischen Dichtern* (1)

Sein Leichenhemd weiß wie Schnee zu seh'n
Johannes Brahms, "Ophelia-Lieder (2)" 1873, WoO posth 22
translated by August Wilhelm Schlegel, from *Hamlet*

Sie senkten ihn in kalten Grund hinab
Johann Rudolf Zumsteeg, "Ophelia" 1802pub
from *Kleine Balladen und Lieder, viertes Heft*

Sie trugen ihn auf der Bahre bloß
Johannes Brahms, "Ophelia-Lieder (4)" 1873, WoO posth 22
translated by August Wilhelm Schlegel, from *Hamlet*
Richard Strauss, "Drittes Lied der Ophelia" 1918, Op67,3
translated by Karl Simrock, from *Hamlet*
from *Drei Lieder der Ophelia*

So wilde Freude nimmt ein wildes Ende
Boris Blacher, "Drei Chansons (3)" 1963pub
from *Drei Chansons aus Shakespeares Romeo und Juliet*

Stoss an Kamerad: es lebe der Soldat!
Johann Rudolf Zumsteeg, "Aus Shakespeare's *Othello*" 1803pub
from *Kleine Balladen und Lieder, fünftes Heft*

Und als ich ein winzig Bübchen war
Robert Schumann, "Schlusslied des Narren" 1840, Op127,5
from *As You Like It*

Und kommt er nicht mehr zurück?
Johannes Brahms, "Ophelia-Lieder (5)" 1873, WoO posth 22
translated by August Wilhelm Schlegel, from *Hamlet*

Und laß der Welt, die noch nicht weiß, mich sagen, wie alles das geschah
Hanns Eisler, "Horatios Monolog" 1956?
translated by A. W. Schlegel

Was ist Sylvia, saget an
Franz Schubert, "Gesag (An Sylvia)" 1826, D891
translated by Eduard von Bauernfeld

Was kriegt er, der den Hirsch erlegt?
Adolph Martin Foerster, "Foresters Lied" 1909, Op57,5
translated by Schlegel and Tieck, from "As You Like It"

Wie erkenn' ich dein Treulieb
Johannes Brahms, "Ophelia-Lieder (1)" 1873, WoO posth 22
translated by August Wilhelm Schlegel, from *Hamlet*
Richard Strauss, "Erstes Lied der Ophelia" 1918, Op67,1
translated by Karl Simrock, from *Hamlet*
from *Drei Lieder der Ophelia*

Wo schweifst du, Herrin, mir so theuer?
Oscar Weil, "Wo schweifst du, Herrin" 1902pub, Op32,3
translated by F. H. Schneider
from *Drei Lieder von Shakespeare* (3)

Woran erkenn' ich deinen Freund
Johann Rudolf Zumsteeg, "Ophelia" 1802pub
from *Kleine Balladen und Lieder, viertes Heft*

Zwei hohe Häuser, gleich an Würdigkeit
Boris Blacher, "Drei Chansons (1)" 1963pub
from *Drei Chansons aus Shakespeares Romeo und Juliet*

Percy Bysshe Shelley (1792-1822)

Der Hagel klirrt nieder, es leuchten die Wogen
Robert Schumann, "Die Flüchtlinge" 1852-3, Op122,2, declamation.pf

Karl Siebel (1836-1868)
Bangt dir mein Lieb? Ich bin ja bei dir
Carl Loewe, "Im Sturme" 1859?, Op145,3
from *Liederkranz für die Bassstimme*

Die Seele träumt und redet leise
George Henschel, "Die Nachtigall" 187-?, Op10,1

Erworben, verdorben! Mein Herz ist schwer
Joachim Raff, "Das verlassene Mädchen" 1855-63, Op98,14
from *Sanges-Frühling*

Es ist mein Herz ein kleines Haus, mitten, mitten im Walde
Carl Loewe, "Die Waldkapelle" 1859, Op130,1

Es ist so still, als wär' es Schlafenszeit
Alexander Zemlinsky, "Frühlingstag" 1894-96, Op2,ii,1

Hätt' es nimmer gedacht, dass ein Strom so heiss
Erik Meyer-Helmund, "Hätt' es nimmer gedacht" 1886-88
August Bungert, "Hätt' es nimmer gedacht!" 1889-91pub, Op32,1
from *Verlorne Liebe, verlornes Leben*

Ich war mal froh vor lange! vor lange! nun pocht mein Herze so!
Joachim Raff, "Abendstimmung" 1855-63, Op98,27
from *Sanges-Frühling*

Mein Herz ist ein Spielmann, ein lustger Gesell'!
Joachim Raff, "Mein Herz" 1855-63, Op98,18
from *Sanges-Frühling*

Mein Herz, o schliess dich ein
Carl Loewe, "Heimlichkeit" 1859?, Op145,4
from *Liederkranz für die Bassstimme*

Sie sass am Rebenfenster im stillen Kämmerlein
Carl Reinecke, "Begegnung" Op81,2

Und als der Mensch geschaffen war
Carl Loewe, "Der Teufel" 1859, Op129,1
after the Koran

Wie viel Sonnenstrahlen fielen golden schwer
Carl Loewe, "Meeresleuchten" 1859?, Op145,1
from *Liederkranz für die Bassstimme*

Johann Petrus Silbert (1772?-1844)
Der Odem Gottes weht
Franz Schubert, "Himmelsfunken" 1819, D651

Still beginnt's im Hain zu thauen
Franz Schubert, "Abendbilder" 1819, D650

"Angelus Silesius:" see Johannes Scheffler

Heinrich Silesius
In meiner Brust eine Glocke klingt
Robert Franz, "O nimm dich in Acht!" 1870?, Op44,1

Karl Joseph Simrock (1802-1876)
An den Rhein, an den Rhein, zieh' nicht an den Rhein
Felix Mendelssohn, "Warnung vor dem Rhein" 184-??

Athme nur leise zieh ich die Kreise
Louis Spohr, "Ständchen" 1836, Op139,1

Blauer Himmel, blaue Wogen
Johannes Brahms, "Auf dem See" 1873, Op59,2

Schnür' den Bündel denn zum Wandern
Carl Loewe, "Zwist und Sühne" 1837

Silbermond, mit bleichen Strahlen
Johannes Brahms, "An den Mond" 1877, Op71,2

Tobias George Smollet (1721-1771)
Leb wohl du Strom, so sanft und schön
Johann Rudolf Zumsteeg, "Lied" 1803pub
from *Kleine Balladen und Lieder, sechstes Heft*

Johann Michael von Soeltl (1797-1888)
Dicht in Blättern eingeschlossen ruht der Knospe stiller Traum
Franz Lachner, "Die Rose" 1837, Op56,2

Otto Sommerstorff (1859-1934)
A' Versle, a' g'spaßig's, hat mei Bua auf mi' g'macht
Max Reger, "Mei Bua" 1903-04, Op76,11, 1v(med).pf
from *Schlichte Weisen, Band 1*

Josef von Spaun (1788-1865)
Die Sonne sinkt, o könnt' ich, o könnt' ich
Franz Schubert, "Der Jüngling und der Tod" 1817, D545

Friedrich von Spee (1591-1635)
Der trübe Winter ist vorbei
Felix Mendelssohn, "Altdeutsches Frühlingslied" 1847, Op86,6

Dietrich Ernst Georg Spiegel, Freiherr von Pickelsheim (1737-1789)
Vor Pavia hat Herr Paliss den Geist einst aufgegeben!
Johann Rudolf Zumsteeg, "Herr Paliss" 1805pub
from *Kleine Balladen und Lieder, siebtes Heft*

Carl Spitteler (1845-1924)
Damals, ganz zuerst am Anfang
Othmar Schoeck, "Das bescheidene Wünschlein" 1910, Op24a,7

Der Denker rechnet wohl einmal
Othmar Schoeck, "Eine Unbekanntschaft" 1910, Op24a,10

Ein junges Glöcklein klagte
Othmar Schoeck, "Glöckleins Klage" 1910, Op24a,8

Schwarzbrauner Hufschmied, ich will dir sagen
Othmar Schoeck, "Der Hufschmied" 1909, Op24a,9

Was huschelt im Garten
Felix Weingartner, "Der Jäger und das Wichtchen" 1905pub, Op37,2
from *Zwei Balladen von C. Spitteler*

Was ist's, das der Gedanken mutigen Tritt
Othmar Schoeck, "Ein Jauchzer" 1910, Op24b,1
Willy Burkhard, "Ein Jauchzer" 1925, Op9,6, 1v(low).pf
from *Frage*

Wenn die Mittagsfrau durch das Kornfeld schleicht
Robert Gund, "Die Mittagsfrau" 1910, Op36,5

Zwölf Engel hielten am Himmelstor
Felix Weingartner, "Die tote Erde" 1905pub, Op37,1
from *Zwei Balladen von C. Spitteler*

Friedrich Ernst (?) Spohr (1776-1840)
Seht ihr's dort funkeln in rosiger Pracht?
Louis Spohr, "Jagdlied" 1856, Op154,2, bar.vn.pf

Anton Matthias Sprickmann (1749-1833)
Es waren, es waren einst glückliche Stunden
Johann Rudolf Zumsteeg, "Trudchen" 1803pub
from *Kleine Balladen und Lieder, sechstes Heft*

Hugo Staacke
see note under Karl Isidor Beck

Ilse von Stach-Lerner (1879-1941)
Bereifte Kiefern, atemlose Seen
Hans Pfitzner, "An die Mark" 1904, Op15,3

Albert Stadler (1794-1888)
Schwüler Hauch weht mir herüber, welkt die Blum' an meiner Brust
Franz Schubert, "Lieb Minne" 1815, D222

Vater, schenk' mir diese Stunde
Franz Schubert, "Namenstagslied" 1820, D695

Stahl
Entfernt von Gram und Sorgen
Joseph Haydn, "Die Landlust" 1781/84, XXVIa Nr.10

Karl Stamm (1890-1919)
Die mit ihrem Strahle mich geblendet, hohe Sonne ist hinweggegangen
Walter Schulthess, "An den Mond" 1928

Die Nacht herauf am Himmel zieht
Walter Schulthess, "Schlummerlied" 1928

Früher Herbst. Die Blätter fallen still mein Herz...? und lausche du!
Walter Schulthess, "Fallende Blätter" 1928

Kein Wandrer sich in diese Schlucht verirrt
Walter Schulthess, "Das letzte Tal" 1928

Still das Sterngeläute ist verklungen
Walter Schulthess, "Morgentau" 1928

Ernst Stauß
Wie war er schön der Maientag, da wir zu Zweien schritten
Frank van der Stucken, "Maientag" 1904pub, Op33,1

August, Freiherr von Steigentesch (1774-1826)

Ein wenig Raum auf grüner Flur
Moriz von Dietrichstein, "Meine Wünsche"

Wir giengen beide Hand in Hand, ihr Auge sprach, was ich empfand
Mauro Giuliani, "Lied" 1817pub, Op89,4, v.pf./guitar

Gretel Stein

Schlaf' ein, mein liebes Kindlein du
Max Reger, "Wiegenlied" 1915, Op142,1
from *Fünf neue Kinderlieder*

Ulrich Steindorff (1888-?)

Sonntag und Frühlingsmorgen
Max Reger, "Frühlingsfeier" 1909, Op111a,2, sop.alt.pf

Hildegard Stern

Nicht den Leib umschlangen unsre Arme
Erich Riede, "Hohe Stunde" Op7,9, sop.pf

Maurice Reinhold von Stern (1860-1938)

Feierlich träumt das Gelände schwimmend in Sonntagsruh'
Rudi Stephan, "Waldnachmittag" 1906

"C. O. Sternau" (Otto Inkermann) (fl.1851)

Heimat! Heimat! wunderbar tönendes Wort!
Johannes Brahms, "An die Heimat" 1864, Op64,1, satb.pf

Wo sich das Meer in weite Fernen
Karl Gottlieb Reissiger, "Felice notte, Marietta" Op206,1

Heinrich Stieglitz (1801-1849)

Deine Stimme lass ertönen, hohe Fürstin meiner Liebe
Carl Loewe, "Ali im Garten" 1833, Op10,ii,2,i
from *Ali und Fatme*

Der Mond blickt über die Haide so freundlich und so mild
Karl Gottlieb Reissiger, "Das Schlachtfeld" Op53,2, bass.pf

Ein Täubchen bringt mir täglich Grüsse von Teheran nach Ferhabad
Carl Loewe, "Taubenpost" 1833, Op10,ii,4
from *Assad und Gulhinde*

Einmal Mekka noch zu sehen, war mein Wunsch
Carl Loewe, "Der verschmachtende Pilger" 1833, Op10,i,2
from *Melek und Maisuna. Arabischer Liederkreis*

Geht nun, ihr Blüthen, meiner Fürstin Freude
Carl Loewe, "Assad mit dem Selam" 1833, Op10,ii,3
from *Assad und Gulhinde*

Heiss glüht der Pfad; am frühen Tag war Melek schon zum Wege wach
Carl Loewe, "Melek in der Wüste" 1833, Op10,i,3
from *Melek und Maisuna. Arabischer Liederkreis*

Hell glüh'n die Sterne im dunkeln Blau
Norbert Burgmüller, "Omars Nachtlied" 1827-36?, Op6,2

Hui! wie die Wolke von Staub und Brand
Carl Loewe, "Die Geister der Wüste" 1833, Op10,i,1
from *Malek und Maisuna. Arabischer Liederkreis*

Ich schaukle leicht mich im grünen Laub
Carl Loewe, "Lied eines Vögleins in der Oasis" 1833, Op10,i,5
from *Melek und Maisuna. Arabischer Liederkreis*

Ihr habt genug getrunken, ihr Herden gross und klein!
Carl Loewe, "Maisuna am Brunnen" 1833, Op10,ii,1
from *Melek und Maisuna. Arabischer Liederkreis*

Lege den Schmuck nun an, schöne Gulhinde
Carl Loewe, "Abendgesang" 1833, Op10,ii,6
from *Assad und Gulhinde*

Meinen Kranz hab' ich gesendet
Carl Loewe, "Fatme vom Balkone" 1833, Op10,ii,2,ii
from *Ali und Fatme*

O wie du schnaubst aus voller Brust und stampfst vor Lust
Carl Loewe, "Melek am Quell" 1833, Op10,i,6
from *Melek und Maisuna. Arabischer Liederkreis*

Reich' mir den Schleier, Emina
Carl Loewe, "Gulhinde am Putztische" 1833, Op10,ii,5
from *Assad und Gulhinde*

Wie lockt der Palmen grünes Dach
Carl Loewe, "Die Oasis" 1833, Op10,i,4
from *Melek und Maisuna. Arabischer Liederkreis*

Karl Stieler (1842-1885)

Als hoch das Feld in Blumen stand, und als die Schwalbe flog in's Land
Ludwig Thuille, "Jahreszeiten" 189-?, Op7,8
from *Von Lieb' und Leid*

Am Waldbach sitz' ich in der Sonnen
Hugo Kaun, "Am Waldbach" 1906?pub, Op68,5

Da drüben im Abendstrahle steht glitzernd des Liebchens Haus!
Josefine Lang, "Im Abendstrahl" WoO

Das ist ein seltsam Gehn: die Schritte schallen
Hugo Kaun, "Nächtiges Wandern" 1906?pub, Op68,1

Das war ein Tag voll Maienwind, da ist auf blauen Wogen
Alexander von Fielitz, "Frauenwörth" 1896pub, Op9,2
from *Eliland*

Die müden Augen, sie tragen's kaum!
Ludwig Thuille, "Nachtlied" 189-?, Op7,3
from *Von Lieb' und Leid*

Ein Fels ragt in den See hinein
Josefine Lang, "Seebild" WoO

Ein Spielmann zog des Wegs einher
Max von Schillings, "Ein Spielmann" 1896

Eine stille Zelle an blauer Welle, das ist mein Leid
Alexander von Fielitz, "Stilles Leid" 1896pub, Op9,1
from *Eliland*

Es klingt der Lärm der Welt, ich hör' ihn nimmer
Ludwig Thuille, "Es klingt der Lärm der Welt" 189-?pub, Op5,3
from *Drei Frauenlieder*

Es schnarcht der alte Müller vor seinem eichenen Tisch
Hugo Kaun, "In der Mühle" 1906?pub, Op68,3

Es zieht das Schiff auf hohen Wogen
Max Bruch, "Flucht" 1892, Op59,4, bar.pf
from *Die Auswanderer* (1)

Gehorchen ist das Erste! Ich hab' mich stumm geneigt
Alexander von Fielitz, "Ergebung" 1896pub, Op9,10
from *Eliland*

Ich bin der Mönch Waltramus
Erik Meyer-Helmund, "Vale Carissima" 1886-88

Ich gab dem Schicksal dich zurück
Josefine Lang, "Ich gab dem Schicksal dich zurück" WoO

Ich lehn' im offenen Gemache, es ist die Stunde still und spät
Ludwig Thuille, "Klage" 189-?pub, Op5,1
from *Drei Frauenlieder*

Ich lieg' an meines Lagers End' und lug' in stille Sterne
Alexander von Fielitz, "Mondnacht" 1896pub, Op9,7
from *Eliland*

Ich wand're heim durch's hohe Feld, die Wolken zieh'n
Ludwig Thuille, "Am Heimweg" 189-?, Op7,7
from *Von Lieb' und Leid*
Hugo Kaun, "Am Heimweg" 1906?pub, Op68,4

Im deutschen Land, daheim am Heerde
Max Bruch, "Heimathbild" 1892, Op59,5, bar.pf
from *Die Auswanderer* (2)

Im Waldesweben ist es Ruh', die Veiglein thun die Augen zu
Ludwig Thuille, "Waldesgang" 189-?, Op7,1
from *Von Lieb' und Leid*

In den Bäumen regt sich's leise
Ludwig Thuille, "Nächtliche Pfade" 189-?, Op7,5
from *Von Lieb' und Leid*
Max Reger, "Nächtliche Pfade" 1899, Op37,5, 1v(med).pf

In der Luft, der schwülen, feuchten, wogt das Feld
Ludwig Thuille, "Julinacht" 189-?, Op7,2
from *Von Lieb' und Leid*

Mein Liebling ist ein Lindenbaum, der steht am Strand
Franz Ries, "Am Strande" Op37,1
Alexander von Fielitz, "Am Strande" 1896pub, Op9,5
from *Eliland*

Mein süsses Lieb, wo weilest du? darf ich dich nicht umfangen?
Ludwig Thuille, "Nicht daheim" 189-?, Op7,6
from *Von Lieb' und Leid*

Mit unsern Fischern war ein Kind gekommen
Alexander von Fielitz, "Kinderstimmen" 1896pub, Op9,6
from *Eliland*

Nun ist wohl Sanges Ende! Wie hart ich davon schied
Alexander von Fielitz, "Anathema" 1896pub, Op9,9
from *Eliland*

O, der Alpen blanke Kette, wie sie glänzt im Morgenblau!
Alexander von Fielitz, "Wanderträume" 1896pub, Op9,8
from *Eliland*

O Irmingard, wie schön bist du, holdseliger ist Keine
Alexander von Fielitz, "Heimliche Grüsse" 1896pub, Op9,4
from *Eliland*

So harrte ich schweigend; durch die Hand, die kalte
Alban Berg, "Im Morgengrauen" 1904

Was ist mir denn geschehen? Bin ich vom Traum erwacht?
Ludwig Thuille, "Sommermorgen" 189-?pub, Op5,2
from *Drei Frauenlieder*

Weisst Du die Rose, die Du mir gegeben?
Richard Strauss, "Rote Rosen" 1883

Wenn's im Thal zu Abend läutet, und es kommt die Dämmerzeit
Ludwig Thuille, "Botschaft" 189-?, Op7,4
from *Von Lieb' und Leid*

Wie wundersam ist dies Verlorengehn
Hugo Kaun, "Wie wundersam" 1906?pub, Op68,2

Wohl manchen Rosenzweig brach ich vom Pfade am grünen Strand
Alexander von Fielitz, "Rosenzweige" 1896pub, Op9,3
from *Eliland*
Charles Edward Ives, "Rosenzweig" 1899?

Julius (Ernst Wilhelm) Stinde (1841-1905)

Auf ein freies Feld bin ich gezogen
Georg Rauchenecker, "Trau, schau, wem." 1940pub, sop.pf
from *Sieben Lieder von J. Stinde* (7)

Dass wir sollen selig sein, will ein lichter Tag erscheinen
Georg Rauchenecker, "Hochzeitsmorgen" 1940pub
from *Lieder der Brautzeit* (2)

Gebleicht sind die Linnen und harren im Schrein
Georg Rauchenecker, "Wie lange noch?" 1940pub, sop.pf
from *Sieben Lieder von J. Stinde* (4)

Ich habe ein Paar Schuhe mit himmelblauem Band
Georg Rauchenecker, "Die Tanzschuhe" 1940pub, sop.pf
from *Sieben Lieder von J. Stinde* (2)

Ihr Heiligen am Kirchenthor aus wettergrauem Stein
Georg Rauchenecker, "Vor der Kirche" 1940pub
from *Lieder der Brautzeit* (3)

Im Schlehendorn, im Schlehendorn, da sitzt ein Vogel und singt
Georg Rauchenecker, "Im Schlehendorn" 1940pub, sop.pf
from *Sieben Lieder von J. Stinde* (1)

Mein lieber Goldschmied, schmiede fein aus laut'rem Gold
Georg Rauchenecker, "Auftrag" 1940pub
from *Lieder der Brautzeit* (1)

Still ist es worden aller Ort
Georg Rauchenecker, "Im Heim" 1940pub
from *Lieder der Brautzeit* (5)

Und ist mein Schatz im fremden Land
Georg Rauchenecker, "Trost" 1940pub, sop.pf
from *Sieben Lieder von J. Stinde* (5)

Was bin ich in's Kloster gegangen und hatt' es doch nicht not?
Georg Rauchenecker, "Gesang der Nonne" 1940pub, sop.pf
from *Sieben Lieder von J. Stinde* (6)

Wo im Wald die klugen Rehe gehen
Georg Rauchenecker, "Waldweg" 1940pub, sop.pf
from *Sieben Lieder von J. Stinde* (3)

Zu diesem Reigen reiche mir die Hand
Georg Rauchenecker, "Hochzeit" 1940pub
from *Lieder der Brautzeit* (4)

Friedrich Leopold, Graf zu Stolberg-Stolberg (1750-1819)

Ach, mir ist das Herz so schwer
Franz Schubert, "Lied in der Abwesenheit" (unfinished), 1816, D416

Brich nur, brich, du armes Herz! Ach wie blutet deine Wunde!
Johann Abraham Peter Schulz, "Lied eines Unglücklichen" 1782-90pub

Des Lebens Tag ist schwer und schwül
Johann Abraham Peter Schulz, "Lied" 1782-90pub
Franz Schubert, "Lied (Die Mutter Erde)" 1823, D788

Groß und rothentflammet schwebet
Franz Schubert, "Abendlied" 1815, D276

Ich hab ein Bächlein funden vom Städtchen ziemlich weit
Johann Rudolf Zumsteeg, "Daphne am Bach" 1803pub
from *Kleine Balladen und Lieder, fünftes Heft*
Louise Reichardt, "Daphne am Bach"
Franz Schubert, "Daphne am Bach" 1816, D411

Ich sehe mit Schmerzen, du kennest die Kerzen
Johann Rudolf Zumsteeg, "Die Mädchen; an einen Jüngling" 1803pub
from *Kleine Balladen und Lieder, sechstes Heft*

In der Väter Hallen ruhte Ritter Rudolphs Heldenarm
Johann Rudolf Zumsteeg, "Romanze" 1803pub
from *Kleine Balladen und Lieder, sechstes Heft*
Franz Schubert, "Romanze" (sketch), 1816, D144

Meine Selinde! denn mit Engelstimme singt die Liebe mir zu
Franz Schubert, "Stimme der Liebe" 1816, D412

Mitten im Schimmer der spiegelnden Wellen
Franz Schubert, "Auf dem Wasser zu singen" 1823, D774
Jan Bedřich Kittl, "Lied auf dem Wasser zu singen" 183-?, Op4,3

Süße heilige Natur, laß mich gehn auf deiner Spur
Johann Abraham Peter Schulz, "An die Natur" 1782-90pub
Franz Schubert, "An die Natur" 1816, D372
Carl Loewe, "An die Natur" before 1826
Ernest Vietor, "An die Natur" 1936, Op14,1

Wenn Aurora früh mich grüsst
Johann Rudolf Zumsteeg, "Morgenlied eines Jünglings" 1803pub
from *Kleine Balladen und Lieder, sechstes Heft*

Willkommen, rothes Morgenlicht!
Franz Schubert, "Morgenlied" 1815, D266

Josef Ludwig Stoll (1778-1815)
Es sitzt die Zeit im weissen Kleid
Carl Maria von Weber, "Die Zeit" 1810, Op13,5, 1v.guit

O dass ich dir vom stillen Auge, in seinem liebevollen Schein
Ludwig van Beethoven, "An die Geliebte" 1811,1814, WoO140
Franz Schubert, "An die Geliebte" 1815, D303

O Liebe, die mein Herz erfüllet
Franz Schubert, "Lambertine" 1815, D301

Wenn im Spiele leiser Töne meine kranke Seele schwebt
Franz Schubert, "Labetrank der Liebe" 1815, D302

Adelheid (Zwierlein) von Stolterfoth (1800-1875)
Allein zu sein! Wie oft mit stillen Thränen hab' ich's erfleht
Eduard Lassen, "Einsamkeit"

Der Sänger ruht auf schroffem Stein
Johann Wenzeslaus Kalliwoda, "Des letzten Kaisers Rheinfahrt" 1846?, Op147,1

Hat ein Schiffer, grau und alt
Johann Wenzeslaus Kalliwoda, "Gisela" 1846?, Op147,2

Wer fühlt's nicht tief im Herzen
Joachim Raff, "Leb' wohl" 1855-63, Op98,5
from *Sanges-Frühling*

"Maria Stona" (Maria Scholz) (1861-1944)
Ach, Liebster, in Gedanken geb' ich dir hin mein Sein
Max Reger, "Ach, Liebster, in Gedanken" 1900, Op48,4, 1v(med).pf

An den Mondesstrahlen gleiten meine Küsse still empor
Max Reger, "Allen Welten abgewandt" 1901, Op55,14, 1v(med).pf

Um Mitternacht blühen die Blumen
Max Reger, "Um Mitternacht blühen die Blumen" 1901, Op79c,i,2

Theodor Storm (1817-1888)

Das aber kann ich nicht ertragen, dass noch wie sonst die Sonne lacht
August Bungert, "Cypresse" 1889-91pub, Op32,4
from *Verlorne Liebe, verlornes Leben*

Das ist die Drossel, die da schlägt
Othmar Schoeck, "April" 1928, Op35,2

Das macht, es hat die Nachtigall die ganze Nacht gesungen
Franz von Holstein, "Die Nachtigall" 1880, Op43,1
Erik Meyer-Helmund, "Das macht, es hat die Nachtigall" 1886-88
Alban Berg, "Die Nachtigall" 1907
from *Sieben frühe Lieder*
Ernest Vietor, "Die Nachtigall" 1936, Op14,12

Einen Brief soll ich schreiben meinem Schatz in der Fern'
Erik Meyer-Helmund, "Der Brief" 1886-88
Max Reger, "Einen Brief soll ich schreiben" 1903-04, Op76,8, 1v(med).pf
from *Schlichte Weisen, Band 1*

Es ist ein Flüstern in der Nacht
Robert Gund, "Es ist ein Flüstern in der Nacht" 1894, Op29,3
Alexander Zemlinsky, "Geflüster der Nacht" 1894-96, Op2,i,3

Heute, nur heute bin ich so schön
Max Reger, "Lied des Harfenmädchens" 1890/91
Reger SW lists this as "Dichter(in) unbekannt".
Franz Schreker, "Lied des Harfenmädchens" 1900?, Op7,8
Ernest Vietor, "Lied des Harfenmädchens" 1937-38, Op16,4

Ich hielt mein Herz verschlossen im engen Kämmerlein
Franz von Holstein, "Vergebliche Mühe" 1880, Op43,4

Ich wand ein Sträußlein morgens früh
Max Reger, "Nelken" 1894, Op15,3, 1v(med).pf
Felix Weingartner, "Nelken" 1900, Op28,3

Meine Mutter hat's gewollt
Robert Franz, "Ach, wär' es nie geschehen!" 1870?pub, Op23,3
Franz lists this as a Volkslied rather than crediting Storm's *Immensee*.
Wilhelm Kienzl, "Meine Mutter hat's gewollt" 189-?, Op39,2

Musikanten wollen wandern, durch die Saiten streicht der Wind
Ernst Krenek, "Musikanten wollen wandern" 1930, Op64,2
from *Fiedellieder aus dem "Liederbuch dreier Freunde"*

Nun ein Scherflein in der Runde
Ernst Krenek, "Nun ein Scherflein in der Runde" 1930, Op64,5
from *Fiedellieder aus dem "Liederbuch dreier Freunde"*

Nun gieb ein Morgenküsschen, du hast genug der Ruh'
Anton Rubinstein, "Morgens" 1864, Op72,4

O lass mich nur von ferne stehn, und hangen stumm an deinem Blick
Frederic Louis Ritter, "Bettler Liebe" 1876pub, Op10,3
Max Reger, "Bettlerliebe" 1890/91

Schließe mir die Augen beide mit den lieben Händen zu
Hermann Goetz, "Schliesse mir die Augen beide" 1868-76, Op12,2

Alban Berg, "Schließe mir die Augen beide" 1900
Joseph Marx, "Schließe mir die Augen beide" 1905, 1v(med).pf
Alban Berg, "Schließe mir die Augen beide" 1925

Sie sass in unserm Mädchenkreise ein Stern im Frauenfirmament
Felix Weingartner, "Eine Fremde" 1893, Op18,4
from *Severa. Sechs ernste Lieder*

So komme, was da kommen mag! Solang du lebest, ist es Tag
Ernest Vietor, "Trost" 1936, Op14,10

Über die Haide hallet mein Schritt, dumpf aus der Erde wandert es mit!
Johannes Brahms, "Über die Heide" 1882pub, Op86,4, 1v(low).pf
August Bungert, "Über die Haide" 1889-91pub, Op32,5
from *Verlorne Liebe, verlornes Leben*

Wohl fühl ich wie das Leben rinnt
Franz Schreker, "Wohl fühl ich wie das Leben rinnt" 189-?, Op4,3

Eleonore van der Straaten

Bächlein, Bächlein, wie du eilen kannst
Erich Wolfgang Korngold, "Das eilende Bächlein" 1935pub
from *Unvergänglichkeit* (2)

Deine edlen weissen Hände legen meine Seel' zur Ruh'
Erich Wolfgang Korngold, "Unvergänglichkeit" 1935pub
from *Unvergänglichkeit* (1,5)

Nimm meinen schweren Dornenkranz aus meinem weissen Haar
Erich Wolfgang Korngold, "Stärker als der Tod" 1935pub
from *Unvergänglichkeit* (4)

Was Du mir bist? Der Ausblick in ein schönes Land
Erich Wolfgang Korngold, "Was Du mir bist..." 1928-29, Op22,1

Wenn du schläfst, ich segne dich, Kind
Erich Wolfgang Korngold, "Das schlafende Kind" 1935pub
from *Unvergänglichkeit* (3)

Moritz, Graf von Strachwitz (1822-1847)

Mein altes Ross, mein Spielgenoss
Robert Schumann, "Mein altes Ross" 1850, Op127,4

's sind heute dreiunddreissig Jahr, dass ich kein Segel sah
Carl Loewe, "Der gefangene Admiral" 1850, Op115

Wie gerne Dir zu Füssen sing ich mein tiefstes Lied
Erik Meyer-Helmund, "Wie gerne Dir zu Füssen" 1886-88

August Stramm (1874-1915)

Aus allen Winkeln gellen Fürchte Wollen
Wolfgang Rihm, "Sturmangriff" 1970, Op1,8

Die Steine feinden Fenster grinst Verrat
Wolfgang Rihm, "Patrouille" 1970, Op1,6

Droben schmettert ein greller Stein
Wolfgang Rihm, "Verzweifelt" 1968-69, Op1,11

Müde webt Stumpfen dämmert Beten
Wolfgang Rihm, "Abend" 1970, Op1,5

Stäbe flehen Kreuze Arme Schrift Zagt blasses Unbekannt
Wolfgang Rihm, "Kriegsgrab" 1970, Op1,7

W. Strauss
O Jugendlust, o Jugendglück, wie seid Ihr doch so weit
Frank van der Stucken, "O Jugendlust, o Jugendglück" 1892pub

Karl Streckfuss (1778-1844)
Du liebes, holdes, himmelsüsses Wesen
Carl Maria von Weber, "Sonett" 1812, Op23,4

August Strindberg (1849-1912)
Schien mir's, als ich sah die Sonne
Anton Webern, "Schien mir's, als ich sah die Sonne" 1915, Op12,3

Regine Strümpell
Mit Neigen ich dich grüße, du blickst so mild in meinen Tag
Emil Mattiesen, "Maria im Rosenhag (gemalt von Stephan Lochner)" 190-?pub, Op11,6
from *Stille Lieder* (6)

Mathilde Gräfin Stubenberg (1863-1927)
Nichts soll, o Herr
Felix Weingartner, "Gottvertrauen" 1913, Op55,1

Christoph Christian Sturm (1740-1786)
Erwacht zum neuen Leben
Wolfgang Amadeus Mozart, "Im Frühlingsanfang" 1791, K597

Segne, Vater, meinen Fleiss
Carl Loewe, "Segne, Vater, meinen Fleiss" before 1829

Sei gnädig mir nach deiner Güte
Carl Loewe, "Busslied (nach dem 51. Psalm)" 1826, 4v

Sieh Jesum Christum leiden!
Carl Loewe, "Jesus auf Golgatha" 1826, 4v

Julius Karl Reinhold Sturm (1816-1896)
Da geht er wieder, der bleiche Knabe
Léander Schlegel, "Zu späte Reue" 1900, Op20,13
from *Deutsche Liebeslieder*
Franz Schreker, "Zu späte Reue" 1900?, Op7,2

Das Meer ist still, die Stürme schlafen
Johann Vesque von Püttlingen, "Willkommene Ruhe" 185-?, Op54,1

Das war die Lisa, die lustige Maid
Erik Meyer-Helmund, "Ein kleines Versehen" 1886-88

Der Bauer steht vor seinem Feld
Felix Weingartner, "Der Bauer und sein Kind" 1904, Op31,3

Der Kukuk hat ein einzig Lied
Franz Schreker, "Die Liebe als Recensentin" 189-?, Op4,4

Der Tag neigt sich zu Ende
Hans Pfitzner, "Abendlied" 1884

Es schwebt um deine zierliche Hand
Felix Weingartner, "Auf ihre Hand" 1900, Op28,4

Freude, wohin mein Auge schaut, duftende Blumen, fröhliche Lieder
Frederic Louis Ritter, "Im Frühling" 1876pub, Op10,5

Genieße still zufrieden den sonnig heitern Tag
Felix Weingartner, "Guter Rat" 1900, Op28,6

Ich sass noch spät in meinem Zimmer
Felix Weingartner, "Frühlingsgespenster" 1894, Op19,4
from *Hilaria. Sechs heitere Lieder*

Im kühlen Schatten, auf sonnigen Höh'n
Carl Reinecke, "Als Mütterchen krank war"
from *Kinderlieder*

Komm, o Nacht, und nimm mich hin, dass ich schlafend mich vergesse
Frederic Louis Ritter, "Komm, o Nacht" 1876pub, Op10,4

Lass nicht dein Auge auf mir ruh'n, o wende deinen Blick von mir!
Frederic Louis Ritter, "Bitte" 1871pub, Op6,5

Mir träumte, die Sonne glühte am blauen Himmelszelt
Felix Weingartner, "Ein Traum" 1894, Op19,3
from *Hilaria. Sechs heitere Lieder*

Schlafe, mein Liebchen, ich dekke dich zu
Franz Schreker, "Wiegenliedchen" 1900?, Op7,1

Schneewittchen hinter den Bergen, bei den sieben Zwergen
Carl Reinecke, "Schneewittchen"
from *Kinderlieder*

Tod, dir zum Raube fiel eine Welt
Felix Weingartner, "Auf einem verfallenen Kirchhof" 1900, Op28,5

Über Nacht, über Nacht kommt still das Leid
Hugo Wolf, "Über Nacht" 1878

Unser Schifflein treibt umher auf des Lebens weitem Meer
Max Reger, "Heimweh" 1900, 1v(med).organ
from *Zwei geistliche Lieder* (2)

Versank die Sonne still im Meere
Felix Weingartner, "Oenothera" 1900, Op28,2

Was nur dadrinnen der Graukopf macht?
Felix Weingartner, "Motten" 1899, Op25,4

Wohin, du rauschender Strom, wohin?
Louis Spohr, "Wohin?" 1856, WoO125

Zur weißen Gans sprach einst vertraulich eine graue
Felix Weingartner, "Zwei Gänse" 1894, Op19,5
from *Hilaria. Sechs heitere Lieder*
Max Reger, "Zwei Gänse 'De Capitolio'" 1901, Op55,8, 1v(med).pf

Johannes Hinrich Suck (1849-1929)
Ehre sei Gott in der Höhe! Ehre sei Gott!
Carl Loewe, "Weihnachts-Cantate" before 1829

Hermann Sudermann (1857-1928)
Du wähnst mich fromm, du wähnst mich weise
Felix Mottl, "Du wähnst mich fromm!" 1896?pub

Margarete Susman (Margarete von Bendemann) (1874-1966)
Im Feld ein Mädchen singt. Vielleicht ist ihr Liebster gestorben
Jean Sibelius, "Im Feld ein Mädchen singt" 1906, Op50,3

Algernon Charles Swinburne (1837-1909)
Die Wellen tragen vom Lande fort mein Schiff und schlagen um seinen Bord
Franz von Holstein, "Seefahrt" 1880, Op43,2
poem from "Chastelard"

Wenzel Swoboda (1764-1822)
Ich sah sie hingesunken
Carl Maria von Weber, "Ich sah sie hingesunken" 1804, J.41

"Carmen Sylva" (Königin Elisabeth von Rumänien) (1843-1916)
Ach, ich küsste dich nur einmal
Wilhelm Kienzl, "Der Kuss" 189-?, Op31,2

Die Blume verblühet auf fliessender Fluth
Hans Sommer, "Die Blume verblühet auf fliessender Fluth" 1884pub, Op6,1
from *Sappho's Gesänge aus Carmen Sylva's Dichtung*

Flieg, Schifflein, flieg!
Felix Weingartner, "Weberlied" 1900, Op28,7

Fragst du mit den Äugelein, was da glänzt am Himmelszelt
Hans Sommer, "Zwei Wiegenlieder, 2" 1891pub, Op15,2

Hört mich, Ihr grausamen Götter
Hans Sommer, "Hört mich, Ihr grausamen Götter" 1884pub, Op6,3
from *Sappho's Gesänge aus Carmen Sylva's Dichtung*

Ich halt' ein Stückchen Leder
Felix Weingartner, "Schuhmacherlied" 1900, Op28,8

Ich singe der Kraft, die die Erde erhält
Hans Sommer, "Ich singe der Kraft, die die Erde erhält" 1884pub, Op6,5
from *Sappho's Gesänge aus Carmen Sylva's Dichtung*

Mein Herz ist die Quelle, die Leben Dir schenkt
Hans Sommer, "Zwei Wiegenlieder, 1" 1891pub, Op15,1

Nicht lange ist's her, da lachte die Welt mir und das Meer
Hans Sommer, "Nicht lange ist's her, da lachte die Welt mir und das Meer" 1884pub, Op6,4
from *Sappho's Gesänge aus Carmen Sylva's Dichtung*

Weine nicht, weil dich die Götter gesendet
Hans Sommer, "Weine nicht, weil dich die Götter gesendet" 1884pub, Op6,6
from *Sappho's Gesänge aus Carmen Sylva's Dichtung*

Wozu soll ich reden? Mein Wort ist so alt!
Hans Sommer, "Wozu soll ich reden? Mein Wort ist so alt!" 1884pub, Op6,2
from *Sappho's Gesänge aus Carmen Sylva's Dichtung*

Ludwig Count von Széchényi (1781-1855)
Es floh die Zeit im Wirbelfluge
Franz Schubert, "Der Flug der Zeit" 1821?, D515

Wirst du halten, was du schwurst
Franz Schubert, "Die abgeblühte Linde" 1821?, D514

"Talvj:" see Therese A. L. von Jacob

Wilhelm Tappert (1830-1907)
Schaust in's Stübchen klein, holder Sonnenschein!
Franz Abt, "An den Sonnenschein" 1870?pub
from *Kinderlieder*

Sara Teasdale (1884-1933)
Ich frag hinauf in die Sterne, was ich dem Liebsten soll schenken
Harald Genzmer, "Nachts bei Amalfi" 1990, sop.pf
from *Sechs Lieder nach angelsächsischen Dichtern* (2)

Lass es sein vergessen, wie eine Blume vergessen
Harald Genzmer, "Lied" 1990, sop.pf
from *Sechs Lieder nach angelsächsischen Dichtern* (3)

Wernher von Tegernsee (fl.1172)
Du bist mein, ich bin dein, dess sollst du gewiss sein (see also "Ich bin dein…")
George Henschel, "Du bist mein" 188-?, Op46,2

Ich bin dein, du bist mein, des sollt du gewiß sein (see also "Du bist mein..")
Peter Cornelius, "Ein Wort der Liebe" 1861-62, Op6,3, sop.bar.pf
Erik Meyer-Helmund, "Altdeutscher Liebesreim" 1886-88
Hermann Behn, "Altes Minnelied" 189-?, Op1,i,2, sop.pf

Esaias Tegnér (1782-1846)
Herbst ist es nun! Nimmer die Stürme des Meeres ruh'n
Max Bruch, "Ingeborg's Klage (aus *Frithjof*)" 1870pub

Nun brennet am Nilstrom die Sonne so sehr
Carl Loewe, "Die Zugvögel" 1837-38, Op74
translated from the Swedish by Johann Carl Schütt

Konrad Telmann (Zitelmann) (1854-1897)
Durch die froh erschrockene Welt
Hugo Kaun, "Lenz" 1905pub, Op61,3

Wilhelm Telschow (1809-1872)
Der Feinde Scharen rüsten sich
Carl Loewe, "Des Königs Zuversicht" 1849, Op118(?)
after Psalm 3

Der Kön'ge Herzen, Rath und Sinn hast du, o Gott, in Händen
Carl Loewe, "Bitte zu Gott um Frieden" 1854, 1v.mch.organ

Gieb ihm dein Herz und breite die Hände nach ihm aus
Carl Loewe, "Gieb ihm dein Herz!" 1848, 4v

Hinauf zu jenen Bergen schau' ich
Carl Loewe, "Hinauf zu jenen Bergen" 1848, 4v
after Psalm 121

Im Lande Uz, dem schönsten Idumäa's, war einst ein Hirtenfürst
Carl Loewe, "Hiob-Idyll" 1848

Mit einem Blicke deiner Augen hast du mir Muth ins Herz gesandt
Carl Loewe, "Des frommen Hirten Liebessang" 1853
from the Oratorio *Das Hohelied Salomonis*

Mög' er ewig wiederkehren
Carl Loewe, "Mög' er ewig wiederkehren" 1853

O dass doch ihr barmherzig wär't
Carl Loewe, "Hiobs Todesschauer" 1848

Siehe, wir preisen selig die erduldet haben!
Carl Loewe, "Siehe, wir preisen selig" 1848, 4v
translated from Jacobus Apostulus

Und Hiobs Hause nahend, sahen sie den ganz Entstellten
Carl Loewe, "Hiobs Todessang" 1848, sop.alt.ten.baß.pf

Alfred, Lord Tennyson (1809-1892)
Süss und sacht, sachte weh', Wind du, vom westlichen Meer
Adolf Jensen, "Süss und sacht" 1873-75, Op52,2
translated by Ferdinand Freiligrath

Weil noch, Sonnenstrahl, leuchte, Glanz, feldein
Franz Liszt, "Weil noch, Sonnenstrahl" 1879
translated from the English by L. Kirschbaum

Thale
Husaren sind gar wack're Truppen
Carl Maria von Weber, "Husarenlied" 1821, Op68,6, 4mv

Erwin Thalhammer (1916-)
Steige aus der Nacht hernieder, Liebste, wie der Mond
Gottfried von Einem, "Das Nachttier" 1983, Op73,10
from *Tag- und Nachtlieder*

Frank Thiess (1890-1977)
Höre mich im Regen rauschen auf die Wipfel, auf die Wiesen
Louis Ferdinand, "Der Tote spricht..." 1952pub

Im Lichte wächst die Weide, vom Wasser lebt das Moos
Louis Ferdinand, "Russisches Volkslied" 1952pub

Lieder, die gleich Regenschauern jagend durch die Lüfte ziehn
Louis Ferdinand, "An die Leserin" 1952pub

Woher ich komme weiß ich nicht
Louis Ferdinand, "Woher ich komme..." 1952pub

Moritz August von Thümmel (1738-1817)
Die Lieb und unser Vogelfang
Leopold Kozeluch, "Vogelstellerlied" 1785?

Hermann Thürauf
Es schaut zum Bauernhaus der Maienbusch heraus
Richard Trunk, "Von den Tauben" 1963pub, Op76,5

(Johann) Ludwig Tieck (1773-1853)
Auf Wogen gezogen, von Klängen, Gesängen
Louis Spohr, "Schifferlied der Wasserfee" 1826, Op72,2

Aus Wolken fällt die frohe Stunde
Paul Hindemith, "Nur Mut" 1925, Op35,i,4, sop.ob.vla.vc
from *Die Serenaden*

Dicht von Felsen eingeschloßen
Louise Reichardt, "Aus *Genoveva*" 1806pub
Friedrich Silcher, "Liebesschmerz"

Durch die bunten Rosenhecken
Louise Reichardt, "Durch die bunten Rosenhecken" 1806pub

Feldeinwärts flog ein Vögelein
Carl Friedrich Zelter, "Herbstlied" 1800

Geliebter, wo zaudert dein irrender Fuß?
Louise Reichardt, "Liebe" 1800pub
Johannes Brahms, "Sulima: Romanzen aus L. Tiecks Magelone (13)" 1862, Op33,13

Im Windsgeräusch, in stiller Nacht
Johann Friedrich Reichardt, "Nacht" 1810?

Keinen hat es noch gereut
Johannes Brahms, "Romanzen aus L. Tiecks Magelone (1)" 1861, Op33,1

Liebe kam aus fernen Landen
Johannes Brahms, "Romanzen aus L. Tiecks Magelone (4)" 1861, Op33,4

Muß es eine Trennung geben
Johannes Brahms, "Romanzen aus L. Tiecks Magelone (12)" 1862-69?, Op33,12

O alte Heimat süß! wo find' ich wieder dich?
Fanny Hensel, "Ferne" 1823, Op9,2

Ruhe, Süßliebchen im Schatten der grünen, dämmernden Nacht
Louis Spohr, "Schlaflied" 1826, Op72,6
Louise Reichardt, "Poesie" 1806pub
Robert Franz, "Schlummerlied" 1843pub, Op1,10
Johannes Brahms, "Romanzen aus L. Tiecks Magelone (9)" 1862-69?, Op33,9

Sind es Schmerzen, sind es Freuden
Carl Maria von Weber, "Sind es Schmerzen, sind es Freuden" 1813, Op30,6
Johannes Brahms, "Romanzen aus L. Tiecks Magelone (3)" 1861, Op33,3

So tönet denn, schäumende Wellen
Johannes Brahms, "Verzweiflung: Romanzen aus L. Tiecks Magelone (10)" 1862-69?, Op33,10

So willst du des Armen dich gnädig erbarmen?
Johannes Brahms, "Romanzen aus L. Tiecks Magelone (5)" 1862, Op33,5

Traun! Bogen und Pfeil sind gut für den Feind
Johannes Brahms, "Romanzen aus L. Tiecks Magelone (2)" 1861, Op33,2

Treue Liebe dauert lange
Johannes Brahms, "Romanzen aus L. Tiecks Magelone (15)" 1869, Op33,15

War es dir, dem diese Lippen bebten
Johannes Brahms, "Romanzen aus L. Tiecks Magelone (7)" 1862-69?, Op33,7

Wie der Quell so lieblich klinget
Felix Mendelssohn, "Minnelied" 1840?pub, Op47,1

Wie froh und frisch mein Sinn sich hebt
Johannes Brahms, "Romanzen aus L. Tiecks Magelone (14)" 1869, Op33,14

Wie ist es denn, daß trüb und schwer so alles kömmt
Franz Schubert, "Abend" 1819, D645

Wie schnell verschwindet so Licht als Glanz
Johannes Brahms, "Romanzen aus L. Tiecks Magelone (11)" 1862-69?, Op33,11

Wie soll ich die Freude, die Wonne denn tragen?
Johannes Brahms, "Romanzen aus L. Tiecks Magelone (6)" 1862, Op33,6

Wir lustigen Bürger in grüner Stadt
Carl Loewe, "Vogelgesang" 1823, Op9,vi,3

Wir müssen uns trennen, geliebtes Saitenspiel
Johannes Brahms, "Romanzen aus L. Tiecks Magelone (8)" 1862-69?, Op33,8

Wohl dem Mann, der in der Stille
Louise Reichardt, "Wohl dem Mann"

Johann Friedrich Tiede (1732-1795)

Wie, wenn die Sonn' aufgehet
Josefine Lang, "Wie, wenn die Sonn' aufgeht" WoO

Christoph August Tiedge (1752-1841)

Alles ruht wie abgeschieden, abgelöst ist jedes Joch
Mauro Giuliani, "Ständchen" 1817pub, Op89,5, v.pf./guitar

Die du so gern in heil'gen Nächten feierst
Ludwig van Beethoven, "An die Hoffnung" 1805, Op32

Königliche Morgensonne
Franz Schubert, "An die Sonne" 1815, D272

Ob ein Gott sei? ob er einst erfülle
Ludwig van Beethoven, "An die Hoffnung" 1815?, Op94

Schöne Minka ich muss scheiden
Ferdinand Ries, "Der Kosack und sein Mädchen" 1829/30pub, Op154,5

Wer lässt hier so lieblich, wer lässt so allein
Louis Spohr, "Wechselgesang" 1838, Op107,2, sop.ten.pf

Wiedersehn! Wiedersehn! Endlich tönt dir mein Willkommen!
Carl Friedrich Zelter, "Wiedersehen" 1807

Aleksei Konstantinovich Tolstoi (1817-1875)

Der Fürst ritt am Morgen mit seinem Geleit
Franz Liszt, "Der blinde Sänger" 1875, declamation.pf

Leo (Lev) Nikolaevich Tolstoi (1828-1910)
Ich sehe Thränen im Aug' dir glänzen
Franz Schreker, "Unendliche Liebe" 189-?, Op4,1

Tosti
Öffne die Augen, Tancredi, die Leichenfeier anzusehen
Friedrich Curschmann, "Canzonetta" 1837, Op16,1,i
translated by J.C.Grünbaum

Peter Toussell
Alles, was war: Tag, Abend und Jahr verweht wie der Wind
Louis Ferdinand, "Das Währende" 1955pub

Albert Träger (1830-1912)
An deinem Finger, dem weissen, schlanken blitzt golden ein schmaler Streif
Adolf Jensen, "An deinem Finger, dem weissen, schlanken–" 1863pub, Op13,4, 1v(low).pf

Aus des Morgenhimmels Blau
Arno Kleffel, "Aus des Morgenhimmels Blau" Op10,1

Der Frühling kehrt alljährlich wieder
Arno Kleffel, "Noch niemals" Op10,2

Der Sonne letzte Strahlen säumen
Arno Kleffel, "Nach dem Sturme" Op10,3

Die Welt weiss deinen Namen nicht
Eduard Lassen, "Im Verborgenen" Op54,5
Arno Kleffel, "Im Verborg'nen" Op10,4

Ihr Sternlein, hoch am Himmelszelt!
Arno Kleffel, "Ihr Sternlein" Op10,5

Ist mir's zu Muthe schwül und bang
Hermann Goetz, "Beruhigung" 1868-76, Op12,6

Kleine Blumen im engen Thal
Arno Kleffel, "Sonnenblicke" Op7,2

Noch liegt der Winter in der Stadt
Hermann Goetz, "Ein Frühlingstraum" 1862-63, Op19,4

Schließe, mein Kind, schließe die Äuglein zu
Max Reger, "Wiegenlied" 1898

Schneeglöckchen läuten leis' im Thal
Arno Kleffel, "Erwachen" Op7,3

Steh' auf, steh' auf und öffne das Fenster schnell
Arno Kleffel, "Morgenständchen" Op12,6

Thut auch das bange Herz dir weh
Hermann Goetz, "Der Frühling kommt!" 1862-63, Op19,5

Und würdest nie die Hand du falten
Arno Kleffel, "Und würdest nie die Hand du falten" Op12,2

Wie Lenzeshauch hast Du mich stets erquickt
Adolf Jensen, "Wie Lenzeshauch" 1863, Op9,1

Georg Trakl (1887-1914)

Abends schweben blutige Linnen
Paul Hindemith, "Abends schweben blutige Linnen" 1922, Op23,2, alt.fl.cl.quart
from *Die junge Magd* (6)

Am Abend, wenn die Glokken Frieden läuten
Felix Wolfes, "Verfall" 1953, 1v(med).pf

Die Bläue meiner Augen ist erloschen in dieser Nacht
Anton Webern, "Nachts" 1919, Op14,5, sop.insts
from *Sechs Lieder* (5)

Dunkler Odem im grünen Gezweig
Anton Webern, "Gesang einer gefangenen Amsel" 1919, Op14,6, sop.insts
from *Sechs Lieder* (6)
Felix Wolfes, "Gesang einer gefangenen Amsel" 1965, 1v(med).pf

Gewaltig endet so das Jahr
Felix Wolfes, "Verklärter Herbst" 1940, 1v(med).pf

Ihr großen Städte Steinern aufgebaut
Anton Webern, "Abendland III" 1917, Op14,4, sop.insts
from *Sechs Lieder* (4)

Immer wieder kehrst du, Melancholie
Felix Wolfes, "In ein altes Stammbuch" 1965, 1v(med).pf

In der Schmiede dröhnt der Hammer
Paul Hindemith, "In der Schmiede dröhnt der Hammer" 1922, Op23,2, alt.fl.cl.quart
from *Die junge Magd* (4)

Mond, als träte ein Totes aus blauer Höhle
Anton Webern, "Abendland I" 1919, Op14,2, sop.insts
from *Sechs Lieder* (2)

Nächtens übern kahlen Anger
Paul Hindemith, "Nächtens übern kahlen Anger" 1922, Op23,2, alt.fl.cl.quart
from *Die junge Magd* (3)

Oft am Brunnen
Paul Hindemith, "Oft am Brunnen" 1922, Op23,2, alt.fl.cl.quart
from *Die junge Magd* (1)

Schmächtig hingestreckt im Bette
Paul Hindemith, "Schmächtig hingestreckt im Bette" 1922, Op23,2, alt.fl.cl.quart
from *Die junge Magd* (5)

So leise sind die grünen Wälder
Anton Webern, "Abendland II" 1919, Op14,3, sop.insts
from *Sechs Lieder* (3)

Sonne, herbstlich dünn und zag
Felix Wolfes, "In den Nachmittag geflüstert" 1961

Stille begegnet am Saum des Waldes ein dunkles Wild
Wolfgang Rihm, "Geistliche Dämmerung" 1969, Op1,2

Stille schafft sie in der Kammer
Paul Hindemith, "Stille schafft sie in der Kammer" 1922, Op23,2, alt.fl.cl.quart
from *Die junge Magd* (2)

Täglich kommt die gelbe Sonne über den Hügel
Anton Webern, "Die Sonne" 1921, Op14,1, sop.insts
from *Sechs Lieder* (1)

Über den weißen Weiher sind die wilden Vögel fort gezogen
Wolfgang Rihm, "Untergang" 1969, Op1,1

Unter verschnittenen Weiden, wo braune Kinder spielen
Paul Hindemith, "Trompeten" 1922, Op18,8

Verflossen ist das Gold der Tage
Wilhelm Grosz, "Rondel" 1922pub, Op11,2

S. Trebitsch
Unter spärlich grünen Blättern
Erich Wolfgang Korngold, "Sommer" 1916, Op9,6

Georg Friedrich Treitschke (1776-1842)
Wenn ich ein Vöglein wär, und auch zwei Flüglein hätt (see also Volkslied)
Ludwig van Beethoven, "Ruf vom Berge" 1816, WoO147

Ella Triebnigg-Pirkhert (Triebnigg) (1874-1938)
Wollt' vorüber gehen, doch es mußt' geschehen
Joseph Marx, "Wie einst" 1910pub, 1v(med).pf

Gertrud Triepel (1863-?)
Im Garten rauscht die Sommernacht
Max Reger, "Sommernacht" 1906, Op98,5, 1v(low).pf

Karl Bernhard Trinius (1778-1844)
Dürft' ich einmal dies Dach durchbrechen!
Carl Loewe, "Feuersgedanken" 1836, Op70

Johannes Trojan (1837-1915)
Marie auf der Wiese, auf der Wiese Marie
Max Reger, "Klein Marie" 1909-10, Op76,44, 1v(med).pf
from *Schlichte Weisen, Band 5, "Aus der Kinderwelt"*

Adolf Ritter von Tschabuschnigg (1809-1877)
Wer ist so spät noch fleissig wach?
Carl Loewe, "Tod und Tödin" 1844, Op105

Hermann Ubell (1876-?)
O presse deine Hand in meine Hand
Max Reger, "Junge Ehe" 1900, Op48,5, 1v(med).pf

Hermann Wilhelm Franz Ueltzen (1759-1808)
Im Arm der Liebe ruht sich's wohl
Ludwig van Beethoven, "Das Liedchen von der Ruhe" 1793, Op52,3

Johann Ludwig Uhland (1787-1862)
Ach Gott, wie weh tut Scheiden! (see also Volkslied)
Erich J. Wolff, "Scheiden" 1914pub, Lieder No.2

Als ich ging die Flur entlang
Othmar Schoeck, "Dichtersegen" 1910, Op20,3

An ihrem Grabe kniet' ich festgebunden
Richard Strauss, "Rückleben" 1900, Op47,3

An jedem Abend geh' ich aus hinauf den Wiesensteg
Edvard Grieg, "Lauf der Welt" 1889, Op48,3

Anzuschauen das Turnei, saßen hundert Frauen droben
Mikhail Glinka, "Der Sieger " (set in Russian), 1832
translated into Russian by Zhukovsky

Aus der Bedrängnis, die mich wild umkettet
Othmar Schoeck, "Auf ein Kind" 1908, Op20,1
Richard Strauss, "Auf ein Kind" 1900, Op47,1

Bei diesem kalten Wehen sind alle Straßen leer
Conradin Kreutzer, "Winterreise" 1811, Op34,6
from *Neun Wanderlieder von Uhland*
Norbert Burgmüller, "Winterreise" 1827-36?, Op3,4
Richard Strauss, "Winterreise" 1871
from *Jugendlieder*
August Bungert, "Bei diesem kalten Wehen" 1889-91pub, Op17,2

Bei einem Wirte wundermild da war ich jüngst zu Gaste
Conradin Kreutzer, "Einkehr" 1811, Op34,8
from *Neun Wanderlieder von Uhland*
Norbert Burgmüller, "Einkehr" 1827-36?, Op3,1
Richard Strauss, "Einkehr" 1871
from *Jugendlieder*
Richard Strauss, "Einkehr" 1900, Op47,4
Othmar Schoeck, "Einkehr" 1955, Op69,2, 2v.pf
from *Zwei zweistimmige Lieder für Kinder- oder Frauenchor*

Da fliegt, als wir im Felde gehn
Felix Weingartner, "Der Sommerfaden" 1891, Op15,5

Da liegen sie alle, die grauen Höhn
Carl Loewe, "Der König auf dem Thurme" 1828, Op9,i,2
Felix Weingartner, "Der König auf dem Turme" 1891, Op15,8

Das Haus benedei' ich und preis' es laut
Robert Schumann, "Brautgesang" 1849, Op146,1, satb

Das ist der Tag des Herrn
Felix Mendelssohn, "Sonntagsmorgen" 1836, Op77,1, 2sop.pf
Felix Weingartner, "Schäfers Sonntagslied" 1891, Op15,1

Das neue Haus ist aufgericht't
Othmar Schoeck, "Zimmerspruch" 1947, o.op43, mch

Der schöne Schäfer zog so nah'
Friedrich Silcher, "Der Schäfer"

Die linden Lüfte sind erwacht
Conradin Kreutzer, "Frühlings-Glaube" 1812, Op33,2
from *Fünf Frühlingslieder von Uhland*
Franz Schubert, "Frühlingsglaube" 1820, D686
Louis Spohr, "Frühlingsglaube" 1826, Op72,1
Friedrich Silcher, "Frühlingsglaube" 4v
Felix Mendelssohn, "Frühlingsglaube" 1830, Op9,8

Friedrich Curschmann, "Frühlingsglaube" 1833, Op5,3
Franz Ries, "Frühlingsglaube" before 1891
Ernest Vietor, "Frühlingsglaube" 1934-35, Op12,3
from *Frühlingslieder*

Die Muse fehlt nicht selten
Felix Weingartner, "Verspätetes Hochzeitslied" 1891, Op15,2

Die Totenglocke tönte mir
Othmar Schoeck, "Nachruf" 1943, o.op42, s.a.b

Droben stehet die Capelle, schauet still in's Thal hinab
Conradin Kreutzer, "Die Kapelle" 1825?pub, Op64,3
Robert Schumann, "Die Capelle" 1849, Op69,6, ssaa.pf or physhar
from *Romanzen für Frauenstimmen I*
Othmar Schoeck, "Die Kapelle" 1905, Op3,2

Du kamst, du gingst mit leiser Spur
Othmar Schoeck, "Auf den Tod eines Kindes" 1907, Op3,6

Ein Goldschmied in der Bude stand
Carl Loewe, "Goldschmieds Töchterlein" 1827, Op8,1

Ein Schifflein ziehet leise den Strom hin seine Gleise
Friedrich Silcher, "Das Schifflein" 4v
Carl Loewe, "Das Schifflein" 1835
Felix Mendelssohn, "Das Schifflein" 1841, Op99,4
Robert Schumann, "Das Schifflein" 1849, Op146,5, satb or sop.fl.hn
Robert Gund, "Das Schifflein" 1914, Op39,3

Einst am schönen Frühlingsmorgen tritt der Räuber vor den Wald
Carl Loewe, "Der Räuber" 1835, Op34,2

Ergehst du dich im Abendlicht
Richard Strauss, "Des Dichters Abendgang" 1900, Op47,2

Es ging wohl über die Heide
Peter Cornelius, "Die Vätergruft" 1874, Op19, bass.satb
words to the Geisterchor by Cornelius

Es reit der Herr von Falkenstein
Johannes Brahms, "Das Lied vom Herrn von Falkenstein" 1857?, Op43,4

Es schritt wohl über die Heide
Franz Liszt, "Die Vätergruft" 1844/1860pub

Es stand in alten Zeiten ein Schloß so hoch und hehr
Ferruccio Busoni, "Des Sängers Fluch" 1879, Op39, alt.pf

Es zogen drei Bursche wohl über den Rhein
Friedrich Silcher, "Der Wirthin Töchterlein"
Carl Loewe, "Der Wirthin Töchterlein" 1823, Op1,2

Gestorben war ich vor Liebeswonne
Franz Liszt, "Gestorben war ich" 1850pub
Nicolai Rimsky-Korsakov, "Gestorben war ich vor Liebeswonne" (set in Russian), 1898, Op55,4, ten.pf

Graf Eberhard im Bart vom Würtemberger Land
Carl Loewe, "Graf Eberhards Weissdorn" 1825, Op9,iv,5

Guckst du mir denn immer nach
Carl Loewe, "Hans und Grete" 1824, Op9,v,2
Max Reger, "Hans und Grete" 1904, Op76,19, 1v(med).pf
from *Schlichte Weisen, Band 2*

Hast du das Schloss gesehen, das hohe Schloss am Meer
Joachim Raff, "Das Schloss am Meer" 1855-63, Op98,1
from *Sanges-Frühling*

Horch! wie brauset der Sturm und der schwellende Strom
Johannes Brahms, "Märznacht" 1859-60?, Op44,12, ssaa.(pf)

Horch, wie der Sturm und der schwellende Strom
Carl Bohm, "Märznacht" 1887cop, Op322,1
text freely adapted

Ich bin so gar ein armer Mann
Conradin Kreutzer, "Lied eines Armen" 1820, Op23,5
Felix Weingartner, "Lied eines Armen" 1891, Op15,3

Ich bin vom Berg der Hirtenknab'
Carl Loewe, "Der Knabe vom Berge" before 1829
Robert Schumann, "Des Knaben Berglied" 1849, Op79,8
from *Lieder-Album für die Jugend*

Ich hatt' einen Kameraden, einen bessern find'st du nit
Friedrich Silcher, "Der gute Kamerad"

Ich hör' meinen Schatz, den Hammer er schwinget
Robert Schumann, "Der Schmidt" 1849, Op145,1, satb
Johannes Brahms, "Der Schmied" 1859, Op19,4
Adolf Jensen, "Der Schmied" 1864, Op24,6

Ich kenne sieben lust'ge Brüder
Richard Strauss, "Von den sieben Zechbrüdern" 1900, Op47,5

Ich reit' ins finstre Land hinein
Conradin Kreutzer, "Nachtreise" 1811, Op34,5
from *Neun Wanderlieder von Uhland*

Ich sass bei jener Linde mit meinem trauten Kinde
Carl Loewe, "Die Zufriedenen" 1824, Op9,v,4

Ich tret in deinen Garten
Felix Weingartner, "Nähe" 1913, Op55,2

Ich will ja nicht in Garten geh'n
Richard Strauss, "Die Drossel" 1877
from *Jugendlieder*

Im schönsten Garten wallten zwei Buhlen Hand in Hand
Robert Schumann, "Der Traum" 1849, Op146,3, satb

Im Sommer such' ein Liebchen dir in Garten und Gefild!
Carl Loewe, "Bauernregel" 1824, Op9,v,3
Erik Meyer-Helmund, "Im Sommer such' ein Liebchen dir!" 1886-88
Max Reger, "Bauernregel" 1892, Op8,5

Im stillen Klostergarten eine bleiche Jungfrau ging
Fanny Hensel, "Die Nonne" 1830pub, Op9,12(FM)

Joachim Raff, "Die Nonne" 1855-63, Op98,21
from *Sanges-Frühling*
Johannes Brahms, "Die Nonne" 1859-60?, Op44,6, ssaa.(pf)

Im Walde geh' ich wohlgemut
Max Reger, "Waldlied" 1892, Op8,1

In der hohen Hall' saß König Sifrid
Carl Loewe, "Die drei Lieder" 1825, Op3,3

In Liebesarmen ruht ihr trunken
Franz Liszt, "Hohe Liebe" 1850pub

Jung Siegfried war ein stolzer Knab'
Leopold Damrosch, "Siegfrieds Schwert"
from *Three Songs without Opus-number, by various authors* (3)

Kein beßre Lust in dieser Zeit
Edvard Grieg, "Jägerlied" 1863-64, Op4,4

Lebe wohl, lebe wohl, mein Lieb! muss noch heute scheiden
Conradin Kreutzer, "Lebewohl" 1807, Op34,1
from *Neun Wanderlieder von Uhland*
Othmar Schoeck, "Lebewohl" 1905?, Op3,4

Leben, das nur Leben scheinet
Hans Pfitzner, "Naturfreiheit" 1886

Lösen sich die ird'schen Bande?
Felix Weingartner, "Gruß der Seelen" 1891, Op15,4

Maria, du Zarte! du bist ein Rosengarte
Erich J. Wolff, "Marienruf" 1914pub, Lieder No.36
from Uhlands *Alte hoch= und niederdeutsche Volkslieder 1844*

Noch ahnt man kaum das Sonnenlicht
Conradin Kreutzer, "Morgenlied" 1811, Op34,4
from *Neun Wanderlieder von Uhland*
Anton Rubinstein, "Morgenlied" 1856, Op33,1

Noch singt den Widerhallen der Knabe sein Gefühl
Robert Schumann, "Der Sänger" 1849, Op145,3, satb

O blaue Luft nach trüben Tagen
Othmar Schoeck, "An einem heitern Morgen" 1910, Op20,2

O brich nicht Steg, du zitterst sehr!
Conradin Kreutzer, "Heimkehr" 1811, Op34,9
from *Neun Wanderlieder von Uhland*
Friedrich Curschmann, "Heimkehr" 1832, Op4,2
Johannes Brahms, "Heimkehr" 1851, Op7,6
Friedrich Gernsheim, "Heimkehr" 1865pub, Op3,6

O legt mich nicht ins dunkle Grab, nicht unter die grüne Erd' hinab!
Conradin Kreutzer, "Frühlings-Ruhe" 1812, Op33,3
from *Fünf Frühlingslieder von Uhland*
Othmar Schoeck, "Frühlingsruhe" 1905, Op20,4

O sanfter, süsser Hauch! schon weckest du wieder
Conradin Kreutzer, "Frühlings-Ahnung" 1812, Op33,1
from *Fünf Frühlingslieder von Uhland*

Jan Bedřich Kittl, "Frühlingsahnung" 183-?, Op4,2

O Winter, schlimmer Winter, wie ist die Welt so klein!
Felix Mendelssohn, "Hirtenlied" 1839, Op57,2

Oh, leget mich nicht ins Grab, unter die Erde
Nikolai Medtner, "Frühlingsberuhigung" 1913-14, Op28,5

Saatengrün, Veilchenduft, Lerchenwirbel, Wachtelschlag
Conradin Kreutzer, "Lob des Frühlings" 1815pub, Op33,5, sop.(t.b.).pf
from *Fünf Frühlingslieder von Uhland*
Joseph Marx, "Lob des Frühlings" 1907
Ernest Vietor, "Lob des Frühlings" 1934-35, Op12,1
from *Frühlingslieder*

Seid gegrüßt mit Frühlingswonne
Fanny Hensel, "Im Herbste" 1846, Op3,3, satb
from *Gartenlieder*
Othmar Schoeck, "Im Herbste" 1908, Op17,2, 1v(med).pf

Sie war ein Kind vor wenig Tagen
Felix Weingartner, "Wunder" 1891, Op15,6

So hab' ich endlich dich gerettet
Carl Loewe, "Die Abgeschiedenen" 1824, Op9,ii,3

So hab' ich nun die Stadt verlassen, wo ich gelebet lange Zeit
Conradin Kreutzer, "Abreise" 1811, Op34,7
from *Neun Wanderlieder von Uhland*
Johann Vesque von Püttlingen, "Abreise" 1836

So soll ich dich nun meiden, du meines Lebens Lust?
Conradin Kreutzer, "Scheiden und Meiden" 1811, Op34,2
from *Neun Wanderlieder von Uhland*
Peter Cornelius, "Scheiden und Meiden" 1847-48, 2sop.pf
Johannes Brahms, "Scheiden und Meiden" 1858, Op19,2
Othmar Schoeck, "Scheiden und Meiden" 1908, Op3,5

Solche Düfte sind mein Leben
Othmar Schoeck, "Wein und Brot" 1910, Op20,5

Stiller Garten, eile nur
Othmar Schoeck, "Der Kirchhof im Frühling" 1908, Op17,3, 1v(med).pf

Süßer goldner Frühlingstag! Inniges Entzücken
Conradin Kreutzer, "Frühlings-Feier" 1811, Op33,4
from *Fünf Frühlingslieder von Uhland*
Othmar Schoeck, "Frühlingsfeier" 1908, Op15,3

Über diesen Strom, vor Jahren, bin ich einmal schon gefahren
Carl Loewe, "Die Überfahrt" 1843, Op94,1

Von dir getrennet, liege ich begraben
Carl Loewe, "Geisterleben" 1819, Op9,i,4

Vor seinem Heergefolge ritt der kühne Held Harald
Carl Loewe, "Harald" 1835, Op45,1

Wann im letzten Abendstrahl
Othmar Schoeck, "Ruhetal" 1903, Op3,1

Was klinget und singet die Straßen herauf?
Carl Loewe, "Abschied" 1825, Op3,1
Othmar Schoeck, "Abschied" 1905?, Op3,3

Was stehst du so in stillem Schmerz
Felix Weingartner, "Mönch und Schäfer" 1891, Op15,7

Was wecken aus dem Schlummer mich für süsse Klänge doch?
Carl Loewe, "Das Ständchen" 1826, Op9,ii,4
Norbert Burgmüller, "Ständchen" 1827-36?, Op10,5
Louis Spohr, "Das Ständchen" 1838, Op105,3
Robert Kahn, "Ständchen" 1892, Op16,4

Wie willst du dich mir offenbaren
Richard Strauss, "Das Thal" 1902, Op51,1, bass.orch

Will ruhen unter den Bäumen hier
Conradin Kreutzer, "In der Ferne" 1806, Op34,3
from *Neun Wanderlieder von Uhland*
Johannes Brahms, "In der Ferne" 1858, Op19,3
Leopold Damrosch, "In der Ferne" Op10,1

Wolken seh' ich abendwärts
Othmar Schoeck, "Abendwolken" 1910, Op20,6

Zu Hirsau in den Träummern da wiegt ein Ulmenbaum
Richard Strauss, "Die Ulme zu Hirsau" 1899, Op43,3

Zu Speier im Saale, da hebt sich ein Klingen
Carl Loewe, "Graf Eberstein" 1826, Op9,vi,5

Titus Ullrich (1813-1891)
Die Fenster klär' ich zum Feiertag
Robert Schumann, "Die Fensterscheibe" 1851-52, Op107,2

Die Weiden lassen matt die Zweige hangen
Robert Schumann, "Herzeleid" 1851-52, Op107,1

Wir gingen einsam durch die Gartenflur in stiller Nacht
Adolf Jensen, "Notturno" 1863pub, Op13,3, 1v(low).pf

Ulrich von Lichtenstein (ca.1200-1275?)
In dem Walde süsse Töne singen kleine Vögelein
Felix Mendelssohn, "Frühlingslied" 1830, Op19,1

Margarete Ungemach
Flieget, ihr Wolken, eilet, ihr Winde
Erich Riede, "Liebeslied" Op23,1, sop.pf

Ich gehöre zu dir wie zum Herzen das Lied
Erich Riede, "Ich gehöre zu dir" Op23,3, sop.pf

Seit ich dir gehöre, ist alles Leid von meinen Schultern gefallen
Erich Riede, "Zueignung" Op23,2, sop.pf

Wie bin ich seltsam tief in dir verankert
Erich Riede, "Verbundenheit" Op23,4, sop.pf

Johann Karl Unger (1771-1836)
Bescheiden verborgen im buschichten Gang
Franz Schubert, “Die Nachtigall” 1821, D724, 2t2b.pf

Wer Lebenslust fühlet, der bleibt nicht allein
Franz Schubert, “Die Geselligkeit” 1818, D609, satb.pf
Schubert’s setting was earlier known as “Lebenslust”

Ungern-Sternberg
Wer des Leidens Kelch geleeret
Emilie Zumsteeg, “Tröstung” 1817pub
from the Hungarian
from *Neun Lieder* (7)

Unzer
Nie will ich meinen Bruder richten
Johann Abraham Peter Schulz, “Verhalten des Christen bei Irrenden” 1786pub

Robert Urban
Des Dorfes heimische Stille tat meinem trotzigen Sinne weh
Adolf Jensen, “Die Heimatglocken” 1880, Op61,5

Anna Barbara Urner (1760-1803)
Goldne Abendsonne, o, wie bist du schön!
Carl Loewe, “Die Abendsonne” before 1829

Johann Peter Uz (1720-1796)
Cypris, meiner Phyllis gleich, sass von Grazien umgeben!
Franz Schubert, “Die Liebesgötter” 1816, D446

Der Herr ist gut! ihr Himmel, höret und jauchzt mir nach
Johann Abraham Peter Schulz, “Dank” 1784pub

Die Munterkeit ist meiner Wangen
Franz Schubert, “An Chloen” (fragment), 1816?, D363

Du Schrecklicher, du Schrecklicher
Franz Schubert, “Gott im Ungewitter” D985, satb.pf

Du verstörst uns nicht, o Nacht! Sieh, wir trinken im Gebüsche
Franz Schubert, “Die Nacht” 1816?, D358

Freude, Königin der Weisen
Wolfgang Amadeus Mozart, “An die Freude” 1786, K53

In seinem schimmernden Gewand hast du den Frühling uns gesandt
Johann Abraham Peter Schulz, “Gott im Frühlinge” 1784pub
Franz Schubert, “Gott im Frühlinge” 1816, D448

O Sonne, Königin der Welt, die unser dunkles Rund
Franz Schubert, “An die Sonne” 1816, D439, satb.pf
Johann Abraham Peter Schulz, “An die Sonne” 1784pub

Singt, singt mit heiligem Entzücken, singt unserm Gott ein neues Lied!
Johann Abraham Peter Schulz, “Lob des Höchsten” 1784pub

Was sorgest du? Sei stille, meine Seele!
Franz Schubert, “Der gute Hirt” 1816, D449

Weiß Chloe mein geheim Verlangen?
Karl Friberth, "An Chloen" 1780pub

Zu Gott, zu Gott, zu Gott flieg' auf
Franz Schubert, "Gott der Weltschöpfer" D986, satb.pf

Lope Félix de Vega Carpio (1562-1635)
Die ihr dort wallet unter den Palmen, heilige Engel!
Eduard Lassen, "Wiegenlied der Jungfrau Maria" Op48,6
See also Geibel's translation, "Die ihr schwebet um diese Palmen"

Paul Verlaine (1844-1896)
Der Himmel, drüben über dem Dach in tiefblauem Schweigen
Helmut Paulsen, "Im Gefängnis"
translated from the French by Cäsar Flaischlen
from *Sieben besinnliche Lieder*

Ich kam so fromm, ein Waisenkind
Felix Wolfes, "Lied Kaspar Hausers" 1926
translated by Richard Dehmel

Leis dem Schmeichellied der Lauten
Othmar Schoeck, "Mandolinen" 1907, Op6,6

Regen über der Stadt und mein Herz steht in Tränen
Joseph Marx, "Regen" 1910, 1v(med).pf

Weich küßt die Zweige der weiße Mond
Conrad Ansorge, "Helle Nacht" 1895-96pub, Op10,1
translated by Richard Dehmel
Max Reger, "Helle Nacht" 1899, Op37,1, 1v(med).pf
Anton Webern, "Helle Nacht" 1906-08
translated by Richard Dehmel
from *Fünf Lieder* (5)
Clemens von Franckenstein, "Helle Nacht" 1913pub, Op34,1
adapted by Richard Dehmel

Berthold Viertel (1885-1953)
Die Leiter blieb noch unterm Feigenbaume stehen
Hanns Eisler, "L'automne californien" 1943

Wer traurig sein will, wird vielleicht mich lesen
Hanns Eisler, "Chanson allemande" 1953

Gisbert, Freiherr von Vincke (1813-1892)
Das macht mir bittre Pein, und treibt mich hin und her
Joachim Raff, "An die Dame (ii)" 1872, Op172,7
translated from the Scottish of Henry Stuart, Lord Darnley
from *Maria Stuart, ein Cyklus von Gesängen* (7)

Herr Jesu Christ, den sie gekrönt mit Dornen
Robert Schumann, "Nach der Geburt ihres Sohnes" 1852, Op135,2
translated from an old English collection
from *Gedichte der Königin Maria Stuart*
Joachim Raff, "Nach der Geburt ihres Sohnes" 1872, Op172,9
translated from the Scottish of Maria Stuart
from *Maria Stuart, ein Cyklus von Gesängen* (9)

Herrin! Dein sterngleich Aug' allein leiht meiner Seele Licht!
Joachim Raff, "David Riccio's letztes Lied" 1872, Op172,8
translated from the English
from *Maria Stuart, ein Cyklus von Gesängen* (8)

Ich zieh' dahin, ade, ade, mein fröhlich Frankenland
Robert Schumann, "Abschied von Frankreich" 1852, Op135,1
translated from an old English collection
from *Gedichte der Königin Maria Stuart*
Joachim Raff, "Maria Stuart's Abschied von Frankreich" 1872, Op172,5
translated from the French of Maria Stuart
from *Maria Stuart, ein Cyklus von Gesängen* (5)

In leisen Trauerklagen entströmt das Lied der Brust
Joachim Raff, "Klage (i)" 1872, Op172,1
translated from the French of Maria Stuart
from *Maria Stuart, ein Cyklus von Gesängen* (1)

Mein Jugendlenz ist nur ein Sorgenfrost
Joachim Raff, "Vor dem Gang zum Schaffot" 1872, Op172,10
translated from the English of Chidiock Tychbourne
from *Maria Stuart, ein Cyklus von Gesängen* (10)

Nichts von den Dingen allen, wie schön sich's immer bot
Joachim Raff, "Klage (iv)" 1872, Op172,4
translated from the French of Maria Stuart
from *Maria Stuart, ein Cyklus von Gesängen* (4)

Nur ein Gedanke, der mich freut und quält
Robert Schumann, "An die Königin Elisabeth" 1852, Op135,3
translated from an old English collection
from *Gedichte der Königin Maria Stuart*

O Gott, mein Gebieter, ich hoffe auf dich!
Robert Schumann, "Gebet" 1852, Op135,5
from *Gedichte der Königin Maria Stuart*
Joachim Raff, "Gebet" 1872, Op172,12
translated from the Latin of Maria Stuart
from *Maria Stuart, ein Cyklus von Gesängen* (12)

Und sei es, wo auch immer: im Wald, am grünen Hang
Joachim Raff, "Klage (iii)" 1872, Op172,3
translated from the French of Maria Stuart
from *Maria Stuart, ein Cyklus von Gesängen* (3)

Was mir einst Lust gewährte, hat Kummer jetzt gebracht
Joachim Raff, "Klage (ii)" 1872, Op172,2
translated from the French of Maria Stuart
from *Maria Stuart, ein Cyklus von Gesängen* (2)

Was nützt die mir noch zugemess'ne Zeit?
Robert Schumann, "Abschied von der Welt" 1852, Op135,4
translated from an old English collection
from *Gedichte der Königin Maria Stuart*
Joachim Raff, "Abschied von der Welt" 1872, Op172,11
translated from the French of Maria Stuart
from *Maria Stuart, ein Cyklus von Gesängen* (11)

Wenn Schmerz uns zieren kann und Trübsinn Witz verleiht
Joachim Raff, "An die Dame (i)" 1872, Op172,6
translated from the Scottish of Henry Stuart, Lord Darnley
from *Maria Stuart, ein Cyklus von Gesängen* (6)

Friedrich Wilhelm Viol (1817-1874)
Es glänzt im Abendsonnengolde der stille Waldesteich
Robert Franz, "Ein Gruss von Ihr!" 1879, Op50,4
Alexander Fesca, "Im Frühling" 1882pub, Op47,1

Friedrich Theodor von Vischer (1807-1887)
Sie haben dich fortgetragen
Wilhelm Kienzl, "Es ist zu spät!" 1926, Op106,6

Wilhelm Vogel (1772-1843)
Was treibt den Waidmann in den Wald
Louis Spohr, "Was treibt den Waidmann in den Wald" 1825, WoO92

(Johann) Heinrich Vogeler (1872-1942)
Ihr lieben Frühlingssänger zieht
Joseph Marx, "Im Frühling" 1901, ten.pf

Johann Nepomuk Vogl (1802-1866)
Ade du lieber Tannenwald, Ade, Ade!
Franz von Holstein, "Abschied" 1853, Op9,6

Das Vöglein hat ein schönes Loos
Franz von Holstein, "Waldvöglein" 1853, Op9,5

Das war der Junker Emerich
Carl Loewe, "Die schwarzen Augen" 1843, Op94,2

Der Sturm ist los, der Sturm ist los und saust und braust im Wald
Franz von Holstein, "Im Sturm" 1853, Op9,3

Ein Mühlrad hör' ich gehen, in einsam stiller Nacht
Joachim Raff, "Zweites Müllerlied" 1855-63, Op98,15
from *Sanges-Frühling.*

Ein Wanderbursch, mit dem Stab in der Hand
Carl Loewe, "Das Erkennen" 1837, Op65,2

Erschaffen schon die Erde lag
Carl Loewe, "Der Gesang" 1836, Op56,2

Es geht ein alter König lustwandeln vor seinem Schloss
Carl Loewe, "Der alte König" 1846, Op116,2

Es reitet schweigend und allein der alte Graf zum Wald hinein
Carl Loewe, "Die verfallene Mühle" 1847, Op109

Es steht der Sachsenführer, Herr Wittekind, gar wild
Carl Loewe, "Karl der Grosse und Wittekind" 1837, Op65,3

Fahr hin! fahr hin! fahr hin für alle Zeiten
Carl Loewe, "Das Vaterland" 1856, Op125,2

Fort, nur fort durch Busch und Zweige eh' die flücht'ge Lust entweicht
Franz von Holstein, "Waldliebe" 1853, Op9,2

Ging Herr Walther hin im Freien
Carl Loewe, "Die Schwanenjungfrau" 1859, Op129,3

Herr Frühling giebt jetzt ein Konzert im Saal zum grünen Wald
Carl Reinecke, "Frühlings-Konzert" 2v.pf
from *Kinderlieder*

Herr Heinrich sitzt am Vogelherd, recht froh und wohlgemuth
Carl Loewe, "Heinrich der Vogler" 1836, Op56,1

Horch, Hörnerklang, horch, Treiberruf
Carl Loewe, "Die Kaiserjagd im Wienerwald" 1846(47?), Op108,1

Im düstern Klostergarten ein einsam Brünnlein steht
Carl Loewe, "Am Klosterbrunnen" 1847, Op110,1

Im Freien, ach im Freien, wie ist's nun grün und licht
Franz von Holstein, "Ausgang" 1852, Op1,1

Ist der alte Schiffsherr endlich heimgekehrt von letzter Fahrt
Carl Loewe, "Der alte Schiffsherr" 1856, Op125,3

Lass mich ganz in dich versinken, Wald
Franz von Holstein, "Waldeslust" 1852, Op1,3

Lustig, lustig, wer zum Wald seine Schritte wendet
Franz von Holstein, "Ermunterung" 1852, Op1,2

Maria sitzt und stimmet die Harfe zum Gesang
Carl Loewe, "Das vergessene Lied" 1837, Op65,1

Morgen wieder, morgen wieder, lieber Wald, muss nun zum Thale nieder
Franz von Holstein, "Morgen wieder" 1852, Op1,6

Nähret Unmuth deine Seele, fliehe nur zum grünen Wald
Franz von Holstein, "Waldes-Trost" 1852, Op1,5

Noch ziehn die Wolken düster, die Erde deckt noch Schnee
Carl Loewe, "Blumenballade (Annunciata)" 1846

Räder klappern, Wasser rauschen und das Glöckchen gellt darein
Joachim Raff, "Erstes Müllerlied" 1855-63, Op98,13
from *Sanges-Frühling*

Sie waren alle zum Tanzplatz hinaus
Carl Loewe, "Urgrossvaters Gesellschaft" 1836, Op56,3

Vöglein ohne Ruh und Rast regt die muntern Schwingen immer
Franz von Holstein, "Nichts ohne Liebe" 1852, Op1,4

Vor dem Schlosse Don Loranca's lehnt Hueska, düster schweigend
Carl Loewe, "Hueska" 1846, Op108,2

Waldesnacht, Waldesnacht, schliesse mich ein
Franz von Holstein, "Waldeinsamkeit" 1853, Op9,4

Welch neues frohes Leben erwacht vom nächt'gen Traum
Franz von Holstein, "Morgens" 1853, Op9,1

Zu Pisa in dem Klostergarten geht ein finstrer Mönch
Carl Loewe, "Der Mönch zu Pisa" 1846, Op114

E. Vogt
O blasen, blasen, blasen, welch eine Freud ist das
Karl Gottlieb Reissiger, "Der wandernde Waldhornist" ten.hn.pf

Christian Friedrich Traugott Voigt (1770-1814)
Zur Freude ward geboren, was unter'm Monde lebt
Carl Maria von Weber, "An eine Freundin" 1812, Op23,6, 1v.ttb.pf

Johanna Voigt: see "Johanna Ambrosius"

Johann Heinrich Voss (1751-1826)
An des Beetes Umbuschung brach sie Rosen zum Kranz
Fanny Hensel, "Der Rosenkranz" 1826, Op9,3

Das Mägdlein, braun von Aug' and Haar
Johann Abraham Peter Schulz, "Der Freier" 1782-90pub

Das Tagewerk ist abgethan. Gieb, Vater, deinem Segen!
Carl Friedrich Zelter, "Abendlied" 1798?
Felix Mendelssohn, "Abendlied" 1828pub, Op8,9

Der Holdseligen sonder Wank sing' ich fröhlichen Minnesang
Johann Abraham Peter Schulz, "Minnelied" 1782-90pub
Carl Maria von Weber, "Minnelied" 1813, Op30,4
Carl Loewe, "Minnelied" 1819, Op9,v,1
Johannes Brahms, "Minnelied" 1860, Op44,1, ssaa.(pf)
George Henschel, "Der Holdseligen" 187-?, Op24,4

Erwacht in neuer Stärke, begrüss' ich, Gott, dein Licht
Carl Friedrich Zelter, "Morgenlied" 1799?
Felix Mendelssohn, "Morgenlied" 1851pub, Op86,2

Frische Flur, du reiner Himmel, frischer atm' ich hier und reiner
Johann Abraham Peter Schulz, "Ländliche Stille" 1782-90pub

Ist es wahr? Ist es wahr?
Felix Mendelssohn, "Frage" 1830pub, Op9,1

O der schöne Maienmond! wenn in Tal und Höhen Blütenbäume wehen
Johann Abraham Peter Schulz, "Mailied" 1782-90pub

Sagt mir an, was schmunzelt ihr?
Carl Maria von Weber, "Reigen" 1813, Op30,5

Schwarz wie Nacht brausest du auf, Meer
Carl Friedrich Zelter, "Die Braut am Gestade" 1811?

Seht den Himmel wie heiter!
Johann Abraham Peter Schulz, "Mailied" 1782-90pub

Trockne deines Jammers Tränen, heitre deinen Blick
Johann Abraham Peter Schulz, "Trost am Grabe" 1786pub

Umweht von Maiduft, unter des Blütenbaums Helldunkel
Fanny Hensel, "Der Maiabend" 1830, Op9,5

Wenn kühl der Morgen atmet, gehn wir schon auf grüner Au
Johann Abraham Peter Schulz, "Heureigen" 1782-90pub

Wie so gelinde die Fluth bewegt!
Felix Mendelssohn, "Scheidend" 1830pub, Op9,6

Willkommen im Grünen! Der Himmel ist blau, und blumig die Au!
Johann Abraham Peter Schulz, "Im Grünen" 1782-90pub
Felix Mendelssohn, "Im Grünen" 1828pub, Op8,11
Carl Loewe, "Frühlingslied" before 1829

Wir bringen mit Gesang und Tanz
Johann Abraham Peter Schulz, "Erntelied" 1782-90pub

"Jaroslav Vrchlický" (Emil Frída) (1853-1912)
Duftreich ist die Erde und die Luft krystallen
Arnold Schönberg, "Ekloge" 189-?

Cäcilie von W.
Dort im Thal hör ich verhallen
Louis Spohr, "Die Stimme der Nacht" 1816, Op37,3

Wär ich ein Vögelein, flög' ich zu ihm!
Louis Spohr, "Liebesschwärmerei" 1816, Op37,5

Wilhelm Wackernagel (1806-1869)
Ich grüne wie die Weide grünt
Arnold Schönberg, "Ich grüne wie die Weide grünt" 189-?

Kommt gezogen, kleine Vögel, kommt geflogen
Wilhelm Taubert, "Wiegenlied"
from *Klänge aus der Kinderwelt*, Vol.2, No7

Schlaf, Kindchen, balde! Die Vögel fliegen im Walde
Friedrich Curschmann, "Wiegenlied" 1833, Op5,4

(Wilhelm) Richard Wagner (1813-1883)
Noch scheint der Mond. Ist's Nacht noch? Ist es Tag?
Wilhelm Kienzl, "Bonapartes Heimkehr" 1896, Op48

"Max Waldau" (Georg von Hauenschild) (1825-1855)
Da sind die bleichen Geister wieder
Robert Franz, "Da sind die bleichen Geister wieder" 1865?, Op13,6

Es klingt in der Luft uralter Sang
Robert Franz, "Es klingt in der Luft" 1865?, Op13,2

Ich habe mir Rosmarin gepflanzt
Robert Franz, "Rosmarin" 1865?, Op13,4

Ich wollte, ich konnte nicht träumen
Robert Franz, "Ich wollte, ich konnte nicht träumen" 1884, Op52,5

Schemen erloschener Flammen fachern über das Moor
Robert Franz, "Ein Friedhof" 1865?, Op13,3

Wenn drüben die Glocken klingen
Robert Franz, "Wenn drüben die Glocken klingen" 1865?, Op13,5

Zwei welke Rosen träumen im Sande zum letztenmal
Robert Franz, "Zwei welke Rosen" 1865?, Op13,1

Wallner
Jüngst sass ich am Grabe der Trauten allein
Carl Maria von Weber, "Wiedersehn" 1804, Op30,1

Walther von der Vogelweide (ca.1170-1228/30)
Heil sei der Stunde, wo ich sie erkannte
Vilhelm Stenhammar, "Heil sei der Stunde" 1897?pub, Op9,2

Könnt' ich doch erleben, dass ich Rosen mit der Minniglichen sollte lesen
Vilhelm Stenhammar, "Ein Kuss von rothem Munde" 1897?pub, Op9,1
translated from Mittelhochdeutsch by Karl Pannier

Unter den Linden, an der Haide
Norbert Burgmüller, "Nach Walther von der Vogelweide" 1827-36?, Op10,1
Louis Spohr, "Die verschwiegene Nachtigall" 1857, WoO126
Wilhelm Kienzl, "Die verschwiegene Nachtigall" 187-?, Op6,1
Ferruccio Busoni, "Unter der Linden" 1885, Op18,2
Edvard Grieg, "Die verschwiegene Nachtigall" 1889, Op48,4
Hans Pfitzner, "Unter der Linden" 1909, Op24,1

Wer gab dir, Minne, die Gewalt
Hans Pfitzner, "Gewalt der Minne" 1909, Op24,2

Wohl mir der Stunde, wo ich sie fand
Joachim Raff, "Geständnis der Liebe" 1855-63, Op98,30
from *Sanges-Frühling*

Johann Christoph Wannovius (1753-?)
Das Leben ist ein Traum, man merkt, man fühlt ihn kaum
Franz Schubert, "Das Leben" 1815, D269, ssa.pf

E. von Warburg
Beim Kerzenlicht in bunten Kreis
George Henschel, "Beim Kerzenlicht" 187-?, Op15,3

Du willst, ich soll ein Lied dir geben
George Henschel, "Das lieblichste Gedicht" 187-?, Op15,1

Vicomte de Wargemont
Herr Puff, an Geld und Jahren reich
Johann Rudolf Zumsteeg, "Le bon ménage" 1805pub
translated by Joh. Chr. Fr. Haug
from *Kleine Balladen und Lieder, siebtes Heft*

Schön, wie die Rose, blüht der Mädchen erste Jugend
Johann Rudolf Zumsteeg, "Das Mädchen und die Rose" 1805pub
translated by Joh. Chr. Fr. Haug
from *Kleine Balladen und Lieder, siebtes Heft*

Theresen lieb' ich, ist das Sünde?
Johann Rudolf Zumsteeg, "Therese" 1805pub
translated by Joh. Chr. Fr. Haug
from *Kleine Balladen und Lieder, siebtes Heft*

Wargentin
Das war ein recht abscheuliches Gesicht
Carl Maria von Weber, "An Sie" 1820, Op80,5

Claire Henrika Weber
Prinzeßlein tanzt durch die Wiese
Max Reger, "Klein-Evelinde" 1915, Op142,4
from *Fünf neue Kinderlieder*

Georg Rudolf Weckherlin (1584-1653)
Ein kleine Weil, da ohn' Gefähr ich Euch in einem Saal gefunden
Ernst Krenek, "Ein Rundum (an eine grosse Fürstin)" 1927, Op53,2
from *Vier Gesänge nach alten Gedichten*

Ihr wisset, was für schwere Klagen
Ernst Krenek, "Ein Anderes" 1927, Op53,3
from *Vier Gesänge nach alten Gedichten*

Frank Wedekind (1864-1918)
Ach, wie brenn' ich vor Verlangen, Galathea
Arnold Schönberg, "Galathea" 1901?
from *Brettl-Lieder*

R. E. Wegener
Lustwandelnd schritt ein Mädchen in kühlem Waldesgrund
Eugen d'Albert, "Das Mädchen und der Schmetterling" 1886, Op3,3

Asta von Wegerer
Es soll mein Gebet dich tragen
Max Reger, "Es soll mein Gebet dich tragen" 1909

Betty Wehrli-Knobel (1904-)
Aus Rosen, Phlox, Zinienflor ragen im Garten Malven empor
Richard Strauss, "Malven" 1948, Op. posth.

Wilhelm Weigand (1862-1949)
Du Sommerabend! Heilig, goldnes Licht!
Anton Webern, "Sommerabend" 1901-04
from *Acht frühe Lieder* (5)

Keine Rose darf ich pflücken
Felix Weingartner, "Rosen" 1909, Op46,1

Merk dir's in vollster Kraft, die man beneidet
Max Reger, "Merkspruch" 1903, Op75,1

Josef Weinheber (1892-1945)
Du, leicht und schön, aus Gottes Traum geboren
Felix Wolfes, "An einen Schmetterling" 1952

Ein Mahl für uns und ein Licht für dich
Richard Strauss, "Sankt Michael" 1942, (Op88,3)

Erste Blume, aus Dunkel und Erde wie ich
Gottfried von Einem, "Erste Blume" 1954-56, Op19,2

Fülle du! Gezier und schöner Geist
Richard Strauss, "Blick vom oberen Belvedere" 1942, (Op88,2)

Stille Blume, erblasst unter herbstlichen Sternen
Felix Wolfes, "An eine Tote" 1960

Christian Weise (1642-1708)
Die Rose blüht, ich bin die fromme Biene
Armin Knab, "Die Rose" 1906
from *Wunderhorn-Lieder* (7)

Emil Rudolf Weiss (1875-1942)
Oft am langen Tage seufz' ich, ach! nach dir
Jean Sibelius, "Sehnsucht" 1906, Op50,2

Christian Felix Weisse (1726-1804)
Ach, an dem Ufer dieser Quelle hab' ich Damöten oft geseh'n
Josef Antonín Štěpán, "Klagen" 1778-79pub

Beschattet von blühenden Ästen
Joseph Haydn, "Die zu späte Ankunft der Mutter" 1781/84, XXVIa Nr.12

Der reiche Tor
Wolfgang Amadeus Mozart, "Die betrogene Welt" 1785, K474

Ein Mädchen, das auf Ehre hielt, liebt' einst ein Edelmann
Johann Adam Hiller, "Ariette" 1768

Ich war bei Chloen ganz allein, und küssen wollt' ich sie
Ludwig van Beethoven, "Der Kuss" 1822?, Op128
Carl Bohm, "Lange nachher" 1887cop, Op326,7

Ihr, Mädchen, flieht Damöten ja!
Wolfgang Amadeus Mozart, "Der Zauberer" 1785, K472

Mein Schäfer, ach! der ist bescheiden!
Max Reger, "Der bescheidene Schäfer" 1906, Op97,4
Joseph Marx, "Der bescheidene Schäfer" 1910, sop.pf

Philint stand jüngst vor Baucis Thür
Joseph Haydn, "Eine sehr gewöhnliche Geschichte" 1781/84, XXVIa Nr.4

Schön sind Rosen und Jasmin, wenn sie noch im Lenzen
Johann Abraham Peter Schulz, "Iris" 1782-90pub

Sobald Damötas Chloën sieht
Wolfgang Amadeus Mozart, "Die Verschweigung" 1787, K518

Warum, geliebtes Veilchen, blühst du so entfernt im Thal?
Johann Rudolf Zumsteeg, "Das Veilchen" 1803pub
from *Kleine Balladen und Lieder, sechstes Heft*

Wie sanft, wie ruhig fühl ich hier
Wolfgang Amadeus Mozart, "Die Zufriedenheit" 1785, K473

Zieht hier ein Krieger stolz geschmükket
Josef Antonín Štěpán, "Der Soldat" 1778-79pub

Karl Weitbrecht (1847-1904)
Wenn ich Abschied nehme, will ich leise gehn
Emil Mattiesen, "Abschied" 190-?pub, Op11,5
from *Stille Lieder* (5)

Johann Sebastian Cammermeyer Welhaven (1807-1873)
Lenznacht, so still und so kühl
Robert Franz, "Norwegische Frühlingsnacht" 1878, Op48,6

Fr. von Weling

Ich liebe dich und will dich ewig lieben

Josefine Lang, "Ich liebe dich und will dich ewig lieben" WoO

Joseph Wenzig (1807-1876)

Ach Mädchen, liebes Mädchen, wie schwartz dein Auge ist!

Johannes Brahms, "So laß uns wandern!" 1877, Op75,3, alt.ten.pf

Ach, mich hält der Gram gefangen

Johannes Brahms, "Abschied" 1877, Op69,3

Ach mir fehlt, nicht ist da

Johannes Brahms, "Klage I" 1877, Op69,1

Brausten alle Berge, sauste rings der Wald

Johannes Brahms, "Verlorene Jugend" 1889pub, Op104,4, satbb

Dunkel, wie dunkel in Wald und in Feld!

Johannes Brahms, "Von ewiger Liebe" 1864, Op43,1

Ei, schmollte mein Vater nicht wach und im Schlaf

Johannes Brahms, "Des Liebsten Schwur" 1877, Op69,4

O Felsen, lieber Felsen, was stürztest du nicht ein

Johannes Brahms, "Klage II" 1877, Op69,2

Wie viel schon der Boten flogen

Johannes Brahms, "Die Boten der Liebe" 1873/74, Op61,4, 2v.pf

Johann August Weppen (1741-1812)

Ein Liedchen vom Lieben verlangst du von mir?

Joseph Haydn, "An Iris" 1781/84, XXVIa Nr.7

Franz Werfel (1890-1945)

Alles, was von uns kommt, wandelt schon andern Raum

Carl Orff, "Ein Liebeslied" 1920

Als mich dein Dasein tränenwärts entrückte

Carl Orff, "Als mich dein Wandeln an den Tod verzückte" 1920

Du, der du keine Gnade kennst

Carl Orff, "Rache" 1920

Gibt's Straß' und Park, wo wir im Traum uns sahn?

Alexander Zemlinsky, "Ahnung Beatricens" 1935

Ich liege in gläsernem Wachen

Carl Orff, "Mondlied eines Mädchens" 1920

Menschen lieben uns, und unbeglückt stehn sie auf vom Tisch

Alma Schindler-Mahler, "Der Erkennende" 1915

Niemals wieder will ich eines Menschen Antlitz verlachen

Paul Hindemith, "Niemals wieder will ich eines Menschen Antlitz verlachen" 1925, Op45,ii,5, 2v.insts

from *Sing-und Spielmusiken für Liebhaber und Musikfreunde*

O die ihr geht am Abend in euer Zimmer ein

Carl Orff, "Nacht" 1920

O Lieb und Leid so überein!

Carl Orff, "Litanei eines Kranken" 1921

Sein ist die Kraft, das Regiment der Sterne
Carl Orff, "Der gute Mensch" 1920

Welchen Weg bist du gegangen, daß du kamst hier herab?
Ernst Krenek, "Elevation" 1922, Op15,3

(Friedrich Ludwig) Zacharias Werner (1768-1823)
Eh' die Sonne früh aufersteht
Franz Schubert, "Morgenlied" 1820, D685

Trarah! Trarah! wir kehren daheim!
Franz Schubert, "Jagdlied" 1817, D521

Paul Wertheimer (1874-1937)
Du weiche Nacht, o komm mich zu umfangen
Alexander Zemlinsky, "Empfängnis" 1894-96, Op2,ii,6

Du weißt, wir bleiben einsam: du und ich
Felix Weingartner, "Seelen" 1909, Op46,4

Hände, viele Hände über der Haide schweben
Joseph Marx, "Tuch der Tränen" 1904

In deiner Näh' ist mir so gut
Alexander Zemlinsky, "Selige Stunde" 1901?, Op10,2
from *Ehetanzlied und andere Gesänge*

Von Melodien, die mich umflieh'n
Alexander Zemlinsky, "Sonntag" 1900?, Op7,5
from *Irmelin Rose und andere Gesänge*

Friedrich August Clemens Werthes (1748-1817)
Allzulange, Wiederhall, tönst du mich zu preisen
Johann Rudolf Zumsteeg, "Die trauernde Rose" 1803pub
from *Kleine Balladen und Lieder, fünftes Heft*

Die Lämmlein springen! die Vögelein singen!
Johann Rudolf Zumsteeg, "Russisches Brautlied" 1801pub, 2v.pf
from *Kleine Balladen und Lieder, drittes Heft*

Es war ein Winterabend und wehte bitter kalt
Johann Rudolf Zumsteeg, "Raymund und Ottilie (Ein Winterstück)" 1800pub
from *Kleine Balladen und Lieder, erstes Heft*

Komm in den Wald! komm an den Fels!
Johann Rudolf Zumsteeg, "Ernestine an Ferdinand" 1800pub
from *Kleine Balladen und Lieder, zweites Heft*

Matt erstirbt der Hoffnung letzter Schimmer
Johann Rudolf Zumsteeg, "Klagelied" 1800pub
from *Kleine Balladen und Lieder, erstes Heft*

Noch hörte mich die Mitternacht um meinen Robert schrey'n
Johann Rudolf Zumsteeg, "Robert und Käthe" 1800pub
from *Kleine Balladen und Lieder, erstes Heft*

O! seht uns arme Kinder ziehn
Johann Rudolf Zumsteeg, "Gesang der vierhundert Kinder, die im Januar 1800 von den verwüsteten Schweizer-Cantonen auswanderten, und in Zürich Hülfe fanden" 1803pub
from *Kleine Balladen und Lieder, fünftes Heft*

Schlummre Knabe! um uns her tobt das aufgewühlte Meer
Johann Rudolf Zumsteeg, "Wiegenlied auf der See" 1805pub
from *Kleine Balladen und Lieder, siebtes Heft*

Wir werden Staub und Asche zu bald seyn
Johann Rudolf Zumsteeg, "An die Flasche" 1800pub
from *Kleine Balladen und Lieder, erstes Heft*

Mathilde Wesendonck (1828-1902)

Hoch gewölbte Blätterkronen, Baldachine von Smaragd
Richard Wagner, "Im Treibhause" 1858, WWV 91
from *Fünf Gedichte für eine Frauenstimme, usw.* (3)

In der Kindheit frühen Tagen
Richard Wagner, "Der Engel" 1857-58, WWV 91
from *Fünf Gedichte für eine Frauenstimme, usw.* (1)

Sag', welch wunderbare Träume
Richard Wagner, "Träume" 1857-58, WWV 91
from *Fünf Gedichte für eine Frauenstimme, usw.* (5)

Sausendes, brausendes Rad der Zeit
Richard Wagner, "Stehe still" 1858, WWV 91
from *Fünf Gedichte für eine Frauenstimme, usw.* (2)

Sonne, weinest jeden Abend dir die schönen Augen rot
Richard Wagner, "Schmerzen!" 1857-58, WWV 91
from *Fünf Gedichte für eine Frauenstimme, usw.* (4)

Ignaz Heinrich Freiherr von Wessenberg (1774-1860)

Franziskus einst, der Heil'ge, sass vor seiner Zell'
Carl Loewe, "Der heilige Franziskus" 1837, Op75,3, alt.pf

Wo blüht das Blümchen, das nie verblüht?
Ludwig van Beethoven, "Das Geheimnis" 1815, WoO146

Adelheid (Humperdinck) Wette (1858-1916)

Das Vöglein singt am Waldessaum: Wiwit, wiwit, wiwit!
Engelbert Humperdinck, "Das Waldvöglein" 1904

Im Grünen, im Walde, da ist es so schön
Engelbert Humperdinck, "Im Freien zu singen" 1888
from *Vier Kinderlieder*

Leise weht's durch alle Lande
Engelbert Humperdinck, "Weihnachten" 1898

Lerchelein, lieb und klein, tirelierst so süß und fein!
Engelbert Humperdinck, "Die Lerche" 1904

Friedrich Gottlob Wetzel (1779-1819)

Im schönen Land Tirol hab ich mir lassen sagen
Carl Loewe, "Das Muttergottesbild" 1834, Op37,1

Schon naht, um uns zu scheiden
Aug. Heinrich von Weyrauch, "(Adieu)" 1824pub

Wenn die Rosen blühen, Hoffe, liebes Herz
Aug. Heinrich von Weyrauch, "Heimweh(?)"
Louise Reichardt, "Heimweh" 1826pub

Lini Wetzler
Fallende Blätter, die Stund' um Stunde rieselnder Regen zu Grabe trägt
Hermann H. Wetzler, "November" 1907

Ich bin getrost, Stern meiner Seele
Hermann H. Wetzler, "Abschied" 1905

Walt Whitman (1819-1892)
Der ich, in Zwischenräumen, in Äonen und Äonen wiederkehre
Paul Hindemith, "Der ich, in Zwischenräumen, in Äonen und Äonen wiederkehre" 1919, Op14,1, bar.pf
from *Drei Hymnen von Walt Whitman*

Ein Kind sagte: "Was ist das Gras?"
Franz Schreker, "Das Gras" 1923
from *Zwei lyrische Gesänge*

Jugend du große, sehnende, liebende!
Joseph Marx, "Jugend und Alter" 1909, 1v(med).orch

O, nun heb du an, dort in deinem Moor
Paul Hindemith, "O, nun heb du an, dort in deinem Moor" 1919, Op14,2, bar.pf
from *Drei Hymnen von Walt Whitman*

Schlagt! Schlagt! Trommeln! Blast, blast, Hörner!
Othmar Schoeck, "Trommelschläge" 1915, Op26, ch.orch
German translation by Johannes Schlaf
Paul Hindemith, "Schlagt! Schlagt! Trommeln!" 1919, Op14,3, bar.pf
from *Drei Hymnen von Walt Whitman*

Wurzeln und Halme sind dies nur
Franz Schreker, "Wurzeln und Halme" 1923
from *Zwei lyrische Gesänge*

Oskar Wiener (1873-?)
Am Dorfsee neigt die Weide ihr kahles Haupt
Max Reger, "Am Dorfsee" 1900, Op48,6, 1v(med).pf

Mein rotes Herz, mein totes Herz
Max Reger, "Mein Herz" 1899-1900, Op43,7, 1v(med).pf

Meine armen, kleinen Lieder
Max Reger, "Abschied" 1899-1900, Op43,4, 1v(med).pf

Sag es nicht, geliebtes Herzchen, sag es nicht
Max Reger, "Sag es nicht" 1899-1900, Op43,8, 1v(med).pf

Adolf von Wilbrandt (Wilbrand) (1837-1911)
Wie glänzt nun die Welt im Abendstrahl
Franz Liszt, "Der Glückliche" 1879pub
Felix Weingartner, "Lied des Glücklichen" 1909, Op46,5

Ernst von Wildenbruch (1845-1909)
Auf meinem Tische stehn Kornblumen, schöne, blaue
Max Reger, "Der Kornblumenstrauß" 1892, Op8,3

Hier von Frühlingsblumen bring' ich einen Strauss
Ingeborg von Bronsart, "Zwei Sträusse" 1899?pub, Op16,3
Hugo Kaun, "Zwei Sträusse" 1905pub, Op15,2

Rosen und duftende Veilchen bring' ich fein Liebchen dir!
Ingeborg von Bronsart, "Ständchen" 1899?pub, Op16,2

Stellt mir den Blumenstrauss in das Glas
Ingeborg von Bronsart, "Der Blumenstrauss" 1899?pub, Op16,4

Unter'm Machandelbaum da ist ein Platz, susala dusala da sitzt mein Schatz
Hans Sommer, "Unter'm Machandelbaum" 1891pub, Op14,1
Wilhelm Kienzl, "Unter'm Machandelbaum" 192-?, Op114,4

Warum so bleich und blaß, geliebtes Angesicht?
Max Reger, "Tränen im Auge" 1892, Op8,2

Wenn du mich einstmals verlassen wirst
Ingeborg von Bronsart, "Letzte Bitte" 1899?pub, Op16,5

Wie ist der Abend stille, wie milde naht die Nacht
Ingeborg von Bronsart, "Abendlied" 1899?pub, Op16,1

Anton Wildgans (1881-1932)

Alles Tagverlangen ist zur Ruh gegangen
Joseph Marx, "Adagio" 1916, 1v(med).vc.pf

Dämm'rung feuchtet die Büsche, Nebel schleiern den Bach
Joseph Marx, "Pan trauert um Syrinx (Eine mythologische Szene)" 1916, 1v(med).fl.pf

Du bist der Garten, wo meine Hände
Joseph Marx, "Du bist der Garten" 1916pub, 1v(med).vn.pf

Durch Einsamkeiten, durch waldwild' Geheg
Joseph Marx, "Durch Einsamkeiten" 1916pub, 1v(med).vla.pf

"Uffo von Wildingen" (Heinrich Gottfried Zitzmann) (1775-1839)

Noch schmückten zarte Blüthen des Knaben weiches Haar
Carl Loewe, "Das Blumenopfer"

Ludwig Karl Eberhard von Wildungen (1754-1822)

Auf, ihr Brüder, auf zum Jagen!
Johann Rudolf Zumsteeg, "Morgenlied des Jägers" 1803pub
from *Kleine Balladen und Lieder, fünftes Heft*

König Friedrich Wilhelm IV von Preußen (1795-1861)

Herr Gott, der du bist! mein Schöpfer, mein Erlöser, mein ewiger Tröster!
Carl Loewe, "Herr Gott, der du bist!" 1863, 4v
after Aurelius Augustinus. Attribution to Wilhelm IV uncertain.

Wie du deine Sonne hast lassen aufgehn
Carl Loewe, "Wie du deine Sonne hast lassen aufgehn" 1863
after Aurelius Augustinus. Attribution to Wilhelm IV uncertain.

Karl Wilhelm

Meine Sehnsucht ist zum Licht
Alban Berg, "Sternenfall" 1902

Karl Wille

Hier auf diesem Blumen Hügel
Ferdinand Ries, "Der Sommerabend in der Schweiz" 1829/30pub, Op154,1

Ich liebte dich, in meiner Seele lebte
Ferdinand Ries, "An Nina" 1811pub, Op35,3

Marianne von Willemer (1784-1860)
Ach, um deine feuchten Schwingen, West, wie sehr ich dich beneide
Carl Friedrich Zelter, "Suleika" 1820
Franz Schubert, "Suleika II" 1824?, D717
Fanny Hensel, "Suleika" 1836
Felix Mendelssohn, "Suleika" 1836pub, Op34,4

Hoch beglückt in deiner Liebe
Hugo Wolf, "Hoch beglückt in deiner Liebe" 1889
from *Goethe Lieder* (40)

Nimmer will ich dich verlieren!
Hugo Wolf, "Nimmer will ich dich verlieren" 1889
from *Goethe Lieder* (48)

Was bedeutet die Bewegung?
Franz Schubert, "Suleika I" 1821, D720
Felix Mendelssohn, "Suleika" 1843pub, Op57,3

Wie, mit innigstem Behagen, Lied, genahr ich deinen Sinn
Robert Schumann, "Lied der Suleika" 1840, Op25,9
3rd strophe, "Ja, mein Herz...," by Goethe
from *Liederkreis*
Giacomo Meyerbeer, "Suleika" 1838

Karl Gottfried Theodor Winkler: see "Theodor Hell"

Franz Wisbacher (1849-1912)
Die Luft ist kühl und trübe
Alban Berg, "Vorüber!" 1903

Carl Wittkowsky
Auf, hinaus aus dem Haus, aus der schwülen Städte luft
Moritz Moszkowski, "Auf, hinaus aus dem Haus" Op26,3
from *Drei Gedichte im Volkston*

Ich frage nicht: "hast Du mich lieb?"
Moritz Moszkowski, "Ich frage nicht" Op26,1
from *Drei Gedichte im Volkston*

O süsseste Noth! O selige Pein!
Moritz Moszkowski, "O süsseste Noth!" Op26,2
from *Drei Gedichte im Volkston*

August Wolf (1816-1861)
Dies eine möcht' ich gerne wissen
Felix Weingartner, "Die Märchen" 1909, Op46,2

Friedrich Wolf (1888-1953)
Als Kinder glaubten wir an Zauberwesen
Boris Blacher, "Die Hexe" 1947pub, Op25,4
from *Vier Lieder nach Texten von Friedrich Wolf*

Erste Kirschen hast du mir gebracht
Boris Blacher, "Kirschkerne" 1947pub, Op25,1
from *Vier Lieder nach Texten von Friedrich Wolf*

Es trabt im Kreis durch die Manege
Boris Blacher, "Das Zirkuspferdchen" 1947pub, Op25,2
from *Vier Lieder nach Texten von Friedrich Wolf*

Man soll seinem Herzen gehorchen
Boris Blacher, "Herzensverstand" 1947pub, Op25,3
from *Vier Lieder nach Texten von Friedrich Wolf*

Pius Alexander Wolf (1784-1828)

Einsam bin ich nicht alleine
Carl Maria von Weber, "Einsam bin ich nicht alleine" 1820, J.279,7
Carl Maria von Weber, "Einsam bin ich nicht alleine (2nd version)" 1820

Julius Wolff (1834-1910)

Alle Blumen möcht ich binden, alle, alle dir zu einem Strauss
Hans Sommer, "Alle Blumen möcht ich binden" 1884pub, Op3,9
from *Mädchenlieder aus Julius Wolff's Waidmannsmär*
Carl Bohm, "Alle Blumen möcht' ich binden" 1887cop, Op326,6

Blaublümlein spiegelten sich im Bach
Hans Sommer, "Blaublümlein spiegelten sich im Bach" 1884pub, Op3,7
from *Mädchenlieder aus Julius Wolff's Waidmannsmär*

Bleib stehn! Dass nur ein Hauch vom Winde
Hans Sommer, "Bleib stehn! Dass nur ein Hauch vom Winde" 1884pub, Op5,7
from *Lieder aus Julius Wolff's Minnesang: Tannhäuser*

Der Lenz ist gekommen ins harrende Land
Hans Sommer, "Der Lenz ist gekommen ins harrende Land" 1884pub, Op5,1
from *Lieder aus Julius Wolff's Minnesang: Tannhäuser*

Der Zaunpfahl trug ein Hütlein weiss
Hans Sommer, "Der Zaunpfahl trug ein Hütlein weiss" 1884pub, Op3,4
from *Mädchenlieder aus Julius Wolff's Waidmannsmär*

Du zähltest wohl die Regentropfen
Hans Sommer, "Du zähltest wohl die Regentropfen" 1884pub, Op5,8
from *Lieder aus Julius Wolff's Minnesang: Tannhäuser*

Ein leises, fernes Rauschen klingt vom Bergeshaupt hernieder
Otto Lessmann, "Waldharfen" 1893?pub, Op30,2

Ein Schwert, das schneidet, ein Falke, der fängt
Hans Sommer, "Ein Schwert, das schneidet, ein Falke, der fängt" 1884pub, Op5,2
from *Lieder aus Julius Wolff's Minnesang: Tannhäuser*

Es wächst ein Kraut im Kühlen
Hans Sommer, "Es wächst ein Kraut im Kühlen" 1884pub, Op3,1
from *Mädchenlieder aus Julius Wolff's Waidmannsmär*

Es wartet ein bleiches Jungfräulein
Hans Sommer, "Es wartet ein bleiches Jungfräulein" 1884pub, Op3,3
from *Mädchenlieder aus Julius Wolff's Waidmannsmär*

Für alle die Schätze, für all die Ehre
Hans Sommer, "Für alle die Schätze, für all die Ehre" 1884pub, Op5,6
from *Lieder aus Julius Wolff's Minnesang: Tannhäuser*

Glockenblumen, was läutet ihr?
Hans Sommer, "Glockenblumen, was läutet ihr?" 1884pub, Op3,5
from *Mädchenlieder aus Julius Wolff's Waidmannsmär*

Ich ging im Wald durch Kraut und Gras
Hans Sommer, "Ich ging im Wald durch Kraut und Gras" 1884pub, Op3,6
from *Mädchenlieder aus Julius Wolff's Waidmannsmär*
Carl Bohm, "Waldtraut's Lied" 1887cop, Op326,2

Im Dorfe blüht die Linde und duftet weit und breit
Hermann Grädener, "Im Dorfe blüht die Linde" 1910pub

Im Grase thaut's, die Blumen träumen von ihrem süssen Honigdieb
Hans Sommer, "Im Grase thaut's, die Blumen träumen" 1884pub, Op3,10
from *Mädchenlieder aus Julius Wolff's Waidmannsmär*
Carl Bohm, "Im Grase thaut's" 1887cop, Op326,5

Immer schaust du in die Ferne, wie die Wolken flieh'n
Hermann Goetz, "Lied der Gertrud (aus dem Rattenfänger von Hameln)" 1868-76, Op12,4

Kukuk! was rufst im Wald mich an?
Erik Meyer-Helmund, "Kukuk" 1886-88

Leer ist der Tag, er geht zu Ende
Hans Sommer, "Leer ist der Tag, er geht zu Ende" 1884pub, Op3,8
from *Mädchenlieder aus Julius Wolff's Waidmannsmär*

Mädchenaug'! Mädchenaug'! Strahlender Schimmer
Moritz Moszkowski, "Mädchenaug'! Mädchenaug'!" 1877pub, Op13,3, bar.pf

Neunerlei Blumen winde zum Kranz
Hans Sommer, "Neunerlei Blumen winde zum Kranz" 1884pub, Op3,2
from *Mädchenlieder aus Julius Wolff's Waidmannsmär*

Offene Arme und pochende Brust
Hans Sommer, "Offene Arme und pochende Brust" 1884pub, Op5,5
from *Lieder aus Julius Wolff's Minnesang: Tannhäuser*

Wie soll ich's bergen, wie soll ich's tragen
Hans Sommer, "Wie soll ich's bergen, wie soll ich's tragen" 1884pub, Op5,4
from *Lieder aus Julius Wolff's Minnesang: Tannhäuser*

Wiege dich, Wind, auf dem wogenden Korn
Hans Sommer, "Wiege dich, Wind, auf dem wogenden Korn" 1884pub, Op5,3
from *Lieder aus Julius Wolff's Minnesang: Tannhäuser*

Louis Wolff-Kassel (1846-?)
Es ist ein hold Gewimmel von Köpflein blond und braun
Hugo Kaun, "Es ist ein hold Gewimmel" 1904pub, Op55,6

Karl Ludwig von Woltmann (1770-1817)
Der Buhle sitzt und ächzet traurig
Johann Rudolf Zumsteeg, "Der Nebelgeist" 1802pub
from *Kleine Balladen und Lieder, viertes Heft*

William Wordsworth (1770-1850)
Die Herde Schafe, die gemächlich zieht
Ernst Pepping, "An den Schlaf" 1949pub
translated by B. Damjakob
from *Haus- und Trostbuch* (19)

Gabriele Fürstin Wrede (1861-?)
Möcht' meine Seele senken ins Waldesgrün hinein
Josef Gänsbacher, "Möcht' meine Seele senken" 1911pub

Fräulein von X
Gleich der Rose welk' ich hin
Johann Rudolf Zumsteeg, "An ein Röschen" 1803pub
from *Kleine Balladen und Lieder, sechstes Heft*

Xenophanes (ca.570BC-ca.478BC)
Die in Lybien denken die Götter
Hanns Eisler, "Die Götter" 1955

Justus Friedrich Wilhelm Zachariä (1726-1777)
Denk ihn hinaus, den schrecklichen Gedanken
Johann Philipp Sack, "Ode" 1760

Die Göttin süßer Freuden, die Nacht stieg aus dem Meer
Karl Friberth, "Das schlafende Mädchen" 1780pub

Friedl Zacharias
Eia, husch, husch, im Fliederbusch sitzt ein feiner Traum
Anna Teichmüller, "Eia, husch, husch!" 1910pub, Op19,2

Ringelringelreigen, mit den jungen Zweigen spielt
Anna Teichmüller, "Ringelreigen" 1907pub, Op17,1
from *Lieder Kindern gesungen*

Schliesst du bald die Äuglein zu, Wirbelköpfchen, Wildfang du
Anna Teichmüller, "Wiegenlied" 1905pub, Op3,6

Joseph Christian Freiherrn von Zedlitz (1790-1862)
Als mein Auge sie fand, als mein Herz sie erkannt
Arnold Schönberg, "Sehnsucht" 189-?

Bahnlos und pfadlos, Felsen hinan stürmet der Mensch, ein Wandersmann
Robert Schumann, "Ungewisses Licht" 1849, Op141,2, 2ch(satb).pf
from *Vier doppelchörige Gesänge*

In einem Dorf, am frühen Morgen, sah ich ein Kirchlein offen stehn
Carl Loewe, "Die Dorfkirche" 1846, Op116,1

Lass, o lass mir deine Hand, zieh' sie nicht so kalt zurücke
Leopold Damrosch, "Trost" Op8,6

Nach oben musst du blicken, gedrücktes, wundes Herz
Robert Schumann, "Zuversicht" 1849, Op141,3, 2ch(satb).pf
from *Vier doppelchörige Gesänge*

Nachts um die zwölfte Stunde verlässt der Tambour sein Grab
Carl Loewe, "Die nächtliche Heerschau" 1832, Op23

Singet die Nachtigall im dunkeln Wald
Louis Spohr, “Lied” 1841, WoO105

Albert Zeller (1804-1877)
Leb’wohl, leb’wohl du schöne Welt!
Josefine Lang, “Leb’wohl, leb’wohl du schöne Welt” 1862, Op29,1

Alois Zettler (1778-1828)
Ihr Freunde und du gold’ner Wein, versüsset mir das Leben
Franz Schubert, “Trinklied” 1815, D183

Christiane Mariane Romanus von Ziegler (?-1752)
Eilt ihr Schäfer aus den Gründen
Josef Antonín Štěpán, “Chloe an Thyrsis” 1778-79pub
Leopold Hofmann, “An Thyrsis” 1780pub
Joseph Haydn, “An Thyrsis” 1781/84, XXVIa Nr.8

Karl Ziegler (“Karlopago”) (1812-1877)
Der Waldbach tost im Tannenthal
Carl Loewe, “Der Hirt auf der Brücke” 1859, Op130,4

Es ist mein Herz verengt, verdorrt
Carl Loewe, “Frühlingsankunft” 1859, Op130,5

Grete Ziegler-Bock
Am kahlen Erdwall, da irgendwo am Hunho ein tükkisch Geschoss schlug auf
Anna Teichmüller, “Mandschurisch” 1906pub, Op10

Ernst Ziel (1841-1921)
Du bist ein Kind und sollst es ewig bleiben
Felix Weingartner, “Du bist ein Kind” 1900, Op28,12

Hehrer bist du und heiliger als die andern Genien alle
Otto Lessmann, “An die Nacht” 1893?pub, Op29

G. Zimmermann
Nur ein lächelnder Blick von deinem strahlenden Auge
Robert Schumann, “Nur ein lächelnder Blick” 1840, Op27,5

Baltasar Friedrich Wilhelm Zimmermann (1807-1878)
Am Bach, am Bach, im flüsternden Gras
Louis Spohr, “Verlust” 1839, WoO99

Julius Wilhelm Zincgref (Zinkgräf) (1591-1635)
Mein feines Lieb ist fern von mir
Carl Friedrich Zelter, “Klage” 1803
Sigismund Neukomm, “Die Trennung” 181-?

Karl Friedrich Bernhard Zinkernagel (1758-1813)
Alles was mich hier umringt, sagt mir, dass ich sterben werde
Johann Rudolf Zumsteeg, “Vom Tode” 1803pub
from *Kleine Balladen und Lieder, sechstes Heft*

W. Zinserling
Sanft mit seligem Entzücken
Carl Loewe, “An die Natur”

Wenn am kleinen Kammerfenster ich euch alle Jahre seh'
Carl Loewe, "Die treuen Schwalben"

Heinrich Gottfried Zitzmann: see "Uffo von Wildingen"

M. A. Zoll
Ich hört' in einem grünen Hag ein silbern Vöglein singen
Erich Riede, "Lied im Maien" Op12,3, sop.pf

Heinrich Zschokke (1771-1848)
Sei mir gegrüßt, o schöne Nacht
Hugo Wolf, "Nacht und Grab" 1875, Op3,1

Anton Wilhelm Florentin von Zuccalmaglio (1803-1869?)
Es flogen drei Schwälbelein über den Rhein
Carl Loewe, "Die verlorene Tochter" 1839, Op78,2

Vinzenz Zusner (1803-1874)
Des Glöckleins Schall durchtönt das Tal
Hugo Wolf, "Abendglöcklein" 1876, Op9,4

Hans Fritz von Zwehl (1883-1966)
Die goldene Waage des Lebens trug
Yrjö Kilpinen, "Lied der Renate" 193-?, Op79,5

Du Trotz des Glaubens! Du behelmtes Haupt!
Yrjö Kilpinen, "Marienkirche zu Danzig im Gerüst" 193-?, Op79,7

Durch alte Marmorhallen streift weicher Wind vom Meer
Yrjö Kilpinen, "Venezianisches Intermezzo" 193-?, Op79,4

Durch hohe Tannen träufelt schon
Yrjö Kilpinen, "Vorfrühling" 193-?, Op79,3

Hier grub man ein
Yrjö Kilpinen, "Grabstein" 1942, Op80,1
from *Grabstein*

In Feindesland die graue Spätherbstnacht
Yrjö Kilpinen, "Nachts auf Posten" 193-?, Op79,6

Mancher Stunden Wehen ist so leuchtend und still
Yrjö Kilpinen, "Mancher Stunden Wehen" 193-?, Op79,1

Nun hat deines Herzens Geige
Yrjö Kilpinen, "Nirwana" 1942, Op80,2
from *Grabstein*

Wandern fremd und unbekannt in der Stadt
Yrjö Kilpinen, "Der Heimatlose" 193-?, Op79,2

Warum kommst du zu mir in der Nacht
Yrjö Kilpinen, "Todsüßes Gespenst" 1942, Op80,3
from *Grabstein*

Wenn der Bann gebrochen und vorbei der Tag
Yrjö Kilpinen, "Wenn der Bann gebrochen und vorbei der Tag" 1942, Op80,4
from *Grabstein*

Stefan Zweig (1881-1942)
Ein Drängen ist in meinem Herzen
Max Reger, "Ein Drängen" 1906, Op97,3
Joseph Marx, "Ein Drängen ist in meinem Herzen" 1909

Linder schwebt der Stunde Reigen
Felix Wolfes, "Abschied vom Leben" 1952

O welch Glühn in fremde Hülle
Max Reger, "Neue Fülle" 1907, Op104,1

Frank Gerhard Zwillinger (1909-1989)
Und wieder spür' ich jenes leise Schwingen
Louis Ferdinand, "Vorgefühl" 1953pub

Anonymous
Ach! es schlägt mein Herz so bange
Josef Antonín Štěpán, "An Minna" 1778-79pub

Ach, wie thut mein Herze weh
Karl Goldmark, "Herzeleid" 1868pub, Op18,12, 1v(med).pf

Ade! Ich muß nun gehen zum Krieg wohl an den Rhein
Friedrich Nietzsche, "Ade! Ich muß nun gehen" 1870, NWV34, satb

Adieu, lieb Mädel, hab dich wohl
J. J. Grünwald, "Suschen" 1785pub

Als die Preussen marschirten vor Prag
Friedrich Silcher, "Die Prager Schlacht"

Als einst mit Weibes Schönheit sich
Joseph Haydn, "Als einst mit Weibes Schönheit" 1796-1800, XXVIa Nr.44

Am Oelberg weiß ich eine Stätte
Emilie Zumsteeg, "Am Oelberg"

An Birkenzweigen blättert der volle Keim herauf
Carl Loewe, "Frühlingslied" before 1829

Auf einem Grab in Stükken liegt ein zerrißner Kranz
Max Reger, "Der zerrißne Grabkranz" 1891, Op4,5, 1v(med).pf

Auf einsam hohem Thurme in trüber Nebelnacht
Johanna Kinkel, "Welt, o Welt! wie liegst du so weit!" Op17,6

Auf! Jeder sei nun froh und sorgenfrei!
Franz Schubert, "Trinklied" 1815, D267, 2t2b.pf

Aufthaute die Erde vom Strahle der Sonne
Carl Loewe, "Maiblümelein"
text by "M.R."

Ave! Ave! Ave maris stella! (see "Meerstern! ich dich grüsse")

Bald wehen uns des Frühlings Lüfte
Joseph Haydn, "Bald wehen uns des Frühlings Lüfte" XXVIa Nr.47

Beim Schmerz der dieses Herz durchwühlet
Joseph Haydn, "Beim Schmerz der dieses Herz durchwühlet" 1795, XXVIa Nr.37

Bist du denn wirklich so fern, lieblicher, glänzender Stern?
Clara Schumann, "Der Abendstern"

Blau der See! Von hohem Schilfe rings umgrenzet
Hans Pfitzner, "Zweifelnde Liebe" 1888/89, Op6,1, 1mv.pf

Bleibe bey uns denn es will Abend werden
Louise Reichardt, "An den Erlöser" 1826pub

Blühe, liebes Veilchen, blühe noch ein Weilchen
Friedrich Curschmann, "Das Veilchen" 1840?, Op27, 2sop.ten.pf

Blümchen der Demuth, unter dichten Blättern birgst
Carl Friedrich Zelter, "Das Veilchen" 1811pub

Brüder, schrecklich brennt die Thräne
Franz Schubert, "Lied" 1817, D535, 1v.insts

Christ, deines Geistes Süßigkeit
Max Reger, "Christ, deines Geistes Süßigkeit" 1914, Op137,6, 1v.pf(harm/org)
from *Zwölf geistliche Lieder*

Da lieg' ich unter den Bäumen
Felix Mendelssohn, "Da lieg' ich unter den Bäumen" 1831, Op84,1

Da schlend'r ich so die Welt hinan
Johann Holzer, "Der Wandrer" 1779pub

Das Schicksal will's ich darf nicht lieben
Norbert Burgmüller, "Das Schicksal will's" 1827-36?, Op12,4

Das Steuer des Bootes im entendurchschwärmten Hafen von Ina
Wilhelm Kienzl, "Schifferlied (Altjapanisches Kagura-Lied)" 189-?, Op47,1

Daß gestern eine Wespe dich in den Finger stach
Arnold Schönberg, "Daß gestern eine Wespe" 189-?

Dem hohen Kaiser-Worte treu
Wolfgang Amadeus Mozart, "Beim Auszug in das Feld" 1788, K552

Denkst du auch so innig meiner
Joseph Haydn, "Antwort auf die Frage eines Mädchen" 1796, XXVIa Nr.46

Der Bergmann lebt beim Grubenlicht
Carl Loewe, "Der Bergmann" before 1829

Der Frühhauch hat gefächelt
Hugo Wolf, "Morgentau" 1877
from *Sechs Lieder für eine Frauenstimme*

Der Frühling ist herangekommen
Louis Spohr, "Räthselhaft" 1841, WoO103, ten.pf(or 4-hand)

Der König Arthur von Engelland, der war ein guter Mann
Carl Reinecke, "Der gute König Arthur"
from the English
from *Kinderlieder*

Der lebt ein Leben wonniglich
Ludwig van Beethoven, "Das Glück der Freundschaft" 1803, Op88

Der Meeresfluth mit Purpurgluth entsteigt der Sonne Strahl
Carl Loewe, "Früh-Lied am Meere" before 1829

Der Sänger zog durch Wald und Flur
Louis Spohr, "Maria" 1842, Op139,2

Der Sternlein Heer am Himmel blinkt
Johann Abraham Peter Schulz, "Der Abendbesuch" 1782-90pub

Der Tag erwacht im Strahlenkranze
Friedrich Curschmann, "Morgenlied" 183-?, 3sop.pf

Des Jahres letzte Stunde ertönt mit ernstem Schlag
Johann Abraham Peter Schulz, "Neujahrslied" 1782-90pub

Des Phöbus Strahlen sind dem Aug' entschwunden
Franz Schubert, "Zur Namensfeier des Herrn Andreas Siller" 1813, D83, 1v.vn.harp

Des stolzen Männerlebens schönste Zeichen
Franz Schubert, "Lied eines Kriegers" 1824, D822, bass.mch.pf

Dich bet' ich an, erstand'ner Held
Carl Loewe, "Dich bet' ich an, erstand'ner Held" 1847, 4v

Die Englein haben das Bettlein gemacht
George Henschel, "Die Englein"
Max Reger, "Beim Schneewetter" 1903-04, Op76,6, 1v(med).pf
from *Schlichte Weisen, Band 1*

Die Feuerschlünde am Seinestrand, auch Königskanonen beigenannt
Carl Loewe, "Der fünfte Mai" 1837

Die frohe neubelebte Flur
Franz Schubert, "Morgenlied" 1816, D381

Die ganze Welt will glücklich sein
Joseph Haydn, "Der schlaue Pudel" 1780-87?, XXVIa Nr.38

Die Lerche sang, die Sonne schien, es färbte sich die Wiese grün
Johann Abraham Peter Schulz, "Frühlingsliebe" 1782-90pub

Die Sonne leuchtet, der Frühling bläht
Franz Abt, "O Jugend, wie bist du so schön" Op428,3

Die Sonne sah die Erde an
Robert Schumann, "Schneeglöckchen" 1850, Op96,2

Dir, kleines Bethlehem, erklang des heil'gen Sehers Lobgesang!
Carl Loewe, "Bethlehem" before 1829

Dir nah ich mich
Joseph Haydn, "Geistliches Lied" 1781/84, XXVIa Nr.17

Dir stets getreu, getreu mit ganzer Seele
Carl Loewe, "Sonaten-Romanze" 1829?
from the piano Sonata in E major Opus 16

Doch der Herr, er leitet die Irrenden recht
Felix Mendelssohn, "Geistliches Lied" Op 112,1

Dort oben auf dem Berge, da steht ein hohes Haus (see also Wunderhorn)
Carl Reinecke, "Dort oben auf dem Berge" Op37
from *Kinderlieder*

Du armes Herz, was wünschest du?
Louis Spohr, "Beruhigung" 1826, Op72,4

Du lieber Gott im Himmel du
Carl Reinecke, "Morgengebet"
from *Kinderlieder*

Du ringst, o Mensch! vergebens, und schaffst dir Sorg' und Müh
Johann Rudolf Zumsteeg, "Lied" 1805pub
from *Kleine Balladen und Lieder, siebtes Heft*

Du schläfst, so will ich leise flehen
Max Reger, "Gute Nacht / Du schläfst" 1890/91

Du siehst mich nun schon drei Tage heut
Max Reger, "Bitte" 1891, Op4,6, 1v(med).pf

Du Unruh', du Unruh', du Unruh' meiner Seelen
Carl Loewe, "Friede und Ruhe in Gott" 1v.organ

Ei, daß ich doch Potz Velten
Paul Hindemith, "Das verfluchte Geld" 1939, 4mv
from *Drei Chöre* (1)

Ei, wenn ich doch ein Maler wär'
Carl Maria von Weber, "Der Sänger und der Maler" 1820, Op80,6

Ein Gärtchen und ein Häuschen drin
Carl Maria von Weber, "Ein Gärtchen und ein Häuschen drin" 1803, J.36, ten.bass

Ein kleines Haus, von Nußgesträuch umgrenzt
Joseph Haydn, "Ein kleines Haus" 1801, XXVIa Nr.45

Ein Mädchen ist's, das früh und spät mir vor der Seele schwebet
Franz Schubert, "Das Bild" 1815, D155

Ein Mägdlein an des Felsen Rand
Carl Loewe, "Erdbeerliedchen" before 1829

Ein Musikus wollt fröhlich sein
Emil Mattiesen, "Der fröhliche Musikus" 1900pub, Op7,2
from *Vier heitere Lieder*

Ein Räppchen zum Reiten, ein Püppchen zum Kleiden
Carl Reinecke, "Ein Räppchen zum Reiten"
from *Kinderlieder*

Ein Stern der Lieb' am Himmelslauf
Bettina von Arnim, "Ein Stern der Lieb' am Himmelslauf" 1842

Eine Brücke kenn' ich, Liebchen
Franz Abt, "Die Brücke" 1873pub, Op220,3

Einmal aus seinen Blicken, von seinem süssen Mund
Felix Mendelssohn, "Romanze" 1828pub, Op8,10
from the Spanish

Elysium, du Land, wo Friede wird
Carl Loewe, "Heimweh"

Entflammt von Liebesqualen, als rings die Nacht noch webte
Bettina von Arnim, "Vision des heiligen Johannes von Cruz" 1842?

Erhebt das Glas mit froher Hand
Ludwig van Beethoven, "Trinklied" 1790?, WoO109

Es fahren die Schiffer auf schlummernder Bahn
Robert Franz, "Der Stern ist die Liebe" 1879, Op50,3

Es flog ein bunter Schmetterling
J. J. Grünwald, "Der Schmetterling und die Biene" 1785pub

Es hat die stille Nacht die Welt zur Ruh gebracht
Franz Abt, "Mond und Kinder" 1870?pub
from *Kinderlieder*

Es ist ein Schnee gefallen und ist es doch nit Zeit (see also Volkslied)
Franz Krause, "Verschneiter Weg" 1972?pub, Op51,ii,5
from *Gedichte aus alter Zeit 2*

Es segeln die Wolken, weiß niemand wohin?
Hugo Wolf, "Wanderlied (Aus einem alten Liederbuche)" 1877

Es sehnt sich das Herz nach Lust und nach Schmerz
Louis Spohr, "Das Herz" 1838, Op108,2, 2sop.pf

Es steht sein Bild noch immer da
Arnold Schönberg, "Gedenken" 190-?

Es tat den Beiden so weh das Scheiden
Othmar Schoeck, "Stummer Abschied" 1905, o.op18

Es wird wohl Winter weit und breit
Carl Loewe, "Trost" before 1826

Fischen schwimmt wohl hin und her
Carl Loewe, "Fischerin und Jägerbursch" (fragment), 1847

Flieg doch fort, du kleines Thier!
Carl Loewe, "Das Vöglein" 1840-50

Frage mich immer– fragest umsonst!
Carl Maria von Weber, "Unbefangenheit" 1813, Op30,3

Frage nicht, wie es gekommen, dass du mich so schnell erkannt
Carl Loewe, "Frage nicht!" before 1836

Frei und froh mit muntern Sinnen
Carl Maria von Weber, "Lebensansicht" 1812, Op66,5

Freund! ich bitte, hüte dich
Joseph Haydn, "Die Warnung" 1796-1801, satb.bc

Frühling ist kommen, lieblicher Lenz!
Stephen Heller, "Frühlings Erwachen" 1830-38?

Frühling und Liebe, sie kehren nun wieder
Johann Abraham Peter Schulz, "Aufforderung" 1782-90pub

Fünf kleine Schwesterchen all' in einer Reih'
Carl Reinecke, "Fünf in einer Reih'"
from *Kinderlieder*

Gelehnet lag ich an dem Baum
Johanna Kinkel, "Abendruhe" Op17,3

Gelobt sei Gott, denn er erhört
Carl Loewe, "Gelobt sei Gott" 1850

Geruhig seines Weges gehn und wo man kann, beglücken
Carl Loewe, "Geruhig seines Weges gehn" before 1826

Gleite hinan die glänzende Bahn!
Carl Loewe, "Kahnlied" before 1829

Gloria in excelsis Deo!/Ehre sei Gott in der Höhe!
Carl Loewe, "Gloria in excelsis" 1859, satb.satb

Golden lacht und glüht der Morgen über maiengrünen Höh'n
Hugo Wolf, "Der goldene Morgen" 1876, Op9,6

Gold'ne Freiheit, gold'ne Freiheit!
Josef Antonín Štěpán, "Gold'ne Freiheit" 1778-79pub

Graf Siegfried einst in Welschland kam
Martin Ruprecht, "Romanze" 1785?

Gute Nacht! Gute Nacht! Im Mondenschein, wenn Keiner mehr wacht
Carl Loewe, "Ständchen"

Hauche milder, Abendluft
Franz Schubert, "Grablied für die Mutter" 1818, D616

Heisse stille Liebe schwebet
Carl Maria von Weber, "Heisse stille Liebe schwebet" 1812, Op23,5, 1v.ttb.pf

Herab kamst du auf Erden, ihr Trost und Heil zu werden
Carl Loewe, "Jesus als Kind" before 1829

Herauf! Herauf! mit deiner purpur Glut'
Peter Cornelius, "Sonnenaufgang" 1843, ttbb

Herzchen, mein Schätzchen, bist tausendmal mein (see also Volkslied)
Max Reger, "Minnelied" 1904, Op76,21, 1v(med).pf
from *Schlichte Weisen, Band 2*

Heute ist Sonntag und Montag ist morgen
Louis Spohr, "Sonntag und Montag" 1835-36, Op94,6

Hie kann nit sein ein böser Mut
Paul Hindemith, "Hie kann nit sein ein böser Mut" 1925, Op45,ii,1, 2v.insts
from *Sing-und Spielmusiken für Liebhaber und Musikfreunde*

Hier sein Grab bei diesen stillen Hügeln
Joseph Haydn, "Auf meines Vaters Grab" 1781/84, XXVIa Nr.24

Hinab, ihr Brüder, in den Schacht!
Franz Schubert, "Bergknappenlied" 1815, D268, 2t2b.pf

Hinaus in weite Ferne, auf Meereswogen hin
Franz Abt, "Mit dir" 1873pub, Op149,1

Hör' auf mein armes Herz so bang zu schlagen
Joseph Haydn, "Die Verlassene" 1781/84, XXVIa Nr.5

Hört ihr die Hörner erschallen, ihr Jäger, eilet herbei
Carl Loewe, "Die Jagd"

Ich bin wie andre Mädchen nicht
Hugo Wolf, "Bescheidene Liebe" 1877

Ich frag' nach dir jedwede Morgensonne
Franz Schreker, "Ich frag nach dir" 1909
from *Tausend und ein Nächten*
from *Fünf Gesänge*

Ich hab' mir eins erwählet, ein Schätzchen
Carl Maria von Weber, "Liebeslied" 1817, Op54,3

Ich habe gar liebliche Sträußchen feil
Johann Abraham Peter Schulz, "Das Blumenmädchen" 1782-90pub
from the French

Ich habe keine Schulden, und hab' noch einen Gulden
Carl Loewe, "Der Sorglose" 1837

Ich schell mein Horn ins Jammertal
Johannes Brahms, "Ich schell mein Horn ins Jammertal" 1860, Op43,3

Ich soll kein Lebewohl dir sagen, dies tröstend süße Trennungswort
Emilie Zumsteeg, "Trennung ohne Abschied" 1819pub

Ich trag' eine Liebe im Herzen, von der wohl Niemand was weiss
Carl Loewe, "Stille Liebe" 185-?

Ich wandelt einsam auf grünem Pfad, zwei Raben hört ich, die hielten Rat
Anna Teichmüller, "Die beiden Raben" 1907pub, Op13,2
from the Scottish

Ihr frühlingstrunk'nen Blumen
Felix Mendelssohn, "Im Frühling" 1829, Op9,4

Ihr mißvergnügten Stunden
Joseph Haydn, "Trost unglücklicher Liebe" 1781/84, XXVIa Nr.9

Im tiefen Wald verborgen, da steht des Försters Haus
Hans Pfitzner, "Im tiefen Wald verborgen" 1888/89, Op2,4

Im Wald auf früher Reise, so morgenfrisch betaut
Anna Teichmüller, "Auf früher Reise" 1907pub, Op9,1

Immer sich rein kindlich erfreu`n
Josefine Lang, "Lied" 1834, Op25,4

In ahnungsvollem Glanze ruht still Neapels tiefes Meer
Johanna Kinkel, "Blaue Augen" Op17,1

In allen Fernen wölbt sich ein Haus
Josefine Lang, "Heimath" WoO

In allen Landen gehet still ein Engelein umher
Carl Reinecke, "Des Kindes Engel"
from *Kinderlieder*

In düstrer Nacht, wenn Gram mein fühlend Herz umziehet
Franz Schubert, "Blondel zu Marien" 1818, D626

In dulci jubilo/nun singet und seid froh!
Carl Loewe, "In dulci jubilo" 1859, satb.satb

In einsamen Stunden drängt Wehmut sich auf
Robert Schumann, "Stiller Vorwurf" 1840, Op77,4

Ja, ja, ich schweige, liebste Seele!
Josef Antonín Štěpán, "Ja, ja, ich schweige, liebste Seele!" 1778-79pub

Ja, wann gleich wär das Firmament
Max Reger, "Böses Weib" 1903, Op75,5

Jeder meint, der Gegenstand
Joseph Haydn, "Jeder meint, der Gegenstand" 1781/84, XXVIa Nr.13
poem possibly by Ph. G. Bader

Jesus nimmt die Sünder an
Carl Loewe, "Jesus nimmt die Sünder an" 1854, 4v
Carl Loewe, "Jesus nimmt die Sünder an (2nd version)" 1855, 4v

Juble, schöne junge Rose
Arnold Schönberg, "Juble, schöne junge Rose" 189-?

Kennst du nicht das Gluthverlangen, diese Qual und diese Lust
Felix Mendelssohn, "Geständniss" 1830pub, Op9,2
Ernst Otto Nodnagel, "Kennst du nicht das Glutverlangen" 1895, Op21,1

Kind, wo bist du hin gewesen
Paul Hindemith, "Die Stiefmutter" 1939, 4mv
from *Drei Chöre* (3)

Klein Vöglein widi widi widi witt witt spricht
Carl Reinecke, "Zugvögelein"
from *Kinderlieder*

Kleine Tropfen, seid ihr Thränen an den Blumenkelchen da?
Robert Schumann, "Mädchen-Schwermuth" 1840, Op142,3

Kleiner, kühler Wiesenquell, silberglänzend rein und hell
Carl Loewe, "Die Quelle" before 1829

Komm, komm, Geselle mein, ich harr' so sehre dein
Max Reger, "Lied eines Mädchens" 1907, Op104,4

Komm, liebe Zither, komm
Wolfgang Amadeus Mozart, "Komm, liebe Zither, komm" 1780-81, K351

Komm mit! beflügle deinen Schritt
Karl Gottlieb Reissiger, "Hornesruf" Op117,1, sop.hn.pf

Komm Schwester zu den Ufern des Garigliano-Strom
Johann Rudolf Zumsteeg, "Romanze" 1803pub
from *Kleine Balladen und Lieder, fünftes Heft*

Komm, und senke die umflorten Schwingen
Franz Schubert, "An den Schlaf" 1816, D447
Poem possibly by Johann Peter Uz

Kommt herzu, ihr seid geladen
Carl Loewe, "Kommt herzu!" 1826, 4v

Kyrie, o Herr Gott Vater, erbarm' dich über uns!
Carl Loewe, "Kyrie, o Herr Gott Vater!"

Lachet nicht, Mädchen, wenn ihr gleich lachet
Joseph Haydn, "Lachet nicht, Mädchen" 1781/84, XXVIa Nr.14

Lasset uns marschiren, rataplan, rataplan
Carl Reinecke, "Rataplan" 2v.pf
from *Kinderlieder*

Lasst uns beten: Vater unser, der du bist im Himmel
Carl Loewe, "Das Gebet des Herrn und die Einsetzungsworte" 1813pub, Op2 (early)
Loewe later assigned "Opus 2" to another group of songs.

Laßt uns das Kindlein wiegen
Max Reger, "Christkindleins Wiegenlied" 1914, Op137,10, 1v.pf(harm/org)
from *Zwölf geistliche Lieder*

Lauter Freude fühl' ich, lauter Liebe hör' ich
Franz Schubert, "Lied eines Kindes" (fragment), 1817, D596

Lebe, liebe, trinke, lärme, kränze dich mit mir
Joseph Haydn, "Alles hat seine Zeit" 1796-1801, satb.bc

Lebe wohl, o mütterliche Erde; birg mich bald in deinem kühlen Schooß
Mauro Giuliani, "Abschied" 1817pub, Op89,3, v.pf./guitar
Giuliani attributed this poem to Schiller

Lebhaft hab ichs oft empfunden
Johann Rudolf Zumsteeg, "Lied" 1803pub
from *Kleine Balladen und Lieder, sechstes Heft*

Leis' wandeln wir wie Geisterhauch
Carl Maria von Weber, "Grablied" 1803, J.37, 1v.ttb.winds

Leucht't heller als die Sonne (see also Wunderhorn)
Felix Mendelssohn, "Minnelied" 1834, Op34,1

Lieben, von ganzer Seele, lieben, herzinniglich
Robert Schumann, "Resignation" 1850, Op83,1

Lieben, warum sollt' ich's nicht?
Louis Spohr, "Warum nicht?" 1838, Op105,6

Liebt er mich? tönt es im Herzensgrund
Louis Spohr, "Liebt er mich?" 1843, WoO109

Loses Herze meiner Schönen
Josef Antonín Štěpán, "Der Mädchenlehrer" 1778-79pub

Luna blickt von ihrem Thron schmachtend auf Endimion
Johann Rudolf Zumsteeg, "Lais an Aristipp" 1803pub
from *Kleine Balladen und Lieder, fünftes Heft*

Mädchen sind wie der Wind
Carl Loewe, "Mädchen sind wie der Wind" 1818, Op9,vi,4
Author of text is identified by Johann André as "v. W."

Mag Thoren hienieden die Fessel aus Gold
Carl Loewe, "Der Liebescheue" 1815-16?

Man geht aus Nacht in Sonne, man geht aus Graus in Wonne
Carl Loewe, "Ein Preussenlied" 1840, 1v.ch.pf

Man strebt die Flamme zu verhehlen
Ludwig van Beethoven, "Man strebt die Flamme zu verhehlen" 1800-02, WoO120

Manchen langen Tag, und manche lange Nacht
Corona Schröter, "Manchen langen Tag" 1786pub

Meerstern! Meerstern! Meerstern ich dich grüsse, Mutter Gottes
Carl Loewe, "Ave maris stella!–Meerstern! ich dich grüsse" 1832, Op22,ii,5, 4v

Mei' Herzensallerliebster das ist en Bettelmann
Peter Cornelius, "Mainzer Mägdelied" 1854, sop.alt

Mein Handwerk geht durch alle Welt
Franz Schubert, "Tischlerlied" 1815, D274

Mein Herz, das ist ein tiefer Schacht
Arnold Schönberg, "Mein Herz, das ist ein tiefer Schacht" 189-?

Mein Leben wälzt sich murrend fort
Franz Schubert, "Der Strom" 1817?, D565

Mein Liebchen ist kein stolzes Schloß
Hans Pfitzner, "Mein Liebchen ist kein stolzes Schloß" 1884-86?, bar.pf

Mein Schatz, der ist auf die Wanderschaft hin (see also Volkslied)
Julius Lammers, "Heimliche Liebe" 1860, Op8,4

Mir ist, als müßt ich dir was sagen
Louis Spohr, "Schottisch Lied" 1809, Op25,2

Mir lächelt kein Frühling
Johannes Brahms, "Mir lächelt kein Frühling" 1881pub, WoO 25, 4fv

Nein, nun hab' ich's fest beschlossen
Franz Anton Hoffmeister, "Der Entschluss"

Nicht mehr so sanft und milde entzücken die Gefilde
Carl Loewe, "Sommerlied" 185-?, 2v.pf

Niemals dich wieder zu sehen
Carl Loewe, "Der Abschied" 1817, sstb.pf
from *Canon-Kranz*

Nimm dies kleine Angedenken
Joseph Haydn, "Abschiedslied"
Attribution to Haydn spurious. Grove credits Gyrowetz.

Nimmer dem liebenden Herzen
Ludwig van Beethoven, "Hoffnung" 1809?, Op82,1

Nimmer lange weil' ich hier, komme bald hinauf zu dir
Franz Schubert, "Trost" 1817, D523

Nimmer trag ich länger dieser Leiden Last
Franz Schubert, "Der Leidende" (2 versions) 1816, D432
poem earlier attributed to Ludwig Hölty
Franz Schubert, "Klage (Nimmer länger trag ich…)" 1817?, D512
attributed to Ludwig Hölty, but not found in his works

Nun holt mir eine Kanne Wein und laßt den Becher sein von Golde
Friedrich Kücken, "Abschied"
Peters edition reads: "Closely imitating Burns and Freiligrath"

Nur bei dir, an deinem Herzen
Ludwig van Beethoven, "An Minna" 1792?, WoO115

Nur die Einsamkeit umschattet
Louise Reichardt, "Stille der Andacht" 1826pub

O Berlin, ich muss dich lassen
Carl Maria von Weber, "Abschied" 1817, Op54,4, 2v.pf

O Fischer auf den Fluten, Fidelin!
Johannes Brahms, "Barcarole" 1860, Op44,3, ssaa.(pf)

O fließ, ja wallend fließ in Zähren
Joseph Haydn, "O fließ, ja wallend fließ in Zähren" 1781/84, XXVIa Nr.19

O Herre Gott, nimm du von mir
Max Reger, "O Herre Gott, nimm du von mir" 1914, Op137,5, 1v.pf(harm/org)
from *Zwölf geistliche Lieder*

O, kennt ihr nicht Emmchen, die Kleine?
Peter Cornelius, "Irisch" 1854, sop.alt

O komm zu mir wenn durch die Nacht
Fanny Hensel, "Gondollied" 1841, Op1,6

O lächle, Freund der Liebe, endlich wieder zu mir herab
Robert Franz, "Abends" 1865?, Op11,6

O Liebe, hast du uns zu kränken
Karl Friberth, "Die unglückliche Liebe" 1780pub

O liebes Mädchen, höre mich!
Josef Antonín Štěpán, "O liebes Mädchen, höre mich!" 1778-79pub
Joseph Haydn, "O liebes Mädchen, höre mich" 1781/84, XXVIa Nr.15

O, meine Blumen, ihr, meine Freude
Carl Loewe, "O, meine Blumen, ihr, meine Freude"

O Ursprung aller Brunnen
Max Reger, "Klage vor Gottes Leiden" 1914, Op137,11, 1v.pf(harm/org)
from *Zwölf geistliche Lieder*

O wie ist es schön in die Schule gehn
Carl Loewe, "Die Schule" before 1829, 2v.pf

Puer natus in Bethlehem/Ein Kind gebor'n zu Bethlehem
Carl Loewe, "Puer natus in Bethlehem" 1859, satb.satb

Quem pastores laudavere/Den die Hirten lobten sehre
Carl Loewe, "Quem pastores laudavere" 1859, satb.satb

Regen, komm' herab! Unsre Saaten stehn und trauern
Johann Abraham Peter Schulz, "Ein Lied um Regen" 1782-90pub, 2v.pf

Rose du am Borne, rote Rose!
Robert Gund, "Die Rose" 1907, Op36,2
translated by Georg Friedrich Daumer

Roter Vogel hinauf dich schwing! bring' mir, bring' mir sieben Ring'!
Anna Teichmüller, "Roter Vogel" 1910pub, Op19,3
poem listed as "Zigeuner-Spruch"

Ruh' von schmerzensreichen Mühen
Robert Schumann, "Requiem" 1850, Op90,7
translated from an old Catholic poem

Ruhe, schönstes Glück der Erde
Franz Schubert, "Ruhe, schönstes Glück der Erde" 1819, D657, 2t2b

Sanft ertönen Morgenglocken
Louis Spohr, "Glockenklänge" 1850, WoO118

Sanft glänzt die Abendsonne auf diese stille Flur
Franz Schubert, "Abendlied" 1816, D382

Schatzerl klein mußt nit traurig sein
Anton Webern, "Schatzerl klein" 1925, Op18,1, sop.cl.guit
from *Drei Lieder* (1)

Schicksalslenker, blicke nieder
Franz Schubert, "Hymne zur Genesung des Herrn Ritter (Des Tages Weihe)" 1822, D763, satb.pf

Schildern, willst du Freund, soll ich dir Elisen?
Ludwig van Beethoven, "Schilderung eines Mädchens" 1783?, WoO107

Schlafe, schlafe, holder, süsser Knabe
Franz Schubert, "Wiegenlied" 1816, D498
poem has been attributed to M. Claudius, but is not to be found in his works

Schlummere, mein süßes Kind
Max Reger, "Schlummerlied" 1893

Schöpfer, deine Herrlichkeit leuchtet auch der Winterzeit
Carl Loewe, "Winterlied" before 1826

Schon deckt die Nacht, von starrem Frost begleitet
Leopold Hofmann, "Die Nacht" 1780pub

Schon milder scheint die Sonne nieder
Norbert Burgmüller, "Frühlingslied" 1827-36?

Schweig o Herz! warum dies bange Sehnen
Louis Spohr, "Lied der Harfnerin" 1835-36, Op94,1

Seh' ich dort die Sternlein blinken
Carl Loewe, "Nachtlied" before 1820

Sei mir gegrüsst! Linderndes Öl!
Josefine Lang, "An die Thräne" WoO

Seid mir gegrüßt, ihr Täler der Gebeine
Josef Antonín Štěpán, "Seid mir gegrüßt, ihr Täler der Gebeine" 1778-79pub

Seid willkommen, stille Haine
Josef Antonín Štěpán, "Das zärtliche Mädchen" 1778-79pub

Selig, o Mutter, wer stirbt!
Carl Friedrich Zelter, "Auf den Tod eines Kindes" 1827pub

Senk dich, o Gram, mit deinen Fantasien tief
Johann Rudolf Zumsteeg, "Nachtgedanken" 1803pub
from *Kleine Balladen und Lieder, fünftes Heft*

Sie steht am Zellenfenster, denkt unablässig sein
Robert Schumann, "Die Nonne" 1849, Op145,2, satb

Sie trug ein Falken auf ihrer Hand
Felix Mendelssohn, "Wartend (Romanze)" 1830pub, Op9,3

So fliehst du mich, du tugendhafte Seele
Franz Anton Hoffmeister, "Arietta"

Sonst konnt' ich dein nicht denken
Carl Loewe, "Gute Nacht!" 1836

Stets sey es Frühling um dich
Emilie Zumsteeg, "Des Freundes Wunsch" 1817pub
from *Neun Lieder* (6)

Still ist die Nacht, nur leise klingen wieder
Franz Abt, "Erinnerung" 1873pub, Op240,1

Stirb immerhin, es welken ja so viele der Freuden
Ludwig van Beethoven, "Elegie auf den Tod eines Pudels" 1792?, WoO110

Süßer Freude heller Bach
Louise Reichardt, "Erinnrung am Bach" 1811pub

Süsser Schlaf umfing den Müden
Carl Loewe, "Jesus mit seinen Jüngern auf dem Meere" 1826
from a biblical folk legend

Tanzt, Paar und Paar, den Ringeltanz am schönen Tag
Johann Abraham Peter Schulz, "Pfingstreihen" 1782-90pub

Tausend goldne Blätter sinken
Joseph Marx, "Herbst" 1914, 1v(med).pf

Töne, lindernder Klang, du kannst nicht nehmen die Schmerzen
Johannes Brahms, "Töne, lindernder Klang" 1872pub, satb

Trachten will ich nicht auf Erden
Joseph Haydn, "Trachten will ich nicht auf Erden" 1790, XXVIa Nr.39

Trauer umfliesst mein Leben, hoffnungslos mein Streben
Franz Schubert, "Klage" 1816, D371
attributed to Ludwig Hölty, but not found in his works

Tretet leise zu meinem Grabe
Fartein Valen, "Tretet leise zu meinem Grabe" 1941, Op39,2
from *Zwei Lieder*

Um die blüthenvollen Äste summen Bienchen, säuseln Weste
Carl Loewe, "Amanda"

Umsonst, umsonst entsagt' ich der lockenden Liebe
Carl Maria von Weber, "Umsonst" 1802, Op71,4

Ungern flieht das Süsse Leben
Carl Maria von Weber, "Die Kerze" 1802, J.27

Uns ist geboren ein Kindelein
Max Reger, "Uns ist geboren ein Kindelein" 1914, Op137,3, 1v.pf(harm/org)
from *Zwölf geistliche Lieder*

Vergangen ist mir Glück und Heil (see also Volkslied)
Johannes Brahms, "Vergangen ist mir Glück und Heil" 1868, Op48,6

Vergangenheit in Luft gewebter Schleier
Emilie Zumsteeg, "Vergangenheit" 1817pub
from *Neun Lieder* (5)

Verschwunden sind die Schmerzen
  Franz Schubert, "Auf den Sieg der Deutschen" 1813, D81, 1v.2vn.vc
  Franz Schubert, "Verschwunden sind die Schmerzen" 1813, D88, ttb

Von allen Zweigen schwingen sich wandernde Vögel empor
  Fanny Hensel, "Nach Süden" 1841, Op10,1

Waldmeisterlein, Waldmeisterlein, Waldmeisterlein!
  Carl Loewe, "Beim Maitrank" 1845

Wann die Kinder schlafen ein
  Carl Reinecke, "Wann die Kinder schlafen ein"

Was gleichet der Lust, die im Busen mir lebt
  Johann Rudolf Zumsteeg, "An Marien" 1802pub
    from *Kleine Balladen und Lieder, viertes Heft*

Was rüttelt die Säulen und schüttelt am Thron?
  Carl Loewe, "Preussentreue" 1848-49?
    Text possibly by Telschow

Was säuselt hier wie banger Seufzer Stöhnen
  Karl Friberth, "Abschied an Adelinen" 1780pub

Was spinnst du? fragte Nachbars Fritz
  Wolfgang Amadeus Mozart, "Die kleine Spinnerin" 1787, K531

Was stehst du lange und sinnest nach?
  Louis Spohr, "Wach auf" 1837, Op103,6, sop.cl.pf

Was trauern doch die Mägdelein?
  Peter Cornelius, "Irisch" 1854, sop.alt

Weisse Lilie, meine Lilie, einsam traurig weil' ich hier
  Franz von Holstein, "Polnisches Lied" 1880, Op42,4

Wenn Eos am Morgen mit rosigem Finger
  Louis Spohr, "Jägerlied" 1845, Op139,3

Wenn fromme Kindlein schlafen geh'n
  Robert Schumann, "Kinderwacht" 1849, Op79,21
    from *Lieder-Album für die Jugend*

Wenn ich der Kaiser wäre
  Maria Therese Paradis, "Wenn ich der Kaiser wäre" 1784-86
    from *Zwölf Lieder auf ihrer Reise in Musik gesetzt*

Wenn im Lenze ringsum Alles lacht
  Louis Spohr, "Liebe" 1838, Op107,3, sop.ten.pf

Wenn Nachts im Wald die Turteltaube klagt
  Alexander Zemlinsky, "Der Liebe Lied" 1894-96, Op2,i,4

Wer die Liebe gepflanzt in die Menschenbrust
  Léander Schlegel, "Spruch" 1900, Op20,15
    from *Deutsche Liebeslieder*

Wer droht unserm deutschen Vaterland?
  Carl Loewe, "Preussisches Hurrahlied" 1848

Wer nicht, wenn warm von Hand zu Hand
  Ludwig van Beethoven, "Punschlied" 1790-92?, WoO111, unis.vv

Wie schön bist du, du güldne Morgenröthe
Franz Schubert, "Lilla an die Morgenröthe" 1815, D273

Wie so trüb, Slimora du!
Johann Rudolf Zumsteeg, "Ossian auf Slimora" 1803pub
from *Kleine Balladen und Lieder, fünftes Heft*

Wie unglücklich bin ich nit
Wolfgang Amadeus Mozart, "Wie unglücklich bin ich nit" 1775-76?, K147

Wieder trüg'risch war der Traum
Wilhelm Kienzl, "Liebeslied (neujapanisch)" 189-?, Op47,4

Winter entflieht, schon der Lenz sich zeigt
Wilhelm Kienzl, "Frühlings-Ankunft (altjapanisch)" 189-?, Op47,3

Wir hatten einander so gerne
Carl Loewe, "Die engste Nähe" 183-?

Wo ich ferne des Mikane hohen Gipfel ragen seh'
Wilhelm Kienzl, "Endlose Liebe (altjapanisch)" 189-?, Op47,2
Joseph Marx, "Japanisches Regenlied" 1909, 1v(med).pf
translated from the Japanese by Pierre Louys

Wo seid ihr hin, ihr stillen frohen Tage?
Johann Holzer, "Das Leiden der Liebe" 1779pub

Wo süss in Frieden ein Herze ruht
Robert Franz, "Das Grab der Liebe" 1878, Op48,2

Wollt Ihr seh'n mein muntres Bäschen
Carl Reinecke, "Das Bäschen"
from *Kinderlieder*

Wozu ist mein langes Haar mir dann
Johannes Brahms, "Fragen" 1860, Op44,4, ssaa.(pf)

Zieht die Lerch im Herbste fort
Carl Friedrich Zelter, "Abschied" 1826

Zirpe, liebe kleine Sängerin der Haine, zirpe nur in Ruh'!
Carl Loewe, "An die Grille" before 1829

Zu dir, dem Weltenmeister, flammt jubelvoll der Lobgesang!
Carl Loewe, "Zu dir, dem Weltenmeister" 1862

Zu meiner Laute Liebesklang, horch auf, horch auf!
Carl Friedrich Zelter, "Ständchen" 1800

Zum Kranz pflückt' ich einst Rosen
Johann Rudolf Zumsteeg, "Lied" 1803pub
from *Kleine Balladen und Lieder, fünftes Heft*

Volkslieder from *Des Knaben Wunderhorn*[8]
Abends, wenn ich schlafen geh, vierzehn Englein bei mir stehn
Armin Knab, "Abendgebet" 1905-20
from *Kinderlieder* (14)

[8]*Des Knaben Wunderhorn: Alte deutsche Lieder* is a volume of several hundred German folk poems assembled by L. Achim von Arnim and Clemens Brentano, first published in Heidelberg and Frankfurt, 1806-08.

Ach hartes Herz, laß dich doch eins erweichen
Erich J. Wolff, "Ach hartes Herz, laß dich doch eins erweichen" 1914pub, Lieder No.3

Ach Mutter, liebe Mutter, ach gebt mir einen Rat!
Johannes Brahms, "Guter Rat" 1877, Op75,2, 2v.pf

Ach wie so schön, wie hübsch und fein sind deine Tritt, Maria rein
Armin Knab, "Zugvögel" 1914
from *Wunderhorn-Lieder* (11)

Ahne, Krahne, wikkele, wahne, wollen wir nit nach England fahren?
Armin Knab, "Abzählreim" 1905-20
from *Kinderlieder* (18)

Als ich kam zur Stube rein, da ist gut wohnen!
Eugen d'Albert, "Hessisch" 1904?pub, Op28,3

Anne Margrittchen! Was willst du, mein Liebchen?
Theodor Streicher, "Weinsüppchen. Ein Kinderlied" 1903pub
from *Dreissig Lieder aus Des Knaben Wunderhorn* (15)

Antonius zur Predigt die Kirche find't ledig!
Gustav Mahler, "Des Antonius von Padua Fischpredigt" 1893, 1v.orch(pf)
from *Des Knaben Wunderhorn*

Bald gras' ich am Nekkar, bald gras' ich am Rhein
Gustav Mahler, "Rheinlegendchen" 1893, 1v.orch(pf)
from *Des Knaben Wunderhorn*

Bei der Nacht ist so finster im Weg
Thorvald Otterström, "Bei Nacht sind alle Kühe schwarz" 1907pub
from *Neun Lieder* (9)

Bin ich nit ein Bürschlein in der Welt?
Armin Knab, "Tanzliedchen" 1905-20
from *Kinderlieder* (5)

Blühe, liebes Veilchen, das so lieblich roch
Eugen d'Albert, "Knabe und Veilchen" 1904?pub, Op28,7
Erich J. Wolff, "Knabe und Veilchen" 1907pub, Op9,4
from *Sechs Gedichte aus "Des Knaben Wunderhorn"*

Büble, wir wollen ausse gehe!
Gustav Mahler, "Verlorne Müh'" 1892, 1v.orch(pf)
from *Des Knaben Wunderhorn*

Buko von Halberstadt, bring' doch meinem Kinde was
Theodor Streicher, "Wiegenlied" 1903pub
from *Dreissig Lieder aus Des Knaben Wunderhorn* (10)
Eugen d'Albert, "Wiegenlied" 1904?pub, Op28,2

Da droben auf jenem Berge, da steht ein goldenes Haus
Theodor Streicher, "Müller's Abschied" 1903pub
from *Dreissig Lieder aus Des Knaben Wunderhorn* (11)

Das Mägdlein will ein' Freier hab'n
Richard Strauss, "Für funfzehn Pfennige" 1897, Op36,2

Der Franz läßt dich grüßen gar hoch und gar fest
Theodor Streicher, "Bayrisches Alpenlied" 1903pub
from *Dreissig Lieder aus Des Knaben Wunderhorn* (20)

Der Kukkuck auf dem Birnbaum saß: Kukkuck
Theodor Streicher, "Kuckuck" 1903pub
from *Dreissig Lieder aus Des Knaben Wunderhorn* (12)

Der Mai will sich mit Gunsten, mit Gunsten beweisen
Theodor Streicher, "Große Wäsche" 1903pub
from *Dreissig Lieder aus Des Knaben Wunderhorn* (22)

Der Mondschein, der ist schon verblichen
Richard Strauss, "Himmelsboten" 1896, Op32,5

Der süße Schlaf, der sonst stillt Alles wohl
Friedrich Silcher, "Sehnsucht"
Erich J. Wolff, "Der süße Schlaf, der sonst stillt alles wohl" 1914pub, Lieder No.14

Des Morgens zwischen drei'n und vieren
Gustav Mahler, "Revelge" 1899, 1v.orch(pf)
from *Des Knaben Wunderhorn*
Armin Knab, "Rewelge" 1914
from *Wunderhorn-Lieder* (8)

Die Gedanken sind frei, wer kann sie errathen
Gustav Mahler, "Lied des Verfolgten im Turm" 1898, 1v.orch(pf)
from *Des Knaben Wunderhorn*

Dort hoch auf jenem Berge
Josefine Lang, "Dort hoch auf jenem Berge" WoO

Dort oben am Berg in dem hohen Haus! (see also Anonymous)
Gustav Mahler, "Wer hat dies Liedlein erdacht?" 1892, 1v.orch(pf)
from *Des Knaben Wunderhorn*

Du Dienerl, du netts, du liegst mir im Herz
Erich J. Wolff, "Tanzreim" 1907pub, Op9,5
from *Sechs Gedichte aus "Des Knaben Wunderhorn"*

Ei! Ei! Wie scheint der Mond so hell
Carl Maria von Weber, "Ei! Ei! Wie scheint der Mond so hell" 1818, Op64,7, ttb
Theodor Streicher, "Ei! Ei!" 1903pub
from *Dreissig Lieder aus Des Knaben Wunderhorn* (29)

Einmal in einem tiefen Thal der Kukuk und die Nachtigall (see also "Einstmals...")
Carl Loewe, "Der Kukuk" 1837, Op64,2
Loewe's text from Herder

Eins, zwei, drei, bicke, backe, hei!
Carl Reinecke, "Wie es in der Mühle aussieht" 2v.pf
from *Kinderlieder*

Einstmals in einem tiefen Thal Kukuk und Nachtigall (see also "Einmal...")
Gustav Mahler, "Lob des hohen Verstands" 1896, 1v.orch(pf)
from *Des Knaben Wunderhorn*

Es blies ein Jäger wohl in sein Horn
Johann Wenzeslaus Kalliwoda, "Der Jäger" 1857?, Op214,4

Es fliegen zwei Schwalben in's Nachbar sein Haus
Robert Schumann, "Die Schwalben" 1849, Op79,20, 2v.pf
from *Lieder-Album für die Jugend*

Es ist ein Schnitter, der heißt "Tod" (see also Volkslied)
  Theodor Streicher, "Erntelied" 1903pub
    from *Dreissig Lieder aus Des Knaben Wunderhorn* (1)

Es ist kein Jäger, er hat ein Schuß
  Theodor Streicher, "Vertraue" 1903pub
    from *Dreissig Lieder aus Des Knaben Wunderhorn* (17)

Es ist kommen, es ist kommen der gewünschte Frühlingsboth'
  Louise Reichardt, "Betteley der Vögel" 1819pub

Es jagt' ein Jäger wohlgemuth, er jagt aus frischem, freiem Muth
  Robert Schumann, "Jäger Wohlgemuth" 1849, Op91,2, ssaa.pf(ad lib)
    from *Romanzen für Frauenstimmen II*
  Friedrich Zipp, "Jägers Wohlgemut" 1935-36, Op5,5, 1v(med).pf
    from *Wunderhorn Lieder*

Es kam ein Herr zum Schlößli auf einem schönen Rößli
  Gustav Mahler, "Um schlimme Kinder artig zu machen" 1887-90
  Theodor Streicher, "Um die Kinder still und artig zu machen" 1903pub
    from *Dreissig Lieder aus Des Knaben Wunderhorn* (18)

Es ritten drei Reiter zum Thore hinaus!
  Gustav Mahler, "Scheiden und Meiden" 1887-90

Es sungen drei Engel einen süssen Gesang
  Gustav Mahler, "Es sungen drei Engel" 1895, 1v.orch(pf)
    from *Des Knaben Wunderhorn*

Es tanzt ein Butze-Butze-Butze-Butzemann in unserm Haus herum
  Wilhelm Taubert, "Butzemann"
    from *Klänge aus der Kinderwelt*, Vol.2, No12

Es war ein Markgraf über dem Rhein (see also Volkslied)
  Theodor Streicher, "Liebesdienst" 1903pub
    from *Dreissig Lieder aus Des Knaben Wunderhorn* (16)

Es wollt das Mädchen früh aufstehn (see also Volkslied)
  Armin Knab, "Der tote Knabe" 1904
    from *Wunderhorn-Lieder* (1)

Es wollt die Jungfrau früh aufstehn (see also Volkslied)
  Johannes Brahms, "Rosmarin" 1874, Op62,1, satb
  Engelbert Humperdinck, "Rosmarin" 1903
  Friedrich Zipp, "Rosmarin" 1935-36, Op5,7, 1v(med).pf
    from *Wunderhorn Lieder*

Es wollt' ein Mägdlein früh aufsteh'n, drei Stündlein vor dem Tag'
  Eugen d'Albert, "Die schweren Brombeeren" 1904?pub, Op28,5

Gar hoch auf jenem Berg allein, da steht ein Rautensträuchelein
  Friedrich Zipp, "Das Rautensträuchelein" 1935-36, Op5,4, 1v(med).pf
    from *Wunderhorn Lieder*

Gleich wie die lieb' Waldvögelein mit ihren Stimmen groß und klein
  Armin Knab, "Der Maria Geburt" 1914-17
    from *Wunderhorn-Lieder* (12)
  Ilse Fromm-Michaels, "Der Maria Geburt" 1921?, Op9,2

Gold'ne Wiegen schwingen und die Mücken singen
Erich J. Wolff, "Goldene Wiegen schwingen" 1907pub, Op9,6
from *Sechs Gedichte aus "Des Knaben Wunderhorn"*

Gott geb' ihm ein verdorben Jahr
Theodor Streicher, "Klosterscheu" 1903pub
from *Dreissig Lieder aus Des Knaben Wunderhorn* (25)

Guten Abend, gut Nacht, mit Rosen bedacht
Johannes Brahms, "Wiegenlied" 1868, Op49,4
Charles Edward Ives, "Wiegenlied" 1900?
second stanza by Georg Scherer, published 1849

Guten Morgen Spielmann, wo bleibst du so lang?
Louise Reichardt, "Hier liegt ein Spielmann begraben" 1819pub
Theodor Streicher, "Hier liegt ein Spielmann begraben" 1903pub
from *Dreissig Lieder aus Des Knaben Wunderhorn* (9)

Hast gesagt, du willst mich nehmen
Gustav Mahler, "Starke Einbildungskraft" 1887-90

Havele, Havele, Hahne, Fastennacht geht ane
Armin Knab, "Havele Hahne" 1905-20
from *Kinderlieder* (20)

Herzlich thut mich erfreuen die fröhliche Sommerzeit
Louise Reichardt, "Frühlingsblumen" 1819pub

Heute marschieren wir! Juchhe, juchhe, im grünen Mai!
Gustav Mahler, "Aus! Aus!" 1887-90

Hier sind wir arme Narrn auf Plätzen und auf Gassen
Theodor Streicher, "Nachtmusikanten" 1903pub
from *Dreissig Lieder aus Des Knaben Wunderhorn* (23)

Hör mich, du arme Pilgerin, die zu wallfahrten hast den Sinn
Armin Knab, "Inschrift" 1914
from *Wunderhorn-Lieder* (10)

Hört wie die Wachtel im Grünen schön schlägt, lobet Gott!
Louise Reichardt, "Wachtelwacht" 1819pub

Ich armer Tamboursg'sell! Man führt mich aus dem G'wölb
Gustav Mahler, "Der Tamboursg'sell" 1901, 1v.orch(pf)
from *Des Knaben Wunderhorn*

Ich armes Käuzlein kleine, wo soll ich fliegen aus
Louise Reichardt, "Käuzlein" 1819pub
Robert Schumann, "Käuzlein" 1849, Op79,10
from *Lieder-Album für die Jugend*

Ich bin gen Baden zogen, zu löschen meine Brunst
Erich J. Wolff, "Ich bin gen Baden zogen" 1914pub, Lieder No.26

Ich eß' nicht gerne Gerste, steh' auch nicht gern früh auf
Theodor Streicher, "Die widerspenstige Braut" 1903pub
from *Dreissig Lieder aus Des Knaben Wunderhorn* (5)
Erich J. Wolff, "Die widerspenstige Braut" 1914pub, Lieder No.29
Robert Gund, "Die widerspenstige Braut" 1914, Op39,6

Ich ging mit Lust durch einen grünen Wald
Gustav Mahler, "Ich ging mit Lust durch einen grünen Wald" 1887-90

Ich hab' emal ein Bettelmädle küßt
Theodor Streicher, "Ach und weh, kein Schmalzele meh!" 1903pub
from *Dreissig Lieder aus Des Knaben Wunderhorn* (28)

Ich habe mein Feinsliebchen so lange nicht geseh'n
Eugen d'Albert, "Auch ein Schicksal" 1904?pub, Op28,4

Ich hatt' nun mei Truschel ins Herz nei geschlosse
Erich J. Wolff, "Don Juan" 1907pub, Op9,1
from *Sechs Gedichte aus "Des Knaben Wunderhorn"*

Ich kann und mag nicht fröhlich sein!
Gustav Mahler, "Der Schildwache Nachtlied" 1892, 1v.orch(pf)
from *Des Knaben Wunderhorn*
Theodor Streicher, "Der Schildwache Nachtlied" 1903pub
from *Dreissig Lieder aus Des Knaben Wunderhorn* (2)

Ich möcht vor tausend Taler nicht, das mir der Kopf ab wär!
Hanns Eisler, "Was möchtst du nicht" 1929

Ich schwing' mein Horn ins Jammertal (see also Volkslied)
Theodor Streicher, "Aufgegebene Jagd. I. Erster Jäger." 1903pub
from *Dreissig Lieder aus Des Knaben Wunderhorn* (13)

Ich soll und muß ein' Buhlen haben, trabe dich Tierlein, trabe
Theodor Streicher, "Sollen und Müssen" 1903pub
from *Dreissig Lieder aus Des Knaben Wunderhorn* (30)

Ich weiss nicht, wie mir ist!
Gustav Mahler, "Selbstgefühl" 1887-90

Ich weiß mir'n Mädchen hübsch und fein, hüt du dich! (see also Volkslied)
Johannes Brahms, "Hüt du dich" 1875, Op66,5, 2v.pf
Eugen d'Albert, "Hüt du dich" 1900?pub, Op22,3
Friedrich Zipp, "Hüt du dich" 1935-36, Op5,6, 1v(med).pf
from *Wunderhorn Lieder*

Ich weiss nicht, wie mir's ist, ich bin nicht krank und bin nicht gesund
Eugen d'Albert, "Selbstgefühl" 1904?pub, Op28,6

Ich wollt', daß der verhindert mich an meinem Glück
Erich J. Wolff, "Ich wollt', daß der verhindert mich an meinem Glück" 1914pub, Lieder No.31

Ich wollte mich zur lieben Maria vermieten
Ilse Fromm-Michaels, "Wiegenlied einer alten frommen Magd" 1921?, Op9,4

In den Garten wollen wir gehen
Johannes Brahms, "Der Überläufer" 1868, Op48,2

Kein Hochgewild ich fahen kann, das muß ich oft entgelten
Theodor Streicher, "Aufgegebene Jagd. II. Zweiter Jäger." 1903pub
from *Dreissig Lieder aus Des Knaben Wunderhorn* (14)

Kling, kling, Glöckchen, im Haus steht ein Döckchen
Armin Knab, "Im Frühling, wenn die Maiglöckchen läuten" 1905-20
from *Kinderlieder* (15)

Kukuk hat sich zu Tode gefallen
Gustav Mahler, “Ablösung im Sommer” 1887-90

Lasset uns scherzen, blühende Herzen
Theodor Streicher, “Ehstand der Freude” 1903pub
from *Dreissig Lieder aus Des Knaben Wunderhorn* (7)

Leucht’t heller denn die Sonne, ihr beiden Äugelein! (see also Volkslied)
Alexander Zemlinsky, “Altdeutsches Minnelied” 1894-96, Op2,ii,2
Theodor Streicher, “Pfauenart” 1903pub
from *Dreissig Lieder aus Des Knaben Wunderhorn* (19)
Friedrich Zipp, “Pfauenart” 1935-36, Op5,1, 1v(med).pf
from *Wunderhorn Lieder*

Margritchen, Margritchen, dein Hemdchen guckt für
Armin Knab, “Ziehs naufi” 1905-20
from *Kinderlieder* (7)

Marienwürmchen, setze dich auf meine Hand (see also Volkslied)
Robert Schumann, “Marienwürmchen” 1849, Op79,13
from *Lieder-Album für die Jugend*

Mein Fleiss und Müh hab ich nie gespart
Arnold Schönberg, “Wie Georg von Frundsberg von sich selber sang” 1899-1903, Op3,1, 1v(med).pf

Mein Kind, sieh an die Brüste mein
Anton Webern, “Erlösung” 1925, Op18,2, sop.cl.guit
from *Drei Lieder* (2)

Mein Schätzle ist fein, ’s könnt feiner nit sein
Armin Knab, “Koseliedchen” 1905-20
from *Kinderlieder* (6)

Mein Vater hat gesagt, ich soll das Kindlein wiegen
Richard Strauss, “Hat gesagt– bleibt’s nicht dabei” 1898, Op36,3
Max Reger, “Hat gesagt– bleibt’s nicht dabei” 1903, Op75,12, 1v(med).pf
Theodor Streicher, “Hat gesagt– bleibt’s nicht dabei” 1903pub
from *Dreissig Lieder aus Des Knaben Wunderhorn* (27)

Mein Vöglein mit dem Ringlein rot
Ilse Fromm-Michaels, “Die Meise” 1921?, Op9,5

Mit Lust tät ich ausreiten durch einen grünen Wald (see also Volkslied)
Theodor Streicher, “Nächtliche Jagd” 1903pub
from *Dreissig Lieder aus Des Knaben Wunderhorn* (8)
Felix Mendelssohn, “Jagdlied” 1834, Op84,3

Mutter, ach Mutter, es hungert mich
Gustav Mahler, “Das irdische Leben” 1892-93, 1v.orch(pf)
from *Des Knaben Wunderhorn*
Erich J. Wolff, “Verspätung” 1914pub, Lieder No.40

Nach meiner Lieb’ viel hundert Knaben trachten
Erich J. Wolff, “Nach meiner Lieb’ viel hundert Knaben trachten” 1914pub, Lieder No.41

Nachtigall, ich hör’ dich singen, das Herz möcht mir im Leib zerspringen
Erich J. Wolff, “Frau Nachtigall” 1907pub, Op9,2
from *Sechs Gedichte aus “Des Knaben Wunderhorn”*
Ilse Fromm-Michaels, “Frau Nachtigall” 1921?, Op9,1

Friedrich Zipp, "Frau Nachtigall" 1935-36, Op5,8, 1v(med).pf
from *Wunderhorn Lieder*

Nun laßt uns singen das Abendlied
Theodor Streicher, "Abendlied" 1903pub
from *Dreissig Lieder aus Des Knaben Wunderhorn* (24)

Nun schürz dich, Gretlein, schürz dich, wohl auf mit mir davon
Armin Knab, "Schürz dich Gretlein" 1906
from *Wunderhorn-Lieder* (4)

O du mein Gott, o du mein Gott
Ilse Fromm-Michaels, "Engelsgesang" 1921?, Op9,3

O Jesulein zart, o Jesulein zart, das Kripplein ist hart
Erich J. Wolff, "Christkindleins Wiegenlied" 1907pub, Op9,3
from *Sechs Gedichte aus "Des Knaben Wunderhorn"*

O Röschen rot! Der Mensch liegt in größter Not
Wilhelm Kienzl, "Urlicht" 1919, Op96,13

Patsche, patsche, patsche, patsche, patsche, patsche Küchelchen
Wilhelm Taubert, "Patsch in's Händchen"
from *Klänge aus der Kinderwelt*, Vol.4, No12

Recht wie ein Leichnam wandle ich umher
Erich J. Wolff, "Recht wie ein Leichnam wandle ich umher" 1914pub, Lieder No.44

Schwer, langweilig ist mir mein Zeit
Arnold Schönberg, "Sehnsucht" 1903-05, Op8,3, 1v.orch
from *Six Orchestral Songs, Opus 8* (Piano acc. by Anton Webern)

Soll ich denn sterben, bin noch so jung?
Erich J. Wolff, "Soll ich denn sterben?" 1914pub, Lieder No.49

Sonne, Sonne, scheine, fahr übern Rheine
Armin Knab, "Sonnenlied" 1905-20
from *Kinderlieder* (4)

Spazieren wollt ich reiten der Liebsten vor die Tür
Friedrich Kücken, "Spazieren wollt ich reiten"
Johannes Brahms, "Von alten Liebesliedern" 1874, Op62,2, satb

Steht auf, ihr lieben Kinderlein (see also Albers)
Armin Knab, "Morgenlied" 1905-20
from *Kinderlieder* (13)
Anton Webern, "Morgenlied" 1922, Op15,2, sop.cham orch
from *Fünf geistliche Lieder*

Storch, Storch, Langbein, wann fliegst du ins Land hinein
Armin Knab, "Klapperstorch" 1905-20
from *Kinderlieder* (17)

Stürmt, reißt und rast, ihr Unglückswinde
Arnold Schönberg, "Das Wappenschild" 1903-05, Op8,2, 1v.orch
from *Six Orchestral Songs, Opus 8* (Piano acc. by Anton Webern)

Und nun ade, mein herzallerliebster Schatz!
Gustav Mahler, "Nicht wiedersehen!" 1887-90

Vögel, tut euch nicht verweilen, kommet, eilet schnell herzu
Eugen d'Albert, "Gedankenstille" 1904?pub, Op28,1

Weine, weine, weine nur nicht, ich will dich lieben, doch heute nicht
Richard Strauss, "Junggesellenschwur" 1900, Op49,6
Theodor Streicher, "Weine nur nicht" 1903pub
from *Dreissig Lieder aus Des Knaben Wunderhorn* (3)
Leo Blech, "Schelmenliedchen" 1909pub

Weinschröter, schlag die Trommel, bis der bittre Bauer kommet
Theodor Streicher, "Weinschröterlied" 1903pub
from *Dreissig Lieder aus Des Knaben Wunderhorn* (21)

Wenn du zu mei'm Schätzel kommst, sag, ich ließ sie grüßen
Thorvald Otterström, "An einen Boten" 1907pub
from *Neun Lieder* (8)
Friedrich Zipp, "An einen Boten" 1935-36, Op5,3, 1v(med).pf
from *Wunderhorn Lieder*

Wenn ich den ganzen Tag geführt hab' meine Klag'
Erich J. Wolff, "Wenn ich den ganzen Tag geführt hab' meine Klag'" 1914pub, Lieder No.55

Wer ist denn draußen und wer klopfet an
Gustav Mahler, "Wo die schönen Trompeten blasen" 1898, 1v.orch(pf)
from *Des Knaben Wunderhorn*

Wer sehen will zween lebendige Brunnen
Johannes Brahms, "Liebesklage des Mädchens" 1868, Op48,3
Erich J. Wolff, "Wer sehen will zween lebendige Brunnen" 1914pub, Lieder No.56

Wer sich auf Ruhm begiebet und freie Tage liebet
Theodor Streicher, "Aurora" 1903pub
from *Dreissig Lieder aus Des Knaben Wunderhorn* (6)

Wie kommts, daß du so traurig bist und gar nicht einmal lachst?
Theodor Streicher, "Unkraut" 1903pub
from *Dreissig Lieder aus Des Knaben Wunderhorn* (26)

Wie schön blüht uns der Maien, der Sommer fährt dahin
Armin Knab, "Abschiedszeichen" 1906
from *Wunderhorn-Lieder* (6)

Will ich in mein Gärtlein gehn
Alexander Zemlinsky, "Das bucklichte Männlein" 1934, Op22,6

Wir geniessen die himmlischen Freuden
Gustav Mahler, "Das himmlische Leben" 1892, 1v.orch(pf)
from *Des Knaben Wunderhorn*

Wohlan! Die Zeit ist kommen!
Gustav Mahler, "Trost im Unglück" 1892, 1v.orch(pf)
from *Des Knaben Wunderhorn*

Zu Koblenz auf der Brükken, da lag ein tiefer Schnee
Friedrich Zipp, "Wassersnot" 1935-36, Op5,2, 1v(med).pf
from *Wunderhorn Lieder*

Zu Strassburg auf der Schanz' (see also Volkslied)
Gustav Mahler, "Zu Strassburg auf der Schanz'" 1887-90

Zum Sterben bin ich verliebt in dich (see also Nikolai)
Theodor Streicher, "Wer's Lieben erdacht" 1903pub
from *Dreissig Lieder aus Des Knaben Wunderhorn* (4)

Other Volkslieder

Ach Elselein, liebes Elselein mein
Johannes Brahms, "Die beiden Königskinder" 1858,1926pub, WoO 32,15
from *Deutsche Volkslieder* (15)
Robert Franz, "Ach Elslein, liebes Elselein mein"
Musical arrangement by Franz
from *Sechs deutsche Lieder aus dem 15.u.16.Jh.* (5)

Ach, englische Schäferin, erhöre mein Bitt
Johannes Brahms, "Ach, englische Schäferin" 1894pub, WoO 33,8
from *Deutsche Volkslieder* (8)

Ach, es bebt der Blütenkeim fliegt der Wandervogel heim
Anna Teichmüller, "Ach, es bebt der Blütenkeim" 1907pub, Op9,4

Ach Gott! wie fällt das Meiden
Robert Franz, "Scheiden und Meiden"
Poem adapted by Osterwald. Musical arrangement by Franz
from *Sechs deutsche Lieder aus dem 15.u.16.Jh.* (1)

Ach Gott, wie weh thut Scheiden (see also Uhland)
Friedrich Silcher, "Erfrorene Blumen"
Johannes Brahms, "Scheiden" 1858,1926pub, WoO 32,16
from *Deutsche Volkslieder* (16)
Johannes Brahms, "Scheiden" 1859-62, WoO posth 37,12, ssaa
from *16 Deutsche Volkslieder*
Johannes Brahms, "Scheiden" 1863/64?, WoO 35,1, satb
from *Deutsche Volkslieder für gemischten Chor* (15)
Johannes Brahms, "Ach Gott, wie weh tut Scheiden" 1894pub, WoO 33,17
from *Deutsche Volkslieder* (17)

Ach, ihr Wälder, dunkle Wälder, Miletiner Wälder
Robert Franz, "Die Verlassene" 1867?, Op40,5

Ach, ihr Wälder, dunkle Wälder, warum lacht im gleichen Grüne
Adalbert von Goldschmidt, "Die Verlassene" 1910pub

Ach könnt ich diesen Abend
Johannes Brahms, "Ach könnt ich diesen Abend" 1894pub, WoO 33,26
from *Deutsche Volkslieder* (26)

Ach lieber Herre Jesu Christ
Johannes Brahms, "Ach lieber Herre Jesu Christ" 1864pub, WoO 34,6, satb
from *Deutsche Volkslieder für gemischten Chor* (6)

Ach, mein Henlein, bi bi bi!
Johannes Brahms, "Die Henne" 1857, WoO 31,3
from *Volks-Kinderlieder* (3)

Ach was Kummer, Qual und Schmerzen
Richard Strauss, "Ach was Kummer, Qual und Schmerzen" 1901, Op49,8

Ach, wenn ich nur ein Liebchen hätte!
Carl Maria von Weber, "Der kleine Fritz an seine jungen Freunde" 1809, Op15,3

All mein Gedanken, die ich hab, die sind bei dir
Johannes Brahms, "All mein Gedanken" 1894pub, WoO 33,30
from *Deutsche Volkslieder* (30)

Alt Mann wollt reiten und hatte kein Pferd (see also "Ull Mann wull...")
Johannes Brahms, "Beim Ritt auf dem Knie" 1857, WoO 31,8b
from *Volks-Kinderlieder* (8b)

Am Sonntag Morgen, zierlich angethan (see also Heyse)
Hermann Goetz, "Am Sonntag Morgen, zierlich angethan" 1866, Op4,5
translated from the Italian by Paul Heyse
from *Sechs Italienische Volksgesänge*

Auf, auf, auf! Schätzelein
Johannes Brahms, "Die Entführung" 1859-62, WoO posth 38,1, ssaa
from *20 Deutsche Volkslieder*

Auf dem Meer bin ich geboren
Friedrich Silcher, "Matrosenlied"

Auf, gebet uns das Pfingstei
Johannes Brahms, "Auf, gebet uns das Pfingstei" 1858,1926pub, WoO 32,4
from *Deutsche Volkslieder* (4)

Bei nächtlicher Weil' an ein's Waldes Born
Friedrich Silcher, "Der Jäger und die Nixe"
Johannes Brahms, "Der Jäger" 1858, WoO 32,2
from *Deutsche Volkslieder* (2)
Johannes Brahms, "Der Jäger" 1859-62, WoO posth 37,11, ssaa
from *16 Deutsche Volkslieder*
Johannes Brahms, "Bei nächtlicher Weil" 1864pub, WoO 34,3, satb
from *Deutsche Volkslieder für gemischten Chor* (3)

Bin ein- und ausgange im ganze Tyrol
Friedrich Silcher, "Bairisches Volksliedchen"

Bin ein Vöglein, das im Schatten zwitschert hier auf grünen Matten
Anna Teichmüller, "Das Vöglein" 1907pub, Op17,2
from *Lieder Kindern gesungen*

Bin i net a lust'ger Schweizerbu
Friedrich Silcher, "Bin i net a lust'ger Schweizerbu"

Blaue Äugle, rothe Bäckle, und ä Grüble im Kinn
George Henschel, "Blaue Äugle" 187-?, Op24,5

Bruder Jakob, schläfst du noch?
Wilhelm Taubert, "Bruder Jakob, schläfst du noch?"
from *Klänge aus der Kinderwelt*, Vol.5, No6

Brüder, Brüder, wir ziehen in den Krieg
Friedrich Silcher, "Beim Ausmarsch"

Da draussen, da draussen, vor der himmlischen Thür
Anna Teichmüller, "Vor der himmlischen Thür" 1905pub, Op3,1

Da drob'n auf jener Linden schlief ich und ruht' des Nachts
Hans Pfitzner, "Untreu und Trost" 1903, 1v(med).pf

Da drunten im tiefen Thale drei hohe Linden steh'n
Friedrich Silcher, "Untreue"

Da steh' i hier oben, schau' abe an See
Friedrich Silcher, "Des Buben Herzleid"

Da unten im Tale läufts Wasser so trüb
Johannes Brahms, "Trennung" 1859-62, WoO posth 37,10, ssa
from *16 Deutsche Volkslieder*
Johannes Brahms, "Da unten im Tale" 1863/64?, WoO 35,5, satb
from *Deutsche Volkslieder für gemischten Chor* (19)
Johannes Brahms, "Trennung" 1885?, Op97,6
Johannes Brahms, "Da unten im Tale" 1894pub, WoO 33,6
from *Deutsche Volkslieder* (6)

Das Lieben bringt groß' Freud'
Friedrich Silcher, "Mein Eigen soll sie sein" 4v

Dem Himmel will ich klagen, mein lieb' Blaublümelein
Friedrich Silcher, "Es muß geschieden sein" 4v
Johannes Brahms, "Dem Himmel will ich klagen" 1894pub, WoO 33,44, satb.(pf)
from *Deutsche Volkslieder* (44)

Der Besen, der Besen! was macht man damit?
Carl Reinecke, "Der Besen und die Ruthe"
from *Kinderlieder*

Der Frühling und der Sonnenschein
George Henschel, "Sonnenblicke" 187-?, Op29,5

Der Jäger in dem Walde sich suchet seinen Aufenthalt
Johannes Brahms, "Der Jäger im Walde" 1857, WoO 31,9
from *Volks-Kinderlieder* (9)

Der Lenz ist angekommen! Habt ihr es nicht vernommen?
Robert Franz, "Frühlings Ankunft" 1870?pub, Op23,5

Der Mai tritt ein mit Freuden
Arnold Schönberg, "Der Mai tritt ein mit Freuden" 1929
from *Vier deutsche Volkslieder*

Der Reiter spreitet seinen Mantel aus
Johannes Brahms, "Der Reiter" 1858,1926pub, WoO 32,6
from *Deutsche Volkslieder* (6)
Johannes Brahms, "Der Reiter" 1894pub, WoO 33,23
from *Deutsche Volkslieder* (23)

Der Tag hat seinen Schmuck auf heute weggethan
Carl Maria von Weber, "Abendsegen" 1819, Op64,5

Der Tag ist vergangen, die Nacht ist schon hier
Anton Webern, "Der Tag ist vergangen" 1915, Op12,1

Des Abends kann ich nicht schlafen gehn
Johannes Brahms, "Gang zur Liebsten" 1858, Op14,6
Johannes Brahms, "Gang zur Liebsten" 1859-62, WoO posth 38,2, ssa
from *20 Deutsche Volkslieder*
Johannes Brahms, "Des Abends" 1863/64?, WoO 35,6, satb
from *Deutsche Volkslieder für gemischten Chor* (20)
Johannes Brahms, "Des Abends kann ich nicht schlafen gehn" 1894pub, WoO 33,38
from *Deutsche Volkslieder* (38)

Dich meiden nein, ach nein!
Robert Franz, "Dich meiden"
Poem adapted by Osterwald. Musical arrangement by Franz from *Sechs deutsche Lieder aus dem 15.u.16.Jh.* (6)

Die Blümelein, sie schlafen schon längst im Mondenschein
Johannes Brahms, "Sandmännchen" 1857, WoO 31,4
from *Volks-Kinderlieder* (4)

Die Heere blieben am Rheine steh'n
Karl Gottlieb Reissiger, "Blücher am Rhein" bar.pf

Die heilige Elisabeth an ihrem Hochzeitsfeste
Johannes Brahms, "Die heilige Elisabeth" 1858,1926pub, WoO 32,7
from *Deutsche Volkslieder* (7)

Die Maid sie wollt 'nen Buhlen wert
Johannes Brahms, "Die Schnürbrust" 1858,1926pub, WoO 32,1
from *Deutsche Volkslieder* (1)

Die Schwälble ziehet fort, ziehet fort
Friedrich Silcher, "Böse Zeit"
Johannes Brahms, "Volkslied" 1852, Op7,4

Die See war wild im Heulen; der Sturm erstöhnt mit Müh
Corona Schröter, "Das Mädchen am Ufer" 1786pub

Die Sonne scheint nicht mehr
Johannes Brahms, "Die Sonne scheint nicht mehr" 1894pub, WoO 33,5
from *Deutsche Volkslieder* (5)

Die Wohllust in den Maien
Johannes Brahms, "Die Wollust in den Maien" 1858,1926pub, WoO 32,27
from *Deutsche Volkslieder* (27)
Johannes Brahms, "Die Wohllust in den Maien" 1859-62, WoO posth 37,9, ssa
from *16 Deutsche Volkslieder*
Johannes Brahms, "Die Wollust in den Maien" 1864pub, WoO 34,11, satb
from *Deutsche Volkslieder für gemischten Chor* (11)

Dort in den Weiden steht ein Haus
Johannes Brahms, "Schifferlied" 1858,1926pub, WoO 32,13
from *Deutsche Volkslieder* (13)
Johannes Brahms, "Schifferlied" 1859-62, WoO posth 38,3, ssaa
from *20 Deutsche Volkslieder*
Johannes Brahms, "Dort in den Weiden" 1863/64?, WoO 35,8, satb
from *Deutsche Volkslieder für gemischten Chor* (22)
Johannes Brahms, "Dort in den Weiden" 1885?, Op97,4
Johannes Brahms, "Dort in den Weiden steht ein Haus" 1894pub, WoO 33,31
from *Deutsche Volkslieder* (31)

Drunten im Unterland, da ist's halt fein
Friedrich Silcher, "Unterländers Heimweh"

Du mein einzig Licht, die Lilg' und Ros' hat nicht
Friedrich Silcher, "Minnelied"
Johannes Brahms, "Du mein einzig Licht" 1894pub, WoO 33,37
from *Deutsche Volkslieder* (37)

Du Mond, i hätt a Bitt' an di
Friedrich Silcher, "Bitte an den Mond"

Durch's Wiesethal gang i jetzt na
Friedrich Silcher, "Untreue"

E bissele Lieb' und e bissele Treu'
Friedrich Silcher, "Schwäbisches Liebesliedchen"

Ein Bursch' und Mägdlein flink und schön
Friedrich Silcher, "Süß' Liebe liebt den Mai" 4v

Ein Jäger aus Kurpfalz
Friedrich Silcher, "Der Jäger aus Kurpfalz"

Ein Sträusschen am Hute, den Stab in der Hand
Friedrich Silcher, "Wanderschaft"

Ein Täubchen, kirr und traut, hatt' ich im Taubenhaus
Friedrich Silcher, "Böhmisches Volkslied"

Einen Engel mit gold'nen Schwingen seh' ich gold'ne Äpfel bringen
Anna Teichmüller, "Gold'ne Äpfel" 1907pub, Op17,5
from *Lieder Kindern gesungen*

Erlaube mir, feins Mädchen, in den Garten zu gehn
Johannes Brahms, "Erlaube mir, feins Mädchen" 1859-62, WoO posth 38,4, ssaa
from *20 Deutsche Volkslieder*
Johannes Brahms, "Erlaube mir" 1863/64?, WoO 35,3, satb
from *Deutsche Volkslieder für gemischten Chor* (17)
Johannes Brahms, "Erlaube mir, feins Mädchen" 1894pub, WoO 33,2
from *Deutsche Volkslieder* (2)

Es fiel ein Reif in Frühlingsnacht (see also Heine)
Armin Knab, "Es fiel ein Reif" 1905
from *Wunderhorn-Lieder* (2)

Es flog ein Täublein weiße vom Himmel herab
Johannes Brahms, "Täublein weiß" 1864pub, WoO 34,5, satb
from *Deutsche Volkslieder für gemischten Chor* (5)

Es geht eine dunkle Wolk' herein
Felix Wolfes, "Es geht eine dunkle Wolk' herein" 1953, 1v(med).pf

Es ging ein Maidlein zarte
Johannes Brahms, "Das Mädchen und der Tod" 1858,1926pub, WoO 32,23
from *Deutsche Volkslieder* (23)
Johannes Brahms, "Es ging ein Maidlein zarte" 1894pub, WoO 33,21
from *Deutsche Volkslieder* (21)

Es ging sich unsre Fraue
Johannes Brahms, "Es ging sich unsre Fraue" 1894pub, WoO 33,47, satb.(pf)
from *Deutsche Volkslieder* (47)

Es gingen zwei Gespielen gut
Arnold Schönberg, "Es gingen zwei Gespielen gut" 1929
from *Vier deutsche Volkslieder*

Es glänzt der Mond nieder
Johannes Brahms, "Der Gang zum Liebchen" 1863, Op31,3, satb.pf
Johannes Brahms, "Der Gang zum Liebchen" 1868, Op48,1

Es ist ein Ros entsprungen
Erich J. Wolff, "Es ist ein Ros entsprungen" 1914pub, Lieder No.19

Es ist ein Schnee gefallen und ist es doch nit Zeit
Felix Wolfes, "Es ist ein Schnee gefallen" 1962, 1v(med).pf

Es ist ein Schnitter, der heißt Tod (see also Wunderhorn)
Felix Mendelssohn, "Erndtelied" 1828pub, Op8,4
Robert Schumann, "Schnitter Tod" 1849, Op75,1, satb
Johannes Brahms, "Schnitter Tod" 1858,1926pub, WoO 32,21
from *Deutsche Volkslieder* (21)
Johannes Brahms, "Schnitter Tod" 1859-62, WoO posth 38,5, ssaa
from *20 Deutsche Volkslieder*
Johannes Brahms, "Schnitter Tod" 1864pub, WoO 34,13, satb
from *Deutsche Volkslieder für gemischten Chor* (13)
Jan Gall, "Es ist ein Schnitter, der heisst Tod" Op26,3
from *Im Herbste* (3)
Erich J. Wolff, "Es ist ein Schnitter" 1914pub, Lieder No.20

Es ist mir wie den kleinen Waldvögelein zu Mut
Robert Franz, "Frühlingswonne" 1870?pub, Op23,2

Es ist nit lang daß 's g'regnet hat
Johann Friedrich Reichardt, "Es ist nit lang daß 's g'regnet hat" 1800pub
from *Lieder aus dem Liederspiel, Lieb' und Treue* (3)

Es pochet ein Knabe sachte
Johannes Brahms, "Der tote Gast" 1858,1926pub, WoO 32,11
from *Deutsche Volkslieder* (11)
Johannes Brahms, "Der tote Knabe" 1859-62, WoO posth 36,3, ssa
from *Acht Deutsche Volkslieder*
Johannes Brahms, "Der tote Knabe" 1864pub, WoO 34,10, satb
from *Deutsche Volkslieder für gemischten Chor* (10)

Es reit ein Herr und auch sein Knecht
Johannes Brahms, "Es reit ein Herr und auch sein Knecht" 1858,1926pub, WoO 32,28
from *Deutsche Volkslieder* (28)
Johannes Brahms, "Es reit ein Herr und auch sein Knecht" 1894pub, WoO 33,28
from *Deutsche Volkslieder* (28)

Es reiten drei Reiter
Johannes Brahms, "Die Bernauerin" 1859-62, WoO posth 38,6, ssaa
from *20 Deutsche Volkslieder*

Es ritt ein Reiter wohl durch das Ried
Johannes Brahms, "Es ritt ein Ritter" 1858,1926pub, WoO 32,24
from *Deutsche Volkslieder* (24)
Johannes Brahms, "Der Ritter" 1859-62, WoO posth 37,15, ssaa
from *16 Deutsche Volkslieder*
Johannes Brahms, "Es ritt ein Ritter" 1894pub, WoO 33,10
from *Deutsche Volkslieder* (10)

Es saß ein schneeweiß Vögelein
Johannes Brahms, "Es saß ein schneeweiß Vögelein" 1894pub, WoO 33,45, satb.(pf)
from *Deutsche Volkslieder* (45)

Es stehen drei Sterne am Himmel
Johannes Brahms, "Das Lied vom eifersüchtigen Knaben" 1859-62, WoO posth 38,7, ssaa
from *20 Deutsche Volkslieder*

Es steht ein Baum in Odenwald
Johannes Brahms, "Der Baum im Odenwald" 1859-62, WoO posth 38,8, ssa
from *20 Deutsche Volkslieder*

Es steht ein Lind in jenem Tal
Johannes Brahms, "Es steht ein Lind" 1894pub, WoO 33,41
from *Deutsche Volkslieder* (41)

Es stunden drei Rosen auf einem Zweig
Johannes Brahms, "Der Ritter und die Feine" 1859-62, WoO posth 37,3, ssa
from *16 Deutsche Volkslieder*
Johannes Brahms, "Der Ritter und die Feine" 1863/64?, WoO 35,10, satb
from *Deutsche Volkslieder für gemischten Chor* (24)
Johannes Brahms, "Es stunden drei Rosen" 1894pub, WoO 33,43, satb.(pf)
from *Deutsche Volkslieder* (43)

Es taget vor dem Walde
Robert Franz, "Es taget vor dem Walde"
Musical arrangement by Franz
from *Sechs deutsche Lieder aus dem 15.u.16.Jh.* (3)

Es wären zwei Königskinder
Johannes Brahms, "Es wären zwei Königskinder" 1859-62, WoO posth 36,6, ssa
from *Acht Deutsche Volkslieder*

Es war ein Markgraf über'm Rhein (see also Wunderhorn)
Friedrich Silcher, "Die drei Schwestern"
Johannes Brahms, "Des Markgrafen Töchterlein" 1858,1926pub, WoO 32,5
from *Deutsche Volkslieder* (5)
Johannes Brahms, "Des Markgrafen Töchterlein" 1859-62, WoO posth 38,9, ssaa
from *20 Deutsche Volkslieder*
Johannes Brahms, "Es war ein Markgraf überm Rhein" 1894pub, WoO 33,29
from *Deutsche Volkslieder* (29)

Es war eine schöne Jüdin
Johannes Brahms, "Es war eine schöne Jüdin" 1894pub, WoO 33,9
from *Deutsche Volkslieder* (9)

Es war eine stolze Jüdin
Johannes Brahms, "Die stolze Jüdin" 1859-62, WoO posth 38,10, ssa
from *20 Deutsche Volkslieder*

Es war einmal ein Zimmergesell
Johannes Brahms, "Der Zimmergesell" 1859-62, WoO posth 38,11, ssa
from *20 Deutsche Volkslieder*
Johannes Brahms, "Der Zimmergesell" 1863/64?, WoO 35,11, satb
from *Deutsche Volkslieder für gemischten Chor* (25)
Johannes Brahms, "Es war einmal ein Zimmergesell" 1894pub, WoO 33,46, satb.(pf)
from *Deutsche Volkslieder* (46)

Es waren einmal drei Reuter gefang'n, gefangen waren sie
Friedrich Silcher, "Treue"

Es wohnet ein Fiedler zu Frankfurt am Main
Johannes Brahms, "Der bucklichte Fiedler" 1859-62, WoO posth 37,6, ssa
from *16 Deutsche Volkslieder*
Johannes Brahms, "Der Fiedler" 1863/64?, WoO 35,4, satb
from *Deutsche Volkslieder für gemischten Chor* (18)
Johannes Brahms, "Der bucklichte Fiedler" 1883?, Op93a,1, satb
Johannes Brahms, "Es wohnet ein Fiedler" 1894pub, WoO 33,36
from *Deutsche Volkslieder* (36)

Es wollt' die Jungfrau früh aufsteh'n (see also Wunderhorn)
Robert Schumann, "Rosmarin" 1849, Op91,1, ssaa.pf(ad lib)
from *Romanzen für Frauenstimmen II*

Es wollt ein Mädchen brechen gehn
Johannes Brahms, "Das Mädchen und die Hasel" 1857, WoO 31,10
from *Volks-Kinderlieder* (10)

Es wollt' ein Mädchen früh aufsteh'n
Robert Schumann, "Vom verwundeten Knaben" 1849, Op75,5, satb
Johannes Brahms, "Vom verwundeten Knaben" 1858, Op14,2

Es wollt gut Jäger jagen
Johannes Brahms, "Der englische Jäger" 1864pub, WoO 34,14, satb
from *Deutsche Volkslieder für gemischten Chor* (14)

Fahret hin, fahret hin, Grillen, geht mir aus dem Sinn!
Friedrich Silcher, "Jägerlied"

Feins Liebchen, trau du nicht
Johannes Brahms, "Klage" 1888?, Op105,3, 1v(low).pf

Feinsliebchen, du sollst mir nicht barfuß gehn
Johannes Brahms, "Die Versuchung" 1858,1926pub, WoO 32,19
from *Deutsche Volkslieder* (19)
Johannes Brahms, "Die Versuchung" 1859-62, WoO posth 37,7, ssa
from *16 Deutsche Volkslieder*
Johannes Brahms, "Feinsliebchen du sollst" 1894pub, WoO 33,12
from *Deutsche Volkslieder* (12)

Frisch auf, frisch auf! Der Bergmann kommt!
Friedrich Silcher, "Bergmannslied"

Frisch auf, Soldatenblut! Fasst einen frischen Muth
Friedrich Silcher, "Soldatenlied"

Früh am Morgen ging die Maid aus der Tür hinaus
Max Reger, "Das Mägdlein und der Spatz" 1907, Op76,38, 1v(med).pf
from *Schlichte Weisen, Band 4*

Fünf Engel haben gesungen, fünf Engel kommen gesprungen
Armin Knab, "Fünf Engel" 1905-20
from *Kinderlieder* (16)

Fürwahr, mein Liebchen, ich will nun frein
Johannes Brahms, "Neckereien" 1863, Op31,2, satb.pf

Gäb's ein einzig Brünnelein auf der weiten, weiten Erde
Max Reger, "Gäb's ein einzig Brünnelein" 1894, Op14,4, sop.alt.pf

Gar lieblich hat sich gesellet
Johannes Brahms, "Liebeslied" 1858,1926pub, WoO 32,25
from *Deutsche Volkslieder* (25)
Johannes Brahms, "Liebeslied" 1859-62, WoO posth 38,12, ssaa
from *20 Deutsche Volkslieder*
Johannes Brahms, "Gar lieblich hat sich gesellet" 1894pub, WoO 33,3
from *Deutsche Volkslieder* (3)

Gegrüßet, Maria, du Mutter der Gnaden
Johannes Brahms, "Der englische Gruß" 1858,1926pub, WoO 32,8
from *Deutsche Volkslieder* (8)

Geh, zartes Blatt, geh, armes Briefchen, hin!
Hermann Goetz, "Geh, zartes Blatt, geh, armes Briefchen, hin!" 1866, Op4,2
translated from the Italian by Paul Heyse
from *Sechs Italienische Volksgesänge*

Gestern Abend in der stillen Ruh'
Max Reger, "Waldeinsamkeit" 1903-04, Op76,3, 1v(med).pf
from *Schlichte Weisen, Band 1*

Gretele, willst tanzen? "O jerum, jo!"
Armin Knab, "Gretele, willst tanzen?" 1905-20
from *Kinderlieder* (1)

Gunhilde lebt gar still und fromm
Johannes Brahms, "Gunhilde" 1858,1926pub, WoO 32,10
from *Deutsche Volkslieder* (10)
Johannes Brahms, "Gunhilde" 1859-62, WoO posth 37,5, ssa
from *16 Deutsche Volkslieder*
Johannes Brahms, "Gunhilde" 1894pub, WoO 33,7
from *Deutsche Volkslieder* (7)

Gut Nacht, gut Nacht, mein feines Lieb, gut Nacht, schlaf' wohl, mein Kind!
Friedrich Silcher, "Gut Nacht"

Gut Nacht, gut Nacht, mein liebster Schatz
Johannes Brahms, "Ständchen" 1858, Op14,7

Guten Abend, guten Abend, mein tausiger Schatz
Johannes Brahms, "Guten Abend" 1858,1926pub, WoO 32,26
from *Deutsche Volkslieder* (26)
Johannes Brahms, "Spannung" 1859-62, WoO posth 36,7, ssaa
from *Acht Deutsche Volkslieder*
Johannes Brahms, "Spannung" 1877-79?, Op84,5, 1or2v.pf
Johannes Brahms, "Guten Abend" 1894pub, WoO 33,4
from *Deutsche Volkslieder* (4)

Guten Abend, mein Schatz, guten Abend, mein Kind
Johannes Brahms, "Vergebliches Ständchen" 1877-79?, Op84,4, 1or2v.pf

Habt ihr sie schon geseh'n, sie, meinen Schatz
Robert Franz, "Habt ihr sie schon geseh'n?" 1862?, Op36,3

Han an em Ort e Blümeli g'seh, e Blümeli roth und wiss
Friedrich Silcher, "'s Blümeli"

Hat dich ein blühendes Blümchen erfreut
Arno Kleffel, "Volkslied" Op7,7

Hatte Liebchen zwei dort im Dorf der Haide
Robert Franz, "Volkslied" 1860?, Op14,4

Herzallerliebstes Schatzerl du, schließ schnell dein Herzenskammerl zu
Friedrich Kücken, "Herzallerliebstes Schatzerl du"

Herzchen, mein Schätzchen, bist tausendmal mein
Carl Maria von Weber, "Herzchen, mein Schätzchen" 1819, Op64,8

Herzerl, was kränkt dich so sehr
Friedrich Silcher, "Hoffe das Beste"

Herziges Schätzle Du hast mer all' mei Ruh' g'stohl'n
Robert Franz, "Herziges Schätzle du" 1879, Op50,1
Verses 2&3 by Wilhelm Osterwald
Erik Meyer-Helmund, "Schwäbisches Volkslied" 1886-88

Hinter jenen dichten Wäldern weilst du
Johannes Brahms, "Sehnsucht" 1868, Op49,3

Hört, wir die Wachtel im Felde dort schlägt
Corona Schröter, "Die Wachtel" 1786pub

I und mein junges Weib können schön tanza
Carl Maria von Weber, "Schwäbisches Bettlerlied" 1812, Op25,4, 1v.guit or 1v.pf

Ich armer Mann was focht mich an
Robert Franz, "Ich armer Mann"
Poem adapted by Osterwald. Musical arrangement by Franz
from *Sechs deutsche Lieder aus dem 15.u.16.Jh.* (4)

Ich bin dir herzengulden gut
Armin Knab, "Ich bin dir herzengulden gut" 1905-20
from *Kinderlieder* (8)

Ich fahr' dahin, wenn es muß sein
Friedrich Silcher, "Altes Minnelied"
Johannes Brahms, "Altes Minnelied" 1858,1926pub, WoO 32,17
from *Deutsche Volkslieder* (17)
Johannes Brahms, "Altes Minnelied" 1859-62, WoO posth 37,8, ssa
from *16 Deutsche Volkslieder*
Johannes Brahms, "Abschiedslied" 1864pub, WoO 34,9, satb
from *Deutsche Volkslieder für gemischten Chor* (9)

Ich ging einmal spazieren
Friedrich Silcher, "Juchhei, dich muss ich haben!"

Ich hab die Nacht geträumet
Johannes Brahms, "Ich hab die Nacht geträumet" 1859-62, WoO posth 36,4, ssa
from *Acht Deutsche Volkslieder*
Erich J. Wolff, "Traum" 1914pub, Lieder No.30

Ich habe den Frühling gesehen
Friedrich Silcher, "Klage"

Ich habe mein Feinsliebchen, so lange nicht gesehen
George Henschel, "Ich habe mein Feinsliebchen" 187-?, Op29,4

Ich hört ein Sichlein rauschen, wohl rauschen durch das Korn
Johannes Brahms, "Ich hörte ein Sichlein rauschen" 1859-62, WoO posth 37,2, ssa
from *16 Deutsche Volkslieder*

Franz von Holstein, "Volkslied" 1880, Op43,3

Ich schwing mein Horn ins Jammertal (see also Wunderhorn)
Johannes Brahms, "Ich schwing mein Horn ins Jammertal" 1861-?, Op41,1, ttbb

Ich stand auf hohem Berge
Johannes Brahms, "Ich stand auf hohem Berge" 1859-62, WoO posth 37,4, ssa
from *16 Deutsche Volkslieder*
Johannes Brahms, "Ich stand auf hohem Berge" 1894pub, WoO 33,27
from *Deutsche Volkslieder* (27)

Ich stund an einem Morgen
Johannes Brahms, "Ich stund an einem Morgen" 1858,1926pub, WoO 32,9
from *Deutsche Volkslieder* (9)

Ich weiss ja, warum ich so traurig bin
Robert Franz, "Das traurige Mädchen" 1870?pub, Op23,4

Ich weiß mir'n Maidlein hübsch und fein (see also Wunderhorn)
Johannes Brahms, "Ich weiß mir'n Maidlein" 1894pub, WoO 33,40
from *Deutsche Volkslieder* (40)

Ihr Hirten, erwacht, seid munter und lacht
Carl Reinecke, "Weihnachtslied"
from *Kinderlieder*

Im Aargäu sind zwei Liebi
Friedrich Silcher, "Die Heimkehr"

Im tiefen Wald im Dornenhag
Johannes Brahms, "Dornröschen" 1857, WoO 31,1
from *Volks-Kinderlieder* (1)

In der finstern Mitternacht
Johannes Brahms, "Der getreue Eckart" 1858,1926pub, WoO 32,18a&b
from *Deutsche Volkslieder* (18a&b)

In meines Vaters Garten da stehen zwei Bäumelein
Max Reger, "Hoffnungstrost" 1902-03, Op70,10

In Polen steht ein Haus
Johannes Brahms, "Das Schlaraffenland" 1857, WoO 31,7
from *Volks-Kinderlieder* (7)

In stiller Nacht, zur ersten Wacht
Johannes Brahms, "Totenklage" 1859-62, WoO posth 36,1, ssaa
from *Acht Deutsche Volkslieder*
Johannes Brahms, "In stiller Nacht" 1864pub, WoO 34,8, satb
from *Deutsche Volkslieder für gemischten Chor* (8)
Johannes Brahms, "In stiller Nacht" 1894pub, WoO 33,42
from *Deutsche Volkslieder* (42)

Jetzt gang i an's Brünnele
Friedrich Silcher, "Die drei Röselein"

Jetzt reisen wir zum Thor hinaus
Friedrich Silcher, "Abschied"

Jung vermähle mich, o Mutter!
Max Reger, "Der Knabe an die Mutter" 1903, Op75,3

Jungfräulein, soll ich mit euch gehn
Johannes Brahms, "Jungfräulein, soll ich mit euch gehn" 1894pub, WoO 33,11
from *Deutsche Volkslieder* (11)

Karlinle, mein Schatz, hat Härle wie Flachs
Armin Knab, "Zwei Liedchen zum Tanz" 1905-20
from *Kinderlieder* (10)

Kein Feuer, kein Kohle
Johannes Brahms, "Heimliche Liebe" 1859-62, WoO posth 38,13, ssa/ssaa (2 ver.)
from *20 Deutsche Volkslieder*

Kein schön'rer Tod ist in der Welt
Friedrich Silcher, "Schlachtlied"

Klein Christel kam vor die Himmelspfort!
Anna Teichmüller, "Klein Christel" 1907pub, Op9,7

Knabe, dir gefiel die duftige Rose
Alban Berg, "Verlassen" 1906

Könnt'st du meine Äugelein seh'n
Robert Franz, "Rote Äugelein" 1870?pub, Op23,6

Komm Mainz, komm Bayrn, komm Österreich
Johannes Brahms, "Vom heiligen Märtyrer Emmerano, Bischoffen zu Regenspurg" 1864pub, WoO 34,4, satb
from *Deutsche Volkslieder für gemischten Chor* (4)

Komm mit mir in's Thäle, 's ist heimlich und still
Friedrich Silcher, "Hirtenliebe"

Komme komme komm herbei, blüthenschwerer, holder Mai
Anna Teichmüller, "Blüthenschwerer Mai" 1905pub, Op3,5

Kommt die Nacht mit ihren Schatten
Leopold Damrosch, "Liebesgruss" Op14,1

Lärchenbaum, mein Lärchenbaum, wer hat dich hierhergebracht?
Anna Teichmüller, "Lärchenbaum, mein Lärchenbaum" 1905pub, Op3,3

Liebchen, ade! Scheiden thut weh!
Friedrich Silcher, "Abschied"

Liegt ein armer Krieger in dem Turm gefangen
Anna Teichmüller, "Der Gefangene" 1906pub, Op8,1

Mädele, ruck, ruck, ruck an meine grüne Seite
Friedrich Silcher, "Die Auserwählte"

Männer suchen stets zu naschen
Wolfgang Amadeus Mozart, "Warnung" 1783
Max Reger, "Warnung" 1907, Op104,2
Joseph Marx, "Warnung" 1909, sop..pf
Marx found the folk poem in a collection by Gorter

Maidle, lass der was verzähle
Friedrich Silcher, "'s Herz"

Maria ging aus wandern
Johannes Brahms, "Marias Wallfahrt" 1858,1926pub, WoO 32,22
from *Deutsche Volkslieder* (22)

Johannes Brahms, "Maria ging aus wandern" 1894pub, WoO 33,14
from *Deutsche Volkslieder* (14)

Maria wollt zur Kirche gehn, da kam sie an den tiefen See (see also Mittler)
Armin Knab, "Maria und der Schiffer" 1914
from *Wunderhorn-Lieder* (9)

Marienwürmchen, setze dich auf meine Hand (see also Wunderhorn)
Johannes Brahms, "Marienwürmchen" 1857, WoO 31,13
from *Volks-Kinderlieder* (13)
George Henschel, "Marienwürmchen" 187-?, Op22,7

Mei Maidle hot e G'sichtle
Friedrich Silcher, "Mei Maidle"

Mei Mueter mag mi net, und kei Schatz han i net (see also "Mein Muter...")
Friedrich Silcher, "Die Trauernde"
Johannes Brahms, "Die Trauernde" 1852, Op7,5
Robert Franz, "Die Trauernde" 1860?pub, Op17,4

Mei Schätzerl, das hat mi verlassen
Robert Franz, "Wird er wohl noch meiner gedenken?" 1870?pub, Op23,1

Mei Schätzerl is hübsch, aber reich is es nit
George Henschel, "Mei Schätzerl is hübsch" 187-?, Op29,3

Mei Schätzle ist fei, 's könnt' feiner net sei
Friedrich Silcher, "Schwäbisches Tanzliedchen"

Mein Herz in steten Treuen
Arnold Schönberg, "Mein Herz in steten Treuen" 1929
from *Vier deutsche Volkslieder*

Mein Herz ist mir gemenget
Arnold Schönberg, "Mein Herz ist mir gemenget" 1929
from *Vier deutsche Volkslieder*

Mein Herzlein thut mir gar zu weh!
Friedrich Silcher, "Herzensweh"
Friedrich Silcher, "Herzensweh" 4v
Johannes Brahms, "Altdeutsches Minnelied" 1859-62, WoO posth 36,5, ssaa
from *Acht Deutsche Volkslieder*
Johannes Brahms, "Altes Liebeslied" 1859-62, WoO posth 38,14, ssa
from *20 Deutsche Volkslieder*

Mein Kindchen ist fein, könnt schöner nicht sein
Max Reger, "Elternstolz" 1902-03, Op70,6

Mein Mädel hat einen Rosenmund
Johannes Brahms, "Mein Mädel hat einen Rosenmund" 1894pub, WoO 33,25
from *Deutsche Volkslieder* (25)

Mein Mützchen schön schwarz und das Schürzchen schön weiss
Carl Reinecke, "Tanzlied" Op135
from *Kinderlieder*

Mein Muter mag mi net, und kein Schatz han i net (see also "Mei Mueter...")
Erich J. Wolff, "Der Trauernde" 1914pub, Lieder No.39

Mein Pferd das ist am Huf so schwer
Robert Franz, "Fahr' hin!"
Poem adapted by Osterwald. Musical arrangement by Franz
from *Sechs deutsche Lieder aus dem 15.u.16.Jh.* (2)

Mein Schätzerl is hübsch
Carl Maria von Weber, "Volkslied" 1818, Op64,1

Mein Schatz, der ist auf die Wanderschaft hin (see also Anonymous)
Friedrich Silcher, "Heimlicher Liebe Pein" 4v
Carl Maria von Weber, "Heimlicher Liebe Pein" 1818, Op64,3

Mein Schatz, ich hab es erfahren
Johannes Brahms, "Dauernde Liebe" 1859-62, WoO posth 38,15, ssaa
from *20 Deutsche Volkslieder*

Mein Schatz ist auf die Wanderschaft hin (see also "Mein Schatz, der...")
Johannes Brahms, "Während die Trennung" 1859-62, WoO posth 38,16, ssaa
from *20 Deutsche Volkslieder*

Mein Schatz ist nicht da, ist weit überm See
Johannes Brahms, "Sehnsucht" 1858, Op14,8

Mein Sohn, wo willst du hin so spät?
Felix Mendelssohn, "Winterlied" 1834pub, Op19,3
Max Reger, "Winterlied (Ballade)" 1888?

Mich dünkt, wir geben einen Ball!
Armin Knab, "Ball der Tiere" 1905-20
from *Kinderlieder* (19)

Mir ist ein schöns brauns Maidelein
Johannes Brahms, "Mir ist ein schöns brauns Maidelein" 1894pub, WoO 33,24
from *Deutsche Volkslieder* (24)

Mir ist's zu wohl ergangen
Friedrich Silcher, "Zu End'"

Mit Lust tät ich ausreiten durch einen grünen Wald (see also Wunderhorn)
Johannes Brahms, "Drei Vögelein" 1858,1926pub, WoO 32,3
from *Deutsche Volkslieder* (3)
Johannes Brahms, "Drei Vögelein" 1859-62, WoO posth 36,8, ssa
from *Acht Deutsche Volkslieder*
Johannes Brahms, "Mit Lust tät ich ausreiten" 1864pub, WoO 34,2, satb
from *Deutsche Volkslieder für gemischten Chor* (2)

Morgen müssen wir verreisen
Friedrich Silcher, "Abschied"

Morgen muß ich fort von hier
Friedrich Silcher, "Lebewohl" 4v
from a 17th century Volkslied, adapted by Wilhelm Müller
Johannes Brahms, "Morgen muß ich fort von hier" 1859-62, WoO posth 38,17, ssa
from *20 Deutsche Volkslieder*

Morgen muss ich weg von hier
Friedrich Silcher, "Lebewohl"

Muss i denn, muss i denn zum Städtele naus
Friedrich Silcher, "Abschied"

Nachtigall, sag was für Grüß
Johannes Brahms, "Nachtigall, sag" 1894pub, WoO 33,48, satb.(pf)
from *Deutsche Volkslieder* (48)

Nichts kann auf Erden verglichen werden des Schäfers Lust
Friedrich Silcher, "Schäferleben"

Nichts Schön'res kann mich erfreuen
Friedrich Silcher, "Schwimm hin, Ringelein"

Nun leb' wohl, du kleine Gasse
Friedrich Silcher, "Nun leb' wohl, du kleine Gasse"

Nur ein Gesicht auf Erden lebt
Johannes Brahms, "Nur ein Gesicht auf Erden lebt" 1894pub, WoO 33,19
from *Deutsche Volkslieder* (19)

O Engel, mein Schutzengel mein
Johannes Brahms, "Dem Schutzengel" 1857, WoO 31,14
from *Volks-Kinderlieder* (14)

O herzensschöns Schätzerl, jetzt komm' i vom Wald
Friedrich Silcher, "Böhmisches Volkslied"

O Maidle, du bist mein Morgestern
Friedrich Silcher, "Werbung"

O Schwälblein, das da fliegt in weite Ferne
Hermann Goetz, "O Schwälblein, das da fliegt in weite Ferne" 1866, Op4,4
translated from the Italian by Paul Heyse
from *Sechs Italienische Volksgesänge*

O Tannenbaum, o Tannenbaum, wie treu sind deine Blätter!
Friedrich Silcher, "O Tannenbaum"

O wie glücklich sind doch Andre!
Anna Teichmüller, "Finnisches Volkslied" 1905pub, Op4,3

O wie herbe ist das Scheiden
Friedrich Silcher, "O wie herbe ist das Scheiden"

Qch Mod'r, ich well en Ding han
Johannes Brahms, "Der Tochter Wunsch" 1858,1926pub, WoO 32,20
from *Deutsche Volkslieder* (20)
Johannes Brahms, "Qch Mod'r, ich well en Ding han" 1894pub, WoO 33,33
from *Deutsche Volkslieder* (33)

Pöppe, Pöppe, danze, schenk di ok en Hohn
Armin Knab, "Puppentanz" 1905-20
from *Kinderlieder* (9)

Prinz Eugenius, der edle Ritter
Friedrich Silcher, "Prinz Eugenius vor Belgrad (1717)"

Ringel, Ringel, Reihe! S'sind der Kinder Zweie
Wilhelm Taubert, "Ringelreihen"
from *Klänge aus der Kinderwelt*, Vol.1, No10

Rosestock, Holderblüth', wenn i mei Dienderl sieh
Friedrich Silcher, "Oberschwäbisches Tanzliedchen"

Rosmarin und Thymian wächst in unserm Garten
Armin Knab, "Rosmarin und Thymian" 1905-20
from *Kinderlieder* (2)

's ist kein verdrüßlicher Lebe als in das Klösterli gehe
Carl Philipp Emanuel Bach, "Nonnelied" 1789

Sagt mir, o schönste Schäf'rin mein
Johannes Brahms, "Sagt mir, o schönste Schäf'rin mein" 1894pub, WoO 33,1
from *Deutsche Volkslieder* (1)

Schätzelein, es kränket mich, deine Eltern leiden's nicht
Friedrich Curschmann, "Altes Volkslied" 1833, Op5,2

Schlaf, Kindlein, balde, schlaf Kindlein, balde
Max Reger, "Wiegenlied" 1909

Schlaf, Kindlein schlaf! Der Vater hüt't die Schaf
Johannes Brahms, "Wiegenlied" 1857, WoO 31,11
from *Volks-Kinderlieder* (11)
Johannes Brahms, "Schlaf, Kindlein, schlaf!" 1891pub, Op113,4, 3fv
from *13 Kanons für Frauenstimmen*

Schlaf', Püppchen, schlaf', schlafe in Ruh'
Carl Reinecke, "Puppenwiegenlied"
from *Kinderlieder*

Schöner Augen schöne Strahlen
Johannes Brahms, "Schöner Augen schöne Strahlen" 1894pub, WoO 33,39
from *Deutsche Volkslieder* (39)

Schönster Herr Jesu, Herrscher aller Enden
Erich J. Wolff, "Schönster Herr Jesu!" 1914pub, Lieder No.45

Schönster Schatz, mein Engel
Johannes Brahms, "Schönster Schatz, mein Engel" 1894pub, WoO 33,20
from *Deutsche Volkslieder* (20)

Schwesterlein, Schwesterlein, wann gehn wir nach Haus?
Johannes Brahms, "Schwesterlein, Schwesterlein" 1859-62, WoO posth 37,1, ssa
from *16 Deutsche Volkslieder*
Johannes Brahms, "Schwesterlein" 1894pub, WoO 33,15
from *Deutsche Volkslieder* (15)

Sind wir geschieden, und ich muss leben ohne dich
Carl Maria von Weber, "Liebesgruss aus der Ferne" 1819, Op64,6
Johannes Brahms, "Scheiden" 1859-62, WoO posth 38,18, ssa
from *20 Deutsche Volkslieder*

Sitzt a schöns Vögerl aufm Dannabaum
Johannes Brahms, "Die Nachtigall" 1857, WoO 31,2
from *Volks-Kinderlieder* (2)
Johannes Brahms, "Sitzt a schöns Vögerl aufm Dannabaum" 1891pub, Op113,3, 4fv
from *13 Kanons für Frauenstimmen*

So geht es in Schnützelputz-Häusel
Carl Maria von Weber, "Quodlibet" 1817, Op54,2, 2v.pf or 1v.pf

So hab ich doch die ganze Woche
Johannes Brahms, "Sonntag" 1868, Op47,3

Max Reger, "Sonntag" 1906, Op98,3, 1v(med).pf

So viel Stern' am Himmel stehen
Friedrich Silcher, "Treue Liebe"

So will ich frisch und fröhlich sein
Johannes Brahms, "Minnelied" 1859-62, WoO posth 36,2, ssaa
from *Acht Deutsche Volkslieder*
Johannes Brahms, "So will ich frisch und fröhlich sein" 1894pub, WoO 33,32
from *Deutsche Volkslieder* (32)

So wünsch ich ihr ein gute Nacht
Johannes Brahms, "So wünsch ich ihr ein gute Nacht" 1894pub, WoO 33,18
from *Deutsche Volkslieder* (18)

Soll sich der Mond nicht heller scheinen
Johannes Brahms, "Vor dem Fenster" 1858, Op14,1
Johannes Brahms, "Vor dem Fenster" 1859-62, WoO posth 38,19, ssaa
from *20 Deutsche Volkslieder*
Johannes Brahms, "Soll sich der Mond nicht heller scheinen" 1894pub, WoO 33,35
from *Deutsche Volkslieder* (35)

Sommer will aus heissem Herzen
Leopold Damrosch, "Der Lindenzweig" Op13,1

Spannenlanger Hansel, nudeldicke Dirn'
Carl Reinecke, "Wie Hansel und Gretel Birnen schütteln"
from *Kinderlieder*

Spinn', Mägdlein, spinn'! so wachsen dir die Sinn'
Robert Schumann, "Spinnlied" 1849, Op79,24, 3v.pf
from *Lieder-Album für die Jugend*
Carl Reinecke, "Spinnlied"
from *Kinderlieder*

Spinn, spinn, mein liebs Nanerl, i kauf dir neue Schuh'
Friedrich Silcher, "Die Spinnerin"

Sprachen Königin und König einstens
Max Reger, "Schlimm für die Männer" 1903, Op75,7

Sternchen mit dem trüben Schein
Johannes Brahms, "Gold überwiegt die Liebe" 1868, Op48,4

Storch, Storch, Steiner, mit de langen Beiner
Carl Reinecke, "Storch, Storch, Steiner"
from *Kinderlieder*

Tanz mit mir, tanz mit mir, ich hab ein schönes Schürzchen für!
Armin Knab, "Aufforderung zum Tanz" 1905-20
from *Kinderlieder* (11)

Tra, ri, ro! Der Sommer, der ist do!
Carl Maria von Weber, "Mailied" 1817, Op64,2, 2v.pf

Tritt auf, tritt auf, den Riegel von der Tür
Johannes Brahms, "Vor der Tür" 1862, Op28,2, alt.bar.pf

Tröst die Bedrängten und hilf den Kranken
Johannes Brahms, "Sankt Raphael" 1864pub, WoO 34,7, satb
from *Deutsche Volkslieder für gemischten Chor* (7)

Ufm Berga da giht dar Wind, da wiegt de Maria ihr Kind
Erich J. Wolff, "Maria auf dem Berge" 1914pub, Lieder No.53

Ull Mann wull riden, wull hat he ken Pärd (see also "Alt Mann wollt…")
Johannes Brahms, "Beim Ritt auf dem Knie" 1857, WoO 31,8a
from *Volks-Kinderlieder* (8a)

Und hast du einen Andern viel lieber als mich
Anna Teichmüller, "Reiterlied" 1907pub, Op12,3

Und schau' ich hin, so schaust du her
Friedrich Silcher, "Liebesqual"

Und wenn ich werd' im Sarg gebettet liegen (see also Heyse)
Hermann Goetz, "Und wenn ich werd' im Sarg gebettet liegen" 1866, Op4,3
translated from the Italian by Paul Heyse
from *Sechs Italienische Volksgesänge*

Uns leuchtet heut der Freude Schein!
Johannes Brahms, "Weihnachten" 1857, WoO 31,12
from *Volks-Kinderlieder* (12)

Vergangen ist mir Glück und Heil (see also Anonymous)
Johannes Brahms, "Vergangen ist mir Glück und Heil" 1874-?, Op62,7, satb or sop.satb

Verstohlen geht der Mond auf, blau, blau, Blümelein!
Johannes Brahms, "Ständchen" 1859-62, WoO posth 38,20, ssaa
from *20 Deutsche Volkslieder*
Johannes Brahms, "Altes Volkslied" 1863/64?, WoO 35,9, satb
from *Deutsche Volkslieder für gemischten Chor* (23)
George Henschel, "Verstohlen geht der Mond auf" 187-?, Op22,1
Johannes Brahms, "Verstohlen geht der Mond auf" 1894pub, WoO 33,49
from *Deutsche Volkslieder* (49)

Vöglein du in meinem Zelt, du mein Liebstes auf der Welt!
Anna Teichmüller, "Vöglein du" 1907pub, Op9,2

Vöglein im Tannenwald pfeifet so hell, tirili
Friedrich Silcher, "Schwäbisch"
George Henschel, "Vöglein im Tannenwald" 187-?, Op22,2

Von allen den Mädchen, so blink und so blank
Friedrich Silcher, "Die Lore"

Von allen schönen Kindern auf der Welt
Felix Mendelssohn, "O Jugend, o schöne Rosenzeit" 1843pub, Op57,4
Rheinisches Volkslied collected by Zuccalmaglio

Von edler Art, auch rein und zart
Johannes Brahms, "Von edler Art" 1864pub, WoO 34,1, satb
from *Deutsche Volkslieder für gemischten Chor* (1)

Wach auf, mein Herzensschöne
Johannes Brahms, "Nachtgesang" 1858,1926pub, WoO 32,14
from *Deutsche Volkslieder* (14)
Johannes Brahms, "Wach auf mein Herzensschöne" 1894pub, WoO 33,16
from *Deutsche Volkslieder* (16)

Wach auf, mein Hort, vernimm mein Wort
Johannes Brahms, "Tageweis von einer schöner Frauen" 1858,1926pub, WoO 32,12
from *Deutsche Volkslieder* (12)
Johannes Brahms, "Wach auf, mein Hort" 1859-62, WoO posth 37,14, ssaa
from *16 Deutsche Volkslieder*
Johannes Brahms, "Wach auf, mein Hort" 1894pub, WoO 33,13
from *Deutsche Volkslieder* (13)

Wach auf, mein Kind, steh auf geschwind
Johannes Brahms, "Morgengesang" 1864pub, WoO 34,12, satb
from *Deutsche Volkslieder für gemischten Chor* (12)

Wach auf, meins Herzens Schöne, Herzallerliebste mein!
Johannes Brahms, "Ständchen" 1859-62, WoO posth 37,16, ssaa
from *16 Deutsche Volkslieder*
Johannes Brahms, "Wach auf!" 1863/64?, WoO 35,2, satb
from *Deutsche Volkslieder für gemischten Chor* (16)
Johannes Brahms, "Wach auf! (2.Bearbeitung)" 1863/64?, WoO 35,7, satb
from *Deutsche Volkslieder für gemischten Chor* (21)

Wach auf, wach auf, du junger Gesell
Johannes Brahms, "Trennung" 1858, Op14,5

War das nicht ein Blick der Liebe
Friedrich Silcher, "Liebe um Liebe"

Was hab' ich denn meinem Feinsliebchen gethan?
Friedrich Silcher, "Untreue"

Weine, weine, weine nur nicht (see also Wunderhorn)
Carl Maria von Weber, "Weine, weine nur nicht" 1818, Op54,7

Wenn alle Brünnlein fliessen, so muss man trinken
Friedrich Silcher, "Heimliche Liebe"

Wenn alle Welt so einig wär'
Max Reger, "Wenn alle Welt so einig wär'" 1904, Op76,17, 1v(med).pf
from *Schlichte Weisen, Band 2*

Wenn der Schnee von der Alma wega geht
Friedrich Silcher, "Die Frühlingszeit"

Wenn du bei mei'm Schätzel kommst
George Henschel, "Wenn du bei mei'm Schätzel kommst" 187-?, Op22,3

Wenn i halt frua afsteh
Friedrich Silcher, "Oesterreichisches Volkslied"

Wenn i zum Brünnle geh
Othmar Schoeck, "Die Verlassene" 1905, Op6,1

Wenn ich an den letzten Abend denk'
Friedrich Silcher, "Wenn ich an den letzten Abend denk'"

Wenn ich ein Vöglein wär, und auch zwei Flüglein hätt (see also Treitschke)
Johann Friedrich Reichardt, "Wenn ich ein Vöglein wär" 1800pub
from *Lieder aus dem Liederspiel, Lieb' und Treue* (8)
Carl Maria von Weber, "Volkslied" 1818, Op54,6
Robert Schumann, "Wenn ich ein Vöglein wär" 1840, Op43,1, sop.alt.pf
George Henschel, "Wenn ich ein Vöglein wär'" 187-?, Op24,6

Wer lieben will, muss leiden
Richard Strauss, "Wer lieben will, muss leiden" 1901, Op49,7

Wer will unter die Soldaten
Friedrich Silcher, "Soldatenlied"

Wie die Blümlein draussen flattern in der Abendlüfte weh'n
Friedrich Silcher, "Herber Abschied"
A. Reichardt, "Liebes Bitte"
Franz Abt, "Bleib bei mir"

Wie han i doch so gern die Zeit
Friedrich Silcher, "Vom Frühjohr"

Wie komm ich denn zur Tür herein?
Johannes Brahms, "Wie komm ich denn zur Tür herein?" 1894pub, WoO 33,34
Brahms includes the Kölnisch, "We kumm ich dann de Po˛o˛z erenn?"
from *Deutsche Volkslieder* (34)

Wie lange schon war immer mein Verlangen (see also Heyse)
Hermann Goetz, "Wie lange schon war immer mein Verlangen" 1866, Op4,6
translated from the Italian by Paul Heyse
from *Sechs Italienische Volksgesänge*

Wie reiten denn die Herren? Trapp, trapp, trapp!
Armin Knab, "Kniereiterliedchen" 1905-20
from *Kinderlieder* (3)

Wie schienen die Sternlein so hell, so hell
Robert Franz, "Abschied" 1865?, Op11,1
Johannes Brahms, "Ade!" 1882, Op85,4
from the Böhmisch (Siegfried Kapper)

Wie traurig sind wir Mädchen dran
Robert Franz, "Dies und Das" 1870?pub, Op30,5

Wille, wille, will, der Mann ist kommen
Johannes Brahms, "Der Mann" 1857, WoO 31,5
from *Volks-Kinderlieder* (5)
Johannes Brahms, "Wille, wille, will" 1891pub, Op113,5, 4fv
from *13 Kanons für Frauenstimmen*

Wir stehen hier zur Schlacht bereit, o Michael!
Johannes Brahms, "Altdeutsches Kampflied" 1863/64?, WoO 35,12, satb
from *Deutsche Volkslieder für gemischten Chor* (26)

Wo e kleins Hüttle steht, ist e kleins Gütle
Friedrich Silcher, "Liebesscherz"

Wo gehst du hin, du Stolze?
Johannes Brahms, "Wo gehst du hin, du Stolze?" 1894pub, WoO 33,22
from *Deutsche Volkslieder* (22)

Wozu, wozu mir sein sollte das Aug'
Robert Franz, "Volkslied" 1870?, Op42,1

Wüsst' ich gewiss, dass es mein Liebster hörte
Hermann Goetz, "Wüsst' ich gewiss, dass es mein Liebster hörte" 1866, Op4,1
translated from the Italian by Paul Heyse
from *Sechs Italienische Volksgesänge*

Z'nächst bin i halt gange über's Bergel in Wald
Friedrich Silcher, "Der Jodeplatz"

Zu dir zieht's mi hin, wo i geh' und wo i bin
Friedrich Silcher, "Der traurige Bua"

Zu Straßburg auf der Schanz, da ging mein Trauern an (see also Wunderhorn)
Friedrich Silcher, "Der Schweizer"
Johannes Brahms, "Zu Straßburg auf der Schanz" 1859-62, WoO posth 37,13, ssaa from *16 Deutsche Volkslieder*
Robert Franz, "Zu Strassburg auf der Schanz" 1860?, Op12,2

Not Yet Identified

Aus schwellenden Blütenkelchen die Engel des Lenzes schau'n
Johann Wenzeslaus Kalliwoda, "Lenz und Liebe" 1851, Op172,5

Ave Maria! Ave Maria, Maria! Neig' dein Angesicht, hochheil'ge Mutter
Heinrich Marschner, "Ave Maria" 184-?pub, Op115,1

Beim Spiele fiel den Kindern ein, Grosseltern wollten sie heute sein
Johannes Doebber, "Grosspapa und Grossmama" 1896?pub, Op22,3
poem possibly by Doebber

Das Herz will mir brechen, Therese
Karl Goldmark, "Franz" 187-?, Op21,4, 1v(low).pf

Das liebe Ränzel ist gespickt, die alten Stiefel sind geflickt
Johann Wenzeslaus Kalliwoda, "Handwerksburschenlied" 1849?, Op154,6

Das Röselein vom Regen gar arg durchnässt
Friedrich Kücken, "Die Rose"

Der Frühling kam! In seinem Hauche athm' ich neues Leben ein
Eugen d'Albert, "Der Frühling kam!" 1889pub, Op9,5

Du fragst mich täglich: "Liebchen, liebst du mich?"
Erik Meyer-Helmund, "Du fragst mich täglich" 1886-88

Du grollest und schmollest und siehst mich nicht an
Erik Meyer-Helmund, "Schätzel Ade!" 1886-88

Düster liegt die Nacht umher, jedes Aug ist schlummerschwer
Christian Gottlob Neefe, "Serenate" 1777

Duftet die Lindenblüth schläfernd zur Nacht
Erik Meyer-Helmund, "Unter dem Lindenbaum" 1886-88

Einsam! einsam! ja, das bin ich wohl
Johann Wenzeslaus Kalliwoda, "Klage" 1838, Op79,3

Es schaukelt so leise der spielende Wind
Erik Meyer-Helmund, "Wiegenlied" 1886-88

Es war dort unter dem Lindenbaum, da träumt' ich seligen Liebestraum
Carl Reinecke, "Leb' wohl, du liebliche Liebe" Op81,8

Es war im Wonnemonat Mai, die Welt, die war so schön
Erik Meyer-Helmund, "Mein Liebchen" 1886-88

Frühlingsahnen Frühlingswehen gleicht dem Lied in stiller Brust
Johann Wenzeslaus Kalliwoda, "Frühlingsahnen" 184-pub, sop.vn.pf

Gedenkst du des Abends, das Meer strahlt' von Golde
August Bungert, "Mir schweben tausend Bilder heiliger Erinnerung warm um's Herz" 1891pub, Op26,4
Title from Goethe
from *An eine schöne Frau: Liebesbriefe in Liedern*

Gleich wie die Sonne hell, heiter auf der Flut lächelnd
August Bungert, "Blühende Lippen" 1889-91pub, Op32,2
translated from the Italian
from *Verlorne Liebe, verlornes Leben*

Herab von den Bergen zum Tale
Johann Wenzeslaus Kalliwoda, "Herab von den Bergen" 1849?, Op154,4

Himmelsmächte, die ihr schirmet holde Mädchen schön und gut
Karl Goldmark, "Marie" 187-?, Op21,2, 1v(low).pf

Hoffnung dein Prangen, Liebe dein Glück
Anna Teichmüller, "Die Reu'" 1904pub, Op2,1

Ich baute dir den stillen Schrein
Johann Wenzeslaus Kalliwoda, "Der Schreiner" 1849?, Op154,5

Ich bin der kleine Postillon, trara
Franz Abt, "Postillon d'amour" Op362,3

Ich hab' noch nie so wie heute mein herziges Schatzerl geliebt
Erik Meyer-Helmund, "Im Volkston" 1886-88

Ich weil' in tiefer Einsamkeit, wo fern der Lärm der Welt verrauscht
Eduard Lassen, "Ich weil' in tiefer Einsamkeit" Op5,ii,4

Im Haine schlagen lustig die muntern Vögelein
Johann Wenzeslaus Kalliwoda, "Geistergruss" 1852, Op177,1

Kikriki! kikriki! Horch, horch! der Hahn ist auch schon wach
Wilhelm Taubert, "Der Hahn"
from *Klänge aus der Kinderwelt*, Vol.1, No8 (Op58,8)

Laß, o laß dein Auge immer in den meinen tief versinken!
Hugo Reichenberger, "Bitte" 1911pub

Mädchen, hör' mich ruhig an
Erik Meyer-Helmund, "Geständniss" 1886-88

Mein Mädel hat Äuglein, so schwarz wie die Kohlen
Erik Meyer-Helmund, "Die Liebe" 1886-88, Op5,3

Mein müdes Auge flieht der Schlaf
George Henschel, "Mein müdes Auge" Op3,1

Nachtigall hüte dich, singe nicht so lieblich
Erik Meyer-Helmund, "Hüte dich!" 1886-88

Niwaschi! Heb' des Kindes Hand! damit es zeig' das Land
Anna Teichmüller, "Zigeunerzauber. 2 kleine Beschwörungen. A.)Niwaschi" 1907pub, Op17,3a
from *Lieder Kindern gesungen*

O Hirtenknab', o Hirtenknab'! du singst so frisch und frei
Johann Wenzeslaus Kalliwoda, "Der Hirtenknabe" 1857?, Op219,1

O wär' ich du, mein Falke du
Eduard Lassen, "O wär' ich du!"

O willst mich nicht mitnehmen, klein Anna Kathrin?
Karl Goldmark, "O willst mich nicht mitnehmen" 1868pub, Op18,11, 1v(med).pf
Original title of poem is "Klein Anna Kathrin"

Sag' an, o Alter! Wem gräbst du dies Grab?
Johann Wenzeslaus Kalliwoda, "Der Totengräber" 1838, Op79,2

Schlaf, mein Kind, schlaf ein! Bald wird Weihnacht sein!
Max Renner, "Wiegenlied" 1899pub, Op3,6

Schleenblüt' und wilde Rose hab' ich mir im Wald gepflückt
Gustave Bley, "Schleenblüt'" 1894?pub, Op16
poem possibly by Bley

Seit er von mir gegangen, wie still die Welt umher!
Max Renner, "Seit er von mir gegangen" 1899pub, Op3,2

Siehst du hinab in die dunkle See
Johann Wenzeslaus Kalliwoda, "Immer dein" 1849?, Op154,3

Ström' leise, du Bächlein, am grünenden Hang
Karl Goldmark, "Ström' leise" 187-?, Op21,1, 1v(low).pf

Wann ich schon schwarz bin d' Schuld ist nicht mein allein
Paul Graener, "Wann ich schon schwarz bin" 1909pub, Op30,2
Poem from "Von Rosen ein Kreutzelein"

Weit, weit sind die Sterne, hin führet kein Steg
Johann Wenzeslaus Kalliwoda, "Nachtlied eines Einsamen" Nachlaß

Weithin durch der Nächte Stille send' ich meine Grüße fort
Johann Wenzeslaus Kalliwoda, "Den Fernen" 1852, Op177,2

Wenn auf zu den Wolken ich schaue in's feucht' umwölkte Blau
August Bungert, "Wer die Schönheit angeschaut mit Augen, ist dem Tode schon anheim gegeben" 1891pub, Op26,2
Title from Platen's "Tristan"
from *An eine schöne Frau: Liebesbriefe in Liedern*

Wenn es Abend wird und still, wird mein Kindchen schläfrig
Wilhelm Taubert, "Müdes Kindchen"
from *Klänge aus der Kinderwelt*, Vol.6, No9

Wespe! Wespe! Wespelein! Kriech du in die Erd' hinein!
Anna Teichmüller, "Zigeunerzauber. 2 kleine Beschwörungen. B.)Wespe" 1907pub, Op17,3b
from *Lieder Kindern gesungen*

Wie ein Sturmwind kamst du in meine Seele Liebe!
Anna Teichmüller, "Wie ein Sturmwind" 1907pub, Op15,2

Wie flüchtig rinnt die Stunde, da in verschwieg'ner Glut
Max Renner, "Lieb' und Leid" 1899pub, Op3,5

Wie ich jüngst mit langem Kusse mich aus deinen Armen wand
Franz Ries, "Abschied" before 1891, Op31,6

Index of First Lines

A' Versle, a' g'spaßig's –*Sommerstorff*
Abend ist's, die Sonne ist verschwunden –*Campe*
Abend ists geworden, Dunkel hüllt uns ein –*Dieffenbach*
Abend, lege deine Hände leise –*C. Lange*
Abendgewölke schweben hell –*Matthisson*
Abendglockenhalle zittern –*Salis-Seewis*
Abendkelch voll Sonnenlicht –*Morgenstern*
Abendlich schon rauscht der Wald –*Eichendorff*
Abendruhe liegt über dem Land –*Maria*
Abends gehn die Liebespaare –*Hesse*
Abends schweben blutige Linnen –*Trakl*
Abends, wenn ich schlafen geh –*Wunderhorn*
Abendschwärmer zogen um die Linden –*Busse*
Aber abseits, wer ist's? –*Goethe*
Aber auch den Föhrenwald –*Keller*
Aber auch ich auf dem letzten Boot –*Brecht*
Aber ein kleiner goldener Stern –*Keller*
Aber Epheu nenn' ich jene Mädchen –*Dahn*
Aber ich will nimmer leben –*Hölderlin*
Aber nun ruhet er eine Weile –*Hölderlin*
Abermal ein Teil vom Jahre –*Günther*
Ach, ach, ich armes Klosterfräulein! –*Kerner*
Ach, alle Blumen neigen das Haupt –*Michalewski*
Ach, an dem Ufer dieser Quelle –*C. Weisse*
Ach, aus dieses Thales Gründen –*Schiller*
Ach! aus Träumen fahr ich in die graue Luft –*Dehmel*
Ach, daß die innre Schöpfungskraft –*Goethe*
Ach dass du kamst, ach dass du kamst –*Osterwald*
Ach, der Gebirgssohn hängt mit kindlicher Lieb' –*Pyrker*
Ach, der Tag – wie so lang! –*Haug*
Ach, des Knaben Augen sind mir so schön –*Heyse*
Ach! die Augen sind es wieder –*Heine*
Ach, die entzückenden Töne –*M. P. Engelhard*
Ach du klar blauer Himmel –*R. Reinick*
Ach Elselein, liebes Elselein mein –*Volkslied*
Ach, englische Schäferin, erhöre mein Bitt –*Volkslied*
Ach, es bebt der Blütenkeim –*Volkslied*
Ach, es ist so dunkel in des Todes Kammer –*M. Claudius*
Ach! es schlägt mein Herz so bange –*Anonymous*
Ach gestern hat er mir Rosen gebracht –*Lingen*
Ach Gott, das druckt das Herz mir ab –*Roquette*
Ach Gott! wie fällt das Meiden –*Volkslied*
Ach Gott, wie weh tut Scheiden –*Volkslied, Uhland*
Ach hartes Herz, laß dich doch eins erweichen –*Wunderhorn*
Ach Herr, wie lange willst du mein –*the Bible*
Ach, ich denke und versenke –*Köstlin*
Ach, ich küsste dich nur einmal –*"Carmen Sylva"*
Ach ich sehnte mich nach Thränen –*Heine*
Ach, ihr lieben Äugelein –*Heyse*
Ach, ihr Wälder, dunkle Wälder –*Volkslied*
Ach im Maien war's im Maien –*Heyse*
Ach, in dem funklenden, träumerisch dunkelnden Aug' –*Longard*
Ach könnt ich diesen Abend –*Volkslied*
Ach, könnt ich, könnte vergessen sie! –*Herder*
Ach Lieb, ich muss nun scheiden –*Dahn*
Ach lieber Herre Jesu Christ –*Volkslied*
Ach Liebste laß uns eilen wir haben Zeit –*Opitz*
Ach, Liebster, in Gedanken geb' ich dir –*Stona*
Ach Mädchen, liebes Mädchen, wie schwartz dein Auge ist! –*Wenzig*
Ach, mein Henlein, bi bi bi! –*Volkslied*
Ach! mein kühler Wasserquell! –*"Talvj"*
Ach, mich hält der Gram gefangen –*Wenzig*
Ach mir fehlt, nicht ist da –*Wenzig*
Ach, mir ist das Herz so schwer –*Stolberg-Stolberg*
Ach mir schallt's dorten –*Sauter*
Ach! mir schallt's dorten so lieblich hervor –*Sauter*
Ach! musstest du denn scheiden –*Osterwald*
Ach Mutter, liebe Mutter, ach gebt mir einen Rat! –*Wunderhorn*
Ach neige, du Schmerzenreiche –*Goethe*
Ach, noch so jung und schon –*E. Scherenberg*
Ach, nun taucht die Klosterzelle –*Lichnowsky*
Ach, um deine feuchten Schwingen –*Willemer*
Ach, und du mein kühles Wasser! –*Kapper*
Ach, uns're leuchtenden Tage –*Jacobowski*
Ach, Vater, sprich, wie fang' ich's an –*Löwenstein*
Ach, wär' doch zu dieser Stund' –*F. Förster*
Ach, wär' ich nur ein Vögelein! –*La Motte Fouqué*
Ach wärst du mein, es wär' ein schönes Leben –*Lenau*
Ach, was bin ich aufgewacht? –*Heyse*
Ach, was ist die Liebe für ein süßes Ding –*F. W. Gotter*
Ach, was ist Leben doch so schwer –*Schorn*
Ach was Kummer, Qual und Schmerzen –*Volkslied*
Ach, was soll der Mensch verlangen? –*Goethe*

Ach, was soll ich beginnen vor Liebe? *–C. W. Schütz*
Ach, was wird uns hier bereitet? *–Kafka*
Ach weh mir unglückhäftem Mann *–Dahn*
Ach, wende diesen Blick *–Daumer*
Ach, wenn du wärst mein eigen *–Hahn-Hahn*
Ach, wenn es nun die Mutter wüsst' *–Paul Remer*
Ach, wenn ich doch ein Immchen wär' *–Osterwald*
Ach, wenn ich nur ein Liebchen hätte! *–Volkslied*
Ach, wenn's nur der König auch wüßt' *–Mörike*
Ach, wer bringt die schönen Tage *–Goethe*
Ach wer heilet die Schmerzen *–Goethe*
Ach, wer möchte einsam trinken *–Lenau*
Ach, wer nimmt von meiner Seele *–Schenkendorf*
Ach, wie brenn' ich vor Verlangen *–Wedekind*
Ach! wie ist es doch gekommen *–Eichendorff*
Ach, wie ist's möglich dann *–Chézy*
Ach, wie lang die Seele schlummert! *–Geibel*
Ach, wie nichtig, ach, wie flüchtig *–M. Franck*
Ach, wie richtete, so klagt' ich *–Hafis*
Ach, wie schnell die Tage fliehen *–Klingemann*
Ach, wie schön ist Carmosenella *–Heyse*
Ach, wie schön ist Nacht und Dämmerschein! *–Hafis*
Ach, wie so bald verhallet der Reigen *–Klingemann*
Ach, wie so gerne bleib' ich euch ferne *–Heyse*
Ach wie so schön, wie hübsch und fein *–Wunderhorn*
Ach, wie süß, wie süß sie duftet! *–Hafis*
Ach, wie thut mein Herze weh *–Anonymous*
Ach, wie wird mir wohl und weh *–Bierbaum*
Ach wüssten's die Blumen, die kleinen *–Heine*
Acht der winzigen Perlen enthält *–R. Graf*
Ade, ade, der Sommer zieht, bis künftig Jahr *–Groth*
Ade denn, du stolze blitzaugige Magd *–Osterwald*
Ade du lieber Tannenwald, Ade, Ade! *–Vogl*
Ade! du muntre, du fröhliche Stadt, Ade! *–Rellstab*
Ade! es muss geschieden sein! *–E. M. Arndt*
Ade! Ich muß nun gehen zum Krieg *–Anonymous*
Ade, mein Schatz, du mocht'st mich nicht *–Eichendorff*
Ade nun, liebes junges Weib! *–Laur*
Adieu, lieb Mädel, hab dich wohl *–Anonymous*
Adieu, Mama, wir fahren auf dem Eise *–Oldenberg*
Ähnlich dem Manne, der Menschen frisset *–Hölderlin*
Ännchen von Tharau ist, die mir gefällt *–Dach*
Aetherische ferne Stimmen *–Candidus*
Ahidi, ich liebe, ahidi, ich liebe! *–Kind*
Ahne, Krahne, wikkele, wahne *–Wunderhorn*
All Abend, bevor ich zur Ruhe geh *–Seyffardt*
All' deine Anmut hab' ich aufgeweckt *–Reisiger*
All mein Gedanken, die ich hab *–Volkslied*
All' mein Gedanken, mein Herz und mein Sinn *–Dahn*
All' mein Leben bist Du! *–Aquinas*
All' mein Wirken, all' mein Leben *–Ehrlich*
All' meine Herzgedanken sind immerdar *–Heyse*
All meine reinen Gedanken, alles, was gut ist an mir *–Michalewski*
Allah giebt Licht in Nächten *–Mahlmann*
Alle Blumen möcht' ich binden *–Wolff*
Alle, die ihr Gott zu Ehren *–Gerhardt*
Alle gingen, Herz, zur Ruh' *–Geibel*
Alle Mädchen erwarten wen *–Rilke*
Alle meine Weisheit hing in meinen Haaren *–Keller*
Alle meine Wünsche schweigen *–P. Schoeck*
Alle Menschen groß und klein *–Goethe*
Alle Sternelein, die am Himmel steh'n *–Holst*
Alle Winde schlafen auf dem Spiegel *–Herder*
Allein, nachdenklich, wie gelähmt vom Krampfe *–Petrarca*
Allein zu sein! Wie oft mit stillen Thränen *–Stolterfoth*
Allen Schmerz hat Gott gezählet *–Klotz-Burr*
Allen weinenden Seelen, aller nahenden Schuld *–Maeterlinck*
Alles, alles in den Wind sagst du mir *–Daumer*
Alles dunkel, alles still *–B. Huber*
Alles endet, was entstehet *–Michelangelo*
Alles geben die Götter, die unendlichen *–Goethe*
Alles in mir glühet, zu lieben *–Gubitz*
Alles ist innig *–Hölderlin*
Alles kündet dich an! Erscheinet die herrliche Sonne *–Goethe*
Alles ruht wie abgeschieden *–Tiedge*
Alles still! es tanzt den Reigen *–Fontane*
Alles still in süsser Ruh *–Hoffmann von Fallersleben*
Alles stille, nur zuweilen *–Rodenberg*
Alles stirbt. Auch die Freunde *–Binding*
Alles Tagverlangen ist zur Ruh gegangen *–Wildgans*
Alles was mich hier umringt *–Zinkernagel*
Alles, was Odem hat, lobe den Herrn! *–Bürde*
Alles, was von uns kommt *–Werfel*
Alles, was war: Tag, Abend und Jahr *–Toussell*
Alles wiegt die stille Nacht *–Körner*
Allnächtlich im Traume seh' ich dich *–Heine*
Allzulange, Wiederhall, tönst du mich zu preisen *–Werthes*
Als bei dem Kreuz Maria stand *–F. Schlegel*
Als das Christkind ward zur Welt *–Anderson*

Als der Frühling sich vom Herzen –*Schober*
Als der Gesandte schied, ging meine Königin –*Schaukal*
Als der Winter die Rosen geraubt –*Mörike*
Als die Linden trieben, weckte süsse Hoffnung –*Osterwald*
Als die Preussen marschirten vor Prag –*Anonymous*
Als du auf Erden, Herr, geweilt –*Cornelius*
Als du frühmorgens gingst –*Hebbel*
Als ein unergründlich Wonnemeer –*Lenau*
Als einst mit Weibes Schönheit sich –*Anonymous*
Als einst von deiner Schöne –*Hafis*
Als endlich sie den Sarg hier abgesetzt –*Keller*
Als er, Sami, mit dir jüngst Blumen brach –*Goethe*
Als hoch das Feld in Blumen stand –*Stieler*
Als ich auf dem Euphrat schiffte –*Goethe*
Als ich das erste Veilchen erblickt –*Ebert*
Als ich dich gebar, schrien deine Brüder –*Brecht*
Als ich dich in meinem Leib trug –*Brecht*
Als ich ein junger Geselle war –*F. Förster*
Als ich, ein Knabe noch –*Loewe and Vocke*
Als ich ging die Flur entlang –*Uhland*
Als ich kam zur Stube rein –*Wunderhorn*
Als ich nachher von dir ging –*Brecht*
Als ich noch ein Knabe war –*Goethe*
Als ich still und ruhig spann –*Goethe*
Als ich von deinem Grabe ging –*Lasker*
Als ich zuerst dich hab' geseh'n –*R. Reinick*
Als ich zum ersten Male dein Angesicht erblickte –*Hafis*
Als ihr Geliebter schied –*Maeterlinck*
Als Kinder glaubten wir an Zauberwesen –*F. Wolf*
Als Lenz die Erde wieder –*"Anastasius Grün"*
Als Maria heut' entwich, heut' vor Jahren –*Rückert*
Als mein Auge sie fand –*Zedlitz*
Als mein Leben voll Blumen hing –*Mahlmann*
Als meine Großmutter die Liese behext –*Heine*
Als mich dein Dasein tränenwärts entrückte –*Werfel*
Als mich die Mama Hänschen küssen sah –*Hagedorn*
Als mir dein Lied erklang –*C. Brentano*
Als mir noch die Thräne –*Reissig*
Als Nachts ich überm Gebirge ritt –*Bierbaum*
Als neuling trat ich ein in dein gehege –*George*
Als Noah aus dem Kasten war –*Kopisch*
Als noch dem blinden Heiden wahn –*J. C. Kugler*
Als noch in jener alten Zeit –*Buri*
Als ob das alles nicht gewesen wäre –*Benn*
Als sie vom Paradiese ward gezwungen –*Lenau*
Als über den Flieder das Mondlicht rann –*Ritter*
Als vom Schlummer leis beschlichen –*Helvig-Imhof*
Als Weibesarm in jungen Jahren –*Giesebrecht*
Als wie ein Feld, das erstes Licht ereilt –*Morgenstern*
Als wir beiden mussten scheiden –*Heyse*
Als wir hinter dem beblümten tore –*George*
Als wir mit deutschen Klingen –*Scheffel*
Als wir noch die Drachen steigen liessen –*Schumacher*
Als wollte Winterqual nicht enden –*E. Scherenberg*
Alsdann kommt Jesus aus Galiläa –*the Bible*
Also ihr lebt noch, alle, alle, ihr –*Morgenstern*
Also lieb' ich Euch, Geliebte –*Geibel*
Alt Heidelberg, du feine –*Scheffel*
Alt Mann wollt reiten und hatte kein Pferd –*Volkslied*
Alte Gruben schaufle um, tiefer werden sie und breiter –*Jacobowski*
Alte Liebe rostet nie –*J. Mayrhofer*
Am Abend, wenn die Glokken Frieden läuten –*Trakl*
Am Abgrund leitet der schwindliche Steg –*Schiller*
Am Bach, am Bach, im flüsternden Gras –*B. W. Zimmermann*
Am Bach viel kleine Blumen steh'n –*Wilhelm Müller*
Am Barbaratage holt' ich drei Zweiglein –*"Martin Greif"*
Am Berge weiß ich trutzen ein Kirchlein –*Rilke*
Am Brunnen vor dem Thore –*Wilhelm Müller*
Am Donaustrande, da steht ein Haus –*Daumer*
Am Dorfsee neigt die Weide ihr kahles Haupt –*Wiener*
Am einsamen Strande plätschert die Flut –*Heine*
Am Felsenvorgebirge schroff –*Platen*
Am Fenster sitzend und schon im Genesen –*Becher*
Am fernen Horizonte erscheint –*Heine*
Am frisch geschnittnen Wanderstab –*Mörike*
Am Gesteine rauscht die Flut –*Daumer*
Am grünen See von Nemi –*Scheffel*
Am Himmel der Wolken er dunkelnder Kranz –*Morgenstern*
Am Himmel wächst der Sonne Glut –*C. F. Meyer*
Am Himmelsantlitz wandelt ein Gedanke –*Lenau*
Am Himmelsgrund schießen so lustig –*Eichendorff*
Am hohen, hohen Thurm, da weht ein kalter Sturm –*Lubi*
Am jüngsten Tag ich aufersteh –*Heyse*
Am kahlen Erdwall, da irgendwo am Hunho –*Ziegler-Bock*
Am Kirchhof ging ich jüngst vorbei –*Michaeli*
Am Kreuzweg da lausche ich –*Eichendorff*
Am Kreuzweg wird begraben –*Heine*

Am langsamsten von allen Göttern *–Mörike*
Am leuchtenden Sommermorgen *–Heine*
Am Markte lag ein totgestürztes Kind *–Ehrler*
Am Morgen, am Mittag, im Abendlicht *–Poe*
Am Morgen spricht die Magd *–Morgenstern*
Am murmelnden Bach, unter schattigen, flüsternden Bäumen *–Gomoll*
Am Oelberg weiß ich eine Stätte *–Anonymous*
Am See, tief zwischen Tannl *–Brecht*
Am Seegestad', in lauen Vollmondsnächten *–Matthisson*
Am Sonntag Morgen zierlich angetan *–Volkslied, Heyse*
am stürzenden Strom, die Städte *–Hölderlin*
Am Ufer blies ich ein lustig Stück *–Scheffel*
Am Ufer des Flusses, des Manzanares *–Geibel*
Am Waldbach sitz' ich in der Sonnen *–Stieler*
Am Waldsaum kann ich lange Nachmittage *–Mörike*
Am Wildbach die Weiden, die schwanken Tag und Nacht *–Heyse*
Am Ziele! ich fühle die Nähe *–Goethe*
Amor, nicht das Kind: der Jüngling *–Goethe*
Amselchen mein, Amselchen mein *–Asenijeff*
An ä Bergli bin i gesässe *–Goethe*
An Babylons Wassern *–Byron*
An baches ranft die einzigen frühen *–George*
An Birkenzweigen blättert der volle Keim herauf *–Anonymous*
An Celia's Baum in stiller Nacht hängt *–Moore*
An deine schneeweiße Schulter *–Heine*
An deinem Finger, dem weissen, schlanken *–Träger*
An dem Brünnele hab' ich oft gelauscht *–Gersdorf*
An dem Ende seiner Tage steht der Kater Hiddigeigei *–Scheffel*
An dem Feuer saß das Kind Amor *–C. Brentano*
An dem Gedanken bin ich oft erwacht *–Hesse*
An dem jungen Morgenhimmel *–La Motte Fouqué*
An dem reinsten Frühlingsmorgen *–Goethe*
An dem Seegestade düster steht der hohe Tannenbaum *–Cornelius*
An dem Spinnrad sitzt das Mädchen *–Dieffenbach*
An den Höhen, an den Wäldern *–Hamerling*
An den Mondesstrahlen gleiten *–Stona*
An den Rhein, zieh' nicht an den Rhein *–Simrock*
An den Ufern jenes Wassers *–Geibel*
An der Brükke stand jüngst ich *–Nietzsche*
An der duftverlor'nen Gränze jener Berge *–Lenau*
An der Quelle sass der Knabe *–Schiller*
An der Rose Busen schmiegt sich *–Hoffmann von Fallersleben*
An der weißgetünchten Wand *–Brecht*
An des Baches stillen Weiden *–Herder*
An des Beetes Umbuschung brach sie Rosen *–Voss*
An des lust'gen Brunnens Rand *–Goethe*
An Dich verschwendet hat mein Herz *–Heyse*
An die blaue Himmelsdecke *–Heine*
An die bretterne Schiffswand *–Heine*
An die Türen will ich schleichen *–Goethe*
An dies Schifflein schmiege, holder See *–Köstlin*
An dieser Stelle war's, wo Herz *–Michelangelo*
An dir allein, an dir hab' ich gesündigt *–Gellert*
An einem Abend, da die Blumen dufteten *–Bethge*
An einem frühen Morgen, lange vor Morgengraun *–Brecht*
An einem lichten Morgen, da klingt es *–Rollet*
An eines Bächleins Rande *–F. Förster*
An hellen Tagen, Herz, welch' ein Schlagen *–Cornelius*
An Himmelshöh'n die Sterne geh'n *–Mahlmann*
An ihrem Grabe kniet' ich festgebunden *–Uhland*
An ihren bunten Liedern klettert *–Lenau*
An jedem Abend geh' ich aus *–Uhland*
An jeder Hand die Finger hatt ich bedeckt *–Daumer*
An meinem Herzen, an meiner Brust *–Chamisso*
An meiner Wand hängt ein japanisches Holzwerk *–Brecht*
An mir vorüber ging ein Geist *–Byron*
An vollen Büschelzweigen, Geliebte *–Goethe*
An wolkenreinem Himmel geht *–C. F. Meyer*
Anders wird die Welt mit jedem Schritt *–Mörike*
And're beten zur Madonna *–Heine*
Anfangs wollt' ich fast verzagen *–Heine*
Angelehnt an die Epheuwand dieser alten Terrasse *–Mörike*
Angst und hoffen wechselnd mich *–George*
Aninka tanzte vor uns im Grase *–Mörike*
Anne Margrittchen! Was willst du *–Wunderhorn*
Ans Auge des Liebsten *–Rückert*
Antonius zur Predigt die Kirche find't ledig! *–Wunderhorn*
Anzuschauen das Turnei, saßen hundert Frauen droben *–Uhland*
Apollo, lebet noch dein hold Verlangen *–Petrarca*
Aprilwind; alle Knospen sind schon aufgesprossen *–Dehmel*
Arbeitsam und wacker *–Salis-Seewis*
Arm am Beutel, krank am Herzen *–Goethe*

Arm in Arm und Kron' an Krone –*Keller*
Armes Bäumchen, dauerst mich –*Hey*
Armes Kind, südlich weht der Wind –*Beer*
As ik hier dit Jaar weer –*Groth*
Athme nur leise zieh ich die Kreise –*Simrock*
Atme, Seele, erhöhter, weil du den Sommer lobst –*Bergengruen*
Auch das schönste Blumenleben –*Gerstenberg*
Auch des Edlen schlummernde Gebeine –*Matthisson*
Auch die sprödeste der Schönen –*F. W. Gotter*
Auch in der Ferne dir so nah! –*Goethe*
Auch kleine Dinge können uns entzücken –*Heyse*
Auch zu mir kommst Du einmal –*Hesse*
Auf a folgt –*Morgenstern*
Auf, auf, auf! Schätzelein –*Volkslied*
Auf, auf, ihr Brüder und seid stark –*C. F. D. Schubart*
Auf, auf, wer deutsche Freiheit liebet –*Opitz*
Auf aus der Ruh! auf aus der Ruh! –*Goethe*
Auf braunen Sammetschuhen geht –*Morgenstern*
Auf, Brüder, auf! der Tag bricht an –*Rudolphi*
Auf das Feuer mit dem goldnen Strahle –*C. F. Meyer*
Auf das Maines grünen Auen –*J.-B. Rousseau*
Auf deinem Bild in schwarzem Rahmen –*Jacobowski*
Auf deinem Grunde haben sie an verborg'nem Ort –*K. Immermann*
Auf dem Dache sitzt der Spatz –*K. Meyer*
Auf dem Dorf' in den Spinnstuben –*Heyse*
Auf dem grünen Balcon –*Heyse*
Auf dem Herd kein Feuer –*Geissler*
Auf dem Hügel sitz' ich spähend –*Jeitteles*
Auf dem Kirchhof unter'm Lindenbaum –*Groth*
Auf dem Land und in der Stadt –*Goethe*
Auf dem Meer bin ich geboren –*Volkslied*
Auf dem Meere meiner Seele –*Morgenstern*
Auf dem See in tausend Sterne –*Köstlin*
Auf dem stillen, schwülen Pfuhle –*F. Freiligrath*
Auf dem Teich, dem regungslosen –*Lenau*
Auf dem Tisch ein kleiner Strauß –*Hesse*
Auf dem Wege vom Tanzsaal nach Haus –*Liliencron*
Auf den Bergen, den Bergen hab' ich gejauchzt –*Lemcke*
Auf den Bergen nur wohnet die Freiheit –*Maltitz*
Auf den Blumen flimmern Perlen –*J. Mayrhofer*
Auf den Schwingen des Windes –*Morgenstern*
Auf den Wällen Salamankas –*Heine*
Auf den Wassern wohnt mein stilles Leben –*A. W. Schlegel*
Auf der Bank im Walde han sich gestern zwei geküßt –*Morgenstern*
Auf der Bank, wo sie sonst sitzet –*Rückert*
Auf der Berge freien Höhen –*Schiller*
Auf der fernen See ein Segel steht –*Bierbaum*
Auf der Flucht vor meinen Landsleuten –*Brecht*
Auf der Haide ist ein Platz –*W. Hertz*
Auf der Heide weht der Wind –*Lemcke*
Auf der Messe, da zieht es –*F. Freiligrath*
Auf der schönen, schönen Wiese –*Boelitz*
Auf der Strasse und in allen Fabriken –*Hesse*
Auf der Treppe sitzen meine Öhrchen –*Morgenstern*
Auf der weiten Welt ist es schlecht bestellt –*C. Breuning*
Auf der Wellen Spiegel schwimmt der Kahn –*J. Mayrhofer*
Auf des Berges höchstem Scheitel –*W. Hertz*
Auf des Gartens Mauerzinne –*Geibel*
Auf des Lagers weichem Kissen –*F. Freiligrath*
Auf die Dächer zwischen blassen Wolken –*Eichendorff*
Auf die Erde voller kaltem Wind –*Brecht*
Auf die Nacht in den Spinnstubn –*Heyse*
Auf die stürm'sche See hinaus –*Dusch*
Auf ein freies Feld bin ich gezogen –*Stinde*
Auf einem Grab in Stükken –*Anonymous*
Auf einem grünen Hügel –*Rollet*
Auf einem hohen Berge –*"Kosten"*
Auf einen Todtenacker –*Wilhelm Müller*
Auf einer Meierei da war einmal ein braves Huhn –*Seidel*
Auf einer Wiese sah ich holde Frauen –*Grisebach*
Auf einsam hohem Thurme in trüber Nebelnacht –*Anonymous*
Auf! es dunkelt, silbern funkelt –*Salis-Seewis*
Auf Flügeln des Gesanges, Herzliebchen –*Heine*
Auf Flügeln rauscht der Wind daher –*Geibel*
Auf frisch gemähtem Weideplatz –*Hermann Gilm*
Auf, gebet uns das Pfingstei –*Volkslied*
Auf geheimem Waldespfade –*Lenau*
Auf goldnem Wagen –*Prittwitz und Gaffron*
Auf, hebe die funkelnde Schale empor zum Mund –*Mackay*
Auf, hinaus aus dem Haus –*Wittkowsky*
Auf hohem Bergesrücken –*J. Mayrhofer*
Auf hohen Burgeszinnen –*Chamisso*
Auf hoher Alp wohnt auch der liebe Gott –*F. A. Krummacher*
Auf, ihr Brüder, auf zum Jagen! –*Wildungen*

Auf ihrem Grab da steht eine Linde *–Heine*
Auf ihrem Leibrößlein, so weiß wie der Schnee *–Mörike*
Auf in das Feld zum Streite! *–Mastalier*
Auf! Jeder sei nun froh und sorgenfrei! *–Anonymous*
Auf jener Flucht, von welcher nun *–Rückert*
Auf Jordan's grünen Borden *–F. Freiligrath*
Auf Jordan's Ufer streifen wilde Horden *–Byron*
Auf Kieseln im Bache da lieg' ich *–Goethe*
Auf langer Haide wallt die Wolke hin und her *–Köstlin*
Auf luft'ger Höh' alleine *–"Martin Greif"*
Auf meinem Tische stehn Kornblumen *–Wildenbruch*
Auf meinen heimischen Bergen *–Leitner*
Auf mondbeschienenen Wegen *–Huggenberger*
Auf morgen ist Sankt Valentin's Tag *–Shakespeare*
Auf, Preussenherz, mit deinen Jubeltönen *–Hildebrandt*
Auf schweigendem Bergesgipfel *–Hamerling*
Auf seinen gold'nen Throne *–J. Mayrhofer*
Auf Wogen gezogen, von Klängen, Gesängen *–Tieck*
Auf zum Himmel steigt die Lerche *–Dieffenbach*
Aufgeschmückt ist der Freudensaal *–Mörike*
Aufs Wohlsein meiner Dame *–Eichendorff*
Aufsteigt der Strahl und fallend gießt *–C. F. Meyer*
Aufthaute die Erde vom Strahle der Sonne *–Anonymous*
Augen ihr, durch allen Schein gegangen *–Ehrler*
Augen, meine lieben Fensterlein *–Keller*
Augen, sagt mir, sagt, was sagt ihr? *–Goethe*
Augenblicke gibt es, zage *–Hamerling*
Aurikelchen stehn auf meinem Beet *–Dehmel*
Aus allen Winkeln gellen Fürchte Wollen *–Stramm*
Aus alten Märchen winkt es *–Heine*
Aus bangen Träumen der Winternacht *–Osterwald*
Aus deinen Augen fliessen meine Lieder *–"D. B. Schwerin"*
Aus dem dunkeln Thor wallt kein Zug *–Candidus*
Aus dem finster'n Schooss der Nacht *–Czermak*
Aus dem Himmel ferne, wo die Eng'lein sind *–Hey*
Aus dem meergrünen Teichea *–Dehmel*
Aus dem Rosenstokke vom Grabe des Christ *–Bierbaum*
Aus dem Walde tritt die Nacht *–Hermann Gilm*
Aus den Himmelsaugen droben *–Heine*
Aus den Trümmern einer hohen Schönheit *–Levetzow*
Aus der Bedrängnis, die mich wild umkettet *–Uhland*
Aus der Eltern Macht und Haus *–C. F. Meyer*
Aus der Erde quellen Blumen *–Groth*
Aus der Ferne schallen Gesänge *–Osterwald*
Aus der Glockenstube überm Dom *–Loerke*
Aus der Heimat hinter den Blitzen rot *–Eichendorff*
Aus der Jugendzeit, aus der Jugendzeit *–Rückert*
Aus der Schiffsbank mach' ich meinen Pfühl *–C. F. Meyer*
Aus der Tiefe tauchte sie nach oben *–Falke*
Aus des Abends weissen Wogen *–Dehmel*
Aus des Meeres tiefem, tiefem Grunde *–Wilhelm Müller*
Aus des Morgenhimmels Blau *–Träger*
Aus dunkler Brandung gährend *–Hesse*
Aus dunkler Nacht ein Brunnenlied *–Flemes*
Aus einem dunklen Forste *–Reiner*
Aus ihrem Bette stürzt sie bleich *–Morgenstern*
Aus meinen großen Schmerzen *–Heine*
Aus meinen Thränen sprießen *–Heine*
Aus meiner Erinn'rung erblüh'n *–Heine*
Aus Rosen, Phlox, Zinienflor *–Wehrli-Knobel*
Aus Sanct Justi Klosterhallen *–"Anastasius Grün"*
Aus schimmernden Zweigen langen und neigen *–Brantl*
Aus schwellenden Blütenkelchen *–Unidentified*
Aus schweren Träumen *–Eichendorff*
Aus silbergrauen Gründen *–Morgenstern*
Aus weißen Bildern wachsen deine Flügel *–Ingrisch*
Aus Wolken fällt die frohe Stunde *–Tieck*
Ausgelitten hast du, ausgerungen *–Reitzenstein*
Ave! Ave! Ave maris stella! *–Anonymous*
Ave Maria! Ave Maria! Neig' dein Angesicht *–Unidentified*
Ave Maria! Jungfrau mild! *–Scott*
Ave Maria! Meer und Himmel ruh'n *–Geibel*
Avends, wenn wi to Bette gaat *–Groth*

Bacchus, feister Fürst des Weins *–Shakespeare*
Bächlein am Wiesenrand, rinnst du noch immer? *–Rodenberg*
Bächlein, Bächlein, wie du eilen kannst *–Straaten*
Bächlein, lass dein Rauschen sein *–Wilhelm Müller*
Bäuerlein, Bäuerlein, tik, tik, tak *–Güll*
Bahnlos und pfadlos, Felsen hinan *–Zedlitz*
Bald gras' ich am Nekkar *–Wunderhorn*
Bald heisst es wieder *–Kannegiesser*
Bald ist der Nacht ein End' gemacht *–R. Reinick*
Bald stösst vom Lande das Schiff geschwinde *–Heyse*
Bald wehen uns des Frühlings Lüfte *–Anonymous*
Bangt dir mein Lieb? Ich bin ja bei dir *–Siebel*
Bau mir die Stadt aus Elfenbein *–Morgenstern*

Bedächtig stieg die Nacht an's Land *–Mörike*
Bedeckt mich mit Blumen, ich sterbe vor Liebe *–Geibel*
Bedekke deinen Himmel, Zeus *–Goethe*
Befiehl du deine Wege und was dein Herze kränkt *–Gerhardt*
Beglückt, beglückt, wer dich erblickt *–L. Hölty*
Begrabt den Leib in seiner Gruft *–Klopstock*
Begrüßet mit Tönen und Liedern den Tag *–Janke*
Bei dem angenehmsten Wetter *–Eichendorff*
Bei dem Glanze der Abendröte *–Goethe*
Bei den Bienenkörben im Garten *–Roquette*
Bei der Abendsonne Wandern *–C. F. Meyer*
Bei der Liebe reinsten Flammen *–Jacobi*
Bei der Nacht ist so finster im Weg *–Wunderhorn*
Bei diesem kalten Wehen sind alle Straßen leer *–Uhland*
Bei dir allein empfind' ich, dass ich lebe *–J. Seidl*
Bei dir ist es traut *–Rilke*
Bei dir sind meine Gedanken *–"Friedrich Halm"*
Bei einem Wirte wundermild *–Uhland*
Bei euren Taten, euren Siegen *–Mörike*
Bei jeder Wendung deiner Lebensbahn *–Mörike*
Bei Nacht im Dorf der Wächter rief: Elfe! *–Mörike*
Bei nächtlicher Weil, an ein's Waldes Born *–Volkslied*
Beim Kerzenlicht in bunten Kreis *–Warburg*
Beim Scheiden der Sonne erschimmert *–Scheffel*
Beim Schmerz der dieses Herz *–Anonymous*
Beim Spiele fiel den Kindern ein *–Unidentified*
Bekehre du mich, Herr *–Bezzel*
Bekränzet die Tonnen und zapfet mir Wein *–L. Hölty*
Bekränzt mit Laub den lieben, vollen Becher *–M. Claudius*
Bemeßt den Schritt! Bemeßt den Schwung! *–C. F. Meyer*
Benedeit die sel'ge Mutter *–Heyse*
Bereifte Kiefern, atemlose Seen *–Stach-Lerner*
Berg' und Burgen schau'n herunter *–Heine*
Berg' und Täler wieder fingen *–Eichendorff*
Berge dein Haupt, wenn ein König *–Keller*
Berggipfel erglühen, Waldwipfel erblühen *–Scheffel*
Beschattet von blühenden Ästen *–C. Weisse*
Bescheiden verborgen im buschichten Gang *–Unger*
Beschwert von Blüten beugen sich *–Kalidasa*
Beugt euch aus euren Wolken nieder *–Macpherson*
Bevor er in die blaue Flut gesunken *–Eichendorff*
Beweint die, so geweint in Babels Land! *–Byron*
Beweint sie, die an Babels Strömen klagen! *–Byron*
Bienchen, Bienchen wiegt sich im Sonnenschein *–Dehmel*
Bienen summen, wie schwer zu tragen *–Giesebrecht*
Bilder der Hoffnung, täuschet mein Herz! *–Goethe*
Bin ein fahrender Gesell *–Baumbach*
Bin ein Feuer hell, das lodert von dem grünen Felsenkranz *–Eichendorff*
Bin ein kleiner Stöpsel noch *–Reinecke*
Bin ein- und ausgange im ganze Tyrol *–Volkslied*
Bin ein Vöglein, das im Schatten *–Volkslied*
Bin i net a lust'ger Schweizerbu *–Volkslied*
Bin ich nit ein Bürschlein in der Welt? *–Wunderhorn*
Bin jung gewesen, kann auch mitreden *–Mörike*
Bin mit Dir im Wald gegangen *–Lenau*
Bin so müde. Alle Nächte trag ich dich auf dem Rükken *–Lasker-Schüler*
Birg, o Veilchen, in deinem blauen Kelche *–L. Hölty*
Birke, Birke, des Waldes Zier *–Pfarrius*
Bist allein im Leeren, glühst einsam, Herz *–Hesse*
Bist du aus einem Traum erwacht? *–Goethe*
Bist du denn wirklich so fern *–Anonymous*
Bist du manchmal auch verstimmt *–Eichendorff*
Bist ja noch ganz allein! *–Enslin*
Bist untreu, Wilhelm, oder tot *–G. A. Bürger*
Bitt' ihn, o Mutter, bitte den Knaben *–Heyse*
Bitte, bitte! einen Blick aus den holden blauen Augen *–Heinrich Schmidt*
Bitteres zu sagen denkst du *–Hafis, Daumer*
Blätter läßt die Blume fallen *–Petöfi*
Blättlein so fein und rund *–"Dilia Helena"*
Blasse Blüten neigen ihre duftende Pracht *–Kamlah*
Blau der See! Von hohem Schilfe *–Anonymous*
Blaublümlein spiegelten sich im Bach *–Wolff*
Blaue Äugle, rothe Bäckle, und ä Grüble im Kinn *–Volkslied*
Blaue Augen hat das Mädchen *–Geibel*
Blaue Augen, holde Sterne *–Erler*
Blauer Himmel, blaue Wogen *–Simrock*
Blaues Sternlein, du sollst schweigen *–Gregorovius*
Bleib' bei uns! wir haben den Tanzplan im Thal *–Eichendorff*
Bleib, mein Bruder, bleib noch *–Giesebrecht*
Bleib stehn! Dass nur ein Hauch vom Winde *–Wolff*
Bleibe bey uns denn es will Abend werden *–Anonymous*
Bleibe, bleibe bei mir, holder Fremdlingbe *–Goethe*
Bleibe hier und singe, liebe Nachtigall! *–Kulmann*
Bleich blickt die föhnige Nacht herein *–Hesse*
Bleich flimmert in stürmender Nacht *–F. L. W. Meyer*

Bleiche, bleiche weisses Lein –*R. Reinick*
Bleiche Blüte, Blüte der Liebe –*Busse*
Bleiches Antlitz, sei gegrüsset –*Rist*
Blicke mir nicht in die Lieder! –*Rückert*
Blindes Schauen, dunkle Leuchte –*Heyse*
Blond ist mein Haar, blau ist mein Blick –*"Klabund"*
Blühe, liebes Veilchen, blühe noch ein Weilchen –*Anonymous*
Blühe, liebes Veilchen, das ich selbst erzog –*Overbeck*
Blühe, liebes Veilchen, das so lieblich roch –*Wunderhorn*
Blühendes Heidekraut, dein Duft –*Heyse*
Blüht denn hier an Tauris Strande –*J. Mayrhofer*
Blümchen der Demuth, unter dichten Blättern birgst –*Anonymous*
Blümlein im Garten, schaut euch doch um –*Schröer*
Blütenblätter wehen, holde Zeit! –*C. Hauptmann*
Blüth' oder Schnee! Lust oder Weh! –*Rückert*
Blumen an den Wegen, Blumen um den Rain –*Lingg*
Blumen der Wiese, dürfen auch diese –*Goethe*
Blumen, Vögel, duftend, singend –*Lenau*
Brächte dich meinem Arm –*L. Hölty*
Brauner Bursche führt zum Tanze –*Conrat*
Braust des Unglücks Sturm empor –*Schober*
Brausten alle Berge, sauste rings der Wald –*Wenzig*
Brecht die schwangern Anmutsnelken –*Günther*
Breit' über mein Haupt dein schwarzes Haar –*Schack*
Brennend rot und schwarz gefleckt –*Ingrisch*
Brennessel steht an Weges Rand –*Conrat*
Brich nur, brich, du armes Herz! –*Stolberg-Stolberg*
Bricht das matte Herz noch immer –*Novalis*
Briefchen schrieb und warf in den Wind ich –*Gregorovius*
Bring' ich der Schönheit –*Michelangelo*
Bring mir keine Geschenke –*Busta*
Bringet des treu'sten Herzens Grüsse –*Ebert*
Bruder Jakob, schläfst du noch? –*Volkslied*
Brüder, Brüder, wir ziehen in den Krieg –*Volkslied*
Brüder, schrecklich brennt die Thräne –*Anonymous*
Brüder! unser Erdenwallen –*Castelli*
Büble, wir wollen ausse gehe! –*Wunderhorn*
Buko von Halberstadt, bring' doch meinem Kinde was –*Wunderhorn*
Bulbuls Nachtlied durch die Schauer –*Goethe*
Bunt sind schon die Wälder –*Salis-Seewis*
Burgen mit hohen Mauern und Zinnen –*Goethe*

Christ, deines Geistes Süßigkeit –*Anonymous*
Christ ist erstanden! Christ ist erstanden! –*Goethe*
Chumm über's Mätteli –*J. Reinhart*
Cidli, du weinest, und ich schlumm're –*Klopstock*
Cupido, loser, eigensinniger Knabe –*Goethe*
Cypris, meiner Phyllis gleich –*Uz*

Da deiner Schönheit Glanz mich hat besiegt –*Michelangelo*
Da der Sommer kommen ist –*Osterwald*
Da die Heimath, o Vater, da Gott –*Byron*
Da die Stunde kam, dass ich Abschied nahm –*Osterwald*
Da die Welt zur Ruh gegangen –*Eichendorff*
Da draußen auf der Aue –*F. Kugler*
Da draussen vor der himmlischen Thür –*Volkslied*
Da droben am Berge, ei, seht doch 'mal an! –*Bulcke*
Da droben auf dem Markte –*Mörike*
Da droben auf jenem Berge –*Goethe*
Da droben auf jenem Berge –*Wunderhorn*
Da drob'n auf jener Linden –*Volkslied*
Da drüben im Abendstrahle –*Stieler*
Da drunten im tiefen Thale –*Volkslied*
Da eben seinen Lauf vollbracht –*Jerusalem*
Da fahr' ich still im Wagen –*Eichendorff*
Da flattert um die Quelle –*Goethe*
Da fliegt, als wir im Felde gehn –*Uhland*
Da geht ein Bach das Thal entlang –*Groth*
Da geht er wieder, der bleiche Knabe –*J. Sturm*
Da hab ich gar die Rose aufgegessen –*Keller*
Da hab' ich viel blasse Leichen –*Heine*
Da ich dich einmal gefunden –*Rückert*
Da ich die Bücher, nach der Grenze hetzend –*Brecht*
Da ich ein Knabe war, rettet' ein Gott mich oft –*Hölderlin*
Da ich nun entsagen müssen Allem –*Geibel*
Da ist die liebe Schwalbe wieder! –*Dieffenbach*
Da kennt so ein Mann nun die halbe Welt –*Ritter*
Da kommt ja der liebliche Mai –*W. Gleim d. J.*
Da lieg' ich denn, ohnmächtiger Geselle –*Keller*
Da lieg' ich unter den Bäumen –*Anonymous*
Da liegen sie alle, die grauen Höhn –*Uhland*
Da liegt, ach Gott, da drunten liegt –*C. F. D. Schubart*
Da liegt der Feinde gestreckte Schaar –*Lenau*
Da meine lippen reglos sind und brennen –*George*
Da mit Sokrates die Freunde tranken –*C. F. Meyer*
Da nachts wir uns küßten, o Mädchen –*Chamisso*
Da nun die Blätter fallen, oh weh –*Bierbaum*
Da nur Leid und Leidenschaft –*Heyse*

Da schlend'r ich so die Welt hinan *–Anonymous*
Da schwimm ich allein auf dem stillen Meer *–F. Freiligrath*
Da sind die bleichen Geister wieder *–"Max Waldau"*
Da sind sie nun! Da habt ihr sie! *–Goethe*
Da sitz ich in der Stube *–G. Lang*
Da sitz' ich ohne Bogen *–J. Mayrhofer*
Da sitz' ich und weine und harre allein *–Pfau*
Da steh' i hier oben, schau' abe an See *–Volkslied*
Da steht der Mond! Verweile *–C. F. D. Schubart*
Da unten im Tale läufts Wasser so trüb *–Volkslied*
Da wächst der Wein, wos Faß ist *–Goethe*
Da war der Lehrer Huber *–Brecht*
Da waren zwei Kinder, jung und gut *–Morgenstern*
Da welkt am Fenster die letzte Rose *–Gottschall*
Da, wo des Tajo grünlich blauer Strom *–Puttkamer*
Da wo die Tausendschönchen blühn *–Jacobi*
Dämmern Wolken über Nacht und Tal *–C. Hauptmann*
Dämmernd liegt der Sommerabend *–Heine*
Dämmerung löscht die letzten Lichter *–Falke*
Dämm'rung feuchtet die Büsche *–Wildgans*
Dämmrung senkte sich von oben *–Goethe*
Dämm'rung will die Flügel spreiten *–Eichendorff*
Daferns geschah, das wir begraben *–Musset*
Damals, ganz zuerst am Anfang *–Spitteler*
Dank, grausender Dank sei dir gebracht *–Loewe and Vocke*
Dar gung en Mann un gung en Fro *–Groth*
Dar kummt en Herr to Peer *–Groth*
Darachna! komm, mein Wunsch *–H. W. Gerstenberg*
Darauf kommt es an, wenn einem ein Schwert *–Kafka*
Das aber kann ich nicht ertragen *–Storm*
Das also, das ist der enge Schrein *–Leitner*
Das alte Wunder ward wieder wahr: *–H. Claudius*
Das Angenehme dieser Welt *–Hölderlin*
Das arme Kind! sie sass und sang *–Shakespeare*
Das arme Veilchen, sieh' o sieh' *–J. W. L. Gleim*
Das Beet, schon lockert sich's in die Höh' *–Goethe*
Das beste Bier im ganzen Nest *–Roquette*
Das dank' ich deiner Güte *–Boelitz*
Das edle Bild der Menschheit *–Schiller*
Das einst ein Kind auf Erden war *–Cornelius*
Das Erste sei, daß man der Welt sich freue *–Hartleben*
Das Fenster klang im Winde *–Evers*
Das Fischergewerbe giebt rüstigen Muth! *–Salis-Seewis*
Das Fischermädchen harret am Ufer *–Pape*
Das Gärtlein dicht verschlossen *–Keller*
Das ganze, nicht das einzelne *–Rückert*
Das Geistige ist wie das Blütenleben *–Jünger*
Das gelbe Laub erzittert *–Heine*
Das Geld ist aus, die Flasche leer *–Hesse*
Das Gescheh'ne, nicht bereut's Hafis *–Hafis*
Das Gesetz der Quadrille ist klar *–Kafka*
Das Glas gefüllt! der Nordwind brüllt *–L. Hölty*
Das glaube mir, so sagte er *–Busch*
Das Glockenspiel der Phantasie *–"Dilia Helena"*
Das Glück ist rund *–K. E. K. Schmidt*
Das Grab, es sprach zur Rose *–Hugo*
Das Grab ist tief und stille *–Salis-Seewis*
Das Haus benedei' ich und preis' es laut *–Uhland*
Das Heimlicht zwischen dir und mir *–H. Claudius*
Das heiss' ich rechte Augenweide *–M. Claudius*
Das Herz ist gewachsen *–Kind*
Das Herz ist mir bedrückt *–Heine*
Das Herz will mir brechen, Therese *–Unidentified*
Das ist der alte Baum nicht mehr *–Eichendorff*
Das ist der Dank für jene Lieder *–Hoffmann von Fallersleben*
Das ist der Tag des Herrn *–Uhland*
Das ist des Abends Segen *–Benzmann*
Das ist des Frühlings traurige Lust! *–Heine*
Das ist die Drossel, die da schlägt *–Storm*
Das ist die sanfte, die heilige *–Dahn*
Das ist die schönste Stunde *–Kuh*
Das ist die Sehnsucht: wohnen im Gewoge *–Rilke*
Das ist die wahre Liebe *–Goethe*
Das ist die Zeit der Rosenpracht *–B. Scholz*
Das ist ein Brausen und Heulen *–Heine*
Das ist ein Flöten und Geigen *–Heine*
Das ist ein lieb Beisammen sein *–Ritter*
Das ist ein Lied für dich allein *–George*
Das ist ein schlechtes Wetter *–Heine*
Das ist ein seltsam Gehn *–Stieler*
Das ist ein Tag, der klingen mag *–Rollet*
Das ist eine Nacht! Eine Wacht! *–Morgenstern*
Das ist im Leben häßlich eingerichtet *–Scheffel*
Das ist nun alles und 's ist nicht genug *–Brecht*
Das ist so süß, das unser rascher Bund *–Mongré*
Das Kind ist krank zu Sterben *–Fontane*
Das Kind ruht aus vom Spielen *–Eichendorff*
Das Kind schläft unter dem Rosenstrauch *–"Eduard Ferrand"*
Das Knäblein nach acht Tagen *–Cornelius*
Das Köhlerweib ist trunken *–Keller*

Das Körnlein springt, der Vogel singt *–Braun*
Das Laub fällt von den Bäumen *–Mahlmann*
Das Leben gleichet der Blume! *–Halem*
Das Leben ist ein Traum *–J. W. L. Gleim*
Das Leben ist ein Traum *–Wannovius*
Das liebe Ränzel ist gespickt *–Unidentified*
Das Lieben bringt groß' Freud' *–Volkslied*
Das lockere saatgefilde lechzet krank *–George*
Das macht das dunkelgrüne Laub *–Roquette*
Das macht, es hat die Nachtigall *–Storm*
Das macht mir bittre Pein *–Vincke*
Das machte dein stiller keuscher Blick *–Schellenberg*
Das Mädchen ging die Wies' entlang *–Kind*
Das Mädchen steht im Grabe *–Ortlepp*
Das Mägdlein, braun von Aug' and Haar *–Voss*
Das Mägdlein sprach: "Lieb Knabe" *–Fischer*
Das Mägdlein trat aus dem Fischerhaus *–Molina*
Das Mägdlein will ein' Freier hab'n *–Wunderhorn*
Das Meer erglänzte weit hinaus *–Heine*
Das Meer erstrahlt im Sonnenschein *–Heine*
Das Meer hat seine Perlen *–Heine*
Das Meer ist für die Fischer auf der Welt *–Heyse*
Das Meer ist still, die Stürme schlafen *–J. Sturm*
Das Meer ist wie flüssige Jade *–Michalewski*
Das Mondschaf sagt sich selbst gut Nacht *–Morgenstern*
Das Mühlrad brauset *–H. Schütz*
Das neue Haus ist aufgericht't *–Uhland*
Das Röselein vom Regen *–Unidentified*
Das Schicksal will's ich darf nicht lieben *–Anonymous*
Das Schilf bückt sich hernieder *–Schüler*
Das schöne beet betracht ich mir im harren *–George*
Das sind die Stunden, da ich mich finde *–Rilke*
Das sind goldne Himmelspfade *–Cornelius*
Das Sonnenfeuer starb Rubingepränge *–"Gerda v. Robertus"*
Das Steuer des Bootes *–Anonymous*
Das süße Zeug ohne Saft und Kraft! *–Mörike*
Das Tagewerk ist abgetan *–Voss*
Das Trauerjahr war vorüber *–Kafka*
Das Veilchen auf der Wiese stand *–Goethe*
Das Vöglein hat ein schönes Loos *–Vogl*
Das Vöglein sang vom grünen Baum *–Rollet*
Das Vöglein singt am Waldessaum *–Wette*
Das Vöglein singt den ganzen Tag *–Eberwein*
Das Volk steht auf, der Sturm bricht los *–Körner*
Das Wandern ist des Müllers Lust *–Wilhelm Müller*
Das war der Junker Emerich *–Vogl*
Das war der Junker Übermut *–Falke*
Das war der Tag der weißen Chrysanthemen *–Rilke*
Das war des Frühlings warmer Hauch *–Sergel*
Das war die junge Königsbraut *–Freudenberg*
Das war die Lisa, die lustige Maid *–J. Sturm*
Das war die Schlacht von Waterloo *–Rückert*
Das war ein recht abscheuliches Gesicht *–Wargentin*
Das war ein Tag der Schmerzen *–Nietzsche*
Das war ein Tag voll Maienwind *–Stieler*
Das war ein Thier, mein Mauleselein! *–Kotzebue*
Das war vor hundert Jahren *–Cornelius*
Das Wasser rauscht', das Wasser schwoll *–Goethe*
Das weiß ich und hab ich erlebt *–Kneip*
Das zarte Knäblein ward ein Mann *–Cornelius*
Dasitzendir gegenüber am Tisch *–Busta*
Daß der Ostwind Düfte *–Rückert*
Dass die Luft mit leisem Wehen *–Geibel*
Dass doch gemalt all' deine Reize wären *–Heyse*
Daß du bei mir magst weilen *–Hesse*
Dass du mein Auge wecktest *–Schiller*
Dass du so krank geworden *–Kerner*
Daß er ganz ein Engel werde *–Holm*
Daß er verrekke, ist mein letzter Wille *–Brecht*
Daß gestern eine Wespe *–Anonymous*
Dass ich an Dich denke immerdar *–M. Jäger*
Dass ich dein auf ewig bliebe *–Meissner*
Dass ich dich verloren habe *–M. Claudius*
Dass ihr steht in Liebesglut *–Geibel*
Daß schon die Maienzeit vorüber *–Christen*
Dass wir sollen selig sein *–Stinde*
Daß zwei sich herzlich lieben *–H. Claudius*
De Dag, de graut, de Katt, de maut *–Groth*
De Wächter geit to blasen alleen in'e Nacht *–Groth*
Dein Angesicht, so lieb und schön *–Heine*
Dein Auge ist mein Himmel *–B. Scholz*
Dein Bildnis wunderselig *–Eichendorff*
Dein blaues Auge hält so still *–Groth*
Dein Gedenken lebt in Liedern fort *–Cornelius*
Dein gedenkend irr' ich einsam *–Lenau*
Dein Herzlein mild, du liebes Bild *–Heyse*
Dein ist mein Herz, mein Schmerz dein eigen *–Lenau*
Dein Leben schliesst, dein Ruhm begann *–Byron*
Dein Liebesfeuer, ach Herr! *–Mörike*
Dein Schlaf ist sanft wie dein Gemüt *–Krais*
Dein Schwert, wie ist's von Blut so rot? *–Herder*
Dein Silber schien durch Eichengrün *–L. Hölty*
Dein süßes Bild o Lyda! *–Klopstock*
Dein Tag ist aus, dein Ruhm fing an *–Byron*
Dein Wille, Herr, geschehe! *–Eichendorff*

Dein Wunsch, nicht mehr zu leiden –*Morgenstern*
Dein Wunsch war immer fliegen! –*Morgenstern*
Deine edlen weissen Hände –*Straaten*
Deine Finger rühren die Saiten –*F. Bodenstedt*
Deine gewölbten Brauen, o Geliebte –*Hafis*
Deine Mutter, süsses Kind –*Heyse*
Deine Rosen an der Brust –*Morgenstern*
Deine Seele hat die meine –*Itzerott*
Deine Sehnsucht ist leer –*Husserl*
Deine Stimme lass ertönen –*Stieglitz*
Deine süßen, süßen Schauer, o Waldesruh –*Leuthold*
Deine weissen Lilienfinger –*Heine*
Deinem Blick mich zu bequemen –*Goethe*
Deinem sanft flötenden Ton, Philomele –*F. Schmidt*
Deiner bunten Blasen Kinderfreude –*Keller*
Deiner hellen Stimme fröhlicher Klang –*K. Henckell*
Deiner Liebe goldene Güte –*Boelitz*
Dem Auge fern, dem Herzen nah! –*Jacobowski*
Dem bist du kind, dem freund –*George*
Dem dunkeln Schoß der heilgen Erde –*Schiller*
Dem Ew'gen unsre Lieder! –*Fink*
Dem Fürsten und dem Bettler –*Jünger*
Dem Herzen ähnlich, wenn es lang –*Schack*
Dem Himmel will ich klagen –*Volkslied*
Dem hohen Kaiser-Worte treu –*Anonymous*
Dem rothen Röslein gleicht mein Lieb' –*Burns*
Dem Schnee, dem Regen, dem Wind entgegen –*Goethe*
Dem Schützen, doch dem alten nicht –*Goethe*
Dem Vater liegt das Kind im Arm –*Bauernfeld*
Dem Wandrer, dem verschwunden –*Kerner*
Den einzigen Psyche, welchen du lieben kannst –*Goethe*
Den Fischer fechten Sorgen und Gram –*Schlechta*
Den Götterverächter schalten sie dich? –*Hölderlin*
Den gordischen Knoten, den Liebe sich band –*Herder*
Den grünen Zeigern, den rothen Wangen –*Lenau*
Den König Wiswamitra' –*Heine*
Den künft'gen Tag und Stunden –*Goethe*
Den kurzen Tag umgab die lange Nacht –*Ehrler*
Den Linden ist zu Füßen tief –*Keller*
Den Säugling an der Brust –*Chamisso*
Den Stab zur Hand genommen –*Reinecke*
Den Strauss, den sie gewunden –*Osterwald*
Den Tag, den ich so himmlisch verbracht –*Heine*
Den Tag hindurch nur einmal –*J. Mayrhofer*
Den Wein, den man mit Augen trinkt –*Giraud*
Den Wirbel schlag ich gar so stark –*Candidus*
Denk ihn hinaus, den schrecklichen Gedanken –*Zachariä*
Denke, denke, mein Geliebter –*Chamisso*
Denkst du auch so innig meiner –*Anonymous*
Denn es gehet dem Menschen wie dem Vieh –*the Bible*
Denn nirgend bleibt er –*Hölderlin*
Denn unsre Liebe hat zu heiß geflammt –*Huch*
Der Abend blüht, Temora glüht –*Kosegarten*
Der Abend dämmert, der Schmied, er hämmert –*Enslin*
Der Abend graut, Herbstfeuer brennen –*Dehmel*
Der Abend ist mein Buch –*Rilke*
Der Abend röthet nun das Thal –*J. Mayrhofer*
Der Abend schaut durchs Fensterlein –*Kayser-Langerhannß*
Der Abend schleiert Flur und Hain –*Matthisson*
Der Abend schließt die samtne Tür –*Kerckhoff*
Der Abend war so dunkel schwer –*Liliencron*
Der Abendthau– es sind die Thränen –*H. Seidel*
Der Adler lauscht auf seinem Horst –*E. Scherenberg*
Der alte Barbarosse, der Kaiser Friederich –*Rückert*
Der alte Turm und die Schwalben –*H. Claudius*
Der arme Peter wankt vorbei –*Heine*
Der Bach hat leise Melodien –*Rilke*
Der Bahnhof steht im Nebel –*Schumacher*
Der Bauer hat ein Taubenhaus –*Güll*
Der Bauer steht vor seinem Feld –*J. Sturm*
Der Bergmann lebt beim Grubenlicht –*Anonymous*
Der Besen! was macht man damit? –*Volkslied*
Der bessre Mensch tritt in die Welt –*Schiller*
Der bleiche, kalte Mond erhob sich in Osten –*Macpherson*
Der Blumen wollt' ich warten –*Geibel*
Der Britte ist der Stern der Nationen –*Shakespeare*
Der Buchenwald ist herbstlich schon gerötet –*Lenau*
Der Buhle sitzt und ächzet traurig –*Woltmann*
Der Dämmrung Schein durchblinkt den Hain –*Matthisson*
Der Damm zerreißt, das Feld erbraust –*Goethe*
Der den Sterngang maß mit Menschenzeichen –*Ehrler*
Der Denker rechnet wohl einmal –*Spitteler*
Der Dichter singt dem Frühling –*Cornelius*
Der du am Sternenbogen –*Geibel*
Der du im Feld die Vöglein nährst –*Cornelius*
Der du mich mit gutem Rate –*Hafis*
Der du so lustig rauschtest –*Wilhelm Müller*
Der du von dem Himmel bist –*Goethe*

Der Duft nach Sandel, den die seidenen Fächer *–Kalidasa*
Der edle Mensch sei hülfreich und gut *–Goethe*
Der Eichwald brauset, die Wolken ziehn *–Schiller*
Der erste Tag im Monat Mai *–H. W. Gerstenberg*
Der erste Tannenbaum, den ich gesehen *–Keller*
Der Ewige segnet der Frommen Tage *–M. Mendelssohn*
Der Feinde Scharen rüsten sich *–Telschow*
Der Fluren Grün, das Abendgold *–Lohbauer*
Der Föhn schreit jede Nacht *–Hesse*
Der Förster ging zu Fest und Schmaus! *–R. Reinick*
Der Franz läßt dich grüßen *–Wunderhorn*
Der Friede sei mit euch! *–Schober*
Der Frost hat mir bereifet des Hauses Dach *–Rückert*
Der Frost in letzter Nacht *–Sergel*
Der Frühhauch hat gefächelt *–Anonymous*
Der Frühling begrüsset die junge Natur *–"Dilia Helena"*
Der Frühling entblühet dem Schoos *–Reissig*
Der Frühling ist erschienen *–Hafis*
Der Frühling ist herangekommen *–Anonymous*
Der Frühling kam! In seinem Hauche *–Unidentified*
Der Frühling kehret wieder *–Hoffmann von Fallersleben*
Der Frühling kehret wieder *–Kulmann*
Der Frühling kehrt alljährlich wieder *–Träger*
Der Frühling naht mit Brausen *–Klingemann*
Der Frühling starb im Dufte der Syringen *–Faktor*
Der Frühling und der Sonnenschein *–Volkslied*
Der Frühlingssonne holdes Lächeln *–A. W. Schlegel*
Der Fürst ritt am Morgen *–A. Tolstoi*
Der Gang war schwer, der Tag war rauh *–Chamisso*
Der ganze Himmel glüht in hellen Morgenrosen *–Falke*
Der Garten des Lebens ist lieblich *–"Rosemann"*
Der Garten trauert, Kühl sinkt *–Hesse*
Der Geisshirt steht am Felsenrand *–Kind*
Der Glükkes Fühle mir verlieh'n *–Cornelius*
Der goldne Morgen kommt herauf *–Laubsch*
Der graue Nebel tropft so still *–Allmers*
Der Hagel klirrt nieder *–Shelley*
Der Hahn hat gekräht, die Lerche singt *–Kurowski-Eichen*
Der Hain widerhallt von der Nachtigall Sang *–Jókai*
Der Hans, der spricht zum Hahn *–R. Reinick*
Der Hans und die Grete tanzen herum *–Heine*
Der Heidebusch voll Knospen stand *–B. P.*
Der Heiland ist für uns gestorben *–G. Nicolai*
Der heilig Geist vom Himmel kam *–Helmbold*
Der Herbst beginnt, schon saust der Wind *–J. G. Schulz*
Der Herbst streut weiße Nebel aus *–Hesse*
Der Herbstwind rüttelt die Bäume *–Heine*
Der Herbstwind schüttelt die Linde *–Eichendorff*
Der Herr erscheint in seiner Höhe *–K. A. Schmid*
Der Herr gab dir ein gutes Augenpaar *–Keller*
Der Herr ist aufs Feld gangen *–Brecht*
Der Herr ist Gott und keiner mehr *–Cramer*
Der Herr ist gut! ihr Himmel *–Uz*
Der Herr ist mein Hirte *–the Bible*
Der Himmel da oben, der freut mich sehr *–R. Reinick*
Der Himmel, drüben über dem Dach *–Verlaine*
Der Himmel glänzt vom reinsten Frühlingslichte *–Mörike*
Der Himmel hat eine Thräne geweint *–Rückert*
Der Himmel hat keine Sterne *–Heyse*
Der Himmel ist so weit und hehr *–Asenijeff*
Der Himmel lacht und heit're Lüfte spielen *–H. Kurz*
Der Himmel strahlend ausgespannt *–"Martin Greif"*
Der Himmel wölbt sich rein und blau *–Anderson*
Der Hirt bläst seine Weise *–Eichendorff*
Der Hoffnung letzter Schimmer sinkt dahin *–S. Breuning*
Der holden Lenzgeschmeide *–Lenau*
Der Holdseligen sonder Wank *–Voss*
Der Husar, trara! was ist die Gefahr? *–Lenau*
Der ich, in Zwischenräumen *–Whitman*
Der ich von den Frauen allen *–Heinrich von Stretlingen*
Der Igel, der ist ein schlimmer Mann *–Schellenberg*
Der Jäger in dem Walde *–Volkslied*
Der jagt dahin, daß die Rosse schnaufen *–Eichendorff*
Der Jüngling hofft des Greises Ziel *–Gellert*
Der junge König Heinrich schlief *–Schwab*
Der junge König und sein Gemahl *–F. Kugler*
Der junge Tag erwacht *–Osterwald*
Der Kirschbaum blüht *–A. v. Arnim*
Der Knabe eilt durch den düstern Hain *–Freudenberg*
Der Knabe seufzt über's grüne Meer *–J. Mayrhofer*
Der Knabe träumt, man schicke ihn fort *–Hebbel*
Der Kön'ge Herzen, Rath und Sinn *–Telschow*
Der König Arthur von Engelland *–Anonymous*
Der König auf dem gold'nen Stuhle *–Giesebrecht*
Der König saß beim frohen Mahle *–F. Bobrik*
Der König thront; es sitzen die Grossen *–Byron*
Der Kuckuck ruft Ku-ku-ku-ku *–Königsbrunn-Schaup*

Der Kuckuck ruft nicht mehr –*Jünger*
Der Kukkuck auf dem Birnbaum saß –*Wunderhorn*
Der Kukuk hat ein einzig Lied –*J. Sturm*
Der lebt ein Leben wonniglich –*Anonymous*
Der leidige Frieden hat lange gewährt –*Lenau*
Der Lenz ist angekommen! –*Volkslied*
Der Lenz ist da und fern und nah –*Leuthold*
Der Lenz ist gekommen ins harrende Land –*Wolff*
Der Lerche wolkennahe Lieder –*J. Mayrhofer*
Der Liebe bangen Sorgen –*Heinrich Schmidt*
Der Löw' ist los! der Löw' ist frei! –*Gruppe*
Der Mai ist auf dem Wege –*Wilhelm Müller*
Der Mai ist gekommen, die Bäume schlagen aus –*Geibel*
Der Mai tritt ein mit Freuden –*Volkslied*
Der Mai will sich mit Gunsten –*Wunderhorn*
Der Maien ist gestorben –*Gerheusser*
Der Mann ist geboren zur Liebe! –*Loewe and Vocke*
Der Marktplatz liegt vom Mond erhellt –*B. Huber*
Der Meeresfluth mit Purpurgluth –*Anonymous*
Der Mensch lebt und bestehet –*M. Claudius*
Der Mensch soll nicht stolz sein –*Himer*
Der Mensch, vom Weibe geboren –*the Bible*
Der Mond blickt über die Haide –*Stieglitz*
Der Mond, der dort am Himmel steht –*Hubalek*
Der Mond, ein blankes Türkenschwert –*Giraud*
Der Mond glüht über'm Garten –*Diederich*
Der Mond hat eine schwere Klag' erhoben –*Heyse*
Der Mond ist aufgegangen –*M. Claudius*
Der Mond ist schlafen gangen –*Osterwald*
Der Mond kommt still gegangen –*Geibel*
Der Mond scheint auf mein Lager –*Falke*
Der Mond schon wandelt am Himmelszelt –*Recke*
Der Mond steht über dem Berge –*F. Kugler*
Der Mond steigt aufwärts –*Sao-han*
Der Mond streut durch die Zweige –*Evers*
Der Mond wird oft noch über den Syringen der Schwermut –*"Klabund"*
Der monddurchbleichte Wald –*Morgenstern*
Der Mondschein, der ist schon verblichen –*Wunderhorn*
Der Mondschein lag auf dem Wasser –*Semler*
Der Mondstrahl ist das Ruder –*Giraud*
Der Morgen blüht; der Osten glüht –*Kosegarten*
Der Morgen glüht, die Rose blüht –*Lafontaine*
Der Morgen steigt und glüht und steigt –*Falke*
Der müde Sommer senkt das Haupt –*Hesse*
Der Nachen dröhnt, Cypressen flüstern –*J. Mayrhofer*
Der Nebel auf dem Weiher spinnt –*Kastropp*
Der Neger, der von der Weltausstellung –*Kafka*
Der Neid, o Kind, zählt unsre Küsse –*Lessing*
Der Nordost weht, der liebste unter den Winden mir –*Hölderlin*
Der Odem Gottes weht –*Silbert*
Der Pfarrer von Assmannshausen sprach –*Scheffel*
Der Pflanze, die dort über dem Abgrund –*Pfau*
Der Rabe Ralf will will hu hu –*Morgenstern*
Der Regen, der Regen, der langentbehrte Segen! –*H. Claudius*
Der Regen rasselt, es saust der Sturm –*Hochwald*
Der reiche Tor –*C. Weisse*
Der Reif hat einen weißen Schein –*Wilhelm Müller*
Der Reimer Thomas lag am Bach –*Fontane*
Der Reiter spreitet seinen Mantel aus –*Volkslied*
Der Rosen Düfte liebeatmend –*"Gerda v. Robertus"*
Der Sabbath hebt, ein gröss'rer Sabbath an –*Giesebrecht*
Der Säemann säet den Samen –*M. Claudius*
Der Sänger geht auf rauhen Pfaden –*Novalis*
Der Sänger hält im Feld die Fahnenwacht –*F. Löwe*
Der Sänger ruht auf schroffem Stein –*Stolterfoth*
Der Sänger zog durch Wald und Flur –*Anonymous*
Der Schäfer putzte sich zum Tanz –*Goethe*
Der Schah von Ormus sah mich nie –*Hafis*
Der Schiffer fährt zu Land –*Rückert*
Der Schlaf entführte mich in deine Gärten –*Lasker-Schüler*
Der Schmerz ist ein Schmied –*Bierbaum*
Der Schmetterling ist in die Rose verliebt –*Heine*
Der Schnee beginnt zu treiben –*Brecht*
Der Schnee, der gestern noch in Flöckchen –*Rückert*
Der Schnee ist zergangen –*Osterwald*
Der Schnee zerrinnt, der Mai beginnt –*L. Hölty*
Der Schneewind packt mich jäh von vorn –*Hesse*
Der Schnitzelmann von Nürenberg –*Güll*
Der schöne Schäfer zog so nah' –*Uhland*
Der schönste Cherub kommt –*Schlaf*
Der schönste Tannenbaum, den ich gesehn –*Keller*
Der See ruht tief im blauen Traum –*Mosen*
Der sei nicht mein Genoß –*Anacreon*
Der Sommer ist so schön –*Burns*
Der Sommer ist vergangen –*Dieffenbach*
Der Sommer ist zu Ende –*Osterwald*
Der Sommer summt –*Rilke*
Der Sonne entgegen in Liebesgluten –*K. Henckell*
Der Sonne letzte Strahlen säumen –*Träger*
Der Sonntag ist da! –*F. A. Krummacher*

Der Sonntag ist gekommen *–Hoffmann von Fallersleben*
Der Spiegel dieser treuen, braunen Augen *–Mörike*
Der Spiegel rief den Mond herein *–Rasche*
Der Spiegel sagt mir, ich bin schön! *–Goethe*
Der Spielmann saß am Felsen *–Körner*
Der Stein zerfließt, der Wald ertrinkt *–Ingrisch*
Der Sternlein Heer am Himmel blinkt *–Anonymous*
Der Strauß, den ich gepflücket *–Goethe*
Der Strom, der neben mir verrauschte *–Platen*
Der Strom glitt einsam hin und rauschte *–Eichendorff*
Der Sturm behorcht mein Vaterhaus *–Dehmel*
Der Sturm geht lärmend um das Haus *–Eichendorff*
Der Sturm ist los, der Sturm ist los *–Vogl*
Der süße Schlaf, der sonst stillt alles wohl *–Wunderhorn*
Der Tag beginnt zu dunkeln *–Osterwald*
Der Tag, der schwüle, verblasst *–Mackay*
Der Tag erwacht im Strahlenkranze *–Anonymous*
Der Tag ging regenschwer und sturmbewegt *–Liliencron*
Der Tag hat seinen Schmuck *–Volkslied*
Der Tag hat sich zur Ruh' gelegt *–E. Koch*
Der Tag ist längst geschieden *–Scherer*
Der Tag ist vergangen *–Volkslied*
Der Tag klingt ab, es gilbt sich Glück *–Nietzsche*
Der Tag neigt sich zu Ende *–J. Sturm*
Der Tag wird kühl, der Tag wird blass *–Heyse*
Der Tannenbaum steht schweigend *–Scheurlin*
Der Tempel ist euch aufgebaut *–Goethe*
Der Thürmer, der schaut zu Mitten der Nacht *–Goethe*
Der Tod, das ist die kühle Nacht *–Heine*
Der Tod ist groß *–Rilke*
Der Traum war so wild *–Lenau*
Der trotzige Mahomet stürzte mit Wut *–Koller*
Der trübe Winter ist vorbei *–Spee*
Der Uhu, der Kauz und zwo Eulen *–Hagedorn*
Der Violine zarte Seele voll *–Giraud*
Der Vogel steigt, ein verkörpertes Lied *–Ebert*
Der volle Mond steigt aus dem Meer herauf *–Bethge*
Der Vollmond strahlt auf Bergeshöh'n *–Chézy*
Der Vorhang schwebet hin und her *–Goethe*
Der Wald beginnt zu rauschen *–Dehmel*
Der Wald ist schwarz, die Luft ist klar *–Redwitz*
Der Wald wird dichter mit jedem Schritt *–Geibel*
Der Wald wird falb, die Blätter fallen *–Eichendorff*
Der Waldbach tost im Tannenthal *–K. Ziegler*
Der Wand'rer, von der Heimat weit *–Eichendorff*
Der Weg an unser'm Zaun entlang *–Groth*
Der Wind aus dem Osten *–Michalewski*
Der Wind der weht *–H. Claudius*
Der Wind des Herbstes weht *–Kalidasa*
Der Wind ist fremd *–Lenau*
Der Wind spielt mit der Wetterfahne *–Wilhelm Müller*
Der Winter hat mit kalter Hand *–G. A. Bürger*
Der Winter ist ein böser Gast *–Feldmann*
Der Winter ist ein rechter Mann *–M. Claudius*
Der Zaunpfahl trug ein Hütlein weiss *–Wolff*
Dereinst, dereinst Gedanke mein *–Geibel*
Derselbe große Engel *–Rilke*
Derweil ich schlafend lag *–Mörike*
Des Abends kann ich nicht schlafen gehn *–Volkslied*
Des Abends Rosen sind abgeblüht *–Jung*
Des Abendsterns ersehnter Schein *–Platen*
Des Berges Gipfel war erschwungen *–Lenau*
Des Dorfes heimische Stille *–Urban*
Des Glöckleins Schall durchtönt das Tal *–Zusner*
Des Himmels frohes Antlitz *–Lenau*
Des Jahres letzte Stunde *–Anonymous*
Des Jünglings Blick erkennt *–H. Fick*
Des lauten Tages wirre Klänge schweigen *–Cornelius*
Des Lebens Schönheit mußt ich tief empfinden *–Glaser*
Des Lebens Tag ist schwer *–Stolberg-Stolberg*
Des Maurers Wandeln, es gleicht dem Leben *–Goethe*
Des Menschen Seele gleicht dem Wasser *–Goethe*
Des Mondes Zauberblume lacht *–Schober*
Des Mondlichts bleiche Blüten *–Giraud*
Des Morgens still ich träume *–Nietzsche*
Des Morgens zwischen drei'n und vieren *–Wunderhorn*
Des Nordens Wunder ist der Winter *–H. Claudius*
Des Phöbus Strahlen sind dem Aug *–Anonymous*
Des Schäfers sein Haus *–Mörike*
Des Sonntags in der Morgenstund' *–R. Reinick*
Des stolzen Männerlebens schönste Zeichen *–Anonymous*
Des Tages laute Stimmen schweigen *–Saar*
Des Tages Licht hat sich verdunkelt *–Haller*
Des Waldes Sänger singen *–Osterwald*
Des Waldes Wipfel rauschen *–Osterwald*
Des Wassermanns sein Töchterlein *–Mörike*
Dessen Fahne Donnerstürme wallte *–Schiller*
Deutschlands Adler liegt gebunden *–Budy*
Dich bet' ich an, erstand'ner Held *–Anonymous*

Dich blendet Kerzenlicht! –*Gerstenberg*
Dich ergriff mit Gewalt –*Goethe*
Dich hat Amor gewiß, o Sängerin –*Goethe*
Dich meiden nein, ach nein! –*Volkslied*
Dich soll mein Lied erheben –*Rüling*
Dich vor allem, heilige Muttersprache –*Leuthold*
Dicht in Blättern eingeschlossen –*Soeltl*
Dicht von Felsen eingeschloßen –*Tieck*
Dichter! was Liebe sei –*Hagn*
Die Abendglocke tönet –*Hüttenbrenner*
Die Abendglocken klangen –*Eichendorff*
Die Ähren nur noch nikken –*Hoffmann von Fallersleben*
Die allerkleinste Schwester –*Reinecke*
Die alten, bösen Lieder –*Heine*
Die Ammer flötet tief im Grund –*Holz*
Die Amsel flötet, es rieselt der Bach –*Rose*
Die andern Mädchen wissen's nicht –*Evers*
Die Angel zuckt, die Ruthe bebt –*J. Mayrhofer*
Die Apfelblüten tun sich langsam –*Borchert*
Die Arbeit ist getan –*Ingrisch*
Die Arme, am Lebensbaum seufzte sie –*Shakespeare*
Die Arme, wie seufzend am Ahorn sass sie! –*Shakespeare*
Die Augen fielen meinem Liebsten zu –*Rona*
Die Bäche rauschen der Frühlingssonne –*Lenau*
Die Bäume blühn, die Vöglein singen –*Lenau*
Die Bäume grünen überall –*Hoffmann von Fallersleben*
Die Bäume rauschen hier noch immer –*Lenau*
Die Bäume tropfen vom Gewitterguß –*Hesse*
Die Bäume wurden gelb –*Cossmann*
Die Berge sind spitz und die Berge sind kalt –*Heyse*
Die Blätter fallen, fallen wie von weit –*Rilke*
Die Bläue meiner Augen ist erloschen –*Trakl*
Die blaue Nacht geht leuchtend –*Evers*
Die blauen Frühlingsaugen –*Heine*
Die Blümelein, sie schlafen –*Volkslied*
Die Blümlein auf der Heide –*Cornelius*
Die Blume verblühet auf fliessender Fluth –*"Carmen Sylva"*
Die Blumen all, die Blüthen all –*Dieffenbach*
Die Bowle fort! und schäume –*Moore*
Die braune Heide starrt mich an –*Osterwald*
Die bretterne Kammer der Todten erbebt –*Matthisson*
Die Burschen, eh sie ihre Mädchen legen –*Brecht*
Die Dämmerung war längst hereingebrochen –*Hebbel*
Die drei Schwestern wollten sterben –*Maeterlinck*
Die du bist so schön und rein –*Heine*
Die du dich an uns verschwendest –*Kamossa*
Die du Gott gebarst, du Reine –*Heyse*
Die du so gern in heil'gen Nächten feierst –*Tiedge*
Die du, über die Sterne weg –*Hebbel*
Die dürre Dirne mit langem Halse –*Giraud*
Die duftenden Gräser auf der Au –*Hoffmann von Fallersleben*
Die Dunkelheit sinkt schwer wie Blei –*Ronsperger*
Die dunklen Wolken hingen –*Lenau*
Die einst'ge Sehnsucht –*Shakespeare*
Die Engel Gottes weinen –*K. E. K. Schmidt*
Die Englein haben's Bett gemacht –*Anonymous*
Die Erde hat nicht Erde genug –*Busta*
Die Erde ist dunkler und satter in den Farben –*Bollmann*
Die Erde ist erschlossen –*Scheffel*
Die Erde ruht, das Herz erwacht –*Mahlmann*
Die Erde schläft, des Mondes Schein –*K. Fick*
Die erste Liebe füllt das Herz –*Fellinger*
Die ersten Blümchen, die ich fand –*S. Albrecht*
Die ersten Tropfen fallen –*"Ernst"*
Die Fahnen flattern im Mitternachtssturm –*Rückert*
Die falben Felder schlafen schon –*Rilke*
Die Feder am Sturmhut in Spiel und Gefahren –*Liliencron*
Die Fenster klär' ich zum Feiertag –*Ullrich*
Die Fenster sonnen, der Winter ist aus –*Scheurlin*
Die fernen, fernen Berge –*Madeleine*
Die Feuerschlünde am Seinestrand –*Anonymous*
Die Finken schlagen, der Lenz ist da –*Dahn*
Die finstre Nacht bricht schnell herein –*Burns*
Die Fischerstochter sitzt am Strand –*Coronini*
Die Flamme hier, die wilde, zu verhehlen –*Hafis*
Die Flamme lodert, milder Schein –*Matthisson*
Die Frauen sind oft fromm und still –*Dahn*
Die frohe neubelebte Flur –*Anonymous*
Die Fürstin zog zu Walde –*F. Freiligrath*
Die ganz' Welt ist in dich verliebt –*Mörike*
Die ganze Welt will glücklich sein –*Anonymous*
Die Gedanken sind frei –*Wunderhorn*
Die Gletscher leuchten im Mondenlicht –*F. Bodenstedt*
Die Glocken gehen bim bam bum –*Reinecke*
Die Göttin süßer Freuden –*Zachariä*
Die goldene Waage des Lebens trug –*Zwehl*
Die grüne Hopfenranke –*Daumer*
Die güldne Sonne voll Freud und Wonne –*Gerhardt*
Die gute Nacht, die ich dir sage –*Rückert*

Die Händler und die Macher –*Kerr*
Die Häuser sollen nicht brennen –*Brecht*
Die Heere blieben am Rheine steh'n –*Volkslied*
Die Heide ist braun –*Müller von Königswinter*
Die heilgen drei König mit ihrem Stern –*Goethe*
Die heil'gen drei Kön'ge aus Morgenland –*Heine*
Die heilige Elisabeth –*Volkslied*
Die heiligen drei König mit ihrem Stern –*Goethe*
Die heil'gen drei Kön'ge aus Morgenland –*Heine*
Die heiligen drei Könige stehn vorm Haus –*Bierbaum*
Die helle Sonne leuchtet –*F. Bodenstedt*
Die Herde Schafe, die gemächlich zieht –*Wordsworth*
Die Himmel rühmen des Ewigen Ehre –*Gellert*
Die Himmel rufen: jeder ehret –*Cramer*
Die Hirten wachen nachts im Feld –*Cornelius*
Die höchste Macht der Erde –*Hafis*
Die Höh'n und Wälder schon steigen –*Eichendorff*
Die ihr an süsser Lieder Schall –*Kalchberg*
Die ihr den Äther mit seligen Schwingen –*Ritter*
Die ihr dort wallet unter den Palmen –*Lope de Vega*
Die ihr einem neuen Grade –*Ratschky*
Die ihr Felsen und Bäume bewohnt –*Goethe*
Die ihr meine Brüder seid –*Hesse*
Die ihr schwebet um diese Palmen –*Geibel*
Die in Lybien denken die Götter –*Xenophanes*
Die Jäger ziehn in grünen Wald –*Eichendorff*
Die Jahre kommen und gehen –*Heine*
Die Jungfrau schläft in der Kammer –*Heine*
Die kleine Welt, mit deren Glanzgestalten –*Mörike*
Die kleinen Hunde öffneten die Augen –*Mistral*
Die Knospe träumte von Sonnenschein –*Sallet*
Die Königin steht im hohen Saal –*Goethe*
Die Königstochter sticket –*Plönnies*
Die kolossale Flut dehnt sich hinaus –*Müller von Königswinter*
Die Krähen rudern schwer im Blut –*Büchler*
Die Krähen schrein und ziehen –*Nietzsche*
Die Künstler sind die Schöpfer –*Kerr*
Die Lämmlein springen! die Vögelein singen! –*Werthes*
Die Lande durchträumt der Schlaf –*Evers*
Die Leiter blieb noch –*Viertel*
Die Lerche grüßt den ersten Strahl –*Eichendorff*
Die Lerche sang, die Sonne schien –*Anonymous*
Die Lerche singt ihr Morgenlied –*Lua*
Die letzten Blumen starben –*Kulmann*
Die Lieb und unser Vogelfang –*Thümmel*
Die Liebe hat gelogen –*Platen*
Die Liebe hemmet nichts –*M. Claudius*
Die Liebe ist die Sonne –*Ambrosius*
Die Liebe ist ein Rosenstrauch –*R. Reinick*
Die Liebe nimmt an, nicht weg –*Busta*
Die Liebe, sagt man, steht am Pfahl gebunden –*Mörike*
Die Liebe saß als Nachtigall –*Geibel*
Die Liebe, sie zerbreche mich –*Hafis*
Die Liebste fragt, warum ich liebe? –*Rückert*
Die Liebste gab mir einen Zweig –*Brecht*
Die Liebste steht mir vor den Gedanken –*Rückert*
Die linden Lüfte sind erwacht –*Uhland*
Die Linien des Lebens sind verschieden –*Hölderlin*
Die Lippe brennt, die Wange glüht –*Kartscher*
Die Lor' sitzt im Garten –*Keller*
Die Lotusblume ängstigt –*Heine*
Die Lüfte werden heller –*Osterwald*
Die Luft ist blau, das Thal ist grün –*L. Hölty*
Die Luft ist kühl und trübe –*Wisbacher*
Die Luft ist trübe, der Wind weht kalt –*Kapff*
Die Mädchen mit den verbundenen Augen –*Maeterlinck*
Die Maid sie wollt 'nen Buhlen wert –*Volkslied*
Die Menschheit ist dahinter kommen –*Lenau*
Die mich hält am Fädchen –*Rückert*
Die mich recht erkennen, Gott! –*Gerstenberg*
Die mir noch gestern glühten –*Hesse*
Die mit ihrem Strahle mich geblendet –*Stamm*
Die Mitternacht zog näher schon –*Heine*
Die müden Augen, sie tragen's kaum! –*Stieler*
Die Mühle, die dreht ihre Flügel –*Chamisso*
Die Mükke sitzt am Fenster –*Hoffmann von Fallersleben*
Die Munterkeit ist meiner Wangen –*Uz*
Die Muse fehlt nicht selten –*Uhland*
Die Mutter betet herzig –*Anderson*
Die Mutter hat mich jüngst gescholten –*J. Seidl*
Die Mutter mahnt mich Abends –*C. F. Meyer*
Die Nacht bricht an –*Pichler*
Die Nacht bricht bald herein –*Scott*
Die Nacht herauf am Himmel zieht –*Stamm*
Die Nacht ist dumpfig und finster –*Macpherson*
Die Nacht ist feucht und stürmisch –*Heine*
Die Nacht ist finster, schwül und bang –*Lenau*
Die Nacht ist heiter und ist rein –*J. Seidl*
Die Nacht ist keines Menschen Freund! –*Ritter*
Die Nacht ist so dunkel –*Kurowski-Eichen*
Die Nacht ist so hell –*Michalewski*
Die Nacht vergeht nach süßer Ruh –*Cornelius*

Die Nacht war kaum verblühet –*Eichendorff*
Die Nacht war schwarz –*Geibel*
Die Nacht war tief, und die Mutter schlief –*Ritter*
Die Nachtigall hat mich vom Schlaf erweckt –*Osterwald*
Die Nachtigall sang ohne Ende –*Bethge*
Die Nachtigall, sie war entfernt –*Goethe*
Die Nachtigall singt überall –*L. Hölty*
Die Nächte stürmen, doch die Seele singt –*J. Grosse*
Die Nebel zerreißen, der Himmel ist helle –*Goethe*
Die Perle, wahrend im Gehäuse –*Ebert*
Die Perlen meiner Seele –*Hafis*
Die Primeln blühn und grüssen –*Morgenstern*
Die Quelle rauscht, die Mükke schwirrt –*Mahlmann*
Die Quellen sangen in tiefer Nacht –*R. Graf*
Die Rechte streckt' ich schmerzlich oft –*C. F. Meyer*
Die Römer, die, vor vielen hundert Jahren –*M. Claudius*
Die Rose blüht, ich bin die fromme Biene –*C. Weise*
Die Rose, die Lilie, die Taube, die Sonne –*Heine*
Die Rose stand im Thau –*Rückert*
Die Rosen leuchten immer noch –*Dehmel*
Die Ruhe zieht durch Haus und Stall –*Groth*
Die Saiten weiß ich zu rühren –*Mommsen*
Die Scheibe friert, der Wind ist rauh –*J. Seidl*
Die schlanke Wasserlilie schaut –*Heine*
Die Schlechten fürchten deine Klaue –*Brecht*
Die Schleiche singt ihr Nachtgebet –*Morgenstern*
Die Schmetterlinge, die fliegen –*Meyer-Helmund*
Die Schnur, die Perl an Perlen –*Daumer*
Die schönen Augen der Frühlingsnacht –*Dr. Mayer*
Die Schwälble ziehet fort, ziehet fort –*Volkslied*
Die Schwalbe, die den Sommer bringt –*Shakespeare*
Die Schwalbe fliegt, der Frühling siegt –*L. Hölty*
Die Schwalbe zieht, der Sommer flieht –*Osterwald*
Die schwarze Erde trinket –*Anacreon*
Die Schwermut senkt mit bräunlichem Gefieder –*Ratschky*
Die See war wild im Heulen –*Volkslied*
Die Seele träumt und redet leise –*Siebel*
Die silbernen Glöckchen der Blume –*Matthisson*
Die Söhne des Glückes beneid ich nicht –*Heine*
Die Sommernacht hat mir's angethan –*Scheffel*
Die Sommernacht ist sanft und milde –*Evers*
Die Sonn' ist hin, wie Lust der Minn' –*Roquette*
Die Sonne kam, im reinsten Glanze –*Köstlin*
Die Sonne kommt! Ein Prachterscheinen! –*Goethe*
Die Sonne leuchtet, der Frühling bläht –*Anonymous*
Die Sonne sah die Erde an –*Anonymous*
Die Sonne sank, der Abend naht –*Hoffmann von Fallersleben*
Die Sonne sank, die Möve zieht nicht mehr –*Felix*
Die Sonne sank, ich wartete lange –*Holz*
Die Sonne sank. Noch schimmert –*K. Henckell*
Die Sonne scheidet –*Bethge*
Die Sonne scheint nicht mehr –*Volkslied*
Die Sonne sengt und dörrt das Land –*Eigenbrodt*
Die Sonne sinkt in's tiefe Meer –*Rochlitz*
Die Sonne sinkt. Jählings schwebt –*Christen*
Die Sonne sinkt, o könnt' ich –*Spaun*
Die Sonne steigt, die Sonne sinkt –*Matthisson*
Die Sonne strahlt auf Wald und Feld –*Freudenberg*
Die Spindel dreht sich auf und ab –*Poeschl*
Die Stachelfrucht hat sich geöffnet –*Busta*
Die Stadt ist nach den Engeln genannt –*Brecht*
Die Steine feinden Fenster grinst Verrat –*Stramm*
Die Sterne flimmern und prangen –*Osterwald*
Die Sterne sah ich am Himmel stehn –*Hepp*
Die Sterne schau'n in stiller Nacht –*Schlippenbach*
Die Sterne sind so hell –*Evers*
Die Sterne tönen ewig hohe Weisen –*Cornelius*
Die stille Lotusblume steigt –*Geibel*
Die stille Nacht heisst –*Rochlitz*
Die stille Nacht umdunkelt –*Reissig*
Die stille Wasserrose steigt –*Geibel*
Die stillen Stunden sind es –*Morgenstern*
Die Straßen, die ich gehe –*Kerner*
Die Ströme zieh'n zum fernen Meer –*Leuthold*
Die Stunde sei gesegnet in Zeit und Ewigkeit –*Scherer*
Die Stunde sei gesegnet, wo ich dir bin begegnet –*Rückert*
Die Stunden eilen — Mitternacht –*Hesse*
Die süsse Dirn' von Inverness –*Burns*
Die süsse Rede hallet noch –*Lasker*
Die Tage rinnen leise hin –*Ritter*
Die tausend Grüsse, die wir dir senden –*Rückert*
Die Todten haben Einen in ihrer Einsamkeit –*Hamerling*
Die Totenglocke tönte mir –*Uhland*
Die Treppe hinunter gesprungen –*Gruppe*
Die Trommel gerühret! –*Goethe*
Die Trommeln und Pfeifen –*Hoffmann von Fallersleben*
Die Vaterstadt, wie find ich sie doch? –*Brecht*
Die Vögel flieh'n geschwind –*Lenau*
Die Vögel im Gesträuch –*Hesse*
Die Vöglein, die so fröhlich sangen –*Eichendorff*

Die Wasserlilie einsam träumet *–Hoffmann von Fallersleben*
Die Wasserlilie kichert leis' *–A. Kaufmann*
Die Wege sind fremd und die Finsternis dicht *–Busta*
Die Weiden lassen matt die Zweige hangen *–Ullrich*
Die Weise guter Zecher ist *–F. Bodenstedt*
Die weiten Wiesen schweigen *–Hausmann*
Die Wellen blinken und fließen dahin *–Heine*
Die Wellen tragen vom Lande fort *–Swinburne*
Die Welt ist schlafen gangen *–Bernstein*
Die Welt ruht still im Hafen *–Eichendorff*
Die Welt verstummt, dein Blut erklingt *–Dehmel*
Die Welt wär' ein Sumpf, faul und matt *–Mörike*
Die Welt weiss deinen Namen nicht *–Träger*
Die Winde sausen am Tannenhang *–E. Schulze*
Die Wipfel säuseln Abendruh' *–Leo*
Die wir dem Licht in Liebe dienen *–R. Goering*
Die Wogen am Gestade schwellen *–Schober*
Die Wohllust in den Maien *–Volkslied*
Die Wolken waren fortgezogen *–Lenau*
Die Wolken ziehen schwarz und hoch *–Dingelstedt*
Die Wolken ziehen so silbern *–Rasmus*
Die Wolken zieh'n vorüber *–F. Förster*
Die Wollust in den Maien *–Volkslied*
Die Wunde brennt, die bleichen Lippen beben *–Körner*
Die Zeit geht nicht, sie stehet still *–Keller*
Die Zeit ist ein Lied *–Ingrisch*
Die Zigeunernonne. Schweigsamkeit *–García Lorca*
Die zwei blauen Augen von meinem Schatz *–Mahler*
Dies aber kann mein Sehnen nimmer fassen *–Ronsperger*
Dies Augenpaar von dunklem Glanz betaut *–Mongré*
Dies eine kann mein Sehnen nimmer fassen *–Ronsperger*
Dies eine möcht' ich gerne wissen *–A. Wolf*
Dies ist ein Herbsttag, wie ich keinen sah! *–Hebbel*
Dies ist ein lied für dich allein *–George*
Dies zu deuten bin erbötig! *–Goethe*
Diese, die noch eben atemlos flohen *–Rilke*
Diese Federn, weiß' und schwarze *–Goethe*
Diese Gondel vergleich' ich *–Goethe*
Diese Rose pflück' ich hier *–Lenau*
Diese Rose von heimlichen Küssen schwer *–Morgenstern*
Diese Stadt hat mich belehrt *–Brecht*
Diese Wolken in den Höhen *–Jeitteles*
Dieser Tag verglüht nun auch *–Fulda*
Dinge gehen vor im Mond *–Morgenstern*
Dioskuren, Zwillingssterne *–J. Mayrhofer*
Dir angetrauet am Altare, o Vaterland *–Mörike*
Dir auch wurde Sehnsucht *–Anacreon*
Dir, kleines Bethlehem, erklang *–Anonymous*
Dir, Mädchen, schlägt mit leisem Beben *–Körner*
Dir nah ich mich *–Anonymous*
Dir stets getreu, getreu mit ganzer Seele *–Anonymous*
Dir zu eröffnen mein Herz verlangt mich *–Goethe*
Dirnen und Burschen hört' ich *–Claude McKay*
Dirnlein kommt vom Maientanz *–Baumbach*
Doch der Herr, er leitet die Irrenden recht *–Anonymous*
Doch hatte niemals tiefre Macht dein Blick *–Dehmel*
Doch vor dem Apostel Thomas *–Rilke*
Don Fadrique bringt ein Ständchen *–C. F. Meyer*
Don Gayseros, Don Gayseros *–La Motte Fouqué*
Dornröschen schlägt zum erstenmal *–Osterwald*
Dort am grünen Hügel glänzen *–J. Müller*
Dort an der Kirchhofmauer *–Mörike*
Dort auf dem hohen Felsen sang *–F. R. Hermann*
Dort bläht ein Schiff die Segel *–Hebbel*
Dort blinket durch Weiden *–Leitner*
Dort hoch auf jenem Berge *–Wunderhorn*
Dort im Thal hör ich verhallen *–Cäcilie von W.*
Dort in den Weiden steht ein Haus *–Volkslied*
Dort ist ihr Grab *–K. A. Engelhardt*
Dort oben am Berg in dem hohen Haus! *–Anon., Wunderhorn*
Dort oben auf dem Berge *–Anon., Wunderhorn*
Dort raget ein Berg aus den Wolken hehr *–Schober*
Dort unten in der Mühle saß ich *–Kerner*
Dort unter'm Lindenbaume *–Osterwald*
Dort werd' ich das im Licht erkennen *–the Bible*
Dort, wo der Morgenstern hergeht *–Rückert*
Dort, wo in reine Lüfte *–Pichler*
Dorthin will ich; und ich traue *–Nietzsche*
Drauss ist alles so prächtig *–F. Richter*
Draussen blinket in silbernem Schein *–Hoffmann von Fallersleben*
Draußen im weiten Krieg *–Morgenstern*
Draußen im Winde *–B. Huber*
Draussen in der weiten Nacht *–J. Seidl*
Draußen weht es bitterkalt *–Boelitz*
Draussen wirbeln viel Blätter im Schein *–C. Hauptmann*
Drei bunte Kühe in guter Ruh *–Falke*
Drei Kön'ge wandern aus Morgenland *–Cornelius*
Drei Masken sah ich am Himmel stehn *–Kerr*
Drei Reiter nach verlorner Schlacht *–Lenau*

Drei Rosen gab sie mir *–Schönaich-Carolath*
Drei Rosen hielt ich in Händen *–Buri*
Drei Seelen hab' ich offenbar *–Lenau*
Drei Sonnen sah ich am Himmel stehn *–Wilhelm Müller*
Drei süsse kleine Dirnen *–K. Freiligrath*
Drei Tage Regen fort und fort *–Mörike*
Drei Zigeuner fand ich einmal *–Lenau*
Dreifach ist der Schritt der Zeit *–Schiller*
Drinnen im Saal eine Geige sang *–Morgenstern*
Droben schmettert ein greller Stein *–Stramm*
Droben stehet die Kapelle *–Uhland*
Dröhnende Hämmer in rußiger Hand *–Boelitz*
Drüben geht die Sonne scheiden *–Lenau*
Drüben hinterm Dorfe steht ein Leiermann *–Wilhelm Müller*
Drüben überm Berge streut sein Licht *–Hesse*
Drum sollst du dulden, Mensch *–Dehmel*
Drunten auf der Gassen stand ich *–Heyse*
Drunten im Unterland *–Volkslied*
Du altes schlafbefang'nes Nest *–Boettcher*
Du arme, arme Kerze giebst *–Chamisso*
Du arme, kleine Nachtigall *–P. Kaufmann*
Du armes Herz, was wünschest du? *–Anonymous*
Du Bächlein silberhell und klar *–Goethe*
Du Baum an meinem Fenster *–Haber*
Du bist betroffen, daß in deinen Händen *–E. Foerster*
Du bist der Garten, wo meine Hände *–Wildgans*
Du bist der schimmernd Edelstein *–Bittner*
Du bist die Herrlichste von Allen *–Dahn*
Du bist die Ruh, der Friede mild *–Rückert*
Du bist ein Kind und sollst es ewig bleiben *–Ziel*
Du bist gestorben und weisst es nicht *–Heine*
Du bist glücklich, o Cicade *–Anacreon*
Du bist im Strahlenkleide die Sonne *–Kauffer*
Du bist ja ein Hamster *–Morgenstern*
Du bist mein Auge! *–Dehmel*
Du bist, mein fernes Tal, verzaubert *–Hesse*
Du bist mein, ich bin dein *–Tegernsee*
Du bist mein Land *–Morgenstern*
Du bist mein Schicksal, das ich wild begehre *–Faktor*
Du bist mir gut! Es hat ein heimlich Singen *–Boelitz*
Du bist Orplid, mein Land! *–Mörike*
Du bist so reich als du tränenreich bist *–Kuckuck*
Du bist vom Schlaf erstanden *–Kerner*
Du bist wie eine Blume *–Heine*
Du bist wie eine Julinacht *–Bittner*
Du bist's, dem Ruhm und Ehre gebühret *–Gellert*
Du blickst herab und scheinst *–M. P. Engelhard*
Du brachst sie nun, die kalte Rinde *–Schober*
Du brachtest mir deiner Seele Trank *–Braungart*
Du, dem kein Epigramm gefällt *–Lessing*
Du denkst mit einem Fädchen mich zu fangen *–Heyse*
Du, der die Menschheit stolz und kühn *–Glücklich*
Du, der Du bist der Geister Hort *–Redwitz*
Du, der du keine Gnade kennst *–Werfel*
Du, der ewig um mich trauert *–F. W. Gotter*
Du, der ich's nicht sage *–Rilke*
Du, deren Kunst die Todten ruft *–Byron*
Du, des Erbarmens Feind, grausamer Tod *–Dante*
Du Diebin mit der Rosenwange *–Lessing*
Du Dienerl, du netts *–Wunderhorn*
Du dunkle Sehnsucht meiner Tage *–W. Hartlieb*
Du dunkler Frühlingsgarten *–Morgenstern*
Du ewig Wandelbare, sieh *–G. H. Goering*
Du ewigkalter Himmel *–Braungart*
Du Färberssohn vom Lech *–Brecht*
Du feuchter Frühlingsabend *–Geibel*
Du fragst mich, du mein blondes Lieb *–Geibel*
Du frag'st mich, Mädchen *–Schack*
Du fragst mich täglich: "Liebchen" *–Unidentified*
Du Frühlingsbote, laue Luft *–Hoschek*
Du gabst mir deine Kette *–Morgenstern*
Du gabst mir immer wieder dein Herz *–"Klabund"*
Du gabst mir längst dein schönes Herz *–"Amalia"*
Du gefällst mir so wohl, mein liebes Kind *–Goethe*
Du gehst und kommst dir aus dem Sinn *–Ingrisch*
Du, gib Ruh', ohne dich, ohne dich *–Boysen*
Du giebst die Freude *–"Dilia Helena"*
Du gleichst dem klaren blauen See *–Kunde*
Du Grabesrose wurzelst wohl *–"Anastasius Grün"*
Du grollest und schmollest *–Unidentified*
Du grüne Rast im Haine *–Osterwald*
Du haderst wohl zuweilen *–Albrecht Goes*
Du hältst uns, Frau, die heiligste der Flammen! *–Bittner*
Du hast Diamanten und Perlen *–Heine*
Du hast es mir vorgesagt *–Busta*
Du hast in meinem Herzen *–Falke*
Du hast mich verlassen Jamie! *–Burns*
Du hast uns oft im Traum gesehen *–Goethe*
Du hattest einen Glanz auf deiner Stirn *–Dehmel*
Du heilest den und tröstest jenen *–Mörike*
Du heilig, glühend Abendroth! *–A. Schreiber*
Du herrlich Glas, nun stehst du leer *–Kerner*
Du holde Kunst, in wieviel grauen Stunden *–Schober*
Du holder Lenz, du Blüthenduft *–Kern*

Du in der Schönheit strahlendem Schein *–Byron*
Du junge, schöne Bleicherin *–Liliencron*
Du junges Grün, du frisches Gras *–Kerner*
Du kamst, du gingst mit leiser Spur *–Uhland*
Du kannst dich zurückhalten *–Kafka*
Du kehrst mir den Rücken *–Pfau*
Du Kindlein weich, im Erdenreich *–C. Hauptmann*
Du klagst, daß bange Wehmut *–Lenau*
Du kleine Biene, verfolg' mich nicht *–Kuh*
Du Kleine bist so lieb und hold *–Pfau*
Du kleine grünumwachs'ne Quelle *–M. Claudius*
Du kleiner Kasten, den ich flüchtend trug *–Brecht*
Du kleiner Mensch im Bettlein klein *–Bittner*
Du kleines blitzendes Sternelein *–Roquette*
Du kömmst vom Kloster Walsingham *–Haug*
Du lehnest wider eine silberweide *–George*
Du, leicht und schön, aus Gottes Traum geboren *–Weinheber*
Du liebe, liebe Sonne, bescheine mich *–H. Claudius*
Du liebe, treue Laute *–Eichendorff*
Du lieber, frommer, heil'ger Christ *–E. M. Arndt*
Du lieber Gott im Himmel du *–Anonymous*
Du liebes Auge, willst dich tauchen *–Roquette*
Du liebes, holdes, himmelsüsses Wesen *–Streckfuss*
Du lieblicher Stern *–Hoffmann von Fallersleben*
Du liebst mich nicht *–Heine*
Du machst mich allein *–Rilke*
Du mein einzig Licht *–Volkslied*
Du, mein Heil, mein Leben *–G. A. Bürger*
Du meine heilige Einsamkeit *–Rilke*
Du meine Seele, du mein Herz *–Rückert*
Du meiner Seele schönster Traum! *–Cornelius*
Du meines Herzens Krönelein *–Dahn*
Du milchjunger Knabe *–Keller*
Du milder, Du schöner, Du herrlicher Geist *–Lecher*
Du Mond, i hätt a Bitt' an di *–Volkslied*
Du mußt nicht meinen *–Dehmel*
Du nächtig todeskranker Mond *–Giraud*
Du nennst mich armes Mädchen *–Kulmann*
Du nicht mehr erhoffter Palmschatten *–Busta*
Du nur bist, du liebes Mädchen *–Petőfi*
Du prophet'scher Vogel du *–Goethe*
Du Rabe, sagte ich, du alter Unglücksrabe *–Kafka*
Du reine Frau aus Licht und Elfenbein *–Kaltneker*
Du Ring an meinem Finger *–Chamisso*
Du ringst, o Mensch! vergebens *–Anonymous*
Du rote Rose, die du in schimmernder Vase *–Leen*
Du sagst, mein liebes Mütterlein *–Enslin*
Du sagst mir, dass ich keine Fürstin sei *–Heyse*
Du sagst,ich hätte die Nachbarn geweckt *–Meyer-Helmund*
Du sagtest, Freund, an diesen Ort *–F. A. Kleinschmidt*
Du sagtest mir es, Mutter *–J. Seidl*
Du sahst durch meine Seele in die Welt *–Dehmel*
Du sahst mich schwelgen oft im Tonregister *–Leuthold*
Du schläfst, so will ich leise flehen *–Anonymous*
Du schläfst, und sachte neig' ich mich *–Falke*
Du schönes Fischermädchen *–Heine*
Du Schrecklicher, du Schrecklicher *–Uz*
Du schweigst und duldest *–Hölderlin*
Du Schwert an meiner Linken *–Körner*
Du siehst mich an *–Hoffmann von Fallersleben*
Du siehst mich, Königin, zurück *–Goethe*
Du siehst mich nun schon drei Tage heut *–Anonymous*
Du, silbernes Mondenlicht *–Gomoll*
Du Sommerabend! Heilig, goldnes Licht! *–Weigand*
Du sprichst, daß ich mich täuschte *–Platen*
Du staunest, o Mensch *–F. Schlegel*
Du tatest mir die Tür auf *–Dehmel*
Du Thurm! zu meinem Leide ragst du *–J. Mayrhofer*
Du trauter Stern! Warum so fern? *–F. Förster*
Du Trotz des Glaubens! Du behelmtes Haupt! *–Zwehl*
Du trüber Nebel, hüllest mir *–Lenau*
Du trüber Tag mit deinen stillen *–Morgenstern*
Du Unruh' meiner Seelen *–Anonymous*
Du Urquell aller Güte *–La Motte Fouqué*
Du verklagest das Weib *–Goethe*
Du verstörst uns nicht, o Nacht! *–Uz*
Du wähnst mich fromm *–Sudermann*
Du warst in dieser götterlosen Zeit *–Huch*
Du warest mir ein täglich Wanderziel *–C. F. Meyer*
Du warst ja meine einzge Blume *–Petőfi*
Du warst mir ein gar trauter, lieber *–Lenau*
Du weiche Nacht, o komm mich zu umfangen *–Wertheimer*
Du weißt, wir bleiben einsam *–Wertheimer*
Du willst, ich soll ein Lied dir geben *–Warburg*
Du wirst im Ehstand viel erfahren *–Mozart*
Du wirst nicht weinen *–Dehmel*
Du Wolke, du Letzte des Sturms *–Pushkin*
Du Wunder, das der Herr uns gab *–Koschnick*
Du wunderbare Frühlingszeit *–B. Huber*
Du wunderholde Maid, ich bin meinem Leben *–Osterwald*

Du zähltest wohl die Regentropfen –*Wolff*
Dürft' ich einmal dies Dach durchbrechen! –*Trinius*
Düster brennt und trüb' die Flamme –*Lingg*
Düster liegt die Nacht umher –*Unidentified*
Düst're Harmonieen hör' ich klingen –*Körner*
Duften nicht die Laubengänge –*Platen*
Duftet die Lindenblüth –*Unidentified*
Duft'ge Mispelblume, zartes Blüthenmeer –*Marzials*
Duftreich ist die Erde –*Vrchlický*
Duld' es still, wenn von den Zweigen –*Jacobowski*
Dulde, gedulde dich fein! –*Heyse*
Dunkel rauscht des Stromes Welle –*A. Schreiber*
Dunkel sind nun alle Gassen –*Hoffmann von Fallersleben*
Dunkel war der Zweig –*H. Claudius*
Dunkel, wie dunkel in Wald und in Feld! –*Wenzig*
Dunkelnd über den See –*Lingg*
Dunkle Giebel, hohe Fenster –*Eichendorff*
Dunkler Lichtglanz, blinder Blick –*Geibel*
Dunkler Odem im grünen Gezweig –*Trakl*
Durch allen Schall und Klang –*Goethe*
Durch alte Marmorhallen –*Zwehl*
Durch Bäume dringt ein leiser Ton –*Keller*
Durch den Hain mit bangem Stoße –*Lenau*
Durch den Wald, den dunkeln –*Lenau*
Durch den Wald im Mondenscheine –*Heine*
Durch den Wald mit raschen Schritten –*C. Brentano*
Durch den Wald, wie schimmert –*R. Reinick*
Durch die abendlichen Gärten –*Schilling*
Durch die bunten Rosenhecken –*Tieck*
Durch die Freundschaft fest verbunden –*J. C. Kugler*
Durch die froh erschrockene Welt –*Telmann*
Durch die Glut, durch die Öde –*Cornelius*
Durch die Lande auf und ab –*Morgenstern*
Durch die Straßen von Granada –*V. A. Huber*
Durch die Straßen von Sevilla –*García Lorca*
Durch die Tannen und die Linden spinnt –*Neun****
Durch die Wälder streif' ich munter –*Sallet*
Durch eine ganze Nacht sich nah zu sein –*Baumberg*
Durch Einsamkeiten, durch waldwild' Geheg –*Wildgans*
Durch Feld und Buchenhallen –*Eichendorff*
Durch Feld und Wald zu schweifen –*Goethe*
Durch Fichten am Hügel –*Matthisson*
Durch hohe Tannen träufelt schon –*Zwehl*
Durch irr' ich Länder noch so fern –*Burns*
Durch Nacht zum Licht! –*Kosegarten*
Durch säuselnde Bäume im Mondenschein –*Osterwald*
Durch Schneegestöber und eisigen Wind –*Marggraff*
Durch schöne Augen hab' ich –*Rückert*
Durch schwankende Wipfel –*Eichendorff*
Durchs Schlüsselloch einkehrt –*Niklos*
Durch's Wiesethal gang i jetzt na –*Volkslied*
Durstig sind wir, lieber Wirt –*Hafis*

E bissele Lieb' und e bissele Treu' –*Volkslied*
Ebenes Paradefeld Kasper in der Mitte –*Colly*
Eh' die Sonne früh aufersteht –*Werner*
Eh' wir uns trennen konnten –*Dehmel*
Eh' wir weiter gehen –*F. Lorenz*
Ehre sei der Hocherhab'nen –*Klopstock*
Ehre sei Gott in der Höhe! –*Anonymous*
Ehre sei Gott in der Höhe! Ehre sei Gott! –*Suck*
Ei, das tanzt, das lärmt und trinket! –*Mickiewicz*
Ei, daß ich doch Potz Velten –*Anonymous*
Ei! Ei! Wie scheint der Mond so hell –*Wunderhorn*
Ei! kennt ihr noch das alte Lied –*Heine*
Ei Mühle, liebe Mühle, wie schaust –*Horn*
Ei, schmollte mein Vater nicht –*Wenzig*
Ei Veilchen, liebes Veilchen –*A. Schults*
Ei, was blüht so heimlich –*Hoffmann von Fallersleben*
Ei, wenn ich doch ein Maler wär' –*Anonymous*
Ei wie langsam kommt der Schneck –*Güll*
Eia, husch, husch, im Fliederbusch –*Zacharias*
"Eia popeia," das ist ein altes Lied –*R. Reinick*
Eia, wie flattert der Kranz –*Rückert*
Eide, so die Liebe schwur –*Heyse*
Eile auf der Morgenröthe Flügeln –*Edward*
Eilende Wellen, spielend im Licht –*Köstlin*
Eilt ihr Schäfer aus den Gründen –*C. M. Ziegler*
Ein Adler saß am Felsenbogen –*Eichendorff*
Ein Alphorn hör' ich schallen –*Kerner*
Ein armer Teufel ist der Schuft –*Keller*
Ein armes Mädchen! vergebt, vergebet! –*Goethe*
Ein Bauernknabe liegt im Wald –*Morgenstern*
Ein betrogen Mägdlein irrt im Walde –*C. F. Meyer*
Ein Bettelmann, schon lange blind –*Percy*
Ein blauer Sommer glanz- und glutenschwer –*Busse*
Ein blendendes Spitzchen –*C. F. Meyer*
Ein Blick von deinen Augen in die meinen –*Goethe*
Ein blondiges Mägdelein, rosig und zart –*Leon*
Ein Blumenglöckchen vom Boden hervor –*Goethe*
Ein Brünnlein im Felde –*Ritter*
Ein Bursch' und Mägdlein –*Volkslied*
Ein Drängen ist in meinem Herzen –*Zweig*
Ein dunkeler Schacht ist Liebe –*Daumer*

Ein Echo kenn' ich, ist weit von hier –*Lehr*
Ein einfaches lichtes Kleid –*Kryzanowski*
Ein Engel zog durch Flur und Haus –*Lutze*
Ein Fels ragt in den See hinein –*Stieler*
Ein feuriges Männlein reit' über die Welt –*Petzold*
Ein Fichtenbaum steht einsam –*Heine*
Ein finstrer Esel sprach einmal –*Morgenstern*
Ein Fräulein klagt' im finstern Thurm –*Matthisson*
Ein Fräulein schaut vom hohen Thurm –*Kenner*
Ein frommer Knecht war Fridolin –*Schiller*
Ein frommer Landmann in der Kirche saß –*Knapp*
Ein Gärtchen und ein Häuschen drin –*Anonymous*
Ein Gems auf dem Stein –*Eichendorff*
Ein Goldschmied in der Bude stand –*Uhland*
Ein Gott, ein wahrer Gott ist nur –*Iffland*
Ein Gras vom Felsen, eine Blume –*C. Hauptmann*
Ein Greis trat lächelnd mir entgegen –*Lenau*
Ein grosses deutsches Volk sind wir –*Friedelberg*
Ein grünes Spinnchen gaukelte –*Cornelius*
Ein guter Ruf ist wie ein wohnlich Haus –*Leuthold*
Ein Häuptling ritt geehrt im Land –*Keller*
Ein Hecht, vom heiligen Anton bekehrt –*Morgenstern*
Ein heilig Säuseln und ein Gesangeston –*L. Hölty*
Ein Himmelreich dein Auge ist *"Dilia Helena"*
Ein Irrsal kam in die Mondscheingärten –*Mörike*
Ein Jäger aus Kurpfalz –*Volkslied*
Ein Jeder hat zu diesem Feste –*Heine*
Ein jeder leide –*Bollmann, Boysen*
Ein jedes Band –*Platen*
Ein Jüngling auf dem Hügel –*Hüttenbrenner*
Ein Jüngling liebt ein Mädchen –*Heine*
Ein jugendlicher Maienschwung –*Schiller*
Ein junger Bursch durchs Kornfeld ging –*Shakespeare*
Ein junges Glöcklein klagte –*Spitteler*
Ein Kind an Mutterbrust –*Kotzebue*
Ein Kind ist uns geboren! –*Kannegiesser*
Ein Kind sagte: "Was ist das Gras?" –*Whitman*
Ein kleine Weil, da ohn' Gefähr –*Weckherlin*
Ein kleiner, hübscher Vogel –*Daumer*
Ein kleiner Hund mit Namen Fips –*Morgenstern*
Ein kleines Haus, von Nußgesträuch –*Anonymous*
Ein Klippeneiland liegt im Meer –*F. Kugler*
Ein König einst gefangen sass –*Castelli*
Ein Körnchen Ambra lasse ich gelten –*Jünger*
Ein Kränzlein sollst du tragen –*Goldtammer*
Ein kühler Hauch. Die Linde träumt –*Falke*
Ein Leben war's im Ährenfeld –*Hoffmann von Fallersleben*
Ein leises, fernes Rauschen –*Wolff*
Ein Licht im Traum hat mich besucht –*Rückert*
Ein Licht tanzt freundlich –*Wilhelm Müller*
Ein Liebchen hatt' ich –*Rückert*
Ein Liedchen vom Lieben –*Weppen*
Ein linder Südhauch sprengt die Riegel –*Boelitz*
Ein lockerer Zeisig, der bin ich –*G. Lang*
Ein Mädchen, das auf Ehre hielt –*C. Weisse*
"Ein Mädchen!" "Ein Mädchen!" –*Ritter*
Ein Mädchen ist's, das früh und spät –*Anonymous*
Ein Mägdlein an des Felsen Rand –*Anonymous*
Ein Mägdlein saß am Meeresstrand –*"Eduard Ferrand"*
Ein Mahl für uns und ein Licht für dich –*Weinheber*
Ein Maler vor dem Zaune sass, aha! –*R. Reinick*
Ein Meister bin ich worden –*Keller*
Ein Menschlein ward geboren –*H. Claudius*
Ein Mühlrad hör' ich gehen –*Vogl*
Ein Müller mahlte Tag und Nacht –*Boelitz*
Ein Münich steht in seiner Zell' –*Leitner*
Ein Musikus wollt fröhlich sein –*Anonymous*
Ein neues Lied! –*Herder*
Ein Obdach gegen Sturm und Regen –*Rückert*
Ein Rabe sass auf einem Meilenstein –*Morgenstern*
Ein Räppchen zum Reiten –*Anonymous*
Ein recht Gemüth springt mit den Nachtigallen –*A. v. Arnim*
Ein Reif ist gefallen ganz über Nacht –*Hepp*
Ein Reiter durch das Bergthal zieht –*Heine*
Ein Reiter muß haben ein Rößlein –*Boelitz*
Ein Röslein zog ich mir –*Hoffmann von Fallersleben*
Ein Rößlein möcht' ich haben –*Eigenbrodt*
Ein Ruder liegt auf dem Dach –*Brecht*
Ein Schäfer sass im Grünen –*La Motte Fouqué*
Ein scheckiges Pferd –*Hoffmann von Fallersleben*
Ein Schifflein ziehet leise –*Uhland*
Ein schlafend Kind! o still, o still! –*Lenau*
Ein Schmeichelkätzchen nenn' ich mein –*Huggenberger*
Ein Schmetterling fliegt über mir –*Morgenstern*
Ein schöner Stern geht auf in meiner Nacht –*Heine*
Ein schwarzer Ritter, Herrin –*Schaukal*
Ein schwarzes Vögelein fliegt über die Welt –*Morgenstern*
Ein Schwert, das schneidet, ein Falke –*Wolff*
Ein sehnend Streben theilt mir das Herz –*F. Schlegel*
Ein solcher ist mein Freund –*Hafis*

Ein Spielmann auf seiner Geige strich *–Schaukal*
Ein Spielmann, der muss reisen *–Monsterberg-Muenckenau*
Ein Spielmann zog des Wegs einher *–Stieler*
Ein Ständchen Euch zu bringen kam ich her *–Heyse*
Ein starker Geist hält seine weiße Hand *–Hesse*
Ein Stern der Lieb' am Himmelslauf *–Anonymous*
Ein Sternlein fiel vom Himmel her *–Marggraff*
Ein Sternlein funkelt am Himmelszelt *–H. Humperdinck*
Ein steter Kampf ist unser Leben *–Müchler*
Ein stilles Wiesental von Schwalben *–Schanderl*
Ein Sträusschen am Hute *–Volkslied*
Ein Stündlein sind sie beisammen gewes't *–Heyse*
Ein Tännlein grünet wo, wer weiss *–Mörike*
Ein Täubchen bringt mir täglich Grüsse *–Stieglitz*
Ein Täubchen, kirr und traut *–Volkslied*
Ein Traum, ein Traum ist unser Leben *–Herder*
Ein unbezwingbar dunkler Hang *–Leuthold*
Ein Vater starb von des Sohnes Hand *–Pfeffel*
Ein Veilchen auf der Wiese stand *–Goethe*
Ein Veilchen blüht im Thale *–Kind*
Ein Vögelein fliegt über den Rhein *–Köstlin*
Ein Vöglein sang die ganze Nacht *–Rodenberg*
Ein Vöglein singt im Wald *–Ritter*
Ein Vöglein singt sein erstes Lied *–C. Lange*
Ein Wändeviereck, blaß, vergilbt *–Hesse*
Ein Wanderbursch, mit dem Stab *–Vogl*
Ein Wand'rer in der Gassen *–Paquet*
Ein Wand'rer läßt sein helles Lied *–Lenau*
Ein Wasser in Oberpommern *–Giesebrecht*
Ein Weg durch Korn *–Schönaich-Carolath*
Ein Weib zu suchen! Wozu *–Kryzanowski*
Ein wenig Raum auf grüner Flur *–Steigentesch*
Ein Wiesel sass auf einem Kiesel *–Morgenstern*
Ein Wolkengebirg' umfließt die Sonne *–Lingg*
Ein Wort in den Winden *–Johnson*
Ein wunderbares Rätselreich die Nacht *–C. Hauptmann*
Ein Wunderland ist oben aufgeschlagen *–Eichendorff*
Eine blasse Wäscherin *–Giraud*
Eine blaue Schürze hast du mir gegeben *–Wilhelm Müller*
Eine Blume weiss ich *–C. F. Scherenberg*
Eine Brücke kenn' ich, Liebchen *–Anonymous*
Eine einzige Nacht an deinem Herzen! *–Goethe*
Eine fromme Magd von gutem Stand *–Ringwald*
Eine Fürstin ist die Schönheit *–Hafis*
Eine Glocke läutet im Grund fernab *–Hesse*
Eine gute, gute Nacht pflegst du mir zu sagen *–Daumer*
Eine Hütte und ein Stück Wald *–Morgenstern*
Eine kleine Geige möcht' ich haben *–Hoffmann von Fallersleben*
Eine Krähe war mit mir *–Wilhelm Müller*
Eine Liebe kenn' ich, die ist treu *–Mörike*
Eine Melodie singt mein Herz *–Huch*
Eine Mühle seh' ich blinken aus *–Wilhelm Müller*
Eine Pappel steht am Karlsplatz *–Brecht*
Eine rote Sonne liegt *–Hesse*
Eine Schale blühender Rosen *–Itzerott*
Eine Schale des Stroms *–L. Hölty*
Eine starke schwarze Barke *–Heine*
Eine stille Melodie, voll von süßer Lust *–T. Schäfer*
Eine stille Zelle an blauer Welle *–Stieler*
Eine Wiese voller Margeriten *–Bierbaum*
Eine wilde Lokomotive schrie in der Nacht *–Eidlitz*
Einen Brief soll ich schreiben *–Storm*
Einen Engel mit gold'nen Schwingen *–Volkslied*
Einen Haushalt klein und fein *–Rückert*
Einen kenn ich, wir lieben ihn nicht *–C. Brentano*
Einen Ring von Golde steckt' ich an die Hand *–Aldrich*
Einen schlimmen Weg ging gestern ich *–Burns*
Einen vergänglichen Tag lebt' ich *–Hölderlin*
Einen weissen Fleck des hellen Mondes *–Giraud*
Eines Dichters Traumgerank *–Hesse*
Eines gibt's, darauf ich mich freuen darf *–Morgenstern*
Eines Tags, am Rand der Felder *–Schumacher*
Einförmig ist der Liebe Gram *–Rückert*
Eingehüllt in graue Wolken *–Heine*
Eingeschlafen auf der Lauer *–Eichendorff*
Eingeschneite stille Felder *–Sergel*
Eingewiegt von Meereswellen *–Heine*
Einmal aus seinen Blicken *–Anonymous*
Einmal in einem tiefen Thal *–Wunderhorn*
Einmal in Kindertagen ging *–Hesse*
Einmal Mekka noch zu sehen *–Stieglitz*
Einmal nach einer lustigen Nacht *–Mörike*
Einmal noch will ich die Kirschenblüten *–Ingrisch*
Einmal wichtig gewesen zu sein *–Busta*
Eins, zwei, drei, bicke, backe, hei! *–Wunderhorn*
Eins, zwei, drei, eins, zwei, drei *–Schellenberg*
Einsam bin ich nicht alleine *–P. A. Wolf*
Einsam bin ich nicht, einzeln! *–C. Hauptmann*
Einsam bin ich und alleine *–Pfau*
Einsam! einsam! ja, das bin ich wohl *–Unidentified*

Einsam hinterm letzten Haus –*Rilke*
Einsam? Nein, das bin ich nicht –*"Theodor Hell"*
Einsam wandelt dein Freund –*Matthisson*
Einsamer Garten, öde und leer –*Gerok*
Einsamkeit, du stummer Bronnen –*C. Brentano*
Einst am diesem Tage hat der Storch –*Reinecke*
Einst am schönen Frühlingsmorgen –*Uhland*
Einst aus meinem Grabe –*Hafis*
Einst gibt ein Tag mir alles Glück –*Ronsperger*
Einst gieng ich meinem Mädchen nach –*Goethe*
Einst hat vor deines Vaters Haus –*Pfau*
Einst kam der Bock als Bote –*Kerr*
Einst träumt' ich im Waldgrün –*Hamerling*
Einst warst du meiner Seele –*Heyse*
Einst wohnten süsse Ruh –*Reissig*
Einst wollt ich einen Kranz –*F. Bodenstedt*
Einstmals in einem tiefen Thal –*Wunderhorn*
Einziger Augenblick, in welchem ich lebte! –*Goethe*
Elysium, du Land, wo Friede wird –*Anonymous*
Empfangen und genähret –*M. Claudius*
Endlich hatte Damon sie gefunden –*Hiemer*
Endlich steh'n die Pforten offen –*Kosegarten*
Endlich winkt der Freund der Müden –*Hermes*
Englein hold im Lockengold –*Bocella*
Entfalte des Kelches Pracht –*Busse*
Entfernt von Gram und Sorgen –*Stahl*
Entflammt von Liebesqualen –*Anonymous*
Entflieh' mit mir und sei mein Weib –*Heine*
Entfliehet schnell von mir –*Seida*
Entflieht auf leichten Kähnen –*George*
Entflohn sind wir der Stadt Gedränge –*Mörike*
Entgegen wandeln wir dem Dorf –*C. F. Meyer*
Entzükket dich ein Wunderhauch –*Hafis*
Er, dem ich einst alles war –*Miller*
Er, der Herrlichste von Allen –*Chamisso*
Er fiel den Tod fürs Vaterland –*Kenner*
Er hat mich im Traum geküßt –*Ehlen*
Er ist erstanden, Jesus Christ –*Münter*
Er ist gekommen in Sturm und Regen –*Rückert*
Er ist uns geschieden vom Berg und vom Walde –*Scott*
Er kam in der Frühe wie der Morgenwind –*Roquette*
Er liegt und schläft an meinem Herzen –*M. Claudius*
Er meckert vor sich hin –*Heym*
Er reitet nachts auf einem braunen Roß –*Eichendorff*
Er sagt' mir so viel –*Groth*
Er schläft so süss –*Ottenwalt*
Er sitzt am Weg und klopft die harten Steine –*Evers*
Er wußte nur vom Tod, was alle wissen: –*Rilke*
Erbarm dich, Herr! mein schwaches Herz –*Cronegk*
Erde, die uns dies gebracht –*Morgenstern*
Erde, du meine Mutter, und du mein Vater –*Herder*
Ergehst du dich im Abendlicht –*Uhland*
Erhalt uns den König –*J. W. L. Gleim*
Erhebt das Glas mit froher Hand –*Anonymous*
Erhebt euch, Freunde –*"Klabund"*
Erhöhet die prächtigen Pforten –*K. A. Schmid*
Erinnerungen, Erinnerungen –*Benn*
Erlaube mir, feins Mädchen –*Volkslied*
Ernst ist der Frühling –*Heine*
Ernst ist der Herbst –*Groth*
Ernst ritt der Kaiser –*Hohlfeld*
Erschaffen schon die Erde lag –*Vogl*
Erscheine noch einmal –*Hoffmann von Fallersleben*
Erschlagen war mit dem halben Heer –*Dahn*
Erst sitzt er eine Weile –*Goethe*
Erste Blume, aus Dunkel und Erde wie ich –*Weinheber*
Erste Kirschen hast du mir gebracht –*F. Wolf*
Erstorben ist in meiner Brust –*Heine*
Ertönet, ihr Saiten, in nächtlicher Ruh' –*E. Schulze*
Erträumter einsamer blauer Engel –*Mayröcker*
Ertrage dus, laß schneiden –*Avenarius*
Erwache Friedericke, vertreib die Nacht –*Goethe*
Erwachen aus dem tiefsten traumes-schoosse –*George*
Erwacht in neuer Stärke, begrüss' ich –*Voss*
Erwacht zum neuen Leben –*C. C. Sturm*
Erworben, verdorben! Mein Herz ist schwer –*Siebel*
Erzeugt von heisser Phantasie –*Baumberg*
Es bebet das Gesträuche –*Daumer*
Es bellen die Hunde –*Wilhelm Müller*
Es blasen die blauen Husaren –*Heine*
Es blies ein Jäger wohl in sein Horn –*Wunderhorn*
Es blinken in der Sonne –*H. Claudius*
Es blinkt der Thau in den Gräsern –*Boddien*
Es blühet das Blümchen –*Floto*
Es blüht ein Blümchen irgendwo –*G. A. Bürger*
Es blüht ein Blümlein rosenrot –*Boelitz*
Es blüht ein schönes Blümchen –*Hoffmann von Fallersleben*
Es blüht eine schöne Blume –*Runge*
Es blüht um mich des Abends Stille –*T. Schäfer*
Es brausen der Liebe Wogen –*F. Schumann*
Es brechen im schallenden Reigen –*Klingemann*
Es brennt mir unter beiden Sohlen –*Wilhelm Müller*
Es deuten die Blumen des Herzens Gefühle –*Platner*
Es donnern die Höh'n, es zittert der Steg –*Schiller*

Es donnert über die Pfaffengaß' *–Keller*
Es drängt sich auf den Beeten *–H. Claudius*
Es dunkelt. Friede im Gemach *–Bittner*
Es fährt der Wind gewaltig *–C. F. Meyer*
Es fällt ein Stern herunter *–Heine*
Es färbte sich die Wiese grün *–Novalis*
Es fahren die Schiffer auf schlummernder Bahn *–Anonymous*
Es faßt mich wieder der alte Mut *–Heine*
Es fiel ein Reif in der Frühlingsnacht *–Heine, Volkslied*
Es fing ein Knab' ein Vögelein *–Goethe*
Es flattert um die Quelle *–Goethe*
Es fliegen zwei Schwalben *–Wunderhorn*
Es fliegt manch Vöglein in das Nest *–Geibel*
Es flimmert der Kranz der Sterne *–Hamerling*
Es flog ein bunter Schmetterling *–Anonymous*
Es flog ein Täublein weiße vom Himmel herab *–Volkslied*
Es flog einmal ein munt'res Fliegel *–Busch*
Es flogen drei Schwälbelein *–Zuccalmaglio*
Es floh die Zeit im Wirbelfluge *–Széchényi*
Es flüstern und rauschen die Wogen *–W. Lorenz*
Es flüstert's der Himmel *–Fanshawe*
Es freut sich Alles *–Hoffmann von Fallersleben*
Es führen mich die Wege *–G. Lang*
Es führen über die Erde *–Hesse*
Es fürchte die Götter das Menschengeschlecht! *–Goethe*
Es gehen zur Kirche die Leute *–Rüeger*
Es geht bei gedämpfter Trommel Klang *–Chamisso*
Es geht der Tag zur Neige *–Pfarrius*
Es geht ein alter König *–Vogl*
Es geht ein Wandrer durch die Nacht *–Nietzsche*
Es geht ein Wehen durch den Wald *–Heyse*
Es geht ein Wind von Westen *–Hesse*
Es geht eine dunkle Wolk' herein *–Volkslied*
Es geht, es weht ein Rauch *–Bartsch*
Es geht mit mir zu Ende *–C. F. Meyer*
Es geht wohl anders, als du meinst *–Eichendorff*
Es g'fallt mer nummen eini *–Hebel*
Es gibt ein stilles Königreich *–Busse*
Es gibt so wundervolle Nächte *–Rilke*
Es giebt geheime Schmerzen *–E. Koch*
Es ging die Riesentochter *–Rückert*
Es ging ein Maidlein zarte *–Volkslied*
Es ging ein Mann zur Frühlingszeit *–Jacobi*
Es ging ein Wind durch's weite Land *–Bierbaum*
Es ging sich unsre Fraue *–Volkslied*
Es ging wohl über die Heide *–Uhland*
Es gingen zwei Gespielen gut *–Volkslied*
Es glänzt der Mond nieder *–Volkslied*
Es glänzt der Tulpenflor *–Eichendorff*
Es glänzt im Abendsonnengolde *–Viol*
Es glänzt so schön die sinkende Sonne *–Heine*
Es graut vom Morgenreif *–Mörike*
Es grünet ein Nussbaum vor dem Haus *–Mosen*
Es grünten die Bäume *–Griesinger*
Es haben die liebjungen Mädchen *–Boelitz*
Es haben viel Dichter gesungen *–Eichendorff*
Es hält der blaue Tag für eine Stunde *–Hesse*
Es hält der Ost, der eitle, sich *–Hafis*
Es hat das Herz des Menschen *–"Anastasius Grün"*
Es hat der schimmernde Sonnenstrahl *–Giesebrecht*
Es hat die Mutter mir gesagt *–Geibel*
Es hat die Rose sich beklagt *–F. Bodenstedt*
Es hat die stille Nacht die Welt *–Anonymous*
Es herrscht' ein König irgendwo *–C. F. Meyer*
Es hing der Reif im Lindenbaum *–Groth*
Es ist bestimmt in Gottes Rat *–Feuchtersleben*
Es ist das Glück ein flüchtig Ding *–Geibel*
Es ist der Tag, wo jedes Leid vergessen *–Bodmann*
Es ist doch im April fürwahr *–Mörike*
Es ist doch meine Nachbarin *–Goethe*
Es ist ein Flüstern in der Nacht *–Storm*
Es ist ein halbes Himmelreich *–L. Hölty*
Es ist ein hold Gewimmel *–Wolff-Kassel*
Es ist ein Ring gebogen *–Jacobowski*
Es ist ein Ros entsprungen *–Volkslied*
Es ist ein Schnee gefallen *–Goethe*
Es ist ein Schnee gefallen *–Volkslied*
Es ist ein Schnitter, der heißt Tod *–Volkslied, Wunderhorn*
Es ist ein Schuß gefallen! *–Goethe*
Es ist ein seliges Prangen *–Evers*
Es ist ein stiller Regentag *–Keller*
Es ist immer derselbe Traum *–Hesse*
Es ist in den Wald gesungen *–Heinrich der Schreiber*
Es ist kein Jäger, er hat ein Schuß *–Wunderhorn*
Es ist kein Mäuschen so jung und klein *–Hey*
Es ist kein Tag so streng und heiß *–Hesse*
Es ist kein Thal so wüst und leer *–H. Seidel*
Es ist kommen, es ist kommen *–Wunderhorn*
Es ist mein Herz ein kleines Haus *–Siebel*
Es ist mein Herz verengt, verdorrt *–K. Ziegler*
Es ist mir wie den kleinen Waldvögelein *–Volkslied*
Es ist mitunter, als wären alle Fäden *–Flaischlen*

Es ist Nacht, und mein Herz kommt zu dir –*Morgenstern*
Es ist nicht Selbstsucht und nicht Eitelkeit –*Keller*
Es ist nit lang daß 's g'regnet hat –*Volkslied*
Es ist schon dunkel um mich her –*Löwenstein*
Es ist schon spät, es ist schon kalt –*Eichendorff*
Es ist schon spät, so um die Mitternacht –*Bittner*
Es ist so angenehm, so süss –*Schiller*
Es ist so still. Alles schläft –*Lentrodt*
Es ist so still, als wär' es Schlafenszeit –*Siebel*
Es ist so still geworden –*G. Kinkel*
Es ist so still, so heimlich um mich –*Leitner*
Es ist so süss, zu scherzen –*Geibel*
Es ist zwar sonsten nicht der Brauch –*Mörike*
Es jagt' ein Jäger wohlgemuth –*Wunderhorn*
Es jagt ein Jäger wohlgemut –*Wunderhorn*
Es kam des Assyrers gewaltige Macht –*Byron*
Es kam ein Herr zum Schlößli –*Wunderhorn*
Es kam zu ihr, leis an die Thür –*Herder*
Es kehret der Maien, es blühet die Au' –*Jeitteles*
Es kehrt die dunkle Schwalbe –*Candidus*
Es klagt im Dunklen irgendwo –*Dehmel*
Es klappert die Mühle am rauschenden Bach –*Anschütz*
Es klingt der Lärm der Welt –*Stieler*
Es klingt eine Regel zwar wunderlich –*Kotzebue*
Es klingt in der Luft uralter Sang –*"Max Waldau"*
Es klingt so prächtig, wenn der Dichter –*Goethe*
Es klingt von den Sternen –*Brockhaus*
Es klopft an das Fenster der Lindenbaum –*Leander*
Es kommen Blätter, es kommen Blüten –*Heyse*
Es kommt der Schmerz gegangen –*Morgenstern*
Es lacht der Mai! Der Wald ist frei –*Goethe*
Es lächelt der See, er ladet zum Bade –*Schiller*
Es läuft ein fremdes Kind –*Rückert*
Es lag auf meiner Stirn –*Löper*
Es lauschte das Laub so dunkelgrün –*Klingemann*
Es lebt ein Ries' im Wald –*Morgenstern*
Es lebt ein Schwur in jeder deutschen Brust –*Cornelius*
Es leiht mir wunderbare Stärke –*Morgenstern*
Es leuchtet die Gottheit aus heiligen Blitzen –*Behn*
Es leuchtet meine Liebe in ihrer dunkeln Pracht –*Heine*
Es leuchtet so schön die Sonne –*Haringer*
Es liebt' in Welschland irgendwo –*L. Hölty*
Es liebte einst ein Hase –*Kerr*
Es liegt der heiße Sommer –*Heine*
Es liegt die Welt in Scherben –*Hesse*
Es liegt ein alter Mühlenstein –*Mayr*
Es lockt und säuselt um den Baum –*J.-B. Rousseau*
Es lockte schöne Wärme –*F. Schlegel*
Es löst ein Blatt sich welk und matt –*B. Huber*
Es lohnet mich heute –*Goethe*
Es lohnet mich heute mit doppelter Beute –*Goethe*
Es lokket und zwitschert –*Hermann Gilm*
Es mahnt der Wald, es ruft der Strom –*J. Mayrhofer*
Es muß das Herz an etwas hangen –*Müchler*
Es muß ein Wunderbares sein –*Redwitz*
Es muß was Wunderbares sein –*Redwitz*
Es pfeift der Wind. –*Morgenstern*
Es pflagen einst drei Knaben –*Baumbach*
Es pochet ein Knabe sachte –*Volkslied*
Es pranget ein Garten im westlichen Strahl –*Justi*
Es preisen dich die Glokken –*Michalewski*
Es ragt der alte Elborus –*F. Bodenstedt*
Es ragt in's Meer der Runenstein –*Heine*
Es rauschen die Bäume –*W. Hensel*
Es rauschen die Tannen und Föhren –*Hamerling*
Es rauschen die Winde –*Rellstab*
Es rauschen die Wipfel –*Eichendorff*
Es rauschet das Wasser –*Goethe*
Es rauscht das rote Laub –*Geibel*
Es rauscht der Strom, es weht der Wind –*Mereau*
Es reden und träumen die Menschen viel –*Schiller*
Es redet und träumet –*Kolumban Schnitzer von Meerau*
Es regnet, es regnet, der Kukuk wird nass –*Fröhlich*
Es reit der Herr von Falkenstein –*Uhland*
Es reit ein Herr und auch sein Knecht –*Volkslied*
Es reiten drei Reiter –*Volkslied*
Es reitet schweigend und allein –*Vogl*
Es rieseln die Sekunden –*Bergengruen*
Es rieselt, klar und wehend –*Salis-Seewis*
Es rinnen die Wasser Tag und Nacht –*F. Kugler*
Es ritt ein Reiter wohl durch das Ried –*Volkslied*
Es ritten drei Reiter zum Thore hinaus! –*Wunderhorn*
Es ruht mit ernstem Sinnen –*Rohrscheidt*
Es sagen mir die Weiber –*Anacreon*
Es sang vor langen Jahren –*C. Brentano*
Es sass die Prinzessin –*Björnson*
Es saß ein Salamander –*Lemcke*
Es saß ein schneeweiß Vögelein –*Volkslied*
Es schauen die Blumen alle –*Heine*
Es schauet der Morgen –*Gramberg*
Es schaukeln die Winde –*Ebeling*
Es schaukelt so leise –*Unidentified*
Es schaut zum Bauernhaus –*Thürauf*

Es schaute in die Wogen *–Plönnies*
Es schienen so golden die Sterne *–Eichendorff*
Es schläft ein stiller Garten *–C. Hauptmann*
Es schliesst der dunkle Wald uns ein *–A. Kaufmann*
Es schlug mein Herz, geschwind zu Pferde! *–Goethe*
Es schlug vom Turm die Mitternacht *–Hesse*
Es schmachtet eine Blume *–Rubinstein*
Es schnarcht der alte Müller *–Stieler*
Es schritt wohl über die Heide *–Uhland*
Es schwebt um deine zierliche Hand *–J. Sturm*
Es segeln die Wolken *–Anonymous*
Es sehnt sich das Herz *–Anonymous*
Es sind die schlecht'sten Früchte nicht *–Ambrosius*
Es singt der Schwan am Ufer des Nachts *–Ballestrem*
Es singt ein Vöglein "Witt,witt,witt." *–Conz*
Es singt in tiefem Tone *–Hamsun*
Es sitzt die Zeit im weissen Kleid *–Stoll*
Es sitzt ein Vogel auf dem Leim *–Busch*
Es soll mein Gebet dich tragen *–von Wegerer*
Es spielen leise die Blüthen *–Ebeling*
Es sprach der Geist: Sieh auf! *–C. F. Meyer*
Es sprechen und blicken die Wellen *–H. Hölty*
Es spricht ein Mann *–Michelangelo*
Es sprießen immerfort *–Mayröcker*
Es stand eine Rose im tieftiefen Grund *–Ritter*
Es stand in alten Zeiten *–Uhland*
Es stand vor eines Hauses Tor *–Busch*
Es stehen drei Sterne am Himmel *–Volkslied, Elwert*
Es stehen unbeweglich die Sterne *–Heine*
Es steh'n in unserm Garten *–Chamisso*
Es steht der Sachsenführer *–Vogl*
Es steht ein altes Gemäuer *–Chamisso*
Es steht ein Baum in jenem Tal *–Hoffmann von Fallersleben*
Es steht ein Baum in Odenwald *–Volkslied*
Es steht ein Berg im Feuer *–Eichendorff*
Es steht ein Blümchen an jenem Rain *–Hoffmann von Fallersleben*
Es steht ein goldnes Garbenfeld *–Dehmel*
Es steht ein Kelch in der Kapelle *–Giesebrecht*
Es steht ein Lied in Nacht und Frost *–Hermann Gilm*
Es steht ein Lind in jenem Tal *–Volkslied*
Es steht eine gold'ne Wiege *–"Anastasius Grün"*
Es steht in der Bibel geschrieben *–Hahn-Hahn*
Es steht sein Bild noch immer da *–Anonymous*
Es streckt der Wald *–Müller von Königswinter*
Es stürmet am Abendhimmel *–Neun*
Es stürmt auf der Flur *–Rochlitz*
Es stürzen der Jugend Altäre *–Morgenstern*
Es stunden drei Rosen auf einem Zweig *–Volkslied*
Es sungen drei Engel *–Wunderhorn*
Es taget vor dem Walde *–Volkslied*
Es tanzen Mond und Sterne *–J. Mayrhofer*
Es tanzt ein Butze-Butze-Butzemann *–Wunderhorn*
Es tat den Beiden so weh das Scheiden *–Anonymous*
Es tönet sein Lob Feld und Wald *–Klopstock*
Es tönt des Nöcken Harfenschall *–Kopisch*
Es tönt in meinem Ohren *–Destinn*
Es trabt im Kreis durch die Manege *–F. Wolf*
Es träumen die Wolken *–J. Mayrhofer*
Es träumte mir, ich sei dir teuer *–Daumer*
Es träumte mir von einer weiten Haide *–Heine*
Es trat ein Himmel in mich ein *–Klotz-Burr*
Es treibt der Wind im Winterwalde *–Rilke*
Es treibt fort von Ort zu Ort *–Heine*
Es treibt mich hin, es treibt mich her! *–Heine*
Es tropft auf die Dächer *–B. Huber*
Es wächst ein Blümchen *–K. L. von Münchhausen*
Es wächst ein Kraut im Kühlen *–Wolff*
Es wälzt der Strom die dunklen Wogen *–B. Huber*
Es wären zwei Königskinder *–Volkslied*
Es wallte so silbernen Scheines *–Chamisso*
Es wandelt, was wir schauen *–Eichendorff*
Es wandert eine schöne Sage *–Keller*
Es war, als hätt der Himmel *–Eichendorff*
Es war dort unter dem Lindenbaum *–Unidentified*
Es war ein alter König *–Heine*
Es war ein Bruder Liederlich *–Calderón*
Es war ein Buhle frech genung *–Goethe*
Es war ein fauler Schäfer *–Goethe*
Es war ein Jäger wohl keck und kühn *–Körner*
Es war ein Kind, das wollte nie *–Goethe*
Es war ein Knabe frech genug *–Goethe*
Es war ein König in Thule *–Goethe*
Es war ein König Lobesam *–G. H. Goering*
Es war ein König Milesint *–Mörike*
Es war ein Markgraf überm Rhein *–Volkslied, Wunderhorn*
Es war ein niedlich' Zeiselein *–Blüthgen*
Es war ein Tag im Maien *–Eschelbach*
Es war ein Winterabend *–Werthes*
Es war eine Ratt' im Kellernest *–Goethe*
Es war eine schöne Jüdin *–Volkslied*
Es war eine stolze Jüdin *–Volkslied*
Es war einmal ein Adler *–Brecht*
Es war einmal ein Bock *–Kerr*
Es war einmal ein Elefant *–Brecht*
Es war einmal ein Gärtner *–Miller*

Es war einmal ein Igel –*Brecht*
Es war einmal ein Kind –*Brecht*
Es war einmal ein König –*Goethe*
Es war einmal ein Lattenzaun –*Morgenstern*
Es war einmal ein Mann –*Brecht*
Es war einmal ein Papagei –*Morgenstern*
Es war einmal ein Pferd –*Brecht*
Es war einmal ein Rabe –*Brecht*
Es war einmal ein Schneidergesell –*"Alexis"*
Es war einmal ein Schwein –*Brecht*
Es war einmal ein Zimmergesell –*Volkslied*
Es war einmal eine Kellerassel –*Brecht*
Es war einmal, ihr Leutchen –*Schall*
Es war einmal 'ne Henne fein –*M. Claudius*
Es war im Wonnemonat Mai –*Unidentified*
Es war in des Maien mildem Glanz –*Kerner*
Es war mal eine Wanze –*Kerr*
Es waren einmal drei Reuter gefang'n –*Volkslied*
Es waren einst zwei Brüder –*P. Pfitzner*
Es waren einst glückliche Stunden –*Sprickmann*
Es waren fünf fette Gänse –*K. Freiligrath*
Es waren mal zwei Mäuschen –*Boelitz*
Es waren Ruhm und Weisheit mein –*Byron*
Es wartet ein bleiches Jungfräulein –*Wolff*
Es webte schön Aennchen –*Hoffmann von Fallersleben*
Es wecket meine Liebe –*Leander*
Es wehet kühl und leise –*F. Schlegel*
Es weht der Wind so kühl –*Lenau*
Es weht um mich Narzissenduft –*Schenkendorf*
Es weicht die Nacht, und über'm Hügel –*Gruppe*
Es weiss und räth es doch Keiner –*Eichendorff*
Es werde Licht! So tönete der Ruf Gottes –*Hafis*
Es will kein Baum so wie die Linde blühen! –*Kryzanowski*
Es winkt und neigt sich seltsam –*Petöfi*
Es wird wohl Winter weit und breit –*Anonymous*
Es wohnet ein Fiedler zu Frankfurt am Main –*Volkslied*
Es wohnt ein kleines Vögelein –*Panizza*
Es wollt' die Jungfrau früh aufsteh'n –*Volkslied, Wunderhorn*
Es wollt ein Mädchen brechen gehn –*Volkslied*
Es wollt' ein Mädchen früh aufsteh'n –*Volkslied, Wunderhorn*
Es wollt gut Jäger jagen –*Volkslied*
Es ziehen die Wolken –*Hamerling*
Es ziehet den Pilgrim rastlos fort –*Binder*
Es ziehn die brausenden Wellen –*Heine*
Es zieht das Schiff auf hohen Wogen –*Stieler*
Es zieht sich eine blut'ge Spur –*Fontane*
Es zog ein Jäger in den Wald –*Boelitz*
Es zog eine Hochzeit den Berg entlang –*Eichendorff*
Es zogen drei Bursche wohl über den Rhein –*Uhland*
Es zogen zwei rüst'ge Gesellen –*Eichendorff*
Es zürnt das Meer, es zürnt die Felsenküste –*Heyse*
Euch bedaur' ich, unglücksel'ge Sterne –*Goethe*
Euch Blümlein will ich senden –*A. Schreiber*
Euer Herz erschrecke nicht –*Giesebrecht*
Euern Helfer, euern Sieger –*Giesebrecht*
Eures Sophrons Seele, Freunde –*G. D. Hartmann*
Ewig muntres Spiel der Wogen! –*Eichendorff*
Ewig trägt im Mutterschoße –*Hölderlin*
Eya popeya, so leise, so lind –*Goechhausen*

Fährmann, ahoi! Ahoi! –*Jünger*
Fänd' ich den Schatten –*Lasker-Schüler*
Fahr hin! fahr hin! –*Vogl*
Fahr wohl, o Vöglein, das nun wandern soll –*Rückert*
Fahren wir froh im Nachen –*Cornelius*
Fahret hin, fahret hin, Grillen –*Volkslied*
Fallende Blätter, die Stund' um Stunde –*Wetzler*
Faulheit, endlich muß ich Dir –*Lessing*
Februarschnee, Februarschnee –*Flaischlen*
Feierlich träumt das Gelände –*M. R. Stern*
Feierlicher Glockenklang hallet –*A. Lange*
Feiger Gedanken bängliches Schwanken –*Goethe*
Fein Rösslein, ich beschlage dich –*Lenau*
Feins Liebchen, trau du nicht –*Volkslied*
Feinsliebchen, du sollst mir –*Volkslied*
Feldblumen, zarte, kleine –*B. Huber*
Feldeinwärts flog ein Vögelein –*Tieck*
Fels auf Felsen hingewälzet –*J. Mayrhofer*
Felsen sollten nicht Felsen –*Goethe*
Felsen stehen gegründet –*Goethe*
Fenster wo ich einst mit dir Abends –*George*
Fensterlein, nachts bist du zu –*Gregorovius*
Fern im Süd' das schöne Spanien –*Geibel*
Fern sei die Ros' und ihre Pracht! –*Hafis*
Fern tobt der Kampf im Palmenthal! –*F. Freiligrath*
Fern und ferner schallt der Reigen –*Droysen*
Fern von dir denk' ich dein –*Honold*
Ferne, ferne flammenhelle Sterne –*C. Heine*
Ferne von der grossen Stadt –*Pichler*
Fest steht mein flammendes Gebot –*Dehmel*
Fetter grüne, du Laub –*Goethe*
Fetter grüne, du Laub, am Rebengeländer –*Goethe*
Finstere Schatten der Nacht –*Daumer*

Finsternisse fallen dichter –*Carossa*
Finstre, schwarze Riesenfalter –*Giraud*
Fischen schwimmt wohl hin und her –*Anonymous*
Fischreiche Wässer, schönbäumige Wälder –*Brecht*
Flack're, ew'ges Licht im Tal –*Keller*
Flamme in Nächten, selig allein –*C. Hauptmann*
Flammenauge, dunkles Haar –*Daumer*
Flatternde Fahnen und frohes Gedränge –*Liliencron*
Flattre, flattr' um deine Quelle –*Herder*
Flieg' auf, Frau Schwalbe mein –*Hersch*
Flieg doch fort, du kleines Thier! –*Anonymous*
Flieg, Schifflein, flieg! –*"Carmen Sylva"*
Fliege, Vögelein, fliege –*Berndes*
Flieget, ihr Wolken, eilet, ihr Winde –*Ungemach*
Fliegt der erste Morgenstrahl –*Eichendorff*
Fliegt der Schnee mir in's Gesicht –*Wilhelm Müller*
Fliegt nur aus, geliebte Tauben! –*Schenkendorf*
Flockendichte Winternacht –*Morgenstern*
Flügel! Flügel! um zu fliegen –*Rückert*
Flügelt ein kleiner blauer Falter –*Hesse*
Fluthenreicher Ebro, blühendes Ufer –*Geibel*
Fort, nur fort durch Busch und Zweige –*Vogl*
Fräulein Gigerlette lud mich ein –*Bierbaum*
Frage mich immer– fragest umsonst! –*Anonymous*
Frage nicht, wie es gekommen –*Anonymous*
Fragst du mich, woher die bange –*Mörike*
Fragst du mit den Äugelein –*"Carmen Sylva"*
Franziskus einst, der Heil'ge –*Wessenberg*
Frau Amme, das Kind ist erwacht! –*Hebbel*
Frau Berte, hört: Ihr dürftet nun –*C. F. Meyer*
Frau Elster hat den Schatz entdeckt –*Kletke*
Frau Erde schläft, Frau Erde träumt –*Ingrisch*
Frau Nachtigall, sagt ihr, "Königin!" –*C. Hauptmann*
Frau Schwalbe ist 'ne Schwätzerin –*Dieffenbach*
Frau Venus, Frau Venus, o lass mich gehn –*Lingg*
Frau X besucht sehr oft –*Lessing*
"Frauenhaar" trag' ich am Hute –*Bierbaum*
Frei und froh mit muntern Sinnen –*Anonymous*
Freiwillige her! Freiwillige her! –*Lemcke*
Freiwillige vor! Auch du –*Kurowski-Eichen*
Fremd bin ich eingezogen –*Wilhelm Müller*
Freud' umblühe dich auf allen Wegen –*Matthisson*
Freude, die im frühen Lenze –*Köpken*
Freude jubelt, Liebe waltet –*Matthisson*
Freude, Königin der Weisen –*Uz*
Freude! schöner Götterfunken! –*Schiller*
Freude, wohin mein Auge schaut –*J. Sturm*
Freuden sonder Zahl blüh'n im Himmelssaal –*L. Hölty*
Freudig war vor vielen Jahren –*Goethe*
Freudig zum Himmel auf blikke mein Herz! –*K. Schweizer*
Freudvoll und leidvoll, gedankenvoll sein –*Goethe*
Freue dich, o Seelenvogel! –*Hafis*
Freund! ich bitte, hüte dich –*Anonymous*
Freund meiner Jugend, zu dir kehr ich –*Hesse*
Freunde, deren Grüfte sich schon bemoosten! –*Matthisson*
Freunde sagt, was wollt ihr trinken? –*Kopisch*
Freunde, sammelt Euch im Kreise –*F. Schäffer*
Freunde, Wasser machet stumm –*Lessing*
Freunde, weihet den Pokal –*A. v. Arnim*
Freundlich ist dein Antlitz –*A. Schreiber*
Fridericus Rex, unser König und Herr –*"Alexis"*
Fried' ist versagt mir –*Petrarca*
Friede auf unserer Erde! –*Brecht*
Friede sei um diesen Grabstein her! –*M. Claudius*
Friedlich bekämpfen Nacht sich und Tag –*Hebbel*
Friedlich lieg' ich hingegossen –*F. Schlegel*
Friedlicher Abend senkt sich aufs Gefilde –*Lenau*
Frisch athmet des Morgens lebendiger Hauch –*Schiller*
Frisch auf, frisch auf! Der Bergmann kommt! –*Volkslied*
Frisch auf, frisch auf mit raschem Flug! –*Körner*
Frisch auf, ihr Jäger, frei und flink! –*Körner*
Frisch auf in Windeseil –*Cornelius*
Frisch auf, Soldatenblut! –*Volkslied*
Frisch, der Wein soll reichlich fließen –*Goethe*
Frisch trabe sonder Ruh' und Rast –*E. Schulze*
Frische Flur, du reiner Himmel –*Voss*
Fröhlich soll mein Herze springen –*Gerhardt*
Fröhlicher Lebensmut braust –*Rellstab*
Froh der süssen Augenweide –*Hölderlin*
Froh kehrt der Schiffer heim –*Hölderlin*
Froh summte nach der süßen Beute –*Lenau*
Frohe Lieder will ich singen –*Hoffmann von Fallersleben*
Früh am Morgen ging die Maid –*Volkslied*
Früh mit der Lerche-Sang wandert ich weit –*Burns*
Früh, wann die Hähne kräh'n –*Mörike*
Früh, wenn Tal, Gebirg' und Garten –*Goethe*
Früher Herbst. Die Blätter fallen –*Stamm*
Frühling, der die Welt umblaut –*C. F. Meyer*
Frühling- Frühling- Frühlingswind –*H. Lang*
Frühling ist gekommen –*Köstlin*
Frühling ist kommen, lieblicher Lenz! –*Anonymous*
Frühling ist's in allen Räumen –*"Anastasius Grün"*

Frühling läßt sein blaues Band *–Mörike*
Frühling schimmert in den Lüften *–Lemayer*
Frühling und Liebe, sie kehren nun wieder *–Anonymous*
Frühlinge und Sommer steigen grün *–Hesse*
Frühlingsahnen Frühlingswehen *–Unidentified*
Frühlingskinder im bunten Gedränge *–Lenau*
Frühmorgens, wenn die Hähne kräh'n *–Dreves*
Fühlt meine Seele das ersehnte Licht *–Michelangelo*
Führ mich, Kind, nach Bethlehem! *–Heyse*
Führe mich zum Rosenhaine *–Gamper*
Führer auf dem Weg des Heiles *–Hafis*
Fülle du! Gezier und schöner Geist *–Weinheber*
Füllest wieder Busch und Tal *–Goethe*
Füllt mir das Trinkhorn! *–F. Bodenstedt*
Füllt noch einmal die Gläser voll *–M. Claudius*
Fünf Engel haben gesungen *–Volkslied*
Fünf kleine Schwesterchen *–Anonymous*
Für alle die Schätze *–Wolff*
Für alle muß vor Freuden *–Eichendorff*
Für Männer uns zu plagen *–Goethe*
Für Maria, meines Lebens Leben *–D. F. Herrmann*
Fürst, Trossbub, Ritter, Gauner *–"Anastasius Grün"*
Fürwahr, mein Liebchen *–Volkslied*

Gäb's ein einzig Brünnelein *–Volkslied*
Gärtner, chum cho d'Schlößli bschnyde! *–Hämmerli-Marti*
Ganz still zuweilen, wie im Traum *–Flaischlen*
Ganz verloren, ganz versunken *–Kosegarten*
Gar fröhlich kann ich scheiden *–Leitner*
Gar hoch auf jenem Berg allein *–Wunderhorn*
Gar lieblich hat sich gesellet *–Volkslied*
Gar tröstlich kommt geronnen *–Leitner*
Gastibelza, der greise, kühne Jäger *–Hugo*
Gazelle, die so wild und schnell *–Byron*
Gebleicht sind die Linnen *–Stinde*
Gebt acht! Gebt acht! Es harrt der Feind *–Lemcke*
Gebt mir meinen Becher! *–Hafis*
Gebt mir zu trinken! *–Rückert*
Gedenk ich noch der Frühlingsnächte *–Eichendorff*
Gedenke mein! die lieben Augen lenke *–Köstlin*
Gedenkst du des Abends *–Unidentified*
Geduld, sagst du und zeigst *–Hermann Gilm*
Gefang'ner Mann, ein armer Mann! *–C. F. D. Schubart*
Gefror'ne Tropfen fallen *–Wilhelm Müller*
Gegen mich selber in Haß entbrannt *–Beer*
Gegen Mitternacht schon war es *–Anacreon*
Gegrüßet, Maria, du Mutter der Gnaden *–Volkslied*
Geh aus, mein Herz, und suche Freud *–Gerhardt*
Geh! gehorche meinen Winken *–Goethe*
Geh', Geliebter, geh' jetzt! *–Geibel*
Geh' nicht, die Gott für mich erschuf! *–C. F. Meyer*
Geh' schlafen, Liebste, lege dich zur Ruh *–Heyse*
Geh schlafen, Tochter, schlafen! *–Hans Schmidt*
Geh unter, schöne Sonne *–Hölderlin*
Geh, zartes Blatt, geh *–Volkslied*
Geheimes Flüstern hier und dort *–Rollet*
Geheimnisvoller Klang *–Lingg*
Gehet nun, gehet nun fort! *–Ehrler*
Geh'n der Nacht die Sterne aus *–Schumacher*
Gehorchen ist das Erste! *–Stieler*
Geht ein grauer Mann durch den stillen Wald *–Schlaf*
Geht nun hin und grabt mein Grab *–E. M. Arndt*
Geht nun, ihr Blüthen, meiner Fürstin Freude *–Stieglitz*
Geiger und Pfeifer, hier habt ihr Geld darauf *–Sauter*
Gekämpft hat meine Barke *–Kulmann*
Gekommen ist der Maie *–Heine*
Gelassen stieg die Nacht an's Land *–Mörike*
Gelb rollt mir zu Füssen *–F. Bodenstedt*
Gelehnet lag ich an dem Baum *–Anonymous*
Geliebter, wo zaudert dein irrender Fuß? *–Tieck*
Gell ja, also Morgen? "Ja freiliwenn's auf stehn" *–Bierbaum*
Gelobt sei Gott, denn er erhört *–Anonymous*
Gemäht sind die Feldert *–Blüthgen*
Gemahnt dein Name mich an deine Züge *–Michelangelo*
General, dein Tank ist ein starker Wagen *–Brecht*
Genieße still zufrieden *–J. Sturm*
Genug gemeistert nun die Weltgeschichte! *–Eichendorff*
Geöffnet sind des Winters Riegel *–A. Pollak*
Gern bin ich allein an des Meeres Strand *–Allmers*
Gern in stillen Melancholieen *–Goethe*
Gern verlaß ich diese Hütte *–Goethe*
Geruhig seines Weges gehn *–Anonymous*
Geschmeidig und wild *–"Gerda v. Robertus"*
Gesegnet sei das Grün und wer es trägt! *–Heyse*
Gesegnet sei, durch den die Welt entstund *–Heyse*
Geselle, woll'n wir uns in Kutten hüllen *–Heyse*
Gespielt mit Regen, Blitz und Sturm *–Lenau*
Gestern Abend in der stillen Ruh' *–Volkslied*
Gestern, als ich vom nächtlichen Lager *–Mörike*
Gestern ein Rieseln im weichen Eise *–Fischer*
Gestern fand ich, räumend *–C. F. Meyer*

Gestern hielt er mich im Arme –*Osterwald*
Gestern liebt' ich, heute leid' ich –*Lessing*
Gestern war ich Atlas, der den Himmel trug –*Rückert*
Gestorben war ich vor Liebeswonne –*Uhland*
Getäuscht hat mich ein Schimmer –*Calatin*
Geuß, lieber Mond –*L. Hölty*
Geuß nicht so laut der liebentflammten Lieder –*L. Hölty*
Gewaltig endet so das Jahr –*Trakl*
Gewiß, so liebt ein Freund den Freund –*Andreas-Salomé*
Gib dich zufrieden und sei stille –*Gerhardt*
Gib dir weiter keine Mühe, mein Sohn –*Bierbaum*
Gib ein Lied mir wieder –*George*
Gib mir deine Hand, nur den Finger –*Dehmel*
Gib mir die Fülle der Einsamkeit! –*J. Mayrhofer*
Gib uns deine milde Hand! –*Hesse*
Gibt es denn wohl bangere Mienen –*Jünger*
Gibt es wo einen Rasen grün –*Hugo*
Gibt's Straß' und Park –*Werfel*
Gieb ihm dein Herz und breite –*Telschow*
Gieb mir deine Hand, nur den Finger –*Dehmel*
Gieb, Schwester, mir die Harf' herab –*Kenner*
Ging Herr Walther hin im Freien –*Vogl*
Ging heut' Morgen über's Feld –*Mahler*
Glaub' es mir, jubelnde Kinderschar –*Faktor*
Glaube, hoffe, liebe! –*Kuffner*
Glaubst du in Gott, den Vater –*Giesebrecht*
Gleich der Rose welk' ich hin –*Fräulein von X*
Gleich einer versunkenen Melodie –*Morgenstern*
Gleich eines Herzens bangen Fieberträumen –*Osterwald*
Gleich wie der Mond so keusch und rein –*Osterwald*
Gleich wie die lieb Waldvögelein –*Wunderhorn*
Gleich wie die Sonne hell –*Unidentified*
Gleich wie Echo frohen Liedern –*Eichendorff*
Gleichtönig, leis und klagend rinnt –*Hesse*
Gleichwie ein Vogel am Fenster vorbei –*Mörike*
Gleite hinan die glänzende Bahn! –*Anonymous*
Glockenblumen, was läutet ihr? –*Wolff*
Glöcklein, Abendglöcklein, läute Frieden –*Güll*
Glokken klingen, Scharen dringen –*"Martin Greif"*
Glück ist wie Blütenduft –*Morgenstern*
Glück und Segen allerwegen –*Reinecke*
Glücklich lebt, vor Noth geborgen –*F. Bodenstedt*
Glücklich, wer zum Liebchen zieht –*Hoefer*
Glühend zwischen dir und mir –*Morgenstern*
Glühwürmchen, steck's Laternchen an! –*R. Reinick*
Göttlicher Morpheus, umsonst bewegst du –*Goethe*
Golden lacht und glüht der Morgen ü –*Anonymous*
Goldene Leier Appolons –*Hölderlin*
Goldene Sonne wie hehr sinkst du –*E. Bürger*
Goldenthronend, ewige Aphrodite –*Sappho*
Goldgrüne Libelle, was fliehest du mich! –*Reinecke*
Goldiger, sonniger Maientag –*Mäding*
Goldne Abendsonne, o, wie bist du schön! –*Urner*
Goldne Brücken seien alle Lieder mir –*Geibel*
Gold'ne Freiheit, gold'ne Freiheit! –*Anonymous*
Gold'ne Wiegen schwingen –*Wunderhorn*
Goldner Schein deckt den Hain –*Matthisson*
Gott, deine Güte reicht so weit –*Gellert*
Gott, deine Himmel sind mir aufgetan –*Bierbaum*
Gott des Schlafes, Freund der Ruh –*Herder*
Gott! Drücke, wenn das Herze bricht –*the Bible*
Gott! erhalte Franz der Kaiser –*Haschka*
Gott geb' ihm ein verdorben Jahr –*Wunderhorn*
Gott grüß dich, Marie! –*Pfau*
Gott grüß'! in die Nachtsee! –*C. Hauptmann*
Gott hiess die Sonne glühen –*F. Bodenstedt*
Gott hilf! im Wasser wächst das Schiff –*Beck*
Gott ist mein Hirt, mir wird nichts mangeln –*Bible*
Gott ist mein Lied! Er ist der Gott der Stärke –*Gellert*
Gott! lass die Glocke glücklich steigen –*Reil*
Gott sei mit euch! Uns ist es nicht beschieden –*Giesebrecht*
Gott sendet Licht in Nächten –*Mahlmann*
Gott! wie herrlich glänzt der Abendhimmel –*Magenau*
Gott woll' dass ich daheime wär' –*Heyse*
Gottes Atem hin und wieder –*Hesse*
Gottes ist der Orient! –*Goethe*
Grab tausend Klafter hinab –*Morgenstern*
Grabe, Spaden, grabe, alles, was ich habe –*L. Hölty*
Grabet in die junge Rinde, Schäfer –*Boie*
Grabt mein verwesliches geheim –*Klopstock*
Graf Eberhard im Bart vom Würtemberger Land –*Uhland*
Graf Siegfried einst in Welschland kam –*Anonymous*
Grau bereits sind meine Schläfen –*Anacreon*
Grausam erweiset sich Amor –*Goethe*
Grausame Frühlingssonne –*Mörike*
Greif' aus, du mein junges –*C. F. Meyer*
Greift zum Becher und laßt das Schelten –*Leuthold*
Gretele, willst tanzen? "O jerum, jo!" –*Volkslied*
Grolle lauter, zürnend Gewitter –*Osterwald*
Grollen die Tomtoms, rollen die Tomtoms –*Hughes*
Groß ist das Leben und reich! –*Hartleben*
Groß ist der Herr! die Himmel ohne Zahl –*Kleist*

Gross ist Jehovah, der Herr *–Pyrker*
Groß und rothentflammet schwebet *–Stolberg-Stolberg*
Groß wuchsen alle Räume *–G. H. Goering*
Große Heilige und kleine *–Rilke*
Grosser Brama, Herr der Mächte! *–Goethe*
Grosser Brama! nun erkenn' ich *–Goethe*
Grosser Thaten that der Ritter *–Scott*
Grosses hast Du mir gegeben *–Levetzow*
Großvater, Großvater, Großvater Stein *–Ingrisch*
Großvater und Großmutter *–"Anastasius Grün"*
Grün ist das Eiland *–Hoffmann von Fallersleben*
Grün ist der Jasminenstrauch *–Rückert*
Grüner wird die Au, und der Himmel blau *–L. Hölty*
Grüss euch aus Herzensgrund *–Eichendorff*
Guckst du mir denn immer nach *–Uhland*
Güldne Sternlein schauen nieder *–Heine*
Gütigster, Bester, Weisester, Größter *–Schubert*
Gunhilde lebt gar still und fromm *–Volkslied*
Gut' Nacht, gut' Nacht, ihr Blumen all' *–Bauer*
Gut Nacht, gut Nacht, mein feines Lieb *–Volkslied*
Gut Nacht, gut Nacht, mein liebster Schatz *–Volkslied*
Gute Nacht, geliebtes Leben *–Heyse*
Gute Nacht! Gute Nacht! Im Mondenschein *–Anonymous*
Gute Nacht! gute Nacht! Unser Tagwerk ist vollbracht *–C. F. D. Schubart*
Gute Nacht! Liebchen sieh *–Mahlmann*
Gute Nacht! Mädchen *–J. W. L. Gleim*
Gute Nacht, mein Herz, und schlumm're ein *–Geibel*
Gute Ruh', gute Ruh', thu' die Augen zu *–Wilhelm Müller*
Guten Abend, gut' Nacht, mit Rosen bedacht *–Wunderhorn*
Guten Abend, guten Abend, mein tausiger Schatz *–Volkslied*
Guten Abend, lieber Mondenschein! *–Wilhelm Müller*
Guten Abend, mein Freund! *–Morgenstern*
Guten Abend, mein Schatz *–Volkslied*
Guten Morgen, du Sonnstagsglockenschall! *–F. Kugler*
Guten Morgen, 's ist Sankt Valentinstag *–Shakespeare*
Guten Morgen, schöne Müllerin *–Wilhelm Müller*
Guten Morgen! sollt' ich sagen *–Lohmeyer*
Guten Morgen, Spielmann *–Wunderhorn*
Gygeli, Gygeli Brotisbei! *–J. Reinhart*
Ha! dort kömmt er mit Schweiß *–Klopstock*
Ha, ich bin der Herr der Welt! *–Goethe*
Ha, Priester, zitt're! nicht verhöhnen *–Anschütz*
Ha! was ist das? Die Sehnen zucken wieder *–Keller*
Hab Erbarmen, hab Erbarmen! *–Heyse*
Hab ich euch denn je geraten *–Goethe*
Hab ich geträumt? Klang hier nicht meine Laute? *–Scheffel*
Hab ich tausendmal geschworen *–Goethe*
Hab' oft ein'n dumpfen düstern Sinn *–Goethe*
Hab' oft im Kreise der Lieben *–Chamisso*
Hab' Singen für mein Leben gern *–Seyboth*
Habe ich dir nicht gesagt *–C. Loewe*
Haben sie von deinen Fehlen *–Goethe*
Habt ihr sie schon geseh'n, sie *–Volkslied*
Hältst mich nun ganz in den Armen *–Evers*
Hände, viele Hände über der Haide schweben *–Wertheimer*
Hänschen möcht ein Reiter sein *–Dieffenbach*
Hänschen will ein Tischler werden *–Löwenstein*
Hänschen will reiten *–R. Reinick*
Hänsel, komm in den Wald *–Busta*
Hänselein, willst du tanzen? *–Hoffmann von Fallersleben*
Härte schwand. Auf einmal legt *–Rilke*
Hätt' es nimmer gedacht *–Siebel*
Hätt ich irgend wohl Bedenken *–Goethe*
Hätt' ich nimmer Sie gesehn *–Cordes*
Hätt' ich tausend Arme zu rühren *–Wilhelm Müller*
Hättest du der Einfalt nicht *–Rilke*
Hain in diesen paradiesen *–George*
Halb Dämmerschein, halb Kerzenlicht *–Cornelius*
Halte dich still, halte dich stumm *–Fontane*
Halte mir einer von euch Laffen mein Pferd *–Schaukal*
Han an em Ort e Blümeli g'seh *–Volkslied*
Hand in Hand und Lipp' auf Lippe! *–Goethe*
Hans Adam war ein Erdenkloß *–Goethe*
Hans und Grethe, Grethe und Hans *–Bierbaum*
Harrt ein Fischer auf der Brücke *–Schlechta*
Hast du das Schloss gesehen *–Uhland*
Hast du den Fischerkindern *–Müller von Königswinter*
Hast du dich je schon ganz allein gefunden *–Lenau*
Hast du ein Tongedicht vollbracht *–Kerr*
Hast du Lianen nicht gesehen? *–J. Mayrhofer*
Hast du nicht Liebe zugemessen *–G. A. Bürger*
Hast du's in meinem Auge nicht gelesen *–Matthisson*

Hast einsam mich verlassen in dieser Öde! *–Geibel*
Hast gesagt, du willst mich nehmen *–Wunderhorn*
Hast viel gespielt und viel gelacht *–Güll*
Hat der alte Hexenmeister *–Goethe*
Hat der junge Geigenmacher *–Falke*
Hat dich die Liebe berührt *–Heyse*
Hat dich ein blühendes Blümchen erfreut *–Volkslied*
Hat ein Schiffer, grau und alt *–Stolterfoth*
Hat einmal ein Mädel die Muhme gefragt *–Ritter*
Hat mit frischem Birkenlaube *–Giesebrecht*
Hat sie's dir denn angetan *–Hebbel*
Hatte Liebchen zwei dort im Dorf *–Volkslied*
Hauche milder, Abendluft *–Anonymous*
Havele, Havele, Hahne *–Wunderhorn*
He! schenket mir im Helme ein! *–Leitner*
He, Zigeuner, greife in die Saiten ein *–Conrat*
Heb' auf dein blondes Haupt *–Heyse*
Hebt ein Falke sich empor *–Kapper*
Heerwagen, mächtig Sternbild der Germanen *–Keller*
Hehrer bist du und heiliger *–Ziel*
Heil! dies ist die letzte Zähre *–Matthisson*
Heil dir, der du hassen kannst *–Morgenstern*
Heil jenem Tag, der dich geboren *–K. Henckell*
Heil sei der Stunde, wo ich sie erkannte *–Walther von der Vogelweide*
Heil und Freude ward mir verheißen *–Cornelius*
Heilge Kreuze sind die Verse *–Giraud*
Heil'ge Liebe, flammend Herz *–Cornelius*
Heil'ge Nacht, du sinkest nieder! *–M. Collin*
Heilig ist mir Dankbarkeit! *–Iffland*
Heilig Wesen! gestört hab' ich *–Hölderlin*
Heilige Nacht! Heilige Nacht! *–C. Brentano*
Heiliges Rätsel, ewige Macht *–Salburg-Falkenstein*
Heimat, Schoß des Heimeslosen *–Ehrler*
Heimat! wunderbar tönendes Wort! *–"C. O. Sternau"*
Heimlich durch's Fenster *–E. Scherenberg*
Hier strecket der wallende Pilger *–Schiller*
Heiss glüht der Pfad *–Stieglitz*
Heiß mich nicht reden, heiß mich schweigen *–Goethe*
Heissa, heia! Stosset an *–Tora zu Eulenburg*
Heisse stille Liebe schwebet *–Anonymous*
Helf' mir Gott, wie fliegen die Gänse *–Malsburg*
Helft mir, ihr Schwestern *–Chamisso*
Hell glüh'n die Sterne *–Stieglitz*
Hell jubeln die Geigen mit Kling *–Busse*
Hell und sieghaft strahlest du *–Behn*
Helle Silberglöcklein klingen aus *–Buddeus*
Helles Klingen in den Lüften *–Gomoll*
Herab kamst du auf Erden *–Anonymous*
Herab läßt sich der Wolke Saum *–Petőfi*
Herab von den Bergen zum Tale *–Unidentified*
Herauf! mit deiner purpur Glut' *–Anonymous*
Heraus in eure Schatten, rege Wipfel *–Goethe*
Herbei, heran, auf die glänzende Bahn! *–Enslin*
Herbst ist es nun! Nimmer die Stürme *–Tegnér*
Herbstlich sonnige Tage *–Geibel*
Herbstsonnenschein! Der liebe Abend *–Schlaf*
Herein, o du Guter! du Alter herein! *–Goethe*
Herolde ritten von Ort zu Ort *–F. Kugler*
Herr Bachus ist ein braver Mann *–G. A. Bürger*
Herr Bäkker, das Brot ist verbakken *–Brecht*
Herr, du bist unsre Zuflucht *–the Bible*
Herr Dýring ritt wohl durch das Land *–"Talvj"*
Herr! ein Mädchen, Herr ein Weibchen *–Goethe*
Herr, es gescheh dein Wille! *–Cronegk*
Herr Frühling giebt jetzt ein Konzert *–Vogl*
Herr Gott, der du bist! *–Wilhelm IV*
Herr Heinrich sitzt am Vogelherd *–Vogl*
Herr! Herr, der du alles wohl gemacht *–Rückert*
Herr! Herr! der du mir das Leben *–Gellert*
Herr, ich liebte aller Dinge *–"Klabund"*
Herr, in dieser Weihestunde *–Koschnick*
Herr Jesu Christ, den sie gekrönt mit Dornen *–Vincke*
Herr Jesu, Gnadensonne *–L. A. Gotter*
Herr, laß dir gefallen dieses kleine Haus! *–Goethe*
Herr, laß mich hungern dann und wann *–Falke*
Herr Lenz springt heute durch die Stadt *–Bodmann*
Herr Oluf reitet spät und weit *–Herder*
Herr Pfarrer hat zwei Fräulchen *–Rückert*
Herr Puff, an Geld und Jahren reich *–Wargemont*
Herr, schicke, was du willt *–Mörike*
Herr, unser Gott! erhöre unser Flehen *–A. Schmidl*
Herr, was trägt der Boden hier *–Heyse*
Herr, wie lange willst du mein so gar vergessen? *–the Bible*
Herr, zu Dir will ich mich retten *–Droysen*
Herrin! Dein sterngleich Aug' allein *–Vincke*
Herrin! sag was heißt das Flüstern? *–Goethe*
Herrlich, was im schönsten Feuer *–Brecht*
Herz, in deinen sonnenhellen Tagen *–Eichendorff*
Herz, lass dich nicht zerspalten *–Körner*
Herz, mein Herz, ermanne dich *–Blankensee*
Herz, mein Herz, sei nicht beklommen *–Heine*
Herz, mein Herz, warum so fröhlich *–Eichendorff*
Herz, mein Herz, was soll das geben? *–Goethe*
Herz, nun so alt und noch immer nicht klug *–Rückert*
Herz! und weisst du selber denn zu sagen *–Mörike*

Herz verzage nicht geschwind *–Heyse*
Herzallerliebstes Schatzerl du *–Unidentified*
Herzchen, mein Schätzchen *–Anonymous, Volkslied*
Herzen, die gen Himmel sich erheben *–Matthisson*
Herzerl, was kränkt dich so sehr *–Volkslied*
Herziges Schätzle Du *–Volkslied*
Herzlaub, holder Honigmund *–Busta*
Herzlich thut mich erfreuen *–Wunderhorn*
Herzliebe gute Mutter *–Castelli*
Hesperus, der blasse Funken *–Lenau*
Heut Nacht erhob ich mich um Mitternacht *–Heyse*
Heut Nacht, mein Lieb, da nehm ich dich *–Binding*
Heut' schwirren Schelmenlieder *–Scheffel*
Heut ward mir bis zum jungen Tag *–C. F. Meyer*
Heute ist Sonntag und Montag ist morgen *–Anonymous*
Heute marschieren wir! Juchhe *–Wunderhorn*
Heute, nur heute bin ich so schön *–Storm*
Heute, Ostersonntag früh *–Brecht*
Heute scheid' ich, heute wander' ich *–F. Müller*
Heute summte mir im Ohr *–Faktor*
Heute tanzt alles, alles, alles tanzt! *–Hafis*
Heute will ich fröhlich, fröhlich sein *–M. Claudius*
Hie kann nit sein ein böser Mut *–Anonymous*
Hie und da ist an den Bäumen *–Wilhelm Müller*
Hielt die allerschönste Herrin *–R. Reinick*
Hielte diesen frühen Segen *–Goethe*
Hier - doch keinem darfst du's zeigen *–C. F. Meyer*
Hier am Hügel heissen Sandes sitz' ich *–Schücking*
Hier auf diesem Blumen Hügel *–Wille*
Hier bin ich, Herr! Gegrüßt das Licht *–Eichendorff*
Hier bring' ich dir ein Blümchen *–Rückert*
Hier ein Weilchen, dort ein Weilchen! *–Schatz*
Hier grub man ein *–Zwehl*
Hier hilft nun weiter kein Bemühn! *–Goethe*
Hier im Schatten, o Batyllos *–Mörike*
Hier in dem Dunkel, auf pfadlosen Mooren *–Rodenberg*
Hier in der öden Fremde *–Hohenberg*
Hier in diesen erdbeklommnen Lüften *–Rückert*
Hier ist Freude, hier ist Lust *–Mörike*
Hier klag' ich verborgen *–Goethe*
Hier lieg' ich auf dem Frühlingshügel *–Mörike*
Hier liegt der Müller Mayhon! *–M. Claudius*
Hier liegt der Sommer begraben– *–Bergengruen*
Hier muss ich sie finden *–Goethe*
Hier ob dem Eingang seid befestiget *–Daumer*
Hier pflegt Natur mit ihren goldnen Auen *–Leuthold*
Hier sass ich, wartend, wartend *–Nietzsche*
Hier scheidet die Klosterpforte *–Leuthold*
Hier sein Grab bei diesen stillen Hügeln *–Anonymous*
Hier sind wir arme Narrn auf Plätzen *–Wunderhorn*
Hier sind wir versammelt zu löblichem Tun *–Goethe*
Hier steh' ich einsam auf dem Fels im Meer *–Kahlert*
Hier umarmen sich getreue Gatten *–Schiller*
Hier und da ist an den Bäumen *–Wilhelm Müller*
Hier unten steht ein Ritter *–Schlechta*
Hier unter dieser Linde saß *–Eichendorff*
Hier von Frühlingsblumen *–Wildenbruch*
Hier, wo ich Abendröte und Tag *–Fuchs*
Hier, wo seine fetten Herden *–Kotzebue*
Hier wo sich die Straßen scheiden *–Köstlin*
Himmel strahlt so helle und klar *–Conrat*
Himmelsluft vom Morgenlande *–Knapp*
Himmelsmächte, die ihr schirmet *–Unidentified*
Hin ist alle meine Kraft *–J. W. L. Gleim*
Hin und wieder fliegen die Pfeile *–Goethe*
Hinab, ihr Brüder, in den Schacht! *–Anonymous*
Hinauf! hinauf! in Sprung und Lauf! *–H. Collin*
Hinauf zu jenen Bergen schau' ich *–Telschow*
Hinaus, hinaus! in freie Luft *–Lasker*
Hinaus in das Lustgeschmetter *–Cornelius*
Hinaus in weite Ferne *–Anonymous*
Hinaus mein Blick! hinaus in's Thal! *–A. W. Schlegel*
Hinter jenen dichten Wäldern weilst du *–Volkslied*
Hinter jenen Epheuranken *–Hamerling*
Hinterm Berge dort, dem grünen *–"Talvj"*
Hinüber wall' ich, und jede Pein *–Novalis*
Hinweg, Kleinmütige, Hinweg *–Petöfi*
Hirschlein ging im Wald spazieren *–Kuh*
Hirten wachen im Feld *–Cornelius*
Hoch am dunklen Himmelsbogen *–Hamann*
Hoch auf dem alten Thurme *–Goethe*
Hoch auf dem Gipfel deiner Gebirge *–Körner*
Hoch auf Stelzen, hoch auf Stelzen *–Dieffenbach*
Hoch gewölbte Blätterkronen *–Wesendonck*
Hoch hing der Mond; das Schneegefild *–Dehmel*
Hoch, hoch sind die Berge *–Geibel*
Hoch in Lüften Vöglein schweben *–Pocci*
Hoch mit den Wolken geht der Vögel Reise *–Eichendorff*
Hoch über mir endlos *–Öhquist*
Hoch über stillen Höhen stand *–Eichendorff*
Hoch, und ehern schier von Dauer *–Bertrand*
Hoch zu Pferd! Stahl auf zartem Leibe *–Burns*
Hochauf strebte mein Geist *–Hölderlin*
Hochbeglückt in deiner Liebe *–Willemer*
Hochgetürmte Rimaflut, wie bist du so trüb *–Conrat*

Hochweiser Rat, geehrte Kollegen! –*Eichendorff*
Höchste Herrscherin der Welt! –*Goethe*
Höchstes Glück ist doch, zu spenden –*Brecht*
Hör' auf mein armes Herz –*Anonymous*
Hör', es klagt die Flöte wieder –*C. Brentano*
Hör' ich das Liedchen klingen –*Heine*
Hör' ich das Pförtchen nicht gehen? –*Schiller*
Hör' ich ein Vöglein singen –*Osterwald*
Hör mein Liebesliedchen ziehn –*Calderón*
Hör mich, du arme Pilgerin –*Wunderhorn*
Hör' uns, Allmächtiger! Hör' uns, Allgütiger! –*Körner*
Hör zu, so wird der letzte Abend sein –*Benn*
Höre den Rat, den die Leier tönt! –*Goethe*
Höre, die Nachtigall singt –*Herder*
Höre mich, Ewiger, höre mich –*Jacobowski*
Höre mich im Regen rauschen –*Thiess*
Höre mir den Prediger –*Hafis*
Höre Schicksal, was ich heische –*Reissig*
Hörnerklänge rufen klagend –*J. Mayrhofer*
Hörst auch du die leisen Stimmen –*Christen*
Hörst du den Vogel singen? –*Kerner*
Hörst du die Gründe rufen –*Eichendorff*
Hörst du nicht die Bäume rauschen –*Eichendorff*
Hörst du nicht die Quellen gehen –*Eichendorff*
Hörst du von den Nachtigallen –*A. W. Schlegel*
Hörst du, wie die Stürme sausen –*Allmers*
Hört an, ihr Mütter alt und jung! –*Ossenfelder*
Hört die Lerche, sie singt! –*F. A. Krummacher*
Hört! ich hatt' einmal ein Blümchen –*Schlotterbeck*
Hört ihn und seht sein dürftig Instrument! –*Mörike*
Hört ihr die Hörner erschallen –*Anonymous*
Hört ihr im Laube des Regens starke Schläge? –*Neun*
Hört ihrs nicht klingen? Leis ganz leis? –*Gomoll*
Hört mich, Ihr grausamen Götter –*"Carmen Sylva"*
Hört wie die Wachtel im Grünen –*Wunderhorn*
Hört wie laut, hört wie laut –*Dieffenbach*
Hört, wir die Wachtel im Felde –*Volkslied*
Hoffährtig seid Ihr, schönes Kind –*Heyse*
Hoffe, liebe, glaube –*Blankensee*
Hoffen und wieder verzagen –*Schack*
Hoffnung dein Prangen –*Unidentified*
Hoffnung, Hoffnung immer grün! –*Herder*
Hoher Berge Schatten liegen auf dem Meer –*Rückert*
Hold bin ich einer Holden –*Haug*
Hold lächelten die Maienhoren –*Haug*
Holde Königin der Geigen –*Falke*
Holde Nacht wie still bist du –*Boelitz*
Holde, schattenreiche Bäume, neiget –*Heyse*
Holder Frühling, kehre wieder –*Behr*
Holder klingt der Vogelsang –*L. Hölty*
Holder, leichtbeschwingter Bote –*Daumer*
Holder Lenz, du bist dahin! –*Lenau*
Holder Lenz, mit reichen Gaben –*Blankenfeldt*
Holder Schein, an deine Spiele –*Hesse*
Holdes Mädchen! unser Leben –*Jacobi*
Horch – endlich zittert es –*Keller*
Horch! Auf der Erde feuchtem Grund –*Mörike*
Horch, der Wind klagt in den Zweigen –*Conrat*
Horch, grausig heult draussen –*L. A. Schubart*
Horch, Hörnerklang, horch, Treiberruf –*Vogl*
Horch, hörst du nicht vom Himmel her –*Hafis*
Horch, horch! die Lerch' im Ätherblau –*Shakespeare*
Horch! Horch, in der wehenden Nacht –*Meynell*
Horch', im Winde säuseln sacht –*Geibel*
Horch! Leise horch, Geliebte! –*Baggesen*
Horch! Rossgestampf! Muss in den Kampf –*Schantz*
Horch! Stimmen und Geschrei –*Keller*
Horch! Welch ein süßes harmonisches Klingen –*Lyser*
Horch! wie brauset der Sturm –*Uhland*
Horch, wie Murmeln des empörten Meeres –*Schiller*
Horch, wie still es wird im dunkeln Hain –*Lenau*
Horchend über schroffe Mauern –*H. Seidel*
Horcht auf! Es schlägt die Stunde –*Rochlitz*
Hüll ein mich in die grünen Dekken –*Keller*
Hüll in deinen Schattenmantel –*Bouterwek*
Hüttelein, still und klein –*Rückert*
Hui! wie die Wolke von Staub und Brand –*Stieglitz*
Husaren müssen reiten –*Hoffmann von Fallersleben*
Husaren sind gar wack're Truppen –*Thale*
Husch, husch! es kommt wer –*Hörmann*

I bi=n i d'Beeri gange dur d'Büsch –*Frey*
I und mein junges Weib können schön tanza –*Volkslied*
I weiß äs Seeli, bodelos –*Lienert*
Ich aber weiß, ich seh dich manche Nacht –*Jacobowski*
Ich ahnte nicht vor kurzer Zeit –*Leixner*
Ich armer Mann was focht mich an –*Volkslied*
Ich armer Tamboursg'sell! –*Wunderhorn*
Ich armer Teufel, Herr Baron –*Goethe*
Ich armes Käuzlein kleine –*Wunderhorn*
Ich armes Klosterfräulein –*Kerner*
Ich atme dich mit allen Sternen aus –*Ingrisch*
Ich atmet' einen Linden Duft –*Rückert*
Ich auf der Erd', am Himmel du –*J. Seidl*

Ich baute dir den stillen Schrein *–Unidentified*
Ich bin auch in Ravenna gewesen *–Hesse*
Ich bin auf Dich böse *–Meyer-Helmund*
Ich bin dein Baum, o Gärtner *–Rückert*
Ich bin dein, du bist mein *–Tegernsee*
Ich bin der Contrabandiste *–Geibel*
Ich bin der kleine Postillon *–Unidentified*
Ich bin der König vom Morgenland *–Schellenberg*
Ich bin der Mönch Waltramus *–Stieler*
Ich bin der Trommelschläger laut *–Moehrcke*
Ich bin der Welt abhanden gekommen *–Rückert*
Ich bin der wohlbekannte Sänger *–Goethe*
Ich bin des Meeres zartweiße *–Hohenlohe*
Ich bin die Blum' im Garten *–Rückert*
Ich bin die Laute *–Rilke*
Ich bin dir herzengulden gut *–Volkslied*
Ich bin dir nie so nah als nachts *–I. Seidel*
Ich bin durch einen schönen Wald gekommen *–Heyse*
Ich bin durch's Leben auf dich zugegangen *–B. von Münchhausen*
Ich bin ein armes Lämpchen nur *–Hafis*
Ich bin ein deutscher Jüngling *–M. Claudius*
Ich bin ein deutsches Mädchen! *–Klopstock*
Ich bin ein Dieb geworden *–Schellenberg*
Ich bin ein einsamer Schaukelstuhl *–Morgenstern*
Ich bin ein Gast auf Erden *–Gerhardt*
Ich bin ein guter Hirte *–the Bible*
Ich bin ein leichter Junggesell *–Pfizer*
Ich bin ein Lust'ger Geselle *–Geibel*
Ich bin ein lust'ger Wandersmann *–F. Förster*
Ich bin ein Spielmann von Beruf *–Leuthold*
Ich bin ein Waller auf der Erde *–Schober*
Ich bin eine Harfe mit goldenen Seiten *–Morgenstern*
Ich bin einmal etwas hinaus spaziert *–R. Reinick*
Ich bin erwacht, ich bin erwacht *–Ott*
Ich bin erwacht! Im Rosenschimmer *–Körner*
Ich bin gekommen in's Niederland *–Burns*
Ich bin gen Baden zogen *–Wunderhorn*
Ich bin getrost, Stern meiner Seele *–Wetzler*
Ich bin häßlich, liebe Mutter *–Kamlah*
Ich bin hinausgegangen des Morgens in der Früh *–R. Reinick*
Ich bin kein Minister *–K. Henckell*
Ich bin mein Lied, mein Lied bin ich *–Eichert*
Ich bin meiner Mutter einzig Kind *–Mörike*
Ich bin so bleich, du bist so roth *–K. Schweizer*
Ich bin so gar ein armer Mann *–Uhland*
Ich bin so gern, so gern daheim *–Pfeil*
Ich bin so müd' und weiß nicht mehr wovon *–Faktor*
Ich bin vergnügt, im Siegeston *–M. Claudius*
Ich bin vergnügt, will ich was mehr? *–J. W. L. Gleim*
Ich bin vom Berg der Hirtenknab' *–Uhland*
Ich bin von aller Ruh' geschieden *–E. Schulze*
Ich bin von lockerem Schlage *–Castelli*
Ich bin wie andre Mädchen nicht *–Anonymous*
Ich blick' in mein Herz *–Geibel*
Ich blicke hinab in die Gasse *–Hebbel*
Ich dachte dein in tiefer Nacht *–Hafis*
Ich danke dir, du stummer Stein *–Morgenstern*
Ich danke Gott und freue mich *–M. Claudius*
Ich darf dir nicht folgen *–Busta*
Ich darf nicht dankend an dir *–George*
Ich denk an dich und gehe aus *–Ehrler*
Ich denke dein, ob auch getrennt *–A. Krafft*
Ich denke dein, wann durch den Hain *–Matthisson*
Ich denke dein, wenn mir der Sonne Schimmer *–Goethe*
Ich denke dein, wenn sich im Blüthenregen *–Brun*
Ich denke oft an's blaue Meer *–Keller*
Ich der Arzt, ich der Arzt *–Giesebrecht*
Ich, der mit flatterndem Sinn *–J. W. L. Gleim*
Ich empfinde fast ein Grauen *–Opitz*
Ich ersehnt' ein Lied *–Cornelius*
Ich eß' nicht gerne Gerste *–Wunderhorn*
Ich esse nun mein Brod nicht trocken mehr *–Heyse*
Ich fahr dahin, wenn es muß sein *–Volkslied*
Ich flüsterte leis in den einsamen Bach *–Pohl*
Ich flüstre deinen Namen in stiller Nacht *–Kletke*
Ich frag hinauf in die Sterne *–Teasdale*
Ich frag' nach dir jedwede Morgensonne *–Anonymous*
Ich frage keine Blume *–Wilhelm Müller*
Ich frage nicht: "hast Du mich lieb?" *–Wittkowsky*
Ich fragte dich, warum dein Auge *–Hesse*
Ich fühle deinen Odem *–F. Bodenstedt*
Ich fürcht' nit Gespenster *–Keller*
Ich fuhr über Meer, ich zog über Land *–Heyse*
Ich gab dem Schicksal dich zurück *–Stieler*
Ich geh' auf stillen Auen *–Boelitz*
Ich geh' auf stillen Wegen *–"Martin Greif"*
Ich geh durch die dunkeln Gassen *–Eichendorff*
Ich geh zu Dir in dunkler Nacht *–Bittner*
Ich gehe des Nachts *–Gregorovius*
Ich gehe fremd durch die Menge hin *–Ritter*
Ich gehe nie vorüber *–Hoffmann von Fallersleben*
Ich gehöre zu dir wie zum Herzen *–Ungemach*
Ich gieng im Walde so für mich hin *–Goethe*
Ich ging an deiner Seite *–Lenau*

Ich ging bei Nacht einst über Land –*Eichendorff*
Ich ging den Weg entlang –*Liliencron*
Ich ging einmal spazieren –*Volkslied*
Ich ging hinaus, um dich zu seh'n –*Cornelius*
Ich ging im Felde so für mich hin –*Goethe*
Ich ging im Wald durch Kraut und Gras –*Wolff*
Ich ging im Walde so für mich hin –*Goethe*
Ich ging mit Lust –*Wunderhorn*
Ich glaube in alten Tagen –*Heyse*
Ich glaubte, die Schwalbe träumte –*Beck*
Ich grolle nicht, und wenn das Herz auch bricht –*Heine*
Ich grüne wie die Weide grünt –*Wackernagel*
Ich grüsse die Sonne –*Mackay*
Ich hab dich ausgetragen –*Brecht*
Ich hab' dich geliebt –*R. Reinick*
Ich hab' die Nacht geträumet –*Volkslied*
Ich hab drei Kränze gewunden –*Hermann Gilm*
Ich hab' eine alte Muhme –*"Anastasius Grün"*
Ich hab ein Bächlein funden –*Stolberg-Stolberg*
Ich hab' ein glühend Messer –*Mahler*
Ich hab' ein heisses junges Blut –*Körner*
Ich hab ein kleines Gärtchen –*Kipper*
Ich hab' ein kleines Hüttchen nur –*J. W. L. Gleim*
Ich hab' ein Liebchen lieb recht von Herzen –*Eichendorff*
Ich hab' ein Mädchen funden –*Kosegarten*
Ich hab' eine alte Muhme –*"Anastasius Grün"*
Ich hab' eine Brieftaub' in meinem Sold –*J. Seidl*
Ich hab eine Wiege so schmuck und nett –*G. P. Schmidt*
Ich hab' emal ein Bettelmädle küßt –*Wunderhorn*
Ich hab' empor gesehen und geglaubt –*Heyse*
Ich hab' es getragen sieben Jahr –*Fontane*
Ich hab' es nicht gewußt, was Liebe ist –*Finckh*
Ich hab' ihn gesehen! –*Goethe*
Ich hab' ihn im Schlafe –*Chamisso*
Ich hab' im Traum geweinet –*Heine*
Ich hab' in Deinem Auge –*Rückert*
Ich hab' in mich gesogen –*Rückert*
Ich hab' in Penna einen Liebsten wohnen –*Heyse*
Ich hab' kein Haus, ich hab' kein Nest –*David*
Ich hab' kein' Mutter, die mich hegt –*Ritter*
Ich hab' mein Herz verloren –*Meyer-Helmund*
Ich hab' mein Sach auf nichts gestellt –*Goethe*
Ich hab' mein Weib allein –*Burns*
Ich hab' mir eins erwählet –*Anonymous*
Ich hab' mir lang' den Kopf zerbrochen –*Heine*
Ich hab' nichts auf Erden –*Koschnick*
Ich hab' noch nie so wie heute –*Unidentified*
Ich hab' zum Brunnen –*"Martin Greif"*
Ich habe allem Leben mit jedem Abendrot –*C. Brentano*
Ich habe bevor der Morgen –*Chamisso*
Ich habe den Frühling gesehen –*Volkslied*
Ich habe dich erlöst –*Ingrisch*
Ich habe dich mit Rosen –*Rückert*
Ich habe Dich schon längst gekannt –*Bittner*
Ich habe ein kleines Lied erdacht –*Boddien*
Ich habe ein Paar Schuhe –*Stinde*
Ich habe ein Röschen gefunden –*Hepp*
Ich habe gar liebliche Sträußchen feil –*Anonymous*
Ich habe geliebet –*Goethe*
Ich habe keine Schulden –*Anonymous*
Ich habe lieb die helle Sonne –*Falke*
Ich habe mein Feinsliebchen –*Volkslied*
Ich habe mein Kindlein in Schlaf gewiegt –*Bern*
Ich habe meine Kerze ausgelöscht –*Hesse*
Ich habe mich dem Heil entschworen –*Hafis*
Ich habe mich neben die Welt –*Schefer*
Ich habe mir Rosmarin gepflanzt –*"Max Waldau"*
Ich habe nicht stets Lust zu lesen –*Lessing*
Ich habe nie vermeint –*"Klabund"*
Ich habe sie selber gezogen –*H. Claudius*
Ich habe was Liebes –*G. A. Bürger*
Ich habe wohl, es sei hier laut –*Hermann Gilm*
Ich hätte wohl, dein Haar zu zieren –*Mörike*
Ich halt' ein Stückchen Leder –*"Carmen Sylva"*
Ich halte dich in meinem Arm –*Keller*
Ich halte ihr die Augen zu –*Heine*
Ich hatt' ein Vöglein, ach wie fein! –*Mörike*
Ich hatt' einen Kameraden –*Uhland*
Ich hatt' einmal ein Mädchen –*C. F. D. Schubart*
Ich hatt' nun mei Truschel –*Wunderhorn*
Ich hatte eine Nachtigall –*Lemcke*
Ich hatte einst ein schönes Vaterland –*Heine*
Ich hielt mein Herz verschlossen –*Storm*
Ich hör' die Bächlein rauschen –*Eichendorff*
Ich hör' ein Vöglein locken –*Böttger*
Ich hör' meinen Schatz –*Uhland*
Ich hört' ein Bächlein rauschen –*Wilhelm Müller*
Ich hört ein Sichlein rauschen –*Volkslied*
Ich hört' in einem grünen Hag –*Zoll*
Ich hörte heute morgen am Klippenhang –*Miegel*
Ich kam so fromm, ein Waisenkind –*Verlaine*
Ich kam zu einer Wiese –*Schlaf*
Ich kann das Wort nicht vergessen –*Liliencron*
Ich kann die Sonne nicht Sonne nennen –*Busta*

Ich kann hier nicht singen –*Eichendorff*
Ich kann und mag nicht fröhlich sein! –*Wunderhorn*
Ich kann wohl manchmal singen –*Eichendorff*
Ich kann's nicht fassen, nicht glauben –*Chamisso*
Ich kenn' ein Blümlein Wunderschön –*Goethe*
Ich kenn', o Jüngling, deine Freude –*Goethe*
Ich kenne einen grossen Garten –*Dieffenbach*
Ich kenne sieben lust'ge Brüder –*Uhland*
Ich kenne wo ein festes Schloß –*Novalis*
Ich komme heim aus dem Sonnenland! –*Ritter*
Ich komme schon durch manches Land –*Goethe*
Ich komme vom Gebirge her –*G. P. Schmidt*
Ich komme vor dein Angesicht –*Gellert*
Ich kose süß mit der und der –*Daumer*
Ich lag auf grünen Matten –*Kosegarten*
Ich lag von sanftem Traum umflossen –*Rückert*
Ich lauscht' dem Fink im grünen Haag –*Ritter*
Ich leb' der Sünde –*Michelangelo*
Ich lebe immer heiter –*C. F. D. Schubart*
Ich legte mein Haupt auf Elvershöh –*Herder*
Ich legte mich unter den Lindenbaum –*Hebbel*
Ich lehn' im offenen Gemache –*Stieler*
Ich lieb' eine Blume –*Heine*
Ich liebe dich, so wie du mich –*Herrosee*
Ich liebe dich und will dich ewig lieben –*Weling*
Ich liebe dich, weil ich dich lieben muß –*Rückert*
Ich liebe die graden Alleen –*Morgenstern*
Ich liebte dich, in meiner Seele lebte –*Wille*
Ich liebte nur Ismenen –*Schlieben*
Ich liebte sie mit innigem Gefühle –*Goethe*
Ich lieg' an meines Lagers End' –*Stieler*
Ich liege in gläsernem Wachen –*Werfel*
Ich liess mir sagen und mir ward erzählt –*Heyse*
Ich lobe mir die Vögelein –*Osterwald*
Ich Mädchen bin aus Schwaben –*C. F. D. Schubart*
Ich möcht vor tausend Taler nicht –*Wunderhorn*
Ich möchte einer werden so wie –*Rilke*
Ich möchte einmal so betauet sein –*Ehrler*
Ich möchte hingehn wie das Abendrot –*Herwegh*
Ich möchte lassen diese glanzumspielte Welt –*Petöfi*
Ich möchte still am Wege stehn –*Flaischlen*
Ich möchte still nach Hause gehn –*Bartels*
Ich möchte wohl der Kaiser sein! –*J. W. L. Gleim*
Ich möchte zieh'n in die Welt hinaus –*Wilhelm Müller*
Ich müh mich ab –*"Friedrich Halm"*
Ich muß hinaus, ich muß zu dir –*Hoffmann von Fallersleben*
Ich pflückte eine kleine Pfirsichblüthe –*Bethge*
Ich raun' dir am Bette in schlafloser Nacht –*Busse*
Ich reit' ins finstre Land hinein –*Uhland*
Ich ritt einmal im Dunkeln –*Hebbel*
Ich roch der Liebe himmlisches Arom –*Hafis*
Ich rühme mir mein Dörfchen hier –*G. A. Bürger*
Ich rufe vom Ufer verlorenes Glück –*Eichendorff*
Ich ruhe still im hohen, grünen Gras –*Allmers*
Ich sag' es jedem, dass er lebt –*Novalis*
Ich sah als Knabe Blumen blühn –*Groth*
Ich sah am liebsten hoch im Turm –*Fischer*
Ich sah den Helikon in Wolkendunst –*Mörike*
Ich sah den Lenz einmal –*Lenau*
Ich sah des Sommers letzte Rose blühn –*Hebbel*
Ich sah' dich einmal –*Mosenthal*
Ich sah dich nachts am Fenster –*Schaukal*
Ich sah die Thräne groß und schwer –*Byron*
Ich sah die volle Thräne glühn –*Byron*
Ich sah eben ein jugendlich Paar –*Mörike*
Ich sah ein Mädchen ohne Mangel –*H. W. Gerstenberg*
Ich sah ein Röschen am Wege stehn –*Müchler*
Ich sah' mein Glück vorüber geh'n –*Heyse*
Ich sah sie hingesunken –*Swoboda*
Ich sah sie nur ein einzigmal –*Rückert*
Ich sah uns alle und empfand –*Morgenstern*
Ich sahe dich im Traume –*Daumer*
Ich sahe eine Tigrin im dunklen Haine –*Kopisch*
Ich sang mich durch das deutsche Land –*Sergel*
Ich sass am einsamen Weiher –*Röser*
Ich saß am Strand und hub an –*Scherer*
Ich sass an einer Tempelhalle –*Baumberg*
Ich sass bei jener Linde –*Uhland*
Ich sass noch spät in meinem Zimmer –*J. Sturm*
Ich sass und träumte Lieder –*Groth*
Ich saß zu deinen Füßen –*Lemcke*
Ich schau' über Forth –*Burns*
Ich schaukle leicht mich im grünen Laub –*Stieglitz*
Ich schell mein Horn ins Jammertal –*Anonymous*
Ich schiess' den Hirsch –*Schober*
Ich schleich umher betrübt und stumm –*Platen*
Ich schnitt' es gern –*Wilhelm Müller*
Ich schreib allzeit nur wenig –*Scheffel*
Ich schwebe wie auf Engelsschwingen –*K. Henckell*
Ich schwing mein Horn ins Jammertal –*Volkslied*
Ich seh durch Tränenbäche –*Hermes*
Ich seh' ein Schifflein fahren –*Reinecke*
Ich seh' von des Schiffes Rande –*Eichendorff*
Ich seh' vor mir ein liebes Bild –*Bittner*
Ich sehe dich in tausend Bildern –*Novalis*

Ich sehe ihn wieder den lieblichen Stern *–A. v. Arnim*
Ich sehe mit Schmerzen *–Stolberg-Stolberg*
Ich sehe oft um Mitternacht *–M. Claudius*
Ich sehe Thränen im Aug' *–L. Tolstoi*
Ich sehe wie in einem Spiegel *–Rückert*
Ich sehe Winterblaß ein Land *–Noehring*
Ich sende einen Gruss wie Duft der Rosen *–Rückert*
Ich singe der Kraft *–"Carmen Sylva"*
Ich sinke dir ans volle Herz *–"Dilia Helena"*
Ich sitz am Strande der rauschenden See *–Lemcke*
Ich sitz' bei der moosigten Quelle *–Macpherson*
Ich sitze hier in dunkler Nacht *–Prechtler*
Ich sitze manchen langen Tag *–Leixner*
Ich soll kein Lebewohl dir sagen *–Anonymous*
Ich soll und muß ein' Buhlen haben *–Wunderhorn*
Ich stand auf Berges Halde *–Rückert*
Ich stand auf hohem Berge *–Volkslied*
Ich stand gelehnet an den Mast *–Heine*
Ich stand in deiner Straße *–B. Huber*
Ich stand in dunkeln Träumen *–Heine*
Ich stand in einer lauen Nacht *–Lemcke*
Ich steh an deiner Krippen hier *–Gerhardt*
Ich stehe hoch überm See *–Lieven*
Ich stehe in Waldesschatten *–Eichendorff*
Ich stellt' ein Lilienstäudlein *–Heyse*
Ich sterbe den Tod des Verräters *–Cornelius*
Ich stund an einem Morgen *–Volkslied*
Ich such' im Schnee vergebens *–Wilhelm Müller*
Ich suchte eine Melodie *–Kotsch*
Ich thät mich einst vermiethen *–Daumer*
Ich träume als Kind mich zurücke *–Chamisso*
Ich träumte von bunten Blumen *–Wilhelm Müller*
Ich trag' ein glückselig Geheimnis *–Ritter*
Ich trag' eine Liebe im Herzen *–Anonymous*
Ich trage meine Minne vor Wonne *–K. Henckell*
Ich trage, wo ich gehe *–J. Seidl*
Ich trat in einen heilig düstern Eichwald *–Lenau*
Ich treibe auf des Lebens Meer *–Senn*
Ich tret in deinen Garten *–Uhland*
Ich tumm'le mich auf der Haide *–Kannegiesser*
Ich unglücksel'ger Atlas *–Heine*
Ich Unglückseliger! Wer gibt mir Nachricht *–Hafis*
Ich verlor die Kraft und das Leben *–Musset*
Ich wache noch in später Nacht *–Morgenstern*
Ich wahrte die Hoffnung tief *–K. Schweizer*
Ich wand ein Sträußchen morgens früh *–Storm*
Ich wand mir einst einen Veilchenkranz *–Mahlmann*
Ich wandelt einsam auf grünem Pfad *–Anonymous*
Ich wandelte unter den Bäumen *–Heine*
Ich wandle einsam, mein Weg ist lang *–Cornelius*
Ich wandle unter Blumen und blühe selber mit *–Heine*
Ich wandre durch die stille Nacht *–Eichendorff*
Ich wand're fort in's ferne Land *–Lenau*
Ich wand're heim durch's hohe Feld *–Stieler*
Ich wandre über Berg und Thal *–E. Schulze*
Ich wandte mich, und sahe an *–the Bible*
Ich war bei Chloen ganz allein *–C. Weisse*
Ich war ein Blatt an grünem Baum *–Cornelius*
Ich war erlöst, jetzt hab ich stark *–W. Scholz*
Ich war erst sechzehn Sommer alt *–M. Claudius*
Ich war mal froh vor lange! *–Siebel*
Ich war mal in dem Dorfe *–Blüthgen*
Ich warf eine Rose ins Meer *–Dehmel*
Ich weil' in tiefer Einsamkeit *–Unidentified*
Ich weiss nicht, wie mir ist! *–Wunderhorn*
Ich weiß: an irgend einem fernen Tag *–Hesse*
Ich weiß, daß Dir und mir bereitet *–Bittner*
Ich weiß ein Mädlein hübsch und fein *–Wunderhorn*
Ich weiss eine Farbe, der bin ich so hold *–Mereau*
Ich weiß es nicht, was es wohl war *–Sergel*
Ich weiß es wohl, und spotte viel *–Goethe*
Ich weiß, ich träume im Grabe *–Jacobowski*
Ich weiß ihr liebt das Dunkel nicht *–Faktor*
Ich weiss ja, warum ich so traurig bin *–Volkslied*
Ich weiß mir'n Mädchen hübsch und fein *–Wunderhorn*
Ich weiß nicht, säuselt in den Bäumen *–Geibel*
Ich weiß nicht, was im Hain *–Rückert*
Ich weiß nicht, was mir gar so bang *–Ritter*
Ich weiß nicht was mir hier gefällt *–Goethe*
Ich weiß nicht, was soll's bedeuten *–Heine*
Ich weiss nicht, wie mir's ist *–Wunderhorn*
Ich weiß nicht, wie's geschieht *–Geibel*
Ich weiß: sie werden über uns lächeln *–Busta*
Ich werde in Ostia sein *–Mayröcker*
Ich werde Mama: und Kinder sind da! *–Rafael*
Ich werde nicht an deinem Herzen satt *–Huch*
Ich werde Soldat, ich werde Soldat! *–Rafael*
Ich will bis in die Sterne *–Hafis*
Ich will dich lieben, meine Krone! *–Scheffler*
Ich will die Fluren meiden *–Rückert*
Ich will die lauten Freuden nicht *–Redwitz*
Ich will dir's nimmer sagen *–Prutz*
Ich will, ein junger Lenzhusar *–Heindl*
Ich will hier am Portale steh'n *–Mosenthal*
Ich will ja nicht in Garten geh'n *–Uhland*
Ich will meine Seele tauchen *–Heine*

Ich will mich im grünen Wald –*Heine*
Ich will nur ihn! Und doch –*Heyse*
Ich will spiegeln mich in jenen Tagen –*Keller*
Ich will von Atreus Söhnen –*Bruchmann*
Ich will von den Atriden –*Anacreon*
Ich will vor deiner Thüre stehn' –*Brunykowski*
Ich wollt', daß der verhindert mich –*Wunderhorn*
Ich wollt' ein Sträußlein binden –*C. Brentano*
Ich wollt' ich wär' ein Fisch –*Goethe*
Ich wollt', ich wär' ein Held –*Falke*
Ich wollt', ich wär' ein morgenklarer See –*Hafis*
Ich wollt', ich wär' eine Blume –*Hesse*
Ich wollt, meine Lieb ergösse sich –*Heine*
Ich wollt' meine Schmerzen ergössen –*Heine*
Ich wollte, ich konnte nicht träumen –*"Max Waldau"*
Ich wollte in die Fremde gehn –*K. Schweizer*
Ich wollte mich zur lieben Maria vermieten –*Wunderhorn*
Ich wünsche dir Glück –*Dehmel*
Ich würd' auf meinem Pfad –*Hermes*
Ich zieh' dahin, ade, ade –*Vincke*
Ich zieh' in's Feld von Lieb' entbrannt –*Reissig*
Ich zieh' so allein –*Müller von Königswinter*
Ich zog meine Fuhre trotz meiner Schwäche –*Brecht*
Ihr Bilder, die die Zeit begrub *Leuthold*
Ihr Blümlein alle, die sie mir gab –*Wilhelm Müller*
Ihr deutschen Länder alle –*Randow & Loewe*
Ihr, die ihr auftauchen werdet –*Brecht*
Ihr, die ihr überlebtet –*Brecht*
Ihr ewigen Sterne –*Sergel*
Ihr fragt, was Großes ich erdenke –*"Theodor Hell"*
Ihr Freunde, hänget, wenn ich gestorben bin –*L. Hölty*
Ihr Freunde und du gold'ner Wein –*Zettler*
Ihr frühlingstrunk'nen Blumen –*Anonymous*
Ihr Glokken von Marling –*Kuh*
Ihr großen Städte Steinern aufgebaut –*Trakl*
Ihr guten Herrn, ihr schönen Frauen –*Goethe*
Ihr habt den Vogel gefangen –*Eichendorff*
Ihr habt genug getrunken –*Stieglitz*
Ihr Heiligen am Kirchenthor –*Stinde*
Ihr Hirten, erwacht, seid munter –*Volkslied*
Ihr hohen Himmlischen, erhöret –*J. Mayrhofer*
Ihr holden Augensterne –*F. Förster*
Ihr Hügel dort am schönen Doon –*Burns*
Ihr, ihr Herrlichen! steht –*Hölderlin*
Ihr in der Ferne seid mir so nah –*L. Hölty*
Ihr jungen Leute, die ihr zieht –*Heyse*
Ihr lichten Sterne –*Hoffmann von Fallersleben*
Ihr Liebe flüsternden Linden! –*J. Kinkel*
Ihr Lieben, die ich Schwermuthsvoll –*Riedinger*
Ihr lieben Frühlingssänger zieht –*Vogeler*
Ihr lieben Mauern hold und traut –*J. Seidl*
Ihr linden Lüfte, Boten Italiens –*Hölderlin*
Ihr, Mädchen, flieht Damöten ja! –*C. Weisse*
Ihr Mädchen seid wie die Gärten –*Rilke*
Ihr Mägdelein, nehmt euch in Acht –*Meyer-Helmund*
Ihr Matten, lebt wohl, ihr sonnigen Weiden! –*Schiller*
Ihr Menschenkinder, seid ihr nicht Laub –*Kraus*
Ihr milden Lüfte, Boten Italiens! –*Hölderlin*
Ihr mißvergnügten Stunden –*Anonymous*
Ihr Mund ist stets derselbe –*A. v. Arnim*
Ihr schwarzen Augen, ihr dürft nur winken –*Daumer*
Ihr seid die Allerschönste –*Heyse*
Ihr Söhne Abrahams, seid einig! –*G. Nicolai*
Ihr Sternlein, hoch am Himmelszelt! –*Träger*
Ihr Sternlein, still in der Höhe –*E. Schulze*
Ihr Stimmen! Was denn ruft ihr mir –*Jünger*
Ihr Thoren wollt das Glück –*Raupach*
Ihr tratet zu dem herde –*George*
Ihr verblühet, süsse Rosen –*Goethe*
Ihr Wälder schön an der Seite –*Hölderlin*
Ihr wandelt droben im Licht –*Hölderlin*
Ihr wisset, was für schwere Klagen –*Weckherlin*
Ihr wunderschönen Augenblicke –*Schenkendorf*
Im Aargäu sind zwei Liebi –*Volkslied*
Im Abendgolde glänzet zu Bärenburg –*Fitzau*
Im Abendschimmer wallt der Quell –*Matthisson*
Im alten loderlohen Glanze –*Hesse*
Im Anfang war's auf Erden nur finster –*M. Claudius*
Im Arm der Liebe ruht sich's wohl –*Ueltzen*
Im Arm der Liebe schliefen wir selig ein –*Hartleben*
Im Dämmer der Nacht, in Mondesluft –*C. Hauptmann*
Im deutschen Land, daheim am Heerde –*Stieler*
Im Dorfe blüht die Linde –*Wolff*
Im düstern Klostergarten –*Vogl*
Im Erlenbusch, im Tannenhain –*Kosegarten*
Im Feld ein Mädchen singt –*Susman*
Im Felde schleich' ich still und wild –*Goethe*
Im Fensterausschnitt mir gegenüber –*Schumacher*
Im Finstern geh ich suchen –*Kopisch*
Im Fliederbusch ein Vöglein saß –*R. Reinick*
Im Föhrenwald wie schwüle! –*Heyse*
Im Freien, ach im Freien –*Vogl*
Im Frühling, als der Märzwind ging –*Falke*
Im Frühlingsschatten fand ich sie –*Klopstock*
Im Garten am Seegestade –*Lemcke*

Im Garten des Pfarrers von Taubenhain
–*G. A. Bürger*
Im Garten Gottes wirft ein Born –*Morgenstern*
Im Garten klagt die Nachtigal –*F. Bodenstedt*
Im Garten meiner Mutter steht –*Hesse*
Im Garten rauscht die Sommernacht –*Triepel*
Im Garten steht die Nonne –*Fröhlich*
Im Gefild zum Strauße wand' wilde Blüt' –*Frey*
Im Grase hingestreckt lausch' ich –*Hesse*
Im Grase lieg' ich manche Stunde –*Osterwald*
Im Grase thaut's, die Blumen träumen –*Wolff*
Im Grünen, im Walde, da ist es so schön –*Wette*
Im Haine schlagen lustig –*Unidentified*
Im heil'gen Land, im Wüstensand –*Scheffel*
Im Herbst verblichen liegt das Land –*Keller*
Im Hofe steht ein Pflaumenbaum –*Brecht*
Im Inselwald, "Zum stillen Kauz" –*Morgenstern*
Im kalten, rauhen Norden –*J. Mayrhofer*
Im Kastanienbaum der Wind –*Hesse*
Im Kreise der Vasallen sitzt der Ritter –*Hebbel*
Im kühlen Schatten, auf sonnigen Höh'n –*J. Sturm*
Im Lande Uz, dem schönsten Idumäa's –*Telschow*
Im Lenz, im Lenz, wenn Veilchen blühn –*Heyse*
Im Lichte wächst die Weide –*Thiess*
Im Meere möcht' ich fahren –*Kopisch*
Im Mondenglanze ruht das Meer –*Heine*
Im Mondenschein' wall' ich auf und ab –*Bruchmann*
Im Mondgeflimmer, im Zauberschimmer –*Leen*
Im Morgengrauen schritt ich fort –*Conradi*
Im morgen-taun trittst du hervor –*George*
Im Mummelsee, im dunkeln See –*Schnezler*
Im Nebel ruhet noch die Welt –*Mörike*
Im Nebelgeriesel, im tiefen Schnee –*Goethe*
Im Palmenhain weht Frieden –*Müller von der Werre*
Im phantast'schen Mondenstrahle –*Giraud*
Im Rhein, im schönen Strome –*Heine*
Im Rosenbusch die Liebe schlief –*Hoffmann von Fallersleben*
Im säuselnden Winde, am murmelnden Bach
–*Herder*
Im Schacht der Adern –*Giesebrecht*
Im Schatten des Waldes, im Buchengezweig –*Geibel*
Im Schlafgemach, entfernt vom Feste –*Goethe*
Im Schlehendorn, im Schlehendorn –*Stinde*
Im Schloss, da brennen der Kerzen viel –*F. Kugler*
Im Schnee und Eis in kalter Nacht –*R. Reinick*
Im Schnee von Blüthenflocken –*Groth*
Im schönen Land Tirol hab ich –*Wetzel*
Im schönsten Garten wallten –*Uhland*
Im schwarzen Wallfisch zu Ascalon –*Scheffel*
Im Sommer such' ein Liebchen dir –*Uhland*
Im Sonnenschimmer, in Luna's flimmer –*Haug*
Im spielenden Bache da lieg ich wie helle! –*Goethe*
Im Städtchen giebt es Jubels viel –*Chamisso*
Im stillen Klostergarten –*Uhland*
Im Süden war's. Zur Nachtzeit –*Morgenstern*
Im tiefen Thale, bei heissem Mittag –*Bone*
Im tiefen Wald im Dornenhag –*Volkslied*
Im tiefen Wald verborgen –*Anonymous*
Im tiefsten Herzen glüht mir eine Wunde –*Cornelius*
Im tiefsten Innern ein süss' Erinnern –*"Betty Paoli"*
Im Traum sah ich die Geliebte –*Heine*
Im trüben Licht verschwinden schon die Berge
–*M. Collin*
Im Wald auf früher Reise –*Anonymous*
Im Wald, im hellen Sonnenschein –*Geibel*
Im Wald, im Wald da grabt mich ein –*J. Mayrhofer*
Im Wald', im Wald' ist's frisch und grün –*Körner*
Im Wald, in grüner Runde –*Pfarrius*
Im Walde blüht der Seidelbast –*Hesse*
Im Walde geh' ich wohlgemut –*Uhland*
Im Walde, im tiefgrünen Wald –*Mommsen*
Im Walde liegt ein stiller See –*Sergel*
Im Walde rauschen dürre Blätter –*Klingemann*
Im Walde rollt der Wagen –*Gruppe*
Im Walde schleich ich still und wild –*Goethe*
Im Walde wandl' ich und weine –*Heine*
Im Waldesweben ist es Ruh' –*Stieler*
Im Weinberg auf der Höhe –*Mörike*
Im Weinberg auf der Höhe –*Mörike*
Im Weizenfeld, im Korn und Mohn –*Liliencron*
Im Welschland, wo die braunen Buben –*Hesse*
Im Winde fächeln, Mutter, die Blätter –*Eichendorff*
Im Winde, im Sturme befahr' ich den Fluss
–*J. Mayrhofer*
Im windes-weben war meine frage –*George*
Im Windsgeräusch, in stiller Nacht –*Tieck*
Im Winterboden schläft, ein Blumenkeim –*Mörike*
Im Wirthshaus geht es aus und ein –*Marées*
Im wunderschönen Monat Mai –*Heine*
Im Zaune klagt die Nachtigall –*Hartleben*
Im zitternden Mondlicht wiegen –*Kastropp*
Immer bin ich ohne Ziel gegangen –*Hesse*
Immer bleibst du lieblich mir –*Falke*
Immer enger, leise, leise ziehen –*Fontane*
Immer leiser wird mein Schlummer –*Lingg*
Immer mag verklingen muntrer Vögel Sang –*Hugo*
Immer schaust du in die Ferne –*Wolff*

Immer schwitzend, immer sitzend *–K. Fick*
Immer sich rein kindlich erfreu`n *–Anonymous*
Immer stiller stehn die Bäume *–Dehmel*
Immer wieder in die Weite *–Goethe*
Immer wieder kehrst du, Melancholie *–Trakl*
Immerdar mit leisem Weben *–Blumauer*
Immortelle! bring' mein "gute Nacht" *–Braun von Braunthal*
In ahnungsvollem Glanze ruht *–Anonymous*
In allen Fernen wölbt sich ein Haus *–Anonymous*
In allen guten Stunden *–Goethe*
In allen Landen gehet still *–Anonymous*
In aller Früh, ach, lang vor Tag *–Mörike*
In Basra eine Wittwe war *–Rückert*
In begrünter Sommerlaube *–Frey*
In dämmrigen Grüften träumte ich lang *–Hesse*
In deine Augen will ich schauen *–"Ernst"*
In deine langen Wellen *–Morgenstern*
In deinem Arm, an deinem Herzen *–Ritter*
In deinen Liedern lebt mein Leben *–Jacobowski*
In deiner Näh' ist mir so gut *–Wertheimer*
In deiner Nähe weil' ich noch *–Cornelius*
In dem Dornbusch blüht ein Röslein *–Osterwald*
In dem Frieden heil'ger Nacht *–Behn*
In dem frischen grünen Walde *Röser*
In dem grünen Kuddelmuddel *–Brecht*
In dem Himmel ruht die Erde *–R. Reinick*
In dem Mondenschein im Walde *–Heine*
In dem Schatten meiner Locken *–Heyse*
In dem stillen Mondenscheine *–Goethe*
In dem Traum siehst du die stillen *–Heine*
In dem Walde süsse Töne singen *–Lichtenstein*
In den Abgrund lass mich schauen *–Hahn-Hahn*
In den Augen liegt das Herz *–Herloßsohn*
In den Bäumen regt sich's leise *–Stieler*
In den blanken Kopf Cassanders *–Giraud*
In den finsteren Zeiten *–Brecht*
In den Garten wollen wir gehen *–Wunderhorn*
In den Hügeln wird Gold gefunden *–Brecht*
In den Lüften schwellendes Gedröhne *–C. F. Meyer*
In den Schlosshof hernieder *–Mickiewicz*
In den Wald bin ich geflüchtet *–C. F. Meyer*
In den Walde spriesst's *–Heine*
In den Wassern der Laguna *–Geibel*
In den Weiden am Sund ruft *–Brecht*
In den Wind sing' ich mein Lied *–C. Hauptmann*
In den Wipfeln des Waldes *–Morgenstern*
In den Wipfeln frische Lüfte *–Eichendorff*
In der Berge Riesenschatten *–Gubitz*
In der Dämmerung, um Glock zwei *–Liliencron*
In der finstern Mitternacht *–Volkslied*
In der Freie will ich leben *–K. Lappe*
In der Früh', wenn die Sonne kommen will *–Leander*
In der hohen Hall' saß König Sifrid *–Uhland*
In der Kindheit frühen Tagen *–Wesendonck*
In der Luft, der schwülen *–Stieler*
In der Mondnacht, in der Frühlingsmondnacht *–Heyse*
In der Nacht, die die Bäume *–C. F. Meyer*
In der Nacht, in der Nacht *–Hahn-Hahn*
In der Ruhe Thal geboren *–Herder*
In der Schmiede dröhnt der Hammer *–Trakl*
In der Seele ein Wachsen und Keimen *–Faktor*
In der Väter Hallen ruhte *–Stolberg-Stolberg*
In der Zeit sprach der Herr Jesus *–the Bible*
In des Meeres kühle Wogen *–Müchler*
In des Pappillons Gestalt *–Goethe*
In des Sees Wogenspiele *–Bruchmann*
In des Südens heissen Zonen *–Goltz*
In des Todes Feierstunde *–Schober*
In die blaue Luft hinaus e *–Dingelstedt*
In die braunen, rauschenden Nächte *–Schlaf*
In die dunkle Bergschlucht *–Dehmel*
In die Städte kam ich zu der Zeit *–Brecht*
In die tiefsten Felsengründe *–Wilhelm Müller*
In diesem Lande und in dieser Zeit *–Brecht*
In diesem Wetter, in diesem Braus *–Rückert*
In diesen Silberhainen von Oliven *–Leuthold*
In diesen Wintertagen *–K. Henckell*
In dieser Rinne will ich sterben! *–Béranger*
In dieser Winterfrühe wie ist mir doch zumut! *–Mörike*
In dieses Thal, in diese Stille *–Giesebrecht*
In düstrer Nacht, wenn Gram *–Anonymous*
In dulci jubilo/nun singet und seid froh! *–Anonymous*
In dunkler Felsenbucht am Rhein *–F. Förster*
In dunkler Nacht, wenn's Aug' noch wacht *–Collignon*
In ein freundliches Städtchen tret' ich ein *–Mörike*
In einem Bächlein helle *–C. F. D. Schubart*
In einem Buche blätternd *–Lenau*
In einem Dorf, am frühen Morgen *–Zedlitz*
In einem kühlen Grunde *–Eichendorff*
In einem leeren Haselstrauch *–Morgenstern*
In einem Rosengärtelein *–Friderici*
In einem stillen Garten *–Dehmel*
In einem Thal bei armen Hirten *–Schiller*
In einem Thal, bei einem Bach *–André*

In einem Thale friedlich stille *–Harring*
In einsamen Stunden drängt Wehmut *–Anonymous*
In Erwägung unser Schwäche *–Brecht*
In Feindesland die graue Spätherbstnacht *–Zwehl*
In frohen Tagen such' ich dich *–B. Huber*
In Frühlings Heiligtume *–Hebbel*
In Gold und Purpur tief verhüllt *–Keller*
In goldnen Abendschein getauchet *–Rückert*
In großen Städten lernen früh *–Goethe*
In Grün will ich mich kleiden *–Wilhelm Müller*
In grüner Landschaft Sommerflor *–Mörike*
In hellen Träumen hab ich Dich *–Gold*
In jüngern Tagen war ich *–Hölderlin*
In leisen Trauerklagen *–Vincke*
In Liebe sich begegnen *–Dr. Bartholdy*
In Liebesarmen ruht ihr trunken *–Uhland*
In Liebeslust, in Sehnsuchtsqual *–Hoffmann von Fallersleben*
In Lust und Schmerzen *–Cornelius*
In Meeres Mitten ist ein offner Laden *–Rückert*
In mein gar zu dunkles Leben *–Heine*
In meine innige Nacht geh' ich ein *–Kaltneker*
In meinem Garten die Nelken *–Geibel*
In meinem Garten lachet *–Mosen*
In meinem Herzen ist's öd' und leer *–Obst*
In meinem Herzen regte *–Cornelius*
In meinem Herzen ruft *–Fankhauser*
In meinem Lebensringe *–F. Bodenstedt*
In meinen Armen wieg' ich dich *–Natorp*
In meiner Brust, da sitzt ein Weh *–Heine*
In meiner Brust eine Glocke klingt *–Silesius*
In meiner Jugend als ich liebte *–Shakespeare*
In meiner Nächte Sehnen, so tief allein *–Daumer*
In meiner Träume Heimat *–C. Hauptmann*
In meines Herzens Mitte *–Wilhelm Müller*
In meines Vaters Garten blühe *–Hartleben*
In meines Vaters Garten da stehen zwei Bäumelein *–Volkslied*
In mir nur Tod, in dir mein Leben ruht *–Michelangelo*
In monderhellten Nächten *–J. Mayrhofer*
In Nachbars Garten duftet *–"Gerda v. Robertus"*
In Nürnberg machten sie ein Gesetz *–Brecht*
In poetischer Epistel ruft ein desperater Wicht *–Mörike*
In Polen steht ein Haus *–Volkslied*
In Schlummer ist der dunkle Wald gesunken *–Lenau*
In schwerer Schuld nur *–Michelangelo*
In seinem schimmernden Gewand *–Uz*
In solchen Nächten wächst *–Rilke*
In Sommertagen rüste den Schlitten *–Rückert*
In Sonnenglut, in Mittagsruh *–Nietzsche*
In Sternennacht, wenn's dämmert sacht *–Heyse*
In stiller Bucht, bei finstrer Nacht *–Eichendorff*
In stiller Nacht, zur ersten Wacht *–Volkslied*
In Stunden der Entmutigung *–F. Bodenstedt*
In tausend Formen magst du dich *–Goethe*
In tiefem Rausch hab' ich *–Faktor*
In tiefer Ruh liegt um mich her *–Rellstab*
In tiefster Erde ruht ein alt Gesetz *–Schober*
In tiefster Schlucht, in Waldesschoss *–Chézy*
In verschwiegener Nacht *–Ritter*
In verschwundnen Rosentagen *–K. F. Reinhardt*
In weite Ferne will ich träumen! *–Heine, Droysen*
Inbrunst, Zärtlichkeit, Verstand *–Ramler*
Inne Buurstraten dar steit en glatt Huus *–Groth*
Inneres Wühlen ewig zu finden *–Goethe*
Ins Grüne, ins Grüne *–Reil*
In's Joch beug' ich den Nacken *–Michelangelo*
Ins Museum bin zu später Stunde *–C. F. Meyer*
In's stille Land!? *–Salis-Seewis*
Irrlichter, die Knaben, die laufen *–Rückert*
Israel hat dennoch Gott zum Trost *–the Bible*
Ist alles eins, was liegt daran! *–Haringer*
Ist auch schmuck nicht mein Rößlein *–Eichendorff*
Ist das der Tod? *–Ingrisch*
Ist das in dir der Mensch *–H. Claudius*
Ist der alte Schiffsherr endlich *–Vogl*
Ist der Frühling über Nacht *–Rollet*
Ist der Gang der Uhr nicht *–Ehrler*
Ist der Himmel darum im Lenz so blau? *–Leander*
Ist der holde Lenz erschienen? *–Schiller*
Ist dies Tauris, wo der Eumeniden Wuth *–J. Mayrhofer*
Ist dir ein getreues, liebevolles *–Hafis*
Ist es wahr? Ist es wahr? *–Voss*
Ist gar ein holder Knabe, er! *–M. Claudius*
Ist mir's doch, als sei mein Leben *–J. Mayrhofer*
Ist mir's zu Muthe schwül und bang *–Träger*
Ist nicht der Himmel so blau? *–Hoffmann von Fallersleben*
Ist nicht heilig mein Herz *–Hölderlin*
Ist schmuck nicht mein Rößlein *–Eichendorff*
Ist's dein Wille, süsse Maid *–Molina*
Ist's möglich, dass ich, Liebchen *–Goethe*
Ist's möglich? sieht ein Mann *–Mörike*

Ja, die Schönst! *–Hoffmann von Fallersleben*

Ja, du bist elend, und ich grolle nicht –*Heine*
Ja, du bist mein! –*Hoffmann von Fallersleben*
Ja, du weisst es teure Seele –*Hermann Gilm*
Ja, freue dich –*Kannegiesser*
Ja, hätt' ich ein verlass'nes Liebchen nun –*Keller*
Ja heil und dank dir die den segen brachte! –*George*
Ja, ich bin krank, ich weiss –*Hafis*
Ja, ich weiss es, diese treue Liebe –*Bernard*
Ja, ja, ich schweige, liebste Seele! –*Anonymous*
Ja, mein Glück, das langgewohnte –*Mörike*
Ja, spanne nur den Bogen –*J. Mayrhofer*
Ja treuster Damon, ich bin überwunden! –*Kleist*
Ja, Vetter, ja! Ja, Vetter, ja –*Ramler*
Ja, wann gleich wär das Firmament –*Anonymous*
Jäger, ruhe von der Jagd! –*Scott*
Jäger, was jagst du die Häselein –*Candidus*
Jahrelang sehnten wir uns –*Falke*
Jauchzet dem Herrn, alle Welt! –*the Bible*
Je höher die Glocke –*Wilhelm Müller*
Je länger du dort bist –*K. L. von Münchhausen*
Jede Blüte will zur Frucht –*Hesse*
Jedem werke bin ich fürder tot –*George*
Jeden Morgen, in der Frühe –*Geibel*
Jeden Morgen, mein Brot zu verdienen –*Brecht*
Jeder meint, der Gegenstand –*Anonymous*
Jedes Ding in jeder Sache –*Gerhardt*
Jedweder Geselle, sein Mädel am Arm –*Heine*
Jehann, nu spann de Schimmels an! –*Groth*
Jesus Christus, wahrer Gottes-Sohn –*Bonn*
Jesus ist mein Hirt, auf Jesum will ich bauen –*J. Hus*
Jesus nimmt die Sünder an –*Anonymous*
Jetzt bist du da, dann bist du dort –*Morgenstern*
Jetzt erklang die Sterbestunde –*Melzer & Hanser*
Jetzt gang i an's Brünnele –*Volkslied*
Jetzt hab ich schon zwei Jahre lang –*Lemcke*
Jetzt ist des Winters grimmer Frost –*Keller*
Jetzt ist die Zeit –*Kalidasa*
Jetzt ist er hinaus in die weite Welt –*Scheffel*
Jetzt kommt der Frühling –*Robert*
Jetzt reisen wir zum Thor hinaus –*Volkslied*
Jetzt steh' ich auf der höchsten Höh' –*Osterwald*
Jetzt wird mein Elend voll –*Rilke*
Jezzund kömmt die Nacht herbei –*Opitz*
Johannes ging am hellen Bach –*Chézy*
John Anderson, mein Lieb! –*Burns*
Juble, schöne junge Rose –*Anonymous*
Juchhei, Blümelein! dufte und blühe! –*E. M. Arndt*
Juchheisa! und ich führ' den Zug –*Eichendorff*
Judäa, hochgelobtes Land –*Kannegiesser*
Jüngst lasest du – ich merkt' es wohl –*Huggenberger*
Jüngst sass ich am Grabe –*Wallner*
Jüngst träumte mir, ich sah auf lichten Höhen –*Körner*
Jugend, dich hab' ich so lieb! –*Hoffmann von Fallersleben*
Jugend du große, sehnende, liebende! –*Whitman*
Jugend, Rausch und Liebe –*Rückert*
Jung Siegfried war ein stolzer Knab' –*Uhland*
Jung stritt ich einst um Accons Schloss –*Giesebrecht*
Jung vermähle mich, o Mutter! –*Volkslied*
Jung Volker, das ist unser Räuberhauptmann –*Mörike*
Junge Hände halfen mich schmücken –*Ritter*
Junges Volk, man rufet euch –*Albert*
Jungfräulein Annika sass –*Rückert*
Jungfräulein, soll ich mit euch gehn –*Volkslied*

Kämpfte er nicht genug? –*Kafka*
Kahl reckt der baum im winterdunst –*George*
Kaiserkron' und Päonien rot –*Eichendorff*
Kalt und schneidend weht der Wind –*Lingg*
Kam ein Schmetterling geflogen –*Mühlbach*
Kampfmüd' und sonnverbrannt –*Scheffel*
Kaninchen, Karnickelchen –*R. Reinick*
Kann auch ein Mensch des andern *Mörike*
Kann ich fürchten, zweifeln, meinen? –*Giesebrecht*
Kannst du rathen wer ich sei? –*Reinecke*
Karlinle, mein Schatz, hat Härle –*Volkslied*
Kaum an dem blaueren Himmel –*Goethe*
Kaum dass ich dich wieder habe –*Goethe*
Kaum sind die ersten Blüten da –*Rafael*
Kehr' ich zum heimischen Rhein –*Cornelius*
Kehre nicht in diesem Kreise –*Goethe*
Kehre zurück zur Arbeit –*Bolliger*
Kein beßre Lust in dieser Zeit –*Uhland*
Kein Blick der Hoffnung –*L. Hölty*
Kein Feuer, kein Kohle –*Volkslied*
Kein Graben so breit –*Groth*
Kein Haus, keine Heimat –*"Friedrich Halm"*
Kein Hochgewild ich fahen kann –*Wunderhorn*
Kein Laut erschallt im öden Wald. –*K. Schaefer*
Kein Meister fällt vom Himmel –*R. Reinick*
Kein Pfad mehr! Abgrund rings –*Nietzsche*
Kein Rosenschimmer leuchtet –*Matthisson*
Kein Schlaf noch kühlt das Auge mir –*Mörike*
Kein schön'rer Tod ist in der Welt –*Volkslied*
Kein Sonnenglanz im Auge meiner Frau –*Shakespeare*
Kein Wandrer sich in diese Schlucht verirrt –*Stamm*

Keine Blumen blühn, nur das Wintergrün *–L. Hölty*
Keine gleicht von allen Schönen *–Byron*
Keine Klage soll erschallen *–Friedelberg*
Keine Lust ohn' treues Lieben! *–F. Förster*
Keine Rose darf ich pflücken *–Weigand*
Keine Sorge verzehre mich um das Künftige *–Hafis*
Keine Stimme hör' ich schallen *–E. Schulze*
Keine von der Erde Schönen *–Byron*
Keinen hat es noch gereut *–Tieck*
Keinen Reimer wird man finden *–Goethe*
Keinen Tropfen im Becher mehr *–Baumbach*
Keinen Vater, der das Kinn mir hebt *–Jacobowski*
Keiner plagt sich gerne, doch wir wissen *–Brecht*
Kennst du das auch, daß manches Mal *–Hesse*
Kennst du das Blümchen auf der Au? *–Aurnhammer*
Kennst du das Land, wo die Citronen blühn *–Goethe*
Kennst du den Fluss *–G. K. A. Richter*
Kennst du die Blume, die märchenhafte *–Dahn*
Kennst du nicht das Gluthverlangen *–Anonymous*
Kennst du nicht das Glutverlangen *–Anonymous*
Kikriki! kikriki! Horch, horch! *–Unidentified*
Kind, wo bist du hin gewesen *–Anonymous*
Kinder, kommt, verzählt euch nicht *–Dehmel*
Kindlein schlaf' ein *–K. Berlepsch*
Klabautermann, Klabauterfrau *–Morgenstern*
Klage, meine Flöte, klage *–Pichler*
Klagen ist der Mond gekommen *–Gregorovius*
Klagt mich nicht an, dass ich vor Leid *–Keller*
Klar und wie die Jugend heiter *–Lenau*
Klaus ist in den Wald gegangen *–Güll*
Klavier und Geige, die ich wahrlich schätze *–Hesse*
Klein Christel kam vor die Himmelspfort! *–Volkslied*
Klein ist mein Kind *–Albrecht Goes*
Klein Lieschen, klein Lieschen *–Gruppe*
Klein Vöglein widi widi widi witt *–Anonymous*
Kleine Blumen im engen Thal *–Träger*
Kleine Blumen, kleine Blätter *–Goethe*
Kleine Blumen wie aus Glas *–Holz*
Kleine Gäste, kleines Haus *–Mörike*
Kleine Schöne, küsse mich *–Lessing*
Kleine Spinnerin hinter deinem Rädchen *–Krauseneck*
Kleine Tränen seh' ich zittern *–Braungart*
Kleine Tropfen, seid ihr Thränen *–Anonymous*
Kleiner blauer Schmetterling *–Eigenbrodt*
Kleiner, kühler Wiesenquell *–Anonymous*
Kleinodien, Zierat, Perlen *–Michelangelo*
Kling' die Nacht durch, klinge *–J. Seidl*
Kling' Glöckchen kling'! *–Enslin*
Kling, kling, Glöckchen *–Wunderhorn*
Kling leise, mein Lied *–Nordmann*
Kling! Meine Seele gibt reinen Ton *–K. Henckell*
Klinge, klinge mein Pandero *–Geibel*
Klingend schlagen hier die Finken *–Frey*
Knabe, dir gefiel die duftige Rose *–Volkslied*
Knabe saß ich Fischerknabe *–Goethe*
Knapp', sattle mir mein Dänenroß *–G. A. Bürger*
König Baumbart, der alte Tann *–Heindl*
König ist spazieren gangen *–Salus*
König Wilhelm, unsre Sonne *–Emsmann*
Königliche Morgensonne *–Tiedge*
Könnt' ich dich in Liedern preisen *–Kerner*
Könnt' ich doch erleben *–Walther von der Vogelweide*
Könnt' ich mit dir dort oben gehn *–Mosen*
Könnt ich zu den Wäldern flüchten *–Eichendorff*
Könnt' ich zu dir, mein Licht *–Pfau*
Könnt ihr die Göttin Freude zwingen *–Haug*
Könnt'st du meine Äugelein seh'n *–Volkslied*
Köpfchen, Köpfchen, nicht gewimmert *–Heyse*
Köpfchen, Köpfchen, nicht gewimmert *–Heyse*
Komm, aller Wesen Freude! *–Haug*
Komm, ambrosische Nacht *–Leuthold*
Komm an mein Feuer, mein Weib *–Dehmel*
Komm ans Fenster, holde Schöne *–Reissig*
Komm, falsche Dirne, laß dich küssen! *–Daumer*
Komm' fein's Liebchen *–Kotzebue*
Komm heil'ger Geist, erhöre *–A. Schmidl*
Komm heraus, komm heraus *–C. Brentano*
Komm herbei, komm herbei, Tod *–Shakespeare*
Komm' ich längs der grünen Wiese *–Falke*
Komm' in aller Tage stille Dunkelheit *–Kamossa*
Komm in den Garten! ich harre dein *–Bassewitz*
Komm in den Wald! komm an den Fels! *–Werthes*
Komm in den Wald, Marie! *–K. Henckell*
Komm' in die stille Nacht *–R. Reinick*
Komm, komm, Geselle mein *–Anonymous*
Komm, komm mit nur einen Schritt! *–"Kurt Aram"*
Komm', komm' zu mir, Lieb' *–Gomoll*
Komm', Liebchen, komm'! die Nacht *–Beer*
Komm, Liebchen, komm! umwinde *–Goethe*
Komm, liebe Zither, komm *–Anonymous*
Komm lieber Mai und mache die Bäume *–Overbeck*
Komm Mädchen an dein Fenster *–Daumer*
Komm Mägdelein' ohne Bangen *–"Dilia Helena"*
Komm Mainz, komm Bayrn, komm Österreich *–Volkslied*
Komm mit! beflügle deinen Schritt *–Anonymous*

Komm mit mir in's Thäle *–Volkslied*
Komm mit, o Schöne, komm mit mir zum Tanze *–Goethe*
Komm' nur mühselig und gebückt! *–the Bible*
Komm, o Bruder, in die helle Sonne *–"Talvj"*
Komm, o Nacht, und nimm mich hin *–J. Sturm*
Komm, o Tod, von Nacht umgeben *–Geibel*
Komm Schwester zu den Ufern *–Anonymous*
Komm, Trost der Welt *–Eichendorff*
Komm und besänftige mir *–Hölderlin*
Komm, und senke die umflorten Schwingen *–Anonymous*
Komm', verhüllte Schöne! komm *–Rückert*
Komm, wir wandeln zusammen *–Cornelius*
Komm zum Garten denn, du Holde! *–Eichendorff*
Komm' zum Garten *–Hoffmann von Fallersleben*
Komme komme komm herbei *–Volkslied*
Kommen und Scheiden, Suchen und Meiden *–Matthisson*
Kommst spät du liebe Nachtigall! *–v.B**n*
Kommt die Nacht mit ihren Schatten *–Volkslied*
Kommt dir manchmal in den Sinn *–Conrat*
Kommt gezogen, kleine Vögel *–Wackernagel*
Kommt herzu, ihr seid geladen *–Anonymous*
Kommt und laßt uns Christum ehren *–Gerhardt*
Kommt, wir wollen uns begeben *–Hoffmann von Fallersleben*
Konnte sie denn anders *–Rilke*
Kornblumen flecht' ich dir zum Kranz *–Geibel*
Kornblumen nenn' ich die Gestalten *–Dahn*
Krank nun vollends und matt! *–Mörike*
Krause, krause Muhme, alte Butterblume *–Dehmel*
Kreuz der Straße wir sind am End' *–George*
Krieger und Feldherrn, ereilt mich der Tod *–Byron*
Kuckuk, Kuckuk ruft *–Hoffmann von Fallersleben*
Kühl in dem Schatten, geküsst von dem Thau *–Felix*
Kühl und stille ist die Nacht *–Bunge*
Kühle auf dem schönen Rheine *–Eichendorff*
Kühlender Abend, steige vom Hügel *–C. F. D. Schubart*
Küss' ich die Mutter Abends *–Hermann Gilm*
Küssen und Kosen steht euch an *–Sergel*
Kukuk hat sich zu Tode gefallen *–Wunderhorn*
Kukuk! was rufst im Wald mich an? *–Wolff*
Kunst! o in deine Arme wie gern *–Mörike*
Kyrie, o Herr Gott Vater *–Anonymous*

Lachen ist des Mundes Sache *–Hamerling*
Lachen und Weinen zu jeglicher Stunde *–Rückert*
Lachet nicht, Mädchen *–Anonymous*
Lächeln ist des Mundes Sache *–Hamerling*
Lächelnd scheidet der Despot *–Heine*
Läg' dort ich unterm Firneschein *–C. F. Meyer*
Läg' ich, wo es Hyänen gibt *–Keller*
Längst schon flog zu Nest der Vogel *–"Ernst"*
Lärchenbaum, mein Lärchenbaum *–Volkslied*
Läuten kaum die Mayenglocken *–Eichendorff*
Lang schon umwanderst Du mich *–Busta*
Lang war die Nacht *–Saar*
Lange begehrten wir ruhig *–Platen*
Lange lieb ich dich schon *–Hölderlin*
Lange waren meine Augen müd' *–Hesse*
Langsam und schimmernd fiel ein Regen *–Keller*
Langsam wird mein Kindchen müde *–Sergel*
Laß Akaziendüfte schaukeln *–Lindner*
Lass' das Zagen, trage mutig *–Schack*
Laß deine Sichel rauschen *–Pfau*
Lass deinen süssen Rubinenmund *–Goethe*
Laß den Jüngling, der dich liebt *–Hebbel*
Lass dich belauschen, du stille Nacht! *–Kerner*
Laß dich genießen, freundliche Frucht *–Goethe*
Lass dich mit gelinden Schlägen *–A. W. Schlegel*
Laß dich nur nichts nicht dauern *–Flemming*
Lass' die Rose schlummern *–Hamerling*
Lass es sein vergessen *–Teasdale*
Lass im Geheim mich zu Dir kommen *–Meissner*
Laß Liebster, wenn ich tot bin *–Kerr*
Laß mein Aug' den Abschied sagen *–Goethe*
Lass mich ganz in dich versinken *–Vogl*
Lass mich ihm am Busen hangen *–Rückert*
Lass mich in den dunklen Grund *–Kastropp*
Lass mich knieen, lass mich schauen *–Goethe*
Laß mich noch einmal dir *–Bierbaum*
Lass mich schlummern, Herzlein *–Kotzebue*
Laß Neid und Mißgunst sich verzehren *–Goethe*
Lass nicht dein Auge auf mir ruh'n *–J. Sturm*
Laß, o laß dein Auge immer *–Unidentified*
Lass, o lass mir deine Hand *–Zedlitz*
Laß, o Welt, o laß mich sein *–Mörike*
Laß schlafen mich und träumen *–Geibel*
Lass sie nur gehn *–Heyse*
Lass stehn die Blume *–Kopisch*
Laß tief in dir mich lesen *–Platen*
Lass uns leise bekennen *–Heyse*
Lass uns noch die Nacht erwarten *–Dehmel*
Lasset die Rosenumkränzeten Stunden *–Helvig-Imhof*
Lasset Gelehrte sich zanken *–Goethe*
Lasset heut im edlen Kreis *–Goethe*

Lasset uns marschiren, rataplan *–Anonymous*
Lasset uns scherzen *–Wunderhorn*
Laßt euch nicht verführen *–Brecht*
Laßt fahren hin das Allzuflüchtige *–Goethe*
Lasst im Morgenstrahl des Mai'n *–Deinhardstein*
Lasst Lautenspiel und Becherklang *–Rückert*
Laßt mich! Laßt mich! ich will klagen *–M. Claudius*
Lasst mich nur auf meinem Sattel gelten! *–Goethe*
Lasst mich, ob ich auch still verglüh' *–F. Gerstenberg*
Laßt mich ruhen *–Hoffmann von Fallersleben*
Lasst sich der Höhle Thor *–Giesebrecht*
Lasst uns beten: Vater unser *–Anonymous*
Laßt uns das Kindlein wiegen *–Anonymous*
Lasst uns, ihr Himmlischen *–J. Mayrhofer*
Lasst uns mit ehrfurchtvollem Dank *–Kraft*
Laue Lüfte, Blumendüfte *–A. W. Schlegel*
Laue Luft kommt blau geflossen *–Eichendorff*
Laue Sommernacht, am Himmel *–Falke*
Laura betet! Engelharfen hallen *–Matthisson*
Laura, über diese Welt *–Schiller*
Laura, Welt und Himmel weggeronnen *–Schiller*
Lausche, lausche! War's ein Säuseln *–Bone*
Lauschende Wolke über dem Wald *–Rilke*
Laut gesungen sei das Feuer *–Gamper*
Lauter Freude fühl' ich *–Anonymous*
Lazarus ward auferwecket *–Giesebrecht*
Leb' wohl, du guter Reiterdienst *–Lingg*
Leb' wohl du schöne Erde *–Pratobevera*
Leb wohl du Strom, so sanft und schön *–Smollet*
Leb' wohl und sehen wir uns wieder *–Rückert*
Lebe, liebe, trinke, lärme *–Anonymous*
Lebe nicht so schnell und stürmisch *–Lenau*
Lebe wohl! Ach, jene Abendstunde *–Lenau*
"Lebe wohl" Du fühlest nicht *–Mörike*
Lebe wohl! Du lieber Freund! *–Schubert*
Lebe wohl! in weite Ferne *–Horváth*
Lebe wohl, mein Lieb! *–Uhland*
Lebe wohl, o mütterliche Erde *–Anonymous*
Lebe wohl! wenn je ein brünstig Flehen *–Byron*
Leben, das nur Leben scheinet *–Uhland*
Leben gibst du, Leben nimmst du *–Barthel*
Lebensfunke vom Himmel entglüht *–Pope*
"Lebewohl" – Du fühlest nicht *–Mörike*
Lebewohl, du Mann der Lust *–G. A. Bürger*
Lebhaft hab ichs oft empfunden *–Anonymous*
Leblos gleitet Blatt um Blatt *–Kalbeck*
Lebt wohl ihr Berge *–Schiller*
Leb'wohl, leb'wohl du schöne Welt! *–Zeller*
Leer ist der Tag, er geht zu Ende *–Wolff*
Leere Zeiten der Jugend! *–Goethe*
Leg' in den Sarg mir mein grünes Gewand *–K. Immermann*
Lege deine Hand auf meine Augen *–Dehmel*
Lege den Schmuck nun an *–Stieglitz*
Legt mir unters Haupt Melissen *–"Martin Greif"*
Lehn' deine Wang' an meine Wang' *–Heine*
Lehnst du deine bleichgehärmte Wange *–Matthisson*
Leichte Segler in den Höhen *–Jeitteles*
Leichte Silberwolken schweben *–Goethe*
Leis dem Schmeichellied der Lauten *–Verlaine*
Leis' in meines Kindleins Träume *–Danz*
Leis, rudern hier, mein Gondolier! *–Moore*
Leis sinkt der Dämmerung Schleier *–"Ernst"*
Leis' wandeln wir wie Geisterhauch *–Anonymous*
Leise deinen Namen flüstern *–Itzerott*
Leise fällt ein Schnee auf das Land *–Mombert*
Leise flehen meine Lieder *–Rellstab*
Leise geht der Tag zu Ende *–B. Huber*
Leise hör' ich dich singen Sankta Maria *–Mombert*
Leise, leise weht ihr Lüfte *–F. Brentano*
Leise Lieder sing' ich dir bei Nacht *–Morgenstern*
Leise, rieselnder Quell *–Salis-Seewis*
Leise schleich' ich mich am Abend *–Mahn*
Leise schwindest du hinter Baum *–Bollmann*
Leise streichen Nebelschleier *–Metternich*
Leise Töne der Brust, geweckt *–Rückert*
Leise tritt auf... Nicht mehr *–Avenarius*
Leise tritt der Mond heraus *–Boelitz*
Leise, um dich nicht zu wecken *–Schack*
Leise weht' es, leise wallte *–Kind*
Leise weht's durch alle Lande *–Wette*
Leise wie ein Hauch *–Ritter*
Leise, windverwehte Lieder *–Leuthold*
Leise zieht durch mein Gemüth *–Heine*
Leiser, leiser, kleine Laute *–Rochlitz*
Leiser nannt' ich deinen Namen *–Jacobi*
Leiser schwanken die Äste *–Schack*
Lenore fuhr um's Morgenrot *–G. A. Bürger*
Lenznacht, so still und so kühl *–Welhaven*
Leon und Castilien waffnen *–Schleifer*
Lerche steiget im Gesang *–Sacken*
Lerche zu des Frühlings Ruhme *–Mickiewicz*
Lerchelein, lieb und klein *–Wette*
Lethe! Brich die Fesseln des Ufers *–Lenau*
Leucht't heller denn die Sonne *–Wunderhorn, Anon.*
Lichtlein schwimmen auf dem Strome *–Goethe*
Lieb' Liebchen, leg's Händchen *–Heine*

Lieb' Seelchen, lass' das Fragen sein –*Hopfen*
Lieb' sei ferne, ist doch immer da –*E. M. Arndt*
Lieb' um Liebe, Stund' um Stunde –*Goethe*
Lieb Vöglein, vor Blüten –*Eichendorff*
Liebchen, ade! Scheiden thut weh! –*Volkslied*
Liebchen fand ich spielend –*C. F. Meyer*
Liebchen, kommen diese Lieder –*Goethe*
Liebchen und der Saft der Reben –*Haug*
Liebchen, was willst du? –*Osterwald*
Liebe, die du mich zum Bilde –*Scheffler*
Liebe, die sonst stets mit Myrten krönet –*Iffland*
Liebe ist ein süsses Licht –*M. Collin*
Liebe ist Wahrheit! –*P. Schoeck*
Liebe kam aus fernen Landen –*Tieck*
Liebe, Liebe, deine Schmerzen –*Raupach*
Liebe mir im Busen zündet einen Brand –*Heyse*
Liebe Mutter, heut Nacht heulte Regen –*"Alexis"*
Liebe rauscht der Silberbach –*Schiller*
Liebe recht tief gehegt –*J.-B. Rousseau*
Liebe säuseln die Blätter –*L. Hölty*
Liebe schwärmt auf allen Wegen –*Goethe*
Liebe Schwalbe, kleine Schwalbe –*Conrat*
Liebe Schwalbe, kleine Schwalbe –*Gregorovius*
Liebe traf mich, meine Augen weinen –*Blumauer*
Lieben Freunde! Es gab schön're Zeiten *Schiller*
Lieben, von ganzer Seele, lieben –*Anonymous*
Lieben, warum sollt' ich's nicht? –*Anonymous*
Liebendes Wort, dich send' ich fort –*Cornelius*
Lieber Gott, du weißt –*Conrat*
Lieber Morgenstern, lieber Abendstern –*Dehmel*
Liebes Häschen, willst du morgen –*G. Lang*
Liebes Haus auf Berges Höh'! –*Gerstenberg*
Liebes, leichtes, luftges Ding –*Herder*
Liebes Mandel, wo ist's Bandel? –*Mozart*
Liebes Töchterlein, liebes Töchterlein –*Seyboth*
Liebesqual verschmäht mein Herz –*Goethe*
Lieblich blühn die Bäume –*Osterwald*
Lieblich in der Rosenzeit –*Hafis*
Lieblich klagend – ein kristallnes Seufzen –*Giraud*
Lieblich wallen durch die Lüfte –*Osterwald*
Lieblich war die Maiennacht –*Lenau*
Liebliches Kind! Liebliches Kind! –*Goethe*
Liebst du um Schönheit –*Rückert*
Liebste! nur dich seh'n –*Rückert*
Liebste, was kann denn uns scheiden? –*Rückert*
Liebster, deine Worte stehlen –*Rückert*
Liebster Freund, und kann's denn sein –*Köstlin*
Liebster, Liebster, schläfst du noch? –*Dietmar von Aiste*
Liebster Schatz, i bitt' di schön –*Hans Schmidt*
Liebt er mich? tönt es im Herzensgrund –*Anonymous*
Lieder, die gleich Regenschauern –*Thiess*
Liegt die Frühlingssonne so goldenhell –*Holstein*
Liegt ein armer Krieger in dem Turm –*Volkslied*
Liegt ein Dorf im Abendleuchten –*Boelitz*
Liegt eine Stadt im Tale –*Dehmel*
Liegt nun so still die weite Welt –*Ritter*
Ließe doch ein hold Geschick –*Lenau*
Lilie der Auen! Herrin im Rosenhag! –*George*
Lilie hat der Zungen zehne –*Hafis*
Lilie sieh' mich Thau umblinkt dich –*A. v. Arnim*
Lilienblüthe! Mädchen schön und zart! –*Cornelius*
Lind duftig hält die Maiennacht –*Scheffel*
Linder schwebt der Stunde Reigen –*Zweig*
Lindes Rauschen in den Wipfeln –*Eichendorff*
Lisch aus, lisch aus, mein Licht! –*Haugwitz*
Litt einst ein Fähnlein große Not –*Morgenstern*
Lobt doch unsre stillen Feste –*Novalis*
Lockenstricke sollst du wissen –*Hafis*
Lösen sich die ird'schen Bande? –*Uhland*
Lokken, haltet mich gefangen –*Goethe*
Lorma sass in der Halle von Aldo –*Macpherson*
Loser, leichter, luft'ger Wind –*Scherer*
Loses Herze meiner Schönen –*Anonymous*
Loset, was i euch will sage! –*Hebel*
Lüttje Finger, gollne Ringer –*Groth*
Luna blickt von ihrem Thron –*Anonymous*
Lust entfloh und hin ist hin! –*Gubitz*
Lust'ge Vögel in dem Wald –*Eichendorff*
Lustig, lustig, wer zum Wald –*Vogl*
Lustwandelnd schritt ein Mädchen –*Wegener*
Lutschemund, Lutschemund –*Boelitz*

Mach' auf, mach' auf deine Thür –*"Alexis"*
Mach auf, mach auf, doch leise –*Schack*
Mächtiger, der brausend die Wipfel –*Rückert*
Mädchen, als du kamst ans Licht –*Goethe*
Mädchen entsiegelten, Brüder –*Matthisson*
Mädchen, hör' mich ruhig an –*Unidentified*
Mädchen Inistores, wein' auf –*Macpherson*
Mädchen mit dem roten Mündchen –*Heine*
Mädchen, seht den Zephyr streichen –*Ramler*
Mädchen, sieh am Wiesenhang –*Lenau*
Mädchen, sieh', der Lenz –*K. Schaefer*
Mädchen sind wie der Wind –*Anonymous*
Mädchen und Jünglinge, Männer –*Haug*
Mädchen von Kola, du schläfst! –*Macpherson*
Mädchen, was trauerst du? –*K. Schaefer*

Mädchenaug'! Mädchenaug'! *–Wolff*
Mädel, halt die Rökke fest *–Busse*
Mädel, laß das Stricken geh *–Dehmel*
Mädel, schau' mir in's Gesicht! *–G. A. Bürger*
Mädel sei kein eitles Ding *–Hochstetter*
Mädel trug des Wegs daher *–R. Reinick*
Mädele, ruck, ruck, ruck *–Volkslied*
Mädle 's ist Winter *–C. F. D. Schubart*
Mägdlein pflücket Beeren *–Odyniec & Mickiewicz*
Männer suchen stets zu naschen *–Volkslied*
Mag auch die Liebe weinen! *–F. A. Krummacher*
Mag auch heiss das Scheiden brennen *–Geibel*
Mag da draussen Schnee sich thürmen *–Heine*
Mag Thoren hienieden die Fessel *–Anonymous*
Magdalena weint am Grabe *–the Bible*
Magst du zu dem Alten halten *–Eichendorff*
Mahadöh, der Herr der Erde *–Goethe*
Mai, Mai! die wunderschöne Zeit *–Heyse*
Maidle, lass der was verzähle *–Volkslied*
Maienblümlein, so schön *–Eckschläger*
Maienglöckchen läutet *–Hoffmann von Fallersleben*
Maienkätzchen, erster Gruß *–Liliencron*
Maiglöckchen läutet *–Hoffmann von Fallersleben*
Maikäfer, summ, summ *–Hoffmann von Fallersleben*
Majestät'sche Sonnenrosse *–Schiller*
Major! Ihr habt zu allen Zeiten *–G. Lenz*
Man geht aus Nacht in Sonne *–Anonymous*
Man lauert, sitzt und sinnt *–Günther*
Man sagt, daß Rosen, die bei Tannen *–Jünger*
Man sagt, durch's Zimmer walle *–Lingg*
Man sagt mir, deine Mutter *–Heyse*
Man soll hören süsses Singen *–Jakob von Warte*
Man soll seinem Herzen gehorchen *–F. Wolf*
Man strebt die Flamme *–Anonymous*
Man weiß oft grade denn *–M. Claudius*
Manch' Bild vergess'ner Zeiten *–Heine*
Manche Thrän' aus meinen Augen *–Wilhelm Müller*
Manchen langen Tag *–Anonymous*
Mancher Stunden Wehen ist *–Zwehl*
Manchmal geschieht es in tiefer Nacht *–Rilke*
Mann merkt, dass der Wein geraten war *–Keller*
Mann und Weib und Kind *–H. Claudius*
Margritchen, Margritchen *–Wunderhorn*
Maria! Du weinst ich weiss *–Rilke*
Maria, du Zarte! du bist ein Rosengarte *–Uhland*
Maria ging aus wandern *–Volkslied*
Maria kam auf ihrer Flucht *–A. Schreiber*
Maria sitzt am Rosenbusch *–Schellenberg*
Maria sitzt am Rosenhag *–Boelitz*
Maria sitzt und stimmet die Harfe *–Vogl*
Maria wollt' zur Kirche gehn *–Mittler, Volkslied*
Marie, am Fenster sitzest du *–Gottschall*
Marie auf der Wiese *–Trojan*
Mariechen sitzt sinnend *–K. Freiligrath*
Marienwürmchen *–Wunderhorn, Volkslied*
Markt und Straßen steh'n *–Eichendorff*
Matt erstirbt der Hoffnung *–Werthes*
Max wollt' aus Augsburg *–"Anastasius Grün"*
Meerstern ich dich grüsse *–Anonymous*
Mei' Herzensallerliebster *–Anonymous*
Mei Maidle hot e G'sichtle *–Volkslied*
Mei Mueter mag mi net *–Volkslied*
Mei Schätzerl, das hat mi verlassen *–Volkslied*
Mei Schätzerl is hübsch *–Volkslied*
Mei Schätzle ist fei *–Volkslied*
Mein altes Ross, mein Spielgenoss *–Strachwitz*
Mein Aug' ist trüb *–Chamisso*
Mein Auge schließ' mit deinem Kusse zu *–Hartwig*
Mein brauner Liebster, sage mir *–Geissler*
Mein Bruder ist ein ganzer Mann *–Reinecke*
Mein Bruder war ein Flieger *–Brecht*
Mein Ende zeigt mir jeder Traum! *–Byron*
Mein Esel sicherlich muss klüger *–Lessing*
Mein federäugiger Liebling! *–Mayröcker*
Mein feines Lieb ist fern *–Zincgref*
Mein Fleiss und Müh hab ich *–Wunderhorn*
Mein Freund Antonius, der Vater *–Herder*
Mein Freund ist mein *–Cornelius*
Mein ganzer Leib ist Traurigkeit *–Ingrisch*
Mein Geist ist trüb' *–Byron*
Mein Geliebter ist ein Sohn *–Macpherson*
Mein Gemüthe blühte gleich *–Rückert*
Mein G'müth ist mir verwirret *–Hassler*
Mein Gott! aus meiner Herden Mitten *–Dumas*
Mein Gretchen ist so kugelrund *–H. Seidel*
Mein Handwerk geht durch alle Welt *–Anonymous*
Mein Haus hat kein' Thür *–Goethe*
Mein Haus steht unter Birken *–Ingrisch*
Mein Heimweh und meine Liebe *–Hesse*
Mein Herz, aus goldnen Jugendtagen *–Lingg*
Mein Herz, das ist ein tiefer Schacht *–Anonymous*
Mein Herz ging auf die Wanderschaft *–Ambrosius*
Mein Herz, ich will dich fragen *–"Friedrich Halm"*
Mein Herz in steten Treuen *–Volkslied*
Mein Herz ist betrübt *–Burns*
Mein Herz ist die Quelle *–"Carmen Sylva"*
Mein Herz ist ein Spielmann *–Siebel*
Mein Herz ist im Hochland *–Burns*

Mein Herz ist leer *–Morgenstern*
Mein Herz ist mir gemenget *–Volkslied*
Mein Herz ist schwer! Auf! *–Byron*
Mein Herz ist schwer, Gott sei's geklagt! *–Burns*
Mein Herz ist schwer, mein Auge wacht *–Geibel*
Mein Herz ist stumm *–Schack*
Mein Herz ist wie die dunkle Nacht *–Geibel*
Mein Herz ist wie ein Saitenspiel *–Leuthold*
Mein Herz ist wie ein See so weit *–Nietzsche*
Mein Herz ist zerrissen *–Platen*
Mein Herz, mein Herz ist traurig *–Heine*
Mein Herz, o schliess dich ein *–Siebel*
Mein Herz schmückt sich mit dir *–F. Bodenstedt*
Mein Herzlein hat allzeit *–Margarethe*
Mein Herzlein tut mir gar zu weh! *–Volkslied*
Mein hochgeborenes Schätzelein *–Rückert*
Mein Hund, du, hat dich bloss beknurrt *–Dehmel*
Mein Jugendlenz ist nur ein Sorgenfrost *–Vincke*
Mein junger Sohn fragt mich *–Brecht*
Mein Kind, in welchem Krieg hast du *–Mörike*
Mein Kind, sieh an die Brüste mein *–Wunderhorn*
Mein Kind, wär ich König *–Hugo*
Mein Kindchen ist fein *–Volkslied*
Mein Knecht! steh' auf, und sattle schnell *–Heine*
Mein Leben wälzt sich murrend fort *–Anonymous*
Mein Lieb, das ist ein Röslein roth *–Burns*
Mein Lieb hat mich verlassen *–Kienzl*
Mein Lieb ist ein Jäger *–"Friedrich Halm"*
Mein Lieb ist eine rothe Ros' *–Burns*
Mein Liebchen ist kein stolzes Schloß *–Anonymous*
Mein Liebchen ist nicht Heliotrop *–Hood*
Mein Liebchen, wir saßen beisammen *–Heine*
Mein Liebe ist ein Segelschiff *–K. Immermann*
Mein lieber Goldschmied *–Stinde*
Mein lieber Herr Reiter *–H. Seidel*
Mein lieber und vertrauter Mann *–Morgenstern*
Mein liebes Herz, was ist dir *–Daumer*
Mein liebes Kind schlaf ein! *–J. Jaeger*
Mein Liebling ist ein Lindenbaum *–Stieler*
Mein Liebster hat zu Tische *–Heyse*
Mein Liebster ist ein Jäger *–R. Reinick*
Mein Liebster ist so klein *–Heyse*
Mein Liebster keck ist ein Matros' *–Leuthold*
Mein Liebster singt am Haus *–Heyse*
Mein Lied ist klein *–Cornelius*
Mein Lied ist wie der Abendhauch *–Hoffmann von Fallersleben*
Mein Liedlein ward ein Büblein *–Michaeli*
Mein Mädel hat Äuglein *–Unidentified*
Mein Mädel hat einen Rosenmund *–Volkslied*
Mein Mädel ward mir ungetreu *–Goethe*
Mein müdes Auge flieht der Schlaf *–Unidentified*
Mein Mützchen schön schwarz *–Volkslied*
Mein Muter mag mi net *–Volkslied*
Mein Pfeifchen traut *–Lenau*
Mein Pferd das ist am Huf *–Volkslied*
Mein Pferdchen gallopirt *–Dieffenbach*
Mein Ross so müd' in dem Stalle *–Scott*
Mein rotes Herz, mein totes Herz *–Wiener*
Mein Schäfer, ach! der ist bescheiden! *–C. Weisse*
Mein Schätzelein ist ein gar köstliches Ding *–Huggenberger*
Mein Schätzerl is hübsch *–Volkslied*
Mein Schätzle ist fein, *–Wunderhorn*
Mein Schatz, der ist auf die Wanderschaft hin *–Volkslied, Anon.*
Mein Schatz, ich hab es erfahren *–Volkslied*
Mein Schatz ist auf der Wanderschaft so lange *–Osterwald*
Mein Schatz ist auf die Wanderschaft hin *–Volkslied*
Mein Schatz ist auf die Wanderschaft wohl *–Seyboth*
Mein Schatz ist nicht da *–Volkslied*
Mein Schatz ist wie ein Schneck *–Pfau*
Mein Schatz will Hochzeit halten *–W. Hertz*
Mein Schiff treibt *–Bethge*
Mein Schifflien schwimmt so wunderschön *–Reiff*
Mein schöner Stern! ich bitte dich *–Rückert*
Mein sind blaue Himmelsstrahlen *–Kamossa*
Mein Sohn, ich hab dir die Stiefel *–Brecht*
Mein Sohn, was immer auch aus dir werde *–Brecht*
Mein Sohn, wo willst du hin so spät? *–Volkslied*
Mein süßer Schatz! du bist zu gut *–Hafis*
Mein süsses Lieb, wo weilest du? *–Stieler*
Mein Täubchen fliegt in Glanz und Duft *–H. Seidel*
Mein Vater hat gesagt *–Wunderhorn*
Mein Vater war ein Gärtner *–H. Hertz*
Mein Vöglein mit dem Ringlein rot *–Wunderhorn*
Mein Wagen rollet langsam *–Heine*
Mein Wappen ist nicht adelig *–Mörike*
Mein Weg ist weit *–B. Huber*
Mein wundes Herz verlangt *–Groth*
Meine armen, kleinen Lieder *–Wiener*
Meine Blüten sind zernagt *–Kosegarten*
Meine Braut führ' ich heim *–Jacobsen*
Meine eingelegten Ruder triefen *–C. F. Meyer*
Meine Freundin hat eine schwarze Katze *–Salus*
Meine fröhliche Liebe hat mich verlassen *–Hesse*
Meine geliebten Tale lächeln mich an *–Hölderlin*

Meine Laute hab' ich gehängt *–Wilhelm Müller*
Meine Laute nehm' ich wieder *–Mommsen*
Meine Lebenszeit verstreicht *–Gellert*
Meine Lebenszeit verstreicht *–Hafis*
Meine Liebe ist grün *–F. Schumann*
Meine Liebe, lange wie die Taube *–G. A. Bürger*
Meine Lieder, meine Sänge *–Löwenstein-Werthheim*
Meine Mutter hat's gewollt *–Storm*
Meine Ruh' ist dahin, meine Freud' *–Rochlitz*
Meine Ruh' ist hin, mein Herz ist schwer *–Goethe*
Meine Schäfchen, morgens früh *–Herder*
Meine scheuen Lieder die sind *–Holst*
Meine Seele, die hat weite Flügel *–Evers*
Meine Seele ist nun stillgeworden *–Hinrichs*
Meine Seele ist still und in sich gekehrt *–F. Bach*
Meine Seele ist still zu Gott *–the Bible*
Meine Sehnsucht ist zum Licht *–Wilhelm*
Meine Selinde! denn mit Engelstimme *–Stolberg-Stolberg*
Meine Töne still und heiter *–Rückert*
Meine Tränen im Bußgewand *–Rückert*
Meine Tränen sind geweint! *–Goekingk*
Meinen Kranz hab' ich gesendet *–Stieglitz*
Meiner lieben trauten Linde *–La Roche*
Meister Oluf, der Schmied *–A. Schreiber*
Melde mir die Nachtgeräusche *–C. F. Meyer*
Menschen lieben uns, und unbeglückt *–Werfel*
Merk dir's in vollster Kraft *–Weigand*
Merkenstein! Wo ich wandle *–Rupprecht*
Mich dünkt, wir geben einen Ball! *–Volkslied*
Mich erfreute der flug aller tiefdunklen pracht *–George*
Mich ergreift, ich weiß nicht wie *–Goethe*
Mich führt mein Weg wohl meilenlang *–Scott*
Mich grüßte erstrahlender Schein *–Leen*
Mich hat der Herbst betrogen *–Rückert*
Mich rief ein Ton aus weiter Ferne *–B. Goetz*
Mich rührt so sehr böhmischen Volkes Weise *–Rilke*
Mich tadelt der Fanatiker *–Keller*
Mich umduftet deine Seele süß *–Evers*
Mich zieht es nach dem Dörfchen hin *–Burns*
Mien leve Hanne Gnegelputt hett allens *–Groth*
Mild umschattet von der Dämmrung Schleier *–Reissig*
Mild und trüb ist mir fern Saum *–George*
Mild wie ein Lufthauch *–Metschorsky*
Millionen öder Jahre lag ich schon *–Hebbel*
Mir bist du tot *–Graf-Bartholemew*
Mir glänzen die Augen *–Keller*
Mir immer wieder unbegreiflich *–C. Hauptmann*
Mir ist, als müßt ich dir was sagen *–Anonymous*
Mir ist, als zögen Arme *–Kuh*
Mir ist, da ich dich habe *–Rückert*
Mir ist die Welt so freudenleer *–Michell*
Mir ist ein schöns brauns Maidelein *–Volkslied*
Mir ist nach einer Heimat weh *–Lienhard*
Mir ist, nun ich Dich habe *–Rückert*
Mir ist so weh ums Herz *–Candidus*
Mir ist so wohl, so weh' *–J. Mayrhofer*
Mir ist wie einem, der im Schlafe schaut *–Dante*
Mir ist's so eng allüberall! *–Neun*
Mir ist's zu wohl ergangen *–Volkslied*
Mir klingt ein Ton so wunderbar *–Cornelius*
Mir lächelt kein Frühling *–Anonymous*
Mir tönt aus fernen Zeiten *–Erler*
Mir träumt', ich bin der liebe Gott *–Heine*
Mir träumt', ich flög gar bange *–Kerner*
Mir träumt', ich komm' ans Himmelstor *–C. F. Meyer*
Mir träumt', ich war ein Vögelein *–L. Hölty*
Mir träumte, die Sonne glühte *–J. Sturm*
Mir träumte einst ein schöner Traum *–F. Bodenstedt*
Mir träumte einst von wildem Liebesglüh'n *–Heine*
Mir träumte: traurig schaute der Mond *–Heine*
Mir träumte von einem Königskind *–Heine*
Mir träumte von einem Myrthenbaum *–Heyse*
Mir tut's so weh im Herzen! *–G. A. Bürger*
Mir ward gesagt, du reisest in die Ferne *–Heyse*
Mir zittern die Saiten *–Hesse*
Mit ausgespannten Armen *–Ambrosius*
Mit deinen blauen Augen *–Heine*
Mit dem grauen Felsensaal *–Keller*
Mit dem Pfeil, dem Bogen *–Schiller*
Mit den Gänsen, weissen Gänsen *–Busse*
Mit der Myrthe geschmückt *–Chamisso*
Mit des Bräutigams Behagen *–Goethe*
Mit dir, wer weiß, würd' ich *–Morgenstern*
Mit Dir zu schweigen still im Dunkel *–Kobald*
Mit edeln Purpurröten *–C. F. Meyer*
Mit einem Blicke deiner Augen *–Telschow*
Mit einem phantastischen Lichtstrahl *–Giraud*
Mit erstorbnem Scheinen steht der Mond *–Schiller*
Mit Fried und Freud ich fahr dahin *–Luther*
Mit geheimnisvollen Düften grüßt *–Geibel*
Mit gelben Birnen hänget *–Hölderlin*
Mit groteskem Riesenbogen *–Giraud*
Mit hellem Sang und Harfenspiel *–Cornelius*
Mit jedem Pulsschlag leb' ich dir *–"Dilia Helena"*

Mit langem Barte, bleich und blass –*Kotzebue*
Mit leisen Harfentönen sei –*Salis-Seewis*
Mit Liebesblick und Spiel und Sang –*Halem*
Mit Lust tät ich ausreiten –*Volkslied, Wunderhorn*
Mit Mädchen sich vertragen –*Goethe*
Mit meinem Gott geh ich zur Ruh –*C. Becker*
Mit meinem Liebchen Hand in Hand –*Huch*
Mit meinem Saitenspiele –*Eichendorff*
Mit Myrthen und Rosen, lieblich und hold –*Heine*
Mit Neigen ich dich grüße –*Strümpell*
Mit Regen und Sturmgebrause –*Schack*
Mit Rheinwein füllt den Becher! –*Rittershaus*
Mit schwarzen Segeln segelt mein Schiff –*Heine*
Mit tausendfacher Schöne begrüsst –*Recke*
Mit Trommeln und Pfeifen –*Liliencron*
Mit unserm Arm ist nichts gethan –*Klopstock*
Mit unsern Fischern war ein Kind –*Stieler*
Mit vierzig Jahren ist der Berg –*Rückert*
Mit vollen Atemzügen saug ich –*Goethe*
Mit wilden Atemstössen wirft –*Morgenstern*
Mittagsruhe haltend auf den Matten –*C. F. Meyer*
Mitten im Schimmer –*Stolberg-Stolberg*
Mitten im Sturm, der mich umbrüllte –*Kotzebue*
Mitten unter deinen Schmerzen –*Recke*
Mitten wir im Leben sind –*Luther*
Mitternachts weint' und schluchzt' ich –*Goethe*
Möcht' im Walde mit dir geh'n –*Cornelius*
Möcht' meine Seele senken –*Wrede*
Möcht' wissen, was sie schlagen –*Eichendorff*
Möcht' wissen, wo der Kerl –*Löwenstein*
Möchte mir ein blondes Glück erkiesen –*Rilke*
Möchten viele Seelen dies verstehen –*Hesse*
Mög' er ewig wiederkehren –*Telschow*
Möge Wasser, springend, wallend –*Goethe*
Mögen alle bösen Zungen –*Geibel*
Mohnblumen sind die runden –*Dahn*
Mond, als träte ein Totes –*Trakl*
Mond, hast du auch gesehen –*Prutz*
Mond, meiner Seele Liebling –*Kulmann*
Mond, sei Zeuge meiner Leiden! –*Leon*
Mond, so gehst du wieder auf –*Lothar*
Mond verhüllt sein Angesicht –*Conrat*
Mondlos hat sich der Teich verdunkelt –*Busta*
Morgen müssen wir verreisen –*Volkslied*
Morgen muß ich fort von hier –*Volkslied*
Morgen wieder, morgen wieder –*Vogl*
Morgenglanz der Ewigkeit, Licht –*Rosenroth*
Morgennebel, Lila, hüllen –*Goethe*
Morgenroth, Morgenroth, leuchtest –*Hauch*
Morgens als Lerche möcht' ich –*R. Reinick*
Morgens steh' ich auf und frage –*Heine*
Morgenwölkchen, leichte, weben –*Grun*
Müde bin ich, geh' zur Ruh' –*L. Hensel*
Müde labend naht der Abend –*K. Schaefer*
Müde schleichen hier die Bäche –*Lenau*
Müde webt Stumpfen dämmert Beten –*Stramm*
Müder Glanz der Sonne! –*Gerok*
Mühlen still die Flügel drehn –*Heyse*
Mühvoll komm' ich und beladen –*Geibel*
Mürrisch braust der Eichenwald –*Lenau*
Mürrisch sitzen sie und maulen –*Eichendorff*
Mund und Augen wissen ihre Pflicht –*H. Claudius*
Murmelndes Lüftchen, Blüthenwind –*Heyse*
Musik des Weltalls und Musik der Meister –*Hesse*
Musik ist alles, was ich sage –*Michalewski*
Musikanten wollen wandern –*Storm*
Muß es eine Trennung geben –*Tieck*
Muss i denn zum Städtele naus –*Volkslied*
Musst nicht allein im Freien –*Osterwald*
Mußt's auch grad' so dunkel –*Ritter*
Mutter, ach Mutter! es hungert mich –*Wunderhorn*
Mutter Beimlein hat ein Holzbein –*Brecht*
Mutter, draußen ist es Frühling
–*Dorr-Ljubljaschtschi*
Mutter geht durch ihre Kammern –*La Motte Fouqué*
Mutter, hilf mir armen Tochter –*Hans Schmidt*
Mutter, ich hab' zwei Äugelein –*Heyse*
Mutter, liebe Mutter, komm rasch –*Schellenberg*
Mutter, Mütterchen, ach sei nicht böse
–*Meyer-Helmund*
Mutter, Mutter! glaube nicht –*Rückert*
Mutter, Mutter, meine Puppe –*Chamisso*
Mutter, o sing' mich zur Ruh'! –*Hemans*
Mutter zum Bienelein –*Heine*
Mutteraug', in deine Bläue –*A. Schults*
Mys Büebli isch erwachet –*J. Reinhart*

Nach all dem Menschenlärm –*Morgenstern*
Nach Corinthus von Athen gezogen –*Goethe*
Nach deinen Lippen sehnen die meinen –*Gomoll*
Nach dem Sturme fahren wir –*Falk*
Nach der Heimath möcht' ich wieder –*Beils*
Nach diesem Frühlingsregen –*Goethe*
Nach diesen trüben Tagen –*Hoffmann von Fallersleben*
Nach Frankreich zogen zwei Grenadier' –*Heine*
Nach Jerusalem, der klaren –*Giesebrecht*
Nach langem Frost, wie weht die Luft –*Lenau*

Nach meiner Lieb' viel hundert Knaben *–Wunderhorn*
Nach Mittage saßen wir *–Goethe*
Nach oben musst du blicken *–Zedlitz*
Nach Oben steigt die Lerche *–Dieffenbach*
Nach Sevilla, nach Sevilla *–C. Brentano*
Nach so vielen trüben Tagen *–Baumberg*
Nach Süden nun sich lenken *–Eichendorff*
Nach Westen zieht der Wind dahin *–Leuthold*
Nacht auf Nacht steh ich am Meere *–Knodt*
Nacht fließt in Tag und Tag in Nacht *–Hart*
Nacht ist es jetzt, und das Gestirn *–Jacobsen*
Nacht ist wie ein stilles Meer *–Eichendorff*
Nacht ist's, und Stürme sausen *–Platen*
Nacht liegt auf den fremden Wegen *–Heine*
Nacht muß es sein, wenn ich sterben will *–Hodel*
Nacht... Nacht... in Nacht sanken wir *–C. Hauptmann*
Nacht umhüllt mit wehendem Flügel *–Grillparzer*
Nacht und Still ist um mich her *–Senf*
Nachtigall hüte dich *–Unidentified*
Nachtigall, ich hör' dich singen *–Wunderhorn*
Nachtigall, o Nachtigall! *–F. Bodenstedt*
Nachtigall, sag was für Grüß *–Volkslied*
Nachtigall, sie singt so schön *–Daumer*
Nachtigallen schwingen *–Hoffmann von Fallersleben*
Nachts bin vom Traum schlaftrunken *–Cornelius*
Nachts durch die stille Runde *–Eichendorff*
Nachts um die zwölfte Stunde *–Zedlitz*
Nachts wenn die Bäume rauschen *–Evers*
Nachts, wenn sich Sturmwind *–Cornelius*
Nachts zu unbekannter Stunde flieht *–Neun*
Nachtviolen, Nachtviolen! *–J. Mayrhofer*
Nachtwandler, tast' ich mich *–Hesse*
Nächtelang, die Stirn in heißer Hand *–Hesse*
Nächtens klang die süsse Laute *–La Motte Fouqué*
Nächtens übern kahlen Anger *–Trakl*
Nächtens wachen auf die irren *–F. Kugler*
Nächtig schwarze Wälder lichtet Euch! *–Kolzow*
Nächtlich dehnen sich die Stunden *–Eichendorff*
Nächtlich macht der Herr die Rund *–Eichendorff*
Nächtlicher Duft weht durch die Luft *–Pushkin*
Nähret Unmuth deine Seele *–Vogl*
Närrchen, sei nicht spröde *–Blumauer*
Nagen am Herzen fühl ich *–Daumer*
Naht die jubelvolle Zeit *–"Martin Greif"*
Natur gab Stieren Hörner *–Anacreon*
Nebel, stiller Nebel über Meer *–Morgenstern*
Nebel trauern über dem See *–Reiner*
Nebel wallen über kahles Land *–Kamossa*
Nebelgrau die weite Welt *–Boelitz*
Neben wohnt Don Henriques *–Heine*
Nehm ich die Harfe, folgend *–Leitner*
Nehmt hin die Welt! *–Schiller*
Neig' schöne Knospe *–F. Bodenstedt*
Neige, neige dich herab *–Giesebrecht*
Nein, es ist nicht auszukommen *–Daumer*
Nein, Geliebter, setze dich *–Daumer*
Nein, ich wiederstrebe *–Klopstock*
Nein, ich will's nicht länger leiden *–F. Förster*
Nein, junger Herr, so treibt man's nicht *–Heyse*
Nein, länger werd' ich diesen Kampf *–Schiller*
Nein, nein, ich liebt' ihn nicht! *–Girardin*
Nein, nun hab' ich's fest beschlossen *–Anonymous*
Nelken wind' ich und Jasmin *–Geibel*
Nennen soll ich, sagt ihr *–Hermann Gilm*
Neu geschmückt lacht die Natur *–Conz*
Neunerlei Blumen winde zum Kranz *–Wolff*
Nicht allein in Rathaussälen *–Leuthold*
Nicht Damen tönt von hohem Rang *–Burns*
Nicht daß ein Engel eintrat *–Rilke*
Nicht, daß ich dies Bestreben *–Leuthold*
Nicht den Leib umschlangen unsre Arme *–H. Stern*
Nicht der Thau und nicht der Regen *–Chamisso*
Nicht deshalb lieb ich *–Bethge*
Nicht die Träne kann es sagen *–Moore*
Nicht düstre, Theosoph, so tief! *–Hafis*
Nicht ein Flügelschlag ging *–Keller*
Nicht ein Lüftchen regt sich leise *–K. Henckell*
Nicht gedacht soll seiner werden! *–Heine*
Nicht Gelegenheit macht Diebe *–Goethe*
Nicht im Schlafe hab ich das geträumt *–Bierbaum*
Nicht länger kann ich singen *–Heyse*
Nicht lange ist's her, da lachte *–"Carmen Sylva"*
Nicht mehr auf Seidenblatt *–Goethe*
Nicht mehr so sanft und milde *–Anonymous*
Nicht mehr zu dir zu gehen *–Daumer*
Nicht mehr zurück? und nicht hinan? *–Nietzsche*
Nicht mit Engeln im blauen Himmelszelt *–F. Bodenstedt*
Nicht so düster und so bleich *–Schlechta*
Nicht so schnelle, nicht so schnelle! *–L'Égru*
Nicht so traurig, nicht so sehr *–Gerhardt*
Nicht unter schwarzer Erdenlast *–Conrad*
Nicht wandle, mein Licht *–Daumer*
Nichts gibt's, was würdig wäre *–Leopardi*
Nichts kann auf Erden verglichen *–Volkslied*
Nichts rundum erforschen des Endlichen Blikke *–Haug*

Nichts Schön'res kann mich erfreuen *–Volkslied*
Nichts soll, o Herr *–Stubenberg*
Nichts unterm Monde gleicht *–Matthisson*
Nichts vom Vergänglichen *–Goethe*
Nichts von den Dingen allen *–Vincke*
Nie hält sich Zephyrus *–Götz*
Nie ward ich, Herrin, müd *–Petrarca*
Nie will ich meinen Bruder richten *–Unzer*
Niemals dich wieder zu sehen *–Anonymous*
Niemals wieder will ich eines Menschen *–Werfel*
Niemand weiß, wie schwer *–Hofmannswaldau*
Nimm die letzten Abschiedsküsse *–Rellstab*
Nimm dies kleine Angedenken *–Anonymous*
Nimm dir ein schönes Weib *–Heyse*
Nimm einen Strahl der Sonne *–Rellstab*
Nimm meinen schweren Dornenkranz *–Straaten*
"Nimm mich! Nimm mich!" Was kriegst *–Sergel*
Nimm sie hin denn, diese Lieder *–Jeitteles*
Nimm sie willig und geduldig *–Geppert*
Nimmer, das glaubt mir *–Schiller*
Nimmer dem liebenden Herzen *–Anonymous*
Nimmer länger trag ich dieser Leiden Last *–Anonymous*
Nimmer lange weil' ich hier *–Anonymous*
Nimmer, nimmer darf ich dir gestehen *–Matthisson*
Nimmer trag ich länger dieser Leiden Last *–Anonymous*
Nimmer werd' ich, nimmer dein vergessen *–L. Hölty*
Nimmer will ich dich verlieren! *–Willemer*
Nina, ninana will ich dir singen *–Heyse*
Niwaschi! Heb' des Kindes Hand! *–Unidentified*
Noch ahnt man kaum der Sonne Licht *–Uhland*
Noch eine Stunde laßt mich hier *–Rückert*
Noch einmal muss ich vor dir stehn *–Gerstenberg*
Noch einmal tön', o Harfe *–Salis-Seewis*
Noch erging sie's leicht im Anbeginne *–Rilke*
Noch fand von Evens Töchterschaaren *–Cowley*
Noch hörte mich die Mitternacht *–Werthes*
Noch hundert Jahre? *–Ingrisch*
Noch immer halt' ich dich umfaßt *–Saul*
Noch immer lag ein tiefes Schweigen *–Lenau*
Noch in meines Lebens Lenze war ich *–Schiller*
Noch ist der Glanz der Frühe *–Bethge*
Noch ist die blühende, goldene Zeit *–Roquette*
Noch liegt der Winter in der Stadt *–Träger*
Noch sass im schwarzen Kleide *–Haug*
Noch scheint der Mond *–Wagner*
Noch schmückten zarte Blüthen *–"Uffo von Wildingen"*
Noch singt den Widerhallen *–Uhland*
Noch spielen die Jagdhunde im Hof *–Kafka*
Noch unverrückt, o schöne Lampe *–Mörike*
Noch weisst du nicht! *–Döhring*
Noch ziehn die Wolken düster *–Vogl*
Noch zwingt mich treue *–George*
Nord oder Süd! Wenn nur im warmen Busen *–K. Lappe*
Nüd schöiners, as wänn's dimm'red *–Lienert*
Nun auf dem fremden Boden *–Giesebrecht*
Nun bevölkert sich das hohe Drüben *–Morgenstern*
Nun, bin ich befreit! Wie behäglich! *–Gubitz*
Nun bin ich dein, du aller Blumen Blume *–Heyse*
Nun bin ich schon damit versöhnt *–Himmelbauer*
Nun bin ich untreu worden *–Keller*
Nun brennet am Nilstrom *–Tegnér*
Nun bricht aus allen Zweigen *–Rodenberg*
Nun da der heiße Tag versank *–Fankhauser*
Nun, da der Tag des Tages müde ward *–Nietzsche*
Nun da die Bäum' in Blüthen stehn *–Osterwald*
Nun, da Schatten niedergleiten *–C. W. Schütz*
Nun, da sie Alle eingeschlafen *–Galli*
Nun, da so warm der Sonnenschein *–Redwitz*
Nun der Tag mich müd' gemacht *–Hesse*
Nun die Schatten dunkeln *–Geibel*
Nun du wie Licht durch meine Träume *–Evers*
Nun ein Scherflein in der Runde *–Storm*
Nun gieb ein Morgenküsschen *–Storm*
Nun grünt der Berg *–Osterwald*
Nun gute Nacht! Es gab so viel *–Blüthgen*
Nun habe Dank für alles *–Björnson*
Nun hängt nur noch am Kirchturmknopf *–Bierbaum*
Nun hast du mir den ersten Schmerz *–Chamisso*
Nun hat das Leid ein Ende *–Osterwald*
Nun hat deines Herzens Geige *–Zwehl*
Nun hat mein Stecken gute Rast *–Osterwald*
Nun hoch den Kopf und den Thränenfluss *–Busse*
Nun holt mir eine Kanne Wein *–Burns, Anon.*
Nun ich der Riesen Stärksten *–Mombert*
Nun, ihr Musen, genug! *–Daumer*
Nun ihr Musen, genug! Vergebens *–Goethe*
Nun ist der Tag verronnen *–Rosenthal*
Nun ist die Nacht gekommen *–Schaukal*
Nun ist ein jeder Nerv in mir *–Bulthaupt*
Nun ist es Herbst, die Blätter fallen *–Lenau*
Nun ist es Zeit, dass ich mit Verstand *–Heine*
Nun ist wohl Sanges Ende! *–Stieler*
Nun kommt die Nacht gegangen *–Braungart*
Nun laß das Lamentieren *–Leuthold*

Nun laß mich träumen –*Cornelius*
Nun lass uns Frieden schliessen –*Heyse*
Nun lasse ganz der Seele Flug –*Cornelius*
Nun laßt uns gehn und treten –*Gerhardt*
Nun laßt uns singen das Abendlied –*Wunderhorn*
Nun leb' wohl, du kleine Gasse –*Volkslied*
Nun legen sich die Wogen –*Eichendorff*
Nun, Liebster, geh', nun scheide! –*Cornelius*
Nun liegen Kränze um die schönen Brüste –*Kalidasa*
Nun mach' mir nicht das Herz –*Groth*
Nun merk' ich erst, wie müd' –*Wilhelm Müller*
Nun quill aus meiner Seele immerfort –*P. Schoeck*
Nun rauscht im Morgenwinde sacht –*Geibel*
Nun reibet euch die Äuglein wach! –*Löwenstein*
Nun rühret die Ähren im Felde –*"Martin Greif"*
Nun ruhst du sanft in meinem Arm –*Braungart*
Nun ruht und schlummert Alles –*Rodenberg*
Nun scheidet vom sterbenden Walde –*Neun*
Nun schmücke mir dein dunkles Haar –*Keller*
Nun schreit' ich aus dem Thore –*Scheffel*
Nun schürz dich, Gretlein –*Wunderhorn*
Nun schweben Dach und Decke –*Morgenstern*
Nun schwirren die Schwalben –*Scherer*
Nun seh' ich wohl, warum –*Rückert*
Nun steh' ich über Grat und Kluft –*Falke*
Nun stehen die Rosen in Blüthe –*Heyse*
Nun verlaß' ich diese Hütte –*Goethe*
Nun wandre, Maria, nun wandre nur fort –*Heyse*
Nun weiß ich doch –*Kraus*
Nun, wer klopft an meine Thür? –*Burns*
Nun will die Sonn' so hell aufgeh'n –*Rückert*
Nun wind um deine Stirne –*Sergel*
Nun wir uns lieben –*Avenarius*
Nun wird es wieder grün –*Lebret*
Nun wollen Berg' und Thale –*Geibel*
Nun wollen Knospen sich entfalten –*Cornelius*
Nun wollen wir uns still –*Morgenstern*
Nun ziehen Tage über die Welt –*Hohenberg*
Nun zieht mit seinem goldnen Schein –*Karstein*
Nunmehr, da Himmel, Erde schweigt –*Petrarca*
Nur bei dir, an deinem Herzen –*Anonymous*
Nur das tut mir so bitterweh' –*Redwitz*
Nur den Abschied schnell genommen –*Köstlin*
Nur die Einsamkeit umschattet –*Anonymous*
Nur ein Gedanke, der mich freut –*Vincke*
Nur ein Gesicht auf Erden lebt –*Volkslied*
Nur ein lächelnder Blick –*G. Zimmermann*
Nur ein Wort, nur eine Bitte –*Kafka*
Nur ein Wörtchen sprich, o Mädchen –*Hamerling*
Nur einen Sommer gönnt –*Hölderlin*
Nur fast so wie im Traum –*Mörike*
Nur fort, du braune Hexe –*Goethe*
Nur Platz, nur Blösse! –*Goethe*
Nur wer die Sehnsucht kennt –*Goethe*
O! A! Kirchengeschichte hör ich –*Nietzsche*
O Abendsonn', o Holde –*Kosegarten*
O alte Heimat süß! –*Tieck*
O alter Duft der Märchenzeit –*Giraud*
O Bänkelsänger Willie –*Burns*
O banger Traum, was flatterst du –*Osterwald*
O Berlin, ich muss dich lassen –*Anonymous*
O Blätter, dürre Blätter! –*Pfau*
O blasen, blasen, blasen –*Vogt*
O blaue Luft nach trüben Tagen –*Uhland*
O blicke, wenn den Sinn –*Rückert*
O brich nicht, Steg, du zitterst sehr –*Uhland*
O Bruder sag, warum bist du gekommen? –*Ehrler*
O Dank, Dank diesen freundlich grünen Bäumen –*Schiller*
O danke nicht für diese Lieder –*Müller von Königswinter*
O dass doch ihr barmherzig wär't –*Telschow*
O dass ich dir vom stillen Auge –*Stoll*
O, der Alpen blanke Kette –*Stieler*
O der schöne Maienmond! –*Voss*
O die du rund, wie meiner Väter Schild –*Hoven*
O die Frauen, o die Frauen –*Daumer*
O die ihr geht am Abend –*Werfel*
O dolce far niente, du bist doch –*Grassmann*
O du, der ich erblühte –*Boelitz*
O du des himmlischen Reiches Kind –*Ebner-Eschenbach*
O du Entriss'ne mir und meinem Kusse! –*Rückert*
O.... du hast es gar zu gut –*J. Kinkel*
O du Land des Wesens –*M. Claudius*
O, du lieber Schatz –*Pfau*
O du mein Alles, mein Alles –*Oser*
O du mein Gott, o du mein Gott –*Wunderhorn*
O du mein Stern, schau dich so gern –*Serre*
O du, wenn deine Lippen mich berühren –*Klenke*
O ein Glöcklein klingelt mir –*Keller*
O Einsamkeit! wie trink' ich gerne –*Lenau*
O Elise, nicht nur für die Freuden –*Jerusalem*
O Engel, mein Schutzengel mein –*Volkslied*
O fände für mich ein Bräutigam sich! –*Goethe*
O falle, mein Schleier, o liege –*Loewe and Vocke*
O Felsen, lieber Felsen –*Wenzig*
O Fischer auf den Fluten, Fidelin! –*Anonymous*

O flaumenleichte Zeit der dunkeln Frühe! *–Mörike*
O fließ, ja wallend fließ in Zähren *–Anonymous*
O Fluß, mein Fluß im Morgenstrahl! *–Mörike*
O frage nicht in bitt'rem Harm *–Nawrocki*
O Freude, o Wonne, wie scheinet die Sonne *–Enslin*
O Freund, mein Schirm, mein Schutz *–Rückert*
O Frühlingsabenddämmerung! *–Candidus*
O Frühlingshauch, o Liederlust *–Leuthold*
O Geliebte! dein vergessen – nein *–Haug*
O gib mir nicht die voll erblühte Rose *–Schönaich-Carolath*
O gieb, vom weichen Pfühle *–Goethe*
O Glokken, böse Glokken, habt schweren *–Holm*
O Gott, mein Gebieter *–Vincke*
O hättest du, begrüßend des Lebens *–Hafis*
O Harfe, die des Gottgeliebten Hand *–Byron*
O harte Sterne! Nie versöhnte *–Hafis*
O hast du dies gewollt *–Rilke*
O Haupt voll Blut und Wunden *–Gerhardt*
O heilig Herz der Völker *–Hölderlin*
O heiliger Augustin im Himmelssaal *–Keller*
O heiliges Band der Freundschaft *–L. F. Lenz*
O Herr, gib jedem seinen eignen Tod *–Rilke*
O Herre Gott, nimm du von mir *–Anonymous*
Das Vöglein auf dem Baum *–Dr. Mayer*
O Herz, sei endlich stille! *–E. Schulze*
O herzensschöns Schätzerl *–Volkslied*
O Hirtenknab', o Hirtenknab'! *–Unidentified*
O Hochland und o Südland! *–Herder*
O höh're Welt, lehrt uns der Schmerz *–Byron*
O Hoffnung! Holde, gütig geschäftige! *–Hölderlin*
O holder Himmelswind *–Ehrler*
O ihr Herren, o ihr werthen *–Rückert*
O Irmingard, wie schön bist du *–Stieler*
O Jesu Christ, wir warten dein *–Albers*
O Jesu Christe, wahres Licht *–Heermann*
O Jesulein zart, o Jesulein zart *–Wunderhorn*
O Jugendlust, o Jugendglück *–W. Strauss*
O, kennt ihr nicht Emmchen *–Anonymous*
O köstlicher Tokayer *–Baumberg*
O komm im Traum, komm in stillester Stunde *–Hugo*
O komm zu mir wenn durch die Nacht *–Anonymous*
O komme, holde Sommernacht *–M. Grohe*
O, konntest du es nicht erraten *–Rassow*
O kühler Wald, wo rauschest du *–C. Brentano*
O Lady Judith, spröder Schatz *–"Alexis"*
O lächle, Freund der Liebe *–Anonymous*
O Lämmlein bleibt, gedenkt *–Giesebrecht*
O Lamm Gottes, welches der Welt *–the Mass*
O lass dich halten, gold'ne Stunde *–Roquette*
O lass, Geliebter, dich erflehen *–Gruppe*
O laß mich nur von ferne stehn *–Storm*
O Lebensfrühling, Blütendrang *–Leuthold*
O, legt mich nicht ins dunkle Grab *–Uhland*
O Lieb', du Wonnemeer! *–C. F. Scherenberg*
O lieb, so lang du lieben *–F. Freiligrath*
O Lieb und Leid so überein! *–Werfel*
O Liebe, die am Kreuze rang *–Wilhelm Müller*
O Liebe, die mein Herz erfüllet *–Stoll*
O Liebe, hast du uns zu kränken *–Anonymous*
O lieber Künstler sei ermahnt *–Kerr*
O liebes Mädchen, höre mich *–Anonymous*
O lieblich klarer Mond *–Leopardi*
O liebliche Wangen *–Flemming*
O Lust am Rheine *–Cornelius*
O Lust, o Lust, vom Berg ein Lied *–Rollet*
O Lust vom Berg zu schauen *–Eichendorff*
O Magdeburg, die Stadt *–Goethe*
O Maidle, du bist mein Morgestern *–Volkslied*
O Maria, meine Liebe, denk ich *–Eichendorff*
O Mariamne, dieses Herz *–Byron*
O Meer im Abendstrahl *–Meissner*
O mein Geliebter – in die Kissen *–Dehmel*
O, meine Blumen, ihr, meine Freude *–Anonymous*
O Mensch, gib acht! *–Nietzsche*
O Menschenherz, was ist dein Glück? *–Lenau*
O Menschheit, o Leben *–Craigher*
O, Mond, o lösch' dein gold'nes Licht *–M. Jäger*
O Muse, mir Vertraute du *–Dionysius*
O Mutter, guten Rat mir leiht *–Goethe*
O Mutter, wie stürmen die Flocken *–Rückert*
O Nacht, du Sternenbronnen *–Morgenstern*
O Nachtigall, dein süßer Schall *–Köstlin*
O nimm mich an als deine Magd! *–"Dilia Helena"*
O, nun heb du an, dort in deinem Moor *–Whitman*
O presse deine Hand in meine Hand *–Ubell*
O Quell, was strömst du rasch und wild *–E. Schulze*
O reine, wundervolle Schau *–Hesse*
O Röschen rot! Der Mensch liegt *–Wunderhorn*
O säh' ich auf der Haide dort *–Burns*
O sähst du mich jetzt beten *–Hess*
O sag' es noch einmal, noch tausendmal *–Oser*
O sagt, ihr Lieben, mir einmal *–Craigher*
O! sanfter süsser Hauch! *–Uhland*
O schau, sie schweben wieder *–Hesse*
O schaudre nicht, laß diesen Blick *–Goethe*
O schauerliche Lebenswirrn *–Morgenstern*
O schick' mich nicht allein *–Heyse*

O schmäht des Lebens Leiden nicht! –*Schack*
O Schmetterling sprich –*Hoffmann von Fallersleben*
O schneller, mein Roß, mit Hast –*Geibel*
O schöne Nacht! Am Himmel märchenhaft –*Daumer*
O schönes Mädchen du –*Goethe*
O Schröpferschwarm, o Händlerkreis –*Kerr*
O Schwälblein, das da fliegt in weite Ferne –*Volkslied*
O Schwarzwald, o Heimat –*Auerbach*
O sehne dich nicht an's graue Meer –*Hamerling*
O sehntest Du dich so nach mir –*Köstlin*
O! seht uns arme Kinder ziehn –*Werthes*
"O sei mein Freund!" so schallt's –*Lenau*
O selig, wem in stiller Nacht –*Hamerling*
O selig wer liebt. Ihm tönet der Wald –*Brun*
O sieh, wie golden die Blümlein –*Hamerling*
O sing, du Schöne, sing mir nicht... –*Pushkin*
O Sommerfrühe blau und hold! –*Geibel*
O Sonn', o Meer, o Rose! –*Rückert*
O Sonne, Königin der Welt –*Uz*
O Sonnenschein, o Sonnenschein! –*R. Reinick*
O Sterne, goldene Sterne! –*Pfau*
O stürzt, ihr Wolkenbrüche –*Lenau*
O süsse Mutter, ich kann nicht spinnen –*Rückert*
O süßer Mai, der Strom ist frei –*A. v. Arnim*
O süsser Mai, o habe du Erbarmen –*K. Henckell*
O süßer Tod, der alle Menschen schrekket –*Platen*
O süßer Zauber im Jugendmut –*Pohl*
O süsseste Noth! O selige Pein! –*Wittkowsky*
O Tannenbaum, o Tannenbaum –*Volkslied*
O tiefstes Wunder, daß mein Leben –*I. Seidel*
O Tod, o Tod, wie bitter bist du –*the Bible*
O unbewölktes Leben! so rein und tief und klar –*J. Mayrhofer*
O Ursprung aller Brunnen –*Anonymous*
O versenk, o versenk dein Leid –*R. Reinick*
O Vögerl, wia singst du lusti –*Rosegger*
O wär' dein Haus durchsichtig wie ein Glas –*Heyse*
O wär es doch! Hinaus in dunkle Wälder –*Liliencron*
O wär ich am Nekkar, o wär ich am Rhein –*Roquette*
O wär' ich du, mein Falke du –*Unidentified*
O wären wir weiter, o wär' ich zu Haus! –*Goethe*
O wärst du mein, es wär' ein schön'res Leben –*Lenau*
O wag' es nicht, mit mir zu scherzen –*Lenau*
O Wand'rer, geh' nicht nach dem Abendstein –*Heindl*
O was muß es die Engel gekostet haben –*Rilke*
O wehe, Heinz von Lüder –*Kopisch*
O weile, süßer Geliebter! –*"Martin Greif"*
O, weint um sie die einst –*Byron*
O welch Glühn in fremde Hülle –*Zweig*
O Welt, ich sag' dir gern Ade –*Cornelius*
O wenn es wahr, daß in der Nacht –*Pushkin*
O wie dringt das junge Leben –*E. Schulze*
O wie du schnaubst aus voller Brust –*Stieglitz*
O wie glücklich sind doch Andre! –*Volkslied*
O wie greulich, wie abscheulich –*Braungart*
O wie herbe ist das Scheiden –*Volkslied*
O wie ist es schön in die Schule gehn –*Anonymous*
O wie lieblich ist das Mädchen –*Geibel*
O, wie meine Lippen beben –*Czermak*
O wie öde, sonder Freudenschall –*G. A. Bürger*
O wie sanft die Quelle –*Daumer*
O, wie schön ist deine Welt –*K. Lappe*
O wie so rein oft rieselt –*Hamerling*
O wie süß ein Duft von oben –*Hafis*
O wie träumt es sich süß –*Leuthold*
O willst mich nicht mitnehmen –*Unidentified*
O Winter, schlimmer Winter –*Uhland*
O Woche, Zeugin heiliger Beschwerde! –*Mörike*
O wüßt ich doch den Weg zurück –*Groth*
O wüsstest du, wie viel ich deinetwegen –*Heyse*
O wunderbare Harmonie, was Er will –*Götz*
O wunderschön ist Gottes Erde –*L. Hölty*
O zürne nicht, wenn mein Begehren –*Dehmel*
Ob auch finstre Blicke glitten –*Heyse*
Ob dein ich bin? Was fragst du mich? –*Leixner*
Ob der Koran von Ewigkeit sei? –*Goethe*
Ob ein Gott sei? ob er einst erfülle –*Tiedge*
Ob ich dich liebe weiss ich nicht –*J. W. L. Gleim*
Ob ich manchmal Dein gedenke? –*Köstlin*
Ob noch die alte Geige singt? –*Brockhaus*
Ob Sie mir je Erfüllung wird –*Morgenstern*
Oben auf des Berges Spitze –*Heine*
Oben drehen sich die grossen –*Fellinger*
Oben in dem Birnenbaum sitzt ein Vögelein –*Schellenberg*
Oben, wo die Sterne glühen –*Heine*
Och Mod'r, ich well en Ding han –*Volkslied*
Ochse, wie bist du so stattlich –*Eichendorff*
Öffne die Augen, Tancredi –*Tosti*
Öffne mir die goldne Pforte –*Cornelius*
Offene Arme und pochende Brust –*Wolff*
Offerus war ein Lanzenknecht –*Kind*
Oft am Brunnen –*Trakl*
Oft am langen Tage seufz' ich, ach! –*E. R. Weiss*
Oft denk' ich, sie sind nur ausgegangen! –*Rückert*

Oft fühl ich in scheuen Schauern *–Rilke*
Oft in einsam stillen Stunden *–"Theodor Hell"*
Oft in meiner Kindheit süssen Träumen *–Lohbauer*
Oft war sie als Kind ihren Dienerinnen *–Rilke*
Oh, das Korn, das wogte so *–Evers*
Oh, daß ich dich fand einzig warm *–I. Seidel*
Oh, leget mich nicht ins Grab *–Uhland*
Oh, schattige Kühle! Einer dunklen Tanne *–Brecht*
Oh Sprengen des Gartens, das Grün *–Brecht*
Oh weh des Scheidens, das er tat *–Rückert*
Oh, wer um alle Rosen wüsste *–Morgenstern*
Ohn' Lieb' bist du durchs Leben kommen *–Cossmann*
Ohne das Schöne, was soll der Gewinn? *–Mörike*
Ohne Liebe lebe, wer da kann *–Lessing*
Orpheus, als du mit Thränen *–H. W. Gerstenberg*
Ostern ist zwar schon vorbei *–Mörike*

Patsche, patsche, patsche Küchelchen *–Wunderhorn*
Perlen der Weisheit sind mir deine Zähne! *–Keller*
Pfeift der Sturm? Keift ein Wurm? *–Morgenstern*
Pflücket Rosen, um das Haar schön *–Kulmann*
Philint stand jüngst vor Baucis Thür *–C. Weisse*
Philosophie oder Liebe? das ist die Frage *–Raupach*
Phöbus, mit lokkerem Zügel *–Kind*
Phyllis, unter diesen Buchen *–J. W. L. Gleim*
Pierrot! Mein Lachen hab ich verlernt! *–Giraud*
Pilger auf Erden, so raste am Ziele *–Cornelius*
Pöppe, Pöppe, danze, schenk di ok *–Volkslied*
Polus, beginne rasch und kühn *–Giesebrecht*
Posthorn, wie so keck und fröhlich *–Eichendorff*
Preis ihm, der alle Dinge *–Overbeck*
Preis ihm! Er schuf und er erhält *–Klopstock*
Primel und Stern und Syringe *–Mörike*
Prinz Eugenius, der edle Ritter *–Volkslied*
Prinz Sisi und die Frau Mama *–K. Freiligrath*
Prinzeßlein tanzt durch die Wiese *–Claire Weber*
Puer natus/Ein Kind gebor'n zu Bethlehem *–Anonymous*
Pulse, höret auf zu schlagen *–Braun von Braunthal*
Purpur malt die Tannenhügel *–Matthisson*
Purpurgluten leuchten ferne *–Serre*
Purpurschimmer tränket die Rebenhügel *–G. Hauptmann*

Quälend ungestilltes Sehnen *–A. W. Schlegel*
Qual über Qual ist uns gesetzt insgesamt *–Hausmann*
Quellen rauschen, Lüfte schweigen *–Itzerott*
Quellende, schwellende Nacht *–Hebbel*
Quem pastores/Den die Hirten lobten *–Anonymous*

Räder klappern, Wasser rauschen *–Vogl*
Rase, Sturmwind, blase *–Kotzebue*
Raste, Krieger, Krieg ist aus *–Scott*
Rausche nur vorüber *–Hebbel*
Rauschender Strom, brausender Wald *–Rellstab*
Rauschendes Bächlein, so silbern und hell *–Rellstab*
Rauschet, ihr Meere, und wehet ihr Winde! *–E. Gross*
Rebhahnruf und Glokkenlaut, ich und du *–Busse*
Recht wie ein Leichnam wandle ich umher *–Wunderhorn*
Rede, Mädchen, allzu liebes *–Daumer*
Regen falle, härter pralle *–B. Huber*
Regen, komm' herab! Unsre Saaten *–Anonymous*
Regen, linder Frühlingsregen *–Rafael*
Regen, Regen druus, wi sitt hier warm *–Groth*
Regen über der Stadt und mein Herz *–Verlaine*
Regentropfen aus den Bäumen fallen *–Groth*
Regenwetter ziehen trübe *–Briesen*
Reglos steht der alte Baum *–Falke*
Regne, regne, Frühlingsregen *–Morgenstern*
Regungslos, ein großer Schweiger *–B. Huber*
Reich' den Pokal mir schäumenden Weines *–R. Reinick*
Reich' mir den Schleier, Emina *–Stieglitz*
Reich' mir die Hand, o Wolke *–Kulmann*
Rein und freundlich lacht der Himmel *–Kumpf*
Reizender Schmetterling, flüchtiges *–Francke*
Ringel Reihe Rosenkranz *–K. Freiligrath*
Ringel, Ringel, Reihe! S'sind der Kinder Zweie *–Volkslied*
Ringel, ringel Reih'n! Wer fröhlich ist *–Mahler*
Ringelringelreigen, mit den jungen Zweigen *–Zacharias*
Ringelringelrosenkranz, ich tanz' *–Bierbaum*
Rings ein Verstummen, ein Entfärben *–Lenau*
Rings Stille herrscht, es schweigt der Wald *–Hersch*
Rings walten Todesstille *–Haug*
Rings waltet heil'ges Schweigen *–Kletke*
Rings weiße Blütendolden *–Sergel*
Ringsum auf allen Plätzen schläft *–G. Kinkel*
Ringsum dunkle Nacht *–Bierbaum*
Ringsum erschallt in Wald und Flur *–Klingemann*
Ringsum ruhet die Stadt *–Hölderlin*
Rinne, rinne leise, meine Thräne du *–Beck*
Ritter, treue Schwesterliebe *–Schiller*
Röschen biß den Apfel an *–Keller*
Röselein! müssen denn Dornen sein? *–Neun*

Röslein dreie in der Reihe blühn so rot *–Conrat*
Rolle, du strömigter Carun *–Macpherson*
Ros' und Lilie morgenthaulich *–Goethe*
Rosa, denkst du an mich? *–Kosegarten*
Rose du am Borne, rote Rose! *–Anonymous*
Rose Marie, Rose Marie, sieben Jahre *–Löns*
Rose, Meer, und Sonne sind *–Rückert*
Rosen auf den Weg gestreut *–L. Hölty*
Rosen brach ich Nachts *–Hans Schmidt*
Rosen! Ein Zypressenhain *–Rückert*
Rosen fliehen nicht allein *–Lenau*
Rosen im Haare, den Becher zur Hand *–Hafis*
Rosen pflücke, Rosen blühn *–J. W. L. Gleim*
Rosen senken ihr Haupt so schwer *–Jacobsen*
Rosen steckt mir an die Mutter *–Daumer*
Rosen und duftende Veilchen bring' ich *–Wildenbruch*
Rosenknöspchen, schön bist du *–Miller*
Rosenzeit, wie schnell vorbei *–Mörike*
Rosestock, Holderblüth' *–Volkslied*
Rosmarin und Thymian wächst *–Volkslied*
Rote Abendwolken ziehn am Firmament *–Conrat*
Rote Flammen so glüht der Mohn *–Müller-Rastatt*
Rote, fürstliche Rubine *–Giraud*
Rote Nelke blüht im Garten *–Hesse*
Rote Rosenknospen künden schon *–Conrat*
Roter Ringelrosenbusch *–"Ernst Rosmer"*
Roter Vogel hinauf dich schwing! *–Anonymous*
Rotkehlchen auf dem Zweige hupft *–Busch*
Rührt die Cymbel, schlagt die Saiten *–Grillparzer*
Rüste abendlich die Schale *–Bergengruen*
Rufst du, Kuckuck? So ganz zur Unzeit *–Jünger*
Ruft die Mutter, ruft der Tochter *–Kapper*
Ruh' dich aus. Mir brauchst Du *–Busta*
Ruh' von schmerzensreichen Mühen *–Anonymous*
Ruhe, heilige Nacht! Dämmerig scheint der Mond *–Fet*
Ruhe, schönstes Glück der Erde *–Anonymous*
Ruhe, Süßliebchen im Schatten *–Tieck*
Ruhig ist des Todes Schlummer *–E. Berlepsch*
Ruh'n in Frieden alle Seelen *–Jacobi*
Ruhn sie? rufet das Horn des Wächters *–Rückert*
Rund um mich Nacht, ich irr' allein *–Macpherson*

's alt Bäni, heißt's, seig gwüss e Häx *–Frey*
's is nichts mit den alten Weibern *–G. Nicolai*
's ist ein so stiller heil'ger Tag *–G. Hauptmann*
's ist kein verdrüßlicher Lebe *–Volkslied*
's ist Krieg! 's ist Krieg! O *–M. Claudius*
's ist nicht dein holdes Angesicht *–Feis*
's ist wahr, mit blanken Scheiben *–Gruppe*
's ist wahrlich besser in Kampf *–Loewe and Vocke*
's sind heute dreiunddreissig Jahr *–Strachwitz*
's war doch wie ein leises Singen *–Eichendorff*
'S war einer, dem's zu Herzen ging *–Chamisso*
's war mal 'ne Katzenkönigin, Ja, ja! *–Chamisso*
Saatengrün, Veilchenduft *–Uhland*
Sachte will's dämmern, mit seinen Lämmern *–Oser*
Säulen, Säulen, immer neue Gänge *–Heinemann*
Säuselnde Lüfte wehend so mild *–Rellstab*
Säusle, liebe Myrthe! Wie still ists *–C. Brentano*
Sag' an, du Träumer am lichten Tag *–Mahler*
Sag' an, o Alter! Wem gräbst du *–Unidentified*
Sag' an, o lieber Vogel mein *–Hebbel*
Sag an, was hinauf zur Drachenkluft *–Lutze*
Sag an, wer lehrt dich Lieder *–J. Mayrhofer*
Sag es nicht, geliebtes Herzchen *–Wiener*
Sag mir, du Siebenschläferlein *–Güll*
Sag mir, wer einst die Uhren erfund *–Heine*
Sag', welch wunderbare Träume *–Wesendonck*
Sag wie kann man Lieb' erkennen? *–H. Schulz*
Sage mir, Vogel im grünen Wald *–Francke*
Sage nicht, ich sei dein Leben *–Rückert*
Saget mir, auf welchem pfade *–George*
Sagt es niemand, nur den Weisen *–Goethe*
Sagt ihm, dass er zu mir komme *–Heyse*
Sagt mir an, was schmunzelt ihr? *–Voss*
Sagt mir, o schönste Schäf'rin mein *–Volkslied*
Sagt, seid Ihr es, feiner Herr *–Heyse*
Sagt, wo sind die Veilchen hin *–Jacobi*
Sagte ein goldener Schmetterling *–Rassow*
Sah dem edlen Bildnis in des Auges *–Daumer*
Sah ein Knab' ein Röslein steh'n *–Goethe*
Sahst du ein Glück vorübergehn *–Lenau*
Sanft ertönen Morgenglocken *–Anonymous*
Sanft glänzt die Abendsonne *–Anonymous*
Sanft mit seligem Entzücken *–Zinserling*
Sanft und lind geht der liebe Abendwind *–Eigenbrodt*
Sanft wehn, im Hauch der Abendluft *–Matthisson*
Sanft, wie deine Seele, Lotte *–G.*
Sanfte Ebbe und hohe Flut tief im Mut *–F. Schlegel*
Sanftes Clavier, sanftes Clavier *–C. F. D. Schubart*
Sanftes Licht, weiche nicht *–Reinbeck*
Sang ein Bettlerpärlein am Schenkentor *–Heyse*
Saphire sind die Augen dein *–Heine*
Sass ein Fink' in dunkler Hecke *–Pfarrius*
Saßen zwei Liebende kosend *–Hamerling*
Sausendes, brausendes Rad der Zeit *–Wesendonck*

Sausewind, Brausewind! dort und hier! *–Mörike*
Schad' um das schöne grüne Band *–Wilhelm Müller*
Schäferin, ach, wie haben sie dich *–Rückert*
Schätzelein, es kränket mich *–Volkslied*
Schäumende Woge rollt immer *–C. Hauptmann*
Schaff', das Tagwerk meiner Hände *–Goethe*
Schatten deckt, vom Thau befeuchtet *–Giesebrecht*
Schatzerl klein mußt nit traurig sein *–Anonymous*
Schau dich im Spiegel der Teiche *–Ingrisch*
Schauet, Priester! schauet, Laien! *–Haug*
Schaukeln und Gaukeln, halb wachender Traum! *–Raabe*
Schaukle auf den grünen Wellen *–Faber*
Schaust in's Stübchen klein *–Tappert*
Schaust so freundlich aus, Gretelein *–Hecker*
Schemen erloschener Flammen fachern *–"Max Waldau"*
Schenk ein, liebe Sonne, dein Licht *–Holz*
Schenk mir deinen goldenen Kamm *–Dehmel*
Scheust dich noch immer, seliges Leben *–Osterwald*
Schicksalslenker, blicke nieder *–Anonymous*
Schien mir's, als ich sah die Sonne *–Strindberg*
Schießgewehr schießt *–Brecht*
Schildern, willst du Freund *–Anonymous*
Schlacht, du brichst an! *–Körner*
Schläfst du noch mein Trauter? *–Dietmar von Aiste*
Schlägt hier ein Menschenherz *–Giesebrecht*
Schlaf ein! Die Nacht ist tief und weit *–Bernus*
Schlaf ein, gewieget an meiner Brust *–Grun*
Schlaf' ein, mein liebes Kindlein du *–G. Stein*
Schlaf' ein, schlaf' ein, mein süsses Kind *–R. Reinick*
Schlaf', Herzenssöhnchen, mein Liebling *–Hiemer*
Schlaf, holder Knabe, süss und mild! *–M. Claudius*
Schlaf, Kindchen, balde! Die Vögel fliegen *–Wackernagel*
Schlaf, Kindlein, balde, schlaf Kindlein *–Volkslied*
Schlaf, Kindlein schlaf! Der Vater hüt't *–Volkslied*
Schlaf, Kindlein, schlaf! *–Morgenstern*
Schlaf', Kindlein, schlaf', wie du schläfst *–Hebbel*
Schlaf, Kindlein, schlafe sanft und süß *–Brun*
Schlaf, mein Kind, der Abendwind weht *–Beer-Hofmann*
Schlaf, mein Kind, schlaf ein! *–Unidentified*
Schlaf, mein Kind, schlaf ein! *–Hoffmann von Fallersleben*
Schlaf mein Kind, schlaf, es ist spät *–Beer-Hofmann*
Schlaf', mein Kindchen, ruhig liege *–Lermontov*
Schlaf, mein liebes Kindlein, schlafe ein *–C. Lange*
Schlaf', Püppchen, schlaf', schlafe in Ruh' *–Volkslied*
Schlaf, Schwester, sanft im Erdenschoos! *–Miller*
Schlaf, Söhnchen! Dein Vater war eisenumhüllt *–Scott*
Schlaf, süßer Schlaf, obwohl dem Tod *–Mörike*
Schlaf' wohl du Himmelsknabe *–C. F. D. Schubart*
Schlaf wohl, schlaf wohl, über dich *–Benz*
Schlafe, Liebchen, weil's auf Erden *–Eichendorff*
Schlafe, mein Liebchen, ich dekke dich zu *–J. Sturm*
Schlafe, müde Seele! Daß dich nichts mehr quäle! *–Flaischlen*
Schlafe, schlafe, holder, süsser Knabe *–Anonymous*
Schlafe, süsser kleiner Donald *–Burns*
Schlafe wohl! Im Thal von Schatten *–Düringsfeld*
Schlafen, schlafen, nichts als schlafen! *–Hebbel*
Schlafend trägt man mich in mein Heimatland *–Mombert*
Schlaflose Nacht, der Regen rauscht *–Lenau*
Schlafloser Augen Sonne trüber Stern *–Byron*
Schlafloser Augen Sonne, zitternd Licht *–Byron*
Schlafloser Sonne, melanchol'scher Stern! *–Byron*
Schlag' die Tschadra zurück *–F. Bodenstedt*
Schlage keinen Nagel in die Wand *–Brecht*
Schlage nicht die feuchten Augen *–Geibel*
Schlagt mein ganzes Glück in Splitter *–Schlechta*
Schlagt! Schlagt! Trommeln! *–Whitman*
Schlange, halt stille! Halt stille *–Goethe*
Schlanke Fatme, hohe Palme, sprich! *–Dahn*
Schleenblüt' und wilde Rose *–Unidentified*
Schlief' die Mutter endlich ein *–Chamisso*
Schließe, mein Kind, schließe *–Träger*
Schließe mir die Augen beide *–Storm*
Schliesst du bald die Äuglein zu *–Zacharias*
Schlitten vorm Haus, steig ein *–Falke*
Schlosser auf, und mache Schlösser *–Daumer*
Schlummere, mein süßes Kind *–Anonymous*
Schlumm're du mein Leben *–Rasmus*
Schlummre Knabe! um uns her tobt *–Werthes*
Schlumm're sanft! Noch an dem Mutterherzen *–Körner*
Schlummre! Schlummre und träume *–Klingemann*
Schmächtig hingestreckt im Bette *–Trakl*
Schmerzen und Freuden reift *–Avenarius*
Schmerzliche Wonnen und wonnige Schmerzen *–Geibel*
Schmück dir das Haar mit wildem Mohn *–Dehmel*
Schmücket die Locken mit duftigen Kränzen *–Schober*

Schmückt das Haus mit grünen Zweigen *–Illaire*
Schnee, du stille weiße Braut *–Ingrisch*
Schneeglöckchen klingen wieder *–Hoffmann von Fallersleben*
Schneeglöckchen läuten leis' im Thal *–Träger*
Schneeglöckchen thut läuten *–R. Reinick*
Schneeglöcklein, o Schneeglöcklein *–Schober*
Schneewittchen hinter den Bergen *–J. Sturm*
Schnell fliehen die Schatten der Nacht *–W. Hensel*
Schnell geniesst die schnellen Stunden *–Heinrich Schmidt*
Schnick, schnack, Dud'lsack *–Fröhlich*
Schnür' den Bündel denn zum Wandern *–Simrock*
Schön ist das Fest des Lenzes *–Rückert*
Schön Klare, zwanzig Sommer alt *–Haug*
Schön prangt im Silbertau die junge Rose *–Mörike*
Schön röthlich die Kartoffeln sind *–M. Claudius*
Schön sind die blumichten Matten *–Ratschky*
Schön sind, doch kalt die Himmelssterne *–Schack*
Schön sind Rosen und Jasmin *–C. Weisse*
Schön Suschen kannt' ich lange Zeit *–G. A. Bürger*
Schön war, das ich dir weihte *–Daumer*
Schön, wie die Rose, blüht der Mädchen *–Wargemont*
Schön wie die Sünden bist du, Kind *–Faktor*
Schön wie Engel voll Walhalla's Wonne *–Schiller*
Schön wie Thirza bist du *–Hafis*
Schöne Himmelssonne, mild und hold *–Kosegarten*
Schöne Minka ich muss scheiden *–Tiedge*
Schöne Sennin, noch einmal singe *–Lenau*
Schöne Welt, wo bist du? Kehre wieder *–Schiller*
Schöne Wiege meiner Leiden *–Heine*
Schöne Zeiten, trübe Zeiten *–Hepp*
Schöner Augen schöne Strahlen *–Volkslied*
Schöner Mai, bist über Nacht *–Osterwald*
Schöner und schöner schmückt sich der Plan *–Grillparzer*
Schönes Leben! Du liegst krank *–Hölderlin*
Schönheit, die du im Mädchen blühst *–Busse*
Schönste Tugend einer Seele *–Goethe*
Schönster Bursch', den je ich traf *–Burns*
Schönster Herr Jesu, Herrscher aller Enden *–Volkslied*
Schönster Schatz, mein Engel *–Volkslied*
Schöpfer, deine Herrlichkeit *–Anonymous*
Schöpferin beseelter Töne! *–Salis-Seewis*
Schon dämmert's leise *–Huggenberger*
Schon deckt die Nacht, von starrem Frost *–Anonymous*
Schon fesselt Lieb' und Ehre mich *–J. Engel*
Schon hat die Nacht den Silberschrein *–Keller*
Schon im bunten Knabenkleide *–L. Hölty*
Schon kehren die Vögel wieder ein *–Eichendorff*
Schon manche selige Nacht *–Hesse*
Schon milder scheint die Sonne nieder *–Anonymous*
Schon naht, um uns zu scheiden *–Wetzel*
Schon sank die Sonne *–Hoffmann von Fallersleben*
Schon seh' ich Hirt' und Herde nimmer *–Lenau*
Schon streckt' ich aus im Bett *–Heyse*
Schon verstummt das Lied der Grille *–Leuthold*
Schon war die letzte Schwalbe fort *–Keller*
Schon will der Abend sinken *–Grun*
Schon zog vom Walde ich ferne wieder *–Lenau*
Schrieb die schöne Adelheid *–Ginzkey*
Schuh um Schuh im Finstern setz ich *–Hesse*
Schwalbe, sag mir an, ists dein alter Mann *–Gruppe*
Schwalben durch den Abend treibend *–Morgenstern*
Schwalbenmütterlein, Schwalbenmütterlein! *–R. Reinick*
Schwand nicht mit Pfeilesschnelle *–Buri*
Schwarz wie Nacht brausest du auf, Meer *–Voss*
Schwarzbrauner Hufschmied *–Spitteler*
Schwarzer Wald, dein Schatten *–Daumer*
Schwarzschattende Kastanie *–C. F. Meyer*
Schweb empor am Himmel *–Kulmann*
Schwebe, mein tanzender Kahn *–Gyr*
Schwebe, schwebe, blaues Auge *–Dingelstedt*
Schwebst du im nächtlichen Raum? *–G. J. Mayerhofer*
Schwebst du nieder aus den Weiten *–Dehmel*
Schweig' einmal still, du garst'ger Schwätzer *–Heyse*
Schweig o Herz! warum dies bange Sehnen *–Anonymous*
Schweig still, du dummes Menschenherz *–Mark*
Schweige, geliebteste Fraue *–Jacobsen*
Schweigen ist ein schönes Ding *–R. Reinick*
Schweigen rings; im Garten der Villa *–Leuthold*
Schweigend geht die junge Frau *–Braungart*
Schweigend sahe der May die bekränzte *–Klopstock*
Schweigsam treibt mein morscher Einbaum *–Scheffel*
Schweigt der Menschen laute Lust *–Eichendorff*
Schwelle die Segel, günstiger Wind! *–Platen*
Schwellen nicht Seufzer *–Kosegarten*
Schwer, langweilig ist mir mein Zeit *–Wunderhorn*
Schwer und Dumpfig, eine Wetterwolke *–Schiller*
Schwerin ist todt, Schwerin, mein General *–"Alexis"*
Schwester von dem ersten Licht *–Goethe*
Schwesterlein, Schwesterlein *–Volkslied*

Schwill an, mein Strom *–Huch*
Schwingt euch auf, Posaunenchöre *–Scheffel*
Schwirrend Tamburin, dich schwing' ich *–Eichendorff*
Schwor ein junges Mädchen *–Kapper*
Schwüle, schwüle Julinacht *–Lingg*
Schwüler Hauch weht mir herüber *–Stadler*
Seele, banger Vogel du *–Hesse*
Seele, vergiß sie nicht, Seele *–Hebbel*
Segne den König, ihn, unsern gütigen *–C. Loewe*
Segne, Herz, den Freudentag *–Cornelius*
Segne, Vater, meinen Fleiss *–C. C. Sturm*
Seh' ich deine kleinen Händchen an *–F. Bodenstedt*
Seh' ich deine zarten Füßchen an *–F. Bodenstedt*
Seh' ich den Pilgrim *–Goethe*
Seh' ich dort die Sternlein blinken *–Anonymous*
Seh' ich im verfall'nen dunklen Haus *–Eichendorff*
Seh ich in das stille Thal *–Kerner*
Sehet ihr am Fensterlein dort *–Mörike*
Sehnsucht aus einsamer Seele *–C. Hauptmann*
Sehnsucht ist Qual! Der Herrin wag *–C. F. Meyer*
Seht auf, ihr Männer *–Rilke*
Seht! da sitzt er auf der Matte *–Schiller*
Seht den Felsenquell, freudehell *–Goethe*
Seht den Himmel wie heiter! *–Voss*
Seht, es war einmal ein König *–Jacobsen*
Seht ihr die zwei Kirschenbäumchen *–Keller*
Seht ihr's dort funkeln in rosiger Pracht? *–F. Spohr*
Seht meine lieben Bäume an *–M. Claudius*
Seht mir doch mein schönes Kind *–G. A. Bürger*
Seht wie die Tage sich sonnig verklären *–Salis-Seewis*
Sei bescheiden, nimm fürliebe *–Rückert*
Sei dennoch unverzagt *–Flemming*
Sei du mein Trost, verschwiegne Traurigkeit! *–Hermes*
Sei gegrüsst, du Frau der Huld *–A. Schreiber*
Sei gegrüsst, Frau Sonne, mir *–Holbein*
Sei gegrüsst, geweihte Stille *–Schlechta*
Sei gesegnet immerdar von allen Tagen *–Petrarca*
Sei gesegnet, König der Magyaren! *–Abrányi*
Sei gnädig mir nach deiner Güte *–C. C. Sturm*
Sei mir gegrüsst in deiner Pracht *–Schwarzenberg*
Sei mir gegrüsst! Linderndes Öl! *–Anonymous*
Sei mir gegrüsst, o Mai *–Kumpf*
Sei mir gegrüßt, o schöne Nacht *–Zschokke*
Sei mir heute nichts zuwider *–Goethe*
Sei nicht traurig, bald ist es Nacht *–Hesse*
Sei rebe die blümt Sei frucht die betört *–George*
Sei sanft wie ihre Seele *–Baumberg*
Sei uns stets gegrüsst, o Nacht! *–J. Seidl*
Sei willkommen, Frühlingswehen *–Naumann*
Sei willkommen, Zwielichtstunde! *–Schack*
Seid gegrüsst, ihr grünen Hallen *–Fitger*
Seid gegrüßt mit Frühlingswonne *–Uhland*
Seid ihr beisammen all'? *–Mörike*
Seid mir gegrüßt, ihr Täler *–Anonymous*
Seid mir gegrüsst ihr Wellen *–"Ernst"*
Seid munter, ihr Mädchen *–Lackner*
Seid willkommen, stille Haine *–Anonymous*
Seid'ne Gewänder, Spangen von Gold *–Schönaich-Carolath*
Sein Bündel Holz am Rücken bringt *–Lenau*
Sein Heer durchwogte das Palmenthal *–F. Freiligrath*
Sein ist die Kraft, das Regiment der Sterne *–Werfel*
Sein Leichenhemd weiß wie Schnee *–Shakespeare*
Seinen Traum, Lind' wob, Frühling kaum *–Rückert*
Seit die Liebste war entfernt *–Heine*
Seit er von mir gegangen *–Unidentified*
Seit ganz mein Aug' ich durft' *–Dahn*
Seit ich dir gehöre, ist alles Leid *–Ungemach*
Seit ich ihn gesehen *–Chamisso*
Seit ich so viele Weiber sah *–Schikaneder*
Seit wann du mein ich weiß es nicht *–Dehmel*
Seitdem dein Aug' in meines schaute *–Schack*
Selbstzweck sei sich die Kunst *–Leuthold*
Sel'ge Abende nieder steigen *–Schröer*
Sel'ge Zeiten sah ich prangen *–Gubitz*
Selig durch die Liebe Götter *–Schiller*
Selig ihr Blinden, die ihr nicht *–Heyse*
Selig, o Mutter, wer stirbt! *–Anonymous*
Selige Nacht! Ich bin nun bei der Liebsten *–Petöfi*
Seliges Blümelein, kann Dir so nahe sein! *–Bartsch*
Seltsam, im Nebel zu wandern! *–Hesse*
Seltsam ist Juanas Weise *–Geibel*
Seltsam schöne Hügelfluchten *–Hesse*
Send' ihr Blumen und Frücht' *–Hölderlin*
Senk dich, o Gram, mit deinen Fantasien tief *–Anonymous*
Senke, strahlender Gott, die Fluren dürsten *–Schiller*
Senkt die Nacht den sanften Fittig nieder *–L'Égru*
Setze mir nicht, du Grobian *–Goethe*
Sey mir gegrüßt mein schmeichelndes Klavier *–Hermes*
Sicheln schallen, Ähren fallen *–L. Hölty*
Sie blasen zum Abmarsch *–Heyse*
Sie fliehet fort! Es ist um mich geschehen! *–Kleist*
Sie floh vor mir wie'n Reh so scheu *–Heine*

Sie führten ihn durch den grauen Hof *–Ammann*
Sie geht in Schönheit und entzücket *–Byron*
Sie haben dich fortgetragen *–Vischer*
Sie haben heut' Abend Gesellschaft *–Heine*
Sie haben mich dazu beschieden *–M. Claudius*
Sie haben mich geheißen *–Chamisso*
Sie haben wegen der Trunkenheit *–Goethe*
Sie hat das Auge, die Hand *–Götz*
Sie hat mich still zum Abschied *–Köstlin*
Sie hatte schüchtern zu ihm aufgesehen *–Amaru*
Sie hüpfte mit mir auf grünem Plan *–J. Mayrhofer*
Sie ist dahin, die Maienlieder tönte *–L. Hölty*
Sie ist gegangen, die Wonnen versanken *–Meissner*
Sie ist herauf gestiegen *–Plönnies*
Sie kam zum Schloß gegangen *–Maeterlinck*
Sie konnte mir kein Wörtchen sagen *–Schiller*
Sie liebt mich! Sie liebt mich! *–Goethe*
Sie liebte ihn, Er liebte sie *–"Alexis"*
Sie liebten sich beide *–Heine*
Sie machte Frieden! Das ist mein Gedicht *–M. Claudius*
Sie sagen, Hafis, du sei'st *–Hafis*
Sie sagen mir, daß meine Wangen *–Heyse*
Sie sagten, ich soll nicht erschrekken *–Ingrisch*
Sie sass am Rebenfenster *–Siebel*
Sie sass in unserm Mädchenkreise *–Storm*
Sie saßen und tranken am Teetisch *–Heine*
Sie saugt mit Gier verrätrisches Getränke *–Goethe*
Sie scheidet. Wie der Mutter Abschiedsblick *–H. Hölty*
Sie scheinen zu spielen voll Leichtsinn *–Goethe*
Sie senkten ihn in kalten Grund hinab *–Shakespeare*
Sie sind in Paris! Die Helden *–Mikan*
Sie sind so schön, die milden *–Ronsperger*
Sie sollen ihn nicht haben *–N. Becker*
Sie spielt mit Blumen im welken Strauss *–Beck*
Sie stand im Boot und fischte *–Wilhelm Müller*
Sie stand wohl am Fensterbogen *–Eichendorff*
Sie steht am Zellenfenster *–Anonymous*
Sie stürzt dem Neck zu Füssen *–Plönnies*
Sie trug den Becher in der Hand *–Hofmannsthal*
Sie trug ein Falken auf ihrer Hand *–Anonymous*
Sie trugen ihn auf der Bahre bloß *–Shakespeare*
Sie wandeln durch des Waldes Grün *–Mombert*
Sie wandelt im Blumengarten *–Klingemann*
Sie wankt dahin, die Abendwinde spielen *–L. Hölty*
Sie war ein Kind vor wenig Tagen *–Uhland*
Sie waren alle zum Tanzplatz hinaus *–Vogl*
Sie wiegen schwankend sich *–H. Claudius*
Sieben kleine Rosenstökke stehn *–Merkel*
Sieben Rosen hat der Strauch *–Brecht*
Sieh, an letzten Himmels Saum *–Bock*
Sieh auf dem Meer den Glanz *–Biegeleben*
Sieh den Abendstern erblinken *–Keller*
Sieh den Nagel in der Wand *–Brecht*
Sieh, der Himmel wird blau *–Dehmel*
Sieh, der Kastanie kindliches Laub *–Mörike*
Sieh Doris wie vom Mond bestrahlt *–Pfeffel*
Sieh' dort den Berg mit seinem Wiesenhange *–Lenau*
Sieh' hier den Bach, anbei die Waldesrose *–Lenau*
Sieh', ich steh' vor deiner Thür *–Lingen*
Sieh Jesum Christum leiden! *–C. C. Sturm*
Sieh', Liebchen, hier im Waldestal *–Hamerling*
Sieh mich, Heil'ger, wie ich bin *–Goethe*
Sieh, wie ist die Welle klar *–Daumer*
Sieh, wie wir zu den Sternen aufsteigen! *–Dehmel*
Siehe, der Frühling währet nicht lang *–Hoffmann von Fallersleben*
Siehe, es scheidet der Tag *–Busta*
Siehe, mein Röschen, der Frühling ist da *–Miller*
Siehe von allen den Liedern *–Mörike*
Siehe, wie die Mondesstrahlen *–Kosegarten*
Siehe, wir preisen selig *–Telschow*
Siehst du am Abend die Wolken ziehn *–Kletke*
Siehst du das Meer? Es glänzt auf seiner Fluth *–Geibel*
Siehst du den Stern im fernsten Blau *–Keller*
Siehst du die Perlen springen *–Hartleben*
Siehst du hinab in die dunkle See *–Unidentified*
Sieht uns der Blick gehoben *–F. Schlegel*
Silberblauer Mondenschein fällt herab *–J. Seidl*
Silbermond, mit bleichen Strahlen *–Simrock*
Silberne Mondesstrahlen glänzen *–Kamlah*
Sind es Schmerzen, sind es Freuden *–Tieck*
Sind wir geschieden, und ich muß leben *–Volkslied*
Sing, mit Sonnenaufgang singe *–F. Bodenstedt*
Sing', o lieblicher Sängermund *–Hafis*
Singe in heiliger Nacht *–Körner*
Singe, Mädchen, hell und klar *–Hans Schmidt*
Singe, Vöglein, singe, singe, Vöglein, singe *–Haase*
Singet die Nachtigall im dunkeln Wald *–Zedlitz*
Singet leise, leise, leise *–C. Brentano*
Singet nicht in Trauertönen *–Goethe*
Singt ein Falk' all die Nacht durch *–"Talvj"*
Singt mein Schatz wie ein Fink *–Keller*
Singt noch ein Lied und denkt euch nur *–Brecht*
Singt, singt mit heiligem Entzücken *–Uz*
Sinke, liebe Sonne, sinke *–Baumberg*

Sinnend stand ich bei dem Grabe Rabby Löv's *–Christen*
Sitz' ich allein. wo kann ich besser sein? *–Goethe*
Sitz' ich im Gras am glatten See *–J. Mayrhofer*
Sitz im Sattel, reite, reite auf die Freite *–Bierbaum*
Sitze hier an lieber Stelle *–J. Kinkel*
Sitzt a schöns Vögerl aufm Dannabaum *–Volkslied*
So bringst du mich um meine Liebe *–Lessing*
So durch die Gassen im Silberlicht *–Geissler*
So ein rechter Soldat fürcht' nicht Kugel *–Boelitz*
So eitel künstlich haben sie verwoben *–Eichendorff*
So fest wie die Hand den Stein hält *–Kafka*
So fliehst du mich, du tugendhafte Seele *–Anonymous*
So fügt sich Blüt'- an Blütezeit *–Heindl*
So geht es in Schnützelputz-Häusel *–Volkslied*
So gross, so rein, so hehr geklart *–Czermak*
So gross, so still, so feierlich *–Christen*
So hab' ich doch die ganze Woche *–Volkslied*
So hab' ich endlich dich gerettet *–Uhland*
So hab' ich nun die Stadt verlassen *–Uhland*
So hab' ich wirklich dich verloren? *–Goethe*
So halt' ich endlich dich umfangen *–Geibel*
So harrte ich schweigend *–Stieler*
So hat noch Niemand mit mir gethan *–J. Grosse*
So ich traurig bin weiss ich nur ein ding *–George*
So ist die Lieb'! So ist die Lieb'! *–Mörike*
So Jemand spricht: Ich liebe Gott! *–Gellert*
So komme, was da kommen mag! *–Storm*
So lang, ach! schon so lang erfüllt *–Leon*
So lang ich werde: "Liebst du mich" *–Rückert*
So lang im deutschen Eichenthale *–Matthisson*
So lang man nüchtern ist *–Goethe*
So lange Schönheit wird bestehn *–Hoffmann von Fallersleben*
So lass' herein nun brechen die Brandung *–Eichendorff*
So lass mich sitzen ohne Ende *–F. Freiligrath*
So laßt mich scheinen, bis ich werde *–Goethe*
So leise sind die grünen Wälder *–Trakl*
So Mancher sieht mit finstrer Miene *–J. Seidl*
So mußt Du allen Dingen Bruder und Schwester sein *–Hesse*
So oft der Herbst die Rosen stahl *–Rückert*
So oft sie kam, erschien mir die Gestalt *–Lenau*
So regnet es sich langsam ein *–Flaischlen*
So ruhig geh' ich meinen Pfad *–Eichendorff*
So sah ich denn auf Erden Engelsfrieden *–Petrarca*
So schlaf in Ruh'! *–Hoffmann von Fallersleben*
So schlafe nun, du Kleine! *–M. Claudius*
So schön sind deine Hände *–Bethge*
So sei gegrüsst viel tausendmal *–Hoffmann von Fallersleben*
So soll ich dich nun meiden *–Uhland*
So stehn wir, ich und meine Weide *–Hafis*
So still und mild der Tag und feierlich *–"Ernst"*
So still zu liegen und an dich zu denken *–Morgenstern*
So stille ruht im Hafen *–C. F. Meyer*
So tanzet und springet in Reihen und Kranz *–Goethe*
So tönet denn, schäumende Wellen *–Tieck*
So trieb sie mich denn grausam fort *–Burns*
So viel Blumen allwärts blühen *–Gerstenberg*
So viel Laub an der Linden ist *–Roquette*
So viel Stern' am Himmel stehen *–Volkslied*
So viele Quellen von den Bergen *–Eichendorff*
So voll und reich wand noch das Leben *–Jacobsen*
So wälz ich ohne Unterlaß *–Goethe*
So wahr die Sonne scheinet *–Rückert*
So wandl' ich wieder den alten Weg *–Heine*
So wart bis ich dies dir noch künde *–George*
So weich und warm hegt dich kein Arm *–Heyse*
So weit gebracht, daß wir bei Nacht *–Goethe*
So wilde Freude nimmt ein wildes Ende *–Shakespeare*
So will ich frisch und fröhlich sein *–Volkslied*
So willst du des Armen dich gnädig erbarmen? *–Tieck*
So willst du treulos von mir scheiden *–Schiller*
So wird der Mann, der sonder Zwang *–J. Mayrhofer*
So wünsch ich ihr ein gute Nacht *–Volkslied*
Sobald Damötas Chloën sieht, so sucht *–C. Weisse*
Sobald Damötas Chloen sieht, wird er *–Leon*
Sohn der Jungfrau, Himmelskind! *–Mörike*
Sohn der Ruhe *–Castelli*
Solang, ach! schon solang erfüllt *–Leon*
Solang' du nach dem Glücke jagst *–Hesse*
Solch ein göttliches Vergnügen *–Haug*
Solche Düfte sind mein Leben *–Uhland*
Soldat sein ist gefährlich *–Eichendorff*
Soll ich denn sterben *–Wunderhorn*
Soll ich dich denn nun verlassen *–Eichendorff*
Soll ich ihn lieben, soll ich ihn lassen *–Heyse*
Soll ich lieben, soll ich ihn lassen *–Heyse*
Soll nach des Volkes *–Byron*
Soll sich der Mond nicht heller *–Volkslied*
Sollt' ich voller Sorg' und Pein *–Eschenburg*

Sollt' man's denken, ist's zu glauben *–Schulte vom Brühl*
Sommer entschwand, Herbstluft durchwehet *–Lua*
Sommer will aus heissem Herzen *–Volkslied*
Sommerfäden hin und wieder *–Candidus*
Sommerruh, wie schön bist du! *–Schad*
Sonn' auf Sonn' sich hellt *–B. Frank*
Sonne der Schlummerlosen *–Byron*
Sonne, du sinkst, Sonne, du sinkst *–Kosegarten*
Sonne hat sich müd gelaufen *–R. Reinick*
Sonne, herbstlich dünn und zag *–Trakl*
Sonne, Sonne, scheine, fahr übern Rheine *–Wunderhorn*
Sonne taucht in Meeresfluthen *–Scheffel*
Sonne über Ähren *–H. Claudius*
Sonne, weinest jeden Abend *–Wesendonck*
Sonnenfädchen spinnt Nixlein im Wald *–Heindl*
Sonnenlicht, Sonnenschein *–A. Becker*
Sonnenstrahlen durch die Tannen *–Bruchmann*
Sonnenuntergang, schwarze Wolken zieh'n *–Lenau*
Sonntag und Frühlingsmorgen *–Steindorff*
Sonntagsfriede liegt heilig *–Bierbaum*
Sonst kam mein Johnnie zur Stadt *–Burns*
Sonst konnt' ich dein nicht denken *–Anonymous*
Sonst plaudert ich mit Euch *–Heyse*
Sophie, mein Henker Mädel, komm *–Morgenstern*
Sorglos über die Fläche weg *–Goethe*
Sorgt für die Zukunft! *–J. F. A. B–r*
Soviel Raben nachts auffliegen *–Lingg*
Spähend nach dem Eisengitter *–J. Seidl*
Späte Rose, in dem hohen Glase *–H. Claudius*
Spätherbstnebel, kalte Träume *–Heine*
Spätnachmittag. Die kleine Straße *–Kuckuck*
Spann dein kleines Schirmchen auf *–Morgenstern*
Spannenlanger Hansel *–Volkslied*
Spazieren wollt ich reiten *–Wunderhorn*
Spende, Veilchen, deine Düfte *–J. Müller*
Spiel ich wo zum Tanze auf *–Sergel*
Spielt die Blues für mich *–Hughes*
Spielt, Mägdlein, unter eurer Weide *–Giesebrecht*
Spinn', Mägdlein, spinn'! *–Volkslied*
Spinn, spinn, mein liebs Nanerl *–Volkslied*
Sprach eine wilde Ros' am Zaun *–"Martin Greif"*
Sprachen Königin und König einstens *–Volkslied*
Sprich, Fräulein, warum härmst du dich? *–Scott*
Sprich nicht immer von dem laub *–George*
Sprich nur, sprich! ich höre die Rede *–Adler*
Springer, der in luft'gem Schreiten *–Eichendorff*
Spute dich, Kronos! Fort *–Goethe*
Stäbe flehen Kreuze Arme Schrift *–Stramm*
Stand das Mädchen, stand am Bergesabhang *–Kapper*
Stark wie der Tod ist die Liebe *–Hafis*
Staunend sahen wir das grosse Pferd *–Kafka*
Staunend schreit' ich durch die Gassen *–Giesebrecht*
Steh' auf, steh' auf und öffne *–Träger*
Steh' balde still und rühr' dich nicht *–Immerman*
Steh' ich im Feld, mein ist die Welt! *–Hebel*
Steh' ich in finst'rer Mitternacht *–Hauch*
Steht auf, ihr lieben Kinderlein! *–Albers, Wunderhorn*
Steht ein Häuschen an der Bahn *–Morgenstern*
Steht ein Mädchen an dem Fenster *–Koch*
Steig auf, geliebter Schatten *–"Friedrich Halm"*
Steig' empor am Himmel, schöner Abendstern *–Kulmann*
Steig, o Mutter aller Schmerzen *–Giraud*
Steige aus der Nacht hernieder *–Thalhammer*
Steigt empor, ihr Wünsche mein *–H. Loewe*
Stell' auf den Tisch die duftenden Reseden *–Hermann Gilm*
Stellt mir den Blumenstrauss *–Wildenbruch*
Sterb' ich, so hüllt in Blumen *–Heyse*
Stern der Liebe! bleich und trübe *–Matthisson*
Stern der Liebe, Glanzgebilde! *–Körner*
Stern, in des Himmels Ferne! *–Rückert*
Sternchen mit dem trüben Schein *–Volkslied*
Sterne mit den goldnen Füßchen *–Heine*
Stets sey es Frühling um dich *–Anonymous*
Steure, Fährmann, deine Barke *–Prechtler*
Still beginnt's im Hain zu thauen *–Silbert*
Still bei Nacht fährt manches Schiff *–Eichendorff*
Still das Sterngeläute ist verklungen *–Stamm*
Still, es ist ein Tag verflossen *–Dehmel*
Still ist die Nacht, es ruhen die Gassen *–Heine*
Still ist die Nacht, nur leise klingen *–Anonymous*
Still ist es worden aller Ort *–Stinde*
Still ist's, wo die Gräber *–"Martin Greif"*
Still min Hanne, hör mi to! *–Groth*
Still schwebt die Nacht in hehrer Größe *–Greiner*
Still sitz' ich an des Hügels Hang *–E. Schulze*
Still, still! 'sist nur ein Traum *–Falke*
Still und ruhig ist des Todes Schlummer *–C. G. Goez*
Still, wie so still! *–Blüthgen*
Stille begegnet am Saum des Waldes *–Trakl*
Stille Blume, erblasst *–Weinheber*
Stille ruht die weite Welt *–"Martin Greif"*
Stille schafft sie in der Kammer *–Trakl*
Stille, stille, dass ich höre *–H. Loewe*

Stille Thränen liebt mein Herz –*Lafontaine*
Stille, träumende Frühlingsnacht –*Bierbaum*
Stillen Geists will ich dir flehen! –*H. W. Gerstenberg*
Stiller Abend sinkt, Sterne blinken leise –*C. Hauptmann*
Stiller Garten, eile nur –*Uhland*
Stirb immerhin, es welken ja –*Anonymous*
Störe nicht den leisen Schlummer –*Kalbeck*
Stoppelfeld, die Wälder leer –*Lenau*
Storch, Storch, Langbein –*Wunderhorn*
Storch, Storch, Steiner –*Volkslied*
Stoss an Kamerad: es lebe der Soldat! –*Shakespeare*
Sträußchen wem zu Ehren –*C. F. D. Schubart*
Strahl, der durch die Gassen geht –*Ehrler*
Strahlt zuweilen auch ein mildes Licht –*Daumer*
Streng ist uns das glück und spröde –*George*
Streu' ich Zucker auf die Speise –*Braun-Prager*
Stricknadeln, blank und blinkend –*Giraud*
Ström' leise, du Bächlein –*Unidentified*
Stromflut dahin rauscht –*Cornelius*
Studieren will nichts bringen –*Eichendorff*
Stürmt, reißt und rast –*Wunderhorn*
Stumm wächst die Einsamkeit –*Ingrisch*
Sturm mit seinen Donnerschlägen –*Lenau*
Sturm, wie lieb ich dich –*Boelitz*
Sünn, Sünn, schiene, kiek ut dien Gardine –*Groth*
Süß duftende Lindenblüte –*Hartleben*
Süß sind mir die Schollen des Tales –*Knodt*
Süß tönt Gesanges Hauch –*Cornelius*
Süss und sacht, sachte weh', Wind du –*Tennyson*
Süsse Ahnung dehnt den Busen –*Reinbeck*
Süsse Augen, klare Bronnen! –*J. Mayrhofer*
Süße Freundin, noch Einen –*Goethe*
Süße heilige Natur, laß mich gehn –*Stolberg-Stolberg*
Süsse Nacht! Wie schweiget –*Heiberg*
Süßer Freude heller Bach –*Anonymous*
Süsser Freund, du blickest mich –*Chamisso*
Süßer, goldner Frühlingstag! –*Uhland*
Süsser Schlaf umfing den Müden –*Anonymous*
Süßes Bild, schwebst mir vor –*Brun*
Süsses Licht! aus goldenen Pforten –*Körner*
Süsses Liebchen! Komm zu mir! –*Körner*
Sum, sum, der Sandmann geht –*Busse*
Summ, summ, summ, Bienchen –*Hoffmann von Fallersleben*
Summ! summ! summ! summ! so schwirrt es um das Bienenhaus –*Eigenbrodt*

Täglich ging die wunderschöne –*Heine*
Täglich kommt die gelbe Sonne –*Trakl*
Täubchen, ihr lieben, lieben Täubchen –*R. Reinick*
Täuscht euch, ihr Augen, nicht –*Michelangelo*
Tag meines Lebens! Die Sonne sinkt –*Nietzsche*
Tag und Regung war entflohen –*Eichendorff*
Tag voll Himmel! da aus Laura's Blicken –*Matthisson*
Tage der Gnade brechen herein –*H. Claudius*
Tage der Wonne, kommt ihr so bald? –*Goethe*
Tage, wie geht ihr dahin –*Jünger*
Tagtäglich bietest du dich dar –*H. Claudius*
Tanz mit mir, tanz mit mir –*Volkslied*
Tanzt, Paar und Paar, den Ringeltanz –*Anonymous*
Tauchst du nieder aus den Weiten –*Dehmel*
Taufrisch glänzen die Blumen –*Drescher*
Tausend Blumen um mich her –*M. Claudius*
Tausend goldne Blätter sinken –*Anonymous*
Tausend goldne Sterne, glänzen –*Saul*
Tausend Menschen ziehen vorüber –*Mackay*
Tausend stille weiße, blaue Blumen –*Sergel*
Tausend Tannenwipfel drohen –*C. Hauptmann*
Tautröpfchen blinkt am Blatt –*Hepp*
Theresen lieb' ich, ist das Sünde? –*Wargemont*
Theures Mädchen, wenn ein andrer Himmel –*Kosegarten*
Theuthold, mein Trauter –*Blumauer*
Thoms saß am hallenden See –*Falk*
Thron der Liebe, Stern der Güte! –*Scheffler*
Thronend auf erhabnem Sitz –*Schiller*
Thu' nicht so spröde, schönes Kind –*F. Bodenstedt*
Thüringens Wälder senden den Waidmann –*Scheffel*
Thut auch das bange Herz dir weh –*Träger*
Tief dunkle Nacht! –*Czermak*
Tief im Gemüt mir Liebe glüht –*Cornelius*
Tief im grünen Frühlingshag –*Geibel*
Tief im Herzen trag' ich Pein –*Geibel*
Tief im Süden Dixies– –*Hughes*
Tief im Talgrund überm Bach –*Huggenberger*
Tief mit blauer Nachtgewalt –*Hesse*
Tiefe Feier schauert um die Welt –*Kosegarten*
Tiefe Stille herrscht im Wasser –*Goethe*
Tiefer liegt die Nacht um mich her –*Goethe*
Tiefer Sehnsucht heil'ges Bangen –*Schubert*
Tiefer sinket schon die Sonne –*F. Schlegel*
Tiefes, tiefes Schweigen –*A. Kleinschmidt*
Tinte! Tinte, wer braucht! –*Mörike*
Tochter des Walds, du Lilienverwandte –*Mörike*
Tod, alter Kapitän, nun säum nicht lange! –*Baudelaire*

Tod, dir zum Raube fiel eine Welt –*J. Sturm*
Tod, du Schrecken der Natur! –*C. F. D. Schubart*
Tod mit Blumen laß dein Tor bereiten –*R. Graf*
Tod, Sünd, Leben und Gnad –*Luther*
Todesstille deckt das Thal –*Jacobi*
Tödtlich graute mir der Morgen –*Mörike*
Töne, lindernder Klang –*Anonymous*
Tollt der Wind über Feld und Wiese –*Falke*
Tonleiterähnlich steiget dein Klaggesang –*Mörike*
Tra, ri, ro! Der Sommer, der ist do! –*Volkslied*
Trachten will ich nicht auf Erden –*Anonymous*
Träume, träume, du mein süßes Leben! –*Dehmel*
Tragt, blaue Träume, mich –*Boelitz*
Trallallala, mein Liebchen –*"Talvj"*
Trallirum larum höre mich! –*G. A. Bürger*
Trara, trara, mein Hörnlein hell –*Rafael*
Trarah! Trarah! wir kehren daheim! –*Werner*
Trau nicht der Liebe, mein Liebster –*Heyse*
Trauer umfliesst mein Leben –*Anonymous*
Traum, den du verwebst –*Michalewski*
Traum der eignen Tage –*Chamisso*
Traun! Bogen und Pfeil sind gut für den Feind –*Tieck*
Traurig, einsam welkst du hin, Blume! –*Haug*
Traurig lehnst du dein Gesicht –*Hesse*
Traurig schau ich von der Klippe –*Burns*
Treibe nur mit Lieben Spott –*Heyse*
Treibe, treibe, Schifflein –*Licht*
Treibt der Sommer seinen Rosen –*Osterwald*
Trenn mich nicht vom Blätterthrone –*Gernss*
Tretet ein, hoher Krieger –*Keller*
Tretet leise zu meinem Grabe –*Anonymous*
Treue Liebe bis zum Grabe –*Hoffmann von Fallersleben*
Treue Liebe dauert lange –*Tieck*
Trink, o Jüngling, heilges Glücke –*Goethe*
Trinkt aus, ihr zechtet zum letztenmal –*V. Klemperer*
Tritt auf, den Riegel von der Tür –*Volkslied*
Triumph er naht, Heil, Heil dem Helden –*Scott*
Trockne deines Jammers Tränen –*Voss*
Trocknet nicht, trocknet nicht –*Goethe*
Tröst die Bedrängten –*Volkslied*
Trom to tom, tom, tom –*Löwenstein*
Trüb verglomm der schwüle Sommertag –*C. F. Meyer*
Trübe wird's die Wolken jagen –*Lenau*
Trübe Wolken, Herbstesluft –*Lenau*
Trug mein Herz ich auf der Hand –*Falke*
Trunken müssen wir alle sein! –*Goethe*
Tu ab den Schmerz, entflieh –*Kaltneker*
Turteltaube, du klagest so laut –*Herder*

Über alle Weiten weht der gleiche Wind –*H. Franck*
Über allen Gipfeln ist Ruh' –*Goethe*
Über Berg und Tal mit lautem Schall –*Mahler*
Über den Bergen, weit zu wandern –*Busse*
Über den Bergen weit zu wandern –*Busse*
Über den Himmel Wolken ziehn –*Hesse*
Über den weißen Weiher –*Trakl*
Über der Erde Stirne –*Morgenstern*
Über die Bäume möcht' ich mich schwingen –*Bone*
Über die Berge mit Ungestüm –*Kotzebue*
Über die Berge steigt schon die Sonne –*Heine*
Über die Berge, über die Wellen –*Herder*
Über die Berge zieht ihr fort –*J. Mayrhofer*
Über die Heide hallet mein Schritt –*Storm*
Über die hellen funkelnden Wellen –*Hoffmann von Fallersleben*
Über die Hügel und über die Berge hin –*Hoffmann von Fallersleben*
Über die See, fern über die See –*Lemcke*
Über die tausend Berge –*Morgenstern*
Über die verhüllten Abendhügel –*Falke*
Über die vier Städte kreisen –*Brecht*
Über die Wellen zieht zagend –*Beckmann*
Über die Welt kommt Stille –*Heyse*
Über diesen Strom, vor Jahren –*Uhland*
Über eine Wiege schaukelt –*Liliencron*
Über gelb' und rote Streifen –*Eichendorff*
Über kahle, fahle Hügel –*Saar*
Über meines Liebchens Äugeln –*Goethe*
Über mir im Blauen reisen Wolken –*Hesse*
Über mir in wolkigen Lüften –*C. Hauptmann*
Über Nacht kommt still das Leid –*J. Sturm*
Über Tal und Fluß getragen –*Goethe*
Über unsre Liebe hängt –*Dehmel*
Über Wiesen und Felder ein Knabe ging –*Bierbaum*
Über Wipfel und Saaten –*Eichendorff*
Über Wolken Herr der Herren –*Dr. Bartholdy*
Überall in dem All, mag ich –*Meier*
Überall, wohin mein Auge blicket –*Kalchberg*
Überblickt man die Jahre –*Benn*
Über'm dunklen Walde steigt –*Heyse*
Überm Strohhut flattern Bänder –*Hepp*
Über'n Garten durch die Lüfte –*Eichendorff*
Übernacht ich im Dorf Albluft –*Hölderlin*
Übers Niederträchtige niemand sich beklage –*Goethe*
Überwunden hat der Herr den Tod! –*Klopstock*
Uffem Kirchhof, am Chor blüeht –*Mörike*

Ufm Berga da giht dar Wind *–Volkslied*
Uf'm Bergli bin i gesässe *–Goethe*
Ull Mann wull riden, wull hat he ken Pärd *–Volkslied*
Ullin trat auf mit der Harfe *–Goethe*
Um bei dir zu sein *–Huch*
Um deine Liebe, zu allen Zeiten *–Gomoll*
Um der fallenden Ruder Spitzen *–Schack*
Um die blüthenvollen Äste *–Anonymous*
Um dies Schifflein schmiege *–Köstlin*
Um meine Weisheit unbekümmert *–Hölderlin*
Um meinen Nakken schliesst sich *–Hart*
Um mich ist Nacht! Nacht! *–Macpherson*
Um Mitternacht blühen die Blumen *–Stona*
Um Mitternacht ging ich *–Goethe*
Um Mitternacht hab' ich gewacht *–Rückert*
Um Mitternacht, ich schlief *–Goethe*
Um Mitternacht ruht die ganze Erde *–Osterwald*
Um Mitternacht, wenn die Menschen *–Goethe*
Um stille Stübel schleicht des Monds *–Morgenstern*
Um zu begreifen, wie sie damals war *–Rilke*
Umflattre mir des liebsten Mädchens Wangen *–v. G.*
Umringt vom mutherfüllten Heere *–Heigel*
Umsonst, daß du ein Herz zu lenken *–Goethe*
Umsonst, umsonst entsagt' ich *–Anonymous*
Umweht von Maiduft, unter des Blütenbaums *–Voss*
Unangeklopft ein Herr tritt Abends *–Mörike*
Unbewegte laue Luft, tiefe Ruhe der Natur *–Daumer*
Und als der Mensch geschaffen war *–Siebel*
Und als ich ein winzig Bübchen war *–Shakespeare*
Und bild' dir nur im Traum nichts ein *–Heyse*
Und bist du jung an Jahren *–Heyse*
Und der Engel sprach und gab sich Müh *–Rilke*
Und der Nachbarssohn, der Ruprecht *–Jacobowski*
Und die mich trug im Mutterleib *–Mörike*
Und die Rosen, die prangen *–Osterwald*
Und die Sonne macht den weiten Ritt *–E. M. Arndt*
Und du kamest in mein Haus *–Dehmel*
Und dürft' ich dich wekken zum Sonnenlicht *–Ritter*
Und endlich stirbt die Sehnsucht doch *–Altenberg*
Und er spützete auf die Erde *–the Bible*
Und es sind die finstern Zeiten *–Brecht*
Und es waren mächtge Zaren *–Brecht*
Und frische Nahrung, neues Blut *–Goethe*
Und gehst du über den Kirchhof *–Heyse*
Und gleichwohl kann ich anders nicht *–Flemming*
Und haben auch im grünen Wald *–Rafael*
Und hast du einen Andern *–Volkslied*
Und hat der Tag all seine Qual *–Jacobsen*
Und heller und heller quollen *–Plönnies*
Und Hiobs Hause nahend *–Telschow*
Und hörst du, kleine Phylis nicht *–Herder*
Und ich werde nicht mehr sehen *–Brecht*
Und ihre Augen irren rings umher *–Kuberzig*
Und ist mein Schatz im fremden Land *–Stinde*
Und kehrt er einst heim *–Maeterlinck*
Und könnt ich auch erwecken dich *–A. Schults*
Und kommt der Frühling wieder her *–Osterwald*
Und kommt er nicht mehr zurück? *–Shakespeare*
Und laß der Welt, die noch nicht weiß *–Shakespeare*
Und morgen fällt Sankt Martins Fest *–Goethe*
Und morgen wird die Sonne wieder scheinen *–Mackay*
Und nimmer schreibst du? *–M. Collin*
Und noch im alten Elternhause *–Dehmel*
Und nun ade, mein herzallerliebster Schatz! *–Wunderhorn*
Und nun ein End' dem Trauern *–Schröer*
Und nun kam die Nacht *–F. Freiligrath*
Und ob auch Sturm das Haus mir umsaust *–Bittner*
Und oft war's nur ein Hauch *–G. H. Goering*
Und ringsum Schnee und Gletschereis *–Hesse*
Und sängen die Vögel dir *–Cornelius*
Und schau' ich hin, so schaust du her *–Volkslied*
Und schläfst du, mein Mädchen *–Geibel*
Und sei es, wo auch immer *–Vincke*
Und sie kamen in ihren Hemden *–Brecht*
Und sitz' ich in der Schenke *–Bowitsch*
Und so finden wir uns wieder *–Schiller*
Und so laßt mich weiter wandern *–Mommsen*
Und steht Ihr früh am Morgen auf *–Heyse*
Und um die Rippen zog er *–Anacreon*
Und wärst du mein Weib *–Busse*
Und was die Sonne glüht *–F. Bodenstedt*
Und weil der Mensch ein Mensch ist *–Brecht*
Und weil Du bist ein Röslein *–Oder*
Und weil ich denn von dannen muss *–W. Hertz*
Und welche Rose Blüthen treibt *–Osterwald*
Und wenn die Primel schneeweiß *–Geibel*
Und wenn es dunkel werden *–Rollet*
Und wenn es einst dunkelt *–Eichendorff*
Und wenn ich werd' im Sarg *–Heyse, Volkslied*
Und werden wir uns nie besitzen *–Morgenstern*
Und wie mag die Liebe dir kommen sein? *–Rilke*
Und wie manche Nacht bin ich aufgewacht *–Carossa*
Und wie sie kam zur Hexe *–Heyse*
Und wieder hatt' ich der Schönsten *–R. Reinick*
Und wieder nehm' ich die Harfe *–Leuthold*
Und wieder schlägt's – ein Viertel erst *–Keller*

Und wieder spür' ich jenes leise Schwingen *–Zwillinger*
Und willst du deinen Liebsten *–Heyse*
Und willst du von mir scheiden *–W. Hertz*
Und wir werden zusammen schweigen *–Morgenstern*
Und wo noch kein Wandrer gegangen *–Eichendorff*
Und wollen mich die klugen Leute fragen *–Heyse*
Und würdest nie die Hand du falten *–Träger*
Und wüssten's die Blumen, die kleinen *–Heine*
Unendlich dehnt sich das brausende Meer *–Glücklich*
Unendliche Freude durchwallet das Herz *–Schiller*
Ungern flieht das Süsse Leben *–Anonymous*
Ungesucht gefunden preis ich *–O. Klemperer*
Unglücklich Herz, und konnt' es sein *–Byron*
Uns ist geboren ein Kindelein *–Anonymous*
Uns ist kein Sein vergönnt *–Hesse*
Uns leuchtet heut der Freude Schein! *–Volkslied*
Unser Feind ist, grosser Gott *–Kerr*
Unser Herzog hat herrliche Thaten *–Giesebrecht*
Unser ist das Los der Epigonen *–Keller*
Unser Schifflein treibt umher *–J. Sturm*
Unsre lieben Hühnerchen *–Hoffmann von Fallersleben*
Unsre Quelle kommt im Schatten *–Chamisso*
Unten Schlacht, doch oben schossen *–Heine*
Unter blühenden Bäumen *–Gensichen*
Unter Blüten des Mai's *–L. Hölty*
Unter den Bäumen ruht das Mädchen *–Geibel*
Unter den blühenden Linden weißt du's noch? *–Ritter*
Unter den grünen Pfefferbäumen *–Brecht*
Unter den Linden, an der Haide *–Walther von der Vogelweide*
Unter den rothen Blumen schlummere *–Bechstein*
Unter den Zweigen in tiefer Nacht *–Heyse*
Unter der Linden, an der Heide *–Walther von der Vogelweide*
Unter die Soldaten ist ein Zigeunerbub' *–Geibel*
Unter spärlich grünen Blättern *–Trebitsch*
Unter verschnittenen Weiden *–Trakl*
Unter'm Machandelbaum, da ist ein Platz *–Wildenbruch*
Unterm schutz von dichten blättergründen *–George*
Unter'm weissen Baume sitzend *–Heine*
Uraltes Wehn vom Meer, Meerwind bei Nacht *–Rilke*
Urnen füllen sich und Krüge *–Jünger*

Vater, du glaubst es nicht *–Leitner*
Vater, ich rufe Dich! Brüllend umwölkt *–Körner*
Vater, schenk' mir diese Stunde *–Stadler*
Vater unser beten wir *–Küster*
Vaterland ist mir das Lied *–Jünger*
Veilchen, Rosmarin, Mimosen *–Hoffmann von Fallersleben*
Veilchen unter Gras versteckt *–Hoffmann von Fallersleben*
Veilchen vom Berg, woran mahnest du *–Lemcke*
Veilchen, wie so schweigend *–Hoffmann von Fallersleben*
Veilchen wollt' ich pflükken *–Max Reger*
Verbirg dich, Sonne *–J. Mayrhofer*
Verbleibst ihm dennoch hold gewogen *–Beck*
Verblichen ist der grüne Wald *–Hirsch*
Verbogen und zerkniffen war *–Keller*
Verdankt sei es dem Glanz *–Hermes*
Verfallen liegt ein Tempeltor *–C. Hauptmann*
Verfließet, vielgeliebte Lieder *–Goethe*
Verflossen ist das Gold der Tage *–Trakl*
Vergangen ist der lange Tag *–W. Hertz*
Vergangen ist der lichte Tag *–Eichendorff*
Vergangen ist mir Glück und Heil *–Volkslied, Anon.*
Vergangenheit in Luft gewebter Schleier *–Anonymous*
Vergeht mir der Himmel vor Staube *–Eichendorff*
Vergessene Lieder, vergessene Lieb' *–Heindl*
Vergiftet sind meine Lieder *–Heine*
Vergiss mein nicht! so lispelt Dir *–"Selmar"*
Vergißmeinnicht hab' ich im Fichtenwald *–Schaukal*
Verglommen ist das Abendrot *–Geibel*
Verhaßt ist mir das Folgen *–Nietzsche*
Verlangend dehntest du dich *–Tora zu Eulenburg*
Verlass dich singend *–C. Hauptmann*
Verlassen hab' ich mein Lieb *–F. Engel*
Vernimm es, Nacht, was Ida dir vertrauet *–Kosegarten*
Verrathen! Verschmähet! *–Gubitz*
Verriet mein blasses Angesicht *–Heine*
Versank die Sonne still im Meere *–J. Sturm*
Verschling' der Abgrund meines Liebsten Hütte *–Heyse*
Verschneit liegt rings die ganze Welt *–Eichendorff*
Verschwunden ist meinem Blick *–Herder*
Verschwunden sind die Schmerzen *–Anonymous*
Verstohlen geht der Mond auf *–Volkslied*
Verstummt ist die Harfe *–Paalzow*
Verstummt sind die Pauken, Posaunen und Zinken *–Heine*
Verteilet Euch nach allen Regionen *–Goethe*
Vertraue dich dem Licht der Sterne *–Hammer*

Vertraue mir, Yoduno! o sage was dir ist –*Haug*
Verwelkte Blätter, entseelte Götter –*Fleischer*
Verwelkte Blume, Menschenkind –*Rückert*
Verzicht, o Herz, auf Rettung –*Daumer*
Vesperzeit, Betgeläut' aus den Dörfern –*Mörike*
Victoria! Victoria! der kleine weisse Zahn –*M. Claudius*
Viel bin ich umhergewandert –*Hafis*
Viel Glück zur Reise, Schwalben! –*Kulmann*
Viel schöne Blumen stehen –*Lehmann*
Viel Thränen flossen in herbem Weh –*Czermak*
Viel Vögel sind geflogen –*Hamerling*
Viele der Blümlein zusammengeknüpfet –*Goethe*
Viele Gäste wünsch ich heut' –*Goethe*
Viele Glokken hör' ich läuten –*Ritter*
Vielfach sind zum Hades die Pfade –*Mörike*
Vier adlige Rosse voran unserm Wagen –*Liliencron*
Vier Elemente, innig gesellt –*Schiller*
Vier Grüße send' ich zu dir auf die Reise –*Heyse*
Vierfach Kleeblatt! Selt'ner Fund! –*Mörike*
Vögel, tut euch nicht verweilen –*Wunderhorn*
Vögelein durchrauscht die Luft –*Daumer*
Vöglein du in meinem Zelt –*Volkslied*
Vöglein einsam in dem Bauer –*Schenkendorf*
Vöglein fliegt dem Nestchen zu –*Cornelius*
Vöglein hüpfet in dem Haine –*F. Förster*
Vöglein, ihr schlauen –*Schwerin-Schwerinburg*
Vöglein im Tannenwald pfeifet so hell –*Volkslied*
Vöglein in den sonn'gen Tagen –*Eichendorff*
Vöglein ohne Ruh und Rast –*Vogl*
Vöglein, Vöglein hüte dich! –*Dieffenbach*
Vöglein vom Zweig gaukelt hernieder –*Hebbel*
Vöglein, wohin so schnell? –*Geibel*
Voll banger Sorge hab ich –*Giesebrecht*
Voll Blüten steht der Pfirsichbaum –*Hesse*
Voll Farben glüht der Garten –*Matt*
Voll glühender Liebeswonne –*Preller*
Voll jener Süße, die, nicht auszudrükken –*Petrarca*
Voll Locken kraus ein Haupt so rund –*Goethe*
Voller, dichter tropft ums Dach da –*Kopisch*
Vom Baum des Lebens fällt mir –*Hesse*
Vom Berg der Knab, der zieht hinab –*Hebbel*
Vom Berg hinabgestiegen –*R. Reinick*
Vom Berge was kommt dort –*Mörike*
Vom Dorfe ab am Raine –*Groth*
Vom Dünnkuchen zum Morgenbrot –*Anacreon*
Vom fernen Klang der Uhren abgemessen –*Brockhaus*
Vom Gebirge Well auf Well –*Daumer*
Vom Himmel ist der Frühlingsregen –*C. Müller*
Vom Himmel zogen rauschend –*Frankl*
Vom Lager stand ich mit dem Frühlicht auf –*Keller*
Vom Meere trennt sich die Welle –*H. Collin*
Vom Taue glänzt der Rasen –*Hölderlin*
Vom Wassergrunde helle grüßt –*Marx*
Vom Wind getroffen –*Bethge*
Von allen Bergen nieder –*Eichendorff*
Von allen den Mädchen –*Volkslied*
Von allen schönen Kindern –*Volkslied*
Von allen schönen Waaren –*Goethe*
Von allen Zweigen schwingen –*Anonymous*
Von deinem Bilde nur umschwebet –*Dr. Mayer*
Von dem Berg, wo zuletzt –*Byron*
Von dem Dome schwer und bang –*Schiller*
Von dem Gartenaltan keucht –*Mickiewicz*
Von dem Rosenbusch, o Mutter –*Geibel*
Von den Bergen zu den Hügeln –*Goethe*
Von der Alpe tönt das Horn –*Proch*
Von der Last des Gedankens –*Altenberg*
Von der Straße her ein Posthorn klingt –*Wilhelm Müller*
Von der Tafel rinnt der Wein –*Hesse*
Von der Wartburg Zinnen nieder –*Cornelius*
Von der zarten Kinder Händen –*Brumm*
Von des Hügels kahlem Rücken –*A. Schreiber*
Von dir getrennet, liege ich begraben –*Uhland*
Von dir schein' ich aufgewacht –*Morgenstern*
Von dunklem Schleier umsponnen –*Schack*
Von edler Art, auch rein und zart –*Volkslied*
Von fern die Uhren schlagen –*Eichendorff*
Von Ferne tönt der Glokkenschlag –*Nietzsche*
Von Händlern wird die Kunst bedroht –*Kerr*
Von mehr als einer Seite verwaist –*Goethe*
Von meines Hauses engen Wänden –*Giesebrecht*
Von Melodien, die mich umflieh'n –*Wertheimer*
Von Nacht übergraut, von Frühe betaut –*Huchel*
Von Porphyr rot –*Bienestein*
Von schön Sicilien war mein Traum –*Marzials*
Von stillem Ort, von kühler Statt –*Cornelius*
Von Taue glänzt der Rasen –*Hölderlin*
Von Wald umgeben ein Blütenbaum –*"Martin Greif"*
Von waldbekränzter Höhe –*Daumer*
Von wem ich's habe, das sag' ich euch nicht –*Goethe*
Von Wolken streifenhaft befangen –*Goethe*
Von zwei Rosen duftet eine anders –*Morgenstern*
Vor allen Leinster Schönen pries –*Haug*
Vor dem Schloss in den Bäumen –*Eichendorff*

Vor dem Schlosse Don Loranca's –*Vogl*
Vor den Mauern von Schiras –*Hafis*
Vor der Tür, im Sonnenscheine –*Busse*
Vor einem grünen Walde –*"Martin Greif"*
Vor Gottes Aug', dem Abendroth –*Hozze*
Vor Kälte ist die Luft erstarrt –*Lenau*
Vor lauter hochadligen Zeugen –*Mörike*
Vor mein Bett wirft der Mond –*Li-Tai-Pe*
Vor meinem Fenster klingt ein deutsches Lied –*Drescher*
Vor meinem Fenster regt die alte Linde –*Osterwald*
Vor meinem Fenster schläft die Nacht –*Boelitz*
Vor meinem Fenster singt ein Vogel –*Holz*
Vor Pavia hat Herr Paliss –*Spiegel*
Vor seinem Heergefolge –*Uhland*
Vor seinem Löwengarten, das Kampfspiel –*Schiller*
VVor seiner Hütte ruhig im Schatten sitzt –*Hölderlin*
Vor Tage weckte mich mein klopfend Herz –*Heyse*
Vor Thebens siebenfach gähnenden Toren –*Körner*
Vorbei, vorbei die dunkle Nacht –*Dieffenbach*
Vorbei, vorbei durch Feld und Wald –*Boddien*
Vorfrühling seufzt in weiter Nacht –*Morgenstern*
Vorüber, ach vorüber –*M. Claudius*
Vorüber der Mai, die selige Zeit –*M. Jäger*
Vorüber die Flut. Noch braust es fern –*Rilke*
Vorüber die stöhnende Klage! –*Schiller*
Vorüber ist der blut'ge Strauß –*Eichendorff*
Vorüber ist der Kampf, vorbei die Trauer –*Ingrisch*
Vorüber, vorüber die stöhnende Klage! –*Schiller*
Vorwärts und nicht vergessen –*Brecht*

Wach' auf, du gold'nes Morgenroth –*F. Förster*
Wach' auf, du schöne Träumerin –*Rodenberg*
Wach' auf, erwache wieder –*Lorenzi*
Wach' auf Geliebte, der Morgen schimmert –*Jean Paul*
Wach auf, mein Herzensschöne –*Volkslied*
Wach auf, mein Hort, vernimm mein Wort –*Volkslied*
Wach auf, mein Kind, steh auf geschwind –*Volkslied*
Wach auf, meins Herzens Schöne –*Volkslied*
Wach auf, wach auf, du junger Gesell –*Volkslied*
Wachst du noch, Liebchen, Gruss und Kuss! –*Burns*
Wälze dich hinweg, du wildes Feuer! –*Jacobi*
Wär' auch mein Lager jener Moor –*Burns*
Wär' ich der gold'ne Sonnenschein –*Rückert*
Wär' ich der Regen –*Mosen*
Wär' ich ein Kind, ein Knäblein klein –*Droste-Hülshoff*
Wär' ich ein muntres Vögelein –*F. A. Kleinschmidt*
Wär ich ein Vögelein, flög' ich –*Cäcilie von W.*
Wär' ich nie aus euch gegangen –*Kerner*
Wär' ich wirklich so falsch –*Byron*
Wären wir zwei kleine, kleine Vögel –*Greiner*
Wär's dunkel, ich läg' im Walde –*Eichendorff*
Wärst du bei mir im Lebensthal –*Scott*
Wärst du nicht, heil'ger Abendschein! –*Kerner*
Wagen musst du und flüchtig erbeuten –*Eichendorff*
Wahre, wahre deinen Sohn, Nachbarin –*Daumer*
Wald du, fieberdurchglutet –*W. Hartlieb*
Wald vor uns, Wies' vor uns –*Bittner*
Waldeinsamkeit! Du grünes Revier –*Eichendorff*
Waldesnacht, du wunderkühle –*Heyse*
Waldesnacht, Waldesnacht –*Vogl*
Waldmeisterlein, Waldmeisterlein! –*Anonymous*
Waldvögelein, wohin ziehst du? –*Leuthold*
Walle, Regen, walle nieder –*Groth*
Waldeinsamkeit, du grünes Revier –*Eichendorff*
Wandelst du auch fern von mir –*Reinwald*
Wandern fremd und unbekannt in der Stadt –*Zwehl*
Wandern lieb' ich für mein Leben –*Eichendorff*
Wandervöglein, leichtes Blut –*Kletke*
Wandl' ich in dem Morgenthau –*Keller*
Wandl' ich in dem Wald des Abends –*Heine*
Wandl' ich sinnend über den lauten Marktplatz –*Hamerling*
Wann der silberne Mond –*L. Hölty*
Wann die goldne Frühe, neu geboren –*G. A. Bürger*
Wann die Kinder schlafen ein –*Anonymous*
Wann die Rosen aufgeblüht –*Rückert*
Wann erscheint der Morgen –*Geibel*
Wann ich schon schwarz bin –*Unidentified*
Wann im letzten Abendstrahl –*Uhland*
Wann in des Abends letztem Scheine –*Matthisson*
Wann meine Grillen schwirren –*K. Lappe*
Wann, o Schicksal, wann wird endlich –*Salis-Seewis*
Wann, wann, erscheint der Morgen –*Geibel*
War das die Liebe –*Morgenstern*
War das nicht ein Blick der Liebe –*Volkslied*
War der schönste Sommermorgen –*Liliencron*
War ein Blümlein wunderfein –*Pfau*
War ein heimathloser Wand'rer –*Keller*
War einst ein hübsch Mädchen –*Melzer & Hanser*
War es also gemeint –*Wilhelm Müller*
War es dir, dem diese Lippen bebten –*Tieck*
War ich gar so jung und dumm –*Ritter*
War schöner als der schönste Tag –*Goethe*
Warm die Lüfte, es sprießt Gras –*Mombert*
Warrrrrrte nur... –*Morgenstern*

Wart', Vöglein, wart'! *–Hoffmann von Fallersleben*
Warte, warte, wilder Schiffsmann *–Heine*
Warum bin ich noch so klein? *–Overbeck*
Warum bist du aufgewacht *–Pfau*
Warum bist du nicht hier *–Kosegarten*
Warum dein Blick so trübe *–Niemeyer*
Warum denn warten von Tag zu Tag? *–Groth*
Warum doch erschallen himmelwärts die Lieder! *–Goethe*
Warum, Geliebte, denk' ich dein *–Mörike*
Warum, geliebtes Veilchen *–C. Weisse*
Warum huldigest du, heiliger Sokrates *–Hölderlin*
Warum ich bleibe, warum ich traurig bin? *–S. Schütze*
Warum kommst du zu mir in der Nacht *–Zwehl*
Warum leckst du dein Mäulchen *–Goethe*
Warum öffnest du wieder *–Macpherson*
Warum sind deine Augen denn so naß? *–Rückert*
Warum sind denn die Rosen so blaß *–Heine*
Warum sind der Tränen unterm Mond *–Overbeck*
Warum so bleich und blaß *–Wildenbruch*
Warum so spät erst, Georgine? *–Hermann Gilm*
Warum soll ich denn wandern *–Christern*
Warum verbirgst du vor mir dein Antlitz *–Cornelius*
Warum versankst du mir so ganz? *–Morgenstern*
Warum willst du and're fragen *–Rückert*
Warum ziehst du mich unwiderstehlich *–Goethe*
Was bedeutet die Bewegung? *–Willemer*
Was bin ich in's Kloster gegangen *–Stinde*
Was blickst du träumend ins verwölkte Land *–Hesse*
Was bricht hervor, wie Blüthen weiss *–F. Gerstenberg*
Was denkst du jetzt? *–Morgenstern*
Was dich ergreift *–A. Schreiber*
Was die Großen Gutes taten *–Goethe*
Was die gute Natur weislich *–Goethe*
Was doch heut Nacht ein Sturm gewesen *–Mörike*
Was drückt, O Holde, dich für Last? *–Justi*
Was du forderst, es gescheh'! *–Hafis*
Was Du mir bist? Der Ausblick *–Straaten*
Was erhoffst du dir, Mädchen, noch?!? *–Altenberg*
Was fällt ihm ein, dem edlen Herrn *–K. Henckell*
Was faßt dich an, o Tochter mein *–Molbech*
Was frag' ich viel nach Geld und Gut *–Miller*
Was freut einen alten Soldaten? *–Lemcke*
Was für ein Lied soll dir gesungen werden *–Heyse*
Was funkelt ihr so mild mich an? *–Fellinger*
Was gehst du, armer bleicher Kopf *–Morgenstern*
Was git's denn do? Was g'seh=n i do? *–Frey*
Was glänzt dort vom Walde *–Körner*
Was gleichet der Lust *–Anonymous*
Was hab' ich denn meinem Feinsliebchen *–Volkslied*
Was haben doch die Gänse getan *–Olorinus*
Was hast du mir gestanden *–Behn*
Was hat des Schlummers Band zerrissen *–I. Kurz*
Was hör' ich draußen vor dem Tor? *–Goethe*
Was huschelt im Garten *–Spitteler*
Was ich dort gelebt, genossen *–Goethe*
Was ich mir still gelobte *–Eisenmayer*
Was ich wollte, liegt zerschlagen *–Eichendorff*
Was im Netze? Schau einmal! *–Mörike*
Was immer mir die Feindschaft *–Leuthold*
Was in der Schenke waren heute *–Goethe*
Was ist der Mensch? halb Thier *–Schiller*
Was ist der Wuchs der Pinie *–F. Bodenstedt*
Was ist des Sängers Vaterland? *–Körner*
Was ist des Vögleins Dach *–Leo*
Was ist die Welt? Ein ewiges Gedicht *–Hofmannsthal*
Was ist es, das die Seele füllt? *–Kosegarten*
Was ist es das im Mutterschoose *–Mahlmann*
Was ist in deiner Seele *–Huch*
Was ist mein Stand, mein Glück *–Gellert*
Was ist mir denn geschehen? *–Stieler*
Was ist mir denn so wehe? *Eichendorff*
Was ist nun doch in mir erwacht! *–Redwitz*
Was ist Sylvia, saget an *–Shakespeare*
Was ist's, das der Gedanken *–Spitteler*
Was ist's, das mir den Athem hemmet *–Robert*
Was Was ist's, o Vater, was ich verbrach? *–Chamisso*
Was kannst du, Süße, wider dies *–Morgenstern*
Was klinget und singet die Straß' herauf? *–Uhland*
Was klopft ans Thor? Über die rothe Heide *–"Alexis"*
Was kriegt er, der den Hirsch erlegt? *–Shakespeare*
Was lachst du so? Mich schmerzt der gelle Ton *–Hesse*
Was machst du mir vor Liebchens Tür *–Goethe*
Was mein Gott will *–Markgraf Albrecht*
Was meine Mutter mir sagte *–Brecht*
Was meinst du, Kunz *–M. Claudius*
Was mich zu Dir so mächtig zog *–Bern*
Was mir einst Lust gewährte *–Vincke*
Was mir wohl übrig bliebe *–Hoffmann von Fallersleben*
Was nennst du deine Liebe schwer und gross *–Kühne*
Was nützt die mir noch zugemessne Zeit? *–Vincke*
Was nur dadrinnen der Graukopf macht? *–J. Sturm*

Was pocht mein Herz so sehr? –*Burns*
Was quälte dir dein banges Herz? –*Mosen*
Was reif in diesen Zeilen steht –*C. Brentano*
Was rüttelt die Säulen? –*Anonymous*
Was säuselt hier wie banger Seufzer Stöhnen –*Anonymous*
Was schauest du so hell und klar –*L. Hölty*
Was schaust du mich so freundlich an –*Schenkendorf*
Was schimmert dort auf dem Berge –*Breidenstein*
Was schläfst und träumst du –*Hölderlin*
Was sich in Zeiten je begeben –*Calé*
Was sie damals empfanden –*Rilke*
Was singt ihr und sagt ihr mir –*Rückert*
Was soll der Zorn, mein Schatz –*Heyse*
Was sorgest du? Sei stille, meine Seele! –*Uz*
Was spinnst du? fragte Nachbars Fritz –*Anonymous*
Was stehst du lange und sinnest nach? –*Anonymous*
Was stehst du so in stillem Schmerz –*Uhland*
Was steht ihr am Wege so müssig –*A.v.N*
Was stürmet die Haide herauf? –*Reinbeck*
Was sucht denn der Jäger –*Wilhelm Müller*
Was that dir, Thor, dein Vaterland? –*Klopstock*
Was tragen wir unsere Leiden –*Braungart*
Was trauern doch die Mägdelein? –*Anonymous*
Was treibst du, Wind, du himmlisches Kind? –*C. F. Meyer*
Was treibt den Waidmann in den Wald –*Vogel*
Was treibt mich hier von hinnen? –*Hebbel*
Was treibt mich hin zu dir mit Macht? –*E. Koch*
Was trinket ihr? Schenkt lustig ein –*J.-B. Rousseau*
Was tut ein Baum den Ganzen Tag? –*Ingrisch*
Was unterm Monde gleicht uns Elfen –*Matthisson*
Was vermeid' ich denn die Wege –*Wilhelm Müller*
Was wecken aus dem Schlummer mich –*Uhland*
Was weht um meine Schläfe –*"Friedrich Halm"*
Was weilst du einsam an dem Himmel –*J. Mayrhofer*
Was weinst du, Blümlein, im Morgenschein? –*Rollet*
Was weinst du, meine Geige? –*Heindl*
Was will die einsame Träne? –*Heine*
Was will dies Klopfen sagen –*C. F. D. Schubart*
Was will in deinen Augen mir –*Dehmel*
Was willst auf dieser Station? –*Eichendorff*
Was zieht mir das Herz so? –*Goethe*
Was zieht zu deinem Zauberkreise –*Müchler*
Wasch dich, mein Schwesterchen –*Mörike*
Wasser holen geht die reine –*Goethe*
Weckst du mich zum neuen Jammer –*Hermes*
Weh, daß ich mußte schauen –*Cornelius*
Weh im Herzen, tiefe Schwerzen –*Boysen*
Weh mir nun sachte, du seufzender Wind –*Guido Gezelle*
Weh, wie zornig ist das Mädchen –*Geibel*
Wehe dem Fliehenden, Welt hinaus Ziehenden! –*Rellstab*
Wehe der, die mir verstrickte –*Heyse*
Wehe, Lüftchen, lind und lieblich –*Hafis*
Wehe mir, mein Rosenkränzlein, weh –*Hafis*
Wehe, so willst du mich wieder –*Platen*
Wehmuth, die mich hüllt –*Kosegarten*
Wehmuth weckt der fernen Wolkenwand'rer Gruss –*J. C. Kugler*
Weh'n im Garten die Arome –*Hafis*
Wehre nicht, o Lieb, wühlen –*Hafis*
Weht, o wehet, liebe Morgenwinde! –*Mörike*
Weich küßt die Zweige der weiße Mond –*Verlaine*
Weiche Flötentöne, tiefverträumtes Girren –*Evers*
Weiche Gräser im Revier –*Daumer*
Weiche nicht, o süsser Traum! –*Preller*
Weichet, Sorgen, von mir! doch ach! –*Goethe*
Weil' auf mir, du dunkles Auge –*Lenau*
Weil es also Gott gefügt –*Lehr*
Weil ich dich nicht legen kann –*Rückert*
Weil ich sterblich bin geboren –*Anacreon*
Weil jetzo alles stille ist –*Eichendorff*
Weil noch, Sonnenstrahl, leuchte –*Tennyson*
Weil nun die Nacht kommt –*Borchert*
Weile Kind, ich will nicht rauben! –*Gubitz*
Weimars Toten will ich's bringen –*Schober*
Wein' aus deine Freude! –*J. C. K.*
Weine du nicht, o, die ich innig liebe –*Klopstock*
Weine nicht, daß ich jetzt gehe –*Lothar*
Weine nicht; es ist der Sieg erkämpfet –*Rüling*
Weine nicht, weil dich die Götter gesendet –*"Carmen Sylva"*
Weine, weine, weine nur nicht –*Volkslied, Wunderhorn*
Weinet, sanfte Mädchen...! –*Altenberg*
Weinschröter, schlag die Trommel –*Wunderhorn*
Weint auch einst kein Liebchen –*Kerner*
Weint, Mädchen, hier bei Amors Grabe! –*Goethe*
Weint nicht, ihr Äuglein! –*Heyse*
Weise nicht von dir mein schlichtes Herz –*Keller*
Weiß Chloe mein geheim Verlangen? –*Uz*
Weiss nicht, woher ich bin gekommen –*Kerner*
Weiß wie Lilien, reine Kerzen –*Goethe*
Weisse Lilie, meine Lilie –*Anonymous*
Weiße Tauben fliegen durch blaue Morgenluft –*Morgenstern*

Weisst Du die Rose, die Du mir gegeben? –*Stieler*
Weißt Du mein kleines Mägdelein –*Leon*
Weißt du noch, mein süßes Herz –*Hafis*
Weisst du noch, weisst du noch? –*Roquette*
Weißt Du noch, wie das war? –*Bittner*
Weisst du noch, wie ich am Fels –*Roquette*
Weisst du warum der Tod im Menschenland –*C. Hauptmann*
Weit aus allen dunklen Talen –*Hesse*
Weit aus den Wäldern drängen die Tiere –*Bollmann*
Weit draussen, einsam im ödem Raum –*Avenarius*
Weit in nebelgrauer Ferne –*Schiller*
Weit über das Feld durch die Lüfte –*F. Bodenstedt*
Weit und breit schaut Niemand mich an –*Conrat*
Weit von meinem Vaterlande –*M. Claudius*
Weit, weit sind die Sterne –*Unidentified*
Weite Wiesen im Dämmergrau –*Bierbaum*
Weithin durch der Nächte Stille –*Unidentified*
Wekke den Amor nicht auf –*Goethe*
Welch ein wunderbares Leben –*Reissig*
Welch Leuchten auf den Wogen –*Gerstenberg*
Welch neues frohes Leben erwacht –*Vogl*
Welche chaotische Haushälterei –*Rückert*
Welche tiefbewegten Lebensläufchen –*Keller*
Welchen Weg bist du gegangen –*Werfel*
Wellen blinkten durch die Nacht –*R. Reinick*
Wellen säuseln, Winde locken –*Prechtler*
Welt der gestalten lang lebewohl! –*George*
Welt ist stille eingeschlafen –*Kobald*
Wem Gott will rechte Gunst erweisen –*Eichendorff*
Wem säng' ich Lieder, wenn nicht Dir? –*Bittner*
Wem so die Nacht die treugewölbten Hände –*Morgenstern*
Wende dich, du kleiner Stern –*Keller*
Wenige wissen das Geheimnis der Liebe –*Novalis*
Wenn alle Blumen träumen –*Muth*
Wenn alle Brünnlein fliessen –*Volkslied*
Wenn alle Nachbarn schlafen gangen –*Hesse*
Wenn alle untreu werden –*Novalis*
Wenn alle Wälder schliefen –*Eichendorff*
Wenn alle Welt so einig wär' –*Volkslied*
Wenn alles eben käme –*La Motte Fouqué*
Wenn am feuchten Maienmorgen –*"Martin Greif"*
Wenn am kleinen Kammerfenster –*Zinserling*
Wenn auf dem höchsten Fels ich steh' –*Chézy, Wilhelm Müller*
Wenn auf Gefilden neues Entzükken keimt –*Hölderlin*
Wenn auf zu den Wolken ich schaue –*Unidentified*
Wenn Aurora früh mich grüsst –*Stolberg-Stolberg*
Wenn aus deinen sanften Blikken –*C. F. D. Schubart*
Wenn aus dem Leben kann –*Hölderlin*
Wenn aus der Ferne, da wir geschieden sind –*Hölderlin*
Wenn, Brüder, wie wir täglich sehen –*Baggesen*
Wenn dein Finger durch die Saiten –*Schiller*
Wenn dein ich denk', dann sinn' ich oft –*Dyherrn*
Wenn dein Mütterlein trit –*Rückert*
Wenn der Bann gebrochen –*Zwehl*
Wenn der Blüten Frühlingsregen –*Goethe*
Wenn der Duft quillt aus der Knospe Schoos –*Liber*
Wenn der Frühling auf die Berge steigt –*F. Bodenstedt*
Wenn der Hahn kräht auf dem Dache –*Eichendorff*
Wenn der holde Frühling lenzt –*Kempner*
Wenn der Regen durch die Gosse tropft –*Dehmel*
Wenn der Schimmer von dem Monde –*Klopstock*
Wenn der Schnee von der Alma wega geht –*Volkslied*
Wenn der silberne Mond –*L. Hölty*
Wenn der Sturm die Blätter jaget –*Schulenburg*
Wenn der uralte heilige Vater –*Goethe*
Wenn der Wein nicht wär –*Sergel*
Wenn dereinst, wo sie versinken –*Hafis*
Wenn des Abends Rosenflügel –*C. F. D. Schubart*
Wenn des Frühlings Wachen ziehen –*A. v. Arnim*
Wenn des Mondes bleiches Licht –*Günther*
Wenn dich die tiefe Sehnsucht rührt –*Boelitz*
Wenn die Abendschatten steigen –*Morgenstern*
Wenn die Buben recht böse sind –*Braungart*
Wenn die Erde leise aufgewacht –*J. Arndt*
Wenn die Felder sich verdunkeln –*Dehmel*
Wenn die Fluthen blau –*J.-B. Rousseau*
Wenn die Hahnen frühe krähen –*Heyse*
Wenn die Klänge nahn und fliehen –*Eichendorff*
Wenn die kleinen Kinder beten –*Rafael*
Wenn die Lieb' aus deinen blauen –*Jacobi*
Wenn die Linde blüh –*Busse*
Wenn die Maien grün sich kleiden –*Kind*
Wenn die Mittagsfrau durch das Kornfeld –*Spitteler*
Wenn die Nacht sich über die Welt –*Hohenberg*
Wenn die Reben wieder blühen –*Goethe*
Wenn die Rosen blühen, Hoffe –*Wetzel*
Wenn die Rosen ewig blühten –*Hebbel*
Wenn die Schwalben heimwärts ziehn –*Herloßsohn*
Wenn die Sommerzeiten enden –*Leen*
Wenn die Sonne lieblich schiene –*Eichendorff*
Wenn die Sonne nieder sinket –*Goeble*

Wenn die Sonne sinkend hinterm Berg *–A. Becker*
Wenn die Vöglein sich gepaart *–Rückert*
Wenn die Wogen unten toben *–Eichendorff*
Wenn dirs in Kopf und Herzen schwirrt *–Goethe*
Wenn drüben die Glocken klingen *–"Max Waldau"*
Wenn du am Abend müde bist *–B. Huber*
Wenn du bei mei'm Schätzel kommst *–Volkslied*
Wenn du dich im Spiegel besiehst *–Goethe*
Wenn du die kleine Hand mir gibst *–Hesse*
Wenn du es wüßtest, was träumen heißt *–Hart*
Wenn du lächelst, wenn du blickst *–Hafis*
Wenn Du, mein Liebster *–Heyse*
Wenn du mich einstmals verlassen wirst *–Wildenbruch*
Wenn du mich lustig machst *–Brecht*
Wenn du mich mit den Augen *–Heyse*
Wenn du noch schläfst, erwach' mein Lieb' *–Marx*
Wenn du nur zuweilen lächelst *–Daumer*
Wenn du schläfst, ich segne dich *–Straaten*
Wenn du schon glaubst *–Haringer*
Wenn du von allem dem *–Lessing*
Wenn du wärst mein eigen *–Kosegarten*
Wenn du zu den Blumen gehst *–Heyse*
Wenn du zu mei'm Schätzel kommst *–Wunderhorn*
Wenn durch Berg' und Thale draussen *–Kerner*
Wenn durch die Piazetta *–Moore*
Wenn ein Gott dir gab fürs Schöne *–Leuthold*
Wenn ein müder Leib begraben *–Groth*
Wenn einem Mädgen das uns liebt *–Goethe*
Wenn einer mäßig trinket *–Hafis*
Wenn einst ich tot bin *–Klopstock*
Wenn einst mein Lebenstag *–F. A. Krummacher*
Wenn Eos am Morgen mit rosigem Finger *–Anonymous*
Wenn es Abend wird und still, *–Unidentified*
Wenn es stürmt auf den Wogen *–C. Brentano*
Wenn etwas leise in dir spricht *–Lingg*
Wenn Fortuna spröde tut *–Eichendorff*
Wenn fremde Blikke wachsam *–A. W. Schlegel*
Wenn fromme Kindlein schlafen geh'n *–Anonymous*
Wenn Gott auch mir vergönnte *–Beck*
Wenn Gott es hätt' gewollt *–Itzerott*
Wenn hell die liebe Sonne lacht *–Schellenberg*
Wenn hier nun kahler Boden wär *–M. Claudius*
Wenn i halt frua afsteh *–Volkslied*
Wenn i zum Brünnle geh *–Volkslied*
Wenn ich Abschied nehme *–Weitbrecht*
Wenn ich an den letzten Abend denk' *–Volkslied*
Wenn ich auf dem Lager liege *–Heine*
Wenn ich, Augenlust zu finden *–Lessing*
Wenn ich dein gedenke *–Goethe*
Wenn ich den ganzen Tag *–Wunderhorn*
Wenn ich der Kaiser wäre *–Anonymous*
Wenn ich dich frage, dem das Leben blüht *–K. Henckell*
Wenn ich dich recht schön bäte *–Reinecke*
Wenn ich dich seh', so lieb und hold *–F. Bodenstedt*
Wenn ich die Blümlein schau' *–Castelli*
Wenn ich durch Busch und Zweig *–J. Seidl*
Wenn ich durch Wald und Fluren geh' *–M. Collin*
Wenn ich ein Vöglein wär *–Dieffenbach*
Wenn ich ein Vöglein wär *–Volkslied, Treitschke*
Wenn ich einst das Ziel errungen habe *–Matthisson*
Wenn ich einst von jenem Schlummer *–Klopstock*
Wenn ich erführe, daß das Alter *–Bethge*
Wenn ich früh in den Garten geh' *–Rückert*
Wenn ich gestorben bin, leg mich *–A. v. Arnim*
Wenn ich gestorben, Liebchen *–Rossetti*
Wenn ich heut nicht deinen leib berühre *–George*
Wenn ich ihn nur habe, lass' ich alles gern *–Novalis*
Wenn ich ihn nur habe, wenn er mein nur ist *–Novalis*
Wenn ich im stillen Friedhof geh' *–Pfau*
Wenn ich in deine Augen seh', *–Heine*
Wenn ich, liebe Lili, dich nicht liebte *–Goethe*
Wenn ich 'mal ungeduldig werde *–Goethe*
Wenn ich mit Menschen- und mit Engelszungen redete *–the Bible*
Wenn ich müde bin einmal, führe *–Friedrich*
Wenn ich nur ein Vöglein wäre *–F. Schlegel*
Wenn ich, o Kindlein, vor dir stehe *–Hebbel*
Wenn ich, o Schöpfer, deine Macht *–Gellert*
Wenn ich von deinem Anschaun *–Mörike*
Wenn ich wüsste, du würdest mein eigen *–Gregorovius*
Wenn ihr Freunde vergeßt *–Hölderlin*
Wenn im braunen Hafen *–Bierbaum*
Wenn im Hauch der Abend kühle *–Lühe*
Wenn im Lenze ringsum Alles lacht *–Anonymous*
Wenn im letzten Dämmrungsstrahle *–Deuern*
Wenn im Spiele leiser Töne *–Stoll*
Wenn im Unendlichen dasselbe *–Goethe*
Wenn immer trüber deine Morgen tagen *–Niemeyer*
Wenn in bangen, trüben Stunden *–Novalis*
Wenn in des Abends letztem Scheine *–Matthisson*
Wenn ins Land die Wetter hängen *–Eichendorff*
Wenn jemand eine Reise thut *–M. Claudius*
Wenn kein Windchen weht *–Leo*

Wenn Kindlein süssen Schlummers Ruh' *–Nostitz-Jänkendorf*
Wenn kühl der Morgen atmet *–Voss*
Wenn Kummer hätte zu töten *–Rückert*
Wenn lichter Mondenschein *–d'Annunzio*
Wenn man beim Wein sitzt *–Kopisch*
Wenn mein Herz beginnt zu klingen *–Frey*
Wenn mein Kindlein in der Wiegen *–Rafael*
Wenn mein Schatz Hochzeit macht *–Mahler*
Wenn mein Stündlein fürhanden ist *–N. Herman*
Wenn meine Blicke hangen *–"Dilia Helena"*
Wenn meine Mutter hexen könnt' *–Mörike*
Wenn mich einsam Lüfte fächeln *–F. Schlegel*
Wenn Nachts im Wald die Turteltaube klagt *–Anonymous*
Wenn, o Mädchen, wenn dein Blut *–G. A. Bürger*
Wenn sanft du mir im Arme schliefst *–Liliencron*
Wenn sanft entzückt mein Auge sieht *–Matthisson*
Wenn schlanke Lilien wandelten *–Keller*
Wenn Schmerz uns zieren kann *–Vincke*
Wenn sich auf dieses Blatt dein Auge senkt *–Geibel*
Wenn sich bei heiliger ruh *–George*
Wenn sich der Abend niedersenkt *–Bethge*
Wenn sich Liebes von dir lösen will *–Bartels*
Wenn sich zwei Herzen scheiden *–Geibel*
Wenn sie nachts lag und dachte *–Brecht*
Wenn sie reiten zur Schwemme *–Huchel*
Wenn so lind dein Auge mir *–Daumer*
Wenn so stolz im Licht der Sterne *–Binding*
Wenn über Berge sich der Nebel breitet *–J. Mayrhofer*
Wenn um den Hollunder *–F. Schumann*
Wenn Vöglein klagen *–Petrarca*
Wenn wir hinauszieh'n am Frühlingssonntag *–Cornelius*
Wenn Worte dir vom Rosenmunde wehen *–Lenau*
Wenn zu den Reihen der Nymphen *–Goethe*
Wenn zu der Regenwand Phöbus *–Goethe*
Wenn zum hellen Glokkenklang *–Koschnick*
Wenn zwei sich ineinander still versenken *–Hebbel*
Wenn zwei sich lieben von ganzem Herzen *–Mosenthal*
Wenn Zwei voneinander scheiden *–Heine*
Wenn's im Thal zu Abend läutet *–Stieler*
Wer auf den Wogen schliefe *–Eichendorff*
Wer bist du doch, o Mädchen? *–Droste-Hülshoff*
Wer bist du, Geist der Liebet *–Kosegarten*
Wer da lebt in Liebesqual *–Heyse*
Wer darf ihn nennen? und wer bekennen *–Goethe*
Wer den Weg nach innen fand *–Hesse*
Wer des Leidens Kelch *–Ungern-Sternberg*
Wer die Liebe gepflanzt *–Anonymous*
Wer die Musik sich erkiest *–Mörike*
Wer die steile Sternenbahn *–Schiller*
Wer droht unserm deutschen Vaterland? *–Anonymous*
Wer einmal tief und durstig *–Eichendorff*
Wer einsam steht im bunten Lebenskreise *–Helene von Orléans*
Wer fühlt's nicht tief im Herzen *–Stolterfoth*
Wer gab dir, Minne, die Gewalt *–Walther von der Vogelweide*
Wer geboren wird, muß sterben *–Michelangelo*
Wer hätte gedacht, daß die Rosen *–Boelitz*
Wer hätte sie gesehn und nicht auch sie geliebt *–Adil*
Wer hat bedacht, daß bis zu ihrem Kommen *–Rilke*
Wer hat das erste Lied erdacht *–Blüthgen*
Wer hat die schönsten Schäfchen? *–Hoffmann von Fallersleben*
Wer hat's doch durchschauet *–Cornelius*
Wer in der Sonne kämpft *–C. F. Meyer*
Wer in die Fremde will wandern *–Eichendorff*
Wer ist denn draußen und wer klopfet an *–Wunderhorn*
Wer ist der Jüngling, lieblich zu schauen? *–Mickiewicz*
Wer ist so spät noch fleissig wach? *–Tschabuschnigg*
Wer ist vor meiner Kammerthür? *–Burns*
Wer kann schlagen-außer der Liebe *–Morgenstern*
Wer Kastor ruft, muß Polydeukos nennen *–Jünger*
Wer klappert am Dache, mein Kindlein? *–Löwenstein*
Wer kommt? wer kauft von meiner Waar? *–Goethe*
Wer lässt hier so lieblich *–Tiedge*
Wer Lebenslust fühlet, der bleibt nicht allein *–Unger*
Wer lenkt nicht gern den heitern Blick *–Burns*
Wer lieben will, muss leiden *–Volkslied*
Wer mir jetzt noch die Hand reicht *–Busta*
Wer möchte noch einmnal durchlaufen *–Raupach*
Wer nicht liebt Weib, Wein und Gesang *–Luther*
Wer nicht, wenn warm von Hand *–Anonymous*
Wer nie sein Brot mit Tränen aß *–Goethe*
Wer ohne Leid, der ist auch ohne Liebe *–Keller*
Wer reitet so spät durch Nacht und Wind? *–Goethe*
Wer rief dich denn? wer hat dich herbestellt? *–Heyse*
Wer sehen will zween lebendige Brunnen *–Wunderhorn*
Wer sein holdes Lieb verloren *–Heyse*
Wer sich auf Ruhm begiebet *–Wunderhorn*
Wer sich der Einsamkeit ergibt *–Goethe*

Wer sich die Musik erkiest –*Luther*
Wer singet im Walde –*Hoffmann von Fallersleben*
Wer sprenget auf dem stolzen Ross –*Schenkendorf*
Wer stets hinter'n Ofen kroch –*Gubitz*
Wer that deinem Füsslein weh? –*Geibel*
Wer traurig sein will –*Viertel*
Wer unter eines Mädchens Hand –*Blumauer*
Wer wagt es, Rittersmann oder Knapp' –*Schiller*
Wer wagt's, wer wagt's, wer wagt's –*Bruchmann*
Wer weiss, woher das Brünnlein quillt –*Heyse*
Wer, wer ist ein freier Mann? –*Pfeffel*
Wer, wer kann gebieten den Vögeln –*Goethe*
Wer will denn alles gleich ergründen! –*Goethe*
Wer will unter die Soldaten –*Volkslied*
Wer wird von der Welt verlangen –*Goethe*
Werde heiter, mein Gemüthe –*Hoffmann von Fallersleben*
Werdet nur nicht ungeduldig –*Heine*
Wespe! Wespe! Wespelein! –*Unidentified*
Wess' Adern leichtes Blut –*Prandstetter*
Wetterleuchten fern im Dunkeln –*Eichendorff*
Wetterleuchten fiebert fern –*Hesse*
Wie aber soll ich dir erwiedern –*Hoffmann von Fallersleben*
Wie an dem Tag, der dich der Welt –*Goethe*
Wie anders, Gretchen, war dir's –*Goethe*
Wie bin ich seltsam tief –*Ungemach*
Wie bist du, meine Königin –*Hafis*
Wie bist du nur, mein Herzensschatz –*Oelschläger*
Wie bist du schön, du tiefer, blauer See! –*Leuthold*
Wie blitzen die Sterne –*Leitner*
Wie blüht es im Thale –*Hoffmann von Fallersleben*
Wie bräutlich glänzt das heilige Rom! –*F. Kugler*
Wie braust durch die Wipfel –*Craigher*
Wie das Gewürm aus unermeßnem Meer –*Meinhold*
Wie das Meer ist die Liebe –*Dehmel*
Wie dem Wanderer in Träumen –*Eichendorff*
Wie der Bäume kühne Wipfel –*Neun*
Wie der Mond sich leuchtend dränget –*Heine*
Wie der Quell so lieblich klinget –*Tieck*
Wie der Tag mir schleichet –*L. A. Gotter*
Wie des Abends schöne Röte –*Daumer*
Wie des Mondes Abbild zittert –*Heine*
Wie deutlich des Mondes Licht –*F. Schlegel*
Wie die Blümlein draussen zittern –*Volkslied*
Wie die jungen Blüthen –*Hoffmann von Fallersleben*
Wie die Nacht mit heil'gem Beben –*Körner*
Wie die Ros' in deinem Haare –*Lenau*
Wie die Wolke nach der Sonne –*Hoffmann von Fallersleben*
Wie dir geschah, so soll's auch mir geschehn –*Kerner*
Wie doch so still dir am Herzen –*Geibel*
Wie du deine Sonne hast lassen aufgehn –*Wilhelm IV*
Wie du mir oft, geliebtes Kind –*Goethe*
Wie du mit gift'gem Stachel fast –*Burns*
Wie ein blasser Tropfen Bluts –*Giraud*
Wie ein Goldadler reißt der Blitz –*Grabbe*
Wie ein Schwan still die Bahn –*"Dilia Helena"*
Wie ein Sturmwind kamst du! –*Unidentified*
Wie ein todeswunder Streiter –*Eichendorff*
Wie eine Lerch' in blauer Luft –*Boddien*
Wie eine trübe Wolke –*Wilhelm Müller*
Wie eine weiße Wolke –*Hesse*
Wie eine Windesharfe sei deine Seele –*G. Hauptmann*
Wie einst den Knaben lacht –*Leuthold*
Wie erhebt sich das Herz –*Klopstock*
Wie erkenn' ich dein Treulieb –*Shakespeare*
Wie erscholl der Gang des lauten Heers –*Kosegarten*
Wie Feld und Au so blinkend im Tau! –*Jacobi*
Wie ferne Tritte hörst du's schallen –*"Martin Greif"*
Wie floß von deiner Lippe milde Güte! –*Leuthold*
Wie flüchtig rinnt die Stunde –*Unidentified*
Wie fremd und wunderlich das ist –*Hesse*
Wie froh und frisch mein Sinn sich hebt –*Tieck*
Wie früh das enge Pförtchen knarre –*Giesebrecht*
Wie Frühlingsahnung weht es –*Grun*
Wie geheimes Lispeln rieselt's –*Evers*
Wie gerne Dir zu Füssen –*Strachwitz*
Wie ging ich durch mein Leben hin –*Bierbaum*
Wie glänzt der helle Mond –*Keller*
Wie glänzt nun die Welt im Abendstrahl –*Wilbrandt*
Wie glänzt so hell dein Auge –*Calatin*
Wie glücklich ist der Morgenwind! –*Hafis*
Wie glücklich, wem das Knabenkleid –*L. Hölty*
Wie gross ist des Allmächt'gen Güte! –*Gellert*
Wie haben sie dich, Baum, verschnitten –*Hesse*
Wie han i doch so gern die Zeit –*Volkslied*
Wie hast du dich in's Herz versenkt –*Czermak*
Wie hat der Sturm zerrissen –*Wilhelm Müller*
Wie heimlicher Weise ein Engelein leise –*Mörike*
Wie heißt König Ringangs Töchterlein? –*Mörike*
Wie herrlich leuchtet mir die Natur –*Goethe*
Wie herrlich wär's, zerschnittner Tannenbaum –*Keller*
Wie ich jüngst mit langem Kusse –*Unidentified*

Wie ich so ehrlich war –*Goethe*
Wie im Morgenglanze –*Goethe*
Wie ist der Abend stillet –*Wildenbruch*
Wie ist die Nacht voll holder Heimlichkeiten! –*Boelitz*
Wie ist doch die Erde so schön –*R. Reinick*
Wie ist es denn, daß trüb und schwer –*Tieck*
Wie ist mein zitterndes Herz entbrannt –*Madeleine*
Wie ist so heiss im Busen mir –*F. Kugler*
Wie kann ich froh und lustig sein? –*P. Kaufmann*
Wie kann ich froh und munter sein –*Burns*
Wie kann, sagten sie, versteckt –*Hugo*
Wie kannst du ruhig schlafen –*Heine*
Wie klag' ich's aus das Sterbegefühl –*Senn*
Wie klingt's so bänglich drüben? –*S. Schmid*
Wie komm ich denn zur Tür herein? –*Volkslied*
Wie kommts, daß du so traurig bist –*Goethe*
Wie kühl schweift sichs bei nächt'ger Stunde –*Goethe*
Wie lächeln die Augen der Liebe –*F. Bodenstedt*
Wie lange schon war immer mein Verlangen –*Heine, Volkslied*
Wie leis die Schwäne gleiten –*Gomoll*
Wie leise scheue Kinder –*Blaauw*
Wie Lenzeshauch hast Du mich –*Träger*
Wie lieb' ich euch ihr Nachtigallen –*Florian*
Wie lieblich und fröhlich, zu schweben –*F. Schlegel*
Wie lockt der Palmen grünes Dach –*Stieglitz*
Wie Melodie aus reiner Sphäre hör' ich –*Hafis*
Wie Melodien zieht es mir –*Groth*
Wie mir geschah, ich weiss es nicht –*F. Förster*
Wie, mit innigstem Behagen –*Willemer*
Wie mochte je mir wohler sein –*Heyse*
Wie nun alles stirbt und endet –*Keller*
Wie oft schon ward es Frühling –*Hoffmann von Fallersleben*
Wie pocht' das Herz mir in der Brust –*C. F. Meyer*
Wie pocht mir vor Lust das Herz –*Gruppe*
Wie poltert es! - Abscheuliches Geroll –*Keller*
Wie rafft ich mich auf in der Nacht –*Platen*
Wie rein Gesang sich windet –*F. Schlegel*
Wie reiten denn die Herren? –*Volkslied*
Wie reizend bist du Montag morgens immer –*Heyse*
Wie sanft, wie ruhig fühl ich hier –*C. Weisse*
Wie Sankt Franciscus schweb' ich –*Morgenstern*
Wie schaust du aus dem Nebelflor –*Kosegarten*
Wie schienen die Sternlein so hell –*Volkslied*
Wie schlafend unterm Flügel –*Keller*
Wie schnell verschwindet so Licht als Glanz –*Tieck*
Wie schön bist du, du güldne Morgenröthe –*Anonymous*
Wie schön bist du, freundliche Stille –*F. W. Krummacher*
Wie schön blüht uns der Maien –*Wunderhorn*
Wie schön geschmückt der festliche Raum! –*Cornelius*
Wie schön ist's im Freien –*Salis-Seewis*
Wie schön sich zu wiegen –*H. Seidel*
Wie sehr ich Dein, soll ich Dir sagen? –*Lenau*
Wie Seide war ihr leiser Tritt –*Lindner*
Wie selig, wer sein Liebchen hat –*G. A. Bürger*
Wie sich der Äuglein kindlicher Himmel –*J. Seidl*
Wie sich Nebelzüge drängend –*Bulthaupt*
Wie sich Rebenranken schwingen –*Hoffmann von Fallersleben*
Wie sie klingeln, die Pfaffen! –*Goethe*
Wie silbernes Geschirr sich stößt –*Jünger*
Wie sind die Tage schwer! –*Hesse*
Wie singt die Lerche schön –*Hoffmann von Fallersleben*
Wie so bleich ich geworden bin? –*Chamisso*
Wie so gelinde die Fluth bewegt! –*Voss*
Wie so innig, möcht' ich sagen –*F. Schlegel*
Wie so schmachtend, glücklich Weibchen –*Döhring*
Wie so trüb, Slimora du! –*Anonymous*
Wie soll den Mut ich finden –*Michelangelo*
Wie soll ich die Freude –*Tieck*
Wie soll ich fröhlich sein –*Heyse*
Wie soll ich meine Seele halten –*Rilke*
Wie soll ich nicht tanzen –*F. Schlegel*
Wie soll ich's bergen –*Wolff*
Wie sollt' ich heiter bleiben –*Goethe*
Wie sollten wir geheim sie halten –*Schack*
Wie still, wie einsam! –*Giesebrecht*
Wie stimmst du mich zur Andacht –*Hafis*
Wie süß der Nachtwind nun die Wiese streift –*Mörike*
Wie tönt an Frühlingstagen –*Seidel*
Wie tönt es mir so schaurig –*Majláth*
Wie trag ich doch in Sinne –*Heyse*
Wie traulich war das Fleckchen –*Groth*
Wie traurig sind wir Mädchen dran –*Volkslied*
Wie treiben die Wolken so finster –*Bertrand*
Wie trübst du, Geliebter! –*Haug*
Wie Uferland, das in der Feuchte blühet –*Jünger*
Wie unglücklich bin ich nit –*Anonymous*
Wie viel besser fuhren wir in der Räuberzeit –*Brecht*
Wie viel schon der Boten flogen –*Wenzig*

Wie viel Sonnenstrahlen fielen golden schwer –*Siebel*
Wie viele Zeit verlor ich, dich zu lieben! –*Heyse*
Wie vieles ist denn Wort geworden –*Morgenstern*
Wie wandelnde Landschaft gehn –*H. Claudius*
Wie war er schön der Maientag –*Stauß*
Wie war so schön doch Wald und Feld! –*Hoffmann von Fallersleben*
Wie war zu Cölln es doch vordem –*Kopisch*
Wie weil' ich so gern –*Deinhardstein*
Wie wenn die alten Wasser –*Hölderlin*
Wie, wenn die Sonn' aufgehet –*Tiede*
Wie wenn im frostgen Windhauch tötlich –*Schack*
Wie willst du dich mir offenbaren –*Uhland*
Wie wir voll Glut uns hier zusammenfinden –*Gubitz*
Wie wohl ist mir im Dunkeln! –*Kosegarten*
Wie wohnst du in des Reiches Städten –*Giesebrecht*
Wie Wolken um die Zeit legt –*Hölderlin*
Wie wundersam ist dies Verlorengehn –*Stieler*
Wie zerrißner Saiten Klingen –*Ritter*
Wieder möcht' ich dir begegnen –*Cornelius*
Wieder schreitet er den braunen Pfad –*Hesse*
Wieder trüg'risch war der Traum –*Anonymous*
Wiederkehrend nach dem Vaterlande –*Platen*
Wiedersehn! Wiedersehn! Endlich –*Tiedge*
Wiederum lebt wohl, ihr Brüder –*Mommsen*
Wiege dich, Wind, auf dem wogenden Korn –*Wolff*
Wiege mich ein, du Mutter –*Heydenreich*
Wie's aussieht im ew'gen Freudenhain –*Hamerling*
Wieviel Wege bin ich schon gegangen? –*Ehrler*
Wild verwachsne dunkle Fichten –*Lenau*
Wilia, sie, der unsre Ström' entsprangen –*Mickiewicz*
Wilkommen schöner froher Tag –*Goethe*
Will die Holde sich ergehen –*"Talvj"*
Will ich in mein Gärtlein gehn –*Wunderhorn*
Will ruhen unter den Bäumen hier –*Uhland*
Will sich Hektor ewig von mir wenden –*Schiller*
Will singen euch im alten Ton –*Jacobi*
Will über Nacht wohl durch das Thal –*Osterwald*
Wille, wille, will, der Mann ist kommen –*Volkslied*
Willkommen, du Gottes Sonne –*Chamisso*
Willkommen im Grünen! der Himmel ist blau –*Voss*
Willkommen, klare Sommernacht –*Keller*
Willkommen, lieber schöner Mai –*L. Hölty*
Willkommen, mein Wald, grünschattiges Haus! –*Roquette*
Willkommen, o silberner Mond –*Klopstock*
Willkommen, rothes Morgenlicht! –*Stolberg-Stolberg*
Willkommen, schöner Jüngling –*Schiller*
Willkommen süsse Kleine –*Rudolphi*
Willst du die Blüten des frühen –*Goethe*
Willst du immer weiter schweifen –*Goethe*
Willst du nicht das Lämmlein hüten? –*Schiller*
Willst du nicht dich schließen –*Keller*
Willst kommen zur Laube –*Moore*
Windes Rauschen, Gottes Flügel –*F. Schlegel*
Windräder gehn die Herbstesharfen sind –*Falke*
Winter entflieht, schon der Lenz –*Anonymous*
Winter vorbei, Herzchen, mein Liebchen! –*"Talvj"*
Wir befanden uns, so träumt' ich –*Hausmann*
Wir beten an, hier unter Brot- und Weingestalten –*Neus*
Wir bevölkerten die abend-düstern –*George*
Wir bringen mit Gesang und Tanz –*Voss*
Wir gehen durch goldenes Ährenfeld –*Sergel*
Wir geniessen die himmlischen Freuden –*Wunderhorn*
Wir giengen beide Hand in Hand –*Steigentesch*
Wir gingen durch die stille, milde Nacht –*Bierbaum*
Wir gingen einsam durch die Gartenflur –*Ullrich*
Wir gingen zusammen zu Feld, mein Hans –*Groth*
Wir graben tief in Trauer –*Giesebrecht*
Wir haben Beide lange Zeit geschwiegen –*Heyse*
Wir haben ein Bett, wir haben ein Kind –*Dehmel*
Wir haben im Lärm der Menge –*"Gerda v. Robertus"*
Wir haben oft beim Wein gesessen –*Falke*
Wir hatten einander so gerne –*Anonymous*
Wir hatten uns ein Haus gebaut von Sand –*Enslin*
Wir helfen gerne, sind nimmer ferne –*Goethe*
Wir Kinder, wir schmecken –*Overbeck*
Wir liegen allesamt im Kattegat –*Brecht*
Wir lustigen Bürger in grüner Stadt –*Tieck*
Wir müssen uns trennen, geliebtes Saitenspiel –*Tieck*
Wir reiten in die Kreuz und Quer –*Goethe*
Wir saßen am Fischerhause und schauten –*Heine*
Wir sassen so traulich beisammen –*Wilhelm Müller*
Wir schreiten in goldener Fülle –*Paul Remer*
Wir Schwestern zwei, wir schönen –*Mörike*
Wir senkten die Wurzeln in Moos und Gestein –*Ritter*
Wir sind durch Not und Freude –*Eichendorff*
Wir sind ja, Kind, im Maie –*Kulmann*
Wir sind nicht droben –*G. H. Goering*
Wir sind zwei Rosen –*Morgenstern*
Wir singen und sagen vom Grafen so gern –*Goethe*
Wir sitzen im Dunkeln –*Morgenstern*

Wir spielen und hüpfen so munter *–Segelbach*
Wir stehen hier zur Schlacht bereit *–Volkslied*
Wir stimmen dir mit Flötensang *–Seckendorf*
Wir träumten von einander *–Hebbel*
Wir tragen alle den Tod im Leib *–H. Claudius*
Wir Vögel singen nicht egal *–M. Claudius*
Wir wähnten lange recht zu leben *–Keller*
Wir wandeln durch die stumme Nacht *–Liliencron*
Wir wandelten, wir zwei zusammen *–Daumer*
Wir waren miteinander nicht befreundet *–Brecht*
Wir waren nie getrennt *–Bittner*
Wir weichen Sklavenbrod in bittre Thränen ein! *–Kotzebue*
Wir werden Staub und Asche zu bald seyn *–Werthes*
Wir wollten mit Kosen und Lieben *–Chamisso*
Wir ziehen treulich auf die Wacht *–Eichendorff*
Wir ziehn nun unsern Zahn heraus *–M. Claudius*
Wirf Rosenblätter in die Flut *–Wilhelm Müller*
Wirklich bist du schon verschwunden *–Bouterwek*
Wirklich, ich lebe in finsteren Zeiten *–Brecht*
Wirklicher Fortschritt ist nicht *–Brecht*
Wirst du halten, was du schwurst *–Széchényi*
Wisse, Herz: Der Tod trommelt hier *–Hughes*
Wissen es die blauen Blumen *–F. Kugler*
Wissen möcht' ich nur wie lange *–Rückert*
Wissen möchtest du, Geliebter *–Behn*
Wißt ihr, wann mein Kindchen *–Conrat*
Wisst ihr, wo ich gerne weil' *–Robert*
Wo aber werd ich sein im künft'gen Lenze? *–Eichendorff*
Wo am Herd ein Brautpaar siedelt *–Geibel*
Wo bist du, Bild, das vor mir stand *–L. Hölty*
Wo bist du? Trunken dämmert die Seele mir *–Hölderlin*
Wo blüht das Blümchen *–Wessenberg*
Wo blüht das Thal wo Liebe sich *–F. Bobrich*
Wo das Reisfeld abgeerntet *–Bethge*
Wo der Mond mit bleichem Schimmer *–Matthisson*
Wo der Weiser steht an der Straß' *–Busse*
Wo die Berge so blau aus dem nebligen Grau *–Jeitteles*
Wo die Rose hier blüht, wo Reben *–Goethe*
Wo die Tannen finstre Schatten werfen *–C. F. Meyer*
Wo die Taub' in stillen Buchen *–Jacobi*
Wo die Wälder Wache halten *–Falke*
Wo dort die alten Gemäuer stehn *–Körner*
Wo du nicht bist und deiner Augen Schimmer *–L. Schroeder*
Wo du triffst ein Mündlein hold *–Saul*
Wo durch dunkle Buchengänge *–Matthisson*
Wo e kleins Hüttle steht *–Volkslied*
Wo eilst du hin, du Bächlein, du? *–Dieffenbach*
Wo ein treues Herze in Liebe vergeht *–Wilhelm Müller*
Wo Engel hausen, da ist der Himmel *–Hafis*
Wo find ich den Liebling der Seele *–C. F. D. Schubart*
Wo fliehst du armes Blättchen hin *–Fischer*
Wo gehst du hin, du schönes Kind? *–Mörike*
Wo gehst du hin, du Stolze? *–Volkslied*
Wo hast du all die Schönheit hergenommen *–Huch*
Wo ich bin, fern und nah, fern und nah *–Asenijeff*
Wo ich bin, fern und nah, stehn zwei Augen da *–Grillparzer*
Wo ich bin, mich rings umdunkelt *–Heine*
Wo ich ferne des Mikane hohen Gipfel *–Anonymous*
Wo ich immer geh' und stehe *–Bittner*
Wo ich sei, und wo mich hingewendet *–Schiller*
Wo im Wald die klugen Rehe gehen *–Stinde*
Wo irr' ich um des Meeresstrand *–F. Müller*
Wo irrst du durch einsame Schatten *–Schlechta*
Wo ist der kleine Jakob geblieben? *–E. M. Arndt*
Wo ist der Ort, an dem du weilst? *–Hafis*
Wo ist mein Vater und Mutter hin *–Arthur*
Wo kein Strahl des Lichts hinblinket *–Lenau*
Wo kommst du her, so bleich und blass *–Mahlmann*
Wo kommst du her? wo kommst du her? *–Gerstenberg*
Wo lebt' ich glücklicher verborgen *–Lohbauer*
Wo liebende Herzen sich innig vermählt *–Scheffel*
Wo mag meine Heimat sein *–Hesse*
Wo noch kein Wand'rer gegangen *–Eichendorff*
Wo reiner Liebe gold'ne Strahlen *–Mecklenburg-Strelitz*
Wo ruhig sich und wilder unstäte Wellen teilen *–Eichendorff*
Wo sah ich, Mädchen, deine Züge *–C. F. Meyer*
Wo schweifst du, Herrin, mir so theuer? *–Shakespeare*
Wo seid ihr hin, ihr stillen frohen Tage? *–Anonymous*
Wo sich das Meer in weite Fernen *–"C. O. Sternau"*
Wo sind all' die Blumen hin? *–Hey*
Wo sind die Stunden der süßen Zeit *–Hofmannswaldau*
Wo süss in Frieden ein Herze ruht *–Anonymous*
Wo über mir die Waldnacht finster *–Leuthold*
Wo weht der Liebe hoher Geist? *–Leon*

Wo weilt er? Im kalten, im schaurigen Land –*Rellstab*
Wo aber werd' ich sein im künftgen Lenze? –*Eichendorff*
Wo willst du, klares Bächlein, hin –*Goethe*
Wo wird einst des Wandermüden –*Heine*
Wo zweie sich küssen zum ersten Mal –*Fischer*
Woget brausend, Harmonien –*J. Mayrhofer*
Woher der Freund so früh und schnelle –*Goethe*
Woher ich komme weiß ich nicht –*Thiess*
Woher, o namenloses Sehnen –*Kosegarten*
Wohin, du rauschender Strom, wohin? –*J. Sturm*
Wohin ich geh' und schaue –*Eichendorff*
Wohin können die Götter weinen –*Benn*
Wohin, o Bächlein, schnelle? –*"Martin Greif"*
Wohin? o Helios! wohin? –*J. Mayrhofer*
Wohin, o Seele, wirst du eilen –*Byron*
Wohin sind all' die Raritäten –*Löwenstein*
Wohin so schnell, so kraus und wild –*Wilhelm Müller*
Wohin? wohin? schöne Müllerin! –*Goethe*
Wohin zieht ihr? Freilich, freilich –*Brecht*
Wohl alle Gedanken des Herzens –*Haug*
Wohl an dem Rasenhügel hin –*Pape*
Wohl auf Kameraden, aufs Pferd! –*Schiller*
Wohl dem Mann, der in der Stille –*Tieck*
Wohl denk' ich allenthalben –*Salis-Seewis*
Wohl denk' ich oft an mein vergang'nes Leben –*Michelangelo*
Wohl endet Tod des Lebens Not –*Rückert*
Wohl fühl ich wie das Leben rinnt –*Storm*
Wohl, ich weiß es, da durchschleicht uns innen –*Goethe*
Wohl in der letzten Stunde –*P. Pfitzner*
Wohl ist es schön, auf fauler Haut –*Leuthold*
Wohl kenn' ich Eueren Stand –*Heyse*
Wohl lag ich einst in Gram und Schmerz –*Geibel*
Wohl manchen Rosenzweig brach ich –*Stieler*
Wohl mir der Stunde, wo ich sie fand –*Walther von der Vogelweide*
Wohl perlet im Glase der purpurne Wein –*Schiller*
Wohl schön bewandt war es vor –*Daumer*
Wohl und immer wohl dem Mann –*Miller*
Wohl viele Tausend Vögelein –*Prutz*
Wohl wandert' ich aus in trauriger Stund' –*Chamisso*
Wohl waren es Tage der Sonne –*Geibel*
Wohl weinen Gottes Engel –*Kosegarten*
Wohl! wer auf rechter Spur –*Goethe*
Wohlan! Die Zeit ist kommen! –*Wunderhorn*
Wohlauf ihr zieren Frauen –*Scheffel*
Wohlauf! im trauten Reih'n –*Haug*
Wohlauf noch getrunken den funkelnden Wein! –*Kerner*
Wohlauf und frisch gewandert –*Kerner*
Wohlauf! Wohlauf! der kühle Winter –*Neidhart*
Wohlauf zum frohen Rundgesang –*Mnioch*
Wolke lichtweiss in dem Blauen –*Giesebrecht*
Wolken, die ihr nach Osten eilt –*R. Reinick*
Wolken, meine Kinder, wandern gehen –*C. F. Meyer*
Wolken seh' ich abendwärts –*Uhland*
Wolken, wälderwärts gegangen –*Eichendorff*
Wolle Keiner mich fragen –*Geibel*
Wollt' er nur fragen, wollt' er nur fragen? –*Burns*
Wollt Ihr seh'n mein muntres Bäschen –*Anonymous*
Wollt ihr sie kennen, soll ich sie nennen –*Lehr*
Wollt ihr wissen, holde Bienen –*G. A. Bürger*
Wollt' vorüber gehen, doch es mußt' geschehen –*Triebnigg*
Wonnelohn getreuer Huldigungen –*G. A. Bürger*
Woran erkenn' ich deinen Freund –*Shakespeare*
Wort des Trostes, o wie schön tönst du –*Mahlmann*
Worte hab' ich nicht, um dir zu sagen –*Otto*
Wozu der Vöglein Chöre belauschen –*Hugo*
Wozu ist mein langes Haar mir dann –*Anonymous*
Wozu noch, Mädchen, soll es frommen –*Schack*
Wozu soll ich reden? –*"Carmen Sylva"*
Wozu, wozu mir sein sollte das Aug' –*Volkslied*
Wüsst ich, dass du mich lieb –*G. A. Bürger*
Wüsst' ich gewiss, dass es mein Liebster hörte –*Volkslied*
Wüßt' ich, wüßt' ich, das Du mich –*G. A. Bürger*
Wunden trägst du mein Geliebter –*Geibel*
Wunderbare Abendhelle, rings die Welt –*Milow*
Wunderbarer Gnadenthron –*Olearius*
Wunderliche Spießgesellen –*Eichendorff*
Wunderlichstes Buch der Bücher –*Goethe*
Wundes Herz, hör auf zu klagen –*Schopenhauer*
Wurzeln und Halme sind dies nur –*Whitman*

Zaghaft vom Gewölk ins Land –*Dehmel*
Zankst du schon wieder, sprach Hans Lau –*Lessing*
Zaubrer bin ich, doch was frommt es? –*R. Reinick*
Zeislein, Zeislein, wo ist dein Häuslein? –*Rückert*
Zeit, Verkündigerin der besten Freuden –*Klopstock*
Zelte, Posten, Werda-Rufer! –*F. Freiligrath*
Zersplittert lag des Schiffes Mast –*Scharrer*
Zeuch uns nach dir, nur für und für –*Funcke*
Zieh hin, du braver Krieger du! –*C. F. D. Schubart*
Zieh mit mir, geliebtes Kind –*George*

Zieh' nicht so schnell vorüber *–Lenau*
Ziehn die Schafe von der Wiese *–Goethe*
Zieht die Lerch im Herbste fort *–Anonymous*
Zieht hier ein Krieger stolz geschmükket *–C. Weisse*
Zierlich ist des Vogels Tritt im Schnee *–Mörike*
Zirpe, liebe kleine Sängerin der Haine *–Anonymous*
Zittr', o Erde, dunkle Macht *–Rückert*
Z'nächst bin i halt gange über's Bergel *–Volkslied*
Zögernd, leise, in des Dunkels *–Grillparzer*
Zu Aachen, in seiner Kaiserpracht *–Schiller*
Zu Augsburg steht ein hohes Haus *–Kerner*
Zu dem Duft, der da würzt die Lenzesluft *–Cornelius*
Zu dem Wettgesange schreiten Minnesänger *–Heine*
Zu den Bergen hebet sich ein Augenpaar *–the Bible*
Zu den winterkahlen Zweigen *–H. Claudius*
Zu der Rose, zu dem Weine komm! *–Hafis*
Zu des Mondes sanftem Schimmer *–J. Seidl*
Zu diesem Reigen reiche mir die Hand *–Stinde*
Zu Dionys, dem Tyrannen, schlich Möros *–Schiller*
Zu dir, dem Weltenmeister *–Anonymous*
Zu dir zieht's mi hin *–Volkslied*
Zu einem Wesen wurden zwei *–Bittner*
Zu fragmentarisch ist Welt und Leben *–Heine*
Zu Golde ward die Welt *–Morgenstern*
Zu Gott, zu Gott, zu Gott flieg' auf *–Uz*
Zu grausem Abendmahle *–Giraud*
Zu Hirsau in den Träummern *–Uhland*
Zu ihr stand all' mein Sehnen *–Ibsen*
Zu Koblenz auf der Brükken *–Wunderhorn*
Zu lieblich ists, ein Wort zu brechen *–Goethe*
Zu Lüttich, im letzten Häuselein *–Oer*
Zu meinen Füssen brichst du dich *–J. Mayrhofer*
Zu meiner Flöte, die aus Jade ist *–Bethge*
Zu meiner Laute Liebesklang *–Anonymous*
Zu meiner Zeit bestand noch Recht *–Hagedorn*
Zu meiner Zeit, zu meiner Zeit *–Hagedorn*
Zu Pisa in dem Klostergarten *–Vogl*
Zu Quedlinburg im Dome ertönet *–Mühler*
Zu Rauch muß werden der Erde Schmelz *–Rückert*
Zu Speier im Saale, da hebt sich ein Klingen *–Uhland*
Zu Strassburg auf der Schanz' *–Wunderhorn, Volkslied*
Zürne nicht des Herbstes Wind *–Rückert*
Zugemessne Rhythmen reizen freilich *–Goethe*
Zum Donaustrom, zur Kaiserstadt *–J. Mayrhofer*
Zum Friedhof schien der Mond herab *–Moore*
Zum Frühling sprach ich: weile! *–Hoffmann von Fallersleben*
Zum Hänschen sprach das Gretchen *–Baumbach*
Zum Kranz pflückt' ich einst Rosen *–Anonymous*
Zum Ossa sprach der Pelion *–Droste-Hülshoff*
Zum Reigen herbei im fröhlichen Mai! *–Hoffmann von Fallersleben*
Zum Sehen geboren, zum Schauen bestellt *–Goethe*
Zum Sterben bin i verliebet in di *–Nikolai, Wunderhorn*
Zum Wasser neigen sich die silbergrauen Weiden *–Ehlers*
Zur Drossel sprach der Fink *–Cornelius*
Zur ew'gen Ruh' sie sangen die schöne Müllerin *–Eichendorff*
Zur Freude ward geboren *–Voigt*
Zur Ruh', zur Ruh'! ihr müden Glieder *–Kerner*
Zur Ruhe, mein Herz zur Ruh *–Lingen*
Zur weißen Gans sprach einst vertraulich *–J. Sturm*
Zuweilen dünkt es mich *–Heine*
Zwar schuf das Glück hienieden *–Reissig*
Zween Mönche von des Indus Strand *–Pfeffel*
Zwei Augen sinds, aus deren Blikken *–Blumauer*
Zwei feine Stieflein hab' ich an *–Kletke*
Zwei Geliebte, treu verbunden *–Keller*
Zwei goldne Ringe hängen *–Morgenstern*
Zwei hohe Häuser, gleich an Würdigkeit *–Shakespeare*
Zwei Könige sassen auf Orkadal *–Geibel*
Zwei Musikanten ziehn daher vom Wald *–Eichendorff*
Zwei Paradieseslauben, sind, Liebste *–Hafis*
Zwei sind der Wege, auf welchen der Mensch *–Schiller*
Zwei Tage reichen sich die Hand *–"Gerda v. Robertus"*
Zwei Tannenwurzeln gross und alt *–Morgenstern*
Zwei welke Rosen träumen *–"Max Waldau"*
Zwei wunderliche Gevattern *–Rückert*
Zwischen Bergen, liebe Mutter! *–Eichendorff*
Zwischen dem Alten, zwischen dem Neuen *–Goethe*
Zwischen Himmel und Erd' hoch in der Lüfte Meer *–Schiller*
Zwischen Mohn und Rittersporn *–Schellenberg*
Zwischen oben, zwischen unten *–Goethe*
Zwischen Weizen und Korn *–Goethe*
Zwitschert nicht vor meinem Fenster *–Hamerling*
Zwölf Engel hielten am Himmelstor *–Spitteler*
Zwölf hat's geschlagen – warum denn Mittag? *–Keller*

Index by Composer, Poet, and First Line

Anonymous
Johann Wolfgang von Goethe
Ich bin der wohlbekannte Sänger

Franz Wilhelm Abt (1819-1885)
Auerbach
O Schwarzwald, o Heimat, wie bist du so schön!
Ludwig Bauer
Gut' Nacht, gut' Nacht, ihr Blumen all'
Rudolph Baumbach
Keinen Tropfen im Becher mehr
Victor Blüthgen
Gemäht sind die Felder, der Stoppelwind weht
Nun gute Nacht! Es gab so viel zu schauen
Rudolf Bunge
Kühl und stille ist die Nacht
Collignon
In dunkler Nacht, wenn's Aug' noch wacht
Peter Cornelius
Hinaus in das Lustgeschmetter der Vögel
Georg Christian Dieffenbach
Abend ists geworden, Dunkel hüllt uns ein
An dem Spinnrad sitzt das Mädchen
Auf zum Himmel steigt die Lerche
Da ist die liebe Schwalbe wieder!
Der Sommer ist vergangen
Die Blumen all, die Blüthen all
Hänschen möcht ein Reiter sein
Hoch auf Stelzen geht mein Büblein kühn dahin
Hört wie laut klingt der Vöglein Chor
Ich kenne einen grossen Garten
Mein Pferdchen gallopirt, Hurrah!
Nach Oben steigt die Lerche
Vöglein, Vöglein hüte dich, hüte dich!
Vorbei, vorbei die dunkle Nacht
Wenn ich ein Vöglein wär
Wo eilst du hin, du Bächlein, du?
Leberecht Dreves
Frühmorgens, wenn die Hähne kräh'n
Ida von Düringsfeld
Schlafe wohl! Im Thal von Schatten singt
A. Faber
Schaukle auf den grünen Wellen
Wilhelm Floto
Es blühet das Blümchen voll Glanz
Francke
Reizender Schmetterling
Sage mir, Vogel im grünen Wald, Kuckuck!
J. L. Haase
Singe, Vöglein, singe, singe, Vöglein, singe
Karl Herloßsohn
In den Augen liegt das Herz
Wenn die Schwalben heimwärts ziehn
Hersch
Flieg' auf, flieg auf, Frau Schwalbe mein
Rings Stille herrscht, es schweigt der Wald
Wilhelm Hertz
Und willst du von mir scheiden
Eduard Kauffer
Du bist im Strahlenkleide die Sonne
August Kopisch
Wenn man beim Wein sitzt
Georg Lang
Da sitz ich in der Stube, da sitz ich in dem Haus
Ein lockerer Zeisig, der bin ich, das weiss ich
Es führen mich die Wege wohl
Liebes Häschen, willst du morgen
Karl Lemcke
Veilchen vom Berg, woran mahnest du mich?
Friedrich Heinrich Oser
O du mein Alles, mein Alles auf der Welt
O sag' es noch einmal, noch tausendmal
Sachte will's dämmern, mit seinen Lämmern
Ludwig Pfau
O Sterne, gold'ne Sterne! wohl scheinet
Pfeil
Ich bin so gern, so gern daheim
Karl Heinrich Preller
Voll glühender Liebeswonne
Weiche nicht, o süsser Traum!
Julius von Rodenberg
Wach' auf, du schöne Träumerin, wach' auf
Otto Roquette
O wär ich am Nekkar, o wär ich am Rhein
Joseph Viktor von Scheffel
Das ist im Leben häßlich eingerichtet
Seyffardt
All Abend, bevor ich zur Ruhe geh
Wilhelm Tappert
Schaust in's Stübchen klein
Anonymous
Die Sonne leuchtet, der Frühling blüht
Eine Brücke kenn' ich, Liebchen
Es hat die stille Nacht die Welt zur Ruh
Hinaus in weite Ferne, auf Meereswogen hin

Still ist die Nacht, nur leise klingen wieder
Volkslied
Wie die Blümlein draussen zittern
Not Yet Identified
Ich bin der kleine Postillon, trara

Eugen (Francis Charles) d'Albert (1864-1932)
Hermann Allmers
Gern bin ich allein an des Meeres Strand
Peter Cornelius
Ich ging hinaus, um dich zu seh'n
Ich war ein Blatt an grünem Baum
Zur Drossel sprach der Fink
Friedrich Hebbel
Quellende, schwellende Nacht
Wilhelm Hertz
Auf der Haide ist ein Platz
Joseph Huggenberger
Schon dämmert's leise; durch's Geäst
Gustav Kastropp
Im zitternden Mondlicht wiegen
Willy Lentrodt
Es ist so still. Alles schläft
Giacomo Leopardi
O lieblich klarer Mond, ich denke dran
Detlev von Liliencron
Der Abend war so dunkel schwer
Du junge, schöne Bleicherin, wo fährst du
War der schönste Sommermorgen
Fritz Rassow
O, konntest du es nicht erraten
Sagte ein goldener Schmetterling
Paul Reiner
Aus einem dunklen Forste drängt sich
Nebel trauern über dem See
R. E. Wegener
Lustwandelnd schritt ein Mädchen
from Des Knaben Wunderhorn
Als ich kam zur Stube rein, da ist gut wohnen!
Blühe, liebes Veilchen, das so lieblich roch
Buko von Halberstadt, bring' doch
Es wollt' ein Mägdlein früh aufsteh'n
Ich habe mein Feinsliebchen
Ich weiss mir'n Mädchen hübsch und fein
Ich weiss nicht, wie mir's ist, ich bin nicht krank
Vögel, tut euch nicht verweilen, kommet
Not Yet Identified
Der Frühling kam! In seinem Hauche athm' ich

(Mary) Frances Allitsen, née Bumpus (1848-1912)
Heinrich Heine
Der Tod, das ist die kühle Nacht
Du hast Diamanten und Perlen
Ein Fichtenbaum steht einsam im Norden
Ein schöner Stern geht auf in meiner Nacht
Mag da draussen Schnee sich thürmen
Mein Knecht! steh' auf, und sattle schnell
Saphire sind die Augen dein, die lieblichen
Seit die Liebste war entfernt

Anna Amalia, Herzogin von Sachsen-Weimar (1739-1807)
Johann Wolfgang von Goethe
Auf dem Land und in der Stadt
Ein Veilchen auf der Wiese stand
Sie scheinen zu spielen voll Leichtsinn und Trug
Sieh mich, Heil'ger, wie ich bin

Johann André (1741-1799)
Gottfried August Bürger
Lenore fuhr ums Morgenrot
Johann Wolfgang von Goethe
Ein Veilchen auf der Wiese stand

Conrad (Eduard Reinhold) Ansorge (1862-1930)
Richard Dehmel
Der Abend graut. Herbstfeuer brennen
Der Wald beginnt zu rauschen
Doch hatte niemals tiefre Macht dein Blick
In die dunkle Bergschlucht kehrt der Mond
Lege deine Hand auf meine Augen
O zürne nicht, wenn mein Begehren dunkel
Still, es ist ein Tag verflossen
Tauchst du nieder aus den Weiten
Und du kamest in mein Haus
Wenn der Regen durch die Gosse tropft
Arno Holz
Schenk ein, liebe Sonne, dein Licht
Friedrich Nietzsche
Tag meines Lebens! die Sonne sinkt
Paul Verlaine
Weich küsst die Zweige der weisse Mond

Hans Erich Apostel (1901-1972)
Stefan George
Mich erfreute der flug aller tiefdunklen pracht
Mild und trüb ist mir fern Saum
Sei rebe die blümt Sei frucht die betört

Bettina von Arnim, née Brentano (1785-1859)
Georg Friedrich Daumer
Holder, leichtbeschwingter Bote
Johann Wolfgang von Goethe
Der du von dem Himmel bist
O schaudre nicht, laß diesen Blick

Anonymous
Ein Stern der Lieb' am Himmelslauf
Entflammt von Liebesqualen

Carl Philipp Emanuel Bach (1714-1788)
Christian Gellert
Gott, deine Güte reicht so weit
Volkslied
's ist kein verdrüßlicher Lebe als in das Klösterli

Gottlob Bachmann (1763-1840)
Johann Wolfgang von Goethe
Wer reitet so spät durch Nacht und Wind

Ernst Bacon (1894-1990)
Joseph von Eichendorff
Nacht ist wie ein stilles Meer
Was ist mir denn so wehe?
Johann Wolfgang von Goethe
Der Du von dem Himmel bist
Über allen Gipfeln ist Ruh
Helene Lecher
Du milder, Du schöner, Du herrlicher Geist
Nikolaus Lenau
Auf dem Teich, dem Regungslosen
Friedrich Rückert
Ich liebe Dich, weil ich Dich lieben muss

Otto Ball
Richard Schaukal
Als der Gesandte schied, ging meine Königin
Halte mir einer von euch Laffen mein Pferd

Moritz Bauer (1875-1932)
Heinrich Heine
Im Mondenglanze ruht das Meer
Nikolaus Lenau
Lethe! Lethe! brich die Fesseln des Ufers

Ludwig van Beethoven (1770-1827)
Stephan von Breuning
Der Hoffnung letzter Schimmer sinkt dahin
Gottfried August Bürger
Es blüht ein Blümchen irgendwo
Hast du nicht Liebe zugemessen
Lebewohl, du Mann der Lust und Schmerzen
Wüsst ich, dass du mich lieb
Matthias Claudius
Wenn jemand eine Reise thut
Johann von Döhring
Noch weisst du nicht! wess Kind du bist
Friedelberg
Ein grosses deutsches Volk sind wir
Keine Klage soll erschallen
Christian Gellert
An dir allein, an dir hab' ich gesündigt
Die Himmel rühmen des Ewigen Ehre
Gott, deine Güte reicht so weit
Gott ist mein Lied! Er ist der Gott der Stärke
Meine Lebenszeit verstreicht
So Jemand spricht: Ich liebe Gott!
Johann Wilhelm Ludwig Gleim
Ich, der mit flatterndem Sinn
H. Goeble
Wenn die Sonne nieder sinket
Johann Wolfgang von Goethe
Der edle Mensch sei hülfreich und gut
Es war einmal ein König
Herz, mein Herz, was soll das geben?
Ich komme schon durch manches Land
Kennst du das Land, wo die Citronen blühn
Kleine Blumen, kleine Blätter streuen mir
Nur wer die Sehnsucht kennt
Trocknet nicht, trocknet nicht
Was zieht mir das Herz so?
Wer reitet so spät durch Nacht und Wind?
Wie herrlich leuchtet mir die Natur
Gerhard Anton von Halem
Mit Liebesblick und Spiel und Sang
Paul Graf von Haugwitz
Lisch aus, lisch aus, mein Licht!
Johann Gottfried Herder
Höre, die Nachtigall singt
Turteltaube, du klagest so laut
Franz Rudolf Hermann
Dort auf dem hohen Felsen sang
K. F. Herrosee
Ich liebe dich, so wie du mich
Ludwig Hölty
Dein Silber schien durch Eichengrün
Aloys Jeitteles
Auf dem Hügel sitz' ich spähend
Diese Wolken in den Höhen
Es kehret der Maien, es blühet die Au'
Leichte Segler in den Höhen
Nimm sie hin denn, diese Lieder
Wo die Berge so blau aus dem nebligen Grau
Friedrich August Kleinschmidt
Du sagtest, Freund, an diesen Ort
Karl Lappe
Nord oder Süd! Wenn nur im warmen Busen
Gotthold Ephraim Lessing
Ohne Liebe lebe, wer da kann
Friedrich von Matthisson
Die Flamme lodert, milder Schein

Einsam wandelt dein Freund im Frühlingsgarten
Freud' umblühe dich auf allen Wegen
Ich denke dein, wenn durch den Hain
Sophie Mereau
Ich weiss eine Farbe, der bin ich so hold
Gottlieb Conrad Pfeffel
Wer, wer ist ein freier Mann?
Christian Ludwig Reissig
Als mir noch die Thräne
Der Frühling entblühet dem Schoos der Natur
Die stille Nacht umdunkelt
Einst wohnten süsse Ruh und goldner Frieden
Ich zieh' in's Feld von Lieb' entbrannt
Welch ein wunderbares Leben
Zwar schuf das Glück hienieden
Johann Baptist Rupprecht
Merkenstein! Wo ich wandle denk' ich dein
Samuel Friedrich Sauter
Ach mir schallt's dorten
Josef Ludwig Stoll
O dass ich dir vom stillen Auge
Christoph August Tiedge
Die du so gern in heil'gen Nächten feierst
Ob ein Gott sei? ob er einst erfülle
G. Friedrich Treitschke
Wenn ich ein Vöglein wär
Hermann Wilhelm Franz Ueltzen
Im Arm der Liebe ruht sich's wohl
Christian Weisse
Ich war bei Chloen ganz allein
Ignaz Heinrich von Wessenberg
Wo blüht das Blümchen, das nie verblüht?
Anonymous
Der lebt ein Leben wonniglich
Erhebt das Glas mit froher Hand
Man strebt die Flamme zu verhehlen
Nimmer dem liebenden Herzen
Nur bei dir, an deinem Herzen
Schildern, willst du Freund, soll ich dir Elisen?
Stirb immerhin, es welken ja so viele
Wer nicht, wenn warm von Hand zu Hand

Hermann Behn (1859?-1927)
Hermann Behn
Es leuchtet die Gottheit aus heiligen Blitzen
Hell und sieghaft strahlest du, golderglühend
In dem Frieden heil'ger Nacht
Was hast du mir gestanden
Wissen möchtest du, Geliebter
Emanuel Geibel
Nun die Schatten dunkeln
Johann Wolfgang von Goethe
Der du von dem Himmel bist
Es war ein König in Thule
Ich ging im Walde so für mich hin
Über allen Gipfeln ist Ruh'
Louisa von Haber
Du Baum an meinem Fenster
Friedrich Hebbel
Die du über die Sterne weg
Heinrich Heine
Aus den Himmelsaugen droben fallen zitternd
Ein Fichtenbaum steht einsam im Norden
Im Rhein, im schönen Strome
Conrad Ferdinand Meyer
Auf das Feuer mit dem goldnen Strahle
Bei der Abendsonne Wandernr
Die Mutter mahnt mich Abends
Du warest mir ein täglich Wanderziel
Ein betrogen Mägdlein irrt im Walde
Entgegen wandeln wir dem Dorf im Sonnenkuß
Es herrscht' ein König irgendwo
Frau Berte, hört: Ihr dürftet nun
Geh nicht, die Gott für mich erschuf!
Greif' aus, du mein junges, mein feuriges Thier!
Heut ward mir bis zum jungen Tag
In den Wald bin ich geflüchtet
In der Nacht, die die Bäume mit Blüten deckt
Ins Museum bin zu später Stunde
Läg' dort ich unterm Firneschein
Liebchen fand ich spielend
Meine eingelegten Ruder triefen
Mir träumt', ich komm an's Himmelsthor
Mit edeln Purpurröten und hellem Amselschlag
Sehnsucht ist Qual! Der Herrin wag ich's
So stille ruht im Hafen
Wer in der Sonne kämpft ein Sohn der Erde
Wernher von Tegernsee
Ich bin dein, du bist mein

Rudolf Bella
Gustav Schüler
Das Schilf bückt sich hernieder

Alban (Maria Johannes) Berg (1885-1935)
Peter Altenberg
Von der Last des Gedankens
Was erhoffst du dir, Mädchen, noch?!?
Weinet, sanfte Mädchen...! So lang ihr weinet
Otto Julius Bierbaum
Auf der fernen See ein Segel steht
Carl Busse
Es gibt ein stilles Königreich

Über den Bergen, weit zu wandern
Joseph von Eichendorff
Es wandelt, was wir schauen
Gustav Falke
Im Frühling, als der Märzwind ging
Ludwig Finckh
Ich hab' es nicht gewußt, was Liebe ist
Johann Georg Fischer
Ich sah am liebsten hoch im Turm
Cäsar Flaischlen
So regnet es sich langsam ein
Siegfried Fleischer
Verwelkte Blätter, entseelte Götter
Emanuel Geibel
Du feuchter Frühlingsabend
Johann Wilhelm Ludwig Gleim
Rosen pflücke, Rosen blühn
Johann Wolfgang von Goethe
Ach, wer bringt die schönen Tage
Kennst du das Land, wo die Zitronen blühn
Wenn der uralte heilige Vater
Christian Dietrich Grabbe
Wie ein Goldadler reißt der Blitz
"Martin Greif" (Friedrich Hermann Frey)
Legt mir unters Haupt Melissen
Still ist's, wo die Gräber sind meiner Liebe
Robert Hamerling
Augenblicke gibt es, zage, wo so grabesstill
Otto Erich Hartleben
Im Arm der Liebe schliefen wir selig ein
Carl Hauptmann
Dämmern Wolken über Nacht und Tal
Friedrich Hebbel
Schlafen, Schlafen, nichts als Schlafen!
Heinrich Heine
Ernst ist der Frühling, seine Träume sind traurig
Mir träumte: traurig schaute der Mond
Spätherbstnebel, kalte Träume
Paul Hohenberg
Hier in der öden Fremde, ach so fern von dir
Nun ziehen Tage über die Welt
Wenn die Nacht sich über die Welt
Arno Holz
Kleine Blumen wie aus Glas seh' ich
Henrik Ibsen
Zu ihr stand all' mein Sehnen
Ludwig Jacobowski
Dem Auge fern, dem Herzen nah!
Karl Ernst Knodt
Süß sind mir die Schollen des Tales
Nikolaus Lenau
Auf geheimem Waldespfade schleich' ich gern
Detlev von Liliencron
Maienkätzchen, erster Gruß
F. Lorenz
Eh' wir weiter gehen, laß uns stille stehen
Alfred Mombert
Nun ich der Riesen Stärksten überwand
Schlafend trägt man mich in mein Heimatland
Sie wandeln durch das Waldes Grün
Warm die Lüfte, es sprießt Gras
Elimar von Monsterberg-Muenckenau
Ein Spielmann, der muss reisen
Rainer Maria Rilke
Alle Mädchen erwarten wen
Das war der Tag der weißen Chrysanthemen
Und wie mag die Liebe dir kommen sein?
Friedrich Rückert
Ich will die Fluren meiden
Rosen! Ein Zypressenhain, alte Brunnen fließen
Georg Scherer
Ich saß am Strand und hub an
Johannes Schlaf
Der schönste Cherub kommt
Geht ein grauer Mann durch den stillen Wald
Herbstsonnenschein. Der liebe Abend blickt
Frida Semler
Der Mondschein lag auf dem Wasser
Karl Stieler
So harrte ich schweigend; durch die Hand
Theodor Storm
Das macht, es hat die Nachtigall
Schließe mir die Augen beide
Karl Wilhelm
Meine Sehnsucht ist zum Licht
Franz Wisbacher
Die Luft ist kühl und trübe
Volkslied
Knabe, dir gefiel die duftige Rose

Ludwig Berger (1777-1839)
Johann Wolfgang von Goethe
So hab' ich wirklich dich verloren?
Wie kommt's, dass du so traurig bist

(Louis-) Hector Berlioz (1803-1869)
Johann Wolfgang von Goethe
Es war ein König in Thule
Es war einmal ein König

Gerald Hugh Tyrwhitt-Wilson, Baron Berners (1883-1950)
Heinrich Heine
Den König Wiswamitra, den treibts ohne Rast
Die heiligen drei Könige aus Morgenland
Du bist wie eine Blume

Günter Bialas (1907-)
Gottfried Benn
Als ob das alles nicht gewesen wäre
Erinnerungen, Erinnerungen, Klänge
Hör zu, so wird der letzte Abend sein
Überblickt man die Jahre von Ur bis El Alamein
Wohin können die Götter weinen
Heinrich Heine
Die Söhne des Glückes beneid ich nicht
Erstorben ist in meiner Brust
Nicht gedacht soll seiner werden!
Wo wird einst des Wandermüden

Julius Bittner (1874-1939)
Julius Bittner
Du bist der schimmernd Edelstein
Du bist wie eine Julinacht, so süß, so weich
Du hältst uns, Frau, die heiligste der Flammen!
Du kleiner Mensch im Bettlein klein
Es dunkelt. Friede im Gemach
Es ist schon spät, so um die Mitternacht
Ich geh zu Dir in dunkler Nacht
Ich habe Dich schon längst gekannt
Ich seh' vor mir ein liebes Bild
Ich weiß, daß Dir und mir bereitet ist ein Haus
Und ob auch Sturm das Haus mir umsaust
Wald vor uns, Wies' vor uns und Blütenpracht
Weißt Du noch, wie das war?
Wem säng' ich Lieder, wenn nicht Dir?
Wir waren nie getrennt und werden nie getrennt
Wo ich immer geh' und stehe
Zu einem Wesen wurden zwei

Boris Blacher (1903-1975)
William Shakespeare
Die einst'ge Sehnsucht, sie liegt nun tot und kalt
So wilde Freude nimmt ein wildes Ende
Zwei hohe Häuser, gleich an Würdigkeit
Friedrich Wolf
Als Kinder glaubten wir an Zauberwesen
Erste Kirschen hast du mir gebracht
Es trabt im Kreis durch die Manege
Man soll seinem Herzen gehorchen

Leo Blech (1871-1958)
Robert Reinick
Vom Berg hinab gestiegen ist nun
from Des Knaben Wunderhorn
Weine, weine nur nicht, ich will dich liebe

Gustave Bley
"Eduard Ferrand" (Eduard Schulz)
Das Kind schläft unter dem Rosenstrauch
Not Yet Identified
Schleenblüt' und wilde Rose hab' ich mir

Carl Bohm (1844-1920)
Rudolph Baumbach
Zum Hänschen sprach das Gretchen
Robert Burns
Wollt' er nur fragen, wollt' er nur fragen
Elisabeth Ebeling
Es spielen leise die Blüthen
Oskar von Redwitz
Es muss was Wunderbares sein
Hans Schmidt
Liebster Schatz, i bitt' di schön
Johann Ludwig Uhland
Horch, wie der Sturm
Christian Weisse
Ich war bei ihr einst ganz allein
Julius Wolff
Alle Blumen möcht' ich binden, alle
Ich ging im Wald durch Kraut und Gras
Im Grase thaut's, die Blumen träumen

Aleksandr Porfirjevich Borodin (1833-1887)
Heinrich Heine
Aus meinen Tränen spriessen
Du schönes Fischermädchen
Vergiftet sind meine Lieder

Johannes Brahms (1833-1897)
"Willibald Alexis" (Wilhelm Häring)
Lieb Mutter, heut Nacht heulte Regen und Wind
O Lady Judith, spröder Schatz
Hermann Allmers
Der graue Nebel tropft so still
Ich ruhe still im hohen grünen Gras
Ludwig Achim von Arnim
O süßer Mai, der Strom ist frei
the Bible
Denn es gehet dem Menschen wie dem Vieh
Herr, wie lange willst du mein so gar vergessen?
Ich wandte mich, und sahe an
O Tod, o Tod, wie bitter, wie bitter bist du
Wenn ich mit Menschen- und mit Engelszungen

Friedrich Bodenstedt
Weit über das Feld durch die Lüfte hoch
Clemens Brentano
Hör, es klagt die Flöte wieder
O kühler Wald, wo rauschest du
Carl Candidus
Aetherische ferne Stimmen
Den Wirbel schlag ich gar so stark
Es kehrt die dunkle Schwalbe
Jäger, was jagst du die Häselein
Mir ist so weh ums Herz
O Frühlingsabenddämmerung!
Sommerfäden hin und wieder
Adelbert von Chamisso
Die Mühle, die dreht ihre Flügel
Hugo Conrat
Brauner Bursche führt zum Tanze
Brennessel steht an Weges Rand
He, Zigeuner, greife in die Saiten ein
Himmel strahlt so helle und klar
Hochgetürmte Rimaflut, wie bist du so trüb
Horch, der Wind klagt in den Zweigen
Kommt dir manchmal in den Sinn
Liebe Schwalbe, kleine Schwalbe
Lieber Gott, du weißt, wie oft bereut ich hab
Mond verhüllt sein Angesicht
Röslein dreie in der Reihe blühn so rot
Rote Abendwolken ziehn am Firmament
Rote Rosenknospen künden schon
Weit und breit schaut Niemand mich an
Wißt ihr, wann mein Kindchen
Georg Friedrich Daumer
Ach, wende diesen Blick
Alles, alles in den Wind sagst du mir
Am Donaustrande, da steht ein Haus
Am Gesteine rauscht die Flut
An jeder Hand die Finger hatt ich bedeckt
Die grüne Hopfenranke, sie schlängelt
Die Schnur, die Perl an Perlen
Ein dunkeler Schacht ist Liebe
Ein kleiner, hübscher Vogel nahm den Flug
Eine gute, gute Nacht pflegst du mir zu sagen
Es bebet das Gesträuche
Es träumte mir, ich sei dir teuer
Finstere Schatten der Nacht
Flammenauge, dunkles Haarn
Hier ob dem Eingang seid befestiget
Ich kose süß mit der und der
Ihr schwarzen Augen, ihr dürft nur winken
In meiner Nächte Sehnen, so tief allein
Mein liebes Herz, was ist dir, was ist dir?
Nachtigall, sie singt so schön
Nagen am Herzen fühl ich ein Gift mir
Nein, es ist nicht auszukommen mit den Leuten
Nein, Geliebter, setze dich mir so nahe nicht!
Nicht mehr zu dir zu gehen
Nicht wandle, mein Licht, dort außen
Nun, ihr Musen, genug!
O die Frauen, o die Frauen, wie sie Wonne
O schöne Nacht! Am Himmel märchenhaft
O wie sanft die Quelle sich durch die Wiese
Rede, Mädchen, allzu liebes
Rosen steckt mir an die Mutter
Sah dem edlen Bildnis in des Auges allzu
Schlosser auf, und mache Schlösser
Schön war, das ich dir weihte
Schwarzer Wald, dein Schatten ist so düster!
Sieh, wie ist die Welle klar
Strahlt zuweilen auch ein mildes Licht
Unbewegte laue Luft, tiefe Ruhe der Natur
Verzicht, o Herz, auf Rettung
Vögelein durchrauscht die Luft
Vom Gebirge Well auf Well
Von waldbekränzter Höhe
Wahre, wahre deinen Sohn, Nachbarin
Weiche Gräser im Revier
Wenn du nur zuweilen lächelst
Wenn so lind dein Auge mir
Wie des Abends schöne Röte
Wir wandelten, wir zwei zusammen
Wohl schön bewandt war es vor ehe
Joseph von Eichendorff
Aus der Heimat hinter den Blitzen rot
Da die Welt zur Ruh gegangen
Ein Gems auf dem Stein, ein Vogel im Flug
Es war, als hätt der Himmel die Erde still geküßt
Gleich wie Echo frohen Liedern
Hoch über stillen Höhen stand in dem Wald
Ich rufe, vom Ufer verlorenes Glück
Lindes Rauschen in den Wipfeln
Sie stand wohl am Fensterbogen
Von allen Bergen nieder so fröhlich Grüßen
Wenn die Klänge nahn und fliehen
"Eduard Ferrand" (Eduard Schulz)
Ein Mägdlein saß am Meeresstrand
Paul Flemming
Laß dich nur nichts nicht dauren
O liebliche Wangen, ihr macht mir Verlangen
Und gleichwohl kann ich anders nicht
Adolf Frey
Wenn mein Herz beginnt zu klingen

Emanuel Geibel
Die ihr schwebet um diese Palmen
Mein Herz ist schwer, mein Auge wacht
Mit geheimnisvollen Düften grüßt vom Hang
Johann Wolfgang von Goethe
Aber abseits, wer ist's?
Dämmrung senkte sich von oben
Ein Blick von deinen Augen in die meinen
Es rauschet das Wasser und bleibet nicht stehn
Feiger Gedanken bängliches Schwanken
Göttlicher Morpheus, umsonst bewegst du
Grausam erweiset sich Amor an mir
Hab ich tausendmal geschworen
Komm mit, o Schöne, komm mit mir zum Tanze
Liebliches Kind, kannst du mir sagen
Sah ein Knab ein Röslein stehn
Warum doch erschallen himmelwärts die Lieder
Wenn zu der Regenwand Phöbus sich gattet
Wie kommts daß du so traurig bist
Melchior Grohe
O komme, holde Sommernacht
Klaus Groth
Aus der Erde quellen Blumen
Dein blaues Auge hält so still
Ernst ist der Herbst. Und wenn die Blätter
Es hing der Reif im Lindenbaum
Ich sah als Knabe Blumen blühn
Mein wundes Herz verlangt nach milder Ruh
O wüßt ich doch den Weg zurück
Regentropfen aus den Bäumen fallen
Walle, Regen, walle nieder
Warum denn warten von Tag zu Tag?
Wenn ein müder Leib begraben
Wie Melodien zieht es mir
Wie traulich war das Fleckchen
Otto Gruppe
Schwalbe, sag mir an, ists dein alter Mann
Hafis
Bitteres zu sagen denkst du
Die Flamme hier, die wilde, zu verhehlen
So stehn wir, ich und meine Weide
Wehe, Lüftchen, lind und lieblich
Wie bist du, meine Königin
"Friedrich Halm" (Münch-Bellinghausen)
Bei dir sind meine Gedanken
Ich müh mich ab und kann nicht verschmerzen
Kein Haus, keine Heimat, kein Weib
Mein Lieb ist ein Jäger, und grün ist sein Kleid
Steig auf, geliebter Schatten
Friedrich Hebbel
Friedlich bekämpfen Nacht sich und Tag
Ich blicke hinab in die Gasse
Ich legte mich unter den Lindenbaum
Heinrich Heine
Dämmernd liegt der Sommerabend
Der Tod, das ist die kühle Nacht
Die Wellen blinken und fließen dahin
Es schauen die Blumen alle
Mein Liebchen, wir saßen beisammen
Nacht liegt auf den fremden Wegen
Johann Gottfried Herder
Ach könnt ich, könnte vergessen sie
Alle Winde schlafen auf dem Spiegel der Flut
Dein Schwert, wie ists von Blut so rot?
Den gordischen Knoten, den Liebe sich band
O Hochland und o Südland!
Über die Berge, über die Wellen
Paul Heyse
All meine Herzgedanken sind immerdar bei dir
Am jüngsten Tag ich aufersteh
Am Sonntag Morgen zierlich angetan
Am Wildbach die Weiden, die schwanken Tag
Auf die Nacht in den Spinnstubn
Dein Herzlein mild, du liebes Bild
Die Berge sind spitz und die Berge sind kalt
Es geht ein Wehen durch den Wald
In dem Schatten meiner Locken
Nun stehn die Rosen in Blüte
Und gehst du über den Kirchhof
Waldesnacht du wunderkühle
Hermann Hölty
Es sprechen und blicken die Wellen
Ludwig Hölty
Birg, o Veilchen, in deinem blauen Kelche
Eine Schale des Stroms
Geuß nicht so laut der liebentflammten Lieder
Holder klingt der Vogelsang
Unter Blüten des Mai's spielt ich mit ihrer Hand
Wann der silberne Mond durch die Gesträuche
Hoffmann von Fallersleben
Ich muß hinaus, ich muß zu dir
Ist nicht der Himmel so blau?
Nachtigallen schwingen lustig ihr Gefieder
So lange Schönheit wird bestehn
Wie die Wolke nach der Sonne
Wie sich Rebenranken schwingen
Max Kalbeck
Leblos gleitet Blatt um Blatt still und traurig
Störe nicht den leisen Schlummer
Siegfried Kapper
Ach, und du mein kühles Wasser!
Hebt ein Falke sich empor

Ruft die Mutter, ruft der Tochter
Schwor ein junges Mädchen
Stand das Mädchen, stand am Bergesabhang
Gottfried Keller
Du milchjunger Knabe, wie schaust du mich an?
Langsam und schimmernd fiel ein Regen
Singt mein Schatz wie ein Fink
Zwei Geliebte, treu verbunden
Justinus Kerner
Ach, ach, ich armes Klosterfräulein!
August Kopisch
Ich sahe eine Tigrin im dunklen Haine
Im Finstern geh ich suchen
Voller, dichter tropft ums Dach da
Franz Kugler
Der Mond steht über dem Berge
Es rinnen die Wasser Tag und Nacht
Nächtens wachen auf die irren
Karl Lemcke
Auf der Heide weht der Wind
Es saß ein Salamander auf einem kühlen Stein
Freiwillige her! Freiwillige her!
Gebt acht! Gebt acht! Es harrt der Feind
Ich saß zu deinen Füßen in Waldeseinsamkeit
Ich sitz am Strande der rauschenden See
Ich stand in einer lauen Nacht
Im Garten am Seegestade uralte Bäume stehn
Jetzt hab ich schon zwei Jahre lang
Über die See, fern über die See
Was freut einen alten Soldaten?
Detlev von Liliencron
Der Tag ging regenschwer und sturmbewegt
Maienkätzchen, erster Gruß
Hermann Lingg
Immer leiser wird mein Schlummer
James Macpherson ("Ossian")
Mädchen von Kola, du schläfst!
Alfred Meissner
Sie ist gegangen, die Wonnen versanken
Eduard Mörike
Angelehnt an die Epheuwand
Rosenzeit, wie schnell vorbei
Wir Schwestern zwei, wir schönen
Wilhelm Müller
Aus des Meeres tiefem, tiefem Grunde
Eine blaue Schürze hast du mir gegeben
August Graf von Platen
Der Strom, der neben mir verrauschte
Du sprichst, daß ich mich täuschte
Ich schleich umher betrübt und stumm
Wehe, so willst du mich wieder
Wie rafft ich mich auf in der Nacht
Christian Reinhold Köstlin
An dies Schifflein schmiege, holder See
Ein Vögelein fliegt über den Rhein
Hier wo sich die Straßen scheiden
O Nachtigall, dein süßer Schall
Robert Reinick
O versenk, o versenk dein Leid, mein Kind
Wie ist doch die Erde so schön, so schön!
Jean-Baptist Rousseau
Es lockt und säuselt um den Baum
Friedrich Rückert
Ans Auge des Liebsten
Einförmig ist der Liebe Gram
Fahr wohl, o Vöglein, das nun wandern soll
Ich weiß nicht, was im Hain die Taube girret
In goldnen Abendschein getauchet
Leise Töne der Brust, geweckt vom Odem
Mit vierzig Jahren ist der Berg erstiegen
Ruhn sie? Ruhn sie? rufet das Horn
Wenn Kummer hätte zu töten
Zu Rauch, zu Rauch muß werden der Erde
Adolf Friedrich von Schack
Leise, um dich nicht zu wecken
Sei willkommen, Zwielichtstunde!
Wie wenn im frostgen Windhauch tötlich
Max von Schenkendorf
Ach, wer nimmt von meiner Seele
Es weht um mich Narzissenduft
Fliegt nur aus, geliebte Tauben!
Ihr wunderschönen Augenblicke
Was schaust du mich so freundlich an
Friedrich von Schiller
Dem dunkeln Schoß der heilgen Erde
Senke, strahlender Gott, die Fluren dürsten
Hans Schmidt
Geh schlafen, Tochter, schlafen!
Mutter, hilf mir armen Tochter
Rosen brach ich Nachts mir am dunklen Hage
Singe, Mädchen, hell und klar
Felix Schumann
Es brausen der Liebe Wogen
Meine Liebe ist grün wie der Fliederbusch
Wenn um den Hollunder der Abendwind kost
William Shakespeare
Auf morgen ist Sankt Valentin's Tag
Sein Leichenhemd weiß wie Schnee zu seh'n
Sie trugen ihn auf der Bahre bloß
Und kommt er nicht mehr zurück?
Wie erkenn' ich dein Treulieb

Karl Simrock
Blauer Himmel, blaue Wogen
Silbermond, mit bleichen Strahlen
"C. O. Sternau" (Otto Inkermann)
Heimat! Heimat! wunderbar tönendes Wort!
Theodor Storm
Über die Heide hallet mein Schritt
Ludwig Tieck
Geliebter, wo zaudert dein irrender Fuß?
Keinen hat es noch gereut
Liebe kam aus fernen Landen
Muß es eine Trennung geben
Ruhe, Süßliebchen, im Schatten
Sind es Schmerzen, sind es Freuden
So tönet denn, schäumende Wellen
So willst du des Armen dich gnädig erbarmen?
Traun! Bogen und Pfeil sind gut für den Feind
Treue Liebe dauert lange
War es dir, dem diese Lippen bebten
Wie froh und frisch mein Sinn sich hebt
Wie schnell verschwindet so Licht als Glanz
Wie soll ich die Freude
Wir müssen uns trennen, geliebtes Saitenspiel
Johann Ludwig Uhland
Es reit der Herr von Falkenstein
Horch! wie brauset der Sturm
Ich hör meinen Schatz
Im stillen Klostergarten
O brich nicht, Steg, du zitterst sehr
So soll ich dich nun meiden
Will ruhen unter den Bäumen hier
Johann Heinrich Voss
Der Holdseligen sonder Wank
Joseph Wenzig
Ach Mädchen, liebes Mädchen
Ach, mich hält der Gram gefangen
Ach mir fehlt, nicht ist da
Brausten alle Berge, sauste rings der Wald
Dunkel, wie dunkel in Wald und in Feld!
Ei, schmollte mein Vater nicht wach
O Felsen, lieber Felsen, was stürztest du
Wie viel schon der Boten flogen
Anonymous
Ich schell mein Horn ins Jammertal
Mir lächelt kein Frühling
O Fischer auf den Fluten, Fidelin!
Töne, lindernder Klang, du kannst nicht
Vergangen ist mir Glück und Heil
Wozu ist mein langes Haar mir dann
from Des Knaben Wunderhorn
Ach Mutter, liebe Mutter, ach gebt mir
Es wollt die Jungfrau früh aufstehn
Guten Abend, gut Nacht, mit Rosen bedacht
Ich weiß ein Mädlein hübsch und fein
In den Garten wollen wir gehen
Spazieren wollt ich reiten der Liebsten
Wer sehen will zween lebendige Brunnen
Volkslied
Ach Elselein, liebes Elselein mein
Ach, englische Schäferin, erhöre mein Bitt
Ach Gott, wie weh tut Scheiden
Ach könnt ich diesen Abend
Ach lieber Herre Jesu Christ
Ach, mein Henlein, bi bi bi!
All mein Gedanken, die ich hab, die sind bei dir
Alt Mann wollt reiten und hatte kein Pferd
Auf, auf, auf! Schätzelein
Auf, gebet uns das Pfingstei
Bei nächtlicher Weil, an ein's Waldes Born
Da unten im Tale läufts Wasser so trüb
Dem Himmel will ich klagen
Der Jäger in dem Walde sich suchet
Der Reiter spreitet seinen Mantel aus
Des Abends kann ich nicht schlafen gehn
Die Blümelein, sie schlafen schon längst
Die heilige Elisabeth an ihrem Hochzeitsfeste
Die Maid sie wollt 'nen Buhlen wert
Die Schwälble ziehet fort, ziehet fort
Die Sonne scheint nicht mehr
Die Wohllust in den Maien
Dort in den Weiden steht ein Haus
Du mein einzig Licht, die Lilj' und Ros
Erlaube mir, feins Mädchen, in den Garten
Es flog ein Täublein weiße vom Himmel herab
Es ging ein Maidlein zarte
Es ging sich unsre Fraue
Es glänzt der Mond nieder
Es ist ein Schnitter, der heißt Tod
Es pochet ein Knabe sachte
Es reit ein Herr und auch sein Knecht
Es reiten drei Reiter
Es ritt ein Ritter wohl durch das Ried
Es saß ein schneeweiß Vögelein
Es stehen drei Sterne am Himmel
Es steht ein Baum in Odenwald
Es steht ein Lind in jenem Tal
Es stunden drei Rosen auf einem Zweig
Es wären zwei Königskinder
Es war ein Markgraf überm Rhein
Es war eine schöne Jüdin
Es war eine stolze Jüdin
Es war einmal ein Zimmergesell

Es wohnet ein Fiedler zu Frankfurt am Main
Es wollt ein Mädchen brechen gehn
Es wollt ein Mädchen früh aufstehn
Es wollt gut Jäger jagen
Feins Liebchen, trau du nicht
Feinsliebchen, du sollst mir nicht barfuß gehn
Fürwahr, mein Liebchen, ich will nun frein
Gar lieblich hat sich gesellet
Gegrüßet, Maria, du Mutter der Gnaden
Gunhilde lebt gar still und fromm
Gut Nacht, gut Nacht, mein liebster Schatz
Guten Abend, guten Abend, mein tausiger
Guten Abend, mein Schatz, guten Abend
Hinter jenen dichten Wäldern weilst du
Ich fahr dahin, wenn es muß sein
Ich hab die Nacht geträumet
Ich hörte ein Sichlein rauschen
Ich schwing mein Horn ins Jammertal
Ich stand auf hohem Berge
Ich stund an einem Morgen
Ich weiß mir'n Maidlein hübsch und fein
Im tiefen Wald im Dornenhag
In der finstern Mitternacht
In Polen steht ein Haus
In stiller Nacht, zur ersten Wacht
Jungfräulein, soll ich mit euch gehn
Kein Feuer, kein Kohle
Komm Mainz, komm Bayrn, komm Österreich
Maria ging aus wandern
Marienwürmchen, setze dich auf meine Hand
Mei Mueter mag mi net, und kei Schatz han i
Mein Herzlein tut mir gar zu weh!
Mein Mädel hat einen Rosenmund
Mein Schatz, ich hab es erfahren
Mein Schatz ist auf die Wanderschaft hin
Mein Schatz ist nicht da, ist weit überm See
Mir ist ein schöns brauns Maidelein
Mit Lust tät ich ausreiten
Morgen muß ich fort von hier
Nachtigall, sag was für Grüß
Nur ein Gesicht auf Erden lebt
O Engel, mein Schutzengel mein
Qch Mod'r, ich well en Ding han
Sagt mir, o schönste Schäf'rin mein
Schlaf, Kindlein schlaf! Der Vater hüt't
Schöner Augen schöne Strahlen
Schönster Schatz, mein Engel
Schwesterlein, Schwesterlein
Sind wir geschieden, und ich muß leben
Sitzt a schöns Vögerl aufm Dannabaum
So hab ich doch die ganze Woche
So will ich frisch und fröhlich sein
So wünsch ich ihr ein gute Nacht
Soll sich der Mond nicht heller scheinen
Sternchen mit dem trüben Schein
Tritt auf, tritt auf, den Riegel von der Tür
Tröst die Bedrängten und hilf den Kranken
Ull Mann wull riden, wull hat he ken Pärd
Uns leuchtet heut der Freude Schein!
Vergangen ist mir Glück und Heil
Verstohlen geht der Mond auf
Von edler Art, auch rein und zart
Wach auf mein Herzensschöne
Wach auf, mein Hort, vernimm mein Wort
Wach auf, mein Kind, steh auf geschwind
Wach auf, meins Herzens Schöne,
Wach auf, wach auf, du junger Gesell
Wie komm ich denn zur Tür herein?
Wie schienen die Sternlein so hell, so hell
Wille, wille, will, der Mann ist kommen
Wir stehen hier zur Schlacht bereit, o Michael!
Wo gehst du hin, du Stolze?
Zu Straßburg auf der Schanz

Reiner Bredemeyer (1929-)

Wilhelm Müller

Am Brunnen vor dem Thore
Auf einen Totenacker hat mich mein Weg
Der du so lustig rauschtest, du heller
Der Reif hat einen weißen Schein
Der Wind spielt mit der Wetterfahne
Drei Sonnen sah ich am Himmel stehn
Drüben hinter'm Dorfe steht ein Leiermann
Ein Licht tanzt freundlich vor mir her
Eine Krähe war mit mir aus der Stadt gezogen
Es bellen die Hunde, es rasseln die Ketten
Es brennt mir unter beiden Sohlen
Fliegt der Schnee mir in's Gesicht
Fremd bin ich eingezogen
Gefrorne Tropfen fallen von meinen Wangen ab
Hier und da ist an den Bäumen
Ich such im Schnee vergebens
Ich träumte von bunten Blumen
In die tiefsten Felsengründe lockte mich
Manche Thrän' aus meinen Augen ist gefallen
Nun merk' ich erst, wie müd' ich bin
Von der Straße her ein Posthorn klingt
Was vermeid' ich denn die Wege
Wie eine trübe Wolke durch heitre Lüfte geht
Wie hat der Sturm zerrissen

Bernhard Theodor Breitkopf (1749-1820)
Johann Wolfgang von Goethe
Da flattert um die Quelle
Da sind sie nun! Da habt ihr sie!
Du hast uns oft im Traum gesehen
Einst gieng ich meinem Mädchen nach
Erst sitzt er eine Weile
Gern verlaß ich diese Hütte
Ich kenn', o Jüngling, deine Freude
Ich weiß es wohl, und spotte viel
Im Schlafgemach, entfernt vom Feste
Im spielenden Bache da lieg ich wie helle!
In des Pappillons Gestalt
In großen Städten lernen früh
O fände für mich ein Bräutigam sich!
Schönste Tugend einer Seele
Schwester von dem ersten Licht
Trink, o Jüngling, heilges Glücke
Umsonst, daß du ein Herz zu lenken
Weint, Mädgen! hier bey Amors Grabe, hier
Wenn einem Mädgen das uns liebt
Wer kömmt! wer kauft von meiner Waar!

(Edward) Benjamin Britten (1913-1976)
Friedrich Hölderlin
Da ich ein Knabe war, rettet' ein Gott mich oft
Die Linien des Lebens sind verschieden
Froh kehrt der Schiffer heim
Ist nicht heilig mein Herz
Mit gelben Birnen hänget
Warum huldigest du, heiliger Sokrates

Rudolf Brömel
Hermann Hesse
An dem Gedanken bin ich oft erwacht
Auf dem Tisch ein kleiner Strauß
Das Geld ist aus, die Flasche leer
Der Herbst streut weiße Nebel aus,
Die ihr meine Brüder seid, arme Menschen
Eine rote Sonne liegt in des Teiches
Es ist kein Tag so streng und heiß
Es schlug vom Turm die Mitternacht
Frühlinge und Sommer steigen grün
Gib uns deine milde Hand!
Gleichtönig, leis und klagend rinnt
Ich weiß: an irgend einem fernen Tag
Im Garten meiner Mutter steht
Im Kastanienbaum der Wind, der Wind
Jede Blüte will zur Frucht, jeder Morgen Abend
Nächtelang, die Stirn in heißer Hand
Nun der Tag mich müd' gemacht
Rote Nelke blüht im Garten
Seltsam schöne Hügelfluchten, dunkle Berge
Solang du nach dem Glücke jagst
Über den Himmel Wolken ziehn,
Voll Blüten steht der Pfirsichbaum
Weit aus allen dunklen Talen kommt
Wenn alle Nachbarn schlafen gangen
Wetterleuchten fiebert fern, der Jasmin
Wie sind die Tage schwer!

Ingeborg (Starck) Bronsart von Schellendorf (1840-1913)
Friedrich Bodenstedt
Die Gletscher leuchten im Mondenlicht
Die helle Sonne leuchtet auf's weite Meer
Gelb rollt mir zu Füssen der brausende Kur
Glücklich lebt, vor Noth geborgen
Ich fühle Deinen Odem mich überall umwehn
Im Garten klagt die Nachtigall
Mir träumte einst ein schöner Traum
Nachtigall, o Nachtigall! Sangeshelle
Nicht mit Engeln im blauen Himmelszelt
Sing, mit Sonnenaufgang singe, Nachtigall
Wenn der Frühling auf die Berge steigt
Wie lächeln die Augen der Liebe willkommen
Ernst von Wildenbruch
Hier von Frühlingsblumen bring' ich
Rosen und duftende Veilchen bring' ich
Stellt mir den Blumenstrauss in das Glas
Wenn du mich einstmals verlassen wirst
Wie ist der Abend stille, wie milde naht

Max Karl August Bruch (1838-1920)
H. Bone
Im tiefen Thale, bei heissem Mittag
Lausche, lausche! War's ein Säuseln
Über die Bäume möcht' ich mich schwingen
Emanuel Geibel
An den Ufern jenes Wassers sah ich Rosen
Goldne Brücken seien alle Lieder mir
Hast einsam mich verlassen in dieser Öde!
Johann Wolfgang von Goethe
Geh, gehorche meinen Winken!
Lasset Gelehrte sich zanken und streiten
Liebliches Kind, kannst du mir sagen
Paul Heyse
Ach, wie schön ist Carmosenella
Bald stösst vom Lande das Schiff geschwinde
Gott woll' dass ich daheime wär'
Mai, Mai, Mai! die wunderschöne Zeit
Wer weiss, woher das Brünnlein quillt
Wie mochte je mir wohler sein

Hermann Lingg
Blumen an den Wegen, Blumen um den Rain
Frau Venus, o lass mich gehn geschwinde
Leb' wohl, du guter Reiterdienst
Eduard Mörike
Gelassen stieg die Nacht an's Land
Joseph Viktor von Scheffel
Kampfmüd und sonnverbrannt
Lind duftig hält die Maiennacht
Sonne taucht in Meeresfluthen
Wohlauf ihr zieren Frauen, lasst euch
Karl Stieler
Es zieht das Schiff auf hohen Wogen
Im deutschen Land, daheim am Heerde
Esaias Tegnér
Herbst ist es nun! Nimmer die Stürme

(Joseph) Anton Bruckner (1824-1896)
Emanuel Geibel
Du feuchter Frühlingsabend wie hab' ich dich

Hugo Brückler (1845-1871)
Friedrich Hebbel
Die du über die Sterne weg
Alexander Kaufmann
Die Wasserlilie kichert leis
Hermann Lingg
Mein Herz, aus goldnen Jugendtagen
Julius Mosen
Der See ruht tief im blauen Traum
Wär' ich der Regen, ich wollte mich legen
Joseph Viktor von Scheffel
Heut' schwirren Schelmenlieder
Schweigsam treibt mein morscher Einbaum

Ignaz Brüll (1846-1907)
Heinrich Heine
Es schauen die Blumen alle
Ich wollt' meine Schmerzen ergössen
Jedweder Geselle sein Mädel am Arm
Manch' Bild vergess'ner Zeiten
Sie liebten sich beide, doch Keiner wollt' es
Wenn ich auf dem Lager liege, in Nachtt
Nikolaus Lenau
Blumen, Vögel, duftend, singend
Die dunklen Wolken hingen herab
Heinrich Leuthold
Deine süssen, süssen Schauer, o Waldesruh'
Mein Liebster keck ist mein Matros'
Eduard Mörike
Früh, wenn die Hähne kräh'n
Joseph Viktor von Scheffel
Schweigsam treibt mein morscher Einbaum

August Brunetti-Pisano (1870-1943)
Friedrich Hebbel
Dort bläht ein Schiff die Segel

(Friedrich) August Bungert (1845-1915)
Karl Beck
Rinne, rinne leise, meine Thräne du
Friedrich Bodenstedt
Wenn ich dich seh', so lieb und hold
Georg Friedrich Daumer
Ich sahe dich im Traume
Ferdinand Gregorovius
Wenn ich wüsste, du würdest mein eigen
Julius Grosse
So hat noch Niemand mit mir gethan
Hafis
Ich dachte dein in tiefer Nacht
Robert Hamerling
O sehne dich nicht an's graue Meer, im Walde
O wie so rein oft rieselt ein Wunderklang
Wandl' ich sinnend über den lauten Marktplatz
Friedrich Hebbel
Die du über die Sterne weg
Heinrich Heine
Der Tod, das ist die kühle Nacht
Lehn' deine Wang' an meine Wang
Nun ist es Zeit, dass ich mit Verstand
Warum sind denn die Rosen so blass?
Thomas Moore
Wenn durch die Piazetta die Abendluft weht
Wolfgang Müller von Königswinter
Die kolossale Flut dehnt sich hinaus
Friedrich Rückert
Ich habe dich mit Rosen so zugedeckt
Ich sende einen Gruss wie Duft der Rosen
Leopold Schefer
Ich habe mich neben die Welt gesetzt
Karl Siebel
Hätt' es nimmer gedacht, dass ein Strom
Theodor Storm
Das aber kann ich nicht ertragen
Über die Haide hallet mein Schritt
Johann Ludwig Uhland
Bei diesem kalten Wehen sind alle Strassen leer
Not Yet Identified
Gedenkst du des Abends, das Meer strahlt'
Gleich wie die Sonne hell, heiter auf der Flut
Wenn auf zu den Wolken ich schaue

(August Joseph) Norbert Burgmüller (1810-1836)
Johann Wolfgang von Goethe
An die Türen will ich schleichen

Wer nie sein Brot mit Tränen aß
Ludwig Andreas Gotter
Wie der Tag mir schleichet
Heinrich Heine
Du bist wie eine Blume
August Graf von Platen
Des Abendsterns ersehnter Schein
Ich schleich' umher betrübt und stumm
Johanna Schopenhauer
Wundes Herz, hör auf zu klagen
Heinrich Stieglitz
Hell glüh'n die Sterne im dunkeln Blau
Johann Ludwig Uhland
Bei diesem kalten Wehen sind alle Straßen leer
Bei einem Wirte wundermild
Was wecken aus dem Schlummer mich
Walther von der Vogelweide
Unter der Linden, an der Heide,
Anonymous
Das Schicksal will's ich darf nicht lieben
Schon milder scheint die Sonne nieder

Willy Burkhard (1900-1955)
Richard Dehmel
Der Abend graut; Herbstfeuer brennen
Immer stiller stehn die Bäume
Joseph von Eichendorff
Dein Bildnis wunderselig hab ich
Alfred Fankhauser
In meinem Herzen ruft ein groß Verlangen
Nun da der heiße Tag versank
Nikolaus Lenau
O Menschenherz, was ist dein Glück?
Wie sehr ich dein, soll ich dir sagen?
Carl Spitteler
Was ist's, das der Gedanken mutigen Tritt

Ferruccio Benvenuto Busoni (1866-1924)
Rudolph Baumbach
Bin ein fahrender Gesell, kenne keine Sorgen
Victor Blüthgen
Wer hat das erste Lied erdacht
Lord Byron
An Babylons Wassern wir weinten und dachten
Ich sah die Thräne groß und schwer
Ernst von Feuchtersleben
Es ist bestimmt in Gottes Rat
Theodor Fontane
Es zieht sich eine blut'ge Spur
Johann Wolfgang von Goethe
Bei dem Glanze der Abendröte
Es war eine Ratt' im Kellernest
Es war einmal ein König
Im Nebelgeriesel, im tiefen Schnee
Keinen Reimer wird man finden
Mitternachts weint und schluchzt ich
Otto von Kapff
Die Luft ist trübe, der Wind weht kalt
Neidhart von Reuenthal
Wohlauf! der kühle Winter ist vergangen
Johann Ludwig Uhland
Es stand in alten Zeiten ein Schloß so hoch
Walther von der Vogelweide
Unter der Linden an der Heide

Domenico Cimarosa (1749-1801)
Johann Wolfgang von Goethe
An dem schönsten Frühlingsmorgen

Franz (Aloys Theodor) Commer (1813-1887)
Heinrich Heine
Ich stand gelehnet an den Mast

(Carl August) Peter Cornelius (1824-1874)
August Becker
Wenn die Sonne sinkend hinterm Berg
the Bible
Zu den Bergen hebet sich ein Augenpaar
Gottfried August Bürger
Du, mein Heil, mein Leben, meine Seele!
Meine Liebe, lange wie die Taube
Wonnelohn getreuer Huldigungen
Adelbert von Chamisso
Da nachts wir uns küßten, o Mädchen
Peter Cornelius
Als du auf Erden, Herr, geweilt
An dem Seegestade düster
An hellen Tagen, Herz, welch' ein Schlagen
Das einst ein Kind auf Erden war
Das Knäblein nach acht Tagen
Das sind goldne Himmelspfade
Das war vor hundert Jahren
Das zarte Knäblein ward ein Mann
Dein Gedenken lebt in Liedern fort
Der du im Feld die Vöglein nährst
Der Glükkes Fühle mir verlieh'n
Des lauten Tages wirre Klänge schweigen
Die Blümlein auf der Heide
Die Hirten wachen nachts im Feld
Die Nacht vergeht nach süßer Ruh
Die Sterne tönen ewig hohe Weisen
Drei Kön'ge wandern aus Morgenland
Durch die Glut, durch die Öde
Ein grünes Spinnchen gaukelte
Es lebt ein Schwur in jeder deutschen Brust

Fahren wir froh im Nachen
Frisch auf in Windeseil
Halb Dämmerschein, halb Kerzenlicht
Heil und Freude ward mir verheißen
Heil'ge Liebe, flammend Herz
Hirten wachen im Feld
Ich sterbe den Tod des Verräters
Ich wandle einsam, mein Weg ist lang
Im tiefsten Herzen glüht mir eine Wunde
In Lust und Schmerzen, in Kampf und Ruh'
In meinem Herzen regte der Liebe Wunsch
Kehr' ich zum heimischen Rhein
Komm, wir wandeln zusammen im Mondschein
Liebendes Wort, dich send' ich fort
Mein Freund ist mein, und ich bin sein!
Mein Lied ist klein, braucht wenig Platz
Mir klingt ein Ton so wunderbar
Mit hellem Sang und Harfenspiel
Möcht' im Walde mit dir geh'n
Nachts bin vom Traum schlaftrunken
Nachts, wenn sich Sturmwind wild erhebt
Nun laß mich träumen, laß mich schwärmen
Nun lasse ganz der Seele Flug
Nun, Liebster, geh', nun scheide!
O Lust am Rheine, am heimischen Strande!
O Welt, ich sag' dir gern Ade
Öffne mir die goldne Pforte
Pilger auf Erden, so raste am Ziele
Segne, Herz, den Freudentag
Stromflut dahin rauscht durch Babels Gefilde
Süß tönt Gesanges Hauch, wenn alles ruht
Tief im Gemüt mir Liebe glüht
Und sängen die Vögel dir laut meine Lieb'
Vöglein fliegt dem Nestchen zu
Von stillem Ort, von kühler Statt
Warum verbirgst du vor mir dein Antlitz
Weh, daß ich mußte schauen
Wenn wir hinauszieh'n am Frühlingssonntag
Wer hat's doch durchschauet
Wie schön geschmückt der festliche Raum!
Zu dem Duft, der da würzt die Lenzesluft

Annette von Droste-Hülshoff
Wär' ich ein Kind, ein Knäblein klein
Wer bist du doch, o Mädchen?
Zum Ossa sprach der Pelion

Joseph von Eichendorff
Der Wandrer, von der Heimat weit
Und wenn es einst dunkelt
Vorüber ist der blut'ge Strauß
Wagen musst du und flüchtig erbeuten

Michael Franck
Ach, wie nichtig, ach, wie flüchtig

Johann Wolfgang von Goethe
Wie kommt's, daß du so traurig bist?

Friedrich Hebbel
Die Dämmerung war längst hereingebrochen
Friedlich bekämpfen Nacht sich und Tag
Hat sie's dir denn angetan im Vorüberschweben
Laß den Jüngling, der dich liebt
Millionen öder Jahre lag ich schon
Seele, vergiß sie nicht, Seele, vergiß nicht
Was treibt mich hier von hinnen?
Wenn ich, o Kindlein, vor dir stehe
Wir träumten voneinander

Heinrich Heine
Der Tod, das ist die kühle Nacht
Es war ein alter König
Warum sind denn die Rosen so blaß?
Was will die einsame Träne?

Paul Heyse
Im Lenz, im Lenz, wenn Veilchen blüh'n
In der Mondnacht, in der Frühlingsmondnacht
In Sternennacht, wenn's dämmert sacht
Köpfchen, Köpfchen, nicht gewimmert
So weich und warm hegt dich kein Arm
Und bist du jung an Jahren
Wenn die Hahnen frühe krähen
Wie trag ich doch in Sinne

Friedrich Hölderlin
Wo bist du? Trunken dämmert die Seele mir

Ludwig Hölty
Ihr Freunde, hänget, wenn ich gestorben bin

Hoffmann von Fallersleben
Die duftenden Gräser auf der Au

Thomas Hood
Mein Liebchen ist nicht Heliotrop

Emil Kuh
Das ist die schönste Stunde
Du kleine Biene, verfolg' mich nicht
Hirschlein ging im Wald spazieren
Mir ist, als zögen Arme mich schaurig

Martin Luther
Mitten wir im Leben sind

Thomas Moore
Nicht die Träne kann es sagen

Julius Mosen
In meinem Garten lachet manch Blümlein

August Graf von Platen
Am Felsenvorgebirge schroff
Lange begehrten wir ruhig allein zu sein

Friedrich Rückert
Jugend, Rausch und Liebe sind gleich
Mächtiger, der brausend die Wipfel du beugst
Johannes Scheffler
Ich will dich lieben, meine Krone!
Liebe, die du mich zum Bilde deiner Gottheit
Thron der Liebe, Stern der Güte!
Friedrich von Schiller
Von dem Dome schwer und bang
William Shakespeare
Komm herbei, komm herbei, Tod
Wernher von Tegernsee
Ich bin dein, du bist mein
Johann Ludwig Uhland
Es ging wohl über die Heide
So soll ich dich nun meiden
Anonymous
Herauf! Herauf! mit deiner purpur Glut'
Mei' Herzensallerliebster das ist en Bettelmann
O, kennt ihr nicht Emmchen, die Kleine?
Was trauern doch die Mägdelein?

César Cui (Tsezar Antonovich Kyui) (1835-1918)
Heinrich Heine
Ich hab im Traum geweinet, mir träumte
Mit deinen blauen Augen

(Karl) Friedrich Curschmann (1805-1841)
Adelbert von Chamisso
Willkommen, du Gottes Sonne
Joseph von Eichendorff
Ich wandle durch die stille Nacht
Übern Garten durch die Lüfte hört' ich
Vergangen ist der lichte Tag
Friedrich Förster
Die Wolken zieh'n vorüber, und Keiner hört
Du trauter Stern! Warum so fern?
Ich bin ein lust'ger Wandersmann
Ihr holden Augensterne, wie möcht ich
Nein, ich will's nicht länger leiden
Wach' auf, du gold'nes Morgenroth
Wie mir geschah, ich weiss es nicht
Johann Wolfgang von Goethe
Das Wasser rauscht, das Wasser schwoll
Der Strauß, den ich gepflükket, grüße dich
Meine Ruh' ist hin, mein Herz ist schwer
Heinrich Heine
Wenn ich in deine Augen seh'
Hoffmann von Fallersleben
Du siehst mich an und kennst mich nicht
Erscheine noch einmal, erscheine!
Ihr lichten Sterne habt gebracht
Schlaf, mein Kind, schlaf ein!
So schlaf in Ruh'! so schlaf in Ruh'!
Wilhelm Müller
Bächlein, lass dein Rauschen sein
Ich schnitt' es gern in alle Rinden ein
War es also gemeint, mein rauschender Freund
August Graf von Platen
Lass tief in dir mich lesen
Friedrich Rückert
Der Schiffer fährt zu Land
Du bist die Ruh', der Frieden mild
Hier bring' ich dir ein Blümchen
Hüttelein, still und klein, blinke sanft
Friedrich von Schiller
Es lächelt der See, er ladet zum Bade
Tosti
Öffne die Augen, Tancredi
Johann Ludwig Uhland
Die linden Lüfte sind erwacht
O brich nicht, Steg, du zitterst sehr!
Wilhelm Wackernagel
Schlaf, Kindchen, balde! Die Vögel fliegen
Anonymous
Blühe, liebes Veilchen, blühe noch
Der Tag erwacht im Strahlenkranze
Volkslied
Schätzelein, es kränket mich

Luigi Dallapiccola (1904-1975)
Johann Wolfgang von Goethe
Der Spiegel sagt mir ich bin schön!
Die Sonne kommt! Ein Prachterscheinen!
In tausend Formen magst du dich verstecken
Ist's möglich, dass ich, Liebchen, dich kose
Kaum dass ich dich wieder habe
Lass deinen süssen Rubinenmund
Möge Wasser, springend, wallend

Bertold Damcke (1812-1875)
Heinrich Heine
Wie des Mondes Abbild zittert

Leopold Damrosch (1832-1885)
Friedrich Bodenstedt
Nicht mit Engeln im blauen Himmelszelt
Seh' ich deine kleinen Händchen an
Wenn der Frühling auf die Berge steigt
Peter Cornelius
Wieder möcht' ich dir begegnen
Emanuel Geibel
Am Ufer des Flusses, am Manzanares
Bedeckt mich mit Blumen, ich sterbe vor Liebe
Dass die Luft mit leisem Wehen

Dereinst, dereinst, Gedanke mein
Geh', Geliebter, geh' jetzt!
Horch', im Winde säuseln sacht, Mutter
Nelken wind' ich und Jasmin
Unter den Bäumen ruht das Mädchen
Von dem Rosenbusch, o Mutter
Wann erscheint der Morgen, wann denn
Johann Wolfgang von Goethe
Füllest wieder Busch und Thal
Ich denke dein, wenn mir der Sonne Schimmer
Kennst du das Land, wo die Citronen blüh'n
Liebchen, kommen diese Lieder jemals wieder
O gieb, vom weichen Pfühle
Klaus Groth
Ich sass und träumte Lieder
Im Schnee von Blüthenflocken
Vom Dorfe ab am Raine
Heinrich Heine
Das Meer erstrahlt im Sonnenschein
Die blauen Frühlingsaugen
Die du bist so schön und rein
Die Wellen blinken und fliessen dahin
Es war ein alter König, sein Herz war schwer
Hör' ich das Liedchen klingen
Ich halte ihr die Augen zu
Ich hatte einst ein schönes Vaterland
Jedweder Geselle, sein Mädel am Arm
Mädchen mit dem rothen Mündchen
Wandl' ich in dem Wald des Abends
Wenn ich auf dem Lager liege
Paul Heyse
Wer da lebt in Liebesqual
Hoffmann von Fallersleben
Wie die jungen Blüthen leise träumen
E. Kern
Du holder Lenz, du Blüthenduft
Ignaz Julius Lasker
Als ich von deinem Grabe ging
Die süsse Rede hallet noch
Nikolaus Lenau
Ach wärst du mein, es wär' ein schönes Leben
Die Bäche rauschen der Frühlingssonne
Ich sah den Lenz einmal
O stürzt, ihr Wolkenbrüche, zum Abgrund
So oft sie kam, erschien mir die Gestalt
Weil' auf mir, du dunkles Auge
Wie die Ros' in deinem Haare, Mädchen
Mikhail Lermontov
Schlaf', mein Kindchen, ruhig liege
Hermann Lingg
Kalt und schneidend weht der Wind
"Novalis" (Friedrich von Hardenberg)
Wenn ich ihn nur habe, lass' ich alles gern
Robert Reinick
Ein Maler vor dem Zaune sass, aha!
Friedrich Rückert
Ich liebe dich, weil ich dich lieben muss
Sage nicht, ich sei dein Leben
Friedrich von Schiller
Es lächelt der See, er ladet zum Bade
Johann Ludwig Uhland
Jung Siegfried war ein stolzer Knab'
Will ruhen unter den Bäumen hier
Freiherr von Zedlitz
Lass, o lass mir deine Hand, zieh' sie nicht
Volkslied
Kommt die Nacht mit ihren Schatten
Sommer will aus heissem Herzen

Joseph A. Dasatièl (Dasatièl-Rinaldini)
Hermann Hesse
In dämmrigen Grüften träumte ich lang

Frederick Theodore Albert Delius (1862-1934)
Friedrich Nietzsche
Dorthin will ich; und ich traue mir fortan
Kein Pfad mehr! Abgrund rings und Totenstille!
Nicht mehr zurück? und nicht hinan?
Verhaßt ist mir das Folgen und das Führen

Paul Dessau (1894-1979)
Bertolt Brecht
Als ich nachher von dir ging
Die Häuser sollen nicht brennen
Die Liebste gab mir einen Zweig
Es war einmal ein Adler, der hatte viele Tadler
Es war einmal ein Elefant
Es war einmal ein Igel, der fiel in einen Tiegel
Es war einmal ein Kind
Es war einmal ein Mann
Es war einmal ein Pferd
Es war einmal ein Rabe
Es war einmal ein Schwein
Es war einmal eine Kellerassel
General, dein Tank ist ein starker Wagen
Herr Bäkker, das Brot ist verbakken
Ihr, die ihr überlebtet in gestorbenen Städten
Im Hofe steht ein Pflaumenbaum
Keiner plagt sich gerne, doch wir wissen
Mein Bruder war ein Flieger
Mein Sohn, ich hab dir die Stiefel
Sieben Rosen hat der Strauch
Singt noch ein Lied und denkt euch nur
Und es waren mächtge Zaren einst

Wenn du mich lustig machst, lustig machst
Wirklicher Fortschritt ist nicht

Joseph Dessauer (1798-1876)
Joseph von Eichendorff
Hörst du nicht die Bäume rauschen
Komm, Trost der Welt, du stille Nacht!

Oskar Dietrich (1888-?)
Nikolaus Lenau
Wenn Worte dir vom Rosenmunde wehen

Moriz von Dietrichstein (1775-1864)
Johann Wolfgang von Goethe
Da droben auf jenem Berge da steh' ich
Trocknet nicht, trocknet nicht!
August von Steigentesch
Ein wenig Raum auf grüner Flur

Hugo Distler (1908-1942)
Paul Brockhaus
Es klingt von den Sternen
Ob noch die alte Geige singt?
Vom fernen Klang der Uhren abgemessen
Eduard Mörike
Ach, wenn's nur der König auch wüßt'
Aninka tanzte vor uns im Grase
Auf ihrem Leibrößlein, so weiß wie der Schnee
Da droben auf dem Markte spazier' ich
Derweil ich schlafend lag
Des Schäfers sein Haus
Dort an der Kirchhofmauer, da sitz' ich
Du heilest den und tröstest jenen
Ein Tännlein grünet wo, wer weiß, im Walde
Entflohn sind wir der Stadt Gedränge
Es war ein König Milesint
Fragst du mich, woher die bange
Früh, wann die Hähne krähn
Frühling läßt sein blaues Band
Gelassen stieg die Nacht ans Land
Herr, schikke, was du willt
Ich hatt' ein Vöglein, ach wie fein!
Im Weinberg auf der Höhe ein Häuslein steht
In aller Früh, ach lang vor Tag
In dieser Winterfrühe wie ist mir doch zumut!
Jung Volker, das ist unser Räuberhauptmann
Kleine Gäste, kleines Haus
Laß, o Welt, o laß mich sein!
"Lebewohl" – Du fühlest nicht, was es heißt
Rosenzeit! Wie schnell vorbei
Sausewind, Brausewind! Dort und hier!
Sehet ihr am Fensterlein dort
Seid ihr beisammen all'? Ihr Freund'
So ist die Lieb'! So ist die Lieb'!
Tonleiterähnlich steiget dein Klaggesang
Uffem Kirchhof, am Chor blüeht
Und die mich trug im Mutterleib
Vierfach Kleeblatt! Selt'ner Fund!
Was im Netze? Schau einmal! Ach
Wasch dich, mein Schwesterchen, wasch dich
Wenn meine Mutter hexen könnt'
Wer die Musik sich erkiest
Wie heißt König Ringangs Töchterlein?
Wo gehst du hin, du schönes Kind?
Zierlich ist des Vogels Tritt im Schnee

Johannes Doebber (1866-1921)
Julius Grosse
So hat noch niemand mir gethan!
Not Yet Identified
Beim Spiele fiel den Kindern ein

Ernő (Ernst von) Dohnányi (1877-1960)
Wilhelm Conrad Gomoll
Du, silbernes Mondenlicht, schleich dich zu ihr!
Hört ihr's nicht klingen? Leis ganz leis?
Komm' zu mir, Lieb', komm' zur Nacht
Nach deinen Lippen sehnen die meinen
Um deine Liebe, zu allen Zeiten
Wie leis die Schwäne gleiten auf dunkler Flut
Victor Heindl
Ich will, ein junger Lenzhusar
König Baumbart, der alte Tann
O Wand'rer, geh' nicht nach dem Abendstein
So fügt sich Blüt'- an Blütezeit
Sonnenfädchen spinnt Nixlein im Wald
Vergessene Lieder, vergessene Lieb'
Was weinst du, meine Geige?

Felix (August Bernhard) Draeseke (1835-1913)
Eduard Mörike
Ein Tännlein grünet wo

Siegfried Drescher
Gustav Falke
Über die verhüllten Abendhügel
"Martin Greif" (Friedrich Hermann Frey)
Glokken klingen, Scharen dringen

Anton Franz Joseph Eberl (1765-1807)
Johann Wolfgang von Goethe
Das Wasser rauscht', das Wasser schwoll
Friedrich Wilhelm Gotter
Ach, was ist die Liebe für ein süßes Ding

Max (Traugott Maximillian) Eberwein (1775-1831)
Johann Wolfgang von Goethe
Hier sind wir versammelt zu löblichem Tun
Mich ergreift, ich weiss nicht wie

Karl Anton Florian Eckert (1820-1879)
Friedrich Förster
An eines Bächleins Rande, gar lieblich anzusehn
Johann Wolfgang von Goethe
Es war ein König in Thule

Gustav Eggers (1835-1861)
Eduard Mörike
Früh, wenn die Hähne krähn
Mit schwarzen Segeln segelt mein Schiff

Wilhelm Ehlers (1774-1845)
Johann Wolfgang von Goethe
Da droben auf jenem Berge da steh ich
Lasset heut im edlen Kreis meine Warnung

Gottfried von Einem (1918-)
Max Bolliger
Kehre zurück zur Arbeit
Walter Bollmann
Die Erde ist dunkler und satter in den Farben
Ein jeder leide, auf daß er glücklich werde
Leise schwindest du hinter Baum
Weit aus den Wäldern drängen die Tiere
Wolfgang Borchert
Die Apfelblüten tun sich langsam
Weil nun die Nacht kommt bleib' ich bei dir
Karola Boysen
Du, gib Ruh', ohne dich, ohne dich ertrage ich
Ein jeder leide, auf daß er glücklich werde
Weh im Herzen, tiefe Schwerzen der Liebe
Christine Busta
Bring mir keine Geschenke. Bring mir nur dich
Dasitzendir gegenüber am Tisch
Die Erde hat nicht Erde genug
Die Liebe nimmt an, nicht weg
Die Stachelfrucht hat sich geöffnet
Die Wege sind fremd und die Finsternis dicht
Du hast es mir vorgesagt
Du nicht mehr erhoffter Palmschatten
Einmal wichtig gewesen zu sein, für jemanden
Hänsel, komm in den Wald
Herzlaub, holder Honigmund summend
Ich darf dir nicht folgen, ich rufe nur heimlich
Ich kann die Sonne nicht Sonne nennen
Ich weiß: sie werden über uns lächeln
Lang schon umwanderst Du mich
Mondlos hat sich der Teich verdunkelt
Ruh' dich aus. Mir brauchst Du das Gras
Siehe, es scheidet der Tag, hingeht die Nacht
Wer mir jetzt noch die Hand reicht
Hans Carossa
Finsternisse fallen dichter auf Gebirg und Stadt
Und wie manche Nacht bin ich aufgewacht
Johann Wolfgang von Goethe
Des Maurers Wandeln, es gleicht dem Leben
Hermann Hesse
Bleich blickt die föhnige Nacht herein
Der Föhn schreit jede Nacht
Die mir noch gestern glühten
Es geht ein Wind von Westen,
Es liegt die Welt in Scherben
Flügelt ein kleiner blauer Falter vom Wind
Ich habe meine Kerze ausgelöscht
Seltsam, im Nebel zu wandern!
Felix Hubalek
Der Mond, der dort am Himmel steht
Peter Huchel
Von Nacht übergraut, von Frühe betaut
Wenn sie reiten zur Schwemme
Lotte Ingrisch
Aus weißen Bildern wachsen deine Flügel
Brennend rot und schwarz gefleckt
Der Stein zerfließt, der Wald ertrinkt
Die Arbeit ist getan. Der Nebel steigt
Die Zeit ist ein Lied, im Herzen entsprungen
Du gehst und kommst dir aus dem Sinn
Einmal noch will ich die Kirschenblüten
Frau Erde schläft, Frau Erde träumt
Großvater, Großvater Stein, alter Zauberer
Ich atme dich mit allen Sternen aus
Ich habe dich erlöst, ich habe deinen Namen
Ist das der Tod? Als wäre nichts geschehen
Mein ganzer Leib ist Traurigkeit
Mein Haus steht unter Birken,
Noch hundert Jahre? Nicht ein einz'ges mehr!
Schau dich im Spiegel der Teiche,
Schnee, du stille weiße Braut
Sie sagten, ich soll nicht erschrekken
Stumm wächst die Einsamkeit
Vorüber ist der Kampf, vorbei die Trauer
Was tut ein Baum den Ganzen Tag?
Friederike Mayröcker
Erträumter einsamer blauer Engel
Es sprießen immerfort die sanften Toten aus
Ich werde in Ostia sein
Mein federäugiger Liebling!

Agnes Miegel
Ich hörte heute morgen am Klippenhang
Johann Niklos
Durchs Schlüsselloch einkehrt
Friedrich Rasche
Der Spiegel rief den Mond herein
Hans Schumacher
Als wir noch die Drachen steigen liessen
Der Bahnhof steht im Nebel
Eines Tags, am Rand der Felder
Geh'n der Nacht die Sterne aus
Im Fensterausschnitt mir gegenüber der Baum
Erwin Thalhammer
Steige aus der Nacht hernieder, Liebste
Josef Weinheber
Erste Blume, aus Dunkel und Erde wie ich

Hanns Eisler (1898-1962)
Peter Altenberg
Und endlich stirbt die Sehnsucht doch
Anacreon
Der sei nicht mein Genoß
Dir auch wurde Sehnsucht nach der Heimat
Grau bereits sind meine Schläfen
Und um die Rippen zog er sich
Vom Dünnkuchen zum Morgenbrot
Johannes R. Becher
Am Fenster sitzend und schon im Genesen
Hans Bethge
Wenn ich erführe, daß das Alter mich besuchen
the Bible
Der Mensch, vom Weibe geboren
Bertolt Brecht
Aber auch ich auf dem letzten Boot
Als ich dich gebar, schrien deine Brüder
Als ich dich in meinem Leib trug
Am See, tief zwischen Tann und Silberpappel
An der weißgetünchten Wand
An einem frühen Morgen
An meiner Wand hängt ein japanisches
Auf der Flucht vor meinen Landsleuten
Auf die Erde voller kaltem Wind kamt ihr alle
Da ich die Bücher, nach der Grenze hetzend
Da war der Lehrer Huber, der war für den Krieg
Das ist nun alles und 's ist nicht genug
Daß er verrekke, ist mein letzter Wille
Der Herr ist aufs Feld gangen
Der Schnee beginnt zu treiben
Die Burschen, eh sie ihre Mädchen legen
Die Schlechten fürchten deine Klaue
Die Stadt ist nach den Engeln genannt
Die Vaterstadt, wie find ich sie doch?
Diese Stadt hat mich belehrt
Du Färberssohn vom Lech
Du kleiner Kasten, den ich flüchtend trug
Ein Ruder liegt auf dem Dach
Eine Pappel steht am Karlsplatz
Fischreiche Wässer, schönbäumige Wälder
Friede auf unserer Erde!
Herrlich, was im schönsten Feuer
Heute, Ostersonntag früh
Ich hab dich ausgetragen
Ich zog meine Fuhre trotz meiner Schwäche
Ihr, die ihr auftauchen werdet aus der Flut
Im Hofe steht ein Pflaumenbaum
In den finsteren Zeiten
In den Hügeln wird Gold gefunden
In den Weiden am Sund ruft
In die Städte kam ich zu der Zeit der Unordnung
In diesem Lande und in dieser Zeit
In Erwägung unser Schwäche
In Nürnberg machten sie ein Gesetz
Jeden Morgen, mein Brot zu verdienen
Mein junger Sohn fragt mich
Mein Sohn, was immer auch aus dir werde
Mutter Beimlein hat ein Holzbein
Oh, schattige Kühle! Einer dunklen Tanne
Oh Sprengen des Gartens
Schießgewehr schießt, und das Spießmesser
Schlage keinen Nagel in die Wand
Sieh den Nagel in der Wand
Singt noch einmal ein Lied und denkt euch nur
Über die vier Städte kreisen die Jagdflieger
Und es sind die finstern Zeiten
Und ich werde nicht mehr sehen das Land
Und sie kamen in ihren Hemden
Und weil der Mensch ein Mensch ist
Unter den grünen Pfefferbäumen
Vorwärts und nicht vergessen
Wenn sie nachts lag und dachte
Wir liegen allesamt im Kattegat
Wirklich, ich lebe in finsteren Zeiten
Matthias Claudius
Ach, es ist so dunkel in des Todes Kammer
So schlafe nun, du Kleine! Was weinest du?
Joseph von Eichendorff
Aus der Heimat hinter den Blitzen rot
Johann Wolfgang von Goethe
Arm am Beutel, krank am Herzen schleppt ich
Von Wolken streifenhaft befangen
Was ich dort gelebt, genossen
Heinrich Heine
Zuweilen dünkt es mich, als trübe

Friedrich Hölderlin
Der Nordost weht, der liebste unter den Winden
Froh kehrt der Schiffer heim
Lange lieb ich dich schon, möchte dich
O heilig Herz der Völker, o Vaterland!
O Hoffnung! Holde, gütig geschäftige!
Um meine Weisheit unbekümmert
Wie wenn die alten Wasser, in anderen Zorn
"Klabund" (Alfred Henschke)
Der Mond wird oft noch über den Syringen
Erhebt euch, Freunde, tanzt mit meinem Wort!
Ich habe nie vermeint, mich selber zu erkennen
Karl Kraus
Nun weiß ich doch, 's ist Frühling wieder
Giacomo Leopardi
Nichts gibt's, was würdig wäre
Eduard Mörike
Schlaf, süßer Schlaf, obwohl dem Tod
William Shakespeare
Und laß der Welt, die noch nicht weiß
Berthold Viertel
Die Leiter blieb noch unterm Feigenbaume
Wer traurig sein will, wird vielleicht mich lesen
Xenophanes
Die in Lybien denken die Götter
from Des Knaben Wunderhorn
Ich möcht vor tausend Taler nicht

Heimo Erbse (1924-)
Eduard Mörike
Es graut vom Morgenreif in Dämmerung
Gelassen stieg die Nacht ans Land
Im Nebel ruhet noch die Welt

Faber-Krause
Hermann Hesse
Auch zu mir kommst Du einmal
Bist allein im Leeren, glühst einsam, Herz
Es führen über die Erde Straßen und Wege viel
Sei nicht traurig, bald ist es Nacht
So mußt Du allen Dingen Bruder und Schwester
Über den Himmel Wolken ziehn

Pierre-Octave Ferroud (1900-1936)
Johann Wolfgang von Goethe
Ach, wer bringt die schönen Tage,
Die ihr Felsen und Bäume bewohnt
Wenn ich 'mal ungeduldig werde

Alexander Ernst Fesca (1820-1849)
Berndes
Fliege, Vögelein, fliege zu der Geliebten hin
Robert Burns
Mein Herz ist im Hochland
Heinrich Heine
Ich wollt', meine Schmerzen ergössen
Otto Prechtler
Ich sitze hier in dunkler Nacht
Robert Reinick
Morgens als Lerche möcht' ich begrüssen
H. Schütz
Das Mühlrad brauset, das Wasser zerstiebt
Wilhelm Viol
Es glänzt im Abendsonnengolde

Alexander von Fielitz (1860-1930)
Paul Heyse
Ach, wie so gerne bleib' ich euch ferne
Der Himmel hat keine Sterne so klar
Der Tag wird kühl, der Tag wird blass
Drunten auf der Gassen stand ich
Mir träumte von einem Myrthenbaum
Soll ich lieben, soll ich ihn lassen
Und bild' dir nur im Traum nichts ein
Und wie sie kam zur Hexe, Dornröschen hold
Karl Stieler
Das war ein Tag voll Maienwind
Eine stille Zelle an blauer Welle
Gehorchen ist das Erste!
Ich lieg' an meines Lagers End'
Mein Liebling ist ein Lindenbaum
Mit unsern Fischern war ein Kind gekommen
Nun ist wohl Sanges Ende!
O, der Alpen blanke Kette, wie sie glänzt
O Irmingard, wie schön bist du, holdseliger
Wohl manchen Rosenzweig brach ich

Christian Fink (1831-1911)
Joseph von Eichendorff
Abendlich schon rauscht der Wald

Gottfried Emil Fischer (1791-1841)
Friedrich Klopstock
Cidli, du weinest, und ich schlumm're sicher

Robert Fischhof (1856-1918)
Edith von Salburg-Falkenstein
Heiliges Rätsel, ewige Macht

Adolph Martin Foerster (1854-1927)
Eufemia Gräfin Ballestrem
Es singt der Schwan am Ufer des Nachts
Friedrich Bodenstedt
Und was die Sonne glüht, was Wind und Welle

Emmy Destinn
Es tönt in meinem Ohren
Joseph von Eichendorff
Ich kann wohl manchmal singen
Carl Felix
Die Sonne sank, die Möve zieht nicht mehr
Kühl in dem Schatten, geküsst von dem Thau
Ernst Foerster
Du bist betroffen, daß in deinen Händen
Johann Wolfgang von Goethe
Tage der Wonne kommt ihr so bald?
Tiefe Stille herrscht im Wasser
Heinrich Heine
Du bist wie eine Blume
Du schönes Fischermädchen, treibe den Kahn
Ein Fichtenbaum steht einsam im Norden
Hör' ich das Liedchen klingen
Im Rhein, im heiligen Strome
Im Walde wandl' ich und weine
So wandl' ich wieder den alten Weg
Wo ich bin, mich rings umdunkelt
Carl Hepp
Die Sterne sah ich am Himmel stehn
Ein Reif ist gefallen ganz über Nacht
Ich habe ein Röschen gefunden
Schönc Zciten, trübe Zeiten sind gekommen
Tautröpfchen blinkt am Blatt
Überm Strohhut flattern Bänder
Nikolaus Lenau
Du trüber Nebel, hüllest mir das Thal
Oskar von Redwitz
Es muß was Wunderbares sein
Robert Reinick
Durch den Wald, wie schimmert es sonnig
Im Schnee und Eis in kalter Nacht
Otto Roquette
Du kleines blitzendes Sternelein, nun sag' mir
Karl Schaefer
Kein Laut erschallt im öden Wald
Mädchen, sieh', der Lenz ist da!
Mädchen, was trauerst du? Lass dir was sagen
Müde labend naht der Abend
William Shakespeare
Was kriegt er, der den Hirsch erlegt?

Josef Bohuslav Foerster (1859-1951)
Gustav Falke
Du hast in meinem Herzen ein reines Feuer
Friedrich Hölderlin
Heilige Wesen! Gestört hab ich
Johann Rochlitz
Leiser, leiser, kleine Laute!
Friedrich Rückert
Verwelkte Blume, Menschenkind

Wolfgang Fortner (1907-1987)
Friedrich Hölderlin
Heilig Wesen! gestört hab ich
Ihr wandelt droben im Licht auf weichem Boden
Nur einen Sommer gönnt, ihr Gewaltigen!
William Shakespeare
Die Arme, am Lebensbaum seufzte sie

Clemens von Franckenstein (1875-1942)
Paul Verlaine
Weich küßt die Zweige der weiße Mond

Robert Franz (Knauth) (1815-1892)
J. Arndt
Wenn die Erde leise aufgewacht
Friedrich Bodenstedt
Die helle Sonne leuchtet auf's weite Meer
Es hat die Rose sich beklagt
Es ragt der alte Elborus so hoch
Wenn der Frühling auf die Berge steigt
Robert Burns
Der Sommer ist so schön
Die süsse Dirn' von Inverness
Du hast mich verlassen Jamie!
Durch irr' ich Länder noch so fern
Einen schlimmen Weg ging gestern ich
Früh mit der Lerche-Sang wandert ich weit
Ihr Hügel dort am schönen Doon
Mein Herz ist im Hochland
Mein Herz ist schwer, Gott sei es geklagt!
Mein Lieb ist eine rothe Ros'
Nun holt mir eine Kanne Wein
O säh' ich auf der Haide dort
So trieb sie mich denn grausam fort
Wär' auch mein Lager jener Moor
Was pocht mein Herz so sehr?
Adelbert von Chamisso
Denke, denke, mein Geliebter
Es geht bei gedämpfter Trommel Klang
Ich habe bevor der Morgen
Nicht der Thau und nicht der Regen
Was ist's, o Vater, was ich verbrach?
Joseph von Eichendorff
Abendlich schon rauscht der Wald
Am Himmelsgrund schiessen
Der Strom glitt einsam hin und rauschte
Die Höh'n und Wälder schon steigen
Die Nacht war kaum verblühet
Durch schwankende Wipfel schiesst
Ich seh' von des Schiffes Rande

Ich wandre durch die stille Nacht
Läuten kaum die Maienglocken
Möcht' wissen, was sie schlagen
Und wo noch kein Wandrer 'gangen
Wohin ich geh' und schaue, in Feld und Wald
Zur ew'gen Ruh' sie sangen die schöne Müllerin

Emanuel Geibel

Ave Maria! Meer und Himmel ruh'n
Der Mond kommt still gegangen
Die stille Lotusblume steigt aus dem blauen See
Es rauscht das rote Laub zu meinen Füssen
Gute Nacht, mein Herz, und schlumm're ein
In meinem Garten die Nelken
Nun die Schatten dunkeln, Stern an Stern
Nun wollen Berg' und Thale wieder blüh'n
Verglommen ist das Abendrot
Vöglein, wohin so schnell?
Wenn sich zwei Herzen scheiden
Wohl waren es Tage der Sonne
Wolle Keiner mich fragen

Johann Wolfgang von Goethe

Alles kündet dich an! Erscheinet
Cupido, loser, eigensinniger Knabe
Dem Schnee, dem Regen, dem Wind entgegen
Ein Blumenglöckchen vom Boden hervor
Trocknet nicht, trocknet nicht
Uf'm Bergli bin i g'sässe
Zwischen Weizen und Korn,

Rudolph von Gottschall

Da welkt am Fenster die letzte Rose
Marie, am Fenster sitzest du

Hafis

Weisst du noch, mein süsses Herz

Ida Gräfin von Hahn-Hahn

Es steht in der Bibel geschrieben
In den Abgrund lass mich schauen
In der Nacht da rauschen die Bäume so traurig

Heinrich Heine

Allnächtlich im Traume seh ich dich
Am fernen Horizonte, erscheint
Am leuchtenden Sommermorgen
An die blaue Himmelsdecke
An die bretterne Schiffswand
Aus den Himmelsaugen droben
Aus meinen grossen Schmerzen
Aus meiner Erinn'rung erblüh'n
Das gelbe Laub erzittert
Das ist des Frühlings traurige Lust!
Das ist ein Brausen und Heulen
Das Meer erstrahlt im Sonnenschein
Das Meer hat seine Perlen,
Deine weissen Lilienfinger
Der Schmetterling ist in die Rose verliebt
Die blauen Frühlingsaugen schau'n
Die du bist so schön und rein
Die Lotusblume ängstigt sich
Die Rose, die Lilie, die Taube, die Sonne
Die schlanke Wasserlilie schaut träumend
Die Wellen blinken und fliessen dahin
Du bist gestorben und weisst es nicht
Durch den Wald im Mondenscheine
Ein Fichtenbaum steht einsam
Ein Jeder hat zu diesem Feste
Ein schöner Stern geht auf in meiner Nacht
Eine starke schwarze Barke segelt trauervoll
Eingewiegt von Meereswellen
Es fällt ein Stern herunter
Es ragt in's Meer der Runenstein
Es träumte mir von einer weiten Haide
Es treibt fort von Ort zu Ort
Es treibt mich hin, es treibt mich her!
Es ziehn die brausenden Wellen
Gekommen ist der Maie
Güldne Sternlein schauen nieder
Hör' ich das Liedchen klingen
Ich hab' im Traume geweinet
Ich lieb' eine Blume, doch weiss ich nicht
Ich stand gelehnet an den Mast
Ich will meine Seele tauchen
Im Rhein, im heiligen Strome
Im wunderschönen Monat Mai
In dem Traum siehst du die stillen
Ja, du bist elend, und ich grolle nicht
Leise zieht durch mein Gemüth
Lieb' Liebchen, leg's Händchen auf's Herze
Mädchen mit dem roten Mündchen
Mein Liebchen, wir sassen beisammen
Mir träumte einst von wildem Liebesglüh'n
Mit schwarzen Segeln segelt mein Schiff
Morgens steh' ich auf und frage
Mutter zum Bienelein: "hüt dich...!"
Sag mir, wer einst die Uhren erfund
Sie floh vor mir wie'n Reh so scheu
Sie liebten sich beide, doch keiner wollt' es
Sterne mit den goldnen Füsschen
Und wüssten's die Blumen, die kleinen
Unter'm weissen Baume sitzend
Wandl' ich in dem Wald des Abends
Was will die einsame Thräne?
Wenn ich auf dem Lager liege
Wenn ich in deine Augen seh'
Wenn Zwei voneinander scheiden

Wie des Mondes Abbild zittert
Zuweilen dünkt es mich
Felicia Hemans
Mutter, o sing' mich zur Ruh'!
Hoffmann von Fallersleben
Grün ist das Eiland, weiss der Strand
Im Rosenbusch die Liebe schlief
Komm' zum Garten, zu dem wohlbekannten
Über die hellen funkelnden Wellen
Zum Frühling sprach ich: weile!
Zum Reigen herbei im fröhlichen Mai!
Johann Georg Jacobi
Wie Feld und Au' so blinkend im Thau!
Maria Jäger
Dass ich an Dich denke immerdar
O, Mond, o lösch' dein gold'nes Licht
Vorüber der Mai, die selige Zeit
Theodor Körner
Im Wald', im Wald' ist's frisch und grün
Lebret
Nun wird es wieder grün auf allen Wiesen
Nikolaus Lenau
An ihren bunten Liedern klettert
Auf dem Teich, dem regungslosen
Auf geheimem Waldespfade
Dic Bäumc blüh'n, die Vöglein singen
Die dunklen Wolken hingen herab so bang
Drüben geht die Sonne scheiden
Du trüber Nebel, hüllest mir das Thal
Durch den Wald, den dunkeln
Frühlingskinder im bunten Gedränge
Horch, wie still es wird im dunkeln Hain
Ich sah den Lenz einmal
Ich trat in einen heilig düstern Eichwald
Ich wand're fort in's ferne Land
Sonnenuntergang, schwarze Wolken zieh'n
Trübe wird's die Wolken jagen
Vor Kälte ist die Luft erstarrt
Weil' auf mir, du dunkles Auge
Wie sehr ich Dein, soll ich Dir sagen?
Zieh' nicht so schnell vorüber
Dr. Mayer
Die schönen Augen der Frühlingsnacht
Das Vöglein auf dem Baum schaut munter
Eduard Mörike
Bedächtig stieg die Nacht an's Land
Derweil ich schlafend lag
Ein Tännlein grünet wo, wer weiss, im Walde
Früh, wenn die Hähne kräh'n
Frühling lässt sein blaues Band
Herz! und weisst du selber denn zu sagen
Jung Volker ist der Räuberhauptmann
Lass', o Welt, o lass' mich sein!
Rosenzeit! wie schnell vorbei
Wolfgang Müller von Königswinter
Die Heide ist braun, einst blühte sie rot
Es streckt der Wald die Zweige so grün
O danke nicht für diese Lieder
Bernhard Natorp
In meinen Armen wieg' ich dich
Wilhelm Osterwald
Ach dass du kamst in Freuden einst gegangen
Ach! musstest du denn scheiden
Ach, wenn ich doch ein Immchen wär'
Ade denn, du stolze blitzaugige Magd
Als die Linden trieben, weckte süsse Hoffnung
Aus bangen Träumen der Winternacht
Aus der Ferne schallen Gesänge
Da der Sommer kommen ist
Da die Stunde kam, dass ich Abschied nahm
Den Strauss, den sie gewunden
Der junge Tag erwacht
Der Mond ist schlafen gangen
Der Schnee ist zergangen
Der Sommer ist zu Ende, ach Liebchen
Der Tag beginnt zu dunkeln
Des Waldes Sänger singen, die rothe Rose blüht
Des Waldes Wipfel rauschen unheimlich
Die Lüfte werden heller
Die Schwalbe zieht, der Sommer flieht
Die Sterne flimmern und prangen
Dornröschen schlägt zum erstenmal die Augen
Dort unter'm Lindenbaume
Du grüne Rast im Haine
Durch säuselnde Bäume im Mondenschein
Gestern hielt er mich im Arme
Gleich eines Herzens bangen Fieberträumen
Gleich wie der Mond so keusch und rein
Grolle lauter, zürnend Gewitter
Hör' ich ein Vöglein singen
Ich lobe mir die Vögelein
Im Grase lieg' ich manche Stunde
In dem Dornbusch blüht ein Röslein
Jetzt steh' ich auf der höchsten Höh'
Liebchen, was willst du? komm ich oft
Lieblich blühn die Bäume voller Schmelz
Mein Schatz ist auf der Wanderschaft so lange
Musst nicht allein im Freien
Nun da die Bäum' in Blüthen stehn
Nun grünt der Berg, nun grünt das Thal
Nun hat das Leid ein Ende
Nun hat mein Stecken gute Rast

O banger Traum, was flatterst du
Scheust dich noch immer, seliges Leben
Schöner Mai, bist über Nacht
Treibt der Sommer seinen Rosen
Um Mitternacht ruht die ganze Erde nun
Und die Rosen, die prangen
Und kommt der Frühling wieder her
Und welche Rose Blüthen treibt
Vor meinem Fenster regt die alte Linde
Will über Nacht wohl durch das Thal
"Betty Paoli" (Barbara Glück)
Im tiefsten Innern ein süss' Erinnern
Sándor Petöfi
Blätter läßt die Blume fallen
Selige Nacht! Ich bin nun bei der Liebsten hier
Robert Eduard Prutz
Wohl viele Tausend Vögelein
Christian Reinhold Köstlin
Ach, ich denke und versenke
Otto Röser
Ich sass am einsamen Weiher
In dem frischen grünen Walde streif' ich leicht
Otto Roquette
Das macht das dunkelgrüne Laub
Die Sonn' ist hin, wie Lust der Minn'
Du liebes Auge willst dich tauchen
Weisst du noch, wie ich am Fels
Willkommen, mein Wald, grünschattiges Haus!
Friedrich Rückert
Der Himmel hat eine Thräne geweint
Durch schöne Augen hab' ich
Er ist gekommen in Sturm und Regen
Hüttelein, still und klein
Ich hab' in Deinem Auge
Ich hab' in mich gesogen den Frühling treu
Leb' wohl und sehen wir uns wieder
J. Schröer
Blümlein im Garten, schaut euch doch um
Sel'ge Abende nieder steigen
Und nun ein End' dem Trauern
Heinrich Silesius
In meiner Brust eine Glocke klingt
Theodor Storm
Meine Mutter hat gewollt
Ludwig Tieck
Ruhe Süssliebchen, im Schatten der grünen,
Wilhelm Viol
Es glänzt im Abendsonnengolde
"Max Waldau" (Georg von Hauenschild)
Da sind die bleichen Geister wieder
Es klingt in der Luft uralter Sang
Ich habe mir Rosmarin gepflanzt
Ich wollte, ich konnte nicht träumen
Schemen erloschener Flammen fachern
Wenn drüben die Glocken klingen
Zwei welke Rosen träumen im Sande
Johann Welhaven
Lenznacht, so still und so kühl
Anonymous
Es fahren die Schiffer auf schlummernder Bahn
O lächle, Freund der Liebe, endlich wieder
Wo süss in Frieden ein Herze ruht
Volkslied
Ach Elslein, liebes Elselein mein
Ach Gott! wie fällt das Meiden
Ach, ihr Wälder, dunkle Wälder
Der Lenz ist angekommen!
Dich meiden nein, ach nein!
Es ist mir wie den kleinen Waldvögelein zu Mut
Es taget vor dem Walde
Habt ihr sie schon geseh'n, sie, meinen Schatz
Hatte Liebchen zwei dort im Dorf der Haide
Herzig's Schätzle du
Ich armer Mann was focht mich an
Ich weiss ja, warum ich so traurig bin
Könnt'st du meine Äugelein seh'n
Mei Mutter mag mi net
Mei Schätzerl, das hat mi verlassen
Mein Pferd das ist am Huf so schwer
Wie schienen die Sternlein so hell, so hell
Wie traurig sind wir Mädchen dran
Wozu, wozu mir sein sollte das Aug'
Zu Strassburg auf der Schanz

Franz Jacob Freystädtler (1761-1841)
Alois Blumauer
Immerdar mit leisem Weben schwebt
Teuthold, mein Trauter ist gangen von hier
von Cronegk
Herr! es gescheh' dein Wille
Gerhard Anton von Halem
Das Leben gleichet der Blume!
Joseph Maria von Koller
Der trotzige Mahomet stürzte mit Wut
Josef Franz von Ratschky
Schön sind die blumichten Matten

Karl Friberth (1736-1816)
Isakschar Falkensohn Behr
Holder Frühling, kehre wieder
Leopold Friedrich Günther von Goekingk
Meine Tränen sind geweint!

Gottlieb von Leon
Mond, sei Zeuge meiner Leiden!
Karl Wilhelm Ramler
Mädchen, seht den Zephyr streichen
Graf von Schlieben
Ich liebte nur Ismenen, Ismenen liebte mich
Johann Peter Uz
Weiß Chloe mein geheim Verlangen?
Friedrich Wilhelm Zachariä
Die Göttin süßer Freuden, die Nacht stieg
Anonymous
O Liebe, hast du uns zu kränken
Was säuselt hier wie banger Seufzer Stöhnen

Friedrich Theodor Fröhlich (1803-1836)
Friedrich Hölderlin
Ihr milden Lüfte, Boten Italiens!

Ilse Fromm-Michaels (1888-1986)
from Des Knaben Wunderhorn
Gleich wie die lieb Waldvögelein
Ich wollte mich zur lieben Maria vermieten
Mein Vöglein mit dem Ringlein rot
Nachtigall, ich hör dich singen
O du mein Gott, o du mein Gott

Johann Evangelist Fuss (János Fusz) (1777-1819)
Karl Müchler
Es muß das Herz an etwas hangen

Christian August Gabler (1770-1839)
Johann Wolfgang von Goethe
Wie herrlich leuchtet mir die Natur!

Josef Gänsbacher (1829-1911)
Gabriele Fürstin Wrede
Möcht' meine Seele senken ins Waldesgrün

Jan Karol Gall (1856-1912)
Heinrich Heine
Mädchen mit dem roten Mündchen
Volkslied
Es ist ein Schnitter, der heisst Tod

Harald Genzmer (1909-)
Hans Bethge
Wenn sich der Abend niedersenkt
Stefan George
Lilie der Auen! Herrin im Rosenhag!
Johann Wolfgang von Goethe
Der du von dem Himmel bist
Ha, ich bin der Herr der Welt!
Lasset Gelehrte sich zanken und streiten
Über allen Gipfeln ist Ruh'
Friedrich Hölderlin
Mit gelben Birnen hänget
Send' ihr Blumen und Frücht'
Lionel Johnson
Ein Wort in den Winden
Alice Meynell
Horch! Horch, in der wehenden Nacht
Gabriela Mistral
Die kleinen Hunde öffneten die Augen
Christian Morgenstern
Ein schwarzes Vöglein fliegt über die Welt
Rainer Maria Rilke
Ich möchte einer werden so wie die
William Shakespeare
Komm herbei, komm herbei Tod
Sara Teasdale
Ich frag hinauf in die Sterne
Lass es sein vergessen, wie eine Blume

Friedrich Gernsheim (1839-1916)
Johann Ludwig Uhland
O brich nicht, Steg, du zitterst sehr!

Mauro Giuseppe Sergio Pantaleo Giuliani (1781-1829)
Johann Wolfgang von Goethe
Zu lieblich ist's, ein Wort zu brechen
Friedrich von Matthisson
Wenn in des Abends letztem Scheine
Christian Ludwig Reissig
Höre Schicksal, was ich heische, höre mich
August von Steigentesch
Wir giengen beide Hand in Hand
Christoph August Tiedge
Alles ruht wie abgeschieden
Anonymous
Lebe wohl, o mütterliche Erde

Aleksandr Konstantinovich Glazunov (1865-1936)
Heinrich Heine
An deine schneeweiße Schulter
Vergiftet sind meine Lieder
Wenn ich in deine Augen seh

Mikhail Ivanovich Glinka (1804-1857)
Johann Wolfgang von Goethe
Meine Ruh' ist hin, mein Herz ist schwer
Friedrich von Schiller
Der Eichwald brauset, die Wolken ziehn
Johann Ludwig Uhland
Anzuschauen das Turnei, saßen hundert Frauen

Christoph Willibald von Gluck (1714-1787)
Friedrich Klopstock
Ich bin ein deutsches Mädchen
Nein, ich wiederstrebe nicht mehr
Schweigend sahe der May die bekränzte
Was that dir, Thor, dein Vaterland?
Wenn der Schimmer von dem Monde
Wie erscholl der Gang des lauten Heers
Willkommen, o silberner Mond

Friedrich Glück (1793-1840)
Joseph von Eichendorff
In einem kühlen Grunde da geht ein Mühlenrad

(Peter) Alexander Goehr (1932-)
Franz Kafka
Darauf kommt es an, wenn einem ein Schwert
Das Gesetz der Quadrille ist klar
Das Trauerjahr war vorüber
Der Neger, der von der Weltausstellung
Du Rabe, sagte ich, du alter Unglücksrabe
Noch spielen die Jagdhunde im Hof
So fest wie die Hand den Stein hält
Staunend sahen wir das grosse Pferd

Johann Valentin Görner (1702-1762)
Johann Wolfgang von Goethe
Erwache Friedericke, vertreib die Nacht

Walter von Goethe (1817-1885)
Johann Wolfgang von Goethe
O gieb vom weichen Pfühle, träumend

Hermann (Gustav) Goetz (1840-1876)
Johann Wolfgang von Goethe
Der du von dem Himmel bist
Hermann Kletke
Wandervöglein, leichtes Blut
L. Liber
Wenn der Duft quillt aus der Knospe Schoos
Eduard Mörike
Früh', wann die Hähne kräh'n
Richard Pohl
Ich flüsterte leis in den einsamen Bach
Christian Friedrich Scherenberg
Eine Blume weiss ich, hegt die Erd'
O Lieb', o Lieb', du Wonnemeer!
Theodor Storm
Schliesse mir die Augen beide
Albert Träger
Ist mir's zu Muthe schwül und bang
Noch liegt der Winter in der Stadt
Thut auch das bange Herz dir weh
Julius Wolff
Immer schaust du in die Ferne
Volkslied
Am Sonntag Morgen, zierlich angethan
Geh, zartes Blatt, geh, armes Briefchen, hin!
O Schwälblein, das da fliegt in weite Ferne
Und wenn ich werd' im Sarg gebettet liegen
Wie lange schon war immer mein Verlangen
Wüsst' ich gewiss, dass es mein Liebster hörte

Karl (Károly) Goldmark (1830-1915)
Robert Burns
Wollt' er nur fragen, wollt' er nur fragen?
Lord Byron
Beweint sie, die an Babels Strömen klagen!
Adelbert von Chamisso
Uns're Quelle kommt im Schatten
Jakob Julius David
Ich hab' kein Haus, ich hab' kein Nest
Emanuel Geibel
Der Wald wird dichter mit jedem Schritt
Schlage nicht die feuchten Augen
Klaus Groth
Ade, ade, der Sommer zieht, der Sommer zieht
Auf dem Kirchhof unter'm Lindenbaum
Die Ruhe zieht durch Haus und Stall
Er sagt' mir so viel und ich sagt' ihm kein Wort
Nun mach' mir nicht das Herz
Wir gingen zusammen zu Feld, mein Hans
Salomon Hermann von Mosenthal
Wenn zwei sich lieben von ganzem Herzen
Aleksandr Pushkin
O wenn es wahr ist, dass in der Nacht
Anonymous
Ach, wie thut mein Herze weh
Not Yet Identified
Das Herz will mir brechen, Therese
Himmelsmächte, die ihr schirmet
O willst mich nicht mitnehmen, klein Anna
Ström' leise, du Bächlein, am grünenden Hang

Adalbert von Goldschmidt (1848-1906)
Volkslied
Ach, ihr Wälder, dunkle Wälder

Hermann Theodor Otto Grädener (1844-1929)
Joseph von Eichendorff
Mürrisch sitzen sie und maulen auf den Bänken
August von Kotzebue
Komm' fein's Liebchen, komm an's Fenster
Julius Wolff
Im Dorfe blüht die Linde und duftet weit

Paul Graener (1872-1944)
Otto Julius Bierbaum
Aus dem Rosenstokke vom Grabe des Christ
Die heiligen drei Könige stehn vorm Haus
Richard Dehmel
Komm an mein Feuer, mein Weib
Hans Friedrich
Wenn ich müde bin einmal, führe, Mutter Erde
Ludwig Fulda
Dieser Tag verglüht nun auch
Eduard Grisebach
Auf einer Wiese sah ich holde Frauen
Otto Erich Hartleben
Im Zaune klagt die Nachtigall
B. P.
Der Heidebusch voll Knospen stand
Anna Ritter
Ich lauscht' dem Fink im grünen Haag
Ich weiß nicht, was mir gar so bang
Leise wie ein Hauch, zärtlich wie ein Lied
Not Yet Identified
Wann ich schon schwarz bin d' Schuld

Edvard Hagerup Grieg (1843-1907)
Friedrich Bodenstedt
Mir träumte einst ein schöner Traum
Adelbert von Chamisso
Die Mühle, die dreht ihre Flügel
Mein Aug ist trüb, mein Mund ist stumm
Sie haben mich geheißen
Wir wollten mit Kosen und Lieben
Emanuel Geibel
Dereinst, Gedanke mein, wirst ruhig sein
Johann Wolfgang von Goethe
Ihr verblühet, süsse Rosen, meine Liebe
Heinrich Heine
Das gelbe Laub erzittert
Ein Fichtenbaum steht einsam
Eingehüllt in graue Wolken
Es ragt ins Meer der Runenstein
Es war ein alter König
Ich stand in dunkeln Träumen
Leise zieht durch mein Gemüth
Johann Ludwig Uhland
An jedem Abend geh' ich aus
Kein beßre Lust in dieser Zeit
Walther von der Vogelweide
Unter den Linden, an der Haide

Charles Tomlinson Griffes (1884-1920)
Joseph von Eichendorff
Bleib' bei uns! wir haben den Tanzplan im Thal
Emanuel Geibel
Der Mond kommt still gegangen
Mein Herz ist wie die dunkle Nacht
So halt' ich endlich dich umfangen
Verglommen ist das Abendrot
Wie doch so still dir am Herzen
Wohl lag ich einst in Gram und Schmerz
Zwei Könige sassen auf Orkadal
Johann Wolfgang von Goethe
Tiefe Stille herrscht im Wasser
Heinrich Heine
Am Kreuzweg wird begraben
Auf ihrem Grab da steht eine Linde
Das ist ein Brausen und Heulen
Entflieh mit mir und sei mein Weib
Es fiel ein Reif in der Frühlingsnacht
Mit schwarzen Segeln segelt mein Schiff
Nacht liegt auf den fremden Wegen
Wo ich bin, mich rings umdunkelt
Nikolaus Lenau
Auf dem Teich, dem regungslosen
Auf geheimem Waldespfade schleich' ich gern
Ich wandre fort in's ferne Land
Julius Mosen
Der See ruht tief im blauen Traum
Könnt' ich mit dir dort oben gehn

Peter Grønland (1761-1825)
Johann Wolfgang von Goethe
Sah ein Knab' ein Röslein stehn

Cor (Cornelius Wilhelm) de Groot (1914-)
Johann Wolfgang von Goethe
Ach, wer bringt die schönen Tage
Der du von dem Himmel bist
Der Strauss den ich gepflücket
Feiger gedanken, bängliches Schwanken
Freudvoll und leidvoll, gedankenvoll seijn
Singet nicht in Trauertönen von der Einsamkeit
Über allen Gipfeln ist Ruh

Wilhelm Grosz (1894-1939)
Georg Trakl
Verflossen ist das Gold der Tage

Gustav Grube
Friedrich Nietzsche
An der Brükke stand jüngst ich in brauner Nacht

J. J. Grünwald (1780fl.)
Gottfried August Bürger
Herr Bachus ist ein braver Mann

Ludwig Hölty
Grabe, Spaden, grabe, alles, was ich habe
Johann Georg Jacobi
Sagt, wo sind die Veilchen hin
Johann Nepomuk von Kalchberg
Die ihr an süsser Lieder Schall
Karl von Lackner
Seid munter, ihr Mädchen, frohlokket ihr Brüder
Anonymous
Adieu, lieb Mädel, hab dich wohl
Es flog ein bunter Schmetterling

Ferdinand Gumbert (1818-1896)
Robert Eduard Prutz
Wohl viele Tausend Vögelein

Robert Gund (1865-1927)
Clemens Brentano
Hör', es klagt die Flöte wieder
Joseph von Eichendorff
Die Jäger ziehn in grünen Wald
Eingeschlafen auf der Lauer oben
Schlafe, Liebchen, weil's auf Erden nun
Hermann Hesse
Im Walde blüht der Seidelbast
Gottfried Keller
Nicht ein Flügelschlag ging durch die Welt
Justinus Kerner
Die Strassen, die ich gehe,
Hermann Lingg
Schwüle, schwüle Julinacht, Südwind küsst
Ferdinand von Saar
Über kahle, fahle Hügel streicht
Johannes Schlaf
Herbstsonnenschein! Der liebe Abend lacht
Ich kam zu einer Wiese im roten Abendschein
Carl Spitteler
Wenn die Mittagsfrau durch das Kornfeld
Theodor Storm
Es ist ein Flüstern in der Nacht
Johann Ludwig Uhland
Ein Schifflein ziehet leise den Strom
Anonymous
Rose du am Borne, rote Rose!
from Des Knaben Wunderhorn
Ich ess' nicht gerne Gerste, steh' auch nicht gern

Johann Christoph Hackel (1758-1814)
Gottlieb Fuchs
Hier wo ich Abendröte und Tag verlöschen sah
Heinrich Christian Leberecht Senf
Nacht und Still ist um mich her

Gustav Hasse (1834-1889)
Heinrich Heine
Dein Angesicht so lieb und schön

Josef Matthias Hauer (1883-1959)
Friedrich Hölderlin
Den Götterverächter schalten sie dich?
Froh kehrt der Schiffer heim
Heilig Wesen! gestört hab ich
Hochauf strebte mein Geist
Ihr wandelt droben im Licht auf weichem Boden
In jüngern Tagen war ich des Morgens froh
Meine geliebten Tale lächeln mich an
Nur einen Sommer gönnt, ihr Gewaltigen!
Schönes Leben! Du liegst krank
Vom Taue glänzt der Rasen
Vor seiner Hütte ruhig im Schatten
Was schläfst und träumst du, Jüngling!
Wo bist du? trunken dämmert die Seele mir

Moritz Hauptmann (1792-1868)
Johann Wolfgang von Goethe
Füllest wieder Busch und Tal
Kennst du das Land? wo die Zitronen blühn
Verfließet, vielgeliebte Lieder

Franz Joseph Haydn (1732-1809)
Anacreon
Natur gab Stieren Hörner
Gottfried August Bürger
Wüßt' ich, wüßt' ich, das Du mich
Johann Jakob Engel
Schon fesselt Lieb' und Ehre mich
Johann Joachim Eschenburg
Sollt' ich voller Sorg' und Pein
Christian Gellert
Der Jüngling hofft des Greises Ziel
Du bist's, dem Ruhm und Ehre gebühret
Herr! Herr! der du mir das Leben
Was ist mein Stand, mein Glück
Johann Wilhelm Ludwig Gleim
Das Leben ist ein Traum
Hin ist alle meine Kraft, alt und schwach bin ich
Ich bin vergnügt, will ich was mehr?
Johann Nikolaus Götz
O wunderbare Harmonie, was Er will
Sie hat das Auge, die Hand, den Mund
Friedrich Wilhelm Gotter
Auch die sprödeste der Schönen
Lorenz Leopold Haschka
Gott! erhalte Franz der Kaiser
Johann Gottfried Herder
Und hörst du, kleine Phylis nicht

Johann Georg Jacobi
Leiser nannt ich deinen Namen
Gottlieb von Leon
Solang, ach! schon solang erfüllt
Weißt Du mein kleines Mägdelein
Gotthold Ephraim Lessing
Faulheit, endlich muß ich Dir
Freunde, Wasser machet stumm
Karl Wilhelm Ramler
Inbrunst, Zärtlichkeit, Verstand
Ja, Vetter, ja! Ja, Vetter, ja: ich fall' euch bei
Stahl
Entfernt von Gram und Sorgen
Christian Weisse
Beschattet von blühenden Ästen
Philint stand jüngst vor Baucis Thür
Johann August Weppen
Ein Liedchen vom Lieben verlangst du von mir?
Christiane Mariane von Ziegler
Eilt ihr Schäfer aus den Gründen
Anonymous
Als einst mit Weibes Schönheit sich
Bald wehen uns des Frühlings Lüfte
Beim Schmerz der dieses Herz durchwühlet
Denkst du auch so innig meiner
Die ganze Welt will glücklich sein
Dir nah ich mich
Ein kleines Haus, von Nußgesträuch umgrenzt
Freund! ich bitte, hüte dich
Hier sein Grab bei diesen stillen Hügeln
Hör' auf mein armes Herz so bang zu schlagen
Ihr mißvergnügten Stunden
Jeder meint, der Gegenstand
Lachet nicht, Mädchen, wenn ihr gleich lachet
Lebe, liebe, trinke, lärme, kränze dich mit mir
Nimm dies kleine Angedenken
O fließ, ja wallend fließ in Zähren
O liebes Mädchen, höre mich
Trachten will ich nicht auf Erden

Hermann Heiss (1897-1966)
Friedrich Hölderlin
Heilig Wesen! gestört hab ich

Stephen (István) Heller (1813-1888)
Johann Wolfgang von Goethe
Ich denke dein, wenn mir der Sonne Schimmer
Heinrich Heine
Du schönes Fischermädchen, treibe den Kahn
In mein gar zu dunkles Leben
Verriet mein blasses Angesicht
Was will die einsame Träne?
Wie kannst du ruhig schlafen
Anonymous
Frühling ist kommen, lieblicher Lenz!

(Isador) Georg Henschel (1850-1934)
Robert Burns
Mein Lieb, das ist ein Röslein roth
Felix Dahn
Erschlagen war mit dem halben Heer
Georg Friedrich Daumer
Komm Mädchen an dein Fenster
Emanuel Geibel
Siehst du das Meer? Es glänzt auf seiner Fluth
Johann Wolfgang von Goethe
Uf 'm Bergli bin i g'sässe
Hafis
Freue dich, o Seelenvogel!
Wie Melodie aus reiner Sphäre hör' ich
Wo Engel hausen, da ist der Himmel
Robert Hamerling
An den Höhen, an den Wäldern
Lachen ist des Mundes Sache
Viel Vögel sind geflogen
Paul Heyse
Vor Tage weckte mich mein klopfend Herz
R. Lehmann
Viel schöne Blumen stehen
Mikhail Lermontov
Schlaf', mein Kindchen, ruhig liege, schlaf'
Gotthold Ephraim Lessing
Du Diebin mit der Rosenwange
G. H. von Oder
Und weil Du bist ein Röslein
Robert Reinick
Bald ist der Nacht ein End' gemacht
Morgens als Lerche möcht' ich begrüssen
Joseph Viktor von Scheffel
Am grünen See von Nemi ein alter Ahorn steht
Die Sommernacht hat mir's angethan
Nun schreit' ich aus dem Thore
Sonne taucht in Meeresfluthen
Karl Siebel
Die Seele träumt und redet leise
Wernher von Tegernsee
Du bist mein, ich bin dein
Johann Heinrich Voss
Der Holdseligen sonder Wank sing' ich
E. von Warburg
Beim Kerzenlicht in bunten Kreis
Du willst, ich soll ein Lied dir geben
Anonymous
Die Englein haben das Bettlein gemacht

Volkslied
Blaue Äugle, rothe Bäckle, und ä Grüble
Der Frühling und der Sonnenschein
Ich habe mein Feinsliebchen
Marienwürmchen setze dich auf meine Hand
Mei Schätzerl is hübsch, aber reich is es nit
Verstohlen geht der Mond auf
Vöglein im Tannenwald pfeifet so hell, tirili
Wenn du bei mei'm Schätzel kommst
Wenn ich ein Vöglein wär'
Not Yet Identified
Mein müdes Auge flieht der Schlaf

Fanny Cäcilie Mendelssohn-Bartholdy Hensel (1805-1847)
Clemens Brentano
Es sang vor langen Jahren
Johann Gustav Droysen
Fern und ferner schallt der Reigen
Joseph von Eichendorff
Abendlich schon rauscht der Wald
Ach! wie ist es doch gekommen
Der Wald wird falb, die Blätter fallen
Es rauschen die Wipfel und schauern
Hörst du nicht die Bäume rauschen
Ich kann wohl manchmal singen
Ich wandre durch die stille Nacht
In den Wipfeln frische Lüfte
Könnt ich zu den Wäldern flüchten
Läuten kaum die Mayenglocken
Nacht ist wie ein stilles Meer, Leid und Lust
O Lust vom Berg zu schauen weit über Wald
Übern Garten durch die Lüfte
Vöglein in den sonn'gen Tagen, Lüfte blau
Emanuel Geibel
Auf des Gartens Mauerzinne
Im Wald, im hellen Sonnenschein
Johann Wolfgang von Goethe
Alles kündet Dich an! Erscheinet
An des lust'gen Brunnens Rand
Auch in der Ferne dir so nah!
Augen, sagt mir, sagt, was sagt ihr?
Dämmrung senkte sich von oben
Der du von dem Himmel bist
Es ist ein Schnee gefallen
Herz mein Herz, was soll das geben
Ihr verblühet süße Rosen
Kennst Du das Land, wo die Zitronen blühen
Leichte Silberwolken schweben
Nur wer die Sehnsucht kennt
Über allen Gipfeln ist Ruh
Und frische Nahrung neues Blut saug ich
Von den Bergen zu den Hügeln
Was zieht mir das Herz so?
Wenn der Blüten Frühlingsregen
Wer sich der Einsamkeit ergibt, ach!
Wie kühl schweift sichs bei nächt'ger Stunde
Franz Grillparzer
Schöner und schöner schmückt sich der Plan
Heinrich Heine
Ach! die Augen sind es wieder
Aus meinen Tränen sprießen
Ein Fichtenbaum steht einsam im Norden
Es fällt ein Stern herunter
Im wunderschönen Monat Mai
Und wüssten's die Blumen, die kleinen
Warum sind denn die Rosen so blaß
Wenn ich in deine Augen sehe
Wilhelm Hensel
Es rauschen die Bäume, es wallen die Düfte
Schnell fliehen die Schatten der Nacht
Ludwig Hölty
Brächte dich meinem Arm
Dein Silber schien durch Eichengrün
Die Nachtigall singt überall auf grünen Reisen
Ihr in der Ferne seid mir so nah
Kein Blick der Hoffnung heitert
Sie wankt dahin, die Abendwinde spielen
Was schauest du so hell und klar
Wenn der silberne Mond, durch die Gesträuche
Friedrich Klopstock
Willkommen o silberner Mond
Nikolaus Lenau
Bin mit dir im Wald gegangen; ach!
Dein ist mein Herz, mein Schmerz dein eigen
Du klagst, daß bange Wehmut dich beschleicht
Friedlicher Abend senkt sich aufs Gefilde
Weil auf mir du dunkles Auge
Wilhelm Müller
Am Bach viel kleine Blumen stehn
Der Mai ist auf dem Wege
Guten Abend, lieber Mondenschein!
Ich frage keine Blume, ich frage keinen Stern
In Grün will ich mich kleiden
O Liebe, die am Kreuze rang, O Liebe
Sie stand im Boot und fischte
Friederike Robert
Was ist's, das mir den Athem hemmet
Friedrich Rückert
Du bist die Ruh, der Friede mild
Friedrich von Schiller
Der Eichwald brauset, die Wolken ziehn

Ludwig Tieck
O alte Heimat süß! wo find' ich wieder dich?
Johann Ludwig Uhland
Im stillen Klostergarten
Seid gegrüßt mit Frühlingswonne
Johann Heinrich Voss
An des Beetes Umbuschung brach sie Rosen
Umweht von Maiduft, unter des Blütenbaums
Marianne von Willemer
Ach! um deine feuchten Schwingen, West
Anonymous
O komm zu mir wenn durch die Nacht
Von allen Zweigen schwingen sich

Gottfried Herrmann (1808-1878)
R. Glaser
Des Lebens Schönheit mußt ich tief empfinden
Heinrich Heine
Du bist wie eine Blume
A. Krafft
Ich denke dein, ob auch getrennt in weiter Ferne

(Leopold) Heinrich Freiherr von Herzogenberg (1843-1900)
Nikolaus Lenau
Du trüber Nebel hüllest mir

Eugen Hildach (1849-1924)
Felix Dahn
Die Finken schlagen, der Lenz ist da
Emanuel Geibel
Es hat die Mutter mir gesagt
Klaus Groth
Der Weg an unser'm Zaun entlang
Paul Heyse
Auf dem Dorf in den Spinnstuben

Ferdinand Hiller (1811-1885)
Johann Wolfgang von Goethe
Über allen Gipfeln ist Ruh
Eduard Mörike
Rosenzeit! wie schnell vorbei

Johann Adam Hiller (1728-1804)
Matthias Claudius
Sie haben mich dazu beschieden
Christian Weisse
Ein Mädchen, das auf Ehre hielt, liebt' einst

Friedrich Heinrich Himmel (1765-1814)
Johann Wolfgang von Goethe
Füllest wieder Busch und Thal
Ich denke dein, wenn mir der Sonne Schimmer
Im Felde schleich ich still und wild

Paul Hindemith (1895-1963)
Curt Bock
Sieh, an letzten Himmels Saum
Hermann Claudius
Mund und Augen wissen ihre Pflicht
Matthias Claudius
Man weiß oft grade denn am meisten
Was meinst du, Kunz
Joseph von Eichendorff
Schweigt der Menschen laute Lust
Adolf Frey
I bi=n i d'Beeri gange dur d'Büsch
's alt Bäni, heißt's, seig gwüss e Häx
Was git's denn do? Was g'seh=n i do?
Guido Gezelle
Weh mir nun sachte, du seufzender Wind
Johann Wilhelm Ludwig Gleim
Phyllis, unter diesen Buchen
Reinhard Goering
Die wir dem Licht in Liebe dienen
Johann Wolfgang von Goethe
Es fing ein Knab' ein Vögelein
Ich denke dein, wenn mir der Sonne Schimmer
Sofie Hämmerli-Marti
Gärtner, chum cho d'Schlößli bschnyde!
Friedrich von Hagedorn
Als mich die Mama Hänschen küssen sah
Friedrich Hebbel
Als du frühmorgens gingst
Ich sah des Sommers letzte Rose blühn
Quellende, schwellende Nacht
R. J. Hodel
Nacht muß es sein, wenn ich sterben will
Friedrich Hölderlin
Das Angenehme dieser Welt hab ich genossen
In jüngern Tagen war ich des Morgens froh
Nur einen Sommer gönnt, ihr Gewaltigen
Von Taue glänzt der Rasen
Vor seiner Hütte ruhig im Schatten sitzt
Wo bist du? trunken dämmert die Seele mir
Gottfried Keller
Wie nun alles stirbt und endet
Jakob Kneip
Das weiß ich und hab ich erlebt
Else Lasker-Schüler
Bin so müde. Alle Nächte trag ich dich
Der Schlaf entführte mich in deine Gärten
Fänd' ich den Schatten eines süßen Herzens
Adolf Licht
Treibe, treibe, Schifflein

Martin Luther
Wer sich die Musik erkiest
August Mahlmann
Gute Nacht! Liebchen sieh
Hans von Matt
Voll Farben glüht der Garten
J. Wilhelm Meinhold
Wie das Gewürm aus unermeßnem Meer
Christian Morgenstern
Auf a folgt
Auf der Treppe sitzen meine Öhrchen
Erde, die uns dies gebracht
Von dir schein' ich aufgewacht
Wie Sankt Franciscus schweb' ich in der Luft
Friedrich Nietzsche
Nun da der Tag des Tages müde ward
Johannes Olorinus
Was haben doch die Gänse getan
A. Ott
Ich bin erwacht, ich bin erwacht
August Graf von Platen
Ein jedes Band
Josef Reinhart
Chumm über's Mätteli. chumm über e Hag!
Gygeli, Gygeli Brotisbei! Lüpfet 's Füessli
Mys Büebli isch erwachet
Rainer Maria Rilke
Derselbe große Engel
Diese, die noch eben atemlos flohen
Doch vor dem Apostel Thomas
Hättest du der Einfalt nicht
Jetzt wird mein Elend voll
Konnte sie denn anders, als auf ihn stolz sein
Nicht daß ein Engel eintrat
Noch erging sie's leicht im Anbeginne
O hast du dies gewollt
O Herr, gib jedem seinen eignen Tod
O was muß es die Engel gekostet haben
Seht auf, ihr Männer
Um zu begreifen, wie sie damals war
Und der Engel sprach und gab sich Müh
Was sie damals empfanden
Wer hat bedacht, daß bis zu ihrem Kommen
Friedrich Rückert
Das ganze, nicht das einzelne
Heinar Schilling
Durch die abendlichen Gärten
Ludwig Tieck
Aus Wolken fällt die frohe Stunde
Georg Trakl
Abends schweben blutige Linnen
In der Schmiede dröhnt der Hammer
Nächtens übern kahlen Anger
Oft am Brunnen
Schmächtig hingestreckt im Bette
Stille schafft sie in der Kammer
Unter verschnittenen Weiden
Franz Werfel
Niemals wieder will ich eines Menschen Antlitz
Walt Whitman
Der ich, in Zwischenräumen, in Äonen
O, nun heb du an, dort in deinem Moor
Schlagt! Schlagt! Trommeln! Blast, blast
Anonymous
Ei, daß ich doch Potz Velten
Hie kann nit sein ein böser Mut
Kind, wo bist du hin gewesen

Karl Höller (1907-1987)
Cäsar Flaischlen
Es ist mitunter, als wären alle Fäden
Ganz still zuweilen, wie im Traum
Ich möchte still am Wege stehn
Schlafe, müde Seele!

Adolf Hoffmann (fl.1887)
Nikolaus Lenau
Weil auf mir, du dunkles Auge

Franz Anton Hoffmeister (1754-1812)
Johann Timotheus Hermes
Ich seh durch Tränenbäche
Karoline Rudolphi
Willkommen süsse Kleine
Heinrich Christian Leberecht Senf
Nacht und Still ist um mich her
Anonymous
Nein, nun hab' ich's fest beschlossen
So fliehst du mich, du tugendhafte Seele

Leopold Hofmann (1738-1793)
Christiane Mariane von Ziegler
Eilt ihr Schäfer aus den Gründen
Anonymous
Schon deckt die Nacht, von starrem Frost

Alexis Holländer (1840-1924)
Joseph von Eichendorff
In einem kühlen Grunde
Johann Wolfgang von Goethe
Ich ging im Wald
Heinrich Heine
Du schönes Fischermädchen, treibe den Kahn

Robert Reinick
"Eia popeia," das ist ein altes Lied
In dem Himmel ruht die Erde, Mond und Sterne
Mein Liebster ist ein Jäger

Franz (Friedrich) von Holstein (1826-1878)
Karl Isidor Beck
Gott hilf, Gott hilf! im Wasser wächst das Schiff
Ich glaube, die Schwalbe träumte schon
Sie spielt mit Blumen im welken Strauss
Verbleibst ihm dennoch hold gewogen
Wenn Gott auch mir vergönnte
Heinrich Bulthaupt
Nun ist ein jeder Nerv in mir und jede Ader
Wie sich Nebelzüge drängend zu Wolken
Joseph von Eichendorff
Hier unter dieser Linde sass ich viel tausendmal
Zwischen Bergen, liebe Mutter
Robert Hamerling
Einst träumt' ich im Waldgrün
O sehne dich nicht an's graue Meer, im Walde
O selig, wem in stiller Nacht erscheint
Zwitschert nicht vor meinem Fenster
Heinrich Heine
Ein schöner Stern geht auf in meiner Nacht
Sterne mit den goldnen Füßchen
H. Hertz
Mein Vater war ein Gärtner
Paul Heyse
Über'm dunklen Walde steigt der Mond empor
F. Hirsch
Verblichen ist der grüne Wald
Hoffmann von Fallersleben
Draussen blinket in silbernem Schein
Franz von Holstein
Liegt die Frühlingssonne so goldenhell
Eduard Mörike
Fragst du mich woher die bange
Friedrich Müller von der Werre
Im Palmenhain weht Frieden
Joseph Viktor von Scheffel
Im heil'gen Land, im Wüstensand
Hugo Staacke
[see note under Karl Beck in Poet Index]
Theodor Storm
Das macht, es hat die Nachtigall
Ich hielt mein Herz verschlossen
Algernon Charles Swinburne
Die Wellen tragen vom Lande fort mein Schiff
Johann Nepomuk Vogl
Ade du lieber Tannenwald, Ade, Ade!
Das Vöglein hat ein schönes Loos
Der Sturm ist los, der Sturm ist los
Fort, nur fort durch Busch und Zweige
Im Freien, ach im Freien, wie ist's nun grün
Lass mich ganz in dich versinken, Wald
Lustig, lustig, wer zum Wald seine Schritte
Morgen wieder, morgen wieder, lieber Wald
Nähret Unmuth deine Seele, fliehe nur
Vöglein ohne Ruh und Rast
Waldesnacht, Waldesnacht, schliesse mich ein
Welch neues frohes Leben erwacht
Anonymous
Weisse Lilie, meine Lilie, einsam traurig
Volkslied
Ich hört ein Sichlein rauschen

Johann Holzer (1779fl.)
Sophie Albrecht
Die ersten Blümchen, die ich fand, Geliebter!
Alois Blumauer
Theuthold, mein Trauter, ist gangen von hier
Zwei Augen sinds, aus deren Blikken
Christian Heinrich Boie
Grabet in die junge Rinde, Schäfer
Gottfried August Bürger
Mädel, schau mir ins Gesicht!
Johann Wilhelm Ludwig Gleim
Ich möchte wohl der Kaiser sein!
Johann Georg Jacobi
Holdes Mädchen! unser Leben
Adolf Julius Laur
Ade nun, liebes junges Weib!
Gottlieb von Leon
So lang, ach! schon so lang erfüllt
Weisst du, mein kleines Mägdelein
Josef Franz von Ratschky
Die Schwermut senkt mit bräunlichem Gefieder
Klamer Eberhard Karl Schmidt
Das Glück ist rund, zur guten Stunde
Anonymous
Da schlend'r ich so die Welt hinan
Wo seid ihr hin, ihr stillen frohen Tage?

Bernhard Hopffer (1840-1877)
Joseph von Eichendorff
Hörst du nicht die Bäume rauschen

Anselm Hüttenbrenner (1794-1868)
Johann Wolfgang von Goethe
Wer reitet so spät durch Nacht und Wind?

Johann Nepomuk Hummel (1778-1837)
Johann Wolfgang von Goethe
Laßt fahren hin das Allzuflüchtige

Engelbert Humperdinck (1854-1921)
Georg Christian Dieffenbach
Frau Schwalbe ist 'ne Schwätzerin
Elisabeth Ebeling
Es schaukeln die Winde das Nest in der Linde
Hedwig Humperdinck
Ein Sternlein funkelt am Himmelszelt
Hella Karstein
Nun zieht mit seinem goldnen Schein
"Ernst Rosmer" (Elsa Bernstein)
Roter Ringelrosenbusch hat mein Hemd
Adelheid Wette
Das Vöglein singt am Waldessaum: Wiwit!
Im Grünen, im Walde, da ist es so schön
Leise weht's durch alle Lande
Lerchelein, lieb und klein, tirelierst so süß
from Des Knaben Wunderhorn
Es wollt' ein' Jungfrau früh aufstehen

Edgar Istel (1880-1948)
Prinzessin Margarethe von Oesterreich
Mein Herzlein hat allzeit Verlangen nach Dir

Charles Edward Ives (1874-1954)
Hermann Allmers
Ich ruhe still im hohen, grünen Gras
Wilhelmine Chézy
Der Vollmond strahlt auf Bergeshöh'n
Peter Cornelius
Mir klingt ein Ton so wunderbar in Herz
Johann Wolfgang von Goethe
Über allen Gipfeln ist Ruh!
Rudolph von Gottschall
Marie, am Fenster sitzest du
Klaus Groth
Wie Melodien zieht es mir leise durch den Sinn
Heinrich Heine
Die blauen Frühlingsaugen schau'n
Du bist wie eine Blume
Ich grolle nicht, und wenn das Herz auch bricht
Leise zieht durch mein Gemüth
Ludwig Hölty
Holder klingt der Vogelsang
Nikolaus Lenau
Weil auf mir, du dunkles Auge
Wolfgang Müller von Königswinter
O danke nicht für diese Lieder
Karl Stieler
Wohl manchen Rosenzweig brach ich
from Des Knaben Wunderhorn
Guten Abend, gute Nacht, mit Rosen bedacht

Emilian Gottfried von Jacquin (1767-1792)
Gottfried August Bürger
Mädel, schau mir ins Gesicht

Philipp Jarnach (1892-1982)
Friedrich Hölderlin
Ewig trägt im Mutterschoße, süße Königin

Adolf Jensen (1837-1879)
Karl Beck
Ich glaubte, die Schwalbe träumte schon
Robert Burns
Die finstre Nacht bricht schnell herein
Die süsse Dirn von Inverness wird nun
Einen schlimmen Weg ging gestern ich
John Anderson, mein Lieb, John
Mein Herz ist im Hochland
Mein Herz ist schwer, Gott sei's geklagt!
O, säh ich auf der Haide dort
Adelbert von Chamisso
Denke, denke, mein Geliebter
Ich hab' ihn im Schlafe zu sehen gemeint
Ich habe, bevor der Morgen im Osten
Nicht der Thau und nicht der Regen dringen
Was ist's, o Vater, was ich verbrach?
Wie so bleich ich geworden bin?
Joseph von Eichendorff
Am Himmelsgrund da schießen so lustig
Es ist schon spät, es wird schon kalt
Über'm Garten, durch die Lüfte
Emanuel Geibel
Am Ufer des Flusses, des Manzanares
Dereinst, dereinst Gedanke mein
Du feuchter Frühlingsabend
Klinge, klinge mein Pandero
Nun die Schatten dunkeln, Stern an Stern
Nun rauscht im Morgenwinde sacht
O schneller, mein Ross, mit Hast, mit Hast!
Und schläfst du, mein Mädchen
Johann Wolfgang von Goethe
Uf'm Bergli bin i g'sässe
Rudolph von Gottschall
Marie, am Fenster sitzest du
Julius Grosse
Die Nächte stürmen, doch die Seele singt
Hafis
Als einst von deiner Schöne
Ich bin ein armes Lämpchen nur
Ich will bis in die Sterne die Fahne der Liebe
Lockenstricke sollst du wissen
Wehe mir, mein Rosenkränzlein, weh
Wehre nicht, o Lieb, wühlen in den Locken

Zu der Rose, zu dem Weine komm!

Johann Ludwig Heiberg

Süsse Nacht! Wie schweiget rings die Luft

Heinrich Heine

Lehn' deine Wang' an meine Wang'

Felicia Hemans

Mutter, o sing mich zur Ruh!

Wilhelm Hertz

Auf des Berges höchstem Scheitel steh' ich

Mein Schatz will Hochzeit halten

Paul Heyse

Ach, ihr lieben Äugelein

Ach, was bin ich aufgewacht?

Als wir beiden mussten scheiden

Auf die Nacht in den Spinnstuben

Dein Herzlein mild, du schönes Bild

Drunten auf der Gassen stand ich

Einst warst du meiner Seele Hoffnungstern

Hab Erbarmen, hab Erbarmen!

Holde, schattenreiche Bäume, neiget

In dem Schatten meiner Locken

Lass uns leise bekennen, dass wir uns kennen

Mühlen still die Flügel drehn

Murmelndes Lüftchen, Blüthenwind

Mutter, ich hab' zwei Äugelein

Nun stehn die Rosen in Blüthe

Ob auch finstere Blicke glitten

Sie blasen zum Abmarsch, lieb Mütterlein

Über die Welt kommt Stille

Unter den Zweigen in tiefer Nacht

Waldesnacht, du wunderkühle

Wenn du zu den Blumen gehst

Gustav Kühne

Was nennst du deine Liebe schwer und gross

Karl Lemcke

Auf den Bergen, den Bergen hab' ich gejauchzt

Chr. F. K. Molbech

Was faßt dich an, o Tochter mein

Thomas Moore

Die Bowle fort! und schäume sie noch

Leis, rudern hier, mein Gondolier!

Wenn durch die Piazzetta

Aleksandr Pushkin

Nächtlicher Duft weht durch die Luft

O sing, du Schöne, sing mir nicht...

Otto Roquette

Bei den Bienenkörben im Garten

Das beste Bier im ganzen Nest

Er kam in der Frühe wie der Morgenwind

Noch ist die blühende goldene Zeit

O lass dich halten, gold'ne Stunde

So viel Laub an der Linden ist

Weißt du noch, wie ich am Felsen

Friedrich Rückert

Da ich dich einmal gefunden

Joseph Viktor von Scheffel

Alt Heidelberg, du feine, du Stadt an Ehrenreich

Berggipfel erglühen, Waldwipfel erblühen

Der Pfarrer von Assmannshausen sprach

Im schwarzen Wallfisch zu Ascalon

Sir Walter Scott

Schlaf, Söhnchen! Dein Vater war eisenumhüllt

Sprich, Fräulein, warum härmst du dich?

Alfred Tennyson

Süss und sacht, sachte weh', Wind du

Albert Träger

An deinem Finger, dem weissen, schlanken

Wie Lenzeshauch hast Du mich stets erquickt

Johann Ludwig Uhland

Ich hör meinen Schatz

Titus Ullrich

Wir gingen einsam durch die Gartenflur

Robert Urban

Des Dorfes heimische Stille tat

Werner (Erich) Josten (1885-1963)

Emanuel Geibel

Der Mond kommt still gegangen

Es ist das Glück ein flüchtig Ding

Ich weiß nicht, wie's geschieht

Johann Wolfgang von Goethe

Ich ging im Walde so für mich hin

Friedrich Hebbel

Quellende, schwellende Nacht

Viktor Junk (1875-1948)

Rudolf Hans Bartsch

Seliges Blümelein, kann Dir so nahe sein!

Erna Heinemann

Säulen, Säulen, immer neue Gänge

Rainer Maria Rilke

Du, der ich's nicht sage, wenn ich bei Nacht

Richard Kahn

Johanna Ambrosius

Mit ausgespannten Armen kommt leis'

Johann Wolfgang von Goethe

An dem reinsten Frühlingsmorgen

Friedrich Hebbel

Wenn die Rosen ewig blühten

Robert Kahn (1865-1951)

Hermann Allmers

Hörst du, wie die Stürme sausen

Gerhart Hauptmann
Purpurschimmer tränket die Rebenhügel
's ist ein so stiller heil'ger Tag
Wie eine Windesharfe sei deine Seele
Paul Heyse
Der Himmel hat keine Sterne so klar
Johann Georg Jacobi
Wie Feld und Au so blinkend im Thau!
Heinrich Leuthold
Leise, windverwehte Lieder, mögt ihr fallen
Mein Liebster keck ist ein Matros'
Hermann Lingg
Düster brennt und trüb' die Flamme
Eduard Mörike
Auf ihrem Leibrösslein, so weiss
Zierlich ist des Vogels Tritt im Schnee
Christian Morgenstern
Leise Lieder sing' ich dir bei Nacht
Julius Mosen
Der See ruht tief im blauen Traum
Friedrich Rückert
Ein Obdach gegen Sturm und Regen
Adolf Friedrich von Schack
Mach auf, mach auf, doch leise mein Kind
Johann Ludwig Uhland
Was wecken aus dem Schlummer mich

Johannes Wenzeslaus Kalliwoda (Jan Křtitel Václav Kalivoda) (1801-1866)
Emanuel Geibel
Nun die Schatten dunkeln, Stern an Stern
Johann Wolfgang von Goethe
Du Bächlein silberhell und klar,
Hoffmann von Fallersleben
Es blüht ein schönes Blümchen
Hermann Kletke
Siehst du am Abend die Wolken ziehn
Friedrich von Matthisson
Durch Fichten am Hügel, durch Erlen am Bach
L. Scharrer
Zersplittert lag des Schiffes Mast
Adelheid von Stolterfoth
Der Sänger ruht auf schroffem Stein
Hat ein Schiffer, grau und alt
from Des Knaben Wunderhorn
Es blies ein Jäger wohl in sein Horn
Not Yet Identified
Aus schwellenden Blütenkelchen
Das liebe Ränzel ist gespickt
Einsam! einsam! ja, das bin ich wohl
Frühlingsahnen Frühlingswehen gleicht
Herab von den Bergen zum Tale
Ich baute dir den stillen Schrein
Im Haine schlagen lustig die muntern Vögelein
O Hirtenknab', o Hirtenknab'! du singst
Sag' an, o Alter! Wem gräbst du dies Grab?
Siehst du hinab in die dunkle See
Weit, weit sind die Sterne, hin führet kein Steg
Weithin durch der Nächte Stille

Sigfrid Karg-Elert (1877-1933)
Gotthold Ephraim Lessing
Der Neid, o Kind, zählt unsre Küsse
Du, dem kein Epigramm gefällt
Frau X besucht sehr oft den jungen Doctor
Gestern liebt' ich, heute leid' ich
Ich habe nicht stets Lust zu lesen
Kleine Schöne, küsse mich, kleine Schöne
Mein Esel sicherlich muss klüger sein als ich!
So bringst du mich um meine Liebe
Wenn du von allem dem, was diese Blätter füllt
Wenn ich, Augenlust zu finden

Hugo Kaun (1863-1932)
Martin Boelitz
Holde Nacht wie still bist du, wie still!
Carl Busse
Entfalte des Kelches Pracht, hörst du
Mit den Gänsen, weissen Gänsen, zog ich
Nun hoch den Kopf und den Thränenfluss
Martin Drescher
Taufrisch glänzen die Blumen
Vor meinem Fenster klingt ein deutsches Lied
Gustav Falke
Der Mond scheint auf mein Lager
Hat der junge Geigenmacher
Jahrelang sehnten wir uns einen Garten
Trug mein Herz ich auf der Hand
Wo die Wälder Wache halten
Theodor Fontane
Das Kind ist krank zum Sterben
Emanuel Geibel
Es fliegt manch Vöglein in das Nest
Wilhelm Conrad Gomoll
Am murmelnden Bach, unter schattigen
Helles Klingen in den Lüften mischt sich
Hört ihrs nicht klingen? Leis ganz leis?
Gustav Kastropp
Der Nebel auf dem Weiher spinnt langsam
Gottfried Keller
Schon hat die Nacht den Silberschrein
Karl Ernst Knodt
Nacht auf Nacht steh ich am Meere

Thekla Lingen
Zur Ruhe, mein Herz zur Ruh
Christian Morgenstern
Leise Lieder sing' ich dir bei Nacht
Karl Müller-Rastatt
Rote Flammen so glüht der Mohn
Ludwig Pfau
O Blätter, dürre Blätter! Wie trauert ihr so sehr!
Anna Ritter
Ich hab' kein' Mutter, die mich hegt
Emil Rudolf Schönaich-Carolath
Ein Weg durch Korn und rothen Klee
Heinrich Seidel
Der Abendthau– es sind die Thränen
Es ist kein Thal so wüst und leer
Horchend über schroffe Mauern
Mein Gretchen ist so kugelrund
Karl Stieler
Am Waldbach sitz' ich in der Sonnen
Das ist ein seltsam Gehn: die Schritte schallen
Es schnarcht der alte Müller
Ich wand're heim, durch's hohe Feld
Wie wundersam ist dies Verlorengehn
Konrad Telmann
Durch die froh erschrockene Welt
Ernst von Wildenbruch
Hier von Frühlingsblumen bring' ich
Louis Wolff-Kassel
Es ist ein hold Gewimmel von Köpflein blond

Philipp Christoph Kayser (1755-1823)
Johann Wolfgang von Goethe
Der du von dem Himmel bist
Ein armes Mädchen! vergebt, vergebet!
Ein Veilchen auf der Wiese stand
Herr! ein Mädchen, Herr ein Weibchen
Ihr verblühet, süsse Rosen, meine Liebe trug
Im Felde schleich ich still und wild
Sieh mich, Heil'ger, wie ich bin

Wilhelm Kempff (1895-1991)
Björnstjerne Björnson
Nun habe Dank für alles seit wir klein
Richard Dehmel
Es steht ein goldnes Garbenfeld
Joseph von Eichendorff
Es steht ein Berg in Feuer
Heinrich Heine
Als meine Großmutter die Liese behext
Ein Fichtenbaum steht einsam
Hoffmann von Fallersleben
Maienglöckchen läutet in dem Tal

Gottfried Keller
Augen, meine lieben Fensterlein
Seidel
Wie tönt an Frühlingstagen so schwermutreich

Johann Christoph Kienlen (1783-1829)
Johann Wolfgang von Goethe
Freudvoll und leidvoll, gedankenvoll sein
Sah ein Knab' ein Röslein stehn

Wilhelm Kienzl (1857-1941)
Rudolph Baumbach
Dirnlein kommt vom Maientanz
Grete Boettcher
Du altes schlafbefang'nes Nest
Wilhelm Czermak
Aus dem finster'n Schooss der Nacht
O, wie meine Lippen beben
So gross, so rein, so hehr geklart
Tief dunkle Nacht! Nur fahler Laternen
Viel Thränen flossen in herbem Weh
Wie hast du dich in's Herz versenkt
Jakob Julius David
Ich hab' kein Haus, ich hab' kein Nest
Richard Dehmel
Komm an mein Feuer, mein Weib
Joseph von Eichendorff
Herz, mein Herz, warum so fröhlich
Markt und Straßen steh'n verlassen
Emanuel Geibel
Kornblumen flecht' ich dir zum Kranz
Johann Wolfgang von Goethe
Ich gieng im Walde so für mich hin
Heinrich Heine
Die Lotusblume ängstigt sich
Karl Heinrich Heydenreich
Wiege mich ein, du Mutter süßen Trostes
Wilhelm Kienzl
Mein Lieb hat mich verlassen
Nikolaus Lenau
Ich wand're fort ins ferne Land
Lethe! brich die Fesseln des Ufers, gieße
Hermann Lingg
Immer leiser wird mein Schlummer
Franz Mäding
Goldiger, sonniger Maientag
Friedrich Marx
Wenn du noch schläfst, erwach' mein Lieb'
Conrad Ferdinand Meyer
Du warest mir ein täglich' Wanderziel
Stefan Milow
Wunderbare Abendhelle, rings die Welt so klar

Christian Morgenstern
So still zu liegen und an dich zu denken
Wilhelm Müller
D'rüben hinter'm Dorfe steht ein Leiermann
Robert Reinick
Ich bin einmal etwas hinausspaziert
Wie ist doch die Erde so schön, so schön
Peter Rosegger
O Vögerl, wia singst du lusti
Friedrich Rückert
Da ich dich einmal gefunden
Die gute Nacht, die ich dir sage
Er ist gekommen in Sturm und Regen
Ich lag von sanftem Traum umflossen
Komm', verhüllte Schöne! komm', komm'!
Mir ist, nun ich dich habe, als müsst' ich sterben
So wahr die Sonne scheinet
Joseph Viktor von Scheffel
Sonne taucht in Meeresfluthen
Franz Schubert
Tiefer Sehnsucht heil'ges Bangen
Schulte vom Brühl
Sollt' man's denken, ist's zu glauben
Theodor Storm
Meine Mutter hat's gewollt
Carmen Sylva
Ach, ich küsste dich nur einmal
Friedrich Theodor Vischer
Sie haben dich fortgetragen
Richard Wagner
Noch scheint der Mond. Ist's Nacht noch?
Walther von der Vogelweide
Unter den Linden, an der Haide
Ernst von Wildenbruch
Unter'm Machandelbaum, da ist ein Platz
Anonymous
Das Steuer des Bootes
Wieder trüg'risch war der Traum
Winter entflieht, schon der Lenz sich zeigt
Wo ich ferne des Mikane hohen Gipfel
from Des Knaben Wunderhorn
O Röschen rot! Der Mensch liegt in größter Not

Yrjö Henrik Kilpinen (1892-1959)
Hermann Hesse
Der müde Sommer senkt das Haupt
Der Schneewind packt mich jäh von vorn
Die Stunden eilen — Mitternacht
Die Vögel im Gesträuch
Drüben überm Berge streut sein Licht
Du bist, mein fernes Tal, verzaubert
Ein starker Geist hält seine weiße Hand
Eine Glocke läutet im Grund fernab
Es führen über die Erde
Es ist immer derselbe Traum
Ich fragte dich, warum dein Auge
Ich wollt', ich wär' eine Blume
Mein Heimweh und meine Liebe
Schon manche selige Nacht hat über mir geblaut
Solang' du nach dem Glücke jagst
Und ringsum Schnee und Gletschereis
Vom Baum des Lebens fällt mir Blatt um Blatt
Von der Tafel rinnt der Wein
Wo mag meine Heimat sein
Berta Huber
Alles dunkel, alles still
Der Marktplatz liegt vom Mond erhellt
Draußen im Winde
Du wunderbare Frühlingszeit
Es löst ein Blatt sich welk und matt
Es tropft auf die Dächer
Es wälzt der Strom die dunklen Wogen
Feldblumen, zarte, kleine
Ich stand in deiner Straße
In frohen Tagen such' ich dich
Leise geht der Tag zu Ende
Mein Weg ist weit
Regen falle, härter pralle
Regungslos, ein großer Schweiger
Wenn du am Abend müde bist
Christian Morgenstern
Also ihr lebt noch, alle, alle, ihr
Auf braunen Sammetschuhen geht der Abend
Auf der Bank im Walde
Das ist eine Nacht! Eine Wacht!
Dein Wunsch war immer fliegen!
Deine Rosen an der Brust
Der monddurchbleichte Wald liegt totenstumm
Diese Rose von heimlichen Küssen schwer
Drinnen im Saal eine Geige sang
Du dunkler Frühlingsgarten
Du trüber Tag mit deinen stillen, grauen Farben
Durch die Lande auf und ab
Ein Schmetterling fliegt über mir
Ein schwarzes Vöglein fliegt über die Welt
Eine Hütte und ein Stück Wald
Eines gibt's, darauf ich mich freuen darf
Es ist Nacht, und mein Herz kommt zu dir
Es stürzen der Jugend Altäre zusammen
Flockendichte Winternacht
Gleich einer versunkenen Melodie
Guten Abend, mein Freund!
Ich danke dir, du stummer Stein

Mein Herz ist leer, ich liebe dich nicht mehr
Mit wilden Atemstössen wirft der Sturm
Nach all dem Menschenlärm
O Nacht, du Sternenbronnen
Ob Sie mir je Erfüllung wird, die Lust
Regne, regne, Frühlingsregen
Über die tausend Berge
Und werden wir uns nie besitzen
Von zwei Rosen duftet eine anders
Was gehst du, armer bleicher Kopf, mich an
Wie vieles ist denn Wort geworden
Wir sind zwei Rosen
Wir sitzen im Dunkeln

Albert Sergel
Das war des Frühlings warmer Hauch
Der Frost in letzter Nacht
Eingeschneite stille Felder
Ich sang mich durch das deutsche Land
Ich weiß es nicht, was es wohl war
Ihr ewigen Sterne
Im Walde liegt ein stiller See
Küssen und Kosen steht euch an
Nun wind um deine Stirne
Rings weiße Blütendolden
Spiel ich wo zum Tanze auf
Tausend stille weiße, blaue Blumen
Wenn der Wein nicht wär
Wir gehen durch goldenes Ährenfeld

Hans Fritz von Zwehl
Die goldene Waage des Lebens trug
Du Trotz des Glaubens! Du behelmtes Haupt!
Durch alte Marmorhallen streift weicher Wind
Durch hohe Tannen träufelt schon
Hier grub man ein
In Feindesland die graue Spätherbstnacht
Mancher Stunden Wehen ist so leuchtend
Nun hat deines Herzens Geige
Wandern fremd und unbekannt in der Stadt
Warum kommst du zu mir in der Nacht
Wenn der Bann gebrochen und vorbei der Tag

Johanna Mockel Kinkel (Johanna Mathieux) (1810-1858)

Adelbert von Chamisso
Die Mühle die dreht ihre Flügel
Ich träume als Kind mich zurücke

Emanuel Geibel
Der Mond kommt still gegangen
Ich blicke in mein Herz
Im Schatten des Waldes, im Buchengezweig

Johann Wolfgang von Goethe
Als ich auf dem Euphrat schiffte
Füllest wieder Busch und Tal
Schwester von dem ersten Licht
Wenn die Reben wieder blühen

Heinrich Heine
Da hab' ich viel blasse Leichen
Es stehen unbeweglich die Sterne in ihrer Höh'
Ich weiss nicht was soll es bedeuten
Ich will meine Seele tauchen
Schöne Wiege meiner Leiden

Alexander Kaufmann
Es schliesst der dunkle Wald uns ein

Gottfried Kinkel
Ringsum auf allen Plätzen schläft unbewegt

Johanna Kinkel
Ihr Liebe flüsternden Linden!
O.... du hast es gar zu gut, lieb Herzenskind
Sitze hier an lieber Stelle

August Kopisch
Freunde sagt, was wollt ihr trinken?
Im Meere möcht' ich fahren, mit Dir

Sebastian Longard
Ach, in dem funklenden, träumerisch...

August Graf von Platen
Lass tief in dir mich lesen

Friedrich Rückert
So wahr die Sonne scheinet

Anonymous
Auf einsam hohem Thurme in trüber Nebelnacht
Gelehnet lag ich an dem Baum
In ahnungsvollem Glanze ruht still

Theodor Fürchtegott Kirchner (1823-1903)

Joseph von Eichendorff
Ich wandre durch die stille Nacht

Jan Bedřich (Johann Friedrich) Kittl (1806-1868)

Ludwig Hölty
Dein Silber schien durch Eichengrün

Hoschek
Du Frühlingsbote, laue Luft, was wekest du

Jean Paul
Wach' auf Geliebte, der Morgen schimmert

H. E. Poeschl
Die Spindel dreht sich auf und ab

Johann von Salis-Seewis
In's stille Land! wer leitet uns hinüber?

Stolberg-Stolberg
Mitten im Schimmer der spiegelnden Wellen

Johann Ludwig Uhland
O! sanfter süsser Hauch! o!

Arno Kleffel (1840-1913)
Ferdinand Braun
Das Körnlein springt, der Vogel singt
Joseph von Eichendorff
Der Hirt bläst seine Weise
Heinrich Heine
Ich will meine Seele tauchen
Mir träumte von einem Königskind
Paul Heyse
All' meine Herzgedanken sind immerdar bei dir
Wenn du zu den Blumen gehst
Hoffmann von Fallersleben
Das ist der Dank für jene Lieder
Frohe Lieder will ich singen
Veilchen, wie so schweigend
Wie aber soll ich dir erwiedern
Wie die jungen Blüthen leise träumen
Franz Kugler
Wissen es die blauen Blumen
Robert Reinick
Wolken, die ihr nach Osten eilt
Hermann Rollet
Das Vöglein sang vom grünen Baum sein Lied
Ist der Frühling über Nacht
Was weinst du, mein Blümlein
Otto Roquette
Weisst du noch, weisst du noch?
Friedrich Rückert
Die Liebste fragt, warum ich liebe?
Wär' ich der gold'ne Sonnenschein
Was singt ihr und sagt ihr mir, Vögelein
Albert Träger
Aus des Morgenhimmels Blau
Der Frühling kehrt alljährlich wieder
Der Sonne letzte Strahlen säumen
Die Welt weiss deinen Namen nicht
Ihr Sternlein, hoch am Himmelszelt!
Kleine Blumen im engen Thal
Schneeglöckchen läuten leis' im Thal
Steh' auf, steh' auf und öffne das Fenster
Und würdest nie die Hand du falten
Volkslied
Hat dich ein blühendes Blümchen erfreut

Bernhard (Joseph) Klein (1793-1832)
Johann Wolfgang von Goethe
Ach neige, du Schmerzenreiche
Wer reitet so spät durch Nacht und Wind
Wie herrlich leuchtet mir die Natur!

Otto Klemperer (1885-1973)
Otto Klemperer
Ungesucht gefunden preis ich meinen Stern

Paul August von Klenau (1883-1946)
Friedrich Hölderlin
Geh unter, schöne Sonne, sie achteten
Ist nicht heilig mein Herz
Nur einen Sommer gönnt ihr Gewaltigen!
Wo bist du? trunken dämmert die Seele mir
Jens Peter Jacobsen
Rosen senken ihr Haupt so schwer von Tau
Schweige, geliebteste Fraue

Armin Knab (1881-1951)
Clemens Brentano
Komm heraus, komm heraus, o du schöne
Richard Dehmel
Aurikelchen, Aurikelchen stehn
Kinder, kommt, verzählt euch nicht
Krause, krause Muhme, alte Butterblume
Joseph von Eichendorff
Die Vöglein, die so fröhlich sangen
Gedenk ich noch der Frühlingsnächte
Ich wandre durch die stille Nacht
Was ist mir denn so wehe?
Wohin ich geh und schaue, in Feld und Wald
Johann Wolfgang von Goethe
Ach, wer bringt die schönen Tage
Als ich noch ein Knabe war
An dem reinsten Frühlingsmorgen
Bei dem Glanze der Abendröte ging ich still
Bleibe, bleibe bei mir, holder Fremdling
Der Strauß, den ich gepflükket, grüße dich
Es ist ein Schnee gefallen
Es war ein fauler Schäfer
Ihr verblühtet, süße Rosen
Kleine Blumen, kleine Blätter streuen mir
Weint, Mädchen, hier bei Amors Grabe!
Wie herrlich leuchtet mir die Natur!
Johann Christian Günther
Brecht die schwangern Anmutsnelken
Friedrich Hölderlin
Ewig trägt im Mutterschoße, süße Königin
Hugo Lang
Frühling- Frühling- Frühlingswind
Christian Weise
Die Rose blüht, ich bin die fromme Biene
from Des Knaben Wunderhorn
Abends, wenn ich schlafen geh
Ach wie so schön, wie hübsch und fein
Ahne, Krahne, wikkele, wahne

Bin ich nit ein Bürschlein in der Welt?
Des Morgens zwischen drein und vieren
Es wollt das Mädchen früh aufstehn
Gleich wie die lieb' Waldvögelein
Havele, Havele, Hahne, Fastennacht geht ane
Hör mich, du arme Pilgerin
Kling, kling, Glöckchen, im Haus steht
Margritchen, Margritchen, dein Hemdchen
Mein Schätzle ist fein, 's könnt feiner nit sein
Nun schürz dich, Gretlein, schürz dich
Sonne, Sonne, scheine, fahr übern Rheine
Steht auf, ihr lieben Kinderlein
Storch, Storch, Langbein, wann fliegst du
Wie schön blüht uns der Maien

Volkslied
Es fiel ein Reif in Frühlingsnacht
Fünf Engel haben gesungen
Gretele, willst tanzen? "O jerum, jo!"
Ich bin dir herzengulden gut
Karlinle, mein Schatz, hat Härle wie Flachs
Maria wollt zur Kirche gehn
Mich dünkt, wir geben einen Ball!
Pöppe, Pöppe, danze, schenk di ok en Hohn
Rosmarin und Thymian wächst
Tanz mit mir, tanz mit mir
Wie reiten denn die Herren? Trapp, trapp, trapp!

Ernst-Lothar von Knorr (1896-1973)
Friedrich Hölderlin
Ist nicht heilig mein Herz, schöneren Lebens

Karl Michael Komma (1913-)
Friedrich Hölderlin
Wenn ihr Freunde vergeßt

Peter Jona Korn (1922-)
Eduard Mörike
Gelassen stieg die Nacht ans Land
Kein Schlaf noch kühlt das Auge mir
Laß, o Welt, o laß mich sein
Und die mich trug im Mutterleib
Was doch heut Nacht ein Sturm gewesen
Zierlich ist des Vogels Tritt im Schnee

Erich Wolfgang Korngold (1897-1957)
Richard Dehmel
Ich wünsche dir Glück. Ich bring dir die Sonne
Joseph von Eichendorff
Auf die Dächer zwischen blassen Wolken
Er reitet nachts auf einem braunen Roß
's war doch wie ein leises Singen
Soll ich dich denn nun verlassen, Erde
E. Honold
Fern von dir denk' ich dein
Hans Kaltneker
Du reine Frau aus Licht und Elfenbein
In meine innige Nacht geh' ich ein
Tu ab den Schmerz, entflieh, Verlangen!
Alfred Kerr
Laß Liebster, wenn ich tot bin
Heinrich Kipper
Ich hab ein kleines Gärtchen
Karl Kobald
Mit Dir zu schweigen still im Dunkel
Welt ist stille eingeschlafen
Koch
Steht ein Mädchen an dem Fenster
Ernst Lothar
Mond, so gehst du wieder auf
Weine nicht, daß ich jetzt gehe
Edith Ronsperger
Dies eine kann mein Sehnen nimmer fassen
William Shakespeare
Kein Sonnenglanz im Auge meiner Frau
Eleonore van der Straaten
Bächlein, Bächlein, wie du eilen kannst
Deine edlen weissen Hände legen meine Seel'
Nimm meinen schweren Dornenkranz
Was Du mir bist? Der Ausblick
Wenn du schläfst, ich segne dich, Kind
S. Trebitsch
Unter spärlich grünen Blättern

Leopold Kozeluch (1747-1818)
Alois Blumauer
Närrchen, sei nicht spröde
Gottlieb Fuchs
Hier, wo ich Abendröte und Tag verlöschen sah
Friedrich Wilhelm Gotter
Auch die Sprödeste der Schönen
Johann Georg Jacobi
Holdes Mädchen! Unser Leben war
Gotthold Ephraim Lessing
Kleine Schöne, küsse mich, kleine Schöne
Moritz August von Thümmel
Die Lieb und unser Vogelfang

Franz Krause
Clemens Brentano
Es sang vor langen Jahren
Was reif in diesen Zeilen steht
Hermann Hesse
Flügelt ein kleiner blauer Falter vom Wind
Freund meiner Jugend, zu dir kehr ich

Gib uns deine milde Hand!
Ich bin auch in Ravenna gewesen
Lange waren meine Augen müd'
Musik des Weltalls und Musik der Meister
Schuh um Schuh im Finstern setz ich
Seltsam, im Nebel zu wandern!
Traurig lehnst du dein Gesicht übers Laub
Über mir im Blauen reisen Wolken
Uns ist kein Sein vergönnt. Wir sind nur Strom
Wieder schreitet er den braunen Pfad
Christian von Hofmannswaldau
Niemand weiß, wie schwer mirs fällt
Wo sind die Stunden der süßen Zeit
Martin Opitz
Ach Liebste laß uns eilen wir haben Zeit
Rainer Maria Rilke
Das sind die Stunden, da ich mich finde
Die Blätter fallen, fallen wie von weit
Einsam hinterm letzten Haus
Es treibt der Wind im Winterwalde
Mich rührt so sehr böhmischen Volkes Weise
Möchte mir ein blondes Glück erkiesen
Anonymous
Es ist ein Schnee gefallen

Ernst Křenek (1900-1991)
Paul Flemming
Sei dennoch unverzagt. Gib dennoch unverloren
Gerd Hans Goering
Du ewig Wandelbare, sieh, du bist die Brükke
Es war ein König Lobesam
Groß wuchsen alle Räume
Und oft war's nur ein Hauch, der Blätter streifte
Wir sind nicht droben, doch wir sind am Ziel
Johann Wolfgang von Goethe
Als ich noch Knabe war, sperrte man mich ein
O Magdeburg, die Stadt, die schöne Mädchen
Von mehr als einer Seite verwaist
Johann Christian Günther
Man lauert, sitzt und sinnt, verändert, schreibt
Franz Kafka
Ach, was wird uns hier bereitet?
Du kannst dich zurückhalten von den Leiden
Kämpfte er nicht genug?
Noch spielen die Jagdhunde im Hof
Nur ein Wort, nur eine Bitte
Friedrich Klopstock
Willkommen, o silberner Mond
Karl Kraus
Ihr Menschenkinder, seid ihr nicht Laub
Ottfried Kryzanowski
Ein einfaches lichtes Kleid, ein leichter Gang
Ein Weib zu suchen! Wozu
Es will kein Baum so wie die Linde blühen!
Theodor Mommsen
Die Saiten weiß ich zu rühren
Im Walde, im Walde, im tiefgrünen Wald
Meine Laute nehm' ich wieder
Und so laßt mich weiter wandern
Wiederum lebt wohl, ihr Brüder
Theodor Storm
Musikanten wollen wandern
Nun ein Scherflein in der Runde
Georg Rudolf Weckherlin
Ein kleine Weil, da ohn' Gefähr
Ihr wisset, was für schwere Klagen
Franz Werfel
Welchen Weg bist du gegangen

Conradin Kreutzer (1780-1849)
Johann Wolfgang von Goethe
Ihr guten Herrn, ihr schönen Frauen
Johann Ludwig Uhland
Bei diesem kalten Wehen sind alle Strassen leer
Bei einem Wirte wundermild
Die linden Lüfte sind erwacht
Droben stehet die Kapelle
Ich bin so gar ein armer Mann
Ich reit' ins finstre Land hinein
Lebe wohl, lebe wohl, mein Lieb!
Noch ahnt man kaum das Sonnenlicht
O brich nicht Steg du zitterst sehr!
O legt mich nicht ins dunkle Grab
O sanfter, süsser Hauch! schon weckest du
Saatengrün, Veilchenduft, Lerchenwirbel
So hab' ich nun die Stadt verlassen
So soll ich dich nun meiden
Süßer goldner Frühlingstag! Inniges Entzücken
Will ruhen unter den Bäumen hier

Niklas von Krufft (1779-1818)
Johannes Falk
Thoms saß am hallenden See
Friedrich von Matthisson
Was unterm Monde gleicht uns Elfen flink
Christian Ludwig Reissig
Komm ans Fenster, holde Schöne
Mild umschattet von der Dämmrung Schleier
Friedrich von Schiller
Der Eichwald brauset, die Wolken ziehn
Hör' ich das Pförtchen nicht gehen?
Weit in nebelgrauer Ferne liegt mir

Friedrich Wilhelm Kücken (1810-1882)
Anton Graf von Brunykowski
Ich will vor deiner Thüre stehn'
Emanuel Geibel
Wenn sich zwei Herzen scheiden
Ida Gräfin von Hahn-Hahn
Ach wenn du wärst mein eigen
L. Hecker
Schaust so freundlich aus, Gretelein!
Heinrich Heine
Du bist wie eine Blume
Ich stand gelehnet an den Mast
Hoffmann von Fallersleben
Alles still in süsser Ruh
Hermann Kletke
Ich flüstre deinen Namen in stiller Nacht
Franz Kugler
Da draußen auf der Aue, da stehn die Blümelein
Wilhelm Osterwald
Du wunderholde Maid, ich bin meinem Leben
Paalzow
Verstummt ist die Harfe, die Saiten entzwei
Otto Roquette
Du kleines blitzendes Sternelein,
Anonymous
Nun holt mir eine Kanne Wein
from Des Knaben Wunderhorn
Spazieren wollt ich reiten der Liebsten
Volkslieder
Herzallerliebstes Schatzerl du
Not Yet Identified
Das Röselein vom Regen gar arg durchnässt

(Daniel) Friedrich (Rudolph) Kuhlau (1786-1832)
Heinrich Wilhelm von Gerstenberg
Der erste Tag im Monat Mai
Ich sah ein Mädchen ohne Mangel
Orpheus, als du mit Thränen deine Geliebte

Friedrich Ludwig Aemilius Kunzen (1761-1817)
Gottfried August Bürger
Bist untreu, Wilhelm, oder tot

Richard Kursch
Adelbert von Chamisso
Mutter, Mutter, meine Puppe hab' ich
Klaus Groth
Jehann, nu spann de Schimmels an!
Justinus Kerner
Ach, ach, ich armes Klosterfräulein!
Eduard Mörike
Derweil ich schlafend lag

Franz Paul Lachner (1803-1890)
Adelbert von Chamisso
Seit ich ihn gesehen, glaub' ich blind zu sein
Heinrich Heine
Auf Flügeln des Gesanges, Herzliebchen
Hermann Kletke
Siehst du am Abend die Wolken zieh'n
Friedrich Klopstock
Wenn ich einst von jenem Schlummer
Johann Michael von Soeltl
Dicht in Blättern eingeschlossen

Karl Lafite (1872-1945
Heinrich Leuthold
Nach Westen zieht der Wind dahin
Richard Schaukal
Ein schwarzer Ritter, Herrin, hält im Burghof

Julius Lammers (1829-1888)
Anonymous
Mein Schatz, der ist auf die Wanderschaft hin

Josefine (Caroline) Lang (1815-1880)
Thomas Aquinas
All' mein Leben bist Du! Ohne Dich nur Tod!
the Bible
Dort werd' ich das im Licht erkennen
Gott! Drücke, wenn das Herze bricht
Komm' nur mühselig und gebückt!
Lord Byron
Mein Ende zeigt mir jeder Traum!
Unglücklich Herz, und konnt' es sein
Agnes von Calatin
Getäuscht hat mich ein Schimmer
Wie glänzt so hell dein Auge
Karl Egon Ebert
Die Perle, wahrend im Gehäuse
L. Feldmann
Der Winter ist ein böser Gast
Carl Gerok
Müder Glanz der Sonne! Blasses Himmelblau!
Johann Wolfgang von Goethe
Ich denke Dein, wenn mir der Sonne Schimmer
Sie liebt mich, sie liebt mich, ja sie liebt mich!
Tage der Wonne, kommt ihr so bald?
Julius Hammer
Vertraue dich dem Licht der Sterne
Heinrich Heine
In weite Ferne will ich träumen!
Mag da draussen Schnee sich thürmen
Und wüssten's die Blumen die kleinen
Wenn ich auf dem Lager liege
Wenn zwei von einander scheiden

Johann Georg Jacobi
Sagt wo sind die Veilchen hin?
J. C. K.
Wein' aus deine Freude!!
Kunde
Du gleichst dem klaren blauen See
Nikolaus Lenau
Als ein unergründlich Wonnemeer
Diese Rose pflück' ich hier
Friedrich von Matthisson
Die silbernen Glöckchen der Blume des Mai's
August Graf von Platen
Duften nicht die Laubengänge
Christian Reinhold Köstlin
Auf dem See in tausend Sterne
Auf langer Haide wallt die Wolke hin und her
Die Sonne kam, im reinsten Glanze
Eilende Wellen, spielend im Licht
Frühling ist gekommen, wie so lieb und hold!
Gedenke mein! die lieben Augen lenke
Liebster Freund, und kann's denn sein
Nur den Abschied schnell genommen
O sehntest Du dich so nach mir
Ob ich manchmal Dein gedenke?
Sie hat mich still zum Abschied angeblickt
Um dies Schifflein schmiege, holder See
Joseph Viktor von Scheffel
Am Ufer blies ich ein lustig Stück
An dem Ende seiner Tage steht der Kater
Max von Schenkendorf
Wer sprenget auf dem stolzen Ross
Karl Stieler
Da drüben im Abendstrahle steht glitzernd
Ein Fels ragt in den See hinein
Ich gab dem Schicksal dich zurück
Johann Friedrich Tiede
Wie, wenn die Sonn' aufgehet
Fr. von Weling
Ich liebe dich und will dich ewig lieben
Albert Zeller
Leb'wohl, leb'wohl du schöne Welt!
Anonymous
Immer sich rein kindlich erfreu`n
In allen Fernen wölbt sich ein Haus
Sei mir gegrüsst! Linderndes Öl!
from Des Knaben Wunderhorn
Dort hoch auf jenem Berge

Eduard Lassen (1830-1904)
Thomas Bailey Aldrich
Einen Ring von Golde steckt' ich an die Hand
Ernst Moritz Arndt
Und die Sonne macht den weiten Ritt
Friedrich Bodenstedt
Die Gletscher leuchten im Mondenlicht
Die helle Sonne leuchtet auf's weite Meer
Ich fühle deinen Odem mich überall umwehn
Wenn der Frühling auf die Berge steigt
Wenn ich dich seh' so lieb und hold
Peter Cornelius
Der Dichter singt dem Frühling, und Allem
Du meiner Seele schönster Traum!
In deiner Nähe weil' ich noch
Lilienblüthe! Mädchen schön und zart!
Nun wollen Knospen sich entfalten
Wieder möcht' ich dir begegnen
Joseph von Eichendorff
Der Hirt bläst seine Weise
Der Wald wird falb, die Blätter fallen
Es steht ein Berg im Feuer
Fliegt der erste Morgenstrahl
Schwirrend Tambourin, dich schwing' ich
W. Eisenmayer
Was ich mir still gelobte, will's halten treu
"Ernst" (Matthias Jakob Schleiden)
Die ersten Tropfen fallen
In deine Augen will ich schauen
So still und mild der Tag und feierlich
J. Feis
's ist nicht dein holdes Angesicht
Emanuel Geibel
Du feuchter Frühlingsabend
Du fragst mich, du mein blondes Lieb
Fern im Süd' das schöne Spanien
In meinem Garten die Nelken
Mein Herz ist wie die dunkle Nacht
Vöglein, wohin so schnell?
Johann Wolfgang von Goethe
Ich denke dein, wenn mir der Sonne Schimmer
Robert Hamerling
Es flimmert der Kranz der Sterne
Es ziehen die Wolken, es wandern die Sterne
Lächeln ist des Mundes Sache
Lass' die Rose schlummern
Nur ein Wörtchen sprich, o Mädchen
O sieh, wie golden die Blümlein
Heinrich Heine
Ei! kennt ihr noch das alte Lied
Ein Fichtenbaum steht einsam
Eine starke, schwarze Barke segelt trauervoll
Ich hab' im Traum geweinet
Ich hatte einst ein schönes Vaterland

Mit deinen blauen Augen
Wandl' ich in dem Wald des Abends
Walther Jung
Des Abends Rosen sind abgeblüht
Friedrich August Leo
Die Wipfel säuseln Abendruh', die Sonne sinkt
Was ist des Vögleins Dach
Wenn kein Windchen weht,
Eduard Mörike
Frühling lässt ein blaues Band
Henriette von Schorn
Ach! was ist leben doch so schwer
Robert Eduard Prutz
Ich will dir's nimmer sagen
Robert Reinick
Komm' in die stille Nacht, Liebchen
Otto Roquette
Noch ist die blühende, goldene Zeit
Bernhard Scholz
Das ist die Zeit der Rosenpracht
Dein Auge ist mein Himmel
E. v. d. Schulenburg
Wenn der Sturm die Blätter jaget
Adelheid von Stolterfoth
Allein zu sein! Wie oft mit stillen Thränen
Albert Träger
Die Welt weiss deinen Namen nicht
Lope de Vega
Die ihr dort wallet unter den Palmen
Not Yet Identified
Ich weil' in tiefer Einsamkeit
O wär' ich du, mein Falke du

Luise Adolphe Le Beau (1850-1927)
Max Bernstein
Die Welt ist schlafen gangen, still ist's in Busch
Peter Cornelius
Zur Drossel sprach der Fink
Rudolf Gernss
Trenn mich nicht vom Blätterthrone
Justinus Kerner
Lass dich belauschen, du stille Nacht!
Wie dir geschah, so soll's auch mir geschehn

Otto Lessmann (1844-1918)
Julius Wolff
Ein leises, fernes Rauschen klingt
Ernst Ziel
Hehrer bist du und heiliger

Gustav Lewin
Victor Blüthgen
Nun gute Nacht! Es gab so viel zu schauen
Martin Boelitz
Wer hätte gedacht, daß die Rosen

Ludwig (Louis) Eduard Liebe (1819-1900)
August Becker
Sonnenlicht, Sonnenschein, fällt mir

Hélène Riese Liebmann (1796-1819+)
Johann Wolfgang von Goethe
Kennst du das Land? wo die Citronen blühn

Ignace Lilien (1897-1964)
Rainer Maria Rilke
Die Blätter fallen, fallen wie von weit

Peter Josef von Lindpaintner (1791-1856)
Feodor Löwe
Der Sänger hält im Feld die Fahnenwacht

Franz (Ferenc) Liszt (1811-1886)
Kornel Abrányi
Sei gesegnet, König der Magyaren!
Pierre Jean de Béranger
In dieser Rinne will ich sterben!
Rüdiger von Biegeleben
Sieh auf dem Meer den Glanz der hohen Sonne
Marchese Cesare Bocella
Englein hold im Lockengold
Friedrich Bodenstedt
Einst wollt ich einen Kranz dir winden
In meinem Lebensringe bist du der Edelstein
In Stunden der Entmutigung
Gottfried August Bürger
Lenore fuhr ums Morgenrot
Peter Cornelius
Von der Wartburg Zinnen nieder
Wieder möcht' ich dir begegnen
Graf Carl Coronini
Die Fischerstochter sitzt am Strand
Franz Dingelstedt
Schwebe, schwebe, blaues Auge
Alexandre Dumas
Mein Gott! aus meiner Herden Mitten
Ferdinand Freiligrath
O lieb, o lieb, so lang du lieben kannst
Und nun kam die Nacht, und wir ritten hindann
Emanuel Geibel
Die stille Wasserrose steigt aus dem blauen See
Frau E. von Girardin
Nein, nein, ich liebt' ihn nicht!
Johann Wolfgang von Goethe
Der du von dem Himmel bist
Es war ein König in Thule

Freudvoll und leidvoll, gedankenvoll sein
Kennst du das Land, wo die Citronen blühn
Über allen Gipfeln ist Ruh
Wer nie sein Brot mit Thränen aß
Charlotte von Hagn
Dichter! was Liebe sei, mir nicht verhehle!
Friedrich Hebbel
In Frühlings Heiligtume, wenn dir ein Duft
Heinrich Heine
Anfangs wollt ich fast verzagen
Du bist wie eine Blume
Ein Fichtenbaum steht einsam
Ich weiß nicht, was soll's bedeuten
Im Rhein, im schönen Strome
Morgens steh ich auf und frage
Vergiftet sind meine Lieder
Helene, Herzogin von Orléans
Wer einsam steht, wer einsam steht
Georg Herwegh
Ich möchte hingehn wie das Abendrot
Hoffmann von Fallersleben
Die duftenden Kräuter auf der Au'
In Liebeslust, in Sehnsuchtsqual
Laßt mich ruhen, laßt mich träumen
Wie singt die Lerche schön
Therese von Hohenlohe
Ich bin des Meeres zartweiße Tochter
P. Horváth
Lebe wohl! Lebe wohl! in weite Ferne
Victor Hugo
Das Grab, es sprach zur Rose
Gastibelza, der greise, kühne Jäger
Gibt es wo einen Rasen grün
Mein Kind, wär ich König
O komm im Traum, komm in stillester Stunde
Wie kann, sagten sie, versteckt hier im Nachen
Moritz Jókai
Der Hain widerhallt von der Nachtigall Sang
Philipp Kaufmann
Du arme, kleine Nachtigall
Emil Kuh
Ihr Glokken von Marling, wie brauset ihr so hell
Nikolaus Lenau
Drei Zigeuner fand ich einmal liegen
Gespielt mit Regen, Blitz und Sturm
Fürst Felix Lichnowsky
Ach, nun taucht die Klosterzelle
Alfred Meissner
O Meer im Abendstrahl in deiner stillen Flut
Fürst Elim Metschorsky
Mild wie ein Lufthauch, ein Lufthauch im Mai
Gustav Michell
Mir ist die Welt so freudenleer
Joseph Müller
Dort am grünen Hügel glänzen
Spende, Veilchen, deine Düfte
Alfred de Musset
Ich verlor die Kraft und das Leben
Johannes Nordmann
Kling leise, mein Lied
Sándor Petőfi
Hinweg, Kleinmütige, Hinweg, Kleinmütige
Francesco Petrarca
Fried' ist versagt mir, vergebens träum' ich
Sei gesegnet immerdar von allen Tagen
So sah ich denn auf Erden Engelsfrieden
Richard Pohl
O süßer Zauber im Jugendmut
Oskar von Redwitz
Es muß ein Wunderbares sein
Ludwig Rellstab
Es rauschen die Winde so herbstlich und kalt
Nimm einen Strahl der Sonne, vom Abendstern
Wo weilt er? Im kalten, im schaurigen Land
Friedrich Rückert
Ich liebe dich, weil ich dich lieben muß
Ferdinand von Saar
Des Tages laute Stimmen schweigen
Joseph Viktor von Scheffel
Als wir mit deutschen Klingen geführt
Beim Scheiden der Sonne erschimmert
Die Erde ist erschlossen
Hab ich geträumt? Klang hier nicht
Ich schreib allzeit nur wenig
Thüringens Wälder senden den Waidmann
Wo liebende Herzen sich innig vermählt
Friedrich von Schiller
Es donnern die Höh'n, es zittert der Steg
Es lächelt der See, er ladet zum Bade
Ihr Matten, lebt wohl, lebt wohl
Franz Schober
Weimars Toten will ich's bringen
Henriette von Schorn
Ach, was ist Leben doch so schwer
Alfred Tennyson
Weil noch, Sonnenstrahl, leuchte, Glanz, feldein
Graf Alexis Tolstoi
Der Fürst ritt am Morgen mit seinem Geleit
Johann Ludwig Uhland
Es schritt wohl über die Heide
Gestorben war ich vor Liebeswonne
In Liebesarmen ruht ihr trunken

Adolf Wilbrandt
Wie glänzt nun die Welt im Abendstrahl

Georg Simon Löhlein (1725-1781)
Johann Wolfgang von Goethe
Wer kommt? wer kauft von meiner Waar?

(Johann) Carl Gottfried Loewe (1796-1869)
Markgraf Albrecht
Was mein Gott will, das g'scheh allzeit
"Willibald Alexis" (Wilhelm Häring)
Es war einmal ein Schneidergesell
Fridericus Rex, unser König und Herr
Liebe Mutter, heut Nacht heulte Regen
Mach' auf deine Thür, charmantestes Kind
Schwerin ist todt, Schwerin, mein General,
Sie liebte ihn, Er liebte sie, sie liebten sich beide
Was klopft ans Thor? Über die rothe Heide
Anacreon
Du bist glücklich, o Cicade
Es sagen mir die Weiber: Anakreon, du greisest
Ich will von den Atriden
Weil ich sterblich bin geboren
Johann André
In einem Thal, bei einem Bach,
Ernst Anschütz
Ha, Priester, zitt're! nicht verhöhnen lässt sich
Ernst Moritz Arndt
Lieb' sei ferne, ist doch immer da
Dr. Bartholdy
In Liebe sich begegnen, das ist der Sorge Tod
Über Wolken Herr der Herren, gütig, weise
Emilie von Berlepsch
Ruhig ist des Todes Schlummer
Christoph Bezzel
Bekehre du mich, Herr, so werd ich
the Bible
Alsdann kommt Jesus aus Galiläa an den Jordan
Herr, du bist unsre Zuflucht für und für!
Ich bin ein guter Hirte, und kenne die Meinen
Israel hat dennoch Gott zum Trost
Magdalena weint am Grabe
Und er spützete auf die Erde
Franz Rudolf Immanuel Binder
Es ziehet den Pilgrim rastlos fort
Otto Blankenfeldt
Holder Lenz, mit reichen Gaben schmückst du
Carl von Blankensee
Hoffe, liebe, glaube, ist des Herren Wort
Hermann Bonn
Jesus Christus, wahrer Gottes-Sohn
Otto von Briesen
Regenwetter ziehen trübe
Pauline Brumm
Von der zarten Kinder Händen
Friedrich Budy
Deutschlands Adler liegt gebunden
Samuel Gottlob Bürde
Alles, was Odem hat, lobe den Herrn!
Robert Burns
Nun, wer klopft an meine Thür?
Lord Byron
An Babylons Wassern gefangen da weinten wir
An mir vorüber ging ein Geist
Auf Jordan's Ufer streifen wilde Horden
Beweint die, so geweint in Babels Land!
Dein Leben schliesst, dein Ruhm begann
Der König thront; es sitzen die Grossen
Du, deren Kunst die Todten ruft
Du in der Schönheit strahlendem Schein
Es kam des Assyrers gewaltige Macht
Es waren Ruhm und Weisheit mein
Gazelle, die so wild und schnell
Ich sah die volle Thräne glühn
Krieger und Feldherrn, ereilt mich der Tod
Lebe wohl! wenn je ein brünstig Flehen
Mein Geist ist trüb'; den Ton der Saiten
O Harfe, die des Gottgeliebten Hand
O höh're Welt, lehrt uns der Schmerz
O Mariamne, dieses Herz, das dein Herz
Schlafloser Augen Sonne, zitternd Licht
Sie geht in Schönheit und entzücket
Soll nach des Volkes und nach Gottes Willen
Von dem Berg, wo zuletzt noch dein Tempel
Wär' ich wirklich so falsch, als der Irrthum
Wohin, o Seele, wirst du eilen
Catholic Mass
O Lamm Gottes, welches der Welt Sünde trägt
Adelbert von Chamisso
An meinem Herzen, an meiner Brust
Du Ring an meinem Finger
Er, der Herrlichste von allen
Helft mir, ihr Schwestern
Ich kann's nicht fassen, nicht glauben
Nun hast du mir den ersten Schmerz gethan
's war mal 'ne Katzenkönigin, Ja, ja!
Seit ich ihn gesehen, glaub' ich blind zu sein
Süsser Freund, du blickest mich verwundert an
Traum der eignen Tage, die nun ferne sind
Wilhelmine Chézy
In tiefster Schlucht, in Waldesschoss
Johannes ging am hellen Bach

Matthias Claudius
Im Anfang war's auf Erden nur finster
Schlaf, holder Knabe, süss und mild!
Victoria! Victoria! der kleine weisse Zahn ist da
Johann Andreas Cramer
Der Herr ist Gott und keiner mehr
Die Himmel rufen: jeder ehret
Dionysius
O Muse, mir Vertraute du, lass klingen
Hugo Emsmann
König Wilhelm, unsre Sonne, Hohenzollern
Karl Enslin
Bist ja noch ganz allein!
Der Abend dämmert, der Schmied, er hämmert
Herbei, heran, auf die glänzende Bahn!
O Freude, o Wonne, wie scheinet die Sonne
Wir hatten uns ein Haus gebaut von Sand
Johannes Falk
Nach dem Sturme fahren wir sicher
Heinrich Fick
Des Jünglings Blick erkennt der Liebe Zeichen
Gottfried Wilhelm Fink
Dem Ew'gen unsre Lieder!
Heinrich Fitzau
Im Abendgolde glänzet zu Bärenburg
Friedrich Förster
Als ich ein junger Geselle war
Theodor Fontane
Der Reimer Thomas lag am Bach
Ich hab' es getragen sieben Jahr
Ludwig August Frankl
Vom Himmel zogen rauschend
Ferdinand Freiligrath
Auf dem stillen, schwülen Pfuhle tanzt
Auf der Messe, da zieht es, da stürmt es
Auf des Lagers weichem Kissen
Auf Jordan's grünen Borden
Da schwimm ich allein auf dem stillen Meer
Die Fürstin zog zu Walde mit Jägern
Fern tobt der Kampf im Palmenthal!
Sein Heer durchwogte das Palmenthal
Zelte, Posten, Werda-Rufer! Lust'ge Nacht
Friedrich Funcke
Zeuch uns nach dir, nur für und für
Christian Gellert
Gott ist mein Lied, er ist der Gott der Stärke
Ich komme vor dein Angesicht
Wenn ich, o Schöpfer, deine Macht
Wie gross ist des Allmächt'gen Güte!
Geppert
Nimm sie willig und geduldig diese Leiden
von Gerstenberg
Auch das schönste Blumenleben
Dich blendet Kerzenlicht! Mich nicht!
Die mich recht erkennen, Gott! erhalte sie mir
Liebes Haus auf Berges Höh'!
Noch einmal muss ich vor dir stehn
So viel Blumen allwärts blühen
Welch Leuchten auf den Wogen
Wo kommst du her? wo kommst du her?
Ludwig Giesebrecht
Als Weibesarm in jungen Jahren
Bienen summen, wie schwer zu tragen
Bleib, mein Bruder, bleib noch eine Stunde!
Der König auf dem gold'nen Stuhle
Der Sabbath hebt, ein gröss'rer Sabbath an
Ein Wasser in Oberpommern
Es hat der schimmernde Sonnenstrahl
Es steht ein Kelch in der Kapelle
Euer Herz erschrecke nicht
Euern Helfer, euern Sieger suchet droben
Glaubst du in Gott, den Vater, Sohn und Geist?
Gott sei mit euch! Uns ist es nicht beschieden
Hat mit frischem Birkenlaube
Ich der Arzt, ich der Arzt für so viel Kranke
Im Schacht der Adern und der Stufen
In dieses Thal, in diese Stille
Jung stritt ich einst um Accons Schloss
Kann ich fürchten, zweifeln, meinen?
Lasst sich der Höhle Thor erschliessen
Lazarus ward auferwecket
Nach Jerusalem, der klaren Mutterstadt
Neige, neige dich herab, unser Flehn zu hören
Nun auf dem fremden Boden mehret
O Lämmlein bleibt, gedenkt an diesen Tag
Polus, beginne rasch und kühn dein Werk!
Schatten deckt, vom Thau befeuchtet
Schlägt hier ein Menschenherz, wie meines
Spielt, Mägdlein, unter eurer Weide
Staunend schreit' ich durch die Gassen
Unser Herzog hat herrliche Thaten vollbracht
Voll banger Sorge hab ich längst bemerkt
Von meines Hauses engen Wänden
Wie früh das enge Pförtchen knarre
Wie still, wie einsam! aber meine Brust
Wie wohnst du in des Reiches Städten
Wir graben tief in Trauer ein Grab hier
Wolke lichtweiss in dem Blauen
Wilhelm Gleim d. J.
Da kommt ja der liebliche Mai
Johann Wolfgang von Goethe
Ach neige, du Schmerzenreiche

Als er, Sami, mit dir jüngst Blumen brach
Arm am Beutel, krank am Herzen
Auf Kieseln im Bache da lieg' ich, wie helle!
Das Beet, schon lockert sich's in die Höh'
Das Wasser rauscht', das Wasser schwoll
Der du von dem Himmel bist
Der Thürmer, der schaut zu Mitten der Nacht
Des Menschen Seele gleicht dem Wasser
Die Königin steht im hohen Saal
Du siehst mich, Königin, zurück
Es flattert um die Quelle die wechselnde Libelle
Es ist ein Schnee gefallen
Es lacht der Mai! Der Wald ist frei
Es war ein Kind, das wollte nie zur Kirche
Gern in stillen Melancholieen
Gottes ist der Orient! Gottes ist der Occident!
Grosser Brama, Herr der Mächte!
Grosser Brama! nun erkenn' ich
Hat der alte Hexenmeister
Herein, o du Guter! du Alter herein!
Ich denke dein, wenn mir der Sonne Schimmer
Ich ging im Felde so für mich hin
Lass mich knieen, lass mich schauen
Mädchen, als du kamst ans Licht
Mahadöh, der Herr der Erde, kommt herab
Mein Haus hat kein' Thür
Meine Ruh' ist hin, mein Herz ist schwer
Nach Corinthus von Athen gezogen
Nur Platz, nur Blösse! wir brauchen Räume
Nur wer die Sehnsucht kennt
O fände für mich ein Bräutigam sich
O gieb, vom weichen Pfühle, träumend
O wären wir weiter, o wär' ich zu Haus!
Seht den Felsenquell, freudehell
Sei mir heute nichts zuwider
Tage der Wonne, kommt ihr so bald?
Über allen Gipfeln ist Ruh'
Ullin trat auf mit der Harfe
Und frische Nahrung, neues Blut
Und Morgen fällt Sanct Martins Fest
Viele der Blümlein zusammengeknüpfet
War schöner als der schönste Tag
Was hör' ich draussen vor dem Thor
Wasser holen geht die reine, schöne Frau
Wenn der Blüthen Frühlingsregen
Wer reitet so spät durch Nacht und Wind?
Wie herrlich leuchtet mir die Natur
Wie im Morgenglanze du rings mich anglühst
Wie kommt's, dass du so traurig bist
Wir singen und sagen vom Grafen so gern
Zum Sehen geboren, zum Schauen bestellt

Fr. Goldtammer
Ein Kränzlein sollst du tragen

Emilie von der Goltz
In des Südens heissen Zonen Blumen giebt

Ludwig Andreas Gotter
Herr Jesu, Gnadensonne
Wie der Tag mir schleichet ohne dich vollbracht

Gerh. Anton Herm. Gramberg
Es schauet der Morgen mit funkelndem Schein

H. Grassmann
O dolce far niente, du bist doch auch etwas!

"Anastasius Grün" (A. A. von Auersperg)
Als Lenz die Erde wieder mit erstem Kuss
Aus Sanct Justi Klosterhallen tönt
Du Grabesrose wurzelst wohl
Es hat das Herz des Menschen ganz
Es steht eine gold'ne Wiege am Fuss
Fürst, Trossbub, Ritter, Gauner
Max wollt' aus Augsburg reiten

Otto Gruppe
Der Löw' ist los! der Löw' ist frei!
Die Trepp' hinunter geschwungen komm' ich
Klein Lieschen, ich hab' dich so lieb
O lass, Geliebter, dich erflehen
's ist wahr, mit blanken Scheiben
Wie pocht mir vor Lust das Herz in der Brust!

"Friedrich Halm" (Münch-Bellinghausen)
Mein Herz, ich will dich fragen

Johannes Heermann
O Jesu Christe, wahres Licht, erleuchte

Heinrich Heine
Die Lotusblume ängstigt sich
Die schlanke Wasserlilie schaut träumend
Du schönes Fischermädchen, treibe den Kahn
Herz, mein Herz, sei nicht beklommen
Ich hab' im Traume geweinet
Im Traum sah ich die Geliebte
Leise zieht durch mein Gemüth
Sie liebten sich beide, doch keiner wollt' es
Täglich ging die wunderschöne Sultanstochter

Heinrich von Stretlingen
Der ich von den Frauen allen

"Dilia Helena" (Helena Branco)
Blättlein so fein und rund
Das Glockenspiel der Phantasie
Der Frühling begrüsset die junge Natur
Du giebst die Freude, du giebst das Leid
Ein Himmelreich dein Auge ist
Ich sinke dir ans volle Herz
Mit jedem Pulsschlag leb' ich dir
O nimm mich an als deine Magd!

Wie ein Schwan still die Bahn zieht der Mond
Helene, Herzogin von Orléans
Wer einsam steht im bunten Lebenskreise
Ludwig Helmbold
Der heilig Geist vom Himmel kam
Johann Gottfried Herder
Dein Schwert, wie ist's von Blut so roth
Es kam zu ihr, leis an die Thür
Herr Oluf reitet spät und weit
Ich legte mein Haupt auf Elvershöh
In der Ruhe Thal geboren, wer verliesse
Liebes leichtes luft'ges Ding, Schmetterling!
Mein Freund Antonius, der Vater mir
Hildebrandt
Auf, Preussenherz, mit deinen Jubeltönen
Ludwig Hölty
O wunderschön ist Gottes Erde
Hoffmann von Fallersleben
Jugend, dich hab' ich so lieb!
Christoph Christian Hohlfeld
Ernst ritt der Kaiser in die heil'gen Hallen
Victor Aimé Huber
Durch die Strassen von Granada
Johannes (Jan) Hus
Jesus ist mein Hirt, auf Jesum will ich bauen
August Kahlert
Hier steh' ich einsam auf dem Fels im Meer
Friedrich Kind
Offerus war ein Lanzenknecht
Ewald Christian von Kleist
Gross ist der Herr! Die Himmel ohne Zahl
Hermann Kletke
Siehst du am Abend die Wolken ziehn
Friedrich Klopstock
Preis ihm! Er schuf und er erhält
Wenn einst ich tot bin
Albert Knapp
Ein frommer Landmann in der Kirche saß
Theodor Körner
Es war ein Jäger wohl keck und kühn
Wo dort die alten Gemäuer stehn
August Kopisch
Es tönt des Nöcken Harfenschall
O wehe, Heinz von Lüder, wie ist um dich
Wie war zu Cölln es doch vordem
Ludwig Kosegarten
Wenn du wärst mein eigen
August von Kotzebue
Das war ein Thier, mein Mauleselein!
Ein Kind an Mutterbrust
Es klingt eine Regel zwar wunderlich
Hier, wo seine fetten Herden
Mit langem Barte, bleich und blass
Mitten im Sturm, der mich umbrüllte
Kraft
Lasst uns mit ehrfurchtvollem Dank
Johann Christian Krauseneck
Kleine Spinnerin hinter deinem Rädchen
Friedrich Adolf Krummacher
Auf hoher Alp wohnt auch der liebe Gott
Der Sonntag ist da! Er kommt uns gesendet
Hört die Lerche, sie singt!
Mag auch die Liebe weinen!
Wenn einst mein Lebenstag sich neiget
Elieser Gottlieb Küster
Vater unser beten wir, der du in dem Himmel
Franz Kugler
Der junge König und sein Gemahl
Ein Klippeneiland liegt im Meer
Guten Morgen, du Sonnstagsglockenschall!
Herolde ritten von Ort zu Ort
Im Schloss, da brennen der Kerzen viel
Wie bräutlich glänzt das heilige Rom!
Wie ist so heiss im Busen mir
Johann C. Kugler
Als noch dem blinden Heiden wahn
Durch die Freundschaft fest verbunden
Wehmuth weckt der fernen Wolkenwand'rer
Friedrich von Kurowski-Eichen
Der Hahn hat gekräht, die Lerche singt
Die Nacht ist so dunkel, der Sturm so laut
Freiwillige vor! Auch du, lieb Mädchen
Ignaz Julius Lasker
Hinaus, hinaus! in freie Luft
Nikolaus Lenau
Weil' auf mir, du dunkles Auge
Gustav Lenz
Major! Ihr habt zu allen Zeiten
Lina Löper
Es lag auf meiner Stirn einst eine Wolke
Carl Loewe
Habe ich dir nicht gesagt, so du glauben würdest
Segne den König, ihn, unsern gütigen
Carl Loewe and [Rechtskandidat] Vocke
Als ich, ein Knabe noch, das heil'ge Land zuerst
Dank, grausender Dank sei dir gebracht
Der Mann ist geboren zur Liebe!
O falle, mein Schleier, o liege, mein Schleier
's ist wahrlich besser in Kampf und Schlacht
Helene Loewe
Steigt empor, ihr Wünsche mein
Stille, stille, dass ich höre,

August Ludwig Lua
Die Lerche singt ihr Morgenlied
Martin Luther
Mit Fried und Freud ich fahr dahin
Tod, Sünd, Leben und Gnad, alles
Arthur Lutze
Ein Engel zog durch Flur und Haus
Sag an, was hinauf zur Drachenkluft
August Mahlmann
Die Erde ruht, das Herz erwacht
Rudolf Marggraff
Durch Schneegestöber und eisigen Wind
Ein Sternlein fiel vom Himmel her
Friedrich von Matthisson
Nichts unterm Monde gleicht uns Elfen
Dr. Mayer
Von deinem Bilde nur umschwebet
Melzer & Hanser
Jetzt erklang die Sterbestunde
War einst ein hübsch Mädchen voll Feuer
Adam Mickiewicz
Ei, das tanzt, das lärmt und trinket!
In den Schlosshof hernieder rief Held Budris
Lerche zu des Frühlings Ruhme
Von dem Gartenaltan keucht zum Schlosse
Wer ist der Jüngling, lieblich zu schauen?
Wilia, sie, der unsre Ström' entsprangen
Moehrcke
Ich bin der Trommelschläger laut
Ernst Adolf von Mühlbach
Kam ein Schmetterling geflogen
Heinrich von Mühler
Zu Quedlinburg im Dome ertönet Glockenklang
Wilhelm Müller
Je höher die Glocke, je heller der Klang
Balthasar Münter
Er ist erstanden, Jesus Christ, der unser Gott
L. G. Naumann
Sei willkommen, Frühlingswehen
Jakob Neus
Wir beten an, hier unter Brot- und Wein-
Gustav Nicolai
Der Heiland ist für uns gestorben
Ihr Söhne Abrahams, seid einig!
August Hermann Niemeyer
Warum dein Blick so trübe, warum dein Herz
Wenn immer trüber deine Morgen tagen
"Novalis" (Friedrich von Hardenberg)
Wenn alle untreu werden, so bleib ich dir
Wenn ich ihn nur habe, wenn er mein nur ist
Anton Odyniec & Adam Mickiewicz
Mägdlein pflücket Beeren in des Waldes Mitten
Max von Oer
Zu Lüttich, im letzten Häuselein
Johannes Olearius
Wunderbarer Gnadenthron
Thomas Percy
Ein Bettelmann, schon lange blind
Gustav Pfizer
Ich bin ein leichter Junggesell
Karoline Pichler
Dort, wo in reine Lüfte der Karmel sich erhebt
August Graf von Platen
Nacht ist's, und Stürme sausen für und für
Luise von Plönnies
Die Königstochter sticket ein gülden Gewand
Es schaute in die Wogen die Maid
Sie ist herauf gestiegen aus der Kristallnen Gruft
Sie stürzt dem Neck zu Füssen
Und heller und heller quollen die Hymnen
Otto Prechtler
Wellen säuseln, Winde locken
Eugen von Puttkamer
Da, wo des Tajo grünlich blauer Strom
Carl Randow & Carl Loewe
Ihr deutschen Länder alle, folgt unserm Ruf
Ernst Raupach
Ihr Thoren wollt das Glück euch wählen
Liebe, deine Schmerzen hab' ich nicht gekannt
Philosophie oder Liebe? das ist die Frage
Wer möchte noch einmnal durchlaufen
Elisa von der Recke
Mit tausendfacher Schöne begrüsst der Lenz
Mitten unter deinen Schmerzen blicktest
Oskar von Redwitz
Der Wald ist schwarz, die Luft ist klar
Du, der Du bist der Geister Hort
Ich will die lauten Freuden nicht
Robert Reinick
Glühwürmchen, steck's Laternchen an!
Christian Ludwig Reissig
Die stille Nacht umdunkelt erquickend Thal
Johann Rist
Bleiches Antlitz, sei gegrüsset
K. Rose
Die Amsel flötet, es rieselt der Bach
"Rosemann" (Johann Klöntrup)
Der Garten des Lebens ist lieblich und schön
Christian Knorr von Rosenroth
Morgenglanz der Ewigkeit, Licht

Karoline Rudolphi
Auf, Brüder, auf! der Tag bricht an
Friedrich Rückert
Als Maria heut' entwich, heut' vor Jahren
Auf der Bank, wo sie sonst sitzet
Auf jener Flucht, von welcher nun
Das war die Schlacht von Waterloo
Die mich hält am Fädchen
Ein Licht im Traum hat mich besucht
Ein Liebchen hatt' ich, das auf einem Aug'
Einen Haushalt klein und fein hab' ich angestellt
Es ging die Riesentochter, zu haben einen Spass
Es läuft ein fremdes Kind am Abend
Herr! Herr, der du alles wohl gemacht
Herr Pfarrer hat zwei Fräulchen
Ich bin die Blum' im Garten
Ich stand auf Berges Halde
In Basra eine Wittwe war
Irrlichter, die Knaben, die laufen und traben
Jungfräulein Annika sass an dem Brückenrande
Mächtiger, der du die Wipfel dir beugst
Mein Gemüthe blühte gleich
Mein hochgeborenes Schätzelein
O Mutter, wie stürmen die Flocken
O süsse Mutter, ich kann nicht spinnen
Schäferin, ach, wie haben sie dich so süss
Sei bescheiden, nimm fürliebe
Welche chaotische Haushälterei,
Zeislein, Zeislein, wo ist dein Häuslein?
Zwei wunderliche Gevattern
Georg Ernst von Rüling
Dich soll mein Lied erheben
Johann von Salis-Seewis
Das Fischergewerbe giebt rüstigen Muth
Sappho
Goldenthronend, ewige Aphrodite
Ernst Scherenberg
Der Adler lauscht auf seinem Horst
Friedrich von Schiller
Ein frommer Knecht war Fridolin
Liebe rauscht der Silberbach
Zu Aachen, in seiner Kaiserpracht
Matthias Schleifer
Leon und Castilien waffnen
Konrad Arnold Schmid
Erhöhet die prächtigen Pforten der Siege!
Friederike Schmidt
Deinem sanft flötenden Ton, Philomele
August Schnezler
Im Mummelsee, im dunkeln See
Alois Schreiber
Maria kam auf ihrer Flucht gen Mittag
Meister Oluf, der Schmied auf Helgoland
Von des Hügels kahlem Rücken
Christian Friedrich Daniel Schubart
Gute Nacht! Unser Tagwerk ist vollbracht
Schlaf wohl, du Himmelsknabe du, schlaf wohl
Joh. Gottlob Schulz
Der Herbst beginnt, schon saust der Wind
Gustav Schwab
Der junge König Heinrich schlief
Friedrich von Schwarzenberg
Sei mir gegrüsst in deiner Pracht
Christian Friedrich Segelbach
Wir spielen und hüpfen so munter
Johann Seidl
Ich trage, wo ich gehe, stets eine Uhr bei mir
William Shakespeare
Die Arme, wie seufzend am Ahorn sass sie!
In meiner Jugend als ich liebte
Komm herbei, komm herbei, Tod
Karl Siebel
Bangt dir mein Lieb? Ich bin ja bei dir
Es ist mein Herz ein kleines Haus
Mein Herz, o schliess dich ein
Und als der Mensch geschaffen war
Wie viel Sonnenstrahlen fielen golden schwer
Karl Simrock
Schnür' den Bündel denn zum Wandern
Heinrich Stieglitz
Deine Stimme lass ertönen, hohe Fürstin
Ein Täubchen bringt mir täglich Grüsse
Einmal Mekka noch zu sehen
Geht nun, ihr Blüthen, meiner Fürstin Freude
Heiss glüht der Pfad; am frühen Tag war Melek
Hui! wie die Wolke von Staub und Brand
Ich schaukle leicht mich im grünen Laub
Ihr habt genug getrunken, ihr Herden gross
Lege den Schmuck nun an, schöne Gulhinde
Meinen Kranz hab' ich gesendet
O wie du schnaubst aus voller Brust
Reich' mir den Schleier, Emina
Wie lockt der Palmen grünes Dach
Stolberg-Stolberg
Süsse heilige Natur, lass mich gehn
Moritz, Graf von Strachwitz
's sind heute dreiunddreissig Jahr
Christoph Christian Sturm
Segne, Vater, meinen Fleiss
Sei gnädig mir nach deiner Güte
Sieh Jesum Christum leiden!

Johannes Hinrich Suck
Ehre sei Gott in der Höhe! Ehre sei Gott!
"Talvj" (Therese A. L. von Jacob)
Ach! mein kühler Wasserquell! Ach!
Herr Dÿring ritt wohl durch das Land
Hinterm Berge dort, dem grünen, tönt
Komm, o Bruder, in die helle Sonne
Singt ein Falk' all die Nacht durch
Trallallala, mein Liebchen, was hast du
Will die Holde sich ergehen
Winter vorbei, Herzchen, mein Liebchen!
Esaias Tegnér
Nun brennet am Nilstrom die Sonne so sehr
Wilhelm Telschow
Der Feinde Scharen rüsten sich
Der Kön'ge Herzen, Rath und Sinn hast du
Gieb ihm dein Herz und breite die Hände
Hinauf zu jenen Bergen schau' ich
Im Lande Uz, dem schönsten Idumäa's
Mit einem Blicke deiner Augen
Mög' er ewig wiederkehren
O dass doch ihr barmherzig wär't
Siehe, wir preisen selig die erduldet haben!
Und Hiobs Hause nahend
Ludwig Tieck
Wir lustigen Bürger in grüner Stadt
Karl Bernhard Trinius
Dürft' ich einmal dies Dach durchbrechen!
Adolf Ritter von Tschabuschnigg
Wer ist so spät noch fleissig wach?
Johann Ludwig Uhland
Da liegen sie alle, die grauen Höhn
Ein Goldschmied in der Bude stand
Ein Schifflein ziehet leise den Strom
Einst am schönen Frühlingsmorgen tritt
Es zogen drei Bursche wohl über den Rhein
Graf Eberhard im Bart vom Würtemberger Land
Guckst du mir denn immer nach
Ich bin vom Berg der Hirtenknab'
Ich sass bei jener Linde
Im Sommer sucht ein Liebchen dir
In der hohen Hall' saß König Sifrid
So hab' ich endlich dich gerettet
Über diesen Strom, vor Jahren
Von dir getrennet, liege ich begraben
Vor seinem Heergefolge ritt der kühne Held
Was klinget und singet die Strassen herauf?
Was wecken aus dem Schlummer mich
Zu Speier im Saale, da hebt sich ein Klingen
Anna Barbara Urner
Goldne Abendsonne, o, wie bist du schön!
Johann Nepomuk Vogl
Das war der Junker Emerich
Ein Wanderbursch, mit dem Stab in der Hand
Erschaffen schon die Erde lag
Es geht ein alter König lustwandeln
Es reitet schweigend und allein der alte Graf
Es steht der Sachsenführer, Herr Wittekind
Fahr hin! fahr hin! fahr hin für alle Zeiten
Ging Herr Walther hin im Freien
Herr Heinrich sitzt am Vogelherd
Horch, Hörnerklang, horch, Treiberruf
Im düstern Klostergarten ein einsam Brünnlein
Ist der alte Schiffsherr endlich heimgekehrt
Maria sitzt und stimmet die Harfe zum Gesang
Noch ziehn die Wolken düster
Sie waren alle zum Tanzplatz hinaus
Vor dem Schlosse Don Loranca's lehnt Hueska
Zu Pisa in dem Klostergarten
Johann Heinrich Voss
Der Holdseligen sonder Wank sing' ich
Willkommen im Grünen! Der Himmel ist blau
Ignaz Heinrich von Wessenberg
Franziskus einst, der Heil'ge
Friedrich Gottlob Wetzel
Im schönen Land Tirol hab ich mir lassen sagen
"Uffo von Wildingen" (Heinrich Zitzmann)
Noch schmückten zarte Blüthen
König Wilhelm IV
Herr Gott, der du bist! mein Schöpfer
Wie du deine Sonne hast lassen aufgehn
Freiherr von Zedlitz
In einem Dorf, am frühen Morgen
Nachts um die zwölfte Stunde
Karl Ziegler ("Karlopago")
Der Waldbach tost im Tannenthal
Es ist mein Herz verengt, verdorrt
W. Zinserling
Sanft mit seligem Entzücken
Wenn am kleinen Kammerfenster
Zuccalmaglio
Es flogen drei Schwälbelein über den Rhein
Anonymous
An Birkenzweigen blättert der volle Keim
Aufthaute die Erde vom Strahle der Sonne
Ave! Ave! Ave maris stella!
Der Bergmann lebt beim Grubenlicht
Der Meeresfluth mit Purpurgluth
Dich bet' ich an, erstand'ner Held
Die Feuerschlünde am Seinestrand
Dir, kleines Bethlehem, erklang
Dir stets getreu, getreu mit ganzer Seele

Du Unruh', du Unruh' meiner Seelen
Ein Mägdlein an des Felsen Rand
Elysium, du Land, wo Friede wird
Es wird wohl Winter weit und breit
Fischen schwimmt wohl hin und her
Flieg doch fort, du kleines Thier!
Frage nicht, wie es gekommen
Gelobt sei Gott, denn er erhört
Geruhig seines Weges gehn und wo man kann
Gleite hinan die glänzende Bahn!
Gloria in excelsis Deo!/Ehre sei Gott
Gute Nacht! Gute Nacht! Im Mondenschein
Herab kamst du auf Erden, ihr Trost und Heil
Hört ihr die Hörner erschallen, ihr Jäger
Ich habe keine Schulden
Ich trag' eine Liebe im Herzen
In dulci jubilo/nun singet und seid froh!
Jesus nimmt die Sünder an
Kleiner, kühler Wiesenquell, silberglänzend
Kommt herzu, ihr seid geladen
Kyrie, o Herr Gott Vater, erbarm' dich über uns!
Lasst uns beten: Vater unser, der du bist
Mädchen sind wie der Wind
Mag Thoren hienieden die Fessel aus Gold
Man geht aus Nacht in Sonne
Meerstern! Meerstern ich dich grüsse
Nicht mehr so sanft und milde entzücken
Niemals dich wieder zu sehen
O, meine Blumen, ihr, meine Freude
O wie ist es schön in die Schule gehn
Puer natus in Bethlehem/Ein Kind gebor'n
Quem pastores laudavere/Den die Hirten lobten
Schöpfer, deine Herrlichkeit leuchtet
Seh' ich dort die Sternlein blinken
Sonst konnt' ich dein nicht denken
Süsser Schlaf umfing den Müden
Um die blüthenvollen Äste summen Bienchen
Waldmeisterlein, Waldmeisterlein!
Was rüttelt die Säulen und schüttelt am Thron?
Wer droht unserm deutschen Vaterland?
Wir hatten einander so gerne
Zirpe, liebe kleine Sängerin der Haine
Zu dir, dem Weltenmeister, flammt jubelvoll

from Des Knaben Wunderhorn
Einmal in einem tiefen Thal

Otto Lohse (1858-1925)

Friedrich Bodenstedt
Neig' schöne Knospe dich zu mir
Joseph von Eichendorff
Am Himmelsgrund schießen so lustig die Stern'
Im Winde fächeln, Mutter, die Blätter
Emanuel Geibel
Laß schlafen mich und träumen
"Anastasius Grün" (A. A. von Auersperg)
Ich hab eine alte Muhme

Victor August Loser

Johann Wolfgang von Goethe
An die Türen will ich schleichen

Louis Ferdinand, Prinz von Preußen (1907-)

Clemens Brentano
Hör', es klagt die Flöte wieder
Adelbert von Chamisso
An meinem Herzen, an meiner Brust
Heinrich Danz
Leis' in meines Kindleins Träume klinge
Joseph von Eichendorff
Dunkle Giebel, hohe Fenster, Türme tief
Wie dem Wanderer in Träumen
Zwei Musikanten zieh'n daher vom Wald
Hans Franck
Über alle Weiten weht der gleiche Wind
Manfred Hausmann
Die weiten Wiesen schweigen im Duft
Käthe Kamossa
Die du dich an uns verschwendest
Komm' in aller Tage stille Dunkelheit
Mein sind blaue Himmelsstrahlen
Nebel wallen über kahles Land
Susanne Kerckhoff
Der Abend schließt die samtne Tür
Rosemarie Klotz-Burr
Allen Schmerz hat Gott gezählet
Es trat ein Himmel in mich ein
Curt Koschnick
Du Wunder, das der Herr uns gab
Herr, in dieser Weihestunde, da sich Herz
Ich hab' nichts auf Erden, ob nah oder fern
Wenn zum hellen Glokkenklang
Carl Lange
Abend, lege deine Hände leise
Ein Vöglein singt sein erstes Lied: Wach auf!
Schlaf, mein liebes Kindlein, schlafe ein
Nikolai von Michalewski
Ach, alle Blumen neigen das Haupt so bang
All meine reinen Gedanken, alles
Das Meer ist wie flüssige Jade
Der Wind aus dem Osten soll mich
Die Nacht ist so hell, ach laß uns zieh'n hinaus
Es preisen dich die Glokken wohl
Musik ist alles, was ich sage
Traum, den du verwebst mit dem Alltagsbild

Eduard Mörike
Frühling, läßt sein blaues Band
Richard Noehring
Ich sehe Winterblaß ein Land
Edgar Allan Poe
Am Morgen, am Mittag, im Abendlicht
Aleksandr Pushkin
Du Wolke, du Letzte des Sturms, der zerstoben!
Frank Thiess
Höre mich im Regen rauschen auf die Wipfel
Im Lichte wächst die Weide
Lieder, die gleich Regenschauern jagend
Woher ich komme weiß ich nicht
Peter Toussell
Alles, was war: Tag, Abend und Jahr
Frank Zwillinger
Und wieder spür' ich jenes leise Schwingen

Edward Alexander MacDowell (1860-1908)
Emanuel Geibel
Der Mond kommt still gegangen
Heinrich Heine
Du liebst mich nicht, du liebst mich nicht
Mein Liebchen, wir saßen beisammen
Oben, wo die Sterne glühen
Friedrich Klopstock
Im Frühlings Schatten fand ich sie

Alma Maria Schindler Mahler (1879-1964)
Otto Julius Bierbaum
Gott, deine Himmel sind mir aufgetan
Ringsum dunkle Nacht, hüllt in Schwarz
Richard Dehmel
Der Wald beginnt zu rauschen
Liegt eine Stadt im Tale, ein blasser Tag vergeht
O zürne nicht, wenn mein Begehren
Wie das Meer ist die Liebe
Gustav Falke
Der ganze Himmel glüht in hellen Morgenrosen
Laue Sommernacht, am Himmel stand
Otto Erich Hartleben
In meines Vaters Garten blühe, mein Herz
Heinrich Heine
Ich wandle unter Blumen und blühe selber mit
"Novalis" (Friedrich von Hardenberg)
Hinüber wall' ich und jede Pein
Wenige wissen das Geheimnis der Liebe
Rainer Maria Rilke
Bei dir ist es traut
Franz Werfel
Menschen lieben uns, und unbeglückt stehn sie

Gustav Mahler (1860-1911)
Richard Leander
Es klopft an das Fenster der Lindenbaum
Es wecket meine Liebe die Lieder
Gustav Mahler
Die zwei blauen Augen von meinem Schatz
Ging heut' Morgen über's Feld
Ich hab' ein glühend Messer
Ringel, ringel Reih'n! Wer fröhlich ist
Sag' an, du Träumer am lichten Tag
Über Berg und Tal mit lautem Schall
Wenn mein Schatz Hochzeit macht
Tirso de Molina
Das Mägdlein trat aus dem Fischerhaus
Ist's dein Wille, süsse Maid
Friedrich Rückert
Blicke mir nicht in die Lieder!
Ich atmet' einen Linden Duft
Ich bin der Welt abhanden gekommen
In diesem Wetter, in diesem Braus
Liebst du um Schönheit, o nicht mich liebe!
Nun seh' ich wohl, warum so dunkle Flammen
Nun will die Sonn' so hell aufgeh'n
Oft denk' ich, sie sind nur ausgegangen!
Um Mitternacht hab' ich gewacht
Wenn dein Mütterlein tritt zur Tür herein
from Des Knaben Wunderhorn
Antonius zur Predigt die Kirche find't ledig!
Bald gras' ich am Nekkar
Büble, wir wollen ausse gehe!
Des Morgens zwischen drei'n und vieren
Die Gedanken sind frei, wer kann sie errathen
Dort oben am Berg in dem hohen Haus!
Einstmals in einem tiefen Thal
Es kam ein Herr zum Schlösseli
Es ritten drei Reiter zum Thore hinaus!
Es sungen drei Engel einen süssen Gesang
Hast gesagt, du willst mich nehmen
Heute marschieren wir! Juchhe, juchhe!
Ich armer Tamboursg'sell!
Ich ging mit Lust durch einen grünen Wald
Ich kann und mag nicht fröhlich sein!
Ich weiss nicht, wie mir ist!
Kukuk hat sich zu Tode gefallen
Mutter, ach Mutter, es hungert mich
Und nun ade, mein herzallerliebster Schatz!
Wer ist denn draußen und wer klopfet an
Wir geniessen die himmlischen Freuden
Wohlan! Die Zeit ist kommen!
Zu Strassburg auf der Schanz'

Heinrich August Marschner (1795-1861)
Clemens Brentano
O kühler Wald, wo rauschest du
Hoffmann von Fallersleben
Die Bäume grünen überall
Ja, du bist mein! Ja, du bist mein!
Ludwig Pfau
O, du lieber Schatz, wir müssen scheiden
Robert Reinick
Der Förster ging zu Fest und Schmaus!
Der Himmel da oben, der freut mich sehr
Die Liebe, die Liebe ist ein Rosenstrauch
Mädel trug des Wegs daher einen Korb
Wie ist doch die Erde so schön, so schön!
Zaubrer bin ich, doch was frommt es?
Julius von Rodenberg
Bächlein am Wiesenrand
Not Yet Identified
Ave Maria! Neig' dein Angesicht

Henri Marteau (1874-1934)
Nikolaus Lenau
Auf dem Teich, dem regungslosen
Auf geheimem Waldespfade schleich' ich gern
Drüben ging die Sonne scheiden
Sonnenuntergang; schwarze Wolken ziehn
Trübe wirds, die Wolken jagent

Donald James Martino (1931-)
Rainer Maria Rilke
Ich bin die Laute. Willst du meinen Leib
In solchen Nächten wächst mein Schwesterlein

Joseph ("Pepo") Marx (1882-1964)
Rudolf Hans Bartsch
Es geht, es weht ein Rauch vor dem Wald
Carl Busse
Schönheit, die du im Mädchen blühst
Walter Calé
Was sich in Zeiten je begeben
Ada Christen
Hörst auch du die leisen Stimmen
Richard Dehmel
Der Wald beginnt zu rauschen
Joseph von Eichendorff
Bleib bei uns! Wir haben den Tanzplatz im Tal
Ich hör die Bächlein rauschen im Walde her
Gustav Falke
Herr, laß mich hungern dann und wann
Windräder gehn die Herbstesharfen sind
Theodor Fontane
Das Kind ist krank zu Sterben
Bruno Frank
Sonn' auf Sonn' sich hellt
Emanuel Geibel
Der Blumen wollt' ich warten
O Sommerfrühe blau und hold!
Max Geissler
Auf dem Herd kein Feuer, kein Rößlein
Mein brauner Liebster, sage mir
So durch die Gassen im Silberlicht
Albert Giraud
Der Violine zarte Seele voll schweigend
Des Mondlichts bleiche Blüten
Im phantast'schen Mondenstrahle
Wie ein blasser Tropfen Blut's
Johann Wolfgang von Goethe
Der du von dem Himmel bist
R. Graf
Acht der winzigen Perlen enthält
Die Quellen sangen in tiefer Nacht
Tod mit Blumen laß dein Tor bereiten
"Martin Greif" (Friedrich Hermann Frey)
Stille ruht die weite Welt
Knut Hamsun
Es singt in tiefem Tone in mir so schwer
Otto Erich Hartleben
Das Erste sei, daß man der Welt sich freue
Groß ist das Leben und reich!
Im Arm der Liebe schliefen wir selig ein
Süß duftende Lindenblüte
Wladimir von Hartlieb
Du dunkle Sehnsucht meiner Tage
Wald du, fieberdurchglutet
Heinrich Heine
Ein Fichtenbaum steht einsam im Norden
E. H. Hess
O sähst du mich jetzt beten
Hermann Hesse
Mir zittern die Saiten und stimmen die Weise an
Wenn du die Hand mir gibst
Paul Heyse
Das Meer ist für die Fischer auf der Welt
Es zürnt das Meer, es zürnt die Felsenküste
Geh' schlafen, Liebste, lege dich zur Ruh
Gute Nacht, geliebtes Leben, ruf' ich dir
Hat dich die Liebe berührt
Ich bin durch einen schönen Wald gekommen
Ich hab' empor gesehen und geglaubt
Ich stellt' ein Lilienstäudlein an mein Fenster
Ich will nur ihn! Und doch, kommt er zu mir
Nimm dir ein schönes Weib
Nina, ninana will ich dir singen

O schick' mich nicht allein zum Brunnen fort
Sie sagen mir, daß meine Wangen schwarz sind
Sonst plaudert ich mit Euch die Zeit entfloh
Und wenn ich werd' im Sarg gebettet liegen
Und wollen mich die klugen Leute fragen
Vier Grüße send' ich zu dir auf die Reise
Wie reizend bist du Montag morgens immer

Arno Holz
Die Sonne sank, ich wartete lange

Ludwig Jacobowski
Ach, uns're leuchtenden Tage
Duld' es still, wenn von den Zweigen

Königsbrunn-Schaup
Der Kuckuck ruft Ku-ku-ku-ku

Thekla Lingen
Ach gestern hat er mir Rosen gebracht

Conrad Ferdinand Meyer
Am Himmel wächst der Sonne Glut

Eduard Mörike
Die Liebe, sagt man, steht am Pfahl gebunden
Im Nebel ruht die weite Welt

Alfred Mombert
Leise hör' ich dich singen Sankta Maria
Schlafend trägt man mich, in mein Heimatland

Paul Mongré
Das ist so süß, das unser rascher Bund
Dies Augenpaar von dunklem Glanz betaut

Alfred de Musset
Daferns geschah, das wir begraben

"Novalis" (Friedrich von Hardenberg)
Ich sehe dich in tausend Bildern

August Graf von Platen
O süßer Tod, der alle Menschen schrekket

Rainer Maria Rilke
Es gibt so wundervolle Nächte

Anna Ritter
Ich komme heim aus dem Sonnenland!

Julius von Rodenberg
Nun bricht aus allen Zweigen

Friedrich Rückert
So lang ich werde: "Liebst du mich, o Liebster"

Sao-han
Der Mond steigt aufwärts

Adolf Friedrich von Schack
Um der fallenden Ruder Spitzen

Emil Rudolf Schönaich-Carolath
O gib mir nicht die voll erblühte Rose

Theodor Storm
Schließe mir die Augen beide

Ella Triebnigg
Wollt' vorüber gehen, doch es mußt' geschehen

Johann Ludwig Uhland
Saatengrün, Veilchenduft, Lerchenwirbel

Paul Verlaine
Regen über der Stadt und mein Herz steht

Heinrich Vogeler
Ihr lieben Frühlingssänger zieht

Christian Weisse
Mein Schäfer, ach! der ist bescheiden!

Paul Wertheimer
Hände, viele Hände über der Haide schweben

Walt Whitman
Jugend du große, sehnende, liebende!

Anton Wildgans
Alles Tagverlangen ist zur Ruh gegangen
Dämm'rung feuchtet die Büsche
Du bist der Garten, wo meine Hände
Durch Einsamkeiten, durch waldwild' Geheg

Stefan Zweig
Ein Drängen ist in meinem Herzen

Anonymous
Tausend goldne Blätter sinken
Wo ich ferne des Mikane hohen Gipfel

Volkslied
Männer suchen stets zu naschen

Karl Marx (1897-1985)

Hermann Claudius
Das alte Wunder ward wieder wahr:
Das Heimlicht zwischen dir und mir
Daß zwei sich herzlich lieben
Der alte Turm und die Schwalben haben
Der Regen, der Regen, der langentbehrte Segen!
Der Wind der weht. Alles vergeht im Winde
Des Nordens Wunder ist der Winter
Du liebe, liebe Sonne, bescheine mich
Dunkel war der Zweig, den du mir brachtest
Ein Menschlein ward geboren
Es blinken in der Sonne die grünen Gräser sehr
Es drängt sich auf den Beeten
Ich habe sie selber gezogen
Ist das in dir der Mensch oder der Christ
Mann und Weib und Kind.
Sie wiegen schwankend sich
Sonne über Ähren du kannst dich nicht
Späte Rose, in dem hohen Glase
Tage der Gnade brechen herein
Tagtäglich bietest du dich dar
Wie wandelnde Landschaft gehn über die Erde
Wir tragen alle den Tod im Leib und helfen ihn
Zu den winterkahlen Zweigen

Johann Wolfgang von Goethe
Da wächst der Wein, wos Faß ist

Dem Schützen, doch dem alten nicht
Felsen sollten nicht Felsen, und Wüsten
Herr, laß dir gefallen dieses kleine Haus!
Hier hilft nun weiter kein Bemühn!
Laß Neid und Mißgunst sich verzehren
Was die Großen Gutes taten
Wenn dirs in Kopf und Herzen schwirrt
Wer, wer kann gebieten den Vögeln
Wer will denn alles gleich ergründen!
Wir reiten in die Kreuz und Quer
Wohl! wer auf rechter Spur sich in der Stille

Rainer Maria Rilke
Das ist die Sehnsucht: wohnen im Gewoge
Ihr Mädchen seid wie die Gärten
Lauschende Wolke über dem Wald
Manchmal geschieht es in tiefer Nacht
Oft fühl ich in scheuen Schauern

Emil Mattiesen (1875-1939)

M. Barthel
Leben gibst du, Leben nimmst du

Clemens Brentano
Singet leise, singt ein flüsternd Wiegenlied

Franz Eichert
Ich bin mein Lied, mein Lied bin ich

Johann Wilhelm Ludwig Gleim
Gute Nacht! Mädchen, das der Liebe lacht

"Martin Greif" (Friedrich Hermann Frey)
Ich geh auf stillen Wegen frühtags

Hermann Hesse
Holder Schein, an deine Spiele sieh
O schau, sie schweben wieder

Ricarda Huch
Mit meinem Liebchen Hand in Hand

Nikolaus Lenau
Diese Rose pflück ich hier, in der fremden Ferne

Detlev von Liliencron
O wär es doch! Hinaus in dunkle Wälder

Conrad Ferdinand Meyer
Es geht mit mir zu Ende

Karl Ludwig von Münchhausen
Je länger du dort bist, um so mehr bist du hier

Friedrich Rückert
Wohl endet Tod des Lebens Not

Seidel
Auf einer Meierei da war einmal

Regine Strümpell
Mit Neigen ich dich grüße, du blickst so mild

Karl Weitbrecht
Wenn ich Abschied nehme, will ich leise gehn

Anonymous
Ein Musikus wollt fröhlich sein

Fried. Mayer

"Martin Greif" (Friedrich Hermann Frey)
Auf luft'ger Höh' alleine ein Wanderbursche

Lise Maria Mayer (1894-)

Hans Bethge
Zu meiner Flöte, die aus Jade ist

"Martin Greif" (Friedrich Hermann Frey)
Der Himmel strahlend ausgespannt

Nikolai Karlovich Medtner (1880-1951)

Adelbert von Chamisso
Hab oft im Kreise der Lieben
Unsre Quelle kommt im Schatten

Joseph von Eichendorff
Es zog eine Hochzeit den Berg entlang
Komm zum Garten denn, du Holde!
Verschneit liegt rings die ganze Welt

Johann Wolfgang von Goethe
Ach, wer bringt die schönen Tage
An dem reinsten Frühlingsmorgen
An die Türen will ich schleichen
Bei dem Glanze der Abendröte
Der du von dem Himmel bist
Der Vorhang schwebet hin und her
Die ihr Felsen und Bäume bewohnt
Die Nebel zerreissen, der Himmel ist helle
Ein Blumenglöckchen vom Boden hervor
Ein Veilchen auf der Wiese stand
Es war ein Knabe frech genug
Hoch auf dem alten Turme steht
Ich denke dein, wenn mir der Sonne Schimmer
Ich ging im Felde so für mich hin
Ich ging im Walde so für mich hin
Im Felde schleich' ich still und wild
Inneres Wühlen ewig zu finden
Liebliches Kind, kannst du mir sagen
Nur wer die Sehnsucht kennt
Sie liebt mich! Sie liebt mich!
Sieh mich, Heil'ger, wie ich bin
So tanzet und springet in Reihen und Kranz
Tiefe Stille herrscht im Wasser
Über allen Gipfeln ist Ruh'
Um Mitternacht, wenn die Menschen
Und frische Nahrung, neues Blut saug' ich
Von wem ich's habe, das sag' ich euch nicht
Wenn im Unendlichen dasselbe
Wenn zu den Reihen der Nymphen
Zwischen Weizen und Korn

Heinrich Heine
Ein Fichtenbaum steht einsam im Norden
Ein Reiter durch das Bergthal zieht

Lieb Liebchen, leg's Händchen auf's Herze
Friedrich Nietzsche
Das war ein Tag der Schmerzen
In Sonnenglut, in Mittagsruh liegt stumm
Von Ferne tönt der Glokkenschlag,
Johann Ludwig Uhland
Oh, leget mich nicht ins Grab, unter die Erde

Arnold Ludwig Mendelssohn (1855-1933)
Heinrich Heine
Lächelnd scheidet der Despot, denn er weiß
Verstummt sind die Pauken, Posaunen

(Jakob Ludwig) Felix Mendelssohn-Bartholdy (1809-1847)
Adolf Böttger
Ich hör' ein Vöglein locken
Robert Burns
O säh ich auf der Heide dort im Sturme dich
Lord Byron
Keine von der Erde Schönen
Schlafloser Augen Leuchte, trüber Stern
Johann Gustav Droysen
Herr, zu Dir will ich mich retten
In weite Fernen will ich träumen
Karl Egon Ebert
Als ich das erste Veilchen erblickt
Bringet des treu'sten Herzens Grüsse
Joseph von Eichendorff
Es weiss und räth es doch Keiner
Laue Luft kommt blau geflossen
Vergangen ist der lichte Tag
Wenn die Sonne lieblich schiene
Wo noch kein Wand'rer gegangen
Wohin ich geh und schaue in Feld und Wald
Ernst von Feuchtersleben
Es ist bestimmt in Gottes Rath
Paul Flemming
Lass dich nur nichts nicht dauern
Emanuel Geibel
Mein Herz ist wie die dunkle Nacht
Wenn sich zwei Herzen scheiden
Johann Wolfgang von Goethe
Ach, wer bringt die schönen Tage
Die Nachtigall, sie war entfernt
Ein Blick von deinen Augen in die meinen
So weit gebracht, daß wir bei Nacht
Heinrich Heine
Allnächtlich im Traume seh' ich dich
Auf Flügeln des Gesanges, Herzliebchen
Der Herbstwind rüttelt die Bäume
Ich stand gelehnet an den Mast
Ich wollt, meine Lieb ergösse sich
In dem Mondenschein im Walde sah ich
Leise zieht durch mein Gemüth
Über die Berge steigt schon die Sonne
Wenn ich auf dem Lager liege
Heinrich der Schreiber
Es ist in den Wald gesungen
Ludwig Hölty
Die Schwalbe fliegt, der Frühling siegt
Holder klingt der Vogelsang
Hoffmann von Fallersleben
Ein Leben war's im Ährenfeld
Es freut sich Alles weit und breit
Maiglöckchen läutet in dem Tal
Werde heiter, mein Gemüthe
Wie war so schön doch Wald und Feld!
Victor Hugo
Wozu der Vöglein Chöre belauschen
Karl Immermann
Leg' in den Sarg mir mein grünes Gewand
Jakob von Warte
Man soll hören süsses Singen
Philipp Kaufmann
Wie kann ich froh und lustig sein?
C. Klingemann
Ach, wie schnell die Tage fliehen
Ach, wie so bald verhallet der Reigen
Der Frühling naht mit Brausen
Es brechen im schallenden Reigen
Es lauschte das Laub so dunkelgrün
Im Walde rauschen dürre Blätter
Ringsum erschallt in Wald und Flur
Schlummre! Schlummre und träume
Sie wandelt im Blumengarten
Nikolaus Lenau
Auf dem Teich, dem regungslosen
Diese Rose pflück' ich hier
Durch den Wald, den dunkeln
Ich wandre fort in's ferne Land
Thomas Moore
An Celia's Baum in stiller Nacht hängt
Wenn durch die Piazzetta die Abendluft weht
Friederike Robert
Jetzt kommt der Frühling, der Himmel isch blau
Wisst ihr, wo ich gerne weil'
Friedrich von Schiller
Der Eichwald brauset, die Wolken ziehn
Albert Graf von Schlippenbach
Die Sterne schau'n in stiller Nacht
Karl Simrock
An den Rhein, an den Rhein, zieh' nicht

Friedrich von Spee
Der trübe Winter ist vorbei
Ludwig Tieck
Wie der Quell so lieblich klinget
Johann Ludwig Uhland
Das ist der Tag des Herrn
Die linden Lüfte sind erwacht
Ein Schifflein ziehet leise den Strom
O Winter, schlimmer Winter, wie ist die Welt
Ulrich von Lichtenstein
In dem Walde süsse Töne singen
Johann Heinrich Voss
Das Tagewerk ist abgethan. Gieb, Vater
Erwacht in neuer Stärke, begrüss' ich, Gott
Ist es wahr? Ist es wahr?
Wie so gelinde die Fluth bewegt!
Willkommen im Grünen! der Himmel ist blau
Marianne von Willemer
Ach, um deine feuchten Schwingen
Was bedeutet die Bewegung?
Anonymous
Da lieg' ich unter den Bäumen
Doch der Herr, er leitet die Irrenden recht
Einmal aus seinen Blicken
Ihr frühlingstrunk'nen Blumen
Kennst du nicht das Gluthverlangen
Leucht't heller als die Sonne
Sie trug ein Falken auf ihrer Hand
from Des Knaben Wunderhorn
Mit Lust thät ich ausreiten
Volkslied
Es ist ein Schnitter, der heisst Tod
Mein Sohn, wo willst du hin so spät?
Von allen schönen Kindern auf der Welt

Erik Meyer-Helmund (1861-1932)
Maximilian Bern
Was mich zu Dir so mächtig zog
Ignaz Franz Castelli
Herzliebe gute Mutter, o grolle nicht mit mir
Felix Dahn
Du bist die Herrlichste von Allen
George von Dyherrn
Wenn dein ich denk', dann sinn' ich oft
Hermann Erler
Mir tönt aus fernen Zeiten ein Wort
Heinrich Heine
Mädchen, Mädchen mit dem rothen Mündchen
Mein Liebchen wir sassen beisammen
Paul Heyse
Soll ich ihn lieben, soll ich ihn lassen
Alexander Kaufmann
Die Wasserlilie kichert leis'
Erik Meyer-Helmund
Die Schmetterlinge, die fliegen von einer Blume
Du sagst,ich hätte die Nachbarn geweckt
Ich bin auf Dich böse, du Liebchen mein
Ich hab' mein Herz verloren
Ihr Mägdelein, nehmt euch in Acht
Mutter, Mütterchen, ach sei nicht böse
Eduard Mörike
Früh, wenn die Hähne krähen
Otto Roquette
Ach Gott, das druckt das Herz mir ab
Joseph Viktor von Scheffel
Das ist im Leben hässlich eingerichtet
Sonne taucht in Meeresfluthen
Karl Siebel
Hätt' es nimmer gedacht, dass ein Strom
Karl Stieler
Ich bin der Mönch Waltramus
Theodor Storm
Das macht, es hat die Nachtigall
Einen Brief soll ich schreiben meinem Schatz
Moritz, Graf von Strachwitz
Wie gerne Dir zu Füssen sing ich
Julius Sturm
Das war die Lisa, die lustige Maid
Wernher von Tegernsee
Ich bin Dein, Du bist mein
Johann Ludwig Uhland
Im Sommer such' ein Liebchen dir
Julius Wolff
Kukuk! was rufst im Wald mich an?
Volkslied
Herziges Schätzle Du hast mer all' mei Ruh'
Not Yet Identified
Du fragst mich täglich
Du grollest und schmollest
Duftet die Lindenblüth schläfernd zur Nacht
Es schaukelt so leise der spielende Wind
Es war im Wonnemonat Mai,
Ich hab' noch nie so wie heute
Mädchen, hör' mich ruhig an
Mein Mädel hat Äuglein, so schwarz
Nachtigall hüte dich, singe nicht so lieblich

Giacomo Meyerbeer (Jakob Liebmann Beer) (1791-1864)
Michael Beer
Armes Kind, südlich weht der Wind
Gegen mich selber in Haß entbrannt
Komm', Liebchen, komm'! die Nacht ist hell

Friedrich Bodenstedt
Die helle Sonne leuchtet auf's weite Meer
Heinrich Heine
Die Rose, die Lilie, die Taube, die Sonne
Du schönes Fischermädchen, treibe den Kahn
Hör' ich das Liedchen klingen
Hermann Kletke
Rings waltet heil'ges Schweigen
Albert Knapp
Himmelsluft vom Morgenlande
Wilhelm Müller
In meines Herzens Mitte
Wirf Rosenblätter in die Flut
Friedrich Rückert
Daß der Ostwind Düfte
Johann Seidl
Zu des Mondes sanftem Schimmer schickt sich
Marianne von Willemer
Wie mit innigstem Behagen, Lied

Peter Mieg (1906-)
Friedrich Hölderlin
Goldene Leier Appolons

Franz Mikorey (1873-1947)
Peter Cornelius
Ich ersehnt' ein Lied wie die Blume den Tau

Franz Mittler (1893-1970)
Carl Busse
Bleiche Blüte, Blüte der Liebe,
Rebhahnruf und Glokkenlaut, ich und du
Wenn die Linde blüht, sind die jungen
Rainer Maria Rilke
Mich rührt so sehr böhmischen Volkes Weise
Anna Ritter
Und dürft' ich dich wekken zum Sonnenlicht

C. Moltke (1783-1831)
Johann Wolfgang von Goethe
Das Wasser rauscht, das Wasser schwoll

Moritz Moszkowski (1854-1925)
Adelbert von Chamisso
Denke, denke, mein Geliebter, meiner alten Lieb
Ich habe bevor der Morgen im Osten
Nicht der Thau und nicht der Regen dringen
Was ist's, o Vater, was ich verbrach?
Wie so bleich ich geworden bin?
Heinrich Heine
Und wüssten's die Blumen, die kleinen
Nikolaus Lenau
Weil auf mir, du dunkles Auge

Carl Wittkowsky
Auf, hinaus aus dem Haus
Ich frage nicht: "hast Du mich lieb?"
O süsseste Noth! O selige Pein!
Julius Wolff
Mädchenaug'! Strahlender Schimmer

Felix Josef Mottl (1856-1911)
Georg Friedrich Daumer
Ich thät mich einst vermiethen zu Sankt Marie
Hermann Lingg
Man sagt, durch's Zimmer walle
Conrad Ferdinand Meyer
Don Fadrique bringt ein Ständchen
Hermann Sudermann
Du wähnst mich fromm, du wähnst mich weise

Wolfgang Amadeus Mozart (1756-1791)
Gabriele von Baumberg
Erzeugt von heisser Phantasie
Alois Blumauer
Wer unter eines Mädchens Hand
Joachim Heinrich Campe
Abend ist's, die Sonne ist verschwunden
Johann Wilhelm Ludwig Gleim
Ich möchte wohl der Kaiser sein
Johann Wolfgang von Goethe
Ein Veilchen auf der Wiese stand
Friedrich von Hagedorn
Zu meiner Zeit, zu meiner Zeit
Johann Timotheus Hermes
Ich würd' auf meinem Pfad
Sei du mein Trost, verschwiegne Traurigkeit!
Verdankt sei es dem Glanz
Ludwig Hölty
Wo bist du, Bild, das vor mir stand
Johann Georg Jacobi
Wenn die Lieb' aus deinen blauen
Ludwig Friedrich Lenz
O heiliges Band der Freundschaft
Johann Martin Miller
Was frag ich viel nach Geld und Gut
Wolfgang Amadeus Mozart
Liebes Mandel, wo ist's Bandel?
Christian Adolf Overbeck
Komm, lieber Mai, und mache die Bäume
Wir Kinder, wir schmecken
Josef Franz von Ratschky
Die ihr einem neuen Grade
Johann Eberhard Friedrich Schall
Es war einmal, ihr Leutchen

Klamer Eberhard Karl Schmidt
Die Engel Gottes weinen
Christoph Christian Sturm
Erwacht zum neuen Leben
Johann Peter Uz
Freude, Königin der Weisen
Christian Weisse
Der reiche Tor
Ihr, Mädchen, flieht Damöten ja!
Sobald Damötas Chloën sieht
Wie sanft, wie ruhig fühl ich hier
Anonymous
Dem hohen Kaiser-Worte treu
Komm, liebe Zither, komm
Was spinnst du? fragte Nachbars Fritz
Wie unglücklich bin ich nit
Volkslied
Männer suchen stets zu naschen

Modest Petrovich Mussorgsky (1839-1881)
Johann Wolfgang von Goethe
An die Türen will ich schleichen
Es war einmal ein König
Heinrich Heine
Aus meinen Tränen spriessen
Ich wollt', meine Schmerzen ergössen
Friedrich Rückert
Hoher Berge Schatten liegen auf dem Meer

Hans Georg Nägeli (1773-1836)
Johann Wolfgang von Goethe
Ach, wer bringt die schönen Tage
Und frische Nahrung, neues Blut saug ich
Friedrich von Matthisson
Goldner Schein deckt den Hain

Christian Gottlob Neefe (1748-1798)
Johann Wolfgang von Goethe
Liebliches Kind! Kannst du mir sagen?
Johann Gottfried Herder
Flattre, flattr' um deine Quelle
Friedrich Klopstock
Ha! dort kömmt er mit Schweiß
Not Yet Identified
Düster liegt die Nacht umher

Sigismund Ritter von Neukomm (1778-1858)
Julius Wilhelm Zincgref
Mein feines Lieb ist fern von mir

Mathieu Neumann (1867-1928)
Anna Ritter
Als über den Flieder das Mondlicht rann
Da kennt so ein Mann nun die halbe Welt
Das ist ein lieb Beisammen sein
Die Tage rinnen leise hin
"Ein Mädchen!" "Ein Mädchen!"
Ich trag' ein glückselig Geheimnis mit mir
In deinem Arm, an deinem Herzen o sag', o sag'
Junge Hände halfen mich schmücken

Friedrich Wilhelm Nietzsche (1844-1900)
Lou Andreas-Salomé
Gewiß, so liebt ein Freund den Freund
Lord Byron
O, weint um sie die einst an Babels Strand
Schlafloser Augen Sonne trüber Stern
Adelbert von Chamisso
Auf hohen Burgeszinnen der alte König stand
Der Gang war schwer, der Tag war rauh
Du arme Kerze giebst fürder keinen Schein
Joseph von Eichendorff
In einem kühlen Grunde da geht ein Mühlenrad
Emanuel Geibel
Herbstlich sonnige Tage
Klaus Groth
Da geht ein Bach das Thal entlang
Der Weg an unserm Zaun entlang
Hoffmann von Fallersleben
Wie sich Rebenranken schwingen
Friedrich Nietzsche
Des Morgens still ich träume und schau
O! A! Kirchengeschichte hör ich nicht
Sándor Petöfi
Du nur bist, du liebes Mädchen
Du warst ja meine einzge Blume
Es winkt und neigt sich seltsam am Fenster
Herab läßt sich der Wolke Saum
Ich möchte lassen diese glanzumspielte Welt
Aleksandr Pushkin
O wenn es wahr, daß in der Nacht
Friedrich Rückert
Aus der Jugendzeit klingt ein Lied mir
Anonymous
Ade! Ich muß nun gehen zum Krieg

Ernst Otto Nodnagel (1870-1909)
Heinrich Heine
Ich hab' mir lang' den Kopf zerbrochen
Otto von Leixner
Ich ahnte nicht vor kurzer Zeit
Ob dein ich bin? Was fragst du mich?
Anonymous
Kennst du nicht das Glutverlangen

Vítězslav Augustín Rudolf Novák (1870-1949)
Otto Julius Bierbaum
Weite Wiesen im Dämmergrau
Richard Dehmel
Wie das Meer ist die Liebe: unerschöpflich
"Martin Greif" (Friedrich Hermann Frey)
Ich geh' auf stillen Wegen frühtags
Otto Erich Hartleben
Siehst du die Perlen springen
Friedrich Hebbel
Wir träumten von einander
Karl Henckell
Komm in den Wald, Marie!

Carl Orff (1895-1982)
Richard Beer-Hofmann
Schlaf mein Kind, schlaf, es ist spät
"Klabund" (Alfred Henschke)
Blond ist mein Haar, blau ist mein Blick
Du gabst mir immer wieder dein Herz
Herr, ich liebte aller Dinge Niederstes
Nikolaus Lenau
Weil auf mir du dunkles Auge
Hermann Lingg
Immer leiser wird mein Schlummer
Friedrich Nietzsche
Mein Herz ist wie ein See so weit
Franz Werfel
Alles, was von uns kommt, wandelt schon
Als mich dein Dasein tränenwärts entrückte
Du, der du keine Gnade kennst
Ich liege in gläsernem Wachen
O die ihr geht am Abend in euer Zimmer ein
O Lieb und Leid so überein!
Sein ist die Kraft, das Regiment der Sterne

Leo Ornstein (1892-)
Richard Dehmel
Bienchen, Bienchen wiegt sich im Sonnenschein
Der Wald beginnt zu rauschen
Paul Remer
Wir schreiten in goldener Fülle

Léon Orthel (1905-1985)
Rainer Maria Rilke
Der Sommer summt. Der Nachmittag
Oft war sie als Kind ihren Dienerinnen

Thorvald Otterström (1868-1942)
Heinrich Heine
Auf ihrem Grab da steht eine Linde
Du bist wie eine Blume
Entflieh' mit mir und sei mein Weib
Es fiel ein Reif in der Frühlingsnacht
Es liegt der heiße Sommer
Still ist die Nacht, es ruhen die Gassen
Friedrich Rückert
Komm, verhüllte Schöne! Komm!
from Des Knaben Wunderhorn
Bei der Nacht ist so finster im Weg
Wenn du zu mei'm Schätzel kommst, sag

Maria Theresia von Paradis (1759-1824)
Gottfried August Bürger
Lenore fuhr um's Morgenroth
Matthias Claudius
Ich bin ein deutscher Jüngling
Johann Nikolaus Götz
Nie hält sich Zephyrus bei einem Vorwurf auf
Johann Timotheus Hermes
Endlich winkt der Freund der Müden
Sey mir gegrüßt mein schmeichelndes Klavier
Weckst du mich zum neuen Jammer
Friedrike Magdalena Jerusalem
Da eben seinen Lauf vollbracht
Friedrich Klopstock
Wenn ich einst von jenem Schlummer
Sophie von La Roche
Meiner lieben trauten Linde
Johann Martin Miller
Es war einmal ein Gärtner, der sang
Wohl und immer wohl dem Mann
Gottlieb Conrad Pfeffel
Sieh Doris wie vom Mond bestrahlt
Johann Riedinger
Ihr Lieben, die ich Schwermuthsvoll
Anonymous
Wenn ich der Kaiser wäre

Casimir von Pászthory (1886-1966)
Hermann Hesse
Es geht ein Wind von Westen
Meine fröhliche Liebe hat mich verlassen
Sei nicht traurig! Bald ist es Nacht
Seltsam, im Nebel zu wandern!
Wenn du die kleine Hand mir gibst
Wie fremd und wunderlich das ist

Helmut Paulsen (1909-)
Rudolf Georg Binding
Heut Nacht, mein Lieb, da nehm ich dich
Hermann Hesse
Bist allein im Leeren, glühst einsam, Herz
Wer den Weg nach innen fand
Kurt Kuberzig
Und ihre Augen irren rings umher

Rainer Maria Rilke
Der Tod ist groß
Uraltes Wehn vom Meer, Meerwind bei Nacht
Paul Verlaine
Der Himmel, drüben über dem Dach

Ernst Pepping (1901-1981)
Werner Bergengruen
Atme, Seele, erhöhter, weil du den Sommer
Es rieseln die Sekunden, an weißen Sand
Hier liegt der Sommer begraben–
Rüste abendlich die Schale, schütte Milch
Käthe Braun-Präger
Streu' ich Zucker auf die Speise
Clemens Brentano
Einen kenn ich, wir lieben ihn nicht
Ich habe allem Leben mit jedem Abendrot
Was reif in diesen Zeilen steht
Matthias Claudius
Bekränzt mit Laub den lieben, vollen Becher
Hier liegt der Müller Mayhon!
Ich sehe oft um Mitternacht
Dante Alighieri
Mir ist wie einem, der im Schlafe schaut
Joseph von Eichendorff
Es wandelt, was wir schauen, Tag sinkt
Ochse, wie bist du so stattlich, bedachtsam
Wir sind durch Not und Freude gegangen
Paul Gerhardt
Alle, die ihr Gott zu Ehren
Befiehl du deine Wege
Die güldne Sonne voll Freud und Wonne
Fröhlich soll mein Herze springen dieser Zeit
Geh aus, mein Herz, und suche Freud
Gib dich zufrieden und sei stille
Ich bin ein Gast auf Erden
Ich steh an deiner Krippen hier
Kommt und laßt uns Christum ehren
Nicht so traurig, nicht so sehr, meine Seele
Nun laßt uns gehn und treten mit Singen
O Haupt voll Blut und Wunden
Johann Wolfgang von Goethe
An vollen Büschelzweigen, Geliebte
Augen, sagt mir, sagt, was sagt ihr?
Der du von dem Himmel bist
Die heilgen drei König mit ihrem Stern
Es ist ein Schnee gefallen
Es klingt so prächtig, wenn der Dichter
Kleine Blumen, kleine Blätter
Mitternachts weint' und schluchzt' ich
Nicht mehr auf Seidenblatt schreib' ich
Sagt es niemand, nur den Weisen
Sie saugt mit Gier verräterisches Getränke
Über allen Gipfeln ist Ruh
Um Mitternacht ging ich, nicht eben gerne
Wunderlichstes Buch der Bücher
Klaus Groth
As ik hier dit Jaar weer, as ik hier dit Jaar weer
Avends, wenn wi to Bette gaat
Dar gung en Mann un gung en Fro
Dar kummt en Herr to Peer
De Dag, de graut, de Katt, de maut
De Wächter geit to blasen alleen in'e Nacht
Inne Buurstraten dar steit en glatt Huus
Lüttje Finger, gollne Ringer, lange Meier
Mien leve Hanne Gnegelputt hett allens
Regen, Regen druus, wi sitt hier warm in Huus!
Still min Hanne, hör mi to!
Sünn, Sünn, schiene, kiek ut dien Gardine
Johann Gottfried Herder
Ein Traum, ein Traum ist unser Leben auf Erden
Erde, du meine Mutter, und du mein Vater
Friedrich Georg Jünger
Das Geistige ist wie das Blütenleben
Dem Fürsten und dem Bettler ziemt nicht
Der Kuckuck ruft nicht mehr, der stete Rufer
Ein Körnchen Ambra lasse ich gelten
Fährmann, ahoi! Ahoi! Hinunter treibt es
Gibt es denn wohl bangere Mienen
Ihr Stimmen! Was denn ruft ihr mir, Flüsterer?
Man sagt, daß Rosen, die bei Tannen
Rufst du, Kuckuck? So ganz zur Unzeit rufst du
Tage, wie geht ihr dahin, o Tage, wie schnell
Urnen füllen sich und Krüge
Vaterland ist mir das Lied
Wer Kastor ruft, muß Polydeukos nennen
Wie silbernes Geschirr sich stößt, so klingen
Wie Uferland, das in der Feuchte blühet
Friedrich de La Motte Fouqué
Wenn alles eben käme, wie du gewollt es hast
Friedrich Nietzsche
Nun, da der Tag des Tages müde ward
William Wordsworth
Die Herde Schafe, die gemächlich zieht

George Perle (1915-)
Rainer Maria Rilke
Der Bach hat leise Melodien
Du meine heilige Einsamkeit

Wilhelm Petersen (1890-1957)
Joseph von Eichendorff
Es zog eine Hochzeit den Berg entlang,
Ich wandre durch die stille Nacht

In den Wipfeln frische Lüfte
Kaiserkron' und Päonien rot
Lieb Vöglein, vor Blüten sieht man dich kaum!
Nun legen sich die Wogen,
Vergangen ist der lichte Tag,
Weil jetzo alles stille ist
Wenn die Wogen unten toben
Johann Wolfgang von Goethe
An dem reinsten Frühlingsmorgen
Bulbuls Nachtlied durch die Schauer
Der Spiegel sagt mir, ich bin schön!
Fetter grüne, du Laub am Rebengeländer
Herrin! sag was heißt das Flüstern?
Ich ging im Walde so für mich hin
O gib vom weichen Pfühle, träumend
Sagt es niemand, nur den Weisen
Zwischen oben, zwischen unten schweb ich

Hans (Erich) Pfitzner (1869-1949)
Adolf Bartels
Wenn sich Liebes von dir lösen will
Adolf Böttger
Ich hör' ein Vöglein locken
Gottfried August Bürger
O wie öde, sonder Freudenschall
Schön Suschen kannt' ich lange Zeit
Wann die goldne Frühe, neu geboren
Wenn, o Mädchen, wenn dein Blut
Wollt ihr wissen, holde Bienen
Carl Busse
Abendschwärmer zogen um die Linden
Ich raun' dir am Bette in schlafloser Nacht
Vor der Tür, im Sonnenscheine
Wo der Weiser steht an der Straß'
Adelbert von Chamisso
'S war einer, dem's zu Herzen ging
Paul Nikolaus Cossmann
Die Bäume wurden gelb, und wir wandelten
Ohn' Lieb' bist du durchs Leben kommen
Richard Dehmel
Liegt eine Stadt im Tale
Träume, träume, du mein süßes Leben
Wir haben ein Bett, wir haben ein Kind
Joseph von Eichendorff
Abendlich schon rauscht der Wald
Am Himmelsgrund schießen so lustig die Stern'
Der Herbstwind schüttelt die Linde
Der Wald wird falb, die Blätter fallen
Die Jäger ziehn in grünen Wald
Dunkle Giebel, hohe Fenster, Türme
Er reitet nachts auf einem braunen Roß
Es glänzt der Tulpenflor, durchschnitten
Es ist schon spät, es wird schon kalt
Herz, mein Herz, warum so fröhlich
Hoch mit den Wolken geht der Vögel Reise
Hörst du nicht die Bäume rauschen
Ich stehe in Waldesschatten
Möcht' wissen, was sie schlagen
Nächtlich macht der Herr die Rund
Seh' ich im verfall'nen dunklen Haus
Und wo noch kein Wandrer gegangen
Wär's dunkel, ich läg' im Walde
Wo aber werd ich sein im künft'gen Lenze?
Wohin ich geh' und schaue in Feld und Wald
Emanuel Geibel
Mein Herz ist wie die dunkle Nacht
O schneller, mein Roß, mit Hast, mit Hast
Johann Wolfgang von Goethe
Der du von dem Himmel bist
Es schlug mein Herz, geschwind zu Pferde
Füllest wieder Busch und Tal
Wie herrlich leuchtet mir die Natur!
Mary Graf-Bartholemew
Mir bist du tot, ob auch deine Wange
"Martin Greif" (Friedrich Hermann Frey)
Wie ferne Tritte hörst du's schallen
James Grun
Morgenwölkchen, leichte, weben märchenhaft
Schlaf ein, gewieget an meiner Brust
Schon will der Abend sinken
Wie Frühlingsahnung weht es durch die Lande
Friedrich Hebbel
Die du, über die Sterne weg
Dies ist ein Herbsttag, wie ich keinen sah!
Wir träumten von einander
Heinrich Heine
Die schlanke Wasserlilie schaut träumend
Ein Fichtenbaum steht einsam im Norden
Es fällt ein Stern herunter
Es faßt mich wieder der alte Mut
Es glänzt so schön die sinkende Sonne
Ich stand gelehnet an den Mast
Ich will mich im grünen Wald ergehn
Sie haben heut' Abend Gesellschaft
Paul Heyse
Dulde, gedulde dich fein! Über ein Stündelein
Friedrich Hölderlin
Heilig Wesen! gestört hab' ich
Ricarda Huch
Denn unsre Liebe hat zu heiß geflammt
Eine Melodie singt mein Herz
Ich werde nicht an deinem Herzen satt
Schwill an, mein Strom, schwill über

Um bei dir zu sein, trüg ich Not und Fährde
Was ist in deiner Seele, was ist in meiner Brust
Wo hast du all die Schönheit hergenommen

Ludwig Jacobowski
Ach, unsre leuchtenden Tage
Ich aber weiß, ich seh dich manche Nacht

Alexander Kaufmann
Die Wasserlilie kichert leis

Gottfried Keller
Du milchjunger Knabe, wie siehst du mich an?
Ich fürcht' nit Gespenster, keine Hexen
Mir glänzen die Augen wie der Himmel so klar
Röschen biß den Apfel an
Singt mein Schatz wie ein Fink
Tretet ein, hoher Krieger
Wandl' ich in dem Morgentau
Wie glänzt der helle Mond

August Kopisch
Als Noah aus dem Kasten war

Richard Leander
In der Früh', wenn die Sonne kommen will
Ist der Himmel darum im Lenz so blau?

Nikolaus Lenau
Auf geheimem Waldespfade schleich ich gern
Lethe! Brich die Fesseln des Ufers

Friedrich Lienhard
Mir ist nach einer Heimat weh

Detlev von Liliencron
Auf dem Wege vom Tanzsaal nach Haus
Ich ging den Weg entlang, der einsam lag

Hermann Lingg
Immer leiser wird mein Schlummer
Kalt und schneidend weht der Wind

Conrad Ferdinand Meyer
Bemeßt den Schritt! Bemeßt den Schwung!
Es geht mit mir zu Ende, mein' Sach'
Geh' nicht, die Gott für mich erschuf!
Meine eingelegten Ruder triefen

Eduard Mörike
Ein Tännlein grünet wo, wer weiß, im Walde
Früh, wann die Hähne krähen

Wolfgang Müller von Königswinter
Hast du den Fischerkindern das alte Märchen

Francesco Petrarca
Voll jener Süße, die, nicht auszudrücken

Oskar von Redwitz
Nun, da so warm der Sonnenschein

Robert Reinick
Ich bin einmal etwas hinaus spaziert

Friedrich Rückert
Herz, nun so alt und noch immer nicht klug
Warum sind deine Augen denn so naß?

Friedrich von Sallet
Durch die Wälder streif' ich munter

Adolf Friedrich von Schack
Mach auf, mach auf, doch leise, mein Kind

Joseph Viktor von Scheffel
Das ist im Leben häßlich eingerichtet

Ilse von Stach-Lerner
Bereifte Kiefern, atemlose Seen

Julius Sturm
Der Tag neigt sich zu Ende

Johann Ludwig Uhland
Leben, das nur Leben scheinet

Walther von der Vogelweide
Unter der Linden, bei der Heide
Wer gab dir, Minne, die Gewalt

Anonymous
Blau der See! Von hohem Schilfe rings
Im tiefen Wald verborgen
Mein Liebchen ist kein stolzes Schloß

Volkslied
Da drob'n auf jener Linden schlief ich

Wilhelm Pohl (1780fl.)

Heinrich Albert
Junges Volk, man rufet euch zu dem Tanz

Johann Gottfried Herder
An des Baches stillen Weiden
Im säuselnden Winde, am murmelnden Bach
Liebes, leichtes, luftges Ding

John H. Powell (1882-1963)

Heinrich Heine
Nacht liegt auf den fremden Wegen

Heinrich Proch (1809-1878)

Heinrich Proch
Von der Alpe tönt das Horn, gar so zaub'risch

Karl Prohaska (1869-1927)

Rainer Maria Rilke
Am Berge weiß ich trutzen ein Kirchlein
Die falben Felder schlafen schon

Sergei Vassilievich Rachmaninoff (1873-1943)

Heinrich Heine
Die schlanke Wasserlilie
Du bist wie eine Blume
Ich hatte einst ein schönes Vaterland

Fürst Antoni Henryk Radziwill (1775-1833)

Johann Wolfgang von Goethe
Es war eine Ratt' im Kellernest

(Joseph) Joachim Raff (1822-1882)

Joseph von Eichendorff

Ich rufe vom Ufer verlorenes Glück

Nachts durch die stille Runde rauschte

"Ernst" (Matthias Jakob Schleiden)

In deine Augen will ich schauen

Längst schon flog zu Nest der Vogel

Leis sinkt der Dämmerung Schleier auf Wiese

Seid mir gegrüsst ihr Wellen,

Freudenberg

Das war die junge Königsbraut

Der Knabe eilt durch den düstern Hain

Die Sonne strahlt auf Wald und Feld

Emanuel Geibel

Auf Flügeln rauscht der Wind daher

Der du am Sternenbogen, als Erstling

Der Mond kommt still gegangen

Ich bin ein lust'ger Geselle

Johann Wolfgang von Goethe

Dem Schnee, dem Regen, dem Wind entgegen

Klaus Groth

Kein Graben so breit, kein Mauer so hoch

"Anastasius Grün" (A. A. von Auersperg)

Frühling ist's in allen Räumen

Heinrich Heine

Ich weiss nicht was soll's bedeuten

"Dilia Helena" (Helena Branco)

Komm Mägdelein' ohne Bangen

Wenn meine Blicke hangen, du Lichtgestalt

Hoffmann von Fallersleben

Es webte schön Aennchen ohn' Unterlass

Ich gehe nie vorüber an ihrem Gartenhag

Karl Siebel

Erworben, verdorben! Mein Herz ist schwer

Ich war mal froh vor lange! vor lange!

Mein Herz ist ein Spielmann

Adelheid von Stolterfoth

Wer fühlt's nicht tief im Herzen

Johann Ludwig Uhland

Hast du das Schloss gesehen

Im stillen Klostergarten

Gisbert, Freiherr von Vincke

Das macht mir bittre Pein, und treibt mich hin

Herr Jesu Christ, den sie gekrönt mit Dornen

Herrin! Dein sterngleich Aug' allein

Ich zieh' dahin, ade, ade

In leisen Trauerklagen entströmt das Lied

Mein Jugendlenz ist nur ein Sorgenfrost

Nichts von den Dingen allen

O Gott, mein Gebieter, stets hofft' ich auf dich!

Und sei es, wo auch immer: im Wald

Was mir einst Lust gewährte

Was nützt die mir noch zugemessne Zeit?

Wenn Schmerz uns zieren kann

Johann Nepomuk Vogl

Ein Mühlrad hör' ich gehen

Räder klappern, Wasser rauschen

Walther von der Vogelweide

Wohl mir der Stunde, wo ich sie fand

Georg Wilhelm Rauchenecker (1844-1908)

Julius Stinde

Auf ein freies Feld bin ich gezogen

Dass wir sollen selig sein

Gebleicht sind die Linnen und harren im Schrein

Ich habe ein Paar Schuhe

Ihr Heiligen am Kirchenthor

Im Schlehendorn, da sitzt ein Vogel und singt

Mein lieber Goldschmied, schmiede fein

Still ist es worden aller Ort

Und ist mein Schatz im fremden Land

Was bin ich in's Kloster gegangen

Wo im Wald die klugen Rehe gehen

Zu diesem Reigen reiche mir die Hand

Max (Johann Baptist Joseph Maximilian) Reger (1873-1916)

Erasmus Albers

O Jesu Christ, wir warten dein

Steht auf, ihr lieben Kinderlein!

Gabriele d'Annunzio

Wenn lichter Mondenschein um wald'ge Gipfel

Ernst Moritz Arndt

Geht nun hin und grabt mein Grab

Elsa Asenijeff

Amselchen mein, Amselchen mein! Sag an!

Der Himmel ist so weit und hehr

Wo ich bin, fern und nah, fern und nah

Rudolph Baumbach

Zum Hänschen sprach das Gretchen

Cornelius Becker

Mit meinem Gott geh ich zur Ruh

Friedrich Benz

Schlaf wohl, über dich hin leuchten rot

Maximilian Bern

Ich habe mein Kindlein in Schlaf gewiegt

the Bible

Meine Seele ist still zu Gott

Otto Julius Bierbaum

Der Schmerz ist ein Schmied

Eine Wiese voller Margeriten

"Frauenhaar" trag' ich am Hute

Laß mich noch einmal dir ins schwarze Auge

Nun hängt nur noch am Kirchturmknopf
Sitz im Sattel, reite, reite auf die Freite
Stille, träumende Frühlingsnacht
Weite Wiesen im Dämmergrau
Wenn im braunen Hafen alle Schiffe schlafen
Wir gingen durch die stille Nacht

Victor Blüthgen
Ich war mal in dem Dorfe
Still, wie so still! 's ist Mitternacht schon

Martin Boelitz
Auf der schönen, schönen Wiese
Das dank' ich deiner Güte, nun geh' ich ganz
Deiner Liebe goldene Güte trägst du
Draußen weht es bitterkalt
Dröhnende Hämmer in rußiger Hand
Du bist mir gut! Es hat ein heimlich Singen
Ein linder Südhauch sprengt die Riegel
Ein Müller mahlte Tag und Nacht
Ein Reiter muß haben ein Rößlein, zu traben
Es blüht ein Blümlein rosenrot
Es haben die liebjungen Mädchen
Es waren mal zwei Mäuschen
Es zog ein Jäger in den Wald, halli, halli!
Ich geh' auf stillen Auen
Leise tritt der Mond heraus, schlafe, Kindchen
Liegt ein Dorf im Abendleuchten
Lutschemund, treib's nur nicht gar zu bunt
Maria sitzt am Rosenhag und wiegt
Nebelgrau die weite Welt, Wolken tief
O du, der ich erblühte, die mich erquickte Tag
So ein rechter Soldat fürcht' nicht Kugel
Sturm, wie lieb ich dich, wilden Gesellen
Tragt, blaue Träume, mich ins Land zurück
Vor meinem Fenster schläft die Nacht
Wenn dich die tiefe Sehnsucht rührt
Wie ist die Nacht voll holder Heimlichkeiten!

Maximilian Brantl
Aus schimmernden Zweigen langen und neigen

Richard Braungart
Du brachtest mir deiner Seele Trank
Du ewigkalter Himmel, ich schreie auf zu dir
Kleine Tränen seh' ich zittern
Nun kommt die Nacht gegangen
Nun ruhst du sanft in meinem Arm
O wie greulich, wie abscheulich ist der Winter
Schweigend geht die junge Frau
Was tragen wir unsere Leiden in diesen Glanz
Wenn die Buben recht böse sind

Fritz Brentano
Leise, leise weht ihr Lüfte, denn mein Kind

Carl Busse
Mädel, halt die Rökke fest
Sum, sum, der Sandmann geht, ach wie dunkel
Wenn die Linde blüht, wenn die Linde blüht

Adelbert von Chamisso
Es steh'n in unserm Garten

Ada Christen
Die Sonne sinkt. Jählings schwebt

Felix Dahn
All' mein Gedanken, mein Herz und mein Sinn
Du meines Herzens Krönelein
Seit ganz mein Aug' ich durft' in deines tauchen

Richard Dehmel
Bienchen, Bienchen wiegt sich im Sonnenschein
Der Wald beginnt zu rauschen
Du sahst durch meine Seele in die Welt
Seit wann du mein ich weiß es nicht
Träume, träume, du mein süßes Leben!

Franz Diederich
Der Mond glüht über'm Garten

C. Dorr-Ljubljaschtschi
Mutter, draußen ist es Frühling worden

Hans Ehlen
Er hat mich im Traum geküßt

Joseph von Eichendorff
Das Kind ruht aus vom Spielen
Dein Wille, Herr, geschehe!
Ich wandre durch die stille, stille Nacht
Was ist mir denn so wehe?

Franz Engel
Verlassen hab' ich mein Lieb

Karl Enslin
Du sagst, mein liebes Mütterlein

Franz Evers
Das Fenster klang im Winde
Der Mond streut durch die Zweige
Die andern Mädchen wissen's nicht
Die Lande durchträumt der Schlaf
Es ist ein seliges Prangen und eine wilde Pracht
Hältst mich nun ganz in den Armen
Meine Seele, die hat weite Flügel
Mich umduftet deine Seele
Nachts wenn die Bäume rauschen
Nun du wie Licht durch meine Träume gehst
Weiche Flötentöne, tiefverträumtes Girren
Wie geheimes Lispeln rieselt's durch die Nacht

Gustav Falke
Aus der Tiefe tauchte sie nach oben
Das war der Junker Übermut
Der Mond scheint auf mein Lager
Der Morgen steigt und glüht und steigt

Drei bunte Kühe in guter Ruh
Du schläfst, und sachte neig' ich mich
Ein kühler Hauch. Die Linde träumt
Holde Königin der Geigen,
Ich habe lieb die helle Sonne
Ich wollt', ich wär' ein Held
Immer bleibst du lieblich mir
Komm' ich längs der grünen Wiese
Nun steh' ich über Grat und Kluft
Still, still! 'sist nur ein Traum
Tollt der Wind über Feld und Wiese
Wir haben oft beim Wein gesessen

K. Fick
Die Erde schläft, des Mondes Schein
Immer schwitzend, immer sitzend

Johann Georg Fischer
Das Mägdlein sprach: "Lieb Knabe"

Bernhard Flemes
Aus dunkler Nacht ein Brunnenlied klang hell

Paul Flemming
Laß dich nur nichts nicht dauern

Adolf Frey
Im Gefild zum Strauße wand' wilde Blüt'

Daniel Friderici
In einem Rosengärtelein

Eugenie Galli
Nun, da sie Alle eingeschlafen

Emanuel Geibel
Du feuchter Frühlingsabend
Wenn sich auf dieses Blatt dein Auge senkt
Wie doch so still dir am Herzen ruhet das Kind!
Wo am Herd ein Brautpaar siedelt

Otto Franz Gensichen
Unter blühenden Bäumen

Rosa Gerheusser
Der Maien ist gestorben in seiner Blütenpracht!

Julius Gersdorf
An dem Brünnele hab' ich oft gelauscht

Hermann Gilm
Es lokket und zwitschert von Haus zu Haus

Franz Karl Ginzkey
Schrieb die schöne Adelheid

Johann Christian Glücklich
Du, der die Menschheit stolz und kühn
Unendlich dehnt sich das brausende Meer

Johann Wolfgang von Goethe
Die ihr Felsen und Bäume bewohnt
Über allen Gipfeln ist Ruh

Leo Greiner
Wären wir zwei kleine, kleine Vögel

"Anastasius Grün" (A. A. von Auersperg)
Ich hab' eine alte Muhme

Ludwig Hamann
Hoch am dunklen Himmelsbogen

Robert Hamerling
Sieh', Liebchen, hier im Waldestal
Wie's aussieht im ew'gen Freudenhain

Otto Erich Hartleben
Im Arm der Liebe schliefen wir selig ein

Dora Hartwig
Mein Auge schließ' mit deinem Kusse zu

Carl Hauptmann
Es schläft ein stiller Garten

Friedrich Hebbel
Die du, über die Sterne weg

Heinrich Heine
Aus den Himmelsaugen droben
Der Tod, das ist die kühle Nacht

Karl Henckell
Ich schwebe wie auf Engelsschwingen

Nikolaus Herman
Wenn mein Stündlein fürhanden ist

Wilhelm Hertz
Und willst du von mir scheiden

C. Himer
Der Mensch soll nicht stolz sein auf Glück

Friedrich Hölderlin
Ihr, ihr Herrlichen! steht wie ein Volk
O Hoffnung, holde! holde! gütig geschäftige!

Ludwig von Hörmann
Husch, husch, husch, husch! es kommt wer

Adolf Holst
Alle Sternelein, die am Himmel steh'n

Joseph Huggenberger
Auf mondbeschienenen Wegen geh' ich bergein
Ein Schmeichelkätzchen nenn' ich mein
Jüngst lasest du – ich merkt' es wohl
Mein Schätzelein ist ein gar köstliches Ding
Tief im Talgrund überm Bach

Marie Itzerott
Deine Seele hat die meine einst so wunderbar
Eine Schale blühender Rosen
Leise deinen Namen flüstern
Quellen rauschen, Lüfte schweigen
Wenn Gott es hätt' gewollt

Ludwig Jacobowski
Alte Gruben schaufle um, tiefer werden sie
Auf deinem Bild in schwarzem Rahmen
Duld' es still, wenn von den Zweigen
Es ist ein Ring gebogen, der ist nicht blank
Höre mich, Ewiger, höre mich, Ewiger

Ich weiß, ich träume im Grabe
In deinen Liedern lebt mein Leben
Keinen Vater, der das Kinn mir hebt
Und der Nachbarssohn, der Ruprecht
Albert Kleinschmidt
Tiefes, tiefes Schweigen waltet ringsum
Isolde Kurz
Was hat des Schlummers Band zerrissen
Frieda Laubsch
Der goldne Morgen kommt herauf mit Glut
Nikolaus Lenau
Weil auf mir, du dunkles Auge
Frau von Lieven
Ich stehe hoch überm See
Detlev von Liliencron
Wenn sanft du mir im Arme schliefst
Hermann Lingg
Geheimnisvoller Klang, für Geister der Luft
John Henry Mackay
Und morgen wird die Sonne wieder scheinen
Marie Madeleine
Die fernen, fernen Berge
A. Mayr
Es liegt ein alter Mühlenstein im Schatten
Lothar Fürst Metternich
Leise streichen Nebelschleier über Flur
Karl Meyer
Auf dem Dache sitzt der Spatz
Otto Michaeli
Am Kirchhof ging ich jüngst vorbei
Mein Liedlein ward ein Büblein
Eduard Mörike
Dir angetrauet am Altare, o Vaterland
Kein Schlaf noch kühlt das Auge mir
Was doch heut Nacht ein Sturm gewesen
Christian Morgenstern
Auf der Bank im Walde han sich gestern
Draußen im weiten Krieg ist blieben
Gleich einer versunkenen Melodie
Heil dir, der du hassen kannst
Leise Lieder sing ich dir bei Nacht
Regne, regne, Frühlingsregen, weine
Über der Erde Stirne, durch Tag und Nacht
Weiße Tauben fliegen durch blaue Morgenluft
Clara Müller
Vom Himmel ist der Frühlingsregen
Franz Alfred Muth
Wenn alle Blumen träumen
Rudolf Nawrocki
O frage nicht in bitt'rem Harm
"Novalis" (Friedrich von Hardenberg)
Ich sehe dich in tausend Bildern
Wenn in bangen, trüben Stunden
Willibald Obst
In meinem Herzen ist's öd' und leer
Wilhelm Osterwald
Die braune Heide starrt mich an
Robert Eduard Prutz
Mond, hast du auch gesehen
Ludwig Rafael
Ich werde Mama: und Kinder sind da!
Ich werde Soldat, ich werde Soldat!
Kaum sind die ersten Blüten da
Regen, linder Frühlingsregen
Trara, trara, mein Hörnlein hell
Und haben auch im grünen Wald
Wenn die kleinen Kinder beten
Wenn mein Kindlein in der Wiegen lächelt
Max Reger
Veilchen wollt' ich pflükken
Robert Reinick
Schwalbenmütterlein, Schwalbenmütterlein!
Anna Ritter
Als über den Flieder das Mondlicht rann
Die ihr den Äther mit seligen Schwingen
Die Nacht war tief, und die Mutter schlief
Ein Vöglein singt im Wald, singt Lieb'
Es stand eine Rose im tieftiefen Grund
Hat einmal ein Mädel die Muhme gefragt
Ich gehe fremd durch die Menge hin
Ich hab' kein' Mutter, die mich hegt
Ich trag' ein glückselig Geheimnis
In verschwiegener Nacht hab' ich
Liegt nun so still die weite Welt
Mußt's auch grad' so dunkel sein
Unter den blühenden Linden weißt du's noch?
Viele Glokken hör' ich läuten
War ich gar so jung und dumm
Wie zerrißner Saiten Klingen
Kurt von Rohrscheidt
Es ruht mit ernstem Sinnen auf mir dein Blick
Otto Roquette
Du liebes Auge willst dich tauchen
Friedrich Rückert
Der Himmel hat eine Träne geweint
Mich hat der Herbst betrogen
Mir ist, da ich dich habe, als müßt ich sterben
D. Saul
Noch immer halt' ich dich umfaßt
Tausend goldne Sterne, glänzen
Wo du triffst ein Mündlein hold

Theo Schäfer
Eine stille Melodie, voll von süßer Lust
Es blüht um mich des Abends Stille
Schatz
Hier ein Weilchen, dort ein Weilchen!
Ernst Ludwig Schellenberg
Das machte dein stiller keuscher Blick
Der Igel, der Igel, der ist ein schlimmer Mann
Eins, zwei, drei, was raschelt da im Heu?
Ich bin der König vom Morgenland
Ich bin ein Dieb geworden, ein bitterböser Dieb
Maria sitzt am Rosenbusch und wiegt
Mutter, liebe Mutter, komm rasch einmal her
Oben in dem Birnenbaum sitzt ein Vögelein
Wenn hell die liebe Sonne lacht
Zwischen Mohn und Rittersporn
Albert Sergel
Langsam wird mein Kindchen müde
Sofie Seyboth
Hab' Singen für mein Leben gern
Liebes Töchterlein, liebes Töchterlein
Mein Schatz ist auf die Wanderschaft wohl
Otto Sommerstorff
A' Versle, a' g'spaßig's, hat mei Bua
Gretel Stein
Schlaf' ein, mein liebes Kindlein du
Ulrich Steindorff
Sonntag und Frühlingsmorgen
Karl Stieler
In den Bäumen regt sich's leise
Marie Stona
Ach, Liebster, in Gedanken geb' ich dir
An den Mondesstrahlen gleiten
Um Mitternacht blühen die Blumen
Theodor Storm
Einen Brief soll ich schreiben meinem Schatz
Heute, nur heute bin ich so schön
Ich wand ein Sträußchen morgens früh
O laß mich nur von ferne stehn
Julius Sturm
Unser Schifflein treibt umher
Zur weißen Gans sprach einst vertraulich
Albert Träger
Schließe, mein Kind, schließe die Äuglein zu
Gertrud Triepel
Im Garten rauscht die Sommernacht
Johannes Trojan
Marie auf der Wiese, auf der Wiese Marie
Hermann Ubell
O presse deine Hand in meine Hand
Johann Ludwig Uhland
Guckst du mir denn immer nach
Im Sommer such ein Liebchen dir in Garten
Im Walde geh' ich wohlgemut
Paul Verlaine
Weich küßt die Zweige der weiße Mond
Claire Henrika Weber
Prinzeßlein tanzt durch die Wiese
Asta von Wegerer
Es soll mein Gebet dich tragen
Wilhelm Weigand
Merk dir's in vollster Kraft, die man beneidet
Christian Weisse
Mein Schäfer, ach! der ist bescheiden!
Oskar Wiener
Am Dorfsee neigt die Weide ihr kahles Haupt
Mein rotes Herz, mein totes Herz
Meine armen, kleinen Lieder
Sag es nicht, geliebtes Herzchen, sag es nicht
Ernst von Wildenbruch
Auf meinem Tische stehn Kornblumen
Warum so bleich und blaß, geliebtes Angesicht?
Stefan Zweig
Ein Drängen ist in meinem Herzen
O welch Glühn in fremde Hülle
Anonymous
Auf einem Grab in Stükken
Christ, deines Geistes Süßigkeit
Die Englein haben's Bett gemacht
Du schläfst, so will ich leise flehen
Du siehst mich nun schon drei Tage heut
Herzchen, mein Schätzchen
Ja, wann gleich wär das Firmament
Komm, komm, Geselle mein
Laßt uns das Kindlein wiegen
O Herre Gott, nimm du von mir
O Ursprung aller Brunnen
Schlummere, mein süßes Kind
Uns ist geboren ein Kindelein
from Des Knaben Wunderhorn
Mein Vater hat gesagt
Volkslied
Früh am Morgen ging die Maid aus der Tür
Gäb's ein einzig Brünnelein
Gestern Abend in der stillen Ruh'
In meines Vaters Garten
Jung vermähle mich, o Mutter!
Männer suchen stets zu naschen
Mein Kindchen ist fein, könnt schöner nicht sein
Mein Sohn, wo willst du hin so spät?
Schlaf, Kindlein, balde, schlaf Kindlein, balde

So hab' ich doch die ganze Woche
Sprachen Königin und König einstens
Wenn alle Welt so einig wär'

A. Reichardt
Volkslied
Wie die Blümlein draussen flattern

Gustav Reichardt (1797-1884)
Harro Paul Harring
In einem Thale friedlich stille

Johann Friedrich Reichardt (1752-1814)
Friederike Brun
O selig wer liebt. Ihm tönet der Wald
Gottfried August Bürger
Lenore fuhr um's Morgenrot
Matthias Claudius
Der Mond ist aufgegangen
Er liegt und schläft an meinem Herzen
Ich danke Gott und freue mich wie's Kind
Florian
Wie lieb' ich euch ihr Nachtigallen
Johann Wolfgang von Goethe
Ach daß die innre Schöpfungskraft
Ach, wer bringt die schönen Tage
Ach wer heilet die Schmerzen
Als ich noch ein Knabe war
Als ich still und ruhig spann
An ä Bergli bin i gesässe
An die Türen will ich schleichen
Arm am Beutel, krank am Herzen
Auf Kieseln im Bache da lieg' ich, wie helle!
Bedekke deinen Himmel, Zeus
Bilder der Hoffnung, täuschet mein Herz!
Bist du aus einem Traum erwacht?
Blumen der Wiese, dürfen auch diese hoffen
Da droben auf jenem Berge,
Das ist die wahre Liebe
Das Veilchen auf der Wiese stand
Das Wasser rauscht', das Wasser schwoll
Dem Schnee, dem Regen, dem Wind entgegen
Den einzigen Psyche, welchen du lieben kannst
Den künft'gen Tag und Stunden
Der Damm zerreißt, das Feld erbraust
Der du von dem Himmel bist
Der Strauß, den ich gepflükket
Der Tempel ist euch aufgebaut
Der Vorhang schwebet hin und her
Dich ergriff mit Gewalt der alte Herrscher
Dich hat Amor gewiß, o Sängerin
Die ihr Felsen und Bäume bewohnt
Die Nebel zerreißen, auf einmal wird's helle
Die Trommel gerühret! Das Pfeifchen gespielt!
Diese Federn, weiß' und schwarze
Du prophet'scher Vogel du
Du verklagest das Weib
Durch Feld und Wald zu schweifen
Ein Veilchen auf der Wiese stand
Einziger Augenblick, in welchem ich lebte!
Es fürchte die Götter das Menschengeschlecht!
Es ist ein Schuß gefallen! Mein!
Es lohnet mich heute mit doppelter Beute
Es schlug mein Herz, geschwind zu Pferde!
Es war ein Knabe frech genug
Es war ein König in Thule
Feiger Gedanken bängliches Schwanken
Felsen stehen gegründet
Fetter grüne, du Laub, am Rebengeländer
Freudvoll und leidvoll, gedankenvoll sein
Frisch, der Wein soll reichlich fließen
Füllest wieder Busch und Tal
Geh! gehorche meinen Winken
Hab' oft ein'n dumpfen düstern Sinn
Hand in Hand und Lipp' auf Lippe!
Heiß mich nicht reden, heiß mich schweigen
Heraus in eure Schatten, rege Wipfel
Herz, mein Herz, was soll das geben?
Hielte diesen frühen Segen
Hier klag' ich verborgen, dem tauenden Morgen
Hier muß ich sie finden
Hoch auf dem alten Turme steht
Ich denke dein, wenn mir der Sonne Schimmer
Ich hab' ihn gesehen! wie ist mir geschehen?
Ich hab mein Sach auf nichts gestellt, Juchhe!
Ich kenn' ein Blümlein Wunderschön
Ich liebte sie mit innigem Gefühle
Ich weiß nicht was mir hier gefällt
Ihr verblühet, süße Rosen
Im Felde schleich ich still und wild
Im Walde schleich ich still und wild
In allen guten Stunden, erhöht von Lieb'
In dem stillen Mondenscheine
Kehre nicht in diesem Kreise neu
Kennst du das Land, wo die Zitronen blühn
Kleine Blumen, kleine Blätter
Komm mit, o Schöne, komm mit mir zum Tanze
Laß dich genießen, freundliche Frucht
Laß mein Aug' den Abschied sagen
Leere Zeiten der Jugend!
Liebchen, kommen diese Lieder
Liebliches Kind! Liebliches Kind!
Mein Mädel ward mir ungetreu
Mich ergreift, ich weiß nicht wie

Mit des Bräutigams Behagen
Mit Mädeln sich vertragen
Mit vollen Atemzügen saug ich, Natur, aus dir
Nach diesem Frühlingsregen, den wir
Nun ihr Musen, genug! Vergebens strebt ihr
Nun verlaß' ich diese Hütte
Nur fort, du braune Hexe
Nur wer die Sehnsucht kennt
O gib vom weichen Pfühle träumend
O schönes Mädchen du
Sah' ein Knab' ein Röslein stehn
Seh ich den Pilgrim
Sieh mich, Heil'ger, wie ich bin
Singet nicht in Trauertönen
So hab' ich wirklich dich verloren?
So laßt mich scheinen bis ich werde
Sorglos über die Fläche weg
Süße Freundin, noch Einen, nur Einen Kuß
Tage der Wonne, kommt ihr so bald?
Tiefe Stille herrscht im Wasser
Tiefer liegt die Nacht um mich her
Trocknet nicht, trocknet nicht
Über Tal und Fluß getragen
Und frische Nahrung, neues Blut
Verfließet, vielgeliebte Lieder
Verteilet Euch nach allen Regionen
Von allen schönen Waren, zum Markte
Warum doch erschallen himmelwärts
Warum ziehst du mich unwiderstehlich
Was die gute Natur weislich nur vielen verteilet
Was hör' ich draußen vor dem Tor?
Was zieht mir das Herz so
Weichet, Sorgen, von mir! doch ach!
Wekke den Amor nicht auf
Wenn die Reben wieder blühen
Wenn ich, liebe Lili, dich nicht liebte
Wer darf ihn nennen? und wer bekennen
Wer nie sein Brot mit Tränen aß
Wer reitet so spät durch Nacht und Wind
Wer sich der Einsamkeit ergibt
Wie du mir oft, geliebtes Kind
Wie herrlich leuchtet mir die Natur!
Wie im Morgenglanze du rings mich anglühst
Wie kommt's, daß du so traurig bist
Wilkommen schöner froher Tag
Willst du immer weiter schweifen
Wir helfen gerne, sind nimmer ferne
Wir singen und sagen vom Grafen so gern
Wo willst du klares Bächlein hin
Woher der Freund so früh und schnelle
Wohin, wohin? schöne Müllerin, wie heißt du?
Wohl, ich weiß es, da durchschleicht uns innen
Zu lieblich ists, ein Wort zu brechen
Zwischen dem Alten, zwischen dem Neuen

Johann Gottfried Herder
Hoffnung, Hoffnung immer grün!
Verschwunden ist meinem Blick

Ludwig Hölty
Grüner wird die Au, und der Himmel blau
Keine Blumen blühn, nur das Wintergrün
Nimmer werd' ich, nimmer dein vergessen
Rosen auf den Weg gestreut

Johann Georg Jacobi
Wie Feld und Au so blinkend im Tau!

Friedrich von Matthisson
Freude jubelt, Liebe waltet, auf, beginnt

Johann von Salis-Seewis
Seht wie die Tage sich sonnig verklären
Wann, o Schicksal, wann wird endlich

Friedrich von Schiller
Am Abgrund leitet der schwindlichte Steg
An der Quelle sass der Knabe
Auf der Berge freien Höhen
Das edle Bild der Menschheit zu verhöhnen
Der bessre Mensch tritt in die Welt
Es reden und träumen die Menschen viel
In einem Tal bei armen Hirt erschien
Laura, über diese Welt zu flüchten
Lebt wohl, ihr Berge, ihr geliebten Triften
Lieben Freunde! Es gab schön're Zeiten
Nimmer, das glaubt mir, erscheinen die Götter
Noch in meines Lebens Lenze
Ritter, treue Schwesterliebe widmet euch
Schön wie Engel voll Walhallas Wonne
So willst du treulos von mir scheiden
Willkommen, schöner Jüngling, du Wonne
Willst du nicht das Lämmlein hüten?
Zu Aachen in seiner Kaiserpracht

Ludwig Tieck
Im Windsgeräusch, in stiller Nacht

Volkslied
Es ist nit lang daß 's g'regnet hat
Wenn ich ein Vöglein wär

Luise Reichardt (1779-1826)

Ludwig Achim von Arnim
Der Kirschbaum blüht, ich sitze da im Stillen
Ein recht Gemüth springt mit den Nachtigallen
Lilie sieh' mich Thau umblinkt dich
Wenn des Frühlings Wachen ziehen
Wenn ich gestorben bin

Clemens Brentano
Durch den Wald mit raschen Schritten

Es sang vor langen Jahren
Hör' es klagt die Flöte wieder
Ich wollt' ein Sträußlein binden
Nach Sevilla, nach Sevilla
Carl Philipp Conz
Es singt ein Vöglein "Witt,witt,witt. Komm mit"
Anselm Karl Elwert
Es stehen drei Stern' am Himmel
"Novalis" (Friedrich von Hardenberg)
Bricht das matte Herz noch immer
Der Sänger geht auf rauhen Pfaden
Es färbte sich die Wiese grün
Hinüber wall' ich, und jede Pein
Ich kenne wo ein festes Schloß
Ich sehe Dich in tausend Bildern
Lobt doch unsre stillen Feste
Wenn ich ihn nur habe, wenn er mein nur ist
Phillip Otto Runge
Es blüht eine schöne Blume
Stolberg-Stolberg
Ich hab ein Bächlein funden
Ludwig Tieck
Dicht von Felsen eingeschloßen
Durch die bunten Rosenhecken
Geliebter, wo zaudert dein irrender Fuß
Ruhe Süßliebchen im Schatten
Wohl dem Mann, der in der Stille
Friedrich Gottlob Wetzel
Wenn die Rosen blühen, Hoffe, liebes Herz
Anonymous
Bleibe bey uns denn es will Abend werden
Nur die Einsamkeit umschattet
Süßer Freude heller Bach
from Des Knaben Wunderhorn
Es ist kommen der gewünschte Frühlingsboth'
Guten Morgen Spielmann
Herzlich thut mich erfreuen
Hört wie die Wachtel im Grünen schön schlägt
Ich armes Käuzlein kleine

Hugo Reichenberger (1873-1938)
Not Yet Identified
Laß, o laß dein Auge immer in den meinen

Aribert Reimann (1936-)
Joseph von Eichendorff
Der jagt dahin, daß die Rosse schnaufen
Die Vöglein, die so fröhlich sangen
Hörst du die Gründe rufen in Träumen
Ich wandre durch die stille Nacht
Vor dem Schloss in den Bäumen
Was ich wollte, liegt zerschlagen
Was ist mir denn so wehe?
Wetterleuchten fern im Dunkeln
Wir ziehen treulich auf die Wacht

Carl (Heinrich Carsten) Reinecke (1824-1910)
Ernst Anschütz
Es klappert die Mühle am rauschenden Bach
Ernst Moritz Arndt
Du lieber, frommer, heil'ger Christ
Ludwig Bechstein
Unter den rothen Blumen schlumm're
Karl Enslin
Kling' Glöckchen kling'!
Käte Freiligrath
Drei süsse kleine Dirnen sassen auf dem Zaun
Es waren fünf fette Gänse
Mariechen sitzt sinnend unter dem Baum
Prinz Sisi und die Frau Mama
Ringel Reihe Rosenkranz
von Fröhlich
Es regnet, es regnet, der Kukuk wird nass
Schnick, schnack, Dud'lsack
Johann Wolfgang von Goethe
Es fing ein Knab' ein Vögelein, hm hm, so so,
Friedrich Güll
Der Schnitzelmann von Nürenberg
Heinrich Heine
Das gelbe Laub erzittert
Luise Hensel
Müde bin ich, geh' zur Ruh'
Wilhelm Hey
Aus dem Himmel ferne, wo die Eng'lein sind
Hoffmann von Fallersleben
Die Sonne sank, der Abend naht
Du lieblicher Stern, du leuchtest so fern
Eine kleine Geige möcht' ich haben
Es blüht ein schönes Blümelein
Maiglöckchen läutet in dem Thal
Summ, summ, summ, Bienchen, summ herum
Unsre lieben Hühnerchen verloren ihren Hahn
Wer hat die schönsten Schäfchen?
August Kopisch
Lass stehn die Blume, geh' nicht ins Korn
Elisabeth Kulmann
Bleibe hier und singe, liebe Nachtigall!
Steig' empor am Himmel, schöner Abendstern
Rudolf Löwenstein
Ach, Vater, sprich, wie fang' ich's an
Möcht' wissen, wo der Kerl nur steckt
Wohin sind all' die Raritäten
Julius Lohmeyer
Guten Morgen! sollt' ich sagen

Thomas Moore
Willst kommen zur Laube, so schattig und kühl?
Friedrich Oldenberg
Adieu, Mama, Adieu, Mama
Gustav Pfarrius
Sass ein Fink' in dunkler Hecke
Franz von Pocci
Hoch in Lüften Vöglein schweben
Carl Reinecke ("Heinrich Carsten")
Bin ein kleiner Stöpsel noch
Den Stab zur Hand genommen
Die allerkleinste Schwester
Die Glocken gehen bim bam bum
Einst am diesem Tage hat der Storch ganz sacht
Glück und Segen allerwegen wünschen wir
Goldgrüne Libelle, was fliehest du mich!
Ich seh' ein Schifflein fahren
Kannst du rathen wer ich sei?
Mein Bruder ist ein ganzer Mann
Wenn ich dich recht schön bäte
Robert Reinick
Im Fliederbusch ein Vöglein sass
Kaninchen, Karnickelchen
Georg Scherer
Der Tag ist längst geschieden
Die Stunde sei gesegnet in Zeit und Ewigkeit
Loser, leichter, luft'ger Wind
Nun schwirren die Schwalben in Lüften
Adolf Schults
Ei Veilchen, liebes Veilchen, so sag'
Mutteraug', in deine Bläue möcht' ich
Und könnt ich auch erwecken dich
Heinrich Seidel
Mein lieber Herr Reiter, nun stoss' er mal an
Mein Täubchen fliegt in Glanz und Duft
Wie schön sich zu wiegen
Karl Siebel
Sie sass am Rebenfenster im stillen Kämmerlein
Julius Sturm
Im kühlen Schatten, auf sonnigen Höh'n
Schneewittchen hinter den Bergen
Johann Nepomuk Vogl
Herr Frühling giebt jetzt ein Konzert im Saal
Anonymous
Der König Arthur von Engelland
Dort oben auf dem Berge
Du lieber Gott im Himmel du
Ein Räppchen zum Reiten
Fünf kleine Schwesterchen all' in einer Reih'
In allen Landen gehet still ein Engelein umher
Klein Vöglein widi widi widi witt witt spricht
Lasset uns marschiren, rataplan, rataplan
Wann die Kinder schlafen ein
Wollt Ihr seh'n mein muntres Bäschen
from Des Knaben Wunderhorn
Eins, zwei, drei, bicke, backe, hei!
Volkslied
Der Besen, der Besen! was macht man damit?
Ihr Hirten, erwacht, seid munter und lacht
Mein Mützchen schön schwarz
Schlaf', Püppchen, schlaf', schlafe in Ruh'
Spannenlanger Hansel, nudeldicke Dirn'
Spinn', Mägdlein, spinn'!
Storch, Storch, Steiner, mit de langen Beiner
Not Yet Identified
Es war dort unter dem Lindenbaum

Karl Martin Reinthaler (1822-1896)
Joseph von Eichendorff
Komm, Trost der Welt, du stille Nacht!

Alfred Reisenauer (1863-1907)
Heinrich Heine
Lieb' Liebchen, leg's Händchen aufs Herze

Karl Gottlieb Reissiger (1798-1859)
Carl Beils
Nach der Heimath möcht' ich wieder
Friedrich Förster
In dunkler Felsenbucht am Rhein
Emanuel Geibel
Fern im Süd das schöne Spanien
Heinrich Heine
Ach ich sehnte mich nach Thränen
Ach wüssten's die Blumen, die kleinen
Nach Frankreich zogen zwei Grenadier'
August Kopisch
Als Noah aus dem Kasten war
Gottfried August von Maltitz
Auf den Bergen nur wohnet die Freiheit
Gustav Rasmus
Die Wolken ziehen so silbern
Schlumm're du mein Leben
Robert Reinick
Ich bin einmal etwas hinaus spaziert
Sir Walter Scott
Ave Maria! Jungfrau mild
"C. O. Sternau" (Otto Inkermann)
Wo sich das Meer in weite Fernen
Heinrich Stieglitz
Der Mond blickt über die Haide
E. Vogt
O blasen, blasen, welch eine Freud ist das

Anonymous
Komm mit! beflügle deinen Schritt
Volkslied
Die Heere blieben am Rheine steh'n

Josef Reiter (1862-1939)
Franz Himmelbauer
Nun bin ich schon damit versöhnt
Wilhelm Raabe
Schaukeln und Gaukeln

Max Renner
Heinrich Heine
Täglich ging die wunderschöne Sultanstochter
Hans von Hopfen
Lieb' Seelchen, lass' das Fragen sein
Ludwig Pfau
O Blätter, dürre Blätter, wie trauert ihr so sehr!
Not Yet Identified
Schlaf, mein Kind, schlaf ein!
Seit er von mir gegangen!
Wie flüchtig rinnt die Stunde

Hermann Reutter (1900-1985)
Matthias Claudius
Ach, es ist so dunkel in des Todes Kammer
Heute will ich fröhlich, fröhlich sein
So schlafe nun, du Kleine! was weinest du?
Hans Heinrich Ehrler
Am Markte lag ein totgestürztes Kind
Augen ihr, durch allen Schein gegangen
Den kurzen Tag umgab die lange Nacht
Der den Sterngang maß mit Menschenzeichen
Gehet nun, gehet nun fort!
Heimat, Schoß des Heimeslosen
Ich denk an dich und gehe aus mir
Ich möchte einmal so betauet sein
Ist der Gang der Uhr nicht ein ganz andrer
O Bruder sag, warum bist du gekommen?
O holder Himmelswind, führ in die Welt
Strahl, der durch die Gassen geht
Wieviel Wege bin ich schon gegangen?
Federico García Lorca
Die Zigeunernonne. Schweigsamkeit von Kalk
Durch die Straßen von Sevilla tanzt
Friedrich Hölderlin
Ringsum ruhet die Stadt
Wo bist du? Trunken dämmert die Seele mir
Langston Hughes
Tief im Süden Dixies– mein Herz
Wisse, Herz: Der Tod trommelt hier

Emil Nikolaus Freiherr von Rezniček (1860-1945)
Karl Henckell
Was fällt ihm ein, dem edlen Herrn und Ritter?

Joseph (Gabriel) Rheinberger (1839-1901)
Joseph von Eichendorff
Nacht ist wie ein stilles Meer

Christof Rheineck (1748-1979)
Matthias Claudius
Der Winter ist ein rechter Mann

Erich Riede (1903-)
Rudolf Georg Binding
Wenn so stolz im Licht der Sterne
Albrecht Goes
Du haderst wohl zuweilen, Liebster, sag'
Klein ist mein Kind, dein erster Schritt
Ricarda Huch
Du warst in dieser götterlosen Zeit
Um bei dir zu sein, trüg ich Not und Fährde
Börries von Münchhausen
Ich bin durch's Leben auf dich zugegangen
"Novalis" (Friedrich von Hardenberg)
Ich sehe dich in tausend Bildern, Maria
Ina Seidel
Ich bin dir nie so nah als nachts
O tiefstes Wunder, daß mein Leben in dir Kraft
Oh, daß ich dich fand einzig warm und fest
Hildegard Stern
Nicht den Leib umschlangen unsre Arme
Margarete Ungemach
Flieget, ihr Wolken, eilet, ihr Winde
Ich gehöre zu dir wie zum Herzen das Lied
Seit ich dir gehöre, ist alles Leid
Wie bin ich seltsam tief in dir verankert
M. A. Zoll
Ich hört' in einem grünen Hag

Ferdinand Ries (1784-1838)
Arthur
Wo ist mein Vater und Mutter hin
Ch. von Breuning
Auf der weiten Welt ist es schlecht bestellt
Johann Wolfgang von Goethe
Als ich still und ruhig spann
Es lohnet mich heute
Hand in Hand und Lipp' auf Lippe
Hier klag' ich verborgen
Hier muss ich sie finden
Ich hab' ihn gesehen!
Mich ergreift ich weiss nicht wie
Nun verlass' ich diese Hütte

Karl Wilhelm Justi
Es pranget ein Garten im westlichen Strahl
Was drückt, O Holde, dich für Last?
Friedrich Klopstock
Grabt mein verwesliches geheim
Friedrich von Matthisson
Ich denke dein, wenn durch den Hain
Laura betet! Laura
Wenn in des Abends letztem Scheine
Ernst Ortlepp
Das Mädchen steht im Grabe
Johann Joseph Reiff
Mein Schifflien schwimmt so wunderschön
Jean-Baptist Rousseau
Auf das Maines grünen Auen
Liebe recht tief gehegt
Was trinket ihr? Schenkt lustig ein
Wenn die Fluthen blau, wenn die Lüfte lau
Friedrich von Schiller
Ach aus dieses Thales Gründen
Und so finden wir uns wieder
Was ist der Mensch? halb Thier, halb Engel
Willkommen, schöner Jüngling
Christoph August Tiedge
Schöne Minka ich muss scheiden
Karl Wille
Hier auf diesem Blumen Hügel
Ich liebte dich, in meiner Seele lebte

Franz Ries (1846-1932)
Friedrich Bodenstedt
Wenn der Frühling auf die Berge steigt
Dorothea Böttcher von Schwerin
Aus deinen Augen fliessen meine Lieder
Peter Cornelius
Hinaus in das Lustgeschmetter
Hermann Erler
Blaue Augen, holde Sterne, sinkt in Schlummer
Emanuel Geibel
In meinem Garten die Nelken
Tief im grünen Frühlingshag
"Anastasius Grün" (A. A. von Auersperg)
Ich hab' eine alte Muhme
Heinrich Heine
Die blauen Frühlingsaugen
Herz, mein Herz, sei nicht beklommen
Hoffmann von Fallersleben
Frohe Lieder will ich singen
Lasst mich ruhen! lasst mich träumen
Veilchen unter Gras versteckt
Gustav Kastropp
Lass mich in den dunklen Grund
Agnes Kayser-Langerhannß
Der Abend schaut durchs Fensterlein
Oskar von Redwitz
Was ist nun doch in mir erwacht!
Emil Rittershaus
Mit Rheinwein füllt den Becher!
Julius von Rodenberg
Ein Vöglein sang die ganze Nacht
Wach' auf, du schöne Träumerin, wach' auf!
Karl Stieler
Mein Liebling ist ein Lindenbaum
Johann Ludwig Uhland
Die linden Lüfte sind erwacht
Not Yet Identified
Wie ich jüngst mit langem Kusse

Wolfgang Michael Rihm (1952-)
Franz Büchler
Die Krähen rudern schwer im Blut
Stefan George
An baches ranft Die einzigen frühen
Georg Heym
Er meckert vor sich hin
Friedrich Hölderlin
Aber ich will nimmer leben
Aber nun ruhet er eine Weile
Ähnlich dem Manne, der Menschen frisset
Alles ist innig
am stürzenden Strom, die Städte
Denn nirgend bleibt er. Es fesselt kein Zeichen
Mit gelben Birnen hänget
Übernacht ich im Dorf Albluft Straße
Wie Wolken um die Zeit legt
Oskar Loerke
Aus der Glockenstube überm Dom
Rainer Maria Rilke
Härte schwand. Auf einmal legt sich Schonung
August Stramm
Aus allen Winkeln gellen Fürchte Wollen
Die Steine feinden Fenster grinst Verrat
Droben schmettert ein greller Stein
Müde webt Stumpfen dämmert Beten
Stäbe flehen Kreuze Arme Schrift Zagt
Georg Trakl
Stille begegnet am Saum des Waldes
Über den weißen Weiher sind die wilden Vögel

Nicolai Andreyevich Rimsky-Korsakov (1844-1908)
Adelbert von Chamisso
Da Nachts wir uns küssten o Mädchen

Heinrich Heine
Aus meinen Tränen sprießen
Ein Fichtenbaum steht einsam
Lehn' deine Wang an meine Wang
Mein Knecht! steh auf und sattle schnell
Mir träumte einst von wildem Liebesglühn
Wenn ich in deine Augen seh
Johann Ludwig Uhland
Gestorben war ich vor Liebeswonne

Frédéric Louis Ritter (1826-1891)
Ludwig Bechstein
Unter den rothen Blumen schlummere
Ferdinand Braun
Das Körnlein springt, der Vogel singt
Ferdinand Freiligrath
So lass mich sitzen ohne Ende
Hafis
Als ich zum ersten Male dein Angesicht
Ich dachte dein in tiefer Nacht
Ist dir ein getreues, liebevolles Kind bescheert
Wenn du lächelst, wenn du blickst
Wo Engel hausen, da ist der Himmel
Zwei Paradieseslauben, sind, Liebste
Hoffmann von Fallersleben
Die Wasserlilie einsam träumet tief
Mein Lied ist wie der Abendhauch
Nikolaus Lenau
Die dunkeln Wolken hingen herab
Ludwig Pfau
Da sitz' ich und weine und harre allein
Hermann Rollet
Und wenn es dunkel werden
J. Schantz
Horch! Rossgestampf! Muss in den Kampf
Theodor Storm
O lass mich nur von ferne stehn
Julius Sturm
Freude, wohin mein Auge schaut
Komm, o Nacht, und nimm mich hin
Lass nicht dein Auge auf mir ruh'n

Andreas Jakob Romberg (1767-1821)
Johann Wolfgang von Goethe
Füllest wieder Busch und Thal
Wer reitet so spät durch Nacht und Wind

Joseph Guy Marie Ropartz (1864-1955)
Heinrich Heine
Am Kreuzweg wird begraben
Mein Liebchen, wir saßen beisammen
Warum sind die Rosen so Blaß
Wo ich bin, mich rings umdunkelt

Ludwig Rottenberg (1864-1930)
Heinrich Heine
And're beten zur Madonna
Das Herz ist mir bedrückt und sehnlich
Das ist ein schlechtes Wetter
Es blasen die blauen Husaren
In mein gar zu dunkles Leben
Mein Herz, mein Herz ist traurig
Nun ist es Zeit daß ich mit Verstand
Sie liebten sich beide, doch keiner wollt' es
So wandl' ich wieder den alten Weg
Warum sind denn die Rosen so blass
Werdet nur nicht ungeduldig
Wie der Mond sich leuchtend dränget

Anton Grigor'yevich Rubinstein (1829-1894)
Gustav von Boddien
Es blinkt der Thau in den Gräsern der Nacht
Vorbei, vorbei durch Feld und Wald
Wie eine Lerch' in blauer Luft
Friedrich Bodenstedt
Die helle Sonne leuchtet auf's weite Meer
Die Weise guter Zecher ist
Es hat die Rose sich beklagt
Gelb rollt mir zu Füssen
Gott hiess die Sonne glühen
Ich fühle deinen Odem, mich überall umweh'n
Mein Herz schmückt sich mit dir
Neig' schöne Knospe, dich zu mir
Nicht mit Engeln im blauen Himmelszelt
Schlag' die Tschadra zurück
Seh' ich deine zarten Füßchen an
Thu' nicht so spröde, schönes Kind
Felix Dahn
Schlanke Fatme, hohe Palme, sprich!
Joseph von Eichendorff
Waldeinsamkeit, du grünes Revier
Emanuel Geibel
Bedeckt mich mit Blumen, ich sterbe vor Liebe
Ich weiß nicht, säuselt in den Bäumen
Klinge, klinge mein Pandero
Nun die Schatten dunkeln, Stern an Stern
Johann Wolfgang von Goethe
Freudvoll und leidvoll, gedankenvoll sein
Laßt mich nur auf meinem Sattel gelten!
Heinrich Heine
Die blauen Frühlingsaugen schau'n
Du bist wie eine Blume
Es war ein alter König, sein Herz war schwer
In den Walde spriesst's und grünt es
Leise zieht durch mein Gemüth
Täglich ging die wunderschöne Sultanstochter

Hoffmann von Fallersleben
An der Rose Busen schmiegt sich
Siehe, der Frühling währet nicht lang
Karl Lemcke
Ich hatte eine Nachtigall, die sang so schön
Thomas Moore
Zum Friedhof schien der Mond herab
Salomon Hermann von Mosenthal
Ich sah' dich einmal, und ich seh' dich immer
Hermann Oelschläger
Wie bist du nur, mein Herzensschatz
Anton Rubinstein
Es schmachtet eine Blume
Th. von Sacken
Lerche steiget im Gesang
Theodor Storm
Nun gieb ein Morgenküsschen
Johann Ludwig Uhland
Noch ahnt man kaum der Sonne Licht

Ernst (Friedrich Karl) Rudorff (1840-1916)
Joseph von Eichendorff
Laue Luft kommt blau geflossen, Frühling

(Joseph) Martin Ruprecht (1758-1800)
Johann Heinrich Reitzenstein
Ausgelitten hast du, ausgerungen
Georg Ernst von Rüling
Weine nicht; es ist der Sieg erkämpfet
Anonymous
Graf Siegfried einst in Welschland kam

Friedrich Wilhelm Rust (1739-1796)
Johann Wolfgang von Goethe
Der du von dem Himmel bist

Johann Philipp Sack (1722-1763)
Friedrich Wilhelm Zachariä
Denk ihn hinaus, den schrecklichen Gedanken

Franz Salmhofer (1900-1975)
Richard Dehmel
Träume, träume, du mein süßes Leben
Johann Wolfgang von Goethe
Trocknet nicht, trocknet nicht
Husserl
Deine Sehnsucht ist leer
Rainer Maria Rilke
Die falben Felder schlafen schon

Josef Schelb (1894-)
Michelangelo Buonarotti
Es spricht ein Mann, es spricht ein Gott
Ich leb' der Sünde, leb' um mir zu sterben
Wer geboren wird, muß sterben

Otto Scherzer (1821-1886)
Eduard Mörike
Derweil ich schlafend lag

Max von Schillings (1868-1933)
Gustav Falke
Trug mein Herz ich auf der Hand
Nikolaus Lenau
Frühlingskinder im bunten Gedränge
Grafin Schwerin-Schwerinburg
Vöglein, ihr schlauen, darf ich euch trauen?
Karl Stieler
Ein Spielmann zog des Wegs einher

Léandre (Leander) Schlegel (1844-1913)
Heinrich Heine
Die du bist so schön und rein
Du bist wie eine Blume
Immerman
Steh' balde still und rühr' dich nicht
Nikolaus Lenau
Bin mit Dir im Wald gegangen
Mürrisch braust der Eichenwald
Weil' auf mir, du dunkles Auge
Alfred Meissner
Dass ich dein auf ewig bliebe
Lass im Geheim mich zu Dir kommen
Wilhelm Osterwald
Die Nachtigall hat mich vom Schlaf erweckt
Lieblich wallen durch die Lüfte
Friedrich Rückert
Mir ist, nun ich Dich habe
Wissen möcht' ich nur wie lange
Julius Sturm
Da geht er wieder, der bleiche Knabe
Anonymous
Wer die Liebe gepflanzt in die Menschenbrust

Louis Schlottmann (1826-1905)
Johann Wolfgang von Goethe
Wer reitet so spät durch Nacht und Wind

Julius Schneider (1805-1885)
Johann Wolfgang von Goethe
Wer reitet so spät durch Nacht und Wind

Othmar Schoeck (1886-1957)
the Bible
Der Herr ist mein Hirte
Jauchzet dem Herrn, alle Welt!
Wilhelm Busch
Das glaube mir, so sagte er

Matthias Claudius
Ach, es ist so dunkel in des Todes Kammer
Das heiss' ich rechte Augenweide
Der Mensch lebt und bestehet
Der Mond ist aufgegangen
Der Winter ist ein rechter Mann
Die Liebe hemmet nichts
Die Römer, die, vor vielen hundert Jahren
Empfangen und genähret
Heute will ich fröhlich, fröhlich sein
Ich sehe oft um Mitternacht
Ich war erst sechzehn Sommer alt
O du Land des Wesens und der Wahrheit
's ist Krieg! 's ist Krieg! O Gottes Engel wehre
Sie machte Frieden! Das ist mein Gedicht
So schlafe nun, du Kleine!
Tausend Blumen um mich her
Weit von meinem Vaterlande
Wir Vögel singen nicht egal
Dante Alighieri
Du, des Erbarmens Feind, grausamer Tod
Richard Dehmel
Wenn die Felder sich verdunkeln
Joseph von Eichendorff
Abendlich schon rauscht der Wald
Aus schweren Träumen
Berg' und Täler wieder fingen
Da fahr' ich still im Wagen
Das Kind ruht aus vom Spielen
Der Hirt bläst seine Weise
Der Sturm geht lärmend um das Haus
Der Wand'rer, von der Heimat weit
Die Abendglocken klangen
Die Lerche grüßt den ersten Strahl
Du liebe, treue Laute
Durch Feld und Buchenhallen
Ein Wunderland ist oben aufgeschlagen
Eingeschlafen auf der Lauer
Es geht wohl anders, als du meinst
Es haben viel Dichter gesungen
Es schienen so golden die Sterne
Es wandelt, was wir schauen
Ewig muntres Spiel der Wogen!
Für alle muß vor Freuden
Genug gemeistert nun die Weltgeschichte!
Herz, in deinen sonnenhellen Tagen
Hier bin ich, Herr! Gegrüßt das Licht
Hochweiser Rat, geehrte Kollegen!
Hörst du die Gründe rufen
Ich hör' die Bächlein rauschen
Ich kann wohl manchmal singen
Juchheisa! und ich führ' den Zug
Komm, Trost der Welt, du stille Nacht!
Kühle auf dem schönen Rheine
Lindes Rauschen in den Wipfeln
Lust'ge Vögel in dem Wald
Magst du zu dem Alten halten
Nach Süden nun sich lenken
Nächtlich dehnen sich die Stunden
Nun legen sich die Wogen
Posthorn, wie so keck und fröhlich
Schon kehren die Vögel wieder ein
So eitel künstlich haben sie verwoben
So ruhig geh' ich meinen Pfad
So viele Quellen von den Bergen rauschen
Soll ich dich denn nun verlassen
Springer, der in luft'gem Schreiten
Tag und Regung war entflohen
Über gelb' und rote Streifen
Vergangen ist der lichte Tag
Verschneit liegt rings die ganze Welt
Von fern die Uhren schlagen
Wär's dunkel, ich läg' im Walde
Waldeinsamkeit! Du grünes Revier
Was willst auf dieser Station?
Weil jetzo alles stille ist
Wem Gott will rechte Gunst erweisen
Wenn der Hahn kräht auf dem Dache
Wer einmal tief und durstig hat getrunken
Wo aber werd' ich sein im künftgen Lenze?
Wo ruhig sich und wilder unstäte Wellen teilen
Wohin ich geh' und schaue
Wunderliche Spießgesellen
Ernst von Feuchtersleben
Es ist bestimmt in Gottes Rat
Adolf Frey
In begrünter Sommerlaube
Klingend schlagen hier die Finken
Gustav Gamper
Führe mich zum Rosenhaine
Laut gesungen sei das Feuer
Johann Wolfgang von Goethe
Ach, wer bringt die schönen Tage
Alles geben die Götter, die unendlichen
An des lust'gen Brunnens Rand
Dämmrung senkte sich von oben
Deinem Blick mich zu bequemen
Dem Schnee, dem Regen, dem Wind entgegen
Diese Gondel vergleich' ich
Ein Veilchen auf der Wiese stand
Eine einzige Nacht an deinem Herzen!
Es klingt so prächtig, wenn der Dichter

Fetter grüne, du Laub
Freudig war vor vielen Jahren
Haben sie von deinen Fehlen
Höre den Rat, den die Leier tönt!
Ihr verblühet, süsse Rosen
Immer wieder in die Weite
Inneres Wühlen ewig zu finden
Kaum an dem blaueren Himmel erblickt' ich
Kehre nicht in diesem Kreise
Keinen Reimer wird man finden
Kleine Blumen, kleine Blätter
Mahadöh, der Herr der Erde
Sagt es niemand, nur den Weisen
Seh' ich den Pilgrim
Ha! Sie liebt mich! Sie liebt mich!
Warum leckst du dein Mäulchen
Wie herrlich leuchtet mir die Natur
Wie ich so ehrlich war
Wie sie klingeln, die Pfaffen!
Hafis
Ach, wie richtete, so klagt' ich
Ach, wie schön ist Nacht und Dämmerschein!
Das Gescheh'ne, nicht bereut's Hafis
Höre mir den Prediger
Horch, hörst du nicht vom Himmel her
Ich habe mich dem Heil entschworen
Ich roch der Liebe himmlisches Arom
Lieblich in der Rosenzeit
Meine Lebenszeit verstreicht
Nicht düstre, Theosoph, so tief!
Sing', o lieblicher Sängermund
Wie stimmst du mich zur Andacht
Friedrich Hebbel
Schlafen, schlafen, nichts als schlafen!
Wenn zwei sich ineinander still versenken
Heinrich Heine
Dämmernd liegt der Sommerabend
Gekommen ist der Maie
Ja, du bist elend, und ich grolle nicht
Vergiftet sind meine Lieder
Warum sind denn die Rosen so blaß
Wo wird einst des Wandermüden
Hermann Hesse
Abends gehn die Liebespaare langsam
Auf der Strasse und in allen Fabriken
Daß du bei mir magst weilen
Die Bäume tropfen vom Gewitterguß
Du bist mein fernes Tal
Ein Wändeviereck, blaß, vergilbt und alt
Eine Glocke läutet im Grund fernab
Es hält der blaue Tag für eine Stunde
Flügelt ein kleiner blauer Falter
Gottes Atem hin und wieder
Ich bin auch in Ravenna gewesen
Im alten loderlohen Glanze
Im Welschland, wo die braunen Buben
Immer bin ich ohne Ziel gegangen
Kennst du das auch, daß manches Mal
Klavier und Geige, die ich wahrlich schätze
Möchten viele Seelen dies verstehen
Seele, banger Vogel du
Seltsam, im Nebel zu wandern!
Tief mit blauer Nachtgewalt
Vom Baum des Lebens fällt mir Blatt und Blatt
Was lachst du so? Mich schmerzt der gelle Ton
Wie eine weiße Wolke
Wie haben sie dich, Baum, verschnitten
Wieder schreitet er den braunen Pfad
Johann Georg Jacobi
Wie Feld und Au
Johannes Jaeger
Mein liebes Kind schlaf ein!
Gottfried Keller
Aber auch den Föhrenwald
Aber ein kleiner goldener Stern
Als endlich sie den Sarg hier abgesetzt
Arm in Arm und Kron' an Krone
Augen, meine lieben Fensterlein
Berge dein Haupt, wenn ein König vorbeigeht
Da hab ich gar die Rose aufgegessen
Da lieg' ich denn, ohnmächtiger Geselle
Deiner bunten Blasen Kinderfreude
Den Linden ist zu Füßen tief
Der erste Tannenbaum, den ich gesehen
Der Herr gab dir ein gutes Augenpaar
Der schönste Tannenbaum, den ich gesehn
Die Zeit geht nicht, sie stehet still
Durch Bäume dringt ein leiser Ton
Ein Meister bin ich worden
Es donnert über die Pfaffengaß'
Es ist ein stiller Regentag
Es ist nicht Selbstsucht und nicht Eitelkeit
Es wandert eine schöne Sage
Flack're, ew'ges Licht im Tal
Ha! was ist das? Die Sehnen zucken wieder
Heerwagen, mächtig Sternbild der Germanen
Horch – endlich zittert es durch meine Bretter!
Horch! Stimmen und Geschrei
Hüll ein mich in die grünen Dekken
Ich halte dich in meinem Arm
Ich will spiegeln mich in jenen Tagen
Im Herbst verblichen liegt das Land

In Gold und Purpur tief verhüllt
Ja, hätt' ich ein verlass'nes Liebchen nun
Jetzt ist des Winters grimmer Frost
Läg' ich, wo es Hyänen gibt, im Sand
Mich tadelt der Fanatiker,
Mit dem grauen Felsensaal
Nun bin ich untreu worden
Nun schmücke mir dein dunkles Haar mit Rosen
O heiliger Augustin im Himmelssaal
Perlen der Weisheit sind mir deine Zähne!
Schon hat die Nacht den Silberschrein
Siehst du den Stern im fernsten Blau
Und wieder schlägt's – ein Viertel erst
Unser ist das Los der Epigonen
Verbogen und zerkniffen war der vordre Rand
Vom Lager stand ich mit dem Frühlicht auf
Wende dich, du kleiner Stern
Wenn schlanke Lilien wandelten
Wer ohne Leid, der ist auch ohne Liebe
Wie herrlich wär's, zerschnittner Tannenbaum
Wie poltert es! - Abscheuliches Geroll
Wie schlafend unterm Flügel ein Pfau
Willkommen, klare Sommernacht
Willst du nicht dich schließen
Wir wähnten lange recht zu leben
Zwölf hat's geschlagen – warum denn Mittag?

Nikolaus Lenau

Ach, wer möchte einsam trinken
Als sie vom Paradiese ward gezwungen
Am Himmelsantlitz wandelt ein Gedanke
Auf geheimem Waldespfade
Dein gedenkend irr' ich einsam
Der Buchenwald ist herbstlich schon gerötet
Der Traum war so wild,
Der Wind ist fremd, du kannst ihn nicht
Des Berges Gipfel war erschwungen
Des Himmels frohes Antlitz
Die Bäume blühn, die Vöglein singen
Die Bäume rauschen hier noch immer
Die dunklen Wolken hingen
Die Menschheit ist dahinter kommen
Die Vögel flieh'n geschwind
Die Wolken waren fortgezogen
Diese Rose pflück' ich hier
Drei Reiter nach verlorner Schlacht
Drei Zigeuner fand ich einmal
Drüben geht die Sonne scheiden
Du warst mir ein gar trauter, lieber
Durch den Hain mit bangem Stoße
Durch den Wald, den dunkeln geht
Ein Greis trat lächelnd mir entgegen
Ein Wand'rer läßt sein helles Lied erklingen
Es weht der Wind so kühl
Froh summte nach der süßen Beute
Hast du dich je schon ganz allein gefunden
Hesperus, der blasse Funken
Holder Lenz, du bist dahin!
Horch, wie still es wird im dunkeln Hain
Ich ging an deiner Seite
Ich sah den Lenz einmal
Ich trat in einen heilig düstern
Ich wand're fort ins ferne Land
In einem Buche blätternd
In Schlummer ist der dunkle Wald gesunken
Klar und wie die Jugend heiter
Lebe nicht so schnell und stürmisch
Lebe wohl! Ach, jene Abendstunde
Lieblich war die Maiennacht
Ließe doch ein hold Geschick
Müde schleichen hier die Bäche
Mürrisch braust der Eichenwald
Noch immer lag ein tiefes Schweigen
O Einsamkeit! wie trink' ich gerne
"O sei mein Freund!" so schallt's
Rings ein Verstummen, ein Entfärben
Rosen fliehen nicht allein
Sahst du ein Glück vorübergehn
Schlaflose Nacht, der Regen rauscht
Schon seh' ich Hirt' und Herde nimmer
Schon zog vom Walde ich ferne wieder
Sein Bündel Holz am Rücken bringt
Sieh' dort den Berg mit seinem Wiesenhange
Sieh' hier den Bach, anbei die Waldesrose
So oft sie kam, erschien mir die Gestalt
Stoppelfeld, die Wälder leer
Trübe wird's, die Wolken jagen
Trübe Wolken, Herbstesluft
Wenn Worte dir vom Rosenmunde weh'n
Wie sehr ich dein, soll ich dir sagen?

Heinrich Leuthold

Der Lenz ist da und fern und nah
Dich vor allem, heilige Muttersprache
Die Ströme zieh'n zum fernen Meer
Du sahst mich schwelgen oft im Tonregister
Ein guter Ruf ist wie ein wohnlich Haus
Ein unbezwingbar dunkler Hang
Greift zum Becher und laßt das Schelten
Hier pflegt Natur mit ihren goldnen Auen
Hier scheidet die Klosterpforte
Ich bin ein Spielmann von Beruf
Ihr Bilder, die die Zeit begrub
In diesen Silberhainen von Oliven

Komm, ambrosische Nacht
Mein Herz ist wie ein Saitenspiel
Nicht allein in Rathaussälen
Nicht, daß ich dies Bestreben nicht erfasse
Nun laß das Lamentieren und halte Maß!
O Frühlingshauch, o Liederlust
O Lebensfrühling, Blütendrang
O wie träumt es sich süß
Schon verstummt das Lied der Grille
Schweigen rings; im Garten der Villa plaudert
Selbstzweck sei sich die Kunst
Und wieder nehm' ich die Harfe zur Hand
Waldvögelein, wohin ziehst du?
Was immer mir die Feindschaft unterschoben
Wenn ein Gott dir gab fürs Schöne
Wie bist du schön, du tiefer, blauer See!
Wie einst den Knaben lacht ihr noch heut
Wie floß von deiner Lippe milde Güte!
Wo über mir die Waldnacht finster
Wohl ist es schön, auf fauler Haut

Li-Tai-Pe

Vor mein Bett wirft der Mond

Lienert

I weiß äs Seeli, bodelos
Nüd schöiners, as wänn's dimm'red

Conrad Ferdinand Meyer

Am Himmel wächst der Sonne Glut
An wolkenreinem Himmel geht
Auf das Feuer mit dem goldnen Strahle
Aufsteigt der Strahl und fallend gießt
Aus der Eltern Macht und Haus
Bei der Abendsonne Wandern
Da mit Sokrates die Freunde tranken
Die Rechte streckt' ich schmerzlich oft
Du warest mir ein täglich Wanderziel
Ein blendendes Spitzchen blickt über den Wald
Es fährt der Wind gewaltig durch die Nacht
Es sprach der Geist: Sieh auf!
Frühling, der die Welt umblaut
Gestern fand ich, räumend
Heut ward mir bis zum jungen Tag
Hier– doch keinem darfst du's zeigen
In den Lüften schwellendes Gedröhne
In der Nacht, die die Bäume mit Blüten deckt
Läg' dort ich unterm Firneschein
Melde mir die Nachtgeräusche, Muse
Mir träumt', ich komm' ans Himmelstor
Mittagsruhe haltend auf den Matten
Schwarzschattende Kastanie
So stille ruht im Hafen
Was treibst du, Wind, du himmlisches Kind?
Wie pocht' das Herz mir in der Brust
Wo die Tannen finstre Schatten werfen
Wo sah ich, Mädchen, deine Züge
Wolken, meine Kinder, wandern gehen

Michelangelo Buonarotti

In mir nur Tod, in dir mein Leben ruht
Ins Joch beug' ich den Nacken demutvoll

Eduard Mörike

Am Waldsaum kann ich lange Nachmittage
Aufgeschmückt ist der Freudensaal
Bei euren Taten, euren Siegen
Bei jeder Wendung deiner Lebensbahn
Das süße Zeug ohne Saft und Kraft!
Der Himmel glänzt vom reinsten Frühlingslichte
Die ganz' Welt ist in dich verliebt
Die kleine Welt, mit deren Glanzgestalten
Die Liebe, sagt man, steht am Pfahl gebunden
Die Welt wär' ein Sumpf, faul und matt
Ein Irrsal kam in die Mondscheingärten
Es ist doch im April fürwahr
Frühling läßt sein blaues Band
Gestern, als ich vom nächtlichen Lager
Gleichwie ein Vogel am Fenster vorbei
Herr! schikke, was du willt
Hier im Schatten, o Batyllos
Hier ist Freude, hier ist Lust
Hört ihn und seht sein dürftig Instrument!
Horch! Auf der Erde feuchtem Grund gelegen
Ich sah den Helikon in Wolkendunst
Im Nebel ruhet noch die Welt
Ist's möglich? sieht ein Mann so heiter aus
Ja, mein Glück, das langgewohnte
Krank nun vollends und matt! Und du
Kunst! o in deine Arme wie gern entflöh' ich
Mein Kind, in welchem Krieg hast du
Mein Wappen ist nicht adelig
Noch unverrückt, o schöne Lampe
Nur fast so wie im Traum ist mir's geschehen
O flaumenleichte Zeit der dunkeln Frühe!
O Fluß, mein Fluß im Morgenstrahl!
Ohne das Schöne, was soll der Gewinn?
Ostern ist zwar schon vorbei
Primel und Stern und Syringe
Rosenzeit, wie schnell vorbei
Schön prangt im Silbertau die junge Rose
Sieh, der Kastanie kindliches Laub
Siehe, von allen den Liedern, nicht eines gilt dir
Tinte! Tinte, wer braucht!
Tonleiterähnlich steiget dein Klaggesang
Vesperzeit, Betgeläut' aus den Dörfern
Vielfach sind zum Hades die Pfade

Weht, o wehet, liebe Morgenwinde!
Wie heißt König Ringangs Töchterlein?
Wie süß der Nachtwind nun die Wiese streift
Wir Schwestern zwei, wir schönen
Wo gehst du hin, du schönes Kind?
Christian Morgenstern
Erde, die uns dies gebracht
"Novalis" (Friedrich von Hardenberg)
Ich sehe dich in tausend Bildern
Anna Ritter
Ein Vöglein singt im Wald
Armin Rüeger
Es gehen zur Kirche die Leute
Paul Schoeck
Alle meine Wünsche schweigen
Liebe ist Wahrheit!
Nun quill aus meiner Seele immerfort
Carl Spitteler
Damals, ganz zuerst am Anfang
Der Denker rechnet wohl einmal
Ein junges Glöcklein klagte
Schwarzbrauner Hufschmied, ich will dir sagen
Was ist's, das der Gedanken mutigen Tritt
Theodor Storm
Das ist die Drossel, die da schlägt
Johann Ludwig Uhland
Als ich ging die Flur entlang
Aus der Bedrängnis, die mich wild umkettet
Bei einem Wirte wundermild
Das neue Haus ist aufgericht't
Die Totenglocke tönte mir
Droben stehet die Kapelle
Du kamst, du gingst mit leiser Spur
Lebe wohl, lebe wohl mein Lieb!
O blaue Luft nach trüben Tagen
O, legt mich nicht ins dunkle Grab
Seid gegrüßt mit Frühlingswonne
So soll ich nun dich meiden
Solche Düfte sind mein Leben
Stiller Garten, eile nur
Süßer, goldner Frühlingstag!
Wann im letzten Abendstrahl
Was klinget und singet die Straß' herauf?
Wolken seh' ich abendwärts
Paul Verlaine
Leis dem Schmeichellied der Lauten
Walt Whitman
Schlagt! Schlagt! Trommeln!
Anonymous
Es tat den Beiden so weh das Scheiden
Volkslied
Wenn i zum Brünnle geh

Arnold (Franz Walter) Schönberg (1874-1951)
Heinrich Ammann
Sie führten ihn durch den grauen Hof
Kurt Aram
Komm, komm mit nur einen Schritt!
Otto Julius Bierbaum
Fräulein Gigerlette lud mich ein zum Tee
Ada Christen
Daß schon die Maienzeit vorüber
Colly
Ebenes Paradefeld Kasper in der Mitte hält
Hermann Conradi
Im Morgengrauen schritt ich fort
Richard Dehmel
Aprilwind; alle Knospen
Aus dem meergrünen Teiche
Du mußt nicht meinen, ich hätte Furcht vor dir
Gieb mir deine Hand, nur den Finger
Lass uns noch die Nacht erwarten
Mädel, laß das Stricken geh
Mein Hund, du, hat dich bloss beknurrt
Schenk mir deinen goldenen Kamm
Emanuel Geibel
In meinem Garten die Nelken
Stefan George
Als neuling trat ich ein in dein gehege
Als wir hinter dem beblümten tore
Angst und hoffen wechselnd mich beklemmen
Da meine lippen reglos sind und brennen
Das schöne beet betracht ich mir im harren
Du lehnest wider eine silberweide
Hain in diesen paradiesen
Ich darf nicht dankend an dir niedersinken
Jedem werke bin ich fürder tot
Saget mir, auf welchem pfade
Sprich nicht immer von dem laub
Streng ist uns das glück und spröde
Unterm schutz von dichten blättergründen
Wenn ich heut nicht deinen leib berühre
Wenn sich bei heiliger ruh in tiefen matten
Wir bevölkerten die abend-düstern
Albert Giraud
Den Wein, den man mit Augen trinkt
Der Mond, ein blankes Türkenschwert
Der Mondstrahl ist das Ruder
Des Mondlichts bleiche Blüten
Die dürre Dirne mit langem Halse
Du nächtig todeskranker Mond
Eine blasse Wäscherin

Einen weissen Fleck des hellen Mondes
Finstre, schwarze Riesenfalter
Heilge Kreuze sind die Verse
In den blanken Kopf Cassanders
Lieblich klagend – ein kristallnes Seufzen
Mit einem phantastischen Lichtstrahl
Mit groteskem Riesenbogen
O alter Duft der Märchenzeit
Pierrot! Mein Lachen hab ich verlernt!
Rote, fürstliche Rubine
Steig, o Mutter aller Schmerzen
Stricknadeln, blank und blinkend
Wie ein blasser Tropfen Bluts
Zu grausem Abendmahle

Johann Wolfgang von Goethe
Zwischen Weizen und Korn

Alfred Gold
In hellen Träumen hab ich Dich oft geschaut

"Martin Greif" (Friedrich Hermann Frey)
Ich hab' zum Brunnen ein Krüglein gebracht

Jakob Haringer
Es leuchtet so schön die Sonne
Ist alles eins, was liegt daran!
Wenn du schon glaubst, es ist ewige Nacht

Julius Hart
Nacht fließt in Tag und Tag in Nacht
Um meinen Nakken schliesst sich

Karl Henckell
In diesen Wintertagen, nun sich das Licht

Paul Heyse
Sang ein Bettlerpärlein am Schenkentor
Waldesnacht, du wunderkühle

Gustav Hochstetter
Mädel sei kein eitles Ding

Hugo von Hofmannsthal
Sie trug den Becher in der Hand

Jens Peter Jacobsen
So voll und reich wand noch das Leben

Gottfried Keller
Ich halte dich in meinem Arm
Weise nicht von dir mein schlichtes Herz
Welche tiefbewegten Lebensläufchen

Viktor Klemperer
Trinkt aus, ihr zechtet zum letztenmal

Nikolaus Lenau
Drüben geht die Sonne scheiden

Karl Freiherr von Levetzow
Aus den Trümmern einer hohen Schönheit
Grosses hast Du mir gegeben

Hermann Lingg
Dunkelnd über den See dämmert das Abendrot
Soviel Raben nachts auffliegen

John Henry Mackay
Tausend Menschen ziehen vorüber

Friedrich Nietzsche
Es geht ein Wandrer durch die Nacht

Francesco Petrarca
Nie ward ich, Herrin, müd, um Euch zu minnen
Voll jener Süße, die, nicht auszudrükken
Wenn Vöglein klagen, und in grünen Zweigen

Ludwig Pfau
Der Pflanze, die dort über dem Abgrund
Du kehrst mir den Rücken
Du Kleine bist so lieb und hold
Einsam bin ich und alleine
Einst hat vor deines Vaters Haus
Gott grüß dich, Marie!
Könnt' ich zu dir, mein Licht
Laß deine Sichel rauschen
Mein Schatz ist wie ein Schneck
War ein Blümlein wunderfein
Warum bist du aufgewacht

Oskar von Redwitz
Nur das tut mir so bitterweh'

Robert Reinick
Im Fliederbusch ein Vöglein saß

Paul Remer
Ach, wenn es nun die Mutter wüsst'

Rainer Maria Rilke
Vorüber die Flut. Noch braust es fern

Hugo Salus
König ist spazieren gangen
Meine Freundin hat eine schwarze Katze

Emanuel Schikaneder
Seit ich so viele Weiber sah

Johannes Schlaf
In die braunen, rauschenden Nächte flittert

"Jaroslav Vrchlický"
Duftreich ist die Erde und die Luft krystallen

Wilhelm Wackernagel
Ich grüne wie die Weide grünt

Frank Wedekind
Ach, wie brenn' ich vor Verlangen, Galathea

Freiherr von Zedlitz
Als mein Auge sie fand

Anonymous
Daß gestern eine Wespe
Es steht sein Bild noch immer da
Juble, schöne junge Rose
Mein Herz, das ist ein tiefer Schacht

from Des Knaben Wunderhorn
Mein Fleiss und Müh hab ich nie gespart

Schwer, langweilig ist mir mein Zeit
Stürmt, reißt und rast, ihr Unglückswinde
Volkslied
Der Mai tritt ein mit Freuden
Es gingen zwei Gespielen gut
Mein Herz in steten Treuen
Mein Herz ist mir gemenget

Fritz Schreiber
Friedrich Hebbel
Friedlich bekämpfen Nacht sich und Tag

Franz Schreker (1878-1934)
Stefan George
Zieh mit mir, geliebtes Kind, in die Wälder
Paul Heyse
An Dich verschwendet hat mein Herz
Es kommen Blätter, es kommen Blüten
Ich glaube in alten Tagen
Ich sah' mein Glück vorüber geh'n
Im Lenz, im Lenz, wenn Veilchen blühn
Mia Holm
Daß er ganz ein Engel werde
O Glokken, böse Glokken, habt schweren
Dora Leen
Du rote Rose, die du in schimmernder Vase
Im Mondgeflimmer, im Zauberschimmer
Mich grüßte erstrahlender Schein
Wenn die Sommerzeiten enden
Karl Freiherr von Lemayer
Frühling schimmert in den Lüften
Alfons Petzold
Ein feuriges Männlein reit' über die Welt
Rainer Maria Rilke
Und wie mag die Liebe Dir kommen sein?
Edith Ronsperger
Die Dunkelheit sinkt schwer wie Blei
Dies aber kann mein Sehnen nimmer fassen
Einst gibt ein Tag mir alles Glück zu eigen
Sie sind so schön, die milden, sonnenreichen
Ferdinand von Saar
Lang war die Nacht; wie auf stygischem Nachen
Ernst Scherenberg
Ach, noch so jung und schon so verblüht
Als wollte Winterqual nicht enden
Heimlich durch's Fenster kam er geflogen
Theodor Storm
Heute, nur heute bin ich so schön
Wohl fühl ich wie das Leben rinnt
Julius Sturm
Da geht er wieder, der bleiche Knabe
Der Kukuk hat ein einzig Lied
Schlafe, mein Liebchen, ich dekke dich zu
Leo Tolstoi
Ich sehe Thränen im Aug' dir glänzen
Walt Whitman
Ein Kind sagte: "Was ist das Gras?"
Wurzeln und Halme sind dies nur
Anonymous
Ich frag' nach dir jedwede Morgensonne

Corona Elisabeth Wilhelmine Schröter (1751-1802)
Johann Wolfgang von Goethe
Als ich noch ein Knabe war
Für Männer uns zu plagen
O Mutter, guten Rat mir leiht
Wer reitet so spät durch Nacht und Wind
Anonymous
Manchen langen Tag, und manche lange Nacht
Volkslied
Die See war wild im Heulen
Hört, wir die Wachtel im Felde dort schlägt

Christian Friedrich Daniel Schubart (1739-1791)
Matthias Claudius
Es war einmal 'ne Henne fein
Christian Friedrich Daniel Schubart
Auf, auf, ihr Brüder und seid stark
Da liegt, ach Gott, da drunten liegt
Da steht der Mond! Verweile, lieber Mond
Gefang'ner Mann, ein armer Mann!
Ich hatt' einmal ein Mädchen
Ich lebe immer heiter und flieh' die Traurigkeit
Ich Mädchen bin aus Schwaben
In einem Bächlein helle, da schoß in froher Eil'
Kühlender Abend, steige vom Hügel
Mädle 's ist Winter; der wollige Schnee
Schlaf wohl, du Himmelsknabe du, schlaf wohl
Sträußchen wem zu Ehren duftest du so süß
Was will dies Klopfen sagen
Wenn aus deinen sanften Blikken
Wenn des Abends Rosenflügel
Wo find ich den Liebling der Seele

Franz Peter Schubert (1797-1828)
Eduard von Bauernfeld
Dem Vater liegt das Kind im Arm
Gabriele von Baumberg
Durch eine ganze Nacht sich nah zu sein
Ich sass an einer Tempelhalle
Nach so vielen trüben Tagen
O köstlicher Tokayer, o königlicher Wein
Sei sanft wie ihre Seele, und heiter wie ihr Blick
Sinke, liebe Sonne, sinke

Josef Karl Bernard
Ja, ich weiss es, diese treue Liebe
Friedrich Bertrand
Hoch, und ehern schier von Dauer
Wie treiben die Wolken so finster und schwer
the Bible
Ach Herr, wie lange willst du mein
Gott ist mein Hirt, mir wird nichts mangeln
In der Zeit sprach der Herr Jesus
Friedrich Bobrik
Der König saß beim frohen Mahle
Franz Bruchmann
Ich will von Atreus Söhnen
Im Mondenschein' wall' ich auf und ab
In des Sees Wogenspiele
Sonnenstrahlen durch die Tannen
Wer wagt's, wer wagt's, wer will mir die Leier
Gottfried August Bürger
Ich rühme mir mein Dörfchen hier
Ignaz Franz Castelli
Brüder! unser Erdenwallen
Herzliebe gute Mutter, o grolle nicht mit mir
Ich bin von lockerem Schlage
Wilhelmine Chézy
Wenn auf dem höchsten Fels ich steh'
Matthias Claudius
Dass ich dich verloren habe
Der Mond ist aufgegangen
Du kleine grünumwachs'ne Quelle
Er liegt und schläft an meinem Herzen
Friede sei um diesen Grabstein her!
Heute will ich fröhlich, fröhlich sein
Ich bin vergnügt, im Siegeston verkünd' es
Ich danke Gott und freue mich wie's Kind
Ich war erst sechszehn Sommer alt
Laßt mich! Laßt mich! ich will klagen
Seht meine lieben Bäume an
Vorüber, ach vorüber
Heinrich von Collin
Hinauf! hinauf! in Sprung und Lauf!
Vom Meere trennt sich die Welle
Matthäus von Collin
Heil'ge Nacht, du sinkest nieder!
Im trüben Licht verschwinden schon die Berge
Liebe ist ein süsses Licht
Und nimmer schreibst du?
Wenn ich durch Wald und Fluren geh'
Abraham Cowley
Noch fand von Evens Töchterschaaren
Jacob Nicolaus Craigher
O Menschheit, o Leben, was soll's?
O sagt, ihr Lieben, mir einmal, welch Ding ist's
Wie braust durch die Wipfel
Johann Ludwig von Deinhardstein
Lasst im Morgenstrahl des Mai'n
Bernhard Ehrlich
All' mein Wirken, all' mein Leben
Karl August Engelhardt
Dort ist ihr Grab, die einst im Schmelz
Johann Georg Fellinger
Die erste Liebe füllt das Herz
Oben drehen sich die grossen unbekannten
Was funkelt ihr so mild mich an?
Friedrich von Gerstenberg
Lasst mich, ob ich auch still verglüh'
Johann Wolfgang von Goethe
Ach neige, du Schmerzenreiche
Ach, wer bringt die schönen Tage
Als ich still und ruhig spann
An die Thüren will ich schleichen
Arm am Beutel, krank am Herzen
Bedecke deinen Himmel, Zeus
Christ ist erstanden! Christ ist erstanden!
Da droben auf jenem Berge, da steh' ich
Das Wasser rauscht', das Wasser schwoll
Dem Schnee, dem Regen, dem Wind entgegen
Der Damm zerreisst, das Feld erbraust
Der du von dem Himmel bist
Des Menschen Seele gleicht dem Wasser
Durch Feld und Wald zu schweifen
Ein Blick von deinen Augen in die meinen
Es ist doch meine Nachbarin
Es schlug mein Herz, geschwind zu Pferde!
Es war ein König in Thule
Freudvoll und leidvoll, gedankenvoll sein
Füllest wieder Busch und Thal
Heiß mich nicht reden, heiß mich schweigen
Hin und wieder fliegen die Pfeile
Hoch auf dem alten Thurme
Ich bin der wohlbekannte Sänger
Ich denke dein, wenn mir der Sonne Schimmer
Ich wollt' ich wär' ein Fisch
Im Felde schleich' ich still und wild
In allen guten Stunden, erhöht von Lieb'
Kennst du das Land, wo die Citronen blühn
Liebe schwärmt auf allen Wegen
Mahadöh, der Herr der Erde, kommt herab
Meine Ruh' ist hin, mein Herz ist schwer
Mich ergreift, ich weiss nicht wie
Nur wer die Sehnsucht kennt
O gieb vom weichen Pfühle, träumend
Ros' und Lilie morgenthaulich blüht im Garten

Sah ein Knab' ein Röslein stehn
Schaff', das Tagwerk meiner Hände
Seht den Felsenquell, freudehell
So hab' ich wirklich dich verloren?
So lasst mich scheinen, bis ich werde
Spute dich, Kronos! Fort, den rasselnden Trott!
Tiefe Stille herrscht im Wasser
Trocknet nicht, trocknet nicht
Über allen Gipfeln ist Ruh'
Über meines Liebchens Äugeln
Über Thal und Fluss getragen
Uf'm Bergli bin i g'sässe, ha de Vögle
Und frische Nahrung, neues Blut
Verfließet, vielgeliebte Lieder
Voll Locken kraus ein Haupt so rund
Von allen schönen Waaren, zum Markte
Was hör' ich draussen vor dem Thor
Was zieht mir das Herz so?
Wenn der uralte heilige Vater
Wer nie sein Brod mit Tränen ass
Wer reitet so spät durch Nacht und Wind?
Wer sich der Einsamkeit ergiebt, ach!
Wie anders, Gretchen, war dir's
Wie im Morgenglanze du rings mich anglüh'st
Wie kommt's, dass du so traurig bist

Friedrich Wilhelm Gotter
Du, der ewig um mich trauert

Franz Grillparzer
Nacht umhüllt mit wehendem Flügel
Rührt die Cymbel, schlagt die Saiten
Zögernd, leise, in des Dunkels nächt'ger Hülle

Johann Christoph Haug
Liebchen und der Saft der Reben

Heinrich Heine
Am fernen Horizonte erscheint
Das Meer erglänzte weit hinaus
Du schönes Fischermädchen, treibe den Kahn
Ich stand in dunkeln Träumen
Ich unglücksel'ger Atlas
Still ist die Nacht, es ruhen die Gassen

C. Heine
Ferne, ferne flammenhelle Sterne

"Theodor Hell" (Karl G. Winkler)
Oft in einsam stillen Stunden

Johann Gottfried Herder
Dein Schwert, wie ist's von Blut so roth

Ludwig Hölty
Beglückt, beglückt, wer dich erblickt
Bekränzet die Tonnen und zapfet mir Wein
Das Glas gefüllt! der Nordwind brüllt
Dein Silber schien durch Eichengrün
Der Schnee zerrinnt, der Mai beginnt
Die Luft ist blau, das Tal ist grün
Die Nachtigall singt überall auf grünen Reisen
Ein heilig Säuseln und ein Gesangeston
Es ist ein halbes Himmelreich
Es liebt' in Welschland irgendwo
Freuden sonder Zahl blüh'n im Himmelssaal
Geuß, lieber Mond, geuß deine Silberflimmer
Geuss nicht so laut der liebentflammten Lieder
Grabe, Spaten, grabe! Alles, was ich habe
Grüner wird die Au und der Himmel blau!
Holder klingt der Vogelsang
Keine Blumen blühn, nur das Wintergrün
Liebe säuseln die Blätter
Mir träumt', ich war ein Vögelein
Nimmer werd' ich, nimmer dein vergessen
Schon im bunten Knabenkleide
Sicheln schallen, Ähren fallen unter Sichelschall
Sie ist dahin, die Maienlieder tönte
Wann der silberne Mond durch die Gesträuche
Was schauest du so hell und klar
Wie glücklich, wem das Knabenkleid
Willkommen, lieber schöner Mai

Heinrich Hüttenbrenner
Die Abendglocke tönet
Ein Jüngling auf dem Hügel

Johann Georg Jacobi
Bei der Liebe reinsten Flammen
Es ging ein Mann zur Frühlingszeit
Ruh'n in Frieden alle Seelen
Todesstille deckt das Thal
Wälze dich hinweg, du wildes Feuer!
Will singen euch im alten Ton ein Lied
Wo die Taub' in stillen Buchen

Johann Nepomuk von Kalchberg
Überall, wohin mein Auge blicket

Josef Kenner
Ein Fräulein schaut vom hohen Thurm
Er fiel den Tod fürs Vaterland
Gieb, Schwester, mir die Harf' herab

Friedrich Kind
Ahidi, ich liebe, ahidi, ich liebe!

Ewald Christian von Kleist
Gross ist der Herr, gross ist der Herr!

Karoline Louise von Klenke
O du, wenn deine Lippen mich berühren

Friedrich Klopstock
Begrabt den Leib in seiner Gruft
Cidli, du weinest, und ich schlumm're sicher
Dein süsses Bild, Edone, schwebt stets
Ehre sei der Hocherhab'nen

Es tönet sein Lob Feld und Wald
Ha, dort kömmt er, mit Schweiss
Ich bin ein deutsches Mädchen!
Im Frühlingsgarten fand ich sie
Mit unserm Arm ist nichts gethan
Überwunden hat der Herr den Tod!
Weine du nicht, o, die ich innig liebe
Wenn der Schimmer von dem Monde
Wie erhebt sich das Herz, wenn es dich
Willkommen, o silberner Mond
Zeit, Verkündigerin der besten Freuden
Friedrich von Köpken
Freude, die im frühen Lenze meinem Haupte
Theodor Körner
Dir, Mädchen, schlägt mit leisem Beben
Du Schwert an meiner Linken
Frisch auf, ihr Jäger, frei und flink!
Hoch auf dem Gipfel deiner Gebirge
Ich hab' ein heisses junges Blut
Jüngst träumte mir, ich sah auf lichten Höhen
Schlacht, du brichst an!
Schlumm're sanft! Noch an dem Mutterherzen
Stern der Liebe, Glanzgebilde
Süsses Licht! aus goldenen Pforten brichst du
Süsses Liebchen! Komm zu mir!
Vater, ich rufe dich! Brüllend umwölkt mich
Vor Thebens siebenfach gähnenden Toren
Was glänzt dort vom Walde im Sonnenschein?
Wie die Nacht mit heil'gem Beben
Kolumban Schnitzer von Meerau
Es redet und träumet die Jugend so viel
Ludwig Kosegarten
Der Abend blüht, der Westen glüht!
Der Abend blüht, Temora glüht
Der Morgen blüht; der Osten glüht
Endlich steh'n die Pforten offen
Ganz verloren, ganz versunken
Ich hab' ein Mädchen funden, sanft, edel
Ich lag auf grünen Matten
Im Erlenbusch, im Tannenhain
Rosa, denkst du an mich?
Siehe, wie die Mondesstrahlen
Sonne, du sinkst, Sonne, du sinkst
Tiefe Feier schauert um die Welt
Vernimm es, Nacht, was Ida dir vertrauet
Warum bist du nicht hier, meine Geliebteste
Was ist es, das die Seele füllt?
Wehmuth, die mich hüllt, welche Gottheit
Wer bist du, Geist der Liebe
Wie schaust du aus dem Nebelflor, o Sonne
Wie wohl ist mir im Dunkeln!
Woher, o namenloses Sehnen
Wohl weinen Gottes Engel
Friedrich Wilhelm Krummacher
Wie schön bist du, freundliche Stille
Christoph Kuffner
Glaube, hoffe, liebe!
Johann Gottfried Kumpf ("Ermin")
Rein und freundlich lacht der Himmel
Sei mir gegrüsst, o Mai
Friedrich de La Motte Fouqué
An dem jungen Morgenhimmel
Don Gayseros, Don Gayseros
Du Urquell aller Güte, du Urquell aller Macht
Ein Schäfer sass im Grünen
Mutter geht durch ihre Kammern
Nächtens klang die süsse Laute
Karl Lappe
In der Freie will ich leben
O, wie schön ist deine Welt
Wann meine Grillen schwirren, bei Nacht
Karl Gottfried von Leitner
Auf meinen heimischen Bergen
Das also, das ist der enge Schrein
Dort blinket durch Weiden
Ein Münich steht in seiner Zell'
Es ist so still, so heimlich um mich
Gar fröhlich kann ich scheiden
Gar tröstlich kommt geronnen der Thränen
He! schenket mir im Helme ein!
Nehm ich die Harfe, folgend dem Drange
Vater, du glaubst es nicht
Wie blitzen die Sterne so hell durch die Nacht!
Gottlieb von Leon
Wo weht der Liebe hoher Geist?
Michael Lubi
Am hohen, hohen Thurm
James Macpherson ("Ossian")
Beugt euch aus euren Wolken nieder
Der bleiche, kalte Mond erhob sich in Osten
Die Nacht ist dumpfig und finster
Ich sitz' bei der moosigten Quelle
Lorma sass in der Halle von Aldo
Mädchen Inistores, wein' auf dem Felsen
Mein Geliebter ist ein Sohn des Hügels
Rolle, du strömigter Carun
Rund um mich Nacht, ich irr' allein
Warum öffnest du wieder, Erzeugter von Alpin
Johann Majláth
Wie tönt es mir so schaurig,
Friedrich von Matthisson
Abendgewölke schweben hell

Am Seegestad', in lauen Vollmondsnächten
Der Abend schleiert Flur und Hain
Der Dämm'rung Schein durchblinkt den Hain
Die bretterne Kammer der Todten erbebt
Die Sonne steigt, die Sonne sinkt
Durch Fichten am Hügel, durch Erlen am Bach
Ein Fräulein klagt' im finstern Thurm
Einsam wandelt dein Freund im Frühlingsgarten
Freunde, deren Grüfte sich schon bemoosten!
Goldner Schein deckt den Hain
Heil! dies ist die letzte Zähre
Herzen, die gen Himmel sich erheben
Ich denke dein, wenn durch den Hain
Im Abendschimmer wallt der Quell
Kein Rosenschimmer leuchtet dem Tag
Kommen und Scheiden, Suchen und Meiden
Laura betet! Engelharfen hallen
Lehnst du deine bleichgehärmte Wange
Mädchen entsiegelten, Brüder, die Flaschen
Nimmer, nimmer darf ich dir gestehen
Purpur malt die Tannenhügel
Sanft wehn, im Hauch der Abendluft
So lang im deutschen Eichenthale
Tag voll Himmel! da aus Laura's Blicken
Wenn ich einst das Ziel errungen habe
Wenn in des Abends letztem Scheine
Wenn sanft entzückt mein Auge sieht

Johann Mayrhofer
Alte Liebe rostet nie
Auf den Blumen flimmern Perlen
Auf der Wellen Spiegel schwimmt der Kahn
Auf hohem Bergesrücken
Auf seinen gold'nen Throne
Blüht denn hier an Tauris Strande
Da sitz' ich ohne Bogen, und starre in den Sand
Den Tag hindurch nur einmal mag ich sprechen
Der Abend röthet nun das Thal
Der Knabe seufzt über's grüne Meer
Der Lerche wolkennahe Lieder
Der Nachen dröhnt, Cypressen flüstern
Die Angel zuckt, die Ruthe bebt
Dioskuren, Zwillingssterne
Du Thurm! zu meinem Leide ragst du
Es mahnt der Wald, es ruft der Strom
Es tanzen Mond und Sterne
Es träumen die Wolken, die Sterne, der Mond
Fels auf Felsen hingewälzet
Gib mir die Fülle der Einsamkeit!
"Hast du Lianen nicht gesehen?"
Hörnerklänge rufen klagend
Ihr hohen Himmlischen, erhöret der Tochter
Im kalten, rauhen Norden ist Kunde
Im Wald, im Wald da grabt mich ein
Im Winde, im Sturme befahr' ich den Fluss
In monderhellten Nächten mit dem Geschick
Ist dies Tauris, wo der Eumeniden Wuth
Ist mir's doch, als sei mein Leben
Ja, spanne nur den Bogen mich zu tödten
Lasst uns, ihr Himmlischen, ein Fest begehen!
Mir ist so wohl, so weh' am stillen Erlafsee
Nachtviolen, Nachtviolen!
O unbewölktes Leben! so rein und tief und klar
Sag an, wer lehrt dich Lieder
Sie hüpfte mit mir auf grünem Plan
Sitz' ich im Gras am glatten See
So wird der Mann, der sonder Zwang gerecht ist
Süsse Augen, klare Bronnen!
Über die Berge zieht ihr fort
Verbirg dich, Sonne, denn die Gluthen
Was weilst du einsam an dem Himmel
Wenn über Berge sich der Nebel breitet
Woget brausend, Harmonien, kehre wieder
Wohin? o Helios! wohin?
Zu meinen Füssen brichst du dich
Zum Donaustrom, zur Kaiserstadt geh' ich

Johann Christian Mikan
Sie sind in Paris! Die Helden

Wilhelm Müller
Am Bach viel kleine Blumen steh'n
Am Brunnen vor dem Thore
Auf einen Todtenacker hat mich mein Weg
Bächlein, lass dein Rauschen sein, Räder
Das Wandern ist des Müllers Lust, das Wandern
Der du so lustig rauschtest
Der Reif hat einen weissen Schein
Der Wind spielt mit der Wetterfahne
Drei Sonnen sah ich am Himmel steh'n
Drüben hinterm Dorfe steht ein Leiermann
Ein Licht tanzt freundlich vor mir her
Eine Krähe war mit mir aus der Stadt gezogen
Eine Mühle seh' ich blinken aus den Erlen
Es bellen die Hunde, es rasseln die Ketten
Es brennt mir unter beiden Sohlen
Fliegt der Schnee mir in's Gesicht
Fremd bin ich eingezogen
Gefror'ne Tropfen fallen von meinen Wangen
Gute Ruh', gute Ruh', thu' die Augen zu
Guten Morgen, schöne Müllerin
Hätt' ich tausend Arme zu rühren
Hie und da ist an den Bäumen
Ich frage keine Blume, ich frage keinen Stern
Ich hört' ein Bächlein rauschen

Ich möchte zieh'n in die Welt hinaus
Ich schnitt' es gern in alle Rinden ein
Ich such' im Schnee vergebens
Ich träumte von bunten Blumen
Ihr Blümlein alle, die sie mir gab
In die tiefsten Felsengründe lockte mich
In Grün will ich mich kleiden
Manche Thrän' aus meinen Augen
Meine Laute hab' ich gehängt an die Wand
Nun merk' ich erst, wie müd' ich bin
Schad' um das schöne grüne Band
Von der Strasse her ein Posthorn klingt
War es also gemeint, mein rauschender Freund
Was sucht denn der Jäger am Mühlbach hier?
Was vermeid' ich denn die Wege
Wenn auf dem höchsten Fels ich steh'
Wie eine trübe Wolke durch heit're Lüfte geht
Wie hat der Sturm zerrissen
Wir sassen so traulich beisammen
Wo ein treues Herze in Liebe vergeht
Wohin so schnell, so kraus und wild

"Novalis" (Friedrich von Hardenberg)

Hinüber wall' ich, und jede Pein
Ich sag' es jedem, dass er lebt
Ich sehe dich in tausend Bildern
Wenige wissen das Geheimniss der Liebe
Wenn alle untreu werden, so bleib' ich dir
Wenn ich ihn nur habe, wenn er mein nur ist

Anton Ottenwalt

Er schläft so süss, der Mutter Blicke hangen

Francesco Petrarca

Allein, nachdenklich, wie gelähmt
Apollo, lebet noch dein hold Verlangen
Nunmehr, da Himmel, Erde schweigt

Gottlieb Conrad Pfeffel

Ein Vater starb von des Sohnes Hand

Karoline Pichler

Die Nacht bricht an, mit leisen Lüften sinket sie
Ferne von der grossen Stadt, nimm mich auf
Klage, meine Flöte, klage

August Graf von Platen

Die Liebe hat gelogen, die Sorge lastet schwer
Mein Herz ist zerrissen, du liebst mich nicht!

Anton Platner

Es deuten die Blumen des Herzens Gefühle

Aaron Pollak

Geöffnet sind des Winters Riegel

Alexander Pope

Lebensfunke vom Himmel entglüht

Martin Josef Prandstetter

Wess' Adern leichtes Blut durchspringt

Adolf von Pratobevera

Leb' wohl du schöne Erde

Johann Ladislaus Pyrker

Ach, der Gebirgssohn hängt mit kindlicher Lieb'
Gross ist Jehovah, der Herr

Friedrich Reil

Gott! lass die Glocke glücklich steigen
Ins Grüne, ins Grüne, da lockt uns der Frühling

Christian Ludwig Reissig

Zwar schuf das Glück hienieden

Ludwig Rellstab

Ade! du muntre, du fröhliche Stadt, Ade!
Es rauschen die Winde so herbstlich und kalt
Fröhlicher Lebensmut braust
In tiefer Ruh liegt um mich her
Leise flehen meine Lieder durch die Nacht
Nimm die letzten Abschiedsküsse
Rauschender Strom, brausender Wald
Rauschendes Bächlein, so silbern und hell
Säuselnde Lüfte wehend so mild
Wehe dem Fliehenden, Welt hinaus Ziehenden!

Johann Rochlitz

Die Sonne sinkt in's tiefe Meer
Horcht auf! Es schlägt die Stunde
Leiser, leiser, kleine Laute
Meine Ruh' ist dahin, meine Freud' ist entfloh'n

Friedrich Rückert

Dass der Ostwind Düfte hauchet in die Lüfte
Der Frost hat mir bereifet des Hauses Dach
Du bist die Ruh, der Friede mild
Lachen und Weinen zu jeglicher Stunde
Meine Tränen im Bußgewand
O du Entriss'ne mir und meinem Kusse!

Johann von Salis-Seewis

Abendglockenhalle zittern
Arbeitsam und wacker, pflügen wir den Acker
Auf! es dunkelt, silbern funkelt dort der Mond
Bunt sind schon die Wälder
Das Fischergewerbe giebt rüstigen Muth!
Das Grab ist tief und stille, und schauderhaft
Es rieselt, klar und wehend, ein Quell
In's stille Land! Wer leitet uns hinüber?
Leise, rieselnder Quell
Mit leisen Harfentönen sei, Wehmut
Noch einmal tön', o Harfe, die nur Gefühlte tönt
Schöpferin beseelter Töne!
Wie schön ist's im Freien, bei grünenden Maien
Wohl denk' ich allenthalben, o du Entfernte

Samuel Friedrich Sauter

Ach! mir schallt's dorten so lieblich hervor

Friedrich Schäffer
Freunde, sammelt Euch im Kreise
Friedrich von Schiller
Ach, aus dieses Thales Gründen
An der Quelle sass der Knabe
Auf der Berge freien Höhen
Der Eichwald braust, die Wolken zieh'n
Dessen Fahne Donnerstürme wallte
Dreifach ist der Schritt der Zeit
Ein jugendlicher Maienschwung
Es ist so angenehm, so süss
Es reden und träumen die Menschen viel
Freude, schöner Götterfunken
Frisch athmet des Morgens lebendiger Hauch
Hier strecket der wallende Pilger
Hier umarmen sich getreue Gatten
Hör' ich das Pförtchen nicht gehen?
Horch, wie Murmeln des empörten Meeres
In einem Thal bei armen Hirten erschien
Ist der holde Lenz erschienen?
Laura, über diese Welt zu flüchten wähn' ich
Liebe rauscht der Silberbach
Majestät'sche Sonnenrosse
Mit erstorbnem Scheinen steht der Mond
Nein, länger werd' ich diesen Kampf
Nimmer, das glaubt mir, erscheinen die Götter
Noch in meines Lebens Lenze war ich
Ritter, treue Schwesterliebe widmet euch
Schön wie Engel voll Walhalla's Wonne
Schöne Welt, wo bist du? Kehre wieder
Schwer und Dumpfig, eine Wetterwolke
Selig durch die Liebe Götter
Sie konnte mir kein Wörtchen sagen
Thronend auf erhabnem Sitz
Unendliche Freude durchwallet das Herz
Vier Elemente, innig gesellt
Vorüber, vorüber die stöhnende Klage!
Weit in nebelgrauer Ferne
Wenn dein Finger durch die Saiten meistert
Wer die steile Sternenbahn
Wer wagt es, Rittersmann oder Knapp'
Will sich Hektor ewig von mir wenden
Willkommen, schöner Jüngling!
Willst du nicht das Lämmlein hüten?
Wo ich sei, und wo mich hingewendet
Wohl perlet im Glase der purpurne Wein
Zu Aachen in seiner Kaiserpracht
Zu Dionys, dem Tyrannen, schlich Möros
Zwei sind der Wege, auf welchen der Mensch
Zwischen Himmel und Erd' hoch in der Lüfte
Franz von Schlechta
Den Fischer fechten Sorgen und Gram
Harrt ein Fischer auf der Brücke
Hier unten steht ein Ritter
Nicht so düster und so bleich, Schläfer
Schlagt mein ganzes Glück in Splitter
Sei gegrüsst, geweihte Stille
Wo irrst du durch einsame Schatten der Nacht
August Wilhelm von Schlegel
Auf den Wassern wohnt mein stilles Leben
Der Frühlingssonne holdes Lächeln
Hinaus mein Blick! hinaus in's Thal!
Hörst du von den Nachtigallen
Lass dich mit gelinden Schlägen rühren
Laue Lüfte, Blumendüfte
Quälend ungestilltes Sehnen pocht mir
Friedrich Schlegel
Als bei dem Kreuz Maria stand
Du staunest, o Mensch, was heilig wir strahlen?
Ein sehnend Streben theilt mir das Herz
Es lockte schöne Wärme, mich an das Licht
Es wehet kühl und leise
Friedlich lieg' ich hingegossen
Sieht uns der Blick gehoben
Tiefer sinket schon die Sonne
Wenn ich nur ein Vöglein wäre
Wenn mich einsam Lüfte fächeln
Wie deutlich des Mondes Licht zu mir spricht
Wie lieblich und fröhlich, zu schweben
Wie rein Gesang sich windet
Wie so innig, möcht' ich sagen
Wie soll ich nicht tanzen, es macht keine Mühe
Windes Rauschen, Gottes Flügel
Adolph Schmidl
Herr, unser Gott! erhöre unser Flehen
Komm heil'ger Geist, erhöre unser Flehen
Georg Philipp Schmidt (von Lübeck)
Ich komme vom Gebirge her
Franz Schober
Als der Frühling sich vom Herzen
Braust des Unglücks Sturm empor
"Der Friede sei mit euch!"
Des Mondes Zauberblume lacht
Die Wogen am Gestade schwellen
Dort raget ein Berg aus den Wolken hehr
Du brachst sie nun, die kalte Rinde
Du holde Kunst, in wieviel grauen Stunden
Ich bin ein Waller auf der Erde
Ich schiess' den Hirsch im grünen Forst
In des Todes Feierstunde
In tiefster Erde ruht ein alt Gesetz

Schmücket die Locken mit duftigen Kränzen
Schneeglöcklein, o Schneeglöcklein

Alois Schreiber
Du heilig, glühend Abendroth!
Euch Blümlein will ich senden
Freundlich ist dein Antlitz
Sei gegrüsst, du Frau der Huld

Christian Friedrich Daniel Schubart
In einem Bächlein helle, da schoss in froher Eil'
Sanftes Clavier, sanftes Clavier
Tod, du Schrecken der Natur!
Zieh hin, du braver Krieger du!

Franz Schubert
Gütigster, Bester, Weisester, Größter
Lebe wohl! lebe wohl! Du lieber Freund!

Clemens August Schücking
Hier am Hügel heissen Sandes sitz' ich

Christian Wilhelm von Schütz
Ach, was soll ich beginnen vor Liebe?
Nun, da Schatten niedergleiten

Ernst Schulze
Die Winde sausen am Tannenhang
Ertönet, ihr Saiten, in nächtlicher Ruh'
Frisch trabe sonder Ruh' und Rast
Ich bin von aller Ruh' geschieden
Ich wandre über Berg und Thal
Ihr Sternlein, still in der Höhe, ihr Sternlein
Keine Stimme hör' ich schallen
O Herz, sei endlich stille! was schlägst du
O Quell, was strömst du rasch und wild
O wie dringt das junge Leben kräftig mir
Still sitz' ich an des Hügels Hang

Sir Walter Scott
Ave Maria! Jungfrau mild!
Die Nacht bricht bald herein
Er ist uns geschieden vom Berg und vom Walde
Grosser Thaten that der Ritter fern
Jäger, ruhe von der Jagd!
Mein Ross so müd' in dem Stalle sich steht
Mich führt mein Weg wohl meilenlang
Raste, Krieger, Krieg ist aus
Triumph er naht, Heil, Heil dem Helden
Wärst du bei mir im Lebensthal

Karl Sigmund von Seckendorf
Wir stimmen dir mit Flötensang

Johann Seidl
Bei dir allein empfind' ich, dass ich lebe
Die Mutter hat mich jüngst gescholten
Die Nacht ist heiter und ist rein
Die Scheibe friert, der Wind ist rauh
Draussen in der weiten Nacht steh' ich
Du sagtest mir es, Mutter
Ich auf der Erd', am Himmel du
Ich hab' eine Brieftaub' in meinem Sold
Ihr lieben Mauern hold und traut
Kling' die Nacht durch, klinge
Sei uns stets gegrüsst, o Nacht!
Silberblauer Mondenschein fällt herab
So Mancher sieht mit finstrer Miene
Wenn ich durch Busch und Zweig
Wie sich der Äuglein kindlicher Himmel

Johann Chrysostomus Senn
Ich treibe auf des Lebens Meer
Wie klag' ich's aus das Sterbegefühl

William Shakespeare
Bacchus, feister Fürst des Weins
Horch, horch! die Lerch' im Ätherblau
Was ist Sylvia, saget an

Johann Petrus Silbert
Der Odem Gottes weht
Still beginnt's im Hain zu thauen

Josef von Spaun
Die Sonne sinkt, o könnt' ich, o könnt' ich

Albert Stadler
Schwüler Hauch weht mir herüber
Vater, schenk' mir diese Stunde

Stolberg-Stolberg
Ach, mir ist das Herz so schwer
Des Lebens Tag ist schwer und schwül
Groß und rothentflammet schwebet
Ich hab' ein Bächlein funden
In der Väter Hallen ruhte Ritter Rudolphs
Meine Selinde! denn mit Engelstimme
Mitten im Schimmer der spiegelnden Wellen
Süsse, heilige Natur, lass mich gehn
Willkommen, rothes Morgenlicht!

Josef Ludwig Stoll
O, dass ich dir vom stillen Auge
O Liebe, die mein Herz erfüllet
Wenn im Spiele leiser Töne meine kranke Seele

Ludwig Széchényi
Es floh die Zeit im Wirbelfluge
Wirst du halten, was du schwurst

Ludwig Tieck
Wie ist es denn, daß trüb und schwer

Christoph August Tiedge
Königliche Morgensonne

Johann Ludwig Uhland
Die linden Lüfte sind erwacht

Johann Karl Unger
Bescheiden verborgen im buschichten Gang
Wer Lebenslust fühlet, der bleibt nicht allein

Johann Peter Uz
Cypris, meiner Phyllis gleich
Die Munterkeit ist meiner Wangen
Du Schrecklicher, du Schrecklicher
Du verstörst uns nicht, o Nacht!
In seinem schimmernden Gewand
O Sonne, Königin der Welt
Was sorgest du? Sei stille, meine Seele!
Zu Gott, zu Gott, zu Gott flieg' auf
Johann Christoph Wannovius
Das Leben ist ein Traum, man merkt
Zacharias Werner
Eh' die Sonne früh aufersteht
Trarah! Trarah! wir kehren daheim!
Marianne von Willemer
Ach, um deine feuchten Schwingen
Was bedeutet die Bewegung?
Alois Zettler
Ihr Freunde und du gold'ner Wein
Anonymous
Auf! Jeder sei nun froh und sorgenfrei!
Brüder, schrecklich brennt die Thräne
Des Phöbus Strahlen sind dem Aug'
Des stolzen Männerlebens schönste Zeichen
Die frohe neubelebte Flur
Ein Mädchen ist's, das früh und spät
Hauche milder, Abendluft
Hinab, ihr Brüder, in den Schacht!
In düstrer Nacht, wenn Gram mein fühlend Herz
Komm, und senke die umflorten Schwingen
Lauter Freude fühl' ich, lauter Liebe hör' ich
Mein Handwerk geht durch alle Welt
Mein Leben wälzt sich murrend fort
Nimmer länger trag ich dieser Leiden Last
Nimmer lange weil' ich hier
Nimmer trag ich länger dieser Leiden Last
Ruhe, schönstes Glück der Erde
Sanft glänzt die Abendsonne auf diese stille Flur
Schicksalslenker, blicke nieder
Schlafe, schlafe, holder, süsser Knabe
Trauer umfliesst mein Leben
Verschwunden sind die Schmerzen
Wie schön bist du, du güldne Morgenröthe

Walter Schulthess (1894-1971)
Christian Morgenstern
Dein Wunsch, nicht mehr zu leiden
Die stillen Stunden sind es
Es leiht mir wunderbare Stärke
Glück ist wie Blütenduft, der dir vorüberfliegt
Glühend zwischen dir und mir Julinächte brüten
Ich wache noch in später Nacht und sinne
Leise Lieder sing ich dir bei Nacht
Nun bevölkert sich das hohe Drüben
Nun wollen wir uns still die Hände geben
War das die Liebe, die mich gestern streifte
Weiße Tauben fliegen durch blaue Morgenluft
Wem so die Nacht die treugewölbten Hände
Wenn die Abendschatten steigen
Wer kann schlagen-außer der Liebe
Zwei goldne Ringe hängen
Karl Stamm
Die mit ihrem Strahle mich geblendet
Die Nacht herauf am Himmel zieht
Früher Herbst. Die Blätter fallen still
Kein Wandrer sich in diese Schlucht verirrt
Still das Sterngeläute ist verklungen

Johann Abraham Peter Schulz (1747-1800)
Friederike Brun
Schlaf, Kindlein, schlafe sanft und süß
Gottfried August Bürger
Der Winter hat mit kalter Hand
Mädel, schau mir ins Gesicht!
Trallirum larum höre mich!
Matthias Claudius
Der Mond ist aufgegangen
Der Säemann säet den Samen
Ich danke Gott und freue mich
Ist gar ein holder Knabe, er!
Wenn hier nun kahler Boden wär
Wir ziehn nun unsern Zahn heraus
von Cronegk
Erbarm dich, Herr! mein schwaches Herz
Herr, es gescheh dein Wille!
Ludwig Hölty
Willkommen, lieber schöner Mai
Johann Georg Jacobi
Sagt, wo sind die Veilchen hin
Ewald Christian von Kleist
Groß ist der Herr! die Himmel ohne Zahl
Christian Adolf Overbeck
Blühe, liebes Veilchen, das ich selbst erzog
Warum sind der Tränen unterm Mond so viel?
Konrad Arnold Schmid
Der Herr erscheint in seiner Höhe
Stolberg-Stolberg
Brich nur, brich, du armes Herz!
Des Lebens Tag ist schwer und schwül
Süße heilige Natur, laß mich gehn
Unzer
Nie will ich meinen Bruder richten
Johann Peter Uz
Der Herr ist gut! ihr Himmel, höret und jauchzt

In seinem schimmernden Gewand
O Sonne, Königin der Welt
Singt, singt mit heiligem Entzücken

Johann Heinrich Voss

Das Mägdlein, braun von Aug' and Haar
Der Holdseligen sonder Wank sing ich
Frische Flur, du reiner Himmel, frischer atm'
O der schöne Maienmond! wenn in Tal
Seht den Himmel wie heiter!
Trockne deines Jammers Tränen
Wenn kühl der Morgen atmet
Willkommen im Grünen! Der Himmel ist blau
Wir bringen mit Gesang und Tanz

Christian Weisse

Schön sind Rosen und Jasmin

Anonymous

Der Sternlein Heer am Himmel blinkt
Des Jahres letzte Stunde ertönt
Die Lerche sang, die Sonne schien
Frühling und Liebe, sie kehren nun wieder
Ich habe gar liebliche Sträußchen feil
Regen, komm' herab! Unsre Saaten stehn
Tanzt, Paar und Paar, den Ringeltanz

Clara Josephine Schumann, née Wieck (1819-1896)

Robert Burns

Traurig schau ich von der Klippe auf die Flut

Emanuel Geibel

Der Mond kommt still gegangen
Die Liebe saß als Nachtigall
Die stille Lotusblume steigt aus dem blauen See

Johann Wolfgang von Goethe

Ein Veilchen auf der Wiese stand

Heinrich Heine

Es fiel ein Reif in der Frühlingsnacht
Ich stand in dunkeln Träumen
Ich weiß nicht, was soll es bedeuten
Sie liebten sich beide, doch keiner wollt' es

Justinus Kerner

Die Straßen, die ich gehe, so oft
Dort unten in der Mühle saß ich in guter Ruh

Johann Peter Lyser

Horch! Welch ein süßes harmonisches Klingen

Hermann Rollet

An einem lichten Morgen, da klingt es hell
Auf einem grünen Hügel, da steht ein Röslein
Das ist ein Tag, der klingen mag
Geheimes Flüstern hier und dort
O Lust, o Lust, vom Berg ein Lied
Was weinst du, Blümlein, im Morgenschein?

Friedrich Rückert

Die gute Nacht, die ich dir sage, Freund
Er ist gekommen in Sturm und Regen
Ich hab' in deinem Auge den Strahl
Liebst du um Schönheit, o nicht mich liebe!
Oh weh des Scheidens, das er tat
Warum willst du and're fragen

Friedrich Serre

O du mein Stern, schau dich so gern
Purpurgluten leuchten ferne

Anonymous

Bist du denn wirklich so fern

Robert Alexander Schumann (1810-1856)

Hans Christian Anderson

Als das Christkind ward zur Welt gebracht
Der Himmel wölbt sich rein und blau
Die Mutter betet herzig

Ludwig Bechstein

Unter den rothen Blumen schlummere

Nikolaus Becker

Sie sollen ihn nicht haben

Ferdinand Braun

Das Körnlein springt, der Vogel singt

Georg Karl Immanuel Buddeus

Helle Silberglöcklein klingen aus der Luft

Robert Burns

Dem rothen Röslein gleicht mein Lieb'
Hoch zu Pferd! Stahl auf zartem Leibe
Ich bin gekommen in's Niederland, o weh!
Ich hab' mein Weib allein, und theil' es
Ich schau' über Forth, hinüber nach Nord
John Anderson, mein Lieb!
Mein Herz ist betrübt, ich sag' es nicht
Mein Herz ist im Hochland
Mich zieht es nach dem Dörfchen hin
Nicht Damen tönt von hohem Rang
O Bänkelsänger Willie, du ziehst zum Jahrmarkt
Schlafe, süsser kleiner Donald
Schönster Bursch', den je ich traf
Sonst kam mein Johnnie zur Stadt vom Land
Wachst du noch, Liebchen, Gruss und Kuss!
Wer ist vor meiner Kammerthür?
Wer lenkt nicht gern den heitern Blick
Wie du mit gift'gem Stachel fast
Wie kann ich froh und munter sein

Lord Byron

Da die Heimath, o Vater, da Gott
Dein Tag ist aus, dein Ruhm fing an
Mein Herz ist schwer! Auf! von der Wand
Schlafloser Sonne, melanchol'scher Stern!

Carl Candidus
Aus dem dunkeln Thor wallt kein Zug
Adelbert von Chamisso
An meinem Herzen, an meiner Brust
Auf hohen Burgeszinnen der alte König stand
Da Nachts wir uns küssten o Mädchen
Den Säugling an der Brust
Du Ring an meinem Finger
Er, der Herrlichste von Allen
Es geht bei gedämpfter Trommeln Klang
Helft mir, ihr Schwestern
Ich kann's nicht fassen, nicht glauben
Im Städtchen giebt es Jubels viel
Mein Aug' ist trüb, mein Mund ist stumm
Mit der Myrthe geschmückt
Nun hast du mir den ersten Schmerz gethan
Schlief' die Mutter endlich ein
Seit ich ihn gesehen, glaub' ich blind zu sein
Süsser Freund, du blickest mich verwundert an
C. Christern
Warum soll ich denn wandern
Joseph von Eichendorff
Aus der Heimath hinter den Blitzen roth
Bin ein Feuer hell, das lodert
Dämm'rung will die Flügel spreiten
Dein Bildniss wunderselig
Eingeschlafen auf der Lauer
Es ist schon spät, es ist schon kalt
Es rauschen die Wipfel und schauern
Es war, als hätt' der Himmel
Es weiss und räth es doch Keiner
Es zog eine Hochzeit den Berg entlang
Es zogen zwei rüst'ge Gesellen
Ich hör' die Bächlein rauschen
Ich kann wohl manchmal singen
In stiller Bucht, bei finstrer Nacht
Komm, Trost der Welt, du stille Nacht!
Schwirrend Tamburin, dich schwing' ich
Still bei Nacht fährt manches Schiff
Über'm Garten durch die Lüfte hört' ich
Wem Gott will rechte Gunst erweisen
Wenn alle Wälder schliefen, er an zu graben hub
Zur ew'gen Ruh' sie sangen die schöne Müllerin
Catherine Maria Fanshawe
Es flüstert's der Himmel, es murrt es die Hölle
von Fröhlich
Im Garten steht die Nonne bei Rosen
Emanuel Geibel
Alle gingen, Herz, zur Ruh'
Also lieb' ich Euch, Geliebte
Bedeckt mich mit Blumen, ich sterbe vor Liebe
Blaue Augen hat das Mädchen
Da ich nun entsagen müssen Allem
Dass ihr steht in Liebesglut
Dereinst, dereinst, o Gedanke mein
Dunkler Lichtglanz, blinder Blick
Es ist so süss, zu scherzen mit Liedern
Fluthenreicher Ebro, blühendes Ufer
Hoch, hoch sind die Berge und steil ist ihr Pfad
Ich bin der Contrabandiste, weiss wohl
Ich bin ein Lust'ger Geselle
Ich blick' in mein Herz
Im Schatten des Waldes, im Buchengezweig
In meinem Garten die Nelken
Jeden Morgen, in der Frühet
Mögen alle bösen Zungen immer sprechen
Nelken wind' ich und Jasmin
O wie lieblich ist das Mädchen
Tief im Herzen trag' ich Pein
Und schläfst du, mein Mädchen, auf!
Und wenn die Primel schneeweiß blickt
Unter die Soldaten ist ein Zigeunerbub'
Von dem Rosenbusch, o Mutter
Wann, wann, erscheint der Morgen
Weh, wie zornig ist das Mädchen
Johann Wolfgang von Goethe
An die Thüren will ich schleichen
Dem Schnee, dem Regen, dem Wind entgegen
Dir zu eröffnen mein Herz verlangt mich
Es war ein Kind, das wollte nie zur Kirche
Es war ein König in Thule
Gottes ist der Orient! Gottes ist der Occident!
Heiss' mich nicht reden, heiss' mich schweigen
Ich denke dein, wenn mir der Sonne Schimmer
Kennst du das Land, wo die Citronen blüh'n
Lasst mich nur auf meinem Sattel gelten!
Nur wer die Sehnsucht kennt
Sah ein Knab' ein Röslein steh'n
Setze mir nicht, du Grobian, mir den Krug
Singet nicht in Trauertönen
Sitz' ich allein. wo kann ich besser sein?
So lasst mich scheinen, bis ich werde
Über allen Gipfeln ist Ruh'
Was hör' ich draussen vor dem Thor
Wer nie sein Brod mit Thränen ass
Wer sich der Einsamkeit ergiebt
Zum Sehen geboren, zum Schauen bestellt
"Anastasius Grün" (A. A. von Auersperg)
Großvater und Großmutter, die saßen
"Friedrich Halm" (Münch-Bellinghausen)
Was weht um meine Schläfe

Friedrich Hebbel
Der Knabe träumt, man schicke ihn fort
Im Kreise der Vasallen sitzt der Ritter
Sag' an, o lieber Vogel mein
Schlaf', Kindlein, schlaf', wie du schläfst
Vöglein vom Zweig gaukelt hernieder

Heinrich Heine
Allnächtlich im Traume seh' ich dich
Am leuchtenden Sommermorgen
Anfangs wollt' ich fast verzagen
Auf ihrem Grab da steht eine Linde
Aus alten Märchen winkt es
Aus meinen Thränen spriessen
Berg' und Burgen schau'n herunter
Das ist ein Flöten und Geigen
Dein Angesicht, so lieb und schön
Der arme Peter wankt vorbei
Der Hans und die Grete tanzen herum
Die alten, bösen Lieder, die Träume bös'
Die Lotusblume ängstigt
Die Mitternacht zog näher schon
Die Rose, die Lilie, die Taube, die Sonne
Du bist wie eine Blume
Ein Jüngling liebt ein Mädchen
Entflieh' mit mir und sei mein Weib
Es fiel ein Reif in der Frühlingsnacht
Es leuchtet meine Liebe in ihrer dunkeln Pracht
Es treibt mich hin, es treibt mich her!
Hör' ich das Liedchen klingen
Ich grolle nicht, und wenn das Herz auch bricht
Ich hab' im Traum geweinet
Ich wandelte unter den Bäumen
Ich will meine Seele tauchen
Im Rhein, im heiligen Strome
Im wunderschönen Monat Mai
In meiner Brust, da sitzt ein Weh
Lehn' deine Wang' an meine Wang'
Lieb' Liebchen, leg's Händchen auf's Herze
Mein Wagen rollet langsam
Mit Myrthen und Rosen, lieblich und hold
Morgens steh' ich auf und frage
Nach Frankreich zogen zwei Grenadier'
Oben auf des Berges Spitze liegt das Schloss
Schöne Wiege meiner Leiden
Und wüssten's die Blumen, die kleinen
Warte, warte, wilder Schiffsmann
Was will die einsame Thräne?
Wenn ich in deine Augen seh'
Wir sassen am Fischerhause
Zu dem Wettgesange schreiten Minnesänger

Paul Heyse
Auf dem Dorf' in den Spinnstuben
Nun stehen die Rosen in Blüthe

Hoffmann von Fallersleben
Der Frühling kehret wieder
Der Sonntag ist gekommen, ein Sträusschen
Du lieblicher Stern, du leuchtest so fern
Ein scheckiges Pferd, ein blankes Gewehr
Kommt, wir wollen uns begeben
Kuckuk, Kuckuk ruft aus dem Wald
Nach diesen trüben Tagen, wie ist so hell
O Schmetterling sprich, was fliehest du mich?
Schneeglöckchen klingen wieder
So sei gegrüsst viel tausendmal
Veilchen, Rosmarin, Mimosen, Engelsüss
Wie blüht es im Thale, wie grünt's

Moritz Horn
Ei Mühle, liebe Mühle, wie schaust so schmuck

Karl Immermann
Auf deinem Grunde haben sie

Justinus Kerner
Dass du so krank geworden
Dem Wandrer, dem verschwunden
Du bist vom Schlaf erstanden
Du herrlich Glas, nun stehst du leer
Du junges Grün, du frisches Gras
Es war in des Maien mildem Glanz
Hörst du den Vogel singen?
Ich armes Klosterfräulein, o Mutter!
Könnt' ich dich in Liedern preisen
Seh ich in das stille Thal
Wär' ich nie aus euch gegangen, Wälder
Wärst du nicht, heil'ger Abendschein!
Weint auch einst kein Liebchen
Wenn durch Berg' und Thale draussen
Wohlauf noch getrunken den funkelnden Wein!
Wohlauf und frisch gewandert
Zu Augsburg steht ein hohes Haus

Gottfried Kinkel
Es ist so still geworden

Hermann Kletke
Zwei feine Stieflein hab' ich an

Friedrich Klopstock
Mit unserm Arm ist nichts gethan

Elisabeth Kulmann
Bleibe hier und singe, liebe Nachtigall!
Der Frühling kehret wieder
Die letzten Blumen starben
Du nennst mich armes Mädchen
Gekämpft hat meine Barke
Mond, meiner Seele Liebling

Pflücket Rosen, um das Haar schön
Reich' mir die Hand, o Wolke
Schweb empor am Himmel, schöner Abendstern
Viel Glück zur Reise, Schwalben!
Wir sind ja, Kind, im Maie, wirf Buch und Heft
Karl Lappe
Nord oder Süd! Wenn nur im warmen Busen
Charles L'Égru
Nicht so schnelle, nicht so schnelle!
Senkt die Nacht den sanften Fittig nieder
Nikolaus Lenau
Da liegt der Feinde gestreckte Schaar
Den grünen Zeigern, den rothen Wangen
Der holden Lenzgeschmeide
Der Husar, trara! was ist die Gefahr?
Der leidige Frieden hat lange gewährt
Die dunklen Wolken hingen herab so bang
Fein Rösslein, ich beschlage dich
Schöne Sennin, noch einmal singe
So oft sie kam, erschien mir die Gestalt
Wild verwachsne dunkle Fichten
Wilhelmine Lorenz
Es flüstern und rauschen die Wogen
August Mahlmann
Das Laub fällt von den Bäumen
Otto von der Malsburg
Helf' mir Gott, wie fliegen die Gänse
Eduard Mörike
Ach, wenn's nur der König auch wüsst'
Auf ihrem Leibrösslein, so weiss
Früh wann die Hähne kräh'n
Frühling lässt sein blaues Band
Und die mich trug im Mutterarm
Wie heisst König Ringang's Töchterlein?
Zierlich ist des Vogels Tritt im Schnee
Thomas Moore
Leis' rudern hier, mein Gondolier, leis', leis'!
Wenn durch die Piazetta die Abendluft weht
Julius Mosen
Der See ruht tief im blauen Traum
Es grünet ein Nussbaum vor dem Haus
Was quälte dir dein banges Herz?
Wolfgang Müller von Königswinter
Ich zieh' so allein in den Wald hinein!
Wilfried von der Neun
Durch die Tannen und die Linden spinnt
Es stürmet am Abendhimmel
Hört ihr im Laube des Regens starke Schläge?
Mir ist's so eng allüberall!
Nachts zu unbekannter Stunde flieht
Nun scheidet vom sterbenden Walde
Röselein, Röselein! müssen denn Dornen sein?
Wie der Bäume kühne Wipfel
Christian Adolf Overbeck
Komm lieber Mai und mache die Bäume
Gustav Pfarrius
Birke, Birke, des Waldes Zier
Es geht der Tag zur Neige
Im Wald, in grüner Runde
August Graf von Platen
Lass' tief in dir mich lesen
Schwelle die Segel, günstiger Wind!
Wiederkehrend nach dem Vaterlande
Robert Reinick
Als ich zuerst dich hab' geseh'n
Bleiche, bleiche weisses Lein
Des Sonntags in der Morgenstund'
Die Liebe ist ein Rosenstrauch
Ich bin hinausgegangen des Morgens
Komm' in die stille Nacht, Liebchen
O Sonnenschein, o Sonnenschein!
Schneeglöckchen thut läuten, klingling!
Und wieder hatt' ich der Schönsten gedacht
Wolken die ihr nach Osten eilt
Friedrich Rückert
Blüth' oder Schnee! Lust oder Weh!
Der Himmel hat eine Thräne geweint
Der Schnee, der gestern noch in Flöckchen
Die gute Nacht, die ich dir sage, Freund
Die Rose stand im Thau, es waren Perlen grau
Die tausend Grüsse, die wir dir senden
Du meine Seele, du mein Herz
Eia, wie flattert der Kranz
Flügel! Flügel! um zu fliegen über Berg
Gebt mir zu trinken! Was in den Sternen steht
Grün ist der Jasminenstrauch Abends
Hier in diesen erdbeklommnen Lüften
Ich bin dein Baum, o Gärtner
Ich bin die Blum' im Garten
Ich hab' in mich gesogen den Frühling treu
Ich sende einen Gruss wie Duft der Rosen
In Meeres Mitten ist ein offner Laden
In Sommertagen rüste den Schlitten
Lass mich ihm am Busen hangen, Mutter
Lasst Lautenspiel und Becherklang nicht rasten
Liebste, was kann denn uns scheiden?
Liebster, deine Worte stehlen aus dem Busen
Mein schöner Stern! ich bitte dich
Meine Töne still und heiter
Mutter, Mutter! glaube nicht
O blicke, wenn den Sinn dir will die Welt
O Freund, mein Schirm, mein Schutz

O ihr Herren, o ihr werthen grossen reichen
O Sonn', o Meer, o Rose! Wie wenn die Sonne
Rose, Meer, und Sonne sind ein Bild
Schön ist das Fest des Lenzes
Seinen Traum, Lind' wob, Frühling kaum
So wahr die Sonne scheinet
Stern, in des Himmels Ferne!
Wenn ich früh in den Garten geh'
Zittr', o Erde, dunkle Macht
Zürne nicht des Herbstes Wind

Christian Schad
Sommerruh, wie schön bist du!

Friedrich von Schiller
Ihr Matten, lebt wohl, ihr sonnigen Weiden!
Mit dem Pfeil, dem Bogen, durch Gebirg'
Vor seinem Löwengarten, das Kampfspiel

Johann Seidl
Spähend nach dem Eisengitter

William Shakespeare
Und als ich ein winzig Bübchen war

Percy Bysshe Shelley
Der Hagel klirrt nieder, es leuchten die Wogen

Moritz, Graf von Strachwitz
Mein altes Ross, mein Spielgenoss

Johann Ludwig Uhland
Das Haus benedei' ich und preis' es laut
Droben stehet die Capelle
Ein Schifflein ziehet leise den Strom
Ich bin vom Berg der Hirtenknab'
Ich hör' meinen Schatz
Im schönsten Garten wallten zwei Buhlen
Noch singt den Widerhallen der Knabe

Titus Ullrich
Die Fenster klär' ich zum Feiertag
Die Weiden lassen matt die Zweige hangen

Gisbert, Freiherr von Vincke
Herr Jesu Christ, den sie gekrönt mit Dornen
Ich zieh' dahin, dahin! Ade
Nur ein Gedanke, der mich freut und quält
O Gott, mein Gebieter, ich hoffe auf dich!
Was nützt die mir noch zugemess'ne Zeit?

Marianne von Willemer
Wie, mit innigstem Behagen

Freiherr von Zedlitz
Bahnlos und pfadlos, Felsen hinan stürmet
Nach oben musst du blicken

G. Zimmermann
Nur ein lächelnder Blick von deinem

Anonymous
Die Sonne sah die Erde an
In einsamen Stunden drängt Wehmut sich auf
Kleine Tropfen, seid ihr Thränen
Lieben, von ganzer Seele, lieben, herzinniglich
Ruh' von schmerzensreichen Mühen
Sie steht am Zellenfenster, denkt unablässig sein
Wenn fromme Kindlein schlafen geh'n

from Des Knaben Wunderhorn
Es fliegen zwei Schwalben in's Nachbar
Es jagt' ein Jäger wohlgemuth
Ich armes Käuzlein kleine
Marienwürmchen, setze dich auf meine Hand

Volkslied
Es ist ein Schnitter der heisst Tod
Es wollt' die Jungfrau früh aufsteh'n
Es wollt' ein Mädchen früh aufsteh'n
Spinn', spinn', Mägdelein, spinn'!
Wenn ich ein Vöglein wär

Kurt Schwaen (1909-)

Bertolt Brecht
In dem grünen Kuddelmuddel sitzt ein Aas
Wir waren miteinander nicht befreundet
Wohin zieht ihr? Freilich wo ihr immer hinzieht

Reinhard Schwarz-Schilling (1904-1987)

the Bible
Jauchzet Gott, alle, alle Lande!

Joseph von Eichendorff
Bevor er in die blaue Flut gesunken
Bist du manchmal auch verstimmt
Durch Feld und Buchenhallen bald singend
O Maria, meine Liebe, denk ich recht im Herzen
Posthorn, wie so keck und fröhlich
Wandern lieb' ich für mein Leben
Wenn die Sonne lieblich schiene
Wenn ins Land die Wetter hängen

"Novalis" (Friedrich von Hardenberg)
Wenn ich ihn nur habe, wenn er mein nur ist

Karl Siegmund Freiherr von Seckendorff (1744-1785)

Johann Wolfgang von Goethe
Am Ziele! ich fühle die Nähe
Auf aus der Ruh! auf aus der Ruh!
Das Wasser rauscht, das Wasser schwoll
Es war ein Buhle frech genung
Es war ein König in Thule
Füllest wieder 's liebe Thal still mit Nebelglanz

Jean (Johan) Julius Christian Sibelius (1865-1957)

Richard Dehmel
Die Rosen leuchten immer noch
Liegt eine Stadt im Tale, ein blasser Tag vergeht

Arthur Fitger
Seid gegrüsst, ihr grünen Hallen
Anna Ritter
Wir senkten die Wurzeln in Moos und Gestein
Margarete Susman
Im Feld ein Mädchen singt
Emil Rudolf Weiss
Oft am langen Tage seufz' ich, ach! nach dir

(Philipp) Friedrich Silcher (1789-1860)
Ernst Moritz Arndt
Ade! es muss geschieden sein!
Juchhei, Blümelein! dufte und blühe!
Ludwig Bowitsch
Und sitz' ich in der Schenke
Adelbert von Chamisso
Es geht bei gedämpfter Trommel Klang
Hab' oft im Kreise der Lieben
Wilhelmine Chézy
Ach, wie ist's möglich dann
Matthias Claudius
Füllt noch einmal die Gläser voll
Simon Dach
Ännchen von Tharau ist, die mir gefällt
Joseph von Eichendorff
In einem kühlen Grunde, da geht ein Mühlenrad
Emanuel Geibel
Der Mai ist gekommen, die Bäume schlagen aus
Es fliegt manch' Vöglein in das Nest
Mag auch heiss das Scheiden brennen
Johann Wolfgang von Goethe
Es war ein König in Thule
Uf'm Bergli bin i g'sesse
Hans Leo Hassler
Mein G'müth ist mir verwirret
Wilhelm Hauch
Morgenroth, leuchtest mir zum frühen Tod?
Steh' ich in finst'rer Mitternacht
Johann Peter Hebel
Es g'fallt mer nummen eini
Loset, was i euch will sage!
Steh' ich im Feld, mein ist die Welt!
Heinrich Heine
Ich weiss nicht, was soll es bedeuten
Hoffmann von Fallersleben
Wer singet im Walde so heimlich allein?
Justinus Kerner
Ach, ach, ich armes Klosterfräulein!
Herman Kurz
Der Himmel lacht und heit're Lüfte spielen
Eduard Mörike
Ach, wenn's nur der König auch wüsst'
Friedrich Müller
Heute scheid' ich, heute wander' ich
Wilhelm Müller
Am Brunnen vor dem Thore
Robert Reinick
Ach du klar blauer Himmel
Fr. Richter
Drauss ist alles so prächtig
Friedrich Rückert
Der alte Barbarosse, der Kaiser Friederich
Alois Schreiber
Dunkel rauscht des Stromes Welle
Ludwig Tieck
Dicht von Felsen eingeschlossen
Johann Ludwig Uhland
Der schöne Schäfer zog so nah'
Die linden Lüfte sind erwacht
Ein Schifflein ziehet leise den Strom
Es zogen drei Bursche wohl über den Rhein
Ich hatt' einen Kameraden
Anonymous
Als die Preussen marschirten vor Prag
from Des Knaben Wunderhorn
Der süsse Schlaf, der sonst stillt Alles wohl
Volkslied
Ach Gott, wie weh thut Scheiden
Auf dem Meer bin ich geboren
Bei nächtlicher Weil' an ein's Waldes Born
Bin ein- und ausgange im ganze Tyrol
Bin i net a lust'ger Schweizerbu
Brüder, Brüder, wir ziehen in den Krieg
Da drunten im tiefen Thale
Da steh' i hier oben, schau' abe an See
Das Lieben bringt groß' Freud'
Dem Himmel will ich klagen
Die Schwälble ziehet fort, ziehet fort
Drunten im Unterland, da ist's halt fein
Du mein einzig Licht, die Lilg' und Ros'
Du Mond, i hätt a Bitt' an di
Durch's Wiesethal gang i jetzt na
E bissele Lieb' und e bissele Treu'
Ein Bursch' und Mägdlein flink und schön
Ein Jäger aus Kurpfalz
Ein Sträusschen am Hute, den Stab in der Hand
Ein Täubchen, kirr und traut
Es war ein Markgraf über'm Rhein
Es waren einmal drei Reuter gefang'n
Fahret hin, Grillen, geht mir aus dem Sinn!
Frisch auf, frisch auf! Der Bergmann kommt!
Frisch auf, Soldatenblut!
Gut Nacht, gut Nacht, mein feines Lieb

Han an em Ort e Blümeli g'seh
Herzerl, was kränkt dich so sehr
Ich fahr' dahin, wenn es muss sein
Ich ging einmal spazieren
Ich habe den Frühling gesehen
Im Aargäu sind zwei Liebi
Jetzt gang i an's Brünnele
Jetzt reisen wir zum Thor hinaus
Kein schön'rer Tod ist in der Welt
Komm mit mir in's Thäle, 's ist heimlich
Liebchen, ade! Scheiden thut weh!
Mädele, ruck, ruck, ruck an meine grüne Seite
Maidle, lass der was verzähle
Mei Maidle hot e G'sichtle
Mei Mutter mag mi net
Mei Schätzle ist fei, 's könnt' feiner net sei
Mein Herzlein thut mir gar zu weh!
Mein Schatz, der ist auf die Wanderschaft hin
Mir ist's zu wohl ergangen
Morgen müssen wir verreisen
Morgen muß ich fort von hier
Morgen muss ich weg von hier
Muss i denn, muss i denn zum Städtele naus
Nichts kann auf Erden verglichen
Nichts Schön'res kann mich erfreuen
Nun leb' wohl, du kleine Gasse
O herzensschöns Schätzerl, jetzt komm' i
O Maidle, du bist mein Morgestern
O Tannenbaum, wie treu sind deine Blätter!
O wie herbe ist das Scheiden
Prinz Eugenius, der edle Ritter
Rosestock, Holderblüth', wenn i mei Dienderl
So viel Stern' am Himmel stehen
Spinn, mein liebs Nanerl, i kauf dir neue Schuh'
Und schau' ich hin, so schaust du her
Vögelein im Tannenwald pfeifet so hell
Von allen den Mädchen, so blink und so blank
War das nicht ein Blick der Liebe
Was hab' ich denn meinem Feinsliebchen
Wenn alle Brünnlein fliessen
Wenn der Schnee von der Alma wega geht
Wenn i halt frua afsteh
Wenn ich an den letzten Abend denk'
Wer will unter die Soldaten
Wie die Blümlein draussen zittern
Wie han i doch so gern die Zeit
Wo e kleins Hüttle steht, ist e kleins Gütle
Z'nächst bin i halt gange über's Bergel in Wald
Zu dir zieht's mi hin, wo i geh' und wo i bin
Zu Strassburg auf der Schanz

Hermann Simon (1896-1948)

Johann Wolfgang von Goethe

Höchste Herrscherin der Welt!
Wie an dem Tag, der dich der Welt verliehen
Zum Sehen geboren, zum Schauen bestellt

(Johann Gustaf) Emil Sjögren (1853-1918)

Elisa von der Recke

Der Mond schon wandelt am Himmelszelt

"Hans Sommer" (Hans Friedrich August Zincke) (1837-1922)

Gustav von Boddien

Ich habe ein kleines Lied erdacht

Hermann Hölty

Sie scheidet. Wie der Mutter Abschiedsblick

Gottfried Keller

Das Köhlerweib ist trunken, und singt im Wald
Die Lor' sitzt im Garten, kehrt den Rücken
Du milchjunger Knabe, wie siehst du mich an?
Mir glänzen die Augen wie der Himmel so klar
Schon war die letzte Schwalbe fort
Singt mein Schatz wie ein Fink
Wandl' ich in dem Morgenthau

Carmen Sylva

Die Blume verblühet auf fliessender Fluth
Fragst du mit den Äugelein
Hört mich, Ihr grausamen Götter
Ich singe der Kraft, die die Erde erhält
Mein Herz ist die Quelle, die Leben Dir schenkt
Nicht lange ist's her, da lachte die Welt mir
Weine nicht, weil dich die Götter gesendet
Wozu soll ich reden? Mein Wort ist so alt!

Ernst von Wildenbruch

Unter'm Machandelbaum da ist ein Platz

Julius Wolff

Alle Blumen möcht ich binden
Blaublümlein spiegelten sich im Bach
Bleib stehn! Dass nur ein Hauch vom Winde
Der Lenz ist gekommen ins harrende Land
Der Zaunpfahl trug ein Hütlein weiss
Du zähltest wohl die Regentropfen
Ein Schwert, das schneidet, ein Falke, der fängt
Es wächst ein Kraut im Kühlen
Es wartet ein bleiches Jungfräulein
Für alle die Schätze, für all die Ehre
Glockenblumen, was läutet ihr?
Ich ging im Wald durch Kraut und Gras
Im Grase thaut's, die Blumen träumen
Leer ist der Tag, er geht zu Ende
Neunerlei Blumen winde zum Kranz
Offene Arme und pochende Brust

Wie soll ich's bergen, wie soll ich's tragen
Wiege dich, Wind, auf dem wogenden Korn

Wilhelm Speidel (1826-1899)
Eduard Mörike
Derweil ich schlafend lag

(Julius August) Philipp Spitta (1841-1894)
Joseph von Eichendorff
Waldeinsamkeit! Du grünes Revier!

Louis Spohr (1784-1859)
Adil
Wer hätte sie gesehn und nicht auch sie geliebt?
Amalia
Du gabst mir längst dein schönes Herz
Karl Bassewitz
Komm in den Garten! ich harre dein
Mathilde Beckmann
Über die Wellen zieht zagend und trauernd
F. Bobrich
Wo blüht das Thal wo Liebe sich ew'ge Kränze
Friedrich Bodenstedt
Deine Finger rühren die Saiten
Füllt mir das Trinkhorn! reicht es herum!
Nicht mit Engeln im blauen Himmelszelt
Karl Johann Braun von Braunthal
Immortelle! bring' mein "gute Nacht" ihr hin
Pulse, höret auf zu schlagen
Christian Karl Buri
Drei Rosen hielt ich in Händen
Adelbert von Chamisso
Was ist's, o Vater, was ich verbrach?
Johann Ludwig von Deinhardstein
Wie weil' ich so gern, wo die Trauer webt
Gottl. von Deuern
Wenn im letzten Dämmrungsstrahle
Franz Dingelstedt
Die Wolken ziehen schwarz und hoch
In die blaue Luft hinaus einen stillen Gruss
Karl Egon Ebert
Der Vogel steigt, ein verkörpertes Lied
Julius Eberwein
Das Vöglein singt den ganzen Tag
"Eduard Ferrand" (Eduard Schulz)
Das Kind schläft unter dem Rosenstrauch
Emanuel Geibel
Ich blick' in mein Herz
In den Wassern der Laguna schwimmt
Wolle Keiner mich fragen warum mein Herz
K. E. K. von Goechhausen
Eya popeya, so leise, so lind, wieg dich
Johann Wolfgang von Goethe
Herz, mein Herz, was soll das geben
Ich hab' meine Sach' auf nichts gestellt, juchhe!
Im Nebelgeriesel, im tiefen Schnee
Kennst du das Land wo die Zitronen blühn
Meine Ruh' ist hin, mein Herz ist schwer
Über Thal und Fluss getragen ziehet rein
Wenn die Reben wieder blühen
Wer reitet so spät durch Nacht und Wind
E. Gross
Rauschet, ihr Meere, und wehet ihr Winde!
Agnes Emerita Gyr
Schwebe, mein tanzender Kahn
Alb. vom Hochwald
Der Regen rasselt, es saust der Sturm
Hoffmann von Fallersleben
Alles still in süsser Ruh
Treue Liebe bis zum Grabe schwör' ich dir
Was mir wohl übrig bliebe
Hozze
Vor Gottes Aug', dem Abendroth
Victor Hugo
Immer mag verklingen muntrer Vögel Sang
Moritz Kartscher
Die Lippe brennt, die Wange glüht
Justinus Kerner
Zu Augsburg steht ein hohes Haus
Friedrich Kind
Das Herz ist gewachsen. Es pocht in der Brust
Ernst Koch
Der Tag hat sich zur Ruh' gelegt
Es giebt geheime Schmerzen
Was treibt mich hin zu dir mit Macht?
Friedrich de La Motte Fouqué
Ach, wär' ich nur ein Vögelein!
Adolph Lange
Feierlicher Glockenklang hallet
August Ludwig Lua
Sommer entschwand, Herbstluft durchwehet
August Mahlmann
Als mein Leben voll Blumen hing
H. Mahn
Leise schleich' ich mich am Abend
Adolf von Marées
Im Wirthshaus geht es aus und ein
Karl von Mecklenburg-Strelitz
Wo reiner Liebe gold'ne Strahlen
D. E. Meier
Überall in dem All, mag ich liegen oder stehen
Wilhelm Müller
Ich schnitt es gern in alle Rinden ein

R. Otto
Worte hab' ich nicht, um dir zu sagen
Robert Reinick
Als ich zuerst dich hab' gesehn
Im Fliederbusch ein Vöglein sass
Schneeglöckchen thut läuten: klinglingling!
Schweigen ist ein schönes Ding
Wellen blinkten durch die Nacht
Johann Rochlitz
Die stille Nacht heisst niedre Sorgen schweigen
Johann von Salis-Seewis
Auf! es dunkelt; silbern funkelt dort der Mond
Georg Scheurlin
Die Fenster sonnen, der Winter ist aus
Heinrich Schmidt
Bitte! einen Blick aus den holden blauen Augen
Der Liebe bangen Sorgen erbleicht
Schnell geniesst die schnellen Stunden
H. Schulz
Sag wie kann man Lieb' erkennen?
Karl Schweizer
Freudig zum Himmel auf blikke mein Herz!
Ich bin so bleich, du bist so roth
Ich wahrte die Hoffnung tief in der Brust
Karl Simrock
Athme nur leise zieh ich die Kreise
Friedrich Spohr
Seht ihr's dort funkeln in rosiger Pracht?
Julius Sturm
Wohin, du rauschender Strom, wohin?
Ludwig Tieck
Auf Wogen gezogen, von Klängen, Gesängen
Ruhe, Süss Liebchen im Schatten
Christoph August Tiedge
Wer lässt hier so lieblich, wer lässt so allein
Johann Ludwig Uhland
Die linden Lüfte sind erwacht
Was wecken aus dem Schlummer
Wilhelm Vogel
Was treibt den Waidmann in den Wald
Cäcilie von W.
Dort im Thal hör ich verhallen
Wär ich ein Vögelein, flög' ich zu ihm!
Walther von der Vogelweide
Unter der Linden an der Haide
Freiherr von Zedlitz
Singet die Nachtigall im dunkeln Wald
Baltasar Wilhelm Zimmermann
Am Bach, am Bach, im flüsternden Gras
Anonymous
Der Frühling ist herangekommen
Der Sänger zog durch Wald und Flur
Du armes Herz, was wünschest du?
Es sehnt sich das Herz nach Lust
Heute ist Sonntag und Montag ist morgen
Lieben, warum sollt' ich's nicht?
Liebt er mich? tönt es im Herzensgrund
Mir ist, als müßt ich dir was sagen
Sanft ertönen Morgenglocken
Schweig o Herz! warum dies bange Sehnen
Was stehst du lange und sinnest nach?
Wenn Eos am Morgen mit rosigem Finger
Wenn im Lenze ringsum Alles lacht

Gasparo Luigi Pacifico Spontini (1774-1851)
Johann Wolfgang von Goethe
Kennst du das Land, wo die Citronen blühn

(Friedrich) Wilhelm Stade (1817-1902)
Johann Wolfgang von Goethe
Wer nie sein Brot mit Tränen aß

Bernhard Stavenhagen (1862-1914)
Heinrich Heine
Sie liebten sich beide, doch keiner wollt' es

(Karl) Vilhelm Eugen Stenhammar (1871-1927)
Heinrich Heine
Ein Fichtenbaum steht einsam im Norden
Ich lieb' eine Blume, doch weiß ich nicht
Sie liebten sich beide, doch keiner wollt' es
Walther von der Vogelweide
Heil sei der Stunde, wo ich sie erkannte
Könnt' ich doch erleben, dass ich Rosen

Josef Antonín Štěpán (1726-1797)
Anacreon
Die schwarze Erde trinket
Gottfried August Bürger
Mir tut's so weh im Herzen! Ich bin so matt
Wie selig, wer sein Liebchen hat
Matthias Claudius
Ich war kaum sechzehn Sommer alt
Johann Wilhelm Ludwig Gleim
Das arme Veilchen, sieh' o sieh'
Johann Wolfgang von Goethe
Ein Veilchen auf der Wiese stand
Friedrich von Hagedorn
Zu meiner Zeit bestand noch Recht
Albrecht von Haller
Des Tages Licht hat sich verdunkelt
Johann Gottfried Herder
Dein Schwert, wie ist's von Blut so rot?
Im säuselnden Winde, am murmelnden Bach

Meine Schäfchen, morgens früh
Und hörst du, kleine Phyllis, nicht
Johann Georg Jacobi
Leiser nannt' ich deinen Namen
Ewald Christian von Kleist
Ja treuster Damon, ich bin überwunden!
Sie fliehet fort! Es ist um mich geschehen!
Friedrich Klopstock
Dein süßes Bild o Lyda!
Im Frühlingsschatten fand ich sie
Karl Mastalier
Auf in das Feld zum Streite!
Johann Martin Miller
Er, dem ich einst alles war
Siehe, mein Röschen, der Frühling ist da
Heinrich August Ossenfelder
Hört an, ihr Mütter alt und jung!
Christian Weisse
Ach, an dem Ufer dieser Quelle hab' ich
Zieht hier ein Krieger stolz geschmükket
Christiane Mariane von Ziegler
Eilt ihr Schäfer aus den Gründen
Anonymous
Ach! es schlägt mein Herz so bange
Gold'ne Freiheit, gold'ne Freiheit!
Ja, ja, ich schweige, liebste Seele!
Loses Herze meiner Schönen
O liebes Mädchen, höre mich!
Seid mir gegrüßt, ihr Täler der Gebeine
Seid willkommen, stille Haine

Rudi Stephan (1887-1915)
Karl von Berlepsch
Kindlein schlaf' ein. Hoch lodern
Otto Julius Bierbaum
Sonntagsfriede liegt heilig über der Stadt.
Richard Dehmel
Und noch im alten Elternhause
Gustav Falke
Reglos steht der alte Baum, alles Leid verwehet
Bruno Goetz
Mich rief ein Ton aus weiter Ferne
"Martin Greif" (Friedrich Hermann Frey)
Naht die jubelvolle Zeit
Leo Greiner
Still schwebt die Nacht in hehrer Größe
Johann Christian Günther
Abermal ein Teil vom Jahre
Friedrich Hebbel
Ich ritt einmal im Dunkeln spät
Hinrich Hinrichs
Meine Seele ist nun stillgeworden
Anton Lindner
Wie Seide war ihr leiser Tritt
"Gerda v. Robertus" (Gertrud Borngräber)
Das Sonnenfeuer starb Rubingepränge
Der Rosen Düfte liebeatmend schwingen
Geschmeidig und wild wie ein junger Panther
In Nachbars Garten duftet die Lindenblüte
Wir haben im Lärm der Menge
Zwei Tage reichen sich die Hand der eine schied
Josef Schanderl
Ein stilles Wiesental von Schwalben überflogen
Maurice Reinhold von Stern
Feierlich träumt das Gelände schwimmend

Richard Sternfeld (1858-1926)
Rudolph Baumbach
Es pflagen einst drei Knaben der Ruh'
Heinrich Heine
Lehn' deine Wang' an meine Wang'

Eduard (Edward) Steuermann (1892-1964)
Bertolt Brecht
Die Vaterstadt, wie find ich sie doch?
In den Weiden am Sund ruft
Schlage keinen Nagel in die Wand
Matthias Claudius
Empfanget und genähret vom Weibe
Johann Wolfgang von Goethe
Der du vom Himmel bist
Des Menschen Seele gleicht dem Wasser

Giorgio Stigelli (1819?-1868)
Heinrich Heine
Du hast Diamanten und Perlen
Thomas Moore
Wenn durch die Piazetta die Abendluft weht

Richard Stöhr (1874-1967)
Dietmar von Aiste
Liebster, Liebster, schläfst du noch?
Joseph von Eichendorff
Ein Adler saß am Felsenbogen
Adolf Holst
Meine scheuen Lieder die sind wie wilde
Toni Mark
Schweig still, du dummes Menschenherz
Eva Merkel
Sieben kleine Rosenstökke stehn im Garten

Richard Georg Strauss (1864-1949)
Ludwig Achim von Arnim
Freunde, weihet den Pokal
Ich sehe ihn wieder den lieblichen Stern

Ihr Mund ist stets derselbe
Hans Bethge
Ich pflückte eine kleine Pfirsichblüthe
Otto Julius Bierbaum
Als Nachts ich überm Gebirge ritt
Es ging ein Wind durch's weite Land
Nicht im Schlafe hab ich das geträumt
Über Wiesen und Felder ein Knabe ging
Weite Wiesen im Dämmergrau
Wir gingen durch die stille, milde Nacht
Emanuel von Bodmann
Es ist der Tag, wo jedes Leid vergessen
Herr Lenz springt heute durch die Stadt
Clemens Brentano
Als mir dein Lied erklang
An dem Feuer saß das Kind Amor
Heilige Nacht! Heilige Nacht!
Ich wollt' ein Sträußlein binden
Säusle, liebe Myrthe! Wie still ists in der Welt
Wenn es stürmt auf den Wogen
Gottfried August Bürger
Seht mir doch mein schönes Kind
Carl Busse
Bleiche Blüte, Blüte der Liebe
Ein blauer Sommer glanz- und glutenschwer
Und wärst du mein Weib
Pedro Calderón de la Barca
Es war ein Bruder Liederlich
Hör mein Liebesliedchen ziehn
Adelbert von Chamisso
Es steht ein altes Gemäuer hervor
Felix Dahn
Aber Epheu nenn' ich jene Mädchen
Ach Lieb, ich muss nun scheiden
Ach weh mir unglückhäftem Mann
All mein Gedanken, mein Herz und mein Sinn
Die Frauen sind oft fromm und still
Du meines Herzens Krönelein
Kennst du die Blume, die märchenhafte
Kornblumen nenn' ich die Gestalten
Mohnblumen sind die runden
Richard Dehmel
Bienchen, Bienchen wiegt sich im Sonnenschein
Der Abend graut, Herbstfeuer brennen
Der Sturm behorcht mein Vaterhaus
Der Wald beginnt zu rauschen
Die Welt verstummt, dein Blut erklingt
Du bist mein Auge! Du durchdringst mich ganz
Du wirst nicht weinen. Leise, leise
Hoch hing der Mond; das Schneegefild
In einem stillen Garten
Träume, träume du, mein süsses Leben
Wir haben ein Bett, wir haben ein Kind
Joseph von Eichendorff
Wir sind durch Not und Freude gegangen
Gustav Falke
Du schläfst und sachte neig' ich mich
Emanuel Geibel
Die Liebe saß als Nachtigall im Rosenbusch
Im Wald, im hellen Sonnenschein
Hermann Gilm
Auf frisch gemähtem Weideplatz
Aus dem Walde tritt die Nacht
Es steht ein Lied in Nacht und Frost
Geduld, sagst du und zeigst mit weißem Finger
Ich habe wohl, es sei hier laut vor aller Welt
Ja, du weisst es teure Seele
Nennen soll ich, sagt ihr, meine Königin
Stell' auf den Tisch die duftenden Reseden
Warum so spät erst, Georgine?
Johann Wolfgang von Goethe
Alle Menschen groß und klein
Das Wasser rauscht' das Wasser schwoll
Du Bächlein silberhell und klar
Durch allen Schall und Klang
Hab ich euch denn je geraten
Hans Adam war ein Erdenkloß
Ich ging im Walde so für mich hin
Knabe saß ich Fischerknabe
Morgennebel, Lila, hüllen deinen Thurm ein
Nichts vom Vergänglichen wie's auch geschah!
Übers Niederträchtige niemand sich beklage
Wer wird von der Welt verlangen
Zugemessne Rhythmen reizen freilich
"Martin Greif" (Friedrich Hermann Frey)
Naht die jubelvolle Zeit, kommt auch mir
Otto Gruppe
Die Treppe hinunter gesprungen
Hafis
Deine gewölbten Brauen, o Geliebte
Die höchste Macht der Erde sitzt
Die Perlen meiner Seele haben keinen
Gebt mir meinen Becher!
Julius Hart
Wenn du es wüßtest, was träumen heißt
Heinrich Heine
Das ist des Frühlings traurige Lust!
Das ist ein schlechtes Wetter
Die heil'gen drei Kön'ge aus Morgenland
Mein Wagen rollet langsam
Mit deinen blauen Augen
Wo ich bin, mich rings umdunkelt Finsternis

Karl Henckell
Der Sonne entgegen in Liebesgluten
Heil jenem Tag, der dich geboren
Ich bin kein Minister, ich bin kein König
Ich schwebe wie auf Engelsschwingen
Ich trage meine Minne vor Wonne
In diesen Wintertagen, nun sich das Licht
Kling! Meine Seele gibt reinen Ton
Nicht ein Lüftchen regt sich leise
O süsser Mai, o habe du Erbarmen
Wenn ich dich frage, dem das Leben blüht
Hermann Hesse
Der Garten trauert, Kühl sinkt in die Blumen
In dämmrigen Grüften träumte ich lang
Nun der Tag mich müd' gemacht
Friedrich Hölderlin
Froh der süssen Augenweide
Ihr linden Lüfte, Boten Italiens
Wenn ihr Freunde vergesst
Hoffmann von Fallersleben
Die Ähren nur noch nikken das Haupt
Die Mükke sitzt am Fenster
Die Trommeln und Pfeifen, die schallen
Ein Röslein zog ich mir im Garten
Husaren müssen reiten überall durch Stadt
Schon sank die Sonne nieder
Justinus Kerner
Ein Alphorn hör' ich schallen
Alfred Kerr
Die Händler und die Macher
Die Künstler sind die Schöpfer
Drei Masken sah ich am Himmel stehn
Einst kam der Bock als Bote
Es liebte einst ein Hase
Es war einmal ein Bock
Es war mal eine Wanze
Hast du ein Tongedicht vollbracht
O lieber Künstler sei ermahnt
O Schröpferschwarm, o Händlerkreis
Unser Feind ist, grosser Gott
Von Händlern wird die Kunst bedroht
Friedrich Klopstock
Im Frühlingsschatten fand ich sie
Zeit, Verkündigerin der besten Freuden
Theodor Körner
Der Spielmann saß am Felsen und blickte
Nikolaus Lenau
Du trüber Nebel hüllst mir das Tal
Frühlingskinder im bunten Gedränge
O wärst du mein, es wär' ein schön'res Leben
Detlev von Liliencron
Die Feder am Sturmhut in Spiel und Gefahren
Ich ging den Weg entlang, der einsam lag
Vier adlige Rosse voran unserm Wagen
Wenn sanft du mir im Arme schliefst
Anton Lindner
Laß Akaziendüfte schaukeln
John Henry Mackay
Auf, hebe die funkelnde Schale
Der Tag, der schwüle, verblasst
Ich grüsse die Sonne, die dort versinkt
Und morgen wird die Sonne wieder scheinen
Conrad Ferdinand Meyer
Aus der Schiffsbank mach' ich meinen Pfühl
Michelangelo Buonarotti
In's Joch beug' ich den Nacken demutvoll
Christian Morgenstern
Leise Lieder sing' ich dir bei Nacht
Oskar Panizza
Es wohnt ein kleines Vögelein
Paul Remer
Wir schreiten in goldener Fülle
Friedrich Rückert
Der Frost hat mir bereifet des Hauses Dach
Die Fahnen flattern im Mitternachtssturm
Die Liebste steht mir vor den Gedanken
Dort, wo der Morgenstern hergeht
Ein Obdach gegen Sturm und Regen
Gestern war ich Atlas, der den Himmel trug
Ich sah sie nur ein einzigmal
Ich sehe wie in einem Spiegel
Noch eine Stunde laßt mich hier
Weil ich dich nicht legen kann
Friedrich von Sallet
Die Knospe träumte von Sonnenschein
Adolf Friedrich von Schack
Breit' über mein Haupt dein schwarzes Haar
Dem Herzen ähnlich, wenn es lang
Du frag'st mich, Mädchen, was flüsternd
Hoffen und wieder verzagen
Lass' das Zagen, trage mutig deine Sorgen
Leiser schwanken die Äste
Mach' auf, mach' auf, doch leise mein Kind
Mein Herz ist stumm, mein Herz ist kalt
Mit Regen und Sturmgebrause
O schmäht des Lebens Leiden nicht!
Schön sind, doch kalt die Himmelssterne
Seitdem dein Aug' in meines schaute
Um der fallenden Ruder Spitzen
Von dunklem Schleier umsponnen
Wie sollten wir geheim sie halten

Wozu noch, Mädchen, soll es frommen
Friedrich von Schiller
Dass du mein Auge wecktest
Christian Friedrich Daniel Schubart
Schlaf' wohl du Himmelsknabe du
William Shakespeare
Guten Morgen, 's ist Sankt Valentinstag
Sie trugen ihn auf der Bahre bloß
Wie erkenn ich mein Treulieb vor andern nun?
Karl Stieler
Weisst Du die Rose, die Du mir gegeben?
Johann Ludwig Uhland
An ihrem Grabe kniet' ich festgebunden
Aus der Bedrängniss, die mich wild umkettet
Bei diesem kalten Wehen sind alle Strassen leer
Bei einem Wirte wundermild
Ergehst du dich im Abendlicht
Ich kenne sieben lust'ge Brüder
Ich will ja nicht in Garten geh'n
Wie willst du dich mir offenbaren
Zu Hirsau in den Träummern da wiegt
Betty Wehrli-Knobel
Aus Rosen, Phlox, Zinienflor ragen im Garten
Josef Weinheber
Ein Mahl für uns und ein Licht für dich
Fülle du! Gezier und schöner Geist
from Des Knaben Wunderhorn
Das Mägdlein will ein' Freier hab'n
Der Mondschein, der ist schon verblichen
Mein Vater hat gesagt,
Weine, weine nur nicht, ich will dich lieben
Volkslied
Ach was Kummer, Qual und Schmerzen
Wer lieben will, muss leiden

Theodor Streicher (1874-1940)
Hafis
Ach, wie süß, wie süß sie duftet
Der du mich mit gutem Rate
Der Schah von Ormus sah mich nie
Die Liebe, sie zerbreche mich
Durstig sind wir, lieber Wirt
Eine Fürstin ist die Schönheit
Es hält der Ost, der eitle, sich
Fern sei die Ros' und ihre Pracht!
Führer auf dem Weg des Heiles
Ich dachte dein in tiefer Nacht
Ich habe mich dem Heil entschworen
Ist dir ein getreues liebevolles Kind beschert
Keine Sorge verzehre mich um das Künftige
Lieblich in der Rosenzeit
Lilie hat der Zungen zehne
Mein süßer Schatz! du bist zu gut
O harte Sterne! Nie versöhnte, rauhe Welt!
Sie sagen, Hafis, du sei'st ein gar so gewalt'ger
Was du forderst, es gescheh'!
Wehe Lüftchen, lind und lieblich
Weh'n im Garten die Arome
Weißt du noch, mein süßes Herz
Wenn dereinst, wo sie versinken
Wenn einer mäßig trinket
Wie glücklich ist der Morgenwind!
Richard Schaukal
Ich sah dich nachts am Fenster stehn
Nun ist die Nacht gekommen
from Des Knaben Wunderhorn
Anne Margrittchen! Was willst du
Buko von Halberstadt, bring' doch
Da droben auf jenem Berge
Der Franz läßt dich grüßen gar hoch und gar fest
Der Kukkuck auf dem Birnbaum saß: Kukkuck
Der Mai will sich mit Gunsten beweisen
Ei, ei, wie scheint der Mond so hell, ei, ei
Es ist ein Schnitter, der heißt "Tod"
Es ist kein Jäger, er hat ein Schuß
Es kam ein Herr zum Schlößli
Es war ein Markgraf über dem Rhein
Gott geb' ihm ein verdorben Jahr
Guten Morgen, Spielmann, wo bleibst du
Hier sind wir arme Narrn auf Plätzen
Ich eß nicht gerne Gerste
Ich hab' emal ein Bettelmädle küßt
Ich kann und mag nicht fröhlich sein
Ich schwing' mein Horn ins Jammertal
Ich soll und muß ein' Buhlen haben
Kein Hochgewild ich fahen kann
Lasset uns scherzen, blühende Herzen
Leucht't heller denn die Sonne
Mein Vater hat g'sagt, ich soll das Kindelein
Mit Lust tät ich ausreiten
Nun laßt uns singen das Abendlied
Weine, weine, weine nur nicht
Weinschröter, schlag die Trommel
Wer sich auf Ruhm begiebet
Wie kommts, daß du so traurig bist
Zum Sterben bin ich verliebt in dich

Frank Valentine van der Stucken (1858-1929)
Friedrich Adler
Sprich nur, sprich! ich höre die Rede rinnen
Hans Christian Anderson
Die Mutter betet herzig und schaut entzückt
Adolf Bartels
Ich möchte still nach Hause gehn

Georg Friedrich Daumer
Komm, falsche Dirne, laß dich küssen!
Dietmar von Aiste
Schläfst du noch mein Trauter?
Joseph von Eichendorff
Das ist der alte Baum nicht mehr
Hans Eschelbach
Es war ein Tag im Maien
Emanuel Geibel
Siehst du das Meer? Es glänzt auf seiner Flut
Johann Wolfgang von Goethe
Trocknet nicht, trocknet nicht
Heinrich Heine
Am Kreutzweg wird begraben
Auf ihrem Grab da steht eine Linde
Aus meinen Thränen spriessen
Die blauen Frühlingsaugen
Die schlanke Wasserlilje schaut träumend
Du bist wie eine Blume
Entflieh mit mir und sei mein Weib
Es fiel eine Reif in der Frühlingsnacht
Lehn' deine Wang' an meine Wang'
Lieb Liebchen, leg's Händchen auf's Herze
Mutter zum Bienelein: "Hüt dich...!"
Was will die einsame Thräne?
Hoffmann von Fallersleben
Es steht ein Blümchen an jenem Rain
Victor Hugo
Wozu der Vöglein Chöre belauschen fern
Theophile Marzials
Duft'ge Mispelblume, zartes Blüthenmeer
Von schön Sicilien war mein Traum
Anna Ritter
Ein Vöglein singt im Wald, singt Lieb'
Unter den blühenden Linden weißt du's noch?
Otto Roquette
O lass' dich halten, gold'ne Stunde
Christina Rossetti
Wenn ich gestorben, Liebchen
Friedrich Rückert
Die Stunde sei gesegnet, wo ich dir bin begegnet
Liebste! nur dich seh'n, dich hören
Mir ist, nun ich dich habe, als müsst' ich sterben
Wann die Rosen aufgeblüht, geht der Lenz
Wenn die Vöglein sich gepaart
Joseph Viktor von Scheffel
Jetzt ist er hinaus in die weite Welt
Ernst Stauß
Wie war er schön der Maientag
W. Strauss
O Jugendlust, o Jugendglück, wie seid Ihr

Karol Maciej Szymanowski (1882-1937)
Karl Bulcke
Da droben am Berge, ei, seht doch 'mal an!
Richard Dehmel
Ach! aus Träumen fahr ich in die graue Luft
Du tatest mir die Tür auf, ernstes Kind
In die dunkle Bergsschlucht kehrt der Mond
Sieh, der Himmel wird blau
Sieh, wie wir zu den Sternen aufsteigen!
Über unsrer Liebe hängt eine tiefe Trauerweide
Und du kamest in mein Haus,
Wenn die Felder sich verdunkeln
Emil Faktor
Ich weiß ihr liebt das Dunkel nicht
Gustav Falke
Dämmerung löscht die letzten Lichter
"Martin Greif" (Friedrich Hermann Frey)
O weile, süßer Geliebter! Es trügt dich nur
Hafis
Der Frühling ist erschienen
Einst aus meinem Grabe werden ungezählte
Heute tanzt alles, alles, alles tanzt!
Ich Unglückseliger! Wer gibt mir Nachricht
Ich wollt', ich wär' ein morgenklarer See
Ja, ich bin krank, ich weiss, doch lasst mich!
Vor den Mauern von Schiras liegt
Ricarda Huch
Was ist in deiner Seele, was ist in meiner Brust
Alfred Mombert
Leise fällt ein Schnee auf das Land
Schlafend trägt man mich in mein Heimatland
Alfons Paquet
Ein Wand'rer in der Gassen
Anna Ritter
Die Nacht ist keines Menschen Freund!

(Karl Gottfried) Wilhelm Taubert (1811-1891)
Ernst Moritz Arndt
Wo ist der kleine Jakob geblieben?
Friedrich Güll
Bäuerlein, Bäuerlein, tik, tik, tak
Der Bauer hat ein Taubenhaus
Ei wie langsam kommt der Schneck
Glöcklein, Abendglöcklein, läute Frieden
Hast viel gespielt und viel gelacht
Klaus ist in den Wald gegangen
Sag mir, du Siebenschläferlein
Wilhelm Hey
Armes Bäumchen, dauerst mich
Es ist kein Mäuschen so jung und klein
Wo sind all' die Blumen hin?

Hoffmann von Fallersleben
Ei, was blüht so heimlich am Sonnenstrahl?
Ein scheckiges Pferd, ein blankes Gewehr
Es steht ein Baum in jenem Tal
Hänselein, willst du tanzen?
Maikäfer, summ, summ, summ, nun sag' mir an
Wart', Vöglein, wart'! Jetzt bist du mein
Hermann Kletke
Frau Elster hat den Schatz entdeckt
Franz Kugler
Da draussen auf der Aue
Rudolf Löwenstein
Es ist schon dunkel um mich her
Hänschen will ein Tischler werden
Nun reibet euch die Äuglein wach!
Trom to tom, tom! Ich bin der beste Trommler
Wer klappert am Dache, mein Kindlein?
Robert Reinick
Der Hans, der spricht zum Hahn
Hänschen will reiten, setzt sich zu Rosse hin
Sonne hat sich müd gelaufen, spricht
Täubchen, ihr lieben, lieben Täubchen
Wilhelm Wackernagel
Kommt gezogen, kleine Vögel, kommt geflogen
from Des Knaben Wunderhorn
Es tanzt ein Butze-Butze-Butze-Butzemann
Patsche, patsche, patsche, patsche Küchelchen
Volkslied
Bruder Jakob, schläfst du noch?
Ringel, Ringel, Reihe! S'sind der Kinder Zweie
Not Yet Identified
Kikriki! kikriki! Horch, horch! der Hahn
Wenn es Abend wird und still

Pyotr Il'yich Tchaikovsky (1840-1893)
Johann Wolfgang von Goethe
Heiss mich nicht reden, heiss mich schweigen
Kennst du das Land, wo die Zitronen blühn
Nur wer die Sehnsucht kennt
Heinrich Heine
Die blauen Frühlingsaugen
Ich wollt' meine Schmerzen ergössen
Warum sind die Rosen so blass?

Anna Teichmüller (1861-1940)
Anacreon
Gegen Mitternacht schon war es um die Stunde
Ferdinand Avenarius
Weit draussen, einsam im ödem Raum
Björnstjerne Björnson
Es sass die Prinzessin im Frau'ngemach
Marianne Blaauw
Wie leise scheue Kinder
Wolrad Eigenbrodt
Die Sonne sengt und dörrt das Land
Ein Rößlein möcht' ich haben
Kleiner blauer Schmetterling
Sanft und lind geht der liebe Abendwind
Summ! summ! summ! summ! so schwirrt es
Carl Hauptmann
Blütenblätter wehen, holde Zeit!
Draussen wirbeln viel Blätter im Schein
Du Kindlein weich, im Erdenreich
Ein Gras vom Felsen, eine Blume
Ein wunderbares Rätselreich die Nacht
Einsam bin ich nicht, einzeln!
Flamme in Nächten, selig allein
Frau Nachtigall, sagt ihr, "Königin!"
Gott grüß'! in die Nachtsee! du kleines Licht
Im Dämmer der Nacht, in Mondesluft
In den Wind, in den Wind sing' ich mein Lied
In meiner Träume Heimat barg ich dich
Mir immer wieder unbegreiflich
Schäumende Woge rollt immer zum Strande her
Sehnsucht aus einsamer Seele auffliehť!
Stiller Abend sinkt, Sterne blinken leise
Tausend Tannenwipfel drohen brausend
Über mir in wolkigen Lüften
Verfallen liegt ein Tempeltor
Verlaß dich singend auf deine heimlichen Feuer
Weisst du warum der Tod im Menschenland
Friedrich Hebbel
Friedlich bekämpfen Nacht sich und Tag
Schlafen, schlafen, nichts als schlafen!
Gottfried Keller
Ein Häuptling ritt geehrt im Land
Klagt mich nicht an, dass ich vor Leid
Kolzow
Nächtig schwarze Wälder lichtet Euch!
Nikolaus Lenau
An der duftverlor'nen Gränze jener Berge
Wo kein Strahl des Lichts hinblinket
Conrad Ferdinand Meyer
Bemesst den Schritt, bemesst den Schwung
Trüb verglomm der schwüle Sommertag
Hans Reisiger
All' deine Anmut hab' ich aufgeweckt
Rainer Maria Rilke
Maria! Du weinst ich weiss
Leopold von Schroeder
Wo du nicht bist und deiner Augen Schimmer

Friedl Zacharias
Eia, husch, husch, im Fliederbusch
Ringelringelreigen, mit den jungen Zweigen
Schliesst du bald die Äuglein zu
Grete Ziegler-Bock
Am kahlen Erdwall, da irgendwo am Hunho
Anonymous
Ich wandelt einsam auf grünem Pfad
Im Wald auf früher Reise
Roter Vogel hinauf dich schwing!
Volkslied
Ach, es bebt der Blütenkeim
Bin ein Vöglein, das im Schatten zwitschert hier
Da draussen, vor der himmlischen Thür
Einen Engel mit gold'nen Schwingen seh' ich
Klein Christel kam vor die Himmelspfort!
Komme komme komm herbei, blüthenschwerer
Lärchenbaum, mein Lärchenbaum
Liegt ein armer Krieger in dem Turm gefangen
O wie glücklich sind doch Andre!
Und hast du einen Andern viel lieber als mich
Vöglein du in meinem Zelt, du mein Liebstes
Not Yet Identified
Hoffnung dein Prangen, Liebe dein Glück
Niwaschi! Heb' des Kindes Hand!
Wespe! Wespe! Wespelein! Kriech du
Wie ein Sturmwind kamst du in meine Seele

Anton Teyber (1756-1822)
Alois Blumauer
Liebe traf mich, meine Augen weinen

Siegfried Thiele (1934-)
Rainer Maria Rilke
Er wußte nur vom Tod, was alle wissen:
Und wie mag die Liebe dir kommen sein?
Wie soll ich meine Seele halten

Ludwig Wilhelm Andreas Maria Thuille (1861-1907)
Otto Franz Gensichen
Unter blühenden Bäumen
Hermann Gilm
Stell' auf den Tisch die duftenden Reseden
Robert Hamerling
Auf schweigendem Bergesgipfel der Knabe
Heinrich Leuthold
Deine süßen, süßen Schauer, o Waldesruh
Hermann Lingg
Immer leiser wird mein Schlummer
Wilhelm Osterwald
Nun grünt der Berg, nun blüht das Thal
Karl Stieler
Als hoch das Feld in Blumen stand
Die müden Augen, sie tragen's kaum!
Es klingt der Lärm der Welt
Ich lehn' im offenen Gemache
Ich wand're heim durch's hohe Feld
Im Waldesweben ist es Ruh'
In den Bäumen regt sich's leise
In der Luft, der schwülen, feuchten
Mein süsses Lieb, wo weilest du?
Was ist mir denn geschehen?
Wenn's im Thal zu Abend läutet

Franz Tischhauser (1921-)
Christian Morgenstern
Du bist ja ein Hamster, ein Hamster bist du
Ein kleiner Hund mit Namen Fips
Es lebt ein Ries' im Wald, der hat ein Ohr
In einem leeren Haselstrauch
Schlaf, Kindlein, schlaf!
Spann dein kleines Schirmchen auf

Ernst Toch (1887-1964)
Otto Julius Bierbaum
Gib dir weiter keine Mühe, mein Sohn
Wilhelm Busch
Es stand vor eines Hauses Tor ein Esel
Ludwiga Kuckuck
Du bist so reich als du tränenreich bist
Spätnachmittag. Die kleine Straße liegt leblos
Christian Morgenstern
Litt einst ein Fähnlein große Not
Steht ein Häuschen an der Bahn
Was denkst du jetzt? Ach, hinter diese Stirne
Rainer Maria Rilke
Der Abend ist mein Buch
Große Heilige und kleine feiert

Václav Jan Křtitel Tomášek (1774-1850)
Gottfried August Bürger
Lenore fuhr um's Morgenrot
Johann Wolfgang von Goethe
Ach! wer bringt die schönen Tage
Als ich still und ruhig spann
An dem reinsten Frühlingsmorgen
Bei dem Glanze der Abendröthe ging ich still
Da droben auf jenem Berge da steh' ich
Das Wasser rauscht, das Wasser schwoll
Dem Schnee, dem Regen, dem Wind entgegen
Der du von dem Himmel bist
Der Vorhang schwebet hin und her
Die Nebel zerreißen, der Himmel wird helle
Du gefällst mir so wohl, mein liebes Kind

Ein Veilchen auf der Wiese stand
Es war ein König in Thule
Füllest wieder Busch und Thal
Heiß mich nicht reden, heiß mich schweigen
Hoch auf dem alten Thurme
Ich bin der wohlbekannte Sänger
Ich denke dein, wenn mir der Sonne Schimmer
Im Felde schleich' ich still und wild
Kehre nicht in diesem Kreise neu
Kennst du das Land, wo die Citronen blühn
Kleine Blumen, kleine Blätter streuen mir
Liebchen, kommen diese Lieder jemahls wieder
Nach Mittage saßen wir junges Volk im Kühlen
Sah ein Knab' ein Röslein stehn
Singet nicht in Trauertönen von der Einsamkeit
So hab' ich wirklich dich verloren?
Tage der Wonne, kommt ihr so bald?
Tiefe Stille herrscht im Wasser
Trocknet nicht, trocknet nicht
Und frische Nahrung, neues Blut
Verfließet, vielgeliebte Lieder
Von allen schönen Waaren, zum Markte
Wenn die Reben wieder blühen
Wer reitet so spät durch Nacht und Wind
Wie herrlich leuchtet mir die Natur
Wie kommt's daß du so traurig bist
Willst du immer weiter schweifen?
Wir singen und sagen vom Grafen so gern
Wo willst du, klares Bächlein, hin so munter?
Wohin? wohin? schöne Müllerin! Wie heißt du?

Friedrich von Schiller

Es donnern die Höhen, es zittert der Steg

Gustav Trautmann

Paul Heyse

Und bild' dir nur im Traum nichts ein

Joseph Viktor von Scheffel

Sonne taucht in Meeresfluthen, Himmel blitzt

Richard Trunk (1879-1968)

Otto Julius Bierbaum

Ach, wie wird mir wohl und weh, süße Dame

Richard Dehmel

Lieber Morgenstern, lieber Abendstern

Paul Ehlers

Zum Wasser neigen sich die silbergrauen

Joseph von Eichendorff

Auf die Dächer zwischen blassen Wolken
Da fahr ich still im Wagen
Die Welt ruht still im Hafen, mein Liebchen
Es schienen so golden die Sterne
Hörst du nicht die Quellen gehen
Wenn die Sonne lieblich schiene
Zwei Musikanten ziehn daher vom Wald

Gustav Falke

Schlitten vorm Haus, steig ein, kleine Maus!

Georg Josef Mayerhofer

Schwebst du im nächtlichen Raum?

Christian Morgenstern

Auf der Bank im Walde han sich gestern

Ludwig Johann Reinwald

Wandelst du auch fern von mir

Albert Sergel

"Nimm mich!" Was kriegst denn du?

Hermann Thürauf

Es schaut zum Bauernhaus der Maienbusch

Viktor Ullmann (1898-1944?)

Friedrich Hölderlin

Vor seiner Hütte ruhig im Schatten sitzt
Wenn auf Gefilden neues Entzükken keimt

(Olav) Fartein Valen (1887-1952)

Johann Wolfgang von Goethe

Der Spiegel sagt mir: ich bin schön!
Weiß wie Lilien, reine Kerzen, Sternen gleich
Willst du die Blüten des frühen
Wo die Rose hier blüht, wo Reben um Lorbeer

Eduard Mörike

Ein Tännlein grünet wo, wer weiss im Walde

Friedrich von Schiller

Horch wie Murmeln des empörten Meeres

Anonymous

Tretet leise zu meinem Grabe

Vanderstucken: see Frank van der Stucken

Aleksandr Egorovich Varlamov (1801-1848)

Johann Wolfgang von Goethe

Über allen Gipfeln ist Ruh

Heinrich Heine

Du bist wie eine Blume
Du schönes Fischermädchen, treibe den Kahn

Giuseppe Verdi (1813-1901)

Johann Wolfgang von Goethe

Ach, neige, du Schmerzenreiche
Meine Ruh' ist hin, mein Herz ist schwer

Johann Vesque von Püttlingen ("J. Hoven") (1803-1883)

Friedrich Bach

Meine Seele ist still und in sich gekehrt

Adelbert von Chamisso

Es wallte so silbernen Scheines nicht immer
's war einer, dem's zu Herzen ging

Joseph von Eichendorff
Es zogen zwei rüstge Gesellen
Ihr habt den Vogel gefangen
Johann Wolfgang von Goethe
Das Wasser rauscht', das Wasser schwoll
Franz Grillparzer
Wo ich bin, fern und nah, stehn zwei Augen da
Heinrich Heine
Am einsamen Strande plätschert die Flut
Auf den Wällen Salamankas sind die Lüfte
Das gelbe Laub erzittert, es fallen die Blätter
Deine weißen Lilienfinger
Den König Wiswamitra, den treibt's ohne Rast
Den Tag, den ich so himmlisch verbracht
Der Mond ist aufgegangen
Die heil'gen drei Kön'ge aus Morgenland
Die Jahre kommen und gehen
Die Jungfrau schläft in der Kammer
Die Nacht ist feucht und stürmisch
Ein Fichtenbaum steht einsam im Norden
Ein Jüngling liebt ein Mädchen
Es war ein alter König, sein Herz war schwer
Mein Herz, mein Herz ist traurig
Mir träumt', ich bin der liebe Gott
Mir träumte von einem Königskind
Neben wohnt Don Henriques
Sie saßen und tranken am Teetisch
Still ist die Nacht, es ruhen die Gassen
Unten Schlacht, doch oben schossen
Wir saßen am Fischerhause und schauten
Zu fragmentarisch ist Welt und Leben
Justinus Kerner
Mir träumt', ich flög gar bange
"Kosten"
Auf einem hohen Berge
Nikolaus Lenau
Diese Rose pflück ich hier in der weiten Ferne
Drüben geht die Sonne scheiden
Weil' auf mir, du dunkles Auge
Johann Martin Miller
Rosenknöspchen, schön bist du
Gustav Pfarrius
Es geht der Tag zur Neige
August Graf von Platen
Laß tief in dir mich lesen, verhehl auch dies
Otto Prechtler
Steure, Fährmann, deine Barke in den Golf
Johann von Salis-Seewis
Abendglokkenhalle zittern dumpf
Karl Schweizer
Ich wollte in die Fremde gehn
Johann Seidl
Ich trage, wo ich gehe, stets eine Uhr bei mir
Julius Sturm
Das Meer ist still, die Stürme schlafen
Johann Ludwig Uhland
So hab ich nun die Stadt verlassen

Ernest Vietor (fl.1905-1930)
Johanna Ambrosius
Die Liebe ist die Sonne, die Freundschaft
Es sind die schlecht'sten Früchte nicht
Mein Herz ging auf die Wanderschaft
Adolf Bartels
Ich möchte still nach Hause gehn
Otto Julius Bierbaum
Da nun die Blätter fallen, oh weh
Gell ja, also Morgen?
Hans und Grethe, Grethe und Hans
Wie ging ich durch mein Leben hin
Clemens Brentano
Hör, es klagt die Flöte wieder
Wilhelm Busch
Es sitzt ein Vogel auf dem Leim
Carl Busse
Über den Bergen weit zu wandern
Hans Carossa
Und wie manche Nacht bin ich aufgewacht
Adelbert von Chamisso
Nun hast du mir den ersten Schmerz getan
Richard Dehmel
Ich warf eine Rose ins Meer
Lieber Morgenstern, lieber Abendstern
Wenn die Felder sich verdunkeln
Joseph von Eichendorff
Es rauschen die Wipfel und schauern
Übern Garten durch die Lüfte hört ich
Johann Georg Fischer
Gestern ein Rieseln im weichen Eise
Wo zweie sich küssen zum ersten Mal
Cäsar Flaischlen
Februarschnee, Februarschnee tut mir nicht weh
Theodor Fontane
Halte dich still, halte dich stumm
Immer enger, leise, leise ziehen sich
Hermann Gilm
Aus dem Walde tritt die Nacht
Albert Giraud
Pierrot! mein Lachen hab ich verlernt!
Johann Wolfgang von Goethe
Dem Schnee, dem Regen, dem Wind entgegen
Feiger Gedanken bängliches Schwanken
Freudvoll und leidvoll, gedankenvoll sein

Geh! gehorche meinen Winken
Ich ging im Walde so für mich hin
"Martin Greif" (Friedrich Hermann Frey)
Nun rühret die Ähren im Felde ein leiser Hauch
Stille ruht die weite Welt, Schlummer fällt
Vor einem grünen Walde, da liegt
Wenn am feuchten Maienmorgen
Wohin, o Bächlein, schnelle? "Hinab ins Tal."
Heinrich Heine
Leise zieht durch mein Gemüth
Karl Henckell
Die dunklen Wolken sausen
Paul Heyse
Blühendes Heidekraut, dein Duft ist wie
Arno Holz
Die Ammer flötet tief im Grund
Gottfried Keller
Das Köhlerweib ist trunken und singt im Wald
Mann merkt, dass der Wein geraten war
Justinus Kerner
Weiss nicht, woher ich bin gekommen
A. Kotsch
Ich suchte eine Melodie seit vierzehn Tagen
Detlev von Liliencron
Flatternde Fahnen und frohes Gedränge
Ich kann das Wort nicht vergessen
Hermann Löns
Rose Marie, Rose Marie, sieben Jahre
Eduard Mörike
Im Nebel ruhet noch die Welt
Alfred Mombert
Sie wandeln durch des Waldes Grün
Christian Morgenstern
Also ihr lebt noch, alle, alle, ihr, am Bach
Am Himmel der Wolken er dunkelnder Kranz
Am Morgen spricht die Magd ganz wild
Auf braunen Sammetschuhen geht der Abend
Auf den Schwingen des Windes
Auf der Bank im Walde han sich gestern
Auf der Treppe sitzen meine Öhrchen
Aus ihrem Bette stürzt sie bleich
Aus silbergrauen Gründen tritt
Bau mir die Stadt aus Elfenbein
Das Mondschaf sagt sich selbst gut Nacht
Der Rabe Ralf will will hu hu
Die Primeln blühn und grüssen
Die Schleiche singt ihr Nachtgebet
Dinge gehen vor im Mond,
Ein Bauernknabe liegt im Wald und liest
Ein Rabe sass auf einem Meilenstein und rief
Ein schwarzes Vöglein fliegt über die Welt
Ein Wiesel sass auf einem Kiesel!
Es pfeift der Wind. Was pfeift er wohl?
Es war einmal ein Lattenzaun
Es war einmal ein Papagei
Ich bin ein einsamer Schaukelstuhl
Ich bin eine Harfe mit goldenen Seiten
Ich liebe die graden Alleen
Ich sah uns alle und empfand
Im Inselwald, "Zum stillen Kauz,"
In deine langen Wellen, tiefe Glocke
Jetzt bist du da, dann bist du dort
Klabautermann, Klabauterfrau, Klabauterkind
Mein lieber und vertrauter Mann
Nebel, stiller Nebel über Meer und Land
O Nacht, du Sternenbronnen, ich bade Leibt
O schauerliche Lebenswirrn, wir hängen hier
Oh, wer um alle Rosen wüsste
Pfeift der Sturm? Keift ein Wurm?
Schlaf, Kindlein, schlaf, am Himmel steht
Sophie, mein Henker Mädel, komm, küsse mir
Spann dein kleines Schirmchen auf
Um stille Stübel schleicht des Monds
Vorfrühling seufzt in weiter Nacht
Warrrrrrte nur... wie viel schon riss ich ab
Warum versankst du mir so ganz?
Weisse Tauben fliegen durch blaue Morgenluft
Zu Golde ward die Welt; zu lange traf der Sonne
Zwei Tannenwurzeln gross und alt
Friedrich Nietzsche
Der Tag klingt ab, es gilbt sich Glück
Die Krähen schrein und ziehen schwirren Flugs
Hier sass ich, wartend, wartend, doch auf nichts
Nun, da der Tag des Tags müde ward
O Mensch! Gib acht! Was spricht
Tag meines Lebens! Die Sonne sinkt
Rainer Maria Rilke
Der Tod ist gross. Wir sind die Seinen
Anna Ritter
Ein Brünnlein im Felde, sechs Linden im Kreis
Friedrich Schlegel
Sanfte Ebbe und hohe Flut tief im Mut
Stolberg-Stolberg
Süsse, heilige Natur, lass mich gehn
Theodor Storm
Das macht, es hat die Nachtigall
Heute, nur heute bin ich so schön
So komme, was da kommen mag!
Johann Ludwig Uhland
Die linden Lüfte sind erwacht
Saatengrün, Veilchenduft, Lerchenwirbel

(Wilhelm) Richard Wagner (1813-1883)
Ernst von Feuchtersleben
Es ist bestimmt in Gottes Rat
Johann Wolfgang von Goethe
Ach neige, du Schmerzenreiche
Burgen mit hohen Mauern und Zinnen
Der Schäfer putzte sich zum Tanz
Es war eine Ratt' im Kellernest
Es war einmal ein König
Meine Ruh' ist hin, mein Herz ist schwer
Was machst du mir vor Liebchens Tür
Heinrich Heine
Nach Frankreich zogen zwei Grenadier
Georg Scheurlin
Der Tannenbaum steht schweigend
Mathilde Wesendonck
Hoch gewölbte Blätterkronen
In der Kindheit frühen Tagen
Sag', welch wunderbare Träume
Sausendes, brausendes Rad der Zeit
Sonne, weinest jeden Abend dir

Rudolf Wagner-Régeny (1903-1969)
Bertolt Brecht
Auf die Erde voller kaltem Wind
Höchstes Glück ist doch, zu spenden
Laßt euch nicht verführen
Was meine Mutter mir sagte
Wie viel besser fuhren wir in der Räuberzeit

Adolf Wallnöfer (1854-1946)
Michael Georg Conrad
Nicht unter schwarzer Erdenlast

Bruno Walter (1876-1962)
Joseph von Eichendorff
Bleib' bei uns! Wir haben den Tanzplan im Tal
Das Kind ruht aus vom Spielen
Hier unter dieser Linde saß ich viel tausendmal
Ich kann hier nicht singen, aus dieser Mauern
Ist schmuck nicht mein Rößlein
Zwei Musikanten ziehn daher vom Wald

(Johann) Ignatz Walter (1755-1822)
Johann Wolfgang von Goethe
Es war einmal ein König, der hat einen Skorpion

Bernhard Anselm Weber (1764-1821)
Johann Wolfgang von Goethe
Im Walde schleich ich still und wild

Carl Maria (Friedrich Ernst) von Weber (1786-1826)
Jens Baggesen
Horch! Leise horch, Geliebte!
Wenn, Brüder, wie wir täglich sehen
Carl von Blankensee
Herz, mein Herz, ermanne dich
Gottfried August Bürger
Mädel, schau' mir in's Gesicht!
Ignaz Franz Castelli
Ein König einst gefangen sass
Sohn der Ruhe
Wenn ich die Blümlein schau', wünsch' ich
Alexander von Dusch
Auf die stürm'sche See hinaus
Joseph August Eckschläger
Maienblümlein, so schön, mag euch gern blühen
Friedrich Förster
Ach, wär' doch zu dieser Stund'
Keine Lust ohn' treues Lieben!
Vöglein hüpfet in dem Haine
Friedrich von Gerstenberg
Was bricht hervor, wie Blüthen weiss
Friedrich Wilhelm Gubitz
Alles in mir glühet, zu lieben
In der Berge Riesenschatten
Lust entfloh und hin ist hin!
Nun, bin ich befreit! Wie behäglich!
Sel'ge Zeiten sah ich prangen
Verrathen! Verschmähet! Wer drängte
Weile Kind, ich will nicht rauben!
Wer stets hinter'n Ofen kroch
Wie wir voll Glut uns hier zusammenfinden
Hafis
Rosen im Haare, den Becher zur Hand
Johann Christoph Haug
Traurig, einsam welkst du hin, Blume!
Max Heigel
Umringt vom mutherfüllten Heere
Johann Gottfried Herder
Ein neues Lied!
Franz Karl Hiemer
Endlich hatte Damon sie gefunden
Schlaf', Herzenssöhnchen, mein Liebling
Franz Ignatz Holbein
Sei gegrüsst, Frau Sonne, mir
Henri Illaire
Schmückt das Haus mit grünen Zweigen
Karl Ludwig Kannegiesser
Bald heisst es wieder
Ein Kind ist uns geboren!

Ich tumm'le mich auf der Haide
Ja, freue dich
Judäa, hochgelobtes Land, und Bethlehem
Friedrich Kind
Das Mädchen ging die Wies' entlang
Der Geisshirt steht am Felsenrand
Ein Veilchen blüht im Thale
Leise weht' es, leise wallte rings der Thau
Wenn die Maien grün sich kleiden
Theodor Körner
Das Volk steht auf, der Sturm bricht los
Die Wunde brennt, die bleichen Lippen beben
Du Schwert an meiner Linken
Düst're Harmonieen hör' ich klingen
Frisch auf, frisch auf mit raschem Flug!
Herz, lass dich nicht zerspalten
Hör' uns, Allmächtiger! Hör' uns, Allgütiger!
Schlacht, du brichst an!
Vater, ich rufe Dich! Brüllend umwölkt mich
Was glänzt dort vom Walde im Sonnenschein?
Was ist des Sängers Vaterland?
August von Kotzebue
Lass mich schlummern, Herzlein, schweige
Rase, Sturmwind, blase
Über die Berge mit Ungestüm
Lehr
Ein Echo kenn' ich, ist weit von hier
Weil es also Gott gefügt
Wollt ihr sie kennen, soll ich sie nennen
Wilhelm von Löwenstein-Werthheim
Meine Lieder, meine Sänge
Friedrich von Matthisson
Ich denke dein, wenn durch den Hain
Karl Müchler
Ein steter Kampf ist unser Leben
Ich sah ein Röschen am Wege stehn
Was zieht zu deinem Zauberkreise
Gustav Nicolai
's is nichts mit den alten Weibern
Clotilde von Nostitz-Jänkendorf
Wenn Kindlein süssen Schlummers Ruh'
Martin Opitz
Ich empfinde fast ein Grauen
Georg von Reinbeck
Sanftes Licht, weiche nicht
Süsse Ahnung dehnt den Busen
Was stürmet die Haide herauf?
Bartolomäus Ringwald
Eine fromme Magd von gutem Stand
Johann Rochlitz
Es stürmt auf der Flur
Samuel Friedrich Sauter
Geiger und Pfeifer, hier habt ihr Geld darauf
Max von Schenkendorf
Vöglein einsam in dem Bauer
Franz Eugen Josef Seida
Entfliehet schnell von mir
Josef Ludwig Stoll
Es sitzt die Zeit im weissen Kleid
Streckfuss
Du liebes, holdes, himmelsüsses Wesen
Wenzel Swoboda
Ich sah sie hingesunken
Thale
Husaren sind gar wack're Truppen
Ludwig Tieck
Sind es Schmerzen, sind es Freuden
Christian Friedrich Voigt
Zur Freude ward geboren, was unter'm Monde
Johann Heinrich Voss
Der Holdseligen sonder Wank
Sagt mir an, was schmunzelt ihr?
Wallner
Jüngst sass ich am Grabe der Trauten allein
Wargentin
Das war ein recht abscheuliches Gesicht
Pius Alexander Wolf
Einsam bin ich nicht alleine
Anonymous
Ei, wenn ich doch ein Maler wär'
Ein Gärtchen und ein Häuschen drin
Frage mich immer– fragest umsonst!
Frei und froh mit muntern Sinnen
Heisse stille Liebe schwebet
Ich hab' mir eins erwählet, ein Schätzchen
Leis' wandeln wir wie Geisterhauch
O Berlin, ich muss dich lassen
Umsonst entsagt' ich der lockenden Liebe
Ungern flieht das Süsse Leben
from Des Knaben Wunderhorn
Ei! Ei! Wie scheint der Mond so hell
Volkslied
Ach, wenn ich nur ein Liebchen hätte!
Der Tag hat seinen Schmuck auf heute
Herzchen, mein Schätzchen
I und mein junges Weib können schön tanza
Mein Schätzerl is hübsch
Mein Schatz, der ist auf die Wanderschaft hin
Sind wir geschieden, und ich muss leben
So geht es in Schnützelputz-Häusel
Tra, ri, ro! Der Sommer, der ist do!
Weine, weine, weine nur nicht

Wenn ich ein Vöglein wär

Anton (Friedrich Wilhelm) von Webern (1883-1945)

Ferdinand Avenarius
Ertrage dus, laß schneiden dir den Schmerz
Leise tritt auf... Nicht mehr in tiefem Schlaf
Nun wir uns lieben, rauscht mein stolzes Glück
Schmerzen und Freuden reift jede Stunde

Hans Bethge
An einem Abend, da die Blumen dufteten

Matthias Claudius
Ach, es ist so dunkel in des Todes Kammer

Richard Dehmel
Aus des Abends weissen Wogen
Die Welt verstummt, dein Blut erklingt
Du hattest einen Glanz auf deiner Stirn
O mein Geliebter – in die Kissen
Schwebst du nieder aus den Weiten
Über unsre Liebe hängt eine tiefe Trauerweide
Zaghaft vom Gewölk ins Land

Gustav Falke
Der Mond scheint auf mein Lager

Stefan George
An baches ranft die einzigen frühen
Das lockere saatgefilde lechzet krank
Dem bist du kind, dem freund
Dies ist ein lied für dich allein
Entflieht auf leichten Kähnen
Erwachen aus dem tiefsten traumes-schoosse
Ihr tratet zu dem herde
Im morgen-taun trittst du hervor
Im windes-weben war meine frage
Ja heil und dank dir die den segen brachte!
Kahl reckt der baum im winterdunst
Noch zwingt mich treue über dir zu wachen
So ich traurig bin weiss ich nur ein ding
So wart bis ich dies dir noch künde
Welt der gestalten lang lebewohl!

Johann Wolfgang von Goethe
Der Strauss, den ich gepflücket
Ein Blumenglöckchen vom Boden hervor
Weiß wie Lilien, reine Kerzen
Ziehn die Schafe von der Wiese

"Martin Greif" (Friedrich Hermann Frey)
Von Wald umgeben ein Blütenbaum

Detlev von Liliencron
In der Dämmerung, um Glock zwei, Glock dreie

Friedrich Nietzsche
Mein Herz ist wie ein See so weit

Rainer Maria Rilke
Du, der ichs nicht sage, daß ich bei Nacht
Du machst mich allein. Dich einzig kann

August Strindberg
Schien mir's, als ich sah die Sonne

Georg Trakl
Die Bläue meiner Augen ist erloschen
Dunkler Odem im grünen Gezweig
Ihr großen Städte Steinern aufgebaut
Mond, als träte ein Totes aus blauer Höhle
So leise sind die grünen Wälder
Täglich kommt die gelbe Sonne über den Hügel

Paul Verlaine
Weich küßt die Zweige der weiße Mond

Wilhelm Weigand
Du Sommerabend! Heilig, goldnes Licht!

Anonymous
Schatzerl klein mußt nit traurig sein

from Des Knaben Wunderhorn
Mein Kind, sieh an die Brüste mein
Steht auf, ihr lieben Kinderlein

Volkslied
Der Tag ist vergangen, die Nacht ist schon hier

Karl Weigl (1881-1949)

Otto Julius Bierbaum
Der Schmerz ist ein Schmied

Oscar Weil (1839?-1921)

Friedrich Bodenstedt
Wenn der Frühling auf die Berge steigt

Friedrich Rückert
So oft der Herbst die Rosen stahl

William Shakespeare
Ein junger Bursch durchs Kornfeld ging
Komm herbei, komm herbei, Tod
Wo schweifst du, Herrin, mir so theuer?

(Paul) Felix Weingartner, Edler von Münzberg (1863-1942)

Hans Benzmann
Das ist des Abends Segen

Hans Bethge
Die Nachtigall sang ohne Ende
Die Sonne scheidet
Mein Schiff treibt
Nicht deshalb lieb ich
Noch ist der Glanz der Frühe
So schön sind deine Hände
Vom Wind getroffen
Wo das Reisfeld abgeerntet

Karl Bienestein
Von Porphyr rot

Friedrich Bodenstedt
Was ist der Wuchs der Pinie

Ada Christen
Sinnend stand ich bei dem Grabe Rabby Löv's
So gross, so still, so feierlich ragen die Bäume
Felix Dahn
Das ist die sanfte, die heilige
Marie von Ebner-Eschenbach
O du des himmlischen Reiches Kind
Franz Evers
Die Sterne sind so hell
Emanuel Geibel
Die Nacht war schwarz, die Luft war schwül
Carl Gerok
Einsamer Garten, öde und leer
Hermann Gilm
Ich hab drei Kränze gewunden
Küss' ich die Mutter Abends
"Martin Greif" (Friedrich Hermann Frey)
Am Barbaratage holt' ich drei Zweiglein
Sprach eine wilde Ros' am Zaun
Otto Gruppe
Es weicht die Nacht, und über'm Hügel
Im Walde rollt der Wagen
Robert Hamerling
Die Todten haben Einen in ihrer Einsamkeit
Es rauschen die Tannen und Föhren
Hinter jenen Epheuranken
Saßen zwei Liebende kosend
Sieh, Liebchen, hier im Waldesthal
Friedrich Hebbel
Rausche nur vorüber
Wilhelm Hertz
Und weil ich denn von dannen muss
Vergangen ist der lange Tag
Paul Heyse
Dulde, gedulde dich fein!
Im Föhrenwald wie schwüle!
Gottfried Keller
Alle meine Weisheit hing in meinen Haaren
Das Gärtlein dicht verschlossen
Ein armer Teufel ist der Schuft
Ich denke oft an's blaue Meer
Ich fürcht' nit Gespenster
Nicht ein Flügelschlag ging durch die Welt
Nun bin ich untreu worden
O ein Glöcklein klingelt mir früh und spät
Schon hat die Nacht den Silberschrein
Seht ihr die zwei Kirschenbäumchen
Sieh den Abendstern erblinken tief im Westen
War ein heimathloser Wand'rer
Weise nicht von dir mein schlichtes Herz
Wende dich, du kleiner Stern
Wenn schlanke Lilien wandelten
Wie glänzt der helle Mond so kalt und fern
Willkommen klare Sommernacht
Nikolaus Lenau
An ihren bunten Liedern klettert
Diese Rose pflück ich dir
Drei Seelen hab' ich offenbar
Du trüber Nebel, hüllest mir das Thal
Hesperus der blasse Funken
In einem Buche blätternd
Mädchen, sieh am Wiesenhang
Mein Pfeifchen traut, mir ist dein Rauch
Sahst du ein Glück vorübergehn
Weil' auf mir, du dunkles Auge
Marie Madeleine
Wie ist mein zitterndes Herz entbrannt
Friedrich Marx
Vom Wassergrunde helle grüßt mich
Eduard Mörike
Als der Winter die Rosen geraubt
Aninka tanzte vor uns
Derweil ich schlafend lag
Es ist zwar sonsten nicht der Brauch
Frühling läßt sein blaues Band
Grausame Frühlingssonne
Herr, schicke was du willt
Ich hätte wohl, dein Haar zu zieren
Ich sah eben ein jugendlich Paar
Jung Volker das ist unser Räuberhauptmann
Siehe von allen den Liedern
Wenn ich von deinem Anschaun
Wie heimlicher Weise ein Engelein leise
Wo gehst du hin, du schönes Kind
Zierlich ist des Vogels Tritt
Christian Morgenstern
Als wie ein Feld, das erstes Licht ereilt
Deine Rosen an der Brust
Du bist mein Land
Ein schwarzes Vöglein fliegt
Es kommt der Schmerz gegangen
Grab tausend Klafter hinab
Im Garten Gottes wirft ein Born
Im Süden war's. Zur Nachtzeit. Eine Gast
In deine langen Wellen
In den Wipfeln des Waldes
Jetzt bist du da, dann bist du dort
Mit dir, wer weiß, würd' ich noch manche Pfade
Nun schweben Dach und Decke
Schwalben durch den Abend treibend
Und wir werden zusammen schweigen
Was kannst du, Süße, wider dies

Salomon Hermann von Mosenthal
Ich will hier am Portale steh'n
Johannes Öhquist
Hoch über mir endlos
Conrad von Prittwitz und Gaffron
Auf goldnem Wagen
Julius von Rodenberg
Alles stille, nur zuweilen
Hier in dem Dunkel, auf pfadlosen Mooren
Fr. Rosenthal
Nun ist der Tag verronnen
Emil Rudolf Schönaich-Carolath
Drei Rosen gab sie mir, drei Küsse
Seid'ne Gewänder, Spangen von Gold
Carl Spitteler
Was huschelt im Garten
Zwölf Engel hielten am Himmelstor
Theodor Storm
Ich wand ein Sträußlein Morgens früh
Sie sass in unserm Mädchenkreise ein Stern
Mathilde Gräfin Stubenberg
Nichts soll, o Herr
Julius Sturm
Der Bauer steht vor seinem Feld
Es schwebt um deine zierliche Hand
Genieße still zufrieden den sonnig heitern Tag
Ich sass noch spät in meinem Zimmer
Mir träumte, die Sonne glühte
Tod, dir zum Raube fiel eine Welt
Versank die Sonne still im Meere
Was nur dadrinnen der Graukopf macht?
Zur weissen Gans sprach einst vertraulich
Carmen Sylva
Flieg, Schifflein, flieg!
Ich halt' ein Stückchen Leder
Johann Ludwig Uhland
Da fliegt, als wir im Felde gehn
Da liegen sie alle die grauen Höh'n
Das ist der Tag des Herrn
Die Muse fehlt nicht selten
Ich bin so gar ein armer Mann
Ich tret in deinen Garten
Lösen sich die ird'schen Bande?
Sie war ein Kind vor wenig Tagen
Was stehst du so in stillem Schmerz
Wilhelm Weigand
Keine Rose darf ich pflücken
Paul Wertheimer
Du weißt, wir bleiben einsam: du und ich
Adolf Wilbrandt
Wie glänzt nun die Welt im Sonnenstrahl
Theodor Winkler
Ihr fragt, was Großes ich erdenke
August Wolf
Dies eine möcht' ich gerne wissen
Ernst Ziel
Du bist ein Kind und sollst es ewig bleiben

Egon Joseph Wellesz (1885-1974)
Hans Bethge
Der volle Mond steigt aus dem Meer herauf
Stefan George
Das ist ein Lied für dich allein
Fenster wo ich einst mit dir Abends
Im Morgentaun trittst du hervor
Im Windesweben war meine Frage
Kahl reckt der Baum im Winterdunst
Kreuz der Straße wir sind am End'

(Eleonore) Sophia Maria Fritscher Westenholz (1759-1838)
Ludwig Kosegarten
Ich lag auf grünen Matten
Friedrich von Matthisson
Hast du's in meinem Auge nicht gelesen

Hermann Hans Wetzler (1870-1943)
Johann Wolfgang von Goethe
Feiger Gedanken bängliches Schwanken
Karl Henckell
Deiner hellen Stimme fröhlicher Klang
Die Sonne sank. Noch schimmert
Lini Wetzler
Fallende Blätter, die Stund' um Stunde
Ich bin getrost, Stern meiner Seele

August Heinrich von Weyrauch (1788-1865)
Friedrich Gottlob Wetzel
Schon naht, um uns zu scheiden
Wenn die Rosen blühen, Hoffe, liebes Herz

Lothar Windsperger (1885-1935)
Friedrich Hölderlin
Einen vergänglichen Tag lebt' ich

Josef Venantius von Wöss (1863-1943)
Joseph von Eichendorff
Ist auch schmuck nicht mein Rößlein
Nacht ist wie ein stilles Meer, Lust und Leid

Hugo (Filip Jakob) Wolf (1860-1903)
Lord Byron
Keine gleicht von allen Schönen
Sonne der Schlummerlosen, bleicher Stern!

Adelbert von Chamisso
Wohl wandert' ich aus in trauriger Stund'
Joseph von Eichendorff
Ade, mein Schatz, du mocht'st mich nicht
Am Kreuzweg da lausche ich
Auf die Dächer zwischen blassen Wolken
Aufs Wohlsein meiner Dame
Bei dem angenehmsten Wetter
Bin ein Feuer hell, das lodert
Da fahr ich still im Wagen
Dein Wille, Herr, geschehe! Verdunkelt
Du liebe, treue Laute
Grüss euch aus Herzensgrund
Hörst du nicht die Quellen gehen
Ich geh durch die dunkeln Gassen
Ich ging bei Nacht einst über Land
Ich hab' ein Liebchen lieb recht von Herzen
Ist auch schmuck nicht mein Rösslein
Komm, Trost der Welt, du stille Nacht!
Mit meinem Saitenspiele, das schön geklungen
Nacht ist wie ein stilles Meer
So lass' herein nun brechen die Brandung
Soldat sein ist gefährlich
Studieren will nichts bringen
Über Wipfel und Saaten in den Glanz hinein
Vergeht mir der Himmel vor Staube schier
Wagen musst du und flüchtig erbeuten
Wandern lieb' ich für mein Leben
Weil jetzo alles stille ist und alle Menschen
Wenn Fortuna spröde tut
Wer auf den Wogen schliefe
Wer in die Fremde will wandern
Wie ein todeswunder Streiter
Wolken, wälderwärts gegangen
Zwischen Bergen, liebe Mutter
Emanuel Geibel
Ach, wie lang die Seele schlummert!
Alle gingen, Herz, zur Ruh
Bedeckt mich mit Blumen, ich sterbe vor Liebe
Dereinst, dereinst Gedanke mein
Die ihr schwebet um diese Palmen
Geh, Geliebter, geh jetzt!
Klinge, klinge, mein Pandero
Komm, o Tod, von Nacht umgeben
Mögen alle bösen Zungen
Mühvoll komm' ich und beladen
Schmerzliche Wonnen und wonnige Schmerzen
Seltsam ist Juanas Weise
Tief im Herzen trag' ich Pein
Und schläfst du, mein Mädchen
Wer that deinem Füsslein weh?
Wunden trägst du mein Geliebter
Johann Wolfgang von Goethe
Ach neige, du Schmerzenreiche
Ach, was soll der Mensch verlangen?
Ach, wer bringt die schönen Tage
Als ich auf dem Euphrat schiffte
Als ich noch ein Knabe war
An dem reinsten Frühlingsmorgen
An die Türen will ich schleichen
Bedekke deinen Himmel, Zeus
Bei dem Glanz der Abendröte
Das Beet, schon lokkert sichs in die Höh!
Das Wasser rauscht', das Wasser schwoll
Der du von dem Himmel bist
Der Strauß, den ich gepflücket
Die heiligen drei König mit ihrem Stern
Dies zu deuten bin erbötig!
Ein Blumenglöckchen vom Boden hervor
Es war ein fauler Schäfer
Feiger Gedanken, bängliches Schwanken
Geh! Gehorche meinen Winken
Großer Brahma! nun erkenn ich
Ha, ich bin der Herr der Welt!
Hätt ich irgend wohl Bedenken
Hans Adam war ein Erdenkloß
Heiss mich nicht reden, heiss mich schweigen
Hoch auf dem alten Turme
Ich armer Teufel, Herr Baron
Ich bin der wohlbekannte Sänger
Kennst du das Land, wo die Zitronen blühn
Komm, Liebchen, komm! umwinde mir
Lasset Gelehrte sich zanken und streiten
Lichtlein schwimmen auf dem Strome
Liebesqual verschmäht mein Herz
Lokken, haltet mich gefangen
Mit des Bräutigams Behagen
Mit Mädchen sich vertragen
Nicht Gelegenheit macht Diebe
Nur wer die Sehnsucht kennt
Ob der Koran von Ewigkeit sei?
Sie haben wegen der Trunkenheit
Singet nicht in Trauertönen
So lang man nüchtern ist
So lasst mich scheinen, bis ich werde
So wälz ich ohne Unterlaß
Trunken müssen wir alle sein!
Und frische Nahrung, neues Blut
Und morgen fällt Sankt Martins Fest
Was hör ich draussen vor dem Tor
Was in der Schenke waren heute
Was zieht mir das Herz so?

Wenn der uralte heilige Vater
Wenn ich dein gedenke, fragt mich gleich
Wenn zu der Regenwand Phöbus sich gattet
Wer nie sein Brot mit Tränen ass
Wer sich der Einsamkeit ergibt
Wie im Morgenglanze du rings mich anglühst
Wie sollt' ich heiter bleiben
Wo die Rose hier blüht, wo Reben um Lorbeer
Zwischen Weizen und Korn

Johann Christian Günther

Wenn des Mondes bleiches Licht

Friedrich Hebbel

Frau Amme, Frau Amme, das Kind ist erwacht!
Vöglein vom Zweig gaukelt hernieder
Vom Berg der Knab, der zieht hinab

Heinrich Heine

Aus meinen großen Schmerzen
Das ist ein Brausen und Heulen
Du bist wie eine Blume
Ernst ist der Frühling, seine Träume sind traurig
Es blasen die blauen Husaren
Es war ein alter König, sein Herz war schwer
Ich stand in dunkeln Träumen
Mädchen mit dem roten Mündchen
Mein Liebchen wir saßen beisammen
Mir träumte von einem Königskind
Mit schwarzen Segeln segelt mein Schiff
Sie haben heut' Abend Gesellschaft
Spätherbstnebel, kalte Träume
Sterne mit den goldnen Füßchen
Wenn ich in deine Augen seh
Wie des Mondes Abbild zittert
Wo ich bin, mich rings umdunkelt
Wo wird einst des Wandermüden

Karl Herloßsohn

Wenn die Schwalben heimwärts ziehn

Paul Heyse

Ach, des Knaben Augen sind mir so schön
Ach im Maien war's im Maien
Auch kleine Dinge können uns entzücken
Auf dem grünen Balcon
Benedeit die sel'ge Mutter
Bitt' ihn, o Mutter, bitte den Knaben
Blindes Schauen, dunkle Leuchte
Da nur Leid und Leidenschaft
Dass doch gemalt all' deine Reize wären
Deine Mutter, süsses Kind
Der Mond hat eine schwere Klag' erhoben
Die du Gott gebarst, du Reine
Du denkst mit einem Fädchen mich zu fangen
Du sagst mir, dass ich keine Fürstin sei
Eide, so die Liebe schwur
Ein Ständchen Euch zu bringen kam ich her
Führ mich, Kind, nach Bethlehem!
Gesegnet sei das Grün und wer es trägt!
Gesegnet sei, durch den die Welt entstund
Geselle, woll'n wir uns in Kutten hüllen
Heb' auf dein blondes Haupt
Herr, was trägt der Boden hier
Herz verzage nicht geschwind
Heut Nacht erhob ich mich um Mitternacht
Hoffährtig seid Ihr, schönes Kind
Ich esse nun mein Brod nicht trocken mehr
Ich fuhr über Meer, ich zog über Land
Ich hab' in Penna einen Liebsten wohnen
Ich liess mir sagen und mir ward erzählt
Ihr jungen Leute, die ihr zieht in's Feld
Ihr seid die Allerschönste
In dem Schatten meiner Locken
Köpfchen, Köpfchen, nicht gewimmert
Lass sie nur gehn, die so die Stolze spielt
Liebe mir im Busen zündet einen Brand
Man sagt mir, deine Mutter woll' es nicht
Mein Liebster hat zu Tische mich geladen
Mein Liebster ist so klein
Mein Liebster singt am Haus
Mir ward gesagt, du reisest in die Ferne
Nein, junger Herr, so treibt man's nicht
Nicht länger kann ich singen
Nun bin ich dein, du aller Blumen Blume
Nun lass uns Frieden schliessen
Nun wandre, Maria, nun wandre nur fort
O wär' dein Haus durchsichtig wie ein Glas
O wüsstest du, wie viel ich deinetwegen
Ob auch finstre Blicke glitten
Sagt ihm, dass er zu mir komme
Sagt, seid Ihr es, feiner Herr
Schon streckt' ich aus im Bett
Schweig' einmal still, du garst'ger Schwätzer
Selig ihr Blinden, die ihr nicht zu schauen
Sie blasen zum Abmarsch
Sterb' ich, so hüllt in Blumen meine Glieder
Trau nicht der Liebe, mein Liebster, gib Acht!
Treibe nur mit Lieben Spott
Und steht Ihr früh am Morgen auf
Und willst du deinen Liebsten sterben sehen
Verschling' der Abgrund meines Liebsten Hütte
Was für ein Lied soll dir gesungen werden
Was soll der Zorn, mein Schatz
Wehe der, die mir verstrickte meinen Geliebten!
Weint nicht, ihr Äuglein!
Wenn Du, mein Liebster, steigst

Wenn du mich mit den Augen streifst und lachst
Wenn du zu den Blumen gehst
Wer rief dich denn? wer hat dich herbestellt?
Wer sein holdes Lieb verloren
Wie lange schon war immer mein Verlangen
Wie soll ich fröhlich sein
Wie viele Zeit verlor ich, dich zu lieben!
Wir haben Beide lange Zeit geschwiegen
Wohl kenn' ich Eueren Stand

Edmund Hoefer
Glücklich, wer zum Liebchen zieht

Hoffmann von Fallersleben
Dunkel sind nun alle Gassen
Ja, die Schönst! ich sagt es offen
Über die Hügel und über die Berge hin
Wie oft schon ward es Frühling wieder

Johann Georg Jacobi
Wie Feld und Au so blinkend im Tau!

Gottfried Keller
Das Köhlerweib ist trunken
Du milchjunger Knabe, wie siehst du mich an?
Singt mein Schatz wie ein Fink
Tretet ein, hoher Krieger
Wandl' ich in dem Morgenthau
Wie glänzt der helle Mond so kalt und fern

Justinus Kerner
Zur Ruh', zur Ruh'! ihr müden Glieder

Theodor Körner
Alles wiegt die stille Nacht

Nikolaus Lenau
Als ein unergründlich Wonnemeer
Bin mit dir im Wald gegangen
Die Nacht ist finster, schwül und bang
Ein schlafend Kind! o still, o still!
Friedlicher Abend senkt sich aufs Gefilde
Horch, wie still es wird im dunklen Hain
Ich sah den Lenz einmal, erwacht
Nach langem Frost, wie weht die Luft so lind!
Nun ist es Herbst, die Blätter fallen
O wag' es nicht, mit mir zu scherzen
Sturm mit seinen Donnerschlägen
Trübe Wolken, Herbstesluft
Wie sehr ich Dein, soll ich Dir sagen?

Lenz Lorenzi
Wach' auf, erwache wieder

August Mahlmann
An Himmelshöh'n die Sterne geh'n

Friedrich von Matthisson
Ich denke dein, wenn durch den Hain

Michelangelo Buonarotti
Alles endet, was entstehet
Fühlt meine Seele das ersehnte Licht von Gott
Wohl denk' ich oft an mein vergang'nes Leben

Eduard Mörike
Am frisch geschnittnen Wanderstab
Anders wird die Welt mit jedem Schritt
Angelehnt an die Epheuwand
Auf ihrem Leibrösslein, so weiss
Bei Nacht im Dorf der Wächter rief: Elfe!
Bin jung gewesen, kann auch mitreden
Dein Liebesfeuer, ach Herr! wie theuer
Der Spiegel dieser treuen, braunen Augen
Derweil ich schlafend lag
Des Schäfers sein Haus
Des Wassermanns sein Töchterlein
Dir angetrauet am Altare
Drei Tage Regen fort und fort
Du bist Orplid, mein Land! das ferne leuchtet
Ein Tännlein grünet wo, wer weiss, im Walde
Eine Liebe kenn' ich, die ist treu
Einmal nach einer lustigen Nacht
Fragst du mich, woher die bange Liebe mir
Früh, wann die Hähne krähn
Frühling lässt sein blaues Band
Gelassen stieg die Nacht an's Land
Grausame Frühlingssonne, du weckst mich
Herr! schicke was du willt
Hier lieg' ich auf dem Frühlingshügel
Ich bin meiner Mutter einzig Kind
Ich hatt ein Vöglein, ach wie fein!
Im Weinberg auf der Höhe
Im Winterboden schläft, ein Blumenkeim
In aller Früh, ach, lang vor Tag
In ein freundliches Städtchen tret' ich ein
In grüner Landschaft Sommerflor
In poetischer Epistel ruft ein desperater Wicht
Kann auch ein Mensch des andern
Kein Schlaf noch kühlt das Auge mir
Kleine Gäste, kleines Haus
Lass, o Welt, o lass mich sein!
"Lebe wohl" Du fühlest nicht
O Woche, Zeugin heiliger Beschwerde!
Rosenzeit! wie schnell vorbei
Sausewind, Brausewind! dort und hier!
Schlaf! süsser Schlaf! obwohl dem Tod
Sehet ihr am Fensterlein dort
So ist die Lieb'! So ist die Lieb'!
Sohn der Jungfrau, Himmelskind!
Tochter des Walds, du Lilienverwandte
Tödtlich graute mir der Morgen
Unangeklopft ein Herr tritt Abends bei mir ein
Vom Berge was kommt dort um Mitternacht

Vor lauter hochadligen Zeugen
Warum, Geliebte, denk' ich dein
Was doch heut Nacht ein Sturm gewesen
Was im Netze? Schau einmal!
Wasch dich, mein Schwesterchen, wasch dich!
Wenn ich, von deinem Anschaun tief gestillt
Wenn meine Mutter hexen könnt
Wie heimlicher Weise ein Engelein leise
Zierlich ist des Vogels Tritt im Schnee

Ludwig Pfau
Wenn ich im stillen Friedhof geh'

Robert Reinick
Ach du klar blauer Himmel, und wie schön
Bald ist der Nacht ein End' gemacht
Hielt die allerschönste Herrin einst mein Herz
In dem Himmel ruht die Erde, Mond und Sterne
Kein Meister fällt vom Himmel
Komm in die stille Nacht! Liebchen
Reich' den Pokal mir schäumenden Weines voll
Schlaf' ein, schlaf' ein,, mein süsses Kind
Schneeglöckchen tut läuten!
Vom Berg hinabgestiegen
Wolken, die ihr nach Osten eilt
Zaubrer bin ich, doch was frommt es?

Otto Roquette
Du liebes Auge, willst dich tauchen

Friedrich Rückert
O süsse Mutter: ich kann nicht spinnen
So wahr die Sonne scheinet

Joseph Viktor von Scheffel
Kampfmüd' und sonnverbrannt
Schwingt euch auf, Posaunenchöre

William Shakespeare
Die Schwalbe, die den Sommer bringt

Julius Sturm
Über Nacht, über Nacht kommt still das Leid

Marianne von Willemer
Hoch beglückt in deiner Liebe
Nimmer will ich dich verlieren!

Heinrich Zschokke
Sei mir gegrüßt, o schöne Nacht

Vinzenz Zusner
Des Glöckleins Schall durchtönt das Tal

Anonymous
Der Frühhauch hat gefächelt
Es segeln die Wolken, weiß niemand wohin?
Golden lacht und glüht der Morgen
Ich bin wie andre Mädchen nicht

Felix Wolfes (1892-1971)

Alexander von Bernus
Schlaf ein! Die Nacht ist tief und weit

Rudolf Georg Binding
Alles stirbt. Auch die Freunde

Clemens Brentano
Einsamkeit, du stummer Bronnen

Wilhelm Busch
Rotkehlchen auf dem Zweige hupft

Richard Dehmel
Liegt eine Stadt im Tale, ein blasser Tag vergeht

Joseph von Eichendorff
Komm, Trost der Welt, du stille Nacht!

Albrecht Goes
Klein ist, mein Kind, dein erster Schritt

Manfred Hausmann
Qual über Qual ist uns gesetzt insgesamt
Wir befanden uns, so träumt' ich, wieder

Friedrich Hebbel
Dies ist ein Herbsttag, wie ich keinen sah!

Johann Gottfried Herder
Ein Traum ist unser Leben auf Erden hier

Hermann Hesse
Aus dunkler Brandung gährend
Eines Dichters Traumgerank mag sich
Einmal in Kindertagen ging ich die Wiese lang
Es führen über die Erde Strassen und Wege viel
Im Grase hingestreckt lausch' ich der Halme
Nachtwandler, tast' ich mich durch Wald
O reine, wundervolle Schau
O schau, sie schweben wieder
Seltsam, im Nebel zu wandern!
Über den Himmel Wolken ziehn
Was blickst du träumend ins verwölkte Land

Hugo von Hofmannsthal
Was ist die Welt? Ein ewiges Gedicht

Frederike Kempner
Wenn der holde Frühling lenzt

Conrad Ferdinand Meyer
Da mit Sokrates die Freunde tranken
Meine eingelegten Ruder triefen
Wer in der Sonne kämpft, ein Sohn der Erde

Eduard Mörike
Am langsamsten von allen Göttern wandeln wir
Es graut vom Morgenreif in Dämmerung
Im Nebel ruhet noch die Welt
Noch unverrückt, o schöne Lampe

Christian Morgenstern
Ein finstrer Esel sprach einmal
Ein Hecht, vom heiligen Anton bekehrt

Wolfgang Amadeus Mozart
Du wirst im Ehstand viel erfahren

Friedrich Nietzsche
An der Brükke stand jüngst ich in brauner Nacht

O Mensch, gib acht! Was spricht

Paul Pfitzner

Es waren einst zwei Brüder, die liebten sich

Wohl in der letzten Stunde

Franz Schober

In des Todes Feierstunde

Wilhelm von Scholz

Ich war erlöst, jetzt hab ich stark und leise

Georg Trakl

Am Abend, wenn die Glokken Frieden läuten

Dunkler Odem im grünen Gezweig

Gewaltig endet so das Jahr

Immer wieder kehrst du, Melancholie

Sonne, herbstlich dünn und zag

Paul Verlaine

Ich kam so fromm, ein Waisenkind

Josef Weinheber

Du, leicht und schön, aus Gottes Traum geboren

Stille Blume, erblasst unter herbstlichen Sternen

Stefan Zweig

Linder schwebt der Stunde Reigen

Volkslied

Es geht eine dunkle Wolk' herein

Es ist ein Schnee gefallen

Erich J. Wolff (1874-1913)

Charles Baudelaire

Tod, alter Kapitän, nun säum nicht lange!

Otto Julius Bierbaum

Aus dem Rosenstokke vom Grabe des Christ

Richard Dehmel

Drum sollst du dulden, Mensch

Eh' wir uns trennen konnten, o wie hielt

Es klagt im Dunklen irgendwo

Fest steht mein flammendes Gebot

Gib mir deine Hand, nur den Finger

Komm an mein Feuer mein Weib

Tora zu Eulenburg

Heissa, heia! Stosset an, seht

Verlangend dehntest du dich aus nach allem

Franz Evers

Die Sommernacht ist sanft und milde

Er sitzt am Weg und klopft die harten Steine

Emil Faktor

Der Frühling starb im Dufte der Syringen

Du bist mein Schicksal, das ich wild begehre

Glaub' es mir, jubelnde Kinderschar

Heute summte mir im Ohr stundenlang

Ich bin so müd' und weiß nicht mehr wovon

In der Seele ein Wachsen und Keimen

In tiefem Rausch hab' ich mein Glück gesegnet

Schön wie die Sünden bist du, Kind

Theodor Fontane

Alles still! es tanzt den Reigen Mondesstrahl

Hafis

Ach, wie süß, wie süß sie duftet!

Bittres mir zu sagen, denkst du

Ein solcher ist mein Freund

Entzükket dich ein Wunderhauch

Es werde Licht! So tönete der Ruf Gottes

Horch, hörst du nicht vom Himmel her

Meine Lebenszeit verstreicht

O hättest du, begrüßend des Lebens

O wie süß ein Duft von oben

Schön wie Thirza bist du

Stark wie der Tod ist die Liebe

Viel bin ich umhergewandert

Wie Melodie aus reiner Sphäre hör' ich

Wo ist der Ort, an dem du weilst?

Carl Hauptmann

Nacht... Nacht... in Nacht sanken wir

Friedrich Hölderlin

Ihr wandelt droben im Licht

Kurt Kamlah

Blasse Blüten neigen ihre duftende Pracht

Ich bin häßlich, liebe Mutter,

Silberne Mondesstrahlen glänzen

Karl Maria

Abendruhe liegt über dem Land

Michelangelo Buonarotti

An dieser Stelle war's, wo Herz

Bring' ich der Schönheit, da ich sie erblickt'

Da deiner Schönheit Glanz mich hat besiegt

Gemahnt dein Name mich an deine Züge

In schwerer Schuld nur, die sie dumpf bedrückt

Kleinodien, Zierat, Perlen und Korallen

Täuscht euch, ihr Augen, nicht

Wie soll den Mut ich finden

Mittler

Maria wollt' zur Kirche gehn

Christian Morgenstern

Aus silbergrauen Gründen tritt

Ein schwarzes Vögelein fliegt über die Welt

Nikolai

Zum Sterben bin i verliebet in di

Johann Ludwig Uhland

Ach Gott, wie weh tut Scheiden!

Maria, du Zarte! du bist ein Rosengarte

from Des Knaben Wunderhorn

Ach hartes Herz, laß dich doch eins erweichen

Blühe, liebes Veilchen, das so lieblich roch

Der süße Schlaf, der sonst stillt alles wohl

Du Dienerl, du netts, du liegst mir im Herz

Gold'ne Wiegen schwingen
Ich bin gen Baden zogen, zu löschen
Ich eß' nicht gerne Gerste
Ich hatt' nun mei Truschel ins Herz
Ich wollt', daß der verhindert mich
Mutter, ach Mutter! es hungert mich
Nach meiner Lieb' viel hundert Knaben trachten
Nachtigall, ich hör' dich singen
O Jesulein zart, das Kripplein ist hart
Recht wie ein Leichnam wandle ich umher
Soll ich denn sterben, bin noch so jung?
Wenn ich den ganzen Tag geführt hab'
Wer sehen will zween lebendige Brunnen
Volkslied
Es ist ein Ros entsprungen
Es ist ein Schnitter, der heißt Tod
Ich hab' die Nacht geträumet
Mein Muter mag mi net, und kein Schatz
Schönster Herr Jesu, Herrscher aller Enden
Ufm Berga da giht dar Wind

Philip Wolfrum (1854-1919)
Johann Wolfgang von Goethe
Der du von dem Himmel bist

Stefan Wolpe (1902-1972)
Friedrich Hölderlin
Ihr Wälder schön an der Seite
Komm und besänftige mir
Mit gelben Birnen hänget und voll
Wenn aus dem Leben kann ein Mensch
Wenn aus der Ferne, da wir geschieden sind

Franz Alfons Wolpert (1917-1978)
Friedrich Hölderlin
Du schweigst und duldest, und sie verstehn

Franz Wüllner (1832-1902)
Johann Wolfgang von Goethe
Lieb' um Liebe, Stund' um Stunde
Karl Immermann
Mein Liebe, mein' Lieb' ist ein Segelschiff
Hermann Lingg
Kalt und schneidend weht der Wind
Wenn etwas leise in dir spricht
Robert Reinick
Ich hab' dich geliebt, du ahntest es nicht
William Shakespeare
Komm herbei, komm herbei, Tod!

Erich Zeisl (1905-1959)
Victor Blüthgen
Ich war mal in dem Dorfe
Wilhelm Busch
Es flog einmal ein munt'res Fliegel
Es stand vor seines Hauses Tor ein Esel
Joseph von Eichendorff
Ich wandre durch die stille Nacht
Walther Eidlitz
Eine wilde Lokomotive schrie in der Nacht
Johann Wolfgang von Goethe
Es war ein fauler Schäfer
Arno Holz
Vor meinem Fenster singt ein Vogel
Gotthold Ephraim Lessing
Zankst du schon wieder, sprach Hans Lau
Hermann Lingg
Ein Wolkengebirg' umfließt die Sonne
Eduard Mörike
Derweil ich schlafend lag
Lily Rona
Die Augen fielen meinem Liebsten zu
Richard Schaukal
Ein Spielmann auf seiner Geige strich
Vergißmeinnicht hab' ich im Fichtenwald

Carl Friedrich Zelter (1758-1832)
Friederike Brun
Ich denke dein, wenn sich im Blüthenregen
Süßes Bild, schwebst mir vor
Johannes Falk
Thoms saß am hallenden See
Paul Gerhardt
Jedes Ding in jeder Sache, was mir träumet
Johann Wilhelm Ludwig Gleim
Erhalt uns den König
Ich hab' ein kleines Hüttchen nur
Johann Wolfgang von Goethe
Ach, dass die innre Schöpfungskraft
Ach! wer bringt die schönen Tage
Amor, nicht das Kind: der Jüngling
An dem reinsten Frühlingsmorgen
An die Türen will ich schleichen
Bei dem Glanze der Abendröthe
Da droben auf jenem Berge, da steh' ich
Das Wasser rauscht, das Wasser schwoll
Dem Schnee dem Regen, dem Wind entgegen
Der du von dem Himmel bist
Der Strauß, den ich gepflücket, grüße dich
Der Thürmer der schaut zu mitten der Nacht
Dir zu eröffnen mein Herz verlangt mich
Durch Feld und Wald zu schweifen
Ein Blumenglöckchen vom Boden hervor
Erst sitzt er eine Weile,i
Es ist ein Schuß gefallen! Mein!

Es war ein König in Thule
Freudvoll, freudvoll und Leidvoll
Füllest wieder Busch und Thal
Hab oft einen dummen düstern Sinn
Hat der alte Hexenmeister
Heiß mich nicht reden, heiß mich schweigen
Herz, mein Herz, was soll das geben?
Hoch auf dem alten Thurme
Ich denke dein, wenn mir der Sonne Schimmer
Ich ging im Walde, so vor mich bin
Ich hab' mein Sach auf nichts gestellt, Juche!
Ich habe geliebet, nun lieb ich erst recht!
Ich wollt' ich wär' ein Fisch
Im Felde schleich ich still und wild
In tausend Formen magst du dich verstekken
Kennst du das Land, wo die Citronen blühn
Mahadöh, der Herr der Erde, kommt herab
Meine Ruh ist hin, mein Herz ist schwer
Mich ergreift, ich weiß nicht wie
Nach Mittage saßen wir junges Volk im Kühlen
Nur wer die Sehnsucht kennt
O gieb, vom weichen Pfühle
So hab ich wirklich dich verloren?
Tage der Wonne kommt ihr so bald?
Trocknet nicht, trocknet nicht
Über allen Gipfeln ist Ruh
Über Tal und Fluß getragen ziehet rein
Uf'm Bergli bin i gesässe
Um Mitternacht ging ich, nicht eben gerne
Viele Gäste wünsch ich heut'
Von allen schönen Waaren, zum Markte
Was hör' ich draußen vor dem Thor
Wenn die Reben wieder blühen
Wer nie sein Brot mit Tränen aß
Wer reitet so spät, durch Nacht und Wind?
Wer sich der Einsamkeit ergiebt, ach!
Wie kommts, daß du so traurig bist
Wir singen und sagen vom Grafen so gern
Wo willst du kleines Bächlein hin
Zwischen Waizen und Korn,

Johann Gottfried Herder
Ach, könnt ich, könnte vergessen sie!

Janke
Begrüßet mit Tönen und Liedern den Tag

Friedrich Kind
Phöbus, mit lokkerem Zügel

Friedrich Klopstock
Im Frühlingsschatten fand ich sie

Ludwig Kosegarten
Meine Blüten sind zernagt

Caroline von der Lühe
Wenn im Hauch der Abend kühle

James Macpherson ("Ossian")
Um mich ist Nacht! Nacht! Verirret steh' ich

Friedrich von Matthisson
Die Flamme lodert, milder Schein
Laura betet! Engelharfen hallen Frieden Gottes
Wann in des Abends letztem Scheine
Wo der Mond mit bleichem Schimmer

Sophie Mereau
Es rauscht der Strom, es weht der Wind

Karl Müchler
In des Meeres kühle Wogen taucht die Sonn

"Rosemann" (Johann Klöntrup)
Der Garten des Lebens ist lieblich und schön

Friedrich von Schiller
Am Abgrund leitet der schwindliche Steg
Der Eichwald brauset, die Wolken ziehn
Nehmt hin die Welt! rief Zeus
So willst du treulos von mir scheiden
Vor seinem Löwengarten, das Kampfspiel

August Wilhelm von Schlegel
Wenn fremde Blikke wachsam uns umgeben

Georg Philipp Schmidt (von Lübeck)
Ich hab eine Wiege so schmuck und nett

Stephen Schütze
Warum ich bleibe, warum ich traurig bin?

Ludwig Tieck
Feldeinwärts flog ein Vögelein

Christoph August Tiedge
Wiedersehn! Wiedersehn! Endlich tönt dir

Johann Heinrich Voss
Das Tagewerk ist abgetan
Erwacht in neuer Stärke, begrüss' ich, Gott
Schwarz wie Nacht brausest du auf, Meer

Marianne von Willemer
Ach, um deine feuchten Schwingen

Julius Wilhelm Zincgref
Mein feines Lieb ist fern von mir

Anonymous
Blümchen der Demuth, unter dichten Blättern
Selig, o Mutter, wer stirbt!
Zieht die Lerch im Herbste fort
Zu meiner Laute Liebesklang, horch auf!

Alexander Zemlinsky (1871-1942)

Amaru
Sie hatte schüchtern zu ihm aufgesehen

Richard Beer-Hofmann
Schlaf, mein Kind, der Abendwind weht

Otto Julius Bierbaum
Ringelringelrosenkranz, ich tanz'

Victor Blüthgen
Es war ein niedlich' Zeiselein
Carl Busse
Hell jubeln die Geigen mit Kling und mit Klang
Richard Dehmel
Schmück dir das Haar mit wildem Mohn
Was will in deinen Augen mir
Joseph von Eichendorff
Zwei Musikanten ziehn daher
Franz Evers
Die blaue Nacht geht leuchtend über'n See
Oh, das Korn, das wogte so
Afanasij Fet
Ruhe, heilige Nacht! Dämmerig scheint
Otto Franz Gensichen
Unter blühenden Bäumen hab'
Stefan George
Gib ein Lied mir wieder
Zieh mit mir, geliebtes Kind, in die Wälder
Johann Wolfgang von Goethe
Der du von dem Himmel bist
Feiger Gedanken bängliches Schwanken
Schlange, halt stille! Halt stille, Schlange!
Um Mitternacht, wenn die Menschen
Zwischen Weizen und Korn
Ferdinand Gregorovius
Blaues Sternlein, du sollst schweigen
Briefchen schrieb und warf in den Wind ich
Fensterlein, nachts bist du zu
Ich gehe des Nachts, wie der Mond thut gehn
Klagen ist der Mond gekommen
Liebe Schwalbe, kleine Schwalbe
Paul Heyse
Ach, was bin ich aufgewacht?
Der Himmel hat keine Sterne
Ein Stündlein sind sie beisammen gewes't
Im Lenz, im Lenz, wenn Veilchen blühn zuhauf
Langston Hughes
Grollen die Tomtoms, rollen die Tomtoms
Spielt die Blues für mich
Jens Peter Jacobsen
Meine Braut führ' ich heim
Nacht ist es jetzt, und das Gestirn
Seht, es war einmal ein König
Und hat der Tag all seine Qual
Kalidasa
Beschwert von Blüten beugen sich
Der Duft nach Sandel, den die seidenen Fächer
Der Wind des Herbstes weht den feinen Duft
Jetzt ist die Zeit, die um die grünen Ränder
Nun liegen Kränze um die schönen Brüste
Otto von Leixner
Ich sitze manchen langen Tag
Detlev von Liliencron
Im Weizenfeld, im Korn und Mohn
Maienkätzchen, erster Gruß
Mit Trommeln und Pfeifen bin ich
Über eine Wiege schaukelt ein blauer
Thekla Lingen
Sieh', ich steh' vor deiner Thür, laß mich ein!
Maurice Maeterlinck
Allen weinenden Seelen, aller nahenden Schuld
Als ihr Geliebter schied
Die drei Schwestern wollten sterben
Die Mädchen mit den verbundenen Augen
Sie kam zum Schloß gegangen
Und kehrt er einst heim
Claude McKay
Dirnen und Burschen hört' ich Beifall rasen
Christian Morgenstern
Abendkelch voll Sonnenlicht
Auf braunen Sammetschuhen geht
Auf dem Meere meiner Seele
Da waren zwei Kinder, jung und gut
Du gabst mir deine Kette
Ein schwarzes Vögelein fliegt über die Welt
Ludwig Pfau
O Blätter, dürre Blätter! Wie trauert ihr so sehr!
O Sterne, goldene Sterne! Wohl scheint ihr
Julius von Rodenberg
Nun ruht und schlummert Alles
Karl Siebel
Es ist so still, als wär' es Schlafenszeit
Theodor Storm
Es ist ein Flüstern in der Nacht
Franz Werfel
Gibt's Straß' und Park, wo wir im Traum
Paul Wertheimer
Du weiche Nacht, o komm mich zu umfangen
In deiner Näh' ist mir so gut
Von Melodien, die mich umflieh'n
Anonymous
Wenn Nachts im Wald die Turteltaube klagt
from Des Knaben Wunderhorn
Leucht't heller als die Sonne
Will ich in mein Gärtlein gehn

Hermann Karl Josef Zilcher (1881-1948)
Ludwig Jacobowski
Ach unsre leuchtenden Tage glänzen
Detlev von Liliencron
Ich kann das Wort nicht vergessen
Wenn sanft du mir im Arme schliefst

Wir wandeln durch die stumme Nacht

Winfried (Petrus Ignatius) Zillig (1905-1963)

Johann Wolfgang von Goethe

Ach, was soll der Mensch verlangen?
Der du von dem Himmel bist
Die ihr Felsen und Bäume bewohnet
Euch bedaur' ich, unglücksel'ge Sterne
Früh, wenn Tal, Gebirg' und Garten
Ich denke dein, wenn mir der Sonne Schimmer
Trocknet nicht, trocknet nicht
Um Mitternacht, ich schlief, im Busen wachte
Weichet, Sorgen, von mir! Doch ach!
Wenn du dich im Spiegel besiehst

Friedrich Zipp (1914-)

from Des Knaben Wunderhorn

Es jagt ein Jäger wohlgemut
Es wollt' die Jungfrau früh aufstehn
Gar hoch auf jenem Berg allein
Ich weiß mir'n Mädchen hübsch und fein
Leucht't heller denn die Sonne
Nachtigall, ich hör dich singen
Wenn du zu mei'm Schätzel kommst, sag
Zu Koblenz auf der Brükken

Emilie Zumsteeg (1796-1857)

Aurnhammer

Kennst du das Blümchen auf der Au?

Karl Breidenstein

Was schimmert dort auf dem Berge so schön

Friederike Brun

Ich denke Dein! wenn sich im Blüthenregen

Elise Bürger

Goldene Sonne wie hehr sinkst du

Johann Georg Fischer

Wo fliehst du armes Blättchen hin

"Theodor Hell" (Karl G. Winkler)

Einsam? Nein, das bin ich nicht

Theodor Körner

Ich bin erwacht! Im Rosenschimmer strahlt mir
Singe in heiliger Nacht

Julius Krais

Dein Schlaf ist sanft wie dein Gemüt

Johann Philipp Karl Lohbauer

Der Fluren Grün, das Abendgold

Rudolf Magenau

Gott! wie herrlich glänzt der Abendhimmel

August Mahlmann

Was ist es das im Mutterschoose

Alois Schreiber

Was dich ergreift, wenn betend zu den Sternen

Ungern-Sternberg

Wer des Leidens Kelch geleeret

Anonymous

Am Oelberg weiß ich eine Stätte
Ich soll kein Lebewohl dir sagen
Stets sey es Frühling um dich
Vergangenheit in Luft gewebter Schleier

Johann Rudolf Zumsteeg (1760-1802)

*v. B**n*

Kommst spät du liebe Nachtigall!

J. F. A. B–r

Sorgt für die Zukunft! sorgt bei Zeiten!

Freidrich Bouterwek

Hüll in deinen Schattenmantel
Wirklich, wirklich bist du schon verschwunden

Gottfried August Bürger

Ich habe was Liebes, das hab ich zu lieb
Im Garten des Pfarrers von Taubenhain
Knapp', sattle mir mein Dänenroß

Christian Karl Buri

Als noch in jener alten Zeit
Schwand nicht mit Pfeilesschnelle

Matthias Claudius

Friede sei um diesen Grabstein her
Ich war erst sechzehn Sommer alt
Schön röthlich die Kartoffeln sind
Weit von meinem Vaterlande
Wir Vögel singen nicht egal

Carl Philipp Conz

Neu geschmückt lacht die Natur

Franz Cordes

Hätt' ich nimmer Sie gesehn

Johann von Döhring

Wie so schmachtend, glücklich Weibchen

Edward

Eile auf der Morgenröthe Flügeln

Magdalena Philippine Engelhard

Ach, die entzückenden Töne der Saiten
Du blickst herab und scheinst zu fragen

v. G.

Umflattre mir des liebsten Mädchens Wangen

G.

Sanft, wie deine Seele, Lotte

Heinrich Wilhelm von Gerstenberg

Darachna! komm, mein Wunsch, mein Lied!
Stillen Geists will ich dir flehen!

Johann Wilhelm Ludwig Gleim

Ob ich dich liebe weiss ich nicht

Johann Wolfgang von Goethe

Hat der alte Hexenmeister
Heiss mich nicht reden, heiss mich schweigen

Ich kenn' ein Blümlein Wunderschön
Über Thal und Fluss getragen
Wenn die Reben wieder blühen
Christian Gottlieb Goez
Still und ruhig ist des Todes Schlummer
Friedrich Wilhelm Gotter
Ach! was ist die Liebe für ein süsses Ding!
Georg August von Griesinger
Es grünten die Bäume, es dufteten fein
Friedrich von Hagedorn
Der Uhu, der Kauz und zwo Eulen
Gottlob David Hartmann
Eures Sophrons Seele, Freunde
Johann Christoph Haug
Ach, der Tag – wie so lang! und mein Herz
Du kömmst vom Kloster Walsingham
Hold bin ich einer Holden
Hold lächelten die Maienhoren
Im Sonnenschimmer, in Luna's flimmer
Könnt ihr die Göttin Freude zwingen
Komm, aller Wesen Freude!
Mädchen und Jünglinge, Männer und Frauen
Nichts rundum erforschen des Endlichen Blikke
Noch sass im schwarzen Kleide
O Geliebte! dein vergessen – nein, bei Gott!
Rings walten Todesstille, und Schlaf
Schauet, Priester! schauet, Laien!
Schön Klare, zwanzig Sommer alt
Solch ein göttliches Vergnügen
Vertraue mir, Yoduno! o sage was dir ist
Vor allen Leinster Schönen pries
Wie trübst du, Geliebter! wie trübst du
Wohl alle Gedanken des Herzens vereine ich
Wohlauf! im trauten Reih'n
Amalie von Helvig-Imhof
Als vom Schlummer leis beschlichen
Lasset die Rosenumkränzeten Stunden
Johann Gottfried Herder
Gott des Schlafes, Freund der Ruh
[David Friedrich?] Herrmann
Für Maria, meines Lebens Leben
Ludwig Hölty
Dein Silber schien durch Eichengrün
Wo bist du Bild das vor mir stand
Friedrich Wilhelm von Hoven
O die du rund, wie meiner Väter Schild
August Wilhelm Iffland
Ein Gott, ein wahrer Gott ist nur
Heilig ist mir Dankbarkeit!
Liebe, die sonst stets mit Myrten krönet
Johann Georg Jacobi
Da wo die Tausendschönchen blühn
Friedrike Magdalena Jerusalem
O Elise, nicht nur für die Freuden
Friedrich August Kleinschmidt
Wär' ich ein muntres Vögelein
Friedrich Klopstock
Dein süsses Bild, o Lida!
Zeit, Verkündigerin der besten Freuden
Ludwig Kosegarten
Durch Nacht zum Licht!
Ich lag auf grünen Matten
O Abendsonn', o Holde, woher so bleich
Schöne Himmelssonne, mild und hold und hehr
Schwellen nicht Seufzer, meine süsse Ida
Theures Mädchen, wenn ein andrer Himmel
Tiefe Feyer schauert um die Welt
Was ist es, das die Seele füllt?
Wie erscholl der Gang des lauten Heers
Wie wohl ist mir im Dunkeln!
August von Kotzebue
Wir weichen Sklavenbrod in bittre Thränen ein!
August Heinrich Julius Lafontaine
Der Morgen glüht, die Rose blüht
Stille Thränen liebt mein Herz
Gottlieb von Leon
Ein blondiges Mägdelein, rosig und zart
Sobald Damötas Chloen sieht
Johann Philipp Karl Lohbauer
Oft in meiner Kindheit süssen Träumen
Wo lebt' ich glücklicher verborgen
Martin Luther
Wer nicht liebt Weib, Wein und Gesang
August Mahlmann
Allah giebt Licht in Nächten
Als mein Leben voll Blumen hieng
Die Quelle rauscht, die Mükke schwirrt
Gott sendet Licht in Nächten
Ich wand mir einst einen Veilchenkranz
Wo kommst du her, so bleich und blass
Wort des Trostes, o wie schön tönst du
Friedrich von Matthisson
Auch des Edlen schlummernde Gebeine
Der Abend schleiert Flur und Hain
Der Dämmrung Schein durchblinkt den Hain
Durch Fichten am Hügel, durch Erlen am Bach
Ich denke dein, wann durch den Hain
Mädchen entsiegelten, Brüder! die Flaschen
Stern der Liebe! bleich und trübe
Wo durch dunkle Buchengänge

Moses Mendelssohn
Der Ewige segnet der Frommen Tage
Friedrich Ludwig Wilhelm Meyer
Bleich flimmert in stürmender Nacht
Johann Martin Miller
Schlaf, Schwester, sanft im Erdenschoos!
Was frag' ich viel nach Geld und Gut
Johann Jakob Mnioch
Wohlauf zum frohen Rundgesang
Friedrich Müller
Wo irr' ich um des Meeresstrand
Karl Ludwig von Münchhausen
Es wächst ein Blümchen irgendwo
A.v.N
Was steht ihr am Wege so müssig
Martin Opitz
Auf, auf, wer deutsche Freiheit liebet
Jezzund kömmt die Nacht herbei
Christian Adolf Overbeck
Preis ihm, der alle Dinge mit unerforschter Kraft
Warum bin ich noch so klein?
Samuel Christian Pape
Das Fischermädchen harret am Ufer auf und ab
Wohl an dem Rasenhügel hin
Gottlieb Conrad Pfeffel
Zween Mönche von des Indus Strand
Karl Friedrich von Reinhardt
In verschwundnen Rosentagen
Georg Karl Alex. Richter
Kennst du den Fluss
Johann von Salis-Seewis
Das Grab ist tief und stille, und schauderhaft
Seht! wie die Tage sich sonnig verklären!
Friedrich von Schiller
Der Eichwald brauset, die Wolken ziehn
Freude! schöner Götterfunken!
Frisch athmet des Morgens lebendiger Hauch
Hör' ich das Pförtchen nicht gehen?
Laura, Welt und Himmel weggeronnen
Lebt wohl ihr Berge, ihr geliebten Triften
O Dank diesen freundlich grünen Bäumen
Ritter, treue Schwesterliebe
Seht! da sitzt er auf der Matte aufrecht
Wohl auf Kameraden, aufs Pferd, aufs Pferd!
Johann Friedrich Schlotterbeck
Hört! ich hatt' einmal ein Blümchen
Siegfried Schmid(t)
Wie klingt's so bänglich drüben?
Ludwig Albrecht Schubart
Horch, grausig heult draussen
"Selmar" (Karl Brinckmann)
Vergiss mein nicht! so lispelt Dir
William Shakespeare
Das arme Kind! sie sass und sang
Der Britte ist der Stern der Nationen
Sie senkten ihn in kalten Grund hinab
Stoss an Kamerad: es lebe der Soldat!
Woran erkenn' ich deinen Freund
Tobias George Smollet
Leb wohl du Strom, so sanft und schön
Dietrich Ernst von Spiegel
Vor Pavia hat Herr Paliss den Geist
Anton Matthias Sprickmann
Es waren, es waren einst glückliche Stunden
Stolberg-Stolberg
Ich hab' ein Bächlein funden
Ich sehe mit Schmerzen, du kennest die Kerzen
In der Väter Hallen ruhte Ritter Rudolphs
Wenn Aurora früh mich grüsst
Vicomte de Wargemont
Herr Puff, an Geld und Jahren reich
Schön, wie die Rose, blüht der Mädchen
Theresen lieb' ich, ist das Sünde?
Christian Weisse
Warum, geliebtes Veilchen, blühst du
Friedrich August Clemens Werthes
Allzulange, Wiederhall, tönst du mich
Die Lämmlein springen! die Vögelein singen!
Es war ein Winterabend und wehte bitter kalt
Komm in den Wald! komm an den Fels!
Matt erstirbt der Hoffnung letzter Schimmer
Noch hörte mich die Mitternacht
O! seht uns arme Kinder ziehn
Schlummre Knabe! um uns her tobt
Wir werden Staub und Asche zu bald seyn
Ludwig Karl Eberhard von Wildungen
Auf, ihr Brüder, auf zum Jagen!
Karl Ludwig Woltmann
Der Buhle sitzt und ächzet traurig
Fräulein von X
Gleich der Rose welk' ich hin
Karl Friedrich Bernhard Zinkernagel
Alles was mich hier umringt, sagt mir
Anonymous
Du ringst, o Mensch! vergebens
Komm Schwester zu den Ufern
Lebhaft hab ichs oft empfunden
Luna blickt von ihrem Thron schmachtend
Senk dich, o Gram, mit deinen Fantasien tief
Was gleichet der Lust, die im Busen mir lebt
Wie so trüb, Slimora du!
Zum Kranz pflückt' ich einst Rosen

Bibliographies

1. Indexes of Settings of Individual Poets

This is a selected list of some useful resources for those who would like more extensive indexes of musical settings of these particular poets. Though they were not used as primary sources for the contents of the current volume, they are interesting and valuable books for anyone researching various song settings.

Johann Wolfgang von Goethe

Willi Schuh. *Goethe-Vertonungen. Ein Verzeichnis.* Zürich: Artemis Verlag, 1952.

Werner-Joachim Düring. *Erlkönig-Vertonungen. Eine historische und systematische Untersuchung.* Kölner Beiträge zur Musikforschung. Herausgegeben von Heinrich Hüschen. Band LXIX. Regensburg: Gustav Bosse Verlag, 1972.

Heinrich Heine

Dichterliebe: Heinrich Heine im Lied. Ein Verzeichnis der Vertonungen von Gedichten Heinrich Heines zusammengestellt zum 175. Geburtstag des Dichters. Hamburg: Hamburger Öffentliche Bücherhallen Musikbücherei, 1972.

Günter Metzner. *Heine in der Musik: Bibliographie der Heine-Vertonungen in Zwölf Bänden.* Tutzing: Hans Schneider, 1989.

Friedrich Hölderlin

Gerhard Schuhmacher. *Geschichte und Möglichkeiten der Vertonung von Dichtungen Friedrich Hölderlins.* Forschungsbeiträge zur Musikwissenschaft. Herausgegeben vom Gustav Bosse Verlag. Band XVIII. Regensburg: Gustav Bosse Verlag, 1967.

Eduard Mörike

Hans-Joachim Erwe. *Musik nach Eduard Mörike. Teil 2: Ein bibliographisches Verzeichnis.* Hamburger Beiträge zur Musikwissenschaft. Herausgegeben von Constantin Floros. Band 35. Hamburg: Verlag der Musikalienhandlung Karl Dieter Wagner, 1987.

Friedrich Rückert

Gernot und Stefan Demel. *Verzeichnis der Rückert-Vertonungen.* 200 Jahre: Friedrich Rückert, 1788-1866, Dichter und Gelehrter. Herausgegeben von Jürgen Erdmann. Coburg: Landesbibliothek Coburg, Stadt Coburg, und Landkreis Coburg, 1988.

2. Biographical sources

These are the major sources of biographical data for the poets and composers found in this volume. It is by no means an exhaustive list of every book consulted for the project, as many of the artists mentioned here refused to give up their Lebensdaten or even their identities without a considerable struggle. But each of the following volumes or sets is remarkable for the amount of pertinent and ready information it contains.

Brockhaus Enzyklopädie. Siebzehnte völlig neu bearbeitete Auflage des Grossen Brockhaus. Wiesbaden: F. A. Brockhaus, 1966-1981.

Franz Brümmer. *Lexikon der deutschen Dichter und Prosaisten vom Beginn des 19. Jahrhunderts bis zur Gegenwart.* Bearbeitet von Franz Brümmer. Sechste völlig neu bearbeitete und stark vermehrte Auflage. Leipzig: Philipp Reclam jun., 1913. Reprint. Nendeln / Liechtenstein: Kraus Reprints, 1975.

Aaron I. Cohen. *International Encyclopedia of Women Composers, second edition.* New York: Books and Music, 1987.

Deutscher Biographischer Index. Herausgegeben von Willi Gorzny. Bearbeitet von Hans-Albrecht Koch, Uta Koch, und Angelika Koller. München: K. G. Saur, 1986.

Anneliese Dühmert. *Von wem ist das Gedicht? Eine bibliographische Zusammenstellung aus 50 deutschsprachigen Anthologien.* Berlin: Haude und Spenersche Verlagsbuchhandlung, 1969?

Karl Goedeke. *Grundrisz zur Geschichte der deutschen Dichtung aus den Quellen, zweite Auflage.* Dresden: Verlag von L. S. Ehlermann, 1884-1966

Otto J. Groeg, editor. *Who's Who in Literature, 1st Edition.* Wörthsee: Who's Who – Book & Publishing, 1979.

The New Grove Dictionary of Music and Musicians. Stanley Sadie, editor. London: Macmillan Publishers Limited, 1980.

Internationale Bibliographie der Zeitschriftenliteratur aus allen Gebieten des Wissens. Register der Schlagwörter 1975-1990. Herausgegeben von Otto und Wolfram Zeller. Osnabrück: Felix Dietrich Verlag, 1991.

Wilhelm Kosch. *Deutsches Literatur-Lexicon.* Biographisch-Bibliographisches Handbuch begründet von Wilhelm Kosch. Dritte, völlig neu bearbeitete Auflage. Bern: Francke Verlag, 1968–.

Die Musik in Geschichte und Gegenwart; allgemeine Enzyklopädie der Musik. Unter Mitarbeit zahlreicher Musikforscher des In- und Auslandes, herausgegeben von Friedrich Blume. Kassel: Bärenreiter Verlag, 1949-1986.

Neue deutsche Biographie. Herausgegeben von der Historischen Kommission bei der Bayerischen Akademie der Wissenschaften. Berlin: Duncker und Humblot, 1953–.

3. Musical Sources

These are the sources for information given about the songs listed in this index. Most are scores, but there are also critical studies, dissertations, recordings, and indexes of individual composers' works. These latter are occasionally used as a shorthand entry where listing the publication data for individual opus numbers would take up an extraordinary amount of space—as, for example, in the case of Robert Franz, where Boonin's *Index* replaces mention of 43 separate publications, all but one of which I have been able to locate.

Franz Abt. *25 Kinderlieder*. London: Augener & Co., 1870. Reprint. New York: Classical Vocal Reprints, 1993?

Franz Abt. *Abt-Album. Sechzehn ausgewählte Lieder für eine Singstimme mit Klavier-Begleitung*. Neuausgabe von Dr. L. Benda. Braunschweig: Henry Litolff's Verlag, [n.d.].

Franz Abt. *Abt-Album. Ausgewählte Lieder für eine Singstimme mit Klavierbegleitung von Franz Abt*. Leipzig: C. F. W. Siegel's Musikalienhandlung, 1873. Reprint. New York: Classical Vocal Reprints, 1992?

Eugen d'Albert. *Fünf Lieder, Opus 17*. Leipzig: C. F. Peters, 1898? Reprint. Huntsville, Texas: Recital Publications, 1982.

Eugen d'Albert. *Vier Lieder, Opus 22*. Leipzig: E. W. Fritzsch, 1900? Reprint. Huntsville, Texas: Recital Publications, 1983.

Eugen d'Albert. *Fünf Lieder nach Gedichten von Detlev von Liliencron und Fritz Rassow, Opus 27*. Berlin: Bote und Bock, 1904.

Eugen d'Albert. *Sieben Lieder im Volkston aus Des Knaben Wunderhorn. Opus 28*. Berlin: Bote und Bock, 1904? Reprint. Huntsville, Texas: Recital Publications, 1992.

Eugen d'Albert. *Fünf Lieder, Opus 9*. Berlin: Bote und Bock. Reprint. Huntsville, Texas: Recital Publications, 1983.

Frances Allitsen. *Acht Gedichte von Heinrich Heine*. New York: G. Schirmer, 1900? Reprint. Huntsville, Texas: Recital Publications, 1985.

Donna K. Anderson. *The Works of Charles T. Griffes: A Descriptive Catalogue*. Studies in Musicology, No.68. George Buelow, Series Editor. Ann Arbor: UMI Research Press, 1983.

Margarete Ansion and Irene Schlaffenberg. *Das Wiener Lied von 1778 bis Mozarts Tod*. Denkmäler der Tonkunst in Österreich, vol. 54. Graz: Akademische Druck- und Verlagsanstalt, 1960.

Conrad Ansorge. *Acht Lieder für eine Singstimme und Klavier, Opus 10*. Berlin: Challier, 1895-96? Reprint. Huntsville, Texas: Recital Publications, 1986.

Conrad Ansorge. *Fünf Lieder, Opus 17. Nach Dichtungen von Richard Dehmel*. Berlin: Eisoldt und Rohkrämer, 1904. Reprint. Huntsville, Texas: Recital Publications, 1991.

Hans Erich Apostel. *Drei Gesänge, Opus 15, aus "Die Lieder von Traum und Tod" von Stefan George*. Wien: Ludwig Doblinger, 1963.

Bettine von Arnim. *Five Lieder by a friend of Beethoven and Goethe*. Edited by Shoshana Shay. Bryn Mawr, Pennsylvania: Hildegard Publications, 1994.

Ernst Bacon. *Ten Songs*. San Francisco: Ernst Bacon, 1928. Reprint. New York: Classical Vocal Reprints, 1992.

Raymond Arthur Barr. *"Carl Friedrich Zelter: A Study of the Lied in Berlin during the Late Eighteenth and Early Nineteenth Centuries."* Ph.D diss., University of Wisconsin, 1968.

Moritz Bauer. *Zwei Lieder für tiefe Stimme mit begleitung des Pianoforte*. München: Alfred Schmid Nachfolger.

Ludwig van Beethoven. *Erlkönig. Gedicht von Goethe.* Nach einer Skizze von Ludwig van Beethoven ausgeführt von Reinhold Becker. Leipzig: J. Schuberth & Co., 1897.

Hermann Behn. *Vier Lieder für eine Singstimme*. Leipzig: Fr. Kistner, [n.d.]. Reprint. Huntsville, Texas: Recital Publications, 1983.

Hermann Behn. *Sieben Lieder für eine Frauenstimme mit Begleitung des Pianoforte, Opus 1*. Leipzig: Fr. Kistner, [n.d.]. Reprint. Huntsville, Texas: Recital Publications, 1994.

Hermann Behn. *Fünf Gesänge für eine mittlere Stimme mit Begleitung des Pianoforte, Opus 2*. Leipzig: Fr. Kistner, [n.d.]. Reprint. Huntsville, Texas: Recital Publications, 1994.

Hermann Behn. *Fünf Gesänge für eine Baritonstimme mit Begleitung des Pianoforte, Opus 3.* Leipzig: Fr. Kistner, [n.d.]. Reprint. Huntsville, Texas: Recital Publications, 1994.

Hermann Behn. *Mädchenlieder. Drei Gedichte für eine hohe Frauenstimme mit Begleitung des Pianoforte, Opus 4.* Leipzig: Fr. Kistner, [n.d.]. Reprint. Huntsville, Texas: Recital Publications, 1994.

Hermann Behn. *Vier Gedichte von Conrad Ferdinand Meyer für eine mittlere Singstimme mit Begleitung des Pianoforte, Opus 5.* Leipzig: Fr. Kistner, [n.d.]. Reprint. Huntsville, Texas: Recital Publications, 1994.

Hermann Behn. *Fünf Gedichte von Conrad Ferdinand Meyer für eine Baritonstimme mit Begleitung des Pianoforte, Opus 7.* Leipzig: Fr. Kistner, [n.d.]. Reprint. Huntsville, Texas: Recital Publications, 1994.

Hermann Behn. *Vier Gedichte von Conrad Ferdinand Meyer für eine Baritonstimme mit Begleitung des Pianoforte, Opus 8.* Leipzig: Fr. Kistner, [n.d.]. Reprint. Huntsville, Texas: Recital Publications, 1994.

Hermann Behn. *Fünf Gedichte von Conrad Ferdinand Meyer für eine mittlere Singstimme mit Begleitung des Pianoforte, Opus 9.* Leipzig: Fr. Kistner, [n.d.]. Reprint. Huntsville, Texas: Recital Publications, 1994.

Alban Berg. *Sieben frühe Lieder.* Wien: Universal Edition, 1928.

Alban Berg. *Jugendlieder Band 1 und 2.* Wien: Universal Edition, 1985 and 1987.

Alban Berg. *Vier Lieder, Opus 2.* Berlin: Schlesinger'sche Buch und Musikhandlung, 1928.

Alban Berg. *Schließe mir die Augen beide.* Wien: Universal Edition, 1955.

Gerald Hugh Tyrwhitt-Wilson, Baron Berners. *Lord Berners, 1883-1950, The Collected Vocal Music.* London: Chester Music, 1982.

Günter Bialas. *O Miserere: Vier Gesänge nach Gedichten von Heinrich Heine für Bariton und Klavier.* Kassel und Basel: Bärenreiter Verlag, 1983.

Günter Bialas. *Überblickt man die Jahre. Fünf Lieder für Tenor und Klavier nach Gedichten von Gottfried Benn.* Kassel und Basel: Bärenreiter Verlag, 1989.

Julius Bittner. *Sechzehn Lieder von Liebe, Treue, und Ehre, von Julius Bittner, Heft I-IV. Dichtungen vom Komponisten.* Wien: Universal Edition, 1923.

Boris Blacher. *Drei Chansons aus Shakespeares Romeo und Juliet, für Gesang und Klavier.* Wien: Universal Edition, 1963.

Boris Blacher. *Vier Lieder nach Texten von Friedrich Wolf, Opus 25.* Berlin: Bote und Bock, 1947.

Carl Bohm. *Lieder Album.* Berlin: N. Simrock, 1887?

Joseph M. Boonin. *An Index to the Solo Songs of Robert Franz.* Music Indexes and Bibliographies, No. 4; George R. Hill, General Editor. Hackensack, New Jersey: Joseph Boonin, Inc, 1970.

Aleksandr Borodin. *Romansi y Pesni.* Edited by Paul Lamm. Moscow, 1967.

Johannes Brahms. *Lieder und Gesänge für eine Singstimme mit Klavierbegleitung I-IV.* Sämtliche Werke; Ausgabe der Gesellschaft der Musikfreunde in Wien. Leipzig: Breitkopf und Härtel, 1926.

Johannes Brahms. *Die Müllerin, Liedfragment für Sopran und Klavier. Text von Adelbert von Chamisso.* Ergänzt und herausgegeben von Joachim Draheim. Wiesbaden: Breitkopf und Härtel, 1983.

Johannes Brahms. *Duette für zwei Singstimmen und Klavier, Opus 20, 61, 66, 75, Band I.* Frankfurt: C. F. Peters.

Johannes Brahms. *Quartette für vier Solostimmen mit Klavierbegleitung.* Herausgegeben von Kurt Soldan. Frankfurt: C. F. Peters.

Johannes Brahms. *Rhapsodie, Opus 53 für Alt, Männerchor, und Orchester, Klavierauszug. Fragment aus Goethes "Harzreise im Winter."* Frankfurt: C. F. Peters.

Johannes Brahms. *Johannes Brahms Sämtliche Werke.* Ausgabe der Gesellschaft der Musikfreunde in Wien. Wiesbaden: Breitkopf und Härtel.

Johannas Brahms. *Zigeunerlieder für vier Singstimmen und Klavier.* Herausgegeben von Kurt Soldan. Frankfurt: C. F. Peters.

Reiner Bredemeyer. *Die Winterreise: Gedichte aus den hinterlassenen Papieren eines reisenden Waldhornisten von Wilhelm Müller, für Bariton, Horn und Klavier, 1984.* Leipzig: VEB Deutscher Verlag für Musik, 1987.

Bernhard Theodor Breitkopf. *Neue Lieder in Melodien gesetzt von B. T. Breitkopf.* Leipzig: Bernhard Christoph Breitkopf und Sohn, 1770. Reprint. Hildesheim: Gerstenberg-Verlag, 1981.

Benjamin Britten. *Sechs Hölderlin Fragmente, Opus 61*. London: Boosey and Hawkes, 1963.

Rudolf Brömel. *Hermann Hesse Lieder für Gesang und Klavier*. Berlin: Richard Birnbach.

Ingeborg von Bronsart. *Sechs Gedichte von Friedrich Bodenstedt mit Begleitung des Pianoforte*. Leipzig: C. F. Kahnt, [n.d.]. Reprint. Huntsville, Texas: Recital Publications, 1983.

Ingeborg von Bronsart. *Fünf Gedichte von Ernst von Wildenbruch für eine Singstimme mit Begleitung des Pianoforte, Opus 16*. Breslau: Julius Hainauer, [n.d.]. Reprint. Huntsville, Texas: Recital Publications, 1983.

Ingeborg von Bronsart. *Sechs Lieder des Mirza-Schaffy von Friedrich Bodenstedt für eine Singstimme mit Begleitung des Pianoforte, Opus 8*. Leipzig: C. F. Kahnt, [n.d.]. Reprint. Huntsville, Texas: Recital Publications, 1983.

Max Bruch. *Vier Lieder für eine Singstimme mit Begleitung des Pianoforte componiert von Max Bruch, Opus 15*. Leipzig: Breitkopf und Härtel, [n.d.]. Reprint. Huntsville, Texas: Recital Publications, 1983.

Max Bruch. *Bruch-Album. 24 ausgewählte Lieder für eine Singstimme mit Klavierbegleitung. (Opus 17, Heft II und III; Opus 33)*. Leipzig: C. F. W. Siegel's Musikalienhandlung, [n.d.]. Reprint. Huntsville, Texas: Recital Publications, 1992.

Max Bruch. *Lieder und Gesänge aus Paul Heyse's Erzählung "Siechentrost," mit Begleitung von Klavier und Sologeige, componiert von Max Bruch, Opus 54*. Leipzig: Breitkopf und Härtel, 1891? Reprint. Huntsville, Texas: Recital Publications, 1986.

Max Bruch. *Fünf Lieder für Baryton componiert von Max Bruch, Opus 59*. Brussels: Schott Frères, 1892? Reprint. Huntsville, Texas: Recital Publications, 1983.

Anton Bruckner. *Im April (E. Geibel); für eine Singstimme mit Pianofortebegleitung componirt und Fräulein Helene Hofmann zugeeignet von Anton Bruckner*. Wien: Ludwig Doblinger, 1979 (1898).

Hugo Brückler. *Sieben Gesänge*. Dresden: L. Hoffarth, 187-? Reprint. Huntsville, Texas: Recital Publications, 1984.

Ignaz Brüll. *Sechs Gesänge nach Dichtungen von Heinrich Heine, Opus 5, vol.1*. Wien: J. P. Gotthard, [n.d.]. Reprint. Huntsville, Texas: Recital Publications, 1986.

Ignaz Brüll. *Drei Gesänge für eine Singstimme mit Begleitung des Pianoforte, Opus 5, vol.2*. Wien: J. P. Gotthard, [n.d.]. Reprint. Huntsville, Texas: Recital Publications, 1986.

Ignaz Brüll. *Drei Gesänge für eine Singstimme mit Begleitung des Pianoforte, Opus 5, vol.3*. Wien: J. P. Gotthard, [n.d.]. Reprint. Huntsville, Texas: Recital Publications, 1986.

August Bungert. *Bungert-Album. Lieder und Gesänge, Band 4 und 5*. Berlin: Friedrich Luckhardt, 1889-1891.

August Bungert. *An eine schöne Frau: Liebesbriefe in Liedern am Pianoforte von August Bungert, Opus 26*. Berlin: Friedrich Luckhardt, 1891.

Norbert Burgmüller. *Ausgewählte Lieder und Gesänge* (Recording), Mitsuko Shirai, mezzo., Hartmut Höll, piano. Detmold: Dabringhaus und Grimm, 1986.

Willy Burkhard. *Frage. Ein Liederzyklus nach Gedichten von Lenau, Eichendorff, Dehmel, Spitteler, Fankhauser, Opus 9 für tiefe Stimme*. Kassel und Basel: Bärenreiter Verlag, 1971.

Peter Cornelius. *Einstimmige Lieder und Gesänge mit Pianofortebegleitung*. Musikalische Werke. Erste Gesamtausgabe im Auftrage seiner Familie, herausgegeben von Max Hasse. Leipzig: Breitkopf und Härtel, 1905?

Peter Cornelius. *Mehrstimmige Lieder und Gesänge: Duette, Männerchöre, Gemischte Chöre*. Musikalische Werke. Erste Gesamtausgabe im Auftrage seiner Familie, herausgegeben von Max Hasse. Leipzig: Breitkopf und Härtel, 1905?

Cesar Cui. *Izbrannye Romansy dlia golosa s fortepiano*. Moscow: Muzyka, 1969.

Friedrich Curschmann. *Favorite Songs with Pianoforte Accompaniment*. Newly revised by Ed. Kremser. Wien: Universal Edition.

Friedrich Curschmann. *Canzonetta und Lied, componiert mit Begleitung des Pianoforte*. Berlin: A. M. Schlesinger, 1830.

Friedrich Curschmann. *Lieder für eine Singstimme, Opus 16*. Berlin: A. M. Schlesinger, 1830.

Luigi Dallapiccola. *Goethe-Lieder per una voce di mezzo soprano e tre clarinetti*. Milano: Edizioni Suvini Zerboni, 1953.

Leopold Damrosch. *Collected Songs of Leopold Damrosch, edited by Frank Damrosch*. English Translations made and selected by Mary L. Webster. New York: G. Schirmer, 1903.

Leopold Damrosch. *Zehn Lieder, Opus 11. Gedichte von Emmanuel Geibel aus dem "Spanisches Liederbuch."* New York: G. Schirmer, 1903? Reprint. Huntsville, Texas: Recital Publications, 1986.

John Deathridge, Martin Geck, and Egon Voss. *Wagner Werk-Verzeichnis: Verzeichnis der musikalischen Werke Richard Wagners und ihrer Quellen. Erarbeitet im Rahmen der Richard Wagner Gesamtausgabe.* Redaktionelle Mitarbeit Isolde Vetter. Mainz: B. Schott's Söhne, 1986.

Norman Del Mar. *Richard Strauss: A Critical Commentary on his Life and Work (vol.3)*. Philadelphia: Chilton Book Co., 1972.

Frederick Delius. *Lieder nach Gedichten von Friedrich Nietzsche für mittlere Stimme und Klavier von Frederick Delius*. Wien: Universal Edition, 1924.

Paul Dessau. *Tierverse von Bertolt Brecht, für Gesang und (präpariertes) Klavier, respektive Gitarre und Violoncello ad libitum. 1973*. Berlin: Bote und Bock, 1975.

Otto Erich Deutsch. *Schubert: Thematic Catalogue of all his Works in Chronological Order*. London: J. M. Dent and Sons, 1951.

Otto Erich Deutsch. *Franz Schubert: Thematisches Verzeichnis seiner Werke in chronologischer Folge.* Neuausgabe in deutscher Sprache bearbeitet und herausgegeben von der Editionsleitung der Neuen Schubert-Ausgabe und Werner Aderhold. Kassel und Basel: Bärenreiter Verlag, 1978.

Deutsches Lieder-Album enthaltend: 50 neuere Lieder mit Klavierbegleitung in zwei Bänden. Band I für hohe Stimme; Band II für mittlere Stimme. Berlin: Adolph Fürstner, 1896?

Hugo Distler. *Drei Lieder für tiefe Frauenstimme und Klavier*. Kassel und Basel: Bärenreiter Verlag, 1967.

Hugo Distler. *Mörike Chorliederbuch*. Kassel und Basel: Bärenreiter Verlag, 1939.

Ernő Dohnáhyi. *Waldelfelein*. Budapest: Editio Musica, 1977.

Ernő Dohnányi. *Sechs Gedichte von Victor Heindl für eine Singstimme mit Klavierbegleitung, Opus 14*. Wien: Ludwig Doblinger, 1908 (1989).

Ernő Dohnányi. *Sechs Gedichte von Wilhelm Conrad Gomoll für eine Singstimme mit Klavierbegleitung, Opus 16*. Wien: Ludwig Doblinger, 1909. Reprint. Huntsville, Texas: Recital Publications, 1991.

K. C. Eberhard Ehmann, editor. *Geistliche Lieder für eine Singstimme mit Begleitung des Pianoforte*. Tübingen: Verlag der H. Laupp'schen Buchhandlung, 1912.

Eichendorff. *Lieder nach Gedichten von Eichendorff. Salzburg Festival 1975*. (Recording) Dietrich Fischer-Dieskau, baritone, Wolfgang Sawallisch, piano. München: Orfeo International Music, 1989.

Gottfried von Einem. *Carmina Gerusena. Acht Gesänge für Singstimme und Klavier*. Wien: Universal Edition, 1982.

Gottfried von Einem. *Leb wohl, Frau Welt. Liederzyklus für mittlere Singstimme und Klavier nach Texten von Hermann Hesse, Opus 43*. London: Boosey and Hawkes, 1975.

Gottfried von Einem. *Sieben Lieder nach verschiedenen Dichtern für eine Singstimme und Klavier, Opus 19*. Berlin: Bote und Bock, 1956.

Gottfried von Einem. *Fünf Lieder für hohe Stimme und Klavier, Opus 25*. Frankfurt: Henry Litolff's Verlag, C. F. Peters, 1958.

Gottfried von Einem. *Lebenstanz. Liederzyklus nach Texten von Lotte Ingrisch für mittlere Stimme und Klavier, Opus 69*. Berlin: Bote und Bock, 1985.

Gottfried von Einem. *Waldviertler Lieder für mittlere Stimme und Klavier nach Gedichten von Lotte Ingrisch, Opus 71*. Wien: Universal Edition, 1983.

Gottfried von Einem. *Zwölf Tag- und Nachtlieder, Opus 73*. Berlin: Robert Lienau, 1986.

Gottfried von Einem. *Inmitten aller Vergänglichkeit. Zwölf Lieder nach Gedichten von Christine Busta für Gesang und Klavier. Opus 77*. Berlin: Bote und Bock, 1989.

Gottfried von Einem. *Meridiane. Fünf Lieder nach Gedichten von Hans Schumacher für Gesang and Klavier, Opus 78*. Berlin: Bote und Bock, 1989.

Gottfried von Einem. *Bald sing' ich das Schweigen. Ein Liederzyklus für Gesang und Klavier nach Gedichten von Lotte Ingrisch, Opus 79*. Berlin: Bote und Bock, 1988.

Hanns Eisler. *Hanns Eisler: Lieder für eine Singstimme und Klavier, vorgelegt von Manfred Grabs*. Gesammelte Werke, Serie I, Bd.16. Leipzig: VEB Deutscher Verlag für Musik, 1976.

Heimo Erbse. *Drei Lieder nach Texten von Eduard Mörike für mittlere Stimme und Klavier, Opus 17*. Frankfurt: Henry Litolff's Verlag, C.F. Peters, 1959.

Reinhard Ermen. *Franz Schreker (1878-1934) zum 50. Todestag, herausgegeben von Reinhard Ermen mit einem Geleitwort von Haidy Schreker-Bures*. Aachen: Rimbaud Press, 1984.

Faber-Krause. *Sechs Lieder für Singstimme und Klavier nach Gedichten von Hermann Hesse*. München: Musikverlag Hans Kasparek, 1946.

Pierre-Octave Ferroud. *Drei traute Gesänge nach Dichtungen von Goethe. (Trois poëmes intimes de Goethe)*. Paris: Durand & Cie., 1932.

Alexander Fesca. *Fesca-Album. Sammlung beliebter Lieder für eine Singstimme mit Pianofortebegleitung*. Leipzig: C. F. Peters, 1882.

Alexander von Fielitz. *Eliland. Ein Sang vom Chiemsee. Gedicht von K. Stieler*. Leipzig: Breitkopf und Härtel, 1896.

Alexander von Fielitz. *Acht Mädchenlieder von Paul Heyse, Opus 40*. Leipzig: Breitkopf und Härtel, 1895. Reprint. Huntsville, Texas: Recital Publications, 1982.

Henry T. Finck, editor. *One Hundred Songs by Ten Masters, vol. 1*. New York: Oliver Ditson, 1917.

Adolph Martin Foerster. *Songs* (individually published songs bound as one volume, Music Division: Research Library for the Performing Arts, New York Public Library).

Franz Jacob Freystädtler. *Sechs Lieder der besten Dichter (Wien 1795)*. Bad Reichenhall: Comes Verlag, 1992.

Max Friedländer, editor. *Gedichte von Goethe in Kompositionen seiner Zeitgenossen*. Weimar: Verlag der Goethe-Gesellschaft, 1896.

Max Friedländer, editor. *Gedichte von Goethe in Kompositionen, zweiter Band*. Weimar: Verlag der Goethe-Gesellschaft, 1916.

Ilse Fromm-Michaels. *[Lieder] Opus 9*. Berlin: Ries und Erler, [n.d.].

Jan Gall. *"Mädchen mit dem roten Mündchen" von Heinrich Heine, Opus 1, No.3*. Leipzig: F. E. C. Leuckart, 19–?

Jan Gall. *Im Herbste, Opus 26*. No.3: "Es ist ein Schnitter, der heisst Tod." Lemberg: Jakubowski & Zadurowicz, [n.d.].

Cord Garben. *Blick auf Alexander Zemlinsky – Ein Plädoyer*. (Recording notes DGG 427 384-2). Hamburg: Deutsche Grammophon GmbH, 1989.

Gems of German Song. A Collection of the most beautiful vocal Compositions, with Accompaniment for the Piano-Forte. Boston: Oliver Ditson, 1865.

Harald Genzmer. *Ausgewählte Lieder (1940-1987) für Bariton und Klavier*. Berlin: Ries und Erler, 1989.

Harald Genzmer. *Ausgewählte Lieder (1940-1990) für Sopran und Klavier*. Berlin: Ries und Erler, 1991.

Mauro Giuliani. *Sechs Lieder Opus 89 for voice and guitar or piano, edited by Thomas F. Heck*. London: Tecla Editions, 1976.

Aleksandr Glazunov. *Romansi i Pesni*. Moscow, 1972.

Mikhail Glinka. *Sochineniia dlia golosa s fortepiano*. Polnoe sobranie sochinenii, vol.10. Moscow: Gos. muzykal'noe izd-vo, 1962.

Aleksandr Goehr. *Das Gesetz der Quadrille, Opus 41. Lieder nach Franz Kafka*. London: Schott & Co. Ltd., 1983.

Hermann Goetz. *Eighteen Songs with pianoforte accompaniment by Hermann Goetz*. London: Novello, Ewer & Co., 188-?

Karl Goldmark. *Goldmark-Album. Lieder und Gesänge für eine Singstimme mit Klavierbegleitung*. Wien: Ludwig Doblinger, 1900.

Paul Graener. *Sechs Lieder, Opus 21 and Opus 30*. Mainz: B. Schott Söhne, 1909. Reprint. Huntsville, Texas: Recital Publications, 1986.

Paul Graener. *Vier Lieder für Gesang und Klavier, Opus 40*. Wien: Universal Edition, 1916.

Edvard Grieg: Verzeichnis seiner Werke mit Einleitung: mein erster Erfolg. Leipzig: C. F. Peters, 1910.

Edvard Grieg. *Romanser og Sanger*. Oslo: Norsk Musik Forlag, 1948-1950.

Cor de Groot. *7 Goethe Lieder voor zangstem en klavier*. Den Haag: Albersen & Co, 194-?

Ernst-Jürgen Dreyer. *Robert Gund (Gound), 1865-1927. Ein vergessener Meister des Liedes mit einem Beiheft: vierundzwanzig ausgewählte Lieder.* Abhandlung zur Kunst-, Musik- und Literaturwissenschaft, Band 375. Bonn: Bouvier Verlag, 1988.

Christopher Hailey. *Franz Schreker, 1878–1934. A cultural biography.* Music in the Twentieth Century. General Editor: Arnold Whittall. Cambridge: Cambridge University Press, 1993.

Josef Matthias Hauer. *Hölderlin Lieder, in vier Bänden, Opus 6, 12, 23, 32, und 40.* Wien: Universal Edition, 1928.

Joseph Haydn. *Einstimmige Gesänge.* Herausgegeben von Paul Mies. Joseph Haydn Werke. München: G. Henle Verlag, 195-?

Joseph Haydn. *Mehrstimmige Gesänge.* Herausgegeben von Paul Mies. Joseph Haydn Werke, vol. 30. München: G. Henle Verlag, 1958.

Stephen Heller. *7 Deutsche Lieder für eine Singstimme mit Begleitung des Klavier.* Herausgegeben von Jean-Jaques Eigeldinger. Berg a.I. / Zürich: Amadeus Verlag, Bernhard Päuler, 1975.

Fritz Hennenberg, editor. *Das große Brecht-Liederbuch. Band 2.* Frankfurt am Main: Suhrkamp Verlag, 1984.

George Henschel: Fifty Songs. The John Church Company, 1905.

Fanny Hensel. *Sechs Lieder mit Begleitung des Pianoforte componiert von Fanny Cäcilia Hensel geboren Mendelssohn-Bartholdy, Opus 9.* Leipzig: Breitkopf und Härtel.

Fanny Hensel. *Ausgewählte Lieder für Singstimme und Klavier, Band I und II.* Herausgegeben von Annette Maurer. Leipzig: Breitkopf und Härtel, 1993.

Fanny Hensel. *[Lieder to texts of Wilhelm Müller]* Edited by Suzanne Summerville. Fairbanks, Alaska: Arts Venture, 1995[projected].

Fanny Hensel. *[Lieder to texts of Ludwig Hölty]* Edited by Suzanne Summerville. Fairbanks, Alaska: Arts Venture, 1995[projected].

Fanny Hensel. *Altes Lied.* Edited by Suzanne Summerville. Fairbanks, Alaska: Arts Venture, 1994.

Fanny Hensel. *Three Duets on Texts by Heinrich Heine.* Edited by Suzanne Summerville. Fairbanks, Alaska: Arts Venture, 1994.

Fanny Hensel. *Faust: Part II of the Tragedy, Act 1 – A Pleasant Landscape.* Edited by Suzanne Summerville. Fairbanks, Alaska: Arts Venture, 1994.

Fanny Hensel. *Ausgewählte Lieder für Singstimme und Klavier.* Herausgegeben von Aloysia Assenbaum. Düsseldorf: Edition Donna, 1991.

Fanny Hensel. *März, April, Mai. Three duets on texts by Johann Wolfgang von Goethe, for Soprano and Alto voices with Piano Accompaniment.* Edited by Suzanne Summerville. Fairbanks, Alaska: Arts Venture, 1994.

Gottfried Herrmann. *Three songs for Clarinet, Soprano or Baritone, and Piano.* Monteux, France: Musica Rara, 1989.

Eugen Hildach. *Lieder für eine Singstimme mit Begleitung des Pianoforte, Opus 9.* Magdeburg: Heinrichshofen's Verlag, 1898.

Eugen Hildach. *Lenz. Opus 19, No.5.* Magdeburg: Heinrichshofen's Verlag, 1894. Reprint. New York: Classical Vocal Reprints, 1993.

Cecil Hill. *Ferdinand Ries: A Thematic Catalogue.* Armidale, Australia: The University of New England, 1977.

Rosemary Hilmar. *Katalog der Musikhandschriften, Schriften und Studien Alban Bergs im Fond Alban Berg und der weiteren handschriftlichen Quellen im Besitz der Österreichischen Nationalbibliothek.* Alban Berg Studien. Herausgegeben von Franz Grasberger und Rudolf Stephan. Wien: Alban Berg Stiftung in der Universal Edition, 1908.

Ernst Hilmer. *Anton Webern 1883-1983.* Eine Festschrift zum hundertsten Geburtstag herausgegeben von Ernst Hilmer mit einer Einleitung von Henri Pousseur. Wien: Universal Edition, 1983.

Paul Hindemith. *Klavierlieder I.* Herausgegeben von Kurt von Fischer. Paul Hindemith: Sämtliche Werke, Band VI,1. Mainz: B. Schott's Söhne, 1983.

Anthony van Hoboken. *Joseph Haydn: Thematisch-bibliographisches Werkverzeichnis zugesammengestellt von Anthony van Hoboken.* Mainz: B. Schott's Söhne, 1957-78.

Hölderlin Gesänge. (Recording) Mitsuko Shirai, mez., Hartmut Höll, piano. Königsdorf: Capriccio, 1994.

Karl Höller. *Cäsar Flaischlen-Zyklus für eine mittlere Singstimme und Klavier, komponiert 1926.* München: Max Hieber Musikverlag, 1985.

Franz von Holstein. *39 Lieder und Gesänge für eine Singstimme mit Begleitung des Pianoforte*. Leipzig: Breitkopf und Härtel, 1884.

Anselm Hüttenbrenner. *"Der Erlkönig," herausgegeben von Andreas Holzer*. Musik Alter Meister, Heft 54. Graz: Akademische Druck- und Verlagsanstalt, 1993.

Engelbert Humperdinck. *Vier Kinderlieder*. Leipzig: Max Brockhaus, 1901.

Engelbert Humperdinck. *Ausgewählte Lieder mit Klavierbegleitung*. Leipzig: Max Brockhaus, 1912.

Engelbert Humperdinck. *Drei Weihnachtslieder für eine Singstimme mit Klavierbegleitung*. Leipzig: Max Brockhaus, 1911. Reprint. New York: Classical Vocal Reprints, 1993.

Charles Ives. *114 Songs by Charles E. Ives*. New York: Associated Music Publishers, Peer International; Bryn Mawr, Theodor Presser, 1975.

Charles Ives. *Forty Earlier Songs*. Critical Edition. Edited by John Kirkpatrick. AMP, Peer International, and Theodor Presser, 1993?

Barbara Garvey Jackson, editor. *Lieder by Women Composers of the Classic Era, Volume 1*. Fayetteville, Arkansas: ClarNan Editions, 1987.

Friedrich Wilhelm Jähns. *Carl Maria von Weber in seinen Werken. Chronologisch-thematisches Verzeichniss seiner sämmtlichen Compositionen*. Berlin: Verlag der Schlesinger'schen Buch- und Musikhandlung (Rob. Lienau), 1871. Reprint. Berlin: Robert Lienau, 1967.

Curt Paul Janz. *Friedrich Nietzsche. Der musikalische Nachlaß*. Herausgegeben im Auftrag der Schweizerischen Musikforschenden Gesellschaft von Curt Paul Janz. Kassel und Basel: Bärenreiter Verlag, 1976.

Adolf Jensen. *Ausgewählte Lieder und Gesänge für eine Singstimme*. Leipzig: F. E. C. Leuckart, 1890.

Adolf Jensen. *Ausgewählte Lieder und Gesänge für eine Singstimme mit Klavierbegleitung*. Nach den ersten Drucken revidiert und mit Anmerkung versehen von Max Friedlaender. Leipzig: C. F. Peters.

Adolf Jensen. *Jensen-Album. 41 ausgewählte Lieder und Gesänge*. Neuausgabe von Schultze-Biesantz. Braunschweig: Henry Litolff's Verlag, 1900.

Adolf Jensen. *Lieder des Hafis, aus dem Persischen von G. Fr. Daumer. Opus 11. Sieben Gesänge am Pianoforte*. Hamburg: Fritz Schuberth, 1863? Reprint. Huntsville, Texas: Recital Publications, 1994.

Adolf Jensen. *Liebeslieder für eine tiefere Stimme mit Begleitung des Pianoforte, Opus 13*. Leipzig: Bartholf Senff, [n.d.]. Reprint. Huntsville, Texas: Recital Publications, 1994.

Adolf Jensen. *Zwölf Gesänge von Paul Heyse für eine mittlere Stimme mit Begleitung des Pianoforte, Opus 22*. Leipzig: C. F. Peters, 1864. Reprint. New York: Classical Vocal Reprints, 1995 (projected).

Adolf Jensen. *Forty Songs by Adolf Jensen*. New York: Oliver Ditson, 1913.

Adolf Jensen. *Lieder-Album für eine mittlere Singstimme mit Klavierbegleitung, herausgegeben von Wilhelm Kienzl*. Leipzig: Breitkopf und Härtel.

Adolf Jensen. *Sieben Lieder von Robert Burns für eine Singstimme und Pianoforte, Opus 49*. Breslau: Julius Hainauer, 1875. Reprint. Huntsville, Texas: Recital Publications, 1989.

Werner Josten. *Fünf Lieder für Gesang und Klavier*. Wien: Universal Edition, 1926.

Robert Kahn. *Auserlesene Lieder für eine Singstimme mit Clavierbegleitung von Robert Kahn*. Leipzig: F. E. C. Leuckart, 1899.

Johannes Wenzeslaus Kalliwoda. *Drei Gesänge für eine Sopran-Stimme mit Begleitung des Pianoforte und der Violine*. Leipzig: C. F. Peters, 184-.

Johannes Wenzeslaus Kalliwoda. *J. W. Kalliwoda Lieder Album, Gesang und Klavier*. Wien: Universal Edition, 1910.

Sigfrid Karg-Elert. *Zehn Epigramme von Gotthold Ephraim Lessing für eine Singstimme mit Klavier, Opus 56*. Berlin: Carl Simon, 1907. Reprint. Huntsville, Texas: Recital Publications, 1989.

Hugo Kaun. *Lieder, Opus 15*. Berlin: Richard Kaun, 1905.

Hugo Kaun. *Sechs Lieder für eine Singstimme und Pianoforte, Opus 25*. Milwaukee, Wisconsin: William Kaun, 1898. Reprint. Huntsville, Texas: Recital Publications, 1986.

Hugo Kaun. *Lieder, Opus 27*. Berlin: Richard Kaun, 1905.

Hugo Kaun. *Vier Dichtungen von Prinz Emil zu Schönaich-Carolath für eine Singstimme und Pianoforte, Opus 33*. Berlin: Breitkopf und Härtel, 1900.

Hugo Kaun. *Drei Lieder für eine Singstimme mit Pianoforte, Opus 37*. Hamburg und Leipzig: D. Rahter, 1902.

Hugo Kaun. *Sechs Lieder für eine Singstimme und Pianoforte, Opus 46*. Hamburg und Leipzig: D. Rahter, 1902. Reprint. Huntsville, Texas: Recital Publications, 1993.

Hugo Kaun. *Fünf Lieder für eine Singstimme, Opus 47*. Hamburg und Leipzig: D. Rahter, 1903.

Hugo Kaun. *Vier Lieder für eine Singstimme, Opus 49*. Hamburg und Leipzig: D. Rahter, 1903.

Hugo Kaun. *Sieben Lieder für eine Singstimme mit Pianoforte, Opus 55*. Leipzig: C. F. Kahnt Nachfolger, 1904.

Hugo Kaun. *Fünf Lieder und Gesänge für eine Singstimme und Pianoforte, Opus 61*. Leipzig: C. F. Kahnt Nachfolger, 1905.

Hugo Kaun. *Sieben Lieder für eine Singstimme und Pianoforte, Opus 68*. Milwaukee, Wisconsin: William Kaun, 1906. Reprint. Huntsville, Texas: Recital Publications, 1986.

Hugo Kaun. *Vier Lieder für eine Singstimme mit Klavier, Opus 79*. Berlin: C. A. Challier & Co., 1908.

Hugo Kaun. *Fünf Gesänge für eine Mezzo-Sopran oder Tenorstimme und Pianoforte, Opus 80*. Magdeburg: Heinrichshofen's Verlag, 1908.

Wilhelm Kempff. *Vier Gesänge, Opus 7*. Berlin: N. Simrock, 1923.

Wilhelm Kempff. *Vier Lieder, Opus 16*. Berlin: N. Simrock, 1923.

Wilhelm Kienzl. *Wilhelm Kienzl: Lieder*. (Recording) Steven Kimbrough, baritone, Dalton Baldwin, piano. Austria: Koch Schwann, 1990.

Wilhelm Kienzl. *Lieder-Album. Eine Auswahl von Liedern und Gesängen für eine Singstimme mit Begleitung des Pianoforte komponiert von Wilhelm Kienzl*. Wien: Universal Edition, ca. 1904.

Wilhelm Kienzl. *Aus Friedrich Rückert's Liebesfrühling: ein Cyclus von sieben Gesängen am Pianoforte von Wilhelm Kienzl, Opus 11*. Leipzig: Breitkopf und Härtel, [n.d.]. Reprint. Huntsville, Texas: Recital Publications, 1989.

Yrjö Kilpinen. *Sechs Lieder nach Gedichten von Christian Morgenstern für mittlere Stimme und Klavier. Opus 59*. Berlin: Bote und Bock, 1934, 1962.

Yrjö Kilpinen. *13 Lieder nach Gedichten von Christian Morgenstern*. Espoo, Finland: Fazer Music Inc., 1991.

Jürgen Kindermann. *Thematisch-chronologisches Verzeichnis der musikalischen Werke von Ferruccio B. Busoni*. Regensburg: Gustav Bosse Verlag, 1980.

Johanna Kinkel. *Sechs Lieder mit Begleitung des Pianoforte von Johanna Mathieux, Opus 6*. Leipzig: Fr. Kistner, [n.d.].

Johanna Kinkel. *Sechs Lieder für eine Singstimme mit Begleitung des Pianoforte von J. Mathieux, Opus 7*. Berlin: M. Bahn Verlag, [n.d.].

Johanna Kinkel. *Das Schloss Boncourt. Gedicht von Adelbert von Chamisso für eine Singstimme mit Begleitung des Pianoforte von J. Mathieux, Opus 9*. Berlin: T. Trautwein, 1838.

Johanna Kinkel. *Sechs Lieder für eine Singstimme mit Pianoforte von J. Mathieux, Opus 10*. Berlin: T. Trautwein (M. Bahn), [n.d.].

Johanna Kinkel. *Sechs Lieder für eine tiefe Stimme mit Begleitung des Pianoforte von J. Mathieux. Opus 17*. Berlin: Bote und Bock, [n.d.].

Johanna Kinkel. *Abschied, for one voice and guitar, Opus 19, No.5*. Köln: M. Schloss.

Georg Kinsky. *Das Werk Beethovens. Thematisch-bibliographisches Verzeichnis seiner sämtlichen vollendeten Kompositionen*. Nach dem Tode des Verfassers abgeschlossen und herausgegeben von Hans Halm. München: G. Henle Verlag, 1955.

Johann Friedrich Kittl. *Sechs Lieder für eine Singstimme mit Begleitung des Pianoforte in Muzik gesetzt*. Wien: Anton Diabelli, 1840?

Arno Kleffel. *30 Lieder und Gesänge für eine Singstimme mit Begleitung des Pianoforte. Opus 7, 10, 12, und 14*. Leipzig: Breitkopf und Härtel, 1890.

Otto Klemperer. *Lied (Otto Klemperer) für eine Singstimme und Klavier*. Mainz: B. Schott's Söhne, 1915.

Paul von Klenau. *Vier Lieder nach Gedichten von Friedrich Hölderlin für tiefe Singstimme und Klavier*. Heidelberg: Willy Müller, Süddeutscher Musikverlag, after 1942.

Armin Knab. *Eichendorff-Lieder. Fünf Gesänge für Alt oder Bariton mit Klavier*. München: F. E. C. Leuckart, 1930.

Armin Knab. *Zwölf Lieder für eine hohe Stimme mit Klavier nach Gedichten von Johann Wolfgang von Goethe*. Mainz: B. Schott's Söhne, 1949.

Armin Knab. *Kinderlieder für eine Singstimme mit Klavier*. Leipzig: Breitkopf und Härtel, 1923?

Armin Knab. *Wunderhorn-Lieder für eine Singstimme mit Klavier*. Leipzig: Breitkopf und Härtel, 1921.

Karl Michael Komma, editor. *Lieder und Gesänge nach Dichtungen von Friedrich Hölderlin*. Mit Einleitung und Erläuterung herausgegeben von Karl Michael Komma. Schriften der Hölderlin-Gesellschaft, Band 5. Tübingen: J. C. B. Mohr (Paul Siebeck), 1967.

Peter Jona Korn. *Der Pfarrer von Cleversulzbach. Sechs Lieder nach Gedichten von Eduard Mörike für eine mittlere Singstimme und Klavier. Opus 24*. Hamburg: N. Simrock, 1964.

Erich Wolfgang Korngold. *Einfache Lieder für eine Singstimme und Klavier, Opus 9*. Mainz: B. Schott's Söhne, 1916. Reprint. New York: Classical Vocal Reprints, 1993.

Erich Wolfgang Korngold. *Lieder des Abschieds, Opus 14*. Mainz: B. Schott's Söhne, 1921.

Erich Wolfgang Korngold. *Drei Gesänge für mittlere Stimme, Opus 18*. Mainz: B. Schott's Söhne, 1925.

Erich Wolfgang Korngold. *Drei Lieder für Gesang und Klavier, Opus 22*. Mainz: B. Schott's Söhne, 1930.

Erich Wolfgang Korngold. *Unvergänglichkeit. Für Singstimme und Klavier*. Mainz: B. Schott's Söhne, 1990.

Erich Wolfgang Korngold. *Fünf Lieder für mittlere Stimme und Klavier, Opus 38*. Mainz: B. Schott's Söhne, 1956.

Franz Krause. *Fünf Gedichte von Hermann Hesse für Gesang und Klavier von Franz Krause. 15. Werk*. Kassel: [s.n.], 196-?

Franz Krause. *Sieben Gedichte von Hermann Hesse für Gesang und Klavier von Franz Krause. 30. Werk*. Kassel: [s.n.], 196-?

Franz Krause. *Sechs Gedichte von Rainer Maria Rilke für Gesang und Klavier von Franz Krause. 47. Werk*. Kassel: [s.n.], 1972?

Franz Krause. *Gedichte aus alter Zeit; für Gesang und Klavier von Franz Krause. 51. Werk*. Kassel: [s.n.], 1972?

Ernst Křenek. *Neun Lieder für Gesang und Klavier, aus Opus 9, 15, und 19*. Wien: Universal Edition, 1927.

Ernst Křenek. *Die Ballade vom König Lobesam, nach dem Gedicht von Gerd Hans Goering. Opus 9, No. 7*. Wien: Universal Edition, 1924.

Ernst Křenek. *Vier Gesänge nach alten Gedichten für Mezzosopran und Klavier, Opus 53*. Die Texte sind der Sammlung "Die Vergessenen", 100 deutsche Gedichte des 17. und 18. Jhdts., ausgewählt von Heinrich Fischer entnommen. Wien: Universal Edition, 1927.

Ernst Křenek. *Drei Gesänge (Goethe) für Bariton und Klavier, Opus 56*. Wien: Universal Edition, 1928.

Ernst Křenek. *Fiedellieder, aus dem "Liederbuch dreier Freunde," Kiel, Schwers'che Buchhandlung, 1843*. Wien: Universal Edition, 1984.

Ernst Křenek. *Die Nachtigall. Aus "Worte in Versen" von Karl Kraus. Musik von Ernst Křenek. Opus 68*. Wien: Universal Edition, 1931.

Ernst Křenek. *Fünf Lieder nach Worten von Franz Kafka für Singstimme und Klavier, Opus 82*. Mainz: B. Schott's Söhne, 1958.

Conradin Kreutzer. *Conradin Kreutzer's Frühlingslieder and Wanderlieder*. A Facsimile Edition with New Translations, by Luise Eitel Peake. Stuyvesant, New York: Pendragon Press, 1989.

Friedrich Kücken. *Kücken-Album. Ausgewählte Lieder für eine Singstimme mit Pianofortebegleitung von Friedrich Kücken*. Leipzig: C. F. Peters, 188-?

Friedrich Kuhlau. *Drey Gedichte aus Gerstenberg's poëtischem Wäldchen für eine Singstimme mit Pianoforte in Musik gesetzt und der Frau Henriette Weiß geboren Schicht zugeeignet von Friedrich Kuhlau*. Leipzig: Breitkopf und Härtel, 1820.

Richard Kursch. *Vier Lieder für eine Singstimme mit Klavierbegleitung, Opus 5*. Leipzig: Mitteldeutscher Musikverlag, 1905?

Franz Lachner. *Frauenliebe und Leben, Opus 82,* and *Lyrisches Intermezzo for Soprano, Clarinet and Piano*. Monteux: Musica Rara, 1981.

Franz Lachner. *Drei deutsche Gesänge für eine Singstimme mit Begleitung des Pianoforte dem Fräulein Sophie Loewe gewidmet von Franz Lachner, 56tes Werk*. München: J. Aibl.

Josephine Lang. *Josephine Lang: Selected Songs.* New Introduction by Judith Tick. New York: Da Capo Press, 1982.

Eduard Lassen. *Eduard Lassen: Song Album.* New York: G. Schirmer, 1883.

Eduard Lassen. *Lassen Album. (in drei Bänden).* Ausgabe mit deutschem und englischem Texte. Breslau: Julius Hainauer, 1891.

Eduard Lassen. *Song Album.* New York: G. Schirmer, 1883. Reprint. Huntsville, Texas: Recital Publications, 1989.

Luise Adolpha LeBeau. *Drei Lieder für eine Altstimme und Violine mit Clavier-Begleitung, Opus 45.* Leipzig: C. F. Kahnt Nachfolger, 1888. Reprint. Fairbanks, Alaska: Arts Venture, 1995.

Lieder der Romantik mit conzertierenden Instrumenten (Recording) Dietrich Fischer-Dieskau, baritone, Dieter Klöcker, piano. Wallendorf, Höll. München: Orfeo International Music GmBH, 1986.

Ignace Lilien. *Ignace Lilien* (Recording) Anja van Wijk, mezzo., Frans van Ruth, piano. Amsterdam: Attaca.

Franz Liszt. *Lieder für eine Singstimme.* Franz Liszts Musikalische Werke. Herausgegeben von der Franz Liszt-Stiftung. Leipzig: Breitkopf und Härtel Reprint. Farnborough, England: Gregg International, 1966.

Carl Loewe. *Carl Loewes Werke: Gesamtausgabe der Balladen, Legenden, Lieder und Gesänge für eine Singstimme im Auftrage der Loeweschen Familie herausgegeben von Dr. Max Runze.* Leipzig: Breitkopf und Härtel, 1898-1904. Reprint. Farnborough, England: Gregg International, 1970.

Otto Lohse. *Fünf Gesänge.* Berlin: Verlag Harmonie, 1910. Reprint. Huntsville, Texas: Recital Publications, 1993.

Louis Ferdinand, Prinz von Preußen. *Lieder, vols. 1-6.* Wilhelmshaven: Heinrichshofens Verlag, 1953-86.

Edward MacDowell. *Five Songs, Opus 11 and 12.* Leipzig: C. F. Kahnt Nachfolger, 1898. Reprint. New York: Classical Vocal Reprints, 1993.

Gunter Maier. *Die Lieder Johann Rudolf Zumsteegs und ihr Verhältnis zu Schubert.* Göppinger Akademische Beiträge Nr.28. Göppingen: Verlag Alfred Kümmerle, 1971.

Dietrich Manicke. *Balladen von Gottfried August Bürger, in Musik gesetzt von André, Kunzen, Zumsteeg, Tomaschek und Reichard, Teil 1.* Herausgegeben von Dietrich Manicke. Das Erbe Deutscher Musik, Band 45 und 46. Mainz: B. Schott's Söhne, 1970.

Heinrich Marschner. *Fünf Lieder von R. Reinick mit Begleitung des Pianoforte componiert und dem Königlich Hannoverschen Hofopernsänger Herrn Hotzmiller zugeeignet von Dr. Heinrich Marschner.* Hannover: Adolph Nagel.

Heinrich Marschner. *Lieder-Album.* Braunschweig: Henry Litolff's Verlag, [n.d.]. Reprint. Huntsville, Texas: Recital Publications, 1985.

Henri Marteau. *Fünf Schilflieder von Nikolaus Lenau für Bariton mit Begleitung des Klaviers und obl. Bratsche, Opus 31.* Berlin: N. Simrock, 1925.

Donald Martino. *Two Rilke Songs, for Mezzo-Soprano and Piano.* Boston: Ione Press, Inc. (E.C.Schirmer, agents), 1970.

Joseph Marx. *Lieder und Gesänge.* Leipzig: Schuberthaus-Verlag (Universal Edition), 1910-1912?

Joseph Marx. *Italienisches Liederbuch, Band 1-2. Nach Gedichten von Paul Heyse.* Leipzig: Schuberthaus-Verlag, 1912. Reprint. New York: Classical Vocal Reprints, 1993.

Joseph Marx. *Adagio (Anton Wildgans) for medium voice, violoncello, and piano.* Leipzig: Universal Edition, 1917? Reprint. New York: Classical Vocal Reprints, 1994.

Joseph Marx. *Durch Einsamkeit (Anton Wildgans) for medium voice, viola and piano.* Wien: Universal Edition, 1916. Reprint. New York: Classical Vocal Reprints, 1993.

Joseph Marx. *Pan trauert um Syrinx (Anton Wildgans) for high voice, flute and piano.* Wien: Universal Edition, 1917. Reprint. New York: Classical Vocal Reprints, 1993.

Joseph Marx. *Du bist der Garten (Anton Wildgans) für mittlere Singstimme mit Klavier und Violine.* Wien: Universal Edition, 1916. Reprint. New York: Classical Vocal Reprints, 1994.

Karl Marx. *Vierzehn Lieder nach Gedichten von Hermann Claudius, Opus 26.* Kassel und Basel: Bärenreiter Verlag, 1948.

Karl Marx. *Neue Lieder nach Gedichten von Hermann Claudius. Opus 29.* Kassel und Basel: Bärenreiter Verlag, 1948.

Karl Marx. *Fünf Rilke-Lieder für eine Singstimme und Klavier*. Kassel und Basel: Bärenreiter Verlag, 1949.

Karl Marx. *Lieder und Sprüche nach Worten von Goethe für hohe Singstimme und Klavier, Opus 49*. Kassel und Basel: Bärenreiter Verlag, 1949.

Hermann Maschek and Hedwig Kraus. *Das Wiener Lied von 1792 bis 1815*. Denkmäler der Tonkunst in Österreich, vol. 79. Graz: Akademische Druck- und Verlagsanstalt, 1960.

Emil Mattiesen. *Vier heitere Lieder für eine Singstimme und Klavier*. Leipzig: C. F. Peters, 1900.

Emil Mattiesen. *Stille Lieder (Hausmusik) für eine Singstimme und Klavier, Opus 11*. Leipzig: C. F. Peters, 190-?

Emil Mattiesen. *Überwindungen. Sieben Gedichte für eine Singstimme und Klavier, Opus 15*. Leipzig: C. F. Peters, 190-?

Margit L. McCorkle. *Johannes Brahms: Thematisch-Bibliographisches Werkverzeichnis.* Herausgegeben nach gemeinsamen Vorarbeiten mit Donald M. McCorkle. München: G. Henle Verlag, 1984.

Nikolai Medtner. *Twenty-six Selected Songs by Nicholas Medtner*. New York: G. Schirmer, 1946.

Nikolai Medtner. *Izhbrannye Romansy dlja golosa s fortepiano*. Moscow: Izdatel'stvo Muzyka, 1971.

Nikolai Medtner. *Sobranie sochinenii*. Moscow: Gos. Muzykal'noe Izd-vo, 1959-1963.

Nikolai Medtner. *Nicolas Medtner plays/spielt/joue* (Recording) Elisabeth Schwarzkopf, soprano. Nikolai Medtner, piano. London: EMI Classics: Composers in Person, 1993.

Nikolai Medtner. *Auf dem See. Worte von W. Göthe. Opus 3, No.3*. Moscow: P. Jurgenson, 1904. Reprint. Moscow: RSFSR. Section Musicale des Editions d'Etat, 1927.

Nikolai Medtner. *Neun Lieder von W. Goethe für Gesang und Klavier, Opus 6*. Moscow: P. Jurgenson, 1906. Reprint. New York: Classical Vocal Reprints, 1992.

Nikolai Medtner. *Drei Gedichte von H. Heine, Opus 12*. Moscow: P. Jurgenson, 190? Reprint. New York: Classical Vocal Reprints, 1992.

Nikolai Medtner. *Zwölf Lieder von W. Goethe, Opus 15*. Moscow: P. Jurgenson, 1910. Reprint. New York: Classical Vocal Reprints, 1992.

Nikolai Medtner. *Sechs Gedichte von W. Goethe, Opus 18*. Berlin: Édition Russe de Musique, 1910. Reprint. New York: Classical Vocal Reprints, 1992.

Nikolai Medtner. *Zwei Gedichte von Nietzsche für eine Singstimme und Klavier. Opus 19a*. Berlin: Édition Russe de Musique, 1910? Reprint. New York: Classical Vocal Reprints, 1992.

Felix Mendelssohn. *Seventy-nine Songs for Voice and Piano*. Melville, New York: Belwin Mills.

Felix Mendelssohn. *Duette für zwei Singstimmen mit Pianoforte-Begleitung*. Felix Mendelssohn Bartholdy's Sämtliche Werke. Frankfurt: C. F. Peters.

Der Merker. Österreichische Zeitschrift für Musik und Theater. Wien, 1909-1914.

Erik Meyer-Helmund. *Songs by Erik Meyer-Helmund, vols. 1 and 2*. New York: G. Schirmer, 1886, 1888.

Giacomo Meyerbeer. *Lieder für eine Singstimme und Klavier. Originalausgabe*. Leipzig: C. F. Peters, 1982.

Giacomo Meyerbeer. *40 Mélodies à une et à plusieurs voix, avec accompagnement de piano*. Paris: Brandus et Cie., 1848-51?

Franz Mittler. *Fünf Lieder*. Wien: Universal Edition, 1911. Reprint. Huntsville, Texas: Recital Publications, 1988.

Hans Joachim Moser, editor. *Das deutsche Sololied und die Ballade.* Mit einer geschichtlichen Einführung von Hans Joachim Moser. Das Musikwerk, Nr.14. Köln: Arno Volk Verlag.

Hans Joachim Moser, editor. *Alte Meister des deutschen Liedes: 46 Gesänge des 17. und 18. Jahrhunderts*. Frankfurt: C. F. Peters, 1960.

Moritz Moszkowski. *Drei Lieder für eine Singstimme mit Begleitung des Pianoforte componiert von Moritz Moszkowski, Opus 13*. Breslau: Julius Hainauer, 1877.

Moritz Moszkowski. *The Vale of Tears (Thränen), a Poem in Five Parts by Adelbert von Chamisso composed for Voice with Pianoforte Accompaniment, Opus 22*. London: Augener & Co., 1888? Reprint. Huntsville, Texas: Recital Publications, 198?

Moritz Moszkowski. *Drei Gedichte im Volkston, Opus 26*. London: Augener & Co. Reprint. New York: Classical Vocal Reprints, 1994.

Wolfgang Amadeus Mozart. *Lieder für eine Singstimme mit Klavier von W. A. Mozart.* Kritisch revidiert und mit Anmerkungen versehen von Max Friedländer. New York: C. F. Peters.

Modest Mussorgsky. *Complete Works. Vols. 8-10,14, edited by Paul Lamm: Lieder und Gesänge.* Reprint. New York: Edwin F. Kalmus.

Mathieu Neumann. *Aus seliger Zeit. Gedichte von Anna Ritter für eine Singstimme mit Pianoforte, Opus 55.* Leipzig: C. F. W. Siegel's Musikalienhandlung, 1904. Reprint. Huntsville, Texas: Recital Publications, 1994.

Vítězslav Novák. *Erotikon. Sechs Lieder für eine Singstimme und Klavier, Opus 46.* Wien: Universal Edition, 1912.

Carl Orff. *Frühe Lieder für eine Singstimme und Klavier.* Einführung: Werner Thomas. Mainz: B. Schott's Söhne, 1982.

Leo Ornstein. *Drei Lieder für eine Singstimme mit Klavierbegleitung, Opus 33.* New York: Carl Fischer, 1915.

Léon Orthel. *Twee Liederen (Rainer Maria Rilke).* Den Haag: Muziekhandel Albersen & Co., 1940?

Thorvald Otterström. *Neun Lieder für eine Singstimme und Klavier.* Kopenhagen: Peder Friis, 1907.

Maria Theresia von Paradis. *Zwölf Lieder auf ihrer Reise in Musik gesetzt (1784-86).* Edited by Hidemi Matsushita. Lieder by Women Composers of the Classic Era. Volume II. Fayetteville, Arkansas: ClarNan Editions, 1987.

Maria Theresia von Paradis. *Lenore: Ballade for soprano and piano, edited by Hidemi Matsushita.* Fayetteville, Arkansas: ClarNan Editions, 1989.

C. v. Pászthory. *Sechs Lieder nach Gedichten von Hermann Hesse.* Braunschweig: Henry Litolff's Verlag, 1936.

Helmut Paulsen. *Sieben besinnliche Lieder nach Texten zeitgenössischer Dichter für mittelhohe Singstimme und Klavier.* Köln: P. J. Tonger Musikverlag.

Ernst Pepping. *Haus- und Trostbuch, für Singstimme und Klavier nach Brentano, Goethe, Bergengruen, Jünger, u.a.* Kassel und Basel: Bärenreiter Verlag, 1949.

Ernst Pepping. *Vaterland. Liederkreis nach Gedichten von Friedrich Georg Jünger für eine Singstimme und Klavier.* Kassel und Basel: Bärenreiter Verlag, 1949.

Ernst Pepping. *Liederbuch nach Gedichten von Paul Gerhardt für Singstimme und Klavier.* Kassel und Basel: Bärenreiter Verlag, 1948.

Ernst Pepping. *As ik hier dit Jaar weer. Liederkreis nach Gedichten und Reimen von Klaus Groth für eine Singstimme und Klavier.* Kassel und Basel: Bärenreiter Verlag, 1948.

George Perle. *Two Rilke Songs.* Hillsdale, New York: Boelke-Bomart Publications, 1986.

Wilhelm Petersen. *Goethe Lieder für hohe Stimme und Klavier, Werk 40.* Heidelberg: Willy Müller, Süddeutscher Musikverlag, 1941.

Wilhelm Petersen. *Der Alte Garten. Zweite Folge der Eichendorff Lieder, Opus 44.* Heidelberg: Willy Müller, Süddeutscher Musikverlag, 1956.

Hans Pfitzner. *Sämtliche Lieder mit Klavierbegleitung (vols. 1 and 2).* Herausgegeben von Hans Rectanus. Mainz: B. Schott's Söhne, 1979.

Sergei Rachmaninoff. *Songs, Volume I, with Piano accompaniment.* London: Boosey and Hawkes, 1922 (1947).

Joachim Raff. *Sanges-Frühling. Dreizig Romanzen, Balladen, Lieder und Gesänge mit Pianoforte Begleitung, Opus 98.* Leipzig: J. Schuberth & Co., 1877.

Joachim Raff. *Maria Stuart, ein Cyklus von Gesängen für eine Singstimme mit Begleitung des Pianoforte, Opus 172.* Leipzig: C. F. W. Siegel's Musikalienhandlung, [n.d]. Reprint. Huntsville, Texas: Recital Publications, 1991.

Georg Rauchenecker. *Sieben Lieder aus dem Roman "Der Liedermacher" von Julius Stinde für Sopran mit Klavierbegleitung.* Wuppertal: Ernst Hugo Becker Verlag, 1940.

Georg Rauchenecker. *Lieder der Brautzeit.* Wuppertal: Ernst Hugo Becker Verlag, 1940.

John Reed. *The Schubert Song Companion.* New York: Universe Books, 1985.

Max Reger. *Sämtliche Werke, vols.30-35,38.* Unter Mitarbeit des Max-Reger-Institutes (Elsa-Reger-Stiftung), Bonn. Wiesbaden: Breitkopf und Härtel.

Nancy B. Reich. *Clara Schumann: The Artist and Woman.* Ithaca, New York: Cornell University Press, 1985.

Johann Friedrich Reichardt. *Lieder aus dem Liederspiel "Lieb' und Treue."* Berlin: Johann Friedrich Unger, 1800.

Johann Friedrich Reichardt. *Lieder und Oden in Auswahl.* Herausgegeben von Fritz Jöde. Hannover: Verlag Adolph Nagel, 1929.

Johann Friedrich Reichardt. *Goethes Lieder, Oden, Balladen und Romanzen mit Musik. Teil I und II.* Herausgegeben von Walter Salmen. Das Erbe Deutscher Musik 58 und 59. München-Duisenburg: G. Henle Verlag, 1964 and 1970.

Johann Friedrich Reichardt. *Schillers lyrische Gedichte in Musik gesetzt und Ihrer Königlichen Hoheit der Prinzessin Wilhelm von Preussen gebohrnen Prinzessin von Hessen-Homburg zugeeignet.* Zweiter Heft. Leipzig: Breitkopf und Härtel, 1809?

Luise Reichardt. *Ausgewählte Lieder.* Herausgegeben und eingeleitet von Gerty Rheinhardt. München: Drei Masken Verlag, 1922.

Luise Reichardt. *Songs.* Compiled and with an introduction by Nancy B. Reich. New York: Da Capo Press, 1981.

Aribert Reimann. *Nachtstück (Joseph von Eichendorff) für Bariton und Klavier (1966).* Mainz: Ars Viva Verlag, 1969.

Aribert Reimann. *Nachtstück II (Joseph von Eichendorff) für Bariton und Klavier.* Mainz: Ars Viva Verlag, 1980.

Carl Reinecke. *Kinderlieder, vols.1 and 2.* Melville, New York: Belwin Mills.

Carl Reinecke. *Acht Lieder, Opus 81.* Leipzig: Breitkopf und Härtel, [n.d.]. Reprint. Huntsville, Texas: Recital Publications, 1989.

Carl Reissiger. *Vier Gesänge für Sopran und Horn mit Begleitung des Pianoforte.* München: Hans Pizka Edition, 1981.

Carl Reissiger. *Reissiger-Album. Sammlung berühmter Lieder und Balladen für eine Singstimme mit Pianofortebegleitung.* Leipzig: C. F. Peters, 1881.

Carl Reissiger. *Der wandernde Waldhornist von E. Vogt für eine Tenorstimme mit Begleitung eines obligaten Waldhorn und des Pianoforte.* München: Hans Pizka Edition, 1983.

Max Renner. *Sechs Lieder für eine Singstimme mit Begleitung des Piano, Opus 3.* Leipzig: August Cranz, 1899?

Hermann Reutter, editor. *Das Zeitgenössische Lied. Ein Querschnitt durch die Liedliteratur des 20. Jahrhunderts. Band I-IV.* Herausgegeben von Hermann Reutter. Mainz: B. Schott's Söhne, 1969.

Hermann Reutter. *Drei Lieder nach Gedichten von Matthias Claudius für hohe Stimme und Klavier.* Mainz: B. Schott's Söhne, 1947.

Hermann Reutter. *Zwölf Lieder nach Gedichten von Hans Heinrich Ehrler (aus "Gesicht und Antlitz") für hohe Stimme und Klavier.* Mainz: B. Schott's Söhne, 1948.

Erich Riede. *Sechzehn Lieder für Sopran und Klavier.* Wiesbaden: Bote und Bock, 1966.

Eva Rieger and Käte Walter. *Frauen komponieren: 25 Lieder für Singstimme und Klavier.* Mainz: B. Schott's Söhne, 1992.

Franz Ries. *Lieder für eine Singstimme mit Clavierbegleitung von Franz Ries, Bd.1.* Berlin: Ries und Erler, 1888.

Franz Ries. *Franz Ries Vocal Album. Nineteen Songs with Piano Accompaniment.* New York: G. Schirmer, 1891.

Wolfgang Rihm. *gesänge, opus 1, für singstimme und klavier (1968-1970).* Wien: Universal Edition, 1992.

Wolfgang Rihm. *Hölderlin-Fragmente für Gesang und Klavier.* Wien: Universal Edition, 1977.

Nicolai Rimsky-Korsakov. *The Complete Works of Rimsky-Korsakov. Songs with Piano Accompaniment.* Melville, New York: Belwin Mills.

Frederic Ritter. *Hafis. Ein Liederkreis aus dessen Gedichten, Opus 1.* Leipzig: J. Schuberth, 1866.

Frederic Ritter. *Zehn Kinder-Lieder für eine Singstimme mit Begleitung des Pianoforte, Opus 3.* Leipzig: J. Schuberth, 1867.

Frederic Ritter. *Six Songs, Opus 6.* Mainz: B. Schott's Söhne, 187-?

Frederic Ritter. *Fünf Lieder, Opus 10.* New York: Edward Schuberth, 1876.

Helmut Rösner. *Paul Hindemith: Katalog seiner Werke. Diskographie. Bibliographie. Einführung in das Schaffen.* Frankfurt am Main: Städtische Musikbibliothek, 1970.

J. Guy Ropartz. *Vingt Oeuvres Vocales.* Paris: Rouart, Lerolle & Cie., 1910.

Ludwig Rottenberg. *Zwölf Lieder von Heinrich Heine.* Mainz: B. Schott's Söhne, 1914. Reprint. Huntsville, Texas: Recital Publications, 1993.

Anton Rubinstein. *Song Album by Anton Rubinstein.* New York: G. Schirmer, 1887.

Anton Rubinstein. *Twelve Songs from the Persian of Mirza-Schaffy, Opus 34*. Leipzig: Fr. Kistner. Reprint. New York: Classical Vocal Reprints, 1994.

Franz Salmhofer. *Vier Lieder, Opus 5, für Gesang und Klavier*. Wien: Universal Edition, 1923.

Ilse Schaefer. *Verzeichnis der Werke von Felix Weingartner.* Auf Grund des Verzeichnisses von Max Boller (Gebr. Hug & Co., Zürich und Laipzig 1927) bearbeitet und ergänzt von Ilse Schaefer. Festschrift für Dr. F. Weingartner. Basel: H. Oppermann, vorm. R. Geering, 1933.

Josef Schelb. *Drei Sonette Michelangelos für eine Singstimme und Klavier, Opus 5*. München: Wunderhornverlag, 1920. Reprint. New York: Classical Vocal Reprints, 1994.

Alma Maria Schindler-Mahler. *Sämtliche Lieder für mittlere Stimme und Klavier*. Wien: Universal Edition, 1984.

Leander Schlegel. *Deutsche Liebeslieder. Ein Cyklus für eine Singstimme und Pianoforte, Op.20*. Leipzig: E. W. Fritzsch.

Arnold Schönberg. *Six Orchestral Songs, Opus 8 Arranged by Anton Webern for Voice and Piano*. Boca Raton, Florida: Masters Music Publications, Inc., 1990.

Arnold Schönberg. *Lieder mit Klavierbegleitung I.* Herausgegeben von Josef Rufer. Sämtliche Werke: Abteilung I: Lieder, Reihe A, Band 1. Mainz: B. Schott's Söhne / Universal Edition AG, 1966.

Arnold Schönberg. *Lieder mit Klavierbegleitung II.* Unter Verwendung der Vorarbeiten von Ivan Vojtěch herausgegeben von Christian Martin Schmidt. Sämtliche Werke: Abteilung I: Lieder, Reihe A, Band 2. Mainz: B. Schott's Söhne / Universal Edition AG, 1988.

Franz Schreker. *Zwei Lieder, Opus 2*. Wien: Josef Eberle, 1904? Reprint. Miami Lakes, Florida: Masters Music Publications, Inc., 1989.

Franz Schreker. *Fünf Gedichte von Paul Heyse für eine Singstimme mit Clavierbegleitung, Opus 3*. Wien: Adolf Robitschek, 1902.

Franz Schreker. *Fünf Lieder, Opus 4*. Wien: Josef Eberle, 1904? Reprint. Miami Lakes, Florida: Masters Music Publications, Inc., 1989.

Franz Schreker. *Zwei Lieder auf den Tod eines Kindes, von Mia Holm, Opus 5*. Wien: Josef Eberle, 1905? Reprint. Miami Lakes, Florida: Masters Music Publications, Inc., 1989.

Franz Schreker. *Acht Lieder, Opus 7*. Wien: Josef Eberle, 190-? Reprint. Miami Lakes, Florida: Masters Music Publications, Inc., 1989.

Franz Schreker. *Fünf Gesänge*. [Texts by Ronsperger and Anonymous, WoO]. Wien: Universal Edition, 1909.

Franz Schreker. *Entführung (Stefan George)*. Der Merker, III/4, 1911.

Franz Schreker. *"Das feurige Männlein" (Petzold)*. Kriegsalmanach 1914-1916. Wien: Kriegshilfsbüro des k. k. Ministeriums des Innern, 1916.

Franz Schreker. *"Und wie mag die Liebe" (Rilke)*. Illustrierte Zeitung. Leipzig, 1920.

Franz Schreker. *Zwei lyrische Gesänge für hohe Singstimme und Klavier nach Dichtungen von Walt Whitman (aus den "Grashalmen")*. Wien: Universal Edition, 1924.

Christian Friedrich Daniel Schubart. *Vergessene Lieder für Singstimme und Klavier in der Bearbeitung von Prof. Wilhelm Krämer*. Herrenberg: Musikverlag Gotthard F. Döring.

Franz Schuberts Werke. Kritische durchgesehene Gesammtausgabe. Leipzig: Breitkopf und Härtel, 1884-1897. Reprint. New York: Dover Publications, 1965.

Walter Schulthess. *Lieder nach Gedichten von Christian Morgenstern für eine Singstimme mit Klavierbegleitung*. Mainz: B. Schott's Söhne, 1967.

Walter Schulthess. *Lieder nach Gedichten von Karl Stamm für eine Singstimme mit Klavierbegleitung*. Mainz: B. Schott's Söhne, 1967.

Johann Abraham Peter Schulz. *Lieder im Volkston bey dem Claviere zu singen (1782-1790)*. Beihefte zum "Musikanten", Nr. 7. Herausgegeben von Fritz Jöde. Wolfenbüttel: Julius Zwißlers Verlag, 1925.

Robert Schumann. *Lieder für eine Singstimme mit Begleitung des Pianoforte*. Robert Schumann's Werke. Serie XIII. Leipzig: Breitkopf und Härtel, 1882-87. Reprint. New York: Edwin F. Kalmus, 1970?

Robert Schumann. *Duette für Gesang und Klavier. Herausgegeben von Max Friedländer*. Frankfurt: C. F. Peters.

Robert Schumann. *Spanisches Liederspiel für eine und mehrere Singstimmen und Klavier, Opus 74.* Frankfurt: C. F. Peters.

Clara Wieck Schumann. *Sämtliche Lieder für Singstimme und Klavier.* Wiesbaden: Breitkopf und Härtel, 1992.

Reinhard Schwarz-Schilling. *Drei Lieder nach Gedichten von Eichendorff für Bariton (Alt) und Klavier.* Kassel und Basel: Bärenreiter Verlag, 1949.

Reinhard Schwarz-Schilling. *Der wandernde Musikant. Lieder nach Gedichten von Eichendorff für Bariton und Klavier.* Kassel und Basel: Bärenreiter Verlag, 1949.

Reinhard Schwarz-Schilling. *Drei Geistliche Lieder für eine Singstimme und Klavier (Orgel) (1949).* Kassel und Basel: Bärenreiter Verlag, 1953.

Jean Sibelius. *Six Songs, Opus 50.* Baton Rouge: Master Music Publications, 1990.

Friedrich Silcher. *100 Volkslieder für eine Singstimme mit Begleitung des Pianoforte revidirt von Alfred Dörffel.* Leipzig: C. F. Peters, 1891.

Friedrich Silcher. *Deutsche Volkslieder.* (Recording) Carus-Quintett. Bietigheim-Bissingen: Bayer-Records, 1988.

Hermann Simon. *Drei Goethe-Gesänge in Musik gesetzt für eine mittlere Männerstimme mit Instrumentalbegleitung.* Wien: Carl Haslinger, 1936?

Victoria Ressmeyer Sirota. *"The Life and Works of Fanny Mendelssohn Hensel"* Ph.D. diss., Boston University, 1981.

John William Smeed, editor. *Famous Poets, Neglected Composers. Songs to Lyrics by Goethe, Heine, Mörike, and Others.* Recent Researches in the Music of the 19th and Early 20th Centuries, v.10. Madison: A-R Editions, Inc., 1992.

Hans Sommer. *Lieder und Gesänge.* Leipzig: C. F. Leede, 1891-1893?

Hans Sommer. *Mädchenlieder aus Julius Wolff's Waidmannsmär: Der wilde Jäger, Opus 3.* Braunschweig: Henry Litolff's Verlag, 1884.

Hans Sommer. *Lieder aus Julius Wolff's Minnesang: Tannhäuser, Opus 5.* Braunschweig: Henry Litolff's Verlag, 1884.

Hans Sommer. *Sappho's Gesänge aus Carmen Sylva's Dichtung, Opus 6.* Braunschweig: Henry Litolff's Verlag, 1884.

Louis Spohr. *The Complete Lieder Sets.* Selected Works of Louis Spohr 1784-1859 vols.8i and 8ii. Edited with Introductions by Clive Brown. New York: Garland Publishing Inc, 1988.

Vilhelm Stenhammar. *Zwei Minnelieder von Walther von der Vogelweide für eine Stimme mit Pianofortebegleitung, Opus 9.* Breslau: Julius Hainauer, 1897?

Vilhelm Stenhammar. *Drei Lieder von Heinrich Heine für eine Singstimme mit Klavierbegleitung, Opus 17.* Copenhagen: Nordisk Musik-Forlag, 19–?

Rudi Stephan. *Ich will dir singen ein Hohenlied. Sechs Gedichte von Gerda von Robertus für eine Singstimme und Klavier.* Aus dem Nachlasse herausgegeben von Dr. Karl Holl. Mainz: B. Schott's Söhne, 1920.

Rudi Stephan. *Sieben Lieder nach verschiedenen Dichtern für eine Singstimme und Klavier.* Mainz: B. Schott's Söhne, 1920?

Rudi Stephan. *Vier Lieder nach verschiedenen Dichtern für eine Singstimme und Klavier.* Audio Graphic, 1988.

Rudi Stephan. *Zwei ernste Gesänge für Bariton und Klavier.* Aus dem Nachlasse herausgegeben von Dr. Karl Holl. Mainz: B. Schott's Söhne, 1920.

Kurt Stephenson. *Romantik in der Tonkunst.* Das Musikwerk, Nr.21. Köln: Arno Volk Verlag Hans Gerig KG.

Eduard Steuermann. *Brecht-Lieder. Three Songs for Low Voice to Poems by Bertolt Brecht.* Northampton, Mass.: New Valley Music Press, Smith College, 1971.

Eduard Steuermann. *Drei Lieder (Three Songs) for Bass Voice and Piano.* New York: Mobart Music Publications, 1985.

Richard Stöhr. *Fünf Lieder für eine Singstimme mit Klavierbegleitung, Opus 28.* Wien: Universal Edition, 1914. Reprint. Huntsville, Texas: Recital Publications, 1992.

Richard Strauss. *Lieder: Gesamtausgabe, vols. 1-3.* Herausgegeben von Dr. Franz Trenner. London: Boosey and Hawkes, 1964.

Richard Strauss. *Wer hat's gethan.* Erstausgabe des Liedes mit vollständigem Faksimile sowie Nachwort von Willi Schuh. Tutzing: Hans Schneider, 1974.

Richard Strauss. *Malven. (Song for Voice and Piano).* London: Boosey and Hawkes, 1985.

Theodor Streicher. *Dreissig Lieder aus Des Knaben Wunderhorn.* Leipzig: Lauterbach und Kuhn, 1904. Reprint. Huntsville, Texas: Recital Publications, 1989.

Theodor Streicher. *Hafis-Lieder.* Six Books in One Volume. With an Introduction by Richard B. Wursten. Leipzig: Breitkopf und Härtel, 1907-08. Reprint. Huntsville, Texas: Recital Publications, 1991.

Frank van der Stucken. *Sieben Lieder: Opus 3 and Opus 4, in one volume.* Leipzig: Fr. Kistner, 1878-79. Reprint. Huntsville, Texas: Recital Publications, 1986.

Frank van der Stucken. *Neun Gesänge für eine Singstimme mit Begleitung des Pianoforte, Opus 5.* Leipzig: Fr. Kistner, 1879? Reprint. Huntsville, Texas: Recital Publications, 1989.

Frank van der Stucken. *Fünf Liebeslieder von Friedrich Rückert für eine Singstimme mit Begleitung des Pianoforte, Opus 16.* Berlin: Friedrich Luckhardt, 1892. Reprint. Huntsville, Texas: Recital Publications, 1991.

Frank van der Stucken. *Acht Lieder für tiefere Singstimme mit Begleitung des Pianoforte.* Leipzig: Luckhardt's Musik Verlag, 1892.

Frank van der Stucken. *Lieder und Gesänge, vols. 1 and 2 (Opus 29, 30, 31, 33, and 34).* Leipzig: Breitkopf und Härtel, 1904. Reprint. Huntsville, Texas: Recital Publications, 1991.

Karol Szymanowski. *Zwölf Lieder, Opus 17, für hohe Stimme und Klavier.* Wien: Universal Edition.

Karol Szymanowski. *Bunte Lieder für eine Singstimme und Klavier, Opus 22.* Wien: Universal Edition, 1912.

Wilhelm Taubert. *Klänge aus der Kinderwelt. Sammlung beliebter Kinderlieder.* Magdeburg: Heinrichshofen's Verlag, 1900.

Pyotr Il'ich Tchaikovsky. *Songs for One Voice and Piano.* Complete Works. Reprint. Melville, New York: Belwin Mills.

Anna Teichmüller. *Fünf Gedichte von Carl Hauptmann, Opus 1.* Berlin: Verlag Helianthus, 1904?

Anna Teichmüller. *Fünf Lieder für eine Singstimme mit Begleitung des Pianoforte, Opus 2.* Berlin: Verlag Helianthus, 1904?

Anna Teichmüller. *Sechs leichte Lieder, Opus 3.* Berlin: Verlag Helianthus, 1905?

Anna Teichmüller. *Drei Lieder, Opus 4.* Berlin: Verlag Helianthus, 1905?

Anna Teichmüller. *Zwei Liebeslieder, Opus 5.* Berlin: Verlag Helianthus, 1905?

Anna Teichmüller. *Drei Lieder, Opus 7.* Berlin: Verlag Dreililien, 1906?

Anna Teichmüller. *Vier Lieder, Opus 8.* Berlin: Verlag Dreililien, 1906?

Anna Teichmüller. *Leichte Lieder, Opus 9.* Berlin: Verlag Dreililien, 1907?

Anna Teichmüller. *Mandschurisch, Opus 10.* Berlin: Verlag Dreililien, 1906?

Anna Teichmüller. *Der Seelchenbaum. Kleine Ballade, Opus 11.* Berlin: Verlag Dreililien, 1906.

Anna Teichmüller. *Vier Lieder, Opus 12.* Berlin: Verlag Dreililien, 1907?

Anna Teichmüller. *Zwei Balladen, Opus 13.* Berlin: Verlag Dreililien, 1907.

Anna Teichmüller. *Fünf Lieder, Opus 15.* Berlin: Verlag Dreililien, 1907?

Anna Teichmüller. *Lieder Kindern gesungen, Opus 17.* Berlin: Verlag Dreililien, 1907?

Anna Teichmüller. *Fünf Lieder für eine Singstimme und Pianoforte, Opus 19.* Berlin: Verlag Dreililien, 1910.

Anna Teichmüller. *Fünf Lieder für eine Singstimme und Pianoforte, Opus 24.* Berlin: Verlag Dreililien, 1910.

Anna Teichmüller. *Drei Lieder für eine Singstimme und Pianoforte, Opus 25.* Berlin: Verlag Dreililien, 1910.

Siegfried Thiele. *Drei Lieder für Alt und Klavier nach Gedichten von Rainer Maria Rilke.* Leipzig: C. F. Peters, ca. 1981.

Ludwig Thuille. *Fünf Lieder, Opus 4; and Drei Frauenlieder, Opus 5.* Leipzig: Breitkopf und Härtel, [n.d.]. Reprint. Huntsville, Texas: Recital Publications, 1993.

Ludwig Thuille. *Von Lieb' und Leid: Ein Liederkreis für eine hohe Singstimme und Pianoforte, Opus 7.* Leipzig: Breitkopf und Härtel, [n.d.]. Reprint. Huntsville, Texas: Recital Publications, 1989.

Jurgen Thym, editor. *100 Years of Eichendorff Songs.* Recent Researches in the Music of the Nineteenth and Early Twentieth Centuries. Volume V. Madison, Wisconsin: A-R Editions, Inc, 1983.

Franz Tischhauser. *Klein Irmchen. Sechs Lieder nach Gedichten von Christian Morgenstern für Sopran und Klavier. (1937).* Winterthur: Amadeus Verlag, 1989.

Ernst Toch. *Neun Lieder für Sopran und Klavier von Ernst Toch, Opus 41.* Mainz: B. Schott's Söhne.

Václav Jan Tomášek. *Dvě Písně (Zwei Lieder).* Praha: Editio Supraphon, 1974.

Václav Jan Tomášek. *Gedichte von Goethe für den Gesang mit Begleitung des Piano-Forte gesetzt von Wenzel J. Tomaschek, Tonsetzer bey Herrn Georg Grafen von Buquoy.* 182-?

Richard Trunk. *Sieben Eichendorff Lieder für eine Stimme mit Klavier, mittel-hoch, Opus 45.* München: F. E. C. Leuckart, 1933.

Richard Trunk. *Vier heitere Lieder für hohe Stimme und Klavier, Opus 63.* München: F. E. C. Leuckart, 1933.

Richard Trunk. *Fünf Lieder mit Klavier, Opus 76.* München: F. E. C. Leuckart, 1963.

Fartein Valen. *Gedichte von Goethe, Opus 6.* Oslo: Norsk Musik Forlag, 1929.

Fartein Valen. *Zwei Lieder für Sopran und Klavier, Opus 31.* Oslo: Harald Lyche & Co's Musikkforlag, 1976.

Fartein Valen. *Zwei Lieder, Opus 39.* Oslo: Harald Lyche & Co's Musikkforlag, 1954.

Aleksandr Varlamov. *Romansi i Pesni, vols.1 and 2.* Moscow, 1974.

Giuseppe Verdi. *Composizioni da camera per canto e pianoforte.* Milano: Ricordi, 1987.

Johann Vesque von Püttlingen. *45 Lieder. Ausgewählt und herausgegeben von Helmut Schultz. Band I: 23 Lieder nach Heinrich Heine. Band II: 22 Lieder nach verschiedenen Dichtern.* Wien: Universal Edition, 1932.

Ernest Vietor. *Five Songs, Opus 3.* [n.p., n.d.: Printed in U.S.A.].

Ernest Vietor. *Four Songs, Opus 4.* [n.p., n.d.: Printed in U.S.A.].

Ernest Vietor. *Five Songs, Opus 5.* [n.p., n.d.: Printed in U.S.A.].

Ernest Vietor. *Six Songs, Opus 6.* [n.p., n.d.: Printed in U.S.A.].

Ernest Vietor. *13 Galgen Lieder, Opus 7. Words by Christian Morgenstern.* [n.p., n.d.: Printed in U.S.A.].

Ernest Vietor. *Eight Songs, Opus 8. Poems from Christian Morgenstern's "Der Ginganz."* [n.p., n.d.: Printed in U.S.A.].

Ernest Vietor. *Six Songs, Opus 9. Poems from Christian Morgenstern's "Melancholie."* [n.p., n.d.: Printed in U.S.A.].

Ernest Vietor. *Five Songs, Opus 10. Poems by Johann Wolfgang von Goethe.* [n.p., n.d.: Printed in U.S.A.].

Ernest Vietor. *Seventeen Songs, Opus 11. Poems by Christian Morgenstern.* [n.p., n.d.: Printed in U.S.A.].

Ernest Vietor. *Sechs Frühlingslieder, Opus 12.* [n.p., n.d.: Printed in U.S.A.].

Ernest Vietor. *Five Songs, Opus 13. Poems by Friedrich Nietzsche.* [n.p., n.d.: Printed in U.S.A.].

Ernest Vietor. *Twelve Songs, Opus 14.* [n.p., n.d.: Printed in U.S.A.].

Ernest Vietor. *Two Songs, Opus 15. Poems by Gottfried Keller.* [n.p., n.d.: Printed in U.S.A.].

Ernest Vietor. *Nine Songs, Opus 16.* [n.p., n.d.: Printed in U.S.A.].

Ernest Vietor. *Six Songs, Opus 17.* [n.p., n.d.: Printed in U.S.A.].

Werner Vogel. *Othmar Schoeck. Leben und Schaffen im Spiegel von Selbstzeugnissen und Zeitgenossenberichten.* Zürich: Atlantis Musikbuch-Verlag, 1976.

Werner Vogel. *Thematisches Verzeichnis der Werke Othmar Schoeck.* Zürich: Atlantis Verlag, 1956.

Bruno Walter. *Sechs Lieder (Joseph von Eichendorff) für eine Singstimme mit Klavier, von Bruno Walter.* Wien: Universal Edition, 1910.

John Warrack. *Carl Maria von Weber, 2nd edition.* Cambridge: Cambridge U P, 1976.

Carl Maria von Weber. *C. M. v. Weber's sämmtliche ein- und zweistimmige Lieder und Gesänge mit Begleitung des Pianoforte. Band I und II.* Berlin: Schlesinger.

Carl Maria von Weber. *Ausgewählte Lieder für eine Singstimme mit Pianofortebegleitung*. Leipzig: C. F. Peters, 1888.

Oscar Weil. *Zwei Lieder für eine Sopranstimme mit Begleitung des Pianoforte und obligater Violine, Opus 10*. Leipzig: Breitkopf und Härtel, 1888?

Oscar Weil. *Drei Lieder von Shakespeare für eine Singstimme mit Pianofortebegleitung, Opus 32*. Deutsche Übersetzung von F. H. Schneider. Deutscher Liederverlag Nr. 3744/45. Leipzig: Breitkopf und Härtel, 1902.

Egon Wellesz. *Lieder nach Dichtungen von Stefan George, Opus 22*. Wien: Ludwig Doblinger, 1982.

Hermann Wetzler. *Fünf Lieder*. Köln: Albert Ahn Verlag, 1908. Reprint. Huntsville, Texas: Recital Publications, 1993.

Josef Wöss. *Das moderne Lied. Eine Sammlung von 50 Gesängen für mittlere Stimme ausgewählt von Josef V. Wöss*. Wien: Universal Edition, 1914.

Hugo Wolf. *Hugo Wolf. Sämtliche Werke, Kritische Gesamtausgabe*. Herausgegeben von der Internationalen Hugo Wolf-Gesellschaft (Hans Jancik). Wien: Musikwissenschaftlicher Verlag.

Felix Wolfes. *Selected Lieder for Voice and Piano, Volumes VI-IX*. Bryn Mawr: Theodore Presser Company, 1987-91.

Erich J. Wolff. *Lieder und Gesänge, Opus 8, 9, 10, and 11*. Berlin: Verlag Harmonie, 1907.

Erich J. Wolff. *Gesammelte Lieder aus dem Nachlass in drei Bänden*. Berlin: Bote und Bock, 1914.

Stefan Wolpe. *Fünf Lieder nach Friedrich Hölderlin für Alt und Klavier, Opus 1*. Hamburg: Peer Musikverlag GmbH, 1991.

Alfred Wotquenne. *Catalogue Thématique des Oeuvres de Chr. W. v. Gluck*. Hildesheim: Georg Olms Verlag, 1967.

Franz Wüllner. *Sechs Lieder für eine Singstimme mit Begleitung des Pianoforte*. Leipzig: C. F. Kahnt Nachfolger, 1857.

Erich Zeisl. *Sechs Lieder für mittlere Stimme und Klavierbegleitung*. Wien: Ludwig Doblinger, 1935.

Erich Zeisl. *Sieben Lieder für Sopran und Klavierbegleitung*. Wien: Ludwig Doblinger, 1936.

Carl Friedrich Zelter. *Sämmtliche Lieder, Balladen und Romanzen für das Pianoforte, Heft I-IV*. Ausgabe Berlin, 1811-12. Reprint. Dokumentation zur Geschichte des deutschen Liedes IV (Siegfried Kross). Hildesheim: Georg Olms Verlag, 1984.

Carl Friedrich Zelter. *Fünfzig Lieder (nach Goethe u.a. für eine Singstimme und Klavier)*. Ausgewählt und mit Unterstützung der Goethe-Gesellschaft herausgegeben von Ludwig Landshoff. Mainz: B. Schott's Söhne, 1932.

Hermann Zilcher. *Vier Lieder für eine hohe Singstimme mit Klavierbegleitung. Opus 12*. Leipzig: Breitkopf und Härtel, 1904. Reprint. Huntsville, Texas: Recital Publications, 1992.

Winfried Zillig. *Zehn Lieder nach Gedichten von Goethe*. Kassel und Basel: Bärenreiter Verlag, 1960.

Friedrich Zipp. *Wunderhorn Lieder. Acht Lieder für mittlere Singstimme und Klavier nach Gedichten aus "Des Knaben Wunderhorn", Werk 5*. Heidelberg: Willy Müller, Süddeutscher Musikverlag, 1964.

Emilie Zumsteeg. *Sechs Lieder mit Begleitung des Pianoforte von Emilie Zumsteeg. Opus 4* (facsimile edition). Mainz: B. Schott's Söhne, 1990.

Emilie Zumsteeg. *Neun Lieder mit Begleitung des Piano-Forte*. Bonn: N. Simrock, 1817?